Sheffield Hallam University
Learning and IT Services
Collegiate Learning Centre
Collegiate Crescent Campus
Sheffield S10 2BP

KT-556-191

101 887 146 2

K LOAN

Sheffield Hallam University
Learning and Information Services
Withdrawn From Stock

AUSTRALIA
Law Book Co.
Sydney

CANADA AND USA
Carswell
Toronto

HONG KONG
Sweet & Maxwell Asia

NEW ZEALAND
Brookers
Wellington

SINGAPORE AND MALAYSIA
Sweet & Maxwell Asia
Singapore and Kuala Lumpur

CRETNEY

PRINCIPLES
OF
FAMILY LAW

EIGHTH EDITION

BY

J.M. MASSON, MA, PhD
Professor of Socio-Legal Studies
University of Bristol

R. BAILEY-HARRIS, MA, BCL
Barrister
Professor Emeritus
University of Bristol

AND

R.J. PROBERT, MA
Associate Professor
University of Warwick

LONDON
SWEET & MAXWELL
2008

First Edition 1974
Second Edition 1976
Third Edition 1979
Fourth Edition 1984
Fifth Edition 1990
Sixth Edition 1997
Reprinted 1998 (twice), 2000
Seventh Edition 2002
Revised edition 2003
Reprinted 2003
Eighth Edition 2008

Published by
Sweet & Maxwell Ltd of
100 Avenue Road,
London NW3 3PF
(http://www.sweetandmaxwell.co.uk)
Typeset by Interactive Sciences Ltd, Gloucester
Printed in the Netherlands
by Krips

No natural forests were destroyed to make this product;
only farmed timber was used and replanted.

British Library Cataloguing in Publication Data
A CIP catalogue record for this book is available
from the British Library.

ISBN 9780421960107

All rights reserved.
Crown copyright material is reproduced with the permission of the Controller of HMSO and the
Queen's Printer for Scotland.
No part of this publication may be reproduced or transmitted in
any form or by any means, or stored in any retrieval system of
any nature without prior written permission, except for permitted fair
dealing under the Copyright, Designs and Patents Act 1988, or in accordance with the terms of a
licence issued by the Copyright Licensing Agency in respect of photocopying and/or reprographic
reproduction. Application for permission for other use of copyright material including permission
to reproduce extracts in other published works shall be made to the publishers. Full
acknowledgment of author, publisher and source must be given.

©
Sweet & Maxwell
2008

PREFACE

The aim of this book continues to be not only to explain the law as it is, but to give an account of its historical background, to analyse the factors underlying its development and to stimulate discussion of its effectiveness as an instrument of social policy in the context of the social realities confronting the legal system early in the twenty-first century.

Providing an account of current family law is a challenge exacerbated by the fast pace of change in family practices and the continued desire by the Government, even after 11 years in power, to leave its mark throughout the statute book. Legislation does not necessarily lead to implementation, as the *volte face* on divorce reform and the abandonment of parts of the Family Law Act 1996 showed. This debacle appears unlikely to be repeated, and the size of the Government's majority suggests that Bills currently before Parliament are likely to be enacted, largely in their current form. There is far more doubt about the future of the Law Commission's proposals for the financial consequences of cohabitation breakdown (Law Com. No. 307). On March 7, 2008, the Justice Minister announced that the Government wanted to examine the cost and efficacy of the Scottish scheme before taking further steps.

The five years since the last edition has been a very productive period for legislators, and has produced some very radical changes to family law and for society. The Civil Partnership Act 2004, together with a much celebrated occasion at the Windsor Guildhall when Elton John and David Furnish formalised their relationship, marked the acceptance in law and broad sections of society of same-sex relationships. The Gender Recognition Act 2004 has allowed transsexual people to change their legal identity and enter into new relationships in their acquired gender. The Domestic Violence Crimes and Victims Act 2004 has criminalised the breach of non-molestation injunctions in an attempt to show the seriousness of such behaviour and provide better protection for victims. Economic changes and government policies promoting employment as a means of tackling child poverty have increased the proportion of parents of young children in employment. Rights to maternity, paternity and parental leave, introduced through EC law, are changing family life radically for many parents. So far as case law is concerned, the courts are still working out the implications of fairness for post-divorce financial arrangements and examining trusts and the family home. The opinions of the House of Lords in *Miller; McFarlane* [2006] UKHL 24 have explored approaches to fairness in big-money cases but have not provided the degree of clarity that could promote settlement; *Stack v Dowden* [2007] UKHL 17 has similarly not had the desired effect of increasing certainty for cohabitants over shares in the family home.

Nor has child law stood still. The Adoption and Children Act 2002 was finally implemented on December 31, 2005; the courts are now beginning to use their powers to make special guardianship orders, providing security for children without the severance entailed by adoption. Almost 20 years after the signing of the United Nations Convention on the Rights of the Child, recognition is being given to children's rights; the Children Act 2004 established the office of Children's Commissioner for England—a similar post but with a broader remit having been established by the Children's Commissioner for Wales Act 2001. The courts are also indicating a greater willingness to allow children to participate in proceedings that are regarding them. In the area of private law, campaigns by mens' organisations, such as Fathers4Justice and concern from the judiciary has focused government attention on the limited ability of the courts to enforce orders for contact in the face of obdurate resistance by the parent with care. The government's response, the Children and Adoption Act 2006 (currently scheduled for implementation in the autumn of 2008), glosses the Children Act 1989 with a sheaf of new provisions, which on close examination involve changes to the law that scarcely justify the paper on which they are printed. In the area of public law, the effects of the Human Rights Act 1998 are continuing to be felt, with the courts giving far more attention to ensuring that local authorities have followed proper procedures in consulting parents. The problem of costs and delay in childcare proceedings remains, but in April 2008, a new system was introduced (the Public Law Outline), which seeks to divert cases from the courts and improve the quality of the applications that are made. However, massive increases in the costs of bringing proceedings from May 1, 2008, ostensibly as part of a policy to make the civil courts self-supporting, are likely to have a much greater effect on the number of proceedings and the protection provided for children in the most adverse circumstances. Further aspects of child law are currently before Parliament, particularly the Child Maintenance and other Payments Bill, which makes further reforms to the child support system, the Children and Young Persons Bill, which seeks to raise the quality of provision for looked-after children, and the Human Fertilisation and Embryology Bill, which amends the law of parentage where children are conceived using assisted reproductive technology, allowing recognition of the second parent in lesbian couples and applying a system of dual consent where donor gametes are used for clinical procedures. These reforms are referred to throughout, although their enactment and date of implementation remain uncertain.

The first edition of this book, published in 1974 and used by the first author as an undergraduate text, was 369 pages long. By the fourth edition it had grown to 1,018 pages. I was pleased to be invited by Stephen Cretney to write the chapters on children for the fifth edition and have continued to do so, also taking over Chapter 6 on State Support for the Family for this eighth edition. Rebecca Bailey-Harris joined Stephen and myself for the seventh edition and has authored Chapters 7, 12 and 13 for this edition. Following Stephen's decision not to continue writing this book after his retirement, I was delighted that my former colleague Rebecca Probert agreed to join the team. She is responsible for the rest of the text. Happily, Stephen Cretney agreed to continue with his important work of identifying a picture for the cover that would capture an aspect of family life in art.

The authors hope that they have done justice to Stephen Cretney's work in completing this edition. The law is stated on the basis of the materials available to them on April 30, 2008.

Judith Masson
May Day, 2008

Valedictory Note by Stephen Cretney

I am deeply grateful to Judith Masson, Rebecca Bailey-Harris and Rebecca Probert. The text of the present edition of this book is entirely theirs, and I am glad that this should be so: family law must keep pace with the social realities that it governs and may influence, and there comes a time when the author of the first edition (published nearly 35 years ago) rightly makes way for new generations.

I have always greatly enjoyed choosing the picture decorating the cover, and the present authors have kindly allowed me to suggest the beautiful image painted by the American artist Cecilia Beaux that appears on this new edition. I believe that many great works of art tell a story, or at least convey messages and different views—whether about the apparent subservience of the nurse (perhaps brutally excluded from the painting as, no doubt, from so much else) or the need of a two-year-old (the artist's niece Ernesta) for what may be a helping but could equally be a restraining hand—will no doubt be held about such issues, as indeed about many of the topics dealt with in the book.

Stephen Cretney
Whit Sunday, 2008

CONTENTS

	page
Preface	v
Table of Cases	xxi
Table of Statutes	xcix
Table of Statutory Instruments	cxxvii

	para
INTRODUCTION: THE FAMILY AND THE LAW	A–001

I. What is "family" law?	A–001
II. Key developments in family law	A–002
A. The availability of alternative opt-in regime	A–003
B. The increase in cohabitation	A–005
C. The encouragement of private ordering	A–006
III. The scope and arrangement of the text	A–007

PART I: THE FAMILY AND FORMAL RELATIONSHIPS

1. MARRIAGE CEREMONIES AND THE REGISTRATION OF CIVIL PARTNERSHIPS	1–001
I. Introduction	1–001
II. Historical development	1–002
A. The canon law of marriage	1–002
B. Problems with the canon law	1–003
C. Lord Hardwicke's Act of 1753	1–004
D. The Marriage Acts of 1823 and 1836	1–005
III. Formalities for marriage—the current law	1–006
A. Preliminaries to marriage	1–007
B. Solemnisation of the marriage	1–031
C. Registration and proof of marriages	1–043
D. Consequences of irregularities	1–044
IV. Formalities for civil partnerships	1–049
V. Conclusion: a need for reform?	1–050

2. CAPACITY TO MARRY OR FORM A CIVIL PARTNERSHIP	2–001
I. Introduction	2–001
II. Historical development	2–002
A. Void and voidable marriages	2–002
B. The need for a decree	2–003

C. Void or non-existent?   2–004
III. The Modern Law of Nullity   2–005
  A. Void marriages   2–006
  B. Voidable marriages   2–023
  C. Bars to a decree   2–047
  D. Effects of a decree   2–052
IV. Void and Voidable Civil Partnerships   2–058
  A. Void civil partnerships   2–059
  B. Voidable civil partnerships   2–060
  C. Bars to a decree   2–061
  D. Effects of an order   2–062
V. Conclusion   2–063

3. THE LEGAL CONSEQUENCES OF MARRIAGE AND CIVIL PARTNERSHIP   3–001

I. Introduction   3–001
II. Common law Doctrines   3–002
  A. The doctrine of legal unity   3–002
  B. The notion of consortium   3–003
  C. The common law right to maintenance   3–004
III. The statutory framework   3–005
  A. Property: ownership and occupation   3–006
  B. Finances: maintenance orders and agreements   3–014
  C. Miscellaneous economic consequences   3–033
  D. Other legal consequences   3–036
IV. Engaged couples   3–041
V. Conclusion   3–042

PART II: FAMILY PROPERTY

4. THE FAMILY AND PROPERTY LAW   4–001

I. Introduction   4–001
II. The socio-economic background   4–003

5. FAMILY ASSETS: OWNERSHIP AND PROTECTION   5–001

I. Introduction   5–001
II. Formal arrangements   5–003
  A. Claims founded on contract   5–004
  B. Legal ownership of the family home   5–008
  C. Ownership of the beneficial interest   5–009
III. Informal trusts   5–013
  A. Resulting trusts   5–014
  B. Constructive trusts   5–018
IV. Proprietary estoppel   5–032
  A. Assurance, promise or representation   5–033

B. Detrimental reliance 5–034
C. The remedy 5–035
D. The relationship between estoppel and the constructive
   trust 5–037
E. Reform? 5–038
V. Resolving disputes between co-owners 5–039
A. Severing the joint tenancy 5–040
B. Disputes as to whether the property should be sold 5–045
C. Dividing the proceeds 5–048
VI. Disputes with third parties 5–049
A. Is the beneficial interest binding on the third party? 5–050
B. Can the transaction be set aside? 5–052
C. Should sale be ordered? 5–057
VII. Personal property 5–062
VIII. Conclusion 5–064

6. STATE SUPPORT FOR FAMILIES 6–001

I. State financial support: the welfare benefit system and family
   breakdown 6–002
A. Historical introduction 6–003
B. Tax credits 6–005
C. Social security benefits 6–008
D. The child trust fund 6–026
II. Work-life balance 6–027
A. Introduction 6–027
B. Childcare 6–028
C. Rights at work 6–029
III. Housing duties and homelessness 6–035
A. Introduction 6–035
B. Homelessness 6–036
IV. Conclusion 6–040

7. DEVOLUTION OF FAMILY PROPERTY ON DEATH 7–001

I. Wills 7–001
A. Effects of marriage, civil partnership, divorce and
   dissolution on wills 7–002
II. Intestacy 7–003
A. Where the intestate leaves a spouse or civil partner and
   issue 7–004
B. Where the intestate leaves a spouse but no issue 7–005
C. Where the intestate leaves no surviving spouse or civil
   partner 7–006
III. The Inheritance (Provision for Family and Dependants) Act
   1975 7–009
A. Not a remedy for unfairness or unjust enrichment 7–010
B. Reform proposals 7–032

8. Reform of Family Property Law: The Future   8–001

   I.   Introduction   8–001
  II. The case for a special scheme for formal Relationships   8–002
 III. Reform of property rights in other relationships   8–005
 IV. The case for a special scheme for unformalised Relationships   8–006

PART III: FAMILY BREAKDOWN

9. Protection from Violence and Harassment   9–001

   I.   Introduction   9–001
  II. The role of the criminal law   9–003
     A. Offences under the general law   9–004
     B. Specific protection against harassment   9–005
 III. The role of the civil law   9–007
     A. Occupation orders   9–009
     B. Orders for personal protection   9–025
 IV. Conclusion   9–043

10. Divorce and Dissolution   10–001

   I.   Introduction   10–001
  II. Trends in divorce   10–002
     A. The significance of divorce rates: cause for concern?   10–003
 III. The evolution of the divorce law 1857–1969   10–004
     A. The doctrine of the matrimonial offence   10–004
     B. The decline of the matrimonial offence doctrine   10–005
     C. The post Second World War campaign for reform   10–006
     D. Irretrievable breakdown: the compromise   10–007
 IV. Divorce: the modern law   10–008
     A. The process of obtaining a divorce   10–008
     B. The ground for divorce   10–015
     C. Judicial interpretation of the five "facts"   10–017
  V. Criticisms and reform initiatives   10–047
     A. Criticisms of the current law   10–047
     B. The recommended reform   10–048
     C. The scheme of the Family Law Act 1996   10–049
     D. Piloting the Family Law Act   10–050
     E. The decision not to implement the Act   10–053
     F. A different approach: FAINs and FAInS   10–054
     G. Where next?   10–055
 VI. Dissolution of civil partnerships   10–057
VII. Conclusion   10–058

11. JUDICIAL SEPARATION AND SEPARATION ORDERS   11–001

    I.   Introduction   11–001
   II.   Judicial separation   11–002
      A. Grounds for judicial separation   11–002
      B. Effects of a decree of judicial separation   11–003
      C. The use made of judicial separation   11–004
  III.   Separation orders   11–005

12. TERMINATION OF MARRIAGE AND CIVIL PARTNERSHIP BY DEATH   12–001

    I.   The presumption of death at common law   12–002
   II.   Decree of presumption of death and dissolution   12–003

13. FINANCIAL CONSEQUENCES OF THE BREAKDOWN OF MARRIAGE
AND CIVIL PARTNERSHIP   13–001

    I.   Introduction   13–001
   II.   The settlement culture   13–003
      A. A conflict of principle: ouster of court's jurisdiction
        contrary to public policy   13–004
      B. Reconciling the conflict of principle: the consent order   13–005
      C. Procedure for obtaining a consent order: the court's role   13–006
      D. Agreements not embodied in a court order   13–008
      E. Facilitating settlement   13–010
      F. Incentives to settle: costs?   13–011
  III.   Financial relief: the legislative framework   13–012
      A. The extent of the court's powers   13–013
  IV.   Working of the law in practice: housing and pensions   13–109
      A. Housing   13–110
      B. Orders dealing with pensions   13–119

14. ENFORCEMENT OF FINANCIAL OBLIGATIONS   14–001

    I.   Introduction   14–001
   II.   Restrictions on the enforcement of maintenance arrears;
      remitting arrears   14–002
  III.   Different courts; different remedies   14–003
  IV.   The superior courts   14–004
      A. Enforcement in the superior courts   14–004
   V.   Magistrates' court   14–015
      A. Enforcement in the magistrates' court   14–015
  VI.   Restricting a contemnor's right to participate in proceedings   14–020

PART IV: CHILD SUPPORT OBLIGATIONS

15. CHILD SUPPORT   15–001

   I. Introduction   15–001
  II. The genesis, passage, criticism and subsequent amendment of
      the Child Support Act 1991   15–002
 III. Support obligations: the formulaic approach   15–005
     A. When does liability arise?   15–006
     B. Who is liable?   15–007
     C. Meeting the responsibility for maintaining a child   15–011
     D. Quantifying child support: the formulae   15–014
     E. Variations from the formula   15–020
     F. Changes and appeals   15–021
     G. Collection and enforcement   15–022
     H. Relevance of the child's welfare   15–026
     I. The impact of child support payments   15–027
     J. Assessing the child support scheme   15–028
  IV. Child maintenance: the role of the courts   15–029
     A. Determining jurisdiction   15–030
     B. The courts' statutory powers   15–039
   V. Capital provision for children   15–042
     A. Orders for children in divorce or dissolution proceedings   15–043
     B. Financial orders for children under the Children Act
        1989   15–046
  VI. Conclusion   15–053

PART V: CHILDREN AND FAMILY LAW

16. CHILDREN   16–001

   I. Introduction   16–001
  II. Children's rights   16–005
     A. Theoretical perspectives   16–005
     B. Children's rights in international law   16–007
 III. Children's rights and English law   16–010
     A. The Gillick case   16–011
     B. The retreat from Gillick   16–015
     C. Children's rights under the European Convention of
        Human Rights   16–017
     D. Children's rights and the Children Act 1989   16–019
     E. Children as parties in legal proceedings   16–020
     F. Rights in other legislation   16–023
     G. Children of unmarried parents   16–024

17. PARENTS   17–001

    I. Introduction—the concepts   17–001
    II. Who are the child's parents?   17–003
        A. Mother   17–003
        B. Father   17–004
        C. Determination of parentage   17–006
    III. What is parental responsibility?   17–013
        A. Rights and powers   17–014
        B. Duties   17–027
    IV. Who has parental responsibility?   17–030
        A. Married parents   17–030
        B. Unmarried parents   17–035
        C. Guardians   17–040
        D. Other persons   17–043
        E. Local authorities   17–047
    V. Where parental responsibility is held by more than one person   17–048
    VI. Revocation of parental responsibility   17–049
    VII. Rights of those without parental responsibility   17–050
        A. Delegation   17–050
        B. De facto carers   17–051
        C. Unmarried fathers   17–052

18. COURT PROCEEDINGS   18–001

    I. Introduction   18–001
    II. Court proceedings—the principles   18–003
        A. The welfare principle   18–004
        B. The "no order" principle   18–005
        C. The principle of no delay   18–006
    III. The family court system   18–007
    IV. Welfare services for the courts   18–009
        A. CAFCASS   18–010
        B. Local authorities   18–011
    V. Family proceedings   18–013
        A. The meaning of "family proceedings"   18–014
        B. Orders that can be made   18–015
        C. Restrictions on making orders   18–029
        D. Children in respect of whom orders can be made   18–030
        E. Who may apply for orders?   18–031
        F. Procedure—the Private Law Programme   18–040
    VI. The court as a welfare agency   18–044
        A. Mediation services   18–045
        B. Contact centres   18–046
        C. Arrangements for children on divorce   18–047
        D. Court ordered investigation   18–048

VII.   Wardship and the inherent jurisdiction of the High court   18–049
     A. The rise and fall of wardship   18–050
     B. Proceedings under the inherent jurisdiction   18–051
     C. Powers under the inherent jurisdiction   18–052
     D. Procedure under wardship and the inherent jurisdiction   18–054
VIII. Enforcement of orders   18–055
     A. Powers of the court   18–056

19. Exercise of the Court's Discretion: The Welfare Principle   19–001

  I.   Child's welfare paramount   19–001
     A. Presumptions and assumptions   19–003
     B. Welfare and the Human Rights Act 1998   19–004
     C. The meaning of the principle   19–005
     D. Application of the welfare principle   19–009
     E. Problems with the welfare principle   19–011
     F. The statutory checklist   19–014
     G. Review of the court's decisions on welfare   19–024

20. Child Abduction   20–001

  I.   Introduction   20–001
  II. Preventing abduction   20–002
     A. Passport control   20–003
     B. All ports warning   20–004
     C. Security for the child's return   20–005
     D. "Mirror" orders   20–006
  III. Tracing children   20–007
  IV. Recovery of the child   20–008
     A. Abduction within England and Wales   20–009
     B. Abduction from one part of the United Kingdom to
       another   20–010
  V.   International abduction   20–012
     A. Role of the Central Authority   20–013
     B. Abduction to a country which has ratified or acceded to
       the Hague Convention   20–014
     C. Abduction under the common law (from or to a
       country that has not ratified the Hague Convention)   20–023
  VI. Enforcing contact decisions   20–024
  VII. Abduction and human rights   20–025
 VIII. Conclusion   20–026

21. Local Authorities   21–001

  I.   Introduction   21–001
     A. The development of children's social care services   21–002
     B. The reform of childcare law   21–004

C. The philosophy of the Children Act 1989   21–005
D. The role of central government   21–006
E. The balance of power between court and social services
    departments   21–007
II.   Modern childcare law—services for children in need   21–008
    A. Family support and prevention   21–008
    B. Local authorities' duties to provide family support   21–009
    C. "Children in need"   21–010
    D. Duty to provide accommodation   21–011
    E. Voluntary agreement   21–013
    F. Co-operation between authorities   21–015
III. The child protection system   21–016
    A. Child abuse and neglect   21–016
    B. Intervention in family life   21–019
    C. The child protection system   21–021
    D. Investigation of child abuse and neglect   21–022
    E. Compulsory measures of care   21–029
    F. Protection of children in emergencies   21–047
    G. Child protection proceedings   21–053
    H. Child protection and the criminal law   21–061
IV. Modern childcare law—the looked-after system   21–067
    A. Local authorities' powers and duties   21–067
    B. The position of parents   21–072
    C. Rights of children   21–073
V.   Modern childcare law—judicial control over local authority
    decision-making   21–074
    A. Decisions requiring court approval   21–074
    B. Challenging local authority decisions   21–081

22. ADOPTION   22–001

I.   Introduction   22–001
    A. The history and development of adoption   22–004
II.   Effects of adoption orders   22–005
    A. Adoption orders   22–005
    B. Registration of adoption   22–010
    C. Access to birth and adoption records   22–011
III. Provision of adoption services   22–014
    A. Organisation of adoption services   22–015
    B. The role of the court   22–017
    C. Eligibility and suitability of adopters   22–018
    D. Adoption support   22–022
IV. Principles in adoption law   22–024
    A. Welfare   22–024
    B. Consent   22–025
    C. Human rights   22–034
    D. Confidentiality   22–035

  V. Modern adoption practice   22–036
     A. The use of adoption   22–036
     B. Relinquishment or baby placement   22–037
     C. Public law adoptions   22–040
     D. Intercountry adoptions   22–046
     E. "In family" adoptions   22–056
     F. Open adoption   22–061
 VI. Orders in adoption proceedings   22–063
     A. Adoption, special guardianship or residence?   22–064
     B. Contact orders   22–066
     C. Other conditions   22–067
     D. Interim orders   22–068
     E. Restrictions on making orders   22–069
VII. Surrogacy   22–070
     A. Introduction   22–070
     B. Surrogacy and adoption   22–072
     C. Enforceability of surrogacy contracts   22–073
     D. Regulation of surrogacy practice   22–074
     E. Acquisition of the status of parent   22–076
     F. Knowledge of origins   22–080

                                                                         page
Index   897

TABLE OF CASES

A, Re (1979) 10 Fam.Law 114 18–012
A, Re [2007] EWCA Civ 1383 18–036
A (A Child) (Adoption: Agreement: Procedure), Re; sub nom. A (A Child) (Adoption:
    Consent), Re [2001] 2 F.L.R. 455; [2001] 2 F.C.R. 174; [2001] Fam. Law 648, CA (Civ
    Div) 22–029, 22–039
A (A Child) (Adoption of a Russian Child), Re [2000] 1 F.L.R. 539; [2000] 1 F.C.R. 673;
    [2000] Fam. Law 596; (2000) 164 J.P.N. 644, Fam Div 22–030, 22–032
A (A Child) (Contact: Risk of Violence), Re [2005] EWHC 851; [2006] 1 F.L.R. 283;
    [2005] Fam. Law 939, Fam Div 18–042
A (A Child) (Contact: Separate Representation), Re; sub nom. A (A Child) (Separate
    Representation in Contact Proceedings), Re; A v A [2001] 1 F.L.R. 715; [2001] 2
    F.C.R. 55, CA (Civ Div) 16–020, 18–008
A (A Child) (Non Accidental Injury: Medical Evidence), Re; sub nom. A (A Child) (Retinal
    Haemorrhages: Non Accidental Injury), Re [2001] 2 F.L.R. 657; [2001] 3 F.C.R. 262;
    [2001] Fam. Law 735, Fam Div 21–022
A (A Minor) (Adoption: Contact Order), Re [1993] 2 F.L.R. 645, CA (Civ Div) 21–075
A (A Minor) (Adoption: Parental Consent), Re; sub nom. A (A Minor) (Wardship:
    Adoption: Custodianship) [1987] 1 W.L.R. 153; [1987] 2 All E.R. 81; (1987) 151 J.P.
    458; [1987] 2 F.L.R. 184; [1987] 1 F.C.R. 9; [1987] Fam. Law 232; (1987) 151 J.P.N.
    191; (1987) 84 L.S.G. 820; (1987) 131 S.J. 194, CA (Civ Div) 22–065, 22–069
A (A Minor) (Child of the Family), Re [1998] 1 F.L.R. 347; [1998] 1 F.C.R. 458; [1998]
    Fam. Law 14, CA (Civ Div) 15–039, 18–034
A (A Minor) (Children: 1959 UN Declaration), Re; sub nom. A (A Minor) (Residence
    Order), Re [1998] 1 F.L.R. 354; [1998] 2 F.C.R. 633; [1998] Fam. Law 72, CA (Civ
    Div) 18–012, 19–006, 19–010
A (A Minor) (Contact Application: Grandparent), Re; sub nom. A (Section 8 Order:
    Grandparent Application), Re; A (A Minor) (Grandparent: Contact), Re [1995] 2
    F.L.R. 153; [1996] 1 F.C.R. 467; [1995] Fam. Law 540; (1995) 159 J.P.N. 812, CA
    (Civ Div) 17–024, 18–020
A (A Minor) (Cultural Background), Re [1987] 2 F.L.R. 429; [1988] Fam. Law 65, Fam
    Div 19–020
A (A Minor) (Paternity: Refusal of Blood Test), Re [1994] 2 F.L.R. 463; [1994] Fam. Law
    622, CA (Civ Div) 15–008, 17–004
A (A Minor) (Supervision Order: Extension), Re [1995] 1 W.L.R. 482; [1995] 3 All E.R.
    401; [1995] 1 F.L.R. 335; [1995] 2 F.C.R. 114; 93 L.G.R. 119; [1995] Fam. Law 178;
    (1995) 159 J.P.N. 230; (1994) 138 S.J.L.B. 228, CA (Civ Div) 21–042
A (A Minor) (Wardship: Police Caution), Re; sub nom. A (A Minor) (Wardship: Criminal
    Proceedings), Re [1989] Fam. 103; [1989] 3 W.L.R. 900; [1989] 3 All E.R. 610; [1990]
    1 F.L.R. 86; [1990] F.C.R. 385; [1990] Fam. Law 63; (1990) 154 J.P.N. 266; (1989)
    86(40) L.S.G. 47, Fam Div 18–052
A (Adoption: Placement Outside Jurisdiction), Re; sub nom. B v Birmingham City Council;
    B (Children) (Adoption: Removal from Jurisdiction), Re [2004] EWCA Civ 515;
    [2005] Fam. 105; [2004] 3 W.L.R. 1207; [2004] 2 F.L.R. 337; [2004] 2 F.C.R. 129;
    [2004] Fam. Law 560, CA (Civ Div) 22–055
A (Application for Leave), Re [1998] 1 F.L.R. 1; [1999] 1 F.C.R. 127; [1998] Fam. Law 71,
    CA (Civ Div) 18–028
A (Care Discharge Application by Child), Re [1995] 1 F.L.R. 599 .... 16–022, 21–045, 21–073
A (Children) (Conjoined Twins: Medical Treatment) (No.1), Re; sub nom. A (Children)
    (Conjoined Twins: Surgical Separation), Re [2001] Fam. 147; [2001] 2 W.L.R. 480;
    [2000] 4 All E.R. 961; [2001] 1 F.L.R. 1; [2000] 3 F.C.R. 577; [2000] H.R.L.R. 721;
    [2001] U.K.H.R.R. 1; 9 B.H.R.C. 261; [2000] Lloyd's Rep. Med. 425; (2001) 57
    B.M.L.R. 1; [2001] Crim. L.R. 400; [2001] Fam. Law 18; (2000) 150 N.L.J. 1453, CA
    (Civ Div) 18–049, 19–001
A (Children) (Conjoined Twins: Medical Treatment) (No.2), Re [2001] 1 F.L.R. 267; [2001]
    1 F.C.R. 313; [2001] Fam. Law 100, CA (Civ Div) 17–021

A (Children) (Contact: Expert Evidence), Re; sub nom. A (Children) (Family Proceedings: Expert Witnesses), Re [2001] 1 F.L.R. 723; (2001) 98(16) L.S.G. 32; (2001) 151 N.L.J. 224, Fam Div 18–042
A (Children) (Specific Issue Order: Parental Dispute), Re; sub nom. A (Children) (Education), Re [2001] 1 F.L.R. 121; [2001] 1 F.C.R. 210; [2001] Fam. Law 22, CA (Civ Div) 17–016, 18–022
A (Contact: Witness Protection Scheme), Re; sub nom. ZA v UZ [2005] EWHC 2189; [2006] 2 F.L.R. 551; [2006] Fam. Law 528, Fam Div 17–024, 18–019, 19–001, 19–008
A (Habitual Residence: Wardship), Re [2007] 1 F.L.R. 1589, Fam Div 18–051
A (Minors) (Abduction: Custody Rights), Re [1992] Fam. 106; [1992] 2 W.L.R. 536; [1992] 1 All E.R. 929; [1992] 2 F.L.R. 14; [1992] 2 F.C.R. 9; [1992] Fam. Law 381, CA (Civ Div) 20–019
A (Minors) (Abduction: Custody Rights) (No.2), Re; sub nom. A (Minors) (Abduction: Acquiescence) (No.2), Re [1993] Fam. 1; [1992] 3 W.L.R. 538; [1993] 1 All E.R. 272; [1993] 1 F.L.R. 396; [1993] Fam. Law 196, CA (Civ Div) 20–018
A (Placement of Child in Contravention of Adoption Act 1976 s.11), Re [2005] 2 F.L.R. 727, Fam Div 21–014
A (Section 8 Order: Grandparent Application), Re. *See* A (A Minor) (Contact Application: Grandparent), Re
A (Security for Return to Jurisdiction), Re; sub nom. A (A Minor) (Holiday in a Non-Convention Country) [1999] 2 F.L.R. 1, Fam Div 20–006
A v A; sub nom. NA v MA [2006] EWHC 2900 (Fam); [2007] 1 F.L.R. 1760; [2007] Fam. Law 295, Fam Div 13–008, 13–009
A v A [2007] EWHC 99 (Fam); [2007] 2 F.L.R. 467; [2007] Fam. Law 791, Fam Div 13–001, 13–066
A v A (A Minor) (Financial Provision) [1994] 1 F.L.R. 657; [1995] 1 F.C.R. 309; [1994] Fam. Law 368, Fam Div 13–018, 15–046, 15–051
A v A (Abduction: Jurisdiction). *See* N (Child Abduction: Jurisdiction)
A v A (Ancillary Relief: Property Division) [2006] 2 F.L.R. 115 13–087
A v A (Children: Shared Residence Order) [1994] 1 F.L.R. 669; [1995] 1 F.C.R. 91; [1994] Fam. Law 431; (1994) 158 J.P.N. 817, CA (Civ Div) 19–025
A v A (Costs Appeal) [1996] 1 F.L.R. 14; [1996] 1 F.C.R. 186; [1996] Fam. Law 79, Fam Div 13–012
A v A (Elderly Applicant: Lump Sum); sub nom. A v A (Duxbury Calculations) [1999] 2 F.L.R. 969; [1999] 3 F.C.R. 433; [1999] Fam. Law 752, Fam Div 13–072, 13–078
A v A (Family: Unborn Child); sub nom. A v A (Child of the Family) [1974] Fam. 6; [1974] 2 W.L.R. 106; [1974] 1 All E.R. 755; (1973) 4 Fam. Law 18; (1973) 118 S.J. 77, Fam Div 15–039, 18–034
A v A (Financial Provision) [1998] 2 F.L.R. 180; [1998] 3 F.C.R. 421; [1998] Fam. Law 393, Fam Div 13–067, 13–078
A v A (Forum Conveniens) [1999] 1 F.L.R. 1; [1999] 3 F.C.R. 376; [1998] Fam. Law 735, Fam Div 20–010
A v A (Maintenance Pending Suit: Provision for Legal Fees); sub nom. A v A (Maintenance Pending Suit: Provision for Legal Costs) [2001] 1 W.L.R. 605; [2001] 1 F.L.R. 377; [2001] 1 F.C.R. 226; [2001] Fam. Law 96; (2000) 97(44) L.S.G. 45; (2000) 144 S.J.L.B. 273, Fam Div 13–037
A v A (No.2) [2008] F.L.R. 206; [2007] F.L.R. 206 13–012
A v A (Shared Residence and Contact); sub nom. A v A (Children: Shared Residence Order) [2004] EWHC 142; [2004] 1 F.L.R. 1195; [2004] 3 F.C.R. 201; [2004] Fam. Law 416, Fam Div 18–017, 18–020, 18–055
A v B (Damages: Paternity) [2007] EWHC 1246 (QB); [2007] 2 F.L.R. 1051; [2007] 3 F.C.R. 861; [2007] Fam. Law 909; (2007) 104(16) L.S.G. 26, QBD 15–009, 17–006
A v B (Financial Relief: Agreements; sub nom. A v B (Ancillary Relief: Separation Agreement) [2005] EWHC 314; [2005] 2 F.L.R. 730, Fam Div 13–008, 13–009
A v Berkshire CC [1989] 1 F.L.R. 273; [1989] F.C.R. 184, CA (Civ Div) 18–051
A v Essex CC [2003] EWCA Civ 1848; [2004] 1 W.L.R. 1881; [2004] 1 F.L.R. 749; [2004] 1 F.C.R. 660; [2004] B.L.G.R. 587; (2004) 7 C.C.L. Rep. 98; [2004] Fam. Law 238; (2004) 148 S.J.L.B. 27, CA (Civ Div) 22–021
A v Hoare; H v Suffolk CC; X v Wandsworth LBC [2006] EWCA Civ 395; [2006] 1 W.L.R. 2320; [2006] 2 F.L.R. 727; [2006] 3 F.C.R. 673; [2006] Fam. Law 533; (2006) 103(18) L.S.G. 29; (2006) 150 S.J.L.B. 536, CA (Civ Div) 21–066
A v J (Nullity) [1989] 1 F.L.R. 110; [1989] Fam. Law 63 2–032

A v L (Contact) [1998] 1 F.L.R. 361; [1998] 2 F.C.R. 204; [1998] Fam. Law 137, Fam
Div 18–019
A v L (Jurisdiction: Brussels II); sub nom. A v C (Jurisdiction: Brussels II) [2002] 1 F.L.R.
1042; [2002] Fam. Law 518, Fam Div 18–051
A v Liverpool City Council [1982] A.C. 363; [1981] 2 W.L.R. 948; [1981] 2 All E.R. 385;
79 L.G.R. 621; (1981) 125 S.J. 396, HL 16–016, 18–035, 18–052, 19–002, 19–023, 21–067,
21–080, 21–085
A v M [2005] EWHC 1721, Fam Div 15–040
A v N (Committal: Refusal of Contact); sub nom. N (A Minor), Re [1997] 1 F.L.R. 533;
[1997] 2 F.C.R. 475; [1997] Fam. Law 233; (1997) 161 J.P.N. 698, CA (Civ Div) 18–057,
18–058
A v United Kingdom [1998] 2 F.L.R. 959; [1998] 3 F.C.R. 597; (1999) 27 E.H.R.R. 611;
5 B.H.R.C. 137; [1998] Crim. L.R. 892; [1998] H.R.C.D. 870; [1998] Fam. Law 733,
ECHR 16–017, 17–017
A v Y (Child's Surname) [1999] 2 F.L.R. 5; [1999] 1 F.C.R. 577; [1999] Fam. Law 443,
Fam Div 18–058
A and B (Minors) (No.2), Re [1995] 1 F.L.R. 351; [1995] 3 F.C.R. 449; [1995] Fam. Law
179, Fam Div 18–008, 21–065
A and D (Non Accidental Injury: Subdural Haematomas), Re [2002] 1 F.L.R. 337; [2002]
Fam. Law 266, Fam Div 21–032
A and W (Minors) (Residence Order: Leave to Apply), Re; sub nom. A (Minors) (Residence
Order), Re [1992] Fam. 182; [1992] 3 W.L.R. 422; [1992] 3 All E.R. 872; [1992] 2
F.L.R. 154; 91 L.G.R. 401; [1992] Fam. Law 439, CA (Civ Div) 18–035, 18–036, 19–002
A Council v B [2007] EWHC 2395 21–036
A Local Authority (Inquiry: Restraint on Publication), Re; sub nom. Local Authority v
Health Authority (Disclosure: Restriction on Publication) [2003] EWHC 2746; [2004]
Fam. 96; [2004] 2 W.L.R. 926; [2004] 1 All E.R. 480; [2004] 1 F.L.R. 541; [2004] 1
F.C.R. 113; [2004] B.L.G.R. 117; (2004) 7 C.C.L. Rep. 426; (2004) 76 B.M.L.R. 210;
[2004] Fam. Law 179; (2004) 101(3) L.S.G. 33, Fam Div 18–053
A Local Authority v D (Chief Constable of Thames Valley Police Intervening) [2006] 2
F.L.R. 1053, Fam Div 21–038
A Local Authority v K [2007] 2 F.L.R. 914, Fam Div 21–038
AB (A Child) (Care Proceedings: Disclosure of Medical Evidence to Police), Re; sub nom.
A Chief Constable v A County Council [2002] EWHC 2198; [2003] 1 F.L.R. 579;
[2003] 2 F.C.R. 385; [2003] Fam. Law 152, Fam Div 21–037
AB (Care Proceedings: Service on Husband Ignorant of Child's Existence), Re. *See* B (A
Child) (Parentage: Knowledge of Proceedings), Re
A-J (Adoption or Special Guardianship), Re [2007] 1 F.L.R. 507, CA 18–028, 22–005, 22–033,
22–060, 22–064, 22–065
A-K (Minors) (Foreign Passport: Jurisdiction), Re; sub nom. A-K (Minors) (Contact), Re
[1997] 2 F.L.R. 569; [1997] 2 F.C.R. 563; [1997] Fam. Law 652, CA (Civ Div) 20–003
AS (Secure Accommodation Order), Re [1999] 1 F.L.R. 103; [1999] 2 F.C.R. 749; [1999]
Fam. Law 20; (2000) 164 J.P.N. 27, Fam Div 18–042
AW (Adoption Application), Re 145 [1993] 1 F.L.R. 62; [1992] Fam. Law 539 22–054
AZ (A Minor) (Abduction: Acquiescence), Re [1993] 1 F.L.R. 682; [1993] 1 F.C.R. 733, CA
(Civ Div) 20–019
Abbey National Bank Plc v Stringer [2006] EWCA Civ 338; [2006] 2 P. & C.R. DG15, CA
(Civ Div) 5–015, 5–022, 5–055
Abbey National Building Society v Cann [1991] 1 A.C. 56; [1990] 2 W.L.R. 833; [1990] 1
All E.R. 1085; [1990] 2 F.L.R. 122; (1990) 22 H.L.R. 360; (1990) 60 P. & C.R. 278;
(1990) 87(17) L.S.G. 32; (1990) 140 N.L.J. 477, HL 5–050, 5–051
Abbott v Abbott [2007] UKPC 53 .... 5–012, 5–018, 5–022, 5–023, 5–029
Abrahams v Trustee in Bankruptcy of Abrahams; sub nom. Abrahams v Abrahams Trustee
in Bankruptcy [1999] B.P.I.R. 637; [2000] W.T.L.R. 593; (1999) 96(31) L.S.G. 38, Ch
D 5–062
Abram (Deceased), Re [1996] 2 F.L.R. 379; [1997] 2 F.C.R. 85; [1997] B.P.I.R. 1; [1996]
Fam. Law 666, Ch D7–014, 7–022, 7–031
Ackerman v Ackerman [1972] Fam. 225; [1972] 2 W.L.R. 1253; [1972] 2 All E.R. 420;
(1972) 116 S.J. 220, CA (Civ Div) 13–082
Adams v Adams [1984] F.L.R. 768 19–017
Adams v Palmer, 51 Maine 480 (1863) A–001

Adoption Application (Non-Patrial: Breach of Procedures), Re [1993] Fam. 125; [1993] 2
W.L.R. 110; [1993] 1 F.L.R. 947; [1993] Fam. Law 275, Fam Div 22–002
Agar-Ellis (No.2), Re; sub nom. Agar-Ellis v Lascelles (No.2) (1883) L.R. 24 Ch. D. 317,
CA 16–003, 17–014
Aggett v Aggett [1962] 1 W.L.R. 183; [1962] 1 All E.R. 190, CA 13–018
Ahmed v Kendrick [1988] 2 F.L.R. 22; (1988) 56 P. & C.R. 120, CA (Civ Div) 5–043
Akintola v Akintola (Transfer of Tenancy) [2001] EWCA Civ 1989; [2002] 1 F.L.R. 701;
[2002] 1 F.C.R. 453; [2002] Fam. Law 263, CA (Civ Div) 13–060, 13–071, 13–117, 13–118
Akram v Akram, 1979 S.L.T. (Notes) 87, OH 2–035
Al Habtoor v Fotheringham [2001] 1 F.L.R. 951 .... 18–051, 20–015
Alawiye v Mahmood (t/a Amsons) [2006] EWHC 277; [2007] 1 W.L.R. 79; [2006] 3 All
E.R. 668, Ch D 14–006
Alhaji Mohamed v Knott; sub nom. M v Knott; Mohamed v Knott [1969] 1 Q.B. 1; [1968]
2 W.L.R. 1446; [1968] 2 All E.R. 563; (1968) 132 J.P. 349; (1968) 112 S.J. 332, DC 2–012
Ali v Khan [2002] EWCA Civ 974; (2002–03) 5 I.T.E.L.R. 232; [2002] 30 E.G. 131 (C.S.);
[2002] 2 P. & C.R. DG19, CA (Civ Div) 5–016
Ali v Lord Grey School Governors; sub nom. A v Headteacher and Governors of Lord Grey
School [2006] UKHL 14; [2006] 2 A.C. 363; [2006] 2 W.L.R. 690; [2006] 2 All E.R.
457; [2006] H.R.L.R. 20; [2006] U.K.H.R.R. 591; 20 B.H.R.C. 295; [2006] E.L.R.
223, HL 16–023
Al-Kandari v JR Brown & Co [1988] Q.B. 665; [1988] 2 W.L.R. 671; [1988] 1 All E.R. 833;
[1988] Fam. Law 382; (1988) 85(14) L.S.G. 50; (1988) 138 N.L.J. Rep. 62; (1988) 132
S.J. 462, CA (Civ Div) 20–002
Al-Khatib v Masry [2004] EWCA Civ 1353; [2005] 1 F.L.R. 381; [2004] 3 F.C.R. 573, CA
(Civ Div) 13–064, 13–066, 13–085, 18–045, 20–005
Allcard v Skinner (1887) L.R. 36 Ch. D. 145, CA 5–055
Alliance & Leicester Plc v Slayford [2004] EWHC 1908, Ch D 5–049
Allied Irish Bank Plc v Byrne [1995] 2 F.L.R. 325; [1995] 1 F.C.R. 430; [1995] Fam. Law
609, Ch D 5–054, 5–056
Allsop v Allsop (1980) 11 Fam. Law 18; (1980) 124 S.J. 710, CA (Civ Div) 3–028
Amalgamated Investment & Property Co Ltd (In Liquidation) v Texas Commerce
International Bank Ltd [1982] Q.B. 84; [1981] 3 W.L.R. 565; [1981] 3 All E.R. 577;
[1982] 1 Lloyd's Rep. 27; [1981] Com. L.R. 236; (1981) 125 S.J. 623, CA (Civ Div) ... 5–034
Amey v Amey [1992] 2 F.L.R. 89; [1992] F.C.R. 289 .... 13–004, 13–103
Ampthill Peerage, The [1977] A.C. 547; [1976] 2 W.L.R. 777; [1976] 2 All E.R. 411; (1976)
120 S.J. 367, HL A–001, 10–023, 17–003, 17–004, 17–012
Andersson (Margareta) v Sweden (A/226) (1992) 14 E.H.R.R. 615, ECHR 21–070, 21–074
Andrews v Salt (1872–73) L.R. 8 Ch. App. 622, CA in Chancery 17–018
Ansah v Ansah [1977] Fam. 138; [1977] 2 W.L.R. 760; [1977] 2 All E.R. 638; (1977) 121
S.J. 118, CA (Civ Div) 9–009
Appleton v Appleton [1965] 1 W.L.R. 25; [1965] 1 All E.R. 44; (1964) 108 S.J. 919, CA 3–007
Aqualina v Aqualina [2004] EWCA Civ 504 9–035
Araghinchi v Araghinchi [1997] 2 F.L.R. 142 13–064
Archer v Archer [1999] 1 F.L.R. 327; [1999] 2 F.C.R. 158; [1999] Fam. Law 141; (1998)
95(46) L.S.G. 34, CA (Civ Div) 10–043
Argar v Holdsworth (1758) 2 Lee 515 1–035
Ash v Ash [1972] Fam. 135; [1972] 2 W.L.R. 347; [1972] 1 All E.R. 582; (1971) 115 S.J.
911, Fam Div 10–024
Ashingdane v United Kingdom (A/93); sub nom. Ashingdane v United Kingdom (8225/78)
(1985) 7 E.H.R.R. 528, ECHR 18–035
Askew-Page v Page [2001] Fam. Law 794, CC (Bath) 15–038, 15–043, 15–052
Associated Provincial Picture Houses Ltd v Wednesbury Corp 888 [1948] 1 K.B. 223;
[1947] 2 All E.R. 680; 63 T.L.R. 623; (1948) 112 J.P. 55; 45 L.G.R. 635; [1948] L.J.R.
190; 177 L.T. 641; (1948) 92 S.J. 26, CA 21–085
Atkinson v Atkinson [1988] Fam. 93; [1988] 2 W.L.R. 204; [1988] 2 F.L.R. 353; [1988]
F.C.R. 356; [1988] Fam. Law 392; (1988) 152 J.P.N. 126; (1988) 132 S.J. 158, CA (Civ
Div) 9–029, 13–068, 13–098
Atkinson v Atkinson; sub nom. A v A (Financial Provision: Variation) [1996] 1 F.L.R. 51;
[1995] 3 F.C.R. 788; [1996] Fam. Law 18; (1995) 159 J.P.N. 813, CA (Civ Div);
affirming; [1995] 2 F.L.R. 356; [1995] 2 F.C.R. 353; [1995] Fam. Law 604, Fam Div ... 13–021
Attar v Attar (No.1) (Discovery) [1985] Fam. Law 252, Fam Div 13–076

Attorney General's Reference (No.1 of 1989), Re [1989] 1 W.L.R. 1117; [1989] 3 All E.R. 571; (1990) 90 Cr. App. R. 141; (1989) 11 Cr. App. R. (S.) 409; [1989] Crim. L.R. 923, CA (Crim Div) 21–062

Austin v Keele [1987] A.L.J.R. 605 5–037

Austin-Fell v Austin-Fell [1990] Fam. 172; [1990] 3 W.L.R. 33; [1990] 2 All E.R. 455; [1989] 2 F.L.R. 497; [1990] F.C.R. 743; [1989] Fam. Law 437; (1989) 139 N.L.J. 1113, Fam Div 14–008

Avis v Turner [2007] EWCA Civ 748 5–058

B, Re [1988] 1 Q.B. 12 22–032

B (A Child) (Adoption Order), Re [2001] EWCA Civ 347; [2001] 2 F.L.R. 26; [2001] 2 F.C.R. 89; [2001] Fam. Law 492; (2001) 165 J.P.N. 565, CA (Civ Div) 22–064, 22–065

B (A Child) (Child Support: Reduction of Contact), Re [2006] EWCA Civ 1574; [2007] 1 F.L.R. 1949; [2007] Fam. Law 114; (2006) 103(47) L.S.G. 28; (2006) 150 S.J.L.B. 1569, CA (Civ Div) 5–018

B (A Child) (Parentage: Knowledge of Proceedings), Re; sub nom. B (A Child) (Adoption Proceedings: Joinder of Presumed Father), Re; AB (Care Proceedings: Service on Husband Ignorant of Child's Existence), Re [2003] EWCA Civ 1842; [2004] 1 F.L.R. 527; [2004] 1 F.C.R. 473; [2004] Fam. Law 178, CA (Civ Div) 17–012, 18–041, 21–054

B (A Child) (Property Transfer), Re; sub nom. B (A Minor) (Consent Order: Property Transfer), Re [1999] 2 F.L.R. 418; [1999] 3 F.C.R. 266; [1999] Fam. Law 535, CA (Civ Div) 15–043

B (A Child) (Section 91(14) Order: Duration), Re [2003] EWCA Civ 1966; [2004] 1 F.L.R. 871; [2004] Fam. Law 242, CA (Civ Div) 18–028, 19–020

B (A Child) (Sexual Abuse: Expert's Report), Re; sub nom. B (A Child) (Sexual Abuse: Independent Expert), Re [2000] 1 F.L.R. 871; [2000] 2 F.C.R. 8; [2000] Fam. Law 479; (2000) 164 J.P.N. 624, CA (Civ Div) 21–065

B (A Child) (Split Hearings: Jurisdiction), Re [2000] 1 W.L.R. 790; [2000] 1 F.L.R. 334; [2000] 1 F.C.R. 297; [2000] Fam. Law 320; (2000) 164 J.P.N. 441; (1999) 96(48) L.S.G. 39; (2000) 144 S.J.L.B. 23, CA (Civ Div) 19–025, 21–030, 21–053

B (A Minor) (Adoption Application), Re [1995] 1 F.L.R. 895; [1995] 2 F.C.R. 749; [1995] Fam. Law 400, Fam Div 17–014, 19–020

B (A Minor) (Adoption Order: Nationality), Re [1999] 2 A.C. 136; [1999] 2 W.L.R. 714; [1999] 2 All E.R. 576; [1999] 1 F.L.R. 907; [1999] 1 F.C.R. 529; [1999] Imm. A.R. 277; [1999] I.N.L.R. 125; [1999] Fam. Law 374; (1999) 96(14) L.S.G. 32; (1999) 143 S.J.L.B. 105, HL 22–001, 22–007, 22–024

B (A Minor) (Adoption: Parental Rights), Re; sub nom. B (Adoption: Father's Objections), Re [1999] 2 F.L.R. 215; [1999] 3 F.C.R. 522; [1999] Fam. Law 440, CA (Civ Div) 22–059

B (A Minor) (Care Order: Criteria), Re; sub nom. B (Child: Interim Care Orders) Re [1993] 1 F.L.R. 815; [1993] 1 F.C.R. 565; [1993] Fam. Law 335 .... 21–034, 21–052

B (A Minor) (Child Abduction: Consent), Re [1994] 2 F.L.R. 249; [1995] 2 F.C.R. 505; [1994] Fam. Law 606; (1994) 91(23) L.S.G. 27; (1994) 138 S.J.L.B. 109, CA (Civ Div) 20–017

B (A Minor) (Contact: Stepfather's Opposition), Re; sub nom. B (A Minor) (Contact: Stepfather's Hostility), Re [1997] 2 F.L.R. 579; [1998] 3 F.C.R. 289; [1997] Fam. Law 720, CA (Civ Div) 18–041, 19–021

B (A Minor) (Disclosure of Evidence), Re; sub nom. B (A Minor) (Confidential Evidence: Disclosure), Re [1993] Fam. 142; [1993] 2 W.L.R. 20; [1993] 1 All E.R. 931; [1993] 1 F.L.R. 191; [1992] 2 F.C.R. 617; [1993] Fam. Law 26, CA (Civ Div) 18–008

B (A Minor) (Secure Accommodation Order), Re [1995] 1 W.L.R. 232; [1994] 2 F.L.R. 707; [1995] 1 F.C.R. 142; [1994] Fam. Law 678; (1995) 159 J.P.N. 112, CA (Civ Div) ... 21–078

B (A Minor) (Supervision Order: Parental Undertaking), Re [1996] 1 W.L.R. 716; [1996] 1 F.L.R. 676; [1996] 3 F.C.R. 446; 94 L.G.R. 244; [1996] Fam. Law 267, CA (Civ Div) 21–013, 21–039, 21–042

B (A Minor) (Wardship: Medical Treatment), Re [1981] 1 W.L.R. 1421; 80 L.G.R. 107; (1981) 125 S.J. 608, CA (Civ Div) 18–051

B (A Minor) (Wardship: Sterilisation), Re [1988] A.C. 199; [1987] 2 W.L.R. 1213; [1987] 2 All E.R. 206; [1987] 2 F.L.R. 314; 86 L.G.R. 417; [1987] Fam. Law 419; (1987) 151 L.G. Rev. 650; (1987) 84 L.S.G. 1410; (1987) 137 N.L.J. 432; (1987) 131 S.J. 625, HL 17–022, 18–001, 18–030, 21–080

B (A Minor: Custody), Re [1991] 2 F.L.R. 405; [1991] F.C.R. 414; [1991] Fam. Law 305, CA (Civ Div) 19–002

B (Abduction: Children's Objections), Re; sub nom. B (Abduction: Views of Children), Re
[1998] 1 F.L.R. 667; [1998] 3 F.C.R. 260; [1998] Fam. Law 308, Fam Div 20–021
B (Adoption Order: Jurisdiction to Set Aside), Re; sub nom. B (Adoption: Setting Aside),
Re [1995] Fam. 239; [1995] 3 W.L.R. 40; [1995] 3 All E.R. 333; [1995] 2 F.L.R. 1;
[1995] 3 F.C.R. 671; [1995] Fam. Law 469; (1995) 92(27) L.S.G. 33; (1995) 139
S.J.L.B. 176, CA (Civ Div) 19–007, 21–009, 22–001, 22–009
B (Agreed Findings of Fact), Re; sub nom. B (Threshold Criteria: Agreed Facts), Re [1998]
2 F.L.R. 968; [1999] 2 F.C.R. 328; [1998] Fam. Law 583; (1999) 163 J.P.N. 994, CA
(Civ Div) 21–036
B (Appeal: Lack of Reasons), Re [2003] EWCA Civ 881; [2003] 2 F.L.R. 1035; [2003]
Fam. Law 716, CA (Civ Div) 19–026
B (Care Proceedings: Expert Witness), Re [2007] 2 F.L.R. 979, CA 21–038, 21–043, 21–055
B (Care Proceedings: Legal Representation), Re [2001] 1 F.L.R. 485; [2001] 1 F.C.R. 512;
[2001] Fam. Law 180, CA (Civ Div) 18–041, 21–056
B (Children) (Leave to Remove: Impact of Refusal), Re; sub nom. B (Children) (Parental
Contact: Relocation), Re; B (Children) (Termination of Contact), Re [2004] EWCA
Civ 956; [2005] 2 F.L.R. 239; [2005] 1 F.C.R. 480; [2005] Fam. Law 462, CA (Civ
Div) 19–025
B (Contact: Child Support), Re [2007] 1 F.L.R. 1949, CA 18–019
B (Contempt: Evidence), Re [1996] 1 F.L.R. 239 17–014
B (Deceased), Re; sub nom. Bouette v Rose [2000] Ch. 662; [2000] 2 W.L.R. 929; [2000]
1 All E.R. 665; [2000] 1 F.L.R. 363; [2000] 1 F.C.R. 385; [2000] W.T.L.R. 403; [2000]
Fam. Law 316; (2000) 150 N.L.J. 20, CA (Civ Div) 7–010, 7–016, 7–017, 7–019, 16–002
B (Disclosure to Other Parties), Re [2001] 2 F.L.R. 1017; [2002] 2 F.C.R. 32; [2001] Fam.
Law 798, Fam Div 21–037
B (L) (otherwise S) v B [1958] 1 W.L.R. 619; [1958] 2 All E.R. 76; (1958) 102 S.J. 421,
PDAD 2–026
B (Minors) (Abduction: Disclosure), Re; sub nom. B (Minors: Abduction), Re [1995] 1
F.L.R. 774; [1995] 2 F.C.R. 601; [1995] Fam. Law 398, CA (Civ Div) 20–002, 20–007
B (Minors) (Care Proceedings: Practice), Re; sub nom. CB and JB (Minors) (Care
Proceedings: Guidelines), Re [1999] 1 W.L.R. 238; [1998] 2 F.L.R. 211; [1998] 2
F.C.R. 313; [1998] Fam. Law 454, Fam Div 18–008, 21–058
B (Minors) (Change of Surname), Re [1996] 1 F.L.R. 791; [1996] 2 F.C.R. 304; [1996] Fam.
Law 346; (1996) 140 S.J.L.B. 28, CA (Civ Div) ... 16–005, 17–025, 18–021, 19–016, 19–018
B (Minors) (Contact), Re [1994] 2 F.L.R. 1; [1994] 2 F.C.R. 812; [1994] Fam. Law 491, CA
(Civ Div) 18–041
B (Minors) (Parentage), Re [1996] 2 F.L.R. 15; [1996] 3 F.C.R. 697; [1996] Fam. Law 536,
Fam Div 17–004, 22–072
B (Minors) (Residence Order), Re; sub nom. B (A Minor) (Residence Order: Ex parte), Re
[1992] Fam. 162; [1992] 3 W.L.R. 113; [1992] 3 All E.R. 867; [1992] 2 F.L.R. 1;
[1992] 1 F.C.R. 555; [1992] Fam. Law 384; (1992) 156 J.P.N. 410, CA (Civ Div) ... 20–009
B (Minors) (Residence Order: Leave to Appeal), Re [1998] 1 F.L.R. 520; [1998] 3 F.C.R.
351; [1998] Fam. Law 258, CA (Civ Div) 19–015, 19–017
B (Minors) (Termination of Contact: Paramount Consideration), Re; sub nom. B (Minors)
(Care: Contact: Local Authority's Plans), Re [1993] Fam. 301; [1993] 3 W.L.R. 63;
[1993] 3 All E.R. 542; [1993] 1 F.L.R. 543; [1993] 1 F.C.R. 363; 91 L.G.R. 311; [1993]
Fam. Law 291; (1993) 137 S.J.L.B. 13, CA (Civ Div) 19–010, 21–075
B (Minors) (Wardship: Power to Detain), Re [1994] 2 F.L.R. 479; [1994] 2 F.C.R. 1142;
[1994] Fam. Law 607, CA (Civ Div) 20–023
B (otherwise H) v B [1901] P. 39, PDAD 2–26
B (Residence Order: Leave to Appeal), Re [1998] 1 F.L.R. 502 19–025
B (Serious Injury: Standard of Proof), Re [2004] 2 F.L.R. 263, CA 21–036
B v Attorney General of New Zealand [2003] UKPC 61; [2003] 4 All E.R. 833; [2003]
Lloyd's Rep. Med. 527, PC (NZ) 22–015, 21–027
B v B [2007] EWHC 2472; [2008] Fam.Law. 111 13–104
B v B; sub nom. D v D [1955] P. 42; [1954] 3 W.L.R. 237; [1954] 2 All E.R. 598; (1954)
98 S.J. 474, PDAD 2–025
B v B (A Minor) (Residence Order) [1992] 2 F.L.R. 327; [1993] 1 F.C.R. 211; [1992] Fam.
Law 490, Fam Div 18–005
B v B (Adult Student: Liability to Support); sub nom. B v B (Financial Provision for Child)
[1998] 1 F.L.R. 373; [1998] 1 F.C.R. 49; [1998] Fam. Law 131, CA (Civ Div) ...15–045, 17–028

B v B (Children: Periodical Payments); sub nom. B v B (Periodical Payments: Variation) [1995] 1 W.L.R. 440; [1995] 1 F.L.R. 459; [1995] 1 F.C.R. 763; [1995] Fam. Law 233; (1995) 159 J.P.N. 194; (1995) 139 S.J.L.B. 24, Fam Div 3–017, 13–068, 15–038

B v B (Consent Order: Variation) [1995] 1 F.L.R. 9; [1995] Fam. Law 70, Fam Div 13–008, 13–009, 13–067, 13–098

B v B (Custody of Child) [1985] F.L.R. 166 19–006

B v B (Financial Provision: Leave to Appeal) [1994] 1 F.L.R. 219; [1994] 1 F.C.R. 885; [1994] Fam. Law 187, Fam Div 13–103, 13–104

B v B (Financial Provision: Welfare of Child and Conduct) [2002] 1 F.L.R. 555; [2002] Fam. Law 173, Fam Div 13–044, 13–058, 13–084, 13–111, 13–116

B v B (Financial Provisions) [1982] 3 F.L.R. 298 .... 13–014, 13–072

B v B (Minors) (Residence and Care Disputes) [1994] 2 F.L.R. 489; [1994] 2 F.C.R. 667; [1994] Fam. Law 613; (1994) 91(21) L.S.G. 40; (1994) 138 S.J.L.B. 119, CA (Civ Div) 19–017, 19–017

B v B (Occupation Order) [1999] 1 F.L.R. 715; [1999] 2 F.C.R. 251; (1999) 31 H.L.R. 1059; [1999] Fam. Law 208, CA (Civ Div) 9–018, 19–002

B v B (Residence: Condition Limiting Geographic Area) [2004] 2 F.L.R. 979; [2004] Fam. Law 651, Fam Div 18–021

B v B (Residence Order: Reasons for Decision); sub nom. B (A Minor) (Residence Order: Reasons), Re [1997] 2 F.L.R. 602; [1998] 1 F.C.R. 409; [1997] Fam. Law 792; (1998) 162 J.P.N. 283, CA (Civ Div) 19–014, 19–026

B v B (Residence Orders: Restricting Applications); sub nom. B v B (Child Orders: Restricting Applications) [1997] 1 F.L.R. 139; [1997] 2 F.C.R. 518; [1997] Fam. Law 236, CA (Civ Div) 18–028

B v C (Maintenance: Enforcement of Arrears) [1995] 1 F.L.R. 467; [1995] 2 F.C.R. 678; [1995] Fam. Law 243, Fam Div 14–002, 14–003

B v H (Habitual Residence: Wardship); sub nom. B v H (Children) (Habitual Residence) [2002] 1 F.L.R. 388; [2002] 2 F.C.R. 329; [2002] Fam. Law 101, Fam Div .. 18–051, 20–015

B v K (Child Abduction) [1993] 1 F.C.R. 382; [1993] Fam. Law 17 20–020

B v M (1852) 2 Rob. Ecc. 580 2–027

B v Miller & Co [1996] 2 F.L.R. 23; [1996] 3 F.C.R. 435, QBD 13–007, 13–008, 13–064

B v P (Adoption by Unmarried Father); sub nom. B (A Child) (Adoption: Natural Parent), Re; B (A Child) (Sole Adoption by Unmarried Parent), Re; B (Adoption by Unmarried Father), Re; B (A Child) v RP; B (A Child) (Adoption by One Natural Parent to the Exclusion of Other), Re [2001] UKHL 70; [2002] 1 W.L.R. 258; [2002] 1 All E.R. 641; [2002] 1 F.L.R. 196; [2002] 1 F.C.R. 150; 11 B.H.R.C. 702; [2002] Fam. Law 168, HL 19–004, 19–022, 22–002, 22–033, 22–034, 22–057

B v Secretary of State for the Home Department [2006] EWCA Civ 1267; (2006) 150 S.J.L.B. 1189, CA (Civ Div) 22–015

B v Secretary of State for Social Security Ex p. Biggin; sub nom. Biggin v Secretary of State for Social Security; R. v Secretary of State for Social Security Ex p. Joint Council for the Welfare of Immigrants [1995] 1 F.L.R. 851; [1995] 2 F.C.R. 595; [1995] C.O.D. 405; (1995) 159 J.P.N. 424, Fam Div 15–026

B v United Kingdom (36337/97); P v United Kingdom (35974/97) [2001] 2 F.L.R. 261; [2001] 2 F.C.R. 221; (2002) 34 E.H.R.R. 19; 11 B.H.R.C. 667; [2001] Fam. Law 506, ECHR 18–008, 18–041, 18–043

B v United Kingdom [2000] 1 F.L.R. 1; [2000] 1 F.C.R. 289; [2000] Fam. Law 88, ECHR 17–035, 20–017, 20–025

B v United Kingdom (36536/02) [2006] 1 F.L.R. 35; [2005] 3 F.C.R. 353; (2006) 42 E.H.R.R. 11; 19 B.H.R.C. 430; [2005] Fam. Law 943, ECHR 22–008

B and L v United Kingdom [2006] 1 F.L.R. 35 2–010

B-J (A Child) (Non Molestation Order: Power of Arrest), Re [2001] Fam. 415; [2001] 2 W.L.R. 1660; [2001] 1 All E.R. 235; [2000] 2 F.L.R. 443; [2000] 2 F.C.R. 599; [2000] Fam. Law 807, CA (Civ Div) 9–032

BM (A Minor) (Wardship: Jurisdiction), Re [1993] 1 F.L.R. 979; [1993] 2 F.C.R. 388; [1993] Fam. Law 516 18–051

B-T v B-T (Divorce: Procedure) [1990] 2 F.L.R. 1; [1990] F.C.R. 654; [1990] Fam. Law 294 .... 13–007, 13–107

Bailey (A Bankrupt), Re; sub nom. Bankrupt (No.25 of 1975), Re; Bailey v Trustee of the Property of the Bankrupt [1977] 1 W.L.R. 278; [1977] 2 All E.R. 26; (1976) 120 S.J. 753, DC 5–059

Bainbrigge v Browne (1880–81) L.R. 18 Ch. D. 188, Ch D 5–055

Baker v Baker [1993] 2 F.L.R. 247; (1993) 25 H.L.R. 408; [1993] E.G. 35 (C.S.); (1993) 137 S.J.L.B. 60; [1993] N.P.C. 32, CA (Civ Div) 5–035, 5–036
Baker v Baker [1995] 2 F.L.R. 829; [1996] 1 F.C.R. 567; [1996] Fam. Law 80, CA (Civ Div) 13–066
Balfour v Balfour [1919] 2 K.B. 571, CA 5–005
Banco Exterior Internacional v Mann 1551 [1995] 1 All E.R. 936; [1995] 1 F.L.R. 602; [1995] 2 F.C.R. 282; (1995) 27 H.L.R. 329; (1995) 145 N.L.J. 179; [1994] N.P.C. 150, CA (Civ Div) 3–013
Banik v Banik (No.1) [1973] 1 W.L.R. 860; [1973] 3 All E.R. 45; (1973) 117 S.J. 507, CA (Civ Div) 10–043, 10–044
Bank Melli Iran v Samadi-Rad [1995] 2 F.L.R. 367; [1995] 3 F.C.R. 735; [1995] Fam. Law 610; [1995] N.P.C. 76, CA (Civ Div) 5–054, 5–056
Bank of Baroda v Dhillon [1998] 1 F.L.R. 524; [1998] 1 F.C.R. 489; (1998) 30 H.L.R. 845; [1998] Fam. Law 138; [1997] N.P.C. 145, CA (Civ Div) 5–049
Bank of Credit and Commerce International SA v Aboody [1990] 1 Q.B. 923; [1989] 2 W.L.R. 759; [1992] 4 All E.R. 955; [1990] 1 F.L.R. 354; [1989] C.C.L.R. 63; [1989] Fam. Law 435; (1988) 132 S.J. 1754, CA (Civ Div) 3–028, 5–055
Bank of Cyprus (London) Ltd v Markou [1999] 2 All E.R. 707; [1999] 2 F.L.R. 17; (1999) 78 P. & C.R. 208; [1999] Fam. Law 385; [1999] E.G. 13 (C.S.); (1999) 96(6) L.S.G. 36, Ch D 5–054, 5–056
Bank of Ireland Home Mortgages Ltd v Bell [2001] 2 All E.R. (Comm) 920; [2001] 2 F.L.R. 809; [2001] 3 F.C.R. 134; [2001] B.P.I.R. 429; [2001] Fam. Law 805; [2000] E.G. 151 (C.S.), CA (Civ Div) 5–060
Bank of Scotland v Bennett [1999] Lloyd's Rep. Bank. 145; [1999] 1 F.L.R. 1115; [1999] 1 F.C.R. 641; (1999) 77 P. & C.R. 447; [1999] Fam. Law 307; [1999] E.G. 1 (C.S.); (1999) 96(3) L.S.G. 33, CA (Civ Div) 5–055, 5–056
Bankers Trust Co v Namdar [1997] E.G. 20 (C.S.); [1997] N.P.C. 22, CA (Civ Div) 5–060
Banks v Banks [1999] 1 F.L.R. 726 .... 9–017, 9–018, 9–033
Barca v Mears [2004] EWHC 2170; [2005] 2 F.L.R. 1; [2005] B.P.I.R. 15; [2005] Fam. Law 444; [2004] N.P.C. 141; [2005] 1 P. & C.R. DG7, Ch D 5–059
Barclays Bank Ltd v Taylor [1974] Ch. 137; [1973] 2 W.L.R. 293; [1973] 1 All E.R. 752; (1973) 25 P. & C.R. 172; (1973) 117 S.J. 109, CA (Civ Div) 14–008
Barclays Bank Plc v Coleman [2001] Q.B. 20; [2000] 3 W.L.R. 405; [2000] 1 All E.R. 385; [2000] Lloyd's Rep. Bank. 67; [2000] 1 F.L.R. 343; [2000] 1 F.C.R. 398; (2001) 33 H.L.R. 8; [2000] Fam. Law 245; [2000] E.G. 4 (C.S.); (2000) 97(3) L.S.G. 37; (2000) 144 S.J.L.B. 42; [2000] N.P.C. 2; (2000) 79 P. & C.R. D28, CA (Civ Div) 5–056
Barclays Bank Plc v Hendricks [1996] 1 F.L.R. 258; [1996] 1 F.C.R. 710; [1996] B.P.I.R. 17; [1996] Fam. Law 148, Ch D 5–060, 14–008
Barclays Bank Plc v Khaira [1993] 1 F.L.R. 343; [1993] Fam. Law 124, CA (Civ Div) 5–020
Barclays Bank Plc v O'Brien [1994] 1 A.C. 180; [1993] 3 W.L.R. 786; [1993] 4 All E.R. 417; [1994] 1 F.L.R. 1; [1994] 1 F.C.R. 357; (1994) 26 H.L.R. 75; (1994) 13 Tr. L.R. 165; [1994] C.C.L.R. 94; [1994] Fam. Law 78; [1993] E.G. 169 (C.S.); (1993) 143 N.L.J. 1511; (1993) 137 S.J.L.B. 240; [1993] N.P.C. 135, HL ...3–004, 3–028, 5–052, 5–054, 5–055, 5–056
Barclays Bank Plc v Rivett [1999] 1 F.L.R. 730; [1998] 3 F.C.R. 304; (1997) 29 H.L.R. 893; [1999] Fam. Law 308; [1997] N.P.C. 18, CA (Civ Div) 5–055
Barder v Barder [1987] 1 F.L.R. 18 .... 13–102, 13–103, 13–104
Barder v Caluori; sub nom. Barder v Barder [1988] A.C. 20; [1987] 2 W.L.R. 1350; [1987] 2 All E.R. 440; [1987] 2 F.L.R. 480; [1988] Fam. Law 18; (1987) 84 L.S.G. 2046; (1987) 137 N.L.J. 497; (1987) 131 S.J. 776, HL 13–103
Barham v Dennis (1600) Cro. Eliz. 770 16–002
Barker v Barker [1952] P. 184; [1952] 1 All E.R. 1128; [1952] 1 T.L.R. 1479; (1952) 96 S.J. 358, CA 13–018
Barnacle v Barnacle [1948] P. 257, PDAD 10–005
Barnardo v Ford; sub nom. R. v Barnardo; Gossage's Case, Re [1892] A.C. 326, HL 17–014
Barnes (RM) v Barnes (GW) [1972] 1 W.L.R. 1381; [1972] 3 All E.R. 872; (1972) 116 S.J. 801, CA (Civ Div) 13–073
Barnett v Hassett [1981] 1 W.L.R. 1385; [1982] 1 All E.R. 80; (1981) 125 S.J. 376, Fam Div 3–013

Barrett v Enfield LBC [2001] 2 A.C. 550; [1998] 1 W.L.R. 277; [1999] 3 W.L.R. 79; [1999]
   3 All E.R. 193; [1999] 2 F.L.R. 426; [1999] 2 F.C.R. 434; (1999) 1 L.G.L.R. 829;
   [1999] B.L.G.R. 473; (1999) 11 Admin. L.R. 839; [1999] Ed. C.R. 833; (1999) 2
   C.C.L. Rep. 203; [1999] P.I.Q.R. P272; (1999) 49 B.M.L.R. 1; [1999] Fam. Law 622;
   (1999) 96(28) L.S.G. 27; (1999) 143 S.J.L.B. 183, HL 21–027, 21–067
Barton v Wray, unreported, May 10, 2002 5–021
Basham (Deceased), Re [1986] 1 W.L.R. 1498; [1987] 1 All E.R. 405; [1987] 2 F.L.R. 264;
   [1987] Fam. Law 310; (1987) 84 L.S.G. 112; (1986) 130 S.J. 986, Ch D 5–033
Bastable v Bastable [1968] 1 W.L.R. 1684; [1968] 3 All E.R. 701; (1968) 112 S.J. 542, CA
   (Civ Div) 10–016
Bateman v Bateman [1979] Fam. 25; [1979] 2 W.L.R. 377; (1978) 9 Fam. Law 86; (1979)
   123 S.J. 201, Fam Div 13–117
Baxtar v Buckley (1752) 1 Lee 42; 161 E.R. 17 1–002
Baxter v Baxter [1948] A.C. 274; [1947] 2 All E.R. 886; 64 T.L.R. 8; 4 A.L.R.2d 216;
   [1948] L.J.R. 479; (1948) 92 S.J. 25, HL 2–025, 2–031, 2–033
Beach v Beach [1995] 2 F.L.R. 160; [1995] 2 F.C.R. 526; [1995] Fam. Law 545, Fam Div 13–008,
                                                                                                                        13–014
Beales v Beales [1972] Fam. 210; [1972] 2 W.L.R. 972; [1972] 2 All E.R. 667; (1972) 116
   S.J. 196, Fam Div 10–041
Beard v Beard [1981] 1 W.L.R. 369; [1981] 1 All E.R. 783; (1980) 11 Fam. Law 84, CA
   (Civ Div) 13–118
Beaumont (Deceased), Re; sub nom. Martin v Midland Bank Trust Co [1980] Ch. 444;
   [1979] 3 W.L.R. 818; [1980] 1 All E.R. 266; (1979) 123 S.J. 803, Ch D 7–016
Begum v Anam [2004] EWCA Civ 578, CA (Civ Div) 9–035
Bellinger v Bellinger [2003] UKHL 21; [2003] 2 A.C. 467; [2003] 2 W.L.R. 1174; [2003]
   2 All E.R. 593; [2003] 1 F.L.R. 1043; [2003] 2 F.C.R. 1; [2003] H.R.L.R. 22; [2003]
   U.K.H.R.R. 679; 14 B.H.R.C. 127; (2003) 72 B.M.L.R. 147; [2003] A.C.D. 74; [2003]
   Fam. Law 485; (2003) 153 N.L.J. 594; (2003) 147 S.J.L.B. 472, HL 2–018, 2–019
Benham v United Kingdom (19380/92) (1996) 22 E.H.R.R. 293, ECHR 9–036
Bennett v Bennett [1969] 1 W.L.R. 430; [1969] 1 All E.R. 539; (1969) 113 S.J. 284,
   PDAD 2–045
Benson v Benson (Deceased) [1996] 1 F.L.R. 692; [1996] 3 F.C.R. 590; [1996] Fam. Law
   351, Fam Div 13–008, 13–103, 13–107
Berkshire CC v B [1997] 1 F.L.R. 171; [1997] 3 F.C.R. 88; [1997] Fam. Law 234; (1997)
   161 J.P.N. 555, Fam Div 19–015
Bernard v Josephs [1982] Ch. 391; [1982] 2 W.L.R. 1052; [1982] 3 All E.R. 162; (1983) 4
   F.L.R. 178; (1982) 126 S.J. 361, CA (Civ Div) 3–041, 5–011
Bernstein v O'Neill [1989] 2 F.L.R. 1; [1989] F.C.R. 79; [1989] Fam. Law 275; (1988) 152
   J.P.N. 802 .... 14–002, 14–003
Best v Samuel Fox & Co Ltd [1952] A.C. 716; [1952] 2 All E.R. 394; [1952] 2 T.L.R. 246;
   (1952) 96 S.J. 494, HL 3–003
Besterman (Deceased), Re; sub nom. Besterman v Grusin [1984] Ch. 458; [1984] 3 W.L.R.
   280; [1984] 2 All E.R. 656; [1984] Fam. Law 203; (1984) 81 L.S.G. 2699; (1984) 128
   S.J. 515, CA (Civ Div) 7–026, 7–031
Bhaiji v Chauhan [2003] 2 F.L.R. 485; [2003] Fam. Law 558, Fam Div 10–056
Billington v Billington [1974] Fam. 24; [1974] 2 W.L.R. 53; [1974] 1 All E.R. 546; (1973)
   118 S.J. 66, Fam Div 14–012
Bird v Syme Thompson [1979] 1 W.L.R. 440; [1978] 3 All E.R. 1027; (1978) 36 P. & C.R.
   435; (1978) 122 S.J. 470, Ch D 5–051
Birmingham City Council v D [1994] 2 F.L.R. 502; [1994] 2 F.C.R. 245; [1994] Fam. Law
   610, Fam Div 21–035
Birmingham City Council v H; sub nom. Birmingham City Council v H (No.2);
   Birmingham City Council v H (No.3) [1994] 2 A.C. 212; [1994] 2 W.L.R. 31; [1994]
   1 All E.R. 12; [1994] 1 F.L.R. 224; [1994] 1 F.C.R. 896; 92 L.G.R. 349; [1994] Fam.
   Law 182; (1994) 158 L.G. Rev. 721; (1994) 144 N.L.J. 17; (1994) 138 S.J.L.B. 13,
   HL 19–001, 21–074, 21–076
Birmingham CC v S; Birmingham CC v R; Birmingham CC v A [2007] 1 F.L.R. 1223, Fam
   Div 22–034, 22–069
Birmingham Midshires Mortgage Services Ltd v Sabherwal (Equitable Interest) (2000) 80
   P. & C.R. 256, CA (Civ Div) 5–050
Bishop, Re; sub nom. National Provincial Bank v Bishop [1965] Ch. 450; [1965] 2 W.L.R.
   188; [1965] 1 All E.R. 249; (1965) 109 S.J. 107, Ch D 5–063

Bishop v Plumley [1991] 1 W.L.R. 582; [1991] 1 All E.R. 236; [1991] 1 F.L.R. 121; [1991] Fam. Law 61; (1990) 140 N.L.J. 1153, CA (Civ Div) 7–010, 7–016

Blackwell v Blackwell [1943] 2 All E.R. 579, CA 3–007

Blunt v Blunt [1943] A.C. 517, HL 10–005

Bolam v Friern Hospital Management Committee [1957] 1 W.L.R. 582; [1957] 2 All E.R. 118; [1955–95] P.N.L.R. 7; (1957) 101 S.J. 357, QBD 21–027

Bond v Leicester City Council [2001] EWCA Civ 1544; [2002] 1 F.C.R. 566; [2002] H.L.R. 6; (2001) 98(47) L.S.G. 27; (2001) 145 S.J.L.B. 259, CA (Civ Div) 6–037

Bosley v Bosley [1958] 1 W.L.R. 645; [1958] 2 All E.R. 167; (1958) 102 S.J. 437, CA 10–030

Bosworthick v Bosworthick [1927] P. 64, CA 13–027

Bouamar v Belgium (A/129) (1989) 11 E.H.R.R. 1, ECHR 21–051, 21–078

Bouette v Rose. *See* B (Deceased), Re

Boylan v Boylan [1988] 1 F.L.R. 282; [1988] F.C.R. 689; [1988] Fam. Law 62; (1988) 152 J.P.N. 770 .... 13–089, 13–090

Bradford, Re; O'Connell, Re [2007] 1 F.L.R. 530, CA 18–020

Bradley v Bradley [1973] 1 W.L.R. 1291; [1973] 3 All E.R. 750; (1973) 117 S.J. 632, CA (Civ Div) 10–026

Bradley-Hole (A Bankrupt), Re [1995] 1 W.L.R. 1097; [1995] 4 All E.R. 865; [1995] B.C.C. 418; [1995] 2 B.C.L.C. 163; [1995] 2 F.L.R. 838; [1996] 2 F.C.R. 259; [1995] Fam. Law 673, Ch D 14–002

Bramley v Bramley [2007] EWCA Civ 1483 9–035

Bremner (A Bankrupt), Re [1999] 1 F.L.R. 912; [1999] B.P.I.R. 185; [1999] Fam. Law 293, Ch D 5–059

Brent v Brent [1975] Fam. 1; [1974] 3 W.L.R. 296; [1974] 2 All E.R. 1211; (1974) 4 Fam. Law 157; (1974) 118 S.J. 442, Fam Div 13–117

Brett v Brett [1969] 1 W.L.R. 487; [1969] 1 All E.R. 1007; (1968) 113 S.J. 204, CA (Civ Div) 13–075

Brewer v Brewer [1989] 2 F.L.R. 251; [1989] F.C.R. 515; [1989] Fam. Law 352, CA (Civ Div) 9–035

Brierley v Brierley and Williams [1918] P. 257 .... 17–005, 17–009

Briggs v Moran (1820) 2 Hag. Con. 324 2–027

Bristol and West Building Society v Henning [1985] 1 W.L.R. 778; [1985] 2 All E.R. 606; (1985) 17 H.L.R. 442; (1985) 50 P. & C.R. 237; (1985) 82 L.S.G. 1788; (1985) 135 N.L.J. 508; (1985) 129 S.J. 363, CA (Civ Div) 5–050

Britannia Building Society v Pugh [1997] 2 F.L.R. 7; [1998] 2 F.C.R. 668; (1997) 29 H.L.R. 423; [1997] Fam. Law 478; [1996] E.G. 128 (C.S.); [1996] N.P.C. 113, CA (Civ Div) 5–056

Brixey v Lynas (No.1); sub nom. B v L (No.1), 1997 S.C. (H.L.) 1; 1996 S.L.T. 908; 1996 S.C.L.R. 856; [1996] 2 F.L.R. 499; [1997] 1 F.C.R. 220; [1997] Fam. Law 10, HL 19–022

Brock v Wollams [1949] 2 K.B. 388; [1949] 1 All E.R. 715; (1949) 93 S.J. 319, CA 22–001

Brodie, Re; sub nom. Brodie v Brodie [1917] P. 271, PDAD 2–032

Brooks v Brooks; sub nom. B v B (Post Nuptial Settlements) (Pension Fund), Re [1996] A.C. 375; [1995] 3 W.L.R. 141; [1995] 3 All E.R. 257; [1995] 2 F.L.R. 13; [1995] 3 F.C.R. 214; [1995] Fam. Law 545; (1995) 145 N.L.J. 995; (1995) 139 S.J.L.B. 165, HL 13–027, 13–119, 13–121, 13–122, 13–123

Brown v Brown (1828) 1 Hag. Ecc. 523 2–027

Brown v Brown [1959] P. 86; [1959] 2 W.L.R. 776; [1959] 2 All E.R. 266; (1959) 103 S.J. 414, CA 13–027

Browne v Browne [1989] 1 F.L.R. 291; [1989] Fam. Law 147, CA (Civ Div) 13–014, 13–066

Buchanan v Milton [1999] 2 F.L.R. 844; (2000) 53 B.M.L.R. 176; [1999] Fam. Law 692, Fam Div 17–026

Buckingham CC v M (1994) 158 L.G. Rev. 256, CA (Civ Div) 21–043

Buckland v Buckland (otherwise Camilleri) [1968] P. 296; [1967] 2 W.L.R. 1506; [1967] 2 All E.R. 300; (1965) 109 S.J. 212; (1967) 111 S.J. 456, PDAD 2–039

Bucknell v Bucknell [1969] 1 W.L.R. 1204; [1969] 2 All E.R. 998; (1969) 113 S.J. 586, PDAD 14–010

Buffery v Buffery [1988] 2 F.L.R. 365; [1988] F.C.R. 465; [1988] Fam. Law 436; (1988) 152 J.P.N. 526, CA (Civ Div) 10–015, 10–017

Buggs v Buggs [2003] EWHC 1538; [2004] W.T.L.R. 799; (2003) 147 S.J.L.B. 1117, Ch D 5–015, 5–022

Bull v Bull [1968] P. 618; [1965] 3 W.L.R. 1048; [1965] 1 All E.R. 1057; (1965) 109 S.J. 50, PDAD 10–005

Bunning (Deceased), Re; sub nom. Bunning v Salmon [1984] Ch. 480; [1984] 3 W.L.R. 265; [1984] 3 All E.R. 1; [1985] Fam. Law 21; (1984) 81 L.S.G. 2623; (1984) 128 S.J. 516, Ch D 7–026

Bunting's Case (1580) Moo. K.B. 303; 72 E.R. 510 1–002

Burden v United Kingdom (13378/05) [2007] S.T.C. 252; [2007] 1 F.C.R. 69; (2007) 44 E.H.R.R. 51; 21 B.H.R.C. 640; 9 I.T.L. Rep. 535; [2007] W.T.L.R. 607; [2007] S.T.I. 106, ECHR A–004, 3–034

Burgess v Burgess [1996] 2 F.L.R. 142 .... 13–044, 13–064

Burgess v Rawnsley [1975] Ch. 429; [1975] 3 W.L.R. 99; [1975] 3 All E.R. 142; (1975) 30 P. & C.R. 221; (1975) 119 S.J. 406, CA (Civ Div) 5–041, 5–042, 5–044

Burke v Burke (1973) [1974] 1 W.L.R. 1063; [1974] 2 All E.R. 944; (1974) 118 S.J. 98, CA (Civ Div) 5–046

Burns v Burns [1984] F.L.R. 216 ....5–023, 5–030, 5–064

Burridge v Burridge [1983] Fam. 9; [1982] 3 W.L.R. 552; [1982] 3 All E.R. 80; (1983) 4 F.L.R. 170; (1982) 12 Fam. Law 152, Fam Div 3–017

Burris v Adzani [1996] 1 F.L.R. 266 9–042

Burrow v Burrow [1999] 1 F.L.R. 508; [1999] 2 F.C.R. 549; [1999] Fam. Law 83, Fam Div 13–122

Burrows v Sharp (1991) 23 H.L.R. 82; [1991] Fam. Law 67; [1989] E.G. 51 (C.S.), CA (Civ Div) 5–036

Burton v Burton [1986] 2 F.L.R. 419; [1986] Fam. Law 330 .... 13–028, 14–005

Butcher v Wolfe [1999] C.P.L.R. 112; [1999] B.L.R. 61; [1999] 1 F.L.R. 334; [1999] 2 F.C.R. 165; [1999] Fam. Law 80; [1998] E.G. 153 (C.S.); (1998) 95(43) L.S.G. 33; (1998) 95(48) L.S.G. 31, CA (Civ Div) 13–012

Butler v Butler [1990] 1 F.L.R. 114; [1990] F.C.R. 336; [1990] Fam. Law 21; (1990) 154 J.P.N. 301 11–004

Button v Button [1968] 1 W.L.R. 457; [1968] 1 All E.R. 1064; (1968) 19 P. & C.R. 257; (1968) 112 S.J. 112, CA (Civ Div) 3–009

Byford (Deceased), Re; sub nom. Byford v Butler [2003] EWHC 1267; [2004] 1 F.L.R. 56; [2004] 2 F.C.R. 454; [2003] B.P.I.R. 1089; [2004] 1 P. & C.R. 12; [2004] Fam. Law 14; (2003) 100(31) L.S.G. 32; (2003) 100(24) L.S.G. 38; [2003] N.P.C. 77, Ch D ... 5–047

C (A Child) (Abduction: Grave Risk of Physical or Psychological Harm) (No.1), Re; sub nom. C (A Minor) (Child Abduction), Re [1999] 2 F.L.R. 478; [1999] 3 F.C.R. 510; [1999] Fam. Law 520, CA (Civ Div) 20–020

C (A Child) (Abduction: Residence and Contact), Re; sub nom. SC (A Child), Re [2005] EWHC 2205; [2006] 2 F.L.R. 277; [2006] Fam. Law 434, Fam Div 19–004

C (A Child) (Care Order or Supervision Order), Re [2001] 2 F.L.R. 466; [2001] Fam. Law 580, Fam Div 21–040

C (A Child) (Financial Provision), Re [2007] 2 F.L.R. 13; [2007] Fam. Law 303, Fam Div 15–051, 15–052

C (A Child) (HIV Testing), Re; sub nom. C (A Minor) (HIV Test), Re [1999] 2 F.L.R. 1004; [2000] Fam. Law 16, CA (Civ Div) 16–009, 18–022, 19–018

C (A Child) (Immunisation: Parental Rights), Re; F (A Child) (Immunisation: Parental Rights), Re; sub nom. C (Welfare of Child: Immunisation), Re; B (A Child) (Immunisation: Parental Rights), Re [2003] EWCA Civ 1148; [2003] 2 F.L.R. 1095; [2003] 3 F.C.R. 156; (2003) 73 B.M.L.R. 152; [2003] Fam. Law 731; (2003) 147 S.J.L.B. 934, CA (Civ Div) 17–022, 17–048, 18–022, 19–004

C (A Child) (Leave to Remove from Jurisdiction), Re; sub nom. C (A Child) (Removal from Jurisdiction), Re [2000] 2 F.L.R. 457; [2000] 2 F.C.R. 40; [2000] Fam. Law 813, CA (Civ Div) 18–026

C (A Child) (Secure Accommodation Order: Representation), Re; sub nom. M (A Child) (Secure Accommodation Order), Re [2001] EWCA Civ 458; [2001] 2 F.L.R. 169; [2001] 1 F.C.R. 692; [2001] Fam. Law 507, CA (Civ Div) 16–022, 21–056, 21–078

C (A Minor) (Adopted Child: Contact), Re; sub nom. A (A Minor), Re (1993); S (Adopted Child: Contact), Re [1993] Fam. 210; [1993] 3 W.L.R. 85; [1993] 3 All E.R. 259; [1993] 2 F.L.R. 431; [1993] 2 F.C.R. 234; [1993] Fam. Law 566, Fam Div .. 18–035, 18–039

C (A Minor) (Adoption Application), Re [1993] 1 F.L.R. 87; [1992] 1 F.C.R. 337; [1992] Fam. Law 538; (1992) 156 L.G. Rev. 566, Fam Div 22–069

C (A Minor) (Adoption: Freeing Order), Re; sub nom. SC (A Minor), Re [1999] Fam. 240; [1999] 1 W.L.R. 1079; [1999] 1 F.L.R. 348; [1999] 1 F.C.R. 145; [1999] Fam. Law 11; (1999) 163 J.P.N. 771; (1998) 95(45) L.S.G. 37; (1998) 142 S.J.L.B. 263, Fam Div 22–041, 22–044

C (A Minor) (Adoption: Illegality), Re; sub nom. C (A Minor) (Adoption: Legality), Re
   [1999] Fam. 128; [1999] 2 W.L.R. 202; [1999] 1 F.L.R. 370; [1998] 2 F.C.R. 641;
   [1998] Fam. Law 724; (1998) 95(22) L.S.G. 28; (1998) 142 S.J.L.B. 151, Fam Div ...22–047,
                                                                                         22–054
C (A Minor) (Adoption Order: Conditions), Re; sub nom. C (A Minor) (Adoption: Contract
   with Sibling), Re [1989] A.C. 1; [1988] 2 W.L.R. 474; [1988] 1 All E.R. 705; [1988]
   2 F.L.R. 159; [1988] F.C.R. 484; [1988] Fam. Law 428; (1988) 152 J.P.N. 430; (1988)
   152 L.G. Rev. 771; (1988) 138 N.L.J. Rep. 64; (1988) 132 S.J. 334, HL 22–062, 22–066,
                                                                                         22–067
C (A Minor) (Adoption: Parental Agreement: Contact), Re [1993] 2 F.L.R. 260; [1994] 2
   F.C.R. 485; [1993] Fam. Law 612, CA (Civ Div) 22–025
C (A Minor) (Adoption: Parties), Re [1995] 2 F.L.R. 483; [1995] Fam. Law 664, CA (Civ
   Div) 17–052
C (A Minor) (Care: Child's Wishes), Re; sub nom. G (A Minor) (Appeal), Re [1993] 1
   F.L.R. 832; [1993] 1 F.C.R. 810; [1993] Fam. Law 400, Fam Div ...16–005, 16–020, 16–022,
                                                                            18–042, 19–017, 21–056
C (A Minor) (Care Proceedings: Disclosure), Re; sub nom. EC (A Minor) (Care
   Proceedings: Disclosure), Re; EC (Disclosure of Material), Re [1997] Fam. 76; [1997]
   2 W.L.R. 322; [1996] 2 F.L.R. 725; [1996] 3 F.C.R. 521; [1997] Fam. Law 160, CA
   (Civ Div) 21–037, 21–038
C (A Minor) (Change of Surname), Re [1998] 2 F.L.R. 656; [1999] 1 F.C.R. 318; [1998]
   Fam. Law 659, CA (Civ Div) 18–006, 18–015
C (A Minor) (Child in Care) (Medical Treatment), Re [1993] Fam. 15 17–022
C (A Minor) (Contribution Notice), Re [1994] 1 F.L.R. 111; [1994] Fam. Law 184, Fam Div ...3–004,
                                                                                         15–015, 21–073
C (A Minor) (Family Assistance Order), Re [1996] 1 F.L.R. 424; [1996] 3 F.C.R. 514;
   [1996] Fam. Law 202; (1996) 160 J.P.N. 697, Fam Div 18–027
C (A Minor) (Leave to Seek Section 8 Orders), Re [1994] 1 F.L.R. 26; [1994] 1 F.C.R. 837;
   (1994) 158 J.P.N. 191, Fam Div 16–005, 18–005, 18–035, 18–038, 19–017
C (A Minor) (Medical Treatment: Court's Jurisdiction), Re; sub nom. C (A Minor)
   (Detention for Medical Treatment), Re [1997] 2 F.L.R. 180; [1997] 3 F.C.R. 49; [1997]
   Fam. Law 474; (1997) 94(13) L.S.G. 29; (1997) 141 S.J.L.B. 72, Fam Div 16–014, 17–018,
                                                                                         18–052, 21–077
C (A Minor) (Secure Accommodation Order: Bail), Re [1994] 2 F.L.R. 922; [1994] 2 F.C.R.
   1153; [1995] Fam. Law 19; (1994) 158 J.P.N. 732, Fam Div 21–077
C (A Minor) (Ward: Surrogacy), Re; sub nom. A Baby, Re [1985] Fam. Law 191; (1985)
   135 N.L.J. 106, Fam Div 22–070
C (A Minor) (Wardship: Contempt), Re [1986] 1 F.L.R. 578; [1986] Fam. Law 187, CA
   (Civ Div) 18–056
C (A Minor) (Wardship: Medical Treatment) (No.1), Re [1990] Fam. 26; [1989] 3 W.L.R.
   240; [1989] 2 All E.R. 782; [1990] 1 F.L.R. 252; [1990] F.C.R. 209; [1990] Fam. Law
   60; (1990) 154 J.P.N. 11; (1989) 86(28) L.S.G. 43; (1989) 139 N.L.J. 612; (1989) 133
   S.J. 876, CA (Civ Div) 18–022
C (Adoption: Disclosure to Father), Re [2005] EWHC 3385; [2006] 2 F.L.R. 589; [2006]
   Fam. Law 624, Fam Div 17–052
C (Adult: Refusal of Medical Treatment), Re [1994] 1 W.L.R. 290; [1994] 1 All E.R. 819;
   [1994] 1 F.L.R. 31; [1994] 2 F.C.R. 151, Fam Div 16–014
C (An Infant), Re [1959] Ch. 363; [1958] 3 W.L.R. 309; [1958] 2 All E.R. 656; (1958) 102
   S.J. 582, Ch D 18–051
C (Breach of Human Rights Damages), Re [2007] 1 F.L.R. 1957 ....21–040, 21–072, 21–086
C (Care: Consultation with Parents not in Child's Best Interests), Re; sub nom. S (A Child),
   Re [2005] EWHC 3390; [2006] 2 F.L.R. 787; [2006] Fam. Law 625, Fam Div 21–072
C (Child Abduction) (Unmarried Father: Rights of Custody), Re; sub nom. C (Child
   Abduction) (Custody Rights: Unmarried Father), Re; G (A Child) (Custody Rights:
   Unmarried Father), Re; G v M [2002] EWHC 2219; [2003] 1 W.L.R. 493; [2003] 1
   F.L.R. 252; [2003] Fam. Law 78; (2002) 99(48) L.S.G. 27, Fam Div 17–052
C (Children Act 1989: Expert Evidence), Re; sub nom. C (Child Cases: Evidence and
   Disclosure Practice), Re [1995] 1 F.L.R. 204; [1995] 2 F.C.R. 97; [1995] Fam. Law
   176; (1995) 159 L.G. Rev. 849, Fam Div 18–041
C (Contact: Moratorium: Change of Gender), Re [2007] 1 F.L.R. 1642, CA 18–019, 18–022,
                                                                                         19–001, 19–019

C (Contact: No Order for Contact), Re [2000] 2 F.L.R. 723; [2000] Fam. Law 699, Fam
Div 18–028, 19–001
C (Deceased: Leave to Apply for Provision), Re [1995] 2 F.L.R. 24; [1995] Fam. Law 479,
Fam Div 7–011
C (Disclosure), Re [1996] 1 F.L.R. 797; [1996] 3 F.C.R. 765; (1996) 160 J.P.N. 732, Fam
Div 17–015, 18–042, 21–059
C (Financial Provision: Leave to Appeal), Re [1993] 2 F.L.R. 799; [1993] Fam. Law 675 13–106,
13–107
C (Minors) (Abduction: Grave Risk of Psychological Harm), Re; sub nom. C (Minors)
(Abduction: Habitual Residence), Re [1999] 1 F.L.R. 1145; [1999] 2 F.C.R. 507;
[1999] Fam. Law 371; (1999) 96(10) L.S.G. 28; (1999) 143 S.J.L.B. 74, CA (Civ
Div) 20–020
C (Minors) (Contact: Jurisdiction), Re; sub nom. C (Minors) (Variation of Contact:
Jurisdiction), Re [1996] Fam. 79; [1995] 3 W.L.R. 30; [1995] 1 F.L.R. 777; [1995] 2
F.C.R. 701; [1995] Fam. Law 403, CA (Civ Div) 18–007, 18–049
C (Minors) (Contempt Proceedings), Re; sub nom. C v C (Contempt: Evidence); C (Minors)
(Hearsay Evidence: Contempt Proceedings), Re [1993] 4 All E.R. 690; [1993] 1 F.L.R.
220; [1993] 1 F.C.R. 820; [1993] Fam. Law 223, CA (Civ Div) 18–042
C (Minors) (Guardian Ad Litem: Disclosure of Report), Re [1996] 1 F.L.R. 61; [1995] 2
F.C.R. 837; [1996] Fam. Law 78; (1995) 159 J.P.N. 558, Fam Div 21–059
C (Minors) (Parental Rights), Re [1992] 2 All E.R. 86; [1992] 1 F.L.R. 1; [1991] F.C.R. 856;
[1992] Fam. Law 153; (1991) 135 S.J.L.B. 100, CA (Civ Div) 17–037
C (Minors) (Wardship: Adoption), Re [1989] 1 F.L.R. 222 22–060
C (Residence: Child's Application for Leave), Re [1995] 1 F.L.R. 927; [1995] Fam. Law
472; (1995) 159 J.P.N. 655, Fam Div 18–038
C (Residence Order), Re [2008] 1 F.L.R. 211, CA 18–058
C (Residence Order: Lesbian Co-parents), Re [1994] Fam.Law 468 19–001
C (Section 8 Order: Court Welfare Officer), Re; sub nom. C (A Minor) (Application for
Residence Order), Re; C (Minor) (Access: Attendance of Court Welfare Officer), Re
[1996] 1 F.L.R. 617; [1995] 2 F.C.R. 276, CA (Civ Div) 18–012
C (Surrogacy: Payments), Re; sub nom. X's Application under s.30 of the Human
Fertilisation and Embryology Act 1990, Re [2002] EWHC 157; [2002] 1 F.L.R. 909;
[2002] Fam. Law 351, Fam Div 22–072, 22–077
C v C [1942] N.Z.L.R. 356 2–042
C v C (1979) 123 S.J. 33, CA (Civ Div) 7–014
C v C (Application for Non Molestation Order: Jurisdiction) [1998] Fam. 70; [1998] 2
W.L.R. 599; [1998] 1 F.L.R. 554; [1998] 1 F.C.R. 11; [1998] Fam. Law 254; (1997)
94(47) L.S.G. 30; (1997) 141 S.J.L.B. 236, Fam Div 9–027, 9–038, 9–042
C v C (Costs: Ancillary Relief) [2003] EWHC 2321; [2004] 1 F.L.R. 291; [2004] Fam. Law
18, Fam Div 13–012
C v C (Financial Provision: Non-Disclosure) [1994] 2 F.L.R. 272; [1995] 1 F.C.R. 75;
[1994] Fam. Law 561, Fam Div 13–106
C v C (Financial Provision: Personal Damages) [1995] 2 F.L.R. 171; [1996] 1 F.C.R. 283;
[1995] Fam. Law 605, Fam Div 13–078, 13–086
C v C (Financial Relief: Short Marriage); sub nom. C v C (Financial Provision: Short
Marriage) [1997] 2 F.L.R. 26; [1997] 3 F.C.R. 360; [1997] Fam. Law 472, CA (Civ
Div) 13–058, 13–076, 13–077, 13–089
C v C (Maintenance Pending Suit: Legal Costs) [2006] 2 F.L.R. 1207; [2006] Fam. Law
739, Fam Div 13–037
C v C (Privilege: Criminal Communications); sub nom. C v C (Evidence: Privilege); GC v
JC; C v C (Custody: Affidavit) [2001] EWCA Civ 469; [2002] Fam. 42; [2001] 3
W.L.R. 446; [2001] 2 F.L.R. 184; [2001] 1 F.C.R. 756; [2001] Fam. Law 496, CA (Civ
Div) 18–043
C v F (Disabled Child: Maintenance Orders); sub nom. C v F (Child Maintenance) [1998]
2 F.L.R. 1; [1999] 1 F.C.R. 39; [1998] Fam. Law 389, CA (Civ Div) 15–036, 17–028
C v Finland (18249/02) [2006] 2 F.L.R. 597; [2006] 2 F.C.R. 195; [2006] Fam. Law 633,
ECHR 17–024, 18–035
C v K (Inherent Powers: Exclusion Order); sub nom. C v K (Ouster Order: Non-Parent)
[1996] 2 F.L.R. 506; [1996] 3 F.C.R. 488; [1997] Fam. Law 16, Fam Div 9–042
C v S (Maintenance Order: Enforcement) [1997] 1 F.L.R. 298; [1997] 3 F.C.R. 423; [1997]
Fam. Law 236; (1997) 161 J.P.N. 629, Fam Div 14–002

C v Salford City Council [1994] 2 F.L.R. 926; [1995] Fam. Law 65, Fam Div 18–035, 18–036,
                                                                    18–051, 18–085, 19–019
C v Solihull MBC [1993] 1 F.L.R. 290; [1993] Fam. Law 189 .... 18–006, 18–016, 19–025, 21–039,
                                                                                         21–043
C and B (Children) (Care Order: Future Harm), Re; sub nom. C and J (Children), Re [2001]
    1 F.L.R. 611; [2000] 2 F.C.R. 614; [2001] Fam. Law 253; (2000) 164 J.P.N. 940, CA
    (Civ Div) 21–035, 21–040, 22–033
C and V (Minors) (Contact: Parental Responsibility Order), Re [1998] 1 F.L.R. 392; [1998]
    1 F.C.R. 52; [1998] Fam. Law 10, CA (Civ Div) 17–037, 18–019
CB (A Minor) (Access), Re [1992] 1 F.C.R. 320; (1992) 156 J.P.N. 234, CA (Civ Div) 18–012
CB (A Minor) (Blood Tests), Re [1994] 2 F.L.R. 762; [1994] 2 F.C.R. 925; [1995] Fam. Law
    20; (1994) 158 J.P.N. 702, Fam Div 17–007
CB (Access: Attendance of Court Welfare Officer), Re [1995] 1 F.L.R. 622 .... 18–019, 19–006
CE (A Minor) (Appointment of Guardian ad Litem), Re; sub nom. CE (Section 37
    Directions), Re [1995] 1 F.L.R. 26; [1995] 1 F.C.R. 387; [1995] Fam. Law 67; (1995)
    159 J.P.N. 179, Fam Div 18–048, 21–058
CE (Section 37 Directions), Re. *See* CE (A Minor) (Appointment of Guardian ad Litem),
    Re
CF v Secretary of State for the Home Department [2004] EWHC 111; [2004] 2 F.L.R. 517;
    [2004] 1 F.C.R. 577; [2004] Fam. Law 639, Fam Div 21–085
CH (Contact: Parentage), Re [1996] 1 F.L.R. 569; [1996] Fam. Law 274, Fam Div 17–024, 18–019
CIBC Mortgages Plc v Pitt [1994] 1 A.C. 200; [1993] 3 W.L.R. 802; [1993] 4 All E.R. 433;
    [1994] 1 F.L.R. 17; [1994] 1 F.C.R. 374; (1994) 26 H.L.R. 90; (1994) 13 Tr. L.R. 180;
    [1994] C.C.L.R. 68; [1993] Fam. Law 79; [1993] E.G. 174 (C.S.); (1993) 143 N.L.J.
    1514; (1993) 137 S.J.L.B. 240; [1993] N.P.C. 136, HL 5–055, 5–056
CR v CR, unreported, June 19, 2007 ....13–052, 13–053, 13–057
Cackett (otherwise Trice) v Cackett [1950] P. 253; [1950] 1 All E.R. 677; 66 T.L.R. (Pt. 1)
    723; (1950) 94 S.J. 256, PDAD 2–033
Cairnes (Deceased), Re; sub nom. Howard v Cairnes (1983) 4 F.L.R. 225; (1982) 12 Fam.
    Law 177 7–024
Calderbank v Calderbank [1976] Fam. 93; [1975] 3 W.L.R. 586; [1975] 3 All E.R. 333;
    (1975) 5 Fam. Law 190; (1975) 119 S.J. 490, CA (Civ Div) 13–012, 13–031
Callaghan (Deceased), Re [1985] Fam. 1; [1984] 3 W.L.R. 1076; [1984] 3 All E.R. 790;
    [1985] Fam. Law 28; (1984) 81 L.S.G. 2775; (1984) 128 S.J. 705, Fam Div ... 7–022, 7–028,
                                                                                         22–001
Cambridge CC v D [1999] 2 F.L.R. 42 .... 18–049, 18–052
Camden LBC v R (A Minor) (Blood Transfusion)ub nom. R (A Minor) (Medical
    Treatment), Re [1993] 2 F.L.R. 757; [1993] 2 F.C.R. 544; 91 L.G.R. 623; [1993] Fam.
    Law 577; (1994) 158 L.G. Rev. 341; (1993) 137 S.J.L.B. 151, Fam Div 16–015, 17–022,
                                                                            18–022, 18–040, 18–051
Cameron v Treasury Solicitor; sub nom. O'Rourke (Deceased), Re [1996] 2 F.L.R. 716;
    [1997] 1 F.C.R. 188; [1996] Fam. Law 723, CA (Civ Div) 7–006, 7–013
Camm v Camm (1983) 4 F.L.R. 577; (1983) 13 Fam. Law 112, CA (Civ Div) 13–007, 13–008
Campbell v Campbell [1922] P. 187, PDAD 14–002
Campbell v Griffin [2001] EWCA Civ 990; [2001] W.T.L.R. 981; [2001] N.P.C. 102; (2001)
    82 P. & C.R. DG23, CA (Civ Div) 5–034
Campbell and Cosans v United Kingdom (A/48) (1982) 4 E.H.R.R. 293, ECHR 16–017
Canon v Canon [2005] 1 F.L.R. 169, CA 20–018
Caparo Industries Plc v Dickman [1990] 2 A.C. 605; [1990] 2 W.L.R. 358; [1990] 1 All E.R.
    568; [1990] B.C.C. 164; [1990] B.C.L.C. 273; [1990] E.C.C. 313; [1955–95] P.N.L.R.
    523; (1990) 87(12) L.S.G. 42; (1990) 140 N.L.J. 248; (1990) 134 S.J. 494, HL 21–027
Capron v Capron [1927] P. 243, PDAD 14–010
Carabott v Huxley [2005] EWCA Civ 1837; (2005) 102(34) L.S.G. 30, CA (Civ Div) 9–037
Carlton v Goodman; sub nom. Goodman v Carlton [2002] EWCA Civ 545; [2002] 2 F.L.R.
    259; [2002] Fam. Law 595; (2002) 99(22) L.S.G. 36; [2002] N.P.C. 61, CA (Civ Div) 5–011,
                                                                            5–015, 5–016, 5–018, 5–022
Carmarthenshire CC v Lewis [1955] A.C. 549; [1955] 2 W.L.R. 517; [1955] 1 All E.R. 565;
    (1955) 119 J.P. 230; 53 L.G.R. 230; (1955) 99 S.J. 167, HL 17–027
Carson v Carson [1983] 1 W.L.R. 285; [1983] 1 All E.R. 478; (1981) 2 F.L.R. 352; (1981)
    125 S.J. 513, CA (Civ Div) 13–116
Carter-Fea v Carter-Fea [1987] Fam. Law 131, CA (Civ Div) 10–023
Cartwright v Cartwright (1982) 12 Fam. Law 252 13–027

Cartwright v Cartwright; sub nom. Cartwright, Re [2002] EWCA Civ 931; [2002] 2 F.L.R. 610; [2002] 2 F.C.R. 760; [2002] B.P.I.R. 895; [2002] Fam. Law 735; (2002) 99(35) L.S.G. 37; (2002) 146 S.J.L.B. 177, CA (Civ Div) 14–005

Catalano v Catalano, 170 A 2d 726 (1961) 2–008

Caunce v Caunce; Lloyds Bank v Caunce [1969] 1 W.L.R. 286; [1969] 1 All E.R. 722; (1969) 20 P. & C.R. 877; (1969) 113 S.J. 204, Ch D 5–051

Chalmers v Johns [1999] 1 F.L.R. 392; [1999] 2 F.C.R. 110; [1999] Fam. Law 16, CA (Civ Div) 9–017, 9–019, 9–020

Chamberlain v Chamberlain [1973] 1 W.L.R. 1557; [1974] 1 All E.R. 33; (1973) 4 Fam. Law 46; (1973) 117 S.J. 893, CA (Civ Div) 15–044

Chan Pui Chun v Leung Kam Ho [2002] EWCA Civ 1075; [2003] 1 F.L.R. 23; [2003] 1 F.C.R. 520; [2003] B.P.I.R. 29; [2003] Fam. Law 25; [2003] 1 P. & C.R. DG2, CA (Civ Div) 5–045, 5–046

Chandler v Secretary of State for Work and Pensions [2007] EWCA Civ 1211; (2007) 104(48) L.S.G. 22; (2007) 151 S.J.L.B. 1564, CA (Civ Div) 15–016

Channon v Lindley Johnstone (A Firm) [2000] 2 F.L.R. 734; [2000] Fam. Law 712, QBD 13–108

Charalambous v Charalambous [2004] 2 F.L.R. 1093 13–027

Chard v Chard (otherwise Northcott) [1956] P. 259; [1955] 3 W.L.R. 954; [1955] 3 All E.R. 721; (1955) 99 S.J. 890, PDAD 12–002

Charman v Charman [2007] EWCA Civ 503; [2007] 1 F.L.R. 1246; [2007] 2 F.C.R. 217; [2007] W.T.L.R. 1151; (2006–07) 9 I.T.E.L.R. 913; [2007] Fam. Law 682; (2007) 157 N.L.J. 814; (2007) 151 S.J.L.B. 710, CA (Civ Div) 4–001

Charman v Charman (No.4) [2007] 2 F.C.R. 217; [2007] 1 F.L.R. 1247 .... 13–002, 13–040, 13–050, 13–053, 13–054, 13–055, 13–056, 13–064, 13–066, 13–076, 13–080

Chater v Mortgage Agency Services Number Two Ltd; sub nom. Charter v Mortgage Agency Services; Mortgage Agency Services Number Two Ltd v Chater [2003] EWCA Civ 490; [2003] H.L.R. 61; [2004] 1 P. & C.R. 4; [2003] 15 E.G. 138 (C.S.); (2003) 147 S.J.L.B. 417; [2003] N.P.C. 48; [2003] 2 P. & C.R. DG9, CA (Civ Div) 5–055, 5–056

Chaudhuri v Chaudhuri [1992] 2 F.L.R. 73; [1992] 2 F.C.R. 426; [1992] Fam. Law 385, CA (Civ Div) 13–103, 13–105

Chechi v Bashier [1999] 2 F.L.R. 489; [1999] 2 F.C.R. 241; [1999] Fam. Law 528; (1999) 143 S.J.L.B. 113, CA (Civ Div) 9–030

Cheni (otherwise Rodriguez) v Cheni [1965] P. 85; [1963] 2 W.L.R. 17; [1962] 3 All E.R. 873, PDAD 2–008

Chesire CC v M [1993] 1 F.L.R. 463 18–041

Chettiar (ARPL Palaniappa) v Chettiar (PLAR Arunasalam); sub nom. Chettiar v Chettiar [1962] A.C. 294; [1962] 2 W.L.R. 548; [1962] 1 All E.R. 494; (1962) 106 S.J. 110, PC (FMS) 5–016

Chhokar v Chhokar [1984] Fam. Law 269; (1983) 80 L.S.G. 3243, CA (Civ Div) 5–050

Chief Adjudication Officer v Bath [2000] 1 F.L.R. 8; [2000] 1 F.C.R. 419; [2001] W.T.L.R. 55; [2000] Fam. Law 91, CA (Civ Div) 1–048

Chief Constable of West Yorkshire v S. *See* S v S (Chief Constable of West Yorkshire Intervening)

Christmas v Hampshire CC (Breach of Duty and Damage) [1998] E.L.R. 1, QBD 21–027

Church Commissioners for England v Al-Emarah 3964 [1997] Fam. 34; [1996] 3 W.L.R. 633; [1996] 2 F.L.R. 544; [1996] 3 F.C.R. 252; (1997) 29 H.L.R. 351; [1996] Fam. Law 725; (1996) 93(22) L.S.G. 27; (1996) 140 S.J.L.B. 129; [1996] N.P.C. 73; (1996) 72 P. & C.R. D45, CA (Civ Div) 13–117

Churchard v Churchard [1984] F.L.R. 635 18–058

Churchill v Roach [2002] EWHC 3230; [2004] 2 F.L.R. 989; [2004] 3 F.C.R. 744; [2003] W.T.L.R. 779; [2004] Fam. Law 720, Ch D 7–016, 7–017, 7–018

Citro (Domenico) (A Bankrupt), Re; Citro (Carmine) (A Bankrupt), Re [1991] Ch. 142; [1990] 3 W.L.R. 880; [1990] 3 All E.R. 952; [1991] 1 F.L.R. 71; [1990] E.G. 78 (C.S.); (1990) 154 N.L.J. 1073; (1990) 134 S.J. 806, CA (Civ Div) 5–059

City of London Building Society v Flegg [1988] A.C. 54; [1987] 2 W.L.R. 1266; [1987] 3 All E.R. 435; [1988] 1 F.L.R. 98; (1987) 19 H.L.R. 484; (1987) 54 P. & C.R. 337; [1988] Fam. Law 17; (1987) 84 L.S.G. 1966; (1987) 137 N.L.J. 475; (1987) 131 S.J. 806, HL 5–050

City of Westminster v IC (By his Litigation Friend the Official Solicitor) and KC and NNC [2007] EWHC 3096, Fam Div 2–037, 2–044

Clark v Chief Land Registrar; Chancery v Ketteringham [1994] Ch. 370; [1994] 3 W.L.R. 593; [1994] 4 All E.R. 96; [1995] 1 F.L.R. 212; [1995] Fam. Law 132; (1994) 91(24) L.S.G. 47; (1994) 138 S.J.L.B. 123; [1994] N.P.C. 61, CA (Civ Div) 14–008
Clark v Clark [1989] 1 F.L.R. 174; [1989] F.C.R. 101; [1989] Fam. Law 111; (1989) 153 J.P.N. 79; (1988) 138 N.L.J. Rep. 101, Fam Div 14–010
Clark v Clark (No.2) [1991] 1 F.L.R. 179; [1990] F.C.R. 953; [1991] Fam. Law 58; (1991) 141 N.L.J. 206 14–010
Clark (George Nowell) v Clark (Julia Oriska) [1999] 2 F.L.R. 498; [1999] 3 F.C.R. 49; [1999] Fam. Law 533, CA (Civ Div) 13–012, 13–084
Clarke v Harlowe [2005] EWHC 3062 (Ch); [2007] 1 F.L.R. 1; [2007] 3 F.C.R. 726; [2006] B.P.I.R. 636; [2005] W.T.L.R. 1473; [2006] Fam. Law 846; [2006] 1 P. & C.R. DG11, Ch D 5–010, 5–011, 5–048
Clarke (otherwise Talbott) v Clarke [1943] 2 All E.R. 540, PDAD 2–025
Claughton v Charalambous [1999] 1 F.L.R. 740; [1998] B.P.I.R. 558; [1999] Fam. Law 205, Ch D 5–059
Clayton v Clayton [2007] 1 F.L.R. 11, CA 17–015, 18–008, 18–016, 18–021
Cleary v Cleary [1974] 1 W.L.R. 73; [1974] 1 All E.R. 498; (1973) 117 S.J. 834, CA (Civ Div) 10–020
Clough v Killey [1996] N.P.C. 38; (1996) 72 P. & C.R. D22, CA (Civ Div) 5–020, 5–027
Clutton v Clutton [1991] 1 W.L.R. 359; [1991] 1 All E.R. 340; [1991] 1 F.L.R. 242; [1991] F.C.R. 265; [1991] Fam. Law 304; (1990) 134 S.J. 1682, CA (Civ Div) 13–021, 13–086, 13–117
Coffer v Coffer (1964) 108 S.J. 465 10–057
Cohen v Cohen [1982] 4 F.L.R. 451; (1982) 12 Fam. Law 251 14–006
Cohen v Sellar [1926] 1 K.B. 536, KBD 3–041
Cole (A Bankrupt), Re; sub nom. Ex p. Trustee v Cole [1964] Ch. 175; [1963] 3 W.L.R. 621; [1963] 3 All E.R. 433; (1963) 107 S.J. 664, CA 5–062
Coles v Coles [1957] P. 68; [1956] 3 W.L.R. 861; [1956] 3 All E.R. 542; (1956) 100 S.J. 842, PDAD 14–010
Collier v Collier [2002] EWCA Civ 1095; [2002] B.P.I.R. 1057; [2003] W.T.L.R. 617; (2003–04) 6 I.T.E.L.R. 270; [2003] 1 P. & C.R. DG3, CA (Civ Div) 5–016
Collins (Deceased), Re [1990] Fam. 56; [1990] 2 W.L.R. 161; [1990] 2 All E.R. 47; [1990] 2 F.L.R. 72; [1990] F.C.R. 433; (1990) 154 J.P.N. 395; (1990) 87(6) L.S.G. 40; (1990) 134 S.J. 262, Fam Div 7–004, 7–008, 7–011, 7–012, 7–017, 7–019
Compton (Marquis of Northampton) v Compton (Marchioness of Northampton) [1960] P. 201; [1960] 3 W.L.R. 476; [1960] 2 All E.R. 70; (1960) 104 S.J. 705, PDAD 13–027
Conran v Conran [1997] 2 F.L.R. 615; [1998] 1 F.C.R. 144; [1997] Fam. Law 724, Fam Div 13–078
Conran v Lowe (1754) 1 Lee 630; 161 E.R. 230 1–003
Cook, Re (1956) 106 L.J. 466 7–019
Cook v Cook [1988] 1 F.L.R. 521; [1988] Fam. Law 163, CA (Civ Div) 13–103, 13–107
Cook v Cook (Matrimonial Home) (No.1) [1962] P. 235; [1962] 3 W.L.R. 441; [1962] 2 All E.R. 811; (1962) 106 S.J. 668, CA 13–027
Coombes v Smith [1986] 1 W.L.R. 808; [1987] 1 F.L.R. 352; [1987] Fam. Law 123; (1986) 130 S.J. 482, Ch D 5–034
Corbett v Corbett [2003] EWCA Civ 559; [2003] 2 F.L.R. 385; [2003] Fam. Law 474, CA (Civ Div) 14–011
Corbett v Corbett (otherwise Ashley) (No.1) [1971] P. 83; [1970] 2 W.L.R. 1306; [1970] 2 All E.R. 33; (1969) 113 S.J. 982, PDAD 2–018, 2–020, 2–021, 2–025, 2–026
Cordle v Cordle [2001] EWCA Civ 1791; [2002] 1 W.L.R. 1441; [2002] 1 F.L.R. 207; [2002] 1 F.C.R. 97; [2002] Fam. Law 174; (2002) 99(1) L.S.G. 19; (2001) 145 S.J.L.B. 262, CA (Civ Div) 13–044, 13–046, 13–058, 13–072, 13–114, 13–116
Cornick v Cornick (No.1) [1994] 2 F.L.R. 530; [1994] 2 F.C.R. 1189; [1994] Fam. Law 617, Fam Div 13–102, 13–103, 13–104, 13–105
Cornick v Cornick (No.2) [1995] 2 F.L.R. 490, CA (Civ Div) 13–098, 13–104
Cornick v Cornick (No.3) [2001] 2 F.L.R. 1240; [2001] Fam. Law 871; (2002) 99(9) L.S.G. 27, Fam Div 13–098, 13–100, 13–104
Cossey v United Kingdom (A/184); sub nom. C v United Kingdom (A/184); Cossey v United Kingdom (10843/84) [1991] 2 F.L.R. 492; [1993] 2 F.C.R. 97; (1991) 13 E.H.R.R. 622; [1991] Fam. Law 362, ECHR 2–018
Costello-Roberts v United Kingdom (A/247-C) [1994] 1 F.C.R. 65; (1995) 19 E.H.R.R. 112, ECHR 16–017

Cotterell v Cotterell [1998] 3 F.C.R. 199, CA (Civ Div) 10–015

Coventry (Deceased), Re; sub nom. Coventry v Coventry [1980] Ch. 461; [1979] 3 W.L.R.
802; [1979] 3 All E.R. 815; (1979) 123 S.J. 606, CA (Civ Div) 7–001, 7–009, 7–010, 7–014,
7–018, 7–019, 7–020, 7–022

Cowan v Cowan [2001] EWCA Civ 679; [2002] Fam. 97; [2001] 3 W.L.R. 684; [2001] 2
F.L.R. 192; [2001] 2 F.C.R. 331; [2001] Fam. Law 498, CA (Civ Div) 13–001, 13–002,
13–045, 13–073, 13–079, 13–105, 13–119

Cowcher v Cowcher [1972] 1 W.L.R. 425; [1972] 1 All E.R. 943; (1972) 116 S.J. 142, Fam
Div 5–011, 5–014

Cox v Jones [2004] EWHC 1006, Ch D 5–001

Cox v Jones [2004] EWHC 1486 (Ch); [2004] 2 F.L.R. 1010; [2004] 3 F.C.R. 693; [2004]
Fam. Law 717, Ch D 3–041, 5–021, 5–025

Crabb v Arun DC [1976] Ch. 179; [1975] 3 W.L.R. 847; [1975] 3 All E.R. 865; (1976) 32
P. & C.R. 70; (1975) 119 S.J. 711, CA (Civ Div) 5–032, 5–035

Crake v Supplementary Benefits Commission; Butterworth v Supplementary Benefits
Commission [1982] 1 All E.R. 498; (1981) 2 F.L.R. 264, QBD 6–012, 6–018, 9–029

Crawford v CPS [2008] EWHC 148, Admin 9–038

Credit Lyonnais Bank Nederland NV v Burch [1997] 1 All E.R. 144; [1996] 5 Bank. L.R.
233; [1997] C.L.C. 95; [1997] 1 F.L.R. 11; [1997] 2 F.C.R. 1; (1997) 29 H.L.R. 513;
(1997) 74 P. & C.R. 384; [1997] Fam. Law 168; (1996) 93(32) L.S.G. 33; (1996) 146
N.L.J. 1421; (1996) 140 S.J.L.B. 158; [1996] N.P.C. 99; (1996) 72 P. & C.R. D33, CA
(Civ Div) 5–055, 5–056

Crossland v Crossland [1993] 1 F.L.R. 175; [1992] 2 F.C.R. 45; [1993] Fam. Law 186,
DC 14–014

Crossley v Crossley [2005] EWCA Civ 1581; [2006] 2 F.L.R. 813; [2006] 1 F.C.R. 655;
[2006] B.P.I.R. 404; [2006] W.T.L.R. 225; [2006] Fam. Law 638; [2006] 2 P. & C.R.
DG1, CA (Civ Div) 5–027

Croydon LBC v A (No.1) [1992] Fam. 169; [1992] 3 W.L.R. 267; [1992] 3 All E.R. 788;
[1992] 2 F.L.R. 341; [1992] Fam. Law 441; (1992) 156 L.G. Rev. 745; (1992) 136
S.J.L.B. 69, Fam Div 18–021

Croydon LBC v A (No.2) [1992] 1 W.L.R. 984; [1992] 2 F.L.R. 348; [1992] 2 F.C.R. 858,
Fam Div 21–046

Croydon LBC v A (No.3) [1992] 2 F.L.R. 350; [1992] 2 F.C.R. 481; [1993] Fam. Law 70,
Fam Div 21–042

Croydon LBC v R; sub nom. R (A Minor) (Child Case: Procedure), Re [1997] 2 F.L.R. 675;
[1997] 3 F.C.R. 704; [1997] Fam. Law 653; (1997) 161 J.P.N. 724, Fam Div 19–014

Crozier v Crozier [1994] Fam. 114; [1994] 2 W.L.R. 444; [1994] 2 All E.R. 362; [1994] 1
F.L.R. 126; [1994] 1 F.C.R. 781; [1994] Fam. Law 244; (1993) 143 N.L.J. 1784, Fam
Div 6–019, 13–087, 13–105

Cruse v Chittum (formerly Cruse) [1974] 2 All E.R. 940; (1974) 4 Fam. Law 152; (1974)
118 S.J. 499, Fam Div 15–010

Cunliffe v Fielden; sub nom. Fielden v Cunliffe [2005] EWCA Civ 1508; [2006] Ch. 361;
[2006] 2 W.L.R. 481; [2006] 2 All E.R. 115; [2006] 1 F.L.R. 745; [2005] 3 F.C.R. 593;
[2006] W.T.L.R. 29; (2005–06) 8 I.T.E.L.R. 855; [2006] Fam. Law 263; (2006) 103(3)
L.S.G. 26, CA (Civ Div) 7–018, 7–026

Curley v Parkes [2004] EWCA Civ 1515; [2005] 1 P. & C.R. DG15, CA (Civ Div) 5–013, 5–015

Currey v Currey [2006] EWCA Civ 1338; [2007] 2 Costs L.R. 227; [2007] 1 F.L.R. 946;
[2007] Fam. Law 12; (2006) 156 N.L.J. 1651; (2006) 150 S.J.L.B. 1393, CA (Civ
Div) 13–037

Curtis v Curtis [1969] 1 W.L.R. 422; [1969] 2 All E.R. 207; (1969) 113 S.J. 242, CA (Civ
Div) 14–005

D (A Child) (Abduction: Rights of Custody), Re; sub nom. D v D; D (A Child) (Abduction:
Foreign Custody Right), Re [2006] UKHL 51; [2006] 3 W.L.R. 989; [2007] 1 All E.R.
783; [2007] 1 F.C.R. 1; [2007] Fam. Law 102; (2006) 103(46) L.S.G. 29; (2006) 156
N.L.J. 1803; (2006) 150 S.J.L.B. 1532, HL 20–016, 20–017, 20–021, 20–022, 20–025

D (A Child) (Grant of Care Order: Refusal of Freeing Order), Re; Kent CC v D; sub nom.
Kent CC v R [2001] 1 F.L.R. 862; [2001] 1 F.C.R. 501, CA (Civ Div) 19–022

D (A Child) (Intractable Contact Dispute: Publicity), Re; sub nom. F v M (Contact Orders)
[2004] EWHC 727; [2004] 1 F.L.R. 1226; [2004] 3 F.C.R. 234; [2004] Fam. Law 490,
Fam Div 19–010

D (A Child) (IVF Treatment), Re; sub nom. D (A Child) (Parental Responsibility: IVF Baby), Re [2001] EWCA Civ 230; [2001] 1 F.L.R. 972; [2001] 1 F.C.R. 481; [2001] Fam. Law 504, CA (Civ Div) 17–037, 19–025, 22–070

D (A Child) (Threshold Criteria: Issue Estoppel), Re [2001] 1 F.L.R. 274; [2001] 1 F.C.R. 124; [2000] Fam. Law 875; (2001) 165 J.P.N. 565, CA (Civ Div) 21–036

D (A Minor) (Adoption Order: Validity), Re [1991] Fam. 137; [1991] 2 W.L.R. 1215; [1991] 3 All E.R. 461; [1991] 2 F.L.R. 66; [1991] F.C.R. 521; [1992] Fam. Law 59; (1991) 135 S.J. 117, CA (Civ Div) 22–008, 22–067

D (A Minor) (Child: Removal from Jurisdiction), Re [1992] 1 W.L.R. 315; [1992] 1 All E.R. 892; [1992] 1 F.L.R. 637; [1992] 2 F.C.R. 41; [1992] Fam. Law 243, CA (Civ Div) 18–021, 20–002

D (A Minor) (Contact: Interim Order), Re; sub nom. D v R (Interim Contact Order) [1995] 1 F.L.R. 495; [1995] 1 F.C.R. 501; [1995] Fam. Law 239; (1995) 159 J.P.N. 268, Fam Div 18–024

D (A Minor) (Contact: Mother's Hostility), Re [1993] 2 F.L.R. 1; [1993] 1 F.C.R. 964; [1993] Fam. Law 465, CA (Civ Div) 18–019

D (A Minor) (Contact Orders: Conditions), Re; sub nom. D v N (Contact Order: Conditions), Re [1997] 2 F.L.R. 797; [1997] 3 F.C.R. 721; [1997] Fam. Law 783; (1997) 94(29) L.S.G. 28; (1997) 141 S.J.L.B. 170, CA (Civ Div) 18–016

D (A Minor) (Justices' Decision: Review), Re [1977] Fam. 158; [1977] 2 W.L.R. 1006; [1977] 3 All E.R. 481; 75 L.G.R. 845; (1977) 7 Fam. Law 138; (1977) 121 S.J. 355, Fam Div 18–050

D (A Minor) (Wardship: Sterilisation), Re [1976] Fam. 185; [1976] 2 W.L.R. 279; [1976] 1 All E.R. 326; (1975) 119 S.J. 696, Fam Div 17–022, 18–051

D (A Minor) v DPP; R (A Minor) v DPP; R. v Burnley Crown Court Ex p. Lancashire CC; R. v Preston Crown Court Ex p. Lancashire CC (1995) 16 Cr. App. R. (S.) 1040; (1996) 160 J.P. 275; [1995] 2 F.L.R. 502; [1995] 3 F.C.R. 725; [1995] Crim. L.R. 748; [1995] C.O.D. 388; [1995] Fam. Law 595, DC 17–027

D (Abduction: Acquiescence: Mother's Removal from Australia to Wales), Re [1998] 2 F.L.R. 335; [1999] 3 F.C.R. 468; [1999] 2 F.C.R. 84; [1998] Fam. Law 512, CA (Civ Div) 20–018

D (Abduction: Discretionary Return), Re [2000] 1 F.L.R. 24; [2000] 1 F.C.R. 208; [2000] Fam. Law 8, Fam Div 20–018

D (Adoption by a Step Parent), Re [1980] 2 F.L.R. 102 22–058

D (An Infant) (Adoption: Parent's Consent), Re [1977] A.C. 602; [1977] 2 W.L.R. 79; [1977] 1 All E.R. 145; (1976) 121 S.J. 35, HL 19–001

D (Care: Natural Parent Presumption), Re; sub nom. D (Minors) (Natural Parent Presumption), Re; D (A Minor) (Residence: Natural Parent), Re [1999] 1 F.L.R. 134; [1999] 2 F.C.R. 118; [1999] Fam. Law 12; (2000) 164 J.P.N. 45, CA (Civ Div) ...19–003, 19–006, 19–026

D (Children) (Adoption: Freeing Order), Re [2001] 1 F.L.R. 403; [2001] Fam. Law 91, Fam Div 22–029

D (Children) (Article 13(b): Non-Return), Re [2006] EWCA Civ 146; [2006] 2 F.L.R. 305; [2006] Fam. Law 438, CA (Civ Div) 20–020

D (Children) (Care: Change of Forename), Re [2003] 1 F.L.R. 339; [2003] Fam. Law 77, Fam Div 17–025, 21–080

D (Children) (Shared Residence Orders), Re; sub nom. D v D (Children) (Shared Residence Orders) [2001] 1 F.L.R. 495; [2001] 1 F.C.R. 147; [2001] Fam. Law 183; (2001) 165 J.P.N. 347, CA (Civ Div) 17–048, 18–016

D (Minors) (Adoption Reports: Confidentiality), Re [1996] A.C. 593; [1995] 3 W.L.R. 483; [1995] 4 All E.R. 385; [1995] 2 F.L.R. 687; [1996] 1 F.C.R. 205; [1996] Fam. Law 8; (1995) 145 N.L.J. 1612, HL 18–042, 19–017, 22–035

D (Minors) (Family Appeals), Re [1995] 1 F.C.R. 301, CA (Civ Div) 19–018

D (No.1), Re (1996) J.P.N. 286 21–077

D v A, 163 E.R. 1039; (1845) 1 Rob. Ecc. 279, Eccl Ct 2–025, 2–029

D v Bury MBC; H v Bury MBC; sub nom. AD v Bury MBC [2006] EWCA Civ 1; [2006] 1 W.L.R. 917; [2006] 2 F.L.R. 147; [2006] 1 F.C.R. 148; [2006] A.C.D. 45; [2006] Fam. Law 348; (2006) 103(6) L.S.G. 30, CA (Civ Div) 21–027

D v D (1974) 5 Fam. Law 61; (1974) 118 S.J. 715 3–030

D v D [2007] EWHC 278 (Fam); [2007] 2 F.L.R. 653; [2007] 1 F.C.R. 603; [2007] Fam. Law 685, Fam Div 13–045

D v D (Access: Contempt: Committal) [1991] 2 F.L.R. 34; [1991] Fam. Law 365, CA (Civ Div) 18–056

D v D (Child of the Family) (1980) 2 F.L.R. 93 18–034
D v D (County Court Jurisdiction: Injunctions) [1993] 2 F.L.R. 802; [1994] Fam. Law 8;
(1993) 137 S.J.L.B. 199, CA (Civ Div) 9–042
D v D (Custody: Jurisdiction) [1996] 1 F.L.R. 574; [1996] 3 F.C.R. 19; [1996] Fam. Law
272; (1996) 146 N.L.J. 917, Fam Div 20–010, 20–015
D v D (Financial Provision: Lump Sum Order) [2001] 1 F.L.R. 633; [2001] 1 F.C.R. 561;
[2001] Fam. Law 254, Fam Div 13–045, 13–046
D v D (Financial Provision: Periodical Payments) [2004] EWHC 445 (Fam); [2004] 1
F.L.R. 988; [2004] Fam. Law 407, Fam Div 13–091, 13–099
D v D (Nullity: Statutory Bar) [1979] Fam. 70; [1979] 3 W.L.R. 185; [1979] 3 All E.R. 337;
(1978) 9 Fam. Law 182; (1979) 123 S.J. 473, Fam Div 2–026, 2–027, 2–050, 2–051, 2–056
D v D and B Ltd [2007] 2 F.L.R. 653 13–087
D v E Berkshire Community Health NHS Trust. *See* JD v East Berkshire Community Health
NHS Trust
D v M (A Minor) (Custody Appeal); sub nom. Dicocco v Milne [1983] Fam. 33; [1982] 3
W.L.R. 891; [1982] 3 All E.R. 897; (1983) 4 F.L.R. 247; (1982) 79 L.S.G. 1175; (1982)
126 S.J. 562, CA (Civ Div) 18–042
D v Registrar General; sub nom. L (A Minor) (Adoption: Disclosure of Information), Re
[1998] Fam. 19; [1997] 2 W.L.R. 739; [1997] 1 F.L.R. 715; [1997] 2 F.C.R. 240; [1997]
Fam. Law 314; (1997) 94(4) L.S.G. 26; (1997) 141 S.J.L.B. 21, CA (Civ Div) 22–011
D v S (Parental Responsibility) [1995] 3 F.C.R. 783, Fam Div 17–037
D and K (Children) (Care Plan: Twin Track Planning), Re; sub nom. D and K (Children)
(Care Plan: Concurrent Planning), Re [2000] 1 W.L.R. 642; [1999] 4 All E.R. 893;
[1999] 2 F.L.R. 872; [1999] 3 F.C.R. 109; [1999] Fam. Law 750; (2000) 164 J.P.N.
244; (1999) 149 N.L.J. 1405, Fam Div 22–042
DB and CB (Minors), Re; sub nom. Southwark LBC v B [1993] 2 F.L.R. 559; [1993] 2
F.C.R. 607; [1994] Fam. Law 73, CA (Civ Div) 19–014, 19–015
DH (A Minor) (Child Abuse), Re; sub nom. DH (A Minor) (Case Proceeding: Evidence and
Orders), Re [1994] 1 F.L.R. 679; [1994] 2 F.C.R. 3; [1994] Fam. Law 433, Fam Div 18–008,
21–036, 21–042
DM (A Minor) (Wardship: Jurisdiction), Re [1986] 2 F.L.R. 122; [1986] Fam. Law 296, CA
(Civ Div) 21–085
DPP v Dziurzynski [2002] EWHC 1380; (2002) 166 J.P. 545; [2002] A.C.D. 88; (2002) 166
J.P.N. 689; (2002) 99(35) L.S.G. 36, QBD (Admin) 9–005
DPP v Hall [2005] EWHC 2612; [2006] 1 W.L.R. 1000; [2006] 3 All E.R. 170; (2006) 170
J.P. 11; (2006) 170 J.P.N. 12, DC 9–040
DPP v Tweddle [2001] EWCA Admin. 188 9–035
Dackham v Dackham [1987] Fam. Law 345, CA (Civ Div) 13–001
Dart v Dart [1996] 2 F.L.R. 286; [1997] 1 F.C.R. 21; [1996] Fam. Law 607, CA (Civ Div) 13–043,
13–072, 13–078
Davenham Trust Plc v CV Distribution (UK) Ltd; sub nom. Taylor (A Bankrupt), Re [2006]
EWHC 3029 (Ch); [2007] Ch. 150; [2007] 2 W.L.R. 148; [2007] 3 All E.R. 638; [2007]
B.P.I.R. 175, Ch D (Manchester) 14–005
Davis v Black (1841) 1 Q.B. 900 1–035
Davis v Davis [1993] 1 F.L.R. 54; [1993] 1 F.C.R. 1002; [1993] Fam. Law 59, CA (Civ
Div) 7–026
Davis v Johnson [1979] A.C. 264; [1978] 2 W.L.R. 553; [1978] 1 All E.R. 1132; (1978) 122
S.J. 178, HL 9–004, 9–023
Davis v Vale [1971] 1 W.L.R. 1022; [1971] 2 All E.R. 1021; (1971) 115 S.J. 347, CA (Civ
Div) 3–008, 3–009
Dawson v Wearmouth [1999] 2 A.C. 308; [1998] 1 W.L.R. 1395; [1999] 2 W.L.R. 960;
[1999] 2 All E.R. 353; [1999] 1 F.L.R. 1167; [1999] 1 F.C.R. 625; [1999] Fam. Law
378; (1999) 96(17) L.S.G. 24; (1999) 143 S.J.L.B. 114, HL 17–025, 18–022, 19–018
De Lasala v De Lasala [1980] A.C. 546; [1979] 3 W.L.R. 390; [1979] 2 All E.R. 1146;
[1980] F.S.R. 443; (1979) 123 S.J. 301, PC (HK) 10–001, 13–005, 13–017, 13–107, 13–108
De Reneville (otherwise Sheridan) v De Reneville [1948] P. 100; [1948] 1 All E.R. 56; 64
T.L.R. 82; [1948] L.J.R. 1761, CA 2–052
Deacock v Deacock [1958] P. 230; [1958] 3 W.L.R. 191; [1958] 2 All E.R. 633; (1958) 102
S.J. 526, CA 12–003
Dean v Stout [2004] EWHC 3315; [2006] 1 F.L.R. 725; [2005] B.P.I.R. 1113; [2006] Fam.
Law 11, Ch D 5–059
Debenham (Deceased), Re [1986] 1 F.L.R. 404; [1986] Fam. Law 101 7–028

Debtor (No.488-IO of 1996), Re; sub nom. JP v Debtor; J (A Debtor), Re; M (A Debtor),
   Re [1999] 2 B.C.L.C. 571; [1999] 1 F.L.R. 926; [1999] 2 F.C.R. 637; [1999] Fam. Law
   293, Ch D 14–005
Delaney v Delaney [1990] 2 F.L.R. 457; [1991] F.C.R. 161; [1991] Fam. Law 22; (1990)
   154 J.P.N. 693, CA (Civ Div) 13–073
Delaney v Delaney [1996] Q.B. 387; [1996] 2 W.L.R. 74; [1996] 1 All E.R. 367; [1996] 1
   F.L.R. 458; [1996] 2 F.C.R. 13; [1996] Fam. Law 207, CA (Civ Div) 9–035
Den Heyer v Newby [2005] EWCA Civ 1311; [2006] 1 F.L.R. 1114; [2006] Fam. Law 260,
   CA (Civ Div) 13–103
Dennis (A Bankrupt), Re; sub nom. Dennis v Goodman [1996] Ch. 80; [1995] 3 W.L.R.
   367; [1995] 3 All E.R. 171; [1995] 2 F.L.R. 387; [1995] 3 F.C.R. 760; [1995] Fam.
   Law 611; [1995] N.P.C. 61, CA (Civ Div) 5–043
Dennis (Deceased), Re; sub nom. Dennis v Lloyds Bank Plc [1981] 2 All E.R. 140; (1980)
   124 S.J. 885, Ch D 7–011, 7–014, 7–022
Dennis v Dennis [2000] Fam. 163; [2000] 3 W.L.R. 1443; [2000] 2 F.L.R. 231; [2000] 2
   F.C.R. 108; [2000] Fam. Law 605, Fam Div 10–012
Dennis v McDonald [1982] Fam. 63; [1982] 2 W.L.R. 275; [1982] 1 All E.R. 590; (1982)
   12 Fam. Law 84; (1982) 126 S.J. 16, CA (Civ Div) 5–046
Densham (A Bankrupt), Re; sub nom. Trustee Ex p. v Densham [1975] 1 W.L.R. 1519;
   [1975] 3 All E.R. 726; (1975) 119 S.J. 774, Ch D 5–022
Denton v Southwark LBC [2007] EWCA Civ 623 6–036
Department of Social Security v Butler [1995] 1 W.L.R. 1528; [1995] 4 All E.R. 193; [1995]
   1 F.C.R. 63; (1995) 159 J.P.N. 796, CA (Civ Div) 15–025
Devon CC v B [1997] 1 F.L.R. 591; [1997] 3 F.C.R. 333; [1997] Fam. Law 399, CA (Civ
   Div) 18–052
Devon CC v S (Wardship: Inherent Jurisdiction) [1994] Fam. 169; [1994] 3 W.L.R. 183;
   [1995] 1 All E.R. 243; [1994] 1 F.L.R. 355; [1994] 2 F.C.R. 409; [1994] Fam. Law 371,
   Fam Div 18–052
Dharamshi v Dharamshi [2001] 1 F.L.R. 736; [2001] 1 F.C.R. 492; [2001] Fam. Law 98, CA
   (Civ Div) 13–045
Dickens v Pattison; sub nom. D v P (1985) 149 J.P. 271; [1985] Fam. Law 163; (1985) 82
   L.S.G. 438; (1985) 129 S.J. 31, Fam Div 14–002
Dickinson v Dickinson; sub nom. Dickinson v Dickinson (otherwise Phillips) [1913] P. 198,
   PDAD 2–024
Dickinson v Jones Alexander & Co [1993] 2 F.L.R. 521; [1990] Fam. Law 137; (1989) 139
   N.L.J. 1525, QBD 13–064
Dimino v Dimino [1989] 2 All E.R. 280, CA (Civ Div) 18–012
Dingmar v Dingmar [2006] EWCA Civ 942; [2006] 3 W.L.R. 1183; [2006] 2 F.C.R. 595;
   [2006] W.T.L.R. 1171; [2006] Fam. Law 1025; [2006] N.P.C. 83; [2007] Ch. 109, CA
   (Civ Div) 5–040
Diplock, Re [1948] Ch. 465 3–009
Dipper v Dipper [1981] Fam. 31; [1980] 3 W.L.R. 626; [1980] 2 All E.R. 722; (1979) 10
   Fam. Law 211; (1981) 145 J.P.N. 391; (1980) 124 S.J. 775, CA (Civ Div) ... 13–035, 13–092
Dixon v Marchant [2008] EWCA Civ.11 13–103
Donohue v Ingram (Trustee in Bankruptcy of Kirkup) [2006] EWHC 282, Ch D 5–059
Dorney-Kingdom v Dorney-Kingdom [2000] 2 F.L.R. 855; [2000] 3 F.C.R. 20; [2000] Fam.
   Law 794; (2000) 97(30) L.S.G. 39, CA (Civ Div) 15–038
Douglas v Hello! Ltd (No.1) [2001] Q.B. 967; [2001] 2 W.L.R. 992; [2001] 2 All E.R. 289;
   [2001] E.M.L.R. 9; [2001] 1 F.L.R. 982; [2002] 1 F.C.R. 289; [2001] H.R.L.R. 26;
   [2001] U.K.H.R.R. 223; 9 B.H.R.C. 543; [2001] F.S.R. 40, CA (Civ Div) 17–015, 18–053
Douglas v Hello! Ltd (No.6); sub nom. Douglas v Hello! Ltd (Trial Action: Breach of
   Confidence) (No.3) [2005] EWCA Civ 595; [2006] Q.B. 125; [2005] 3 W.L.R. 881;
   [2005] 4 All E.R. 128; [2005] E.M.L.R. 28; [2005] 2 F.C.R. 487; [2005] H.R.L.R. 27;
   (2005) 28(8) I.P.D. 28057; (2005) 155 N.L.J. 828, CA (Civ Div) 17–015
Downing v Downing [1976] Fam. 288; [1976] 3 W.L.R. 335; [1976] 3 All E.R. 474; (1976)
   6 Fam. Law 222; (1976) 120 S.J. 540, Fam Div 13–015, 15–045, 17–028
Doyle v White City Stadium Ltd [1935] 1 K.B. 110, CA 16–004
Drake v Whipp [1996] 1 F.L.R. 826; [1996] 2 F.C.R. 296; (1996) 28 H.L.R. 531; [1995]
   N.P.C. 188; (1996) 71 P. & C.R. D32, CA (Civ Div) 5–013, 5–022, 5–028
Draper's Conveyance, Re; sub nom. Nihan v Porter [1969] 1 Ch. 486; [1968] 2 W.L.R. 166;
   [1967] 3 All E.R. 853; (1968) 19 P. & C.R. 71; 204 E.G. 693; (1967) 111 S.J. 867, Ch
   D 5–040, 5–041

Dredge v Dredge (otherwise Harrison) [1947] 1 All E.R. 29; 63 T.L.R. 113; [1947] W.N. 71,
PDAD 2–025
Du Toit v Minister for Welfare and Population Development, 13 B.H.R.C. 187, Const Ct
(SA) 22–019
Dunbar Bank Plc v Nadeem [1998] 3 All E.R. 876; [1998] 2 F.L.R. 457; [1998] 3 F.C.R.
629; (1999) 31 H.L.R. 402; [1998] Fam. Law 595; (1999) 77 P. & C.R. D8, CA (Civ
Div) 5–056
Dunhill (An Infant), Re (1967) 111 S.J. 113 18–051
Durham v Durham; Hunter v Edney (otherwise Hunter); Cannon v Smalley (otherwise
Cannon) (1885) L.R. 10 P.D. 80, PDAD 2–036
Duxbury v Duxbury [1987] 1 F.L.R. 7; [1987] Fam. Law 13, CA (Civ Div) 13–021
Dyer v Dyer, 30 E.R. 42; (1788) 2 Cox Eq. Cas. 92, KB 5–014
Dyson Holdings Ltd v Fox [1976] Q.B. 503; [1975] 3 W.L.R. 744; [1975] 3 All E.R. 1030;
(1976) 31 P. & C.R. 229; 239 E.G. 39; (1975) 119 S.J. 744, CA (Civ Div) A–001
E (A Minor) (Abduction), Re [1989] 1 F.L.R. 135; [1989] Fam. Law 105, CA (Civ Div) 20–018
E (A Minor) (Adopted Child: Contact: Leave), Re [1995] 1 F.L.R. 57; [1995] 2 F.C.R. 655;
[1995] Fam. Law 117, Fam Div 18–039, 22–062
E (A Minor) (Care Order: Contact), Re [1994] 1 F.L.R. 146; [1994] 1 F.C.R. 584; [1993]
Fam. Law 671, CA (Civ Div) 21–074
E (A Minor) (Wardship: Medical Treatment), Re [1993] 1 F.L.R. 386; [1994] 5 Med. L.R.
73, Fam Div 16–014, 19–016
E (Abduction: Non Convention Country), Re. *See* Osman v Elasha
E (Family Assistance Order), Re [1999] 2 F.L.R. 512; [1999] 3 F.C.R. 700; [1999] Fam.
Law 529; (2000) 164 J.P.N. 762, Fam Div 18–027, 22–067
E (Minors) (Residence: Imposition of Conditions), Re; sub nom. E (Minors) (Residence
Orders), Re [1997] 2 F.L.R. 638; [1997] 3 F.C.R. 245; [1997] Fam. Law 606; (1997)
161 J.P.N. 937, CA (Civ Div) 18–016
E (Parental Responsibility: Blood Tests), Re [1995] 1 F.L.R. 392; [1994] 2 F.C.R. 709;
[1995] Fam. Law 121, CA (Civ Div) 17–007, 17–037
E (SA) (A Minor) (Wardship: Court's Duty), Re [1984] 1 W.L.R. 156; [1984] 1 All E.R.
289; 82 L.G.R. 257; (1984) 128 S.J. 80, HL 18–016, 18–052
E v C (Calculation of Child Maintenance) [1996] 1 F.L.R. 472; [1996] 1 F.C.R. 612; [1996]
Fam. Law 205, Fam Div 3–017, 13–058, 15–040
E v E (Financial Provision) [1990] 2 F.L.R. 233; [1989] F.C.R. 591; [1990] Fam. Law 297;
(1989) 153 J.P.N. 722 .... 13–027, 13–058
E v United Kingdom (33218/96) [2003] 1 F.L.R. 348; [2002] 3 F.C.R. 700; (2003) 36
E.H.R.R. 31; [2003] Fam. Law 157, ECHR 21–001
E v X LBC [2005] EWHC 2811; [2006] 1 F.L.R. 730; [2006] Fam. Law 187, Fam Div 18–049
ES, Re [2007] N.I.O.B. 58 21–049
Eadie v Inland Revenue Commissioners [1924] 2 K.B. 198, KBD 3–004
Eastham v Eastham and Eastham [1982] C.L.Y. 2141 17–027
Edgar v Edgar [1980] 1 W.L.R. 1410; [1980] 3 All E.R. 887; (1981) 2 F.L.R. 19; (1980) 11
Fam. Law 20; (1980) 124 S.J. 809, CA (Civ Div) 3–032, 13–007, 13–008, 13–009
Edmonds v Edmonds [1990] 2 F.L.R. 202; [1990] F.C.R. 856, CA (Civ Div) 13–104, 14–012
Edwards v Edwards [1986] 1 F.L.R. 187 19–003
Edwards v Lloyds TSB Bank Plc [2004] EWHC 1745; [2005] 1 F.C.R. 139; [2004] B.P.I.R.
1190, Ch D 5–060
Elder v Elder [1986] 1 F.L.R. 610; [1986] Fam. Law 190, CA (Civ Div) 18–042
Elkington and Co Ltd v Amery [1936] 2 All E.R. 86 3–041
Elliott v Elliott [2001] 1 F.C.R. 477, CA (Civ Div) 13–058, 13–116
Elsholz v Germany (25735/94) [2000] 2 F.L.R. 486; [2000] 3 F.C.R. 385; (2002) 34
E.H.R.R. 58; [2000] Fam. Law 800, ECHR 18–012, 19–004
Elwes, Re, Application of D Elwes, *The Times*, July 30, 1958 18–051
Emmanuel v Emmanuel [1981] 2 F.L.R. 319 13–064
England v Supplementary Benefits Commission [1981] 3 F.L.R. 222 6–023
Equity & Law Home Loans Ltd v Prestridge [1992] 1 W.L.R. 137; [1992] 1 All E.R. 909;
[1992] 1 F.L.R. 485; [1992] 1 F.C.R. 353; (1992) 24 H.L.R. 76; (1992) 63 P. & C.R.
403; [1992] Fam. Law 288; (1992) 89(2) L.S.G. 31; [1991] N.P.C. 103, CA (Civ
Div) 5–050
Eriksson v Sweden (A/156); sub nom. Eriksson v Sweden (11919/86) (1990) 12 E.H.R.R.
183, ECHR 21–0
Eski v Austria [2007] 1 F.L.R. 1650 .... 22–034, 22

Espinosa v Bourke; Espinosa v Isaacs; Espinosa v Wilson [1999] 1 F.L.R. 747; [1999] 3
F.C.R. 76; [1999] Fam. Law 210, CA (Civ Div) 7–014, 7–018, 7–024
Essex CC v B [1993] 1 F.L.R. 866; [1993] 1 F.C.R. 145; [1993] Fam. Law 457; (1993) 157
L.G. Rev. 507 21–032
Essex CC v F [1993] 1 F.L.R. 847; [1993] 2 F.C.R. 289; [1993] Fam. Law 337; (1994) 158
L.G. Rev. 27 ....21–046, 21–048, 21–049
Essex CC v Mirror Group Newspapers Ltd [1996] 1 F.L.R. 585; [1996] 2 F.C.R. 831; [1996]
Fam. Law 270, Fam Div 18–051
Ette v Ette [1964] 1 W.L.R. 1433; [1965] 1 All E.R. 341; (1964) 108 S.J. 181, PDAD 14–011
Ettenfield v Ettenfield [1940] P. 96, CA 17–004
Evans v Amicus Healthcare Ltd; Hadley v Midland Fertility Services Ltd [2004] EWCA
Civ 727; [2005] Fam. 1; [2004] 3 W.L.R. 681; [2004] 3 All E.R. 1025; [2004] 2 F.L.R.
766; [2004] 2 F.C.R. 530; (2004) 78 B.M.L.R. 181; [2004] Fam. Law 647; (2004) 148
S.J.L.B. 823, CA (Civ Div) 17–014
Evans v Evans, 161 E.R. 466; (1790) 1 Hag. Con. 35, KB 10–003
Evans v Evans (1989) 153 J.P. 78; [1989] 1 F.L.R. 351; [1989] F.C.R. 153; (1989) 153 J.P.N.
169, CA (Civ Div) 13–084
Evans v United Kingdom (6339/05) [2006] 2 F.L.R. 172; [2006] 1 F.C.R. 585; (2006) 43
E.H.R.R. 21; [2006] Fam. Law 357; (2006) 156 N.L.J. 456, ECHR 16–017, 17–014
Evers Trust, Re; sub nom. Papps v Evers [1980] 1 W.L.R. 1327; [1980] 3 All E.R. 399;
(1980) 10 Fam. Law 245; (1980) 124 S.J. 562, CA (Civ Div) 5–046
Eves v Eves [1975] 1 W.L.R. 1338; [1975] 3 All E.R. 768; (1975) 119 S.J. 394, CA (Civ
Div) 5–021, 5–025
F (A Child) (Indirect Contact), Re [2006] EWCA Civ 1426; [2006] 3 F.C.R. 553; [2007]
Fam. Law 109; (2006) 150 S.J.L.B. 1465, CA (Civ Div) 19–001
F (A Child) (Mental Health Act: Guardianship), Re; sub nom. F (A Child) (Care Order:
Sexual Abuse), Re [2000] 1 F.L.R. 192; [2000] 1 F.C.R. 11; (1999) 2 C.C.L. Rep. 445;
(2000) 51 B.M.L.R. 128; [2000] Fam. Law 18; (1999) 96(39) L.S.G. 38, CA (Civ
Div) 18–051
F (A Minor) (Blood Tests: Paternity Rights), Re [1993] Fam. 314; [1993] 3 W.L.R. 369;
[1993] 3 All E.R. 596; [1993] 1 F.L.R. 598; [1993] 1 F.C.R. 932; [1993] 4 Med. L.R.
268; [1993] Fam. Law 407; (1993) 143 N.L.J. 472, CA (Civ Div) 17–007, 19–007
F (A Minor) (Child Abduction), Re; sub nom. AF (A Minor) (Abduction), Re [1992] 1
F.L.R. 548; [1992] F.C.R. 269; [1992] Fam. Law 195, CA (Civ Div) 20–015, 20–018
F (A Minor) (Child Abduction: Rights of Custody Abroad), Re; sub nom. F (A Minor)
(Child Abduction: Risk if Returned), Re [1995] Fam. 224; [1995] 3 W.L.R. 339; [1995]
3 All E.R. 641; [1995] 2 F.L.R. 31; [1995] Fam. Law 534, CA (Civ Div) 20–016, 20–020
F (A Minor) (Contact: Child in Care), Re [1995] 1 F.L.R. 510; [1994] 2 F.C.R. 1354; [1995]
Fam. Law 231; (1994) 158 J.P.N. 856, Fam Div ..16–020, 17–024, 18–019, 18–020, 18–029,
19–001, 21–076
F (A Minor) (Contact: Enforcement: Representation of Child), Re [1998] 1 F.L.R. 691;
[1998] 3 F.C.R. 216; [1998] Fam. Law 319, CA (Civ Div) 18–041, 18–058
F (A Minor) (Immigration: Wardship), Re [1990] Fam. 125; [1989] 3 W.L.R. 691; [1989]
1 All E.R. 1155; [1989] 1 F.L.R. 233; [1989] F.C.R. 165; [1988] Fam. Law 474; (1989)
153 J.P.N. 306; (1989) 133 S.J. 1088, CA (Civ Div) 18–016, 18–052
F (A Minor) (Parental Responsibility Order), Re [1994] 1 F.L.R. 504 17–037
F (A Minor) (Publication of Information), Re; sub nom. A (A Minor), Re [1977] Fam. 58;
[1976] 3 W.L.R. 813; [1977] 1 All E.R. 114; (1976) 120 S.J. 753, CA (Civ Div) 18–050,
18–052
F (A Minor) (Wardship: Appeal), Re [1976] Fam. 238; [1976] 2 W.L.R. 189; [1976] 1 All
E.R. 417; (1975) 6 Fam. Law 147, CA (Civ Div) 17–014, 19–024, 19–026
F (Abduction: Unborn Child), Re [2007] 1 F.L.R. 627, Fam Div 20–015
F (Adoption: Natural Parents), Re [2007] 1 F.L.R. 363, CA 22–035
F (Children) (Care: Termination of Contact), Re; sub nom. F (Children) (Care Proceedings:
Contact), Re [2000] 2 F.C.R. 481; [2000] Fam. Law 708; (2000) 164 J.P.N. 703, Fam
Div 21–004
F (Children) (Shared Residence Order), Re [2003] EWCA Civ 592; [2003] 2 F.L.R. 397;
[2003] 2 F.C.R. 164; [2003] Fam. Law 568, CA (Civ Div) 18–016
F (Contact: Lack of Reasons), Re [2007] 1 F.L.R. 65, CA 19–010
F (Family Proceedings: Section 37 Investigation), Re; sub nom. C v C [2005] EWHC 2935;
[2006] 1 F.L.R. 1122; [2006] Fam. Law 261, Fam Div 18–048

F (In Utero), Re [1988] Fam. 122; [1988] 2 W.L.R. 1288; [1988] 2 All E.R. 193; [1988] 2
F.L.R. 307; [1988] F.C.R. 529; [1988] Fam. Law 337; (1988) 152 J.P.N. 538; (1988)
138 N.L.J. Rep. 37; (1988) 132 S.J. 820; (1989) 133 S.J. 1088, CA (Civ Div) 18–050, 18–051
F (Indirect Contact), Re [2007] 1 F.L.R. 1015, CA 18–019, 19–008, 19–022
F (Minors) (Contact), Re; sub nom. F (Minors) (Denial of Contact), Re [1993] 2 F.L.R. 677;
[1993] 1 F.C.R. 945; [1993] Fam. Law 673, CA (Civ Div) 18–019
F (Minors) (Contact: Mother's Anxiety), Re [1993] 2 F.L.R. 830; [1994] 1 F.C.R. 712;
[1994] Fam. Law 251, CA (Civ Div) 18–019
F (Minors) (Specific Issue: Child Interview), Re; sub nom. F (Minors) (Solicitors
Interviews), Re [1995] 1 F.L.R. 819; [1995] 2 F.C.R. 200, CA (Civ Div) 18–022, 21–065
F (Paternity: Jurisdiction) [2008] 1 F.L.R. 246 18–022
F (R) (An Infant), Re [1970] 1 Q.B. 385; [1969] 3 W.L.R. 853; [1969] 3 All E.R. 1101;
(1969) 113 S.J. 835, CA (Civ Div) 22–032
F (Residence Order: Jurisdiction), Re [1995] 2 F.L.R. 518; [1995] Fam. Law 668, Fam
Div 18–030
F (Wardship: Sterilisation), Re [1990] 2 A.C. 1 21–080
F v Cambridgeshire CC [1995] 1 F.L.R. 516; [1995] 2 F.C.R. 804; [1995] Fam. Law 240;
(1995) 159 J.P.N. 476, Fam Div 18–048
F v F; sub nom. Foard v Foard [1967] 1 W.L.R. 793; [1967] 2 All E.R. 660; (1967) 111 S.J.
474, PDAD 13–018
F v F (Ancillary Relief: Substantial Assets) [1995] 2 F.L.R. 45; [1996] 2 F.C.R. 397; [1995]
Fam. Law 546, Fam Div 13–001, 13–037, 13–043, 13–072, 13–078
F v F (Clean Break: Balance of Fairness) [2003] 1 F.L.R. 847; [2003] Fam. Law 311, Fam
Div 13–045
F v F (Duxbury Calculation: Rate of Return) [1996] 1 F.L.R. 833, Fam Div 13–012, 13–072,
13–078
F v G (Child: Financial Provision) [2004] EWHC 1848; [2005] 1 F.L.R. 261, Fam Div 15–050,
15–051
F v Kent CC [1993] 1 F.L.R. 432; [1993] 1 F.C.R. 217; [1993] Fam. Law 132; (1992) 89(34)
L.S.G. 39; (1992) 136 S.J.L.B. 258, Fam Div 21–075
F v Lambeth LBC; sub nom. F (Children: Care Planning), Re [2002] 1 F.L.R. 217; [2001]
3 F.C.R. 738; [2002] Fam. Law 8, Fam Div 21–039
F v Leeds City Council [1994] 2 F.L.R. 60; [1994] 2 F.C.R. 428; [1994] Fam. Law 610, CA
(Civ Div) 19–001
F v Wirral MBC; sub nom. Fitzpatrick v Wirral MBC [1991] Fam. 69; [1991] 2 W.L.R.
1132; [1991] 2 All E.R. 648; [1991] 2 F.L.R. 114; [1991] Fam. Law 299, CA (Civ
Div) 16–002, 17–015, 17–019, 17–051
F and R (Section 8 Order: Grandparents' Application), Re [1995] 1 F.L.R. 524; [1995] Fam.
Law 235, Fam Div 18–020
Fairpo v Humberside CC; sub nom. F v Humberside CC; R. v Special Educational Needs
Tribunal Ex p. Fairpo (No.2) [1997] 1 All E.R. 183; [1997] 1 F.L.R. 339; [1997] 3
F.C.R. 181; [1997] E.L.R. 12; (1997) 161 J.P.N. 748, QBD 17–016
Farley v Child Support Agency; sub nom. Farley v Secretary of State for Work and Pensions
(No.2) [2006] UKHL 31; [2006] 1 W.L.R. 1817; [2006] 3 All E.R. 935; (2006) 170 J.P.
650; [2006] 2 F.L.R. 1243; [2006] 2 F.C.R. 713; [2006] Fam. Law 735; (2007) 171
J.P.N. 105; (2006) 103(28) L.S.G. 28; (2006) 150 S.J.L.B. 889, HL 15–024
Farrow (Deceased), Re [1987] 1 F.L.R. 205; [1987] Fam. Law 14 7–013
Fender v St John Mildmay; sub nom. Fender v Mildmay [1938] A.C. 1, HL 3–027, 5–007
Fessi v Whitmore [1999] 1 F.L.R. 767; [1999] Fam. Law 221, Ch D 17–027
Field v Field [2003] 1 F.L.R. 376; [2003] Fam. Law 76, Fam Div 14–008, 14–009
Fielder v Smith (1816) 2 Hag. Con. 193; 161 E.R. 712 1–005
Figgis, Re; sub nom. Roberts v MacLaren [1969] 1 Ch. 123; [1968] 2 W.L.R. 1173; [1968]
1 All E.R. 999; (1968) 112 S.J. 156, Ch D 5–063
First National Bank Plc v Achampong [2003] EWCA Civ 487; [2004] 1 F.C.R. 18; (2003)
147 S.J.L.B. 419; [2003] N.P.C. 46; [2003] 2 P. & C.R. DG11, CA (Civ Div) 5–060
First National Bank Plc v Walker [2001] 1 F.L.R. 505; [2001] 1 F.C.R. 21; [2001] Fam. Law
182, CA (Civ Div) 5–056
First National Securities Ltd v Hegerty [1985] Q.B. 850; [1984] 3 W.L.R. 769; [1984] 3 All
E.R. 641; (1984) 48 P. & C.R. 200; [1984] Fam. Law 316; (1984) 81 L.S.G. 2543;
(1984) 128 S.J. 499, CA (Civ Div) 5–043, 14–008
Fischer v Adams, 38 N.W. 2d 337 (1949) .... 2–03●

Fitzpatrick v Sterling Housing Association Ltd [2001] 1 A.C. 27; [1999] 3 W.L.R. 1113; [1999] 4 All E.R. 705; [2000] 1 F.L.R. 271; [1999] 2 F.L.R. 1027; [2000] 1 F.C.R. 21; [2000] U.K.H.R.R. 25; 7 B.H.R.C. 200; (2000) 32 H.L.R. 178; [2000] L. & T.R. 44; [2000] Fam. Law 14; [1999] E.G. 125 (C.S.); (1999) 96(43) L.S.G. 3; [1999] N.P.C. 127; (2000) 79 P. & C.R. D4, HL A–001, 9–029

Flavell v Flavell [1997] 1 F.L.R. 353; [1997] 1 F.C.R. 332; [1997] Fam. Law 237, CA (Civ Div) 13–090, 13–091, 13–097, 13–098, 13–099

Fleming v Fleming [2003] EWCA Civ 1841; [2004] 1 F.L.R. 667; [2004] Fam. Law 174, CA (Civ Div) 13–021, 13–098, 13–099

Fleming v Fleming [2006] 2 F.L.R. 1186 13–090

Flemming v Pratt (1823) 1 L.J. (O.S.) K.B. 195 17–014

Flint (A Bankrupt), Re [1993] Ch. 319; [1993] 2 W.L.R. 537; [1993] 1 F.L.R. 763; (1992) 136 S.J.L.B. 221, Ch D 14–005

Flintshire v K [2001] 2 F.L.R. 476, Fam Div 21–079, 22–053

Ford v Ford [1987] Fam. Law 232, CC (Croydon) 2–031

Ford v Stier [1896] P. 1, PDAD 2–042

Foster v Foster [2003] EWCA Civ 565; [2003] 2 F.L.R. 299; [2005] 3 F.C.R. 26; [2003] Fam. Law 562; (2003) 100(26) L.S.G. 37, CA (Civ Div) 13–049

Foulkes v Chief Constable of Merseyside [1998] 3 All E.R. 705; [1998] 2 F.L.R. 789; [1999] 1 F.C.R. 98; [1998] Fam. Law 661, CA (Civ Div) 3–010

Fournier v Fournier [1998] 2 F.L.R. 990; [1999] 2 F.C.R. 20; [1998] Fam. Law 662, CA (Civ Div) 13–072

Fowler v Fowler (1981) 2 F.L.R. 141, OH 14–002, 14–017

Francis v Manning [1997] EWCA 1231, CA 15–051

Frary v Frary [1993] 2 F.L.R. 696; [1994] 1 F.C.R. 595; [1993] Fam. Law 628, CA (Civ Div) 13–021

Frette v France (36515/97) [2003] 2 F.L.R. 9; [2003] 2 F.C.R. 39; (2004) 38 E.H.R.R. 21; [2003] Fam. Law 636, ECHR 22–018, 22–019

Fricker v Personal Representatives of Fricker [1981] 3 F.L.R. 228 7–031

Fullard (Deceased), Re; sub nom. Fuller (Deceased), Re [1982] Fam. 42; [1981] 3 W.L.R. 743; [1981] 2 All E.R. 796; (1981) 11 Fam. Law 116, CA (Civ Div) 7–013, 7–018, 7–024

Fuller v Fuller [1973] 1 W.L.R. 730; [1973] 2 All E.R. 650; (1973) 117 S.J. 224, CA (Civ Div) 10–001, 10–037

G (A Child), Re; sub nom. G (A Child) (Parental Responsibility Order), Re [2006] EWCA Civ 745; [2006] 2 F.L.R. 1092; [2006] Fam. Law 744; (2006) 150 S.J.L.B. 666, CA (Civ Div) 17–037

G (A Child) (Care Order: Threshold Criteria), Re; sub nom. G (A Child) (Care Proceedings: Split Trials), Re [2001] 1 F.L.R. 872; [2001] 1 F.C.R. 165, CA (Civ Div) 18–042, 21–030, 21–053

G (A Child) (Contempt: Committal Order), Re; sub nom. PG v LMR [2003] EWCA Civ 489; [2003] 1 W.L.R. 2051; [2003] 2 F.L.R. 58; [2003] 2 F.C.R. 231; [2003] Fam. Law 470; (2003) 100(24) L.S.G. 35, CA (Civ Div) 18–057

G (A Child) (Custody Rights: Unmarried Father), Re. *See* C (Child Abduction) (Unmarried Father: Rights of Custody), Re

G (A Child) (Domestic Violence: Direct Contact), Re [2000] 2 F.L.R. 865; [2001] 2 F.C.R. 134; [2000] Fam. Law 789; (2001) 165 J.P.N. 526, Fam Div 17–037

G (A Child) (Interim Care Order: Residential Assessment), Re; sub nom. G (A Child) (Interim Care Orders: Inpatient Assessment), Re; Kent CC v G [2005] UKHL 68; [2006] 1 A.C. 576; [2005] 3 W.L.R. 1166; [2006] 1 All E.R. 706; [2006] 1 F.L.R. 601; [2005] 3 F.C.R. 621; [2006] Fam. Law 91; (2005) 102(47) L.S.G. 28, HL 21–043

G (A Child) (Maintenance Pending Suit), Re [2006] EWHC 1834 (Fam); [2007] 1 F.L.R. 1674; [2007] Fam. Law 215, Fam Div 13–037

G (A Child) (Parental Responsibility Order), Re. *See* G (A Child), Re

G (A Child) (Secure Accommodation Order), Re [2001] 1 F.L.R. 884; [2001] 3 F.C.R. 47; [2001] Fam. Law 263, Fam Div 21–077

G (A Minor) (Adoption: Freeing Order), Re [1997] A.C. 613; [1997] 2 W.L.R. 747; [1997] 2 All E.R. 534; [1997] 2 F.L.R. 202; [1997] 2 F.C.R. 289; [1997] Fam. Law 596; (1997) 94(22) L.S.G. 31; (1997) 141 S.J.L.B. 106, HL 22–044

G (A Minor) (Blood Tests), Re; sub nom. CG (A Minor) (Blood Tests), Re [1994] 1 F.L.R. 495; [1994] 2 F.C.R. 889; [1994] Fam. Law 310; (1994) 158 J.P.N. 682, Fam Div ... 17–007

G (A Minor) (Care Orders: Threshold Conditions), Re; sub nom. G (A Minor) (Care
    Proceedings), Re [1995] Fam. 16; [1994] 3 W.L.R. 1211; [1994] 2 F.L.R. 69; 93 L.G.R.
    162; [1994] Fam. Law 485, Fam Div 18–042
G (A Minor) (Child Abuse: Standard of Proof), Re [1987] 1 W.L.R. 1461; [1988] 1 F.L.R.
    314; [1988] Fam. Law 129; (1987) 84 L.S.G. 3415; (1987) 131 S.J. 1550, Fam Div 21–036
G (A Minor) (Enforcement of Access Abroad), Re; sub nom. G (A Minor) (Hague
    Convention: Access), Re; G (A Minor) (Convention on the Civil Aspects of
    International Child Abduction: Access), Re [1993] Fam. 216; [1993] 2 W.L.R. 824;
    [1993] 3 All E.R. 657; [1993] 1 F.L.R. 669; [1993] 2 F.C.R. 485; [1993] Fam. Law 340,
    CA (Civ Div) 20–024
G (A Minor) (Parental Responsibility: Education), Re [1994] 2 F.L.R. 964; [1995] 2 F.C.R.
    53; [1994] Fam. Law 492, CA (Civ Div) 17–048, 18–005, 18–015
G (A Minor) (Role of the Appellate Court), Re [1987] 1 F.L.R. 164; [1987] Fam. Law 52,
    CA (Civ Div) 19–025
G (A Minor) (Witness Summons), Re [1988] 2 F.L.R. 396; [1989] Fam. Law 67, Fam Div ... 18–052
G (Abduction: Striking Out Application), Re [1995] 2 F.L.R. 410; [1995] Fam. Law 662,
    Fam Div 20–018
G (Child Abductionsychological Harm), Re [1995] 1 F.L.R. 64; [1995] 2 F.C.R. 22; [1995]
    Fam. Law 116, Fam Div 20–020
G (Children) (Care Order: Evidence), Re; sub nom. G (Children) (Care Order: Threshold
    Criteria), Re; G (Care Proceedings: Threshold Conditions), Re [2001] EWCA Civ 968;
    [2001] 1 W.L.R. 2100; [2001] 2 F.L.R. 1111; [2001] 2 F.C.R. 757; [2001] Fam. Law
    727; (2001) 98(29) L.S.G. 37; (2001) 145 S.J.L.B. 166, CA (Civ Div) 21–033
G (Children) (Care Proceedings: Wasted Costs), Re; sub nom. G, S and M (Children)
    (Wasted Costs), Re; G, S and H (Care Proceedings: Wasted Costs), Re [2000] Fam.
    104; [2000] 2 W.L.R. 1007; [1999] 4 All E.R. 371; [2000] 1 F.L.R. 52; [1999] 3 F.C.R.
    303; [2000] Fam. Law 24, Fam Div 18–041
G (Children) (Residence: Making of Order), Re [2005] EWCA Civ 1283; [2006] 1 F.L.R.
    771; [2006] Fam. Law 93, CA (Civ Div) 18–005, 19–023
G (Children) (Residence: Same Sex Partner), R; sub nom. CG v CW [2006] UKHL 43;
    [2006] 1 W.L.R. 2305; [2006] 4 All E.R. 241; [2006] 2 F.L.R. 629; [2006] 3 F.C.R. 1;
    [2006] Fam. Law 932; (2006) 103(32) L.S.G. 21; (2006) 156 N.L.J. 1252; (2006) 150
    S.J.L.B. 1021, HL 19–003, 19–005
G (Contact), Re [2007] 1 F.L.R. 1663, CA 18–016, 19–007
G (Decree Absolute: Prejudice), Re [2002] EWHC 2834; [2003] 1 F.L.R. 870; [2003] Fam.
    Law 306, Fam Div 10–012
G (Foreign Adoption: Consent), Re [1995] 2 F.L.R. 528, Fam Div 22–029
G (Foreign Contact Order: Enforcement), Re [2004] 1 F.L.R. 394, CA 20–024
G (Minors) (Care: Leave to Place Outside Jurisdiction), Re [1994] 2 F.L.R. 301; [1994] 2
    F.C.R. 359; [1994] Fam. Law 568, Fam Div 19–002, 21–041, 21–079
G (Minors) (Celebrities: Publicity), Re [1999] 1 F.L.R. 409; [1999] 3 F.C.R. 181; [1999]
    Fam. Law 141, ... CA (Civ Div) 18–008, 18–049
G (Minors) (Ex parte Interim Residence Order), Re [1993] 1 F.L.R. 910; [1993] Fam. Law
    460, CA (Civ Div) 18–024, 18–040, 20–009
G (Minors) (Welfare Report: Disclosure), Re [1993] 2 F.L.R. 293; [1994] 1 F.C.R. 37;
    [1993] Fam. Law 576, CA (Civ Div) 18–012
G (Parentage: Blood Sample), Re; sub nom. G (A Minor) (Paternity: Blood Tests), Re
    [1997] 1 F.L.R. 360; [1997] 2 F.C.R. 325; [1997] Fam. Law 243; (1997) 161 J.P.N.
    434, CA (Civ Div) 17–008
G (Wardship)(Jurisdiciton: Power of Arrest) (1983) 4 F.L.R. 538 18–052
G and B (Children), Re [2007] 2 F.L.R. 140, CA 22–033
G and R (Child Sexual Abuse: Standard of Proof), Re [1995] 2 F.L.R. 867, CA (Civ Div) 21–036
G v Child Support Agency [2006] EWHC 423; [2006] 2 F.L.R. 857; [2006] Fam. Law 523,
    Fam Div 15–024
G v F (Non Molestation Order: Jurisdiction); sub nom. G v G (Non Molestation Order:
    Jurisdiction) [2000] Fam. 186; [2000] 3 W.L.R. 1202; [2000] 2 F.L.R. 533; [2000] 2
    F.C.R. 638; [2000] Fam. Law 519; [2000] Fam. Law 703; (2000) 97(25) L.S.G. 40,
    Fam Div 9–028, 9–029
G v F (Shared Residence: Parental Responsibility); sub nom. G v F (Contact and Shared
    Residence: Applications for Leave) [1998] 2 F.L.R. 799; [1998] 3 F.C.R. 1; [1998]
    Fam. Law 587, Fam Div 18–039
G v G [1924] A.C. 349; 1924 S.C. (H.L.) 42; 1924 S.L.T. 248, HL 2–026

G v G [1952] V.L.R. 402 .... 2–025, 2–033
G v G [1964] P. 133; [1964] 2 W.L.R. 250; [1964] 1 All E.R. 129, PDAD 10–031
G v G (1981) 1 Fam.Law 148 18–016
G v G [2006] EWCA Civ 1670; (2006) 103(44) L.S.G. 30; (2006) 150 S.J.L.B. 1466, CA
    (Civ Div) 9–035
G v G (Contempt: Committal) [1992] 2 F.C.R. 145; [1993] Fam. Law 335, CA (Civ Div) 9–035
G v G (Financial Provision: Equal Division) [2002] EWHC 1339 (Fam); [2002] 2 F.L.R.
    1143; [2003] Fam. Law 14, Fam Div 13–080
G v G (Financial Provision: Separation Agreement); sub nom. Wyatt-Jones v Goldsmith
    [2004] 1 F.L.R. 1011, CA (Civ Div) 13–004, 13–008, 13–075, 13–083
G v G (Maintenance Pending Suit: Legal Costs) [2002] EWHC 306 (Fam); [2003] 2 F.L.R.
    71; [2002] 3 F.C.R. 339; [2003] Fam. Law 393, Fam Div 13–037
G v G (Matrimonial Property: Rights of Extended Family) [2005] EWHC 1560 (Fam);
    [2006] 1 F.L.R. 62; [2005] Fam. Law 764, Fam Div 4–001, 13–066
G v G (Minors: Custody Appeal) [1985] 1 W.L.R. 647; [1985] 2 All E.R. 225; [1985] F.L.R.
    894; [1985] Fam. Law 321; (1985) 82 L.S.G. 2010; (1985) 83 L.S.G. 2010; (1985) 135
    N.L.J. 439; (1985) 129 S.J. 315, HL 19–020, 19–024, 19–025, 19–026, 21–046, 22–064
G v G (Occupation Order: Conduct) [2000] 2 F.L.R. 36; [2000] 3 F.C.R. 53; [2000] Fam.
    Law 466, CA (Civ Div) 9–017, 9–018, 9–019, 9–020
G v G (Periodical Payments: Jurisdiction to Vary) [1998] Fam. 1; [1997] 2 W.L.R. 614;
    [1997] 1 All E.R. 272; [1997] 1 F.L.R. 368; [1997] 1 F.C.R. 441; [1996] Fam. Law
    722; (1997) 161 J.P.N. 86, CA (Civ Div) 13–097
G v G (Role of FDR Judge) [2006] EWHC 1993 (Fam); [2007] 1 F.L.R. 237; [2006] Fam.
    Law 922, Fam Div 13–012
G v M (1884–85) L.R. 10 App. Cas. 171, HL 2–026, 2–050
GW v RW (Financial Provision: Departure from Equality) [2003] EWHC 611; [2003] 2
    F.L.R. 108; [2003] 2 F.C.R. 289; [2003] Fam. Law 386, Fam Div ...13–012, 13–049, 13–058,
                                                                                              15–040
Gage v King (Quantum) [1961] 1 Q.B. 188; [1960] 3 W.L.R. 460; [1960] 3 All E.R. 62;
    (1960) 104 S.J. 644, QBD 5–063
Galloway v Galloway (1914) 30 T.L.R. 531 3–028
Gandhi v Patel; sub nom. Ghandi v Patel [2002] 1 F.L.R. 603; [2002] Fam. Law 262, Ch
    D 1–048
Garcia v Garcia [1992] Fam. 83; [1992] 2 W.L.R. 347; [1991] 3 All E.R. 451; [1992] 1
    F.L.R. 256; [1991] F.C.R. 927; [1992] Fam. Law 103, CA (Civ Div) 10–046
Garner v Garner [1992] 1 F.L.R. 573; [1992] Fam. Law 331; (1992) 156 J.P.N. 202, CA (Civ
    Div) 13–098
Gascoigne v Gascoigne [1918] 1 K.B. 223, KBD 5–016
Gatehouse v Robinson [1986] 1 W.L.R. 18; [1986] 1 F.L.R. 504; [1986] Fam. Law 158;
    (1986) 83 L.S.G. 118; (1986) 130 S.J. 13, DC 22–002
Gault, Re, 387 U.S. 1 (1967) 18–050
Gay v Sheeran; sub nom. Enfield LBC v Gay [2000] 1 W.L.R. 673; [1999] 3 All E.R. 795;
    [1999] 2 F.L.R. 519; [1999] 2 F.C.R. 705; (1999) 31 H.L.R. 1126; [1999] Fam. Law
    619; (1999) 96(30) L.S.G. 29; [1999] N.P.C. 70, CA (Civ Div) 13–118
George v George [1986] 2 F.L.R. 342 9–027
Gereis v Yagoub [1997] 1 F.L.R. 854; [1997] 3 F.C.R. 755; [1997] Fam. Law 475, Fam
    Div 1–048
Gibson v Austin [1992] 2 F.L.R. 437; [1993] 1 F.C.R. 638; [1993] Fam. Law 20, CA (Civ
    Div) 19–002
Giles, Re; sub nom. Giles v Giles [1972] Ch. 544; [1971] 3 W.L.R. 640; [1971] 3 All E.R.
    1141; (1971) 115 S.J. 428, Ch D 7–004
Gillett v Holt [2001] Ch. 210; [2000] 3 W.L.R. 815; [2000] 2 All E.R. 289; [2000] 2 F.L.R.
    266; [2000] 1 F.C.R. 705; [2000] W.T.L.R. 195; [2000] Fam. Law 714; (2000) 97(12)
    L.S.G. 40; (2000) 144 S.J.L.B. 141; [2000] N.P.C. 25; (2000) 80 P. & C.R. D3, CA
    (Civ Div) 5–032, 5–033, 5–034, 5–035
Gillick v West Norfolk and Wisbech AHA [1986] A.C. 112; [1985] 3 W.L.R. 830; [1985]
    3 All E.R. 402; [1986] Crim. L.R. 113; (1985) 82 L.S.G. 3531; (1985) 135 N.L.J. 1055;
    (1985) 129 S.J. 738, HL ... 16–002, 16–003, 16–004, 16–005, 16–011, 16–014, 16–015, 16–019,
                              16–023, 17–001, 17–014, 17–015, 17–021, 18–017, 18–021, 19–002, 19–016,
                                                                        19–017, 21–012, 21–073
Gissing v Gissing [1971] A.C. 886; [1970] 3 W.L.R. 255; [1970] 2 All E.R. 780; (1970) 21
    P. & C.R. 702; (1970) 114 S.J. 550, HL 5–001, 5–013, 5–022, 5–023, 5–025

Glaser v United Kingdom [2001] 1 F.L.R. 153 ....18–055, 19–004
Glass v United Kingdom (61827/00) [2004] 1 F.L.R. 1019; [2004] 1 F.C.R. 553; (2004) 39
    E.H.R.R. 15; (2005) 8 C.C.L. Rep. 16; (2004) 77 B.M.L.R. 120; [2004] Fam. Law 410,
    ECHR 17–022
Gloucestershire CC v P; sub nom. P (A Minor) (Residence Orders), Re [2000] Fam. 1;
    [1999] 3 W.L.R. 685; [1999] 2 F.L.R. 61; [1999] 3 F.C.R. 114; [1999] Fam. Law 444;
    (1999) 96(20) L.S.G. 39, CA (Civ Div) 18–007, 18–014, 18–029, 18–030, 19–023
Gojkovic v Gojkovic (No.2) [1992] Fam. 40; [1991] 3 W.L.R. 621; [1992] 1 All E.R. 267;
    [1991] 2 F.L.R. 233; [1991] F.C.R. 913; [1991] Fam. Law 378, CA (Civ Div) ...13–001, 13–012,
                                                                                13–043, 13–072, 13–078
Gollins v Gollins [1964] A.C. 644; [1963] 3 W.L.R. 176; [1963] 2 All E.R. 966; (1963) 107
    S.J. 532, HL 10–005
Goodchild v Goodchild; sub nom. Goodchild (Deceased), Re [1997] 1 W.L.R. 1216; [1997]
    3 All E.R. 63; [1997] 2 F.L.R. 644; [1997] 3 F.C.R. 601; [1997] Fam. Law 660; (1997)
    147 N.L.J. 759, CA (Civ Div) 7–010, 7–014, 7–022
Goodinson v Goodinson [1954] 2 Q.B. 118; [1954] 2 W.L.R. 1121; [1954] 2 All E.R. 255;
    (1954) 98 S.J. 369, CA 13–004
Goodman v Gallant [1986] Fam. 106; [1986] 2 W.L.R. 236; [1986] 1 All E.R. 311; [1986]
    1 F.L.R. 513; (1986) 52 P. & C.R. 180; [1986] Fam. Law 59; (1985) 135 N.L.J. 1231;
    (1985) 129 S.J. 891, CA (Civ Div) 5–010
Goodridge v Department of Public Health (2003) SJC–08860 .... A–004
Goodwin v United Kingdom (28957/95) [2002] I.R.L.R. 664; [2002] 2 F.L.R. 487; [2002]
    2 F.C.R. 577; (2002) 35 E.H.R.R. 18; 13 B.H.R.C. 120; (2002) 67 B.M.L.R. 199;
    [2002] Fam. Law 738; (2002) 152 N.L.J. 1171, ECHR 2–018, 17–010
Gora v Treasury Solicitor [2003] Fam. Law 93, CC 7–028
Gore and Snell v Carpenter (1990) 60 P. & C.R. 456, Ch D 5–044
Gorgulu v Germany (74969/01) [2004] 1 F.L.R. 894; [2004] 1 F.C.R. 410; [2004] Fam. Law
    411, ECHR 22–034
Gorman (A Bankrupt), Re [1990] 1 W.L.R. 616; [1990] 1 All E.R. 717; [1990] 2 F.L.R. 284;
    (1990) 87(19) L.S.G. 41, DC 5–022, 5–044, 5–057
Gorman v Gorman [1964] 1 W.L.R. 1440; [1964] 3 All E.R. 739; (1964) 108 S.J. 878, CA ... 3–032
Gosling v Gosling [1968] P. 1; [1967] 2 W.L.R. 1219; [1967] 2 All E.R. 510; (1967) 111
    S.J. 192, CA (Civ Div) 10–005
Gotham v Doodes; sub nom. Doodes v Gotham [2006] EWCA Civ 1080; [2007] 1 W.L.R.
    86; [2007] 1 All E.R. 527; [2006] B.P.I.R. 1178; [2007] Fam. Law 15; (2006) 156
    N.L.J. 1325; [2006] N.P.C. 89, CA (Civ Div) 5–059
Gould v Gould [1970] 1 Q.B. 275; [1969] 3 W.L.R. 490; [1969] 3 All E.R. 728; (1969) 113
    S.J. 508, CA (Civ Div) 3–027, 5–005, 13–004
Graeme v United Kingdom [2000] 1 Fam.Law 188 18–028
Graham v Graham [1992] 2 F.L.R. 406, CA 14–011
Grant v Edwards [1986] Ch. 638; [1986] 3 W.L.R. 114; [1986] 2 All E.R. 426; [1987] 1
    F.L.R. 87; [1986] Fam. Law 300; (1986) 83 L.S.G. 1996; (1986) 136 N.L.J. 439;
    (1986) 130 S.J. 408, CA (Civ Div) 5–021, 5–025, 5–034, 5–037
Gray (otherwise Formosa) v Formosa; sub nom. Formosa v Formosa [1963] P. 259; [1962]
    3 W.L.R. 1246; [1962] 3 All E.R. 419; (1962) 106 S.J. 629, CA 3–002
Greasley v Cooke [1980] 1 W.L.R. 1306; [1980] 3 All E.R. 710; (1980) 124 S.J. 629, CA
    (Civ Div) 5–034, 5–035
Greaves v Greaves (1869–72) L.R. 2 P. & D. 423, Ct of Probate 1–045
Green v Green [2006] EWHC 2010, Fam Div 4–001, 5–016
Greensill v Greensill [2007] EWCA Civ 680 9–035
Greenwich LBC v S [2007] EWHC 820 (Fam); [2007] 2 F.L.R. 154, Fam Div 22–055
Greig Middleton & Co Ltd v Denderowicz (No.2); Olaleye-Oruene v London Guildhall
    University [1998] 1 W.L.R. 1164; [1997] 4 All E.R. 181; (1997) 94(31) L.S.G. 36;
    (1997) 147 N.L.J. 1097, CA (Civ Div) 13–102, 13–105
Griffin v Griffin [2000] C.P.L.R. 452; [2000] 2 F.L.R. 44; [2000] 2 F.C.R. 302; [2000] Fam.
    Law 531; (2000) 97(20) L.S.G. 42; (2000) 144 S.J.L.B. 213, CA (Civ Div) 9–035
Griffith v Griffith [1944] I.R. 35 2–039
Griffiths v Dawson & Co [1993] 2 F.L.R. 315; [1993] 2 F.C.R. 515; [1993] Fam. Law 476,
    QBD 13–027, 13–064, 13–070
Griffiths v Griffiths (Improvements to Matrimonial Home) [1974] 1 W.L.R. 1350; [1974] 1
    All E.R. 932; (1973) 5 Fam. Law 59; (1973) 118 S.J. 810, CA (Civ Div) 3–009, 13–014
                                                                                                13–0

Grimes (otherwise Edwards) v Grimes [1948] P. 323; [1948] 2 All E.R. 147; 64 T.L.R. 330; [1948] L.J.R. 1471; (1948) 92 S.J. 325, PDAD 2–033

Gubay v Kington (Inspector of Taxes); sub nom. Gubay v Kingston [1984] 1 W.L.R. 163; [1984] 1 All E.R. 513; [1984] S.T.C. 99; 57 T.C. 601; (1984) 81 L.S.G. 900; (1984) 134 N.L.J. 342; (1984) 128 S.J. 100, HL 3–034

Gull v Gull [2007] EWCA Civ 900 9–035

Gully v Dix; sub nom. Dix (Deceased), Re [2004] EWCA Civ 139; [2004] 1 W.L.R. 1399; [2004] 1 F.L.R. 918; [2004] 1 F.C.R. 453; [2004] W.T.L.R. 331; [2004] Fam. Law 334; (2004) 101(6) L.S.G. 32; (2004) 148 S.J.L.B. 116, CA (Civ Div) 7–016, 7–017

Gunn-Russo v Nugent Care Society; sub nom. R. (on the application of Gunn-Russo) v Nugent Care Society [2001] EWHC Admin 566; [2002] 1 F.L.R. 1; [2001] U.K.H.R.R. 1320; [2001] A.C.D. 86; [2002] Fam. Law 92; (2001) 151 N.L.J. 1250, QBD (Admin) 22–011

H, Re (1994) 158 J.P.N. 211 21–042

H (A Child), Re [2007] 2 F.L.R. 317, CA 18–026

H (A Child) (Abduction: Habitual Residence: Consent), Re; sub nom. H (Child Abduction: Wrongful Retention), Re [2000] 2 F.L.R. 294; [2000] 3 F.C.R. 412; [2000] Fam. Law 590, Fam Div 20–015

H (A Child) (Adoption: Consultation of Unmarried Fathers), Re; G (A Child) (Adoption: Disclosure), Re; sub nom. H (A Child) (Adoption: Disclosure), Re [2001] 1 F.L.R. 646; [2001] 1 F.C.R. 726; [2001] Fam. Law 175, Fam Div 22–034

H (A Child) (Contact: Domestic Violence), Re [2005] EWCA Civ 1404; [2006] 1 F.L.R. 943; [2006] 1 F.C.R. 102; [2006] Fam. Law 439, CA (Civ Div) 18–020, 19–021

H (A Child) (First Name), Re [2002] EWCA Civ 190; [2002] 1 F.L.R. 973; [2002] Fam. Law 340; (2002) 99(11) L.S.G. 35; (2002) 146 S.J.L.B. 44, CA (Civ Div) 17–025

H (A Minor) (Abduction: Rights of Custody), Re; sub nom. H (A Child) (Removal from Jurisdiction), Re [2000] 2 A.C. 291; [2000] 2 W.L.R. 337; [2000] 2 All E.R. 1; [2000] 1 F.L.R. 374; [2000] 1 F.C.R. 225; [2000] Fam. Law 310; (2000) 97(7) L.S.G. 40; (2000) 144 S.J.L.B. 101, HL 17–035, 20–016, 20–017

H (A Minor) (Adoption: Non-Patrial) (1982), Re (1982) 12 Fam. Law 142, CA (Civ Div) 22–007

H (A Minor) (Adoption: Non-Patrial), Re; sub nom. A (A Minor) (Adoption: Non-Patrial), Re [1997] 1 W.L.R. 791; [1996] 4 All E.R. 600; [1996] 2 F.L.R. 187; [1996] 3 F.C.R. 1; [1996] Fam. Law 602; (1996) 93(20) L.S.G. 30; (1996) 140 S.J.L.B. 128, CA (Civ Div) 22–005

H (A Minor) (Blood Tests: Parental Rights), Re [1997] Fam. 89; [1996] 3 W.L.R. 506; [1996] 4 All E.R. 28; [1996] 2 F.L.R. 65; [1996] 3 F.C.R. 201; (1996) 160 J.P.N. 576; (1996) 146 N.L.J. 406, CA (Civ Div) 17–007

H (A Minor) (Care Proceedings: Child's Wishes), Re [1993] 1 F.L.R. 440; [1993] Fam. Law 200, Fam Div 16–021, 16–022, 21–058

H (A Minor) (Contact: Enforcement), Re [1996] 1 F.L.R. 614; [1996] 2 F.C.R. 784; [1996] Fam. Law 348; (1996) 160 J.P.N. 482, Fam Div 18–056

H (A Minor) (Foreign Custody Order: Enforcement), Re [1994] Fam. 105; [1994] 2 W.L.R. 269; [1994] 1 All E.R. 812; [1994] 1 F.L.R. 512; [1994] Fam. Law 366, CA (Civ Div) 20–024

H (A Minor) (Guardian ad Litem: Requirement), Re; sub nom. H (A Minor) (Role of Official Solicitor), Re; H (A Minor) (Independent Representative), Re [1994] Fam. 11; [1993] 3 W.L.R. 1109; [1994] 4 All E.R. 762; [1993] 2 F.L.R. 552; [1993] 2 F.C.R. 437; [1993] Fam. Law 614, Fam Div 16–021

H (A Minor) (Parental Responsibility), Re [1993] 1 F.L.R. 484; [1993] 1 F.C.R. 85; [1993] Fam. Law 272, CA (Civ Div) 17–037

H (A Minor) (Parental Responsibility), Re; sub nom. RH (A Minor) (Parental Responsibility), Re [1998] 1 F.L.R. 855; [1998] 2 F.C.R. 89; [1998] Fam. Law 325, CA (Civ Div) 17–037

H (A Minor) (Section 37 Direction), Re; sub nom. H (Child's Circumstances: Direction to Investigate) Re [1993] 2 F.L.R. 541; [1993] 2 F.C.R. 277; [1993] Fam. Law 205; (1993) 157 L.G. Rev. 861 .... 18–048, 21–035, 22–075, 22–076, 22–079

H (Abduciton), Re [2007] 1 F.L.R. 242, CA 20–021, 20–022

H (Adoption: Disclosure of Information), Re [1995] 1 F.L.R. 236; [1995] 1 F.C.R. 546; [1995] Fam. Law 174, Fam Div 22–011

H (Child Abduction: Whereabouts Order to Solicitors), Re [2000] 1 F.L.R. 766; [2000] 1 F.C.R. 499; [2000] Fam. Law 392, Fam Div 20–002, 20–007

H (Children) (Contact Order) (No.2), Re [2002] 1 F.L.R. 22; [2001] 3 F.C.R. 385; [2001]
  Fam. Law 795, Fam Div 18–024
H (Children: Residence Order: Relocation), Re; sub nom. H (Children) (Residence Order:
  Condition), Re [2001] EWCA Civ 1338; [2001] 2 F.L.R. 1277; [2001] 3 F.C.R. 182;
  [2001] Fam. Law 870, CA (Civ Div) 18–005, 18–016, 18–021
H (Children) (Termination of Contact), Re; sub nom. H (Children) (Terminating Contact
  Orders: Local Authorities Powers), Re [2005] EWCA Civ 318; [2005] 2 F.L.R. 408;
  [2005] 1 F.C.R. 658; [2005] Fam. Law 526; (2005) 149 S.J.L.B. 179, CA (Civ Div) 21–075
H (Conciliation: Welfare Reports), Re [1986] 1 F.L.R. 476; [1986] Fam. Law 193; (1986)
  83 L.S.G. 525; (1986) 130 S.J. 128 18–012
H (Contact: Domestic Violence), Re [2000] 2 F.L.R. 334, CA 19–022
H (Contact: Principles), Re [1994] 2 F.L.R. 969; [1994] 2 F.C.R. 249; [1993] Fam. Law 673,
  CA (Civ Div) 18–019
H (Deceased), Re [1990] 1 F.L.R. 441; [1990] Fam. Law 175 7–004
H (Minors) (Access), Re [1992] 1 F.L.R. 148; [1992] F.C.R. 70; [1992] Fam. Law 152, CA
  (Civ Div) 19–015, 19–026
H (Minors) (Local Authority: Parental Rights) (No.3), Re; sub nom. H (Minors) (Adoption:
  Putative Father's Rights) (No.3), Re [1991] Fam. 151; [1991] 2 W.L.R. 763; [1991] 2
  All E.R. 185; [1991] 1 F.L.R. 214; [1991] F.C.R. 361; 89 L.G.R. 537; [1991] Fam. Law
  306; (1991) 135 S.J. 16, CA (Civ Div) 17–037
H (Minors) (Parental Responsibility Order: Maintenance), Re [1996] 1 F.L.R. 867; [1996]
  3 F.C.R. 49; [1996] Fam. Law 402; (1996) 160 J.P.N. 696, CA (Civ Div) 17–037
H (Minors: Prohibited Steps Order), Re [1995] 1 W.L.R. 667; [1995] 4 All E.R. 110; [1995]
  1 F.L.R. 638; [1995] 2 F.C.R. 547, CA (Civ Div) 18–021, 18–029, 21–044
H (Minors) (Sexual Abuse: Standard of Proof), Re; sub nom. H and R (Child Sexual Abuse:
  Standard of Proof), Re; H (Minors) (Child Abuse: Threshold Conditions), Re [1996]
  A.C. 563; [1996] 2 W.L.R. 8; [1996] 1 All E.R. 1; [1996] 1 F.L.R. 80; [1996] 1 F.C.R.
  509; [1996] Fam. Law 74; (1995) 145 N.L.J. 1887; (1996) 140 S.J.L.B. 24, HL 19–021,
                                                                21–034, 21–035, 21–036, 21–062
H (Minors) (Wardship: Surety), Re [1991] 1 F.L.R. 40; [1991] F.C.R. 45, CA (Civ Div) 20–005
H (Minors) (Welfare Reports), Re [1990] 2 F.L.R. 172; [1991] F.C.R. 866; (1990) 154 J.P.N.
  708, CA (Civ Div) 18–012
H (Paternity: Welfare of Child), Re [2007] 1 F.L.R. 1064 .... 19–001, 19–007
H (Residence Order: Child's Application for Leave), Re [2000] 1 F.L.R. 780; [2000] Fam.
  Law 404, Fam Div 16–019, 16–020, 18–038, 19–017
H (Residence Order: Placement out of Jurisdiction), Re [2004] EWHC 3243; [2006] 1
  F.L.R. 1140; [2006] Fam. Law 349, Fam Div 18–016, 21–042
H (Shared Residence: Parental Responsibility), Re [1995] 2 F.L.R. 883; [1996] 3 F.C.R.
  321; [1996] Fam. Law 140, CA (Civ Div) 18–016
H v H; sub nom. Harris v Hawkins [1947] K.B. 463; [1947] 1 All E.R. 312; 63 T.L.R. 207;
  (1947) 111 J.P. 160; [1948] L.J.R. 349; 176 L.T. 281, DC 22–025
H v H [1954] P. 258; [1953] 3 W.L.R. 849; [1953] 2 All E.R. 1229; (1953) 97 S.J. 782,
  PDAD 2–039, 2–042
H v H [1988] 2 F.L.R. 114; [1988] Fam. Law 293 7–013
H v H [2007] EWHC 459 (Fam); [2007] 2 F.L.R. 548; [2007] Fam. Law 578; (2007) 151
  S.J.L.B. 503, Fam Div 13–054, 13–056
H v H (Child Abduction: Acquiescence); sub nom. H (Minors) (Abduction: Acquiescence),
  Re [1998] A.C. 72; [1997] 2 W.L.R. 563; [1997] 2 All E.R. 225; [1997] 1 F.L.R. 872;
  [1997] 2 F.C.R. 257; [1997] Fam. Law 468, HL 20–019
H v H (Financial Provision: Application to Terminate Wife's Right to Periodical Payments);
  sub nom. Horsman v Horsman [1993] 2 F.L.R. 35; [1993] 2 F.C.R. 357, Fam Div ... 14–002
H v H (Financial Provision: Short Marriage) (1981) 2 F.L.R. 392 13–076
H v H (Financial Relief: Attempted Murder as Conduct) [2005] EWHC 2911 (Fam); [2006]
  1 F.L.R. 990; [2006] Fam. Law 264, Fam Div 13–084
H v H (Financial Relief: Conduct); sub nom. H v H (Financial Provision: Conduct) [1998]
  1 F.L.R. 971; [1999] 1 F.C.R. 225; [1998] Fam. Law 395, Fam Div 13–058
H v H (Financial Relief: Costs) [1997] 2 F.L.R. 57; [1998] 2 F.C.R. 27; [1997] Fam. Law
  537, Fam Div 13–012
H v H (Financial Relief: Non-disclosure: Costs) [1994] 2 F.L.R. 94; [1994] 2 F.C.R. 301;
  [1994] Fam. Law 497, Fam Div 13–008
H v H (Forum Conveniens) [1993] 1 F.L.R. 959 20–023

H v H (Pension Sharing: Rescission of Decree Nisi) [2002] EWHC 767; [2002] 2 F.L.R. 116; [2002] Fam. Law 591, Fam Div 13–124

H v H (Residence Order: Leave to Remove from Jurisdiction) (Note) [1995] 1 F.L.R. 529; [1995] 2 F.C.R. 469; [1995] Fam. Law 238, CA (Civ Div) 19–014

H v M (Property: Beneficial Interest) [1992] 1 F.L.R. 229; [1991] F.C.R. 938; [1991] Fam. Law 473, Fam Div 5–021

H v M (Property Occupied by Wife's Parents); sub nom. JH v AM [2004] EWHC 625; [2004] 2 F.L.R. 16; [2004] Fam. Law 485, Fam Div 4–001

H v O (Contempt of Court: Sentencing) [2004] EWCA Civ 1691; [2005] 2 F.L.R. 329; [2005] Fam. Law 532; (2005) 149 S.J.L.B. 59, CA (Civ Div) 9–001, 9–035

H v P (Illegitimate Child: Capital Provision) [1993] Fam. Law 515 15–052

H v Trafford MBC [1997] 3 F.C.R. 113; (1997) 161 J.P.N. 556, Fam Div 19–020

H v United Kingdom (A/120); sub nom. H v United Kingdom (9580/81) (1988) 10 E.H.R.R. 95, ECHR 18–006, 19–020

H and A (Children) (Paternity: Blood Tests), Re [2002] EWCA Civ 383; [2002] 1 F.L.R. 1145; [2002] 2 F.C.R. 469; [2002] Fam. Law 520, CA (Civ Div) 15–008, 17–007

HB (Abduction: Children's Objections) (No.1), Re [1998] 1 F.L.R. 422; [1998] 1 F.C.R. 398; [1998] Fam. Law 128, CA (Civ Div) 19–017, 19–025

HB (Abduction: Children's Objections) (No.2), Re [1998] 1 F.L.R. 654, CA (Civ Div) ... 20–021

HG (Specific Issue: Sterilisation), Re [1993] 1 F.L.R. 587; [1993] 1 F.C.R. 553; [1993] Fam. Law 403 17–022

Haas v Netherlands (36983/97) [2004] 1 F.L.R. 673; [2004] 1 F.C.R. 147; (2004) 39 E.H.R.R. 41; [2004] Fam. Law 245, ECHR 17–035

Haase v Germany (11057/02) [2004] 2 F.L.R. 39; [2004] 2 F.C.R. 1; (2005) 40 E.H.R.R. 19; [2004] Fam. Law 500, ECHR 21–045, 21–050

Hackshaw v Hackshaw; sub nom. Hacksaw v Hacksaw [1999] 2 F.L.R. 876; [1999] 3 F.C.R. 451; [1999] Fam. Law 697; (2000) 164 J.P.N. 326, Fam Div 14–014

Hadjimilitis v Tsavliris (Divorce: Irretrievable Breakdown) [2003] 1 F.L.R. 81; [2002] Fam. Law 883, Fam Div 10–016

Hadkinson v Hadkinson [1952] P. 285; [1952] 2 All E.R. 567; [1952] 2 T.L.R. 416, CA 14–020

Hager v Osborne; sub nom. H v O [1992] Fam. 94; [1992] 2 W.L.R. 610; [1992] 2 All E.R. 494; [1992] 1 F.L.R. 282; [1992] F.C.R. 125; (1992) 4 Admin. L.R. 147; [1992] Fam. Law 105; (1991) 155 J.P.N. 655; (1991) 135 S.J.L.B. 76, Fam Div 17–012

Haldane (Dorothy) v Haldane (George Christopher) [1977] A.C. 673; [1976] 3 W.L.R. 760; (1976) 120 S.J. 703, PC (NZ) 13–045

Hale v Tanner [2000] 1 W.L.R. 2377; [2000] 2 F.L.R. 879; [2000] 3 F.C.R. 62; [2000] Fam. Law 876; (2000) 164 J.P.N. 861; (2001) 165 J.P.N. 184, CA (Civ Div) 9–035, 9–038

Hall v Hall (1908) 24 T.L.R. 756 2–042

Hall v Hall [1962] 1 W.L.R. 1246; [1962] 3 All E.R. 518; (1962) 106 S.J. 650, CA 10–027

Hall and Co v Simms [2000] 2 F.L.R. 545, HL 13–108

Hamilton Jones v David & Snape (A Firm) [2003] EWHC 3147; [2004] 1 W.L.R. 924; [2004] 1 All E.R. 657; [2004] 1 F.L.R. 774; [2004] 1 F.C.R. 243; [2004] P.N.L.R. 21; [2004] Fam. Law 246; (2004) 101(4) L.S.G. 31; (2004) 154 N.L.J. 55, Ch D 17–015, 17–026, 20–003

Hammerton v Hammerton [2007] EWCA Civ 248; [2007] 2 F.L.R. 1133, CA (Civ Div) 9–001, 9–035, 9–036, 18–020, 18–057

Hancock (Deceased), Re; sub nom. Snapes v Aram [1998] 2 F.L.R. 346; [1999] 1 F.C.R. 500; [1998] Fam. Law 520; (1998) 95(20) L.S.G. 35; (1998) 142 S.J.L.B. 167, CA (Civ Div) 7–014, 7–023, 7–024

Hanlon v Hanlon [1978] 1 W.L.R. 592; [1978] 2 All E.R. 889; (1978) 122 S.J. 62, CA (Civ Div) 13–111, 13–116

Hanlon v Law Society [1981] A.C. 124; [1980] 2 W.L.R. 756; [1980] 2 All E.R. 199; (1980) 124 S.J. 360, HL 13–013

Hansen v Turkey (36141/97) [2004] 1 F.L.R. 142; [2003] 3 F.C.R. 97; (2004) 39 E.H.R.R. 18; [2003] Fam. Law 877, ECHR 18–055

Harb v Aziz (No.2); sub nom. Harb v King Fahd Bin Abdul Aziz (No.2) [2005] EWCA Civ 1324; [2006] 1 W.L.R. 578; [2006] 1 F.L.R. 825; [2006] W.T.L.R. 609; [2006] Fam. Law 96; (2005) 102(45) L.S.G. 28, CA (Civ Div) 3–015, 3–020

Hardy v Hardy [1981] 1 F.L.R. 321 13–067

Haringey LBC v C; Haringey LBC v E [2007] 1 F.L.R. 1035 18–043

Harman v Glencross [1986] Fam. 81; [1986] 2 W.L.R. 637; [1986] 1 All E.R. 545; [1986]
2 F.L.R. 241; [1986] Fam. Law 215; (1986) 83 L.S.G. 870; (1986) 136 N.L.J. 69;
(1986) 130 S.J. 224, CA (Civ Div) 14–008
Harnett v Harnett [1974] 1 W.L.R. 219; [1974] 1 All E.R. 764; (1974) 118 S.J. 34, CA (Civ
Div) 3–008
Harouki v Kensington and Chelsea LBC [2007] EWCA 1000 6–037
Haroutunian v Jennings (1977) 7 Fam. Law 210; (1977) 121 S.J. 663, DC 15–051
Harrington v Gill (1983) 4 F.L.R. 265, CA (Civ Div) 7–016, 7–019, 7–022, 7–029
Harris v Goddard [1983] 1 W.L.R. 1203; [1983] 3 All E.R. 242; (1983) 46 P. & C.R. 417;
[1984] Fam. Law 242; (1983) 80 L.S.G. 2517; (1983) 133 N.L.J. 958; (1983) 127 S.J.
617, CA (Civ Div) 5–040, 5–041
Harris v Harris [2001] 1 F.C.R. 68, CA (Civ Div) 13–098
Harris v Harris; sub nom. Attorney General v Harris [2001] 2 F.L.R. 895; [2001] 3 F.C.R.
193; [2001] Fam. Law 651, Fam Div 18–055
Harris v Harris (Contempt of Court: Application to Purge) [2001] EWCA Civ 1645; [2002]
Fam. 253; [2002] 2 W.L.R. 747; [2002] 1 All E.R. 185; [2002] 1 F.L.R. 248; [2001] 3
F.C.R. 640; [2002] Fam. Law 93; (2002) 99(2) L.S.G. 27; (2001) 145 S.J.L.B. 270, CA
(Civ Div) 9–035, 9–036, 13–099, 13–100, 18–056
Harris (formerly Manahan) v Manahan [1996] 4 All E.R. 454; [1997] 1 F.L.R. 205; [1997]
2 F.C.R. 607; [1997] Fam. Law 238, CA (Civ Div) 13–005, 13–107, 13–108
Harrods Ltd v Tester [1937] 2 All E.R. 236 5–063
Harthan v Harthan [1949] P. 115; [1948] 2 All E.R. 639; [1949] L.J.R. 115; (1948) 92 S.J.
586, CA 2–028
Harvey v Harvey (1982) 3 F.L.R. 141, CA 13–117
Harwood v Harwood [1991] 2 F.L.R. 274; [1992] F.C.R. 1; [1991] Fam. Law 418, CA (Civ
Div) 5–011, 5–016
Havering LBC v S [1986] 1 F.L.R. 489; [1986] Fam. Law 157, Fam Div 18–052
Haviland v Haviland (1863) 32 L.J.P.M. & A. 65 10–030
Hawes v Evenden [1953] 1 W.L.R. 1169; [1953] 2 All E.R. 737, CA A–001
Hawkins Ex p. Hawkins, Re [1894] 1 Q.B. 25, QBD 14–005
Hawkins v Attorney General [1966] 1 W.L.R. 978; [1966] 1 All E.R. 392, PDAD 17–031
Haydon v Gould (1711) 1 Salk 119; 91 E.R. 113 1–003
Hayes v Watts (1819) 3 Phill. Ecc. 43; 161 E.R. 1252 1–005
Heard v Heard [1995] 1 F.L.R. 970; [1996] 1 F.C.R. 33; [1995] Fam. Law 477, CA (Civ
Div) 13–104
Hedderwick, Re; sub nom. Morton v Brinsley [1933] Ch. 669, Ch D 14–002
Hedges v Hedges [1991] 1 F.L.R. 196; [1990] F.C.R. 952; [1991] Fam. Law 267, DC 13–076
Hemming v Price (1701) 12 Mod 432; 88 E.R. 1430 1–002
Henderson, Re (1888) L.R. 20 Q.B.D. 509, CA 14–005
Hepburn v Hepburn [1989] 1 F.L.R. 373; [1989] F.C.R. 618; [1989] Fam. Law 271; (1989)
153 J.P.N. 465, CA (Civ Div) 13–021
Herczegfalvy v Austria (A/242-B) (1993) 15 E.H.R.R. 437, ECHR 16–016
Heseltine v Heseltine [1971] 1 W.L.R. 342; [1971] 1 All E.R. 952; (1970) 114 S.J. 972, CA
(Civ Div) 5–063
Hewer v Bryant [1970] 1 Q.B. 357; [1969] 3 W.L.R. 425; [1969] 3 All E.R. 578; (1969) 113
S.J. 525, CA (Civ Div) 3–001, 16–003, 17–019
Hewison v Hewison (1977) 7 Fam. Law 207, CA (Civ Div) 19–020
Hewitson v Hewitson [1995] Fam. 100; [1995] 2 W.L.R. 287; [1995] 1 All E.R. 472; [1995]
1 F.L.R. 241; [1995] 2 F.C.R. 588; [1995] Fam. Law 129; (1994) 91(41) L.S.G. 41;
(1994) 144 N.L.J. 1478; (1994) 138 S.J.L.B. 211, CA (Civ Div) 10–001, 13–103
Hickerton v Child Support Agency [2006] EWHC 61, Fam Div 15–024
Hildebrand v Hildebrand [1992] 1 F.L.R. 244; [1992] Fam. Law 235 13–064
Hill v Hill [1959] 1 W.L.R. 127; [1959] 1 All E.R. 281; (1959) 103 S.J. 111, PC (Bar) 2–036
Hill v Hill [1998] 1 F.L.R. 198; [1997] 3 F.C.R. 477; [1997] Fam. Law 657, CA (Civ Div) ... 13–103
Hill v Turner (1737) 1 Atk 516; 26 E.R. 326 1–003
Hipgrave v Jone; sub nom. Jones v Hipgrave [2004] EWHC 2901; [2005] 2 F.L.R. 174;
[2005] A.C.D. 67; [2005] Fam. Law 453; (2005) 102(6) L.S.G. 33. QBD 9–007, 9–039
Hirani v Hirani (1983) 4 F.L.R. 232, CA (Civ Div) 2–040, 2–041
Hoddinott v Hoddinott [1949] 2 K.B. 406; 65 T.L.R. 266; (1949) 93 S.J. 286, CA ... 3–007, 5–063
Hodgkiss v Hodgkiss & Walker [1985] Fam. Law 87; (1984) 148 J.P.N. 283; (1984) 81
L.S.G. 658; (1984) 128 S.J. 332, CA (Civ Div) 17–007

Hodgson v Marks [1971] Ch. 892; [1971] 2 W.L.R. 1263; [1971] 2 All E.R. 684; (1971) 22
P. & C.R. 586; (1971) 115 S.J. 224, CA (Civ Div) 5–014
Hoffman v Austria (1993) 17 E.H.R.R. 293 .... 19–004, 19–006
Hokkanen v Finland (A/299-A); sub nom. K v Finland (19823/92) [1996] 1 F.L.R. 289;
[1995] 2 F.C.R. 320; (1995) 19 E.H.R.R. 139; [1996] Fam. Law 22, ECHR 16–017, 17–024,
18–055
Holliday (A Bankrupt), Re [1981] Ch. 405; [1981] 2 W.L.R. 996; [1980] 3 All E.R. 385;
(1980) 77 L.S.G. 340; (1981) 125 S.J. 411, CA (Civ Div) 5–059
Holman v Howes [2005] EWHC 2824; [2006] 1 F.L.R. 1003; [2005] 3 F.C.R. 474; [2006]
B.P.I.R. 722; [2006] Fam. Law 176, Ch D 5–026, 5–046
Holmes v Mitchell (Inspector of Taxes) [1991] S.T.C. 25; [1991] 2 F.L.R. 301; [1991]
F.C.R. 512; 63 T.C. 718; [1991] B.T.C. 28; [1991] Fam. Law 217, Ch D 3–004, 3–034
Holmes-Moore v Richmond LBC [2007] EWCA Civ 970 6–037
Holmes-Moorhouse v Richmond LBC [2007] EWCA Civ 970 18–005
Hope v Hope (1856) 22 Beav. 35 13–003
Hopes v Hopes [1949] P. 227; [1948] 2 All E.R. 920; 64 T.L.R. 623; (1949) 113 J.P. 10; 46
L.G.R. 538; [1949] L.J.R. 104; (1948) 92 S.J. 660; (1949) 93 S.J. 141, CA 10–037
Hope-Smith v Hope-Smith [1989] 2 F.L.R. 56; [1989] F.C.R. 785; [1989] Fam. Law 268;
(1989) 153 J.P.N. 630; (1989) 139 N.L.J. 111, CA (Civ Div) 13–103, 13–105
Horner v Horner [1982] Fam. 90; [1982] 2 W.L.R. 914; [1982] 2 All E.R. 495; (1983) 4
F.L.R. 50; (1982) 12 Fam. Law 144, CA (Civ Div) 9–027
Horton v Horton [1947] 2 All E.R. 871; 64 T.L.R. 62; [1948] W.N. 3; [1948] L.J.R. 396;
(1948) 92 S.J. 95, HL 2–031
Horton v Sadler [2006] UKHL 27; [2006] 2 W.L.R. 1346; [2006] 3 All E.R. 1177; [2006]
R.T.R. 27; [2006] P.I.Q.R. P30; (2006) 91 B.M.L.R. 60; (2006) 103(26) L.S.G. 27;
(2006) 156 N.L.J. 1024; (2006) 150 S.J.L.B. 808, HL 21–066
Hosking v Michaelides (2004) 101(3) L.S.G. 32, Ch D 3–008, 3–009, 5–059
Howard v Howard [1945] P. 1, CA 13–066
Howlett v Holding [2006] EWHC 41; (2006) 150 S.J.L.B. 161, QBD 9–005
Hudson v Hudson [1995] 2 F.L.R. 72; [1996] 1 F.C.R. 19; [1995] Fam. Law 550, CA (Civ
Div) 9–035
Hulley v Thompson [1981] 1 W.L.R. 159; [1981] 1 All E.R. 1128; (1981) 125 S.J. 47, DC 6–019,
13–087
Hulton v Hulton (Maintenance) [1916] P. 57, CA 13–018
Humberside CC v B; sub nom. B v Humberside CC [1993] 1 F.L.R. 257; [1993] Fam. Law
61 .... 9–017, 21–032
Humberside CC v R; sub nom. Humberside CC v DPR (An Infant) [1977] 1 W.L.R. 1251;
[1977] 3 All E.R. 964; 76 L.G.R. 121; (1977) 7 Fam. Law 171; (1977) 121 S.J. 693,
QBD 18–008
Hunt v Soady [2007] EWCA Civ 366 5–033
Hunter v Babbage [1994] 2 F.L.R. 806; [1995] 1 F.C.R. 569; (1995) 69 P. & C.R. 548;
[1994] Fam. Law 765; [1994] E.G. 8 (C.S.), Ch D 5–042
Hunter v Canary Wharf Ltd; sub nom. Hunter v London Docklands Development Corp
[1997] A.C. 655; [1997] 2 W.L.R. 684; [1997] 2 All E.R. 426; [1997] C.L.C. 1045; 84
B.L.R. 1; 54 Con. L.R. 12; [1997] Env. L.R. 488; [1997] 2 F.L.R. 342; (1998) 30
H.L.R. 409; [1997] Fam. Law 601; [1997] E.G. 59 (C.S.); (1997) 94(19) L.S.G. 25;
(1997) 147 N.L.J. 634; (1997) 141 S.J.L.B. 108; [1997] N.P.C. 64, HL 3–012, 9–038
Hunter v Hunter [1973] 1 W.L.R. 958; [1973] 3 All E.R. 362; (1973) 117 S.J. 544, CA (Civ
Div) 13–031
Hunter v Murrow; sub nom. H v M (Abduction: Rights of Custody) [2005] EWCA Civ 976;
[2005] 2 F.L.R. 1119; [2005] 3 F.C.R. 1; [2005] Fam. Law 762, CA (Civ Div) 20–016,
20–017, 20–024
Huntingford v Hobbs [1993] 1 F.L.R. 736; (1992) 24 H.L.R. 652; [1992] Fam. Law 437;
[1992] E.G. 38 (C.S.); [1992] N.P.C. 39, CA (Civ Div) 5–010, 5–011, 5–017, 5–028
Hurst v Supperstone; sub nom. Supperstone v Hurst [2005] EWHC 1309; [2006] 1 F.L.R.
1245; [2006] 1 F.C.R. 352; [2005] B.P.I.R. 1231; [2006] Fam. Law 101; [2005] 25 E.G.
192 (C.S.); [2005] 2 P. & C.R. DG21, Ch D 5–022, 5–027
Hussey v Palmer [1972] 1 W.L.R. 1286; [1972] 3 All E.R. 744; (1972) 116 S.J. 567, CA
(Civ Div) 5–013
Hyde v Hyde; sub nom. Hyde v Hyde and Woodmansee (1865–69) L.R. 1 P. & D. 130;
[1861–73] All E.R. Rep. 175, Divorce Ct 2–015, 2–021
Hyman v Hyman; Hughes v Hughes [1929] A.C. 601, HL 5–007, 13–004, 13–008

Hypo-Mortgage Services Ltd v Robinson [1997] 2 F.L.R. 71; [1997] 2 F.C.R. 422; [1997]
Fam. Law 544, CA (Civ Div) 5–051
I v United Kingdom (25680/94) [2002] 2 F.L.R. 518; [2002] 2 F.C.R. 613; (2003) 36
E.H.R.R. 53; [2002] Fam. Law 740; (2002) 152 N.L.J. 1171, ECHR 2–018
I and H (Minors) (Contact: Right to Give Evidence), Re; sub nom. I v H (Contact Hearing:
Procedure) [1998] 1 F.L.R. 876; [1998] 2 F.C.R. 433; [1998] Fam. Law 327, CA (Civ
Div) 18–012, 18–041
Iglesias Gil v Spain (56673/00); sub nom. Gil v Spain (56673/00) [2005] 1 F.L.R. 190;
[2005] 1 F.C.R. 210; (2005) 40 E.H.R.R. 3; [2005] Fam. Law 20, ECHR 20–025, 25–026
Ignaccolo-Zenide v Romania (31679/96) (2001) 31 E.H.R.R. 7, ECHR 19–016, 20–025
Ikimi v Ikimi (Divorce: Habitual Residence) [2001] EWCA Civ 873; [2002] Fam. 72;
[2001] 3 W.L.R. 672; [2001] 2 F.L.R. 1288; [2001] 2 F.C.R. 385; [2001] Fam. Law
660; (2001) 98(27) L.S.G. 38; (2001) 145 S.J.L.B. 163, CA (Civ Div) 15–010
Independiente Ltd v Music Trading On-Line (HK) Ltd [2007] EWCA Civ 111; [2007] 4 All
E.R. 736; (2007) 151 S.J.L.B. 159, CA (Civ Div) 14–011
Inland Revenue Commissioners v Mills (Hayley); sub nom. Mills (Hayley) v Inland
Revenue Commissioners [1975] A.C. 38; [1974] 2 W.L.R. 325; [1974] 1 All E.R. 722;
[1974] S.T.C. 130; 49 T.C. 367; [1974] T.R. 39; (1974) 118 S.J. 205, HL 17–025
Inze v Austria (A/126); sub nom. Inze v Austria (8695/79) (1988) 10 E.H.R.R. 394, ECHR 16–024,
17–035
Ivett v Ivett (1930) 94 J.P. 237 2–056
Ivin v Blake (Property: Beneficial Interest) [1995] 1 F.L.R. 70; [1994] 2 F.C.R. 504; (1994)
67 P. & C.R. 263; [1995] Fam. Law 72; [1993] E.G. 104 (C.S.); [1993] N.P.C. 87, CA
(Civ Div) 5–017
J (A Child) (Adoption: Appointment of Guardian ad Litem), Re [1999] 2 F.L.R. 86; [1999]
3 F.C.R. 456; [1999] Fam. Law 375, CA (Civ Div) 21–058
J (A Child) (Custody Rights: Jurisdiction), Re; sub nom. Jomah v Attar; J (Child Returned
Abroad: Human Rights), Re; J (A Child) (Return to Foreign Jurisdiction: Convention
Rights), Re; J (A Child) (Child Returned Abroad: Convention Rights) [2005] UKHL
40; [2006] 1 A.C. 80; [2005] 3 W.L.R. 14; [2005] 3 All E.R. 291; [2005] 2 F.L.R. 802;
[2005] 2 F.C.R. 381; [2005] Fam. Law 689; (2005) 155 N.L.J. 972; (2005) 149 S.J.L.B.
773, HL 19–002, 19–024, 20–023
J (A Child) (Freeing for Adoption), Re; sub nom. JS, Re; J (A Child) (Adoption: Revocation
of Freeing Order), Re [2000] 2 F.L.R. 58; [2000] 2 F.C.R. 133; [2000] Fam. Law 598;
(2000) 164 J.P.N. 606; (2000) 97(24) L.S.G. 39, Fam Div 21–079
J (A Child) (Leave to Issue Application for Residence Order), Re [2002] EWCA Civ 1346;
[2003] 1 F.L.R. 114; [2003] Fam. Law 27, CA (Civ Div) 18–035, 18–039
J (A Child) (Restrictions on Applications), Re [2008] 1 F.L.R. 369, CA 18–028
J (A Minor), Re [1984] F.L.R. 535 18–052
J (A Minor) (Abduction: Custody Rights), Re; sub nom. C v S (Minors) (Abduction:
Illegitimate Child) [1990] 2 A.C. 562; [1990] 3 W.L.R. 492; [1990] 2 All E.R. 961;
[1990] 2 F.L.R. 442; [1991] F.C.R. 129; [1991] Fam. Law 57; (1990) 154 J.P.N. 674;
(1990) 87(35) L.S.G. 39; (1990) 140 N.L.J. 1191; (1990) 134 S.J. 1039, HL 15–010, 20–014
J (A Minor) (Adoption Order: Conditions), Re [1973] Fam. 106; [1973] 2 W.L.R. 782;
[1973] 2 All E.R. 410; (1973) 117 S.J. 372, Fam Div 22–067
J (A Minor) (Change of Name), Re [1993] 1 F.L.R. 699; [1993] Fam. Law 399; (1993) 157
L.G. Rev. 281 .... 21–041, 21–080
J (A Minor) (Contact), Re [1994] 1 F.L.R. 729; [1994] 2 F.C.R. 741; [1994] Fam. Law 316,
CA (Civ Div) 19–001, 19–025
J (A Minor) (Interim Custody), Re [1989] 2 F.L.R. 304 18–057
J (A Minor) (Prohibited Steps Order: Circumcision), Re; sub nom. J (A Minor) (Specific
Issue Orders: Muslim Upbringing and Circumcision), Re; J (Specific Issue Orders:
Child's Religious Upbringing and Circumcision), Re [2000] 1 F.L.R. 571; [2000] 1
F.C.R. 307; (2000) 52 B.M.L.R. 82; [2000] Fam. Law 246; (1999) 96(47) L.S.G. 30,
CA (Civ Div) 17–018, 17–048, 18–015, 18–021, 19–020
J (A Minor) (Specific Issue Order: Leave to Apply), Re [1995] 1 F.L.R. 669; [1995] 3 F.C.R.
799; [1995] Fam. Law 403; (1995) 159 J.P.N. 387, Fam Div 18–022, 18–035, 21–010
J (A Minor) (Wardship: Jurisdiction), Re [1984] 1 W.L.R. 81; [1984] 1 All E.R. 29; 82
L.G.R. 60; (1983) 13 Fam. Law 258; (1983) 127 S.J. 616, CA (Civ Div) 21–045
J (Abduction: Acquiring Custody Rights by Caring for Child), Re [2005] 2 F.L.R. 791;
[2005] Fam. Law 605, Fam Div 20–017
J (Care Assessment: Fair Trial), Re [2007] 1 F.L.R. 77, CA 21–056, 21–087, 22–042

J (Income Support: Cohabitation), Re [1995] 1 F.L.R. 660 .... 6–017, 9–029
J (Leave to Remove: Urgent Case), Re [2006] 1 F.L.R. 2033, CA 18–026
J (Minors) (Care: Care Plan), Re [1994] 1 F.L.R. 253, Fam Div 21–030, 21–039
J (Minors) (Ex Parte Orders), Re [1997] 1 F.L.R. 606; [1997] 1 F.C.R. 325; [1997] Fam.
    Law 317; (1997) 161 J.P.N. 111, Fam Div 18–057, 20–009
J (Parental Responsibility), Re [1999] 1 F.L.R. 784; [1999] Fam. Law 216, Fam Div 17–037
J (SR) v J (DW); sub nom. SRJ v DWJ [1999] 2 F.L.R. 176; [1999] 3 F.C.R. 153; [1999]
    Fam. Law 448, CA (Civ Div) 13–048, 13–086, 13–096
J v C [1970] A.C. 668 ....17–014, 19–001, 19–005
J v C (Child: Financial Provision) [1999] 1 F.L.R. 152; [1998] 3 F.C.R. 79; [1999] Fam.
    Law 78, Fam Div 13–058, 13–062, 15–041, 15–050, 15–051, 15–052
J v C (Void Marriage: Status of Children) [2006] EWCA Civ 551; [2007] Fam. 1; [2006]
    3 W.L.R. 876; [2006] 2 F.L.R. 1098; [2006] Fam. Law 742, CA (Civ Div) 2–021, 2–056
J v J [1955] P. 236 13–066
J v J; sub nom. J (Otherwise B) PC v J (Otherwise B) AF [1955] P. 215; [1955] 3 W.L.R.
    72; [1955] 2 All E.R. 617; 48 R. & I.T. 644; [1955] T.R. 193; (1955) 99 S.J. 399, CA ... 14–011
J v J (A Minor) (Property Transfer); sub nom. J (A Minor) (Property Transfer), Re [1993]
    2 F.L.R. 56; [1993] Fam. Law 461; (1992) 136 S.J.L.B. 316, Fam Div 7–015, 15–039
J v Lancashire CC, unreported, May 25, 1993 21–056
J v ST (formerly J) (Transsexual: Ancillary Relief); sub nom. ST v J (Transsexual: Void
    Marriage) [1998] Fam. 103; [1997] 3 W.L.R. 1287; [1998] 1 All E.R. 431; [1997] 1
    F.L.R. 402; [1997] 1 F.C.R. 349; [1997] Fam. Law 239, CA (Civ Div) 2–021, 2–056, 13–084
J v V (Disclosure: Offshore Corporations) [2003] EWHC 3110 (Fam); [2004] 1 F.L.R.
    1042; [2004] Fam. Law 398, Fam Div 13–064
JA (A Minor) (Child Abduction: Non-Convention Country), Re; sub nom. A (A Minor)
    (Abduction: Non-Convention Country), Re [1998] 1 F.L.R. 231; [1998] 2 F.C.R. 159;
    [1997] Fam. Law 718, CA (Civ Div) 20–023
JC (Committal Proceedings), Re [2007] EWCA Civ 896 9–035
JD v East Berkshire Community Health NHS Trust; K v Dewsbury Healthcare NHS Trust;
    RK v Oldham NHS Trust; sub nom. MAK v Dewsbury Healthcare NHS Trust; D v
    East Berkshire Community Health NHS Trust [2005] UKHL 23; [2005] 2 A.C. 373; [2005] 2
    W.L.R. 993; [2005] 2 All E.R. 443; [2005] 2 F.L.R. 284; [2005] 2 F.C.R. 81; (2005)
    8 C.C.L. Rep. 185; [2005] Lloyd's Rep. Med. 263; (2005) 83 B.M.L.R. 66; [2005]
    Fam. Law 615; (2005) 155 N.L.J. 654, HL 16–002, 16–017, 21–027, 21–027
JS (A Child) (Contact: Parental Responsibility), Re [2002] EWCA Civ 1028; [2003] 1
    F.L.R. 399; [2002] 3 F.C.R. 433; [2003] Fam. Law 81, CA (Civ Div) 17–037
JS (A Minor) (Declaration of Paternity), Re [1981] Fam. 22; [1980] 3 W.L.R. 984; [1980]
    1 All E.R. 1061; (1980) 10 Fam. Law 121; (1980) 124 S.J. 881, CA (Civ Div) ...17–012, 18–052
JS (Private International Adoption), Re [2000] 2 F.L.R. 638; [2000] Fam. Law 787, Fam
    Div 20–016
Jackson v Bell [2001] EWCA Civ 387; [2001] B.P.I.R. 612; [2001] Fam. Law 879, CA (Civ
    Div) 5–059
Jackson v Watson & Sons [1909] 2 K.B. 193, CA 3–003
Jacobs v Davis [1917] 2 K.B. 532, KBD 3–041
James v James [1964] P. 303; [1963] 3 W.L.R. 331; [1963] 2 All E.R. 465; (1963) 127 J.P.
    352; (1963) 107 S.J. 116, DC 14–002
James v Thomas [2007] EWCA Civ 1212 ....5–018, 5–020, 5–022, 5–023, 5–026, 5–033
Jansen v Jansen [1965] P. 478; [1965] 3 W.L.R. 875; [1965] 3 All E.R. 363; (1965) 109 S.J.
    612, CA 3–008
Jelley v Iliffe [1981] Fam. 128; [1981] 2 W.L.R. 801; [1981] 2 All E.R. 29; (1981) 125 S.J.
    355, CA (Civ Div) 7–010, 7–016, 7–024
Jenkins v Jenkins (1978) 9 Fam. Law 215, CA (Civ Div) 18–057
Jenkins v Livesey (formerly Jenkins) [1985] A.C. 424; [1985] 2 W.L.R. 47; [1985] 1 All
    E.R. 106; [1985] Fam. Law 310; (1985) 82 L.S.G. 517; (1985) 134 N.L.J. 55, HL 13–006,
                                                        13–013, 13–064, 13–103, 13–107, 14–011
Jennings (Deceased), Re; sub nom. Harlow v National Westminster Bank Plc [1994] Ch.
    286; [1994] 3 W.L.R. 67; [1994] 3 All E.R. 27; [1994] 1 F.L.R. 536; [1995] 1 F.C.R.
    257; [1994] Fam. Law 439; (1994) 91(7) L.S.G. 33; (1994) 138 S.J.L.B. 31, CA (Civ
    Div) 7–011, 7–014, 7–017, 7–022, 7–024
Jennings v Rice [2002] EWCA Civ 159; [2003] 1 F.C.R. 501; [2003] 1 P. & C.R. 8; [2002]
    W.T.L.R. 367; [2002] N.P.C. 28; [2002] 2 P. & C.R. DG2, CA (Civ Div) ...5–033, 5–034, 5–035,
                                                                                    5–036

Jessel v Jessel [1979] 1 W.L.R. 1148; [1979] 3 All E.R. 645; (1979) 123 S.J. 404, CA (Civ
Div) 3–031, 13–004, 13–021, 13–096
Jessop v Jessop [1992] 1 F.L.R. 591; [1992] 2 F.C.R. 253; [1992] Fam. Law 328, CA (Civ
Div) 7–024
Jodla v Jodla (otherwise Czarnomska) [1960] 1 W.L.R. 236; [1960] 1 All E.R. 625; (1960)
104 S.J. 233, PDAD 2–032
Johansen v Norway (17383/90) (1997) 23 E.H.R.R. 33, ECHR 16–017, 17–024, 17–048, 18–026,
19–004, 21–041, 21–045, 21–070, 21–074, 22–040
Johnson v Calvert, 5 Cal. 4th 84 (1993) 17–003
Johnson v Walton [1990] 1 F.L.R. 350; [1990] F.C.R. 568; [1990] Fam. Law 260; (1990)
154 J.P.N. 506, CA (Civ Div) 9–027
Johnson's Will Trusts, Re; sub nom. National Provincial Bank v Jeffrey [1967] Ch. 387;
[1967] 2 W.L.R. 152; [1967] 1 All E.R. 553; (1966) 110 S.J. 811, Ch D 3–028
Johnston v Ireland (A/112); sub nom. Johnston v Ireland (9697/82) (1987) 9 E.H.R.R. 203,
ECHR 17–035
Johnston v Parker (1819) 3 Phill. Ecc. 39; 161 E.R. 1251 1–005
Johnston v Wellesley Hospital (1970) 17 D.L.R. (3d) 139 16–012
Jones v Challenger [1961] 1 Q.B. 176; [1960] 2 W.L.R. 695; [1960] 1 All E.R. 785; (1960)
104 S.J. 328, CA 5–046
Jones v Garnett (Inspector of Taxes) [2007] UKHL 35; [2007] 1 W.L.R. 2030; [2007] 4 All
E.R. 857; [2007] S.T.C. 1536; [2007] I.C.R. 1259; [2007] 3 F.C.R. 487; [2007] B.T.C.
476; [2007] W.T.L.R. 1229; [2007] S.T.I. 1899; (2007) 157 N.L.J. 1118; (2007) 151
S.J.L.B. 1024, HL 3–034
Jones v Jones [1993] 2 F.L.R. 377; [1993] 2 F.C.R. 82; [1993] Fam. Law 519, CA (Civ
Div) 9–035
Jones v Jones [1997] Fam. 59; [1997] 2 W.L.R. 373; [1997] 1 F.L.R. 27; [1997] 1 F.C.R. 1;
(1997) 29 H.L.R. 561; [1997] Fam. Law 164, CA (Civ Div) 13–117, 13–118
Jones v Jones (Periodical Payments) [2001] Fam. 96; [2000] 3 W.L.R. 1505; [2000] 2 F.L.R.
307; [2000] 2 F.C.R. 201; [2000] Fam. Law 607; (2000) 97(17) L.S.G. 34; (2000) 144
S.J.L.B. 203, CA (Civ Div) 13–097, 13–098
Jones v Maynard [1951] Ch. 572; [1951] 1 All E.R. 802; [1951] 1 T.L.R. 700; (1951) 95 S.J.
442, Ch D 5–063
Jones v Padavatton [1969] 1 W.L.R. 328; [1969] 2 All E.R. 616; (1968) 112 S.J. 965, CA
(Civ Div) 5–005
Jones (John Keith) v Roberts (John Ronald) [1995] 2 F.L.R. 422; [1995] Fam. Law 673, Ch
D 7–004
Joram Developments v Sharratt; sub nom. Carega Properties SA (Formerly Joram
Developments) v Sharratt [1979] 1 W.L.R. 928; (1980) 39 P. & C.R. 76; (1979) 252
E.G. 163; (1979) 123 S.J. 505, HL 22–001
Joseph v Joseph [1953] 1 W.L.R. 1182; [1953] 2 All E.R. 710; (1953) 97 S.J. 586, CA 10–030
Judd v Brown; sub nom. Bankrupts (Nos.9587 and 9588 of 1994), Re [1999] 1 F.L.R. 1191;
[1999] B.P.I.R. 517; (2000) 79 P. & C.R. 491; [1999] Fam. Law 523, CA (Civ Div) 5–059
Julian v Julian (1972) 116 S.J. 763 10–045
K, Re; sub nom. A local authority v N [2005] EWHC 2956 (Fam); [2007] 1 F.L.R. 399;
[2007] Fam. Law 298; [2007] Fam. Law 211, Fam Div 1–010, 1–011, 2–012, 2–013, 2–043
K (A Child) (Secure Accommodation Order: Right to Liberty), Re; sub nom. W BC v DK;
W BC v AK [2001] Fam. 377; [2001] 2 W.L.R. 1141; [2001] 2 All E.R. 719; (2001)
165 J.P. 241; [2001] 1 F.L.R. 526; [2001] 1 F.C.R. 249; [2001] H.R.L.R. 13; (2001) 3
L.G.L.R. 39; [2001] A.C.D. 41; [2001] Fam. Law 99; (2001) 165 J.P.N. 585; (2000)
97(48) L.S.G. 36; (2000) 144 S.J.L.B. 291, CA (Civ Div) 16–018, 16–020, 17–017, 18–042,
21–034, 21–051, 21–077, 21–078
K (A Minor), Re (1978) 122 S.J. 626 17–014
K (A Minor) (Adoption: Foreign Child), Re; sub nom. K (Adoption and Wardship), Re
[1997] 2 F.L.R. 221; [1997] 2 F.C.R. 389; [1997] Fam. Law 316, CA (Civ Div) 18–052,
19–019, 19–020, 22–009, 22–049
K (A Minor) (Contact: Psychiatric Report), Re [1995] 2 F.L.R. 432; [1995] Fam. Law 597,
CA (Civ Div) 18–008, 18–012, 19–016
K (A Minor) (Removal from Jurisdiction: Practice), Re [1999] 2 F.L.R. 1084; [1999] 3
F.C.R. 673; [1999] Fam. Law 754; (1999) 96(33) L.S.G. 29, CA (Civ Div) 18–026
K (A Minor) (Residence Order: Securing Contact), Re [1999] 1 F.L.R. 583; [1999] 3 F.C.R.
365; [1999] Fam. Law 220, CA (Civ Div) 20–002

K (A Minor) (Ward: Care and Control), Re [1990] 1 W.L.R. 431; [1990] 3 All E.R. 795; [1990] 2 F.L.R. 64; [1990] F.C.R. 553; [1990] Fam. Law 256; (1990) 154 J.P.N. 411; (1990) 134 S.J. 49, CA (Civ Div) 19–003

K (Adoption: Disclosure of Information), Re [1997] 2 F.L.R. 74; [1998] 2 F.C.R. 388, Fam Div 22–035

K (Adoption: Permission to Advertise), Re [2007] 2 F.L.R. 326 22–004

K (Application to Remove Children from Jurisdiction), Re [1998] 2 F.L.R. 1006; [1999] 2 F.C.R. 410; [1998] Fam. Law 584, Fam Div 18–026

K (Care Order), Re [2007] 2 F.L.R. 1066, CA 21–038, 21–043, 21–055

K (Children) (Care: Threshold Criteria), Re [2005] EWCA Civ 1226; [2006] 2 F.L.R. 868; [2006] Fam. Law 626, CA (Civ Div) 21–032

K (Children) (Contact: Committal Order), Re; sub nom. K (Children) (Committal Proceedings), Re [2002] EWCA Civ 1559; [2003] 1 F.L.R. 277; [2003] 2 F.C.R. 336; [2003] Fam. Law 11, CA (Civ Div) 9–035

K (Children) (Procedure: Family Proceedings Rules), Re [2004] EWCA Civ 1827; [2005] 1 F.L.R. 764; [2005] Fam. Law 275; (2005) 149 S.J.L.B. 29, CA (Civ Div) 18–040

K (Contact: Mother's Anxiety), Re [1999] 2 F.L.R. 703; [1999] Fam. Law 527, Fam Div 19–007, 19–022

K (Minors) (Care or Residence Order), Re [1995] 1 F.L.R. 675; [1996] 1 F.C.R. 365; (1995) 159 J.P.N. 691, Fam Div 18–001, 18–014, 19–023

K (Minors) (Children: Care and Control), Re; sub nom. K (Minors) (Wardship: Care and Control), Re [1977] Fam. 179; [1977] 2 W.L.R. 33; [1977] 1 All E.R. 647, CA (Civ Div) 19–006, 19–022

K (Minors) (Incitement to Breach Contact Order), Re [1992] 2 F.L.R. 108; [1992] 2 F.C.R. 529; [1993] Fam. Law 530 20–002

K (Specific Issue Order), Re [1999] 2 F.L.R. 280; [1999] Fam. Law 455, Fam Div 19–021

K v Finland (25702/94) (No.2); sub nom. T v Finland (25702/94) (No.2) [2001] 2 F.L.R. 707; [2001] 2 F.C.R. 673; (2003) 36 E.H.R.R. 18; [2001] Fam. Law 733, ECHR 17–029, 17–051, 18–034, 18–035, 21–001, 21–050

K v H (Child Maintenance) [1993] 2 F.L.R. 61; [1993] 1 F.C.R. 684; [1993] Fam. Law 464, Fam Div 18–005

K v K [1961] 1 W.L.R. 802; [1961] 2 All E.R. 266; (1961) 105 S.J. 231, CA 3–032

K v K (Financial Provision: Conduct) [1988] 1 F.L.R. 469, CA (Civ Div) 13–067, 13–084

K v K (Financial Relief: Widow's Pension) [1997] 1 F.L.R. 35; [1996] 3 F.C.R. 158; [1997] Fam. Law 162, Fam Div 13–121

K v K (Minors: Property Transfer); sub nom. Kelly v Kelly [1992] 1 W.L.R. 530; [1992] 2 All E.R. 727; [1992] 2 F.L.R. 220; [1992] 2 F.C.R. 253; (1993) 25 H.L.R. 229; [1992] Fam. Law 336; (1992) 136 S.J.L.B. 69, CA (Civ Div) 15–049, 19–002

K v K (Periodical Payment: Cohabitation) [2005] EWHC 2886; [2006] 2 F.L.R. 468; [2006] Fam. Law 518, Fam Div 13–021, 13–068, 13–098

K v M (Paternity: Contact) [1996] 1 F.L.R. 312; [1996] 3 F.C.R. 517; [1996] Fam. Law 206; (1996) 160 J.P.N. 731, Fam Div 17–007, 17–024, 18–019

K v P (Children Act Proceedings: Estoppel) [1995] 1 F.L.R. 248; [1995] 2 F.C.R. 457; [1995] Fam. Law 178, Fam Div 21–036

K and A (Local Authority: Child Maintenance), Re [1995] 1 F.L.R. 688; [1995] Fam. Law 407, Fam Div 21–009

K and H, Re [2007] 1 F.L.R. 2043, CA 21–046

K and S (Minors) (Wardship: Immigration), Re [1992] 1 F.L.R. 432; [1992] 1 F.C.R. 385; [1992] Fam. Law 239 18–052

KD (A Minor) (Ward: Termination of Access), Re [1988] A.C. 806; [1988] 2 W.L.R. 398; [1988] 1 All E.R. 577; [1988] 2 F.L.R. 139; [1988] F.C.R. 657; [1988] Fam. Law 288; (1988) 152 J.P.N. 558; (1988) 132 S.J. 301, HL 17–024, 18–016, 18–019, 19–001, 19–004

KR (A Child) (Abduction: Forcible Removal by Parents), Re; sub nom. KR (A Minor) (Abduction: Forcible Removal), Re [1999] 4 All E.R. 954; [1999] 2 F.L.R. 542; [1999] 2 F.C.R. 337; [1999] Fam. Law 545, Fam Div 17–018, 18–052, 20–001, 20–023, 21–032

KR v Bryn Alyn Community (Holdings) Ltd (In Liquidation); sub nom. Various Claimants v BACHL; Various Claimants v Bryn Alyn Community (Holdings) Ltd (In Liquidation) [2003] EWCA Civ 85; [2003] Q.B. 1441; [2003] 3 W.L.R. 107; [2004] 2 All E.R. 716; [2003] 1 F.L.R. 1203; [2003] 1 F.C.R. 385; [2003] Lloyd's Rep. Med. 175; [2003] Fam. Law 482, CA (Civ Div) 21–066

KW and H (Minors) (Medical Treatment), Re [1993] 1 F.L.R. 854; [1993] Fam. Law 280; (1993) 157 L.G. Rev. 267 16–016

Kali *L/1* v Chawla [2007] EWHC 2357 (Ch), Ch D 5–008, 5–012, 5–029
Kassim (*otherwise* Widmann) v Kassim (otherwise Hassim) (Carl and Dickson cited) [1962]
 P. 224; [1960] 3 W.L.R. 865; [1962] 3 All E.R. 426; (1962) 106 S.J. 632, PDAD 2–042
Katz v Katz [1972] 1 *W*.L.R. 955; [1972] 3 All E.R. 219; (1972) 116 S.J. 546, Fam Div 10–023,
 10–024
Kaur v Gill [1988] Fam. 110; [1988] 3 W.L.R. 39; [1988] 2 All E.R. 288; [1988] 2 F.L.R.
 328; [1988] F.C.R. 540; (1988) 56 P. & C.R. 450; [1988] Fam. Law 479; (1988) 138
 N.L.J. Rep. 95; (1988) 132 S.J. 852, CA (Civ Div) 3–012, 3–013
Kaur v Secretary of State for Social Services [1981] 3 F.L.R. 237 6–012
Kaur v Singh [1972] 1 W.L.R. 105; [1972] 1 All E.R 292; (1971) 115 S.J. 967, CA (Civ
 Div) 2–032, 2–040
Kean v Kean [2002] 2 F.L.R. 28; [2002] Fam. Law 508, Fam Div 13–104
Keeber v Keeber [1995] 2 F.L.R. 748; [1996] 1 F.C.R. 199; [1996] Fam Law 24; (1995) 159
 J.P.N. 778, CA (Civ Div) 18–057
Keegan v Ireland (16969/90) [1994] 3 F.C.R. 165; (1994) 18 E.H.R.R. 342, ECHR 17–035, 17–052
Kelly v BBC [2001] 1 F.L.R. 197 .... 18–049, 18–053
Kelly v Kelly (1932) 49 T.L.R. 99 2–042
Kent CC v C [1993] Fam. 57; [1992] 3 W.L.R. 808; [1993] 1 All E.R. 719; [1993] 1 F.L.R.
 308; [1993] Fam. Law 133, Fam Div 21–014
Kerr v Kennedy [1942] 1 K.B. 409, KBD 10–057
Kerr v Kerr [1897] 2 Q.B. 439, QBD 14–005
Khan v Khan [1980] 1 W.L.R. 355; [1980] 1 All E.R. 497; (1981) 11 Fam. Law 19; (1980)
 124 S.J. 239, Fam Div 3–017
Khorasandjian v Bush [1993] Q.B. 727; [1993] 3 W.L.R. 476; [1993] 3 All E.R. 669; [1993]
 2 F.L.R. 66; (1993) 25 H.L.R. 392; [1993] Fam. Law 679; (1993) 137 S.J.L.B. 88, CA
 (Civ Div) 9–038
Kiely v Kiely [1988] 1 F.L.R. 248; [1988] Fam. Law 51, CA (Civ Div) 13–113, 15–044, 15–051
Kimber v Kimber; sub nom. K v K (Enforcement) [2000] 1 F.L.R. 383; [2000] Fam. Law
 317, Fam Div 9–029
Kimber v Kimber [2001] 1 F.L.R. 232 .... 6–012, 6–013
Kinch v Bullard [1999] 1 W.L.R. 423; [1998] 4 All E.R. 650; [1999] 1 F.L.R. 66; [1998] 3
 E.G.L.R. 112; [1998] 47 E.G. 140; [1998] Fam. Law 738; [1998] E.G. 126 (C.S.);
 [1998] N.P.C. 137; (1999) 77 P. & C.R. D1, Ch D 5–041
King v Bunyon [2008] Fam.Law. 308 14–002
Kingsnorth Finance Co Ltd v Tizard; sub nom. Kingsnorth Trust Ltd v Tizard [1986] 1
 W.L.R. 783; [1986] 2 All E.R. 54; (1986) 51 P. & C.R. 296; (1986) 83 L.S.G. 1231;
 (1985) 130 S.J. 244, Ch D 5–051
Kingston upon Thames RLBC v Prince [1999] 1 F.L.R. 593; (1999) 31 H.L.R. 794; [1999]
 B.L.G.R. 333; [1999] L. & T.R. 175; [1999] Fam. Law 84; [1998] E.G. 179 (C.S.);
 (1999) 96(2) L.S.G. 28; (1999) 143 S.J.L.B. 45; [1998] N.P.C. 158, CA (Civ Div) 16–001,
 16–002
Kinnear v Department of Health and Social Security [1989] Fam. Law 146 17–021
Kirby, Re [1981] 3 F.L.R. 249 .... 7–016, 7–019
Kirklees MBC v S (Contact to Newborn Babies); sub nom. S (A Child) (Care Proceedings:
 Contact), Re [2006] 1 F.L.R. 333; [2005] Fam. Law 768, Fam Div 21–074
Kleinwort Benson Ltd v Lincoln City Council; Kleinwort Benson Ltd v Birmingham City
 Council; Kleinwort Benson Ltd v Southwark LBC; Kleinwort Benson Ltd v Kensing-
 ton and Chelsea RLBC [1999] 2 A.C. 349; [1998] 3 W.L.R. 1095; [1998] 4 All E.R.
 513; [1998] Lloyd's Rep. Bank. 387; [1999] C.L.C. 332; (1999) 1 L.G.L.R. 148;
 (1999) 11 Admin. L.R. 130; [1998] R.V.R. 315; (1998) 148 N.L.J. 1674; (1998) 142
 S.J.L.B. 279; [1998] N.P.C. 145, HL 13–108
Klentzeris v Klentzeris [2007] EWCA Civ 533 .... 19–016, 20–021
Knibb v Knibb [1987] 2 F.L.R. 396; [1987] Fam. Law 346; (1987) 84 L.S.G. 1058; (1987)
 131 S.J. 692, CA (Civ Div) 13–113
Knowles v Knowles [1962] P. 161; [1962] 2 W.L.R. 742; [1962] 1 All E.R. 659; (1961) 105
 S.J. 1011, PDAD 17–030
Kokosinski v Kokosinski; sub nom. K v K [1980] Fam. 72; [1980] 3 W.L.R. 55; [1980] 1
 All E.R. 1106; (1979) 10 Fam. Law 91; (1980) 124 S.J. 16, Fam Div 13–063
Koniarska v United Kingdom (Admissibility) (33670/96); sub nom. Koniarski v United
 Kingdom (Admissibility) (33670/96) (2000) 30 E.H.R.R. CD139, ECHR 21–077, 21–078
Kosmopoulou v Greece (60457/00) [2004] 1 F.L.R. 800; [2004] 1 F.C.R. 427; [2004] Fam.
 Law 330, ECHR 18–0

Kotke v Saffarini [2005] EWCA Civ 221; [2005] 2 F.L.R. 517; [2005] 1 F.C.R. 642; [2005]
    P.I.Q.R. P26; [2005] Fam. Law 535; (2005) 155 N.L.J. 414, CA (Civ Div) 7–017
Kourgky v Lusher (1983) 4 F.L.R. 65; (1982) 12 Fam. Law 86, Fam Div 7–016, 7–023
Kowalczuk v Kowalczuk [1973] 1 W.L.R. 930; [1973] 2 All E.R. 1042; (1973) 117 S.J. 372,
    CA (Civ Div) 3–008, 5–022
Krishnan v Sutton LBC [1970] Ch. 181; [1969] 3 W.L.R. 683; [1969] 3 All E.R. 1367;
    (1969) 113 S.J. 774, CA (Civ Div) 21–013
Kroon v Netherlands (A/297-C) [1995] 2 F.C.R. 28; (1995) 19 E.H.R.R. 263, ECHR 17–007,
    17–035
Krubert (Deceased), Re; sub nom. Krubert v Rutherford Davies [1997] Ch. 97; [1996] 3
    W.L.R. 959; [1997] 1 F.L.R. 42; [1996] 3 F.C.R. 281; [1997] Fam. Law 165; (1996)
    93(27) L.S.G. 28; (1996) 140 S.J.L.B. 167, CA (Civ Div) 7–026
Kurma v Kurma, *The Times,* April 30, 1958 2–042
Kusminow v Barclays Bank Trust Co Ltd [1989] Fam. Law 66 .... 7–022, 7–026
Kuwait Oil Tanker Co SAK v Qabazard; sub nom. Kuwait Oil Tanker Co SAK v UBS AG
    [2003] UKHL 31; [2004] 1 A.C. 300; [2003] 3 W.L.R. 14; [2003] 3 All E.R. 501;
    [2003] 2 All E.R. (Comm) 101; [2003] 1 C.L.C. 1206; [2003] I.L.Pr. 45; (2003)
    100(28) L.S.G. 32; (2003) 147 S.J.L.B. 750, HL 14–006
L, Re [2007] EWCA Civ 196 .... 17–046, 22–064
L (A Child), Re [2007] EWHC 3404 21–055
L (A Child) (Care: Assessment: Fair Trial), Re; sub nom. C (A Child) (Care Proceedings:
    Disclosure of Local Authority's Decision Making Process), Re [2002] EWHC 1379;
    [2002] 2 F.L.R. 730; [2002] 2 F.C.R. 673; [2002] Fam. Law 802, Fam Div 21–086
L (A Child) (Contact: Domestic Violence), Re; M (A Child) (Contact: Domestic Violence),
    Re; V (A Child) (Contact: Domestic Violence), Re; H (Children) (Contact: Domestic
    Violence), Re [2001] Fam. 260; [2001] 2 W.L.R. 339; [2000] 4 All E.R. 609; [2000]
    2 F.L.R. 334; [2000] 2 F.C.R. 404; [2000] Fam. Law 603; (2000) 164 J.P.N. 918;
    (2000) 144 S.J.L.B. 222, CA (Civ Div) ...17–024, 18–019, 18–027, 19–001, 19–003, 19–008,
    19–016, 19–021, 19–022
L (A Child) v Reading BC [2001] EWCA Civ 346; [2001] 1 W.L.R. 1575; [2001] 2 F.L.R.
    50; [2001] 1 F.C.R. 673; [2001] P.I.Q.R. P29; [2001] Fam. Law 421; (2001) 98(18)
    L.S.G. 44; (2001) 145 S.J.L.B. 92, CA (Civ Div) 21–027
L (A Child) v United Kingdom (Disclosure of Expert Evidence) [2000] 2 F.L.R. 322; [2000]
    2 F.C.R. 145; [2000] Fam. Law 708, ECHR 18–043, 21–037
L (A Minor) (Adoption: Parental Agreement), Re [1987] 1 F.L.R. 400; [1988] F.C.R. 92;
    [1987] Fam. Law 156; (1987) 151 J.P.N. 638; (1988) 152 L.G. Rev. 250 22–032
L (A Minor) (Police Investigation: Privilege), Re; sub nom. L (Minors) (Disclosure of
    Medical Reports), Re; L (Minors) (Police Investigation: Privilege), Re [1997] A.C. 16;
    [1996] 2 W.L.R. 395; [1996] 2 All E.R. 78; [1996] 1 F.L.R. 731; [1996] 2 F.C.R. 145;
    (1996) 32 B.M.L.R. 160; [1996] Fam. Law 400; (1996) 160 L.G. Rev. 417; (1996)
    93(15) L.S.G. 30; (1996) 146 N.L.J. 441; (1996) 140 S.J.L.B. 116, HL 18–043,
    21–037
L (A Minor) (Residence Order: Justices Reasons), Re [1995] 2 F.L.R. 445; [1995] 3 F.C.R.
    684; [1995] Fam. Law 598; (1995) 159 J.P.N. 625, Fam Div 18–043, 19–025
L (A Minor) (Section 37 Direction), Re [1999] 1 F.L.R. 984; [1999] 3 F.C.R. 642; [1999]
    Fam. Law 307; (2000) 164 J.P.N. 546; (2000) 164 J.P.N. 781, CA (Civ Div) 18–048
L (Abduction: Pending Criminal Proceedings), Re [1999] 1 F.L.R. 433; [1999] 2 F.C.R. 604;
    [1999] Fam. Law 140, Fam Div 20–018
L (Care: Confidentiality), Re [1999] 1 F.L.R. 165; [1999] Fam. Law 81, Fam Div 21–037
L (Care: Threshold Criteria), Re [2007] 1 F.L.R. 2064 21–032
L (Child Abduction) (Psychological Harm), Re [1993] 2 F.L.R. 401; [1993] 2 F.C.R. 509;
    [1993] Fam. Law 514 ....20–020, 21–033, 21–035
L (Children) (Care Proceedings: Threshold Criteria), Re [2006] 3 F.C.R. 301; [2007] Fam.
    Law 17; (2006) 103(36) L.S.G. 36; (2006) 150 S.J.L.B. 1152, CA (Civ Div) 17–027, 21–020
L (Contact: Transsexual Applicant), Re [1995] 2 F.L.R. 438; [1995] 3 F.C.R. 125; [1995]
    Fam. Law 599, Fam Div 17–004, 17–037, 18–027, 19–019
L (Family Proceedings Court) (Appeal: Jurisdiction), Re [2003] EWHC 1682; [2005] 1
    F.L.R. 210; [2005] Fam. Law 23, Fam Div 15–024, 17–012
L (Infants), Re [1962] 1 W.L.R. 886; [1962] 3 All E.R. 1; (1962) 106 S.J. 686, CA 19–005
L (Medical Treatment: Gillick Competence), Re; sub nom. L (A Minor), Re [1998] 2 F.L.R.
    810; [1999] 2 F.C.R. 524; (2000) 51 B.M.L.R. 137; [1998] Fam. Law 591, Fam Div 16–014
(Minors), Re (1979) (1979) 123 S.J. 404 13–068

L (Minors) (Sexual Abuse: Standard of Proof), Re; sub nom. L (Minors) (Care Proceedings: Appeal), Re [1996] 1 F.L.R. 116; [1996] 2 F.C.R. 352; [1996] Fam. Law 73; (1995) 159 J.P.N. 812, CA (Civ Div) 21–075

L (Minors) (Wardship: Jurisdiction), Re; sub nom. L Minors, Re [1974] 1 W.L.R. 250; [1974] 1 All E.R. 913; (1973) 4 Fam. Law 94; (1973) 118 S.J. 22, CA (Civ Div) 20–023

L (Removal from Jurisdiction: Holiday), Re [2001] 1 F.L.R. 241; [2001] Fam. Law 9, Fam Div 18–026, 20–005

L (Residence: Jurisdiction), Re [2007] 1 F.L.R. 1686 18–030

L v Bromley LBC; sub nom. L (Minors) (Care Proceedings: Contact), Re [1998] 1 F.L.R. 709; [1998] 3 F.C.R. 339; [1998] Fam. Law 251; (1997) 161 J.P.N. 960, Fam Div ... 21–074

L v Finland [2000] 2 F.L.R. 118; [2000] 3 F.C.R. 219; (2001) 31 E.H.R.R. 30; [2000] Fam. Law 536, ECHR 21–070

L v L [2006] EWHC 956 .... 13–012, 13–098, 13–102

L v L [2008] Fam.Law 11 .... 13–054, 13–055, 13–056, 13–057

L v L (Child Abuse: Access) [1989] 2 F.L.R. 16; [1989] F.C.R. 697; [1989] Fam. Law 311; (1989) 153 J.P.N. 738, CA (Civ Div) 18–019

L v L (Lump Sum: Interest) [1994] 2 F.L.R. 324; [1995] 2 F.C.R. 60; [1994] Fam. Law 620, Fam Div 13–024

L v L (otherwise W) (1882) L.R. 7 P.D. 16, PDAD 2–026

L v L (School Fees: Maintenance: Enforcement); sub nom. L v L (Payment of School Fees) [1997] 2 F.L.R. 252; [1997] 3 F.C.R. 520; [1997] Fam. Law 658, CA (Civ Div) 15–035

L and H (Residential Assessment), Re [2007] 1 F.L.R. 1370, CA 21–043

LM v Medway Council; sub nom. M (A Child) (Care Proceedings: Witness Summons), Re [2007] EWCA Civ 9; [2007] 1 F.C.R. 253; (2007) 157 N.L.J. 142; (2007) 151 S.J.L.B. 124, CA (Civ Div) 18–042, 21–038

LR v Witherspoon [2000] 1 F.L.R. 82; [1999] 3 F.C.R. 202; [1999] Lloyd's Rep. P.N. 401; [1999] P.N.L.R. 776; [2000] Fam. Law 19, CA (Civ Div) 18–006

Laing v Laing [2005] EWHC 3152 (Fam); [2007] 2 F.L.R. 199, Fam Div 14–020

Lambert v Lambert; sub nom. L v L (Financial Provision: Contributions) [2002] EWCA Civ 1685; [2003] Fam. 103; [2003] 2 W.L.R. 631; [2003] 4 All E.R. 342; [2003] 1 F.L.R. 139; [2002] 3 F.C.R. 673; [2003] Fam. Law 16, CA (Civ Div) 13–045, 13–079

Lancashire CC v B (A Child) (Care Orders: Significant Harm); sub nom. B and W (Children) (Threshold Criteria), Re; Lancashire CC v W (A Child) (Care Orders: Significant Harm); Lancashire CC v A (A Child); BW (Care Orders), Re [2000] 2 A.C. 147; [2000] 2 W.L.R. 590; [2000] 2 All E.R. 97; [2000] 1 F.L.R. 583; [2000] 1 F.C.R. 509; [2000] B.L.G.R. 347; [2000] Fam. Law 394; (2000) 164 J.P.N. 426; (2000) 97(13) L.S.G. 42; (2000) 150 N.L.J. 429; (2000) 144 S.J.L.B. 151, HL 21–034

Langley v Liverpool City Council [2005] EWCA Civ 1173; [2006] 1 W.L.R. 375; [2006] 2 All E.R. 202; [2006] 1 F.L.R. 342; [2005] 3 F.C.R. 303; [2006] B.L.G.R. 453; [2006] Fam. Law 94, CA (Civ Div) 21–051

Langton v Langton [1995] 2 F.L.R. 890; [1995] 3 F.C.R. 521; [1996] Fam. Law 86, Ch D 5–055

Larson v Sweden (33250/96) 20–026

Laskar v Laskar, unreported, February 7, 2008 .... 5–012, 5–014, 5–017

Lau v DPP [2000] 1 F.L.R. 799; [2000] Crim. L.R. 580; [2000] Fam. Law 610, DC 9–006

Lauder v Lauder [2007] EWHC 1227 (Fam); [2007] 2 F.L.R. 802, Fam Div 13–053, 13–098

Lavelle v Lavelle [2004] EWCA Civ 223; [2004] 2 F.C.R. 418, CA (Civ Div) 5–016

Lawrence v Pembrokeshire CC [2007] 2 F.L.R. 705, CA 21–027

Layton v Martin [1986] 2 F.L.R. 227; [1986] Fam. Law 212, Ch D 5–033

Le Brocq v Le Brocq [1964] 1 W.L.R. 1085; [1964] 3 All E.R. 464; (1964) 108 S.J. 501, CA 10–028

Le Foe v Le Foe; Woolwich Plc v Le Foe [2001] EWCA Civ 1870, CA (Civ Div) 3–008, 5–023, 13–083

Leach (Deceased), Re; sub nom. Leach v Linderman [1986] Ch. 226; [1985] 3 W.L.R. 413; [1985] 2 All E.R. 754; [1985] Fam. Law 319; (1985) 82 L.S.G. 2081; (1985) 135 N.L.J. 392; (1985) 129 S.J. 318, CA (Civ Div) 7–028

Leadbeater v Leadbeter [1985] F.L.R. 789 13–067

Lebens v Lebens [2003] W.T.L.R. 251, CC (Central London) 5–023

Ledger-Beadell v Peach [2006] EWHC 2940 (Ch); [2007] 2 F.L.R. 210; [2007] Fam. Law 595; [2006] 48 E.G. 230 (C.S.), Ch D 3–041, 5–013, 5–016, 5–022

Leeds County Council v C [1993] 1 F.L.R. 269; [1993] 1 F.C.R. 585; [1993] Fam. Law 73 .....18–016, 18–019

Leeds Teaching Hospital NHS Trust v A [2003] 1 F.L.R. 1091, Fam Div 17–004

Legge v Legge [2006] EWCA Civ 1484, CA (Civ Div) 9–035
Leicestershire CC v G [1994] 2 F.L.R. 329; [1995] 1 F.C.R. 205; [1994] Fam. Law 486;
    (1995) 159 J.P.N. 80, Fam Div 19–025
Levermore v Levermore [1979] 1 W.L.R. 1277; [1980] 1 All E.R. 1; (1979) 10 Fam. Law
    87; (1979) 123 S.J. 689, Fam Div 14–009, 14–017
Levy v Legal Services Commission (formerly Legal Aid Board); sub nom. Levy v Legal
    Aid Board [2001] 1 All E.R. 895; [2001] 1 F.L.R. 435; [2001] 1 F.C.R. 178; [2000]
    B.P.I.R. 1065; [2001] Fam. Law 92; (2000) 97(46) L.S.G. 39; (2000) 150 N.L.J. 1754,
    CA (Civ Div) 14–005
Lewis v Lewis [1977] 1 W.L.R. 409; [1977] 3 All E.R. 992; (1976) 6 Fam. Law 111; (1977)
    121 S.J. 271, CA (Civ Div) 13–098
Lewisham LBC v Lewisham Juvenile Court Justices [1980] A.C. 273; [1979] 2 W.L.R. 513;
    [1979] 2 All E.R. 297; 77 L.G.R. 469; (1979) 123 S.J. 270, HL 21–013
Lightfoot v Lightfoot-Brown [2005] EWCA Civ 201; [2005] 2 P. & C.R. 22; [2005]
    W.T.L.R. 1031; [2005] 2 P. & C.R. DG4, CA (Civ Div) 5–022
Linton v Linton (1884–85) L.R. 15 Q.B.D. 239, CA 14–002, 14–005
Lissimore v Downing [2003] 2 F.L.R. 308; [2003] Fam. Law 566, Ch D 5–033, 5–034
Lister v Hesley Hall Ltd [2001] UKHL 22; [2002] 1 A.C. 215; [2001] 2 W.L.R. 1311;
    [2001] 2 All E.R. 769; [2001] I.C.R. 665; [2001] I.R.L.R. 472; [2001] Emp. L.R. 819;
    [2001] 2 F.L.R. 307; [2001] 2 F.C.R. 97; (2001) 3 L.G.L.R. 49; [2001] E.L.R. 422;
    [2001] Fam. Law 595; (2001) 98(24) L.S.G. 45; (2001) 151 N.L.J. 728; (2001) 145
    S.J.L.B. 126; [2001] N.P.C. 89, HL 21–066, 21–067
Livingstone-Stallard v Livingstone-Stallard [1974] Fam. 47; [1974] 3 W.L.R. 302; [1974] 2
    All E.R. 766; (1974) 4 Fam. Law 150; (1974) 118 S.J. 462, Fam Div 10–023
Lloyds Bank Plc v Byrne [1993] 1 F.L.R. 369; [1993] 2 F.C.R. 41; (1991) 23 H.L.R. 472;
    [1991] E.G. 57 (C.S.), CA (Civ Div) 14–008
Lloyds Bank Plc v Rosset [1991] 1 A.C. 107; [1990] 2 W.L.R. 867; [1990] 1 All E.R. 1111;
    [1990] 2 F.L.R. 155; (1990) 22 H.L.R. 349; (1990) 60 P. & C.R. 311; (1990) 140 N.L.J.
    478, HL 5–020, 5–021, 5–022, 5–023, 5–024, 5–025, 5–027, 5–028, 5–037
Loades-Carter v Loades-Carter, 197 E.G. 361; (1966) 110 S.J. 51, CA 5–016
Local Authority X v MM [2007] EWHC 2003 (Fam), Fam Div 2–013, 2–036, 2–037
Lohia v Lohia [2001] EWCA Civ 1691, CA (Civ Div) 5–014
Lomas v Parle [2003] EWCA Civ 1804; [2004] 1 W.L.R. 1642; [2004] 1 All E.R. 1173;
    [2004] 1 F.L.R. 812; [2004] 1 F.C.R. 97; [2004] Fam. Law 243, CA (Civ Div) 9–043
Lonslow v Henning [1986] 2 F.L.R. 378 19–006
Loosemore v McDonnell, unreported, November 15, 2007, CA (Civ Div) 5–014
Lord Lilford v Glynn; sub nom. L v G [1979] 1 W.L.R. 78; [1979] 1 All E.R. 441; (1978)
    9 Fam. Law 81; (1978) 122 S.J. 433, CA (Civ Div) 15–044
Lort-Williams v Lort-Williams [1951] P. 395; [1951] 2 All E.R. 241; [1951] 2 T.L.R. 200;
    (1951) 95 S.J. 529, CA 13–027
Lough v Ward [1945] 2 All E.R. 338 17–019
Loughran v Pandya [2005] EWCA Civ 1720, CA (Civ Div) 9–035
Lowson v Coombes [1999] Ch. 373; [1999] 2 W.L.R. 720; [1999] 1 F.L.R. 799; [1999] 2
    F.C.R. 731; [1999] Fam. Law 91; (1999) 96(1) L.S.G. 23; (1999) 77 P. & C.R. D25,
    CA (Civ Div) 5–016
Luscombe v Luscombe (Westminster Bank Ltd, Garnishee) [1962] 1 W.L.R. 313; [1962] 1
    All E.R. 668; (1962) 106 S.J. 152, CA 14–002
M (A Child), Re [2007] EWCA Civ 260, CA (Civ Div) 20–021
M (A Child) (Care Order: Freeing Application), Re; sub nom. M (Care Order: Freeing for
    Adoption), Re [2003] EWCA Civ 1874; [2004] 1 F.L.R. 826; [2004] 1 F.C.R. 157;
    [2004] Fam. Law 322; (2004) 101(5) L.S.G. 27, CA (Civ Div) 19–019
M (A Child) (Contact Order: Committal for Contempt), Re; sub nom. M (Children), Re
    [2005] EWCA Civ 615; [2005] 2 F.L.R. 1006; [2005] Fam. Law 694, CA (Civ Div) 18–057,
                                                                                            18–058
M (A Child) (Contact: Parental Responsibility), Re [2001] 2 F.L.R. 342; [2001] 3 F.C.R.
    454; [2001] Fam. Law 594, Fam Div 16–001, 16–019, 17–037, 17–044, 18–019, 18–030,
                                                                                    19–001, 19–003
M (A Child) (Interim Contact: Domestic Violence), Re [2000] 2 F.L.R. 377; [2000] Fam.
    Law 604, CA (Civ Div) 18–024
M (A Child) (Refusal of Medical Treatment), Re; sub nom. M (A Child) (Medical
    Treatment: Consent) [1999] 2 F.L.R. 1097; [1999] 2 F.C.R. 577; (2000) 52 B.M.L.R.
    124; [1999] Fam. Law 753, Fam Div 18–049, 19–017

M (A Minor), Re (1980) 10 Fam. Law 184, CA (Civ Div) 18–034
M (A Minor) (Access Application), Re; sub nom. M (A Minor) (Child in Care: Access:
   Appeal), Re (1988) 152 J.P. 629; [1988] 1 F.L.R. 35; [1988] F.C.R. 450; [1988] Fam.
   Law 13; (1988) 152 J.P.N. 398, CA (Civ Div) 17–027, 19–019
M (A Minor) (Adoption or Residence Order), Re [1998] 1 F.L.R. 570; [1998] 1 F.C.R. 165;
   [1998] Fam. Law 188, CA (Civ Div) 18–028, 22–033
M (A Minor) (Appeal: Interim Care Order) (No.1), Re [1994] 1 F.L.R. 54; [1994] 1 F.C.R.
   1; [1994] Fam. Law 373; (1993) 158 L.G. Rev. 121, CA (Civ Div) 21–040, 21–046
M (A Minor) (Care Order: Threshold Conditions), Re; sub nom. M (A Minor) (Care Order:
   Significant Harm), Re [1994] 2 A.C. 424; [1994] 3 W.L.R. 558; [1994] 3 All E.R. 298;
   [1994] 2 F.L.R. 577; [1994] 2 F.C.R. 871; 92 L.G.R. 701; [1994] Fam. Law 501; (1994)
   158 J.P.N. 651; (1994) 91(37) L.S.G. 50; (1994) 138 S.J.L.B. 168, HL 21–032, 21–033,
                                                                                          21–040
M (A Minor) (Care Proceedings: Appeal), Re [1994] 1 F.L.R. 59; [1995] 1 F.C.R. 417;
   [1994] Fam. Law 374, CA (Civ Div) 19–025, 21–040
M (A Minor) (Child's Upbringing), Re [1996] 2 F.L.R. 441; [1996] 2 F.C.R. 473, CA (Civ
   Div) 18–049, 19–005, 19–006, 19–020
M (A Minor) (Contact Order), Re; sub nom. M (Section 94 Appeals), Re [1995] 1 F.L.R.
   546; [1995] 2 F.C.R. 435; [1995] Fam. Law 236; (1995) 159 J.P.N. 438, CA (Civ Div) ...19–007,
                                                                           19–020, 19–025, 19–026
M (A Minor) (Contact: Supervision), Re [1998] 1 F.L.R. 727; [1998] Fam. Law 70, CA (Civ
   Div) 18–019
M (A Minor) (Custodianship: Jurisdiction), Re [1987] 1 W.L.R. 162; [1987] 2 All E.R. 88;
   [1987] 1 F.L.R. 465; [1987] Fam. Law 92; (1987) 151 L.G. Rev. 832, CA (Civ Div) 22–065
M (A Minor) (Custody Appeal), Re [1990] 1 F.L.R. 291; [1990] F.C.R. 424; [1990] Fam.
   Law 99; (1990) 154 J.P.N. 379, CA (Civ Div) 19–006
M (A Minor) (Disclosure), Re [1998] 1 F.L.R. 734; [1998] 3 F.C.R. 517; [1998] Fam. Law
   189, CA (Civ Div) 21–025
M (A Minor) (Justices Discretion), Re; sub nom. M (Child) (Ascertaining Wishes and
   Feelings), Re [1993] 2 F.L.R. 706; [1993] Fam. Law 616 19–017
M (A Minor) (Secure Accommodation Order), Re [1995] Fam. 108; [1995] 2 W.L.R. 302;
   [1995] 3 All E.R. 407; [1995] 1 F.L.R. 418; [1995] 2 F.C.R. 373; 93 L.G.R. 127; [1995]
   Fam. Law 180; (1995) 159 J.P.N. 407; (1994) 138 S.J.L.B. 241, CA (Civ Div) 19–002,
                                                                                          21–077, 21–078
M (Abduction: Consent: Acquiescence), Re [1999] 1 F.L.R. 171; [1999] 1 F.C.R. 5; [1999]
   Fam. Law 8, Fam Div 20–019
M (Adoption: Rights of Natural Father), Re [2001] 1 F.L.R. 745; [2001] Fam. Law 252, Fam
   Div 17–052, 22–034
M (An Infant), Re [1961] Ch. 328; [1961] 2 W.L.R. 350; [1961] 1 All E.R. 788; (1961) 125
   J.P. 278; (1961) 105 S.J. 153, CA 21–085
M (Care Order: Parental Responsibility), Re; sub nom. MM (Care Order: Abandoned Baby),
   Re [1996] 2 F.L.R. 84; [1996] 2 F.C.R. 521; [1996] Fam. Law 664, Fam Div 17–042, 21–035
M (Care Proceedings Bet Evidence), Re [2007] 1 F.L.R. 1006, CA 18–043
M (Care Proceedings: Judicial Review), Re [2003] EWHC 850; [2003] 2 F.L.R. 171; [2004]
   1 F.C.R. 302; [2003] Fam. Law 479, QBD (Admin) 21–074
M (Care: Challenging Decisions by Local Authority), Re [2001] 2 F.L.R. 1300; [2001] Fam.
   Law 868, Fam Div 18–029, 19–002, 21–039, 21–086
M (Child Support Act: Parentage), Re [1997] 2 F.L.R. 90; [1997] 3 F.C.R. 383; [1997] Fam.
   Law 536, Fam Div 17–004
M (Children), Re [2004] EWCA Civ 1413, CA (Civ Div) 15–018
M (Children) (Contact: Long Term Best Interests), Re; sub nom. M (Children) (Intractable
   Contact Dispute: Court's Positive Duty), Re [2005] EWCA Civ 1090; [2006] 1 F.L.R.
   627; [2005] Fam. Law 938, CA (Civ Div) 18–019, 18–020, 19–001, 19–010, 19–016
M (Children) (Interim Care Order: Removal), Re [2005] EWCA Civ 1594; [2006] 1 F.C.R.
   303; [2006] Fam. Law 258; (2005) 149 S.J.L.B. 1355, CA (Civ Div) 21–043
M (Children) (Residence), Re [2004] EWCA Civ 1574; [2005] 1 F.L.R. 656; [2005] Fam.
   Law 216, CA (Civ Div) 18–012
M (Contact: Family Assistance: McKenzie Friend), Re; sub nom. M (Contact: Parental
   Responsiblity: McKenzie Friend), Re [1999] 1 F.L.R. 75; [1999] 1 F.C.R. 703; [1998]
   Fam. Law 727; (1999) 163 J.P.N. 795, Fam Div 18–027
M (Disclosure), Re [1998] 2 F.L.R. 1028; [1999] 1 F.C.R. 492; [1998] Fam. Law 729, CA
   (Civ Div) 18–041

M (Family Proceedigns: Affadavits), Re [1995] 2 F.L.R. 100 18–042
M (Intractable Contact Dispute: Interim Care Order), Re; sub nom. CDM v CM [2003]
    EWHC 1024; [2003] 2 F.L.R. 636; [2003] Fam. Law 719, Fam Div 18–048, 21–032
M (K) v M (H) (1992) 96 D.L.R. 596 17–027
M (Leave to Remove from Jurisdiction), Re [1999] 2 F.L.R. 334, Fam Div 18–026
M (Minors) (Abduction: Non-Convention Country), Re [1995] 1 F.L.R. 89; [1995] 2 F.C.R.
    265; [1995] Fam. Law 8, CA (Civ Div) 20–020
M (Minors) (Abduction: Peremptory Return Order), Re [1996] 1 F.L.R. 478; [1996] 1
    F.C.R. 557; [1996] Fam. Law 203, CA (Civ Div) 20–023
M (Minors) (Abduction: Psychological Harm), Re [1997] 2 F.L.R. 690; [1998] 2 F.C.R. 488;
    [1997] Fam. Law 780, CA (Civ Div) 20–018
M (Minors) (Adoption), Re [1991] 1 F.L.R. 458; [1990] F.C.R. 785; [1991] Fam. Law 222;
    (1990) 154 J.P.N. 675, CA (Civ Div) 22–009
M (Minors) (Breach of Contact Order: Committal), Re; sub nom. M (A Minor) (Contempt
    of Court: Committal of Court's Own Motion), Re [1999] Fam. 263; [1999] 2 W.L.R.
    810; [1999] 2 All E.R. 56; [1999] 1 F.L.R. 810; [1999] 1 F.C.R. 683; [1999] Fam. Law
    208; (1999) 96(6) L.S.G. 33; (1999) 143 S.J.L.B. 36, CA (Civ Div) 18–057, 18–058
M (Minors) (Care Proceedings: Child's Wishes), Re [1994] 1 F.L.R. 749; [1994] 1 F.C.R.
    866; [1994] Fam. Law 430, Fam Div 16–005, 16–021, 16–022
M (Minors) (Children's Welfare: Contact), Re [1995] 1 F.L.R. 274; [1995] 1 F.C.R. 753;
    [1995] Fam. Law 174; (1995) 159 J.P.N. 248, CA (Civ Div) 17–024, 18–019, 19–016
M (Minors) (Contact: Violent Parent), Re [1999] 2 F.L.R. 321; [1999] 2 F.C.R. 56; [1999]
    Fam. Law 380; (1999) 163 J.P.N. 651; (1998) 95(45) L.S.G. 37, Fam Div 18–019
M (Minors) (Residence Order: Jurisdiction), Re [1993] 1 F.L.R. 495; [1993] 1 F.C.R. 718;
    [1993] Fam. Law 285, CA (Civ Div) 15–010, 20–010
M (Minors in Care) (Contact: Grandmother's Application), Re [1995] 2 F.L.R. 86; [1995]
    3 F.C.R. 551; [1995] Fam. Law 540; (1995) 159 J.P.N. 757, CA (Civ Div) .. 18–020, 18–039,
                                                                                        21–074, 21–075
M (Minors: Interview), Re; sub nom. M (Minors) (Solicitors Interviews), Re; M (Care:
    Leave to Interview Child), Re [1995] 1 F.L.R. 825; [1995] 2 F.C.R. 643; [1995] Fam.
    Law 404, Fam Div 18–049, 21–065, 21–080
M (Official Solicitor's Role), Re [1998] 2 F.L.R. 815; [1998] 3 F.C.R. 315; [1998] Fam.
    Law 594; (1998) 95(27) L.S.G. 26, CA (Civ Div) 18–048
M (Petition to European Commission of Human Rights), Re [1997] 1 F.L.R. 755; [1996] 3
    F.C.R. 377; [1997] Fam. Law 12, Fam Div 18–049
M (Prohibited Steps Order: Application for Leave), Re [1993] 1 F.L.R. 275; [1993] 1 F.C.R.
    78; [1993] Fam. Law 76 18–039
M (Section 94 Appeals), Re. See M (A Minor) (Contact Order), Re
M (Terminating Appointment of Guardian ad Litem), Re [1999] 2 F.L.R. 717; [1999] 2
    F.C.R. 625; [1999] Fam. Law 541, Fam Div 21–058
M (Threshold Criteria: Parental Concessions), Re [1999] 2 F.L.R. 728; [1999] Fam. Law
    524, CA (Civ Div) 21–036
M v B [2005] EWHC 1681; [2006] 1 F.L.R. 117; [2005] Fam. Law 860; (2005) 102(34)
    L.S.G. 31, Fam Div 2–042
M v B (Ancillary Proceedings: Lump Sum). See Marshall v Beckett
M v Birmingham City Council [1994] 2 F.L.R. 141; [1995] 1 F.C.R. 50; [1994] Fam. Law
    557; (1994) 158 J.P.N. 836, Fam Div 19–002, 21–034, 21–078
M v H [2008] EWHC 324, Fam Div 18–016
M v H (Costs: Residence Proceedings) [2000] 1 F.L.R. 52 18–041
M v M (1977) 7 Fam.Law 17 19–017
M v M (Contempt: Committal) [1997] 1 F.L.R. 762; [1997] 3 F.C.R. 288; [1997] Fam. Law
    321, CA (Civ Div) 9–035
M v M (Defined Contact Application) [1998] 2 F.L.R. 244; [1998] Fam. Law 456, Fam Div ...18–005,
                                                                                                      18–024
M v M (Divorce: Jurisdiction: Validity of Marriage); sub nom. A-M v A-M (Divorce:
    Jurisdiction: Validity of Marriage) [2001] 2 F.L.R. 6; [2001] Fam. Law 495, Fam Div 1–044,
                                                                                                      1–048
M v M (Enforcement: Judgment Summons) [1993] Fam. Law 469 .... 13–006, 14–011
M v M (Financial Provision) [1987] 2 F.L.R. 1; [1987] Fam. Law 195 13–090
M v M (Minor: Custody Appeal); sub nom. M v M (Transfer of Custody: Appeal) [1987]
    1 W.L.R. 404; [1987] 2 F.L.R. 146; [1988] F.C.R. 37; [1987] Fam. Law 237; (1987)
    151 J.P.N. 446; (1987) 84 L.S.G. 981; (1987) 131 S.J. 408, CA (Civ Div) 19–025

M v M (No.1); E v E; B v B and T; B v B and D; M v M (No.2); W v W [1967] P. 313; [1967] 2 W.L.R. 1333, PDAD 10–005

M v M (Parental Responsibility); sub nom. J (A Minor) (Parental Responsibility), Re [1999] 2 F.L.R. 737; [1999] Fam. Law 538, Fam Div 17–037, 18–019

M v M (Prenuptial Agreement) [2002] 1 F.L.R. 654; [2002] Fam. Law 177, Fam Div 2–038, 13–058, 13–067, 13–072, 13–084

M v M (Specific Issue: Choice of School) [2007] 1 F.L.R. 251, Fam Div 18–022

M v Newham LBC [1995] A.C. 648, HL 21–027

M v Secretary of State for Work and Pensions; Langley v Bradford MDC; sub nom. Secretary of State for Work and Pensions v M [2006] UKHL 11; [2006] 2 A.C. 91; [2006] 2 W.L.R. 637; [2006] 4 All E.R. 929; [2006] 2 F.L.R. 56; [2006] 1 F.C.R. 497; [2006] H.R.L.R. 19; [2006] U.K.H.R.R. 799; 21 B.H.R.C. 254; [2006] Fam. Law 524; (2006) 150 S.J.L.B. 363, HL A–001, 2–017

M v W (Non Molestation Order: Duration) [2000] 1 F.L.R. 107; [2000] Fam. Law 13, Fam Div 9–033

M v Warwickshire CC [1994] 2 F.L.R. 593; [1994] 2 F.C.R. 121; [1994] Fam. Law 611, Fam Div 21–041

M v Warwickshire CC [2007] EWCA Civ 1084 22–024

M v Wigan MBC; sub nom. M (Review of Care Order), Re [1980] Fam. 36; [1979] 3 W.L.R. 244; [1979] 2 All E.R. 958; 77 L.G.R. 556; (1979) 9 Fam. Law 186; (1979) 123 S.J. 284, DC 17–027

M and J (Children) (Abduction: International Judicial Collaboration), Re [2000] 1 F.L.R. 803; [1999] 3 F.C.R. 721; [2000] Fam. Law 81, Fam Div 20–018

M, T, P, K and B (Children) (Care: Change of Name), Re [2000] 2 F.L.R. 645; [2000] Fam. Law 601, Fam Div 17–025, 19–016, 21–080

MB v KB; sub nom. B v B [2007] EWHC 789 (Fam); [2007] 2 F.L.R. 586; [2007] Fam. Law 801, Fam Div 15–044

MD and TD (Minors) (No.2), Re [1994] Fam. Law 489, Fam Div 21–045

MDC v GW; MDC v PW [2007] 2 F.L.R. 597 18–043

M-H (Assessment: Father of Half-Brother), Re [2007] 2 F.L.R. 715, CA 19–022

MH v GP (Child: Emigration); sub nom. Harris v Pinnington [1995] 2 F.L.R. 106; [1995] 3 F.C.R. 35; [1995] Fam. Law 542, Fam Div 19–002

M-J (Adoption Orders or Special Guardianship), Re [2007] 1 F.L.R. 691, CA 22–033, 22–064, 22–065

MT v MT (Financial Provision: Lump Sum) [1992] 1 F.L.R. 362; [1991] F.C.R. 649; [1992] Fam. Law 99 13–069

M-T v T [2006] EWHC 2494, Fam Div 15–052

MW (Adoption: Surrogacy), Re [1995] 2 F.L.R. 789; [1996] 3 F.C.R. 128; [1995] Fam. Law 665, Fam Div 22–002, 22–029, 22–072, 22–077

Mabon v Mabon [2005] EWCA Civ 634; [2005] Fam. 366; [2005] 3 W.L.R. 460; [2005] 2 F.L.R. 1011; [2005] 2 F.C.R. 354; [2005] H.R.L.R. 29; [2006] U.K.H.R.R. 421; (2005) 8 C.C.L. Rep. 412; [2005] Fam. Law 696, CA (Civ Div) 16–020, 16–021, 19–011, 19–017

McBroom (Deceased), Re [1992] 2 F.L.R. 49; [1992] Fam. Law 376 ....5–040, 7–011, 7–024

McC, In the Estate of (1978) 9 F.L.R. 26 7–014

MacDarmaid v Attorney General [1950] P. 218; [1950] 1 All E.R. 497; 66 T.L.R. (Pt. 1) 543; (1950) 94 S.J. 211, PDAD 12–004

Macdonald v MacDonald [1964] P. 1; [1963] 3 W.L.R. 350; [1963] 2 All E.R. 857; (1963) 107 S.J. 630, CA 13–097

McFarlane v McFarlane; Parlour v Parlour [2004] 2 F.L.R. 1093; [2005] Fam. 171 ....13–047, 13–098

McGrath v Wallis [1995] 2 F.L.R. 114; [1995] 3 F.C.R. 661; [1995] Fam. Law 551; (1995) 92(15) L.S.G. 41, CA (Civ Div) 5–016

McKee (Mark) v McKee (Evelyn) [1951] A.C. 352; [1951] 1 All E.R. 942; [1951] 1 T.L.R. 755; (1951) 95 S.J. 316, PC (Can) 20–024

McKenzie v McKenzie [2003] 2 P. & C.R. DG6, Ch D 5–012, 5–013, 5–015

McMichael v United Kingdom (A/308); sub nom. McMichael v United Kingdom (16424/90) [1995] 2 F.C.R. 718; (1995) 20 E.H.R.R. 205; [1995] Fam. Law 478, ECHR 18–041

Macey v Macey (1981) 11 Fam. Law 248, DC 13–068

Mahadervan v Mahadervan; sub nom. Mahadevan v Mahadevan [1964] P. 233; [1963] 2 W.L.R. 271; [1962] 3 All E.R. 1108; (1962) 106 S.J. 533, PDAD 1–045

Mahoney v Purnell [1996] 3 All E.R. 61; [1997] 1 F.L.R. 612; [1997] Fam. Law 169, QBD 5–055, 5–0

Malone v Harrison [1979] 1 W.L.R. 1353; (1979) 123 S.J. 804, Fam Div 7–020, 7–024
Manchester City Council v F [1993] 1 F.L.R. 419; [1993] 1 F.C.R. 1000 21–074
Manchester CC v T; sub nom. T (A Minor) (Guardian ad Litem: Case Record), Re [1994]
    Fam. 181; [1994] 2 W.L.R. 594; [1994] 2 All E.R. 526; [1994] 1 F.L.R. 632; [1994] 3
    F.C.R. 81; (1994) 144 N.L.J. 123, ...CA (Civ Div) 21–039, 21–058, 22–035
Manchester City Council v Worthington [2000] 1 F.L.R. 411; [2000] Fam. Law 238, CA
    (Civ Div) 9–035
Mandla, Re [1993] Fam. 183 18–052
Manser v Manser [1940] P. 224, PDAD 12–003
March v March (Marriage Settlement: Allotment of Income); sub nom. March v March &
    Palumbo (1865–69) L.R. 1 P. & D. 440, Divorce Ct 13–026
Marckx v Belgium (A/31) (1979–80) 2 E.H.R.R. 330, ECHR 16–017, 16–024, 17–035
Marsh v Von Sternberg [1986] 1 F.L.R. 526; [1986] Fam. Law 160 ....3–041, 5–017, 5–028
Marshall v Beckett; sub nom. M v B (Ancillary Proceedings: Lump Sum) [1998] 1 F.L.R.
    53; [1998] 1 F.C.R. 213; [1998] Fam. Law 75, CA (Civ Div) 13–058, 13–072, 13–114
Marshall v Crutwell; sub nom. Marshal v Crutwell (1875) L.R. 20 Eq. 328, Ct of
    Chancery 5–063
Martin v Martin [1995] 2 F.L.R. 160 13–083
Martin (BH) v Martin (D) [1978] Fam. 12; [1977] 3 W.L.R. 101; [1977] 3 All E.R. 762;
    (1977) 7 Fam. Law 175; (1977) 121 S.J. 335, CA (Civ Div) 13–117
Martin v Myers [2004] EWHC 1947, Ch D 1–044
Martin-Dye v Martin-Dye [2006] EWCA Civ 681; [2006] 1 W.L.R. 3448; [2006] 4 All E.R.
    779; [2006] 2 F.L.R. 901; [2006] 2 F.C.R. 325; [2006] Fam. Law 731; (2006) 156
    N.L.J. 917, CA (Civ Div) 13–119
Martin-Sklan v White [2006] EWHC 3313, Ch D 5–059
Masarati v Masarati [1969] 1 W.L.R. 393; [1969] 2 All E.R. 658; (1969) 113 S.J. 205, CA
    (Civ Div) 10–005
Masefield v Alexander (Lump Sum: Extension of Time) [1995] 1 F.L.R. 100; [1995] 2
    F.C.R. 663; [1995] Fam. Law 130, CA (Civ Div) 13–113
Maskell v Maskell [2001] EWCA Civ 858; [2003] 1 F.L.R. 1138; [2001] 3 F.C.R. 296;
    [2003] Fam. Law 391, CA (Civ Div) 13–104, 13–108, 13–119
Massey v Midland Bank Plc [1995] 1 All E.R. 929; [1994] 2 F.L.R. 342; [1995] 1 F.C.R.
    380; (1995) 27 H.L.R. 227; [1994] Fam. Law 562; [1994] N.P.C. 44, CA (Civ Div) 5–054
Matharu v Matharu [1994] 2 F.L.R. 597; [1994] 3 F.C.R. 216; (1994) 26 H.L.R. 648; (1994)
    68 P. & C.R. 93; [1994] Fam. Law 624; [1994] E.G. 87 (C.S.); (1994) 91(25) L.S.G.
    31; (1994) 138 S.J.L.B. 111; [1994] N.P.C. 63, CA (Civ Div) 5–035
Mawji v R [1957] A.C. 126 3–037
Mawson v Mawson [1994] 2 F.L.R. 985; [1994] 2 F.C.R. 852; [1995] Fam. Law 9, Fam
    Div 13–086, 13–089
May v May [1986] 1 F.L.R. 325; [1986] Fam. Law 106 ....19–006, 19–018
Medway Council v BBC [2002] 1 F.L.R. 104; [2001] Fam. Law 883, Fam Div 18–051, 18–052
Mehta (otherwise Kohn) v Mehta [1945] 2 All E.R. 690; 174 L.T. 63, PDAD 2–042
Mercantile Credit Co Ltd v Fenwick; Mercantile Credit Co Ltd v Speechly Bircham [1999]
    2 F.L.R. 110; [1999] Lloyd's Rep. P.N. 408; [1999] Fam. Law 453; [1999] E.G. 22
    (C.S.); (1999) 96(10) L.S.G. 30; (1999) 143 S.J.L.B. 74, CA (Civ Div) 5–056
Mercier v Mercier [1903] 2 Ch. 98, CA 5–016
Merritt v Merritt [1970] 1 W.L.R. 1211; [1970] 2 All E.R. 760; (1970) 114 S.J. 455, CA
    (Civ Div) 3–027, 5–005
Mesher v Mesher [1980] 1 All E.R. 126 (Note), CA (Civ Div) 13–116, 13–117
Messina (formerly Smith otherwise Vervaeke) v Smith (Messina Intervening); Messina
    (formerly Smith otherwise Vervaeke) v Smith (Queen's Proctor Showing Cause);
    Messina (formerly Smith otherwise Vervaeke) v Smith (Member of Public Showing
    Cause) [1971] P. 322; [1971] 3 W.L.R. 118; [1971] 2 All E.R. 1046; (1971) 115 S.J.
    467, PDAD
Michael v Michael [1986] 2 F.L.R. 389; [1986] Fam. Law 334; (1986) 83 L.S.G. 2488;
    (1986) 130 S.J. 713, CA (Civ Div) 13–069
Middleton v Middleton [1998] 2 F.L.R. 821; [1999] 2 F.C.R. 681; [1998] Fam. Law 589, CA
    (Civ Div) 13–104, 13–105, 13–106, 13–107
Midland Bank Plc v Cooke [1995] 4 All E.R. 562; [1997] 6 Bank. L.R. 147; [1995] 2 F.L.R.
    915; [1996] 1 F.C.R. 442; (1995) 27 H.L.R. 733; [1995] Fam. Law 675; (1995) 145
    N.L.J. 1543; (1995) 139 S.J.L.B. 194; [1995] N.P.C. 116, CA (Civ Div) 3–008, 5–001, 5–021,
                                                     5–022, 5–024, 5–026, 5–028, 5–029, 5–030

Midland Bank Plc v Dobson [1986] 1 F.L.R. 171; [1986] Fam. Law 55; (1985) 135 N.L.J.
    751, CA (Civ Div) 5–021, 5–025
Midland Bank Trust Co Ltd v Green (No.3) [1982] Ch. 529; [1982] 2 W.L.R. 1; [1981] 3
    All E.R. 744; (1981) 125 S.J. 554, CA (Civ Div) 3–002
Miller v Miller; McFarlane v McFarlane; sub nom. M v M (Short Marriage: Clean Break)
    [2006] UKHL 24; [2006] 2 A.C. 618; [2006] 2 W.L.R. 1283; [2006] 3 All E.R. 1;
    [2006] 1 F.L.R. 1186; [2006] 2 F.C.R. 213; [2006] Fam. Law 629; (2006) 103(23)
    L.S.G. 28; (2006) 156 N.L.J. 916; (2006) 150 S.J.L.B. 704, HL 13–001, 13–002, 13–013,
                            13–040, 13–041, 13–047, 13–048, 13–049, 13–051, 13–052, 13–053, 13–054,
                            13–055, 13–056, 13–074, 13–075, 13–076, 13–079, 13–080, 13–081, 13–083,
                                                                                            13–086, 13–090
Mills (Hayley) v Inland Revenue Commissioners. *See* Inland Revenue Commissioners v
    Mills (Hayley)
Millward v Shenton; sub nom. Millward v Shenton and British Empire Cancer Campaign
    for Research [1972] 1 W.L.R. 711; [1972] 2 All E.R. 1025; (1972) 116 S.J. 355, CA
    (Civ Div) 7–022
Minton v Minton [1979] A.C. 593; [1979] 2 W.L.R. 31; [1979] 1 All E.R. 79; (1978) 122
    S.J. 843, HL 13–086
Minwalla v Minwalla [2004] EWHC 2823 (Fam); [2005] 1 F.L.R. 771; [2006] W.T.L.R.
    311; (2004–05) 7 I.T.E.L.R. 457; [2005] Fam. Law 357, Fam Div 13–066
Mir v Mir; sub nom. M v M (Sequestration: Sale of Property) [1992] Fam. 79; [1992] 2
    W.L.R. 225; [1992] 1 All E.R. 765; [1992] 1 F.L.R. 624; [1992] 1 F.C.R. 227; [1992]
    Fam. Law 378; (1992) 89(4) L.S.G. 33; (1992) 136 S.J.L.B. 10, Fam Div 14–010, 18–056,
                                                                                            20–005
Mitchell v Allardyce; sub nom. Mitchell v St Mungo Lodge of Ancient Shepherds, 1916
    S.C. 689; 1916 1 S.L.T. 365, IH (2 Div) 2–042
Mnguni v Mnguni (1979) 123 S.J. 859, CA (Civ Div) 18–012
Mohamed Arif (An Infant), Re; Nirbhai Singh (An Infant), Re; S(N) (An Infant), Re; Singh
    v Secretary of State for Home Affairs; sub nom. A (An Infant), Re; Hanif v Secretary
    of State for Home Affairs [1968] Ch. 643; [1968] 2 W.L.R. 1290; [1968] 2 All E.R.
    145, CA (Civ Div) 18–052, 19–002
Mollo v Mollo; sub nom. Mollo v Diez [2000] W.T.L.R. 227; [1999] E.G. 117 (C.S.), Ch
    D 5–020
Moody v Stevenson; sub nom. Moody (Deceased), Re [1992] Ch. 486; [1992] 2 W.L.R. 640;
    [1992] 2 All E.R. 524; [1992] 1 F.L.R. 494; [1992] F.C.R. 107; [1992] Fam. Law 284;
    (1991) 135 S.J.L.B. 84, CA (Civ Div) 7–009, 7–019, 7–026
Moore v Moore [2004] EWCA Civ 1243; [2005] 1 F.L.R. 666; [2004] 3 F.C.R. 461; [2005]
    H.L.R. 5, CA (Civ Div) 3–011, 9–010, 9–035
Mordant (A Bankrupt), Re (1993); sub nom. Mordant v Halls [1996] 1 F.L.R. 334; [1997]
    2 F.C.R. 378; [1996] B.P.I.R. 302; [1996] Fam. Law 211, Ch D 14–005
Morgan v Hill; sub nom. Hill v Morgan [2006] EWCA Civ 1602; [2007] 1 W.L.R. 855;
    [2007] 1 F.L.R. 1480; [2006] 3 F.C.R. 620; [2007] Fam. Law 112; (2006) 150 S.J.L.B.
    1605, CA (Civ Div) 15–039, 15–048, 15–049, 15–051
Morgan v Morgan (1973) 117 S.J. 223 10–027
Morgan v Morgan; sub nom. M v M (Financial Misconduct: Subpoena against Third Party);
    M v M (Third Party Subpoena: Financial Conduct) [2006] EWCA Civ 1852, CA (Civ
    Div) 13–083
Morgan v Morgan (otherwise Ransom) [1959] P. 92; [1959] 2 W.L.R. 487; [1959] 1 All E.R.
    539; (1959) 103 S.J. 313, PDAD 2–028, 2–032
Morris v Morris (1986) 150 J.P. 7; [1985] F.L.R. 1176; [1986] Fam. Law 24, CA (Civ
    Div) 13–086
Mortgage Corp v Shaire; Mortgage Corp v Lewis Silkin (A Firm) [2001] Ch. 743; [2001]
    3 W.L.R. 639; [2001] 4 All E.R. 364; [2000] 1 F.L.R. 973; [2000] 2 F.C.R. 222; [2000]
    B.P.I.R. 483; (2000) 80 P. & C.R. 280; [2000] 3 E.G.L.R. 131; [2000] W.T.L.R. 357;
    [2000] Fam. Law 402; [2000] E.G. 35 (C.S.); (2000) 97(11) L.S.G. 37, Ch D 5–017, 5–021,
                                                                            5–022, 5–027, 5–031, 5–046
Mortimer v de Mortimer-Griffin [1986] 2 F.L.R. 315; [1986] Fam. Law 305, CA (Civ Div) 13–112,
                                                                                            13–116
Moses-Taiga v Taiga; sub nom. Taiga v Taiga [2005] EWCA Civ 1013; [2006] 1 F.L.R.
    1074; [2006] Fam. Law 266, CA (Civ Div) 13–037
Moss v Moss (otherwise Archer) [1897] P. 263, PDAD 2–042, 2–045

Mossop v Mossop [1989] Fam. 77; [1988] 2 W.L.R. 1255; [1988] 2 All E.R. 202; [1988] 2 F.L.R. 173; [1988] Fam. Law 334; (1988) 138 N.L.J. Rep. 86, CA (Civ Div) 3–041
Mouncer v Mouncer [1972] 1 W.L.R. 321; [1972] 1 All E.R. 289; (1971) 116 S.J. 78, Fam Div 10–037
Moynihan, Re [2000] 1 F.L.R. 113 17–031
Moynihan v Moynihan (Nos.1 and 2; Moynihan, Re [1997] 1 F.L.R. 59; [1997] Fam. Law 88, Fam Div 10–011, 16–024, 17–007
Mubarak v Mubarak (No.1); Mubarak v Wani; Mubarak v Dianoor International Ltd; Mubarak v Dianoor Jewels Ltd; sub nom. Mubarak v Mubarik; Murbarak v Murbarak [2001] 1 F.L.R. 698; [2001] 1 F.C.R. 193; [2001] Fam. Law 178, CA (Civ Div) 14–001, 14–003, 14–011, 14–020
Mullard v Mullard [1982] F.L.R. 330, CA 13–028
Mullin v Richards [1998] 1 W.L.R. 1304; [1998] 1 All E.R. 920; [1998] P.I.Q.R. P276, CA (Civ Div) 16–002
Murphy v Gooch [2007] EWCA Civ 603 .... 5–047, 5–048
N, Re [2007] EWCA Civ 1053 .... 22–072, 22–073
N (A Child) (Adoption: Foreign Guardianship), Re; sub nom. AGN (Adoption: Foreign Adoption), Re [2000] 2 F.L.R. 431; [2000] 2 F.C.R. 512; [2000] Fam. Law 694, Fam Div 22–026
N (A Child) (Contact: Leave to Defend and Remove Guardian), Re [2003] 1 F.L.R. 652; [2003] Fam. Law 154, Fam Div 18–038
N (A Child) (Leave to Withdraw Care Proceedings), Re [2000] 1 F.L.R. 134; [2000] 1 F.C.R. 258; [2000] Fam. Law 12, Fam Div 21–055
N (A Child) (Residence Order: Procedural Mismanagement), Re; sub nom. N (A Child) (Residence: Appointment of Solicitor: Placement with Extended Family), Re [2001] 1 F.L.R. 1028; [2001] Fam. Law 423, CA (Civ Div) 18–008, 18–039, 19–025
N (A Minor) (Adoption), Re [1990] 1 F.L.R. 58; [1990] F.C.R. 241; (1990) 154 J.P.N. 313 .....19–002, 19–020
N (Child Abduction: Habitual Residence), Re; sub nom. N v N (Child Abduction: Habitual Residence) [2000] 2 F.L.R. 899; [2000] 3 F.C.R. 84; [2000] Fam. Law 786, Fam Div ... 20–015
N (Child Abduction: Jurisdiction), Re; sub nom. A v A (Abduction: Jurisdiction) [1995] Fam. 96; [1995] 2 W.L.R. 233; [1995] 2 All E.R. 417; [1995] 1 F.L.R. 341, [1995] 2 F.C.R. 605; [1995] Fam. Law 230, Fam Div 20–014
N (Minors) (Child Abduction), Re [1991] 1 F.L.R. 413; [1991] F.C.R. 765; [1991] Fam. Law 367, Fam Div 20–018
N (Minors) (Contested Care Application), Re; sub nom. N (Minors) (Care Order: Termination of Parental Contact), Re [1994] 2 F.L.R. 992; [1994] 2 F.C.R. 1101; [1995] Fam. Law 63; (1994) 158 J.P.N. 731, Fam Div 18–043
N (Minors) (Residence Orders: Sexual Abuse), Re; sub nom. N (Minors) (Residence: Hopeless Appeals), Re [1995] 2 F.L.R. 230; [1996] 1 F.C.R. 244; [1995] Fam. Law 600, CA (Civ Div) 19–021, 19–025
N (Sexual Abuse Allegations: Professionals Not Abiding by Findings of Fact), Re [2005] 2 F.L.R. 340; [2005] Fam. Law 529, Fam Div 18–048, 21–032
N v N (Abduction: Article 13 Defence) [1995] 1 F.L.R. 107; [1995] 1 F.C.R. 595; [1995] Fam. Law 116, Fam Div 20–020
N v N (Consent Order: Variation) [1993] 2 F.L.R. 868; [1994] 2 F.C.R. 275; [1993] Fam. Law 676, CA (Civ Div) 13–008, 13–086, 13–089, 13–091
N v N (Financial Provision: Sale of Company) [2001] 2 F.L.R. 69, Fam Div 13–024, 13–045
NA v MA. *See* A v A
NS v MI [2006] EWHC 1646 (Fam); [2007] 1 F.L.R. 444; [2007] 2 F.C.R. 748; [2006] Fam. Law 839, Fam Div 2–038, 2–040
Napier v Napier (otherwise Goodban) [1915] P. 184, CA 2–027, 2–030
Nash v Nash; sub nom. N v N [1965] P. 266; [1965] 2 W.L.R. 317; [1965] 1 All E.R. 480; (1965) 109 S.J. 73, PDAD 10–005
National Provincial Bank Ltd v Ainsworth; sub nom. National Provincial Bank Ltd v Hastings Car Mart Ltd [1965] A.C. 1175; [1965] 3 W.L.R. 1; [1965] 2 All E.R. 472; (1965) 109 S.J. 415, HL 3–010, 4–002
National Westminster Bank Ltd v Stockman; sub nom. National Westminster Bank Ltd v Stockton [1981] 1 W.L.R. 67; [1981] 1 All E.R. 800; (1980) 124 S.J. 810, QBD 14–008
National Westminster Bank Plc v Morgan [1985] A.C. 686; [1985] 2 W.L.R. 588; [1985] 1 All E.R. 821; [1985] F.L.R. 266; (1985) 17 H.L.R. 360; (1985) 82 L.S.G. 1485; (1985) 135 N.L.J. 254; (1985) 129 S.J. 205, HL 5–055

Negus v Bahouse [2007] EWHC 2628 (Ch.) 5–033
Neil v Ryan [1998] 2 F.L.R. 1068; [1999] 1 F.C.R. 241; [1998] Fam. Law 728, CA (Civ
Div) 9–035
Nessa v Chief Adjudication Officer [1999] 1 W.L.R. 1937; [1999] 4 All E.R. 677; [1999]
2 F.L.R. 1116; [1999] 3 F.C.R. 538; [2000] Fam. Law 28; (1999) 96(42) L.S.G. 42;
(1999) 149 N.L.J. 1619; (1999) 143 S.J.L.B. 250, HL 20–015
Neville v Wilson [1997] Ch. 144; [1996] 3 W.L.R. 460; [1996] 3 All E.R. 171; [1996] 2
B.C.L.C. 310, CA (Civ Div) 5–010
Newlon Housing Trust v Al-Sulaimen; sub nom. Newlon Housing Trust v Alsulaimen
[1999] 1 A.C. 313; [1998] 3 W.L.R. 451; [1998] 4 All E.R. 1; [1998] 2 F.L.R. 690;
[1998] 3 F.C.R. 183; (1998) 30 H.L.R. 1132; [1999] L. & T.R. 38; [1998] Fam. Law
589; (1998) 95(35) L.S.G. 35; (1998) 148 N.L.J. 1303; (1998) 142 S.J.L.B. 247, HL 13–117
Newton v Newton [1990] 1 F.L.R. 33; [1989] F.C.R. 521; [1990] Fam. Law 25; (1989) 153
J.P.N. 642, CA (Civ Div) 13–066
Nicholls v Lan [2006] EWHC 1255; [2006] B.P.I.R. 1243; [2006] Fam. Law 1020, Ch D 5–059
Nicholson (Deceased), Re; sub nom. Nicholson v Perks [1974] 1 W.L.R. 476; [1974] 2 All
E.R. 386; (1973) 118 S.J. 133, Ch D 3–008, 3–009
Nielsen v Denmark (A/144); sub nom. Nielsen v Denmark (10929/84) (1989) 11 E.H.R.R.
175, ECHR 16–018, 17–017
Niersmans v Pesticcio. *See* Pesticcio v Huet
Norman v Norman [1983] 1 W.L.R. 295; [1983] 1 All E.R. 486; (1983) 4 F.L.R. 446; (1983)
13 Fam. Law 17; (1983) 80 L.S.G. 30; (1983) 133 N.L.J. 132; (1982) 126 S.J. 707,
Fam Div 13–028
Norris v Norris; Haskins v Haskins [2003] EWCA Civ 1084; [2003] 1 W.L.R. 2960; [2003]
4 Costs L.R. 591; [2003] 2 F.L.R. 1124; [2003] 3 F.C.R. 136; [2003] Fam. Law 721;
(2003) 100(36) L.S.G. 37, CA (Civ Div) 13–012
North v North [2007] EWCA Civ 760; [2007] 2 F.C.R. 601; (2007) 151 S.J.L.B. 1022, CA
(Civ Div) 13–096, 13–098
Northamptonshire CC v Islington LBC; sub nom. Northampton CC v Islington LBC [2001]
Fam. 364; [2000] 2 W.L.R. 193; [1999] 2 F.L.R. 881; [1999] 3 F.C.R. 385; [2000]
B.L.G.R. 125; [1999] Fam. Law 687; (2000) 164 J.P.N. 166, CA (Civ Div) 21–015
Northamptonshire CC v S [1993] Fam. 136; [1992] 3 W.L.R. 1010; [1993] 1 F.L.R. 574;
[1993] 1 F.C.R. 351; [1993] Fam. Law 274, Fam Div 21–033
Northrop v Northrop [1968] P. 74; [1967] 3 W.L.R. 907; [1967] 2 All E.R. 961; (1967) 111
S.J. 476, CA (Civ Div) 3–017
Nottingham CC v H [1995] 1 F.L.R. 115 21–058
Nottingham City Council v October Films Ltd [1999] 2 F.L.R. 347; [1999] 2 F.C.R. 529;
[1999] Fam. Law 536; (1999) 163 J.P.N. 929; (1999) 96(23) L.S.G. 33, Fam Div 17–015
Nottinghamshire CC v P; sub nom. P v Nottinghamshire CC [1994] Fam. 18; [1993] 3
W.L.R. 637; [1993] 3 All E.R. 815; [1993] 2 F.L.R. 134; [1994] 1 F.C.R. 624; 92
L.G.R. 72; [1994] Fam. Law 9; (1994) 158 L.G. Rev. 421; (1993) 137 S.J.L.B. 147, CA
(Civ Div) 18–021, 18–029, 18–048, 18–049
Nugent-Head v Jacob [1948] A.C. 321; [1948] 1 All E.R. 414; 64 T.L.R. 127; 30 T.C. 83;
[1948] T.R. 23; [1948] L.J.R. 759; (1948) 92 S.J. 193, HL 3–004
Nutley v Nutley [1970] 1 W.L.R. 217; [1970] 1 All E.R. 410; (1970) 114 S.J. 72, CA (Civ
Div) 10–030
Nwogbe v Nwogbe [2000] 2 F.L.R. 744; [2000] 3 F.C.R. 345; [2000] Fam. Law 797, CA
(Civ Div) 3–013, 9–023
O (A Child) (Contact: Withdrawal of Application), Re; sub nom. O (A Child) (Termination
of Contact), Re [2003] EWHC 3031; [2004] 1 F.L.R. 1258; [2004] 1 F.C.R. 687;
[2004] Fam. Law 492, Fam Div 18–020
O (A Child) (Supervision Order: Future Harm), Re [2001] EWCA Civ 16; [2001] 1 F.L.R.
923; [2001] 1 F.C.R. 289; (2001) 165 J.P.N. 606, CA (Civ Div) 18–005, 19–004, 21–040,
21–042, 22–033
O (A Minor) (Care Proceedings: Education), Re; sub nom. O v Berkshire CC; O (A Minor)
(Care Order: Education: Procedure), Re [1992] 1 W.L.R. 912; [1992] 4 All E.R. 905;
[1992] 2 F.L.R. 7; [1992] 1 F.C.R. 489; [1992] Fam. Law 487; (1992) 156 J.P.N. 364;
(1992) 156 L.G. Rev. 845; (1992) 89(21) L.S.G. 26, Fam Div 17–016, 21–032
O (A Minor) (Child Abduction: Custody Rights), Re [1997] 2 F.L.R. 702; [1997] 2 F.C.R.
465; [1997] Fam. Law 781; (1997) 94(25) L.S.G. 34, Fam Div 20–017
O (A Minor) (Contact: Imposition of Conditions), Re [1995] 2 F.L.R. 124; [1995] Fam. Law
541; (1995) 159 J.P.N. 540, CA (Civ Div) 17–024, 17–048, 18–018, 18–019, 18–052, 19–003

O (A Minor) (Medical Treatment), Re [1993] 2 F.L.R. 149; [1993] 1 F.C.R. 925; [1993] 4
Med. L.R. 272; [1993] Fam. Law 454; (1993) 157 L.G. Rev. 165; (1993) 137 S.J.L.B.
107, Fam Div 17–022, 18–022, 18–054

O (A Minor) (Wardship: Adopted Child), Re; sub nom. O'B (A Minor), Re [1978] Fam.
196; [1977] 3 W.L.R. 725; [1978] 2 All E.R. 27, CA (Civ Div) 21–009

O (Care: Discharge of Care Order), Re [1999] 2 F.L.R. 119; [1999] Fam. Law 442, Fam
Div 21–040

O (Child Abduction: Re-Abduction), Re; sub nom. O (Minors) (Abduction), Re; O (Child
Abduction: Competing Orders), Re [1997] 2 F.L.R. 712; [1998] 1 F.C.R. 107; [1997]
Fam. Law 719, Fam Div

O (Child Abduction: Undertakings), Re [1994] 2 F.L.R. 349; [1995] 1 F.C.R. 721; [1994]
Fam. Law 482, Fam Div 20–020

O (Children) (Care Proceedings: Evidence), Re [2003] EWHC 2011 (Fam); [2004] 1 F.L.R.
161; [2004] Fam. Law 16; (2003) 100(39) L.S.G. 37, Fam Div 16–022

O (Minors) (Adoption: Injunction), Re; sub nom. O (Adoption Order: Effect on Injunction),
Re [1993] 2 F.L.R. 737; [1993] 2 F.C.R. 746; [1994] Fam. Law 14 .... 18–049, 22–067

O (Minors) (Contempt: Committal), Re [1995] 2 F.L.R. 767; [1996] 2 F.C.R. 89; [1996]
Fam. Law 26, CA (Civ Div) 22–067

O (Minors) (Leave to Seek Residence Order), Re [1994] 1 F.L.R. 172; [1993] 2 F.C.R. 482;
[1994] Fam. Law 127, Fam Div 18–040

O (Transracial Adoption: Contact), Re; sub nom. O (A Minor) (Adoption), Re [1995] 2
F.L.R. 597; [1996] 1 F.C.R. 540; [1996] Fam. Law 138, Fam Div 18–018, 19–007, 22–064

O v Governor of Holloway Prison; sub nom. O v Governor of Brixton Prison [2000] 1 Cr.
App. R. 195; [2000] 1 F.L.R. 147; [2000] Fam. Law 10, QBD 20–002

O v L (Blood Tests); sub nom. L (A Minor) (Blood Tests), Re; W v Official Solicitor [1995]
2 F.L.R. 930; [1996] 2 F.C.R. 649; [1996] Fam. Law 82, CA (Civ Div) 17–008, 17–024,
18–019

O and J (Children) (Blood Tests: Constraint), Re; sub nom. O and J (Children) (Paternity:
Blood Tests), Re; J (A Child) (Blood Tests), Re [2000] Fam. 139; [2000] 2 W.L.R.
1284; [2000] 2 All E.R. 29; [2000] 1 F.L.R. 418; [2000] 1 F.C.R. 330; (2000) 55
B.M.L.R. 229; [2000] Fam. Law 324; (2000) 164 J.P.N. 839; (2000) 97(6) L.S.G. 35;
(2000) 144 S.J.L.B. 85, Fam Div 17–012

O'Rourke v Camden LBC [1998] A.C. 189 21–081

Oakley v Walker (1977) 121 S.J. 619 3–003

O'Connor v A and B; sub nom. A&B, Petitioners; A v B & C [1971] 1 W.L.R. 1227; [1971]
2 All E.R. 1230; 1971 S.C. (H.L.) 129; 1971 S.L.T. 258; (1971) 115 S.J. 586, HL 22–001

O'D v O'D; sub nom. O'Donnell v O'Donnell [1976] Fam. 83; [1975] 3 W.L.R. 308; [1975]
2 All E.R. 993; (1975) 119 S.J. 560, CA (Civ Div) 13–043, 13–072, 13–078

Odievre v France (42326/98) [2003] 1 F.C.R. 621; (2004) 38 E.H.R.R. 43; 14 B.H.R.C. 526,
ECHR 22–034

Official Solicitor v K; sub nom. K (Infants), Re [1965] A.C. 201; [1963] 3 W.L.R. 408;
[1963] 3 All E.R. 191; (1963) 107 S.J. 616, HL 18–041

Oldham MBC v E [1994] 1 F.L.R. 568; 92 L.G.R. 615; [1994] Fam. Law 494, CA (Civ
Div) 19–014, 21–031, 21–040

Olsson v Sweden (A/130); sub nom. Olsson v Sweden (10465/83) (1989) 11 E.H.R.R. 259,
ECHR 21–001, 21–074, 21–079

Olsson v Sweden (No.2) (A/250) (1994) 17 E.H.R.R. 134, ECHR 21–070, 21–074

Omielan v Omielan [1996] 2 F.L.R. 306; [1996] 3 F.C.R. 329; [1996] Fam. Law 608, CA
(Civ Div) 13–028, 13–100

O'Neill v O'Neill [1975] 1 W.L.R. 1118; [1975] 3 All E.R. 289; (1975) 5 Fam. Law 159;
(1975) 119 S.J. 405, CA (Civ Div) 10–024

Orford v Orford (1979) 10 Fam. Law 114, CA (Civ Div) 18–022

Osman v Elasha; sub nom. E (Abduction: Non Convention Country), Re [2000] Fam. 62;
[2000] 2 W.L.R. 1036; [1999] 2 F.L.R. 642; [1999] 3 F.C.R. 497; [1999] Fam. Law
610; (1999) 96(30) L.S.G. 29, CA (Civ Div) 20–013, 20–023

Osman v United Kingdom (23452/94) [1999] 1 F.L.R. 193; (2000) 29 E.H.R.R. 245; 5
B.H.R.C. 293; (1999) 1 L.G.L.R. 431; (1999) 11 Admin. L.R. 200; [1999] Crim. L.R.
82; [1998] H.R.C.D. 966; [1999] Fam. Law 86; (1999) 163 J.P.N. 297, ECHR 21–027

Ottey v Grundy (Andreae's Executor); sub nom. Grundy v Ottey [2003] EWCA Civ 1176;
[2003] W.T.L.R. 1253, CA (Civ Div) 5–034

Owo-Samson v Barclays Bank Plc (No.1); sub nom. Owo-Sampson v Barclays Bank Plc
[2003] EWCA Civ 714; [2003] B.P.I.R. 1373; (2003) 100(28) L.S.G. 30; (2003) 147
S.J.L.B. 658, CA (Civ Div) 5–061
Oxford University v Broughton [2008] EWHC 75, QBD 9–005
Oxfordshire CC v L and F [1997] 1 F.L.R. 235; [1997] 3 F.C.R. 124; [1997] Fam. Law 249,
Fam Div 17–015
Oxfordshire CC v M [1994] 1 F.L.R. 175 .... 18–008, 18–043, 18–053
Oxfordshire CC v P (A Minor) [1995] Fam. 161; [1995] 2 W.L.R. 543; [1995] 2 All E.R.
225; [1995] 1 F.L.R. 552; [1995] 2 F.C.R. 212; 93 L.G.R. 336; (1995) 159 J.P.N. 302,
Fam Div 21–037
Oxley v Hiscock; sub nom. Hiscock v Oxley [2004] EWCA Civ 546; [2005] Fam. 211;
[2004] 3 W.L.R. 715; [2004] 3 All E.R. 703; [2004] 2 F.L.R. 669; [2004] 2 F.C.R. 295;
[2004] W.T.L.R. 709; (2003–04) 6 I.T.E.L.R. 1091; [2004] Fam. Law 569; [2004] 20
E.G. 166 (C.S.); (2004) 101(21) L.S.G. 35; (2004) 148 S.J.L.B. 571; [2004] N.P.C. 70;
[2004] 2 P. & C.R. DG14, CA (Civ Div) 4–001, 5–026, 5–031
P, Re [2007] EWCA Civ 1053 19–022
P (A Child) (Abduction: Custody Rights), Re; sub nom. P (A Child) (Abduction: Consent),
Re; P (A Child) (Abduction: Acquiescence), Re [2004] EWCA Civ 971; [2005] Fam.
293; [2005] 2 W.L.R. 201; [2004] 2 F.L.R. 1057; [2004] 2 F.C.R. 698; [2004] Fam.
Law 711; (2004) 101(35) L.S.G. 33, CA (Civ Div) 20–017
P (A Child) (Care Orders: Injunctive Relief), Re [2000] 2 F.L.R. 385; [2000] 3 F.C.R. 426;
[2000] Fam. Law 696, Fam Div 9–042, 17–016, 21–032, 21–041
P (A Child) (Children Act 1989, ss.22 and 26: Local Authority Compliance), Re [2000] 2
F.L.R. 910; [2000] Fam. Law 792, Fam Div 17–048, 21–072
P (A Child) (Financial Provision), Re; sub nom. P v T [2003] EWCA Civ 837; [2003] 2
F.L.R. 865; [2003] 2 F.C.R. 481; [2003] Fam. Law 717; (2003) 100(33) L.S.G. 27, CA
(Civ Div) 15–046, 15–050, 15–051, 15–052
P (A Child) (Mirror Orders), Re; sub nom. P (Jurisdiction: Mirror Orders), Re [2000] 1
F.L.R. 435; [2000] 1 F.C.R. 350; [2000] Fam. Law 240, Fam Div 18–030, 20–006
P (A Child) (Parental Dispute: Judicial Determination), Re [2002] EWCA Civ 1627; [2003]
1 F.L.R. 286; [2003] Fam. Law 80, CA (Civ Div) 18–022
P (A Minor), Re [1990] 1 F.L.R. 96; [1990] F.C.R. 260; [1990] Fam. Law 66; (1990) 154
J.P.N. 311; (1989) 139 N.L.J. 1265, CA (Civ Div) 19–020
P (A Minor) (Abduction: Minor's Views), Re [1998] 2 F.L.R. 825; [1999] 1 F.C.R. 739;
[1998] Fam. Law 580, CA (Civ Div) 19–017, 20–021
P (A Minor) (Child Abduction: Declaration), Re [1995] 1 F.L.R. 831; [1995] Fam. Law 398,
CA (Civ Div) 18–019, 20–016
P (A Minor) (Contact), Re [1994] 2 F.L.R. 374; [1994] 1 F.C.R. 285; [1994] Fam. Law 484,
Ch D 17–027, 19–007
P (A Minor) (Education: Child's Views), Re [1992] 1 F.L.R. 316; [1992] F.C.R. 145; [1992]
Fam. Law 108, CA (Civ Div) 17–016, 19–016
P (A Minor) (Ex parte Interim Residence Order), Re [1993] 1 F.L.R. 915; [1993] 2 F.C.R.
417; [1993] Fam. Law 462, CA (Civ Div) 18–024, 18–040
P (A Minor) (Parental Responsibility), Re [1998] 2 F.L.R. 96; [1998] 3 F.C.R. 98; [1998]
Fam. Law 461, CA (Civ Div) 17–037
P (A Minor) (Parental Responsibility Order), Re [1994] 1 F.L.R. 578; [1994] Fam. Law 378,
Fam Div 17–001, 17–037
P (A Minor) (Residence Order: Child's Welfare), Re; sub nom. P (Section 91(14)
Guidelines: Residence and Religious Heritage), Re [2000] Fam. 15; [1999] 3 W.L.R.
1164; [1999] 3 All E.R. 734; [1999] 2 F.L.R. 573; [1999] 2 F.C.R. 289; [1999] Fam.
Law 531; (1999) 163 J.P.N. 712; (1999) 96(21) L.S.G. 38; (1999) 149 N.L.J. 719;
(1999) 143 S.J.L.B. 141, CA (Civ Div) 17–018, 18–028, 18–036, 19–003, 19–019, 21–075
P (Adoption), Re [2004] EWHC 1954; [2005] 1 F.L.R. 303, Fam Div 21–014
P (Care Proceedings: Father's Application to be Joined as Party), Re [2001] 1 F.L.R. 781;
[2001] 3 F.C.R. 279, Fam Div 17–052
P (Children) (Shared Residence Order), Re. *See* Pengelly v Enright-Redding
P (Committal for Breach of Contact Order: Reasons), Re [2007] 1 F.L.R. 1820, CA 18–058
P (Contact: Supervision), Re; sub nom. P (Minors) (Contact: Parental Hostility), Re [1996]
2 F.L.R. 314; [1997] 1 F.C.R. 458; [1996] Fam. Law 532; (1996) 160 J.P.N. 544, CA
(Civ Div) 19–014, 19–025
P (Emergency Protection Order), Re [1996] 1 F.L.R. 482; [1996] 3 F.C.R. 637; [1996] Fam.
Law 273; (1997) 161 J.P.N. 40, Fam Div 21–046, 21–049

P (Medical Treatment: Best Interests), Re; sub nom. P (A Child), Re [2003] EWHC 2327;
[2004] 2 F.L.R. 1117; [2004] Fam. Law 716, Fam Div 16–016
P (Minors) (Adoption by Step-parent), Re [1989] 1 F.L.R. 1; [1988] F.C.R. 401; [1989]
Fam. Law 70, CA (Civ Div) 22–059
P (Minors) (Children Act: Diplomatic Immunity), Re [1998] 1 F.L.R. 624; [1998] 2 F.C.R.
480; [1998] Fam. Law 12, Fam Div 18–051
P (Minors) (Contact with Children in Care), Re [1993] Fam. Law 394 .... 18–019, 21–074
P (Minors) (Parental Responsibility Order), Re; sub nom. P (Minors) (Parental Responsibil-
ity: Change of Name), Re [1997] 2 F.L.R. 722; [1997] 3 F.C.R. 739; [1997] Fam. Law
723; (1997) 161 J.P.N. 976, CA (Civ Div) 17–037
P (Minors) (Sexual Abuse: Standard of Proof), Re [1996] 2 F.L.R. 333; [1996] 3 F.C.R. 714;
[1996] Fam. Law 531; (1996) 160 J.P.N. 1102, CA (Civ Div) 19–021
P (Minors) (Wardship: Surrogacy), Re [1987] 2 F.L.R. 421; [1988] F.C.R. 140; [1987] Fam.
Law 414; (1987) 151 J.P.N. 334 .... 19–020, 22–073
P (Section 91(14) Guidelines: Residence and Religious Heritage), Re. *See* P (A Minor)
(Residence Order: Child's Welfare), Re
P (Terminating Parental Responsibility), Re [1995] 1 F.L.R. 1048; [1995] 3 F.C.R. 753;
[1995] Fam. Law 471; (1995) 159 J.P.N. 675, Fam Div 17–049
P v B (Paternity: Damages for Deceit) [2001] 1 F.L.R. 1041; [2001] Fam. Law 422, QBD 15–009,
18–034
P v P (Consent Order: Appeal Out of Time) [2002] 1 F.L.R. 743, Fam Div 13–107, 13–108
P v P (Contempt of Court: Mental Capacity) [1999] 2 F.L.R. 897; [1999] 3 F.C.R. 547;
[1999] Fam. Law 690, CA (Civ Div) 9–033, 9–036
P v P (Divorce: Financial Provision: Clean Break) [2002] EWCA Civ 1886; [2003] 1 F.L.R.
942; [2003] 1 F.C.R. 97; [2003] Fam. Law 314, CA (Civ Div) 13–045
P v P (Financial Relief: Non-Disclosure) [1994] 2 F.L.R. 381; [1994] 1 F.C.R. 293; [1994]
Fam. Law 498, Fam Div 13–084
P v R (Forced Marriage: Annulment: Procedure) [2003] 1 F.L.R. 661; [2003] Fam. Law 162,
Fam Div 2–038, 2–040
P v Serial No 52/2006 [2007] EWCA Civ 616 ....22–024, 22–029, 22–033, 22–039
P v United Kingdom (56547/00) [2002] 2 F.L.R. 631; [2002] 3 F.C.R. 1; (2002) 35 E.H.R.R.
31; 12 B.H.R.C. 615; [2002] Fam. Law 811, ECHR 16–017, 18–006, 21–001, 21–049,
21–050, 21–056, 21–072, 22–034, 22–040, 22–043
P v W; sub nom. Patterson v Walcot [1984] Fam. 32; [1984] 2 W.L.R. 439; [1984] 1 All E.R.
866; (1984) 148 J.P. 161; [1984] Fam. Law 208; (1984) 81 L.S.G. 735; (1984) 128 S.J.
171, Fam Div 18–056
P-B (Placement Order), Re [2007] 1 F.L.R. 1106, CA 22–017, 22–033, 22–043
PC (Change of Surname), Re; sub nom. C (Minors) (Change of Surname), Re; P (Change
of Surname: Parent's Rights), Re [1997] 2 F.L.R. 730; [1997] 3 F.C.R. 310; [1997]
Fam. Law 722, Fam Div 17–025, 17–048, 18–005
PJ (Adoption: Practice on Appeal), Re; sub nom. P-J (Minors) (Adoption Order: Practice on
Appeal), Re [1998] 2 F.L.R. 252; [1998] Fam. Law 453, CA (Civ Div) 22–059
Pace (Formerly Doe) v Doe [1977] Fam. 18; [1976] 3 W.L.R. 865; [1977] 1 All E.R. 176;
(1976) 120 S.J. 818, Fam Div 3–032
Paddington Building Society v Mendelsohn (1985) 50 P. & C.R. 244; [1987] Fam. Law 121,
CA (Civ Div) 5–050
Page v Page (1981) 2 F.L.R. 198, CA (Civ Div) 13–043, 13–072, 13–078
Palau-Martinez v France (64927/01) [2004] 2 F.L.R. 810; (2005) 41 E.H.R.R. 9; [2004]
Fam. Law 413, ECHR 19–020
Palmer (Gavin) (Deceased) (A Debtor), Re; sub nom. Gavin Hilary Palmer Estate Trustee
v Palmer [1994] Ch. 316; [1994] 3 W.L.R. 420; [1994] 3 All E.R. 835; [1994] 2 F.L.R.
609; [1995] 1 F.C.R. 320; [1994] Fam. Law 566; [1994] E.G. 52 (C.S.); (1994) 138
S.J.L.B. 72; [1994] N.P.C. 41; (1994) 68 P. & C.R. D13, CA (Civ Div) 5–040, 5–043
Panchal v Panchal, unreported, 2000 9–010
Papouis v Gibson-West; sub nom. Bennett (Florence Lilian), In the Estate of [2004] EWHC
396; [2004] W.T.L.R. 485, Ch D 5–055, 5–062
Paquine v Snary [1909] 1 K.B. 688, CA 14–002
Park, In the Estate of; sub nom. Park v Park [1954] P. 112; [1953] 3 W.L.R. 1012; [1953]
2 All E.R. 1411; (1953) 97 S.J. 830, CA 2–035, 2–036
Parkash v Irani Finance Ltd [1970] Ch. 101; [1969] 2 W.L.R. 1134; [1969] 1 All E.R. 930;
(1969) 20 P. & C.R. 385; (1969) 113 S.J. 106, Ch D 14–101

Parker v Parker [1972] Fam. 116; [1972] 2 W.L.R. 21; [1972] 1 All E.R. 410; (1971) 115
  S.J. 949, Fam Div 13–018
Parker v Parker; sub nom. Macclesfield v Parker [2003] EWHC 1846; [2003] N.P.C. 94, Ch
  D 5–033
Parkinson v Parkinson [1939] P. 346, PDAD 12–003
Parojcic (otherwise Ivetic) v Parojcic [1958] 1 W.L.R. 1280; [1959] 1 All E.R. 1; (1958) 102
  S.J. 938, PDAD 1–050, 2–042
Pascoe v Turner [1979] 1 W.L.R. 431; [1979] 2 All E.R. 945; (1978) 9 Fam. Law 82; (1979)
  123 S.J. 164, CA (Civ Div) 5–035, 5–036
Pasmore v Oswaldtwistle Urban DC (No.2); sub nom. Peebles v Oswaldtwistle Urban DC
  (No.2) [1898] A.C. 387, HL 21–084
Patel v Patel [2007] EWCA Civ 384 .... 9–035, 9–042
Paterson v Ritchie (Mary Jane), 1934 J.C. 42; 1934 S.L.T. 281, HCJ 6–012
Paul v Constance [1977] 1 W.L.R. 527; [1977] 1 All E.R. 195; (1976) 7 Fam. Law 18;
  (1977) 121 S.J. 320, CA (Civ Div) 5–062
Pavlou (A Bankrupt), Re [1993] 1 W.L.R. 1046; [1993] 3 All E.R. 955; [1993] Fam. Law
  629, Ch D 3–008, 5–047
Payne v Payne; sub nom. P v P (Removal of Child to New Zealand) [2001] EWCA Civ 166;
  [2001] Fam. 473; [2001] 2 W.L.R. 1826; [2001] 1 F.L.R. 1052; [2001] 1 F.C.R. 425;
  [2001] H.R.L.R. 28; [2001] U.K.H.R.R. 484; (2001) 165 J.P.N. 466; (2001) 98(10)
  L.S.G. 41; (2001) 145 S.J.L.B. 61, CA (Civ Div) 18–026, 19–004, 19–026, 20–025, 21–079
Pazpena de Vire v Pazpena de Vire [2001] 1 F.L.R. 460; [2001] Fam. Law 95, Fam Div 1–044
Peacock v Peacock [1984] 1 W.L.R. 532; [1984] 1 All E.R. 1069; [1984] Fam. Law 112;
  (1984) 128 S.J. 116, Fam Div 13–037
Pearce (Deceased), Re [1998] 2 F.L.R. 705; [1999] 2 F.C.R. 179; [1998] Fam. Law 588, CA
  (Civ Div) 7–014
Pearce v Pearce [2003] EWCA Civ 1054; [2004] 1 W.L.R. 68; [2003] 2 F.L.R. 1144; [2003]
  3 F.C.R. 178; [2003] Fam. Law 723; (2003) 100(36) L.S.G. 39, CA (Civ Div) 13–100
Pearson v Franklin (Parental Home: Ouster) [1994] 1 F.L.R. 246 .... 9–042, 15–049, 18–022
Pearson v Pearson (Queen's Proctor Showing Cause) [1971] P. 16; [1969] 3 W.L.R. 722;
  [1969] 3 All E.R. 323; (1969) 113 S.J. 639, PDAD 10–005
Pelling v Bruce-Williams [2004] EWCA Civ 845; [2004] Fam. 155; [2004] 3 W.L.R. 1178;
  [2004] 3 All E.R. 875; [2004] 2 F.L.R. 823; [2004] 3 F.C.R. 108; [2004] Fam. Law 784,
  CA (Civ Div) 18–041
Pengelly v Enright-Redding; sub nom. P (Children) (Shared Residence Order), Re [2005]
  EWCA Civ 1639; [2006] 2 F.L.R. 347; [2006] 1 F.C.R. 309; [2006] Fam. Law 447, CA
  (Civ Div) 18–016
Penn v Bristol and West Building Society; sub nom. Brill & Co v Penn [1997] 1 W.L.R.
  1356; [1997] 3 All E.R. 470; [1997] 3 F.C.R. 789; [1997] P.N.L.R. 607; (1997) 74 P.
  & C.R. 210; [1997] E.G. 54 (C.S.); (1997) 94(18) L.S.G. 32; (1997) 141 S.J.L.B. 105;
  [1997] N.P.C. 58, CA (Civ Div) 5–043
Penrose v Penrose [1994] 2 F.L.R. 621; [1994] 2 F.C.R. 1167; [1994] Fam. Law 618, CA
  (Civ Div) 13–024, 13–093, 13–101, 13–103, 13–104
Pepper v Pepper [1960] 1 W.L.R. 131; [1960] 1 All E.R. 529; (1960) 124 J.P. 184; (1960)
  104 S.J. 190, DC 14–012
Pereira v Keleman [1995] 1 F.L.R. 428; [1994] 2 F.C.R. 635; [1995] Fam. Law 182, QBD 17–027,
  21–066
Perry v Perry [1964] 1 W.L.R. 91; [1963] 3 All E.R. 766; (1963) 107 S.J. 739, PDAD ... 10–032
Pesticcio v Huet; sub nom. Niersmans v Pesticcio [2004] EWCA Civ 372; [2004] W.T.L.R.
  699; (2004) 154 N.L.J. 653; (2004) 148 S.J.L.B. 420; [2004] N.P.C. 55, CA (Civ Div) 5–052,
  5–055
Peters' Executors v Inland Revenue Commissioners [1941] 2 All E.R. 620, CA 3–027, 3–030
Pettitt v Pettitt; sub nom. P v P [1970] A.C. 777; [1969] 2 W.L.R. 966; [1969] 2 All E.R.
  385; (1969) 20 P. & C.R. 991; (1969) 113 S.J. 344, HL 2–028, 3–006, 3–027, 5–001, 5–014,
  5–016, 5–045
Pheasant v Pheasant [1972] Fam. 202; [1972] 2 W.L.R. 353; [1972] 1 All E.R. 587; (1971)
  116 S.J. 120, Fam Div 10–024, 10–034
Phelps (Deceased), Re; sub nom.Wells v Phelps [1980] Ch. 275; [1980] 2 W.L.R. 277;
  [1979] 3 All E.R. 373; (1980) 124 S.J. 85, CA (Civ Div) 7–007
Phillips v Peace [1996] 2 F.L.R. 230; [1996] 2 F.C.R. 237; [1996] Fam. Law 603, Fam Div 15–042,
  15–049, 15–051, 15–05⁀

Phippen v Palmers (A Firm) [2002] 2 F.L.R. 415; [2002] Fam. Law 593, Fam Div 13–086, 13–090, 13–108

Piglowska v Piglowski [1999] 1 W.L.R. 1360; [1999] 3 All E.R. 632; [1999] 2 F.L.R. 763; [1999] 2 F.C.R. 481; [1999] Fam. Law 617; (1999) 96(27) L.S.G. 34; (1999) 143 S.J.L.B. 190, HL ... 8–001, 13–001, 13–002, 13–040, 13–041, 13–043, 13–058, 13–063, 13–072, 13–112

Pilcher v Pilcher (No.2) [1956] 1 W.L.R. 298; [1956] 1 All E.R. 463; (1956) 120 J.P. 127; (1956) 100 S.J. 227, PDAD 14–002, 14–017

Pink v Lawrence (1978) 36 P. & C.R. 98, CA (Civ Div) 5–010

Place v Searle [1932] 2 K.B. 497, CA 3–003

Plant v Plant (1982) (1983) 4 F.L.R. 305; (1982) 12 Fam. Law 179, CA (Civ Div) 18–016, 19–018

Plimmer v Wellington Corp; sub nom. Plimmer v Mayor, Councillors, and Citizens of the City of Wellington (1883–84) L.R. 9 App. Cas. 699, PC (NZ) 5–035

Pluck v Pluck [2007] EWCA Civ 1250 9–010

Portsmouth NHS Trust v Wyatt; sub nom. Wyatt (A Child) (Medical Treatment: Parents Consent), Re [2004] EWHC 2247; [2005] 1 F.L.R. 21; (2005) 84 B.M.L.R. 206; [2004] Fam. Law 866; (2004) 154 N.L.J. 1526, Fam Div 17–022

Portsmouth NHS Trust v Wyatt; sub nom. Wyatt (A Child) (Medical Treatment: Continuation of Order), Re [2005] EWCA Civ 1181; [2005] 1 W.L.R. 3995; [2006] 1 F.L.R. 554; [2005] 3 F.C.R. 263; (2006) 9 C.C.L. Rep. 131; [2005] Lloyd's Rep. Med. 474; (2005) 86 B.M.L.R. 173; [2006] Fam. Law 13, CA (Civ Div); [2005] EWHC 693; [2005] 2 F.L.R. 480; [2005] Fam. Law 614, Fam Div 17–022, 19–018

Potter v Potter (1975) 5 F.L.R. 16 2–031

Pounds v Pounds [1994] 1 W.L.R. 1535; [1994] 4 All E.R. 777; [1994] 1 F.L.R. 775; [1994] Fam. Law 436; (1994) 144 N.L.J. 459, CA (Civ Div) 10–010, 13–004, 13–005, 13–006, 13–007, 13–009, 13–013

Powell v Benney [2007] EWCA Civ 1283 5–035

Powell v Osbourne [1993] 1 F.L.R. 1001; [1993] 1 F.C.R. 797; [1993] Fam. Law 287, CA (Civ Div) 7–024, 7–026

Practice Direction [1989] 1 F.L.R. 307 20–007

Practice Direction [1992] 2 F.L.R. 87 18–054

Practice Direction [2007] 2 F.L.R. 625 18–010

Practice Direction (CA: Consolidation: Notice of Consolidation) [1999] 1 W.L.R. 1027; [1999] 2 All E.R. 490, CA (Civ Div) 19–024, 19–025

Practice Direction (Fam Div: Access: Supervised Access) [1980] 1 W.L.R. 334; [1980] 1 All E.R. 1040, Fam Div 18–018

Practice Direction (Fam Div: Ancillary Relief Procedure) [2000] 1 W.L.R. 1480; [2000] 3 All E.R. 379; [2000] 1 F.L.R. 997; [2000] 2 F.C.R. 216, Fam Div 13–009

Practice Direction (Fam Div: Children Act 1989: Applications by Children: Leave) [1993] 1 W.L.R. 313; [1993] 1 All E.R. 820; [1993] 1 F.L.R. 668, Fam Div 18–038

Practice Direction (Fam Div: Children: Removal from Jurisdiction) [1986] 1 W.L.R. 475; [1986] 1 All E.R. 983; [1986] 2 F.L.R. 89, Fam Div 20–004

Practice Direction (Fam Div: Conciliation); sub nom. Practice Direction (Child: Custody: Conciliation) [2004] 1 W.L.R. 1287; [2004] 2 All E.R. 463; [2004] 1 F.L.R. 974; [2004] 1 F.C.R. 781, Fam Div 18–040

Practice Direction (Fam Div: Exclusion Requirement: Procedure on Arrest); sub nom. Practice Direction (Fam Div: Children Act 1989: Exclusion Requirement) [1998] 1 W.L.R. 475; [1998] 2 All E.R. 928; [1998] 1 F.L.R. 495; [1998] 1 F.C.R. 338, Fam Div 21–044

Practice Direction (Fam Div: Family Proceedings: Allocation of Costs); sub nom. Practice Direction (Fam Div: Civil Procedure Rules 1998: Allocation of Cases: Costs); Practice Direction (Fam Div: Family Proceedings: Costs) [1999] 1 W.L.R. 1128; [1999] 3 All E.R. 192; [1999] 1 F.L.R. 1295; [1999] 2 F.C.R. 1, Fam Div 18–041

Practice Direction (Fam Div: Family Proceedings: Allocation to Judiciary 1999) [1999] 2 F.L.R. 799, Fam Div 18–054

Practice Direction (Fam Div: Family Proceedings: Case Management) [1995] 1 W.L.R. 332; [1995] 1 All E.R. 586; [1995] 1 F.L.R. 456, Fam Div 18–041

Practice Direction (Fam Div: Family Proceedings: Representation of Children) [2004] 1 W.L.R. 1180; [2004] 2 All E.R. 459; [2004] 1 F.L.R. 1188; [2004] 2 F.C.R. 124, Fam Div 16–020, 18–007, 18–008

Practice Direction (Fam Div: Human Rights Act 1998: Citation of Authorities); sub nom. Practice Direction (Fam Div: Proceedings: Human Rights) [2000] 1 W.L.R. 1782; [2000] 4 All E.R. 288; [2000] 2 F.L.R. 429; [2000] 2 F.C.R. 768, Fam Div 18–007
Practice Direction (Fam Div: Maintenance Orders: Service Personnel: Disclosure of Addresses) [1995] 2 F.L.R. 813, Fam Div 20–007
Practice Direction (Fam Div: Variation Orders: Form 11); sub nom. Practice Direction (Fam Div: Divorce: Financial Provision) [1984] 1 W.L.R. 1300; [1984] 3 All E.R. 640, Fam Div 20–023
Practice Direction of 10 March 2000 (Family Proceedings: Court Bundles) [2000] 1 F.L.R. 536 13–012
Practice Note (1987) 17 Fam.Law. 263 20–005
Practice Note (Officers of CAFCASS Legal Services and Special Casework: Appointment in Family Proceedings) [2001] 2 F.L.R. 151; [2001] 2 F.C.R. 562 ...17–022, 18–011, 18–054, 21–056
Practice Note (Official Solicitor: Appointment in Family Proceedings) [2001] 2 F.L.R. 155; [2001] 2 F.C.R. 566 18–054
Pratt v Inman (1890) L.R. 43 Ch. D. 175, Ch D 14–010
Prescott (otherwise Fellowes) v Fellowes [1958] P. 260; [1958] 3 W.L.R. 288; [1958] 3 All E.R. 55; (1958) 102 S.J. 581, CA 13–027
President's Direction (Fam Div: HIV Testing of Children); sub nom. Practice Note: (Fam Div: HIV Testing of Children) [2003] 1 F.L.R. 1299, Fam Div 18–007
Preston v Preston [1982] Fam. 17; [1981] 3 W.L.R. 619; [1982] 1 All E.R. 41; (1981) 125 S.J. 496, CA (Civ Div) 13–043, 13–072, 13–087
Primavera v Primavera [1991] 1 F.L.R. 16; [1992] F.C.R. 77; [1991] Fam. Law 471, CA (Civ Div) 13–098
Pritchard Englefield (A Firm) v Steinberg [2004] EWHC 1908; [2005] 1 P. & C.R. DG2, Ch D 5–060
Purba v Purba [2000] 1 F.L.R. 444; [2000] 1 F.C.R. 652; [2000] Fam. Law 86, CA (Civ Div) 14–002
Q (A Minor) (Parental Order), Re [1996] 1 F.L.R. 369; [1996] 2 F.C.R. 345; [1996] Fam. Law 206, Fam Div 17–004, 22–072
Quick v Quick [1953] V.R. 224 1–043
Quoraishi v Quoraishi [1985] Fam. Law 308, CA (Civ Div) 10–031
R, Re [2006] EWCA Civ 1748 17–046
R (A Child) (Adoption: Father's Involvement), Re; sub nom. S (A Child) (Adoption Proceedings: Joinder of Father), Re [2001] 1 F.L.R. 302; [2001] 1 F.C.R. 158; [2001] Fam. Law 91, CA (Civ Div) 17–052, 22–032, 22–034, 22–039
R (A Child) (Care Proceedings: Disclosure), Re [2000] 2 F.L.R. 751; [2000] Fam. Law 793; (2001) 165 J.P.N. 104; (2000) 97(30) L.S.G. 39, CA (Civ Div) 21–037
R (A Child) (Care Proceedings: Teenage Pregnancy), Re; sub nom. R (A Child) (Care Proceedings: Teenage Mother), Re [2000] 2 F.L.R. 660; [2000] 2 F.C.R. 556; [2000] Fam. Law 791, Fam Div 22–042
R (A Child) (Care: Disclosure: Nature of Proceedings), Re [2002] 1 F.L.R. 755; [2002] Fam. Law 253, Fam Div 22–035
R (A Child) (IVF: Paternity of Child), Re; sub nom. R (A Child) (Contact: Human Fertilisation and Embryology Act 1990) (No.2), Re; D (A Child) (IVF: Paternity of Child), Re; R (A Child) (Parental Responsibility: IVF Baby), Re; B v R [2005] UKHL 33; [2005] 2 A.C. 621; [2005] 2 W.L.R. 1158; [2005] 4 All E.R. 433; [2005] 2 F.L.R. 843; [2005] 2 F.C.R. 223; [2005] Fam. Law 701; (2005) 102(21) L.S.G. 33; (2005) 155 N.L.J. 797, HL 17–004
R (A Minor) (Abduction), Re [1992] 1 F.L.R. 105; [1991] Fam. Law 475 20–021
R (A Minor) (Contact), Re [1994] 2 F.L.R. 441 19–001
R (A Minor) (Contempt: Sentence), Re [1994] 1 W.L.R. 487; [1994] 2 All E.R. 144; [1994] 2 F.L.R. 185; [1994] 2 F.C.R. 629; [1994] Fam. Law 435, CA (Civ Div) 18–056
R (A Minor) (Inter-Country Adoptions: Practice) (No.1), Re [1999] 1 F.L.R. 1014; [1999] 1 F.C.R. 385; [1999] Fam. Law 289, Fam Div 19–019, 22–054
R (A Minor) (Medical Treatment), Re. *See* Camden LBC v R (A Minor) (Blood Transfusion)
R (A Minor) (Residence: Contact: Restricting Applications), Re; sub nom. R (A Minor) (Leave to Make Applications), Re [1998] 1 F.L.R. 749; [1998] 2 F.C.R. 129; [1998] Fam. Law 247, CA (Civ Div) 18–028

R (A Minor) (Residence Order: Financial Considerations), Re; sub nom. R (A Minor) (Residence Order: Finance), Re; R (A Minor) (Shared Residence Order), Re [1995] 2 F.L.R. 612; [1995] 3 F.C.R. 334; [1995] Fam. Law 601, CA (Civ Div) 15–018

R (A Minor) (Residence: Religion), Re; sub nom. R (A Minor) (Religious Sect), Re [1993] 2 F.L.R. 163; [1993] 2 F.C.R. 525; [1993] Fam. Law 460, CA (Civ Div) 19–017, 19–018, 19–020

R (A Minor) (Wardship: Consent to Treatment), Re [1992] Fam. 11; [1991] 3 W.L.R. 592; [1992] 1 F.L.R. 190; [1992] 2 F.C.R. 229; [1992] 3 Med. L.R. 342; [1992] Fam. Law 67, CA (Civ Div) 16–014, 16–015, 16–019, 18–052

R (Abduction: Consent), Re; sub nom. R (Minors) (Abduction: Acquiescence), Re [1999] 1 F.L.R. 828; [1999] 1 F.C.R. 87; [1999] Fam. Law 288, Fam Div 20–019

R (Adoption), Re [1967] 1 W.L.R. 34; [1966] 3 All E.R. 613; (1967) 131 J.P. 1; 65 L.G.R. 65; (1966) 110 S.J. 652, Ch D 22–032

R (Child Abuse: Video and Expert Evidence), Re [1995] 1 F.L.R. 451; [1995] 2 F.C.R. 573; [1995] Fam. Law 237, Fam Div 18–043

R (Children) (Residence: Shared Care: Children's Views), Re [2005] EWCA Civ 542; [2006] 1 F.L.R. 491; [2006] Fam. Law 15, CA (Civ Div) 18–016, 19–024

R (Minors) (Custody), Re [1986] 1 F.L.R. 6; [1986] Fam. Law 15, CA (Civ Div) 19–001

R (Minors) (Wardship Jurisdiction), Re (1981) 2 F.L.R. 416 19–005

R (Minors: Child Abduction), Re [1995] 1 F.L.R. 716; [1995] 2 F.C.R. 609, CA (Civ Div) ... 20–019

R (PM) (An Infant), Re; sub nom. R (PM) (An Infant), Re [1968] 1 W.L.R. 385; [1968] 1 All E.R. 691 (Note); 66 L.G.R. 613; (1968) 112 S.J. 189, Ch D 18–052

R (Recovery Orders), Re [1998] 2 F.L.R. 401; [1998] 3 F.C.R. 321; [1998] Fam. Law 401, Fam Div 20–009

R and G (Minors) (Interim Care or Supervision Order), Re; sub nom. Hereford and Worcester CC v R and G [1994] 1 F.L.R. 793; [1994] 2 F.C.R. 981; [1994] Fam. Law 314; (1994) 158 J.P.N. 730, Fam Div 21–040, 21–042

R and G (Minors) (Wardship), Re; sub nom. G and R (Wards) (Police Interviews), Re [1990] 2 All E.R. 633; [1990] 2 F.L.R. 347; [1990] F.C.R. 495; [1991] Fam. Law 64, Fam Div 18–052

R. v Alass [2007] EWCA Crim 2504 9–005

R. v Avon CC Ex p. Crabtree [1996] 1 F.L.R. 502; [1996] 3 F.C.R. 773; [1996] Fam. Law 277; (1996) 160 J.P.N. 730, CA (Civ Div) 21–085

R. v Barnardo (1889) L.R. 23 Q.B.D. 305, CA 17–014

R. v Barnet LBC Ex p. B [1994] 1 F.L.R. 592; [1994] 2 F.C.R. 781; [1994] Fam. Law 185, QBD 21–009, 21–082

R. v Barnet LBC Ex p. Shah (Nilish); Akbarali v Brent LBC; Abdullah v Shropshire CC; Shabpar v Barnet LBC; Shah (Jitendra) v Barnet LBC; Ablack v Inner London Education Authority; R. v Shropshire CC Ex p. Abdullah [1983] 2 A.C. 309; [1983] 2 W.L.R. 16; [1983] 1 All E.R. 226; 81 L.G.R. 305; (1983) 133 N.L.J. 61; (1983) 127 S.J. 36, HL 15–010

R. v Bham (Usuf Arif) [1966] 1 Q.B. 159; [1965] 3 W.L.R. 696; [1965] 3 All E.R. 124; (1965) 49 Cr. App. R. 355; (1965) 109 S.J. 573, CCA 1–048

R. v Birmingham City Council Ex p. A (A Minor) [1997] 2 F.L.R. 841; [1997] 2 F.C.R. 357; [1998] Fam. Law 23, Fam Div 21–085

R. v Birmingham Justices Ex p. Bennett [1983] 1 W.L.R. 114; (1983) 147 J.P. 279; [1983] Crim. L.R. 259; (1983) 127 S.J. 35, DC 14–017

R. v Bolton MBC Ex p. B, 84 L.G.R. 78; [1985] Fam. Law 193; (1985) 82 L.S.G. 1086, QBD 19–019

R. v Brent LBC Ex p. Awua; sub nom. Awua v Brent LBC [1996] A.C. 55; [1995] 3 W.L.R. 215; [1995] 3 All E.R. 493; [1995] 2 F.L.R. 819; [1995] 3 F.C.R. 278; (1995) 27 H.L.R. 453; [1996] Fam. Law 20; (1996) 160 L.G. Rev. 21; (1995) 145 N.L.J. 1031; (1995) 139 S.J.L.B. 189; [1995] N.P.C. 119, HL 6–037

R. v Brent LBC Ex p. Sawyers; sub nom. R. v Brent LBC Ex p. S; Sawyers v Brent LBC [1994] 1 F.L.R. 203; [1994] 2 F.C.R. 996; [1994] C.O.D. 416; [1994] Fam. Law 249, CA (Civ Div) 21–082, 21–084

R. v Bristol Justices Ex p. Hodge; sub nom. R. v Bristol Magistrates Court Ex p. Hodge [1997] Q.B. 974; [1997] 2 W.L.R. 756; [1996] 4 All E.R. 924; [1997] 1 F.L.R. 88; [1997] 1 F.C.R. 412; [1997] Fam. Law 89; (1997) 161 J.P.N. 87, QBD 14–003

R. v Brown (Anthony Joseph); R. v Laskey (Colin); R. v Lucas (Saxon); R. v Carter
(Christopher Robert); R. v Jaggard (Roland Leonard); R. v Cadman (Graham William)
[1994] 1 A.C. 212; [1993] 2 W.L.R. 556; [1993] 2 All E.R. 75; (1993) 97 Cr. App. R.
44; (1993) 157 J.P. 337; (1993) 157 J.P.N. 233; (1993) 143 N.L.J. 399, HL 9–004
R. v Cannings (Angela) [2004] EWCA Crim 1; [2004] 1 W.L.R. 2607; [2004] 1 All E.R.
725; [2004] 2 Cr. App. R. 7; [2004] 1 F.C.R. 193; [2005] Crim. L.R. 126; (2004) 101(5)
L.S.G. 27; (2004) 148 S.J.L.B. 114, CA (Crim Div) 21–036
R. v Cardiff Justices Ex p. Salter [1986] 1 F.L.R. 162; [1986] Fam. Law 53; (1985) 149
J.P.N. 619, DC 14–017
R. v Cardiff Magistrates Court Ex p. Czech [1999] 1 F.L.R. 95; [1999] 1 F.C.R. 721; [1998]
C.O.D. 392; [1998] Fam. Law 658; (1999) J.P.N. 555, Fam Div 14–003
R. v Chief Constable of Chesire, Ex p. K [1990] 1 F.L.R. 70 18–057
R. v Chief Constable of North Wales Ex p. AB; sub nom. R. v Chief Constable of North
Wales Ex p. Thorpe [1999] Q.B. 396; [1998] 3 W.L.R. 57; [1998] 3 All E.R. 310;
[1998] 2 F.L.R. 571; [1998] 3 F.C.R. 371; [1998] Fam. Law 529; (1998) 95(17) L.S.G.
29, CA (Civ Div) 21–028
R. v Clarke (1857) 7 El. & Bl. 186 19–016
R. v Colohan [2001] EWCA Crim 1251 .... 9–005, 9–038
R. v Cornwall CC Ex p. Cornwall and Isles of Scilly Guardians ad litem and Reporting
Officers Panel [1992] 1 W.L.R. 427; [1992] 2 All E.R. 471; [1992] 1 F.L.R. 270; [1992]
1 F.C.R. 511; 90 L.G.R. 159; [1992] Fam. Law 110; (1992) 156 L.G. Rev. 666; (1992)
89(4) L.S.G. 33; (1991) 135 S.J.L.B. 204, QBD 21–085
R. v Cornwall CC Ex p. LH; sub nom. R. v Cornwall CC Ex p. L; R. v Cornwall CC Ex
p. H [2000] 1 F.L.R. 236; [2000] 1 F.C.R. 460; [2000] B.L.G.R. 180; (2000) 3 C.C.L.
Rep. 362; [2000] C.O.D. 26; [2000] Fam. Law 89; (1999) 96(45) L.S.G. 31; (1999) 143
S.J.L.B. 282, QBD 21–025, 21–085
R. v Creamer (Wilbert Roy) [1919] 1 K.B. 564; (1920) 14 Cr. App. R. 19 3–004
R. v D (Ian Malcolm) [1984] A.C. 778; [1984] 3 W.L.R. 186; [1984] 2 All E.R. 449; (1984)
79 Cr. App. R. 313; [1984] Crim. L.R. 558; [1984] Fam. Law 311; (1984) 81 L.S.G.
2458, HL 16–013, 19–002
R. v D (Sexual Offences Prevention Order) [2005] EWCA Crim 3660; [2006] 1 W.L.R.
1088; [2006] 2 All E.R. 726; [2006] 2 Cr. App. R. (S.) 32; [2006] 1 F.L.R. 1085; [2006]
Crim. L.R. 364; [2006] Fam. Law 273, CA (Crim Div) 18–019
R. v Derby Magistrates Court Ex p. B [1996] A.C. 487; [1995] 3 W.L.R. 681; [1995] 4 All
E.R. 526; [1996] 1 Cr. App. R. 385; (1995) 159 J.P. 785; [1996] 1 F.L.R. 513; [1996]
Fam. Law 210; (1995) 159 J.P.N. 778; (1995) 145 N.L.J. 1575; [1995] 139 S.J.L.B.
219, HL 21–037
R. v Devon CC Ex p. O (Adoption); sub nom. R. v Devon CC Ex p. B [1997] 2 F.L.R. 388;
[1997] 3 F.C.R. 411; [1997] C.O.D. 369; [1997] Fam. Law 390, QBD ..21–073, 21–085, 22–045
R. v Devon Ex p. Baker and Johns (1992) 11 B.M.L.R. 141 21–084
R. v Ealing LBC Ex. P Sidhu (1983) 3 F.L.R. 438 6–037
R. v East Sussex CC Ex p. W (A Minor) [1998] 2 F.L.R. 1082; [1999] 1 F.C.R. 536; [1999]
C.O.D. 55; [1998] Fam. Law 736; (1999) 163 J.P.N. 495, QBD 16–019, 21–085
R. v Eastleigh BC Ex p. Beattie (No.2) (1985) 17 H.L.R. 168, QBD 6–037
R. v Edwards (Danny Michael) [2005] EWCA Crim 1738, CA (Crim Div) 9–041
R. v Evans (Dorothy Gertrude) [2004] EWCA Crim 3102; [2005] 1 W.L.R. 1435; [2005] 1
Cr. App. R. 32; (2005) 169 J.P. 129; [2005] Crim. L.R. 654; (2005) 169 J.P.N. 222;
(2005) 102(7) L.S.G. 26, CA (Crim Div) 9–040
R. v Exeter Juvenile Court Ex p. H and H [1988] 2 F.L.R. 214 18–006
R. v Gloucestershire CC Ex p. Barry; R. v Lancashire CC Ex p. Royal Association for
Disability and Rehabilitation; R. v Islington LBC Ex p. McMillan; R. v Gloucestershire
CC Ex p. Grinham; R. v Gloucestershire CC Ex p. Dartnell; sub nom. R. v
Gloucestershire CC Ex p. Mahfood [1997] A.C. 584; [1997] 2 W.L.R. 459; [1997] 2
All E.R. 1; (1997) 9 Admin. L.R. 209; (1997–98) 1 C.C.L. Rep. 40; (1997) 36
B.M.L.R. 92; [1997] C.O.D. 304; (1997) 94(14) L.S.G. 25; (1997) 147 N.L.J. 453;
(1997) 141 S.J.L.B. 91, HL 21–009
R. v Gyngall [1893] 2 Q.B. 232, CA 18–052, 16–003
R. v H (Assault of Child: Reasonable Chastisement) [2001] EWCA Crim 1024; [2002] 1 Cr.
App. R. 7; [2001] 2 F.L.R. 431; [2001] 3 F.C.R. 144, CA (Crim Div) 17–017
R. v Hammersmith and Fulham LBC Ex p. D [1999] 1 F.L.R. 642; [1999] 2 F.C.R. 401;
(1999) 31 H.L.R. 786; [1999] B.L.G.R. 575; (1999) 2 C.C.L. Rep. 18; [1999] Fam.
Law 213; (1999) 96(2) L.S.G. 28, QBD 21–009, 21–012, 21–085

R. v Hampshire CC Ex p. H [1999] 2 F.L.R. 359; [1999] 3 F.C.R. 129; [1999] Fam. Law
537; (2000) 164 J.P.N. 405; (1998) 95(29) L.S.G. 27; (1998) 142 S.J.L.B. 188, CA (Civ
Div) 21–025, 21–026, 21–085
R. v Hampshire CC Ex p. K [1990] 2 Q.B. 71; [1990] 2 W.L.R. 649; [1990] 2 All E.R. 129;
[1990] 1 F.L.R. 330; [1990] F.C.R. 545; [1990] 2 Med. L.R. 84; [1990] Fam. Law 253;
(1990) 154 J.P.N. 457; (1990) 87(4) L.S.G. 68; (1989) 133 S.J. 1605, DC 21–037, 21–053
R. v Harrow LBC Ex p. D [1990] Fam. 133; [1989] 3 W.L.R. 1239; [1990] 3 All E.R. 12;
[1990] 1 F.L.R. 79; [1989] F.C.R. 729; 88 L.G.R. 41; (1989) 2 Admin. L.R. 48; [1990]
C.O.D. 31; [1990] Fam. Law 18; (1989) 153 J.P.N. 153; (1989) 86(42) L.S.G. 42;
(1989) 139 N.L.J. 1153; (1989) 133 S.J. 1514, CA (Civ Div) 19–002, 21–025, 21–085
R. v Hill [2001] 1 F.L.R. 580 9–006
R. v Hills [2001] 1 F.L.R. 185 .... 9–006, 9–038
R. v Hopley (1860) 2 F. & F. 202 17–017
R. v Howes, 121 E.R. 467; (1860) 3 El. & El. 332, QB 16–003
R. v Human Fertilisation and Embryology Authority Ex p. Blood; sub nom. R. v Human
Fertilisation and Embryology Authority Ex p. DB [1999] Fam. 151; [1997] 2 W.L.R.
807; [1997] 2 All E.R. 687; [1997] 2 C.M.L.R. 591; [1997] Eu. L.R. 370; [1997] 2
F.L.R. 742; [1997] 2 F.C.R. 501; (1997) 35 B.M.L.R. 1; [1997] C.O.D. 261; [1997]
Fam. Law 401; (1997) 147 N.L.J. 253, CA (Civ Div) 17–004
R. v Immigration Appeal Tribunal Ex p. Iqbal (Iram) [1993] Imm. A.R. 270; (1993) 5
Admin. L.R. 561; [1993] C.O.D. 226, QBD 3–040
R. v Inland Revenue Commissioners Ex p. National Federation of Self Employed and Small
Businesses Ltd; sub nom. Inland Revenue Commissioners v National Federation of
Self Employed and Small Businesses Ltd [1982] A.C. 617; [1981] 2 W.L.R. 722;
[1981] 2 All E.R. 93; [1981] S.T.C. 260; 55 T.C. 133; (1981) 125 S.J. 325, HL 21–085
R. v Ireland (Robert Matthew); R. v Burstow (Anthony Christopher) [1998] A.C. 147;
[1997] 3 W.L.R. 534; [1997] 4 All E.R. 225; [1998] 1 Cr. App. R. 177; (1997) 161 J.P.
569; [1998] 1 F.L.R. 105; [1997] Crim. L.R. 810; [1998] Fam. Law 137; (1997) 161
J.P.N. 816; (1997) 147 N.L.J. 1273; (1997) 141 S.J.L.B. 205, HL 9–006, 9–038
R. v Islington LBC Ex p. Rixon [1997] E.L.R. 66; (1997–98) 1 C.C.L. Rep. 119; (1996) 32
B.M.L.R. 136, QBD 21–006
R. v Jackson [1891] 1 Q.B. 671, CA 3–003, 9–004
R. v Kingston upon Thames RLBC Ex p. T; sub nom. R. v Kingston upon Thames RLBC
Ex p. X [1994] 1 F.L.R. 798; [1994] 1 F.C.R. 232; [1993] C.O.D. 470; [1994] Fam.
Law 375, Fam Div 21–010, 21–082, 21–085
R. v Lambeth LBC Ex p. Caddell; sub nom. R. v Lambeth LBC Ex p. C [1998] 1 F.L.R. 253;
[1998] 2 F.C.R. 6; [1998] Fam. Law 20; (1997) 94(30) L.S.G. 30; (1997) 141 S.J.L.B.
147, QBD 21–015
R. v Legal Aid Board Ex p. W (Children); sub nom. W (Children) v Legal Services
Commission [2000] 1 W.L.R. 2502; [2000] 2 F.L.R. 821; [2000] 3 F.C.R. 352; [2000]
Fam. Law 802; (2000) 97(38) L.S.G. 44; (2000) 150 N.L.J. 1453; (2000) 144 S.J.L.B.
252, CA (Civ Div 16–022, 21–056
R. v Liddle (Mark) (Appeal against Sentence); R. v Hayes (Andrew Michael) [1999] 3 All
E.R. 816; [2000] 1 Cr. App. R. (S.) 131; [1999] Crim. L.R. 847; (1999) 96(23) L.S.G.
34, CA (Crim Div) 9–005
R. v Local Authority in the Midlands Ex p. LM [2000] 1 F.L.R. 612; [2000] 1 F.C.R. 736;
[2000] U.K.H.R.R. 143; (2000) 2 L.G.L.R. 1043; [2000] C.O.D. 41; [2000] Fam. Law
83, QBD 21–085
R. v Luton Magistrates Court Ex p. Sullivan [1992] 2 F.L.R. 196; [1992] F.C.R. 475; [1992]
Fam. Law 380; (1992) 156 J.P.N. 426 .... 14–016, 14–017
R. v Maher [2007] EWCA Crim 3296 9–005
R. v Miller [2007] EWCA Crim 2852 9–005
R. v Millis, 8 E.R. 844; (1844) 10 Cl. & F. 534, HL 1–002
R. v Mole Valley DC Ex p. Burton (1988) 20 H.L.R. 479; [1989] Fam. Law 64, QBD 6–037
R. v Molyneux [2007] EWCA Crim. 3417 9–005
R. v North Devon DC Ex p. Lewis; sub nom. Lewis v North Devon DC [1981] 1 W.L.R.
328; [1981] 1 All E.R. 27; 79 L.G.R. 289; (1980) 124 S.J. 742, QBD 6–037
R. v North Yorkshire CC Ex p. M (No.1) [1989] Q.B. 411; [1988] 3 W.L.R. 1344; [1989]
1 All E.R. 143; (1989) 153 J.P. 390; [1989] 1 F.L.R. 203; [1989] F.C.R. 128; [1989]
C.O.D. 190; [1989] Fam. Law 102; (1989) 153 J.P.N. 288; (1989) 153 L.G. Rev. 652;
(1989) 86(5) L.S.G. 42; (1988) 132 S.J. 1731, QBD 21–058

R. v North Yorkshire CC Ex p. M (No.2); sub nom. R. v North Yorkshire CC Ex P. BM
[1989] 2 F.L.R. 79; [1989] F.C.R. 394; [1989] Fam. Law 350; (1989) 153 J.P.N. 390,
QBD 21–058
R. v Northavon DC Ex p. Smith; sub nom. Northavon DC v Smith; Smith v Northavon DC
[1994] 2 A.C. 402; [1994] 3 W.L.R. 403; [1994] 3 All E.R. 313; [1994] 2 F.L.R. 671;
[1994] 2 F.C.R. 859; (1994) 26 H.L.R. 659; 92 L.G.R. 643; [1994] C.O.D. 492; [1995]
Fam. Law 16; (1994) 158 J.P.N. 651; (1994) 158 L.G. Rev. 990; (1994) 91(38) L.S.G.
42; (1994) 144 N.L.J. 1010; (1994) 138 S.J.L.B. 178; [1994] N.P.C. 113, HL 6–039, 21–015,
22–023, 21–085
R. v Norwood [2007] EWCA Crim 2669 9–005
R. v Nottingham County Court Ex p. Byers [1985] 1 W.L.R. 403; [1985] 1 All E.R. 735;
[1985] Fam. Law 278; (1985) 82 L.S.G. 518, QBD 10–001
R. v Nottinghamshire CC [1993] Fam.Law 543 18–041
R. v Oldham MBC Ex p. Garlick; R. v Bexley LBC Ex p. Bentum; R. v Tower Hamlets LBC
Ex p. Begum (Ferdous); sub nom. R. v Oldham MBC Ex p. G; R. v Bexley LBC Ex
p. B [1993] A.C. 509; [1993] 2 W.L.R. 609; [1993] 2 All E.R. 65; [1993] 2 F.L.R. 194;
[1993] 2 F.C.R. 133; (1993) 25 H.L.R. 319; 91 L.G.R. 287; (1993) 143 N.L.J. 437;
(1993) 137 S.J.L.B. 109, HL 6–038
R. v Oxfordshire CC (Secure Accommodation Order) [1992] Fam. 150; [1992] 3 W.L.R. 88;
[1992] 3 All E.R. 660; [1992] 1 F.L.R. 648; [1992] Fam. Law 338; (1992) 156 L.G.
Rev. 906, Fam Div 19–014, 21–006, 21–078
R. v Pearce (Gary James) [2001] EWCA Crim 2834; [2002] 1 W.L.R. 1553; [2002] 1 Cr.
App. R. 39; (2002) 166 J.P. 103; [2002] 3 F.C.R. 75; (2002) 166 J.P.N. 190; (2002)
99(8) L.S.G. 34; (2002) 146 S.J.L.B. 37, CA (Crim Div) 3–039
R. v Portsmouth Hospitals NHS Trust Ex p. G [1999] 2 F.L.R. 905; [1999] 3 F.C.R. 145;
(1999) 11 Admin. L.R. 991; [1999] Lloyd's Rep. Med. 367; (1999) 50 B.M.L.R. 269;
[2000] C.O.D. 54; [1999] Fam. Law 696; (1999) 96(32) L.S.G. 31; (1999) 143 S.J.L.B.
220, CA (Civ Div) 18–051
R v R (Costs: Child Case) [1997] 2 F.L.R. 92 19–025
R v R (Financial Provision: Reasonable Need) [1994] 2 F.L.R. 1044; [1995] Fam. Law 15,
Fam Div 13–043, 13–072
R v R (Lump Sum Repayments) [2003] EWHC 3197 (Fam); [2004] 1 F.L.R. 928; [2004]
Fam. Law 333, Fam Div 13–024, 13–066
R. v R (otherwise F) [1952] 1 All E.R. 1194; [1952] 1 T.L.R. 1201; [1952] W.N. 236; (1952)
96 S.J. 362, PDAD 2–025
R. v R (Rape: Marital Exemption); sub nom. R. v R (A Husband) [1992] 1 A.C. 599; [1991]
3 W.L.R. 767; [1991] 4 All E.R. 481; (1992) 94 Cr. App. R. 216; (1991) 155 J.P. 989;
[1992] 1 F.L.R. 217; [1992] Crim. L.R. 207; [1992] Fam. Law 108; (1991) 155 J.P.N.
752; (1991) 141 N.L.J. 1481; (1991) 135 S.J.L.B. 181, HL 3–037, 9–004
R. v Registrar General Ex p. Segerdal [1970] 2 Q.B. 697; [1970] 3 W.L.R. 479; [1970] 3
All E.R. 886; (1970) 114 S.J. 703, CA (Civ Div) 1–040
R. v Registrar General Ex p. Smith [1991] 2 Q.B. 393; [1991] 2 W.L.R. 782; [1991] 2 All
E.R. 88; [1991] 1 F.L.R. 255; [1991] F.C.R. 403; [1991] C.O.D. 232; (1991) 88(2)
L.S.G. 32; (1991) 135 S.J. 52, CA (Civ Div) 22–011
R. v Reid (Samuel Percival) [1973] Q.B. 299; [1972] 3 W.L.R. 395; [1972] 2 All E.R. 1350;
(1972) 56 Cr. App. R. 703; [1972] Crim. L.R. 553; (1972) 116 S.J. 565, CA (Crim Div) ...3–003,
9–004
R. v Richards [2007] EWCA Crim 2516 9–005
R. v Rossiter (Ethel Amelia) [1994] 2 All E.R. 752; (1992) 95 Cr. App. R. 326; (1992) 142
N.L.J. 824, ...CA.(Crim.Div) 9–004
R. v Rushmoor BC Ex p. Barrett [1989] Q.B. 60; [1988] 2 W.L.R. 1271; [1988] 2 All E.R.
268; [1988] 2 F.L.R. 252; (1988) 20 H.L.R. 366; 86 L.G.R. 481; [1988] Fam. Law 335;
(1988) 152 L.G. Rev. 791, CA (Civ Div) 13–028
R. v Salford City Council Ex p. Devenport; sub nom. Devenport v Salford City Council
(1983) 8 H.L.R. 54; 82 L.G.R. 89; (1983) 127 S.J. 306, CA (Civ Div) 6–037
R. v Secretary of State for Health Ex p. Luff [1992] 1 F.L.R. 59; [1991] F.C.R. 821; [1991]
Imm. A.R. 382; (1991) 3 Admin. L.R. 797; [1991] Fam. Law 472 22–051
R. v Secretary of State for Social Security Ex p. Lloyd [1995] 1 F.L.R. 856; [1995] 3 F.C.R.
97; [1995] Fam. Law 406, QBD 15–026

R. v Secretary of State for the Environment Ex p. Ward [1984] 1 W.L.R. 834; [1984] 2 All
E.R. 556; 82 L.G.R. 628; (1984) 48 P. & C.R. 212; [1984] J.P.L. 90; (1984) 128 S.J.
415, QBD 21–084
R. v Secretary of State for Social Services Ex p. Ward [1990] 1 F.L.R. 119; [1990] F.C.R.
361; [1990] C.O.D. 139; [1990] Fam. Law 58; (1990) 154 J.P.N. 301; (1989) 133 S.J.
1133, DC 2–053, 10–001
R. v Secretary of State for the Home Department Ex p. Gangadeen; R. v Secretary of State
for the Home Department Ex p. Khan (Khalid); sub nom. Gangadeen v Secretary of
State for the Home Department; Khan (Khalid) v Secretary of State for the Home
Department [1998] 1 F.L.R. 762; [1998] 2 F.C.R. 96; [1998] Imm. A.R. 106; [1998]
I.N.L.R. 206; [1998] C.O.D. 216; [1998] Fam. Law 248; (1998) 95(1) L.S.G. 24;
(1998) 142 S.J.L.B. 27, CA (Civ Div) 19–002
R. v Secretary of State for the Home Department Ex p. Teame; Teame v Aberash; sub nom.
T (Political Asylum), Re; [1995] 1 F.L.R. 293; [1995] 3 F.C.R. 1; [1994] Imm. A.R.
368; [1995] Fam. Law 124, CA (Civ Div) 18–016
R. v Slough Justices Ex p. Lindsay; sub nom. R. v Petty Sessional Divisions of Slough and
Windsor Ex p. Lindsay [1997] 1 F.L.R. 695; [1997] 2 F.C.R. 636; [1997] Fam. Law
322; (1997) 161 J.P.N. 648; (1996) 140 S.J.L.B. 239, QBD 14–017
R. v Somerset CC Ex p. Prospects Care Services Ltd [2000] 1 F.L.R. 636; (1999) 2 C.C.L.
Rep. 161; [1999] C.O.D. 268, QBD 21–085
R. v Tameside MBC Ex p. J (A Child) [2000] 1 F.L.R. 942; [2000] 1 F.C.R. 173; (2000) 3
C.C.L. Rep. 402; [2000] Fam. Law 90, QBD 21–013, 21–067
R. v Tower Hamlets LBC Ex p. Begum (Ferdous); R. v Tower Hamlets LBC Ex p. Rahman
(Luftur) [1993] Q.B. 447; [1993] 2 W.L.R. 9; [1993] 1 All E.R. 447; (1992) 24 H.L.R.
715, CA (Civ Div) 21–015
R. v Tower Hamlets LBC Ex p. Byas (1992) 25 H.L.R. 109 21–015
R. v W (Stephen) (1993) 14 Cr. App. R. (S.) 256; [1992] Crim. L.R. 905, CA (Crim Div) 9–004
R. v Wallwork (William Evans) (1958) 42 Cr. App. R. 153; (1958) 122 J.P. 299, CCA ... 21–064
R. v Wandsworth LBC Ex p. Hawthorne [1994] 1 W.L.R. 1442; [1995] 2 All E.R. 331;
[1995] 2 F.L.R. 238; [1995] 1 F.C.R. 539; (1995) 27 H.L.R. 59; 93 L.G.R. 20; [1995]
C.O.D. 70; [1995] Fam. Law 608; (1994) 158 L.G. Rev. 961, (1994) 91(37) L.S.G. 50;
(1994) 138 S.J.L.B. 178; [1994] N.P.C. 107; (1994) 68 P. & C.R. D11, CA (Civ Div) 6–037
R. v Watling [2007] EWCA Crim 2307 9–005
R. v Wealden DC Ex p. Wales [1995] N.P.C. 145 .... 21–009, 21–085
R. v Woods (1921) 85 S.J. 272 17–017
R. v Yacoob (David Shik) (1981) 72 Cr. App. R. 313; [1981] Crim. L.R. 248, CA (Crim
Div) 2–003, 2–015
R v United Kingdom (A/136-E) [1988] 2 F.L.R. 445; (1991) 13 E.H.R.R. 457, ECHR 21–001,
21–004
R. (on the application of A) v Enfield LBC [2002] 2 F.L.R. 1, QBD 21–009
R. (on the application of A) v Lambeth LBC; sub nom. R. v Lambeth LBC Ex p. A; A v
Lambeth LBC [2001] EWCA Civ 1624; [2002] 1 F.L.R. 353; [2001] 3 F.C.R. 673;
[2002] H.L.R. 13; [2002] B.L.G.R. 163; (2001) 4 C.C.L. Rep. 486; (2002) 64 B.M.L.R.
88; [2002] A.C.D. 18; [2002] Fam. Law 179; [2001] N.P.C. 158, CA (Civ Div) 21–009
R. (on the application of Anton) v Secretary of State for the Home Department [2004]
EWHC 2730; [2005] 2 F.L.R. 818; [2005] Fam. Law 442, QBD (Admin) 18–052
R. (on the application of Axon) v Secretary of State for Health [2006] EWHC 37 (Admin);
[2006] Q.B. 539; [2006] 2 W.L.R. 1130; [2006] 2 F.L.R. 206; [2006] 1 F.C.R. 175;
[2006] H.R.L.R. 12; (2006) 88 B.M.L.R. 96; [2006] A.C.D. 58; [2006] Fam. Law 272;
(2006) 103(8) L.S.G. 25, QBD (Admin) 16–011, 16–013, 16–014, 17–015
R. (on the application of B) v Medway Council; sub nom. R. (on the application of BG) v
Medway Council [2005] EWHC 1932; [2006] 1 F.L.R. 663; [2005] 3 F.C.R. 199;
[2006] H.L.R. 6; (2005) 8 C.C.L. Rep. 448; [2006] Fam. Law 97, QBD (Admin) 21–085
R. (on the application of Baiai) v Secretary of State for the Home Department; R. (on the
application of Trzcinska) v Secretary of State for the Home Department; R. (on the
application of Tilki) v Secretary of State for the Home Department; R. (on the
application of Bigoku) v Secretary of State for the Home Department [2007] EWCA
Civ 478; [2007] 3 W.L.R. 573; [2007] 4 All E.R. 199; [2007] 2 F.L.R. 627; [2007] 2
F.C.R. 421; [2007] H.R.L.R. 29; [2007] U.K.H.R.R. 771; [2007] Fam. Law 806; (2007)
104(23) L.S.G. 33; (2007) 151 S.J.L.B. 711, CA (Civ Div) 1–015

R. (on the application of Begum) v Denbigh High School Governors; sub nom. R. (on the application of SB) v Denbigh High School Governors [2006] UKHL 15; [2007] 1 A.C. 100; [2006] 2 W.L.R. 719; [2006] 2 All E.R. 487; [2006] 1 F.C.R. 613; [2006] H.R.L.R. 21; [2006] U.K.H.R.R. 708; 23 B.H.R.C. 276; [2006] E.L.R. 273; (2006) 103(14) L.S.G. 29; (2006) 156 N.L.J. 552, HL 16–018, 16–023

R. (on the application of Berhe) v Hillingdon LBC; R. (on the application of Kidane) v Hillingdon LBC; R. (on the application of Munir) v Hillingdon LBC; R. (on the application of Ncube) v Hillingdon LBC; sub nom. R. (on the application of Behre) v Hillingdon LBC [2003] EWHC 2075; [2004] 1 F.L.R. 439; (2003) 6 C.C.L. Rep. 471; [2003] Fam. Law 872; (2003) 100(39) L.S.G. 38, QBD (Admin) 21–012, 21–068, 21–085

R. (on the application of CD) v Isle of Anglesey CC; sub nom. CD (A Child) v Isle of Anglesey CC [2004] EWHC 1635; [2005] 1 F.L.R. 59; [2004] 3 F.C.R. 171; (2004) 7 C.C.L. Rep. 589; [2004] Fam. Law 865, QBD (Admin) 21–085

R. (on the application of Conville) v Richmond upon Thames LBC; sub nom.: Conville v Richmond upon Thames LBC [2006] EWCA Civ 718; [2006] 1 W.L.R. 2808; [2006] 4 All E.R. 917; [2006] H.L.R. 45; (2006) 103(25) L.S.G. 30; (2006) 150 S.J.L.B. 811; [2006] N.P.C. 70, CA (Civ Div) 6–037

R. (on the application of Cowl) v Plymouth City Council; sub nom. Cowl v Plymouth City Council; Cowl (Practice Note), Re [2001] EWCA Civ 1935; [2002] 1 W.L.R. 803; [2002] C.P. Rep. 18; (2002) 5 C.C.L. Rep. 42; [2002] A.C.D. 11; [2002] Fam. Law 265; (2002) 99(8) L.S.G. 35; (2002) 146 S.J.L.B. 27, CA (Civ Div) .,..................... 21–085

R. (on the application of the Crown Prosecution Service) v Registrar General of Births, Deaths and Marriages; sub nom. J and B, Re [2002] EWCA Civ 1661; [2003] Q.B. 1222; [2003] 2 W.L.R. 504; [2003] 1 All E.R. 540; [2003] 1 F.C.R. 110; [2003] Prison L.R. 100; (2003) 100(3) L.S.G. 33, CA (Civ Div) 3–039

R. (on the application of Daly) v Secretary of State for the Home Department; sub nom. R. v Secretary of State for the Home Department Ex p. Daly [2001] UKHL 26; [2001] 2 A.C. 532; [2001] 2 W.L.R. 1622; [2001] 3 All E.R. 433; [2001] H.R.L.R. 49; [2001] U.K.H.R.R. 887; [2001] A.C.D. 79; (2001) 98(26) L.S.G. 43; (2001) 145 S.J.L.B. 156, HL 21–085

R. (on the application of Davies) v Commissioners Office [2008] EWHC 334, QBD (Admin) 15–021

R. (on the application of Denson) v Child Support Agency [2002] EWHC 154; [2002] 1 F.L.R. 938; [2002] 1 F.C.R. 460; [2002] Fam. Law 516, QBD (Admin) 15–024

R. (on the application of G) v Barnet LBC; R. (on the application of W) v Lambeth LBC; R. (on the application of A) v Lambeth LBC [2003] UKHL 57; [2004] 2 A.C. 208; [2003] 3 W.L.R. 1194; [2004] 1 All E.R. 97; [2004] 1 F.L.R. 454; [2003] 3 F.C.R. 419; [2004] H.R.L.R. 4; [2004] H.L.R. 10; [2003] B.L.G.R. 569; (2003) 6 C.C.L. Rep. 500; [2004] Fam. Law 21; (2003) 100(45) L.S.G. 29; [2003] N.P.C. 123, HL ..6–036, 6–039, 21–085, 22–023

R (on the application of G) v Nottingham CC [2008] EWHC 400 21–014

R. (on the application of G) v Barnet LBC; R. (on the application of W) v Lambeth LBC; R. (on the application of A) v Lambeth LBC [2003] UKHL 57; [2004] 2 A.C. 208; [2003] 3 W.L.R. 1194; [2004] 1 All E.R. 97; [2004] 1 F.L.R. 454; [2003] 3 F.C.R. 419; [2004] H.R.L.R. 4; [2004] H.L.R. 10; [2003] B.L.G.R. 569; (2003) 6 C.C.L. Rep. 500; [2004] Fam. Law 21; (2003) 100(45) L.S.G. 29; [2003] N.P.C. 123, HL 21–009

R. (on the application of the Howard League for Penal Reform) v Secretary of State for the Home Department (No.2) [2002] EWHC 2497; [2003] 1 F.L.R. 484; (2003) 6 C.C.L. Rep. 47; [2003] Fam. Law 149; (2003) 100(3) L.S.G. 30; (2003) 147 S.J.L.B. 61, QBD (Admin) 21–003

R. (on the application of Howes) v Child Support Commissioners [2007] EWHC 559 (admin); [2007] Fam. Law 980, QBD (Admin) 15–021

R. (on the application of Isiko) v Secretary of State for the Home Department; sub nom. Secretary of State for the Home Department v Isiko; R. v Secretary of State for the Home Department Ex p. Isiko [2001] 1 F.L.R. 930; [2001] 1 F.C.R. 633; [2001] H.R.L.R. 15; [2001] U.K.H.R.R. 385; [2001] Imm. A.R. 291; [2001] I.N.L.R. 175; [2001] A.C.D. 39; [2001] Fam. Law 419, CA (Civ Div) 18–016

R. (on the application of J) v Caerphilly CBC [2005] EWHC 586; [2005] 2 F.L.R. 860; [2005] 2 F.C.R. 153; (2005) 8 C.C.L. Rep. 255; [2005] A.C.D. 80; [2005] Fam. Law 611; [2005] Fam. Law 528, QBD (Admin) 21–071

R. (on the application of J) v West Sussex CC; sub nom. J v West Sussex CC [2002] EWHC
1143; [2002] 2 F.L.R. 1192; [2003] Fam. Law 22, QBD (Admin) 21–028
R. (on the application of Kehoe) v Secretary of State for Work and Pensions; sub nom.
Secretary of State for Work and Pensions v Kehoe; Kehoe v Secretary of State for
Work and Pensions [2005] UKHL 48; [2006] 1 A.C. 42; [2005] 3 W.L.R. 252; [2005]
4 All E.R. 905; [2005] 2 F.L.R. 1249; [2005] 2 F.C.R. 683; [2005] H.R.L.R. 30; [2006]
U.K.H.R.R. 360; [2005] Fam. Law 850; (2005) 155 N.L.J. 1123; (2005) 149 S.J.L.B.
921, HL 15–001, 15–006, 15–025, 17–028, 18–058
R. (on the application of L (A Child)) v Manchester City Council; R. (on the application of
R (A Child)) v Manchester City Council [2001] EWHC Admin 707; [2002] 1 F.L.R.
43; (2002) 5 C.C.L. Rep. 268; [2002] A.C.D. 45; [2002] Fam. Law 13, QBD (Admin) 21–058,
21–068, 21–086
R. (on the application of M) v Gateshead MBC [2006] EWCA Civ 221; [2006] Q.B. 650;
[2006] 3 W.L.R. 108; [2006] 2 F.L.R. 379; (2006) 9 C.C.L. Rep. 337; [2006] Fam. Law
444; (2006) 103(13) L.S.G. 25; [2006] N.P.C. 31, CA (Civ Div) 21–077
R. (on the application of M) v Islington LBC; sub nom. M v Islington LBC [2004] EWCA
Civ 235; [2005] 1 W.L.R. 884; [2004] 4 All E.R. 709; [2004] 2 F.L.R. 867; [2004] 2
F.C.R. 363; [2004] B.L.G.R. 815; (2004) 7 C.C.L. Rep. 230; [2004] Fam. Law 645, CA
(Civ Div) 6–036
R. (on the application of Mellor) v Secretary of State for the Home Department; sub nom.
R. v Secretary of State for the Home Department Ex p. Mellor [2001] EWCA Civ 472;
[2002] Q.B. 13; [2001] 3 W.L.R. 533; [2001] 2 F.L.R. 1158; [2001] 2 F.C.R. 153;
[2001] H.R.L.R. 38; (2001) 59 B.M.L.R. 1; [2001] Fam. Law 736; (2001) 98(22)
L.S.G. 35; (2001) 145 S.J.L.B. 117, CA (Civ Div) 22–074
R. (on the application of National Association of Guardians ad Litem and Reporting
Officers) v Children and Family Court Advisory and Support Service [2001] EWHC
Admin 693; [2002] 1 F.L.R. 255; [2002] A.C.D. 44; [2001] Fam. Law 877, QBD
(Admin) 18–010
R. (on the application of O) v Haringey LBC [2004] EWCA Civ 535; [2004] 2 F.L.R. 476;
[2004] 2 F.C.R. 219; [2004] H.L.R. 44; [2004] B.L.G.R. 672; (2004) 7 C.C.L. Rep.
310; [2004] Fam. Law 634, CA (Civ Div) 21–009
R. (on the application of Plymouth City Council) v HM Coroner for Devon; sub nom.
Plymouth City Council v County of Devon Coroner [2005] EWHC 1014; [2005] 2
F.L.R. 1279; [2005] 2 F.C.R. 428; [2005] A.C.D. 83; [2005] Fam. Law 699, QBD
(Admin) 21–033
R. (on the application of Qazi (Hamid)) v Secretary of State for Work and Pensions [2004]
EWHC 1331, QBD (Admin) 15–020
R. (on the application of Rose) v Secretary of State for Health; sub nom. Rose v Secretary
of State for Health [2002] EWHC 1593; [2002] 2 F.L.R. 962; [2002] 3 F.C.R. 731;
[2002] U.K.H.R.R. 1329; (2003) 69 B.M.L.R. 83; [2003] A.C.D. 6; [2003] Fam. Law
19; (2002) 99(39) L.S.G. 38, QBD (Admin) 22–002, 22–080
R. (on the application of S) v Haringey LBC; sub nom. S v Haringey LBC (Habeas Corpus)
[2003] EWHC 2734; [2004] 1 F.L.R. 590; [2004] Fam. Law 100; (2004) 101(1) L.S.G.
21, QBD (Admin) 21–049, 21–078
R (on the application of S) v Sutton LBC [2007] 2 F.L.R. 849, QBD 21–010
R. (on the application of S) v Swindon BC; sub nom. R. v Swindon BC Ex p. S; S (Sexual
Abuse Allegations: Local Authority Response), Re [2001] EWHC Admin 334; [2001]
2 F.L.R. 776; [2001] 3 F.C.R. 702; [2001] B.L.G.R. 318; [2001] Fam. Law 659, QBD
(Admin) 21–004, 21–022, 21–036
R. (on the application of S) v Wandsworth LBC [2001] EWHC Admin 709; [2002] 1 F.L.R.
469; (2001) 4 C.C.L. Rep. 466; [2002] Fam. Law 180, QBD (Admin) 21–015
R. (on the application of Spink) v Wandsworth LBC [2005] EWCA Civ 302; [2005] 1
W.L.R. 2884; [2005] 2 All E.R. 954; [2005] 1 F.C.R. 608; [2005] H.L.R. 41; [2005]
B.L.G.R. 561; (2005) 8 C.C.L. Rep. 272; (2005) 84 B.M.L.R. 169; (2005) 102(19)
L.S.G. 34; (2005) 149 S.J.L.B. 390, CA (Civ Div) 21–006
R. (on the application of Sturton) v Office of the Social Security and Child Support
Commissioners [2007] EWHC 2957 (Admin), QBD (Admin) 15–021
R. (on the application of Thomson) v Minister of State for Childrenub nom. R. (on the
application of Charlton Thomson) v Secretary of State for Education and Skills [2005]
EWHC 1378; [2006] 1 F.L.R. 175; [2005] 2 F.C.R. 603; [2005] Fam. Law 861, QBD
(Admin) 22–050

R. (on the application of W) v Lambeth LBC [2002] EWCA Civ 613; [2002] 2 All E.R. 901;
[2002] 2 F.L.R. 327; [2002] 2 F.C.R. 289; [2002] H.L.R. 41; [2002] B.L.G.R. 351;
(2002) 5 C.C.L. Rep. 203; [2002] Fam. Law 592; (2002) 146 S.J.L.B. 125, CA (Civ
Div) 21–009
R. (on the application of Williamson) v Secretary of State for Education and Employment;
sub nom. Williamson v Secretary of State for Education and Employment [2005]
UKHL 15; [2005] 2 A.C. 246; [2005] 2 W.L.R. 590; [2005] 2 All E.R. 1; [2005] 2
F.L.R. 374; [2005] 1 F.C.R. 498; [2005] H.R.L.R. 14; [2005] U.K.H.R.R. 339; 19
B.H.R.C. 99; [2005] E.L.R. 291; [2005] Fam. Law 456; (2005) 102(16) L.S.G. 27;
(2005) 155 N.L.J. 324; (2005) 149 S.J.L.B. 266, HL 16–017, 16–018, 17–017, 17–018
RJ (Foster Placement), Re; sub nom. R-J (Minors) (Fostering: Person Disqualified), Re
[1999] 1 W.L.R. 581; [1999] 1 F.L.R. 605; [1998] 3 F.C.R. 579; [1999] Fam. Law 19;
(1998) 95(39) L.S.G. 34; (1998) 148 N.L.J. 1550; (1998) 142 S.J.L.B. 259, CA (Civ
Div) 18–036
RJ (Wardship), Re [1999] 1 F.L.R. 619 .... 18–036, 18–052
RP v RP [2006] EWHC 3409 (Fam); [2007] 1 F.L.R. 2105; [2007] Fam. Law 581, Fam
Div 13–052, 13–053, 13–057
Rafiq v Muse [2000] 1 F.L.R. 820; [2000] Fam. Law 396, CA (Civ Div) 9–035
Rajabally v Rajabally [1987] 2 F.L.R. 390; [1987] Fam. Law 314, CA (Civ Div) 7–022
Rampal v Rampal (Ancillary Relief); sub nom. Rampal v Rampal (No.2) [2001] EWCA Civ
989; [2002] Fam. 85; [2001] 3 W.L.R. 795; [2001] 2 F.L.R. 1179; [2001] 2 F.C.R. 552;
[2001] Fam. Law 731; (2001) 98(29) L.S.G. 37; (2001) 151 N.L.J. 1006; (2001) 145
S.J.L.B. 165, CA (Civ Div) 2–056, 13–014, 13–084
Ramsden v Dyson; Ramsden v Thornton (1866) L.R. 1 H.L. 129, HL 5–032
Randall v Randall [2004] EWHC 2258; [2005] W.T.L.R. 119; (2004–05) 7 I.T.E.L.R. 340;
[2005] 1 P. & C.R. DG4, Ch D 5–055
Ranson v Ranson (Ancillary Relief) [2001] EWCA Civ 1929; [2002] 1 F.C.R. 261, CA (Civ
Div) 14–009
Ratcliffe v Ratcliffe [1962] 1 W.L.R. 1455; [1962] 3 All E.R. 993; (1962) 106 S.J. 900,
CA 3–032
Raval, Re [1998] 2 F.L.R. 718; [1998] B.P.I.R. 389; [1998] Fam. Law 590, Ch D 5–059
Rawlings v Rawlings [1964] P. 398; [1964] 3 W.L.R. 294; [1964] 2 All E.R. 804; (1964) 108
S.J. 424, CA 5–046
Rees v United Kingdom (A/106); sub nom. Rees v United Kingdom (9532/81) [1987] 2
F.L.R. 111; [1993] 2 F.C.R. 49; (1987) 9 E.H.R.R. 56; [1987] Fam. Law 157, ECHR 2–018
Regan v Regan [1977] 1 W.L.R. 84; [1977] 1 All E.R. 428; 75 L.G.R. 257; (1976) 7 Fam.
Law 17; (1977) 121 S.J. 84, Fam Div 13–117
Reiterbund v Reiterbund [1975] Fam. 99; [1975] 2 W.L.R. 375; [1975] 1 All E.R. 280;
(1974) 118 S.J. 831, CA (Civ Div) 6–03, 10–043
Richards v Richards [1972] 1 W.L.R. 1073; [1972] 3 All E.R. 695; (1972) 116 S.J. 599, Fam
Div 10–015
Richards v Richards [1984] A.C. 174; [1983] 3 W.L.R. 173; [1983] 2 All E.R. 807; (1984)
12 H.L.R. 68; (1983) 13 Fam. Law 256, HL 3–010, 9–007, 19–001, 19–002
Richardson v Richardson [1989] Fam. 95; [1989] 3 W.L.R. 865; [1989] 3 All E.R. 779;
[1990] 1 F.L.R. 186; [1990] F.C.R. 232; (1990) 154 J.P.N. 233, Fam Div 14–010, 18–056,
20–005
Richardson v Richardson (No.1) [1994] 1 W.L.R. 186; [1994] 1 W.L.R. 187; [1993] 4 All
E.R. 673; [1994] 1 F.L.R. 286; [1994] 1 F.C.R. 53; [1994] Fam. Law 188, Fam Div 13–097
Richardson v Richardson (No.2) [1996] 2 F.L.R. 617; [1997] 2 F.C.R. 453; [1997] Fam.
Law 14, CA (Civ Div) 13–058, 13–062, 13–089, 15–041
Rickards v Rickards [1990] Fam. 194; [1989] 3 W.L.R. 748; [1989] 3 All E.R. 193; [1990]
1 F.L.R. 125; [1990] F.C.R. 409; (1990) 154 J.P.N. 346; (1989) 86(41) L.S.G. 39;
(1989) 139 N.L.J. 899, CA (Civ Div) 13–103
Ritchie v Ritchie [1996] 1 F.L.R. 898; [1996] 3 F.C.R. 609, CA (Civ Div) 13–104
Ritchie v Ritchie, unreported, August 17, 2007 ....5–012, 5–015, 5–029
Roberts (Deceased), Re [1978] 1 W.L.R. 653; [1978] 3 All E.R. 225; (1978) 122 S.J. 264,
CA (Civ Div) 2–002, 2–005
Robertson v Robertson (1983) 4 F.L.R. 387; (1982) 12 Fam. Law 181, Fam Div 13–076
Robins v Robins [1907] 2 K.B. 13, KBD 14–002
Robinson, Re (1884) L.R. 27 Ch. D. 160, CA 14–002
Robinson v Murray; sub nom. Murray v Robinson [2005] EWCA Civ 935; [2006] 1 F.L.R.
365; [2005] 3 F.C.R. 504; [2005] Fam. Law 859, CA (Civ Div) 9–037, 9–038

SC (A Minor) (Leave to Seek Residence Order), Re [1994] 1 F.L.R. 96; [1994] 1 F.C.R. 609; [1993] Fam. Law 618, Fam Div 18–035, 18–038

SH (Care Order: Orphan), Re [1995] 1 F.L.R. 746; [1996] 1 F.C.R. 1; (1995) 159 J.P.N. 757, Fam Div 17–042

SK (An Adult) (Forced Marriage: Appropriate Relief), Re; sub nom. SK (Proposed Plaintiff), Re [2004] EWHC 3202; [2006] 1 W.L.R. 81; [2005] 3 All E.R. 421; [2005] 2 F.L.R. 230; [2005] 2 F.C.R. 459; [2005] Fam. Law 460, Fam Div 2–043

SW v RC [2008] EWHC 73, Fam Div 15–052

SW (A Minor) (Wardship: Jurisdiction), Re [1986] 1 F.L.R. 24; [1985] Fam. Law 322 18–030

SY v SY (otherwise W); sub nom. S v S; Symonds v Symonds [1963] P. 37; [1962] 3 W.L.R. 526; [1962] 3 All E.R. 55; (1962) 106 S.J. 467, CA 2–025, 2–026

Sahin v Germany (30943/96) [2002] 1 F.L.R. 119; [2002] 3 F.C.R. 321; (2003) 36 E.H.R.R. 43; [2002] Fam. Law 94, ECHR 16–017, 17–024, 17–035, 19–011, 20–025

Salgueiro da Silva Mouta v Portugal (33290/96) [2001] 1 F.C.R. 653; (2001) 31 E.H.R.R. 47; 2001 Fam. L.R. 2, ECHR 19–004, 19–006

Salmon (Deceased), Re; sub nom. Coard v National Westminster Bank Ltd [1981] Ch. 167; [1980] 3 W.L.R. 748; [1980] 3 All E.R. 532; (1980) 124 S.J. 813, Ch D 7–011

Samuel's Trustee v Samuel (1975) 233 E.G. 149 3–008

Sanctuary Housing Association v Campbell [1999] 1 W.L.R. 1279; [1999] 3 All E.R. 460; [1999] 2 F.L.R. 383; [1999] 2 F.C.R. 657; (2000) 32 H.L.R. 100; [1999] L. & T.R. 425; [1999] 2 E.G.L.R. 20; [1999] Fam. Law 449; (1999) 149 N.L.J. 521; [1999] N.P.C. 39; (1999) 78 P. & C.R. D15, CA (Civ Div) 3–013

Sanderson v McManus; sub nom. S v M (A Minor: Access Order); Sanderson v MacManus, 1997 S.C. (H.L.) 55; 1997 S.L.T. 629; 1997 S.C.L.R. 281; [1997] 1 F.L.R. 980; 1997 G.W.D. 6–220, HL 17–024

Sandford v Sandford [1986] 1 F.L.R. 412; [1986] Fam. Law 104, CA (Civ Div) 13–091

Sansom v Sansom [1966] P. 52 11–004

Santos v Santos [1972] Fam. 247; [1972] 2 W.L.R. 889; [1972] 2 All E.R. 246; (1972) 116 S.J. 196, CA (Civ Div) 3–004, 10–035, 10–037, 10–038, 10–039

Savage v Dunningham [1974] Ch. 181; [1973] 3 W.L.R. 471; [1973] 3 All E.R. 429; (1973) 26 P. & C.R. 177; (1973) 117 S.J. 697, Ch D 5–022

Savill v Goodall [1993] 1 F.L.R. 755; [1994] 1 F.C.R. 325; (1993) 25 H.L.R. 588; [1993] Fam. Law 289; [1992] N.P.C. 153, CA (Civ Div) 5–027

Scheeres v Scheeres [1999] 1 F.L.R. 241; [1999] F.C.R. 476; [1999] Fam. Law 18, CA (Civ Div) 13–072

Scott v Scott (otherwise Fone) [1959] P. 103 (Note); [1959] 2 W.L.R. 497 (Note); [1959] 1 All E.R. 531; (1959) 103 S.J. 313, PDAD 2–032

Scott v Sebright; sub nom. Scott (otherwise Sebright) v Sebright (1887) L.R. 12 P.D. 21, PDAD 2–038, 2–039

Scott v United Kingdom (34745/97) [2000] 1 F.L.R. 958; [2000] 2 F.C.R. 560; 2000 Fam. L.R. 102; [2000] Fam. Law 538, ECHR 19–022, 21–025, 21–039, 22–034, 22–042

Seaford, Re; sub nom. Seaford v Seifert [1968] P. 53; [1968] 2 W.L.R. 155; [1968] 1 All E.R. 482; (1967) 111 S.J. 981, CA (Civ Div) 7–004

Sears Tooth v Payne Hicks Beach [1997] 2 F.L.R. 116; [1998] 1 F.C.R. 231; [1997] Fam. Law 392; (1997) 94(5) L.S.G. 32; (1997) 141 S.J.L.B. 37, Fam Div 13–037

Secretary of State for Social Security v Harmon; Secretary of State for Social Security v Carter; Secretary of State for Social Security v Cocks [1999] 1 W.L.R. 163; [1998] 2 F.L.R. 598; [1999] 1 F.C.R. 213; [1998] Fam. Law 519; (1999) 163 J.P.N. 192; (1998) 95(25) L.S.G. 32; (1998) 142 S.J.L.B. 183, CA (Civ Div) 15–012

Secretary of State for Work and Pensions v Jones [2003] EWHC 2163; [2004] 1 F.L.R. 282; [2003] Fam. Law 881; (2003) 100(35) L.S.G. 34, Fam Div 15–008, 17–008

Secretary of State for Work and Pensions v Roach [2006] EWCA Civ 1746 15–012

Sekhon v Alissa [1989] 2 F.L.R. 94; [1989] Fam. Law 355, Ch D 5–014

Shah v Baverstock [2008] 1 P. & C.R. DG3, CC (Bournemouth) 5–012, 5–024

Shaw v DPP [2005] EWHC 1215, QBD 9–040

Shaw v Fitzgerald [1992] 1 F.L.R. 357; [1992] F.C.R. 162 3–041

Shaw v Shaw [1954] 2 Q.B. 429; [1954] 3 W.L.R. 265; [1954] 2 All E.R. 638; (1954) 98 S.J. 509, CA 2–056

Shearn v Shearn [1931] P. 1, PDAD 13–018

Sheffield and Horsham v United Kingdom [1998] 2 F.L.R. 928 2–018

Sheffield City Council v E; sub nom. E (Alleged Patient), Re [2004] EWHC 2808 (Fam);
[2005] Fam. 326; [2005] 2 W.L.R. 953; [2005] 1 F.L.R. 965; [2005] Lloyd's Rep. Med.
223; [2005] Fam. Law 279; (2005) 102(9) L.S.G. 30, Fam Div 2–036, 3–003
Sheffield CC v V (Legal Services Commission Intervening) [2007] 1 F.L.R. 279, Fam Div ... 21–043
Shorthouse v Shorthouse (1898) 78 L.T. 687 13–018
Sichel v Lambert (1864) 15 C.B. (N.S.) 781; 143 E.R. 992 1–045
Sidaway v Board of Governors of the Bethlem Royal Hospital [1985] A.C. 871; [1985] 2
W.L.R. 480; [1985] 1 All E.R. 643; (1985) 82 L.S.G. 1256; (1985) 135 N.L.J. 203;
(1985) 129 S.J. 154, HL 16–012
Sillett v Meek [2007] EWHC 1169, Ch D 5–062
Silver v Silver [1958] 1 W.L.R. 259; [1958] 1 All E.R. 523; (1958) 102 S.J. 174, CA 2–042, 5–016
Silverwood v Silverwood (1997) 74 P. & C.R. 453; (1997) 74 P. & C.R. D9, CA (Civ Div) ... 5–016
Simpson v Simpson [1992] 1 F.L.R. 601; [1989] Fam. Law 20, Ch D 3–028, 5–063
Singer v Sharegin [1984] F.L.R. 114 13–012
Singh v Bhakar & Bhakar [2007] 1 F.L.R. 880 .... 9–038, 9–039
Singh v Singh [1971] P. 226; [1971] 2 W.L.R. 963; [1971] 2 All E.R. 828; (1971) 115 S.J.
205, CA (Civ Div) 2–026, 2–040, 2–041
Singh (Pawandeep) v Entry Clearance Officer (New Delhi) [2004] EWCA Civ 1075; [2005]
Q.B. 608; [2005] 2 W.L.R. 325; [2005] 1 F.L.R. 308; [2004] 3 F.C.R. 72; [2004] Imm.
A.R. 672; [2004] I.N.L.R. 515; [2005] Fam. Law 9; (2004) 101(36) L.S.G. 33, CA (Civ
Div) 22–001, 22–046
Sivyer (Deceased), Re; sub nom. Sivyer v Sivyer [1967] 1 W.L.R. 1482; [1967] 3 All E.R.
429, Ch D 7–008, 7–019
Slater v Simm [2007] EWHC 951 (Ch); [2007] W.T.L.R. 1043, Ch D 5–010, 5–016
Slater v Slater [1953] P. 235; [1953] 2 W.L.R. 170; [1953] 1 All E.R. 246; (1953) 97 S.J.
46, CA 2–051
Sledmore v Dalby (1996) 72 P. & C.R. 196; [1996] N.P.C. 16, CA (Civ Div) 5–035
Smallman v Smallman [1972] Fam. 25; [1971] 3 W.L.R. 588; [1971] 3 All E.R. 717; (1971)
115 S.J. 527, CA (Civ Div) 13–004
Smith v McInerney [1994] 2 F.L.R. 1077; [1994] 2 F.C.R. 1086; [1995] Fam. Law 10, Fam
Div 13–008
Smith v Smith (1973) 4 Fam. Law 24; (1973) 118 S.J. 184, Fam Div 10–023
Smith v Smith; sub nom. Smith (Deceased), Re [1992] Fam. 69; [1991] 3 W.L.R. 646;
[1991] 2 All E.R. 306; [1991] 2 F.L.R. 432; [1991] F.C.R. 791; [1991] Fam. Law 412;
(1991) 141 N.L.J. 309, CA (Civ Div) 7–026, 13–103, 13–106
Smith v Smith; sub nom. Smith v Secretary of State for Work and Pensions [2006] UKHL
35; [2006] 1 W.L.R. 2024; [2006] 3 All E.R. 907; [2007] 1 F.L.R. 166; [2006] 2 F.C.R.
487; [2006] Fam. Law 834; (2006) 103(30) L.S.G. 31; (2006) 150 S.J.L.B. 986, HL 13–122,
15–016
Smith v Smith [2007] Fam.Law 795 13–075
Smith (Letitia) v Smith (Richard) [2000] 3 F.C.R. 374, CA (Civ Div) 13–008
Snoeck (Deceased), Re [1982] 13 F.L.R. 18 7–024
Snowman (otherwise Bensinger) v Snowman [1934] P. 186, PDAD 2–025
Society of Lloyd's v Khan; sub nom. Lloyd's of London v Khan [1999] 1 F.L.R. 246; [1998]
3 F.C.R. 93; [1999] Fam. Law 92; (1998) 162 J.P.N. 321, QBD (Comm) 5–056
Soderback v Sweden [1999] 1 F.L.R. 250; (2000) 29 E.H.R.R. 95; 1999 Fam. L.R. 104;
[1998] H.R.C.D. 958; [1999] Fam. Law 87, ECHR 22–034, 22–059
Solicitor (Wasted Costs Order), Re [1993] 2 F.L.R. 959; [1993] Fam. Law 627; (1993) 137
S.J.L.B. 107, CA (Civ Div) 13–064
Sommerfield v Germany [2002] 1 F.L.R. 119 16–020
Sorrell v Sorrell [2005] EWHC 1717 (Fam); [2006] 1 F.L.R. 497; [2006] 1 F.C.R. 75; [2006]
Fam. Law 12, Fam Div 13–079, 13–080, 13–083
Soulsbury v Soulsbury [2007] EWCA Civ 969; [2007] 3 F.C.R. 811; [2007] W.T.L.R. 1841,
CA (Civ Div) 13–004
South Glamorgan CC v B; sub nom. South Glamorgan CC v W and B [1993] 1 F.C.R. 626;
[1993] Fam. Law 398 .... 16–019, 18–049
South Place Ethical Society, Re; sub nom. Barralet v Attorney General [1980] 1 W.L.R.
1565; [1980] 3 All E.R. 918; 54 T.C. 446; [1980] T.R. 217; (1980) 124 S.J. 774, Ch
D 1–040
Southwark LBC v B. *See* DB and CB (Minors), Re
Southwark LBC v D [2007] 1 F.L.R. 2181, CA 21–012, 21–068

Spence (Deceased), Re; sub nom. Spence v Dennis [1990] Ch. 652; [1990] 2 W.L.R. 1430;
  [1990] 2 All E.R. 827; [1990] 2 F.L.R. 278; [1990] F.C.R. 983, CA (Civ Div) 2–003, 2–055,
          17–031, 17–032
Springette v Defoe [1992] 2 F.L.R. 388; [1992] 2 F.C.R. 561; (1992) 24 H.L.R. 552; (1993)
  65 P. & C.R. 1; [1992] Fam. Law 489; [1992] N.P.C. 34, CA (Civ Div) 5–011, 5–015, 5–020,
          5–021, 5–024, 5–026, 5–028
Stack v Dowden; sub nom. Dowden v Stack ....[2007] UKHL 17; [2007] 2 W.L.R. 831; [2007] 2 All
          E.R. 929; [2007] 1 F.L.R. 1858; [2007] 2 F.C.R. 280; [2007] B.P.I.R. 913; [2007]
          W.T.L.R. 1053; (2006–07) 9 I.T.E.L.R. 815; [2007] Fam. Law 593; [2007] 18
          E.G. 153 (C.S.); (2007) 157 N.L.J. 634; (2007) 151 S.J.L.B. 575; [2007]
          N.P.C. 47; [2007] 2 P. & C.R. DG11; [2007] 2 A.C. 432, HL 5–001, 5–010,
          5–011, 5–012, 5–013, 5–014, 5–016, 5–018, 5–022, 5–023, 5–024, 5–026,
          5–028, 5–029, 5–030, 5–031, 5–037, 5–047, 5–064
Staffordshire CC v B [1998] 1 F.L.R. 261; [1999] 2 F.C.R. 333; [1998] Fam. Law 8, Ch D ... 22–006
Stallwood v Tredger (1815) 2 Phill. Ecc. 287; 161 E.R. 1147 1–005
Standen v Standen (1791) Peake 45; 170 E.R. 73 1–005
Staples v Lee [1998] 1 F.L.R. 138 5–055
Stewart v Engel (Permission to Amend) [2000] 1 W.L.R. 2268; [2000] 3 All E.R. 518;
  [2001] C.P. Rep. 9; [2001] E.C.D.R. 25, CA (Civ Div) 13–009
Stock v Brown [1994] 1 F.L.R. 840; [1994] 2 F.C.R. 1125; [1994] Fam. Law 254, Fam
  Div 7–011
Stocker v Stocker [1966] 1 W.L.R. 190 2–049
Stockford v Stockford [1981] 3 F.L.R. 58 3–017
Stockholm Finance Ltd v Garden Holdings Inc [1995] N.P.C. 162, Ch D 5–051
Stockport MBC v B; Stockport MBC v L [1986] 2 F.L.R. 80; [1986] Fam. Law 187, Fam
  Div 18–006
Stoeckert v Geddes (No.2); sub nom. Stoekert v Geddes (No.2) [2004] UKPC 54; (2004–05)
  7 I.T.E.L.R. 506; (2005) 149 S.J.L.B. 57, PC (Jam) 5–062, 5–063
Stokes v Anderson [1991] 1 F.L.R. 391; [1991] F.C.R. 539; [1991] Fam. Law 310, CA (Civ
  Div) 5–017, 5–031
Stonor v Fowle; sub nom. R. v Brompton County Court Judge (1888) L.R. 13 App. Cas. 20,
  HL 14 011
Stringer v Stringer [2007] 1 F.L.R. 1532, CA 18–028
Stubbings v United Kingdom (22083/93) [1997] 1 F.L.R. 105; [1997] 3 F.C.R. 157; (1997)
  23 E.H R.R. 213; 1 B.H.R.C. 316; [1997] Fam. Law 241, ECHR 21–066
Stubbings v Webb [1993] A.C. 498; [1993] 2 W.L.R. 120; [1993] 1 All E.R. 322; [1993] 1
  F.L.R. 714; [1993] P.I.Q.R. P86; [1993] Fam. Law 342; (1993) 137 S.J.L.B. 32, HL 17–027,
          21–066
Subpoena (Adoption: Commissioner for Local Administration), Re; sub nom. Subpoena at
  the Request of the Commissioner for the Local Authority, Re; Subpoena issued by the
  Commissioner for Local Administration, Re [1996] 2 F.L.R. 629; [1996] 3 F.C.R. 190;
  (1996) 8 Admin. L.R. 577; [1996] Fam. Law 663; (1996) 140 S.J.L.B. 108, QBD ... 21–083
Sullivan v Sullivan, 161 E.R. 728; (1818) 2 Hag. Con. 238, KB 2–042
Sullivan v Sullivan [1958] N.Z.L.R. 912 10–038
Surtees v Kingston upon Thames RBC; Surtees v Hughes [1991] 2 F.L.R. 559; [1992]
  P.I.Q.R. P101; [1991] Fam. Law 426, CA (Civ Div) 17–027
Suss v Germany [2006] 1 F.L.R. 522 17–024
Suter v Suter [1987] Fam. 111; [1987] 3 W.L.R. 9; [1987] 2 All E.R. 336; (1987) 151 J.P.
  593; [1987] 2 F.L.R. 232; [1987] Fam. Law 239; (1987) 151 J.P.N. 174; (1987) 84
  L.S.G. 1142; (1987) 131 S.J. 471, CA (Civ Div) 13–060, 13–068, 13–089, 19–002
Sutton v Mishcon de Reya [2003] EWHC 3166 (Ch); [2004] 1 F.L.R. 837; [2004] 3 F.C.R.
  142; [2004] Fam. Law 247, Ch D 5–007
Sutton v Sutton [1984] Ch. 184; [1984] 2 W.L.R. 146; [1984] 1 All E.R. 168; [1984] Fam.
  Law 205; (1984) 81 L.S.G. 591; (1984) 128 S.J. 80, Ch D 3–030, 5–007, 13–003, 13–004
Swindale v Forder; sub nom. Forder v Forder [2007] EWCA Civ 29; [2007] 1 F.L.R. 1905;
  [2007] 1 F.C.R. 220; [2007] Fam. Law 392; (2007) 151 S.J.L.B. 197, CA (Civ Div) 13–117
Sylvester v Austria (36812/97); Sylvester v Austria (40104/98) [2003] 2 F.L.R. 210; [2003]
  2 F.C.R. 128; (2003) 37 E.H.R.R. 17; [2003] Fam. Law 638, ECHR 20–025
Symmons v Symmons [1993] 1 F.L.R. 317; [1993] 2 F.C.R. 247; [1993] Fam. Law 135 ...13–006,
          14–011
Szczepanski v Szczepanski [1985] Fam. Law 120, CA (Civ Div) 18–057

Szechter v Szechter [1971] P. 286; [1971] 2 W.L.R. 170; [1970] 3 All E.R. 905, PDAD 2–035, 2–038, 2–040, 2–041

T, Petitioner; sub nom. AMT, Petitioners, 1997 S.L.T. 724; 1996 S.C.L.R. 897; [1997] Fam. Law 225; [1997] Fam. Law 8, IH (1 Div) 22–019

T (A Child) (Order for Costs), Re [2005] EWCA Civ 311; [2005] 2 F.L.R. 681; [2005] 1 F.C.R. 625; [2005] Fam. Law 534, CA (Civ Div) 18–058

T (A Minor) (Adoption: Contact Order), Re [1995] 2 F.L.R. 251; [1995] 2 F.C.R. 537; [1995] Fam. Law 536, CA (Civ Div) 22–062

T (A Minor) (Care or Supervision Order), Re [1994] 1 F.L.R. 103; [1994] 1 F.C.R. 633; [1994] Fam. Law 75; (1994) 158 J.P.N. 153, CA (Civ Div) 21–040

T (A Minor) (Care Order: Conditions), Re [1994] 2 F.L.R. 423; [1994] Fam. Law 558; (1994) 158 J.P.N. 680; (1994) 91(21) L.S.G. 40, CA (Civ Div) 17–048, 18–016, 21–041, 21–042

T (A Minor) (Change of Surname), Re [1998] 2 F.L.R. 620; [1999] 1 F.C.R. 476; [1998] Fam. Law 531; (1998) 95(27) L.S.G. 26; (1998) 142 S.J.L.B. 190, CA (Civ Div) 17–025

T (A Minor) (Child: Representation), Re [1994] Fam.49, CA 16–014, 16–019, 16–020, 16–021

T (A Minor) (Parental Responsibility: Contact), Re [1993] 2 F.L.R. 450; [1993] 1 F.C.R. 973; [1993] Fam. Law 572, CA (Civ Div) 18–019

T (A Minor) (Wardship: Medical Treatment), Re; sub nom. T (A Minor) (Liver Transplant: Consent), Re; C (A Minor) (Medical Treatment: Refusal of Parental Consent), Re [1997] 1 W.L.R. 242; [1997] 1 All E.R. 906; [1997] 1 F.L.R. 502; [1997] 2 F.C.R. 363; [1997] 8 Med. L.R. 166; (1997) 35 B.M.L.R. 63; (1996) 93(42) L.S.G. 28; (1996) 146 N.L.J. 1577; (1996) 140 S.J.L.B. 237, CA (Civ Div) 19–018, 19–025

T (A Minor) (Wardship: Representation), Re; sub nom. CT (A Minor) (Wardship: Representation), Re [1994] Fam. 49; [1993] 3 W.L.R. 602; [1993] 4 All E.R. 518; [1993] 2 F.L.R. 278; [1993] 2 F.C.R. 445; [1993] Fam. Law 568; (1993) 143 N.L.J. 776, CA (Civ Div) 16–021, 18–038, 18–051, 18–054, 22–009

T (Accommodation by Local Authority), Re [1995] 1 F.L.R. 159; [1995] 1 F.C.R. 517; [1995] Fam. Law 125, QBD 21–010, 21–012, 21–085

T (Children) (Abduction: Child's Objections to Return), Re; sub nom. T (Children) (Abduction: Custody Rights), Re [2000] 2 F.L.R. 192; [2000] 2 F.C.R. 159; [2000] Fam. Law 594, CA (Civ Div) 19–016, 20–018, 20–021, 20–025

T (Judicial Review: Local Authority Decisions Concerning Child in Need), Re [2004] 1 F.L.R. 601; [2004] Fam. Law 176, QBD (Admin) 21–010, 21–085

T (Minors) (Adopted Children: Contact), Re [1996] Fam. 34; [1995] 3 W.L.R. 793; [1996] 1 All E.R. 215; [1995] 2 F.L.R. 792; [1996] 2 F.C.R. 118; [1996] Fam. Law 9; (1995) 159 J.P.N. 826, CA (Civ Div) 18–035, 18–039

T (Minors) (Convention on the Civil Aspects of International Child Abduction: Access), Re [1993] 1 W.L.R. 1461; [1993] 3 All E.R. 127; [1993] 2 F.L.R. 617, Fam Div 20–024

T (Minors) (Termination of Contact: Discharge of Order), Re; sub nom. T (Children in Care: Contact), Re [1997] 1 W.L.R. 393; [1997] 1 All E.R. 65; [1997] 1 F.L.R. 517; [1997] 3 F.C.R. 73; [1997] Fam. Law 230; (1997) 161 J.P.N. 236, CA (Civ Div) 21–075

T (Paternity: Ordering Blood Tests), Re [2001] 2 F.L.R. 1190; [2001] 3 F.C.R. 577; [2001] Fam. Law 738, Fam Div 15–008

T (Staying Contact in Non-Convention Country), Re; sub nom. T (A Minor) (Contact: Non-Convention Country), Re [1999] 1 F.L.R. 262; [1998] 3 F.C.R. 574; [1999] Fam. Law 15, Fam Div 20–006

T v Child Support Agency [1998] 1 W.L.R. 144; [1997] 4 All E.R. 27; [1997] 2 F.L.R. 875; [1998] 1 F.C.R. 62; [1998] Fam. Law 9, Fam Div 15–024

T v T (1974) 4 Fam. Law 190, CA (Civ Div) 19–006

T v T (Consent Order: Procedure to Set Aside) [1996] 2 F.L.R. 640; [1997] 1 F.C.R. 282; [1997] Fam. Law 15, Fam Div 13–107

T v T (Financial Relief: Pensions) [1998] 1 F.L.R. 1072; [1998] 2 F.C.R. 364; [1998] O.P.L.R. 1; [1998] Fam. Law 398, Fam Div 13–119, 13–122

T v T (Interception of Documents) [1994] 2 F.L.R. 1083; [1995] 2 F.C.R. 745; [1995] Fam. Law 15, Fam Div 13–064

T v T (Joinder of Third Parties) [1996] 2 F.L.R. 357; [1997] 1 F.C.R. 98; [1996] Fam. Law 669, Fam Div 13–027

T v United Kingdom (24724/94); V v United Kingdom (24888/94) [2000] 2 All E.R. 1024 (Note); (2000) 30 E.H.R.R. 121; 7 B.H.R.C. 659; [1999] Prison L.R. 189; 12 Fed. Sent. R. 266; [2000] Crim. L.R. 187, ECHR 16–017

T and E (Proceedings: Conflicting Interests), Re; sub nom. S (Minors) (Proceedings:
    Conflicting Interests), Re [1995] 1 F.L.R. 581; [1995] 3 F.C.R. 260; [1995] Fam. Law
    232, Fam Div 19–001
TA v DPP [1997] 1 Cr. App. R. (S.) 1; (1996) 160 J.P. 736; [1997] 2 F.L.R. 887; [1996]
    Crim. L.R. 606; [1997] Fam. Law 654; (1996) 160 J.P.N. 966, DC 17–027
TB (Minors) (Care Proceedings: Criminal Trial), Re [1995] 2 F.L.R. 801; [1996] 1 F.C.R.
    101; (1995) 159 J.P.N. 796, CA (Civ Div) 18–006, 21–065
TB v JB (formerly JH) (Abduction: Grave Risk of Harm) [2001] 2 F.L.R. 515; [2001] 2
    F.C.R. 497; [2001] Fam. Law 576, CA (Civ Div) 20–020, 20–021
TL v ML (Ancillary Relief: Claim against Assets of Extended Family) [2005] EWHC 2860
    (Fam); [2006] 1 F.L.R. 1263; [2006] 1 F.C.R. 465; [2006] Fam. Law 183, Fam Div 13–037,
                                                                                                13–066
TP v United Kingdom (28945/95) [2001] 2 F.L.R. 549; [2001] 2 F.C.R. 289; (2002) 34
    E.H.R.R. 2; (2001) 3 L.G.L.R. 52; (2001) 4 C.C.L. Rep. 398; [2001] Fam. Law 590,
    ECHR 16–017, 17–015, 18–041, 21–027, 21–037
TSB Bank Plc v Camfield [1995] 1 W.L.R. 430; [1995] 1 All E.R. 951; [1995] 1 F.L.R. 751;
    [1995] 2 F.C.R. 254; (1995) 27 H.L.R. 205; (1995) 92(3) L.S.G. 37; (1995) 145 N.L.J.
    215; (1995) 139 S.J.L.B. 15, CA (Civ Div) 5–054, 5–056, 12–002
Tackaberry v Hollis [2007] EWHC 2633 (Ch); [2007] N.P.C. 121, Ch D 5–001, 5–011, 5–014,
                                                                                    5–018, 5–020
Tameside MBC v Grant [2002] Fam. 194; [2002] 2 W.L.R. 376; [2002] 1 F.L.R. 318; [2002]
    3 F.C.R. 238; [2002] Fam. Law 106; (2001) 98(41) L.S.G. 34; (2001) 145 S.J.L.B. 237,
    Fam Div 9–042
Tandy v Tandy, unreported, October 24, 1986 13–086
Tavoulareas v Tavoulareas [1998] 2 F.L.R. 418; [1999] 1 F.C.R. 133; [1998] Fam. Law 521,
    CA (Civ Div) 13–012
Taylor (A Bankrupt), Re. *See* Davenham Trust Plc v CV Distribution (UK) Ltd
Taylor Fashions Ltd v Liverpool Victoria Trustees Co Ltd; Old & Campbell Ltd v Liverpool
    Victoria Friendly Society [1982] Q.B. 133; [1981] 2 W.L.R. 576; [1981] 1 All E.R.
    897; [1981] Com. L.R. 34; (1979) 251 E.G. 159, Ch D 5–032
Taylor v Dickens [1998] 1 F.L.R. 806; [1998] 3 F.C.R. 455; [1998] Fam. Law 191, Ch D 5–033
Taylor v Taylor [1967] P. 25; [1965] 2 W.L.R. 779; [1965] 1 All E.R. 872, PDAD 12–002
Taylor's Application, Re [1972] 2 Q.B. 369 17–021
Tee v Tee; Tee v Hillman [1999] 2 F.L.R. 613; [1999] 3 F.C.R. 409; [1999] Fam. Law 534,
    CA (Civ Div) 3–006, 4–001
Teeling v Teeling [1984\ F.L.R. 808, CA .... 18–034}
Telecom Plus Plc v Hatch [2005] EWHC 1523, Ch D 5–060
Thain (An Infant), Re; sub nom. Thain v Taylor [1926] Ch. 676, CA 19–008, 21–004
Thomas v Fuller-Brown [1988] 1 F.L.R. 237; [1988] Fam. Law 53, CA (Civ Div) 5–023
Thomas v News Group Newspapers Ltd; sub nom. Thomas v News Group International Ltd;
    Thomas v Hughes [2001] EWCA Civ 1233; [2002] E.M.L.R. 4; (2001) 98(34) L.S.G.
    43; (2001) 145 S.J.L.B. 207, CA (Civ Div) 9–005, 9–042
Thomas v Thomas [1995] 2 F.L.R. 668; [1996] 2 F.C.R. 544; [1995] Fam. Law 672, CA
    (Civ Div) 13–013, 13–066
Thompson v Thompson [1956] P. 414; [1956] 2 W.L.R. 814; [1956] 1 All E.R. 603; (1956)
    100 S.J. 247, PDAD 12–004
Thompson v Thompson (1985) [1986] Fam. 38; [1985] 3 W.L.R. 17; [1985] 2 All E.R. 243;
    [1986] Fam. Law 195; (1985) 82 L.S.G. 2906; (1985) 135 N.L.J. 155; (1985) 129 S.J.
    284, CA (Civ Div) 13–028, 13–116
Thompson v Thompson [1986] 1 F.L.R. 212 18–012
Thompson v Thompson (1986) 150 J.P. 625; [1987] Fam. Law 89; (1986) 150 J.P.N. 686 19–015
Thompson v Thompson (Financial Provision) [1991] 2 F.L.R. 530; [1992] 1 F.C.R. 368;
    [1992] Fam. Law 18; [1991] N.P.C. 95, CA (Civ Div) 13–104
Thompson v Thompson (Costs) [1993] 2 F.L.R. 464; [1994] 1 F.C.R. 97; [1993] Fam. Law
    626, CA (Civ Div) 13–012
Thompson (Sheila) v Thompson [1976] Fam. 25; [1975] 2 W.L.R. 868; [1975] 2 All E.R.
    208; 73 L.G.R. 488; (1975) 30 P. & C.R. 91; (1975) 5 Fam. Law 162; (1975) 119 S.J.
    255, CA (Civ Div) 13–117
Thompson and Venables v News Group Newspapers [2001] 1 F.L.R. 791, Fam Div 18–053
Thorner v Curtis [2007] EWHC 2422 (Ch) 5–033, 5–034, 5–035, 5–036
Thornley (Deceased), Re; sub nom. Thornley v Palmer [1969] 1 W.L.R. 1037; [1969] 3 All
    E.R. 31, CA (Civ Div) 7–024

Thorpe v Thorpe [1998] 2 F.L.R. 127; [1998] 2 F.C.R. 384; [1998] Fam. Law 320, CA (Civ
Div) 9–035
Thurlow v Thurlow [1976] Fam. 32; [1975] 3 W.L.R. 161; [1975] 2 All E.R. 979; (1975)
5 Fam. Law 188; (1975) 119 S.J. 406, Fam Div 10–023, 10–025
Thwaite v Thwaite [1982] Fam. 1; [1981] 3 W.L.R. 96; [1981] 2 All E.R. 789; (1981) 125
S.J. 307, CA (Civ Div) 3–032, 10–001, 13–005, 13–107, 13–108
Tilley v Tilley (1979) 10 Fam. Law 89, CA (Civ Div) 13–024, 13–093, 13–101
Tindall v Tindall [1953] P. 63; [1953] 2 W.L.R. 158; [1953] 1 All E.R. 139; (1953) 97 S.J.
47, CA 2–051
Tinker v Tinker (No.1) [1970] P. 136; [1970] 2 W.L.R. 331; [1970] 1 All E.R. 540; (1970)
21 P. & C.R. 102; (1969) 114 S.J. 32, CA (Civ Div) 5–016
Tinsley v Milligan [1994] 1 A.C. 340; [1993] 3 W.L.R. 126; [1993] 3 All E.R. 65; [1993]
2 F.L.R. 963; (1994) 68 P. & C.R. 412; [1993] E.G. 118 (C.S.); [1993] N.P.C. 97, HL 5–014,
5–016
Titheradge v Titheradge (1983) 4 F.L.R. 552 3–017
Tommey v Tommey [1983] Fam. 15; [1982] 3 W.L.R. 909; [1982] 3 All E.R. 385; (1983)
4 F.L.R. 159; (1982) 12 Fam. Law 148; (1982) 126 S.J. 243, Fam Div 13–108
Tribe v Tribe [1996] Ch. 107; [1995] 3 W.L.R. 913; [1995] 4 All E.R. 236; [1995] C.L.C.
1474; [1995] 2 F.L.R. 966; [1996] 1 F.C.R. 338; (1996) 71 P. & C.R. 503; [1996] Fam.
Law 29; (1995) 92(28) L.S.G. 30; (1995) 145 N.L.J. 1445; (1995) 139 S.J.L.B. 203;
[1995] N.P.C. 151; (1995) 70 P. & C.R. D38, CA (Civ Div) 5–016
Trippas v Trippas [1973] Fam. 134; [1973] 2 W.L.R. 585; [1973] 2 All E.R. 1; (1973) 117
S.J. 204, CA (Civ Div) 13–031, 13–063
Tweney v Tweney [1946] P. 180, PDAD
Tymosczuk v Tymoszuk (1964) 108 S.J. 656 3–007
Tyrer v United Kingdom (1978) 2 E.H.R.R. 175 16–017
U (Care Proceedings: Criminal Conviction: Refusal to Give Evidence), Re [2006] EWHC
372; [2006] 2 F.L.R. 690; [2006] Fam. Law 520, Fam Div 21–037, 21–062
U v W (Attorney General Intervening) (No.2) [1998] Fam. 29; [1997] 3 W.L.R. 739; [1997]
2 C.M.L.R. 431; [1997] Eu. L.R. 350; [1997] 2 F.L.R. 282; [1998] 1 F.C.R. 526; (1997)
38 B.M.L.R. 54; (1997) 141 S.J.L.B. 57, Fam Div 17–004, 22–070, 22–075
Uglow v Uglow [2004] EWCA Civ 987; [2004] W.T.L.R. 1183, CA (Civ Div) 5–033
Ulrich v Ulrich and Felton [1968] 1 W.L.R. 180; [1968] 1 All E.R. 67; (1968) 19 P. & C.R.
669; (1967) 111 S.J. 889, CA (Civ Div) 13–026
Ungurian v Lesnoff [1990] Ch. 206; [1989] 3 W.L.R. 840; [1990] 2 F.L.R. 299; [1990]
F.C.R. 719; [1990] Fam. Law 93; (1989) 133 S.J. 948, Ch D 5–021
V (A Child) (Care Proceedings: Human Rights Claims), Re [2004] EWCA Civ 54; [2004]
1 W.L.R. 1433; [2004] 1 All E.R. 997; [2004] 1 F.L.R. 944; [2004] 1 F.C.R. 338;
[2004] Fam. Law 328; (2004) 101(11) L.S.G. 33, CA (Civ Div) 21–086
V (A Child) (Jurisdiction: Habitual Residence), Re; sub nom. VP (Loss of Child's Habitual
Residence), Re [2001] 1 F.L.R. 253; [2001] 1 F.C.R. 712; [2000] Fam. Law 874, Fam
Div 20–015, 20–023
V (A Minor) (Care or Supervision Order), Re [1996] 1 F.L.R. 776; [1996] 2 F.C.R. 555;
[1996] Fam. Law 269, CA (Civ Div) 21–032, 21–040, 21–042
V (Residence Order: Finance), Re [1995] 2 F.L.R. 612, CA 19–011
V (Residence: Review), Re; sub nom. V (Residence Order), Re [1995] 2 F.L.R. 1010;
[1996] 3 F.C.R. 101; [1996] Fam. Law 78, CA (Civ Div) 19–016, 19–026
V v V (Ancillary Relief: Power to Order Child Maintenance) [2001] 2 F.L.R. 799; [2001]
Fam. Law 649, Fam Div 15–038, 15–040, 15–050, 15–051
V v V (Children) (Contact: Implacable Hostility [2004] EWHC 1215; [2004] 2 F.L.R. 851;
[2004] Fam. Law 712, Fam Div 18–058
VB v JP [2008] EWHC 112 .... 13–053, 13–098
Van Laethem v Brooker [2005] EWHC 1478; [2006] 2 F.L.R. 495; [2006] 1 F.C.R. 697;
[2006] Fam. Law 537; [2005] N.P.C. 91, Ch D 5–033
Vandervell's Trusts (No.2), Re; sub nom. White v Vandervell Trustees [1974] Ch. 269;
[1974] 3 W.L.R. 256; [1974] 3 All E.R. 205; (1974) 118 S.J. 566, CA (Civ Div) 5–014
Vasey v Vasey (1985) 149 J.P. 219; [1985] Fam. Law 158; (1984) 81 L.S.G. 3500; (1985)
129 S.J. 17, CA (Civ Div) 3–017
Vaughan v Vaughan [1973] 1 W.L.R. 1159; [1973] 3 All E.R. 449; (1973) 4 Fam. Law 123;
(1973) 117 S.J. 583, CA (Civ Div) 9–010, 9–027
Vaughan v Vaughan [2008] Fam.Law. 15 13–056

Vernon v Bosley (No.1) [1997] 1 All E.R. 577; [1997] R.T.R. 1; [1998] 1 F.L.R. 297; [1997] P.I.Q.R. P255; (1997) 35 B.M.L.R. 135; [1997] Fam. Law 476; (1996) 146 N.L.J. 589, CA (Civ Div) 19–016

Vernon v Bosley (No.2) [1999] Q.B. 18; [1997] 3 W.L.R. 683; [1997] 1 All E.R. 614; [1997] R.T.R. 275; [1998] 1 F.L.R. 304; [1997] P.I.Q.R. P326; (1997) 35 B.M.L.R. 174; [1997] Fam. Law 476; (1997) 94(4) L.S.G. 26; (1997) 147 N.L.J. 89; (1997) 141 S.J.L.B. 27, CA (Civ Div) 18–043, 19–016

Vervaeke v Smith [1983] 1 A.C. 145; [1982] 2 W.L.R. 855; [1982] 2 All E.R. 144; (1982) 126 S.J. 293, HL 2–035

Vicary v Vicary [1992] 2 F.L.R. 271; [1993] 1 F.C.R. 533; [1992] Fam. Law 428, CA (Civ Div) 13–072, 13–078, 13–107

Vigreux v Michel [2006] 2 F.L.R. 1180 .... 20–021, 20–022

W (A Child) (Care Proceedings: Leave to Apply), Re [2004] EWHC 3342; [2005] 2 F.L.R. 468; [2005] Fam. Law 527, Fam Div 16–020, 18–041, 21–054

W (A Child) (Contact Application: Procedure), Re; sub nom. W (A Child) (Contact: Leave to Apply), Re [2000] 1 F.L.R. 263; [2000] 1 F.C.R. 185; [2000] Fam. Law 82, Fam Div 18–020

W (A Child) (Illegitimate Child: Change of Surname), Re; A (A Child) (Change of Name), Re; B (Children) (Change of Name), Re; sub nom. W (A Child) (Change of Name), Re [2001] Fam. 1; [2000] 2 W.L.R. 258; [1999] 2 F.L.R. 930; [1999] 3 F.C.R. 337; [1999] Fam. Law 688; (1999) 96(33) L.S.G. 29, CA (Civ Div) 17–025, 18–022

W (A Child) (Parental Contact: Prohibition), Re; sub nom. W (A Child) (Section 34(2) Orders), Re [2000] Fam. 130; [2000] 2 W.L.R. 1276; [2000] 1 F.L.R. 502; [2000] 1 F.C.R. 752; [2000] Fam. Law 235; (2000) 97(3) L.S.G. 36, CA (Civ Div) 21–074

W (A Child) (Section 34(2) Orders), Re. *See* W (A Child) (Parental Contact: Prohibition), Re

W (A Minor) (Access), Re [1989] 1 F.L.R. 163; [1989] Fam. Law 112 19–019

W (A Minor) (Adoption or Custodianship), Re [1988] 1 F.L.R. 175; [1988] F.C.R. 129; [1988] Fam. Law 92; (1988) 152 J.P.N. 142; (1987) 84 L.S.G. 2193; (1987) 84 L.S.G. 2530; (1987) 131 S.J. 915, CA (Civ Div) 22–060, 22–065

W (A Minor) (Adoption: Homosexual Adopter), Re [1998] Fam. 58; [1997] 3 W.L.R. 768; [1997] 3 All E.R. 620; [1997] 2 F.L.R. 406; [1997] Fam. Law 597; (1997) 94(24) L.S.G. 32; (1997) 141 S.J.L.B. 137, Fam Div 22–019

W (A Minor) (Adoption: Non-Patrial), Re [1986] Fam. 54; [1985] 3 W.L.R. 945; [1985] 3 All E.R. 449; [1986] 1 F.L.R. 179; [1986] Fam. Law 57; (1985) 135 N.L.J. 964; (1985) 129 S.J. 794, CA (Civ Div) 21–007, 22–001

W (A Minor) (Child: Contact), Re [1994] 1 F.L.R. 843; [1993] 2 F.C.R. 731; [1994] Fam. Law 376, Fam Div 18–043, 19–017

W (A Minor) (Contact), Re [1994] 2 F.L.R. 441; [1994] 2 F.C.R. 1216; [1994] Fam. Law 614; (1994) 158 J.P.N. 817, CA (Civ Div) 18–019, 19–007, 19–024

W (A Minor) (Contact Orders: Medical Reports), Re; sub nom. W (Contact: Parent's Delusional Beliefs), Re [1999] 1 F.L.R. 1263; [1999] Fam. Law 298, CA (Civ Div) 18–019

W (A Minor) (Medical Treatment: Court's Jurisdiction), Re; sub nom. J (A Minor) (Consent to Medical Treatment), Re [1993] Fam. 64; [1992] 3 W.L.R. 758; [1992] 4 All E.R. 627; [1992] 3 Med. L.R. 317; (1992) 142 N.L.J. 1124, CA (Civ Div) ...16–014, 16–015, 16–019, 17–022, 18–022, 18–049, 19–002, 19–016, 21–042, 21–043

W (A Minor) (Residence Order), Re [1992] 2 F.L.R. 332; [1992] 2 F.C.R. 461; [1992] Fam. Law 493; (1992) 156 J.P.N. 476, CA (Civ Div) 18–016, 19–015, 19–018, 19–020, 22–073

W (A Minor) (Residence Order), Re [1993] 2 F.L.R. 625; [1993] 2 F.C.R. 589; [1993] Fam. Law 573, CA (Civ Div) 19–018, 19–025

W (A Minor) (Secure Accommodation Order), Re; sub nom. W v North Yorkshire CC [1993] 1 F.L.R. 692; [1993] 1 F.C.R. 693; [1993] Fam. Law 345; (1993) 157 J.P.N. 249, Fam Div 21–078

W (A Minor) (Secure Accommodation Order: Attendance at Court), Re [1994] 2 F.L.R. 1092; [1994] 3 F.C.R. 248; [1995] Fam. Law 19; (1994) 158 J.P.N. 731, Fam Div 16–020, 16–022, 21–056

W (A Minor) (Staying Contact), Re [1998] 2 F.L.R. 450; [1998] 2 F.C.R. 453, CA (Civ Div) 19–025

W (A Minor) (Wardship: Jurisdiction), Re; sub nom. W v Hertfordshire CC [1985] A.C. 791; [1985] 2 W.L.R. 892; [1985] 2 All E.R. 301; (1985) 149 J.P. 593; 83 L.G.R. 669; [1985] Fam. Law 326; (1985) 82 L.S.G. 2087; (1985) 135 N.L.J. 483; (1985) 129 S.J. 347, HL 18–052, 21–085

W (A Minor) (Wardship: Restrictions on Publication), Re; sub nom. W (A Minor) (Wardship: Freedom of Publication), Re [1992] 1 W.L.R. 100; [1992] 1 All E.R. 794; [1992] 1 F.L.R. 99; [1992] F.C.R. 231; [1992] Fam. Law 69; (1992) 156 L.G. Rev. 350, CA (Civ Div) 18–053

W (A Minor) (Welfare Reports: Appeals), Re [1995] 2 F.L.R. 142; [1995] 3 F.C.R. 793; [1995] Fam. Law 544; (1995) 159 J.P.N. 703, CA (Civ Div) 18–012

W (An Infant), Re [1971] A.C. 682; [1971] 2 W.L.R. 1011; [1971] 2 All E.R. 49; (1971) 115 S.J. 286, HL 22–024

W (Assessment of Child), Re; sub nom. W (A Minor) (Care Proceedings: Assessment), Re [1998] 2 F.L.R. 130; [1998] 1 F.C.R. 287; [1998] Fam. Law 318, CA (Civ Div) 21–043

W (Children) v Legal Services Commission. *See* R. v Legal Aid Board Ex p. W (Children)

W (Children: Removal into Care), Re [2005] EWCA Civ 642; [2005] 2 F.L.R. 1022; [2005] Fam. Law 767, CA (Civ Div) 21–040

W (Exclusion: Statement of Evidence), Re; sub nom. W v A Local Authority (Exclusion Requirement); W v Middlesbrough BC (Exclusion Order: Evidence) [2000] 2 F.L.R. 666; [2000] 2 F.C.R. 662; [2000] Fam. Law 705, Fam Div 21–044

W (Minors) (Abduction: Father's Rights), Re; B (A Minor) (Abduction: Father's Rights), Re; sub nom. W (A Minor) (Unmarried Father), Re; B (A Minor) (Unmarried Father), Re [1999] Fam. 1; [1998] 3 W.L.R. 1372; [1998] 2 F.L.R. 146; [1998] 2 F.C.R. 549; [1998] Fam. Law 452; (1998) 95(21) L.S.G. 24; (1998) 142 S.J.L.B. 131, Fam Div 20–016

W (Minors) (Residence Order), Re [1999] 1 F.L.R. 869; [1998] 1 F.C.R. 75; [1999] Fam. Law 220, CA (Civ Div) 19–006, 19–018, 19–025

W (Minors) (Sexual Abuse: Standard of Proof), Re [1994] 1 F.L.R. 419; [1994] 2 F.C.R. 759; [1994] Fam. Law 427, CA (Civ Div) 21–036

W (Minors) (Surrogacy), Re [1991] 1 F.L.R. 385; [1991] Fam. Law 180 22–076

W (otherwise K) v W [1967] 1 W.L.R. 1554; [1967] 3 All E.R. 178 (Note); (1967) 111 S.J. 926, PDAD 2–025

W (RJ) v W (SJ) [1972] Fam. 152; [1972] 2 W.L.R. 371; [1971] 3 All E.R. 303; (1971) 116 S.J. 58, Assizes (Devon) 18–034

W (Residence), Re [1999] 2 F.L.R. 390; [1999] 3 F.C.R. 274; [1999] Fam. Law 454, CA (Civ Div) 18–012, 19–006

W (Wardship: Discharge: Publicity), Re [1995] 2 F.L.R. 466; [1995] Fam. Law 612, CA (Civ Div) 18–001, 18–052

W (Wardship: Relatives Rejected as Foster Carers), Re [2003] EWHC 2206; [2004] 1 F.L.R. 415; [2003] Fam. Law 883, Fam Div 18–052

W v D [1980] 1 F.L.R. 393 18–057

W v Essex CC [2001] 2 A.C. 592; [2000] 2 W.L.R. 601; [2000] 2 All E.R. 237; [2000] 1 F.L.R. 657; [2000] 1 F.C.R. 568; [2000] B.L.G.R. 281; (2000) 53 B.M.L.R. 1; [2000] Fam. Law 476; (2000) 164 J.P.N. 464; (2000) 97(13) L.S.G. 44; (2000) 144 S.J.L.B. 147, HL 21–027

W v H (Child Abduction: Surrogacy) (No.1) [2002] 1 F.L.R. 1008; [2002] Fam. Law 345, Fam Div 17–003, 20–015, 22–073

W v H (Family Division: Without Notice Orders); sub nom. W v H (Ex Parte Injunctions); W (Ex Parte Orders), Re [2001] 1 All E.R. 300; [2000] 2 F.L.R. 927; [2000] 3 F.C.R. 481; [2000] Fam. Law 811, Fam Div 20–005

W v Hertfordshire CC [1993] 1 F.L.R. 118; [1992] 2 F.C.R. 865; [1993] Fam. Law 75; (1992) 136 S.J.L.B. 259, Fam Div 19–026

W v J (A Child) (Variation of Financial Provision) [2003] EWHC 2657 (Fam); [2004] 2 F.L.R. 300; [2004] Fam. Law 568, Fam Div 15–052

W v Official Solicitor. *See* S (An Infant) v S

W v P (Justices Reasons) [1988] 1 F.L.R. 508; [1988] F.C.R. 349; [1988] Fam. Law 391; (1988) 152 J.P.N. 238; (1987) 84 L.S.G. 3501; (1988) 138 N.L.J. Rep. 18; (1987) 131 S.J. 1589, Fam Div 19–025

W v S (otherwise W) [1905] P. 231, PDAD 2–026

W v United Kingdom (A/121); sub nom. W v United Kingdom (9749/82) (1988) 10 E.H.R.R. 29, ECHR 16–017, 21–025, 21–074

W v W (Ancillary Relief: Practice) [2000] Fam. Law 473, Fam Div 13–012, 13–072

W v W (Child Abduction: Acquiescence) [1993] 2 F.L.R. 211; [1993] Fam. Law 451 20–019

W v W (Child of the Family) [1984] F.L.R. 796 18–034

W v W (Divorce Proceedings: Withdrawal of Consent before Perfection of Order) [2002] EWHC 1826; [2002] 2 F.L.R. 1225; [2002] Fam. Law 885, Fam Div 13–124

W v W (Joinder of Trusts of Land and Children Act Applications) [2004] 2 F.L.R. 865 15–051
W v W (Judicial Separation: Ancillary Relief); sub nom. W v W (Financial Provision)
    [1995] 2 F.L.R. 259; [1996] 3 F.C.R. 641; [1995] Fam. Law 548, Fam Div 13–078
W v W (Nullity: Gender); sub nom. W v W (Physical Inter-sex) [2001] Fam. 111; [2001]
    2 W.L.R. 674; [2001] 1 F.L.R. 324; (2001) 58 B.M.L.R. 15; [2001] Fam. Law 104, Fam
    Div 2–020, 10–001
W v W (Periodical Payments: Pensions) [1996] 2 F.L.R. 480; [1997] 2 F.C.R. 126, Fam
    Div 13–027
W v W [1952] P. 152; [1952] 1 All E.R. 858; [1952] 1 T.L.R. 879, CA 2–051
WB (Residence Orders), Re [1995] 2 F.L.R. 1023; [1993] Fam. Law 395, Fam Div ...18–016, 18–021
W H-J v H H-J [2002] 1 F.L.R. 415 ....13–045, 13–073, 13–079
WM (Adoption: Non-Patrial), Re [1997] 1 F.L.R. 132; [1997] 2 F.C.R. 494; [1997] Fam.
    Law 84, Fam Div 22–019
Wachtel v Wachtel (No.2) [1973] Fam. 72; [1973] 2 W.L.R. 366; [1973] 1 All E.R. 829;
    (1973) 117 S.J. 124, CA (Civ Div) 3–009, 5–001, 13–031, 13–078, 13–080, 13–083, 13–112
Wales v Wadham [1977] 1 W.L.R. 199; [1977] 1 All E.R. 125; (1976) 7 Fam. Law 19;
    (1977) 121 S.J. 154, Fam Div 3–028
Walker v Hall [1984] Fam. Law 21; (1983) 80 L.S.G. 2139; (1983) 127 S.J. 550, CA (Civ
    Div) 5–011, 5–017, 5–028
Wallbank v Price [2007] EWHC 3001 (Ch), Ch D 5–010, 5–042
Warr v Warr [1975] Fam. 25; [1975] 2 W.L.R. 62; [1975] 1 All E.R. 85; (1974) 5 Fam. Law
    18; (1974) 118 S.J. 715, Fam Div 10–035
Warren v Warren (1983) 4 F.L.R. 529, CA 13–104
Warwickshire CC v M [2007] EWCA Civ 1048 22–043
Waterman v Waterman [1989] 1 F.L.R. 380; [1989] F.C.R. 267; [1989] Fam. Law 227, CA
    (Civ Div) 13–058, 13–089, 13–091
Watkins, Re; sub nom. Watkins v Watkins [1953] 1 W.L.R. 1323; [1953] 2 All E.R. 1113;
    (1953) 97 S.J. 762, Ch D 12–002
Watkins v Watkins [1896] P. 222, CA 14–002
Watson (Deceased), Re [1999] 1 F.L.R. 878; [1999] 3 F.C.R. 595; [1999] Fam. Law 211;
    (1999) 96(2) L.S.G. 28; (1999) 143 S.J.L.B. 51, Ch D 9–029
Way v Way [1950] P. 71 2–042
Wayling v Jones [1995] 2 F.L.R. 1029; [1996] 2 F.C.R. 41; (1995) 69 P. & C.R. 170; [1996]
    Fam. Law 88; [1993] E.G. 153 (C.S.), CA (Civ Div) 5–033, 5–034, 5–035
Webster (A Child), Re; sub nom. Norfolk CC v Webster [2006] EWHC 2733; [2007]
    E.M.L.R. 7; [2007] H.R.L.R. 3, Fam Div 17–015, 18–008
Wehmeyer v Wehmeyer [2001] 2 F.L.R. 84; [2001] B.P.I.R. 548; [2001] Fam. Law 493, Ch
    D 14–005
Wellesley v Beaufort (1827) 2 Russ. 1 18–050
Wellesley v Wellesley (1828) 2 Bligh (N.S) 124 18–050
Wells v Pickering; sub nom. Pickering v Wells [2002] 2 F.L.R. 798; [2002] Fam. Law 812;
    (2002) 99(26) L.S.G. 38; [2002] 2 P. & C.R. DG23, Ch D 5–061
Wells v Wells (1992) [1992] 2 F.L.R. 66; [1992] 2 F.C.R. 368; [1992] Fam. Law 386, CA
    (Civ Div) 13–103
Wennhak v Morgan (1888) L.R. 20 Q.B.D. 635, QBD 3–038
Westbury v Sampson [2001] EWCA Civ 407; [2002] 1 F.L.R. 166; [2001] 2 F.C.R. 210;
    [2002] Fam. Law 15; (2001) 98(20) L.S.G. 44, CA (Civ Div) 13–024, 13–093, 13–101
Westcar v Westcar [2006] EWCA Civ 1414, CA (Civ Div) 9–033
Westminster City Council v RA [2005] EWHC 970; [2005] 2 F.L.R. 1309; [2005] Fam. Law
    687, Fam Div 21–025
Whiston v Whiston [1995] Fam. 198; [1995] 3 W.L.R. 405; [1998] 1 All E.R. 423; [1995]
    2 F.L.R. 268; [1995] 2 F.C.R. 496; [1995] Fam. Law 549, CA (Civ Div) 10–001, 13–084
White v White [1983] Fam. 54; [1983] 2 W.L.R. 872; [1983] 2 All E.R. 51; (1983) 13 Fam.
    Law 149, CA (Civ Div) 10–024
White v White; sub nom. W v W (Joinder of Trusts of Land Act and Children Act
    Applications) [2003] EWCA Civ 924; [2004] 2 F.L.R. 321; [2004] Fam. Law 572, CA
    (Civ Div) 5–046, 5–060
White (otherwise Berry) v White [1948] P. 330; [1948] 2 All E.R. 151; 64 T.L.R. 332;
    [1948] L.J.R. 1476; (1948) 92 S.J. 325, PDAD 2–025, 2–033

White (Pamela) v White (Martin) [2001] 1 A.C. 596; [2000] 3 W.L.R. 1571; [2001] 1 All
E.R. 1; [2000] 2 F.L.R. 981; [2000] 3 F.C.R. 555; [2001] Fam. Law 12; (2000) 97(43)
L.S.G. 38; (2000) 150 N.L.J. 1716; (2000) 144 S.J.L.B. 266; [2000] N.P.C. 111, HL ...4–001,
7–026, 8–001, 13–001, 13–002, 13–012, 13–040, 13–041, 13–043, 13–044,
13–045, 13–045, 13–046, 13–050, 13–054, 13–055, 13–058, 13–063, 13–072,
13–073, 13–075, 13–078, 13–079, 13–081, 13–105, 13–116
Whiting v Whiting [1988] 1 W.L.R. 565; [1988] 2 All E.R. 275; [1988] 2 F.L.R. 189; [1988]
F.C.R. 569; [1988] Fam. Law 429; (1988) 152 J.P.N. 574; (1988) 138 N.L.J. Rep. 39;
(1988) 132 S.J. 658, CA (Civ Div) 13–086
Wickham v Enfield (1633) Cro Car 351; 79 E.R. 908 1–003
Wigmore's Case (1707) Holt K.B. 460; 90 E.R. 1153 1–003
Wilcox v Tait [2006] EWCA Civ 1867, CA (Civ Div) 5–048
Wilkinson (Deceased), Re; sub nom. Neale v Newell [1978] Fam. 22; [1977] 3 W.L.R. 514;
[1978] 1 All E.R. 221; (1977) 7 Fam. Law 176; (1977) 121 S.J. 375, Fam Div 7–016
Wilkinson v Kitzinger [2006] EWHC 835 (Fam); [2006] 2 F.L.R. 397; [2006] 2 F.C.R. 537;
[2006] Fam. Law 526; (2006) 103(19) L.S.G. 26, Fam Div A–004, 2–017, 13–001
Wilkinson v Payne (1791) 4 Term Rep 468; 100 E.R. 1123 1–005
Williams v Hensman (1861) 1 John. & H. 546 ....5–042, 5–044
Williams v Johns [1988] 2 F.L.R. 475; [1988] Fam. Law 257, DC 7–023
Williams v Staite [1979] Ch. 291; [1978] 2 W.L.R. 825; [1978] 2 All E.R. 928; (1978) 36
P. & C.R. 103; (1978) 122 S.J. 333, CA (Civ Div) 5–037
Williams v Williams (1881–82) L.R. 20 Ch. D. 659, Ch D 17–026
Williams v Williams (Insanity as Defence to Cruelty) [1964] A.C. 698; [1963] 3 W.L.R.
215; [1963] 2 All E.R. 994; (1963) 107 S.J. 533, HL 10–005
Williams v Williams (Sale of Matrimonial Home); sub nom. Williams (JW) v Williams
(MA) [1976] Ch. 278; [1976] 3 W.L.R. 494; [1977] 1 All E.R. 28; (1976) 120 S.J. 434,
CA (Civ Div) 5–046
Williams (LA) v Williams (EM) [1974] Fam. 55; [1974] 3 W.L.R. 379; [1974] 3 All E.R.
377; (1974) 4 Fam. Law 159; (1974) 118 S.J. 580, Fam Div 13–067
Williams & Glyn's Bank Ltd v Boland; Williams & Glyn's Bank Ltd v Brown [1981] A.C.
487; [1980] 3 W.L.R. 138; [1980] 2 All E.R. 408; (1980) 40 P. & C.R. 451; (1980) 124
S.J. 443, HL 3–006, 3–010, 5–013, 5–051, 8–003
Wills v Wills [1984] F.L.R. 672 13–014
Wilson v Webber [1998] 1 F.L.R. 1097 9–035
Wilson v Wilson (Rectification of Deed) [1969] 1 W.L.R. 1470; [1969] 3 All E.R. 945;
(1969) 20 P. & C.R. 780; (1969) 113 S.J. 625, Ch D 5–010
Wing v Taylor (1861) 2 Sw. & Tr. 278 2–009
Winkworth v Edward Baron Development Co Ltd [1986] 1 W.L.R. 1512; [1987] 1 All E.R.
114; (1987) 3 B.C.C. 4; [1987] B.C.L.C. 193; [1987] 1 F.L.R. 525; [1987] 1 F.T.L.R.
176; (1987) 53 P. & C.R. 378; [1987] Fam. Law 166; (1987) 84 L.S.G. 340; (1986) 130
S.J. 954, HL 5–016
Witkowska v Kaminski [2006] EWHC 1940; [2006] 3 F.C.R. 250; [2006] W.T.L.R. 1293;
[2007] Fam. Law 115, Ch D 7–017
Wolverhampton MBC v DB (A Minor); sub nom. B (A Minor) (Treatment and Secure
Accommodation), Re; A MBC v DB [1997] 1 F.L.R. 767; [1997] 1 F.C.R. 618; (1997)
37 B.M.L.R. 172; [1997] Fam. Law 400; (1997) 161 J.P.N. 413, Fam Div 21–077
Wood v Wood (Foreign Divorce: Maintenance Order) [1957] P. 254; [1957] 2 W.L.R. 826;
[1957] 2 All E.R. 14; (1957) 121 J.P. 302; (1957) 101 S.J. 356, CA 3–019
Woodcock and Woodcock, Re p1957] N.Z.L.R. 960 2–01
Woodland v Woodland (otherwise Belin) [1928] P. 169, PDAD 2–047
Woodley v Woodley (Committal Order) (No.1) [1992] 2 F.L.R. 417; [1993] 1 F.C.R. 701;
[1993] Fam. Law 24, CA (Civ Div) 14–005, 14–011
Woolf v Pemberton (1877) L.R. 6 Ch. D. 19, CA 17–021
Worlock v Worlock [1994] 2 F.L.R. 689; [1994] 2 F.C.R. 1157; [1994] Fam. Law 619, CA
(Civ Div) 13–103, 13–104
Wright v Jess [1987] 1 W.L.R. 1076; [1987] 2 All E.R. 1067; [1987] 2 F.L.R. 373; [1987]
Fam. Law 380; (1987) 84 L.S.G. 1241; (1987) 131 S.J. 942, CA (Civ Div) 9–035
Wright v Johnson [2001] EWCA Civ 1667; [2002] 2 P. & C.R. 15, CA (Civ Div) 5–048
Wright v Wright (1980) 2 F.L.R. 276 19–020
Wroth v Tyler [1974] Ch. 30; [1973] 2 W.L.R. 405; [1973] 1 All E.R. 897; (1973) 25 P. &
C.R. 138; (1972) 117 S.J. 90, Ch D 3–010, 3–012
Wyatt, Re [2006] 2 F.L.R. 111 17–022

X, Re; sub nom. Barnet LBC v Y [2006] 2 F.L.R. 998; [2006] Fam. Law 740, CC (Barnet) ... 21–039

X (A Child: Emergency Protection Orders), Re [2006] EWHC 510; [2006] 2 F.L.R. 701; [2006] Fam. Law 627, Fam Div 21–048

X (A Minor) (Adoption Details: Disclosure), Re; sub nom. X (A Minor) (Adoption Order), Re [1994] Fam. 174; [1994] 3 W.L.R. 327; [1994] 3 All E.R. 372; [1994] 2 F.L.R. 450; [1995] 1 F.C.R. 135; 92 L.G.R. 656; [1994] Fam. Law 555; (1995) 159 J.P.N. 80, CA (Civ Div) 18–049, 18–052, 21–080, 21–010, 22–067

X (A Minor) (Wardship: Jurisdiction), Re; sub nom. X (A Minor) (Wardship: Restriction on Publication), Re [1975] Fam. 47; [1975] 2 W.L.R. 335; [1975] 1 All E.R. 697, CA (Civ Div) 19–002

X (Care: Notice of Proceedings), Re [1996] 1 F.L.R. 186; [1996] 3 F.C.R. 91; [1996] Fam. Law 139; (1996) 160 J.P.N. 732, Fam Div 21–054

X (Children) (Adoption: Confidential Procedure), Re; sub nom. X (Children) (Adoption by Foster Parents: Disclosure), Re; X (Children) (Adoption: Confidentiality), Re [2002] EWCA Civ 828; [2002] 2 F.L.R. 476; [2002] 3 F.C.R. 648; [2002] Fam. Law 653, CA (Civ Div) 22–035

X (Children) (Care Proceedings: Parental Responsibility), Re; sub nom. X (A Child) (Parental Responsibility Agreement: Child in Care), Re [2000] Fam. 156; [2000] 2 W.L.R. 1031; [2000] 2 All E.R. 66; [2000] 1 F.L.R. 517; [2000] 1 F.C.R. 379; [2000] Fam. Law 244; (2000) 97(1) L.S.G. 23; (2000) 144 S.J.L.B. 25, Fam Div 17–038, 17–047, 21–041

X (Disclosure of Information), Re [2001] 2 F.L.R. 440; [2001] Fam. Law 586, Fam Div 21–038

X (Leave to Remove from Jurisdiction: No Order Principle), Re [2001] 2 F.L.R. 118; [2001] 2 F.C.R. 398, Fam Div 18–005

X (Minors) v Bedfordshire CC; M (A Minor) v Newham LBC; E (A Minor) v Dorset CC (Appeal); Christmas v Hampshire CC (Duty of Care); Keating v Bromley LBC (No.2) [1995] 2 A.C. 633; [1995] 3 W.L.R. 152; [1995] 3 All E.R. 353; [1995] 2 F.L.R. 276; [1995] 3 F.C.R. 337; 94 L.G.R. 313; (1995) 7 Admin. L.R. 705; [1995] Fam. Law 537; (1996) 160 L.G. Rev. 123; (1996) 160 L.G. Rev. 103; (1995) 145 N.L.J. 993, HL 16–017, 21–001, 21–027, 21–081, 21–082

X City Council v MB [2006] EWHC 168 (Fam); [2006] 2 F.L.R. 968; [2007] 3 F.C.R. 371; [2006] Fam. Law 637, Fam Div 2–037, 2–042

X Local Authority v B [2005] 1 F.L.R. 341, Fam Div 21–048

X v Netherlands (A/91); Y v Netherlands (A/91); sub nom. X and Y v Netherlands (8978/80) (1986) 8 E.H.R.R. 235, ECHR 19–004

X v United Kingdom (1978) 2 E.H.R.R. 63 16–024

X v X [2002] 1 F.L.R. 508; [2002] Fam. Law 98, Fam Div 13–004, 13–007, 13–008, 13–009, 13–014, 13–040, 13–066, 13–068

X, Y and Z v United Kingdom (21830/93) [1997] 2 F.L.R. 892; [1997] 3 F.C.R. 341; (1997) 24 E.H.R.R. 143; (1998) 39 B.M.L.R. 128; [1997] Fam. Law 605; (1997) 94(17) L.S.G. 25, ECHR 17–004, 17–010, 18–035

Xydhias v Xydhias [1999] 2 All E.R. 386; [1999] 1 F.L.R. 683; [1999] 1 F.C.R. 289; [1999] Fam. Law 301; (1999) 96(6) L.S.G. 34; (1999) 149 N.L.J. 52, CA (Civ Div) 13–004, 13–005, 13–009

Y (Child Orders: Restricting Applications), Re [1994] 2 F.L.R. 699; [1994] 2 F.C.R. 367; [1994] Fam. Law 615, Fam Div 18–028, 21–075

Y (Children) (Occupation Order), Re; sub nom. Y (Children) (Matrimonial Home: Vacation), Re [2000] 2 F.C.R. 470, CA (Civ Div) 9–019

Yaxley v Gotts; sub nom. Yaxley v Gott [2000] Ch. 162; [1999] 3 W.L.R. 1217; [2000] 1 All E.R. 711; [1999] 2 F.L.R. 941; (2000) 32 H.L.R. 547; (2000) 79 P. & C.R. 91; [1999] 2 E.G.L.R. 181; [1999] Fam. Law 700; [1999] E.G. 92 (C.S.); (1999) 96(28) L.S.G. 25; (1999) 143 S.J.L.B. 198; [1999] N.P.C. 76; (1999) 78 P. & C.R. D33, CA (Civ Div) 5–002, 5–006, 5–037

Young v Lauretani [2007] EWHC 1244 (Ch); [2007] Fam. Law 906; [2007] 2 P. & C.R. DG12, Ch D 5–011, 5–048

Young v Young [1984] F.L.R. 375 5–017

Young v Young (Costs: Order Nisi) [1998] 2 F.L.R. 1131; [1999] 3 F.C.R. 36; [1998] Fam. Law 660, CA (Civ Div) 13–012

Young v Young (Settlement: Variation) [1962] P. 27; [1961] 3 W.L.R. 1109; [1961] 3 All E.R. 695; (1961) 105 S.J. 665, CA 13–027

Yousef v Netherlands (33711/96) [2003] 1 F.L.R. 210; [2002] 3 F.C.R. 577; (2003) 36 E.H.R.R. 20; [2003] Fam. Law 89, ECHR 16–017, 19–004

Z (A Minor) (Freedom of Publication), Re; sub nom. Z (A Minor) (Identification: Restrictions on Publication), Re [1997] Fam. 1; [1996] 2 W.L.R. 88; [1995] 4 All E.R. 961; [1996] 1 F.L.R. 191; [1996] 2 F.C.R. 164; [1996] Fam. Law 90, CA (Civ Div) 17–015, 18–021, 18–053

Z and A (Children) (Contact: Supervision Order), Re [2000] 2 F.L.R. 406; [2000] Fam. Law 700, Fam Div 21–042

Z v United Kingdom (29392/95) [2001] 2 F.L.R. 612; [2001] 2 F.C.R. 246; (2002) 34 E.H.R.R. 3; 10 B.H.R.C. 384; (2001) 3 L.G.L.R. 51; (2001) 4 C.C.L. Rep. 310; [2001] Fam. Law 583, ECHR 16–017, 21–001, 21–027, 21–066

Zaffino v Zaffino [2006] 1 F.L.R. 410, CA 20–021

Zawadka v Poland (48542/99); sub nom. Zawadkaw v Poland (48542/99) [2005] 2 F.L.R. 897; [2006] 1 F.C.R. 371; (2007) 44 E.H.R.R. 9; [2005] Fam. Law 774, ECHR 18–026, 18–055

TABLE OF STATUTES

1533 Ecclesiastical Licences Act (25 Hen.8 c.21) 1–029
1601 Statute of Elizabeth s.6 15–001
1695 Marriage Duty Act s.102 1–003
1753 Clandestine Marriages Act (26 Geo.2 c.33) ..1–004, 1–005, 3–041
1772 Royal Marriages Act (12 Geo.3 c.11) 1–005, 1–008, 2–005
1774 Life Assurance Act (14 Geo.3 c.48) 3–002
1823 Marriage Act (4 Geo.4 c.76) ... 1–005
    s.22 1–005
1836 Marriage Act (6 & 7 Will.4 c.85) 1–005, 1–013, 1–032
    s.45 1–032
    Births and Deaths Registration Act (6 & 7 Will.4 c.86) ... 1–013
1837 Wills Act (7 Will.4 & Vict.1 c.26) 7–001, 7–002
    s.7 16–002
    s.11 16–002
    s.18 .... 7–002, 17–041
    s.18A 17–041
     (1) 11–003
     (2) 7–002
    s.18B 7–002
    s.18C(3) 7–002
1838 Judgment Act (1 & 2 Vict.c.26) 13–024
1844 Poor Law Amendment Act (7 & 8 Vict.c.101) 15–001
1846 Fatal Accidents Act (8 & 9 Vict.c.93) 3–038
1857 Matrimonial Causes Act (20 & 21 Vict.c.85) 10–004, 11–001
    s.6 10–004
    s.45 15–001
1861 Offences against the Person Act (24 & 25 Vict.c.100)
    s.18 9–004
    s.20 9–004
    s.42 9–004
    s.43 9–004
    s.47 9–004
1869 Debtors Act (32 & 33 Vict.c.62) 14–011
    s.5(2) 14–011
1870 Wages Attachment (Abolition) Act (33 & 34 Vict.c.30) 14–012
1874 Infants Relief Act (37 & 38 Vict.c.62) 16–002
1878 Matrimonial Causes Act (41 & 42 Vict.c.19) 15–001

1882 Married Women's Property Act (45 & 46 Vict.c.75) 3–002, 3–006
    s.17 ....3–006, 3–041, 5–045
1884 Matrimonial Cause Act (47 & 48 Vict.c.68)
    s.5 10–004
1886 Guardianship of Infants Act (49 & 50 Vict.c.27) 19–001
1889 Prevention of Cruelty to Children Act (52 & 53 Vict.c.44) 16–001, 21–061
1891 Custody of Children Act (54 & 55 Vict.c.3)
    s.4 19–016
1894 Prevention of Cruelty to Children Act (57 & 58 Vict.)
    s.4 21–047
    s.10 21–047
1898 Marriage Act (61 & 62 Vict. c.58) 1–039
1907 Deceased Wife's Sister's Marriage Act (7 Edw.7 c.47) ... 2–009
1918 Wills (Soldiers and Sailors) Act (7 & 8 Geo.5 c.58) 17–020
1921 Deceased Brother's Widow's Marriage Act (11 & 12 Geo.5 c.24) 2–009
1923 Matrimonial Cause Act (13 & 14 Geo.5 c.19) 10–004
1925 Law of Property Act (15 & 16 Geo.5 c.20) 5–006, 5–010
    s.1(6) 5–040, 16–002
    s.36(2) 5–008, 5–040, 5–041
    s.52 5–008
    s.53(1)(b) 5–010, 5–012, 5–027
     (c) 5–010, 5–029, 5–063
     (2) 5–010, 5–012
    s.184 5–040
    s.196(3) 5–041
     (4) 5–041
    s.199 5–051
     (1) 5–051
    Administration of Estates Act (15 & 16 Geo.5 c.23) 7–003, 7–004
    s.46(i) 17–020
     (iii) 17–020
     (1)(vi) 7–006
    s.47 7–004
    s.55(1)(x) 7–004
    Guardian of Infants Act (15 & 16 Geo.5 c.45) 17–001, 19–001
    s.1 19–001
    s.2 17–001

Widows' Orphans and Old Age
Contributory Pensions Act
(15 & 16 Geo.5 c.70) 6–003,
6–024
Criminal Justice Act (15 & 16
Geo.5 c.86)
s.47 3–037
1926 Adoption of Children Act (16
& 17 Geo.5 c.29) ...22–001, 22–004
s.2(3) 22–004, 22–032
s.5(2) 22–004
Legitimacy Act (16 & 17 Geo.5
c.70) 16–024
1933 Children and Young Persons
Act (23 & 24 Geo.5 c.12)
s.1 19–002
(1)(e) 16–017
s.3 19–002
s.4 19–002
s.11 19–002
ss.18–21 16–002
s.34A 17–027
s.40 21–047
s.42 21–064
s.43 21–064
s.44 19–002
s.50 16–002
Sch.1 .... 21–032, 21–062
1935 Law Reform (Married Women
and Tortfeasors) Act (25 &
26 Geo.5 c.30)
s.1 3–038
1937 Matrimonial Causes Act (1
Edw.8 & 1Geo.6 c.57) 2–045,
10–004, 10–005, 12–003
s.1 10–009
s.2 10–004
s.7(1) 2–052
(2) 2–052
s.8 12–003
1938 Inheritance (Family Provision)
Act (1 & 2 Geo.6 c.45) 7–001,
7–009
1939 Adoption of Children (Regulation) Act (2 & 3 Geo.6
c.27) 17–004
1944 Education Act (7 & 8 Geo.6
c.31) 6–028
1948 National Assistance Act (11 &
12 Geo.6 c.29)
s.1 6–003
s.29 21–010
Children Act (11 & 12 Geo.6
c.43) 21–002, 21–007, 21–011,
21–013
s.1 21–011
s.39 21–002
s.41 21–002
1949 Representation of the People
Act (12, 13 & 14 Geo.6
c.68)
s.1(1)(c) 16–002

Sch.2 16–002
Law Reform (Miscellaneous
Provisions) Act (12, 13 &
14 Geo.6)
s.4 2–052
Marriage Act (12, 13 & 14
Geo.6 c.76) ...1–006, 1–008, 1–019,
1–025, 1–032, 1–042,
1–044, 1–045, 1–047,
1–048, 1–049
Pt IV 1–039
Pt V 1–031
s.2 2–012
s.3 .... 1–006, 2–012
(1)(a) 1–010
(b) 1–010, 17–023, 21–080
(1A) 17–048, 18–005, 21–080
(a) 1–009
(b) 1–009, 17–048, 18–005
(c) 1–009
(d) 1–009, 17–048
(e) 1–009
(f) 1–009
(g) 1–009
(h) 1–009
(3) 1–008
(5) 17–023
(6) 1–009
s.4 1–038
s.5(d) 1–013, 1–020
s.5A 1–035
(b) 1–035
s.5B 1–035
s.6 1–022
(4) 1–022
s.7(1) 1–123
(2) 1–123
(3) 10123
s.11 .... 1–029, 1–036
s.12 .... 1–029, 1–036
(1) 1–022
s.15(1) 1–126
ss.15–16 1–125
s.16 1–027
(2) 1–028
s.22 1–037
s.25 .... 1–005, 1–045
s.26(1)(bb) 1–033
(d) 1–038
s.27(1) 1–014
s.27A 1–018
s.28A 1–014, 1–123
s.29 1–015
s.30 1–015
s.31(1) 1–014
(2) 1–015
(5A) 1–016
s.33 1–016
s.35 1–040
(2A) 1–033
s.41(1) 1–040
s.43 1–041

s.44(1) 1–042
(2) 1–042
(3) 1–034, 1–042
(3A) 1–034
(a) 1–034
(b) 1–034
s.45 1–034
(1) 1–034
(2) 1–034
s.46(1) 1–029
(2) 1–029
s.46B(1) 1–034
(3) 1–034
(4) 1–034
s.47 1–038
(1) 1–038
s.48 .... 1–046, 2–012
s.49 .... 1–005, 1–045
s.52 1–034
s.65 1–043
s.72 .... 1–022, 1–126
s.74(2) 1–004
s.75(1) 1–047
(a) 1–038
(2)(a) 1–048
s.78(1) 1–033
s.79(5) 1–032
(6) 1–029, 1–047
Sch.1 Pt I 2–008, 2–009, 22–008
Pt III 2–010
Sch.2 17–023
Adoption of Children Act (12,
    13 & 14 Geo.6 c.98) 22–006
s.3(4) 22–030
s.5 22–004
s.7(2) 22–004
s.9 22–004
s.10 22–004

1952 Intestates' Estates Act (15 & 16
        Geo.6 & 1 Eliz.2 c.64)
      Sch.2 7–007

1953 Births and Deaths Registration
        Act (1 & 2 Eliz.2 c.20) ... 17–010
      s.1(2) 17–010
      s.2 17–010
      (b) 17–010
      s.10 .... 17–010, 17–025
      (1) 17–010
      (a) 17–010
      (b) 17–010
      (c) 17–010
      (d) 17–010
      (f) 17–010
      (1A) 17–010
      s.10A(1) 17–010
      (f) 17–010
      (1A) 17–010
      s.10ZA 17–004
      s.14A 17–010, 17–012
      s.33 .... 17–010, 22–010
      s.34 12–001
      (2) 17–009

(6) 17–011
s.36 17–010

1956 Sexual Offences Act (4 & 5
        Eliz.2 c.69) 16–011
      s.5 16–011
      s.6(1) 16–011
      s.14 .... 16–011, 16–012
      s.28(1) 16–011
      (2) 16–011

1957 Maintenance Agreements Act
        (5 & 6 Eliz.2 c.35) 3–029
      Affiliation Proceedings Act (5
        & 6 Eliz.2 c.55) 15–046

1958 Adoption Act (7 & 8 Eliz.2
        c.5) 22–004
      s.3 22–004
      s.15 22–057
      Marriage Acts Amendment Act
        (7 & 8 Eliz.2 c.35)
      s.1(1) 1–040

      Maintenance Orders Act (7 & 8
        Eliz.2 c.39) 14–014, 14–015
      s.1 14–014
      (6) 14–015
      s.2(1) 14–014
      s.4(2) 14–014
      Matrimonial Proceedings (Chil-
        dren) Act (7 & 8 Eliz.2
        c.40) 18–044
      s.7 3–041

1959 Legitimacy Act (7 & 8 Eliz.2
        c.73) 16–024

1960 Marriage (Enabling) Act (8 & 9
        Eliz.2 c.29) 2–009
      Administration of Justice Act
        (8 & 9 Eliz.2 c.65)
      s.12 18–008

1962 Law Reform (Husband and
        Wife) Act (8 & 9 Eliz.2
        c.48) 3–002

1963 Betting, Gaming and Lotteries
        Act (11 Eliz.2 c.2)
      s.21 16–001
      Children and Young Persons
        Act (11 Eliz.2 c.37) 21–008
      s.16 16–002
      Matrimonial Cause Act (11
        Eliz.2 c.45)
      s.1 10–005
      s.2 10–005
      s.4 10–005

1964 Married Women's Property Act
        (11 Eliz.2 c.19) 3–007

1965 Law Commissions Act (11
        Eliz.2 c.22)
      s.3(1)(e) 10–007
      Matrimonial Causes Act (11
        Eliz.2 c.72)
      s.8(2)(b) 1–035

1967 Matrimonial Homes Act (11
    Eliz.2 c.75) ...3–010, 3–011, 3–012,
               9–007
    Abortion Act (11 Eliz.2 c.87) ... 22–037
1968 Guardianship Act
    s.5(4)(b) 18–019
    Theft Act (11 Eliz.2 c.60)
    s.30(1) 3–037
    Civil Evidence Act (11 Eliz.2
      c.64) 7–023
    s.12 17–012
1969 Children and Young Persons
    Act (11 Eliz.2 c.54)
    s.1(2)(b) 21–032
      (bb) 21–032
      (e) 21–032
      (f) 21–032
    s.2 21–027
    s.28 ....21–047, 22–070
      (2) 21–047
    Tatooing of Minors Act (11
      Eliz.2 c.64)
    s.1 16–001
    Family Law Reform Act (11
      Eliz.2 c.46) 1–011, 16–002
    s.1(1) 16–001
      (3) 16–024
    s.2 16–024
      (1)(c) 1–011
      (3) 1–023
    s.8 17–022
      (1) 16–012
      (3) 16–015
    s.14 16–024
    s.16 16–024
    s.18 16–024
    ss.18–20 16–025
    s.20 15–008
      (1) 17–007
      (1A) 17–008
    s.21 17–008
      (3) 15–008, 17–008
    s.23 17–004
      (1) 17–008
    s.26 17–004
    s.28 16–024
    Sch.12 para.6(2) 17–010
    Divorce Reform Act (11 Eliz.2
      c.55) 10–001, 10–002, 10–007,
            10–015, 10–017, 10–020,
            10–027, 10–042, 10–047,
            10–048, 11–001, 11–002,
            13–003, 13–032, 13–033,
                      13–082
    s.1(2)(d) 13–003
1970 Income and Corporation Taxes
    Act (11 Eliz.2 c.10)
    s.31(1) 3–034
    Administration of Justice Act
      (11 Eliz.2 c.31) 14–011, 18–050
    s.1(2) 18–049
    s.11 14–011

    Sch.8 ....14–012, 14–015
      para.2A 14–011
    Law Reform (Miscellaneous
      Provisions) Act (11 Eliz.2
      c.33) 2–057, 3–003, 3–041,
             16–003, 17–019
    s.2 3–006
      (1) 3–041
      (2) 3–041
    s.3(1) 3–041
      (2) 3–041
    s.5 17–019
    Marriage (Registrar General's
      Licence) Act (11 Eliz.2
      c.34) 1–016, 1–019
    s.1 1–019
    s.8(1) 1–047
    s.19 1–029
    Equal Pay Act (c.41) 4–003
    Local Authority Social Services
      Act (11 Eliz.2 c.42) 21–002,
                     21–006
    s.2 21–002
    s.3 21–002
    s.6 21–002
    s.7B 21–025
    Sch.1 21–021
    Matrimonial Proceedings and
      Property Act (11 Eliz.2
      c.45) 3–008, 3–041, 13–031,
             13–033, 13–034
    s.37 ....3–008, 3–009, 3–041
    s.39 3–006
    s.40 3–038
1971 Guardianship of Minors Act
    (11 Eliz.2 c.3) 17–040
    s.1 19–001
    s.14A 18–033
    Attachment of Earnings Act (11
      Eliz.2 c.32) 14–012
    s.3 14–012
      (3A) 14–012
    s.6(1) 14–012
      (b) 14–012
      (5) 14–012
      (a) 14–012
      (b) 14–012
      (6)(b) 14–012
      (7) 14–012
      (9) 14–012
    s.7(4)(a) 14–012
    s.9(4) 14–012
    s.13 14–012
    s.14(1) 14–012
      (b) 14–012
      (2) 14–012
    s.15 14–012
    s.24(1) 14–012
      (2) 14–012
    s.25(3) 14–012
    Sch.3 Pt I 14–012
      Pt II 14–012

para.3 14–012
para.6(2) 14–012
   (3) 14–012
   (4) 14–012
Nullity of Marriage Act (11
   Eliz.2 c.44) ...2–005, 2–021, 2–034,
                  2–044, 2–047
s.3(4) 2–028, 2–050
Immigration Act (11 Eliz.2
   c.77)
s.1(1) 3–040
s.3(1) 3–040
   (2) 3–040
1972 Matrimonial Proceedings (Po-
    lygamous Marriages) Act
    (c.38)
s.1 2–022
Land Charges Act (c.61) 3–012,
                           14–008
s.2(7) 3–012
s.4(8) 3–012
1973 Matrimonial Causes Act (c.18) ...2–005,
             2–021, 2–028, 2–047,
             2–050, 4–001, 6–013,
             7–024, 10–001, 10–015,
             10–016, 10–042, 11–003,
             11–005, 12–003, 13–001,
             13–002, 13–006, 13–021,
             13–024, 13–031, 13–070,
             13–080, 13–086, 13–124,
             15–001, 15–007, 15–028,
             18–014, 18–044
Pt II 9–022, 13–001, 13–040, 13–023
s.1(2) 10–015
   (a) 10–038
   (b) 10–019
   (b)–(e) 10–057
   (c) 10–033
   (d) 10–027, 10–034, 10–038
   (e) 10–027, 10–034, 10–038
   (4) 10–015
s.2(1) 10–021, 10–026
   (2) 10–021
   (3) 10–026
   (4) 10–032
   (5) 10–033
   (6) 10–037
   (7) 10–041
s.3(1) 10–009
   (2) 10–009
s.5 .... 10–040, 10–042, 11–003
s.6 10–015
   (2) 10–016
s.7(1)(a) 2–030
s.8 10–011
s.10(1) 10–041
   (2) 10–027, 10–046
s.10A 10–014
s.11 .... 2–006, 17–031
   (c) 2–017
   (d) 2–022
s.12 2–023

   (a) 2–024
   (b) 2–030
   (c) 2–034
   (d) 2–045
   (e) 2–045
   (f) 2–045
   (g) 2–019, 2–046
   (h) 2–046
s.13(1) 2–028, 2–050
   (2) 2–048
   (2A) 2–049
   (3) 2–049
   (4) 2–048
s.15 2–052
s.16 .... 2–052, 17–031
s.17(1) 10–032, 11–002
   (2) 11–002
s.18(1) 11–005
   (2) 11–003
s.19(1) 12–003
   (3) 12–003
   (4) 12–003
   (6) 12–003
s.21 13–017
   (1)(a) 13–018
   (b) 13–018
   (c) 13–024
   (2)(a) 13–025, 13–026
   (c) 13–027
s.21A 13–017, 13–029
   (1) 13–124
   (b) 13–125
s.22 .... 13–030, 13–037
s.23 ....2–056, 3–025, 13–101
   (1) 13–001
   (a) 13–018, 15–038
   (b) 13–018
   (d) 15–039
   (e) 15–039
   (f) 15–043
   (3)(a) 15–043
   (b) 15–043
   (c) 13–024
   (6) 13–024
ss.23–24D 13–030
ss.23–25A 13–013
s.24 .....2–056, 13–023, 13–101, 13–118
   (1) 13–001
   (a) 13–025, 15–043
   (b) 13–026, 15–043
   (c) 13–027, 13–123, 15–043
   (d) 13–027, 13–123, 15–043
s.24A 13–023, 13–027, 13–028,
                       15–043
   (1) 13–027
s.24B 13–017, 13–029
   (1) 13–001, 13–030, 13–124
   (2) 13–124
   (3) 13–122, 13–124
   (4) 13–122, 13–124
   (5) 13–122, 13–124

s.25 ... 13–006, 13–008, 13–040, 13–041,
         13–043, 13–044, 13–046, 13–047,
         13–048, 13–050, 13–053, 13–056,
         13–072, 13–098, 13–119, 13–122
  (1) 13–008, 13–035, 13–039,
         13–051, 13–057, 13–072, 15–001,
              15–026, 15–040, 19–002
    (d) 7–027
    (f)..7–027
  (2) 13–008, 13–039, 13–040,
         13–043, 13–045, 13–046, 13–051,
                     13–057, 13–063
    (a) 13–051, 13–063, 13–066,
                     13–071, 13–021
    (b) 13–043, 13–048, 13–053,
                                  13–071
    (c) 13–053, 13–074
    (d) 13–053, 13–055, 13–075
    (e) 13–053, 13–077
    (f) 7–030, 13–044, 13–045,
         13–048, 13–055, 13–078, 13–079
    (g) 7–024, 13–008, 13–055,
         13–080, 13–082, 13–083, 13–084
    (h) 13–085, 13–021
  (3) ... 7–028, 13–039, 15–044, 17–028,
                                  18–034
  (4) 7–028, 15–044, 17–028
  (6) 13–027
s.25A 13–022, 13–039, 13–086
  (1) 13–088
  (2) 13–023, 13–089
  (3) 13–092
s.25B(1) 13–121
  (4) 13–101
  (5) 13–122
  (7B) 13–122
ss.25B–25D 13–122
s.25D(2)(e) 13–119
s.27 .... 3–015, 3–021, 10–009
  (3) 3–022
  (6)(b) 3–023
  (c) 3–023
s.28 3–024
  (1)(a) 3–023, 13–020, 13–021
  (b) 3–023, 13–020
  (1A) 13–091
s.29(1) 15–032
  (2) 15–041
    (a) 15–041
    (b) 15–041
  (3) 15–032, 15–041
  (4) 15–041
s.31 .... 13–101, 15–045
  (1) 13–095
  (2) 13–101
    (dd) 13–093, 13–122
    (f) 13–028
    (g) 13–093
  (2A) 14–002
  (4) 13–101
  (7) 13–098
    (a) 13–099

    (7A) 13–104
      (b) 13–100
    (7A)–(7G) 13–100
    (7B)(a)–(c) 13–100
      (c) 13–100
    (10) 13–097
s.32 14–002
  (1) 14–002
s.33A(1) 13–007
  (3) 13–005
s.34(1) 3–031, 13–004
  (2) 3–030, 3–031
s..34–36 3–029
s.35 .... 3–032, 13–004
  (2) 3–032
  (3) 3–032
s.36 3–032
s.41 .... 2–051, 18–044, 18–047
  (1) 10–013
  (2) 10–013
s.43 .... 18–044, 18–048
s.47 2–022
s.52(1) 13–060, 15–039, 17–028
Sch.1 para.6 2–005
Guardianship Act (c.29) 17–001
  s.1 19–001
    (1) 17–048
  s.2(2)(b) 18–044
Domicile and Matrimonial Pro-
      ceedings Act (c.45) 15–010
  s.1 3–002
1974 Local Government Act (c.7)
  s.26 21–083
      Juries Act (c.23)
  s.7(2)(a) 16–002
1975 Child Benefit Act (c.61) 6–023
      Inheritance (Provision for Fam-
      ily and Dependents) Act
      (c.63) A–005, 7–001, 7–002,
                 7–006, 7–008, 7–009,
                 7–011, 7–013, 7–020,
                 7–023, 7–024, 7–026,
                 7–031, 7–032, 11–003,
                                  13–092
  s.1 16–024
    (b)(a) 7–017
    (ba) 7–032
    (1)(a) 2–057, 7–012
      (b) 2–056, 7–013
      (d) 22–001
      (e) 7–016
    (1A) 7–017, 7–032
    (1B) 7–017
    (2)(a) 7–021
      (aa) 7–021
      (b) 7–022
    (3) 7–016
  s.2(1)(a) 7–031
    (b) 7–031
    (c) 7–031
    (d) 7–031
    (e) 7–031

(f) 7–031
(g) 7–031
(4) 7–031
s.3 .... 7–015, 7–019
(1) 7–023, 7–031, 7–032
(a)–(f) 7–030
(2) 7–026
(2A) 7–017, 7–030, 7–032
(3) 7–015, 7–028
(a) 7–028
(b) 7–028
(c) 7–028
(4) 7–029
(5) 7–023
s.8 7–024
s.10 7–031
s.11 7–031
s.15 7–013
(1) 7–014
s.15A 7–013
s.15B 7–013
s.15ZA 7–013
ss.16–18 7–031
s.19 7–031
(2) 7–031
s.20 7–031
s.21 7–023
s.25 7–024
(1) 2–056, 16–024
(b) 7–014
(4) 2–057, 7–012
(5) 7–013
Sex   Discrimination   Act
(c.65) 6–030
Children Act (c.72) 17–001, 17–043,
21–004, 21–011, 21–017,
22–004, 22–006, 22–011,
22–038, 22–040, 22–056,
22–057, 22–058
s.10(3) 17–043, 22–004
s.11(4) 17–043
s.14 .... 21–005, 22–004, 22–038
s.26 22–011
s.33 21–005
s.34(1)(a) 18–033
(5) 18–044
s.56 21–011
s.57 21–005
s.85(1) 17–001, 17–024
s.86 16–012
(1) 17–002
s.87(1) 17–001
Sch.1 .... 16–024, 22–006
para.5 22–004
Sch.3 para.8 22–008
1976 Congenital Disabilities (Civil
Liability) Act (c.28)
s.1(1) 17–027
s.2 17–027
Fatal Accidents Act (c.30) 7–017,
12–001, 16–024
s.1A 3–003

Legitimacy Act (c.31) 16–024,
17–031, 17–032
s.1 .... 2–055, 16–024, 17–031
(2) 17–031
(3) 17–031
(4) 17–031
s.2 17–032
s.2A 17–032
s.4 17–032
s.8 16–024
s.9 17–010
Adoption Act (c.36) 9–018, 22–004,
22–022, 22–057
s.1 .... 22–004, 22–022
s.6 22–024
s.11 22–002
s.12 22–001
(1) 22–005
(2) 22–005
(3) 17–049
(4) 22–005
(6) 22–067
s.14(3) 17–043, 22–004
s.15(3)(b) 19–004
(4) 17–043
s.16(2) 22–024
(a) 22–032
s.18 .... 21–005, 22–004, 22–038
s.19 22–029
s.20 22–029
s.24(2) 22–029, 22–069
s.25 22–068
s.26 22–004
(1) 18–044
s.28 22–045
s.30 22–069
s.39 ...22–001, 22–005, 22–006, 22–007,
22–078
(1) 22–006
s.42 22–006
ss.42–46 22–078
s.43 22–006
s.47(1) 22–008
s.50 22–078
(1) 22–010
(2) 22–010
(3) 22–010
(4) 22–011
(5) 22–011
s.51(2) 22–008
(7) 22–011
(8) 22–011
s.51A 22–004, 22–013
s.56A 22–051
s.57 22–022
(4) 22–004
s.57A 22–004, 22–022
s.58 22–004
s.63(2) 22–078
Sch.1 para.1 22–010
para.3 22–010

Domestic Violence and Matrimonial Proceedings Act (c.50) 9–007, 9–022
Supplementary Benefits Act (c.71)
s.1(1) 6–003
1977 Marriage (Scotland) Act (c.15)
s.2 2–008
Sch.1 2–008
Rent Act (c.42)
Sch.1para.3 9–029
Criminal Law Act (c.45)
s.2(2)(a) 3–002, 3–037
National Health Service Act (c.49) 16–011
s.84 21–017
1978 Domestic Proceedings and Magistrates Courts Act (c.22) 3–015, 3–016, 3–018, 9–007, 13–014, 14–014, 15–001, 15–028, 18–014
Pt 1 15–007
s.1 3–017
s.2 3–017
(2) 3–017
s.3(2) 3–017
(3) 3–017
(4) 3–017
s.4(2) 3–019
s.6 3–017
(1)(a) 3–018
(b) 3–018
s.7 3–016
s.10(1) 18–044
s.14 18–033
s.20(1) 3–020
(3) 3–020
(6) 3–020
(7) 3–020
s.22 3–017
s.25(1) 3–019
(2) 3–019
s.32(4) 14–002
s.88(3) 3–019
Adoption (Scotland) Act (c.28)
s.45(5) 22–011
1979 Charging Orders Act (c.53) 5–060, 14–008, 14–009
s.1 14–008
s.2 14–008
(1)(b) 14–008
s.3(5) 14–008
1980 Childcare Act (c.5) 21–013
s.1 .... 21–007, 21–027
(2) 21–013
s.2 .... 21–005, 21–007, 21–011
s.3 .... 21–005, 21–041
(1)(b) 17–027
(v) 17–027
s.10(2) 17–001
ss.12A–12F 21–074
s.13 21–011

s.18 21–027
s.76 21–017
Magistrates Courts Act (c.43)
s.59(1) 14–018
(2) 14–018
(3)(c) 14–015
(d) 14–018
s.59B 14–019
s.63 21–042
(1) 9–035
(3) 17–048, 18–056
s.65(1)(j) 3–015
s.67 3–015
s.75(1) 3–017
s.76 14–017
(1) 14–016
(2) 14–016
(3) 14–016
s.77(1) 14–016
(2) 14–017
s.93(2) 14–017
(5) 14–017
(6) 14–017
(b) 14–017
(c) 14–017
(7) 14–017
(8) 14–017
s.94 14–017
s.95 14–002
s.132 14–017
s.150 14–015
Sch.4 para.3 14–017
Housing Act (c.51) 13–118
Limitation Act (c.58) 21–066
1981 Matrimonial Homes and Property Act (c.24)
s.8(1) 13–028
Contempt of Court Act (c.49)
s.14 18–056
(1) 9–035
(2) 9–035
s.17 18–056
(2) 18–056
Sch.3 18–056
Supreme Court Act (c.54)
s.37 .... 9–042, 14–009
s.41(2) 18–054
s.42 18–028
s.51 20–002
s.61 18–050
s.90 18–009
s.116 17–026
s.138(3A) 14–005
Sch.1 18–050
British Nationality Act (c.61) ... 16–025, 22–007
s.1 22–052
(1) 16–025
(5) 22–007
s.2(1) 16–025
s.3(1) 22–007
s.6(2) 3–040

s.50(9)(b) 16–025
   (9A) 16–025
Sch.1 para.3 3–040
1982 Social Security and Housing
       Benefits Act (c.24) 6–020
     Forfeiture Act (c.34) 7–004
     Administration of Justice Act
       (c.53) 3–003, 7–002, 11–003,
                                      17–019
     Pt IV 7–001
     s.1(5)(b) 16–024
     s.2(b) 17–019
     s.3 3–003
        (1) 3–038
     s.18 7–002
        (2) 7–002
     s.18B 7–002
     s.18C 7–002
     s.53 14–012
     s.76(11) 7–002
1983 Representation of the People
       Act (c.2)
     s.9B 9–005
     Matrimonial Homes Act (c.19) ...3–010,
                                 9–007, 9–010
     s.1(11) 9–015
     Mental Health Act (c.20) 2–023,
                        2–045, 16–016, 17–018,
                                      21–077
     s.1(1)(a) 3–010
        (2) 2–045
     s.131 16–016
     Sch.4 para.34 2–045
     Marriage Act (c.32) 1–018, 1–019
     s.1 1–031
     Sch.1 para.12 1–029
     Health and Social Services and
       Social Security Adjudica-
       tions Act (c.41) 16–017
1984 County Courts Act (c.28)
     s.38 ....9–042, 14–009, 18–056
     s.74 13–024
     s.107 14–009
     Child Abduction Act (c.37) 17–014,
                  20–002, 20–004, 20–016
     ss.1(1)–(3) 18–005
        (2) 20–002
        (3) 20–002
        (4A) 20–002
     s.2 ....17–014, 17–051, 20–002
        (3)(a) 20–002
     Matrimonial and Family Pro-
       ceedings Act (c.42) 7–013,
               11–005, 13–006, 13–031,
               13–036, 13–067, 13–074,
               13–083, 13–124, 15–001,
                                      18–054
     Pt III 18–014
     s.1 10–009
     s.2(2) 2–048
        (3) 2–048
     s.7 13–007

s.10 3–017
s.17L 7–013
s.38(2)(b) 18–050, 18–054
   (5) 18–050
Inheritance Tax Act (c.51)
s.18 3–034
s.22 3–034
Police and Criminal Evidence
  Act (c.60)
s.17(1)(e) 21–024, 21–049
s.24 ....9–004, 20–002
s.80 9–004
   (2) 3–039
   (3) 3–039
   (4) 3–039
1985 Family Law (Scotland) Act
       (c.37)
     ss.9–10 13–002
     Surrogacy Arrangements Act
       (c.49) 22–070
     s.1 22–071
     s.1A 22–072
     s.2 22–071
     Child Abduction and Custody
       Act (c.60) 20–007, 20–012
     Pt I 20–014
     s.1 20–014
     s.3 20–013
     s.14 20–013
     s.24A 20–007
     Housing Act (c.68) 6–039, 13–118
1986 Marriage (Prohibited Degrees
       of Relationship) Act (c.16) ...2–008,
                          2–009, 22–008
     s.3 1–035
     s.6(2) 2–007
     s.78 2–008
     Insolvency Act (c.45) 5–058, 5–059,
                          7–031, 14–005
     s.264 14–005
     s.279 14–005
     s.281 14–005
     s.283 5–058
        (2)(a) 5–058
        (b) 5–058
     s.283A 5–058
     s.284 ....5–058, 14–005
     s.285(3)(b) 14–005
     s.306 14–005
     s.324 14–005
     s.335A 5–058
        (2) 5–058
        (3) 5–058
     s.336 5–058
     s.337 5–058
        (5) 5–059
     s.339 3–038
     s.423 3–038
     Family Law Act (c.55) 17–010,
               18–051, 20–007, 20–008,
                                      20–010
     Pt III 17–012

s.1 .... 18–051, 20–010
  (1)(a) 18–030, 20–010
s.2 20–010
  (1) 18–030, 20–010
  (3) 20–010
    (b) 18–051
s.2A 18–030, 18–051, 20–010
  (1) 20–010
  (2) 20–010
s.3 .... 18–030, 20–010
  (1) 18–051
  (2) 18–051
s.4 18–030
s.5 20–011
s.13 20–010
s.14 .... 17–010, 20–011
s.15 20–010
s.20(2A) 17–007
s.21 20–010
s.22 20–011
s.25 20–010
s.27 20–011
s.29 20–011
s.30 20–011
s.31 20–011
s.32(1) 20–011
s.33 18–049
  (1) 20–007
  (2) 20–007
s.34 ....18–049, 18–057, 20–010
s.37 .... 18–049, 20–003
s.41 20–011
s.42(1) 20–010
  (2) 20–010
  (3) 20–010
s.55 .... 2–005, 17–012
  (1) 2–056, 17–012
  (2) 17–012
  (3) 17–012
s.55A 15–008, 17–004, 17–007,
                           17–012
  (2) 17–012
  (3) 17–012
  (4) 17–012
  (5) 17–012
  (7) 17–012
s.56 ...15–008, 17–007, 17–010, 17–012
  (1) 17–012
  (2) 17–012
  (4) 17–012
s.58(1) 17–012
  (2) 17–012
s.59 17–012
Education (No.2) Act (c.61)
s.15(4) 16–002
Public Order Act (c.64)
s.4A 9–005
1987 Crossbows Act (c.32)
s.1 16–001

Family Law Reform Act (c.42) 2–021,
        15–001, 16–024, 17–003,
        17–004, 17–030, 17–036,
                       22–080
s.1 17–030
  (1) 16–024
  (3) 17–029, 17–035
s.18 7–004
  (2) 17–020
s.20(1) 17–003
  (2) 17–003
s.22 .... 2–005, 17–012
s.23 .... 17–003, 17–007
  (1) 17–003
s.26 17–010
s.27 .... 2–021, 17–003
s.28 .... 2–055, 17–031
  (1) 17–031
1988 Social Security Act (c.7)
s.4(1) 16–002
Malicious Communications Act
  (c.27) 9–005
Criminal Justice Act (c.33)
s.34(2) 21–064
Finance Act (c.39)
s.32 3–034
1989 Law of Property (Miscellane-
  ous Provisions) Act (c.34)
s.2 5–006
  (5) 5–006
Children Act (c.41) 2–021, 5–046,
      6–028, 6–039, 9–008,
      9–017, 9–018, 10–009,
      10–013, 15–031, 15–039,
      15–046, 15–051, 16–001,
      16–003, 16–009, 16–012,
      16–015, 16–016, 16–019,
      16–021, 16–022, 17–002,
      17–012, 17–022, 17–024,
      17–027, 17–030, 17–036,
      17–040, 17–043, 17–044,
      17–047, 17–048, 17–051,
      18–001, 18–004, 18–008,
    18–013—18–016, 18–023,
      18–031, 18–040, 18–044,
      18–047, 18–052, 18–054,
      19–002, 19–003, 19–012,
      19–019, 19–020, 19–023,
      20–008, 21–001, 21–007,
      21–013, 21–015, 21–017,
      21–019, 21–020, 21–027,
      21–038, 21–043, 21–044,
      21–046, 21–053, 21–067,
      21–068, 21–070, 21–071,
      21–075, 21–079, 21–081,
      21–082, 21–085, 22–003,
      22–004, 22–005, 22–013,
      22–022, 22–024, 22–026,
      22–033, 22–034, 22–040,
      22–056, 22–058, 22–060,
              22–063, 22–073
Pt I 18–014, 20–007

Pt II 18–014, 21–008
Pt III 16–001, 21–010, 21–013,
  21–020, 21–035, 22–023, 22–064
Pt IV 16–022, 17–015, 18–006,
  18–014, 18–015, 18–029, 19–015,
  21–020
Pt V 16–022, 18–014, 21–020
Pt VI–VIII 21–068
Pt IX 22–054
s.1 ....16–006, 16–009, 16–019, 17–002,
  17–007, 17–014, 17–015, 17–024,
  17–025, 17–042, 18–053, 19–001,
  19–002, 21–074
  (1) 13–060, 15–026, 18–028,
  19–003, 22–063
  (2) 18–006, 19–019
  (3) 16–004, 16–019, 19–002,
  19–013, 21–030
  (4) 19–015, 21–030
  (b) 21–045
  (5) 17–037, 18–005, 19–023,
  21–030, 21–032, 21–043
s.2 ......1–009, 17–027, 19–012, 22–058,
  22–063
  (1) 17–030
  (1A) 17–030
  (6) 17–037
  (7) 17–037, 17–048, 18–005,
  18–015, 18–016, 18–030
  (8) 17–002, 17–015, 17–048,
  18–015, 18–016
  (9) 17–038, 17–045, 17–050,
  22–001, 22–073
  (10) 17–050
  (11) 17–050, 22–001
s.3 ......1–009, 16–003, 17–027, 17–029,
  22–005, 22–058, 22–064, 22–066
  (1) 17–002, 17–013
  (2) 17–020
  (5) 17–001, 17–014, 17–038,
  17–051, 18–016, 21–013, 21–067,
  22–001
s.4 ....17–002, 17–036, 17–037, 18–016,
  18–017, 21–041, 22–064, 22–066,
  22–075
  (1)(a) 17–036, 17–039
  (b) 17–036
  (1A) 17–039
  (2) 17–038, 17–039
  (2A) 17–037, 17–039
  (3) 17–037, 17–039, 17–049
s.4A 17–002, 17–043, 17–045,
  18–032, 21–041, 22–059, 22–063
  (1)(b) 22–059
  (3) 17–049
s.4ZA 17–037
  (1)(a) 17–039
  (b) 17–038
s.5 .... 17–029, 22–005
  (1) 17–040, 17–041, 17–042,
  17–049
  (b) 18–016

(1)–(5) 17–040
(2) 17–041, 17–042, 17–049
(3) 17–029, 17–041, 18–016
(3A) 17–041
(4) 17–029, 17–040, 17–041,
  18–016, 22–060
(5) 17–041
(6) 17–001, 17–040, 19–024
(7) 17–040, 17–041, 18–005
  (b) 18–016
(7)–(9) 18–005
(8) 17–041
(9) 18–016
(10) 17–041
(11) 17–020, 17–042
(12) 17–042
s.6(1) 17–041
(2) 17–041
(3) 17–041
(4) 17–041
(5) 17–041
(6) 17–041
(7)(a) 21–041
s.7 ....17–042, 18–008, 18–010, 18–011,
  18–012, 18–013, 18–042, 18–048,
  19–017, 21–006
(1) 18–008
(4)(b) 18–012
s.7A 21–006
s.8 ......9–031, 16–001, 16–015, 16–019,
  17–002, 17–022, 17–024, 17–025,
  17–028, 17–029, 17–044, 17–048,
  17–052, 18–001, 18–014, 18–015,
  18–020, 18–029, 18–030, 18–036,
  18–037, 18–047, 18–051, 18–052,
  18–056, 18–057, 19–002, 19–010,
  19–012, 19–023, 20–002, 20–007,
  21–040, 21–073, 21–074, 21–079,
  22–019, 22–043, 22–063, 22–066
(1) 16–003, 18–015, 18–016,
  18–018, 18–021, 18–022, 18–030,
  18–031, 18–032, 19–020, 21–040,
  21–045, 21–067
(3) 18–001, 21–040, 22–059
  (a) 18–049
(4) 18–001
  (a) 21–040
(5A) 18–031
s.9(1) 16–016, 18–020, 18–029,
  18–030, 21–040
(1)–(3) 18–029
(2) 16–019, 19–030, 21–040,
  21–080
(3) 17–044, 18–014, 18–030,
  18–036, 22–060
  (b) 18–037
(5) 16–019, 19–023, 21–013,
  21–040, 21–080
  (a) 18–029
  (b) 18–029
(6) 16–019, 17–027, 17–044,
  18–017, 18–030

(7) 16–001, 17–027, 18–024
s.10 ....17–022, 18–005, 21–045
  (c)(ii) 18–036
  (1) 17–044, 18–001, 18–007,
     18–014, 18–030, 19–023, 21–040,
     22–059, 22–060, 22–077
    (a) 19–002
    (b) 18–030, 22–063
  (2) 17–044, 18–001
    (b) 18–030
  (4) 17–024, 18–021, 18–032,
     21–006
    (a) 17–052
    (b) 17–052
  (5) 17–014, 17–024, 17–029,
     17–044, 18–033, 22–060, 22–073
    (a) 18–030, 18–033
    (c) 18–005, 18–033
  (5A) 17–014, 17–029, 17–044,
     18–033, 22–045
  (5B) 18–033, 18–037
  (6) 16–019, 18–033
  (7) 18–033
  (7A) 22–064
  (8) 16–001, 16–003, 16–019,
     18–030, 18–035, 18–038, 21–006
  (9) 16–020, 18–020, 18–030,
     18–035, 19–002, 21–074
    (a) 18–039
    (c) 18–039
    (d) 18–036
  (10) 17–014
s.11(1) 18–024, 19–019
  (4) 18–016
  (5) 18–017
  (6) 18–020
  (7) 18–018, 18–021, 18–058,
     19–023
    (b) 17–048, 20–002
    (c) 18–024
    (d) 18–024
s.11A 17–027, 18–018
  (5) 18–010, 18–058
  (6) 18–045, 18–058
  (7) 18–058
s.11A–11G 17–048
s.11B 17–027
  (1) 18–058
s.11C 18–018
s.11G(2) 18–010
s.11H(2) 18–010, 18–058
  (3) 18–058
s.11I 18–058
s.11J 18–058
  (2) 18–058
s.11L(2) 18–058
  (7) 18–058
s.11O 18–058
  (11) 18–058
s.12 19–024
  (1) 17–002, 18–016, 18–017
  (1A) 17–037, 18–016

(2) 16–003, 17–001, 17–002,
     21–041
  (3) 17–048
  (4) 17–037, 18–016
  (5) 16–019, 17–027, 17–044,
     18–017, 18–024, 22–060, 22–064
  (6) 17–027, 17–044, 18–017,
     22–060, 22–064
  (8) 19–023
s.13 ....17–025, 17–026, 19–024
  (1) 16–019, 17–048, 18–016,
     18–021, 18–022
    (a) 17–025
    (b) 20–017, 21–079
  (2) 18–016, 18–026, 20–002,
     20–015, 20–017
  (3) 17–048
s.14 .... 17–048, 18–056
  (2) 18–056
s.14A 17–029
  (2)–(5) 17–046
  (3)(b) 17–046
  (5) 22–060
    (b) 22–060
    (c) 22–060
  (6) 22–060
    (b) 17–046, 22–059, 22–063
  (7) 17–046
  (8) 22–069
  (9) 17–046, 22–069
  (11) 22–069
ss.14A–14G ...17–043, 17–046, 22–001,
     22–005, 22–019
s.14C 17–046, 17–048
  (1)(a) 17–002
    (b) 17–040
  (3) 21–079, 22–064
  (4) 17–048
  (5) 17–026
s.14D 17–046, 22–064
  (2) 17–049
  (5) 17–049
  (6) 17–049
s.14F 17–046, 22–066
  (1) 22–023
  (2) 22–023
s.14G 17–046
  (4)(b) 22–060
s.16 ...16–019, 17–042, 18–010, 18–011,
     18–013, 18–018
  (1) 18–014, 18–027
  (2) 18–027
    (b) 22–033
  (3) 18–027
  (4) 18–027
  (4A) 18–027
  (6) 18–027
s.16A 18–010, 18–040, 18–057
s.17 ....6–039, 17–044, 18–022, 21–003,
     21–009, 21–010, 21–012, 21–027,
     21–012, 21–015, 21–085, 22–023
  (1) 21–009, 21–085

(a) 17–027, 19–002
(2) 21–009
(3) 21–010
(4) 21–006
(4A) 16–019
(5) 21–009
(6) 6–039, 21–009
(7)–(9) 21–009
(10) 21–010
(11) 21–010
s.17A 21–009
s.18 6–028
s.20 ....6–037, 18–036, 21–009, 21–012,
        21–014, 21–049, 21–067
(1) 21–012
(2) 21–085
(3) 21–012
(4) 21–012
(5) 21–012, 21–077
(5)–(8)(a) 22–028
(6) 16–019
(7) 21–013
(7)–(9) 18–029
(7)–(10) 21–013
(8) 16–019, 17–015, 18–005
(9) 17–015, 18–005, 18–029,
                                        21–013
(10) 18–029
(11) 16–019, 21–012, 21–013,
                                        21–073
s.21 21–021
(1) 21–049
s.22 22–039
(1) 17–048, 21–067
(b) 18–030
(2) 18–030
(3) 17–027, 21–067
(a) 19–002, 21–068
(3)–(5) 18–036, 22–045
(3A) 21–067
(4) 16–004, 16–017, 17–048,
                                21–039, 21–068
(a) 21–073
(b) 16–019, 21–072
(c) 21–072
(d) 17–051
(5) 16–004, 16–017, 21–039,
                                        21–068
(a) 16–019, 21–073
(b) 21–072
(c) 19–020, 22–024
(6) 19–002
s.22A 21–068
ss.22A–F 21–041
s.22B 21–068
s.22C 21–039, 21–068, 21–070
(5)–(9) 21–068
(6)(a) 18–037, 21–068
(7)(a) 18–037
(8)(c) 21–076
(10) 21–068
(11) 21–068

s.23 .... 21–021, 21–068
(1) 21–068
(5) 21–068
(6) 21–071
(7) 21–068
(b) 19–015, 21–076
(8) 21–068
s.23A 6–037
ss.23A–24D 21–041, 22–064
ss.23A–24E 21–012, 21–071
s.23CA 21–071
s.23D 21–071
s.24 21–003
(1) 21–067, 21–071
ss.24–24D 21–045
s.24B 21–071
s.24D 21–082
s.25 ...16–022, 17–017, 18–014, 19–002,
                                        21–078
(1) 21–077
(4) 21–078
(5) 21–078
(9) 21–078
s.25A(1) 21–069
ss.25A–25C 21–069
s.26 ...17–048, 17–048, 18–020, 21–069
(2)(k) 21–007, 21–040
(2A) 21–007, 21–040
(2B) 21–007, 21–040
(2C) 21–007, 21–040
(3) 21–004, 21–010, 21–082
(a) 21–073
(a)–(c) 21–082
(b) 21–072
(d) 21–082
(e) 21–082
(3A) 21–082
(3B) 21–082, 22–020
(4) 21–082
(6) 22–043
(7) 21–082
s.26A 16–004, 21–082
s.27 .... 6–039, 22–023
(2) 21–015, 21–085
(3) 21–015
s.29(3) 17–048
s.31 ...16–022, 17–015, 17–016, 17–022,
        17–027, 18–015, 19–023, 21–054
(1) 18–048, 21–030, 21–040
(2) 16–001, 18–029, 19–002,
        19–002, 19–021, 19–023, 21–031,
                        22–033, 22–043
(3) 16–001, 17–027, 21–030
(3A) 21–039
(4) 18–048
(7) 21–030
(9) ...9–017, 19–021. 21–021, 21–030,
                                        21–032
(10) 9–017, 21–032
s.31A 21–039
s.32 .... 18–006, 19–019
s.33 ...16–015, 17–022, 18–029, 22–058

(3) 17–002, 17–048, 21–041
  (b) 17–047, 21–072
(4) 17–002, 17–047, 21–041,
                     21–072
(6) 17–048
  (a) 21–041
  (b) 21–041
(7) 21–041
  (a) 21–080
  (b) 21–079
(8) 21–041
s.34 ...16–017, 16–022, 17–024, 17–047,
   17–048, 18–020, 18–029, 18–039,
   19–010, 21–007, 21–073, 22–043
(1) 17–029, 17–052, 18–018
(2) 19–001, 21–074
(3) 21–074
(4) 19–001
(6) 21–074
s.35 18–029
  (1)(a) 21–042
  (b) 21–042
  (c) 21–042
s.36 ....17–010, 21–032
s.37 ...18–011, 18–013, 18–027, 18–048,
                     18–049
(1) 18–048, 21–043
(2) 18–048
(3) 18–048
(4) 18–048
(5) 18–048
s.38 ....18–027, 18–048, 21–046
(1) 21–017, 21–043
  (b) 18–048
  (c) 18–048
(2) 18–048, 21–043
  (c) 18–048
(3) 21–042, 21–043
(4) 21–043
(5) 21–043
(6) 16–016, 17–047, 21–017,
                 21–043, 21–058
s.38A 21–004
  (2)(a) 21–044
  (b) 21–044
  (3) 21–044
  (5) 21–044
  (10) 21–044
s.38B 21–044
  (3) 21–044
s.39 ....16–022, 21–042, 21–045
  (1)(b) 21–073
s.40 21–046
(1) 21–046
(4) 21–046
(5) 21–046
(6) 21–046
s.41 ...16–020, 16–022, 18–042, 18–047,
                    21–056
(1) 18–047
(2) 18–047
(6) 18–008, 18–048, 21–004

(11) 21–038
s.42 21–037
(1) 21–058
(6) 22–077
s.43 ....18–014, 21–048, 21–077
(1) 21–052
(3) 21–052
(4) 21–052
(5)–(7) 21–052
(8) 16–001, 16–016
(9) 21–052
(11) 21–052
s.44 ....17–022, 18–014
  (1)(a) 21–048
  (b) 21–048
  (c) 21–048
  (4) 21–048
  (b) 21–048
  (c) 17–047
  (5)(a) 21–049
  (b) 21–049
  (6) 21–017, 21–058
  (6)–(9) 21–049
  (7) 16–001
  (8) 16–016
  (10) 21–048
  (12) 21–048
  (13) 21–048
  (15) 21–048
ss.44–45B 21–048
ss.44–46 21–014
s.44A 21–049
  (10) 21–049
s.44B 21–049
  (3) 21–049
s.45(1) 21–049, 21–052
  (2) 21–049
  (5) 21–049
  (8)–(11) 21–049
  (8A) 21–049
  (8B) 21–049
  (9) 21–049
  (10) 21–049
s.46 ....17–014, 20–002, 21–051
(1) 21–024, 21–051
(2) 21–051
(3) 21–051
(4) 21–051
(7) 21–051
(8) 21–051
(10) 21–046, 21–051
s.47 ....21–009, 21–010, 21–027
(1) 21–022
  (b) 18–027
(4) 18–048, 21–022, 21–048
  (a) 21–023
(5A) 16–019, 21–023
(9)–(11) 21–022, 21–023
s.48 21–049
s.50 ....17–014, 20–009
s.51 17–014
s.52(10) 17–048

s.58 16–017
s.61 22–039
s.62 21–003
s.63(1) 9–021
s.64 21–003
s.66 22–075
s.67 21–003
s.68 21–062
s.81 21–006
s.82 21–006
s.83(6) 21–006
s.84 .... 21–082, 21–084
s.85 21–003
   (3) 17–048
ss.85–87 21–003
s.88 .... 22–013, 22–022
s.91(1) 17–044, 17–048, 17–049,
      18–029, 21–0208, 21–040, 21–045
   (2) 17–048, 17–049, 21–041
   (4) 18–052
   (5A) 21–045
   (7) 21–075
   (10) 16–001, 16–019, 17–044
   (12) 21–041
   (14) 17–046, 18–028, 21–075,
                                        22–064
s.92 .... 18–001, 21–030
   (1) 18–007
s.94 19–026
   (1) 21–046
s.95 .... 18–042, 21–056
   (1) 16–022
s.96(1) 21–038
   (2) 21–038
   (3) 18–042, 21–038
s.97(2) 18–008
s.100 .... 18–050, 19–023, 21–013,
             21–080, 21–085, 21–086
   (1) 18–049, 18–052
   (2) 16–019, 18–049, 18–052
   (a) 18–029
   (b) 18–029, 21–013
   (d) 18–029
   (3)–(5) 18–051
   (4) 16–015, 21–080, 22–067
   (5) 16–015, 21–080
s.104 .... 21–006, 22–039
s.105 9–017
   (1) 16–001, 17–027, 18–030,
                          18–033, 19–002
Sch.1 .... 13–015, 13–017, 14–012,
      15–001, 15–007, 15–028, 15–036,
      15–049, 17–010, 17–040, 19–018
   para.1 .... 15–047, 17–028
   (2) 15–039, 18–022
   para.2(1) 15–032, 17–028
   para.3(2) 17–028
   para.4 19–002
   (1) 15–050
   (2) 15–050
   para.5 15–052
   (1) 15–049

para.6 17–028
para.10(3) 15–049
   (b) 15–049
para.15 ....5–046, 17–044, 18–036,
                        21–013, 22–064
para.16 .... 17–028, 18–052
   (2) 15–047
Sch.2 ....21–006, 21–008, 21–009
Pt 1 21–009
Pt 3 ....21–009, 21–072, 22–049
para.1(2) 21–009
para.1A 21–009
para.3 21–010
para.4 21–021
para.5 21–044
para.9(2) 21–079
para.12A–12F 21–068
para.15 .... 16–017, 21–074
   (1) 17–024, 18–018
   (2)(b) 21–072
para.16 21–074
para.17 16–019
para.19 ....17–026, 17–047, 19–002,
           21–007, 21–041, 21–079
   (3) 16–019, 21–041
   (4) 21–041, 21–079
   (5) 21–041, 21–079
   (6) 21–079
paras.19A–19C 21–071
para.20 17–026
para.21(3) 17–028
Sch.3 Pt I 18–027
Pt II 18–027
Pt III 21–032, 22–009
para.1 21–042
paras 2–5 21–042
para.3 21–042
   (1) 21–042
para.4 21–042
   (4) 16–016
para.5 21–042
   (5) 16–016
para.6 21–042
para.7 21–042
para.8 21–042
para.9 21–042
Sch.5 para.15 21–013
Sch.7 para.5 21–082
Sch.10 para.3 22–004
para.21 .... 22–004, 22–013
para.25 22–022
Sch.11 18–001
Sch.12 17–048
para.5 .... 1–008, 17–023
para.6 17–010
   (2) 17–010
   (3) 17–010
para.31 11–003
Sch.13 para.62 18–051
Sch.A1 18–058

1990   National Health Service and
         Community   Care   Act
         (c.19)
       s.42(1) 21–003
       s.47(1)(a) 21–010
       Human Fertilisation and Em-
         bryology Act (c.37) 2–021,
               15–007, 15–008, 17–003,
               17–005, 18–014, 22–071
       s.2 22–070
       s.3 22–070
         (1) 22–073
       s.4(1) 22–073
       s.5 22–071
       s.8 22–071
       s.13(5) 22–072, 22–074
       s.27 ...15–007, 15–008, 17–003, 22–070
       ss.27–29 22–071
       s.28 ...15–007, 15–008, 16–025, 17–010,
               22–070, 22–072, 22–075, 22–077
         (2) 17–004, 17–005, 22–070,
                                        22–075
         (3) 17–004, 17–005, 22–070,
                                        22–075
         (5A)–(5I) 17–004
         (6) 17–004, 22–072
           (a) 17–004, 17–004
           (b) 17–004
         (7)(b) 2–021
       s.29(1) 17–030
       s.30 ...15–008, 17–003, 17–034, 22–071,
                                 22–076, 22–077
         (1) 22–077
         (2) 22–077
         (3) 22–077
         (5) 22–077
         (6) 22–077
         (7) 22–077
         (8)(a) 18–014, 22–077
         (9) 22–072
       s.31 22–080
         (4) 22–080
         (5) 22–080
       s.31ZA 22–080
       s.31ZB 22–080
       s.31ZC 22–080
       s.31ZD 22–080
       s.31ZE 22–080
       s.31ZF 22–080
       s.33 22–074
       s.36 22–073
       s.37 22–075
       Sch.2 22–071
       Courts and Legal Services Act
         (c.41) 9–042
       s.9 18–007
       s.15(1) 14–005
       s.125(2) 14–012
1991   Maintenance Enforcement Act
         (c.17) 14–012, 14–018, 14–019
       s.1(1) 14–012
         (2) 14–012

         (3) 14–012
         (4) 14–012
         (5) 14–012
         (8) 14–012
         (10) 14–012
       Child Support Act (c.48) 3–017,
               6–003, 6–019, 13–016,
               13–058, 13–073, 14–012,
               15–002, 15–004, 15–005,
               15–008, 15–009, 15–010,
               15–012, 15–014, 15–015,
               15–020, 15–022, 15–023,
               15–025, 15–026, 15–029,
               15–030, 15–032, 15–038,
               15–040, 15–042, 17–028,
                       19–002, 22–058
       s.1 17–028
         (1) 15–007, 15–011
         (2) 15–011, 17–028
         (3) 15–011, 17–028
       s.2 .... 15–026, 19–002
       s.3(1) 15–006
         (2) 15–006
         (3) 15–006
           (c) 15–006
       s.4(1) 15–011
           (aa) 15–013
         (2) 15–026
         (10)(a) 15–038
       s.6 .... 6–019, 15–012
       s.8(1) ...3–017, 15–033, 17–028, 18–014
         (3) 15–030, 15–052
         (5) 15–038
         (6) 15–034
         (7) 15–035
         (8) 15–036
         (9) 15–036
         (10) 15–037
         (11) 3–017, 15–030
       s.9 15–037
       s.10 15–027
       s.11 15–026
         (1) 15–026
         (6) 15–016
       s.16 15–021
       s.17 15–021
       s.20(8) 15–021
       s.24 15–021
       s.25 15–021
       s.26(1) 15–008
         (2) 15–008, 17–004, 17–005,
                                        17–006
       s.27 .... 15–008, 17–012
         (1A) 15–008
       s.27A 15–008
         (4) 15–008
       s.28A(1) 15–020
         (3) 15–020
       s.28F(1) 15–020
         (2) 15–020
       s.33(2) 15–014
         (3) 15–024

s.35 15–024
s.36 15–024
s.39A 15–024, 17–028
s.40 17–028
　(3) 15–024
　(6)(b) 15–024
s.40B 15–024, 17–028
s.42 15–019
s.44 15–033
　(1) 15–010
　(2A) 15–010
s.46(3) 15–012
s.52 15–026
s.54 15–007
s.55 .... 15–006, 15–026, 15–036
　(1) 15–032, 15–035
　(3) 15–035
Sch.1 15–016
　Pt 1 15–019
　para.2 15–019
　　(1) 15–016
　　(2) 15–017
　para.3 15–016
　　(3) 15–019
　para.4 15–016
　　(1) 15–017, 15–019
　para.5 15–016
　para.6 15–018
　para.7 15–016
　para.8 15–016
　para.10 15–016
　　(3) 15–019, 15–034
Sch.4B para.2(1) 15–020
　para.3 15–020
Age of Legal Capacity (Scot-
　　land) Act (c.50) 16–002
s.1 .... 16–003, 17–027
s.2(1) 16–002
　(2) 16–002
s.3 17–027
s.4 17–027
Criminal Justice Act (c.53) 21–064
1992　Social Security Contributions
　　and Benefits Act (c.4) 6–004,
　　　　6–019, 6–020, 6–023,
　　　　6–025
ss.2A–2C 6–021
s.35(2) 6–030
s.44(3) 13–124
s.45B 13–125
s.77 6–024
　(2) 6–024
s.78 17–028
　(6) 6–019
s.105 ....6–019, 15–012, 17–028
　(3) 6–019
s.106 17–028
s.124(1) 16–023
　(4) 6–009
s.130A 6–020
s.130B 6–021
s.134 6–012

　(2) 6–009
s.136(1) 17–019
s.137 6–012
s.138 6–021
s.141 6–021
s.143 6–023
s.144 6–023
s.165(1) 6–030
s.171EZA 6–031
s.171ZA 6–031
s.171ZL 6–032
Sch.9 para.1 6–023
Sch.10 6–023
　para.2 6–023
　para.3 6–023
　para.4(2) 6–023
　para.5 6–023
Social Security Administration
　　Act (c.5) 6–004
Taxation of Chargeable Gains
　　Act (c.12)
s.58 3–034
Human Fertilisation and Em-
　　bryology (Disclosure of
　　Information) Act
s.1 22–077
1993　National Lottery etc Act (c.39)
s.12 16–001
1994　Criminal Justice and Public
　　Order Act (c.33) 21–009
s.32 21–064
s.142 .... 3–035, 9–004
s.154 9–005
Marriage Act (c.34) 1–006, 1–033,
　　　　1–051
s.1(1) 1–033
s.2(1) 1–033
Sch.1 para.8 1–033
1995　Jobseekers Act (c.18) 6–004
s.1 6–010
s.16 16–023
s.35 6–012
Pensions Act (c.26) 13–119, 13–122
s.166 13–122
s.168 2–052
Child Support Act (c.34) 15–003,
　　　　15–004, 15–020
Sch.2 15–020
Children (Scotland) Act (c.36) ...16–001,
　　　　17–024, 17–027, 22–003
s.1 .... 16–003, 17–027
　(1) 17–013
　　(a) 17–026
　　(c) 17–027
　(2)(b) 17–027
s.2 16–003
　(1) 17–001, 17–013
　　(b) 17–015
　　(c) 17–024
　(4) 17–015
　(7) 17–027
s.6 ....16–004, 17–015, 18–047

(1) 16–001, 19–017
s.11 18–047
Law Reform (Succession) Act
  (c.41) 11–003
s.2(4) 7–030
s.3 7–002
s.4 7–002
  (1) 17–041
Private International Law (Miscellaneous Provisions) Act
  (c.42)
Sch. para.2(2) 2–022
Disability Discrimination Act
  (c.50)
s.28K(2) 16–023
1996 Employment Rights Act (c.18)
s.55 6–030
s.56 6–030
s.75A 6–032
s.80A 6–031
s.80AA 6–030
s.80F(4) 6–034
ss.80F–80I 6–034
s.80G 6–034
s.80H 6–034
s.84 6–030
s.96 6–030
Family Law Act (c.27) ... 3–011, 3–012,
                6–037, 9–009, 9–015,
                9–017, 9–019, 9–023,
                9–025, 9–026, 9–027,
                9–028, 9–029, 9–030,
                9–031, 9–032, 9–033,
                9–034, 9–038, 9–042,
                10–003, 10–048, 10–049,
                10–052, 10–053, 10–055,
                13–100, 13–118, 18–014,
                18–016, 18–045, 18–047,
                20–001, 21–044
Pt I 9–018, 9–027
Pt II 10–055
Pt III 10–051, 10–055
Pt IV 3–010, 5–045, 9–008, 9–009,
                9–029, 9–030, 9–042, 10–009,
                11–003, 11–005, 18–022, 18–049,
                19–002, 22–067
s.1 .... 10–049, 10–055
s.3 9–033
  (1)(a) 10–049
  (c) 10–049
s.5(1) 10–049
  (d) 10–049
s.7(1) 10–049
  (2) 10–049
s.8 10–049
s.9 10–049
s.10 10–049
s.11(4)(c) 18–018, 19–003
s.13(1) 18–045
s.16 13–123
s.22 .... 10–050, 10–055
s.29 .... 10–051, 18–045

s.30(1) 3–011
  (a) 9–010
  (2) 3–010
  (3) 3–013
  (5) 3–013, 9–010
  (7) 3–010
  (8) 9–010
  (9) 3–011, 9–013
s.31(1) 3–012
  (2) 3–012
  (3) 3–012
  (10) 3–012
  (b) 3–012
s.33 .... 5–045, 9–018, 9–019
  (a)–(d) 9–020
  (1)(a) 9–012
  (b) 9–010
  (3) 9–010
  (4) 9–010
  (5) 3–012
  (a) 9–022
  (6) 9–018
  (7) 9–017, 9–019, 19–002
  (9) 9–022
  (b) 9–022
  (10) 9–022
ss.33–41 21–044
s.35 9–015
  (3) 9–020
  (4) 9–020
  (5) 9–020
  (6) 9–020
  (g) 9–020
  (8) 9–020, 19–002
  (10) 9–022
  (11) 9–013, 9–015
  (12) 9–013, 9–015
s.36 9–015
  (6)(a)–(d) 9–021
  (e) 9–021
  (e)–(i) 9–021
  (8) 9–021, 19–002
  (10) 9–022
  (11) 9–013, 9–015
  (12) 9–013, 9–015
s.37 9–010
  (5) 9–022
s.38 9–010
  (6) 9–022
s.39(2) 9–008
  (a) 9–028
  (3) 9–015
  (4) 9–015
s.40 3–013
  (1)(b) 9–023
  (c)–(e) 9–023
  (2) 9–023
s.41 9–021
s.42 9–027
  (2) 21–044, 21–049
  (a) 9–028
  (b) 9–031, 9–032

(3) 21–049
(4A) 9–024
(5) 9–033
    (a) 9–033
(6) 9–032
(7) 9–032
(8) 9–032
s.42A(1) 9–037
(3) 9–037
(4) 9–037
(5) 9–037
s.43 9–010
s.44(1) 9–028
(2) 9–028
s.45(1) 9–009, 9–028
(2) 9–009
(3) 9–009
s.46(2) 9–033
(3A) 9–033
s.47 9–024
(2) 21–044
s.50 9–035
s.51 9–035
s.52 21–049
s.53 .... 4–001, 9–022, 15–049
ss.54–56 3–013
s.57(1) 9–008, 9–009
s.59 18–001
(1) 9–008
s.60 .... 9–028, 21–044
s.62 9–029
(1)(a) 9–015, 9–029
(2) 9–018, 9–031, 9–033, 19–002
(3) 6–037, 9–028, 9–029
(ea) 9–030
(4) 9–028
(5) 9–028
(6) 9–028
s.63(1) 3–010, 9–013, 9–016, 9–028
(a) 9–029
(b) 9–029
(2) 9–028
(3) 9–017
(5) 9–020
s.63A(1) 2–043
(6) 2–040
s.63B 2–043
(3) 2–043
s.63C(2) 2–043
s.64 16–020
Sch.2 2–056
Sch.4 para.2 3–010
    para.3 3–013
    para.5 3–013
    para.6 3–013
Sch.6 21–049
Sch.7 .... 4–001, 9–022, 15–049
    para.5 9–022
    para.10 9–022
Sch.8 para.16(5) 13–100
    (6) 13–100
    (7) 13–100

para.41 17–041
Sch.10 para.6(2) 13–100
Community Care (Direct Pay-
    ments) Act (c.30) 21–009
Marriage Ceremony (Pre-
    scribed Words) Act
    (c.34) 1–034
Trusts of Land and Appoint-
    ment of Trustees Act
    (c.47) 4–001, 5–009, 5–045,
                5–048, 5–060, 5–061,
                                15–051
s.12 ....5–009, 9–013
(1) 5–045
s.13 5–045
(5) 5–047
(6) 5–047
(7) 5–045
s.14 ....5–045, 5–060
(1) 5–045
(2) 5–045
s.15 ....5–047, 5–058, 5–060
(1) 5–045
(2) 5–045
(3) 5–045
(4) 5–058
s.17(2) 5–045
Sch.1 16–002
Housing Act (c.52) 6–037, 6–039
Pt 6 6–036
Pt 7 6–036
s.159 6–036
s.167 6–036
s.175(1) 6–037
(3) 6–037
s.177(1) 6–037
(1A) 6–037
s.178 6–037
s.179 6–037
s.185 6–036
s.188 ....6–037, 21–012
s.189(1)(a) 6–037
(b) 6–037
(c) 6–037
s.190 ....6–037, 21–015
s.191(1) 6–037
s.192 6–037
s.193 ....6–037, 6–038, 19–018
(2) 6–037
Education Act (c.56) ... 17–016, 19–018
s.7 17–016
s.9 ....16–023, 17–016
s.325 17–016
s.326 17–016
s.352 17–016
s.405 ....16–023, 17–016
s.437 17–016
s.442 16–023
s.443 17–016
ss.443–444 21–032
s.444 17–016
s.497A 21–082, 21–082

s.537 17–016
s.548 .... 16–017, 17–017
s.549 16–017
s.576 17–016
   (1)(b) 17–016
Sch.27 para.8(3) 17–016
1997 Adminstration of Justice Act
    s.28(1) 7–004
    Protection from Harassment
       Act (c.40) 9–005, 9–008, 9–025,
                9–030, 9–037, 9–038,
                9–039, 9–042, 9–042,
                18–016, 22–067
    s.1 9–039
      (1) 9–005
      (2) 9–005
    s.2 .... 9–005, 9–039
      (1) 9–005
      (2) 9–005
    s.3 9–039
      (1) 9–039
      (2) 9–039
      (3) 9–041
      (6) 9–040
      (7) 9–041
      (8) 9–041
      (9) 9–041
    s.4 .... 9–005, 9–039
      (1) 9–006
      (2) 9–005
    s.5(1) 9–039
      (2) 9–039
      (3) 9–040
      (4) 9–040
      (5) 9–040
      (6) 9–040
    s.5A 9–039
    s.7(3) 9–006
      (4) 9–005
1998 Social Security Act (c.14) 6–004
    s.86(1) 15–033
    Sch.7 para.41 15–033
    Data Protection Act (c.29) 16–014
    Sch.3 para.7(1)(b) 21–022
    School Standards and Frame-
      work Act (c.31)
    s.71 .... 17–016, 17–018
      (1) 16–023
      (8) 16–023
    s.86 .... 16–023, 17–016
    s.92 17–016
    s.94 .... 16–023, 17–016
    s.114A 16–001
    s.131 17–017
    Crime and Disorder Act
      (c.37) 18–014
    s.8 17–027
      (1)(d) 17–016
      (4) 18–014
    s.9 17–027
    s.11 18–014
    s.12 18–014

s.34 16–002
Human Rights Act (c.42) 14–011,
      16–018, 16–023, 17–017,
      18–007, 18–020, 19–001,
      19–004, 21–001, 21–027,
      21–039, 21–054, 21–069,
      21–085, 21–087, 22–032
    s.3 19–004
    s.4(2) 21–086
    s.6 ....17–029, 20–0258, 21–027
      (1) 16–017
    s.7 .... 18–029, 21–085
      (1) 21–085, 21–086
        (a) 21–027
        (b) 21–086
    s.8 .... 18–029, 21–027, 21–086
      (4) 21–086
    s.12(3) 18–053
      (4) 18–053
    s.15 17–016
1999 Protection of Children Act
      (c.14) 19–003, 21–006, 21–017
    ss.2–2C 21–028
    s.3 21–028
    s.7 21–028
    Adoption (Intercountry As-
      pects) Act (c.18) ...22–002, 22–051,
                22–051
    s.2(1) 22–052
      (2) 22–052
      (3) 22–052
      (4) 22–052
    s.7 .... 22–007, 22–052
    s.9 22–046
    Access to Justice Act (c.22) 10–051
    s.8 18–045
    Youth Justice and Criminal Evi-
      dence Act (c.23) 21–064
    s.24 21–064
    s.27(2) 21–064
      (5)(b) 21–065
      (7) 21–065
    s.28 21–064
    s.29 21–064
    s.35 21–064
    s.53 21–064
    s.55 21–064
    Welfare Reform and Pensions
      Act (c.30) 6–004, 13–017,
          13–027, 13–029, 13–119,
               13–122, 13–123
    Pt III 13–123
    Pt IV 13–123
    s.19 .....3–025, 13–029, 13–086, 13–123
    s.26(1) 13–124
    s.27 13–124
    s.29 .... 13–124, 13–125
      (1) 13–125
      (2) 13–125
      (4) 13–125
      (5) 13–125
    s.30 13–125

s.33 13–125
s.34 13–125
s.47(2) 13–124
s.49(1) 13–125
s.52 6–020
s.55A 13–124
s.85(2)(a) 13–123
  (4) 13–123
Sch.3 .... 13–027, 13–029, 13–123
  para.1 .... 13–029, 13–086
  para.2 .... 3–025, 13–029
  para.4 13–029
  para.6 13–086
Schs 3–6 13–123
Sch.5 13–125
  para.1(3) 13–125
  para.2 13–125
  para.3 13–125
Sch.6 13–125
Immigration and Asylum Act
  (c.33) 1–006, 1–014, 1–023
s.24 1–017
s.115(9) 6–007
  (10) 6–007
s.122(4) 21–009
s.160 1–013
  (4) 1–015
  (6) 1–016
s.161(1) 1–014
s.162 .... 1–014, 1–023

2000 Powers of Criminal Courts
  (Sentencing) Act (c.6) 21–077
s.137 17–027
s.150 17–027
Care Standards Act (c.14) 21–084,
                                    22–016
Pt V 21–073
s.4(7A) 22–014
s.22 21–017
s.23 21–006
s.72A 16–004
s.72B 21–084
s.73 21–084
s.74 .... 21–081, 21–084
s.75A 16–004
s.81 21–006
Child Support, Pensions and
  Social Security Act (c.19) ...6–004,
              15–004, 15–008, 15–012,
              15–016, 15–017, 15–019,
              15–027, 15–038
s.1(2) 15–008, 15–011, 15–033
s.2(3) 15–013
s.5(5) 15–020
s.15 ...17–004, 17–005, 17–006, 17–008
s.16 15–024
s.22 15–033
s.82 17–008
  (2) 17–008
  (3) 15–008
s.83 17–012
  (3) 17–012

Sch.1 para.2(3) 15–011
Sch.3 para.11(2) 15–011, 15–033
  (9) 15–008
Sch.4 para.3(3) 15–019
  para.10 15–019
Sch.8 para.18 17–012
Local Government Act (c.22)
s.92 21–081
Regulation of Investigatory
  Powers Act (c.23) 21–036
Children (Leaving Care) Act
  (c.35) 21–041, 21–071
s.6 16–023
Criminal Justice and Court
  Services Act (c.43)
ss.11–17 18–010
ss.11–23 21–057
s.12(1) 18–010
s.15 18–010
s.26 21–062
s.28 .... 21–028, 21–062
s.29 21–028
s.35 21–028
s.36 21–028
Sch.2 .... 18–010, 21–057
Sch.4 .... 21–027, 21–062

2001 Regulatory Reform Act (c.6) 1–051
Adoption (Intercountry As-
  pects) Act (Northern Ire-
  land) (c.11)
Children's Commissioner for
  Wales Act (c.18) ...16–004, 21–073,
                                    21–084

2002 Homelessness Act (c.7)
s.1 6–035
s.3 6–035
ss.6–8 19–018
s.10(1) 6–037
s.12 6–039
Land Registration Act (c.9) 3–012,
                            3–012, 14–008
s.11 5–051
s.12 5–051
s.25(1) 5–011
Sch.3 para.2 5–051
Tax Credits Act (c.21)
s.3 6–005
s.6 6–005
s.8 6–005
s.9 6–007
ss.10–12 6–007
s.12 6–006
s.22 6–005
s.49(1)(b) 6–023
Employment Act (c.22) ..6–004, 6–031,
                                    6–034
s.47 6–034
Divorce (Religious Marriages)
  Act (c.27) 10–014
Education Act (c.32) 17–016
s.52 16–023
s.175 21–023

Adoption and Children Act
   (c.38) 9–018, 9–028, 17–005,
      17–034, 17–036, 17–043,
      17–045, 17–046, 17–048,
      18–014, 18–031, 19–002,
      19–016, 21–007, 21–068,
      22–001, 22–002, 22–003,
      22–005, 22–019, 22–019,
      22–023, 22–024, 22–025,
      22–031, 22–034, 22–039,
      22–043, 22–045, 22–051,
      22–058, 22–059, 22–063,
      22–077
Ch.3 22–054
s.1 .... 19–002, 22–051
   (1) 22–042
   (2) 19–002, 22–042, 22–060,
      22–063
   (3) 19–019, 22–033
   (4) 19–013, 22–042
     (a) 22–024
     (c) 22–024, 22–063
     (f) 22–024
   (5) 17–018, 22–024
   (6) 22–043, 22–058, 22–059,
      22–060, 22–063
   (7) 22–024, 22–043, 22–063
   (8)(a) 22–024
s.2 .... 22–016, 22–051
   (8) 22–046, 22–052
s.3 .... 22–014, 22–052
   (1) 22–023
   (2) 22–023
   (3) 22–004
s.4 ....22–004, 22–015, 22–051
   (1) 22–023
   (3) 22–023
   (4) 22–023
   (7) 22–023
     (a) 22–023
   (9)–(11) 22–023
s.5 .... 22–014, 22–051
s.7 22–051
s.8 22–014
   (1) 22–016
s.9 .... 22–014, 22–016
s.10 22–016
s.12 .... 22–012, 22–020
s.18(1) 22–038
s.19 ...17–048, 18–016, 22–038, 22–039
   (1) 22–025, 22–028
   (3) 22–025
s.20(1) 22–029, 22–039
   (2) 22–029
   (3) 22–029, 22–039
   (4) 22–029, 22–039
s.21 .... 21–041, 22–028
   (2) 21–035, 21–042
     (c) 22–043
   (3) 22–028, 22–043
s.22 .... 22–015, 22–039
   (1) 22–025, 22–043

   (2) 22–043
   (5) 22–043
s.24 18–049
   (1) 22–044
   (1)–(4) 22–043
   (2) 22–043, 22–044
   (3) 22–043
   (4) 22–044
s.25 17–033
   (1) 22–039, 22–043
   (3) 22–068
   (4) 17–033, 22–039, 22–043
s.26 .... 18–020, 18–049, 22–043
   (1) 18–020, 22–043
   (2) 18–030
     (a) 18–031, 22–043
   (3) 22–039
   (3B) 22–023
   (4) 22–039
s.27 22–043
   (4) 22–026, 22–043
   (5) 22–043
s.28(3) 17–025
s.29 18–035
   (1) 22–044
   (2) 18–020
   (3) 18–030, 18–031
   (3)–(5) 22–043
   (4) 18–030
s.30 17–014
   (1) 22–025, 22–030
   (3) 22–025
   (8) 22–025
s.31 22–025
s.32 22–025
   (1) 22–039
s.34(1) 22–043
s.35 22–069
s.38(2) 22–028, 22–045
   (3) 22–028, 22–045
   (5)(b) 22–028
s.42(4) 18–036, 22–028, 22–045
   (3) 22–058
   (5) 22–054, 22–060, 22–076
   (6) 22–060
   (7) 22–054, 22–058
s.44 .... 22–045, 22–069
   (1) 22–006, 22–079
   (2)–(5) 22–060
   (5) 22–054, 22–079
   (6) 22–079
s.46 .... 18–035, 22–001
   (1) 22–005
   (2) 17–049
     (d) 22–005
   (3)(a) 17–033
     (b) 22–005
   (4) 22–005
   (5) 22–009
   (6) 22–026, 22–062, 22–066
s.47 .... 17–048, 22–028
   (2) 22–029,

(b)	22–029
(c)	22–033
(2)–(7)	22–039
(3)	22–029, 22–033
(4)	22–043
(b)	22–029
(c)	22–033
(5)	22–029, 22–030, 22–033, 22–043
(6)	22–028
(7)	22–033
(9)	22–001
s.48	22–069
s.49(2)	22–019
(3)	22–019
(4)	22–001
s.50	22–019
(2)(a)	22–058
s.51(2)	17–033, 22–005
(3)	22–019
(4)	22–057
s.52	18–016, 22–028
(1)	22–025
(a)	22–031
(b)	21–019, 22–024, 22–033
(2)	22–058
(3)	22–030, 22–039
(4)	22–026, 22–039
(5)	22–029, 22–062
(6)	17–029, 17–052
(7)	22–029
(9)	22–026
(10)	22–026
s.54	22–012
ss.54–65	22–035
s.57(1)–(3)	22–012
(5)	22–012
s.58(2)	22–012
s.60(2)(b)	22–012
(3)	22–012
(4)	22–012
s.61	22–012
s.62	22–012
s.64(4)	22–013
s.65(1)	22–013
s.67	17–033, 22–001, 22–004, 22–007
(1)–(3)	22–005
(2)(b)	22–005, 22–058
(3)(b)	22–005
(4)	22–006, 22–057
s.69	22–006
(2)	22–006
(4)	22–006
s.71	22–006
s.74(1)	22–007
(a)	2–008
(2)	22–007
s.75	22–059
s.77(2)	22–010
(4)	22–010
(5)	22–010
s.79	22–011
(2)	22–010
(7)	22–008
s.80	22–004
(2)	22–013
(5)	22–013
(6)	22–013
(a)	22–013
s.81	22–004
(3)	22–013
(6)	22–054
s.83(1)(b)	22–053
(3)	22–053
(4)	22–054
(5)	22–054
(7)	22–051, 22–053
(8)	22–051
s.84	22–055
s.85	21–079, 22–055
s.87(1)	22–053
(2)(b)	22–053
s.88	22–001
(2)	22–029
s.89	22–069
(1)	22–052
s.91	22–052
s.92	22–002
(1)	22–014, 22–029, 22–071
(4)	22–029, 22–071, 22–076
ss.92–94	22–051
s.93	22–002
(1)	22–014
s.94	22–051
s.95	22–069
(3)	22–029
s.98	22–012, 22–013
(2)	22–013
(3)	22–013
s.102	22–063
(1)	22–029
s.103	21–058
s.111	17–036, 17–039
s.112	17–043, 17–045, 22–059
s.113	17–044
s.114	18–017, 22–060
(1)	16–019
s.115	17–046, 22–001, 22–056, 22–064
s.116	6–039
s.117	21–082
s.118	21–007
s.120	9–017, 21–032
s.122	16–020, 16–022
s.123	22–004, 22–051
s.125	22–003
s.141(3)	22–063
(4)	22–063
s.144	22–060
(1)	22–026
(4)	17–046, 22–019
(4)–(7)	22–005
Sch.1	22–051
para.1	22–010

Sch.2 22–012
Sch.3 21–045
    para.3 1–008
    para.56 22–045
        (d) 22–064
Sch.4 para.17 22–006
Sch.5 22–039
Enterprise Act (c.40)
s.261(1) 5–058
Nationality, Immigration and
    Asylum Act (c.41) 16–025
s.9 16–025

2003 Criminal Justice (Scotland) Act
        (asp 7)
    s.51 17–017
Communications Act (c.21)
Sch.17 para.90 9–005
Human Fertilisation and Em-
    bryology (Deceased Fa-
    thers) Act (c.24) 17–004
Courts Act (c.39) 18–002
s.1 18–002
ss.75–81 18–002
s.81 18–002
Extradition Act (c.41) 20–023
Sexual Offences Act (c.42) 2–011,
                                                2–037
Pt 2 .... 21–028, 21–062
s.1 .... 3–037, 9–004
s.9 16–011
    (1) 16–011
s13 16–011
s.25 .... 2–011, 22–008
s.25 2–011
s.26 16–012
s.27(1) 22–008
    (2)(b) 2–011
    (3)(a) 2–011
        (b) 2–011
    (5)(e) 2–011
s.28(1) 2–011
s.30 2–037
s.64 2–011
Sch.3 21–028
Health and Social Care (Com-
    munity Health and Stan-
    dards) Act (c.43)
s.42 21–084
s.44 21–084

2004 Child Trust Funds Act (c.6) 6–026
s.2(1) 6–026
s.3(8) 6–026
s.5 6–026
s.6 6–026
s.8 6–026
s.9 6–026
s.10 6–026
s.19 6–026

Gender Recognition Act (c.7) 1–035,
                2–019, 2–020, 2–021,
                2–023, 2–026, 2–046,
                2–048, 2–048, 2–049,
                                        17–010
s.2 2–019
    (2) 2–019
s.3 2–019
s.4(3) 2–019
s.6(1) 2–047
s.9 .... 2–019, 17–004
    (1) 2–046
s.12 17–004
Sch.4 Pt 1 para.3 1–035
Asylum and Immigration
    (Treatment of Claimants,
    etc.) Act (c.19)
s.19(2)(b) 1–014
    (3) 1–017
Domestic Violence, Crime and
    Victims Act (c.28) ..9–021, 9–024,
                9–028, 9–029, 9–030,
                9–033, 9–034, 9–037,
                                        9–039
s.1 9–037
s.2(1) 9–021
s.4 .... 9–028, 9–030
s.9 9–004
s.12(1) 9–039
    (5) 9–039
s.32 9–003
Sch.1 para.2(1) 9–028
Sch.10 para.36 9–024
    para.37 9–033
    para.41 9–029
Human Tissue Act (c.30)
s.2 17–008
s.45 .... 17–007, 17–008
Sch.4 para.5(1) 17–008
Civil Partnership Act (c.33) A–001,
                A–003, A–004, A–005,
                1–049, 2–017, 2–017,
                2–059, 2–060, 3–001,
                3–002, 3–009, 3–015,
                3–034, 3–041, 7–001,
                7–003, 7–009, 8–004,
                9–015, 9–029, 9–030,
                10–057, 11–001, 11–005,
                12–004, 13–001, 13–021,
                13–029, 13–086, 13–100,
                13–118, 13–119, 13–123,
                13–124, 17–005, 18–014,
                                        22–059
Pt 1 12–001
Pt 2 12–001
s.2(1) 1–049
    (5) 1–049
s.3 2–059
s.4 .... 1–049, 17–023
s.6(1)(b) 1–049
    (2) 1–033
s.8 1–049

s.18 1–049
s.19 1–049
ss.21–27 1–049
s.37(1) 12–004
s.38 10–057
  (1) 12–004
s.39 10–057
s.40 10–057
s.41 10–057
s.43 .... 13–005, 13–007
s.44(1) 10–057
  (5) 10–057
s.47 10–057
s.48 10–057
s.49 2–059
  (b) 1–049
s.50 2–060
s.53 13–117
s.55(1) 12–004
  (2) 12–004
s.56(1) 11–005
s.57 11–005
s.65 3–008
s.66 3–006
s.69 3–002
s.72 7–024
  (1) 13–001
s.73 9–028
s.74 3–008
  (2) 3–041
  (3) 3–041
  (5) 3–041
s.75 17–045
s.83 3–038
s.84 3–039
s.135 13–060
s.215 2–017
s.253 3–002
s.254 6–012
Sch.1 Pt 1 .... 1–049, 2–059
Sch.2 Pt 1 17–023
  Pts 2–4 17–023
Sch.4 .... 7–001, 7–008
  paras 1–5 7–002
  paras 7–14 7–002
  para.13 7–007
  para.15 7–017
  paras 15–27 7–009
  para.17 7–026
  para.27 7–012
Sch.5 ....3–015, 7–024, 9–022, 9–028,
          13–001, 13–040, 18–014
  para.1 13–017
    (1) 3–025, 13–001
    (2) 13–001
  paras 1–37 13–030
  para.2 ....13–017, 15–038, 15–043
    (1) 13–017, 13–023
  para.3 13–023
    (1) 15–043
    (2) 15–043
    (3) 13–024

  (5) 13–024
para.4 13–017
para.6(1) 13–001
paras 6–9 13–023
para.7(1) 13–025, 13–026, 13–027,
                                          15–043
  (3) 13–027
para.10 15–043
paras 10–14 .... 13–023, 13–028
para.14 3–028
para.15 3–025
  (1) 13–001, 13–030, 13–124
paras 15–19 .... 13–017, 13–029,
                                          13–123
para.16(1) 13–124
para.18(1) 13–124
  (2) 13–124
  (3) 13–124
para.19(1) 13–124
para.20 .... 13–039, 13–057
para.21 ....13–050, 13–053, 13–057,
                            13–020, 13–055
  (1) 13–008
  (2) 13–008, 13–039, 13–048,
    13–063, 13–077, 13–080, 13–082,
                            13–083, 13–121
para.22 13–039
  (2) 15–044
  (3) 15–044
para.23 ....13–022, 13–039, 13–088
  (2) 13–086
  (3) 13–089
  (4) 13–092
para.24(1) 13–121
  (2) 13–121
para.25(2) 13–101
  (3) 13–122
  (8) 13–122
paras 25–29 13–122
para.30 13–121
paras 31–37 13–122
para.34 ....13–017, 13–029, 13–123
para.38 .... 13–030, 13–037
para.39 3–021
para.41(1) 3–023
para.43(3) 3–022
para.47(2) 3–024, 13–020, 13–021
  (3) 3–023, 13–020
para.49(1) 15–032
  (3) 15–041
  (5) 15–032, 15–041
  (6) 15–041
para.50(1) ...13–093, 13–101, 13–122
  (2) 13–093
para.51 15–045
  (1) 13–095
para.53 13–100
  (1) 13–100
  (2) 13–100
para.56 13–101
para.59(2) 13–098
  (4) 13–099

para.61(1) 13–097
para.66 13–007
para.67(1) 3–030
    (2) 3–030, 3–031
para.68 13–004
    (a) 3–031
paras 68–70 .... 3–029, 3–031
para.69 .... 3–032, 13–004
    (2) 3–032
    (4) 3–032
para.70 3–032
para.73 3–032
para.80(2) 15–039
Sch.6 .... 3–015, 3–016, 18–014
    para.1 3–017
    para.3(1) 3–017
    para.5(2) 3–017
    para.6(2) 3–017
        (3) 3–017
    para.9 3–017
        (2) 3–017
    para.15 3–016
    para.26(2) 3–019
    para.29(1) 3–019
        (2) 3–019
        (4) 3–019
    para.30(1) 3–020
        (b) 3–020
        (2) 3–020
    para.31(1) 3–020
        (3) 3–020
    para.41 3–017
Sch.9 para.1 9–010
    (6) 9–010
    (9) 9–010
    para.4(4) 9–029
    para.13 9–028
        (2) 9–015, 9–028
Sch.23 1–049
Sch.24 para.46 6–012
    para.124 6–012
Sch.27 3–036
    para.56 3–002
    para.72 3–040
    para.97 3–039
    para.119 3–038
    para.121 3–038
Children Act (c.34) 16–004, 17–017,
                           21–002, 21–017
Pt 1 21–073
s.2(1) 16–004
    (7) 21–081
s.4(1) 21–084
ss.6–8 16–004
s.9 21–073
s.10 .... 21–002, 21–010, 21–015
    (6) 21–015
    (7) 21–015
    (8) 21–006
s.11 .... 19–002, 21–018, 21–021
s.12 21–026
s.13 21–021

ss.13–16 21–018
s.14 21–021
s.18 21–002
s.19 21–002
s.28 19–002
ss.35–43 21–057
s.50 .... 21–082, 21–084
s.58 .... 16–017, 17–017
Pensions Act (c.35) 13–119, 13–124
2005 Constitutional   Reform   Act
        (c.4)
    s.9 18–002
    Sch.2 Pt 1 18–002
        para.9 18–002
    Sch.17 para.213 18–007
    Child Benefit Act (c.6) .. 6–023, 15–006
    Finance Act (c.7)
    s.103 3–034
    Mental Capacity Act (c.9) 2–036,
                              2–037, 2–045
    s.1(3) 2–036
    s.3(1) 2–036
    s.27 2–036
    Inquiries Act (c.12)
    s.1 .... 21–006, 21–017, 21–084
    Serious Organised Crime and
        Police Act (c.15) 20–002
    s.110 9–004
    Sch.17(2) para.1 9–005
2006 Family   Law   Amendment
        (Shared Residence) Act
    Sch.2 18–057
    Family Law (Scotland) Act
        (asp 2) 7–032, 8–007
    s.23 17–036
    s.28 8–007
    Work and Families Act (c.18) 6–004,
                              6–031, 6–034
    s.1 6–030
    s.3 6–030
    s.6 .... 6–030, 6–031
    Children and Adoption Act
        (c.20) 15–024, 17–024, 17–027,
                    17–048, 18–018, 18–058
    Pt 2 .... 22–050, 22–051
    s.1 18–045
    s.7 18–058
    Childcare Act (c.21) 6–004
    s.6 18–027
        (1) 6–028
    s.7 18–010
    s.8 6–028
        (3) 6–028
    s.12(2) 6–028
    s.27 6–028
    s.28 6–028
    s.29 6–028
    s.31 6–028
    s.32 6–028
    Electoral Administration Act
        (c.22)
    s.10 9–005

Education and Inspections Act
(c.40) 16–001, 21–084
s.43 16–023
s.55 16–023
s.93 17–017
s.103 17–017
s.120 .... 16–004, 21–073
s.135 21–003
s.147 22–015
s.148 22–015
Safeguarding Vulnerable
Groups Act (c.47) 17–042,
21–006, 21–017
s.58(1) 17–042
2007 Income Tax Act (c.3)
s.1011 3–034
Adoption and Children (Scot-
land) Act (asp 4) 22–001
s.29 22–058
s.30 22–058
s.32 22–026
Welfare Reform Act (c.5) 6–020,
6–021, 6–025
Mental Health Act (c.12)
s.43 16–016
Tribunals, Courts and Enforce-
ment Act (c.15) 14–001, 14–003
Pt 3 14–006
Pt 4 .... 14–008, 14–013
Forced Marriage (Civil Protec-
tion) Act (c.20) 2–043
s.1 ....2–040, 2–043, 20–001
Registration Services Act
s.70 1–013
Child Maintenance and Other
Payments Bill 15–019
cl.18 15–020
cl.22 15–024
cl.23 15–024
cl.26 15–024
cl.27 15–024
cl.28 15–024
cl.40 15–024
cl.54 22–072
cl.55 22–072
Sch.4 para.2 15–019
para.3(1) 15–019
para.4 15–019
para.10 15–034
Education and Skills Bill
cl.1 15–041
2008 Children and Young Persons
Bill 18–031, 18–037, 18–045,
21–001, 21–003, 21–004,
21–006, 21–009, 21–010,
21–012, 21–039, 21–067,
21–069, 21–076

cl.9 .... 18–037, 21–068, 21–070
cl.11 21–069
(1) 21–069
cl.20 21–041
cl.22 21–071
cl.23 21–071
cl.30 21–049
cl.36 .... 18–031, 18–037
cl.37 18–017
(1) 18–030
Sch.1 21–068
Human Fertilisation and Em-
bryology Bill 17–003, 17–039,
18–016, 22–071, 22–076,
22–080
cl.14(2) 22–074
cl.24 22–080
cl.33 17–003
cl.35(1) 17–004
cl.36 17–004
(1) 17–004
cl.37 17–004
cl.38 17–004
cl.39 17–004
cl.40 17–004
cl.41(1) 17–004
cl.42 17–005
(1) 18–034
cl.43 17–005
cls 43–45 18–034
cl.44 17–005
cl.47 17–010
cl.48 17–049
(1) 17–005
cl.49 17–049
cl.54 .... 17–034, 22–076
(1) 17–030, 22–076
(2) 17–003
(3)–(5) 22–077
(6) 22–077
cl.55 17–034
(1) 22–077
cl.59 22–071
Sch.6 para.15 17–032
para.17 17–031
para.19 17–030
para.21 17–037
para.25 17–030
para.26 ....17–037, 17–038, 17–039

TABLE OF STATUTORY INSTRUMENTS

1947 Matrimonial Causes Rules 18–044
1952 Marriage (Authorised Persons) Regulations (SI 1952/ 1869) 1–034
1964 Prison Rules (SI 1964/388) r.43 21–062
1968 Birth Certificate (Shortened Form) Regulations (SI 1968/2050) 17–011
1973 Adoption (Designation of Overseas Adoption) Order (SI 1973/19) 22–053
1981 Magistrates' Court Rules (SI 1981/1552)
　　r.54(1)(b) 14–016
　　　　(c) 14–016
　　　　(2) 14–016
　　　　(4) 14–016
　　　　(8) 14–016
1983 Succession (Interest and Capitalisation) Order (SI 1983/1374) 9–004
　　Adoption Agencies Regulations (SI 1983/1964)
　　reg.15 22–012
1986 Insolvency Rules (SI 1986/1925)
　　r.12.3 14–005
　　Statutory Maternity Pay (General) Regulations (SI 1986/1960) 6–030
1987 Social Security (Maternity Allowance) Regulations (SI 1987/416) 6–030
　　Income Support (General) Regulations (SI 1987/1967)
　　reg.2 6–009
　　reg.4 6–009
　　reg.6 6–009
　　reg.35 6–011
　　reg.36 6–011
　　reg.45 6–011
　　reg.47 6–011
　　reg.53 6–011
　　Sch.2 16–023
　　Sch.3 para.1 6–009
　　　　(2) 6–009
　　　　para.6 6–009
　　　　paras 8–12 6–009
　　　　para.11(4) 6–009
　　　　(5) 6–009
　　　　para.15 6–009
　　Sch.8 para.5 6–009
　　　　para.6 6–011
　　　　para.9 6–011

　　Sch.9 6–011
　　Sch.10 6–011
　　Registration of Births and Deaths Regulations (SI 1987/2088) 17–010, 17–025
　　reg.64 22–010
　　Adoption (Northern Ireland) Order (SI 1987/2203) 22–001
1988 Social Fund Cold Weather Payments (General) Regulations (SI 1988/1724) 6–021
1991 Attachment of Earnings (Employer's Deduction) Order (SI 1991/356) 14–012
　　Arrangements for Placement of Children (General) Regulations (SI 1991/890) 21–068
　　reg.3 21–072
　　reg.13 21–012
　　Sch.4 21–072
　　Contact with Children Regulations (SI 1991/891)
　　reg.2 21–074
　　reg.3 21–074
　　Placement of Children with Parents etc Regulations (SI 1991/893) 18–048, 21–040, 21–068, 21–071
　　reg.7 21–072
　　Review of Children's Cases Regulations (SI 1991/895) 21–069
　　reg.2A 21–069
　　　　(6) 21–045
　　reg.3 21–045
　　reg.7 21–072
　　Sch.2 21–045
　　County Courts (Interest on Judgment Debts) Order (SI 1991/1184) 13–024
　　Family Proceedings Rules (SI 1991/1247) 10–039, 13–012, 13–064, 14–011, 18–001, 18–007
　　Pt VII 14–005
　　r.1.2(1) 13–001
　　r.1.3(1) 14–003
　　r.2.6(1)(e) 13–012
　　　　(1A) 13–122
　　　　(3) 13–122
　　r.2.6B(1) 13–064
　　　　(2) 13–064
　　r.2.24(3) 10–039, 11–002
　　r.2.28 18–008
　　r.2.36 .... 10–010, 10–057

r.2.39 18–047
  (1) 18–047
r.2.40 18–047
r.2.51A–2.70 13–001
r.2.51B(1) 13–009
  (5) 13–009
  (6) 13–009
r.2.53(1)(d) 13–124
r.2.54 13–015
r.2.61 .... 13–007, 13–064
rr.2.61A–2.69F 13–009
r.2.61B(1) 13–107
  (2) 13–107
r.2.62 13–064
r.2.69 13–012
r.2.69B 13–012
r.2.69D 13–012
r.2.71 13–012
r.4.2(2) 16–020, 18–008
r.4.3 .... 18–035, 18–040, 18–051
r.4.4 .... 18–040, 18–054
  (4) 18–040, 18–054
r.4.5 21–055
r.4.6 18–041
r.4.7 .... 18–030, 18–040
  (2) 18–041
r.4.8 18–040
  (8) 21–054
r.4.10 .... 16–020, 21–056
  (9) 21–058
r.4.11 .... 16–020, 18–008
  (1) 19–002, 19–015, 21–058
  (2) 21–058
  (4)(b) 19–017
r.4.11A 16–020
  (1) 21–058
    (a) 21–058
    (b) 21–058
    (e) 21–058
  (4) 21–058
  (6) 21–058
  (7) 21–059
  (8) 21–058
  (10) 21–059
r.4.11B(2) 18–012
r.4.12 .... 16–020, 21–056
  (1)(a) 21–058, 21–060
r.4.13 .... 18–008, 18–011
  (1) 18–012
r.4.14 21–058
  (2)(a) 18–006
  (f) 18–007
  (3)(g) 18–012
r.4.15 19–019
  (2) 18–006
r.4.16(2) 18–042, 21–056
  (7) 18–041
r.4.17 .... 18–041, 18–054
r.4.18 .... 18–042, 21–038, 21–058
r.4.21 18–041
r.4.22 21–046
r.4.23(1) 18–012

r.4.24 21–044
r.4.24A 21–044
r.5.1(2) 18–051
r.7 14–011
r.7.2 14–011
r.7.4 14–011
  (9)(b) 14–011
rr 7.4–7.8 14–011
rr 7.22–7.29 14–014
r.8.1 13–093
r.9(2A) 16–020, 18–054
r.9.2 16–021
r.9.2A 16–003, 17–021, 18–051
r.9.5 .... 16–020, 18–027, 18–048
r.10.20A 18–008, 18–012, 18–042,
                                        21–038
r.14(3)(g) 18–012
r.21(5) 18–043
Sch.2 21–052
Appendix 1 10–041
Appendix 1A Form E
  Form M1
Appendix 2 18–040
Appendix 3 21–054
Family Proceedings Courts
    (Children Act 1989) Rules
    (SI 1991/1395) 18–001, 18–007,
                                        21–039
r.2.5(a) 21–048
r.3 21–048
r.4.4 21–048
r.4.11(4)(b) 19–017
r.5 21–055
r.11(1) 19–002
r.15 19–019
r.24 21–044
Appendix 2 21–054
Emergency Protection Order
    (Transfer of Responsibili-
    ties) Regulations (SI
    1991/1414) 17–047, 21–048
Children (Secure Accommoda-
    tion) Regulations (SI
    1991/1505) 17–017, 21–068,
                                        21–077
reg.4 21–077
reg.5(1) 21–077
  (2) 21–077
reg.6 21–077
reg.11 21–078
reg.12 21–078
reg.15 21–078
reg.16 21–078
Children's Homes Regulations
    (SI 1991/1506)
reg.11 21–041
Children (Allocation of Pro-
    ceedings) Order (SI
    1991/1677) 18–002, 18–006,
                                        18–007
art.7(1)(b) 18–048
art.9 18–007

art.14 22–017
Family Law Act 1986 (Dependent Territories) Order (SI 1991/1723) 20–010
Family Proceedings (Costs) Rules (SI 1991/1832) 18–041
r.15 18–041
Adoption Allowance Regulations (SI 1991/2030) 22–004, 22–022
Children (Secure Accommodation) (No. 2) Regulations (SI 1991/2034) 17–017
1992 Child Support (Maintenance Assessment Procedure) Regulations (SI 1992/ 1813)
reg.51 15–006
Sch.1 15–006
Child Support (Collection and Enforcement) Regulations (SI 1992/1989) 15–024
regs 30–32 15–024
Child Support (Maintenance Arrangements and Jurisdiction) Regulations (SI 1992/2645) 15–010
reg.20 15–017
1993 Child Maintenance (Written Agreements) Order (SI 1993/620) 15–038
Children (Admissibility of Hearsay Evidence) Order (SI 1993/621) 18–012, 18–042, 18–054, 21–038
Family Provision (Intestate Succession) Order (SI 1993/2906) 9–004, 9–005
1994 National Lottery Regulations (SI 1994/189)
r.3 16–001
Enrolment of Deeds (Change of Name) Regulations (SI 1994/604) 17–025
Parental Orders (Human Fertilisation and Embryology) Regulations (SI 1994/ 2767) 17–003, 17–034, 22–072, 22–076
Sch.1 22–077
para.2 22–077
para.3 22–077
para.4(a) 22–077
(b) 22–080
para.5(b) 22–077
1995 Children (Secure Accommodation) (Amendment) Regulations (SI 1995/139) 21–077
Marriages (Approved Premises) Regulations (SI 1995/510)
Sch.1para.2 1–033

Sch.2 para.7 1–033
para.9 1–033
para.11 1–035
Child Support and Income Support (Amendment) Regulations (SI 1995/1045) 15–003
1996 Jobseeker's Allowance Regulations (SI 1996/207) 6–010
Pt IV 16–023
reg.98 6–011
reg.107 6–011
reg.116 6–011
Sch.2 para.1(2) 6–010
para.10(3) 6–010
(4) 6–010
para.12 6–010
para.14 6–010
Sch.6 6–011
para.6 6–011
paras 11–12 6–011
Sch.7 6–011
Children Act 1989 (Amendment) (Children's Services Planning) Order (SI 1996/785) 21–009
Family Proceedings (Amendment) (No.2) Rules (SI 1996/1674)
r.3 13–122
Child Support Departure Direction and Consequential Amendments Regulations (SI 1996/2907) 15–020
Social Security (Child Maintenance Bonus) Regulations (SI 1996/3195) 15–027
1997 Family Homes and Domestic Violence (Northern Ireland) Order 18–019
Family Law Act 1996 (Commencement No.1) Order (SI 1997/1077) 10–051
1998 Children (Protection at Work) Regulations (SI 1996/ 276) 16–002
Working Time Regulations (SI 1998/1833) 6–029
Civil Procedure Rules (SI 1998/3132) 13–012, 18–002
r.2.1(2) 14–003
r.20.12 17–042
Pt 21 .... 16–020, 17–021
r.21.2(3) 16–021, 17–021
r.21.10(1) 17–021
r.44.3(1) 13–012
(1)–(5) 13–012
(2) 13–012
(4) 13–012
(5) 13–012
r.48.7 18–041
r.52.4(2) 13–093
r.54 21–085

Pts 70–73 14–003
Pt 71 14–011
Pt 72 14–006
Sch.1 .... 13–093, 14–003,
  14–005—14–011, 18–008, 18–054,
              18–056, 21–046
Sch.2 .... 14–005, 14–006, 14–008,
  14–009, 14–012, 14–013, 21–046
1999 Family Proceedings (Miscella-
      neous Amendments) Rules
      (SI 1999/1012)
      r.4 13–012
      Family Proceeding Rules (SI
        1999/1247) 18–007
      r.2.54 15–045
      Maternity and Parental Leave
        etc Regulations (SI
        1999/3312) 6–033
      reg.13 6–033
      reg.15(c) 6–033
      reg.19 6–033
      reg.20 6–033
      Sch.2 6–033
      Family Proceedings (Amend-
        ment No.2) Rules (SI
        1999/3491) 13–009
2000 Social Fund Winter Fuel Pay-
      ment Regulations (SI
      2000/729) 6–021
      Pensions on Divorce etc (Provi-
        sion of Information) Reg-
        ulations (SI 2000/1048) ... 13–123
      reg.3 .... 13–119, 13–125
      reg.5 13–125
      Pensions on Divorce etc.
        (Charging) Regulations
        (SI 2000/1049) 13–123
      Pension Sharing (Valuation)
        Regulations (SI
        2000/1052) 13–119, 13–123,
                              13–124
      Pension Sharing (Implementa-
        tion and Discharge of Lia-
        bility) Regulations (SI
        2000/1053) 13–123, 13–125
      Pension Sharing (Pension Cred-
        it Benefit) Regulations (SI
        2000/1054) 13–123
      Welfare Reform and Pensions
        Act 1999 (Commence-
        ment No.5) Order (SI
        2000/1116) 13–123
      Divorce etc. (Pensions) Regula-
        tions (SI 2000/1123) 13–123
      reg.3 13–119
        (1)(a) 13–119, 13–125
        (b) 13–125
      Part-time Workers (Prevention
        of Less Favourable Treat-
        ment) Regulations (SI
        2000/1551) 6–029

Children (Protection at Work)
  (No. 2) Regulations (SI
  2000/2548) 16–002
Pension Sharing (Consequen-
  tial and Miscellaneous
  Amendments) Regulations
  (SI 2000/2691) 13–123
reg.4 22–023
reg.5 22–023
reg.13 22–023
Reporting of Suspicious Mar-
  riages and Registration of
  Marriages (Miscellaneous
  Amendments) Regulations
  (SI 2000/3164) 1–014, 1–017
Prescription Only Medicines
  (Human Use) Amendment
  (No. 3) Order (SI
  2000/3231) 16–001
2001 Child Support (Maintenance
      Calculations and Special
      Cases) Regulations (SI
      2001/155)
      reg.3 15–016
      reg.4 15–016
      reg.5 15–016
      reg.7A 15–017
      reg.8 15–006
      Child Support (Variations) Reg-
        ulations (SI 2001/156) 15–020
      reg.18 15–020
      reg.19 15–020
      reg.20 15–020
      reg.21(1)(a) 15–020
        (2) 15–020
      Child Support (Maintenance
        Calculation Procedure)
        Regulations (SI 2001/
        157) 15–023
      reg.21(1) 15–006
      Pension Sharing (Excepted
        Schemes) Order (SI
        2001/358) 13–124
      Blood Tests (Evidence of Pater-
        nity) (Amendment) Reg-
        ulations (SI 2001/773) 17–007,
                                    17–008
      Family Proceedings Courts
        (Family Law Act 1986)
        Rules (SI 2001/778) 17–012
      Parental Responsibility Agree-
        ment (Amendment) Reg-
        ulations (SI 2001/2261) ... 17–038
      Children's Commissioner for
        Wales Regulations (SI
        2001/2787) 21–081
      Children (Leaving Care) (Eng-
        land) Regulations (SI
        2001/2874) 21–071
      Children (Leaving Care) Social
        Security Benefits Regula-
        tions (SI 2001/3074) 21–071

Children's Homes Regulations
(SI 2001/3967)
reg.17(5) 17–017
Welfare Reform and Pensions
Act 1999 (Commence-
ment No.12) Order (SI
2001/4049) 13–123

2002 Fostering Services Regulations
(SI 2002/57) 21–041, 21–068
reg.13 17–017
reg.36 .... 21–013, 22–045
reg.37 21–012
Sch.5 21–068
Children's Homes (Wales) Reg-
ulations (SI 2002/327) 17–017
Civil Procedure (Modification
of Enactments) Order (SI
2002/439) 14–011
Deregulation (Correction of
Birth and Death Entries in
Registers or Other Re-
cords) Order (SI
2002/1419) 17–010, 21–069
Working Tax Credit (Entitlement and Maximum Rate)
Regulations (SI 2002/
2005) 6–006
Child Tax Credit Regulations
(SI 2002/2007) 6–007
reg.3 6–007
Tax Credits (Claims and Notifi-
cations) Regulations (SI
2002/2014) 6–005
Homelessness (Priority Need
for Accommodation)
(England) Order (SI
2002/2051) 6–037
regs. 3–6 6–037
Education (Pupil Referral
Units) (Appeals Against
Permanent Exclusion)
(England) Regulations (SI
2002/2550) 16–023
Paternity and Adoption Leave
Regulations (SI 2002/
2788)
reg.4(2) 6–031
reg.6 6–031
(2) 6–031
reg.8 6–032
reg.17 6–032
reg.18 6–032
Flexible Working (Procedural
Requirements) Regula-
tions (SI 2002/3207) 6–034
Flexible Working (Eligibility,
Complaints and Reme-
dies) Regulations (SI
2002/3236)
reg.5 6–034

2003 Intercountry Adoption (Hague
Convention) Regulations
(SI 2003/118) 22–051
Family Proceedings (Amend-
ment) Rules (SI 2003/
184)
r.11 14–011
Fostering Services (Wales)
Regulations (SI
2003/237) 17–017, 21–012
Guardian's Allowance (Gener-
al) Regulations (SI
2003/495) 6–024
reg.5 6–024
Land Registration Rules (SI
2003/1417)
reg.23 5–011
reg.58 5–011
Occupational Pension Schemes
(Transfer Values and Mis-
cellaneous Amendments)
Regulations (SI 2003/
1727) 13–123
Social Security (Jobcentre Plus
Interviews for Partners)
Regulations (SI 2003/
1886) 6–010
Day Care and Child Minding
(National Standards)
(England) Regulations (SI
2003/1996)
reg.5 17–017
Registration of Births and
Deaths (Amendment)
Regulations (SI 2003/
3048) 17–004
Child Support (Information,
Evidence and Disclosure)
Amendment Regulations
(SI 2003/3206) 15–010
Education (Information About
Individual Pupils) (Wales)
Regulations (SI 2003/
3237) 16–023

2004 Advocacy Services and Representations Procedure
(Children) (Amendment)
Regulations SI 2004/
719) 21–082
Advocacy Services and Representations Procedure
(Children) (Wales) Regu-
lations (SI 2004/1448) 21–082
Child Trust Funds Regulations
(SI 2004/1450) 6–026
Pt 2 6–026
reg.5 6–026
reg.8A 6–026
reg.33A 6–026

Human Fertilisation and Embryology Authority (Disclosure of Donor Information) Regulations (SI 2004/1511) 17–004, 22–072, 22–080

Child Trust Funds (Amendment) Regulations (SI 2004/2676) 6–026

2005 Adoption Agencies Regulations (SI 2005/389) 22–003, 22–014, 22–016, 22–039
Pt 2 22–016
regs 11–17 22–015
reg.14(1)(a) 22–039
(c) 22–034
(4) 17–052, 22–034
reg.17(1)(d) 22–034
regs.18–20 22–021
reg.19 .... 22–016, 22–020
reg.23 22–019
reg.25 22–020
(6) 22–051
reg.26 22–020
(4) 22–020
reg.28 22–020
reg.29 22–020
reg.33 22–020
(1) 22–016
reg.35(4) 22–039
reg.41 22–035
reg.45 22–039
reg.46(3)(a) 22–034
Sch.3 22–019
Adoptions with a Foreign Element Regulations (SI 2005/392) 22–003, 22–051, 22–052, 22–055
reg.4(4) 22–054
reg.5(4) 22–051
reg.9 22–054
Adoption Support Services Regulations (SI 2005/691) 22–004, 22–015, 22–023, 22–064
reg.3(1)(c) 22–066
Disclosure of Adoption Information (Post-Commencement Adoptions) Regulations (SI 2005/888) 22–012
r.8 22–012
r.15 22–012
r.16 22–012
r.17 22–012
Adoption Information and Intermediary Services (Pre-Commencement Adoptions) Regulations (SI 2005/890) 22–012, 22–013
reg.4 22–013
reg.7 22–013
reg.16 22–035

reg.17 22–013
Adopted Children and Adoption Contact Registers Regulations (SI 2005/924) 22–054
reg.7 22–013
reg.9 22–013
Special Guardianship Regulations (SI 2005/1109) 17–046, 21–006, 22–069
reg.3(1)(c) 22–066
reg.11 17–046
Adoption Support Services (Local Authorities) (Wales) Regulations (SI 2005/1512) 22–064
Adoptions with a Foreign Element Regulations (SI 2005/1711) 22–003, 22–051
Suitability of Adopters Regulations (SI 2005/1712) 22–003
reg.5 22–020
Family Proceedings (Amendment No 4) Rules (SI 2005/1976) 18–008
Civil Partnership (Amendments to Registration Provisions) Order (SI 2005/2000) 1–049
Family Procedure (Adoption) Rules
r.23 17–052
r.29 22–063
r.32 22–063
r.36 22–063
r.59 22–063
r.73 .... 22–062, 22–063
r.74 22–062
Adoption and Children Act 2002 (Commencement No.9) Order (SI 2005/2213) 22–001, 22–003
Adoption Support Agencies (England) and Adoption Agencies (Miscellaneous Amendments) Regulations (SI 2005/2720) 22–014
Family Procedure (Adoption) Rules (SI 2005/2795) 22–003, 22–017
Pt 6 22–032
Pt 8 22–035
r.20 22–035
r.21 22–035
r.28 22–035
r.29 22–035
r.32 22–035
r.39 22–032
r.84 .... 22–012, 22–013
Family Proceedings (Amendment) (No.5) Rules (SI 2005/2922)
r.29 10–057

Social Fund Maternity and Funeral Expenses (General) Regulations (SI 2005/3061) 6–021

Domestic Violence, Crime and Victims Act 2004 (Commencement Order No.5) Order (SI 2005/3196) 9–021, 9–029

Mariages and Civil Partnerships (Approved Premises) Regulations (SI 2005/3168 1–033
Sch.1 para.1 1–033
  para.5 1–033
Sch.2 para.11(3) 1–034
  para.12 1–034

Electronic Commerce Directive (Adoption and Children Act 2002) Regulations (SI 2005/3222) 22–051

Tax and Civil Partnership Regulations (SI 2005/3229) ... 3–034
reg.7 3–034
reg.8 3–034
reg.107 3–034

Representations Procedure (Children) (Wales) Regulations (SI 2005/3365) 21–082

2006 Local Safeguarding Children Boards Regulations (SI 2006/90) 21–021

Guardian's Allowance (General) (Amendment) Regulations (SI 2006/204) 6–024

Housing Benefit Regulations (SI 2006/213) 6–020

Child Benefit (General) Regulations (SI 2006/223) 6–023
reg.16 6–024

Family Proceedings (Amendment) Rules (SI 2006/352) 13–012

British Nationality (Proof of Paternity) Regulations (SI 2006/1496)
reg.3 16–025

Child Support (Miscellaneous Amendments) Regulations (SI 2006/1520)
reg.6 15–023

Children Act 1989 Representations Procedure (England) Regulations (SI 2006/1738) 21–082
regs 2–5 21–082
reg.6 21–082
reg.8 21–082
reg.9 21–082
reg.13 21–081
reg.14 21–082
reg.15 21–082

reg.17 21–082
reg.19 21–082
reg.23 21–082

Statutory Maternity Pay, Social Security (Maternity Allowance) and Social Security (Overlapping Benefits) (Amendment) Regulations (SI 2006/2379) 6–030

Registration of Births and Deaths (Amendment) Regulations (SI 2006/2827) 17–010

Children (Secure Accommodation) (Amendment) (Wales) Regulations (SI 2006/2986) 21–077

Child Trust Funds (Amendment No. 2) Regulations (SI 2006/3382) 6–026

2007 Marriage Act 1949 (Remedial) Order (SI 2007/438) 1–035, 2–009

Office for Standards in Education, Children's Services and Skills (Children's Rights Director) Regulations(SI 2007/460) 21–073

Lasting Powers of Attorney, Enduring Powers of Attorney and Public Guardian Regulations (SI 2007/1253)
reg.15 22–018

Equality Act (Sexual Orientation) Regulations (SI 2007/1263)
reg.15 22–004

Human Fertilisation and Embryology (Quality and Safety) Regulations (SI 2007/1522) 22–074

Domestic Violence, Crime and Victims Act 2004 (Commencement No.9 and Transitional Provisions) Order (SI 2007/1845) 9–024, 9–030, 9–033, 9–037

Child Support (Miscellaneous Amendments) Regulations (SI 2007/1979)
reg.4 15–016
reg.5 15–016

Tribunals, Courts and Enforcement Act 2007 (Commencement No. 1) Order (SI 2007/2709) 14–001

Tribunals, Courts and Enforcement Act 2007 (Commencement No. 2) Order (SI 2007/3613) 14–001

2008 Allocation and Transfer of Pro-
      ceedings Order
      art.2 18–007
      art.5(2)(d) 21–054
         (3) 21–054
         (4) 21–054
      arts 5–8 18–007
      art.6 18–007
         (a)
      arts 13–19 18–007
      art.15 21–054
      art.18 21–054
      arts 24–26 18–007

     Tribunals, Courts and Enforce-
        ment Act 2007 (Com-
        mencement No. 3) Order
        (SI 2008/749) 14–001
     Social Security (Miscellaneous
        Amendments) (No.2) Reg-
        ulations (SI 2008/1042)
     reg.3 15–027
     reg.5 15–027
     Family Proceedings Fees Order
        (SI 2008/1054) 21–054
     Tribunals, Courts and Enforce-
        ment Act 2007 (Com-
        mencement No. 4) Order
        (SI 2008/1158) 14–001

INTRODUCTION

THE FAMILY AND THE LAW

I. What is "Family" Law?

For many years "family law"[1] could quite simply be defined as the laws affecting **A–001**
the family,[2] and "the family" consisted of a husband and wife and their
dependent children.[3] This focus could easily be justified since it was by marriage
that rights to support were conferred (and certain legal disabilities were
imposed[4]); in addition, it was through marriage that the status of the parties'
children was defined. Marriage—although originating in an agreement between
the parties—created a status, that is to say "the condition of belonging to a class
in society to which the law ascribes peculiar rights and duties, capacities and
incapacities".[5] Also the law was reluctant to allow the parties to the marriage to
vary the rights and responsibilities attaching to that status. As one nineteenth-
century American judge explained:

> "When the contracting parties have entered into the married state, they have
> not so much entered into a contract as into a new relation, the rights, duties
> and obligations of which rest, not upon their agreement, but upon the
> general law of the State, statutory or common, which defines and prescribes
> those rights, duties and obligations . . . They can neither be modified nor
> changed by any agreement."[6]

---

[1] On the history of the term itself, see R. Probert, "Family law—a modern concept?" [2004] Fam.
Law 901.
[2] See, for example, Lord Evershed's foreword to R.H. Graveson and F.R. Crane, *A Century of Family
Law* (London: Sweet & Maxwell, 1957), p.vii, which defined "family law" as "a convenient means
of reference to so much of our law . . . as directly affects that essential unit of the English social
structure, the family".
[3] Lord Evershed's foreword, p.vii (see fn.2); see also P. Bromley, *Family Law* (London: Butterworths,
1957), p.1. The focus was, however, very much on adult relationships: a mere two chapters of *A
Century of Family Law* dealt with the position of children.
[4] See further Ch.3.
[5] *The Ampthill Peerage* [1977] A.C. 547 at 577, *per* Lord Simon of Glaisdale.
[6] *Adams v Palmer* 51 Maine 480, (1863) at 483, *per* Appleton C.J.

1

Today, however, matters are rather more complicated. First, while marriage still forms a central part of family life and family law,[7] the fact that two persons are married has relatively little impact on their rights while the relationship is ongoing[8]; secondly, since the Civil Partnership Act 2004, marriage is no longer the only formal legal relationship available in this jurisdiction; and thirdly, at least some rights have been conferred on couples who have not formalised their relationship at all.[9] Legal decisions have, step by step, first recognised that cohabiting couples with children could be regarded as "family",[10] then that heterosexual couples without children might also be so regarded,[11] and finally that same-sex couples fall within the scope of the term.[12]

At the same time, there has been an increase in the number of relationships that break down[13]: within the past 50 years, family law has changed from a discipline concerned with rights and responsibilities within the intact family[14] to one that largely focuses on the aftermath of relationship breakdown—for example in providing protection in cases of domestic violence,[15] determining how the parties' assets should be divided[16] and resolving disputes between parents regarding the upbringing of their children.[17] Such disputes bring children— whose interests are often conflated with their parents in intact families—to the forefront of family law.[18] The increasing number of children born outside marriage, and the changes to the law that have been effected in response to this, have meant that parenthood, rather than marriage, is in many ways the key status within family law today.[19]

So any definition of modern family law has to encompass a wide variety of forms and functions. Much of family law is concerned with issues of status—for example determining who may marry or enter into a civil partnership,[20] how such

---

[7] Despite gloomy prognostications regarding the decline of marriage, it remains the case that the majority of marriages are ended by death rather than divorce (see "Proportion of marriages ending in divorce" (2008) 131 *Population Trends* 28).

[8] See further Ch.3 for the remaining legal consequences of formalising a relationship.

[9] For examples see Ch.7 (rights on the death of a partner) and Ch.9 (protection from domestic violence). On proposals for reform, see Ch.8.

[10] *Hawes v Evenden* [1953] 1 W.L.R. 1169.

[11] *Dyson Holdings v Fox* [1976] Q.B. 503.

[12] *Fitzpatrick v Sterling Housing Authority Ltd* [2001] 1 A.C. 27. Note, however, that this does not mean that such couples enjoy "family life" for the purposes of art.8 of the European Convention on Human Rights, it being held by the House of Lords in *Secretary of State for Work and Pensions v M* [2006] UKHL 11 that "family life" was an autonomous Convention concept that did not yet extend to same-sex couples.

[13] See Ch.11.

[14] On this shift, see R. Probert (ed.), *Family Life and the Law: Under One Roof* (Aldershot: Ashgate, 2007).

[15] See further Ch.9.

[16] See further Ch.13.

[17] See further Ch.18.

[18] A trend reflected in the nomenclature of the new Department for Children, Schools and Families, established on June 28, 2007.

[19] See further G. Douglas, "Marriage, cohabitation and parenthood—from contract to status?" in S. Katz, J. Eekelaar and M. Maclean, *Cross Currents: Family Law and Policy in the US and England* (Oxford: Oxford University Press, 2000).

[20] See further Ch.2.

relationships come into being[21] and how they are legally terminated[22]; or how the law determines who is to be regarded as the legal parent of a child (a question of no little difficulty in light of developments in assisted reproduction[23]) and the circumstances in which legal parenthood may be transferred through adoption.[24] Family law is also concerned with setting out the rights and responsibilities flowing from the status of being a spouse, civil partner or parent, although there is considerable debate as to what those rights and responsibilities should be and whether the parties should be able to alter them by private agreement.[25] And a third key element in family law is the protection of the weaker members of the family—for example in providing remedies for adults who suffer violence at the hands of other family members[26] and in allowing state intervention to protect children who are suffering at the hands of their parents or other family members.[27]

II. KEY DEVELOPMENTS IN FAMILY LAW

Family law is a fast-moving area, and few aspects have been untouched since the last edition of this work. In this introductory section it may be helpful to highlight some of the key changes—whether legal, demographic or social—that have implications for family law as a whole. The introduction of civil partnerships, for example, has implications for issues such as the allocation of legal parenthood as well as for the parties themselves; the increase in the number of couples cohabiting outside marriage raises questions about the way in which the law should treat such couples and their children if the relationship breaks down. There is also an issue as to whether the law has a role to play at all in determining the consequences of relationship breakdown: one key theme in current legal policy is that individuals should resolve matters for themselves as far as possible.
A–002

A. The availability of an alternative opt-in regime
One of the most significant developments in family law in recent years has been the passage of the Civil Partnership Act 2004.[28] This provided same-sex couples with the opportunity to register a civil partnership and thereby gain access to virtually all of the same rights and responsibilities of married couples. The Act came into force on December 5, 2005, and by the end of the year almost 2,000
A–003

---

[21] See further Ch.1.
[22] See further Ch.10.
[23] See further Ch.17.
[24] See further Ch.22.
[25] See further Ch.13 (on pre-nuptial agreements); Ch.15 (on child maintenance obligations).
[26] See further Ch.9.
[27] See further Ch.21.
[28] For an account of the background to the passage of the Act, see M. Harper et al. *Civil Partnership—The New Law* (Bristol: Family Law, 2005).

civil partnerships had been celebrated across the United Kingdom.[29] By the end of 2006, the number of civil partnerships registered in the United Kingdom had risen to over 18,000.[30]

The 2004 Act was part of a growing trend, both within Europe and elsewhere, to offer same-sex couples the chance of opting into a legally recognised relationship akin to marriage.[31] In 1989 Denmark was the first jurisdiction to offer the option of a registered partnership to same-sex couples,[32] and the other Nordic countries followed relatively swiftly.[33] From 1999, same-sex couples in France could register a *pacte civil de solidarité*, and in Germany the option of registering a *Lebenspartnerschaft* became available in 2001.

Such developments pose two key questions. First, if the new form of relationship is modelled on marriage, why not simply extend marriage to same-sex couples? Secondly, if it, by contrast, provides a different set of rights and responsibilities to those conferred by marriage, why should it be confined to same-sex couples?

A–004   The ease with which the 2004 Act passed on to the statute book suggests one tactical reason for distinguishing between marriage and civil partnership—namely that providing same-sex couples with a form of relationship that parallels marriage is less controversial than allowing them to marry. The key theme in the Government's proposals was that of equality: it was, as the Women and Equality Unit noted, "proposing the creation of a new legal status of civil partnerships for reasons of general equality and social justice".[34] However, a small but growing number of jurisdictions have adopted the view that providing same-sex couples with a separate form of legal relationship is not to treat them equally.[35] Thus the Netherlands, having introduced registered partnerships for both same-sex and

---

[29] This number is all the more dramatic given that December 5 was the first day on which a couple could give notice of their intention to form a civil partnership; given the legal waiting period between giving notice and registration, the first day on which a civil partnership could be registered in England and Wales was December 21, although 18 civil partnerships were registered under special arrangements (as to which see para.1–049).

[30] Office for National Statistics, "News release: more than 18,000 civil partnerships formed", June 28, 2007.

[31] See, for example, K. Waaldijk (ed.), *More or Less Together: Levels of Legal Consequences of Marriage, Cohabitation and Registered Partnership for Different-sex and Same-sex Partners* (Paris: INED, 2005); I. Curry-Sumner, *All's well that ends registered? The Substantive and Private International Law Aspects of Non-marital Registered Relationships in Europe* (Antwerp: Intersentia, 2005).

[32] See, for example, L. Nielson, "Family rights and the registered partnership in Denmark" (1990) 4 I.J.L.F. 297; M. Broberg, "The registered partnership for same-sex couples in Denmark" (1996) 8 C.F.L.Q. 149. For an analysis of its impact, see I. Lund-Anderson, "The Danish Registered Partnership Act, 1989: has the Act meant a change in attitudes?", in R. Wintemute and M. Andenæs (eds), *Legal Recognition of Same-Sex Partnerships* (Oxford: Hart Publishing, 2001); W. Eskridge Jr and D. Spedale, *Gay Marriage: For Better or For Worse? What We've Learned from the Evidence* (Oxford: Oxford Univesity Press, 2006).

[33] Legislation was passed by Norway in 1993, Sweden in 1994, Iceland in 1996 and Finland in 2001.

[34] Women and Equality Unit, *Response to Civil Partnership: A Framework for the Legal Recognition of Same-sex Couples* (November 2003), p.16.

[35] See also L. Crompton, "Civil Partnerships Bill 2004: the illusion of equality" [2004] Fam. Law 888.

opposite-sex couples in 1998, opened up marriage to same-sex couples in 2001.[36] Same-sex marriage was subsequently introduced in Belgium in 2003, in the US state of Massachusetts in 2004, in Spain and Canada in 2005,[37] and in South Africa in 2006. The case of Massachusetts is particularly interesting: following a decision that it would be unconstitutional to prevent same-sex couples from entering into civil marriage,[38] the legislature instead proposed the option of civil unions that would offer same-sex couples the same rights and responsibilities as if they were married. The Justices of the Supreme Court of Massachusetts took the view that this was not an adequate response:

> "The dissimilitude between the terms 'civil marriage' and 'civil union' is not innocuous; it is a considered choice of language that reflects a demonstrable assigning of same-sex, largely homosexual couples to second-class status."[39]

This is certainly the view taken by some same-sex couples, and the courts have already dealt with the first—but almost certainly not the last—challenge to the approach adopted in the Civil Partnership Act.[40] Others, however, take a more negative view of marriage, and welcome civil partnerships precisely because the concept does not have the same connotations as marriage.[41]

This leads on to the second issue, which is whether an alternative to marriage should be made available to others, such as heterosexual couples or those in other relationships. A number of European jurisdictions have enacted legislation providing an alternative institution for those who do not wish to (or cannot) marry. Some of these alternatives—such as the registered partnership in the Netherlands—are closely modelled on marriage; others, such as the French *pacte civil de solidarité*,[42] offer a more radical alternative.[43] It has been suggested that the law should move towards offering a range of options,[44] but offering an

---

[36] K. Waaldijk, "Small change: how the road to same-sex marriage got paved in the Netherlands", in Wintemute and Andenæs (eds), *Legal Recognition of Same-Sex Partnerships*.

[37] See, for example, Wade K. Wright, "The tide in favour of equality: same-sex marriage in Canada and England and Wales" (2006) 20 I.J.L.P.F. 249.

[38] *Goodridge v Department of Public Health* (2003) SJC-08860.

[39] "Opinions of the Justices of the Massachusetts Supreme Judicial Court to the Senate regarding same sex marriage" (2004), in S. Cretney, *Same-Sex Relationships: From "Odious Crime" to "Gay Marriage"* (Oxford: Oxford University Press, 2006), p.280.

[40] *Wilkinson v Kitzinger* [2006] EWHC 2022 (Fam.); see further para.2–017.

[41] See, for example, the discussion by R. Auchmuty, "Same-sex marriage revived: feminist critique and legal strategy" (2004) *Feminism & Psychology* 101.

[42] See, for example, A. Barlow and R. Probert, "Reforming the rights of cohabitants: lessons from across the channel" [199] Fam. Law 477; E. Steiner, "The spirit of the new French registered partnership law—promoting autonomy and pluralism or weakening marriage?" (2000) 12 C.F.L.Q. 1; R. Probert and A. Barlow, "Displacing marriage—diversification and harmonisation within Europe?" (2000) 12 C.F.L.Q. 153; C. Martin and I. Thery, "The Pacs and marriage and cohabitation in France" (2001) 15 I.J.L.P.F. 135.

[43] Although some couples would prefer it to be more closely modelled on marriage: see G. Ignasse, *Les pacsé-e-s: Enquête sur les signataires d'un pacte civil de solidarité* (Paris: L'Hamilton, 2002).

[44] See, for example, A. Barlow, C. Burgoyne and J. Smithson, *The Living Together Campaign—An Investigation of its Impact on Legally Aware Cohabitants* (Ministry of Justice Research Series 5/07, 2007), p.50.

alternative to marriage for those who can marry would be more politically controversial than offering a new institution to those who do not have that option. Questions will inevitably arise, however, as to the status to be accorded to a registered partnership entered into overseas by an opposite-sex couple: at present, English law has no equivalent status to offer such a couple.

During the debates on the Civil Partnership Bill in the House of Lords, an amendment was passed that would have allowed family members who had lived together for at least 12 years since attaining adulthood to register a civil partnership.[45] The argument put forward in support of this amendment was that carers and other home-sharers were also in need of legal protection to recognise the contributions each had made to the relationship.[46] The House of Commons subsequently rejected the amendment, not because this particular group did not need legal protection but rather because the registration of a civil partnership was not thought to be an appropriate means of achieving such protection.[47] Subsequently, two elderly sisters challenged UK law before the European Court of Human Rights.[48] Their complaint was that when one of them died the other would have to sell the jointly-owned home in which they had spent most of their lives in order to meet the inheritance tax bill. This, they argued, was discriminatory, since if they had been in a civil partnership the survivor would not have had to pay any inheritance tax. Their claim was rejected, but by a surprisingly small margin. The passage of the Civil Partnership Act has clearly left many issues still to be resolved.

B. The increase in cohabitation

A–005 Perhaps the most significant challenge for family law today is how to deal with those couples who choose not to formalise their relationship at all. The Civil Partnership Act 2004 equated the position of same-sex cohabitants with that of heterosexual couples, but this simply conferred on the former a patchwork of legal rights. In some contexts cohabiting couples are treated as if they were married[49]; in others they are accorded lesser legal rights[50]; and in yet others they are ignored altogether.

It is clear that current levels of cohabitation are unprecedented,[51] and it appears that they are set to increase.[52] This being the case, what should the response of the law be? Should it treat cohabiting couples as if they were married, or should

---

[45] *Hansard*, HL Vol.662, col.1389. The amendment was passed by 148 votes to 130.
[46] See, for example, the arguments advanced by Baroness O'Cathain, who proposed the amendment: *Hansard*, HL Vol.662, col.1363 (June 24, 2004).
[47] *Hansard*, HC Standing Committee, col.007 (October 19, 2004).
[48] *Burden and Burden v UK* [2007] 1 F.C.R. 69.
[49] Notably in the context of entitlement (or rather disentitlement) to means-tested benefits: see para.6–012.
[50] See, for example, Inheritance (Provision for Family and Dependants) Act 1975, discussed at para.7–017.
[51] For discussion of the extent of cohabitation in previous centuries, see R. Probert, "Common law marriage: myths and misunderstandings" (2008) 20 C.F.L.Q. 1.
[52] J. Haskey, "Cohabitation in Great Britain: past, present and future trends—and attitudes" (2001) 103 *Population Trends* 4.

it refuse to extend any extra rights to cohabitants on the basis that they have deliberately rejected the roles and responsibilities associated with marriage?[53] The appropriate solution may lie somewhere between the two: the evidence that the majority of cohabiting couples mistakenly believe that they already enjoy rights under a "common law marriage" suggests that cohabitation does not involve a deliberate rejection of marriage-like responsibilities,[54] while empirical studies of separating cohabitants show that current law and practice do not seem to offer sufficient protection to children and those who assume responsibility for their care.[55]

The fact that those studies also showed that many couples were unaware of their legal rights, and that one party often received less than he or she might have done had the case gone to court, is also relevant to the next development within family law—namely, the encouragement of private ordering.

C. The encouragement of private ordering

In recent years there has been growing concern that litigation—particularly in its **A–006** more adversarial form—is an inappropriate means of dealing with many family disputes. Couples are encouraged to settle the consequences of separation—in relation to both the division of property[56] and the challenges of post-separation parenting[57]—between themselves or with the assistance of a mediator. This policy is now to be extended to child maintenance, in the hope that this will reduce the administrative burden on the new agency being set up to deal with this issue.[58] Of course, unnecessary litigation should be avoided, but it may be questioned whether the emphasis on couples sorting out matters for themselves is wholly beneficial. There is a risk that individuals may agree to accept inadequate financial support—either for themselves or for their children—or be pressured into accepting unsafe contact arrangements. After all, if people could be relied upon to behave well to each other, would we need a system of family law at all?

II. The Scope and Arrangement of the Text

The focus of this book is the domestic family law of England and Wales. This **A–007** should not obscure the fact that many of the issues examined in the following

---

[53] See, for example, R. Deech, "The case against the legal recognition of cohabitation" (1980) I.C.L.Q. 480.
[54] See A. Barlow, C. Burgoyne and J. Smithson, "Cohabitation and the law: myths, money and the media", in A. Park et al. (eds), *British Social Attitudes: The 24th Report* (London: Sage Publications, 2008).
[55] See, for example, R. Tennant, J. Taylor and J. Lewis, *Separating from Cohabitation: Making Arrangements for Finances and Parenting* (DCA Research Series 7/06, 2006); G. Douglas, J. Pearce and H. Woodward, *A Failure of Trust: Resolving Property Disputes on Cohabitation Breakdown* (Cardiff Law School Research Papers No.1, 2007).
[56] See further para.13–003.
[57] See further para.18–045.
[58] See further para.15–004.

chapters have an international element. Many couples choose to marry or enter into other legally recognised relationships overseas, and the courts may be asked to determine the status of such unions.[59] Some may seek to adopt a child from overseas.[60] Others may move to this country and then seek the assistance of the law if their relationship breaks down; in such cases the courts may need to determine whether they have jurisdiction to hear the case. The breakdown of a relationship may cause one party to wish to relocate to another jurisdiction, whether to return to their country of origin or to make a fresh start in another country with a new job or new partner; if the parties have children then such relocation may prove problematic in terms of contact with the non-residential parent.[61] Some relocations turn into abductions, and in the past 30 years or so there has been a growing body of case law on the approach to be taken to such cases.[62] In the following chapters we shall deal with such issues insofar as they relate to domestic family law, but not with the conflicts of law rules that determine which country's laws are to be applied when determining a particular point,[63] nor with the rules setting out the circumstances in which a domestic court has jurisdiction to hear a case with an international element.

Part I deals with **The Family and Formal Relationships**. This covers the formal processes with which a couple must comply in order to create a legally recognised relationship (Ch.1); the rules restricting who may marry or enter into a civil partnership, and the circumstances in which a marriage or civil partnership may be annulled or regarded as void from the outset (Ch.2); and the legal consequences that flow from entering into either a marriage or civil partnership (Ch.3).

Part II deals with **Family Property**. It begins by identifying the circumstances in which the ownership of assets may need to be determined and the socio-economic factors that affect family life (Ch.4). It then goes on to examine how ownership of real and personal property will be determined in case of dispute and the extent to which family property is protected in the case of a dispute with a creditor (Ch.5). Chapter 6 explains the nature and extent of state support for families through the tax and benefit system, and Ch.7 deals with the devolution of family property on death. Part II closes with a consideration of the options for the reform of family property, whether within formal relationships or not (Ch.8).

In **Part III** we turn to the issue of **Family Breakdown**. This focuses on the way in which the law deals with the status of—and legal remedies available to—adults whose relationship breaks down. In some cases—for example the

---

[59] See further para.2–017, and see also J. Masson, "International families: making new relationships at home and away" in R. Probert (ed.), *Family Life and the Law: Under One Roof* (Aldershot: Ashgate, 2007).
[60] See further para.22–046.
[61] See further para.18–026.
[62] See further Ch.20.
[63] On this, reference should be made to J. Murphy, *International Dimensions in Family Law* (Manchester: Manchester University Press, 2005).

legal remedies available in the context of domestic violence, dealt with in Ch.9—the differences between formal and informal relationships are relatively slight. In others, however, they are far more significant. Chapter 10 sets out the circumstances in which a formal relationship may be terminated either by divorce or by dissolution, and Ch.11 provides a brief account of the alternative remedy of judicial separation. Chapter 12 addresses the problems that may arise where the death of a spouse or civil partner is suspected but not known, and Ch.13 provides a detailed examination of the powers of the court to reallocate assets between the parties when a marriage or civil partnership comes to an end. Chapter 14 deals with the ways in which the court's orders may be enforced.

Part IV deals with **Child Support Obligations**, which, unlike the financial obligations discussed in the previous chapter, are not dependent on the parents having formalised their relationship.   **A–008**

Finally, **Part V** is devoted to the issue of **Children and Family Law**. In recent years there has been growing awareness of children as independent actors within the family unit, and Ch.16 is devoted to an examination of children's rights. Chapter 17 addresses the fundamental question of who is a child's parent, and the distinct and no-less-important question of who has parental responsibility for a child and what this means in terms of their rights and responsibilities. Chapter 18 examines the orders that may be made by a court in relation to a child's upbringing where the child's parents or carers are unable to agree on the best course of action, and Ch.19 discusses the welfare principle that governs the making of such orders. Chapter 20 deals with the specific problem of child abduction and the developments that have occurred at an international level to address it. Since not all children have parents who are able or willing to care for them, the law needs to determine what support parents may need to carry out their role and the level at which legal intervention to remove the child is necessary; these issues are considered in Ch.21. Sometimes children may be removed from their families for relatively short periods of time to enable particular issues to be addressed; in other cases, rehabilitation with the birth parent(s) is not an option, and the possibility of finding a new family—through adoption—will be explored in Ch.22.

PART I

THE FAMILY AND FORMAL RELATIONSHIPS

MARRIAGE CEREMONIES AND THE REGISTRATION OF CIVIL PARTNERSHIPS

I.	INTRODUCTION	1–001		A. Preliminaries to marriage	1–007
II.	HISTORICAL DEVELOPMENT	1–002		B. Solemnisation of the marriage	1–031
	A. The canon law of marriage	1–002		C. Registration and proof of marriages	1–043
	B. Problems with the canon law	1–003		D. Consequences of irregularities	1–044
	C. Lord Hardwicke's Act of 1753	1–004	IV:	FORMALITIES FOR CIVIL PARTNERSHIPS	1–049
	D. The Marriage Acts of 1823 and 1836	1–005	V.	CONCLUSION: A NEED FOR REFORM?	1–050
III.	FORMALITIES FOR MARRIAGE—THE CURRENT LAW	1–006			

I. INTRODUCTION

Novels often close with a wedding—"Reader, I married him"[1]; family law **1–001** textbooks, by contrast, begin with weddings, on the basis that they mark the moment at which the two persons involved assume a new status and particular legal rights and responsibilities. The former carries the promise that the parties live happily ever after; the latter, by contrast, would be considerably slimmer if this were the case.

We tend to think of a wedding as a social event—"the dress, the cake, and the drunk uncle" as Bob Geldof put it[2]—but it is, of course, also an important legal event. Because of the legal rights and responsibilities that flow from marriage— and now from a civil partnership—it is important that there should be no uncertainty as to whether two persons have formalised such a relationship, either for the parties themselves or for the state. The process of marrying or registering a civil partnership is therefore tightly regulated in order to reduce such uncertainty as far as possible. At the same time, the law recognises the importance of allowing people to make their commitment to each other in a form that is meaningful to them, and therefore offers a range of ways in which a

---

[1] C. Bronte, *Jane Eyre* (1847), Ch.38.
[2] *Geldof on Marriage: The Dress, The Cake, and The Drunk Uncle*, Channel Four, October 11, 2004.

marriage may be contracted. Same-sex couples, however, have a more restricted range of options.

This chapter deals with the formalities required to establish the legal relationship of husband and wife, or of civil partners. To create such a relationship, however, it is not sufficient that the parties should have observed these rules; it is also necessary that each of them should have had legal capacity to marry or enter into a civil partnership. The rules governing capacity are discussed in Ch.2; for present purposes, their relevance lies in the fact that the formal procedures should offer an opportunity for any impediments to be discovered before the ceremony takes place.

The modern law can only be understood in its historical context, and it is therefore essential to begin with an outline of the development of the law. This chapter will go on to examine the modern law, focusing primarily on the more complex law relating to marriages and then briefly outlining the simpler procedure for registering a civil partnership. It will conclude with an assessment of what reforms might be necessary to address the sometimes conflicting objectives of achieving certainty, ensuring that impediments are uncovered and providing a meaningful occasion for the parties.

II. Historical Development

A. The canon law of marriage

1–002   For centuries the regulation of marriage was largely a matter for the Church: marriage law was part of canon law.[3] The early Church debated what was necessary to create a marriage: should consummation be necessary or would consent alone suffice?[4] To require consummation was problematic with regard to the marriage of Joseph and the Virgin Mary who, according to one view, had exchanged vows of lifelong chastity.[5] In the twelfth century, therefore, it became accepted that consent without consummation was sufficient.[6] An exchange of vows in the present tense (e.g. "I take you as my wife/husband") would therefore be binding on the parties without any further ceremony, as was a promise of marriage that was followed by sexual intercourse (such intercourse, in this context, being interpreted as evidence of the parties' present consent to marriage).[7]

Yet marriage has always had a public as well as a private dimension. At the very time that consent was accepted as the basis of marriage, attempts were made

---

[3] Since the nineteenth century the pre-statutory requirements have been described as "the common law of marriage" but this usage has led to a number of misunderstandings: see R. Probert, "Common-law marriage: myths and misunderstandings" (2008) 20 C.F.L.Q. 1.

[4] See, for example, Thomas Aquinas, *Summa Theologiae*, quoted in C. McCarthy (ed.) *Love, Sex and Marriage in the Middle Ages: A Sourcebook* (London: Routledge, 2004).

[5] J.A. Brundage, *Law, Sex and Christian Society in Medieval Europe* (Chicago: University of Chicago Press, 1987), p.274.

[6] Brundage, *Law, Sex and Christian Society*, pp.268–269.

[7] See, for example, Henry Swinburne, *A Treatise of Spousals, or Matrimonial Contracts*, 2nd edn (London, 1711), p.226.

to ensure that marriages were celebrated with due formality. Papal decrees and local legislation directed that all marriages should take place in church and be preceded by the calling of banns.[8] In addition, although an exchange of vows was viewed as creating a marriage "before God", or "in conscience", only those that could be proved to the satisfaction of the ecclesiastical courts were *legally* binding. Since in any disputed case the ecclesiastical courts insisted on witnesses or written evidence,[9] sweet nothings breathed between passionate lovers in private might create a marriage "in conscience" but would not be sufficient to do so in law.[10] Nor did a simple exchange of vows carry the same legal rights as a marriage celebrated in church: contracted couples were not meant to anticipate the church ceremony by engaging in sexual intercourse and could be punished by the Church courts for doing so[11]; the parties did not acquire any rights to or interests in each other's property until the marriage had been solemnised[12]; and a later marriage with a third party was voidable, rather than void,[13] and did not constitute the crime of bigamy.[14] Research by scholars of the medieval and early modern periods suggests that people attached considerable weight to the actual solemnisation of marriage and did not regard an informal exchange of vows as sufficient justification to set up home together.[15]

In fact, the most important legal consequence of an exchange of vows in words of the present tense was that the parties were thenceforth bound to solemnise marriage with each other, and the Church courts would enforce the contract if either party proved recalcitrant.[16] Such an exchange should perhaps be regarded as akin to the modern contract for the purchase of land, in that it was binding on

---

[8] K. Stevenson, *Nuptial Blessing: A Study of Christian Marriage Rites* (London: SPCK, 1982), discusses the evolution of the church ceremony in detail, providing evidence of rituals dating back to Anglo-Saxon England; see pp.42–43, 63. The option of dispensing with the banns by obtaining a licence was introduced by the Ecclesiastical Licences Act of 1533. See para.1–025 below on the modern requirements.

[9] Swinburne, *A Treatise of Spousals*; T. Salmon, *A Critical Essay concerning Marriage* (London, 1724) pp.199–200.

[10] As early as the twelfth century it was held that an unwitnessed promise of marriage would be null if denied by either party: see M. Sheehan, *Marriage, Family and the Law in Medieval Europe: Collected Studies* (Cardiff: University of Wales Press, 1996 (eds J. Farge and J. Rosenthal)), Ch.8.

[11] See, for example, *Bunting's case* (1580) Moo. K.B. 303; 72 E.R. 510, in which it was noted that the parties would be guilty of contempt of the church's edict prohibiting carnal copulation before the marriage had been solemnised in church.

[12] Salmon, *A Critical Essay*, p.180. See also Swinburne, *A Treatise of Spousals*, p.235. This meant, for example, that a woman would not be entitled to dower if the man with whom she had contracted died before solemnisation: Swinburne, pp.233–234.

[13] E. Coke, *The First Part of the Institutes of the Laws of England. Or, a Commentary on Littleton*, 10th edn (London, 1703), p.33. Cf *Hemming v Price* (1701) 12 Mod 432; 88 E.R. 1430, referring to the fact that a marriage entered into while a previous spouse was still alive was void.

[14] See the judgment of Lord Lyndhurst in *R. v Millis* (1844) 10 Cl. & F. 534, HL; 8 E.R. 844.

[15] R.H. Helmholz, *Marriage Litigation in Medieval England* (Cambridge: Cambridge University Press, 1975), p.32; D. Cressy, *Birth, Marriage and Death: Ritual, Religion and the Life-Cycle in Tudor and Stuart England* (Oxford: Oxford University Press, 1997), p.316.

[16] See, for example, *Baxtar v Buckley* (1752) 1 Lee 42; 161 E.R. 17. Various legal mechanisms existed to reinforce the order that the contracted couple should solemnise their union: in ascending order of severity, these were admonition, excommunication and imprisonment; Salmon, *A Critical Essay*, p.202; Swinburne, *A Treatise of Spousals*, p.231; P. Floyer, *The Proctor's Practice in the Ecclesiastical Courts* (London, 1744), p.78.

the parties, and specifically enforceable, but needed to be completed by solemnisation.

B. Problems with the canon law

1–003   The canon law of marriage did, however, have a number of disadvantages. First, there was the possibility that a marriage duly celebrated in church might be invalidated by evidence that one of the parties had previously contracted to marry another. While this was kept in check by the requirement that the earlier exchange of vows be proved by two witnesses, it still remained a potential threat to the security of long-standing unions.

Secondly, hasty and ill-considered marriages were facilitated. A marriage could be valid even if it did not comply with the canons governing the preliminaries to—and celebration of—matrimony. And from the start of the seventeenth century it was accepted that a marriage did not have to be celebrated in church in order for the parties to acquire property rights: marriage before an Anglican minister would suffice.[17] In the later seventeenth century a number of churches became notorious for celebrating marriages without the stipulated preliminaries, but this practice was ended by legislation fining clergymen who married couples in this way.[18] Unfortunately, new and more problematic practices emerged in the search to find loop-holes in the law: clergymen who had no livings (and therefore little to lose) congregated in the area surrounding the Fleet prison in London and married couples without banns or licence (and without asking too many questions).[19]

The case of *Hill v Turner*[20] shows exactly why Fleet marriages were regarded with disfavour by the ruling elite. A 17-year old lad who was entitled to substantial property was taken to an ale-house in the vicinity of the Fleet, was intoxicated and married to a woman "in mean circumstances and of bad character". Since he was a ward of court, the assistance of the Court of Chancery was sought. It held that the validity of the marriage could not be impugned, and Lord Hardwicke, presiding over the court as Lord Chancellor, noted the "misfortune [of] . . . the want of a sufficient law to restrain such clandestine marriages".

It is understandable that patrician parents would be nervous about the possibility of their offspring entering into unsuitable unions in this way. But marriages celebrated in the Fleet could also pose problems for the parties themselves: courts attached little weight to the word of—or registers kept

---

[17] *Wickham v Enfield* (1633) Cro Car 351; 79 E.R. 908 confirmed that a wife so married would still be entitled to dower. *Wigmore's* case (1707) Holt K.B. 460; 90 E.R. 1153 and *Haydon v Gould* (1711) 1 Salk 119; 91 E.R. 113 emphasised that the marriage had to be celebrated according to Anglican rites.

[18] Marriage Duty Act 1695 s.102.

[19] See R. Lee Brown, "The rise and fall of the fleet marriage", Ch.6 in R.B. Outhwaite, *Marriage and Society* (London: Europa Publications, 1981).

[20] (1737) 1 Atk 516; 26 E.R. 326.

by—Fleet parsons, and those who had married in this way might have a hard task persuading the court of the fact.[21]

C. Lord Hardwicke's Act of 1753

The Clandestine Marriages Act of 1753 (almost always called Lord Hardwicke's   **1–004**
Act after its main proponent) attempted to address these problems: it set out to channel marriages into a standard form, to increase parental control over the marriages of minors and to improve the registration of marriages. It therefore stipulated that marriages should only take place in church after the calling of banns on three successive Sundays or the obtaining of a licence (common or special). The consent of a minor's parents or guardians had to be obtained and the marriage had to be recorded in the parish register. None of these requirements were novel; what was new was the provision that marriages that did not comply with certain formalities would be void.

The Act applied to all persons except members of the Royal Family,[22] Quakers and Jews.[23] Thus Protestant dissenters and Roman Catholics were compelled to marry according to the Anglican rite, or not at all.[24]

D. The Marriage Acts of 1823 and 1836

For many years the 1753 Act worked tolerably well. The courts adopted a   **1–005**
purposive approach when interpreting the legislation, upholding marriages that did not flout the spirit of the Act while striking down those that were clearly intended to evade its provisions.[25] In the early decades of the nineteenth century, however, a new problem emerged: cases in which one spouse argued that a marriage celebrated many years earlier had not complied with the requirements of the law and was therefore invalid.[26] The courts did their best to prevent the law of nullity from being used as a substitute for divorce—then available only by an

---

[21] See, for example, *Conran v Lowe* (1754) 1 Lee 630; 161 E.R. 230, in which it was stated that a Fleet register "was not evidence".

[22] The freedom of members of the Royal Family to contract marriages was subsequently restricted by the Royal Marriages Act 1772, but otherwise this exemption from the formal requirements of the law appears to have been preserved; see the Marriage Act 1949 s.74(2), and para.1–032 below.

[23] Quakers and Jews were the only groups—apart from Catholics, who were in any case not allowed to worship freely—who regularly married according to their own rites before 1754. Questions had, however, been raised about the status of such marriages and, since the 1753 Act did not specifically state that they would be valid, continued to be asked.

[24] There is evidence that the vast majority did comply with the law: see R. Probert and L. D'Arcy Brown, "Catholics and the Clandestine Marriages Act of 1753" (2008) *Local Population Studies* 78.

[25] See, for example, *Standen v Standen* (1791) Peake 45; 170 E.R. 73; *Wilkinson v Payne* (1791) 4 Term Rep. 468; 100 E.R. 1123; *Stallwood v Tredger* (1815) 2 Phill. Ecc. 287; 161 E.R. 1147, and the cases reviewed in R. Probert, "The judicial interpretation of Lord Hardwicke's Act 1753" (2002) 23 *Journal of Legal History* 129.

[26] See, for example, *Johnston v Parker* (1819) 3 Phill. Ecc. 39; 161 E.R. 1251 (22 years of marriage and 7 children); *Hayes v Watts*, (1819) 3 Phill. Ecc. 43; 161 E.R. 1252 (18-year marriage); and *Fielder v Smith* 1816) 2 Hag. Con. 193; 161 E.R. 712 (19-year marriage and 12 children).

Act of Parliament—but there was only so much that could be done through judicial interpretation. Legislation was therefore passed to ensure that a failure to comply with the requisite formalities would only invalidate a marriage if the parties had "knowingly and wilfully" contravened the law.[27] This remains the terminology used in the current legislation.[28]

But more fundamental change was necessitated by the changing nature of English society. Increasing numbers of individuals were worshipping outside the Church of England,[29] and attitudes to such dissent were changing. In 1836 the law was changed to confirm the validity of marriages celebrated according to Quaker and Jewish rites and to allow marriages to be celebrated in other places of worship.[30] The Act also made provision for a purely secular form of marriage: civil marriage. An attempt was even made to introduce uniform civil preliminaries for all marriages, but this was rejected by the House of Lords. As a result, the Act simply provided that all marriages except those celebrated according to Anglican rites had to be preceded by civil preliminaries.

As a result of the Marriage Act of 1836, there were a number of different routes to a valid marriage, depending on the parties' status,[31] wealth and religious affiliation. The somewhat complex system it established—with distinctions being drawn not only between religious and civil marriages but also between different types of religious marriage—remains, in essence, that which operates today, as we shall see.

III. FORMALITIES FOR MARRIAGE—THE CURRENT LAW

1–006   There are three separate elements to the celebration of a marriage: first, certain preliminaries, designed to bring the marriage to public attention and uncover any impediments; secondly, the ceremony itself, the timing and location of which may be regulated to reflect the fact that marriage is a public event; and, thirdly, registration, which ensures that the State has a record of the marriage and provides a simple means of proving that the marriage did indeed take place. The current law is largely contained in the Marriage Act 1949, which consolidated earlier legislation, although, as will be seen, a number of amendments have been made to the original text over the past six decades.[32]

---

[27] Marriage Act 1823 s.22.
[28] Marriage Act 1949 ss.25 and 49; and see para.1–045 below.
[29] By 1830 the Church of England "was on the point of becoming a minority religious Establishment": A.D. Gilbert, *Religion and Society in Industrial England: Church, Chapel and Social Change, 1740–1914* (London: Longman, 1976), p.27.
[30] Although for some time such marriages remained subject to considerably more regulation than other religious marriages: see R. Floud and P. Thane, "The incidence of civil marriage in Victorian England and Wales" (1979) 84 *Past and Present* 146.
[31] See para.1–032 below on members of the Royal family.
[32] Notably by the Marriage Act 1994 and by the Asylum and Immigration Act 1999.

A. Preliminaries to marriage

Every couple must observe certain preliminaries before they marry in England   **1–007**
and Wales, whatever form their marriage is to take. Those under the age of 18
must, in addition, obtain parental consent to the proposed marriage.

i. Parental consent

Under the 1949 Marriage Act, "parental" consent is, in principle, required for the   **1–008**
marriage of a person who is under 18[33] (and not a widow or widower[34]); but a
marriage solemnised without such consent will be valid.[35]

(1) Whose consent is required?

The law on this point is somewhat complex,[36] but basically gives effect to the   **1–009**
principle that the consent required should be that of the person or persons who
have had actual day-to-day care of a child. Consent is required from the following:

- Each of the child's parents who has "parental responsibility" for the
  child,[37] and each guardian of a child.[38]

- If the child is the subject of a care order,[39] then the consent of the local
  authority designated in the order is required *in addition* to the consents of
  the parents and guardians.[40] Special provisions also apply to children who
  are in the process of being adopted.[41]

---

[33] See the Marriage Act 1949 s.3, as amended by the Children Act 1989 Sch.12 para.5 and the
Adoption and Children Act 2002 Sch.3 para.3. Consent is only a statutory prerequisite to a marriage
after civil preliminaries or by common licence; parental consent is not formally required to a marriage
after the calling of banns, but the parent or other third party may object: Marriage Act 1949 s.3(3).
Moreover, Anglican clergy are prohibited from solemnising a marriage "otherwise than in
accordance with the requirements of the law relating to the consent of parents or guardians in the case
of a person under 18 years of age": *The Canons of the Church of England* 6th edn (London: Church
House, 2000), B32.

[34] Consent is thus required in the unlikely event of a minor's previous marriage having been
terminated by divorce or annulment.

[35] By contrast, under the Royal Marriages Act 1772 the consent of the Sovereign in Council is
required to the marriage of descendants of George II, and a marriage contracted in defiance of the Act
is void: note the illuminating articles by T.B. Pugh and A. Samuels, "The Royal Marriages Act 1772;
its defects and the case for repeal" (1994) 15 *Statute Law Review* 46; S.M. Cretney, "The Royal
Marriage Act 1772: a footnote" (1995) 16 *Statute Law Review* 195 and "Royal marriages: some legal
and constitutional issues" (2008) 124 L.Q.R. 218.

[36] For the history of this requirement, see R. Probert, "Parental responsibility and consent to
marriage" in R. Probert, S. Gilmore and J. Herring (eds) *Parental Responsibility and Responsible
Parenting* (Oxford: Hart Publishing, 2009, forthcoming).

[37] As defined in the Children Act 1989 ss.2, 3; see Ch.17.

[38] Marriage Act 1949 s.3(1A)(a).

[39] See para.21–041 for a definition of such an order.

[40] Marriage Act 1949 s.3(1A)(c).

[41] If an adoption agency has been authorised to place the child for adoption, its consent will be
required: Marriage Act 1949 s.3(1A)(e). If a placement order is in force, the consent of the
appropriate local authority will be necessary: s.3(1A)(f). And if the child has been placed for adoption
with prospective adopters, their consent will be required in addition: s.3(1A)(g).

- If a special guardianship order is in force with respect to the child,[42] the consent of the child's special guardian(s) will be necessary *in substitution* for that of the parents or guardians.[43]

- Similarly, if a residence order[44] is in force, the consent of the person or persons with whom the child is to live under the terms of that order is required, rather than that of the parents or guardians.[45]

- If the child is a ward of court, the consent of the court is required in addition to that of any person specified above.[46]

(2) Dispensing with parental consent

1–010   Consent may be dispensed with in two groups of cases:

(1) Where consent of a prescribed person "cannot be obtained by reason of absence or inaccessibility or by reason of his being under any disability". In such circumstances either the consent may be dispensed with by the superintendent registrar, or the court may consent.[47]

(2) If a person whose consent is required refuses to give it, in which case application can be made to the court.[48]

It should, however, be noted that few teenagers avail themselves of this procedure: indeed, in *Re K; A Local Authority v N*[49] Munby J. described this jurisdiction—together with the use of wardship to control the marriages of minors[50]—as "little more than dead letters".

(3) Should the requirement of parental consent be retained?

1–011   The age for "free marriage" was reduced from 21 to 18 by the Family Law Reform Act 1969.[51] Discussions regarding the need to retain any requirement of parental consent to the marriage of teenagers now have a somewhat dated flavour. Far from rushing into marriage in late adolescence, the trend has been

---

[42] See para.17–046 for a definition of such an order.
[43] Marriage Act 1949 s.3(1A)(d).
[44] See para.18–016 for a definition of such an order.
[45] Marriage Act 1949 s.3(1A)(b). If there is no residence or care order in force, but a residence order was in force immediately before the child reached the age of 16, the consent of a person or persons with whom he or she was to live under that residence order is required: s.3(1A)(h).
[46] Marriage Act 1949 s.3(6).
[47] Marriage Act 1949 s.3(1), proviso (a).
[48] Marriage Act 1949 s.3(1), proviso (b).
[49] [2005] EWHC 2956 (Fam); [2007] 1 F.L.R. 399, para.80.
[50] See para.18–049 on wardship, and see Probert, above, fn.36, on the past use of the wardship jurisdiction to control the marriages of minors.
[51] Family Law Reform Act 1969 s.2(1)(c), giving effect to the recommendations of the Committee on the Age of Majority (Chairman: The Hon. Mr Justice Latey) Cmnd.3342 (1965) (subsequently cited as the *Latey Report*). In 2004 only 667 females and 100 males married under this age: *Marriage, Divorce and Adoption Statistics*, Tables 3.18 and 3.19.

towards marriage much later in life. The average age for first marriage by women was 22.6 in 1971 but had risen to 29.5 in 2005[52]; and whereas in 1971 nearly a third of all brides married as teenagers, by 2005 the proportion had fallen to less than 2 per cent.[53] Insofar as teenage marriages constituted a problem, it is one that has solved itself. And parents wishful of exercising control over their child's choice of partner are unlikely to find the requirement of parental consent to marriage of much assistance: it may delay the *marriage*, but is of little use in preventing the *relationship*.[54] The need to retain the requirement of parental consent is therefore open to question.[55]

ii. Notice of the intended marriage

The legal preliminaries are primarily designed to ensure that notice of the **1–012** intended marriage is given, thus providing publicity and an opportunity for objections to be made (e.g. by a parent who believes his or her consent should be obtained, or by a person who claims to be married to one of the parties). In recent years the process has also aimed to identify "sham" marriages entered into by parties who have no intention of cohabiting but who wish to enhance their immigration status by marrying.

The suggestion that there should be uniform civil preliminaries for all marriages is one that has been advanced on a number of occasions: in 1836, when new ways of celebrating marriage were first introduced[56]; in 1973, when the Law Commission reviewed the law in this area[57]; and in 2002, when the Blair Government issued a White Paper proposing wide-ranging changes to the law of marriage.[58] To date, however, no reform to this effect has been enacted, which means that two systems—the traditional, Church administered, Anglican proce-

---

[52] See C. Gibson, "Changing family patterns in England and Wales", in S.N. Katz, J. Eekelaar and M. Maclean (eds), *Cross Currents* (2000), Table 2.1; "Report: marriages in England and Wales, 2005" (2007) 127 *Population Trends* 61, Table 5. The average age for first marriage amongst men in 2005 was 31.7.

[53] "Report: marriages in England and Wales, 2005" (2007) 127 *Population Trends* 61, Table 5. Among young men the proportion was even lower: indeed, in 2004 more men married over the age of 85 than under the age of 18: *Marriage, Divorce and Adoption Statistics*, Series FM2 No.32 (London: ONS, 2007), Table 3.19.

[54] As Munby J. noted in *Re K; A Local Authority v N* [2005] EWHC 2956 (Fam); [2007] 1 FLR 399 the "unintended but nonetheless foreseeable" consequence of restricting the girl's marriage in that case might be to push her into less desirable forms of behaviour—such as absconding or entering into a sexual relationship outside marriage. Such behaviour is far more common than teenage marriage: in 2005 there were some 42,200 conceptions to women under 18 (almost half of which led to abortion): "Report: marriages in England and Wales" (2007) 129 *Population Trends* 49, Table 4.1.

[55] See further Probert, above, fn.36.

[56] See above at para.1–005.

[57] Law Com. No.53 (1973).

[58] *Civil Registration: Vital Change*, Cm.5355. This was subsequently followed by a more detailed consultation paper published by the Office for National Statistics: *Civil Registration: Delivering Vital Change* (2003). For comment on the proposals see C. Barton, "White Paper weddings—the beginnings, muddles and ends of wedlock" [2002] Fam. Law 431 and R. Probert, "Lord Hardwicke's Marriage Act 250 years on: vital change?" [2004] Fam. Law 583.

dures and the state-administered registrars' procedure introduced in 1836—
continue to exist side by side.

(1) Civil preliminaries

1–013 All non-Anglican marriages,[59] whether civil or religious, must be preceded by
civil preliminaries whereby notice is given to the superintendent registrar[60] of the
district(s) where the parties reside. There are now only two[61] different procedures: first, the superintendent registrar's certificate, which will usually be the
appropriate preliminary; secondly, the registrar-general's licence, which is used
where one party is seriously ill and not expected to recover.

(a) Superintendent registrar's certificate. The main requirements are:

1–014 *(i) Notice.* Each party must give notice in a prescribed form[62] to the superintendent registrar of the district or districts where he or she has resided for at
least seven days.[63] All notices are recorded in a marriage notice book, which is
open to public inspection. The notice must be "suspended or affixed" for 15 days
on a noticeboard in "some conspicuous place" in the superintendent registrar's
office.[64]

1–015 *(ii) Objections and inquiries.* The superintendent registrar will seek to satisfy
him- or herself that, on the basis of the evidence provided, the parties are free to
marry. For example, if one party states that she is a widow or has been divorced,
proof of the relevant death or divorce will have to be produced.

Members of the public may object to an intended marriage: any person may
enter a caveat with the superintendent registrar,[65] and any person whose consent
is required to the marriage of a minor may forbid the issue of a certificate by
writing "forbidden" by the entry and signing it with a statement of the capacity

[59] References to the Church of England should be read as including the Church in Wales. Marriages
in the Church of England may be preceded by one variant of the civil preliminaries (i.e. the issue of
a superintendent registrar's certificate) rather than by ecclesiastical preliminaries: Marriage Act 1949
s.5(d). But the reverse is not true: Anglican preliminaries cannot be used for any other than Anglican
marriages.
[60] The office of superintendent registrar of births, death and marriages was created by the 1836
legislation: see the Births and Deaths Registration Act 1836 and the Marriage Act 1836. Under the
Statistics and Registration Services Act 2007 s.70, superintendent registrars are now employed
directly by the local authority.
[61] A third option—which, on payment of a higher fee, allowed a marriage to take place after the
expiration of one whole day from the giving of notice—was abolished by the Immigration and
Asylum Act 1999 s.160 (with effect from January 1, 2001).
[62] The notice must give details of the parties' age, marital status, place of residence, nationality, etc.:
see the Reporting of Suspicious Marriages and Registration of Births Deaths and Marriages
(Miscellaneous Amendments) Regulations 2000 (SI 2000/3164). The 1999 Act introduced a
requirement that a person giving notice should provide evidence of the prescribed matters if required
to do so: Marriage Act 1949 s.28A inserted by Immigration and Asylum Act 1999 s.162. Persons
giving notice are warned that to make a false declaration will expose them to prosecution.
[63] Marriage Act 1949 s.27(1), as amended by Immigration and Asylum Act 1999 s.161(1). From
February 1, 2005 those who are subject to immigration control have been required to give notice at
one of the 76 specially designated register offices: Asylum and Immigration (Treatment of Claimants,
Etc) Act 2004 s.19(2)(b).
[64] Marriage Act 1949 s.31(1), as amended by the Immigration and Asylum Act 1999 s.160(4).
[65] Marriage Act 1949 s.29.

in which he or she purports to act.[66] The validity of the objection will then be investigated.

(iii) Waiting time. At the end of 15 days[67] from the giving of notice, the **1–016** superintendent registrar will issue a certificate that authorises the solemnisation of the marriage.[68] If there are "compelling reasons" for reducing the 15-day waiting period because of the "exceptional circumstances of the case"—it was suggested that a call to military service abroad might be such a reason—the Registrar General may, on application, reduce the period.[69]

(iv) Special provisions for those subject to immigration control. The super- **1–017** intendent registrar is under an obligation to report to the Home Office Immigration Department any proposed marriages that do not appear to be genuine.[70] In addition, in 2005 new rules were implemented for persons subject to immigration control. These provided that such persons would not be granted a certificate enabling the marriage to take place unless they had been given entry clearance for this purpose, or had the written permission of the Secretary of State.[71] The fact that such consent would only be given in a narrow range of circumstances attracted criticism, since many genuine marriages were affected by these extra restrictions.[72] The future of the scheme is currently in question: the Court of Appeal has declared it to be in breach of the European Convention on Human Rights,[73] on the basis that the scheme was not a proportionate response to the legitimate aim of controlling immigration, and the original scheme has been modified in the light of its criticisms.[74] However, it is the intention of the Home Office to appeal to the House of Lords.

(v) Special provisions for marriage of the house-bound and detained. The law **1–018** makes special provision for persons who are house-bound by reason of illness or disability or detained in prison or under certain legislation relating to mental health. Such persons may be married[75] at their place of residence or detention by

---

[66] Marriage Act 1949 s.30.
[67] Marriage Act 1949 s.31(2), as amended by the Immigration and Asylum Act 1999 s.160(4).
[68] Marriage Act 1949 s.33. The marriage must take place within three months of the date when notice was entered in the marriage notice book.
[69] Marriage Act 1949 s.31(5A), as inserted by Immigration and Asylum Act 1999 s.160(6). Note also the provisions of the Marriage (Registrar-General's Licence) Act 1970: see below.
[70] Immigration and Asylum Act 1999 s.24; Reporting of Suspicious Marriages and Registration of Births Deaths and Marriages (Miscellaneous Amendments) Regulations 2000 (SI 2000/3164).
[71] Or fell within certain other categories to be specified by regulations: Asylum and Immigration (Treatment of Claimants, Etc) Act 2004 s.19(3).
[72] For discussion see H. Toner, "Immigration law and family life—a happy marriage?", Ch.12 in R. Probert (ed.), *Family Life and the Law: Under One Roof* (Aldershot: Ashgate, 2007).
[73] *Secretary of State for the Home Department v Baiai* [2007] EWCA Civ 478.
[74] Home Office Border & Immigration Authority, "Important information regarding certificate of approval for marriage or civil partnership applications", para.3.3: *http://www.ukba.homeoffice.gov.uk/ sitecontent/documents/visitingtheuk/coaguidance.pdf* [Accessed July 21, 2008]. It is still necessary for those subject to immigration control to obtain a certificate of approval, but the scheme no longer prescibes the circumstances in which permission will be given.
[75] According to religious or civil rites.

means of a superintendent registrar's certificate, but in order to take advantage of these provisions, the notice must be accompanied either by an official certificate giving details of the detention or by a doctor's certificate stating that by reason of illness or disability the person concerned ought not to move or be moved from the place where he or she is at the time, and that the position is unlikely to change for at least three months.[76]

But the drafting of the legislation is not without its problems: for example, a person who is likely to die within a few days or weeks will not remain house-bound for the stipulated minimum period of three months. A separate procedure—the registrar-general's licence—may be invoked in such a case.

1–019   **(b) Registrar-general's licence.** As we shall see below, the law exercises considerable control over where a marriage may be celebrated. This caused hardship where the parties wanted to contract a so-called "death-bed marriage". The only way of doing this was to obtain a special licence from the Archbishop of Canterbury[77]; but a licence would only be given for an Anglican marriage, and, it would appear in practice, only to those who were free to marry by Anglican canon law.[78]

The Marriage (Registrar-General's Licence) Act 1970 accordingly provided a civil procedure analogous to the Archbishop's special licence. The registrar-general's[79] licence may be issued if there is evidence that one of the persons to be married is seriously ill and not expected to recover, and that he or she cannot be moved to a place at which marriages can be solemnised under the 1949 Act.[80] It is specifically provided—presumably in order to avoid any interference with the traditional use of the Archbishop's licence—that the procedure shall not be used as a preliminary to an Anglican wedding.

In practice, the restrictively drawn provisions of this Act might be thought to have been rendered largely superfluous by the enactment of the Marriage Act 1983, which establishes a simpler and more far-reaching procedure whereby those who are ill or disabled may marry. But, in fact, it appears that more marriages take place under its provisions than under those of the 1983 Act.[81] It seems regrettable that the opportunity was not taken to draw the 1983 Act in terms wide enough to permit the repeal of the 1970 Act.

---

[76] Marriage Act 1949 s.27A, as amended by the Marriage Act 1983.

[77] See below, para.1–029.

[78] Thus, a special licence would not normally be available where one of the parties had been divorced so long as the former spouse were still alive; nor would a special licence be granted if neither party had been baptised: General Synod of the Church of England, *Just Cause or Impediment? A Report from the Review of Aspects of Marriage Law Working Group* (2001), para.37.

[79] Despite the name, it is the superintendent registrar of the relevant district who is responsible for issuing the licence.

[80] Marriage (Registrar-General's Licence) Act 1970 s.1.

[81] According to the Office for National Statistics each year approximately 100 marriages take place according to the provisions of the 1983 Act, and 220 by Registrar-General's licence: *Civil Registration: Delivering Vital Change* (Office for National Statistics 2003), paras 3.5.1 and 3.6.1. In 2004, 337 registrar-general's licences were issued: *Marriage, Divorce and Adoption Statistics*, Table 3.34.

(2) Anglican preliminaries

Three procedures (administered exclusively by the church authorities) are 1–020
available only[82] as a preliminary to marriage according to the rites of the Church
of England: banns, common licence, and special licence. At present the special
procedure to be observed by those who are subject to immigration control does
not apply if the marriage is to be celebrated according to Anglican rites, but the
Government has indicated that Anglican marriages are to be brought within its
scope.[83]

(a) Banns. The calling of banns in the parish church is an ancient procedure that 1–021
can be traced back as far as the first millennium. It involves the incumbent
announcing the intended marriage during a church service on three successive
Sundays. This procedure is used in 90 per cent of Anglican weddings.[84] The main
features of the law are as follows:

(i) Residence. If the parties reside in the same parish, the banns must be published 1–022
there[85]; if in different parishes, in each of them.[86] They may also be published in
any parish church or authorised chapel that is the usual place of worship of one
or both of the parties,[87] but this will only be necessary if the parties are to be
married there.[88]

There is no specific requirement as to length of prior residence or as to what
constitutes residence.[89]

(ii) Publicity. The banns are entered in a register, and must be published 1–023
therefrom[90] "in an audible manner and in accordance with the form of words

---

[82] However, it should be noted that an Anglican marriage can take place on the authority of a
superintendent registrar's licence (Marriage Act 1949 s.5(d)). It seems that relatively few marriages
are celebrated in reliance on a registrar's certificate, and for many years such marriages were
extremely rare. However in 2004 there were 1,013 (albeit only 1.6 per cent of the total of Anglican
marriages). It appears that some clergy encourage this procedure as an alternative to the calling of
banns in cases in which they have agreed to solemnise a wedding involving a divorced person:
General Synod of the Church of England, *Just Cause or Impediment?*, p.13.
[83] Home Office Border & Immigration Authority, "Important information regarding certificate of
approval for marriage or civil partnership applications", para.5.1.
[84] In 2004, 55,552 out of 62,006 Anglican marriages were preceded by banns: *Marriage, Divorce and
Adoption Statistics*, Table 3.34. Banns may, of course, be called in Roman Catholic or Non-
conformist churches, but they have no legal significance in such cases.
[85] There is a great deal of case law on the proper publication of banns; see J. Jackson, *The Formation
and Annulment of Marriage* (London: Butterworths, 1969), pp.169–182.
[86] Marriage Act 1949 s.6.
[87] Marriage Act 1949 s.6(4).
[88] Marriage Act 1949 s.12(1). In order to qualify for this purpose, the applicant must be enrolled on
the church electoral roll: Marriage Act 1949 s.72.
[89] The Church of England's own guidance notes that the law on this point is "very unclear", but
emphasises that residence must be genuine and cannot be satisfied merely by "leaving a suitcase" or
a temporary stay in a hotel: *Diocesan Handbook* (D12). However, the Church's proposal to expand
the circumstances in which a person may marry in a particular church will obviate the need to
fabricate residence in many cases.
[90] "and not from loose papers": Marriage Act 1949 s.7(3).

prescribed by the rubric prefixed to the office of matrimony in the Book of Common Prayer" on three Sundays preceding the solemnisation.[91]

The theory is that banns are primarily:

> "[A]ddressed to Parents and Guardians, to excite their vigilance, and afford them fit opportunities of protecting those lawful rights which may be avoided by clandestinity."[92]

However, whereas in the case of civil preliminaries the registrar may now require the production of evidence that any necessary consents have been obtained,[93] there is no analogous provision in relation to marriage after banns.[94]

1–024 *(iii) Waiting time.* The marriage cannot take place until the banns have been published three times. The waiting time will depend on whether or not the incumbent requires seven days' notice before the first publication: the absolute minimum would be 15 days if publication were sought and made without prior notice on a Sunday, in which event the marriage could take place after the banns had been called on the two following Sundays, but, in practice, the waiting time will almost invariably be in excess of 21 days.

1–025 **(b) Common licence.** This is the ecclesiastical counterpart of the superintendent registrar's certificate and licence. Basic rules are laid down in the Marriage Act 1949,[95] but the details are matters of ecclesiastical law and practice.[96] Common Licences are granted by Diocesan Registrars (or by a surrogate appointed by the Chancellor of the Diocese). The main requirements are:

1–026 *(i) Residence.* The licence can only permit a marriage in either the parish where one of the parties has had their usual place of residence for 15 days immediately before the grant of the licence or in the church that is "the usual place of worship" of either or both parties.[97]

---

[91] Marriage Act 1949 s.7(1)(2).

[92] T. Poynter, *A Concise View of the Doctrine and Practice of the Ecclesiastical Courts*, 2nd edn (1824), p.27.

[93] This power was only introduced by the Family Law Reform Act 1969 s.2(3), although it had prior to this been the practice of registrars to ask for such written consent; see *Latey Report*, para.185. The Immigration and Asylum Act 1999 gave civil registrars (but not the clergy) power to require the production of documentary evidence: Marriage Act 1949 s.28A, inserted by Immigration and Asylum Act 1999 s.162.

[94] Although Canon B32 prohibits a clergyman from celebrating marriages in defiance of the parental consent requirement.

[95] Marriage Act 1949 ss.15–16.

[96] Since the grant of a licence is a matter for discretion, it is open to the church to impose conditions, for example that no licence will be issued unless one party is a baptised Christian: *An Honourable Estate* (1988), para.178. It is not the practice to issue a licence where a party to the intended marriage is divorced and the former spouse is still living: General Synod of the Church of England, *Just Cause or Impediment?*, p.12.

[97] Marriage Act 1949 s.15(1). To qualify, the party's name must be on that church's electoral roll: s.72.

(ii) Declaration. In contrast to the procedure by banns, a common licence can **1–027** only be granted if one of the parties swears an affidavit[98] that he or she believes there to be no lawful impediment, that the residential qualification is satisfied, and (where one of the parties is a minor and not a widow or a widower) that the requisite consents have been obtained or dispensed with.[99]

(iii) Publicity, discovery of impediments and waiting time. A caveat may be **1–028** entered against the grant of a licence; if it is, no licence can be issued until the caveat has been withdrawn or the ecclesiastical judge certifies that the caveat should not obstruct the grant of a licence.[100]

There is no waiting time: once the licence is issued the marriage can take place immediately. In practice, the formalities for obtaining a licence usually take some time; but there is virtually no publicity or opportunity for objection. The cost is more than for the normal procedure by banns, and only 5 per cent or so of Anglican marriages take place on the authority of a common licence.[101]

(c) Special licence. The Archbishop of Canterbury has the power[102] to license **1–029** marriages at any hour of the day or night in any church or chapel or other meeting and convenient place, whether consecrated or not. Originally, we are told, licences "were intended exclusively for the use of persons of noble and illustrious quality",[103] and the number granted remained low until relatively recently. However, for a variety of reasons the use of the special licence procedure increased in the last quarter of the twentieth century. In 2004, 2,226 Anglican marriages (3.6 per cent of the total) were by Archbishop's licence.[104] In practice, they are today usually granted to permit marriages in places such as college chapels at Oxford and Cambridge and in churches with which neither party has the connections stipulated for marriage after banns or by licence.[105] It has been said[106] that the authorities exercise the jurisdiction to grant special licences "sparingly", and that they will only normally be used to permit a marriage outside the parish in which one or other of the parties resides if a "clear justification" is shown, and that normally there must be a clear connection between the parties and the place in question.

---

[98] And may therefore be punished for perjury if he or she knows that its contents are untrue.
[99] Marriage Act 1949 s.16.
[100] Marriage Act 1949 s.16(2).
[101] *Marriage, Divorce and Adoption Statistics*, Table 3.34.
[102] Conferred by the Ecclesiastical Licences Act 1533, and see also the express savings in the Marriage Act 1949 s.79(6): Marriage (Registrar-General's Licence) Act 1970 s.19. The Act provides a right of appeal to the Lord Chancellor against a refusal without reasonable cause to grant a licence: Ecclesiastical Licences Act 1533 ss.11, 12.
[103] Poynter, *A Concise View*, p.50.
[104] *Marriage, Divorce and Adoption Statistics*, Table 3.34.
[105] An alternative is to go through a civil ceremony and then follow this with a religious service: Marriage Act 1949 s.46(1), as amended by the Marriage Act 1983 Sch.1 para.12. In such a case the couple are in law married by the civil ceremony, and there is no legal need for the religious service: Marriage Act 1949 s.46(2). New proposals on the "qualifying connection" necessary for a person to marry in a particular parish may reduce the need for such expedients: see below, para.1–036.
[106] General Synod of the Church of England, *Just Cause or Impediment?*, para.37. The Faculty Office publishes the criteria that are applied in deciding on the grant of Archbishop's licences on its website: *http://www.facultyoffice.org.uk* [Accessed May 23, 2008].

(3) Do the current procedures for giving notice serve their purpose?

1–030 In these days of "larger, more mobile and more anonymous populations",[107] the statutory provisions wholly fail to achieve publicity for the intended union. The conditions that made the calling of banns in rural English parishes a hundred or more years ago an important and talked about event have vanished, never to reappear, whilst the Efficiency Scrutiny's investigations confirmed that the main use made of the register office's marriage notice boards is by photographers, florists, "salesmen of insurance, babyware and marital aids" in order to identify potential customers.[108] Only one superintendent registrar had ever heard of the display of a notice leading to a valid objection, "and that by pure chance".[109]

B. Solemnisation of the marriage

1–031 After the necessary preliminaries have been observed, the couple may proceed to the actual solemnisation of the marriage. There are four main categories of marriage ceremony in English law: civil marriage, marriage according to the rites of the Church of England, Quaker and Jewish marriages, and marriage according to another non-Anglican religious ceremony.

It should be noted, however, that there is by no means an equal split between these different categories. Civil marriages constituted around 68 per cent of all marriages in England and Wales in 2004, continuing a long-established trend towards the secular, while marriages according to the rites of the Church of England accounted for 23 per cent, Quaker and Jewish marriages for a tiny proportion (0.3 per cent and 0.02 per cent respectively) and other non-Anglican marriages for 9 per cent.[110] Although the trend towards civil marriage has been influenced by the refusal of many religious bodies to celebrate marriages if either party had been divorced and had a former spouse living,[111] in 2004 over half of civil marriages involved persons who had never previously been married.[112] It is possible that the statistics will continue to be influenced by the increased readiness of some religious bodies to provide facilities for remarriage after divorce,[113] and by the registration of religious premises for the solemnisation of marriage,[114] but it seems clear that marriage has now, for the majority of the population, become a secular event.

---

[107] Efficiency Scrutiny of the Registration Service (1985) PRO RG41/79.

[108] Efficiency Scrutiny of the Registration Service (1985).

[109] Efficiency Scrutiny of the Registration Service (1985).

[110] *Marriage, Divorce and Adoption Statistics*, Tables 3.29 and 3.40.

[111] Non-conformist churches are less reluctant than the Established and Roman Catholic churches to solemnise the marriages of the divorced: slightly more than half of the marriages by Methodist ceremonies in 2004 involved a divorced person. In contrast, some 17% of Anglican weddings involved a divorced person (a percentage which has increased in recent years and seems still to be increasing) whereas the Roman Catholic Church seems still to uphold its traditional discipline in this matter, with fewer than 7% of marriages involving a divorcé(e): *Marriage, Divorce and Adoption Statistics*, Table 3.31.

[112] 94,203 out of a total of 184,913: see *Marriage, Divorce and Adoption Statistics*, Table 3.30.

[113] Including the Church of England: in July 2002 the General Synod passed a motion recognising "[t]hat some marriages regrettably do fail" and that "there are exceptional circumstances in which a divorced person may be married in church during the lifetime of a former spouse". New advice to the clergy was issued accordingly: "Advice to the Clergy", Annex 1 of GS 1449.

[114] See below.

Three questions arise in relation to each mode of marrying: who may marry in this way? where will the marriage take place? and what form will the ceremony take?[115]

i. Civil marriage

(1) Who may marry in a civil ceremony?
One would imagine that a civil ceremony would be open to anyone, and certainly **1–032** there are no specific restrictions on who may marry in this way. However, the Act that introduced civil marriage in 1836 specifically provided that it did not extend to the marriages of members of the Royal family.[116] It was therefore assumed that members of the Royal family would not be able to marry according to any of the forms of marriage introduced by the 1836 Act, and that this was not affected by the consolidation of the law by the Marriage Act 1949.[117] Until 2005 the only members of the Royal family to marry in a civil ceremony did so outside England and Wales.[118] In April 2005, however, the Prince of Wales married Camilla Parker-Bowles in a civil ceremony, after the then Lord Chancellor, Lord Falconer, controversially opined that the earlier interpretation of the law had been "over-cautious".[119] While no challenge to the validity of this marriage has been made, it remains a moot point whether members of the Royal family can, or could, marry in a form that was not available before 1836.

(2) Location
Before 1995 civil marriages could be celebrated in only a single place in each **1–033** registration district: namely, the register office. In accordance with the then Conservative government's general philosophy, the principle was adopted that people should have a choice of building in which their marriage may be celebrated.[120] As a result of the Marriage Act 1994,[121] a civil marriage may now also take place in a register office located in a different district[122] or on

---

[115] There are special provisions relating to marriages in naval, military or air force chapels (Marriage Act 1949 Pt V), as well as to the marriages of those who are housebound or detained (Marriage Act 1983 s.1).
[116] Marriage Act 1836 s.45.
[117] The 1949 Act specifically provided that "[n]othing in this Act shall affect any law or custom relating to the marriages of members of the Royal Family": s.79(5).
[118] See R. Probert, "The wedding of the Prince of Wales: royal privileges and human rights" (2005) 17 C.F.L.Q. 363.
[119] For discussion of this point see S. Cretney, "Royal marriages: the law in a nutshell" [2005] Fam. Law 317 and "Royal marriages: some legal and constitutional issues" (2008) 124 L.Q.R. 218.
[120] *Registration: Proposals for Change*, Cm.939 (1990) (criticised by A. Bradney [1989] Fam. Law 408).
[121] The relevant provisions came into force on April 1, 1995: see the Marriage Act 1994 (Commencement No.2) Order 1995 (SI 1995/424).
[122] The Marriage Act 1994 allowed a superintendent registrar to issue a certificate for the solemnisation of the marriage in the office of another superintendent registrar, notwithstanding that the office is not within a registration district in which either of the parties resides: Marriage Act 1949 s.35(2A), inserted by the Marriage Act 1994 s.2(1).

"approved premises",[123] i.e. premises approved by the local authority in accordance with regulations made by the Secretary of State.[124]

The Regulations[125] require the local authority to satisfy itself that the premises provide a "seemly and dignified venue" for the solemnisation of marriages[126]; that they will be regularly available to the public for the purpose of solemnising marriages[127]; that they are not "religious premises",[128] and that the room or rooms in which ceremonies of marriage will be solemnised are identifiable by description as a distinct part of the building.[129] It is further stipulated that the marriage room be separate "from any other activity on the premises at the time of the proceedings",[130] and precautions are taken against some of the fears expressed about the availability of alcoholic drink at marriages by the requirement that no food or drink be sold or consumed in the room in which a marriage ceremony takes place for one hour prior to the ceremony or during the ceremony.[131]

Since the passage of the 1994 Act, a wide range of venues have been approved for the solemnisation of marriage, including numerous hotels, stately homes, castles and, perhaps more surprisingly, shops.[132] Those of a more adventurous disposition might want to tie the knot at Brighton Sea Life Centre, London Zoo, or Sir Francis Drake's *Golden Hinde*, or to take a trip on the London Eye, which is apparently "timed perfectly so that vows are exchanged at the top of the eye".[133] However, as yet it is not possible to marry in the open air.[134]

---

[123] Marriage Act 1949 s.26(1)(bb), as inserted by Marriage Act 1994 s.1(1).

[124] Marriage Act 1949 s.78(1), as amended by Marriage Act 1994 Sch.1 para.8.

[125] Marriages and Civil Partnerships (Approved Premises) Regulations 2005 (SI 2005/3168).

[126] Marriages and Civil Partnerships (Approved Premises) Regulations 2005 (SI 2005/3168) Sch.1 para.1.

[127] It is not possible to obtain a "one-off" approval for a specific marriage: an approval is valid for three years. This requirement (then contained in the Marriage (Approved Premises) Regulations 1995 (SI 1995/510) Sch.1 para.2 and Sch.2 para.7) was overlooked when it was initially announced that the Prince of Wales was to marry Camilla Parker-Bowles in a civil ceremony at Windsor Castle. As Stephen Cretney has commented, "[t]he improbability of the Royal Family wishing to have such provisions applying to Windsor Castle immediately suggested . . . that the Clarence House announcement had not taken into account all the legal considerations". (Cretney, "Royal marriages: the law in a nutshell".)

[128] As defined by the Civil Partnership Act 2004 s.6(2): namely, premises that are used solely or mainly for religious purposes, or that have been so used in the past and have not subsequently been used for other purposes.

[129] Marriages and Civil Partnerships (Approved Premises) Regulations 2005 (SI 2005/3168) Sch.1 para.5.

[130] Marriages and Civil Partnerships (Approved Premises) Regulations 2005 (SI 2005/3168) Sch.2 para.9.

[131] Marriages and Civil partnerships (Approved Premises) Regulations 2005 (SI 2005/3168) Sch.2 para.7.

[132] See, for example, the report in the *Daily Telegraph*, "Couple walk down aisle at Selfridges", March 5, 2003. Civil marriages may also take place at Fortnum and Mason in London, and a branch of Asda in York: *http://www.civilvenuesuk.com* [Accessed May 23, 2008], and see "Checkout couple in Britain's first superstore wedding", *Independent on Sunday*, February 29, 2004.

[133] In 2007 58 couples chose to marry or register a civil partnership in this fashion: communication from the London Eye Press Office.

[134] Mr Gyles Brandeth MP, the sponsor of the Marriage Act 1994, stated that it was a basic tenet of English law that marriages should take place in a building, and that while the idea of a wedding in a garden might seem attractive, it might be difficult to give a sufficiently specific description of the place in which an outdoor wedding is to be celebrated. "We do not want to encourage people to get married behind the bushes" (he said): *Hansard*, HC Vol.250, col.1330.

The possibility of marrying on approved premises has been a major factor in the increased popularity of civil marriage. It was not until the mid 1990s that the number of civil marriages exceeded the number celebrated according to religious rites; by contrast, a mere decade after the coming into force of the Marriage Act 1994 there were more marriages on approved premises than either register-office marriages or religious marriages.[135]

(3) The content of the ceremony

The public dimension of marriage is reflected in the requirement that the public **1–034** should have access to the ceremony.[136] The marriage must be celebrated in the presence of two witnesses, the superintendent registrar and a registrar of the registration district in which the premises are situated.[137]

At some stage in the proceedings the parties are required[138] to declare (in a set form of words[139]) that they do not know of any reason why they may not marry[140] and that they take the other party as their husband or wife.[141] However, there is no requirement that these declarations be translated for those who do not speak English.[142]

Registrars sometimes declare that it is their duty to remind the parties "of the solemn and binding character" of the marriage vows and that marriage "according to the law of this country is the union of one man with one woman, voluntarily entered into, for life, to the exclusion of all others".[143] Since a

---

[135] "Report: marriages in England and Wales, 2005" (2007) 127 *Population Trends* 61, Table 1. 88,710 marriages were celebrated on approved premises, 71,560 in a register office and 84,440 in a religious ceremony. This trend may have been encouraged by the conversion of certain marriage rooms into approved premises: see B. Wilson and S. Smallwood, "Understanding recent trends in marriage" (2007) 128 *Population Trends* 24.

[136] In the case of a marriage in a register office, it is prescribed that the ceremony should take place "with open doors": Marriage Act 1949 s.45 (although according to the form of instructions for the solemnisation of marriages in a registered building, the "doors need not actually be open provided they are not so closed as to prevent persons from entering that part of the building": SI 1952/1869 Form 12 para.3). In the case of a marriage on approved premises, it is a condition of approval that "[p]ublic access to any proceedings in approved premises must be permitted without charge": SI 2005/3168 Sch.2 para.12.

[137] Marriage Act 1949 s.45(1) (marriage in register office) and s.46b(1) (marriage on approved premises).

[138] Marriage Act 1949 s.45(1) (marriage in register office) and s.46B(3) (marriage on approved premises).

[139] A choice of two alternatives is available: that set out in s.44(3) of the Marriage Act 1949 and the more modernised version set out in s.44(3A), as inserted by the Marriage Ceremony (Prescribed Words) Act 1996.

[140] Either "I do solemnly declare that I know not of any lawful impediment why I, A.B., may not be joined in matrimony to C.D." (Marriage Act 1949 s.44(3)), or "I declare that I know of no legal reason why I [name] may not be joined in marriage to [name]" (s.443A(a)). Alternatively, the parties may simply answer "I am" to the question "Are you [name] free lawfully to marry [name]?" (s.443A(b)).

[141] Either "I call upon these persons here present to witness that I, A.B., do take thee, C.D., to be my lawful wedded wife [or husband]" (Marriage Act 1949 s.44(3)), or "I [name] take you [or thee] [name] to be my wedded wife [or husband]" (s.44(3A)).

[142] Although provision is made for the vows to be exchanged in Welsh: Marriage Act 1949 s.52.

[143] The practice was intended to meet criticisms made by the Committee on Procedure in Matrimonial Causes (under the chairmanship of Denning J.), Cmd.7024 (1947).

divorced person is involved in almost half of all civil ceremonies,[144] the parties may feel this allocution to be inappropriate, but the words should be interpreted as an ideal rather than as a legal definition of marriage.[145]

The ceremony—whether in a register office or on approved premises—must not include any religious service.[146] Readings from sacred texts and the singing of hymns are also prohibited, although "the proceedings may include readings, songs, or music that contain an incidental reference to a god or deity in an essentially non-religious context".[147]

ii. Marriage according to the rites of the Church of England

(1) Who may marry in the Church of England?

1–035　It is commonly believed that a cleric of the Church of England is bound to solemnise the marriage of a parishioner irrespective of the religion (or lack of it) of the parties,[148] but, by statute, members of the clergy are entitled to refuse to marry any person whose former marriage has been dissolved (on whatever ground) if the former spouse is still living, or any person whose gender reassignment has been legally recognised under the Gender Recognition Act 2004,[149] and they may refuse to celebrate marriages permitted by the civil law between persons who are related by affinity.[150] They may also refuse to allow such marriages to be solemnised in their churches.[151]

(2) Place of marriage

1–036　The wedding must be solemnised in one of the churches where the banns have been published.[152] As noted in the discussion of Anglican preliminaries, a special licence is necessary in order for an Anglican marriage to take place in a parish

---

[144] In 2004, 90,710 of the 184,913 civil marriages involved one or two divorced persons: *Marriage, Divorce and Adoption Statistics*, Table 3.31.

[145] R. Probert "*Hyde v Hyde*: defining or defending marriage?" (2007) 19 C.F.L.Q. 322.

[146] Marriage Act 1949 s.45(2) (marriage in register office) and s.46B(4) (marriage on approved premises).

[147] The Marriages and Civil Partnerships (Approved Premises) Regulations 2005 (SI 2005/3168) Sch.2 para.11(3). This modified the previous requirement that any readings or music be "secular in nature" (Marriages (Approved Premises) Regulations 1995 (SI 1995/510) Sch.2 para.11). There was evidence that this was sometimes interpreted restrictively, with Shakespearean sonnets, Aretha Franklin's "I say a little prayer" and Robbie Williams' "Angels" being banned on the basis that they contained religious references: General Register Office, *Content of Civil Marriage Ceremonies: A Consultation Document on Proposed Changes to Regulation and Guidance to Registration Officers* (June 2005).

[148] *Argar v Holdsworth* (1758) 2 Lee 515; *Davis v Black* (1841) 1 Q.B. 900; *An Honourable Estate* (1988), App. I.

[149] Marriage Act 1949 s.5B, as inserted by the Gender Recognition Act 2004 Sch.4 Pt 1 para.3.

[150] Marriage Act 1949 s.5A, as inserted by the Marriage (Prohibited Degrees of Relationship) Act 1986 s.3 and amended by the Marriage Act 1949 (Remedial) Order 2007 (SI 2007/438).

[151] Matrimonial Causes Act 1965 s.8(2)(b) (divorced persons); Marriage Act 1949 s.5A(b), as inserted by the Marriage (Prohibited Degrees of Relationship) Act 1986 s.3 (persons related by affinity).

[152] Certificates must be provided of the publication of banns in the other relevant churches: Marriage Act 1949 s.11. The marriage must take place within three months of completion of publication: s.12.

where neither party resides. In July 2007, however, the General Synod of the Church of England approved a measure that would enable a couple to be married in a parish where neither party was resident but with which one or both had a "qualifying connection". A person would have such a connection with the parish where he or she was baptised, was resident or had habitually worshipped (for a period of six months or more), or where his or her parent had married, was resident or had habitually worshipped, or where his or her grandparent had married.[153] The measure will need to be confirmed by Parliament before it becomes law, but is likely to reduce demand for special licences. Even if the requirements are liberalised in this way, those marrying according to Anglican rites will still have a narrower choice of venues and locations than those who choose to marry in a civil ceremony.

(3) The ceremony
The marriage must be celebrated by a member of the clergy in the presence of two or more witnesses[154] according to the rite prescribed in the Book of Common Prayer or other authorised form of service.

1–037

iii. Quaker and Jewish marriages
In terms of who can marry according to Jewish or Quaker rites, the former must be between "two persons professing the Jewish religion",[155] but there is no comparable requirement in the case of Quaker marriages, provided that the Society of Friends' general rules permit the marriage.[156]

1–038

Quaker and Jewish marriages were exempted from the provisions of Lord Hardwicke's Act in 1753, but since 1836 it has been necessary for civil preliminaries to be completed.[157] Apart from this, the celebration of Jewish and Quaker marriages is entirely a matter for the rules of those religions. They need not be celebrated in a registered building, by an authorised person, or in public, and there is no restriction on the time of day at which such marriages may take place.[158] There are, however, special rules for the registration of such marriages.[159]

iv. Marriage according to another non-Anglican religious ceremony
The possibility of marrying in another form of non-Anglican ceremony is—so far as eligibility is concerned—a matter for each particular religion. However, a

1–039

---

[153] Draft Church of England Marriage Measure, GS 1616B.
[154] Marriage Act 1949 s.22.
[155] Marriage Act 1949 s.26(1)(d).
[156] Marriage Act 1949 s.47(1).
[157] In the case of Quaker marriages ("marriages according to usages of Society of Friends"), a special declaration has to be made when giving notice: Marriage Act 1949 s.47.
[158] Cf. Marriage Act 1949 s.75(1)(a); s.4.
[159] See Marriage Act 1949 Pt IV.

degree of state control is exercised over the preliminaries to such a marriage,[160] where it can take place and who can solemnise it.

(1) Location: "registered building"

1–040 Since 1836 it has been possible for non-Anglican places of worship to be registered for the solemnisation of matrimony. The marriage must take place in a registered building, normally in the district where at least one of the parties resides.[161] If a building is to qualify for registration, it must be a "separate building"[162] that is "a place of meeting for religious worship". It has been judicially stated[163] that religious worship usually means reverence or veneration of God or of a supreme being, and that the expression used in the legislation connotes a place where people come together as a congregation or assembly to do reverence to a deity. Applying this test, the court upheld the registrar-general's refusal to register a chapel of the Church of Scientology. Sikh and Hindu temples and Muslim mosques are entitled to be registered, although in fact only a comparatively small number are registered for marriage.[164] Those who wish to celebrate their marriage in a place of worship that has not been registered for marriage must go through an additional civil ceremony in order to be legally married.

(2) Celebrant: registrar or "authorised person"

1–041 When this form of marriage was first made available, the ceremony was conducted by a civil official. In 1898, however, it made possible for congregations to nominate a person (usually a minister of the group concerned) to celebrate marriages without the presence of the registrar in order to reduce discrimination against religious groups outside the established church. An "authorised person" is therefore a person whose authorisation by the trustees or governing body of the building has been duly notified to the authorities.[165] Although it remains possible for a registrar to conduct the ceremony, it is now far more common for the celebrant to be an authorised person.[166]

---

[160] The parties must comply with the civil preliminaries, as set out above. The certificate will state where the marriage is to be held: Marriage Act 1898.

[161] But there is power to designate a building elsewhere if this is the nearest place in which a particular form of religious ceremony can be conducted, or if it is the usual place of worship of one or both parties: Marriage Act 1949 s.35.

[162] Marriage Act 1949 s.41(1), unless it is a Roman Catholic chapel: Marriage Acts Amendment Act 1958 s.1(1).

[163] *R. v Registrar-General Ex p. Segerdal* [1970] 2 Q.B. 697 at 707 *per* Lord Denning M.R.; and see further *Re South Place Ethical Society* [1980] 1 W.L.R. 1565; St. J. Robilliard [1981] Conv. 150.

[164] In 2004 there were only 141 mosques in which marriages might be solemnised (out of a total of 708 certified places of worship), whereas marriages might be solemnised in 152 of the 190 Sikh temples: *Marriage, Divorce and Adoption Statistics*, Table 3.42.

[165] Marriage Act 1949 s.43.

[166] In 2004 22,795 religious marriages were celebrated by authorised persons and only 2,534 by registrars (*Marriage, Divorce and Adoption Statistics*, Table 3.35).

(3) The ceremony

The Act provides that the marriage shall be celebrated with open doors in the **1–042** presence of two or more witnesses.[167] Subject to one important qualification, the marriage may be solemnised "according to such form and ceremony as [the parties] may see fit to adopt",[168] (e.g. according to Hindu or Islamic form). The qualification is that it is essential that at some stage in the proceedings the parties make the same statements (in English) that are prescribed for those marrying in a civil ceremony.[169]

C. Registration and proof of marriages

All marriages, however celebrated, must be registered, although non-registration **1–043** does not affect the validity of the union.[170] The objects of a system of registration are to ensure that[171]:

> "[T]here is a public record of an event which has important legal consequences both for the parties themselves and for third parties and for the State. The parties need such a record as evidence of their marriage and so that they can present proof of it to others. Third parties need it so that they can determine the status of the parties and the status (e.g. legitimacy) of themselves and others in so far as that is dependent on the marriage of the parties. The State needs it because upon it may depend rights and obligations owed by or to the State in relation, for example, to tax, social security, and allegiance. An effective system of registration affords means of proof or disproof and avoids uncertainty where certainty is essential. In addition registration provides statistics regarding marriage which are vital for any serious research into legal, social or demographical problems."

There are statutory provisions facilitating proof of marriage by production of a certified copy of the relevant entry in the register of marriages.[172] Where no such evidence is available, the court may, on evidence that the couple had cohabited for such a length of time and in such circumstances as to acquire the reputation of being husband and wife, presume that a marriage ceremony has

---

[167] Marriage Act 1949 s.44(2).

[168] Marriage Act 1949 s.44(1).

[169] Marriage Act 1949 s.44(3). When the marriage is in the presence of an authorised person (instead of a registrar) the formula "I, A.B., do take thee, C.D., to be my wedded wife (or husband)" may be substituted.

[170] The reason is that the parties are already married by the time that they sign the register, although it is not entirely clear at what point in the service the marriage is complete. It may well be that the crucial moment is the formal exchange of consent, as in the Australian case of *Quick v Quick* [1953] V.R. 224: in this case the parties had exchanged the marriage promises but as the man was putting the ring on the woman's finger (and before the priest had joined their hands or pronounced them man and wife) she pulled it off, hurled it to the ground and, with the words "I will not marry you", ran out of the church. It was held that the parties had been validly married.

[171] Law Com. No.53 (1973) Annex para.104.

[172] See Marriage Act 1949 s.65.

taken place and that the ceremony complied with the necessary formalities.[173] However, as was pointed out in one recent case, most of the authorities "either pre-date the present system of registration of marriages in this country or concern parties who may have been married abroad", and the absence of any marriage certificate is itself "strong evidence" that the parties are not married "unless marriage abroad is a real possibility".[174]

The system of registration introduced into English law in 1836 has provided a reasonably effective means whereby the parties can prove that they have contracted a valid marriage. There are plans to modernise registration facilities, making the central database the legal record of a marriage.[175] Some of the more minor changes can be effected under existing legislation; the more ambitious ones—including the creation of a "through life record"—will require new legislation.[176]

D. Consequences of irregularities

1–044 There are three categories of irregularity within the statutory scheme: (1) those that render the marriage void; (2) those that have no effect on the validity of the marriage; and (3) those as to the consequence of which the legislation is silent. In some cases, however, the form of the ceremony differs so fundamentally from the form prescribed by the 1949 Act that the marriage is deemed to be outside the statutory scheme altogether and is neither valid nor void but a "non-marriage".

i. Defects invalidating the marriage

1–045 In contrast to the system originally introduced by Lord Hardwicke's Act,[177] the general principle of modern English law is that only contumacious disregard of the marriage formalities will invalidate a marriage. The Marriage Act 1949 provides that if the parties "knowingly and wilfully" disregard certain requirements, the marriage shall be void.[178] It has never been determined whether it is sufficient that the parties know that in fact the formality has not been observed, or whether they must also know that the defect will, in law, invalidate the marriage.[179]

---

[173] See, for example, *Pazpena de Vire v Pazpena de Vire* [2001] 1 F.L.R. 460; *A-M v A-M (Divorce: Jurisdiction: Validity of Marriage)* [2001] 2 F.L.R. 6. For discussion, see A. Borkowski, "The presumption of marriage" [2002] C.F.L.Q. 251 and R. Probert, "When are we married? Void, non-existent and presumed marriages" [2002] L.S. 398.

[174] *Martin v Myers* [2004] EWHC 1947 (Ch), para.23(a).

[175] *Civil Registration: Vital Change*, Cm.5355 (2002); General Register Office, *Registration Modernisation: A Position and Consultation Paper on the Delivery of the Local Registration Service in England and Wales* (November 2005).

[176] For a full analysis of the steps needed, see General Register Office, *Registration Modernisation*.

[177] Under which failure to comply with certain of the stipulated procedures made the purported marriage void.

[178] Marriage Act 1949 s.25 (Anglican marriages) and s.49 (marriage under certificate).

[179] *Greaves v Greaves* (1872) L.R. 2 P. & D. 423 at 424–425, *per* Lord Penzance.

Examples of irregularities falling within this class (in the case of Anglican marriages) are: (a) marriages celebrated other than in a church or chapel where banns may be published; (b) failure properly to carry out the necessary preliminaries; (c) marriages after parental objection has been duly made or after expiry of the banns; and (d) marriages performed by persons not in Holy Orders.

Examples in respect of other marriage procedures are: (a) marriages without due notice or without a certificate; (b) marriages after the certificate has expired; (c) marriages in a place other than that specified in the certificate; and (d) marriages in the absence of a registrar, where such presence is required.[180]

It should be noted that the onus is on the person impugning the validity of the marriage to prove that the parties "knowingly and wilfully" flouted the relevant formalities, and if a ceremony was followed by cohabitation as husband and wife, there is a strong presumption that all was "rightly done".[181]

ii. Defects not affecting the validity of the marriage

The legislation specifies certain defects, evidence of which is not to be given in **1–046** proceedings touching the validity of the marriage; and it would seem to follow that such defects cannot invalidate the marriage. This class includes: (a) failure to obtain parental consent; and (b) failure to comply with the requirements as to the parties' residence.[182]

iii. Other defects

The Marriages Act 1949 is silent as to the consequences of certain irregularities; **1–047** these include the requirements that the ceremony take place between 8 am and 6 pm,[183] that it be celebrated with open doors, and that certain prescribed words be used. It seems probable that such irregularities do not affect the validity of the marriage,[184] but it is unsatisfactory that this is a matter of inference.

iv. Non-marriage

The fact that the legislation states that certain defects only render a marriage void **1–048** if the parties "knowingly and wilfully" failed to comply with formalities raises the question as to how the law should deal with a couple who innocently failed to comply with any of the required formalities. The possibility of this occurring would have seemed remote in 1823, when the only valid way of marrying

---

[180] Marriage Act 1949 s.25 (Anglican marriages) and s.49 (marriage under certificate).
[181] *Sichel v Lambert* (1864) 15 C.B. (N.S.) 781; 143 E.R. 992; *Mahadervan v Mahadervan* [1964] P. 233.
[182] Marriage Act 1949 s.48.
[183] However, except in the case of Quaker and Jewish marriages, and marriages by special or registrar-general's licence, it is an offence knowingly and wilfully to celebrate a marriage save between 8 am and 6 pm: Marriage Act 1949 ss.75(1), 79(6); Marriage (Registrar-General's Licence) Act 1970 s.8(1).
[184] See the Law Commission's Report on *Solemnisation of Marriage in England and Wales*, Law Com. No.53 (1973), Annex. para.120.

was—except for Quakers and Jews—according to the rites of the Church of England. But multiplying the permissible modes of marrying is likely to create confusion, especially since reports of marriages in "approved premises" may give the misleading impression that it is possible to marry anywhere.

In the absence of statutory provision, it has been left to the courts to determine this point, and a general principle has emerged that in English law a marriage can only be created by something that can be described as "a ceremony in a form known to and recognised by our law as capable of producing ... a valid marriage".[185] In a series of recent cases the courts have been required to consider the status of ceremonies that departed—sometimes very markedly—from the form prescribed by the Marriage Act: in *Gereis v Yagoub*,[186] a marriage conducted by a Coptic Orthodox priest in a Coptic Orthodox church that had not been licensed for marriage; in *Chief Adjudication Officer v Bath*,[187] a marriage in a Sikh temple that was similarly unlicensed; in *A-M v A-M (Divorce: Jurisdiction: Validity of Marriage)*,[188] a Muslim ceremony of marriage in the couple's flat; and, in *Gandhi v Patel*,[189] a Hindu ceremony of marriage in a restaurant. The ceremony in *Gereis v Yagoub* was held to be sufficiently close to the form prescribed by the legislation to escape relegation to the non-status of non-marriage, on the basis that it "had the hallmarks of a marriage that would be recognised as a marriage but for the formal requirements of the Marriage Act 1949".[190] The marriage in *Chief Adjudication Officer v Bath* was upheld by some rather creative reasoning[191] but the latter two were, by contrast, thought to be outside the statutory scheme altogether.[192] While the dividing line is not entirely clear, it would appear that a ceremony of marriage will be sufficiently close to the form prescribed by the Marriage Act if it purports to be a marriage,[193] and is celebrated in a place that was capable of falling within the statutory scheme in a form that is recognisably one of marriage.

---

[185] *R. v Bham* [1966] 1 Q.B. 159, in which a prosecution under the Marriage Act 1949 s.75(2)(a) failed because the potentially polygamous marriage in accordance with Islamic law that the defendant had solemnised in a private house was not in a form known to and recognised by English law as capable of creating the status of marriage between the parties.

[186] [1997] 1 F.L.R. 854.

[187] [2000] 1 F.L.R. 8.

[188] [2001] 2 F.L.R. 6.

[189] [2001] 1 F.L.R. 603.

[190] [1997] 1 F.L.R. 854, at 858. However, the marriage was held to be void because the parties knew that they had failed to comply with the relevant formalities.

[191] Robert Walker L.J. (with whom Schiemann L.J. agreed) noted that there had been "a manifold non-compliance" with the requisite formalities and doubted whether the parties would have been regarded as validly married had they separated shortly after the ceremony; however, since they had cohabited for a long period of time "it would be contrary to the general policy of the law to refuse to extend to the parties the benefit of a presumption which would apply to them if there were no evidence of any ceremony at all". (p.23). The problem with this reasoning is that if the presumption is rebutted by showing that the initial ceremony was invalid, the court is effectively presuming that a second valid marriage took place even though the parties would not have perceived the need to do so. For a discussion of the case law on the presumption, see Probert, "When are we married?"; Borkowski, "The presumption of marriage".

[192] Although the marriage in *A-M v A-M* was eventually upheld by a rather tortuous application of the presumption in favour of marriage.

[193] This would therefore exclude marriage ceremonies conducted on stage in the course of a play, as suggested by counsel in *Gereis v Yagoub* [1997] 1 F.L.R. 854.

The significance of the distinction between a marriage that is void and one that is non-existent is considered further in Ch.2.

IV. FORMALITIES FOR CIVIL PARTNERSHIPS

The formalities for registering a civil partnership can be stated much more **1–049** briefly, since they are modeled[194] on those for civil marriage.[195] Intending civil partners must comply with the required preliminaries,[196] and the registration of a civil partnership must take place either in a register office or on approved premises. [197] The Act also replicates the provisions of the law of marriage to deal with the civil partnerships of prisoners and those in psychiatric hospitals,[198] the house-bound,[199] and those who are terminally ill and not expected to recover.[200]

However, there are certain key differences between civil marriage and the registration of a civil partnership. There are no prescribed vows that have to be exchanged by civil partners: the Act simply states that:

"[T]wo people are to be regarded as having registered as civil partners of each other once each of them has signed the civil partnership document".[201]

One could scarcely imagine a more pared-down celebration: signing the register is consent, ceremony and proof all rolled into one. In practice, of course, just as civil weddings generally involve much more than the bare legal formalities, it is likely that civil partnerships will be accompanied by readings and music, and a wide range of venues have been approved for the celebration of civil partnerships.[202]

The consequences of failing to comply with the required formalities are the same for civil partners as for married couples, although the language of the

---

[194] It should be noted that the original text of the Civil Partnership Act 2004 was drafted on the basis of what it was presumed the law of marriage would be by the time the Act was implemented. When it became clear that the planned reforms to the law of marriage would be delayed, the relevant provisions of the 2004 Act had to be amended to bring them into line with the existing law of marriage: Civil Partnership (Amendments to Registration Provisions) Order 2005 (SI 2005/2000).

[195] Registration cannot take place in religious premises (Civil Partnership Act 2004 s.6(1)(b)), and no religious service is permitted (s.2(5)). However, some churches are willing to provide a blessing for civil partners.

[196] Civil Partnership Act 2004 s.8. Parental consent is required for the civil partnership of a minor: Civil Partnership Act 2004 s.4; Sch.1 Pt I. In addition, those subject to immigration control must comply with additional requirements: see Civil Partnership Act 2004, Sch.23.

[197] The criteria for determining whether premises may be approved for the registration of civil partnerships are the same as those for civil marriages: see para.1–033 above.

[198] Civil Partnership Act 2004 s.19.

[199] Civil Partnership Act 2004 s.18.

[200] Civil Partnership Act 2004 ss.21–27.

[201] Civil Partnership Act 2004 s.2(1).

[202] See S. Cretney, "Relationships: law content and form", in C. Thorpe and J. Trowell, *Re-rooted Lives: Inter-disciplinary Work within the Family Justice System* (Bristol: Jordan Publishing Ltd, 2007) for a discussion.

legislation has been updated.[203] Presumably a ceremony between two same-sex partners that failed to comply with any of the required formalities would be deemed to be a "non-existent" civil partnership. Whether the courts will develop presumptions in favour of civil partnerships akin to those that operate in the context of marriage remains to be seen. It would be sensible if the registration of a civil partnership, followed by cohabitation, were to raise a presumption that the relevant formalities had been observed but by contrast, it would be inappropriate to extend the out-dated presumption based solely on cohabitation and reputation to a new context.

V. Conclusion: A Need for Reform?

1–050 One obvious criticism of the current laws is their complexity. As long ago as 1988 a Government Green Paper[204] noted that "many of the procedures [relating to marriage] are unnecessarily complex and restrictive and reflect the needs and social conditions of the early nineteenth century rather than those of the late twentieth century"; indeed, the Law Commission went so far as to suggest that "the law is not understood by members of the public or even by all those who have to administer it".[205]

Such complexity would matter less if the law achieved the purpose for which it was enacted. But, as pointed out above, the current system of preliminaries does little to ensure that the intended union is publicised; the concept of a "non-marriage" involves the courts in a value judgment as to whether any given ceremony was "close enough" to the prescribed form to be accorded some legal status; and it is not clear at what point a couple become married. In addition, current procedures do little to ensure that the parties understand the implications[206] or even the nature[207] of the ceremony, and the parties' choice as to where they may marry remains restricted.

What reforms could be put in place to address these deficiencies? It would be difficult to devise a simple and easily-administered system that would achieve adequate publicity for every marriage or civil partnership, but a national database of civil status would at least ensure that the relevant authorities could check whether the parties were free to marry each other.[208]

---

[203] The 2004 Act states that a civil partnership will be void if both parties "know" that certain formalities have not been observed (Civil Partnership Act s.49(b), as amended by the Civil Partnership (Amendments to Registration Provisions) Order 2005 (SI 2005/2000)), but it seems unlikely that this is intended to connote any different state of mind from the term "knowingly and wilfully" used in the Marriage Act 1949.

[204] *Registration: A Modern Service*, Cm.531, para.3.2.

[205] Law Com. No.53, Annex para.6.

[206] An individual might (reasonably but wrongly) be under the impression that Islamic law governs a marriage contracted in a mosque in England.

[207] Given the lack of any requirement that the crucial parts of the ceremony be conducted in a language that the parties understand, it is possible that they may not even realise the nature of the ceremony: see, for example, *Parojcic v Parojcic* [1958] 1 W.L.R. 1280 (marriage of Yugoslavs in Oxford register office).

[208] See *Report of the Departmental Committee on the Marriage Law of Scotland*, Cmnd. 4011 (1968–9), para.128 and the cogent criticism in Law Com. No.53 (1973), Annex paras 116–117.

The law could also set out the minimum requirements for a marriage or civil **1–051** partnership, in order to clarify how far a ceremony may depart from the prescribed form before it loses any legal status, and specify the point at which a couple become married.[209]

It might be asked whether (as in many foreign countries) a civil ceremony should become the only legally effective way of contracting a marriage. This would bring the law of marriage into line with that governing civil partnerships, and the parties would of course remain free subsequently to go through any religious ceremony they pleased. There is a long history of proposals for reform along these lines, but an equally long history of their being rejected (often, it would seem, on no better ground than that the foreign overtones of such a procedure would, as a Royal Commission put it in 1868, be "opposed to the habits and feelings of the great majority of the people of Great Britain").[210] In addition, the trend of reforms has been to increase the choices—of venue, ceremony and form—available to those who wish to marry.[211]

The most recent proposals for reform would increase this choice still further. In 2002 a White Paper, *Civil Registration: Vital Change*,[212] set out plans to update the legislation governing the celebration and registration of marriages. The scheme involved the registration of *celebrants* rather than of the *places* where weddings can take place. While these proposals would have led to many improvements, much was left uncertain, and to date there has been no attempt to introduce the legislation necessary to bring about such change.[213]

---

[209] The consultation paper on civil registration envisaged that a couple would be married once the celebrant had declared this to be the case: *Civil Registration: Delivering Vital Change*, para.3.4.97. An alternative would be to bring the law of marriage into line with that pertaining to civil partnerships and to make the signing of the register the crucial moment.

[210] *Report of the Royal Commission on the Laws of Marriage* (1868, BPP 1867–1868), Vol.32 p.35. It appears that the current government is well aware of the need to ensure the approval of the Church of England (and no doubt other groups) to proposals for reform: see General Synod of the Church of England, *Just Cause or Impediment?*, pp.2–6.

[211] See, for example, Marriage Act 1994; above, para.1–033; and note the proposals of the Church of England that the residence requirements for Anglican marriages should be relaxed; para.1–036.

[212] *Civil Registration: Vital Change*, Cm.5355 (2002) para.3.12.

[213] It had initially been intended that the reforms could and would be carried out by means of delegated legislation under the Regulatory Reform Act 2001. However, when related reforms to the registration of births and deaths were proposed, the select committees appointed to consider them concluded that this would be inappropriate: House of Commons Select Committee on Regulatory Reform, *Second Report* HC 118; House of Lords Select Committee on Delegated Powers and Regulatory Reform, *Third Report* HL 14. The Government accepted this (Ministerial Statement on the Modernisation of Civil Registration, *Hansard,* HC Vol.431, col.77WS), but has failed to indicate what steps—if any—it plans to take.

CHAPTER TWO

CAPACITY TO MARRY OR FORM A CIVIL PARTNERSHIP

I.	INTRODUCTION	2–001		D. Effects of a decree	2–052
II.	HISTORICAL DEVELOPMENT	2–002	IV.	VOID AND VOIDABLE CIVIL	
	A. Void and voidable marriages	2–002	PARTNERSHIPS		2–058
	B. The need for a decree	2–003		A. Void civil partnerships	2–059
	C. Void or non-existent?	2–004		B. Voidable civil partnerships	2–060
III.	THE MODERN LAW OF NULLITY	2–005		C. Bars to a decree	2–061
	A. Void marriages	2–006		D. Effects of an order	2–062
	B. Voidable marriages	2–023	V.	CONCLUSION	2–063
	C. Bars to a decree	2–047			

I. INTRODUCTION

An individual's right to marry is enshrined in art.12 of the European Convention **2–001** on Human Rights. Yet this is only a qualified right (being a right to marry "according to national laws governing the exercise of this right"), and domestic law sets out minimum requirements that an individual must satisfy in the form of grounds on which a marriage may be set aside. These can broadly be divided into those that affect the individual (such as age or the capacity to understand what marriage entails) and those that affect the couple (such as whether the parties are of the same sex or related to one another). Some may straddle the two categories; incapacity to consummate, for example, may be either general (an inability to engage in sexual intercourse at all) or particular (an inability to have sexual intercourse with one's spouse).

The reader may wonder why the sexual difficulties of a couple should be relevant to the question of whether there is a marriage. The answer is that—like the formalities for creating a marriage—this is an area weighed down with history, and much of the current law of nullity has been inherited from the canon law that governed marriage for many centuries. Yet it would be wrong to view the law of nullity as no more than an historical artifact. New grounds have been added in recent years, while others have been applied to new (or rather revived) social problems such as forced marriages.[1] In addition, the small number of

---

[1] For earlier examples, see A. Fraser, *The Weaker Vessel* (London: Weidenfeld and Nicolson, 1984), Ch.1.

nullity suits that actually come before the courts—a mere 406 petitions in 2006, with 243 decrees absolute being made[2]—belies the importance of the topic; for every marriage that is annulled, there are many more that do not take place because of the legal restrictions on who may marry whom. The same is now true of civil partnerships, to which similar—although not identical—restrictions apply. The main role of the rules set out in this chapter is therefore to prevent certain types of unions from being solemnised in the first place.

This chapter will set out the rules governing the legal capacity to marry, and will then go on to consider those relevant to civil partnerships. Separate consideration needs to be given to the two sets of rules, since slight terminological differences make any description that attempts to encompass both somewhat cumbersome. In addition, although the rules relating to civil partnerships were based on those relating to marriage, there are some significant differences between the grounds on which a civil partnership, as opposed to a marriage, may be annulled. First, however, a brief discussion of the historical development of the law is necessary in order to explain certain key concepts.

II. Historical Development[3]

A. Void and voidable marriages

2–002   The key distinction in this area of the law is between marriages that are void and marriages that are voidable, and the origins of this can be traced back to the Reformation.

Until the Reformation, a marriage was either valid or void. The existence of any of the impediments recognised by the canon law (e.g. that either party was already married, or incapable of consummating the marriage) would invalidate a purported marriage. It made no difference that the couple had been through a solemn marriage ceremony and had thereafter lived together as man and wife for many years: in the eyes of the law, there never had been a marriage between them; and their relationship could create none of the legal consequences of marriage. In addition, anyone who had an interest in the matter (such as a relative entitled to property in default of legitimate issue) could dispute the validity of the marriage, perhaps many years after the death of the parties.[4]

---

[2] Ministry of Justice, *Judicial and Court Statistics 2006* (2007), Table 5.5.

[3] See generally J. Jackson, *The Formation and Annulment of Marriage* 2nd edn (London: Butterworths, 1969), pp.7–58; and (for the canon law and its impact), J.A. Brundage, *Law, Sex and Christian Society in Medieval Europe* (Chicago: University of Chicago Press, 1987), p.274. L. Stone, *Uncertain Unions, Marriage in England 1660–1753* (Oxford: Oxford University Press, 1992) contains interesting case studies; and reference may be made to the same author's *Road to Divorce* (Oxford: Oxford University Press, 1990) for useful contextual material. For the concept of the voidable marriage, see F.H. Newark (1945) 8 M.L.R. 203; E.J. Cohn (1948) 64 L.Q.R. 324; D. Tolstoy (1964) 27 M.L.R. 385. The development of English law was greatly influenced by the matrimonial problems of Henry VIII: for illuminating accounts, see J. Scarisbrick, *Henry VIII* 2nd edn (New Haven: Yale University Press, 1997), Ch.7.

[4] There were certain limited exceptions: see Jackson, *The Formation and Annulment of Marriage*, pp.44–53. S.M. Waddams's, *Law, Politics and the Church of England: The Career of Stephen Lushington 1782–1873* (Cambridge: Cambridge University Press, 1992) is a source of much useful information about the working of the ecclesiastical law in practice.

This was unsatisfactory, and after the Reformation, the common law courts began to prohibit the ecclesiastical courts from impeaching the validity of marriages on certain grounds[5] after the death of either party. This practice effectively created the main conceptual distinction between void and voidable marriages: a decree could be pronounced in relation to a void marriage at any time, even after the death of the parties, but voidable marriages could only be attacked while both parties were still living.

The distinctions between the two categories can conveniently be tabulated as follows:

Void	*Voidable*
No valid marriage ever existed.	The marriage is valid unless annulled.
Any interested person[6] may take proceedings.	Only the parties to the marriage can take proceedings.
A decree is not necessary since the marriage does not exist.	Unless a decree is obtained, the marriage remains in force.
There are no bars to a decree.	In certain circumstances, a decree may be barred.
Can be challenged after death of either party.	Cannot be challenged after death of either party.

Behind this formal legal distinction between a marriage that is void and one that is merely voidable lies a deeper perception that certain elements are so fundamental to the concept of marriage that without them no marriage can come into existence, while other factors should give the parties themselves the right to challenge the marriage but are not so inimical to the very existence of the marriage.[7] An example of the first is the minimum age prescribed by the law; the fact that a marriage under the prescribed age is void takes priority over the wishes of the parties themselves. An example of the second is the inability of one of the parties to consummate the marriage: if both parties are content with a sexless marriage then it is not the role of the law to intervene. In this way one can, by way of inference, work out what is fundamental to the concept of marriage in English law.

B. The need for a decree

The distinction between the void and merely voidable still remains of practical importance, not least because it is never *necessary* to obtain a decree annulling a void marriage. But it will now often be in a petitioner's interest to obtain a decree in respect of a purported marriage that is void in law. This is because (in   **2–003**

---

[5] Those subsequently termed "canonical disabilities" (i.e. impotence, marriage within the prohibited degrees, lack of age or pre-contract).

[6] As to what constitutes a sufficient interest, see Jackson, *The Formation and Annulment of Marriage*, pp.100–102.

[7] See *Re Roberts dec'd* [1978] 1 W.L.R. 653 at 656, *per* Walton J.

order to avoid hardship), many of the incidents of a valid marriage have by statute been attached to void marriages provided that a decree of nullity is obtained. Consider, for example, the case of a marriage that is void because the "husband" was already married to a third party[8]: unless and until a decree is granted, the "wife" has none of the legal rights normally attaching to that status, for the simple reason that she is not married. But if a decree is granted,[9] she becomes entitled to apply for financial relief orders in the same way as a wife whose marriage has been dissolved. In effect, therefore, a decree declaring a marriage void gives the parties at least some of the rights and duties flowing from a legal status that they never had.[10]

C. Void or non-existent?

2–004 The fact that a decree relating to a void marriage has these consequences highlights the importance of the distinction between a marriage that is void and one that is non-existent. As discussed in the previous chapter, there are certain purported unions that do not even qualify as void marriages, being conducted altogether outside the statutory scheme set out in the Marriage Acts.[11] The real issue in these cases will usually be whether the court has the power to grant financial relief to the parties: if the marriage was non-existent, it has no such power.

III. The Modern Law of Nullity

2–005 For much of the twentieth century, the law of nullity consisted of a mixture of the old canon law and new statutory grounds. In the wake of a comprehensive review by the Law Commission,[12] it was codified in the Nullity of Marriage Act 1971[13] and subsequently consolidated in the Matrimonial Causes Act 1973. The grounds set out in the legislation are exhaustive; there is no other ground on which a

---

[8] See, for example, the remarkable facts of *R. v Yacoob* [1981] Crim. L.R. 248, set out at fn.67 below. In practice, if the existence of the "void" marriage is disclosed, it will be necessary to satisfy the authorities of its invalidity.

[9] As to the position if the other party dies before a decree is obtained, see below, para.2–057.

[10] The statement by Nourse L.J. in *Re Spence dec'd* [1990] Ch. 652 that a void marriage is "only an idle ceremony [that] achieves no change in the status of the participants [and] achieves nothing of substance" is an impeccable statement of the position at common law, but is not literally true of the current law.

[11] See para.1–048.

[12] *Report on Nullity of Marriage* Law Com. No.33.

[13] Thereby displacing the earlier canon law. It should, however, be noted that the legislation (see now Matrimonial Causes Act 1973 Sch.1 para.6) provided that nothing in the Act affected any law or custom relating to the marriage of members of the Royal Family, and thereby preserved the rule that purported marriages contrary to the provisions of the Royal Marriages Act 1772 remain void notwithstanding the fact that the 1772 Act is not mentioned: for another case where the provisions of the 1772 Act were preserved without that fact being expressly adverted to in parliamentary discussion, see S.M. Cretney, "The Royal Marriages Act 1772: a footnote" (1995) 16 *Statute Law Review* 195.

decree of nullity can be obtained.[14] The text examines each ground in turn and then goes on to consider the effects of making a decree.

A. Void marriages

Section 11 of the 1973 Act now[15] provides that a marriage taking place after July 31, 1971 will be void on the following grounds only:

2–006

> "(a) that it is not a valid marriage under the provisions of the Marriage Acts 1949 to 1986 (that is to say where—
>
> > (i) the parties are within the prohibited degrees of relationship;
> >
> > (ii) either party is under the age of sixteen; or
> >
> > (iii) the parties have intermarried in disregard of certain requirements as to the formation of marriage);
>
> (b) that at the time of the marriage either party was already lawfully married;
>
> (c) that the parties are not respectively male and female.
>
> (d) in the case of a polygamous marriage entered into outside England and Wales, that either party was at the time of the marriage domiciled in England and Wales".[16]

i. Prohibited degrees

The Marriage Acts 1949–1986[17] declare that marriages between certain relatives are void.[18] We shall first consider the existing restrictions on who may marry whom and then go on to examine the underlying policy considerations and the extent to which the prohibitions on marriage are echoed in the criminal law.

2–007

(1) The restrictions

There are broadly three types of restrictions. First, there are restrictions on marriages between certain blood relations: the law states that a person may not marry his or her parent, grandparent,[19] child or grandchild, sibling, uncle or aunt,

2–008

---

[14] See *Re Roberts dec'd* [1978] 1 W.L.R. 653, 658 (but see fn.13 above). See also Family Law Act 1986 s.55 (as substituted by Family Law Reform Act 1987 s.22), which now governs the court's power to grant declarations.

[15] The text as set out below includes the amendments and additions made by later statutes.

[16] Matrimonial Causes Act 1973 s.11.

[17] The legislation may now be so described: Marriage (Prohibited Degrees of Relationship) Act 1986 s.6(2).

[18] This classification has changed over time. Before the Reformation, such marriages, as explained above, were void. After the Reformation, they were merely voidable. However, Lord Lyndhurst's Act of 1835 (passed in that year for reasons that are obscure and may have been discreditable) declared any future marriage within the prohibited degrees to be void: see S. Wolfram, *In-laws and Outlaws* (London: Croom Helm, 1987).

[19] The draftsman of the English legislation evidently did not think it necessary to prohibit marriages with a great-grandparent (or indeed with a great-grandchild). Compare the more cautious approach of the Marriage (Scotland) Act 1977 s.2 and Sch.1.

nephew or niece.[20] One might imagine that restrictions based on consanguinity would be uniform across different legal systems, but this is far from being the case. For example, under English law, first cousins are entitled to marry, whereas such marriages are prohibited in parts of the United States[21]; by contrast, under English law, a man is not entitled to marry his niece, whereas Jewish law permits uncle/niece marriages without restriction[22] and some systems based on canon law allow such marriages, provided a dispensation is obtained.[23]

Secondly, there are restrictions arising out of the making of an adoption order. A child who is adopted remains within the same prohibited degrees in respect of the natural parents and other relatives as if the adoption order had never been made.[24] An adoptive parent and the adopted person are deemed to be within the prohibited degrees, and they continue to be so notwithstanding that someone else subsequently adopts the adopted child[25]; but there is no other prohibition arising by reason of adoption. Hence, otherwise unrelated persons who have been adopted by the same parents may marry each other or other relatives of their adoptive parents.

Thirdly, there are restrictions arising as a result of a previous marriage or civil partnership. Following a series of reforms, the only remaining restrictions relate to potential marriages between stepparent and stepchild, and since the Marriage (Prohibited Degrees of Relationship) Act 1986 even these are not absolute. A person may marry the child of a former spouse or civil partner if two conditions are satisfied: (1) both parties to the marriage must be 21 or over; and (2) the younger party must not at any time before attaining the age of 18 have "lived in the same household as that person and been treated by that person as a child of his family"[26] in relation to the other party.[27] The case of *Smith v Clerical Medical and General Life Assurance Society*[28] offers an illustration of how this prohibition would operate:

> In this case, a man married the mother of a 13-year-old girl. Six years after the marriage he left the matrimonial home with the girl and they set up house together, holding themselves out as a married couple. It was apparently intended that they should marry, but it seems clear that the provisions of the 1986 Act could not validate such a marriage (since the girl

---

[20] Marriage Acts 1949–1986 Sch.1 Pt I.
[21] See generally H.D. Krause, *Family Law* (St Paul, Minnesota: West Publishing, 1995), pp.49–51; C. Hamilton, *Family, Law and Religion* (London: Sweet & Maxwell, 1995), p.4.
[22] See *Cheni v Cheni* [1965] P. 85.
[23] See, for example *Catalano v Catalano* 170 A 2d 726 (1961) (uncle/niece marriage valid under Italian law but not recognised in Connecticut); and see further, *per* Sir J. Simon P., in *Cheni v Cheni* [1965] P. 85.
[24] Adoption and Children Act 2002 s.74(1)(a).
[25] Marriage Acts 1949–1986 Sch.1 Pt I. For the background to this apparently unsatisfactory rule, see S.M. Cretney, "From status to contract?" in F.D. Rose (ed.), *Consensus ad Idem* (London: Sweet & Maxwell, 1996).
[26] Marriage Acts 1949–1986 s.78. On the concept of a "child of the family" see para.7–015.
[27] However, it is unlikely that there can be any realistic investigation into the parties' declaration that the younger party has not been a child of the family in relation to the other.
[28] [1993] 1 F.L.R. 47.

had, before attaining the age of 18, lived in the same household with the intended husband, and he had treated her as a child of his family).

(2) The policy of the law[29]

There are three sets of justifications for rules prohibiting marriages between **2–009** certain persons that have been relied upon at different periods: religious, genetic and social.

The prohibited degrees, like much of the law of nullity, originated in the canon law.[30] For the church, marriage[31] made a man and woman one flesh; accordingly, it was held that it was just as wrong to marry a former spouse's brother or sister as it would be to marry one's own brother or sister. Since one's brother or sister would be within the prohibited degrees of consanguinity, a spouse's sibling would be within the (correspondingly prohibited) degrees of affinity. This led to a complex series of restrictions, and it was not until 1907 that the first steps were taken to relax the rules by allowing a marriage between a man and his deceased wife's sister.[32] Further reforms followed over the course of the century,[33] but it was not until 2007 that the last of the restrictions on marriages between former in-laws was removed.[34]

Concern about the potential risks to the offspring of those who are closely related long predates the modern understanding of genetics. It is now understood that the probability of recessive genetic defects being transmitted to a child is more likely if the parents are closely related.[35] Yet some marriages are permitted even where there are such increased risks, while in the past the law has prohibited marriages between those related by affinity, to whom no such considerations would apply. Nor does the law prohibit marriages solely on the basis that one party has a disease that is likely to be transmitted to a child.

The main justification that has been relied upon in more recent times is that the **2–010** prohibition on marriage may discourage certain sexual relationships within the family circle. This argument was once used to justify the prohibition on marriage

---

[29] A fuller discussion can be found in the fifth edition of this work at pp.36 *et seq.*

[30] Canon law was based on the rather obscure prohibitions contained in Ch.18 of the Book of Leviticus and elsewhere in the Pentateuch.

[31] Or even sexual intercourse outside marriage: *Roger Donington's Case*, 2 Co. Inst. 684 (marriage invalid because H had previously had intercourse with third cousin of his future wife). This rule was abolished at the Reformation: Marriage Act 1540; *Wing v Taylor* (1861) 2 Sw. & Tr. 278.

[32] Deceased Wife's Sister's Marriage Act 1907.

[33] See, for example, Deceased Brother's Widow's Marriage Act 1921; the Marriage (Enabling) Act 1960, which allowed marriage with the former spouse of a divorced brother or sister; and the Marriage (Prohibited Degrees of Relationship) Act 1986, which (in certain limited circumstances) allowed marriages between a former stepparent and stepchild and between a former parent-in-law and son- or daughter-in-law. For a comprehensive discussion, see S. Cretney, *Family Law in the Twentieth Century: A History* (Oxford: Oxford University Press, 2003), pp.47–56.

[34] See the Marriage Act 1949 (Remedial Order) 2007 (SI 2007/438), which removed the legal barriers to a marriage between a former parent-in-law and son- or daughter-in-law. Some couples were quick to take advantage of this liberalisation: see, for example, M. Acton, "Jest married. It may sound like a joke but . . . I've just married my mother-in-law!", March 18, 2007 *The News of the World* p.11. I am grateful to Corey Gooding for this reference.

[35] For a cross-cultural review, see R. Bennett *et al*, "Genetic counseling and screening of consanguineous couples and their offspring: recommendations of the National Society of Genetic Counselors" (2002) 11 *Journal of Genetic Counseling* 97.

between a man and his deceased wife's sister.[36] If a man could look on his wife's sister as a potential spouse, the trusting, intimate but asexual relationship of brother and sister might well (it was argued) be destroyed. It has also been used to justify the current prohibition on marriage between a stepparent and stepchild. There is, of course, a very strong argument that the law should protect young persons from the danger—increasingly recognised as a very real danger—of sexual abuse by those in authority over them.[37] Yet does the prohibition on *marriage* really provide such protection? One might well doubt whether an abusive stepparent would be deterred by the prospect of being unable to formalise a relationship with the stepchild in the future. Similar objections may be made to the argument that marriages between those previously related by marriage should be discouraged because they are likely to cause a confusion of roles within the family. Preventing a marriage does not necessarily prevent the relationship, and the confusion of roles may result from a cohabiting relationship as much as from marriage. Indeed, this was a factor influencing the decision of the European Court of Human Rights in the recent case of *B and L v United Kingdom*[38]:

> In this case, a man and his former daughter-in-law had formed a relationship, each having been divorced from their former spouses. They were living together with the woman's child from her marriage to her new partner's son, and the child had begun to address his grandfather as "Dad". They wished to marry but were unable to do so under the law as it then stood.[39] The European Court of Human Rights upheld their claim that the law breached their right to marry under art.12: the law did not prevent the relationship,[40] and the fact that it was possible to obtain a private Act of Parliament allowing such a marriage to take place undermined the apparent rationale for the restriction.[41]

---

[36] See the evidence of the Church of England to the Morton Commission (*Report of the Royal Commission on Marriage and Divorce*, Cmnd. 9676 (1951–5) cited at para.1162). *Re Woodcock and Woodcock* [1957] N.Z.L.R. 960, *per* Finlay A.C.J.; and the speech of then Bishop of Durham on the Marriage (Enabling) Bill, February 25, 1981 (*Hansard*, HL Vol.417, col.1121).

[37] See, for example, the speeches of Lord Denning (*Hansard*, HL Vol.469, col.47); Lord Mishcon, at col.54; the Bishop of Birmingham (*Hansard*, HL Vol.470, col.950); and Lord Simon of Glaisdale (*Hansard*, HL Vol.470, col.953).

[38] [2006] 1 F.L.R. 35.

[39] This provided that such a marriage could only take place if both parties had attained the age of 21, and the former spouse of the younger party and his or her other parent had both died: Marriage Act 1949 Sch.1 Pt III (as amended).

[40] For criticism of the decision, and the argument that there is an important distinction between not preventing a particular relationship and allowing couples the public stamp of approval of marriage, see S. Cretney, "Marriage, mothers-in-law and human rights" (2006) 122 L.Q.R. 8.

[41] This last point was particularly influential: as the European Court of Human Rights noted that "[t]he inconsistency between the stated aims of the incapacity and the waiver applied in some cases undermines the rationality and logic of the measure ... there is no indication of any detailed investigation into family circumstances in the Parliamentary procedure and ... in any event, a cumbersome and expensive vetting procedure of this kind would not appear to offer a practically accessible or effective mechanism for individuals to vindicate their rights" ([2006] 1 F.L.R. 35, para.40).

It should also be noted that there is no general restriction on a marriage between persons simply on the basis that their relationship has effectively been that of parent and child. So, although restrictions exist on marriages between parents and their biological children, adopted children, or stepchildren who have lived in the same household, there are no restrictions on marriages between a person and the children of his or her cohabitant, or children that he or she has fostered. However, in such cases, the criminal law has a role to play.

(3) The prohibited degrees and the criminal law

Until recently there was a considerable disjunction between the laws governing the range of persons an individual was prohibited from marrying and the range of persons with whom sexual intercourse would constitute a sexual offence, the latter group being more narrowly defined than the former. The Sexual Offences Act 2003 has in some respects brought these two sets of rules into closer alignment, replacing the old crime of incest with a new set of more specific offences. The offence of "sex with an adult relative" makes it an offence for a person to have penetrative sex with his or her adult child, grandchild, parent, grandparent, sibling (whether full or half), aunt, uncle, nephew or niece,[42] a list identical to that of persons with whom marriage is prohibited on the basis of consanguinity.[43] The Act also introduced a new offence of "sexual activity with a child family member".[44] This criminalises sexual activity between those who are prohibited from marrying, including a stepparent and a minor stepchild who live in the same household, a step which can be seen as reinforcing the policy underpinning the remaining restrictions on marriages between such persons.[45] However, the offence is much wider in scope, encompassing, inter alia, sexual activity between a foster parent and foster child[46] and between cousins who have lived in the same household,[47] and no prohibition on marriage exists in either of these cases.[48] Indeed, the potential for marriage is recognised in the provision that conduct that would otherwise constitute an offence under this section will not be an offence between married couples.[49] No such defence applies to those who are intending to marry: courting cousins must therefore be either chaste or criminal.[50]

2–011

---

[42] Sexual Offences Act 2003 s.64.

[43] Although, as noted above, not all jurisdictions prohibit such marriages, a couple validly married in another country might find themselves prosecuted in this jurisdiction for engaging in marital intercourse.

[44] Sexual Offences Act 2003 s.25.

[45] Sexual Offences Act 2003 s.27(3)(a). The definition of stepparent is, however, wider than that in the Marriage Acts, encompassing as it does the unmarried partner of a parent as well as one in a formal relationship (marriage or civil partnership) with a parent: s.27(5)(e).

[46] Sexual Offences Act 2003 s.27(2)(b).

[47] Sexual Offences Act 2003 s.27(3)(b).

[48] One could argue, however, that there is the same justification for prohibiting a marriage between a foster parent and foster child as between adopter and adoptee, or between stepparent and stepchild, especially given the vulnerability of many children in foster care.

[49] Sexual Offences Act 2003 s.28(1).

[50] See J.R. Spencer, "The Sexual Offences Act 2003: (2) child and family offences" (2004) Crim. Law. Rev. 347.

ii. Minimum age

2–012 A marriage is void if either party is under the age of 16.[51] This rule should be distinguished from that requiring parental consent if either party is aged between 16 and 18,[52] failure to comply with which has no effect on the validity of the marriage.[53]

In considering the policy underpinning this rule,[54] there are three issues that need consideration. First, what is the purpose of imposing a minimum age for marriage? Secondly, what should that age be? Thirdly, what should be the legal consequences of a purported marriage that infringes the rule?

The reasons for imposing a minimum age for marriage have varied over time. At one time, parentally approved marriage between two persons who had attained the age of puberty may well have seemed unobjectionable: age as such was not important. Informed opinion then became concerned with problems of child sexual abuse and prostitution, which were thought to be related to the age at which marriage was permitted.[55] More recently, the focus of concern has moved towards promoting the stability of marriage, and in the 1960s it was often suggested that the age at which marriage was permitted should be raised.[56] However, since the early 1970s there has been a general upward trend in the age of first marriage in this country, and (as already noted[57]) the problem of youthful marriage seems to have solved itself.

2–013 The law's view as to what the appropriate minimum age at marriage should be has also changed over time. Before 1929 a boy could marry at 14, and a girl at 12; marriages where one or both parties were under the relevant age were not void but voidable. Either party could avoid the marriage on attaining majority, but unless and until this was done, the marriage remained valid.[58] The current choice of 16 as the minimum age at which an individual may marry is linked to the age at which consent may be given to sexual intercourse. When the matter was considered in the 1960s, the view was taken that to raise the age of marriage above the age of consent would send a message that sex outside marriage was legally approved, while to raise the age of consent would simply create a large

---

[51] Marriage Act 1949 s.2. A party's capacity to marry is governed by the law of their domicile, and so English law may recognise a marriage celebrated abroad by younger persons as long as they have attained the age at which the law of their domicile states they may marry: *Alhaji Mohamed v Knott* [1969] 1 Q.B. 1.

[52] Marriage Act 1949 s.3, as amended.

[53] Marriage Act 1949 s.48. This requirement is regarded as part of the formalities of the marriage ceremony: see para.1–008.

[54] The policy arguments are considered in more detail in the fourth edition of this work at pp.56–61.

[55] See the sources cited in the fourth edition of this work at pp.56–57, and note also *Re K; A Local Authority v N* [2005] EWHC 2956 (Fam); [2007] 1 F.L.R. 399, in which a 15-year-old girl who went through a ceremony of marriage with an older man later alleged that she had been raped and beaten by him.

[56] *Committee on the Age of Majority*, Cmnd.3342 (1965) ("*Latey Report*"), paras 102–103 and 166–177; *Kilbrandon Report*, paras 14–21.

[57] See para.1–011 above.

[58] See Jackson, *The Formation and Annulment of Marriage*, p.26, W. Blackstone, *Commentaries on the Laws of England* (1765), Vol.1, Ch.15, p.424.

number of criminals.[59] Yet, in *Re MM (an adult); Local Authority X v MM*[60] it was recognised that an individual "may have capacity to consent to sexual relations whilst lacking capacity to decide more complex questions about long-term relationships", and it can be argued that the same reasoning is applicable to the level of maturity needed in these different contexts.

The question of whether an under-age marriage should be void or voidable is rather more difficult.[61] The present law may well cause some hardship, particularly if the parties—perhaps immigrants from a country with an unreliable birth registration system—believed that they were of age.[62] However, there seems no realistic likelihood of change being made in the law; the issue is not usually of great importance. If the parties discover the defect, and still wish to be married, they can go through a further marriage ceremony and thereby, for most purposes, remedy the situation; in any event, the law now attaches many of the legal incidents of marriage to a void marriage, provided a decree of nullity is obtained or other appropriate legal action is taken.

iii. Defective formalities

The circumstances in which failure to comply with the formalities laid down by the Marriage Acts 1949–1986 will invalidate a marriage have been explained in detail in ch.1. In brief, a marriage will only be void if the parties "knowingly and willfully" fail to comply with certain formalities, while non-compliance with other less-fundamental formalities has no effect on the validity of the marriage. A *total* failure to comply with any of the relevant formalities, by contrast, will lead to what is termed a "non-marriage".[63] **2–014**

iv. Existing marriage or civil partnership

In English law, marriage is traditionally regarded as "the voluntary union for life of one man and one woman to the exclusion of all others".[64] Hence, a purported marriage is void if it is proved that, at the time of the ceremony, either party was already lawfully married to, or in a civil partnership with, a third party.[65] **2–015**

It should be stressed that the marriage will still be void even if the parties had believed on reasonable grounds that the third party was dead.[66] It should also be

---

[59] *Latey Report*, para.103.

[60] [2007] EWHC 2003 (Fam), at para.95.

[61] The arguments in favour of preserving the existing rule that under-age marriages are void are cogently summarised in Law Com. No.33, paras 17–19, but for the view that these arguments are unconvincing, see the fourth edition of this work at pp.60–61.

[62] Or believed that they were entitled to marry at a younger age: see *Re K; A Local Authority v N* [2005] EWHC 2956 (Fam), in which the marriage did not comply with the formal requirements and therefore the erroneous belief was not identified.

[63] See para.1–048.

[64] *Hyde v Hyde* (1866) L.R. 1 P. & D. 130 *per* Lord Penzance at 133; see the stimulating analysis by S. Poulter, "The Definition of marriage in English law" (1979) 42 M.L.R. 4.

[65] Matrimonial Causes Act 1973 s.11(b); as to proof of the existence of a prior marriage, see below.

[66] This means that the marriage will be void even if there is a defence to the criminal offence of bigamy.

noted that the crucial date is that of the ceremony.[67] If the former spouse or civil partner subsequently dies, the later "marriage" remains void (although the parties could regularise their position by going through a second marriage ceremony, which they would then be free to do).

v. Parties of same sex

2–016 Statute provides that a marriage is void if the parties are not respectively male and female[68]; to date, English law has refused to recognise a union between two persons of the same sex—wherever celebrated—as constituting a valid marriage. Three different situations need to be considered: first, the legal status of same-sex marriages validly celebrated overseas; secondly, options available to those who have undergone gender reassignment; and thirdly, the legal treatment of those who are physically intersex. There is also a question about the precise classification of a marriage celebrated between two persons of the same sex.

(1) Same-sex marriages celebrated overseas

2–017 A small but growing number of jurisdictions allow same-sex couples to enter into marriages,[69] and English law has therefore had to address the status such marriages will have within this jurisdiction. It is laid down by statute that a same-sex marriage celebrated overseas will not be recognised as a marriage in this jurisdiction, but will instead have the status of a civil partnership.[70] In *Wilkinson v Kitzinger*,[71] this rule was challenged by an English woman who had married another woman in Canada and then sought a declaration that their marriage was valid. It was argued that the current law—as contained in the 2004 Act and in s.11(c) of the Matrimonial Causes Act 1973—was in breach of arts 8 and 12 (combined with art.14) of the European Convention on Human Rights. The President of the Family Division, Sir Mark Potter, rejected these arguments: first, the right conferred by art.12 was the right to marry "in the traditional sense (namely as a marriage between a man and a woman)"[72]; secondly, withholding the title of marriage from same-sex partnerships was not an interference with

---

[67] See, for example, the complicated facts of *R. v Yacoob* [1981] Crim. L.R. 248, in which the question was whether an intended witness ("W") was the defendant's wife. The facts were that W's marriage to H1 was ended by divorce in 1964; in 1965 she "married" H2, who (unknown to her) was already married to X; in 1968, she married H3, but did not see him after the ceremony: in 1969 she "married" H4, who disappeared. In 1970 she obtained a decree of nullity in respect of the marriage to H2, and (in 1971) "married" the defendant. It was held that this marriage was void, since that marriage to H3 was valid.

[68] Matrimonial Causes Act 1973 s.11(c).

[69] At the time of writing, these were Belgium, Canada, Massachusetts, The Netherlands, South Africa and Spain.

[70] Civil Partnership Act 2004 s.215. For a detailed discussion of the conflicts of laws points raised by this rule, see K. McK.Norrie, "Recognition of foreign relationships under the Civil Partnerships Act 2004" (2006) *Journal of Private International Law* 137.

[71] [2006] EWHC 2022 (Fam).

[72] At para.55.

their private or family[73] life[74]; and thirdly, that the difference in treatment had a legitimate aim, was reasonable and proportionate, and fell within the margin of appreciation accorded to Convention States.[75]

Three factors appeared to be particularly influential in reaching this decision. The first two acknowledged the policy choices made at both an international and national level: (1) the divergence in policy across Europe with regard to same-sex partnerships; and (2) the fact that Parliament had only recently passed the Civil Partnership Act 2004, which had adopted the course of extending the rights but not the label of marriage to those same-sex couples who wished to register a partnership. The third factor was the perception that same-sex relationships "are indeed different",[76] although precisely what differences existed, other than the obvious physical ones, was not made clear.[77] It may be that at some point in the future, as more jurisdictions confer the label of marriage on same-sex partnerships, the policy behind the Civil Partnership Act will appear less justifiable, but the case indicates that the recognition of same-sex marriage in English law is still some way off.[78]

(2) Gender reassignment

Problems may also arise in determining whether two persons are in fact of the   **2–018**
same sex. A number of individuals are affected by gender identity dysphoria—
that is to say, "discontent with being a person of the sex to which one was born
and discontent with living in the gender role consistent with that birth sex".[79]

[73] Note the current paradox that while same-sex couples may be regarded as "family" within English law, they do not enjoy "family life" for the purpose of art.8 of the European Convention since—according to the House of Lords in *M v Secretary of State for Work and Pensions* [2006] UKHL 11—the concept of family life is an autonomous Convention concept with a single meaning across the Council of Europe.

[74] "In my view, by declining to recognise a same-sex partnership as a marriage in legislation the purpose and the thrust of which is to enhance their rights, the state cannot be said improperly to intrude on or interfere with the private life of a same-sex couple who are living in a close loving and monogamous relationship": [2006] EWHC 2022 (Fam), para.85.

[75] At para.122. It has, however, been pointed out that it is the role of the European Court of Human Rights to decide whether the law of any given country exceeds the "margin of appreciation", and that the appropriate task of the domestic court is to consider whether to defer to the policy adopted by the executive or legislature within its "discretionary area of judgment": see N. Bamforth, "'The benefits of marriage in all but name'? Same-sex couples and the Civil Partnership Act 2004" (2007) 19 C.F.L.Q. 133.

[76] At para.121.

[77] It was noted, for example, that marriage was regarded as "an age-old institution, valued and valuable, respectable and respected, as a means not only of encouraging monogamy but also the procreation of children and their development and nurture in a family unit in which both maternal and paternal influences are available in respect of their nurture and upbringing" (para.118). Sir Mark Potter presumably did not intend to imply that civil partnerships were less "respectable" than marriages. Moreover, many married couples choose not to have children, while same-sex couples may well be bringing up children.

[78] See further Bamforth, above fn.75.

[79] See the evidence of Professor Green, Consultant Psychiatrist and Research Director of the Gender Identity Clinic Charing Cross Hospital, as cited in *Bellinger v Bellinger* [2001] 2 F.L.R. 1048 at 1055.

Members of the "trans" community may seek to adopt the gender roles of the opposite sex, while "transgender" individuals seek to live as members of the opposite sex.[80] For many years, medical procedures have been available to address the dissonance between psychological sex and physiological structure,[81] ranging from hormone treatment to surgical reconstruction,[82] and "transsexuals" seek medical treatment to bring their physical body into greater harmony with their psychological sex.[83]

What is the legal position if a male-to-female transsexual wishes to marry a man? The traditional view of English law was that a person's sex was fixed for all time at birth, and the only relevant tests of sexual identity were biological.[84] Thus, persons born with male chromosomes, gonads and genitalia would be regarded as male for the purpose of marriage, even if this was not in accordance with their self-perception and even after undergoing extensive surgery to bring their body into alignment with their psychological sex. Psychological and other secondary sexual characteristics would only be taken into account if the chromosomal, gonadal and genital factors were not congruent.

Over time, however, this approach met with increasing criticism,[85] and, as other countries changed their laws on this issue, the pressure for reform mounted. In 2002 the European Court of Human Rights finally[86] held that the failure to recognise the reassigned sex of a transsexual was in breach of arts 8 and 12 of the European Convention on Human Rights:

> In *Goodwin v United Kingdom*,[87] a post-operative male-to-female trans-sexual claimed that her rights under art.12 had been breached, as English law did not allow her to marry her (male) partner. The European Court of Human Rights held that while the right to marry was subject to the national laws of the contracting states, "the limitations thereby introduced must not restrict or reduce the right in such a way or to such an extent that the very essence of the right is impaired".[88] In the case before it, the applicant "lives

---

[80] S. Whittle, *Respect and Equality: Transsexual and Transgender Rights* (London: Cavendish, 2002), pp.xxii–xxiii.

[81] A. Bradney [1987] Fam. Law 350.

[82] For example, plastic surgery may be used to remove male genitalia and construct an artificial vagina.

[83] The popular term "sex change" is, however, somewhat misleading, as Lord Nicholls pointed out in *Bellinger v Bellinger* [2003] UKHL 21, para.8: "Hormonal treatment can change a person's secondary sexual characteristics. Irreversible surgery can adapt or remove genitalia and other organs, external and internal . . . But there are still limits to what can be done. Gonads cannot be constructed. The creation of replica genital organs is particularly difficult with female to male gender reassignment surgery. Chromosomal patterns remain unchanged. The change of body can never be complete."

[84] *Corbett v Corbett* [1971] P. 83.

[85] See, for example, Whittle, *Respect and Equality*, and the powerful dissent by Thorpe L.J. in *Bellinger v Bellinger* [2001] 2 F.L.R. 1048.

[86] It had on previous occasions held that there was no such breach, but by diminishing majorities and with injunctions to keep the law under review in the light of continuing developments: see *Rees v United Kingdom* [1987] 2 F.L.R. 111; *Cossey v United Kingdom* [1991] 2 F.L.R. 492; *Sheffield and Horsham v United Kingdom* [1998] 2 F.L.R. 928.

[87] [2002] 2 F.L.R. 487. See also *I v United Kingdom* [2002] 2 F.C.R. 612.

[88] At para.99.

as a woman, is in a relationship with a man and would only wish to marry a man. She has no possibility of doing so."[89] It was therefore the court's view that "the very essence of her right to marry ha[d] been infringed".[90]

Legislation[91] was subsequently passed to bring the law into line with the European Convention. The Gender Recognition Act 2004 established a new body—the Gender Recognition Panel—to decide whether applications for gender recognition certificates should be granted. It stipulated that the Panel must[92] grant an application if the applicant has or has had gender identity dysphoria,[93] "has lived in the acquired gender throughout the period of two years ending with the date on which the application is made" and "intends to continue to live in the acquired gender until death".[94] Under this statutory procedure, psychological factors—largely ignored by the common law—become paramount; there is not even a requirement that the applicant should have undergone surgery.

2–019

If the applicant is married, however, the panel can only grant an interim gender recognition certificate.[95] The marriage must be annulled before a full certificate can be granted,[96] since otherwise the granting of a certificate would effectively bring a same-sex marriage into being.[97] When the decree of nullity has been made absolute, a full gender recognition certificate will be issued and "the person's gender becomes for all purposes the acquired gender".[98]

The pressure group Press For Change has reported that around 2,200 people have applied to the Gender Recognition Panel for legal recognition, of whom 97.5 per cent were successful.[99] This number is very close to the official estimate of the total number of transsexual persons in the United Kingdom as a whole.[100] It should, however, be noted that there is no obligation on an individual who has undergone the physical process of gender reassignment to seek legal recognition of this change, and the common law rules continue to apply to those who have not successfully applied for a gender recognition certificate.

---

[89] At para.101.
[90] At para.101.
[91] It was held by the House of Lords that the law as it stood could not be interpreted in a manner that would enable a transsexual to marry in his or her acquired gender: see *Bellinger v Bellinger* [2003] UKHL 21. For criticism, see A. Bradney, "Developing human rights? The Lords and transsexual marriages" [2003] Fam. Law 585.
[92] Gender Recognition Act 2004 s.2(2).
[93] This must be established by medical evidence: s.3 requires that the applicant produce reports from two medical practitioners, or one medical practitioner and a chartered psychologist, diagnosing gender dysphoria.
[94] Gender Recognition Act 2004 s.2.
[95] Gender Recognition Act 2004 s.4(3).
[96] The grant of an interim certificate is itself a ground on which a marriage is voidable: see Matrimonial Causes Act 1973 s.12(g) and para.2–046 below.
[97] The parties to the former marriage may of course enter into a civil partnership, but a marriage cannot simply be converted into a civil partnership.
[98] Gender Recognition Act 2004 s.9.
[99] As of September 2007: see *http://www.pfc.org.uk* [Accessed May 26, 2008].
[100] The *Report of the Interdepartmental Working Group on Transsexual People* (Home Office, April 2000), para.1.3, estimated that there are between 1,300 and 2,000 male-to-female and 250 female-to-male transsexual people in the UK.

(3) Intersex individuals

2–020   A further problem arises in relation to those who are physically "intersex". The simple binary distinction between male and female is imposed on a more complex biological reality. An individual may be born with genitalia that cannot be classified as either "male" or "female" or that are at odds with his or her chromosomes or internal anatomical structure. However, an individual has to be either male or female for the purposes of marriage, and so a decision will need to be made.[101]

The approach set out in *Corbett v Corbett* was applied in a modified form to the only case of this kind to have been reported: *W v W (Physical Inter-sex)*.[102] In this case, the judge held that the biological factors were not "congruent" in the sense that that term was used in *Corbett*,[103] and that, therefore, other factors— psychological and hormonal factors and secondary sexual characteristics—could be taken into account. This bears some similarities to the approach eventually taken under the Gender Recognition Act, and in most cases an intersex individual will therefore not need to make an application to the Gender Recognition Tribunal.[104]

(4) The classification of a marriage between two persons of the same sex

2–021   It has been questioned whether a "marriage" between two persons of the same sex should be categorised as "non-existent" rather than as a void marriage.[105] Since the Matrimonial Causes Act 1973 declares such a marriage to be void, it is clear that the court may grant a decree making a declaration to this effect. But, as noted above, the real significance of classifying a marriage as void or non-existent lies in the consequences of such classification. In *S-T (formerly J) v J*,[106] which involved a "marriage" between a female-to-male transsexual and a woman, the court assumed that it had the same power to make orders for financial provision as it did when granting any decree of nullity or divorce, although on the facts of the case it held that it would be contrary to public policy to do so. By contrast, a different approach was taken in the sequel to this case:

---

[101] For a critical view, see P.-L. Chau and J. Herring, "Defining, assigning and designing sex" (2002) 16 I.J.L.P.F. 327.

[102] [2001] 1 F.L.R. 324.

[103] Charles J. noted that it would be "an incorrect application" of the test in *Corbett* "to take each of the criteria and ask which side of the line between male and female they fell and if (however near the line) all of them fell on one side of it that determined a person's sex for the purposes of marriage" (p.357).

[104] Whether any such individual would be able to make such an application would depend on whether they were regarded as having gender identity dysphoria: see, for example, the *Diagnostic and Statistical Manual of Mental Disorders ("DSM-IV")*.

[105] It seems clear from the Parliamentary debates on the relevant provision of the Nullity of Marriage Act 1971 that the promoters did not intend to give even the recognition implicit in granting a decree of nullity to relationships between persons who were, and knew themselves to be, unequivocally of the same sex: see *Hansard,* HC Vol.814, col.1838 (Mr Leo Abse); and *Hansard,* HL Vol.317, cols 816–817 (Lord Chancellor Hailsham). But cf. *Bellinger v Bellinger* [2001] 2 F.L.R. 1048 at 1086–1087, *per* Thorpe L.J.

[106] [1997] 1 F.L.R. 402.

In *J v C and E (a child)*,[107] J, a female-to-male transsexual, had gone through a ceremony of marriage with C, a woman, who subsequently gave birth to two children as the result of artificial insemination. After the "marriage" had been declared void, J sought orders under s.8 of the Children Act 1989 to regulate what the children were told about the reasons for the breakdown of the marriage. Whether the leave of the court was necessary for such an application depended on whether J was a "parent", which in the circumstances depended on the application of s.27 of the Family Law Reform Act 1987 (which provided that the other party to a void marriage would be treated as the father of a child conceived by artificial insemination by donor as long as at least one of the parties believed the marriage to be valid).[108] The Court of Appeal held that J, being a woman at the material time,[109] could not be said to be a party to a marriage with a female and that therefore there was no marriage at all.

The reasoning in this case is, however, open to criticism; first, because it arguably attaches too much weight to the judicial dictum that marriage is "the union of one man and one woman"[110] and too little to the plain words of the statute; and secondly, because it introduces considerable uncertainty into the law as to the consequences of a void marriage. The status of a marriage, once determined, should be the same for all purposes.

vi. Polygamous marriages

While it is not possible to contract a polygamous marriage in England and Wales, **2–022** some countries do allow such marriages, and the courts of this jurisdiction may therefore be required to determine their status. For a long time, English law refused to recognise both marriages that were actually polygamous (i.e. where a person had concurrent spouses) and marriages that were only *potentially* polygamous (i.e. that had been celebrated under a system that permitted polygamy). Gradually, a more liberal approach prevailed whereby recognition was accorded to marriages (whether actually or potentially polygamous) between persons domiciled in a country that permitted polygamy[111] and to potentially polygamous marriages celebrated by persons domiciled in this country.[112] Today,

---

[107] [2006] EWCA Civ 551.
[108] The current governing legislation is s.28(7)(b) of the Human Fertilisation and Embryology Act 1990, but the provisions of the 1987 Act were applicable in this case because of the date when artificial insemination occurred. Wall L.J. did suggest, however, that the same interpretation would apply to the equivalent provisions of the 1990 Act.
[109] The events at the heart of the case pre-dated the Gender Recognition Act 2004, but J subsequently acquired a gender recognition certificate and is now legally a man.
[110] *Hyde v Hyde* (1866) L.R. 1 P. & D. 130.
[111] The Matrimonial Proceedings (Polygamous Marriages) Act 1972 s.1 allowed a court to grant matrimonial relief or to make a declaration concerning the status of a marriage even if it is polygamous (now see Matrimonial Causes Act 1973 s.47).
[112] Matrimonial Causes Act 1973 s.11(d), as amended by the Private International Law (Miscellaneous Provisions) Act 1995 Sch., para.2(2).

therefore, it is only actually polygamous marriages celebrated by persons domiciled in this country that are void under English law.[113]

B. Voidable marriages

2–023   Voidable marriages are governed by s.12 of the 1973 Act, which (as amended) provides that a marriage which has taken place after July 31, 1971 is voidable on the following grounds only:

"(a) that the marriage has not been consummated owing to the incapacity of either party to consummate it;

(b) that the marriage has not been consummated owing to the wilful refusal of the respondent to consummate it;

(c) that either party to the marriage did not validly consent to it, whether in consequence of duress, mistake, unsoundness of mind or other-wise;

(d) that at the time of the marriage either party, though capable of giving a valid consent, was suffering (whether continuously or intermittently) from mental disorder within the meaning of the Mental Health Act 1983, of such a kind or to such an extent as to be unfitted for mar-riage;

(e) that at the time of the marriage the respondent was suffering from venereal disease in a communicable form;

(f) that at the time of the marriage the respondent was pregnant by some person other than the petitioner;

(g) that an interim gender recognition certificate under the Gender Recognition Act 2004 has, after the time of the marriage, been issued to either party to the marriage;

(h) that the respondent is a person whose gender at the time of the marriage had become the acquired gender under the Gender Recognition Act 2004".[114]

i. Incapacity to consummate

2–024   A marriage is voidable if, owing to the incapacity of either party, it has not been consummated.[115] Statute thus codifies a basic principle of the earlier canon law: although marriage was formed simply by consent, the contract of marriage implied that the parties had the capacity to consummate it.[116] If this capacity

---

[113] For a more detailed discussion, see J. Murphy, *International Dimensions in Family Law* (Manchester: Manchester University Press, 2005), pp.71–79.
[114] Matrimonial Causes Act 1973 s.12, as amended by the Mental Health Act 1983 and Gender Recognition Act 2004.
[115] Matrimonial Causes Act 1973 s.12(a).
[116] *Dickinson v Dickinson* [1913] P. 198 at 205, *per* Sir Samuel Evans.

were lacking, the rule prior to the Reformation was that the marriage was void, and thereafter that it was voidable.

Apart from two matters (considered below), the present law is unchanged from the canon law administered in the ecclesiastical court.

(1) What was required by way of consummation?

The case law[117] establishes that what is required is capacity for intercourse that **2–025** is "ordinary and complete" and not "incipient, imperfect and unnatural".[118] More precisely, "ordinary" means penile-vaginal sex, and "complete" means that there must be erection and penetration for a reasonable length of time.[119] However, it is not necessary for either party to be capable of orgasm[120] or to be capable of procreation.[121]

The act of consummation must take place after the wedding,[122] and the fact that the parties have had normal intercourse prior to the marriage ceremony is irrelevant. Only one act of sexual intercourse is required, and the subsequent incapacity of either party to engage in sexual relations is irrelevant.

(2) When is an individual incapable of consummation?

It is for the petitioner to prove that the incapacity exists. The court has power to **2–026** order a medical examination, and may draw adverse inferences against a party who refuses to be examined.[123] The question is whether this particular individual is capable of having capacity to engage in sexual intercourse with his or her spouse. It matters not that he or she is capable of engaging in sexual relations with other persons.[124] The law recognises that sexual difficulties may arise either as a result of impotence, physical incompatibility,[125] or what is termed "invincible repugnance".[126] However, it would seem that a rational decision not to

---

[117] *D v A* (1845) 1 Rob.Eccl. 279; *Snowman v Snowman* [1934] P. 186; *Clarke v Clarke* [1943] 2 All E.R. 540; *White v White* [1948] P. 330; *R. v R.* [1952] 1 All E.R. 1194; *G v G* [1952] V.L.R. 402; *B v B* [1955] P. 42; *SY v SY* [1963] P. 37; *W v W* [1967] 1 W.L.R. 1554; *Corbett v Corbett* [1971] P. 83.

[118] *D v A* (1845) 1 Rob.Eccl 279 at 298, 299 *per* Dr Lushington. It follows from the accepted definition of consummation that a decree of nullity may be obtained on the ground of incapacity even although a child has been conceived by *fecundatio ab extra*: *Clarke v Clarke* [1943] 2 All E.R. 540.

[119] *R. v R.* [1952] 1 All E.R. 1194; *W v W* [1967] 1 W.L.R. 1554; cf. the definition of sexual intercourse for adultery and rape in which penetration for however short a period suffices.

[120] *SY v SY* [1963] P. 37.

[121] This is true even if the inability to procreate results from the voluntary act of the respondent (e.g. in undergoing a vasectomy or sterilisation) that has not been disclosed to the other: *Baxter v Baxter* [1948] A.C. 274.

[122] *Dredge v Dredge* [1947] 1 All E.R. 29.

[123] *B v B* [1901] P. 39; *W v W* [1905] P. 231; Marriage Causes Act 1973 r.30.

[124] See, for example, *G v M* (1885) 10 App.Cas. 171 at 176, where medical evidence was given that if the husband were "encouraged and had plenty of time and was not nervous, and if a little champagne were given him beforehand, he might succeed with any other woman".

[125] On which see, for example, Sir R. Burton and F.F. Arbuthnot (trans.), *The Kama Sutra* (London: Diamond Books, 1993), pp.127–128.

[126] *G v G* [1924] A.C. 349.

permit intercourse is insufficient; there must be some element of psychiatric or physical aversion.[127] Thus, in *Singh v Singh*[128]:

> The petitioner, a 17-year-old Sikh girl, reluctantly went through a marriage ceremony arranged by her parents with a man she had never previously met. According to Karminski L.J., she "never submitted to the physical embraces of the husband, because . . . it does not appear that she saw him again. Having taken the view . . . that she did not want to be married to him, it is understandable that she did not want to have sexual intercourse with him; but that . . . seems to be a very long way from an invincible repugnance."

It must also be shown that the incapacity is both permanent and incurable. Thus, a bridegroom who has imbibed too much champagne at the wedding reception and is unable to perform on his wedding night will not be regarded as incapable of consummating the marriage by virtue of this.[129] A spouse's capacity will be deemed to be incurable if any remedial operation is dangerous or if the respondent refuses to undergo an operation.[130]

The narrow legal definition of consummation may pose particular problems for transsexuals who marry in their reassigned sex.[131] The Gender Recognition Act 2004 made no mention of this particular issue, and the only decision to deal directly with the point is that of *Corbett v Corbett*.[132] This held a male-to-female transsexual to be incapable of consummation on the basis that intercourse using an artificially constructed cavity did not constitute "ordinary and complete" intercourse. There were, however, earlier dicta suggesting that the mode of creation was immaterial,[133] and it can be argued that a more generous interpretation of the requirement would be consistent with the policy underpinning the 2004 Act.

(3) Supervening incapacity sufficient?

2–027 It is necessary to emphasise that the theory was that incapacity prevented a marriage from coming into existence at all, and that physical capacity was as much a basic requirement of marriage as the intellectual capacity to consent. For the canon law, there was a vast theoretical difference between, on the one hand, recognising that the marriage was a nullity in cases where incapacity existing at

---

[127] *Singh v Singh* [1971] P. 226, *per* Karminski L.J. at 232.

[128] [1971] P. 226.

[129] Indeed, it used to be the practice to require the parties to cohabit for three years before either could petition on this ground, but this is no longer the case: see, for example, *B v B* [1958] 1 W.L.R. 619 (cohabitation for one week).

[130] *S v S* [1956] P. 1; *L v L (falsely called W)* (1882) 7 P.D. 16. If the respondent refuses to undergo an operation, a petition may also be founded on wilful refusal: see *D v D (Nullity: Statutory Bar)* [1979] Fam. 70 at 72.

[131] For discussion of this point, see R. Probert, "How would Corbett v Corbett be decided today?" [2005] Fam. Law 382.

[132] [1971] P. 83.

[133] In *SY v SY* [1963] P. 37, at 59, Willmer L.J. suggested that it was difficult to see "why the enlargement of a vestigial vagina should be regarded as producing something different in kind from a vagina artificially created from nothing".

the time of the marriage could be proved and, on the other, dissolving a valid marriage because of some supervening cause.

While it is clear that the codification of the law in 1971 was not intended to effect any change,[134] the legislation does not explicitly require that the incapacity should have existed "at the time of the celebration of the marriage". Could a wife whose husband is made impotent as a result of a car accident on the way from the church to the honeymoon therefore petition successfully for nullity on this ground? Perhaps the courts would interpret the provision in the light of the classical concept of the distinction between nullity and divorce,[135] and refuse a decree. But this is by no means certain; in particular, it cannot now be argued that nullity is restricted to those cases in which the condition existed at the time of the marriage, since the grounds of wilful refusal to consummate and the grant of a gender recognition certificate subsequent to the marriage are an exception to that principle.

(4) Petitioner's knowledge of own incapacity not a bar?

Either party to the marriage can petition; there is nothing in the words of the Act **2–028** to prevent a spouse who is incapable basing a petition on his or her own incapacity. It is true that, before 1971, such a spouse could not obtain a decree if, at the time of the marriage, he or she knew of the incapacity or if it would, in all the circumstances, be unjust to allow the petition to succeed.[136] However, this rule was (it is submitted) an application of the old bar of approbation, which was abolished in 1971.[137] If this is correct, a petitioner who knew of the incapacity is entitled to a decree on that ground unless the respondent can establish the modern statutory bar of approbation laid down in the Matrimonial Causes Act 1973.[138]

(5) Should incapacity to consummate be a ground for nullity?

Why was consummation required? The cases can be said to have been based on **2–029** a primitive version of the theory—now underlying the ground on which divorce is permitted[139]—that marriages should be decently buried if they have irretrievably broken down: if the parties do not find sexual satisfaction in marriage, they will be tempted to find solace elsewhere. In the words of Dr Lushington:

---

[134] See the explanatory notes to the Law Commission's draft bill: Law Com. No.33, p.47, para.2. The report was referred to by Dunn J. in *D v D (Nullity: Statutory Bar)* [1979] Fam. 70 at 77.
[135] *Briggs v Morgan* (1820) 2 Hag. Con. 324 at 331; *Brown v Brown* (1828) 1 Hag. Ecc. 523; *B v M* (1852) 2 Rob. Ecc. 580; *Napier v Napier* [1915] P. 184 at 189–190; *S v S* [1963] P. 162.
[136] H.K. Bevan, "Limitations on the right of an impotent spouse to petition for nullity" (1960) 76 L.Q.R. 267; *Harthan v Harthan* [1949] P. 115; *Pettit v Pettit* [1963] P. 177; *Morgan v Morgan* [1959] P. 92. In this last case a man of 72 married a woman of 59 on the basis that their relationship was to be one of companionship only. The husband's subsequent petition on the ground of his own impotence was rejected because, having regard to the agreement, it would have been contrary to justice and public policy to allow him to succeed.
[137] The Nullity of Marriage Act 1971 s.3(4) provided that the statutory bar of approbation (now to be found in Matrimonial Causes Act 1973 s.13(1)) "replaces . . . any rule of law whereby a decree may be refused by reason of approbation, ratification or lack of sincerity on the part of the petitioner or on similar grounds".
[138] Matrimonial Causes Act 1973 s.13(1): see below, para.2–050, and see further the fourth edition of this work at p.65.
[139] See para.10–007.

> "[W]hen the *coitus* itself is absolutely imperfect, and I must call it unnatural, there is not a natural indulgence of natural desire; almost of necessity disgust is generated, and the probable consequences of other connections with men of ordinary self control become almost certain . . . no man ought to be reduced to this state of quasi unnatural connection and consequent temptation".[140]

However, the law failed to develop a general doctrine that would have permitted a marriage to be terminated if the parties were incapable of forming a normal sexual relationship, and the fact that only one act of sexual intercourse was required for the purposes of consummation hardly guaranteed sexual satisfaction in marriage. Given that the vast majority of modern spouses will have tested their sexual compatibility prior to the marriage, the significance of this ground has diminished still further. Yet it may still have a role to play for those who have entered into an arranged marriage, or those whose religious beliefs preclude sexual experience outside marriage, especially since divorce is less likely to be acceptable to such groups.

ii. Wilful refusal to consummate

2–030   A marriage is voidable if it has not been consummated owing to the wilful refusal of the respondent to consummate it.[141] This ground did not form part of the canon law, but was added by statute in 1937.[142] Indeed, it was not a ground that the canon law could have accommodated: by definition, wilful refusal is something that happens after the marriage; to have accepted it as a ground for annulment would have offended the basic principle of the canon law that nullity is "granted for some defect or incapacity existing at the date of the marriage".[143]

A decree can only be granted if the respondent has made "a settled and definite decision . . . without just excuse"[144] not to consummate marriage.

(1) Settled and definite decision

2–031   Whether the respondent has made a settled and definite decision not to consummate the marriage is a question of fact that may involve an examination of the whole history of the marriage. For example:

> In *Ford v Ford*,[145] the marriage had taken place whilst H was serving a sentence of five years' imprisonment. H and W were left alone on visits for periods of up to two hours. W had heard from other visitors that it was not

---

[140] *D v A* (1845) 1 Rob.Eccl. 279 at 299.
[141] Matrimonial Causes Act 1973 s.12(b).
[142] Matrimonial Causes Act 1937 s.7(1)(a).
[143] Morton Commission, para.89. See also *Napier v Napier* [1915] P. 184 at 189, *per* Pickford L.J. However, attempts (by the Church of England amongst others) to have wilful refusal removed from the grounds for annulment have been unsuccessful: see Law Com. No.33, para.27; *Hansard* HL Vol.318, col.940.
[144] *Horton v Horton* [1947] 2 All E.R. 871.
[145] (1987) 17 Fam. Law 232.

unusual in such circumstances for intercourse to take place; but H refused. Moreover, he showed no interest in living with W, and when he was granted a home visit he insisted that W take him to a former girlfriend's home. A circuit judge granted a decree on the grounds of wilful refusal. H's behaviour indicated that he had no intention of pursuing a married life with W, even though the refusal to have intercourse (in breach of the Prison Rules) in prison would not by itself have justified the finding that he had wilfully refused to consummate the marriage.

In another case, a husband's claim that his wife had wilfully refused to consummate the marriage failed because the court considered that he had not used appropriate tact, persuasion and encouragement.[146] Also:

In *Potter v Potter*,[147] the failure to consummate the marriage originally resulted from a physical defect in the wife. This was cured by surgery, and the husband then made one further attempt to consummate the marriage. The wife's emotional state following the operation was such that this was unsuccessful, and thereafter the husband refused to make any further attempts. The wife failed in a petition alleging his wilful refusal. The court held that his failure to consummate resulted from natural and not deliberate loss of ardour. The wife would also, presumably, have failed had she pursued a petition based on the husband's incapacity since, at the date of the marriage, he apparently did have capacity, and it is immaterial that he subsequently became impotent in relation to his wife.[148]

(2) Absence of "just excuse"

A wilful refusal petition must be dismissed if the respondent can show a "just excuse" for the refusal to consummate.[149] For example, if the parties have agreed that a civil marriage shall be followed by a religious ceremony, it is a "just excuse" for refusing to consummate the marriage that the religious ceremony has not taken place. Indeed, the courts have held that one party's refusal to go through the religious ceremony is a failure to implement the agreement and thus itself amounts to wilful refusal to consummate the marriage[150]:   **2–032**

In *Kaur v Singh*,[151] a marriage was arranged between two Sikhs. A civil ceremony took place, but by Sikh religion and practice (as the parties well

---

[146] *Baxter v Baxter* [1947] 1 All E.R. 387 at 388, *per* Lord Greene M.R.
[147] (1975) 5 Fam. Law 161.
[148] See *S v S* [1956] P. 1.
[149] For the view that the requirement of "just excuse" is based on dubious authority, has not received sufficient judicial analysis, has been expressed in alternative and confusing terms and that its application has been rare; see A. Borkowski [1994] Fam. Law 685.
[150] *Jodla v Jodla* [1960] 1 W.L.R. 236; *Singh v Kaur* [1972] 1 W.L.R. 105. In *A v J* (*Nullity Proceedings*) [1989] 1 F.L.R. 110, it was held that a wife's uncompromising insistence on the postponement of a religious ceremony because she was disappointed by the husband's cool and inconsiderate behaviour to her constituted a wilful refusal on her part to consummate the marriage.
[151] [1972] 1 W.L.R. 105.

knew), a religious ceremony was necessary in order to perfect the marriage. It was the husband's duty to arrange the religious ceremony, but he refused to make the necessary arrangements. The court held that the wife was entitled to a decree on the grounds of his wilful refusal to consummate. The result would apparently be the same if the husband had tried to have intercourse but the wife refused.[152]

Would it be a "just excuse" that the parties had agreed not to have intercourse? Such agreements are sometimes said to be invalid as being contrary to public policy,[153] but this has been held not to be a valid objection if the parties are elderly[154] or there is some other good reason for their having made the agreement.

(3) Consummation

2–033 Consummation involves sexual intercourse; the word intercourse must be interpreted as generally understood in the light of social circumstances known to exist when the legislation was passed. Hence, the House of Lords held[155] that a refusal to have intercourse unless a condom were used was not a refusal to consummate. Conflicting decisions exist[156] as to whether a marriage is consummated by *coitus interruptus*, but the weight of authority seems to favour the view that it is.[157]

If the respondent is physically unable to consummate the marriage, he or she will nevertheless be held wilfully to have refused to do so if he or she has refused to undergo straightforward curative treatment.

iii. Lack of consent: duress, mistake, insanity, etc.

2–034 There are many reasons why the question of whether the parties have consented to the marriage may arise. Young men and women may be put under considerable pressure to marry a person of their family's choosing. Individuals suffering particular conditions may lack the mental capacity to appreciate what a marriage entails. Those who go through a ceremony conducted in a language with which they are unfamiliar may not realise the nature of that ceremony. And someone

---

[152] *Jodla v Jodla* [1960] 1 W.L.R. 236.
[153] *Brodie v Brodie* [1917] P. 271 (although note that in this case the agreement between the parties was not to live together at all).
[154] *Morgan v Morgan* [1959] P. 92; *Scott v Scott* [1959] P. 103.
[155] *Baxter v Baxter* [1948] A.C. 274. It should be noted that the decision was based on the fact that this ground for annulment is statutory; the question was not, therefore, to be solved exclusively by reference to the construction given by the courts to the word "consummation" in the (then non-statutory) ground of incapacity. For a criticism of the decision, see Gower (1948) 11 M.L.R. 176 and *G v G* [1952] V.L.R. 402.
[156] *Cackett v Cackett* [1950] P. 253; *White v White* [1948] P. 330; cf. *Grimes v Grimes* [1948] P. 323.
[157] It is unlikely that any court will need to resolve this point, given that divorce is now more freely available. In both *Cackett v Cackett* and *White v White* the court held that although the marriage had been consummated, a divorce should be granted on the basis of cruelty, the practice of *coitus interruptus* being regarded as injurious to the health of the wife in these cases.

under the influence of alcohol or other drugs may not be aware of their actions. Issues of consent are, therefore, still a significant problem in the twenty-first century.

But what status should the marriage have if either party did not consent? For the canon law, consent was essential to marriage; if there were no true consent, there could be no marriage.[158] Hence, until the Nullity of Marriage Act 1971, lack of consent (whether arising from duress, mistake or insanity) made a marriage void. However, as a result of the 1971 Act, a marriage celebrated after July 31, 1971 is voidable (rather than void) if either party did not validly consent to it, whether in consequence of duress, mistake, unsoundness of mind or otherwise.[159]

Here, we first of all examine the substance of the law; we then consider the reasons why the law was changed in 1971.

(1) Outward and inward consent

If there is no outward indication of consent, the formalities prescribed by English law[160] cannot have been completed. More difficult is the situation where an outward expression of consent is not accompanied by the necessary intention. Such cases present an acute juristic dilemma.[161] If the apparent consent is not real, there should in principle be no marriage; marriage depends on a true consent. But to allow an apparently valid marriage to be avoided by one of the parties alleging the existence of a state of mind or belief that was not evident at the time of the ceremony was traditionally thought to jeopardise the security of marriage.

2–035

English law[162] seeks to resolve this dilemma. On the one hand, the law does not allow private reservations or motives to vitiate an ostensibly valid marriage; on the other hand, it accepts that there may be cases in which there has been no consent at all.

The application of this subtle distinction can give rise to difficulties in practice; the cases can best be considered under the three categories alluded to in the legislation: (1) mental capacity; (2) duress and fear; and (3) mistake and fraud.

(2) Mental capacity

Whether or not an individual has capacity to engage in various actions (e.g. marrying, making a will, or consenting to medical treatment) is judged according

2–036

---

[158] But the doctrine of ratification might in some cases prevent the validity of the marriage being challenged.

[159] See now Matrimonial Causes Act 1973 s.12(c).

[160] *Szechter v Szechter* [1971] P. 286 at 294–295, *per* Sir Jocelyn Simon P. See para.1–034 on the words of contracting in which consent is indicated.

[161] The issues are fully explored, with the aid of much comparative material, by J.H. Wade, "Limited purpose marriages" (1982) 45 M.L.R. 159.

[162] Other systems adopt a conceptual approach that places greater emphasis on the need for a genuine consent: see *Vervaeke (formerly Messina) v Smith* [1983] 1 A.C. 145; *Akram v Akram* 1979 S.L.T. 87.

to the particular issue, with the result that a person may have capacity to make certain decisions but not others.[163] However, although the assessment of an individual's capacity to marry is *issue*-specific, it is not *person*-specific: if a person has capacity to marry, then he or she has the capacity to marry anyone. As Munby J. pointed out in *Sheffield City Council v E*, the courts are concerned with the question of whether an individual has capacity to marry, not the wisdom of a particular marriage.[164]

The law of capacity has recently been overhauled by the Mental Capacity Act 2005. This provides that a person will lack capacity in relation to a specific issue if he or she cannot (i) understand the information relevant to the decision; (ii) retain that information; (iii) use or weigh that information as part of the process of making the decision; or (iv) communicate any decision made (whether by talking, using sign language or any other means).[165] The Code of Practice on the Act makes it clear, however, that this approach is intended to reflect, rather than replace, the tests that have been devised by the courts in specific contexts.[166] We can therefore turn to the common law for illumination as to what is required.

The courts have consistently taken the view that marriage is a very simple contract, which does not require a high degree of intelligence to understand.[167] Mental illness or lack of mental capacity will only affect the validity of consent if either spouse was, at the time of the ceremony, by reason of the illness or deficiency, incapable of understanding the nature[168] of marriage and the duties and responsibilities it creates.[169] This test of capacity was recently endorsed in *Sheffield City Council v E*,[170] in which Munby J. summarised the modern duties and responsibilities of marriage as follows:

> "Marriage . . . confers on the parties the status of husband and wife, the essence of the contract being an agreement between a man and a woman to live together, and to love one another as husband and wife, to the exclusion of all others. It creates a relationship of mutual and reciprocal obligations, typically involving the sharing of a common home and a common domestic

---

[163] See, for example, *Re Park* [1954] P. 112; *Sheffield City Council v E* [2004] EWHC 2808, at para.49.

[164] [2004] EWHC 2808, at para.84. See also *Re MM (an adult); Local Authority X v MM* [2007] EWHC 2003 (Fam).

[165] Mental Capacity Act 2005 s.3(1).

[166] *Mental Capacity Act 2005: Code of Practice*, para.4.33, discussed in *Re MM (an adult); Local Authority X v MM* [2007] EWHC 2003 (Fam), para.80. It should be noted, however, that the suggestion by Munby J. that the Court of Protection is not concerned with decision-making in relation to marriage or sexual relations may overstate the case: certainly, as s.27 of the 2005 Act makes clear, it is not possible for a person to consent to marriage or sexual relations on behalf of a person who is incapable of doing so, but this does not mean that the Court cannot declare that an individual lacks capacity to give such consent in his or her own right.

[167] *Durham v Durham* (1885) 10 P.D. 80 at 82, *per* Sir J. Hannen P.: see also *per* Hodson L.J., in *Re Park* [1954] P. 112 at 136, and *per* Munby J. in *Sheffield City Council v E* [2004] EWHC 2808, para.68.

[168] As opposed to its implications: *Sheffield City Council v E* [2004] EWHC 2808, para.85.

[169] *Re Park* [1954] P. 112; *Hill v Hill* [1959] 1 W.L.R. 127; and see *Fischer v Adams* 38 N.W. 2d 337 (1949).

[170] [2004] EWHC 2808.

life and the right to enjoy each other's society, comfort and assistance."[171]

As a legal definition of marriage, this is open to criticism,[172] but it does capture **2–037** the essence of what marriage usually entails in a social and emotional sense, and it would be asking too much for any intending spouses to have a precise knowledge of the legal consequences of marriage. It should also be noted that the 2005 Act states that a person "is not to be treated as unable to make a decision unless all practicable steps to help him to do so have been taken without success",[173] which will presumably require information about the rights and duties of marriage to be given to a person whose capacity is in question.

The courts have further held that capacity to marry "must include the capacity to consent to sexual relations"[174] on the basis that a sexual relationship is usually implicit in marriage, and one spouse may commit offences under the Sexual Offences Act 2003 if the other is unable to consent.[175] An individual may, however, have the capacity to consent to sexual relations without having capacity to marry.[176]

The recent cases that have come before the court have required an assessment of whether an individual would have capacity to marry, rather than the annulment of marriages that have already taken place.[177] The possibility of a marriage taking place where one of the parties lacks capacity to consent to it will depend on the extent of their impairment. In *City of Westminster v IC (By his Litigation Friend the Official Solicitor) and KC and NNC*, it was suggested that those responsible for drafting the legislation probably had in mind conditions that would not be immediately obvious, and that if one of the parties demonstrably lacked the capacity to consent, "it would . . . be repugnant to public policy . . . to proceed with such a ceremony".[178]

(3) Duress and fear
The underlying principle of the law is that true consent has not been given if one **2–038** party's consent was "brought about by force, menace or duress—a yielding of the lips, not of the mind".[179] In applying this, however, the key question is what level of duress a petitioner needs to show, and in answering it the law needs to

---

[171] At para.132.
[172] See, for example, the analysis by R. Gaffney-Rhys, "Sheffield City Council v E and Another—capacity to marry and the rights and responsibilities of married couples" [2006] 18 C.F.L.Q. 139.
[173] Mental Capacity Act 2005 s.1(3).
[174] *X City Council v MB, NB and MAB (By His Litigation Friend the Official Solicitor)* [2006] EWHC 168 (Fam), para.53.
[175] See Sexual Offences Act 2003 s.30 (sexual activity with a person with a mental disorder impeding choice).
[176] See, for example, *Re MM (an adult); Local Authority X v MM* [2007] EWHC 2003 (Fam).
[177] See below, para.2–043.
[178] [2007] EWHC 3096 (Fam).
[179] J.P. Bishop, *Commentaries on the Law of Marriage and Divorce* 6th edn (Boston: Little, Brown & Co., 1881), p.177, cited in *Szechter v Szechter* [1971] P. 286.

accommodate a variety of competing considerations. The view that marriages should not be lightly set aside[180] might suggest that a high level of duress must be shown before a marriage is set aside, while the emphasis on consent as the basis of marriage would suggest a lower level. Similarly, respect for the tradition of arranged marriages within certain ethnic minority cultures might indicate that the law should tolerate a considerable element of parental involvement, while the emphasis placed by modern Western European societies on freedom of personal choice would dictate that those who believe their choice to have been constrained should be able to free themselves from an unwanted marriage.

In recent years there has been increased official awareness of the problem of forced marriages[181] and a greater appreciation of the pressures that a young man or woman may face.[182] Forced marriages have been distinguished from arranged marriages,[183] and it has been emphasised that the former cannot be justified on either religious or cultural grounds.[184] The wider availability of divorce means that courts may today be less committed to the principle of upholding the institution of marriage as an overriding aim[185]; at the same time, the fact that divorce may not be an appropriate solution for those with strong religious beliefs[186]—who are perhaps the most susceptible to family and religious pressure—justifies the development of the law of duress.

2-039   **(a) The source of the pressure.** The pressure on an individual to enter into marriage may emanate from a variety of sources. It may result from threats made by the other party,[187] one's parents or wider family, or the parents of the other party. There are even a number of Cold War cases in which threats to life and liberty by totalitarian regimes were held to suffice.[188] These do, however, appear somewhat questionable because the parties were not being forced to marry by the authorities[189] but rather chose to marry in order to be able to leave the country.

---

[180] *Scott v Sebright* (1886) 12 P.D. 21 at 24, *per* Butt J.
[181] See, for example, the joint papers issued by the Home Office and the Foreign and Commonwealth Office: *A Choice by Right: The Report of the Working Group on Forced Marriage* (HMSO, 2000); *Forced Marriage: A Wrong Not a Right* (HMSO, 2005); and see also *Hansard*, HL Vol.688, col.1319 for discussion on the Forced Marriage (Civil Protection) Bill. For obvious reasons it is difficult to assess the precise extent of the problem, since the pressures that force a young man or woman into marriage may also prevent them from seeking legal redress, but it has been suggested that a thousand cases each year would be "a reasonable, if anything rather a conservative, estimate": see Sir P. Singer, "When is an arranged marriage a forced marriage?" [2001] I.F.L. 30.
[182] See, for example, *NS v MI* [2006] EWHC 1646 (Fam), para.34.
[183] The distinction, as the working group on forced marriage noted, "lies in the right to choose. In the tradition of arranged marriages, the families of both spouses take a leading role in arranging the marriage, but the choice whether to solemnise the arrangement remains with the spouses.": *A Choice by Right*, p.10.
[184] *A Choice by Right*, p.10. The report also noted that it might be misleading to describe forced marriages as a "religious" issue, since "no major world faith condones forced marriages" (p.6).
[185] See, by way of analogy, *M v M (Prenuptial Agreement)* [2002] 1 F.L.R. 654.
[186] *P v R (Forced Marriage: Annulment: Procedure)* [2003] 1 F.L.R. 661.
[187] *Scott v Sebright* (1886) 12 P.D. 31.
[188] *H v H* [1954] P. 258; *Szechter v Szechter* [1971] P. 286.
[189] Cf. *Buckland v Buckland* [1968] P. 296, in which a young man was wrongly accused of defiling a young girl and was advised that the alternatives were marriage or prison.

Although the parties were no doubt frightened, their decision to marry was in each case a conscious and indeed a rational one.[190]

It is sometimes said that the fear must not be justly imposed. A petition will on this view fail if, for example, the petitioner who had had unlawful sexual intercourse with the bride went through a marriage ceremony with her because he was frightened that he might otherwise be imprisoned.[191] However, it is submitted that this view is wrong. It is illogical (because the justice of the threat has nothing to do with the subjective question of whether the threatened person did in fact consent) and it is contrary to principle (because canon law held a marriage void even if the petitioner had been subjected to a just fear arising as a consequence of his own fault).

(b) The nature of the pressure. There are a number of authorities[192] that seemed **2–040** to suggest that nothing less than a threat of immediate danger to life, limb or liberty could be sufficient to justify a finding of lack of consent. More recent authorities[193] have held that the nature of the pressure is irrelevant, and that it is the impact on the petitioner that is important; therefore, if the petitioner's will has been overborne by the pressure, then no true consent has been given. While the conflict between the two views has never been formally resolved,[194] precedent, principle and practice all suggest that the latter test should be regarded as the appropriate one. First, it has been doubted whether the requirement that there be a threat to life, limb or liberty was in line with earlier authorities.[195] Secondly, the imposition of any such rigid requirement seems inconsistent with principle, since what is in issue is simply whether or not there was a true consent. Modern decisions show a greater appreciation of the more subtle and insidious forms of pressure that may be exerted to force an unwilling child into marriage.[196] Thirdly, the "overborne will" test has been applied by the lower courts[197] and has been identified as the appropriate test in official documents.[198] Current legislation in place to protect the victims of forced marriages explicitly provides that force includes coercion "by threats or other psychological means",[199] which echoes the approach taken in the modern case law.

---

[190] Indeed, *Szechter v Szechter* had a surprising sequel: Szymon Szechter, having divorced his wife to go through a ceremony of marriage with Nina Karsov to facilitate her leaving Poland, remarried his first wife after the annulment but then divorced her again to marry Nina.

[191] The man is free to elect between scandal and possible punishment on the one hand, and marriage to the girl he has wronged on the other; *per* Haugh J., *Griffith v Griffith* [1944] I.R. 35 at 43; *Buckland v Buckland* [1968] P. 296. On this view, a decree may only be granted if the accusation is shown to be false, as it was in *Buckland*.

[192] *Szechter v Szechter* [1971] P. 286; *Singh v Singh* [1971] P. 226; *Singh v Kaur* [1972] 1 W.L.R. 105.

[193] *Hirani v Hirani* (1982) 4 F.L.R. 232.

[194] For discussion, see, for example, A. Bradney, "Duress, family law and the coherent legal system" (1994) 57 M.L.R. 963.

[195] See *NS v MI* [2006] EWHC 1646 (Fam), paras 27–29.

[196] *NS v MI* [2006] EWHC 1646 (Fam).

[197] *P v R (Forced Marriage: Annulment: Procedure)* [2003] 1 F.L.R. 661; *NS v MI* [2006] EWHC 1646 (Fam).

[198] See, for example, *A Choice by Right*, p.7.

[199] Family Law Act 1996 s.63A(6), as inserted by the Forced Marriage (Civil Protection) Act 2007 s.1.

2–041   **(c) The effect on the petitioner.** The test to be applied is a subjective one; the
question is not whether a person of ordinary courage and resolution would yield
to the fear but whether the petitioner did so yield.[200] The will of a weak or
vulnerable person may be overcome by threats or pressure that would not have
affected the more resolute. Thus:

> In *Hirani v Hirani*,[201] a 19-year-old Hindu girl, who was found to be wholly
> dependent on her parents, was told by them to break off a friendship she had
> formed with a young Muslim and to marry a Hindu selected by them: "You
> had better marry somebody we want you to—otherwise pick up your
> belongings and go." The daughter did as she was told and went through a
> marriage ceremony with the respondent (whom neither she nor her parents
> had seen before the wedding). After living with him for six weeks, she left
> and went to her former boy-friend's house. It was held that this was "as
> clear a case as one could want of the overbearing of the will of the petitioner
> and thus invalidating or vitiating her consent".[202] The petitioner had been
> forced into the marriage, and a decree was granted.

By contrast, the courts have refused to annul marriages deliberately entered
into in order to escape from a disagreeable situation such as penury or social
degradation[203] or out of a sense of obligation to family or religious tradition. The
distinction may be a fine one, as is evident from a comparison of the facts of
Hirani with those of *Singh v Singh*.[204] In the latter case:

> A marriage was arranged by the parents of two Sikhs: a girl aged 17 and a
> boy aged 21. The bride had never seen her husband before the marriage, and
> only went through the register office ceremony out of a "proper respect" for
> her parents and the traditions of her people. She then refused to go through
> the usual religious ceremony or to live with the husband. The court declined
> to annul the marriage as there was no evidence of fear.

While the court in *Singh* reached this result by applying the requirement that
there must be some threat to life, limb or liberty, it is arguable that the application
of the "overborne will" test would produce the same result. It is one thing to take
into account the subtle forms of pressure that may overbear the will of an
individual; it is quite another to hold that a marriage may be annulled where there
is no overt pressure and no contemporaneous evidence that the petitioner did not
consent to the marriage. Of course, in family law, context is all, and it is possible

---

[200] It is true that in *Szechter v Szechter* [1971] P. 286 at 297–298, Simon P. said that the will of one
of the parties must be shown to have been overborne by "genuine and reasonably held" fear.
However, Lord Simon apparently had second thoughts about the validity of this way of formulating
the matter: see (1983) 99 L.Q.R. 353.
[201] (1982) 4 F.L.R. 232.
[202] At 234, *per* Ormrod L.J.
[203] *Szechter v Szechter* [1971] P. 286.
[204] [1971] P. 226 (cogently criticised by S. Poulter (1979) 42 M.L.R. 408 at 410–418).

to envisage cases in which the petitioner was so cowed by his or her family that specific threats were unnecessary and any protest dangerous: in such cases, no doubt a court would make a finding of duress.

(4) Mistake and fraud

Generally, neither mistake nor fraud avoids a marriage. The cynic may say that **2–042** the maxim *caveat emptor* applies just as much to marriage as it does to other contracts. Fraud is only a vitiating factor if it procures the appearance without the reality of consent, and it is not sufficient that fraud has induced a genuine consent.[205]

There are, in fact, only two groups of cases, in which mistake has been held sufficient to vitiate consent to marriage:

(1) Mistake as to the person (as distinct from mistake as to that person's attributes). If A marries B under the belief that she is C, this is sufficient to found a petition. In contrast, if A marries B erroneously, believing her to be a chaste virgin of good family and possessed of ample wealth, the marriage will be unimpeachable.[206]

(2) Mistake as to the nature of the ceremony. It is sufficient to avoid the marriage if one party believes that he or she is, for example, appearing in a police court, or that the ceremony is a betrothal[207] or religious conversion ceremony,[208] or if one of the parties is so drunk (or under the influence of drugs) as not to know what is happening.[209]

These principles have been applied to cases where a "sham" marriage has been contracted in order to acquire a nationality or immigration status. If the parties intend to contract a marriage (even though the marriage is only to be for

---

[205] *Moss v Moss* [1897] P. 263 at 269, *per* Sir F.H. Jeune P.

[206] There are fine distinctions. In a New Zealand case (*C v C* [1942] N.Z.L.R. 356) H represented to W that he was a well-known featherweight pugilist. Her mistake was as to his attributes and not as to his identity; she intended to marry the man physically present, and his name was not an essential condition of the marriage. Hence the petition failed. In an Australian case, however, where W believed that H was a member of a particular family with which she was acquainted, there was held to be a mistake of identity as against a mere mistake of name: *Allardyce v Mitchell* (1869) 6 W.W. & A'B. 45.

[207] *Hall v Hall* (1908) 24 T.L.R. 756 (where an English woman, who thought that marriages could only be celebrated in church, went through a marriage ceremony in Kensington Register Office believing that she was merely registering her name); *Kelly v Kelly* (1932) 49 T.L.R. 99; *Parojcic v Parojcic* [1958] W.L.R. 1280; *Ford v Stier* [1896] P. 1.

[208] *Mehta v Mehta* [1945] 2 All E.R. 690.

[209] *Sullivan v Sullivan* (1812) 2 Hag.Con. 238 at 246 (*per* Sir W. Scott). A mistake as to the effects of the relationship produced by the marriage is insufficient: a petition failed where H thought the marriage was polygamous, entitling him to take further wives (*Kassim v Kassim* [1962] P. 224) and also where H erroneously assumed that his Russian wife would be allowed to leave the Soviet Union and live with him: *Way v Way* [1950] P. 71.

that limited purpose), it will, in the absence of fear or duress,[210] be unimpeach-able[211] in English law:

> In *Messina v Smith*,[212] W went through with a marriage ceremony, knowing that it was such a ceremony, and that the purpose of it was to enable her to obtain British nationality and a British passport and thereby protect herself against the risk of deportation for offences incidental to her engaging in prostitution. A petition to annul the marriage on the ground that the parties had had no intention to cohabit as husband and wife, and that there had thus been no true consent to the marriage, failed.[213]

(5) Preventative steps

2–043 Annulments undo marriages that have taken place, and in cases of mistake and fraud there is little else that the law can do by way of prevention (other than making sure that the relevant words of consent are spoken in a language that both parties understand). However, recent years have seen a greater emphasis on preventative steps in relation to both those who lack capacity and those who are being forced into a marriage.[214] The High Court has developed a protective role on the basis of its inherent declaratory jurisdiction, and has granted injunctions to prevent marriages from taking place if one of the parties does not have the necessary ability to consent[215] or is being forced into a marriage.[216] The Forced Marriage (Civil Protection) Act 2007 will extend the range of courts[217] entitled to make an order to prevent a person from being forced into a marriage, as well as orders protecting those who have been forced into such marriages.[218] Application may be made by the victim or by a relevant third party,[219] and the

---

[210] *H v H* [1954] P. 258; see also *Kurma v Kurma, The Times*, April 30, 1958.

[211] *Silver v Silver* [1958] 1 W.L.R. 259; *Vervaeke (formerly Messina) v Smith* [1983] 1 A.C. 145.

[212] [1971] P. 322. For subsequent proceedings, see *Vervaeke (formerly Messina) v Smith* [1983] 1 A.C. 145.

[213] *Messina v Smith* [1971] p.322, *per* Ormrod J., as cited and approved by Lord Hailsham of St. Marylebone. *Vervaeke (formerly Messina) v Smith* [1983] 1 A.C. 145 at 152.

[214] See, for example, *A Choice by Right*, pp.17–26.

[215] See, for example, *M v B, A, and S (By Her Litigation Friend the Official Solicitor)* [2005] EWHC 1681 (23-year-old woman who suffered from a severe learning disability: injunction granted to prevent her parents from taking her to Pakistan to be married); *X City Council v MB, NB and MAB (By His Litigation Friend the Official Solicitor)* [2006] EWHC 168 (Fam), para.53 (25-year-old autistic man: undertakings from parents that they would not cause or permit him to undergo any form of marriage ceremony or take him out of the jurisdiction); *Re SA (Vulnerable Adult with Capacity: Marriage)* [2005] EWHC 2942 (Fam) (17-year-old girl who was profoundly deaf and unable to speak but did have capacity: order that she be properly informed about any proposed match).

[216] See *Re SK (Proposed Plaintiff) (An Adult by way of her Litigation Friend)* [2004] EWHC 3202 (Fam); *Re SA (Vulnerable Adult with Capacity: Marriage)* [2005] EWHC 2942 (Fam); *Re K (A Local Authority) v N* [2005] EWHC 2956 (Fam).

[217] Previously, only the High Court, in the exercise of its inherent jurisdiction, could make orders preventing a marriage from going ahead; application for the new orders, by contrast, may be made in the county courts.

[218] Family Law Act 1996 s.63A(1), as inserted by the Forced Marriage (Civil Protection) Act 2007 s.1. The Government has, however, resolved against making it a criminal offence to force another person into a marriage: see *Forced Marriage: A Wrong Not a Right: Summary of Responses to the Consultation on the Criminalisation of Forced Marriage* (2006).

[219] Family Law Act 1996 s.63C(2), as inserted by the Forced Marriage (Civil Protection) Act 2007 s.1.

court has wide powers to impose restrictions or requirements on a range of respondents.[220]

The need to protect individuals from being forced into a marriage is obvious. But the taking of preventative steps in relation to those who lack capacity raises an interesting question: if a marriage entered into without full consent is only voidable, and can only be annulled upon the petition of one of the parties, should it be possible for a third party, such as a local authority, to prevent the marriage from going ahead in the first place?

(6) Should lack of consent make a marriage void or voidable?

This leads to the question of whether lack of consent should render a marriage void or voidable. As noted above, the canon law rule that a marriage was void[221] if one party had not truly consented survived until the Nullity of Marriage Act 1971 rendered such marriages merely voidable. The modern rule is no doubt convenient, but it is conceptually astonishing.[222] The result of holding such a marriage to be merely voidable is that a person who does not understand what he or she is doing may become legally bound to a relationship whose whole juridical basis is the consent of both parties.[223] Moreover, that relationship has important legal consequences, including, for example, the right of intestate succession. A man—such as an attendant in a nursing home—may go through a marriage ceremony with a rich elderly woman whose mental faculties are so impaired that she has no idea what is happening; such a "marriage" will, since 1971, effectively revoke the will she had made some years previously in favour of her family, whilst her "husband" will have extensive succession rights on her death intestate.[224] It has also been suggested that classifying a forced marriage as void would send a stronger message that it is not acceptable to force another person into a marriage.

2–044

iv. Pregnancy by another, venereal disease and mental illness

These three grounds originate in the Matrimonial Causes Act 1937, and were introduced because of the lack of matrimonial relief for fraudulent or wilful concealment of material facts.[225]

2–045

---

[220] Family Law Act 1996 s.63B, as inserted by the Forced Marriage (Civil Protection) Act 2007 s.1. The Act provides that the order may relate to persons who are or may be involved in forcing another into a marriage: their involvement does not need to be direct but may take the form of "aiding, abetting, counselling, procuring, encouraging or assisting another to force, or to attempt to force, a person to enter into a marriage" or conspiring to bring about a forced marriage (s.63B(3)).

[221] There is some judicial support for the view that marriages affected by force, fear, fraud or drunkenness were traditionally voidable only, but this view is convincingly refuted by D. Tolstoy (1963) 27 M.L.R. 385: see Jackson, *Formation and Annulment of Marriage* p.285.

[222] A full account of the policy considerations is given in the fourth edition of this work at pp.79–81; and reference should be made to the Law Commission's Report on *Nullity of Marriage*, Law Com. No.33.

[223] Although there are indications in *KC, NNC v City of Westminster Social and Community Services Department, IC (a protected party, by his litigation friend the Official Solicitor)* [2008] EWCA Civ. 198 that the courts would refuse to recognise a marriage if one of the parties demonstrably lacked capacity.

[224] See Ch.7, below.

[225] Morton Commission, para.267.

Previously, a husband who discovered that his wife was carrying another man's child had no ground of matrimonial relief, since deceit was not a ground for annulment[226] and the pregnancy could not prove that she had, since the marriage, committed adultery. The ability of a husband to petition for a decree of nullity[227] on the basis that at the time of the ceremony he was unaware of the fact that his wife was pregnant by a third party does address this specific deceit, but one should perhaps ask whether it is the only deceit that merits such a remedy, and whether a wife who discovers that her husband has impregnated another woman shortly before their wedding should not be entitled to similar redress.

The justification for being able to obtain a decree of nullity on the basis that the respondent is "suffering from venereal disease in a communicable form"[228] is also open to question. The seriousness of many venereal diseases in the 1930s—before the possibility of a cure by means of antibiotics—was very different from the position today. In addition, the increase in sexually transmitted infections in recent years[229] raises the possibility[230] that a large number of marriages are technically voidable on this ground.

The third ground, that of mental illness, is also a creature of its time; there is more than a hint of eugenicist concerns in the concept of a person being "unfit" for marriage. There are two elements to it: (1) that the affected party is suffering from a "mental disorder" at the time of the ceremony; and (2) that he or she is thereby "unfitted for marriage".[231] The first element is broadly defined[232]; the second, by contrast, has been given a narrow interpretation in the case law: the court is to ask "is this person capable of living in a married state and of carrying out the ordinary duties and obligations of marriage?"[233] In such cases the marriage is voidable even though the party in question was capable of giving a valid consent (and even if he or she is later capable of bringing an action to annul the marriage, since this ground may be relied upon by either party to the marriage).

v. Gender reassignment

2–046   The final two grounds on which a marriage is voidable were added by the Gender Recognition Act 2004. The first deals with the situation where a married person seeks legal recognition of a change of gender. As noted above, a married person who applies for a gender recognition certificate is only entitled to an interim

---

[226] *Moss v Moss* [1897] P. 263.

[227] Under Matrimonial Causes Act 1973 s.12(f).

[228] Matrimonial Causes Act 1973 s.12(e).

[229] Diagnoses of sexually transmitted diseases at genitourinary clinics in the UK increased by 63% between 1997 and 2006: the biggest increase was in diagnoses of syphilis, which increased by 1,607% within this period, while chlamydia was responsible for the highest number of infections.

[230] The precise scope of this provision has not been tested, and it remains uncertain whether all sexually transmitted disease would fall within its scope.

[231] Matrimonial Causes Act 1973 s.12(d), as amended by Mental Health Act 1983 Sch.4 para.34.

[232] For these purposes, "mental disorder" has the same meaning as in the Mental Health Act 1983, and is defined as "mental illness, arrested or incomplete development of mind, psychopathic disorder, and any other disorder or disability of mind": Mental Health Act 1983 s.1(2). This has not been altered by the Mental Capacity Act 2005.

[233] *Bennett v Bennett* [1969] 1 W.L.R. 430, at 434.

certificate[234]; the granting of such a certificate is, however, a ground upon which the marriage may be annulled upon the application of either party.[235]

The second ground deals with the situation where a person marries after having undergone gender reassignment and obtained a gender recognition certificate. If the spouse of such a person was ignorant of this fact at the time of the ceremony, he or she may petition for a decree of nullity on the basis that the respondent had undergone gender reassignment prior to the marriage.[236] It has been argued that such a provision is necessary on the basis that gender is an aspect of identity, and that a mistake as to the other spouse's gender would be a relevant mistake rendering the marriage voidable.[237] It may be contended, however, that the mistake relates only to what the respondent's gender once *was*, rather than what it has been legally determined to be. In addition, this provision is perhaps at odds with the statement in the Gender Recognition Act that a person's reassigned gender is to be recognised as their gender for all purposes.[238]

C. Bars to a decree

The fact that a petitioner has established one of the grounds set out above does   2–047
not mean that a decree will automatically be granted. This is because in certain circumstances there may be a bar to the granting of the relief sought. While there are no longer[239] any bars to the granting of a decree on the ground that a marriage is void, the legislation[240] sets out three factors that may prevent a decree being granted where the marriage is merely voidable.

i. Time

It is an absolute bar to the granting of a decree on the ground of lack of consent,   2–048
venereal disease, pregnancy by a third party, or gender reassignment preceding the marriage that proceedings were not instituted within three years of the marriage.[241] Exceptionally, the court may give leave for proceedings to be

---

[234] See para.2–019 above.
[235] Matrimonial Causes Act 1973 s.12(g).
[236] Matrimonial Causes Act 1973 s.12(h).
[237] N. Lowe and G. Douglas, *Bromley's Family Law*, 10th edn (Oxford: Oxford University Press, 2006), p.90.
[238] Gender Recognition Act 2004 s.9(1).
[239] Prior to the Nullity of Marriage Act 1971 (see s.6(1)), collusion was a bar to the grant of a decree even where the marriage was void; see Law Com. No.33, paras 37, 38. There may also be cases where a party is estopped from putting the validity of a marriage in issue: *Woodland v Woodland* [1928] P. 169: see generally, Tolstoy, "Marriage by estoppel or an excursion into res judicata" (1968) 84 L.Q.R. 245, but note that the divorce courts' jurisdiction is inquisitorial in nature and that the scope for such doctrines is accordingly restricted: see *W v W (Physical Inter-sex)* [2001] 1 F.L.R. 324 (concession correctly made that neither estoppel nor laches applicable in a case in which a court had previously granted a respondent to nullity petition decree absolute of divorce in respect of the marriage).
[240] The three bars were codified in the Nullity of Marriage Act 1971 and subsequently consolidated in the Matrimonial Causes Act 1973. The bars of "time" and "knowledge" apply only to marriages celebrated after July 31, 1971; that of "approbation", however, applies to proceedings instituted after that date.
[241] Matrimonial Causes Act 1973 s.13(2), as substituted by Matrimonial and Family Proceedings Act 1984 s.2(2) and amended by the Gender Recognition Act 2004.

instituted after the expiration of three years if the petitioner has at some time during the three-year period suffered from mental disorder, and it would in all the circumstances be just to give leave.[242] Where the petition is based on the issue of a gender recognition certificate to a married person, the time limit is shorter, (only six months), and there is no provision for it to be extended.[243]

ii. Knowledge of defect

2–049　A petition founded on venereal disease, pregnancy by a third party or gender reassignment pre-dating the ceremony will fail unless the petitioner can satisfy the court that, at the time of the marriage, the petitioner was ignorant of the facts alleged.[244] A husband's knowledge that the wife is pregnant is not in itself a bar; he must also know that she was pregnant by someone other than himself.[245]

iii. "Approbation"[246]

2–050　For the ecclesiastical courts,[247] approbation could be defined as conduct on the part of the petitioner that so plainly implied a recognition of the existence and validity of the marriage as to render it inequitable and contrary to public policy that he or she should subsequently question the validity of the marriage.[248]

In 1971 these uncertain and obscure rules were replaced with a statutory code.[249] In proceedings instituted after July 31, 1971 the court must not[250] grant a decree of nullity on the ground that a marriage is voidable if the respondent satisfies the court:

> "(a) that the petitioner, with knowledge that it was open to him to have the marriage avoided, so conducted himself in relation to the respondent as to lead the respondent reasonably to believe that he would not seek to do so; and
>
> (b) that it would be unjust to the respondent to grant the decree".[251]

---

[242] Matrimonial Causes Act 1973 s.13(4) as inserted by Matrimonial and Family Proceedings Act 1984 s.2(3). For the reasons, see the Law Commission's *Report on Time Restrictions on Presentation of Divorce and Nullity Petitions*, Law Com. No.116.

[243] Matrimonial Causes Act 1973 s.13(2A), as inserted by the Gender Recognition Act 2004.

[244] Matrimonial Causes Act 1973 s.13(3), as amended by the Gender Recognition Act 2004.

[245] *Stocker v Stocker* [1966] 1 W.L.R. 190.

[246] As the following discussion will show, the bar of approbation has been replaced by a specific statutory bar that does not use this specific term, but "approbation" remains a convenient way of summing up the substance of the bar.

[247] For full discussions of the pre-1971 law, see D. Lasok, "Approbation of marriage in English law and the doctrine of validation" (1963) 26 M.L.R. 249; Jackson, *Formation and Annulment of Marriage*, Ch.8. The old law can be of no more than historical interest, because the new rules now embodied in Matrimonial Causes Act 1973 apply to all proceedings instituted after July 31, 1971 (whenever the marriage was celebrated): Nullity of Marriage Act 1971 s.3(4).

[248] *G v M* (1885) 10 App. Cas. 171, at p.186, *per* Lord Selborne L.C.

[249] *D v D (Nullity: Statutory Bar)* [1979] Fam. 70 at 72.

[250] The bar is absolute and not discretionary: *D v D (Nullity: Statutory Bar)* [1979] Fam. 70 at 76. For the reasons, see Law Com. No.33, para.43.

[251] Matrimonial Causes Act 1973 s.13(1).

Hence, three separate matters must be proved[252]: first, that the petitioner has behaved towards the respondent in such a way that the latter reasonably believes that no steps will be taken to annul the marriage; secondly, that the petitioner knows, at the time of the conduct relied on, that the marriage could be annulled; and thirdly, that the respondent would suffer injustice if a decree were to be granted.

There has been no reported case in which this statutory bar has been **2–051** successfully pleaded; a spouse wishing to resist the granting of a decree has formidable hurdles to overcome. Even if the petitioner did lead the respondent to believe that no annulment would be sought, knowing that this was a possibility, it will often be impossible for a respondent to show that he or she would suffer injustice if a decree were granted. This is because any spouse will usually be able, in time, to have the marriage terminated by divorce,[253] and the respondent in that case will have the same rights to apply for financial provision and property adjustment orders as in nullity proceedings.[254]

Finally, it should be noted that public policy is no longer a consideration directly relevant to the operation of the bar.[255] Thus:

> In *D v D (Nullity: Statutory Bar)*,[256] a couple had adopted two young children, thereby representing to the court that they were validly married. A decree of nullity was granted: the fact that the couple had held themselves out as married was no longer relevant; nor was it relevant that it might be contrary to public policy to allow a couple who had acted in this way to have their marriage annulled.[257]

D. Effects of a decree[258]

At common law, none of the legal consequences associated with marriage could **2–052** flow from a void marriage, which by definition had no legal existence.[259] The

---

[252] The requirements of the section are cumulative: *D v D (Nullity: Statutory Bar)* [1979] Fam 70, 78.

[253] See Ch.10, below.

[254] *D v D (Nullity: Statutory Bar)* [1979] Fam. 70 at 78.

[255] *D v D (Nullity: Statutory Bar)* [1979] Fam. 70. Under the old law there was authority for the view that the court might hold that a marriage had been approbated in spite of the absence of injustice to the parties if public policy so required (see *Tindall v Tindall* [1953] P. 63 at 72; *Slater v Slater* [1953] P. 235 at 244); for the policy underlying the change, see Law Com. No.33, para.44—a passage cited by Dunn J. in *D v D (Nullity: Statutory Bar)* [1979] Fam. 70 at 77, who added (at 78): "parties are to be encouraged to resolve their differences, and to do that, certainty in the law is a requisite, untrammelled by considerations of public policy which may vary from judge to judge".

[256] [1979] Fam. 70.

[257] Contrast *W v W* [1952] P. 152 (a decision under the old law). It is submitted that the change in the law was clearly desirable: the policy of protecting the child in such cases is better secured by the statutory requirement that the court consider whether to exercise its powers to make residence or other orders, in respect of the children (Matrimonial Causes Act 1973 s.41) rather than by asserting the continuance of the marriage.

[258] Every decree is in the first instance a decree nisi that is not generally to be made absolute before the end of six weeks from its grant: Matrimonial Causes Act 1973 s.15. It follows that a voidable marriage will not be legally terminated until the decree nisi has been made absolute; quite what effect a decree nisi has on the status of the parties to a marriage held to be void is not clear.

[259] Thus, for example, any children of a void marriage would be illegitimate because their parents had never been married.

same consequences followed if the marriage were voidable. This was because, although the marriage would be valid until avoided, the decree, when made, operated retrospectively and declared the marriage "to have been and to be absolutely null and void to all intents and purposes whatsoever",[260] and once the decree had been pronounced, the marriage became void ab initio.[261]

Over the years the law has been reformed, and the position is now radically different in relation to both voidable and void marriages.

i. Voidable marriages

2–053   The fact that a decree operated retroactively was anomalous and inconvenient, and created hardship. In 1971 the law was changed, and it now provides that a decree operates to annul the marriage only as respects any time after it has been made absolute, and that "the marriage shall, notwithstanding the decree, be treated as if it had existed up to that time".[262] This new rule undoubtedly removes anomalies, but its application will not always produce a result that seems conspicuously just. For example:

> In *Ward v Secretary of State for Social Services*,[263] the widow of an army officer went through a ceremony of marriage, but the marriage was a disaster and lasted for less than a week. It was never consummated and, in due course, a decree of nullity was granted on that basis. But it was held that the marriage which had been annulled brought to an end the petitioner's status as a widow, and that she had therefore lost her entitlement to an army widow's pension.

ii. Void marriages

2–054   Even more striking is the fact that a void marriage may now have some of the legal consequences of a valid marriage.

(1) Legitimacy of children

2–055   Since 1959 English law has accepted that the offspring of a void marriage may be "treated as" the parent's legitimate child if, at the time of conception (or the time of the marriage ceremony if later), both or either of the parties reasonably believed that the marriage was valid.[264]

---

[260] *De Reneville v De Reneville* [1948] P. 100 at 111.

[261] However, the legitimacy of the children of a voidable marriage was preserved notwithstanding the fact that the parents' marriage had been declared never to have existed: see Matrimonial Causes Act 1937 s.7(1) (2) and Law Reform (Miscellaneous Provisions) Act 1949 s.4.

[262] Matrimonial Causes Act 1973 s.16.

[263] [1990] 1 F.L.R. 119. The Pensions Act 1995 s.168 preserves the rights of women whose remarriage is terminated by death, divorce or annulment to certain war pensions, but it does not affect the general principle stated in the text.

[264] The rule is now contained in Legitimacy Act 1976 s.1, as amended by Family Law Reform Act 1987 s.28. But this provision only applies to a child born *after* the void marriage has taken place: *Re Spence (dec'd)* [1990] Ch. 652. For the history of the law's refusal to recognise the canon law doctrine of the putative marriage, see: F.H. Newark (1944) 8 M.L.R. 203; E.J. Cohn (1948) 64 L.Q.R. 324.

(2) Financial provision after decree[265] of nullity

If a "marriage" does not exist, it logically follows that none of the rights and   **2–056**
duties of marriage subsist between the parties. If a man fails to maintain his
"wife", it was at common law an answer to her claim for maintenance that the
"marriage" was void (and it is still an answer if a spouse seeks maintenance in
proceedings under the Domestic Proceedings and Magistrates' Courts Act 1978
or in the High Court on the ground of failure to provide reasonable maintenance).[266] This is because those remedies depend upon the existence of the
relationship of husband and wife. However, provided that a decree of nullity is
obtained, the court now[267] has exactly the same powers[268] to order one party to
make financial provision for the other as it would have when dissolving a valid
marriage.[269] Similarly, a "wife" or "husband" who has obtained such a decree
can apply to the court for reasonable provision out of the estate after the other's
death.[270]

(3) Financial provision from estate if no decree

If an impediment was only discovered after the other spouse's death, the survivor   **2–057**
would have no right to succeed on intestacy, and it would be too late to obtain a
decree that would enable an application to be made to the court under the
legislation referred to above.[271] In 1970 legislation[272] dealt with this problem: a
person who in good faith entered into a void marriage with a person since
deceased may apply to the court for reasonable provision out of the deceased's
estate in exactly the same way as if the applicant were the deceased's surviving
spouse (or a person who had obtained a decree of nullity carrying with it the right
to be considered for financial provision).

---

[265] An applicant cannot effectively oust the court's jurisdiction to make such ancillary orders by seeking a bare declaration that the marriage was void ab initio: see Family Law Act 1986 s.55(1) and, for a full discussion of the background, the Law Commission's *Report on Declarations in Family Matters*, Law Com. No.132.

[266] Relief is only available to a "party to a marriage", and a party to a void union is not such: see *Ivett v Ivett* (1930) 94 J.P. 237; 143 L.T. 680. On the powers of the court to award maintenance, see para.3–014.

[267] Matrimonial Causes Act 1973 ss.23, 24, as substituted by the Family Law Act 1996 Sch.2.

[268] *D v D (Nullity: Statutory Bar)* [1979] Fam. 70.

[269] In *S-T (formerly J) v J* [1997] 1 F.L.R. 402, a majority of the Court of Appeal (whilst denying in that case the applicant's claim for relief) nonetheless favoured a flexible approach to applications even when the applicant had been guilty of some wrongdoing (e.g. making a false declaration when giving notice for the marriage) in contracting it. See also *Rampal v Rampal* [2001] EWCA Civ 989.

[270] Inheritance (Provision for Family and Dependants) Act 1975 ss.1(1)b, 25(1) (and see further Ch.7). This presupposes that a person whose void marriage has been annulled is within the definition of former spouse (i.e. "a person whose marriage with the deceased was . . . annulled"). The case of *J v C and E (a child)* [2006] EWCA Civ 551 suggests that in certain cases it may be argued that there has never been a marriage capable of being annulled: see above para.2–021.

[271] In some cases the survivor might have been able to recover damages for breach of contract from the estate: *Shaw v Shaw* [1954] 2 Q.B. 429; see Law Com. No.26.

[272] Law Reform (Miscellaneous Provisions) Act 1970; see now Inheritance (Provision for Family and Dependants) Act 1975 ss.1(1)(a), 25(4).

IV. VOID AND VOIDABLE CIVIL PARTNERSHIPS

2–058 The grounds on which an order may be sought to annul a civil partnership are virtually identical to those examined above, but there are a number of significant differences.

A. Void civil partnerships

2–059 The grounds on which a civil partnership is void are as follows[273]:

- that the parties are within the prohibited degrees[274];

- that either party is under the age of 16;

- that the parties both know that they have failed to comply with certain stipulated formalities;

- that either party is already in an existing formal relationship (civil partnership or marriage);

- that the parties are not of the same sex.

It was, of course, unnecessary for the 2004 Act to make provision for the recognition of "polygamous" civil partnerships contracted overseas, since no jurisdiction in the world recognises multiple civil partnerships. It should also be noted that a person who enters into concurrent civil partnerships in this country does not commit the offence of bigamy[275]—which remains applicable only to individuals who contract concurrent marriages—but would be guilty of perjury, since he or she would have made a formal and untruthful declaration that there were no impediments to the civil partnership. The second civil partnership would of course be void.

B. Voidable civil partnerships

2–060 The grounds on which a civil partnership is voidable are[276]:

- lack of consent;

- mental disorder;

- respondent was pregnant by a third party;

- the issue of an interim gender reassignment certificate to either party;

---

[273] Civil Partnership Act 2004 ss.3 and 49.
[274] These are set out in Sch.1 Pt 1 of the Act, and echo the prohibited degrees of relationship for the purposes of marriage.
[275] Cf. the report in *The Times*, July 10, 2007 of a case in which a married woman entered into a civil partnership with another woman: "Mother is first lesbian guilty of bigamy".
[276] Civil Partnership Act 2004 s.50.

- respondent had undergone gender reassignment prior to the civil partnership.

There are three omissions from this list (and one inclusion) that require some explanation. It is not possible to annul a civil partnership on the basis of either non-consumption (whether due to incapacity or wilful refusal) or the fact that one party suffers from a communicable venereal disease. As noted above, the legal definition of "consummation" is explicitly heterosexual, and the government took the view that it should not be extended to same-sex couples. The Women and Equality Unit responsible for the reform further stated that it was not "appropriate in present day circumstances to include [transmission of a venereal disease] as a ground to nullify a civil partnership".[277] It did not explain why it remains appropriate in the context of marriage.

As a result, the provisions relating to void and voidable civil partnerships suffer from a lack of coherence. To prohibit a civil partnership within certain degrees of relationship implies that the relationship of the parties is assumed to be sexual, yet there is nothing in the Act that requires a sexual relationship as a precondition for validity or even acknowledges that the parties are likely to be engaging in such a relationship. One can appreciate the difficulties facing a draftsman trying to define consummation within same-sex relationships, but this does not explain why suffering from a communicable venereal disease was omitted.

It is, however, recognised that the parties may have been having a sexual relationship with a third party, since the 2004 Act allows a civil partnership to be annulled on the basis that the respondent was pregnant by a third party at the time of registration. Of course, it is also possible that the respondent may have become pregnant as the result of artificial insemination, although the deception in such a case would be less significant.

C. Bars to a decree

An order annulling a voidable civil partnership may be barred in the circum-   **2–061**
stances set out above in relation to marriages.

D. Effects of an order

The effects of an order annulling a civil partnership mirror those of a decree   **2–062**
annulling a marriage.

V. CONCLUSION

The law of nullity is an inevitable concomitant of the fact that the law defines   **2–063**
who can legally formalise a relationship; if, for example, a marriage or civil

---

[277] Woman and Equality Unit, *Response to Civil Partnership: A Framework for the Legal Regulation of Same-sex Couples* (November 2003).

partnership between close relations or two 15-year-olds were *not* void, then the prohibition would be an empty one.

Yet the fact that some rules are necessary does not mean that all of the current grounds are required. It is sometimes suggested that there would be much to be said for abolishing the concept of the voidable marriage (with the attendant full hearings and sometimes unpleasant medical examination) and allowing the parties to seek a divorce based on the breakdown of their marriage, as has been done in Australia. However, the Law Commission has rejected this proposal, and it seems unlikely that further reform of the law governing the annulment of marriage will be on the agenda in the foreseeable future. Indeed, it may be that reform of the law of nullity has become less likely in recent years because of the awareness that it is a more acceptable solution than divorce to certain ethnic minorities and those of strong religious belief.

As we have seen, even a void marriage or civil partnership may carry legal consequences; precisely what legal consequences flow from formalising a relationship is the subject of the next chapter.

CHAPTER THREE

THE LEGAL CONSEQUENCES OF MARRIAGE AND CIVIL PARTNERSHIP

I.   INTRODUCTION.............................. 3–001
II. COMMON LAW DOCTRINES.......... 3–002
     A. The doctrine of legal unity........... 3–002
     B. The notion of consortium.............. 3–003
     C. The common law right to
        maintenance...................................... 3–004
III. THE STATUTORY FRAMEWORK... 3–005
     A. Property: ownership   and
        occupation 3–006

     B. Finances: maintenance orders and
        agreements.. 3–014
     C. Miscellaneous economic conse-
        quences.. 3–033
     D. Other legal consequences............... 3–036
IV. ENGAGED COUPLES 3–041
V.   CONCLUSION.................................... 3–042

I. INTRODUCTION

In the opening pages of this book, the emphasis traditionally given to marriage in expositions of family law was explained by the fact that marriage created a status from which certain legal rights and duties automatically stemmed. The same is now true of civil partnerships. The reader, having learned in the preceding chapters how such relationships come into existence in English law, might therefore reasonably expect now to be told what those rights and duties are. After all, if one looks at the codified systems of law in force in many of the other countries of the European Union,[1] one finds statements (albeit often cast in rather general terms[2]) about the rights and duties of couples who have formalised their relationship, dealing with such matters as the choice of the family home,[3] as well as the effects of the relationship in relation to the parties' property.[4] This chapter should surely contain the English counterpart.

3–001

It has to be admitted at once that (notwithstanding the commitment once made by the Law Commission to the systematic reform and eventual codification of

---

[1] See, for example, the French *Code Civil*, Ch.VI.
[2] See, for example, *Code Civil*, art.212: "Les epoux se doivent mutuellement fidélité secours, assistance".
[3] *Code Civil*, art.215.
[4] *Code Civil*, Title V.

family law,[5] and the cascade[6] of legislation[7] affecting the family) no such comprehensive statement is to be found. Civil partners have the advantage that the law applicable to their relationship is set out in one statute, rather than scattered through many, but they would search its 264 sections and 30 Schedules in vain for any general statement of principle. Indeed, those coming to the English legal system from a different cultural background might well describe English family law as:

> "[L]ittle more than a jumble of procedures, couched almost entirely in terms of remedies rather than rights, moving directly from the formation of marriage to divorce or death, pausing only to give the parties the right to apply to the court for protection from violence."[8]

From this jumble of procedures certain general duties may be inferred, but the statute book is silent on certain basic points.

The failure to develop a systematic code is not unique to family law and can in part be attributed to the influence of certain common law doctrines, which were sufficiently all-encompassing to be applied to a variety of practical situations. How far these remain relevant to spouses, and indeed to civil partners,[9] and how far they have been supplanted or curtailed by statute is thus an appropriate starting point in considering the legal consequence of formalising a relationship. The chapter will then consider the existing statutory framework and will close with a brief discussion of the legal consequences of agreeing to formalise a relationship.

II. COMMON LAW DOCTRINES

A. The doctrine of legal unity

3–002 At common law, husband and wife were said[10] to be one person; and (as Blackstone put it):

---

[5] *Second Programme of Law Reform* (Law Com. No.14 (1967)), Item XIX. However, the Law Commission gradually retreated from the commitment to provide a comprehensive and logical formulation of the law governing family support obligations (see Working Paper No.9, 1967 and note S.M. Cretney, "The codification of family law" (1981) 44 M.L.R. 1 at 11, n.56), although it remains committed to the notion of codification in the sense of the systematic examination of various topics.

[6] *Hewer v Bryant* [1970] Q.B. 357 at 371, *per* Sachs L.J.

[7] The achievements of the Law Commission are summarised in the Commission's *Twenty-Eighth Annual Report 1993* (Law Com. No.233 (1994)), Pt III and see also Dame B. Hale, "Family law reform: whither or wither?" (1995) C.L.P. 217. Since that date the only family law project undertaken by the Commission has been that relating to the rights of cohabiting couples: see Ch.8.

[8] The words put into the mouth of a foreign enquirer by Cretney, "The codification of family law" at 9; cf. Hale "Family law reform".

[9] It is unlikely that any court would extend these doctrines to civil partnerships, which are a statutory creation with no common law past. However, an understanding of these common law doctrines is necessary to understand certain provisions of the 2004 Act, which effectively extend to civil partners the application of those statutes curtailing these doctrines.

[10] The doctrine in reality imperfectly represented the common law: see G. Williams, "The legal unity of husband and wife" (1947) 10 M.L.R. 16, at 18; *Midland Bank Trust Co Ltd v Green (No.3)* [1979] Ch. 496.

"[The] very being or legal existence of the woman is suspended during the marriage, or at least is incorporated and consolidated into that of the husband: under whose wing, protection, and *cover* she performs every-thing ... Upon this principle, of an union of person in husband and wife, depend almost all the legal rights, duties, and disabilities, that either of them acquire by marriage."[11]

In reality, the doctrine was not consistently applied, but it did provide an attractively simple explanation for many of the distinctive rules relating to the legal relations between spouses ranging from the common law rule that one spouse could not sue the other in tort[12] to the rule that a married woman automatically had the same legal domicile as her husband.[13] For years the unity doctrine continued to rear its head "hydra-like"[14]: as recently as 1978 the courts had to decide whether it was a good defence to a tort action in conspiracy that those involved were husband and wife and thus one person (it was held that it was not).[15] It is certainly true that the unity doctrine was a legal fiction, and it has been said that it had been so eroded by the judges (who created exception after exception to it) and cut down by statute after statute that "little of it remains".[16] But, this statement encapsulates one of the difficulties of providing a coherent account of the law; although it is true that usually answers will be found to questions about the legal consequences of marriage in one or more of a range of ill-related statutes, the difficulty is to know how much the "little" that remains of the doctrine of unity is still significant. Moreover, those aspects of the doctrine of unity that have been put on a statutory basis have been extended to civil partners.[17] For example, the 2004 Act prescribes that a civil partner cannot be prosecuted for conspiring with his or her partner,[18] thus extending to such

---

[11] W. Blackstone, *Commentaries on the Laws of England* (1765), Vol.1, p.430. This explains the use until well into the twentieth century of the Norman French expression "feme covert" to refer to a married woman. "Feme sole" meant an unmarried woman, whether spinster, widow or divorced.

[12] Abolished by the Law Reform (Husband and Wife) Act 1962, giving effect to recommendations of the Law Reform Committee (*9th Report*, Cmnd.1268); for civil partners, see Civil Partnership Act 2004 s.69. However, the court has a discretionary power to stay an action in certain circumstances (e.g. if it appears that no substantial benefit would accrue to either party from the continuance of the proceedings, or if the action relates to property and could more conveniently be disposed of by an application under the Married Women's Property Act 1882); and the legislation thus reflects a cautious approach to the desirability of litigation within the family. It seems that most actions between spouses are, in substance, actions by the two of them to recover compensation from an insurance company.

[13] Described as "the last barbarous relic of a wife's servitude": *Gray v Formosa* [1963] P. 259 at 267, *per* Lord Denning M.R. The rule was abolished by the Domicile and Matrimonial Proceedings Act 1973 s.1.

[14] S.N. Grant-Bailey, *Lush on the Law of Husband and Wife*, 4th edn (London: Stevens & Sons, 1933), p.58.

[15] *Midland Bank Trust Co Ltd v Green (No.3)* [1982] Ch. 529.

[16] *Midland Bank Trust Co Ltd v Green (No.3)* [1982] Ch. 529 at 538, *per* Lord Denning M.R.

[17] See, for example, the principle that one spouse has an unlimited insurable interest in the life of the other (so that a spouse may insure the other's life and recover the sum insured without needing to prove that the death has caused any financial loss): Life Assurance Act 1774; Civil Partnership Act 2004 s.253.

[18] Civil Partnership Act 2004 Sch.27 para.56, amending Criminal Law Act 1977 s.2(2)(a).

couples what has been described as "perhaps the last surviving application of the medieval axiom".[19] Its survival is, however, under threat: the Law Commission recently described the fact that spouses or civil partners who conspire with each other to commit a crime cannot be convicted of the crime of conspiracy as a "conspicuous anomaly"[20] and recommended the abolition of the rule.

B. The notion of consortium

3–003   The difficulty of giving a coherent account of the common law rules relating to the legal consequences of marriage is well exemplified by an attempt to state the contemporary relevance of the rather nebulous common law doctrine that husband and wife[21] became entitled to one another's *consortium*—in effect the right to the other's society, assistance, comfort and protection.[22] At one time the right to a spouse's company was enforceable against a recalcitrant spouse (by means of a decree for restitution of conjugal rights[23]) and against any third party who interfered with the relationships (by claiming damages of enticement, harbouring and adultery), but all of these actions were abolished in 1970,[24] by which time they had long been obsolete. And until 1982 the doctrine did have some practical significance as the basis on which a husband might bring an action in tort for the loss of the services or society of his wife when the latter had been injured by the negligent act of another.[25] This action, too, has now been abolished.[26]

But no statute has ever abolished the principle that spouses are entitled to consortium, and this principle may still be relevant in some circumstances. For example, in interpreting statutes in which the expression "living together" has

---

[19] S. Cretney, *Same-Sex Relationships: From 'Odious Crime' to 'Gay Marriage'* (Oxford: Oxford University Press, 2006), p.29.

[20] Law Commission, *Conspiracy and Attempts: A Consultation Paper* (Law Com. CP No.183 (2007)), para.1.42.

[21] Although, as Munby J. points out in *Sheffield City Council v E* [2004] EWHC 2808, para.125, in earlier centuries "the view would probably have been taken that although the husband had the right to his wife's consortium, she had not so much a reciprocal right to her husband's consortium as a correlative duty to give him her society and her services". Reciprocal rights to consortium were, however, confirmed in *Place v Searle* [1932] 2 K.B. 497.

[22] *Best v Samuel Fox & Co Ltd* [1952] A.C. 716 at 729, *per* Lord Goddard, and at 735, *per* Lord Reid. An echo of this—couched in terms of expectation rather than entitlement—may be found in the more recent case of *Sheffield City Council v E* [2004] EWHC 2808, para.132.

[23] Self-help was, however, discouraged (*R. v Jackson* [1891] 1 Q.B. 671) and it was held in *R. v Reid* [1973] Q.B. 299 that a husband no longer had any right to control his wife by physical force, and would be guilty of the crime of kidnapping if he forcibly removed her from the place where she wished to remain.

[24] By the Law Reform (Miscellaneous Provisions) Act 1970.

[25] See, for example, *Oakley v Walker* (1977) 121 S.J. 619.

[26] Administration of Justice Act 1982. There may apparently still be liability for loss of a wife's services if the loss is attributable to breach of contract: *Jackson v Watson & Sons* [1909] 2 K.B. 193. The question of whether damages should be available for the loss of a relative's society was a controversial one; the Administration of Justice Act 1982 followed the recommendation of the Law Commission (Law Com. No.56) that a spouse or parent should be entitled to a fixed sum of damages for "bereavement" against a person who had wrongfully caused death: Fatal Accidents Act 1976 s.1A, inserted by the Administration of Justice Act 1982 s.3.

been used (in the criminal law[27] and in relation to taxation[28] as well as in divorce matters[29]) it has been said[30] that:

"[The] law has regard to what is called the consortium of husband and wife, which is a kind of association only possible between husband and wife. A husband and wife are living together, not only when they are residing together in the same house, but also when they are living in different places, even if they are separated by the high seas, provided the consortium has not been determined."

The difficulty is, therefore, that under the case law system, judges may still reach decisions on the basis that the relationship of husband and wife (and perhaps[31] now that of civil partners) is in some sense "special"[32]; but it is not always easy to predict when they will do so. Nor is it likely that modern judges would be willing to echo their predecessors' views regarding the nature of the obligations that consortium entailed. As Munby J. pointed out in *Sheffield City Council v E*[33]:

"[T]o describe the 'natural relations' which spring from marriage as being 'protection on the part of the man, and submission on the part of the woman' sounds almost ludicrous to the modern ear ... Insofar as the concept of consortium—the sharing of a common home and a common domestic life, and the right to enjoy each other's society, comfort and assistance—still has any useful role to play, the rights of husband and wife must surely now be regarded as exactly reciprocal."

C. The common law right to maintenance

One aspect of the common law that remained of real significance until well into **3–004** the twentieth century was the principle (perhaps flowing from the doctrines of property law under which a husband became entitled to substantial interests in his wife's property[34]) that a husband had an obligation, "whether he wished that result or no", to support his wife "according to his estate and condition".[35]

---

[27] *R. v Creamer* [1919] 1 K.B. 564.
[28] *Eadie v IRC* [1924] 2 K.B. 198; *Nugent-Head v Jacob* [1948] A.C. 321; *Holmes v Mitchell* [1991] 2 F.L.R. 301.
[29] See, for example, *Santos v Santos* [1972] Fam. 247.
[30] *R. v Creamer* [1919] 1 K.B. 564 at 569, *per* Darling J.
[31] The equation (or not) of marriage and civil partnership in this respect would depend on why marriage is regarded as "special". Is it special simply because it is marriage? Or because the parties have formalised their relationship? Or because, in practice, married couples are perceived as behaving in a particular way? The first would preclude any similar treatment of civil partnerships, the second would require it and the third would depend on the empirical evidence—or rather judicial perceptions—regarding civil partners.
[32] See notably the decision in *Barclays Bank Plc v O'Brien* [1994] 1 A.C. 180.
[33] [2004] EWHC 2808, at para.130–1.
[34] See below, para.3–006.
[35] On the difficulties in enforcing this obligation, see the seventh edition of this work at pp.73–74.

Whereas the curtailment of the doctrine of unity and the concept of consortium occurred because they were increasingly anachronistic in view of the greater equality between spouses, this same trend led to legislation conferring mutual rights to maintenance between spouses (and now civil partners) and creating more effective enforcement mechanisms.[36] Such specific statutory obligations have now rendered the common law doctrines largely irrelevant. As Ward J. has put it[37]:

> "The strange state of our law is that there may be a so-called common law duty to maintain, but when one analyses what that duty is it seems effectively to come to nothing. Like so many rights, the right extends only so far as the remedy to enforce it extends ... the common law has no remedy. The remedies to enforce a duty to maintain are the statutory remedies which are variously laid down in numerous statutes."

III. THE STATUTORY FRAMEWORK

3–005   As noted in the introduction, there has been no comprehensive codification of English family law, and there are surprisingly large areas in which statute remains silent. Whilst English statutes seek to provide answers to all possible questions on issues within the scope of a particular Act of Parliament, they do not seek to lay down general principles that might be used as the basis for solving problems not part of the draftsman's remit at the time. This means that in many areas it is difficult to state the law save by reference to the underlying principle—implicit in the doctrine of the rule of law as conventionally expounded—that the law permits anything that is not expressly prohibited.[38] For these reasons, the reader cannot conscientiously be advised that the law governing the position of husband and wife, or even civil partners, is entirely founded on statute; but the statutory framework remains the main source of law. The following sections consider the statutory rights and duties imposed on spouses and civil partners in relation to property and finances, and then highlights some of the more important legal consequences of formal relationships in areas such as criminal law, contract, and tort.

A. Property: ownership and occupation
3–006   Under many legal systems the coming into existence of marriage has an important effect on the parties' property rights; in particular, in many systems,

---

[36] See below, para.3–014. In addition, it is important to note the continued relevance of one of the concerns that underpinned the husband's common law duty to maintain; namely, that individuals should not be allowed to abandon their families to be cared for at public expense: see Ch.6. On the details of the social security legislation, see N. Wikeley, "Family law and social security", in R. Probert (ed.) *Family Life and the Law: Under One Roof* (Aldershot: Ashgate, 2007).
[37] *Re C (A Minor) (Contribution Notice)* [1994] 1 F.L.R. 111 at 116.
[38] Thus, for example, there is no rule that a married woman must assume the name of her husband, or that a divorced woman may not use that of her husband, as long as no fraud is intended.

some or all of the parties' property becomes, as a result of their marriage, subjected to legal joint ownership.

English law never accepted a community regime in this sense; however, until the late nineteenth century, marriage had a most profound effect on property entitlement at common law, since husband and wife became legally one— although as Lord Denning put it in *Williams & Glyn's Bank Ltd v Boland*,[39] the husband was that one. In the absence of specific provision by settlement, much of the wife's property was vested in her husband; but in compensation she acquired a right to be supported by the husband and she also had certain rights to property after his death. In the nineteenth century there was a powerful movement of opinion[40] against the injustice caused by the common law rules, and in a series of enactments culminating in the Married Women's Property Act 1882, Parliament adopted the regime of "separate property", which had long been familiar to the upper and middle classes whose marriage settlements provided that the wife's capital should remain her separate property and not become subject to the common law rules. One result of the 1882 reform was that marriage no longer had any immediate effect on entitlement to property.[41]

The 1882 reform was intended to be beneficial to married women, and the introduction of separate property certainly did have advantages—for example, a married woman's earnings were thenceforth her own to do with as she wished, whereas at common law her earnings had belonged to her husband. Nevertheless, the Act introduced only a system of formal equality between husband and wife in respect of legal capacity to acquire and retain property, leaving untouched the socio-economic background whereby the respective roles conventionally taken by spouses determined their respective capacities to benefit from the legal system. The Act's shortcomings in achieving fairness in economic terms at the time of divorce eventually necessitated the creation of a statutory adjustive jurisdiction.[42] However, as Thorpe L.J. observed in *Tee v Tee and Hillman*,[43] the general principles of property law continue to be of primary importance to married couples when the dispute involves a third party (e.g. a creditor of one spouse). The creditor may be able to enforce his or her legal rights of recovery against the property of the debtor spouse; but he or she will not usually be entitled to attack property that is beneficially owned by the other spouse unless the spouse has joined in the transaction or done something else to justify the imposition of liability. In such cases the question of whether the non-debtor spouse has any proprietary interest in the family home assumes considerable importance.[44]

---

[39] [1979] Ch. 312 at 432.

[40] The fourth edition of this work, pp.625–634, contains a fuller account with more extensive references. For an account of the movement for reform in the nineteenth century, see L. Holcombe, *Wives and Property* (Oxford: Martin Robertson, 1983); and, for an excellent brief account, W.R. Cornish and G. de N. Clark, *Law and Society in England 1750–1950* (London: Sweet and Maxwell, 1989), pp.398–402.

[41] However, there is one long-standing non-statutory presumption that applies to transfer from husband to wife and fiancé to fiancée (but not between civil partners): namely, the presumption of advancement. This is considered in Ch.5.

[42] See Ch.13.

[43] [1999] 2 F.L.R. 613 at 619.

[44] On the rules to be applied in this context, see Ch.5.

It should be noted, however, that the purity of the regime of separation of property during marriage in English law has been eroded by a number of piecemeal statutory reforms of the latter part of the twentieth century; in addition to provisions dealing with housekeeping allowances and the impact of improvements to the shared home, the law has also created statutory "home rights". The first, being sex-specific, has not been extended to civil partners; the latter two, in common with other statutory provisions relating to spouses, have. It should also be noted that a special summary procedure is available[45] for the determination of disputes about the title to or possession of property between would-be,[46] current or former[47] spouses and civil partners,[48] irrespective of the value of the property in issue. The Married Women's Property Act procedure does not enable the court to vary property rights,[49] but it is said[50] that the summary procedure will be quicker, simpler and cheaper than an ordinary action.[51]

i. Housekeeping Allowances

3–007 At common law, if a husband provided his wife with an allowance out of his income for housekeeping, any sums not spent on this purpose remained his, and he was entitled to any property bought with such savings.[52]

This rule seemed symptomatic of the injustices done to married women (particularly those who devoted their lives to looking after the home). The Morton Commission[53] therefore recommended that savings made out of a housekeeping allowance should belong half to the husband and half to the wife. The Married Women's Property Act 1964 accordingly provided:

> "If any question arises as to the right of a husband or wife to money derived from any allowance made by the husband for the expenses of the matrimonial home or for similar purposes, or to any property acquired out of such money, the money or property shall, in the absence of any agreement between them to the contrary, be treated as belonging to the husband and wife in equal shares."

---

[45] Married Women's Property Act 1882 s.17.

[46] Law Reform (Miscellaneous Provisions) Act 1970 s.2.

[47] Matrimonial Property and Proceedings Act 1970 s.39.

[48] Civil Partnerships Act 2004 s.66.

[49] *Pettitt v Pettitt* [1970] A.C. 777.

[50] By the Law Commission in its *Report on Domestic Violence and Occupation of the Family Home* (Law Com. No.207 (1992)), para.6–014.

[51] In 1995 the Government accepted the Law Commission's recommendation that the summary procedure should be made available to cohabitants and former cohabitants, and provision to that effect was included in the Family Homes and Domestic Violence Bill. However, this provision came to be seen by some as symptomatic of that Bill's failure to uphold the institution of marriage, and it is not reproduced in the 1996 Act. It may be that opposition to the proposed change did not appreciate its extremely limited scope.

[52] *Blackwell v Blackwell* [1943] 2 All E.R. 579; *Hoddinott v Hoddinott* [1949] 2 K.B. 406. The law was reviewed by the Law Commission, *Matrimonial Property* (Law Com. No.175 (1989)).

[53] *Royal Commission on Marriage and Divorce Report 1951–1955* (Cmd.9678 (1956)), para.701.

This provision therefore confers a genuine proprietary interest in such savings; it applies both during the marriage and when it comes to an end, and may assume some importance on death and insolvency. However, the ambit of the provision is unclear[54]; it is uncertain what would count as an "allowance"[55] or an "expense"[56] for these purposes, or what would fall within the scope of property "acquired out of" the money in question.[57] Even when the legal effect of the Act is clear, the consequences sometimes seem bizarre. First, the Act creates a tenancy in common, so that the fund will be held jointly by the spouses during their lives, but on death the share passes under the deceased's will or intestacy. Secondly, if a wife buys something obviously intended for her own personal use (e.g. jewellery), the Act apparently entitles the husband to a half share in it (unless the courts find there is an implied agreement to the contrary).

Although the Act has been on the statute book for over four decades, it has rarely been referred to and seems to have had little effect on decisions. In practical terms, the ancillary relief jurisdiction that operates on divorce is the principal forum in which disputes over property between husband and wife are determined.[58] Moreover, while the legislation may have met a particular grievance of married women at the time it was passed, the assumptions on which it was based now appear somewhat outdated; it perpetuates the stereotype under which a husband provides an allowance for his wife.[59] Because of its sex-specific nature (it has no effect on provision made by a wife for her husband), it has not been extended to civil partners, and it has been argued that it should be repealed.[60]

ii. Improvements to the home

One of the ways in which the courts tried to give effect to the partnership idea of marriage was to hold that a spouse who contributed in money or in labour to the improvement of the matrimonial home should be given credit on any realisation of the house for a proportion of the value, insofar as it was attributable to the work done in improving the property.[61] However, it was never clear on

3–008

---

[54] The defects of the law were fully analysed by the Law Commission in PWP No.90, *Transfer of Money between Spouses* (1985).

[55] For example, would it cover the case where the wife has a power to draw on the husband's bank account?

[56] It is not, for example, clear whether payment of mortgage instalments is to be regarded as "an expense of the matrimonial home" or an expense of acquiring it: *Tymosczuk v Tymosczuk* (1964) 108 S.J. 656.

[57] For example, if part of the allowance is "invested" in a ticket in the National Lottery, are any winnings "derived from" the allowance? Cf. *Hoddinott v Hoddinott* [1949] 2 K.B. 406.

[58] Discussed in Ch.13.

[59] On the prevalence of this practice, see J. Pahl, *Money and Marriage* (London: Macmillan, 1989), Table 5.3; C. Vogler, M. Brockmann, and R. Wiggins, "Intimate relationships and changing patterns of money management at the beginning of the twenty-first century" (2006) 57 *The British Journal of Sociology* 455; C. Burgoyne et al., "'All my worldly goods I share with you?' Managing money at the transition to heterosexual marriage" (2006) 54 *The Sociological Review* 619.

[60] See Ch.8.

[61] See *Appleton v Appleton* [1965] 1 W.L.R. 25 at 28 and 29; *Jansen v Jansen* [1965] P. 478.

precisely what juristic basis such a claim could be founded,[62] and the Matrimonial Proceedings and Property Act 1970 was an attempt to remove uncertainty.[63] Section 37 provides:

> "It is hereby declared that where a husband or wife contributes in money or money's worth to the improvement of real or personal property in which or in the proceeds of sale of which either or both of them has or have a beneficial interest, the husband or wife so contributing shall, if the contribution is of a substantial nature and subject to any agreement between them to the contrary express or implied, be treated as having then acquired by virtue of his or her contribution a share or an enlarged share, as the case may be, in that beneficial interest of such an extent as may have been then agreed or, in default of such agreement, as may seem in all the circumstances just to any court before which the question of the existence or extent of the beneficial interest of the husband or wife arises (whether in proceedings between them or in any other proceedings)."

This rule does not alter the basic law of property as to the effect of improvements[64] since it applies only to contributions by a spouse or civil partner[65] (or by persons who have agreed to marry or enter into a civil partnership).[66] It does, however, allow the court to confer a genuine proprietary right that will be recognised in bankruptcy or for succession[67] purposes. It is also relevant to all types of property, real or personal. Since it is not limited to a house bought as a home for the parties, there seems to be no reason why it should not be invoked in relation to business assets, for example—although no doubt in the nature of things it is most likely to be invoked in respect of home improvements.[68]

The limitations of the provision should, however, be noted. The focus on "improving" the property would seem to exclude day-to-day maintenance or repairs.[69] It has also been held that the contribution must be identifiable with the relevant improvement; mere general contributions to looking after the home will

---

[62] Although see the explanation given by Lord Denning M.R. in *Davis v Vale* [1971] 1 W.L.R. 1022 at 1025–1026.

[63] See Law Com. No.25 (1969), para.56. The Act is declaratory, and in a number of cases the significance of improvements has been determined without any specific reference to the legislation: see, for example, *Re Pavlou (A Bankrupt)* [1993] 2 F.L.R. 751; *Midland Bank v Cooke* [1995] 2 F.L.R. 915.

[64] On which see para.5–023.

[65] Civil Partnerships Act 2004, s.65.

[66] Law Reform (Miscellaneous Provisions) Act 1970 s.2(1); Civil Partnerships Act 2004 s.74.

[67] *Re Nicholson, (dec'd)* [1974] 1 W.L.R. 476. Cf. *Samuel's Trustee v Samuel* (1975) 233 E.G. 149.

[68] *Kowalczuk v Kowalczuk* [1973] 1 W.L.R. 930. It was not referred to in relation to the enhancement of the home for the purposes of running a bed-and-breakfast business in *Le Foe v Le Foe and Woolwich plc* [2001] 2 F.L.R. 970.

[69] In *Re Nicholson (dec'd)* [1974] 1 W.L.R. 476 Pennycuick V.C. suggests that a replacement may not constitute an improvement. This must, however, be a question of degree. The distinction may result in some curious anomalies: if a husband who is a jobbing builder takes time off from work to carry out extensive repairs to the roof or structure of the house, or is an electrician who rewires the house, neither of these expensive services seems to give him any claim under the Act. But he does have a claim if he installs a prefabricated garage, although the value of this work is much less.

not suffice.[70] A change to the property may be regarded as an "improvement" even if it has not increased the value of the property; however, whether or not it has increased its value may be taken into account in deciding whether it is "just" to grant the contributor a beneficial interest.[71]

In addition, the contribution must be "of a substantial nature". This is intended **3–009** to prevent a claim arising in the case of the minor "do-it-yourself job which husbands often do".[72] It is not, however, necessary that the claimant should have personally carried out the work; sums expended in paying a contractor to carry out the work will also be regarded as a relevant contribution for these purposes.[73]

The provisions of the Act yield to agreement between the parties, whether express or implied from their conduct. The agreement may be negative (i.e. that, notwithstanding the work, no interest shall be acquired) or positive (e.g. that the shares shall be a certain percentage of the proceeds of sale). On the strict wording of the Act, the agreement must be contemporaneous with the improvement.

In evaluating the share or enhanced share[74] that is to be awarded to the party making the contribution, the court's discretion is limited,[75] and it seems that the court will, in principle, assess the outcome by reference to the increase in the value of the property that can be attributed to the improvements.[76] In practice, s.37 has rarely been invoked: it may assume some significance if there is a dispute as to the parties' respective property rights and the only contribution made by the claimant is an improvement to the property; but, on divorce, the courts have consistently indicated a preference for exercising their wide powers to reallocate property without determining the parties' precise property interests.[77]

---

[70] *Harnett v Harnett* [1973] Fam. 156 (appeal dismissed [1974] 1 W.L.R. 219); *Kowalczuk v Kowalczuk* [1974] 1 W.L.R. 933.

[71] *Hosking v Michaelides* [2004] All E.R. (D) 147.

[72] *Button v Button* [1968] 1 W.L.R. 457 at 461, *per* Lord Denning M.R. The Act has been held to apply to payments made to have a house connected to the electricity supply, and for installing a water heater, sink unit, three fireplaces, a wall and iron gates (*Davis v Vale* [1971] 1 W.L.R. 1022) and to the installation of a central heating system (*Re Nicholson (dec'd)* [1974] 1 W.L.R. 476).

[73] *Griffiths v Griffiths* [1974] 1 W.L.R. 1350 and *Re Nicholson (dec'd)* [1974] 1 W.L.R. 476.

[74] If the parties are joint tenants, the acquisition of an enlarged share under the Act would apparently operate to sever the joint tenancy by destroying the unity of interest.

[75] Law Com. No.25 (1969), para.58, and explanatory note to draft cl.27.

[76] *Re Nicholson (dec'd)* [1974] 1 W.L.R. 1350; *Griffiths v Griffiths* [1973] 1 W.L.R. 1454 (Arnold J.). Strictly, it may be that the court should assess the value of the property prior to each improvement calculate the increase in value then brought about by the improvement and enlarge the share of the improving spouse accordingly. But a calculation of this kind would be difficult to carry out in cases where there has been a series of improvements, and particularly if there is no satisfactory evidence of value. In such cases the court will probably "look at the situation in the round, to see what has been achieved by means of the improvements" in relation to the value of the house: *Griffiths v Griffiths* [1973] 1 W.L.R. 1454 at 1457, *per* Arnold J.; and see *Re Nicholson, (dec'd)* [1974] 1 W.L.R. 1350 at 482–483. Of course, improvements "may add not one penny to the value of the house (see, for example, *Hosking v Michaelides* [2004] All E.R. (D) 147). Indeed, the alteration may even lower its value, "for the alteration, though convenient to the owner, may be highly inconvenient in the eyes of a purchaser", *per* Lord Greene M.R., *Re Diplock* [1948] Ch. 465 at 546.

[77] See, for example, *Wachtel v Wachtel* [1973] 2 W.L.R. 84; *Griffiths v Griffiths* [1974] 1 W.L.R. 1350.

iii. Occupation of the home

3–010   At common law, a wife had a right to be provided by her husband with a suitable home; but in 1965 the House of Lords held[78] that this right was a purely personal right, not attaching to any particular house and of its nature incapable of binding third parties. A man might, therefore, without consulting his wife, mortgage the family home, and the wife would—unless she could establish that she was entitled to a beneficial interest that bound the purchasers[79]—have no defence to an action for possession brought by the lender to enforce the security. The Matrimonial Homes Act 1967 was enacted to remedy this situation, which it did by conferring on a spouse who lacked any proprietary interest in the matrimonial home a right not to be evicted or excluded from the home without leave of the court, and by providing machinery whereby that right could, by registration, be made to bind purchasers (such as mortgagees) or other third parties. Those rights (now called "home rights" and extended to civil partners) are now contained in Pt IV of the Family Law Act 1996, being defined as[80]:

- if in occupation, a right[81] not to be evicted or excluded from the dwelling house[82] or any part of it by the other spouse or civil partner except with the leave of the court;

- if not in occupation, a right with the leave of the court so given to enter into and occupy the dwelling house.

We will meet such rights again when considering the jurisdiction of the court to make an "occupation order"[83] and the protection afforded to a home in case of bankruptcy.[84] This section focuses on those rights unique to spouses and civil partners; namely, the way in which such persons may protect their occupation rights against third parties dealing with the property.

---

[78] *National Provincial Bank Ltd v Ainsworth* [1965] A.C. 1175.
[79] Usually under the doctrines of implied, resulting or constructive trust: see *Williams & Glyn's Bank Ltd v Boland* [1981] A.C. 487, and Ch.5.
[80] Family Law Act 1996 s.30(2). The definition is in substance identical to the definition of "rights of occupation" contained in the Matrimonial Homes Act 1983 s.1(1)(a). For a penetrating analysis of the concept, see *Wroth v Tyler* [1974] Ch. 30, *per* Megarry J.
[81] The nature of which was discussed by Thorpe L.J. in *Foulkes v Chief Constable of Merseyside Police* [1998] 2 F.L.R. 789 at 796.
[82] "Dwelling house" is defined as including "(a) any building or part of a building which is occupied as a dwelling, (b) any caravan, house-boat or structure which is occupied as a dwelling, and any yard, garden, garage or outhouse belonging to it and occupied with it": Family Law Act 1996 s.63(1). Home rights do not arise in respect of a house that has at no time been, and which was at no time intended by the parties to be, their home: s.30(7). A spouse or civil partner may be entitled to home rights in respect of more than one house (e.g. a town house and a country cottage), but registration may only be effected in respect of one of them: Family Law Act 1996 Sch.4 para.2.
[83] It was held in *Richards v Richards* [1984] 1 A.C. 174 that the legislation—then the Matrimonial Homes Act 1983—codified the jurisdiction of the court in relation to ouster proceedings between spouses, and that applications during the marriage for orders relating to the occupation of the matrimonial home should accordingly be made under that Act. The jurisdiction of the court in this regard is discussed in Ch.9.
[84] See Ch.5.

(1) Who is entitled to home rights?

As explained above, the concern of the Matrimonial Homes Act 1967 was to **3–011** protect a spouse (usually a wife) who was vulnerable because she had no recognised property right in the home; this concern is reflected in the definition now embodied in the Family Law Act 1996. A spouse or civil partner has home rights if the other party "is entitled to occupy a dwelling house by virtue of a beneficial estate or interest or contract"[85] or "by virtue of any enactment giving that [party] the right to remain in occupation" and the applicant spouse or civil partner is not so entitled.[86] In effect, therefore, it is only a "non-owning" spouse or civil partner who is entitled to home rights.[87]

(2) Making home rights bind third parties

Although, on a strict analysis, home rights are personal in nature[88] (so that they **3–012** cannot be assigned[89] and will come to an end on termination of the relationship by death or legal process[90] unless the court has otherwise ordered[91]), the legislation provides machinery whereby they may be protected—almost as if they were property rights—against third parties. The legislation[92] provides that where at any time during the subsistence of a marriage or civil partnership one of the parties is entitled to occupy a dwelling house by virtue of a beneficial estate or interest, then the other's home rights[93] are a charge on that estate or interest that has the same priority:

> "[A]s if it were an equitable interest created at whichever is the latest of the following dates—
>
> (a) the date on which the [entitled spouse or civil partner] acquires the estate or interest,
> (b) the date of the marriage or formation of the civil partnership, and
> (c) January 1, 1968 . . . "[94]

---

[85] See, for example, *Moore v Moore* [2004] EWCA Civ 1243.
[86] Family Law Act 1996 s.30(1).
[87] In principle, a beneficial interest will bind third parties. However, Family Law Act 1996 s.30(9) provides that a spouse or civil partner who has only an equitable interest shall be treated "for the purpose only of determining whether he has home rights as not being entitled to occupy the dwelling-house by virtue of that interest", thus ensuring that such a person will be entitled to home rights capable of protection by registration. For the evolution of the law, see the fourth edition of this work at pp.247–248.
[88] Considered in the context of entitlement to bring an action in private nuisance by the House of Lords in *Hunter v Canary Wharf Ltd* [1997] A.C. 666; for a critical comment on the decision, see S. Cretney [1997] Fam. Law 601.
[89] *Wroth v Tyler* [1974] Ch. 30 at 45, *per* Megarry J.
[90] *O'Malley v O'Malley* [1982] 1 W.L.R. 244.
[91] Family Law Act 1996 s.33(5).
[92] Family Law Act 1996 s.31(1), (2), (3).
[93] Family Law Act 1996 includes a number of complex provisions dealing with the (unusual) case where the dwelling house is a trust property and a married couple, or civil partners, are living there because one of them is a beneficiary. These refinements are ignored in the explanation given in the text.
[94] The date of the commencement of the Matrimonial Homes Act 1967.

The charge must, if it is to bind third parties, be protected by registering[95] a notice under the Land Registration Act 2002[96] or (if the title is not registered) by registering it as a Class F Land Charge under the provisions of the Land Charges Act 1972.[97] Unless and until so registered, the charge will be void against a purchaser (including a mortgagee) of the land or of any interest therein.[98]

The legislation thus reconciles the conflicting policies of giving protection to a non-owning spouse or civil partner and yet enabling transactions in land to take place without the purchaser having to make difficult and embarrassing inquiries about the vendor's matrimonial status. An intending purchaser searches for land charges as a matter of routine. If the search[99] reveals no charge, the purchaser can be confident that no home right can be asserted against the title.

3–013   It may be helpful to give an illustration of the working of these provisions:

> Suppose that H (who is married to W) buys[100] Blackacre as a matrimonial home. At that moment a charge attaches to it in W's favour. But if, as is commonly done, H immediately on the same day mortgages the property to a building society, the wife's charge will not bind the building society.[101] This is because the charge was not protected by registration at the time that the mortgage was created. Hence, if H defaults on the mortgage payments, the building society will be entitled to enforce the mortgage by possession, sale or other means.[102]
>
> If W does register a Class F charge after completion of the purchase and mortgage, her right will bind subsequent purchasers so that if, for example, H were to contract a second mortgage, the second mortgagee would take subject to W's rights.

In practice it is of course most improbable that a mortgagee would knowingly grant a mortgage subject to another's rights of occupation.[103] Accordingly, in

---

[95] Notice of the registration will be served upon the registered proprietor: see Form MH1.

[96] Family Law Act 1996 s.31(10).

[97] Land Charges Act 1972 s.2(7).

[98] Land Charges Act 1972 s.4(8). It is expressly provided that home rights do not constitute an interest that overrides under the Land Registration Act 2002: Family Law Act 1996 s.31(10)(b).

[99] A purchaser will only be protected by an official certificate of search: cf. *Kaur v Gill* [1988] Fam. Law 110, where a purchaser who relied on a telephone inquiry was not protected. For a discussion of the advantages and disadvantages of the registration requirement, see the fourth edition of this work at pp.259–260.

[100] Note that the protection afforded to a tenant is also limited in the absence of registration: *Sanctuary Housing v Campbell* [1999] 2 F.L.R. 383.

[101] Although the wife will be entitled to meet the mortgage payments (Family Law Act 1996 s.30(5)) and has certain procedural protection in possession proceedings: see Family Law Act 1996 ss.54–56.

[102] However, the legislation contains important provisions whereby a spouse may make payments of mortgage instalments, rent and other outgoings which (in effect) have to be accepted as if made by the mortgagor or tenant; a spouse may thus be able to avoid a default situation arising: see now Family Law Act 1996 s.30(3). The court has power to order a party to make payments (s.40), although this provision is apparently unenforceable: *Nwogbe v Nwogbe* [2000] 2 F.L.R. 744. The Act also confers certain procedural protection in respect of mortgage enforcement: see ss.54–56.

[103] But for an unusual case in which a purchaser was bound by the wife's matrimonial home right, see *Kaur v Gill* [1988] Fam. 110 (in which, under the legislation then in force, the Court of Appeal refused to make an order in favour of the wife giving her an exclusive right to occupy).

practice—even if not in theory—registration of one party's rights may well prevent the other from dealing with the property at all without the consent of the first.[104] One party may, therefore, be tempted to register a charge as a tactical device to exert pressure on the other to come to some financial arrangement. To act in this way is to misuse the legislation,[105] but it is not easy to ensure that such misuse does not occur.

B. Finances: maintenance orders and agreements

The court has wide powers to make financial orders when a marriage or civil **3–014** partnership is annulled or brought to an end.[106] This chapter, by contrast, is concerned with those powers that are available while a marriage or civil partnership is still subsisting.[107] We will look first at the court's powers to make maintenance orders, and then turn to the extent to which agreements between spouses will be upheld by the courts.

i. Maintenance orders

The importance of the parties' status in this context was emphasised by Wall L.J. **3–015** in *Harb v King Fahd*[108]:

"That the right to make a claim for financial relief in matrimonial proceedings is exclusively dependent upon the status of the applicant is also demonstrated by the fact that whereas an unmarried heterosexual couple living together as man and wife may well create a situation in which one is dependent upon the other, the dependent party has no common law right to financial support from the other during the latter's lifetime. Many think this creates an injustice, but it will require legislation to correct it, in the same way that it has required the Civil Partnership Act 2004 to extend such rights to same-sex couples."

Three procedures are available:

(1) Application may be made under the Domestic Proceedings and Magistrates' Courts Act 1978, or under Sch.6 of the Civil Partnership Act 2004, to magistrates sitting as a family proceedings court.[109]

(2) Application may be made to a County Court or High Court under s.27 of the Matrimonial Causes Act 1973, or Sch.5 of the Civil Partnership

---

[104] The legislation provides that a person entitled to a charge may postpone or release it: Family Law Act 1996 Sch.4 paras 5, 6 (and, for an example of a case in which this was done, see *Banco Exterior Internacional v Mann* [1995] 1 F.L.R. 602). The Act also contains a provision protecting the position of a contracting purchaser; Sch.4 para.3.

[105] *Barnett v Hassett* [1981] 1 W.L.R. 1385

[106] See Ch.13, below.

[107] It should be noted that the practical significance of these powers is much reduced now that divorce is more widely available.

[108] [2005] EWCA Civ 1324, para.59.

[109] Magistrates' Courts Act 1980 ss.65(1)(j), 67, as amended.

Act 2004, on the ground that the respondent has failed to provide reasonable maintenance for the applicant or for a child of the family.

(3) A spouse may seek a decree of judicial separation, or a civil partner a separation order, and the court may exercise wide powers to make orders for financial provision and property adjustment in such cases.

As noted above, spouses and civil partners now owe each other reciprocal obligations of support, so either may apply for an order via any of these three procedures.

(1) Financial Orders in Magistrates' Courts[110]

3–016   The court has power to make financial[111] orders if the applicant can establish one of the grounds set out in the Domestic Proceedings and Magistrates' Courts Act 1978, or (for civil partners) in Sch.6 of the 2004 Act. The court is also given power to make certain financial orders in cases where the parties are living apart by agreement,[112] and to make consent orders in relation to payments that have been agreed by the parties.

3–017   **(a) Applications under s.1.** An applicant may seek a financial order on the grounds that the other party has failed to provide reasonable maintenance for the applicant; or has failed to provide, or to make proper contribution towards, reasonable maintenance for any child of the family[113]; or has behaved in such a way that the applicant cannot reasonably be expected to live with the other party; or has deserted[114] the applicant.[115]

---

[110] For the history, see the *Report of the Committee on One-Parent Families* (Cmnd.5629 (1974)); and for a brief account, the fifth edition of this work at p.353. The Domestic Proceedings and Magistrates' Courts Act 1978 gave effect to recommendations made by the Law Commission in its *Report on Matrimonial Proceedings in Magistrates' Courts* (Law Com. No.77 (1976)).

[111] For the court's powers to make residence and other orders relating to children, see Pt V.

[112] The 1978 Act introduced a complex provision empowering the court to make an order in favour of a spouse living apart from the other by agreement for periodical payments of a similar amount to those made voluntarily in the previous three months: Domestic Proceedings and Magistrates' Courts Act 1978 s.7. However, it appears that this well-intentioned provision is rarely invoked in practice, and for that reason it is not discussed in the text of this edition. For the background and a brief discussion see the fifth edition of this book at pp.361–362; for the equivalent provision in the Civil Partnership Act, see Sch.6 para.15.

[113] The expression "child of the family" is very widely defined in the Act (see s.88) and extends to any child of the parties and to other children—most obviously, stepchildren—"treated" as a child of the spouses' family. In practice, orders will now rarely be made in favour of a child of the parties because of the provisions of the Child Support Act 1991 s.8(1). However, it seems that the court could make an order in favour of the mother on proof that there had been neglect of the child (see *Northrop v Northrop* [1968] P. 74), and that its power to do so is not affected by the fact that a child support officer has jurisdiction to make a maintenance assessment: see Child Support Act 1991 s.8(11) defining "maintenance order" in terms of orders "to or for the benefit of the child".

[114] Desertion has the same meaning as in the law of divorce (see para.10–027), but under the 1978 Act no minimum period of desertion need be satisfied.

[115] Domestic Proceedings and Magistrates' Courts Act 1978 s.1 and Civil Partnerships Act 2004 Sch.6 para.1.

If the applicant satisfies the court of a ground of complaint, the court may[116] make an order for periodical payments[117] or for a lump sum.[118] However, the powers of the magistrates' court are significantly more limited than those of the divorce court: there is no power to order that the periodical payment be secured, and any lump sum ordered (whether for the applicant or a child of the family[119]) may not exceed £1,000.[120]

It is provided that where an application is made for a financial order on one of the grounds set out above the court must have regard to all the circumstances of the case, first consideration being given to the welfare, while a minor, of any child of the family who has not attained the age of 18. The Act also sets out a number of factors—similar to those governing the exercise of the court's powers when reallocating assets on divorce or dissolution[121]—to which the court is required to have particular regard.[122] The emphasis is, in practice, likely to be on determining how the reasonable needs of the family can best be met in the light of the resources that are available.[123]

(b) Consent orders. The 1978 Act gives magistrates the power to make consent **3–018** orders. Either party may apply to the court on the ground that the applicant or the other party has agreed to make financial provision for the other or a child of the family.[124] The court may order that the agreed financial provision be made,[125]

---

[116] Domestic Proceedings and Magistrates' Courts Act 1978 s.2; Civil Partnerships Act 2004 Sch.6 para.1.

[117] The court has a flexible power to make weekly, monthly or other periodical orders; any order may be for a limited or unlimited period (see, e.g., *Khan v Khan* [1980] 1 W.L.R. 355). On the enforcement of orders, see generally Ch.14.

[118] For the purpose of enabling any liability or expenses reasonably incurred in maintaining the applicant, or any child of the family, before the making of the order to be met: Domestic Proceedings and Magistrates' Courts Act 1978 s.2(2); Civil Partnerships Act 2004 Sch.6 para.3(1).

[119] A lump sum may be ordered in favour of a child even if a child support officer has jurisdiction to make an assessment under the Child Support Act 1991: see further Ch.15.

[120] It has been held that the power to award a lump sum is not to be limited to cases where the other party has capital available, since in an appropriate case the payment could be made out of earnings: *Burridge v Burridge* [1983] Fam. 9. The court may order payment by instalments (Magistrates' Courts Act 1980 s.75(1)), and the instalments may be varied (Domestic Proceedings and Magistrates' Courts Act 1978 s.22; Civil Partnerships Act 2004 Sch.6 para.41).

[121] See further Ch.13.

[122] Domestic Proceedings and Magistrates' Courts Act 1978 s.3(2) and (in relation to orders in favour of children of the family) s.3(3), (4); Civil Partnerships Act 2004 Sch.6 paras 5(2), 6(2) and 6(3). The court should make findings in respect of each of the matters referred to in the statute: *Vasey v Vasey* [1985] F.L.R. 596 at 603.

[123] *Stockford v Stockford* [1981] 3 F.L.R. 58 at 63, *per* Ormrod L.J. See, for example, *Titheradge v Titheradge* (1983) 4 F.L.R. 552; *E v C (Child Maintenance)* [1996] 1 F.L.R. 472; and *B v B (Periodical Payments: Transitional Provisions)* [1995] 1 F.L.R. 459, discussed in more detail in the seventh edition of this work at pp.81–82.

[124] Domestic Proceedings and Magistrates' Courts Act 1978 s.6 (as amended by Matrimonial and Family Proceedings Act 1984 s.10, to enable an order to be made on the application of either the payer or the payee); Civil Partnerships Act 2004 Sch.6 para.9. At one time, the making of a consent order could result in significant tax savings, but changes in tax law have now virtually extinguished this advantage. A consent order does still give the payee the advantage of having a comparatively easily enforceable right and it gives the payer some limited security against allegations that he has failed to provide for the family. But these advantages will rarely justify incurring the expense involved in obtaining a court order.

[125] Domestic Proceedings and Magistrates' Courts Act 1978 s.6(1)(a); Civil Partnerships Act 2004 Sch.6 para.9(2).

provided: (1) that there is proof of the agreement[126]; and (2) that the court has no reason to think that it would be contrary to the interests of justice to do so.[127]

3–019   **(c) Effect of cohabitation, divorce and remarriage.** An order can be obtained notwithstanding that the parties are living with each other at the date of the making of the order.[128] However, if they continue to live with each other, or subsequently resume living with each other for a continuous period of six months or more, any periodical payment order for a spouse or civil partner[129] ceases to be enforceable.[130] Orders do not automatically come to an end on divorce[131] or dissolution, and in the past they were often allowed to continue in force. However, periodical payment orders in favour of a spouse or civil partner (but not those in favour of a child) do automatically come to an end if he or she formalises a new relationship,[132] even if the new union is void or voidable.[133]

3–020   **(d) Variation of orders.** The court has power to vary or revoke periodical payment orders[134] (including interim orders),[135] but it has no power to vary a lump sum order. It may increase or decrease periodical payments and add a lump sum order[136] (not exceeding the maximum of £1,000).[137] There is power to suspend any periodical payments order[138] (e.g. while the other party is unemployed[139]) and subsequently to revive it.

---

[126] Domestic Proceedings and Magistrates' Courts Act 1978 s.6(1)(a); s.6(8); Civil Partnerships Act 2004 Sch. 6 para.9(2)(a).
[127] Domestic Proceedings and Magistrates' Courts Act 1978 s.6(1)(b); Civil Partnerships Act 2004 Sch.6 para.9(2)(b).
[128] Domestic Proceedings and Magistrates' Courts Act 1978 s.25(1); Civil Partnerships Act 2004 Sch.6 para.29(1), (2).
[129] But not orders for children unless the court otherwise directs: Domestic Proceedings and Magistrates' Courts Act 1978 s.25(2); Civil Partnerships Act 2004 Sch.6 para.29(4).
[130] The question of whether the court should have the power to make an order whilst the parties were living under the same roof was for a long time controversial: see S.M. Cretney, *Law, Law Reform and the Family* (Oxford: Clarendon Press, 1998), p.172; and see the discussion in Law Com. No.77 (1976), paras 2.58–2.65.
[131] *Wood v Wood* [1957] P. 254.
[132] Domestic Proceedings and Magistrates' Courts Act 1978 s.4(2); Civil Partnerships Act 2004 Sch.6 para.26(2).
[133] Domestic Proceedings and Magistrates' Courts Act 1978 s.88(3).
[134] Domestic Proceedings and Magistrates' Courts Act 1978 s.20(1); Civil Partnerships Act 2004 Sch.6 para.30(1).
[135] Domestic Proceedings and Magistrates' Courts Act 1978 s.20(3); Civil Partnerships Act 2004 Sch.6 para.30(2).
[136] Domestic Proceedings and Magistrates' Courts Act 1978 s.20(1); Civil Partnerships Act 2004 Sch.6 para.31(1).
[137] Or such larger amounts as may be specified at the time: Domestic Proceedings and Magistrates' Courts Act 1978 s.20(7); Civil Partnerships Act 2004 Sch.6 para.31(3).
[138] Domestic Proceedings and Magistrates' Courts Act 1978 s.20(6); Civil Partnerships Act 2004 Sch.6 para.30(1)(b).
[139] Law Com. No.77 (1976) para.4.53.

(2) Orders in the High Court and County Court on the Ground of Failure to Provide Reasonable Maintenance[140]

Either party to a subsisting marriage or civil partnership may apply to the court   **3–021**
for an order on the ground that the other party has failed to provide reasonable maintenance for the applicant or to provide (or to make a proper contribution towards) reasonable maintenance for any child of the family.[141]

(a) Factors to be taken into account. In exercising this discretion, the court is   **3–022**
directed to have regard to all the circumstances of the case (specifically including those factors to be taken into account when a court is considering what order to make in relation to the parties' assets on divorce or dissolution). Where an application is also made in respect of a child of the family under 18, first consideration must be given to the child's welfare.[142]

(b) Orders that can be made. The court may make orders for periodical   **3–023**
payments, unrestricted in amount, secured or unsecured. If secured, payments may continue during the applicant's life.[143] The court may also order payment of a lump sum.[144] The powers of the High Court and county court are thus wider than those of the magistrates, since in the superior courts there is no restriction on the size of lump sum awards. But the courts' powers are narrower than those available in divorce or dissolution in that there is no power to make any other capital provision order (e.g. to transfer a house or shares).

(c) Duration of orders. The fact that the parties cohabit after the making of an   **3–024**
order is not a bar to its being enforced. Orders do not automatically come to an end on divorce, but a subsequent marriage or civil partnership automatically brings any order for periodical payments to an end.[145]

(3) Orders in judicial separation
The court has power to make financial provision and property adjustment orders   **3–025**
in judicial separation proceedings in the same way as in divorce proceedings.[146] However, there is no power to make pension sharing orders in judicial separation proceedings.[147]

ii. Separation and maintenance agreements
A couple whose relationship is in difficulties might prefer to separate and to   **3–026**
regulate their financial affairs by private agreement rather than taking legal

---

[140] This jurisdiction is very little used: see, for example, *Harb v King Fahd* [2005] EWCA Civ 1324, para.29.
[141] Matrimonial Causes Act 1973 s. 27; Civil Partnerships Act 2004 Sch.5 para.39.
[142] Matrimonial Causes Act 1973 s.27(3); Civil Partnerships Act 2004 Sch.5 para.43(3).
[143] Matrimonial Causes Act 1973 s.27(6)(b), s.28(1)(b); Civil Partnerships Act 2004 Sch.5 para.47(3)(a).
[144] Matrimonial Causes Act 1973 s.27(6)(c); Civil Partnerships Act 2004 Sch.5 para.41(1)(c).
[145] Matrimonial Causes Act 1973 s.28; Civil Partnerships Act 2004 Sch.5 para.47(2)(b).
[146] Matrimonial Causes Act 1973 s.23; Civil Partnerships Act 2004 Sch.5 para.1(1).
[147] Welfare Reform and Pensions Act 1999 s.19 Sch.3 para.2; Civil Partnerships Act 2004 Sch.5 para.15.

proceedings; this was particularly true before divorce became readily available and acceptable.[148] However, should the law uphold a contract that seeks to vary rights and duties that have been conferred by statute? The general principle that has emerged is that husbands and wives may make legally enforceable agreements regulating their financial affairs, but that any such agreement may be varied by the court; the same approach is likely to be taken to civil partners. It is not possible by private agreement to oust the court's jurisdiction, but the outcome of the conflicting pressures that have led to this result is that the law governing the enforceability of separation and maintenance agreements is by no means straightforward.

(1) An enforceable contract?

3–027   The first question to be asked is whether the agreement is entitled to be regarded as an enforceable contract.[149] Although the initial assumption is that couples do not, in their ordinary day-to-day lives, usually intend to enter into enforceable contracts with one another,[150] if a couple decide, to separate and make an agreement to govern their future financial relationship, the court will usually be prepared to impute to them an intention to create legal relations.[151]

(2) Public policy

3–028   Maintenance agreements between spouses are also susceptible to attack on the ground that a particular provision is contrary to public policy,[152] and the authorities seem to support the following propositions. First, agreements or dispositions that tend to encourage the violation of the marriage tie are void.[153] Secondly, it is said to follow from this that an agreement between husband and wife whereby they make arrangements in the event of a future separation is void. Thirdly, if the husband and wife, while living apart, agree to resume cohabitation, enforceable financial arrangements may be made in the same agreement to take effect in the event of a future separation. This exception to the general principle is justified on the basis that such an agreement will promote rather than hinder reconciliation. The same policy considerations arguably apply to civil partners.

---

[148] For the position on divorce or dissolution, and the relevance of agreements between the parties in that context, see Ch.13.

[149] See para.5–004 on the requirements of a valid contract.

[150] *Pettitt v Pettitt* [1970] A.C. 777 at 816, *per* Lord Upjohn. For discussion and criticism, see C. Barton, "Contract—a justifiable taboo?", Ch.6 in R. Probert (ed.) *Family Life and the Law*, and see further para.5–005.

[151] *Merritt v Merritt* [1970] 1 W.L.R. 1211 (but cf. *per* Lord Denning M.R. at 1213, presumption in such circumstances of intention to create legal relations, and *per* Widgery L.J. at 1214, no presumption against creating such a relationship). See also *Peters (Executors) v IRC* [1941] 2 All E.R. 620; *Gould v Gould* [1970] 1 Q.B. 275.

[152] See, generally, *Fender v St John-Mildmay* [1938] A.C. 1.

[153] See, for example, *Re Johnson's Will Trusts* [1967] Ch. 387: provision providing that an annuity to the testator's daughter would be increased if she were divorced or separated held to be void because the condition might well influence the daughter's mind if she were contemplating separation or divorce.

Finally, an agreement may be attacked by one of the parties on the ground that it had been obtained by fraud,[154] duress, undue influence or by misrepresentation[155] (and in some circumstances that the agreement was vitiated by mistake[156]). In practice, however, the existence of the statutory power to vary maintenance agreements, coupled with the statutory rule that an agreement ousting the jurisdiction of the court is void (both of which matters are dealt with below) mean that it is rarely necessary to invoke these contractual doctrines in order to obtain a review of a private agreement.

(3) Final and conclusive?

Although the object of making a maintenance agreement was traditionally to settle the extent of a husband's obligations to his wife once and for all, whilst giving her the assurance that, come what may, she would be entitled to the stipulated provision, the law now makes it impossible to achieve such finality by private agreement. The statutory power[157] to vary maintenance agreements reflects the belief that, in principle, maintenance agreements should be binding and enforceable, but that either party should be able to seek a variation if fresh circumstances making the agreement inequitable had arisen.

3–029

(a) The meaning of "maintenance agreement". In brief, a maintenance agreement is an agreement in writing[158] made between spouses or civil partners and dealing with their financial arrangements or separation.[159] "Financial arrangements" are for this purpose given a broad definition,[160] encompassing "the making or securing of payments or the disposition or use of any property".[161]

3–030

(b) Void provisions. Any provisions purporting to restrict the right to apply to the court for financial provision are void,[162] but any other financial arrangements contained in the agreement are valid (unless they are void or unenforceable for

3–031

---

[154] *Allsop v Allsop* (1980) 124 S.J. 710.

[155] See *Barclays Bank plc v O'Brien* [1994] 1 A.C. 180; *Simpson v Simpson* [1992] 1 F.L.R. 602; *Bank of Commerce and Credit International SA v Aboody* [1990] 1 Q.B. 923; and see *Wales v Wadham* [1977] 1 W.L.R. 199.

[156] *Galloway v Galloway* (1914) 30 T.L.R. 531.

[157] Now contained in Matrimonial Causes Act 1973 ss.34–36; Civil Partnerships Act 2004 Sch.5 paras 68–70. Provision for the variation of agreements was first made by the Maintenance Agreements Act 1957, enacted to give effect to the recommendations of the Royal Commission on Marriage and Divorce (Cmd.9678 (1956)), Pt X.

[158] An oral maintenance agreement is enforceable (see *Peters v IRC* [1941] 2 All E.R. 620) but falls outside the provisions of the Act. Of much greater practical importance is the doctrine that the legal effect of an agreement that has been embodied in an order of the court derives from the *order*; and the terms of such an order cannot be varied in the same way as a maintenance agreement: see generally Ch.13 below.

[159] Matrimonial Causes Act 1973 s.34(2); Civil Partnerships Act 2004 Sch.5 para.67(1).

[160] Matrimonial Causes Act 1973 s.34(2); Civil Partnerships Act 2004 Sch.5 para.67(2).

[161] This would, for example, include an agreement about furnishings: see *D v D* (1974) 118 S.J. 715 (agreement to pay instalments for half-share of matrimonial home); *Sutton v Sutton* [1984] Ch. 184.

[162] See, for example, *Jessel v Jessel* [1979] 1 W.L.R. 1148 at 1152.

some other reason).[163] The agreement need not be made for the purpose of the parties living separately.[164]

3–032   **(c) Power to vary agreements.** It is provided[165] that if a maintenance agreement is for the time being subsisting,[166] either party[167] may apply to the court for a variation order. The court's powers on such an application are sweeping.[168] It may vary or revoke "financial arrangements" contained in the agreement or insert such arrangements for the benefit of a spouse or civil partner, or for a child of the family,[169] but as a condition precedent to the exercise of these powers, the court must be satisfied either that there has been a change in the circumstances in the light of which the agreement was made or that the agreement does not contain proper financial arrangements with respect to any child of the family.[170] However, the court may act even if the parties had directed their minds to the possibility of a particular change of circumstances.[171] A spouse or civil partner who has chosen to accept a lower but consistent income in preference to a higher but perhaps speculative and problematical income will be entitled to apply for a variation if the choice turns out to have been the wrong one. However, the fact that there is jurisdiction to entertain the application does not mean that it will be granted; the court will not act unless the change of circumstances has made the agreement unjust,[172] and, generally, the courts are reluctant to interfere with freely negotiated agreements entered into on the basis of a full knowledge of the relevant circumstances and on proper advice.[173]

C. Miscellaneous economic consequences

3–033   The above discussion has focused on the financial consequences of formalising a relationship in the context of disputes between the parties. Formal relationships, however, also have important consequences in terms of the financial benefits that flow from the status of the parties.

---

[163] Matrimonial Causes Act 1973 s.34(1); Civil Partnerships Act 2004 Sch.5 para.68(a).

[164] Matrimonial Causes Act 1973 s.34(2); Civil Partnerships Act 2004 Sch.5 para.67(1)(a). However, the definition of "financial arrangements" still stipulates that they be provisions governing the rights of the parties "towards one another when living separately": Matrimonial Causes Act 1973 s.34(2); Civil Partnerships Act 2004 Sch.5 para.67(2).

[165] Matrimonial Causes Act 1973 s.35; Civil Partnerships Act 2004 Sch.5 para.69.

[166] See *Pace (formerly Doe) v Doe* [1977] Fam. 18 at 22. Whether a maintenance agreement is "subsisting" is to be determined at the time of the application. An agreement is no longer "subsisting" for the purposes of this definition if its terms have been embodied in a court order: see *Thwaite v Thwaite* [1982] Fam. 1.

[167] If one party has died, provision is made for application by personal representatives: Matrimonial Causes Act 1973 s.36; Civil Partnerships Act 2004 Sch.5 para.73.

[168] Although note that a magistrates' court can only vary provisions relating to periodical payments: Matrimonial Causes Act 1973 s.35(3); Civil Partnerships Act 2004 Sch.5 para.70.

[169] Matrimonial Causes Act 1973 s.35(2); Civil Partnerships Act 2004 Sch.5 para.69(4). For the extent of the court's powers, see *Pace (formerly Doe) v Doe* [1977] Fam. 18 at 23.

[170] Matrimonial Causes Act 1973 s.35(2); Civil Partnerships Act 2004 Sch.5 para.69(2).

[171] cf. *K v K* [1961] 1 W.L.R. 802; *Ratcliffe v Ratcliffe* [1962] 1 W.L.R. 1455.

[172] Hence voluntary reduction in earning capacity would not justify a variation: *K v K* [1961] 1 W.L.R. 802; *Gorman v Gorman* [1964] 1 W.L.R. 1440.

[173] See, generally, *Edgar v Edgar* [1980] 1 W.L.R. 1410, and see further para.13–008.

i. Taxation

The influence of the common law doctrine that husband and wife became one **3–034** person was for many years exemplified by the statutory provision that the income of a married woman living with her husband was "deemed for income tax purposes to be his income and not to be her income".[174] It was widely (but erroneously[175]) thought that this rule imposed a tax on marriage, and, in any event, the fact that a married woman's existence was often ignored by the Revenue—who would[176] communicate with her husband about a woman's financial affairs—seemed offensive to many. After protracted campaigning, the rule was eventually abolished from 1990.[177] However, the tax system has not adopted a consistent policy of neutrality as between couples who have formalised their relationship[178] and those who have not.[179]

Transfers (whether on death or by way of lifetime gift) between spouses or civil partners are exempt from inheritance tax,[180] whereas transfers between a cohabiting couple are not. A transfer between spouses or civil partners does not give rise to a chargeable gain for the purposes of capital gains tax,[181] but there is no comparable provision for transfers between those who have not formalised their relationship. Conversely, there are certain situations in which spouses or civil partners are treated less favourably than other couples.[182] Many of these rules have their origins in specific responses to particular needs (or abuses) rather than in any coherent policy towards the taxation of the family unit. Why, for example, should a husband and wife—who may have been married for only days—be entitled to an exemption from inheritance tax, but not siblings who have lived together in the same house since birth?[183]

---

[174] Income and Corporation Taxes Act 1970 s.31(1). See D. Salter, "Income tax and family life" in Probert (ed.), *Family Life and the Law* for a discussion of the development of the law.

[175] A married couple would pay less tax than an unmarried couple in the same financial position unless either their income took them into the higher rates of tax or a substantial part of their income was derived from investments: see the explanation in the fourth edition of this book at p.956.

[176] At least until administrative changes were introduced in 1979: see [1979] B.T.R. 481.

[177] Finance Act 1988 s.32. Thereafter, each spouse became responsible for making a return of income and paying the relevant tax.

[178] The position of spouses and civil partners is stated on the basis that they are living together: see Income Tax Act 2007 s.1011; *Gubay v Kington* [1984] 1 W.L.R. 163; *Holmes v Mitchell* [1991] F.L.R. 301.

[179] The Civil Partnership Act 2004 did not address the tax consequences of forming a civil partnership, but it was subsequently provided in the Finance Act 2005 s.103 that the Treasury had the power to make regulations to ensure that civil partners and spouses were treated equally. The relevant statutory provisions were accordingly amended by the Tax and Civil Partnership Regulations 2005 (SI 2005/3229).

[180] Inheritance Taxes Act 1984 s.18, as amended by the Tax and Civil Partnership Regulations 2005 (SI 2005/3229) reg.7. There are also limited exemptions from inheritance tax in respect of gifts in consideration of marriage or civil partnership: Inheritance Taxes Act 1984 s.22, as amended by the Tax and Civil Partnership Regulations 2005 (SI 2005/3229) reg.8.

[181] Taxation of Chargeable Gains Act 1992 s.58, as amended by the Tax and Civil Partnership Regulations 2005 (SI 2005/3229) reg.107.

[182] See, for example, *Jones v Garnett* [2005] EWCA Civ 1553, para.70, discussed in Salter, above fn.174.

[183] See, for example, *Burden v UK* [2007] F.C.R. 69 in which the European Court of Human Rights found that the current law did not breach the parties' human rights, but only by the narrowest of margins.

ii. Pensions

3–035 Legislation makes provision for the payment by the state of pensions to a surviving spouse or civil partner (i.e. to the person who was married to, or in a civil partnership with, the deceased at the date of death).[184] No comparable provision is made for those who have not formalised a relationship.

D. Other legal consequences

3–036 Since, as was noted in the introduction, there is no one single code setting out the rights and responsibilities of married couples, one needs a knowledge of many different areas of the law in order to provide a comprehensive statement of the legal consequences that flow from marriage. This section highlights a few of the most relevant, but an appreciation of the full range can be gained from a perusal of Sch.27 of the Civil Partnership Act 2004, which provides a useful compendium of the more obscure statutory provisions applicable to spouses and, by that Act, extended to civil partners.

i. The criminal law

3–037 At common law, a husband could not be convicted of rape on his wife, but in 1991 the House of Lords held that the supposed marital exemption today forms no part of the law of England.[185] Again, at one time neither husband nor wife could be convicted of stealing the other's property, but under the modern law, husband and wife[186] are to be regarded as separate persons (although prosecutions for "marital theft" usually require the consent of the Director of Public Prosecutions). However, it remains the law that spouses and civil partners cannot be convicted of the criminal offence of conspiring with one another[187] (although as we have seen they can be held liable for the tort of conspiracy[188]), and there are circumstances in which a wife will be able to escape criminal liability on the ground that she committed the offence in the presence of and under the coercion of her husband.[189]

ii. Contract and tort

3–038 Statute[190] now provides that a married woman is capable of rendering herself and being rendered liable in respect of any contract, debt or obligation, and of suing and being sued in contract as if she were a feme sole.[191] The same statute also provided that a married woman should be equally liable to enforcement and

---

[184] On the extension to civil partners of the privileges accorded to spouses in private sector occupational pensions, see M. Harper et al., *Civil Partnership: The New Law* (Bristol: Jordans Publishing, 2005), pp.103–104.

[185] *R. v R* [1992] 1 A.C. 599. This was confirmed by the Criminal Justice and Public Order Act 1994 s.142, and see now Sexual Offences Act 2003 s.1.

[186] And civil partners: Theft Act 1968 s.30(1), as amended.

[187] Criminal Law Act 1977 s.2(2)(a); *Mawji v R.* [1957] A.C. 126.

[188] See above, para.3–002.

[189] Criminal Justice Act 1925 s.47.

[190] Law Reform (Married Women and Tortfeasors) Act 1935 s.1.

[191] See above, para.3–002.

bankruptcy proceedings.[192] No statute has interfered with the common law rule under which it was presumed that a wife had her husband's authority to pledge his credit for necessary goods and services,[193] but changes in the provision of credit have effectively rendered this option redundant.

We have seen that, in principle, spouses are liable to one another and to third parties in tort without regard to their marital status, but it is possible that some relics of the unity theory that can be justified by broader policy considerations (e.g. the rule that a spouse who communicates a defamatory statement about a third party to the other spouse is not liable to be sued by the third party[194]) will linger on.

Since the passage of the Fatal Accidents Act 1846, certain specified categories of dependant have had the right to sue a person whose wrongful act, neglect or default brought about a death that has caused the claimant financial loss. The category of dependant has always included a surviving spouse, and has now been extended to civil partners. Unlike many of the rights and responsibilities considered in this chapter, it is no longer confined to those who have formalised their relationship: in 1982 the class was extended to enable an unmarried partner who satisfied certain conditions to sue in respect of the loss flowing from the death,[195] and in 2004 same-sex cohabiting couples were added to the list.[196]

iii. Evidence

The common law rule that denied the competence of spouses to give evidence for or against each other has been whittled away over the years; in addition, spouses are now *compellable* witnesses for the accused in all[197] cases, as are civil partners.[198] However, a spouse or civil partner is only compellable to give evidence for the prosecution if the offence charged involves an assault on, or injury or a threat of injury to, the person concerned (typically wife battering) or on a person under the age of 16; or if the offence charged is a sexual offence against a person under the age of 16; or the offence charged consists of an attempt to commit such an offence or conspiring, aiding and abetting, etc. the commission of such an offence.[199] Cohabitants, by contrast, are competent and compellable witnesses for either the defence or the prosecution.[200]

3–039

---

[192] There are certain provisions that evidently seek to prevent spouses (and now civil partners) from obtaining unfair advantages against creditors: Insolvency Act 1986 ss.339, 423, as amended by Civil Partnerships Act 2004 Sch.27 paras 119, 121.

[193] As distinct from her agency of necessity, abolished by Matrimonial Proceedings and Property Act 1970 s.40, and see the seventh edition of this work at p.74.

[194] *Wennhak v Morgan* (1888) 20 Q.B.D. 635.

[195] Administration of Justice Act 1982 s.3(1).

[196] Civil Partnerships Act 2004 s.83.

[197] Except where they are charged jointly: Police and Criminal Evidence Act 1984 s.80(4), as amended by the Civil Partnerships Act 2004 Sch.27 para.97.

[198] Civil Partnerships Act 2004 s.84.

[199] Police and Criminal Evidence Act 1984 s.80(2), and (3), as amended by the Civil Partnerships Act 2004 Sch.27 para.97.

[200] See, for example, *R. v Pearce* [2001] EWCA Crim 2834, in which the claim that this infringed the art.8 rights of the accused was dismissed. The authorities may not prevent a couple from marrying to take advantage of the exemptions in s.80: *Rota CPS v Registrar General of Births, Deaths and Marriages* [2002] EWCA Civ 1661.

iv. Citizenship and immigration

3–040 Entering into a formal relationship with a British citizen confers no automatic right to British citizenship, but a person married to, or in a civil partnership with, a British citizen may apply for naturalisation under conditions that are less onerous than those governing applications by others.[201]

Similarly, although British citizens have the right of abode—that is, "the right to live in, and to come and go into and from, the United Kingdom without let or hindrance"[202]—it does not follow that a citizen's spouse or civil partner has the same right, and a spouse or civil partner who is not a British citizen may only enter and remain in the United Kingdom in accordance with rules made by the Home Secretary.[203] Current restrictions prevent the entry of a spouse or civil partner under the age of 18, or multiple spouses, and there is a requirement that the couple should intend to continue living together as husband and wife. These attempts to distinguish between genuine marriages and marriages of convenience have given rise to difficulty, particularly in cases in which the parties come from a culture in which arranged marriages are the norm.[204]

IV. ENGAGED COUPLES

3–041 At one time, entering into an engagement to marry had important legal consequences. As Ch.1 discussed, a vow made in words of the present tense was binding on the parties, as was a promise to marry that was followed by sexual intercourse, and the ecclesiastical courts had extensive powers to compel the parties to solemnise their union. After the Clandestine Marriages Act of 1753, this was no longer possible, but there remained an action at common law whereby a jilted fiancé(e) could obtain damages for breach of promise of marriage. This action was finally abolished by the Law Reform (Miscellaneous Provisions) Act 1970,[205] which introduced a special code to deal with some of the proprietary problems that may arise when an agreement to marry[206] is

---

[201] British Nationality Act 1981 s.6(2) and Sch.1 para.3, as amended by the Civil Partnerships Act 2004 Sch.27 para.72.

[202] Immigration Act 1971 s.1(1).

[203] Immigration Act 1971 s.3(1), (2). For discussion, see H. Toner, "Immigration law and family life—a happy marriage?", Ch.12 in Probert (ed.) *Family Life and the Law.*

[204] See, for example, *R. v Immigration Appeal Tribunal Ex p. Iqbal* [1993] Imm. A.R. 270 (absence of passionate relationship or indeed of being "in love" not of itself indicative of it being primary purpose of marriage to obtain admission to the United Kingdom: "Marie Antoinette married Louis XVI for dynastic reasons rather than as a love match but no one would regard that fact was indicating that the primary purpose of the marriage was for her to secure admission to France", *per* Schiemann J.).

[205] The Act gives rise to a large number of problems of interpretation, but since the Act is, in practice, rarely invoked, those difficulties are not dealt with in this or the previous edition: see, for a detailed consideration, the fourth edition of this work at pp.689–692; and Cretney (1970) 33 M.L.R. 534.

[206] The mere possibility of ultimate marriage being in a party's mind is insufficient to bring the provisions of the Act into play; what is required is a clear agreement or common fixed intention: *Bernard v Josephs* [1982] Ch. 391 at 406, *per* Kerr L.J. However, it has been held to be immaterial that the agreement might have been unenforceable before 1970 (e.g. on the ground that one or both parties were married to others at the relevant time): see *Shaw v Fitzgerald* [1992] 1 F.L.R. 357.

terminated. The Civil Partnership Act 2004 subsequently made similar provision for same-sex couples who had agreed to enter a civil partnership.

The relevant provisions are complex. First, there are rules dealing with gifts between those who have agreed to marry or enter into a civil partnership. The gift of an engagement ring[207] is rebuttably[208] presumed to be absolute,[209] but other gifts may be recovered if they were conditional on the marriage or civil partnership taking place.[210] Secondly, the Act applies s.17 of the Married Women's Property Act 1882[211]:

> "[T]o any dispute between, or claim by, one [*sic*] of them in relation to property in which either or both had a beneficial interest while the agreement was in force"[212]

provided that proceedings are instituted within three years of the termination of the agreement. However, this provision is of somewhat limited effect[213] and does no more than to make the advantages of a summary procedure[214] available.

The relevant provisions also apply the rules of law governing the property rights of spouses or civil partners to the determination of beneficial interests in property acquired during an engagement.[215] These rules include not only the presumption of advancement[216] but also the statutory principle embodied in the Matrimonial Proceedings and Property Act 1970[217] whereby a substantial contribution in money or money's worth to the improvement of property may entitle the contributor to a beneficial interest in the property. What the Act does *not* do is give the parties any right to apply to the court for financial relief or property adjustment orders, since those powers are only exercisable upon divorce, dissolution or annulment.[218]

---

[207] The term "engagement ring" is not defined: cf. *Elkington and Co Ltd v Amery* [1936] 2 All E.R. 86.

[208] The difficulties of rebutting this presumption may be illustrated by *Cox v Jones* [2004] EWHC 1486 (Ch) in which contradictory evidence was given by the parties: the judge held that, in the context of a romantic holiday, it was implausible that Mr Jones had told Miss Cox that the gift was conditional.

[209] Law Reform (Miscellaneous Provisions) Act 1970 s.3(2). There is no equivalent provision of the 2004 Act on this point.

[210] See Law Reform (Miscellaneous Provisions) Act 1970 s.3(1); Civil Partnerships Act 2004 s.74(5). In this respect the 1970 Act preserved the effect of earlier rules: see *Cohen v Sellar* [1926] 1 K.B. 536; *Jacobs v Davis* [1917] 2 K.B. 532.

[211] As extended by s.7 of the Matrimonial Proceedings (Property and Maintenance) Act 1958.

[212] Law Reform (Miscellaneous Provisions) Act 1970 s.2(2); *Marsh v von Sternberg* [1986] 1 F.L.R. 526; Civil Partnerships Act 2004 s.74(3).

[213] *Mossop v Mossop* [1988] 2 F.L.R. 173.

[214] *Marsh v von Sternberg* [1986] 1 F.L.R. 526; *Mossop v Mossop* [1988] 2 F.L.R. 173 at 178, *per* Sir Frederick Lawton.

[215] Law Reform (Miscellaneous Provisions) Act 1970, s.2(1); Civil Partnerships Act 2004 s.74(2).

[216] *Mossop v Mossop* [1988] 2 F.L.R. 173 at 176, *per* Balcombe L.J. See also *Ledger-Beadell v Peach* [2006] EWHC 2940 (Ch) in which it was held that the presumption was rebutted on the facts.

[217] Matrimonial Proceedings and Property Act 1970 s.37 (above para.3–008). *See Mossop v Mossop* [1988] 2 F.L.R. 173 at 176, *per* Balcombe L.J.

[218] *Mossop v Mossop* [1988] 2 F.L.R. 173 at 176–177, *per* Balcombe L.J.; cf. *Bernard v Josephs* [1982] Ch. 391 at 403, 406.

CHAPTER FOUR

THE FAMILY AND PROPERTY LAW

I.   INTRODUCTION.............................. 4–001   II.   THE   SOCIO-ECONOMIC   BACK-
                                                             GROUND 4–003

I. INTRODUCTION

Having considered the specific legal consequences that flow from a marriage or **4–001** civil partnership (including those relating to the finances and assets of the parties[1]), we can now turn to the broader issue of family property. As noted in Ch.3, formalising a relationship has no automatic impact on the parties' property rights.[2] As the President of the Family Division, Sir Mark Potter, pointed out in one recent case[3]:

> "Almost uniquely our jurisdiction does not have a marital property regime and it is scarcely appropriate to classify our jurisdiction as having a marital regime of separation of property. More correctly we have no regime, simply accepting that each spouse owns his or her own separate property during the marriage but subject to the court's wide distributive powers in prospect upon a decree of judicial separation, nullity or divorce."

It is true that on divorce or dissolution the court has extensive powers— considered in Part III of this book—to reallocate assets between the parties,[4] but even in this context it may be necessary to resolve issues of ownership in order to determine whether certain assets belong to the spouses or to third parties (such

---

[1] See Ch.3.
[2] At para.3–006.
[3] *Charman v Charman* [2007] EWCA Civ 503, para.124.
[4] And once the Matrimonial Causes Act 1973 has been invoked, it is dominant in determining the spouses' respective rights and interests, and the general law (either common law, equity or statute) should not be invoked: note the comments of Thorpe L.J. in *Tee v Tee and Hillman* [1999] 2 F.L.R. 613 at 618, where there was a "diversionary excursion" into the Trusts of Land Act 1996, the case being described as "about as appalling a litigation history as it would be possible to discover".

as parents or members of the extended family[5]). More generally, while the relationship is subsisting, the interests of the parties fall to be determined by the general rules of property law: thus, a court may need to decide who owns what if there is a dispute with a third party such as a bank or building society. It should also be borne in mind that the majority of marriages are terminated by death rather than by divorce, and it is the rules of property law that determine what assets form the estate of the deceased.

For cohabiting couples, there is currently no basis on which capital assets or income may be reallocated between the parties,[6] and so such couples need to rely on property law both when engaged in a dispute with a third party and when disputing the ownership of the property upon breakdown or death.

4–002   Both property law and the principles applicable on divorce or dissolution invoke the concept of "fairness"[7]; however, as we shall see, this means very different things in different contexts. Indeed, the underlying theme of this part of the book is not so much the legal concept of "family property" in England and Wales—since there is no such concept—but rather the context-specific nature of such rights that do exist. Each of the chapters in this part offers a different interpretation of this issue of family property—not only a different way of dealing with property, or different types of property,[8] but also a different interpretation of the term "family". Under the general law of property, as Ch.5 will show, the relevance of the familial status of the parties is a much-debated question. The state's definition of the family for the purposes of the welfare benefit system, considered in Ch.6, varies according to the context; thus, a cohabiting couple may be treated in the same way as a married couple in the context of means-tested benefits but are not given the same rights to other benefits. The circle of persons who may make a claim for provision on the death of a family member is different again, as Ch.7 will discuss. Whether the law should be reformed, and what direction future reform might take, is discussed in Ch.8.

The remainder of this introductory chapter will provide some background evidence about the context in which these different systems operate. Such evidence will enable the reader to evaluate the impact of the rules outlined in the following chapters and to assess the arguments in favour of the proposed reforms outlined in Ch.8.

---

[5] See, for example, *H v M (Property Occupied by Wife's Parents)* [2003] EWHC 625 (Fam); *G v G (Matrimonial Property: Rights of Extended Family)* [2005] EWHC 1560 (Fam); *Green v Green* [2006] EWHC 2010 (Fam).

[6] But see the transfer of certain tenancies under the Family Law Act 1996 s.53 and Sch.7, discussed in Ch.13.

[7] See, for example, *White v White* [2001] 1 A.C. 596 (discussed at para.13–045) and *Oxley v Hiscock* [2004] EWCA Civ 546 (discussed at para.5–026).

[8] The classic definition of a property right, as *per* Lord Wilberforce in *National Provincial Bank v Ainsworth* [1965] A.C. 1175 at 1248, is that it must be "definable, identifiable by third parties, capable in its nature of assumption by third parties, and have some degree of permanence or stability". Such a definition would exclude welfare benefits, but it has been argued that these have become as important to some families as conventional assets: see, for example, M.A. Glendon, *The New Family and the New Property* (Toronto: Butterworths, 1981).

II. THE SOCIO-ECONOMIC BACKGROUND

If men and/or women who chose to live together as a couple were autonomous, **4–003** independent individuals, unencumbered by family responsibilities and with equal access to the labour market, then there might be no need for any special system of family property, but all too often this is not the case. If the parties have children, they may decide that one of them should cease paid employment or reduce the number of hours they work in order for care for them; similarly, responsibilities for caring for elderly parents or other relatives may reduce the ability of the carer to engage in paid employment.

The Law Commission has noted the "tendency for most parents to specialise to some extent in their breadwinning and child-caring functions".[9] More often than not it is the female partner who reduces her working hours to take on child care. Although 71 per cent of married or cohabiting mothers were in paid work in 2006, only 30 per cent were in full-time work.[10] Women's rates of participation in paid work depend largely on the age of their youngest child: only 56 per cent of mothers with a child under the age of 5 were in paid employment, but this rose to 71 per cent for those whose youngest child was aged between 5 and 10, and still higher for mothers of older children.[11] By contrast, 91 per cent of married or cohabiting fathers were in paid employment, and 87 per cent worked full time.[12] In addition, mothers are more likely than fathers to adopt a flexible working pattern[13] or to work from home.[14] Women also bear the brunt of other caring responsibilities, accounting for 58 per cent of the 6 million who provide unpaid care for a friend or relative, and 61 per cent of those carers who provide over 50 hours' care per week.[15]

How far such role specialisation is the result of individual preferences, and how far it is determined by external constraints such as the availability of child care, the gender pay gap[16] and the attitudes of the other parties involved, is a matter of debate.[17] What is clear is that it has a profound impact on lifetime earnings. The earning shortfall that is likely to be experienced by an individual as a result of taking time out of paid employment for caring responsibilities is not

---

[9] *Cohabitation: The Financial Consequences of Relationship Breakdown: A Consultation Paper*, Law Com. No.179 (HMSO, 2006), para.4.15.

[10] *Social Trends 37* (2007), Table 4.12.

[11] *Social Focus on Gender* (ONS, 2006).

[12] *Social Trends 37* (2007), Table 4.12.

[13] *Social Trends 37* (2007), Table 4.13.

[14] *Labour Market Review 2006* (ONS, 2006).

[15] Office for National Statistics, *Focus on Health* (2006), Ch.12, p.152.

[16] Despite the fact that almost four decades have passed since the Equal Pay Act 1970, the median weekly earnings of women remain lower than those of men in comparable professions (see, e.g., *Social Trends 37* (2007), Table 5.7). The gender pay gap—based on median hourly earnings—has narrowed, but is still significant: in 2007 the gap between men's and women's median hourly earnings was 12.6% (*2007 Annual Survey of Hours and Earnings* (ONS, 2007), p.6). Moreover, the gap between men's and women's median weekly earnings is wider than that between their respective hourly earnings because women tend to work fewer hours per week than men.

[17] For a review of the literature, see G. Moffat, "Work-life balance and employment law: cultural change or *Mission: Impossible*?", in R. Probert, *Family Life and the Law: Under One Roof* (Aldershot: Ashgate, 2007).

merely due to pay foregone at the time but also because of the impact on subsequent earning levels "through loss of promotion prospects . . . downward occupation mobility, or depletion of skill on return after a gap".[18]

4–004   During the relationship the negative effects may not be evident, since the income of the breadwinner will be available to support the family. However, if the relationship ends:

> "[T]hat support is lost, and the primary carer is exposed to the economic consequences of the role-specialisation which the parties adopted during their relationship. In particular, that individual may have an impaired earning capacity and reduced pension-savings. Moreover, if the children are still dependent on separation, whichever parent is primarily responsible for them thereafter may be unable to engage in full-time employment for a time, either at all or without engaging professional child-care."[19]

If, in that eventuality, the rights of the parties are to be determined in accordance with strict rules of property law, how far does property law take account of these different types of contributions? The answer is by no means simple, and will depend upon the precise combination of contributions made, as the next chapter will demonstrate.

---

[18] K. Rake, *Women's Incomes over the Lifetime* (London: TSO, 2000), p.117.
[19] *Cohabitation: The Financial Consequences of Relationship Breakdown*, para.4.20.

CHAPTER FIVE

FAMILY ASSETS: OWNERSHIP AND PROTECTION

I.	INTRODUCTION	5–001
II.	FORMAL ARRANGEMENTS	5–003
	A. Claims founded on contract	5–004
	B. Legal ownership of the family home	5–008
	C. Ownership of the beneficial interest	5–009
III.	INFORMAL TRUSTS	5–013
	A. Resulting trusts	5–014
	B. Constructive trusts	5–018
IV.	PROPRIETARY ESTOPPEL	5–032
	A. Assurance, promise or representation	5–033
	B. Detrimental reliance	5–034
	C. The remedy	5–035
	D. The relationship between estoppel and the constructive trust	5–037
	E. Reform?	5–038
V.	RESOLVING DISPUTES BETWEEN CO-OWNERS	5–039
	A. Severing the joint tenancy	5–040
	B. Disputes as to whether the property should be sold	5–045
	C. Dividing the proceeds	5–048
VI.	DISPUTES WITH THIRD PARTIES.	5–049
	A. Is the beneficial interest binding on the third party?	5–050
	B. Can the transaction be set aside?	5–052
	C. Should sale be ordered?	5–057
VII.	PERSONAL PROPERTY	5–062
VIII.	CONCLUSION	5–064

I. INTRODUCTION

The term "family assets" is here used in a non-technical sense, simply to denote: **5–001**

> "[T]hose things which are acquired by one or other or both of the parties, with the intention that there should be continuing provision for them and their children during their joint lives, and used for the benefit of the family as a whole."[1]

The term itself has been said to have "no legal meaning" as a method of solving questions of title[2]; in determining who owns which assets, it is to the general principles of property law that we must turn.

---

[1] *Wachtel v Wachtel* [1973] Fam. 72 at 90, *per* Lord Denning M.R. For another definition of "family assets", see *Gissing v Gissing* [1971] A.C. 886, *per* Lord Diplock at 904.
[2] *Pettitt v Pettitt* [1970] A.C. 777 at 809, 810, 817; *Gissing v Gissing* [1971] A.C. 886 at 899.

There is, however, an important issue as to the extent to which these general principles take into account the context of any dispute over family assets. Quite apart from the debate as to whether general principles of property law *should* be applied to the family home,[3] there is the question as to whether the courts *do* in fact take a different approach when faced with a family dispute. At the very minimum, the inferences drawn by the court about the intentions of the parties will be affected by their status; as Lord Upjohn put it in *Pettitt v Pettitt*:

> "[T]he rights of the parties must be judged on the general principles applicable in any court of law when considering questions of title to property... while making full allowances in view of [their] relationship."[4]

Indeed, certain rules of property law were directly influenced by the status of the parties: equity developed the presumption of advancement, under which the purchase of property by a husband in the name of his wife (or by a father in the name of his child) was presumed to be a gift.[5] It has also been argued that in actual fact the courts have already developed a set of principles that have no application outside the family home while paying lip-service to the idea that they are applying strict rules of property law.[6] In *Stack v Dowden*,[7] the majority of the House of Lords went further still, arguing that a different approach was called for when dealing with family relationships. As Baroness Hale noted:

> "[A]n outcome which might seem just in a purely commercial transaction may appear highly unjust in a transaction between husband and wife or between cohabitant and cohabitant."[8]

Furthermore, it was suggested that it was the role of the courts to bring about "the evolution of the law of property to take account of changing social and economic circumstances".[9] Yet the lower courts continue to reiterate the old orthodoxy that they are applying general principles of property law,[10] and, as we shall see, the application of the approach advocated in *Stack v Dowden* is not without its difficulties.

---

[3] For the argument that an alternative approach is necessary, see, for example, A. Barlow and C. Lind, "A matter of trust: the allocation of rights in the family home" (1999) 19 L.S. 153.
[4] *Pettitt v Pettitt* [1970] A.C. 777, at 813. For examples of cases in which the parties' relationship affected the inferences drawn by the court see, for example, *Midland Bank v Cooke* [1995] 4 All E.R. 562.
[5] See further below, para.5–016.
[6] J. Dewar, "Land, law and the family home", Ch.13 in S. Bright and J. Dewar (eds), *Land Law: Themes and Perspectives* (Oxford: Oxford University Press, 1998), at p.335. Some cases do display evidence of cross-fertilisation: see, for example, *Yaxley v Gotts* [2000] Ch. 162; *Cox v Jones* [2004] EWHC 1486 (Ch).
[7] [2007] UKHL 17.
[8] At para.42. Note also Lord Hope at para.3.
[9] At para.46, *per* Baroness Hale. Such a development had been advocated by the Law Commission in *Sharing Homes*; see further Ch.8.
[10] See, for example, *Tackaberry v Hollis* [2007] EWHC 2633 (Ch), para.80.

Turning to the types of assets that may be in question, usually the most **5–002** important family asset—and hence the one that has attracted the most litigation—is the family home.[11] Over the past half-century there has been an increase both in home-ownership and in the value—or cost—of a home. In 1953 less than one-third of dwellings were owner-occupied, but by the start of the 1980s this proportion had risen to over half,[12] and today 7 in 10 households in England and Wales are owner-occupied.[13] Two factors have been important in contributing to this growth: first, the availability of building-society and bank credit to finance the purchase of a home; secondly, the sale of social-sector housing to tenants under the right-to-buy legislation of the 1980s.[14] At the same time there has also been an increase in the cost of housing: in 1986 the average price of a house was £36,276; 10 years later this had almost doubled, to £70,626; and by 2006 it had more than doubled again, to £204,813.[15] Early in 2008 it was reported that the total value of housing in Britain had reached £4 trillion.[16]

Each of these developments has left its imprint in the law reports: the increase in the value of housing has made litigation between former home-sharers worthwhile, while the use of mortgage finance has paved the way for disputes between lenders and borrowers over the priority of different kinds of interest in the family home, the circumstances in which one party's consent to a mortgage may be set aside and the situations in which the sale of the home may be ordered.

The family home is also different from other family assets—such as cars, bank accounts or furniture—in that the formalities required for the creation of an interest in land are far more demanding than those required in the context of personal property.[17] This inevitably means that there are a greater number of cases in which family members have failed to comply with those formalities, and the courts have developed a number of means by which an interest may, in certain circumstances, be acquired *informally.*

This chapter looks first at the variety of means by which one person may acquire an interest in the family home—whether formally or informally, and whether the home is in joint or sole legal ownership—and at how disputes between co-owners are resolved when the relationship comes to an end. It then

---

[11] Pension and life assurance funds have at certain periods outstripped the value of residential housing in terms of their financial significance, but the family home, in providing the base for family life, has a significance to the family beyond its financial value: see, for example, L. Fox, *Conceptualising Home: Theories, Laws and Policies* (Oxford: Hart Publishing, 2007), Ch.4.

[12] G. Jones, "Assessing the success of the sale of social housing in the UK" (2007) 29 J.S.W.F.L. 135.

[13] Department of Communities and Local Government, *Housing in England 2005/6* (2007), Table 1.9.

[14] See Jones, "Assessing the success of the sale of housing in the UK".

[15] See *http://www.communities.gov.uk/documents/housing/xls/141272* [Accessed May 27, 2008].

[16] "Value of all homes in Britain tops £4 trillion for first time", *The Times*, January 12, 2008.

[17] The imposition of formal requirements on legal transactions has a number of objectives: the achievement of certainty, the provision of evidence of intention and an indication to the parties of the serious nature of the transaction and its consequences: M. Howard and J. Hill, "The informal creation of interests in land" (1995) 15 L.S. 356 at 357.

goes on to consider the extent to which the home is protected against claims by third parties, and concludes with a brief discussion of personal property.

II. FORMAL ARRANGEMENTS

5–003   A couple may decide to regulate their affairs in relation to family property either by a contract or by a declaration of trust. In addition, the fact that the property is conveyed into joint names may provide the opportunity for the parties to clarify their beneficial interests; even if they do not, the fact that it is in joint names may justify the courts in drawing inferences about their intentions.

A. Claims founded on contract
5–004   In order to establish a contract there must be a genuine meeting of minds between the parties (i.e. an offer and an acceptance), the terms of the agreement must be sufficiently precise, and they must have intended to create a legally enforceable relationship. In addition, unless the agreement is contained in a deed or document under seal, there must be consideration, and any additional formal requirement prescribed by law in respect of the subject matter of the contract must be satisfied. Finally, the contract must not be affected by fraud, duress or undue influence, and the terms that it is sought to enforce must not be illegal or contrary to public policy.

These are general rules applicable to all contracts, but a number of them are of particular significance in the context of agreements relating to family property and therefore require further explanation.

i. Intention to create legal relations
5–005   There is a presumption that family members do not intend their agreements to take the form of legally binding contracts, at least while the relationship is ongoing.[18] As Salmon L.J. explained in *Jones v Padvatton*, this is a presumption of fact, rather than of law, and:

> "[D]erives from experience of life and human nature which shows that in such circumstances men and women usually do not intend to create legal rights and obligations, but intend to rely solely on family ties of mutual trust and affection."[19]

However, much will depend on the circumstances of the case. An oral assurance to a family member that is couched in vague terms is unlikely to be regarded as

---

[18] *Balfour v Balfour* [1919] 2 K.B. 571. Once the parties are no longer living in amity this is no longer the case: *Merritt v Merritt* [1970] 1 W.L.R. 1211.
[19] [1969] 1 W.L.R. 328 at 332.

a legally-binding contract[20]; by contrast, a formal document, drawn up with professional advice and contained in a deed, may well be. In addition, the nature of the agreement may well be relevant: while an agreement relating to the property rights or maintenance obligations of the parties is likely to be regarded as giving rise to legally enforceable obligations, agreements relating to the parties' domestic duties during an ongoing relationship are likely to pose more difficult questions in relation to enforcement.[21]

ii. Formal requirements for contracts relating to land

If the contract relates to an interest in land, then it must be in writing and signed **5–006** by both parties.[22] Any contract that does not comply with this requirement is void.[23] However, the legislation also provides that this formal requirement does not affect "the creation or operation of resulting, implied or constructive trusts",[24] and so the lack of writing will not preclude a finding that such a trust has arisen out of an informal arrangement.[25] An informal agreement may also, in appropriate circumstances, give rise to a claim based on proprietary estoppel.[26]

iii. Rules of public policy

The contractual resolution of the parties' finances appeals in principle to the **5–007** interests of party autonomy, individual responsibility and diversity. The circumstances of family relationships are so diverse that a particular rather than a generalised solution has obvious attractions; moreover, such contracts may, if carefully drawn, achieve clarity in the definition of legal rights. However, inherent problems are also readily apparent. If the parties wish to contract out of a statutory regime such as that which exists on divorce or dissolution, rather than simply to clarify their respective property rights, a conflict arises between State paternalism and party autonomy. A statutory regime may be seen as the expression of community norms, and a system of unqualified contractual freedom may lead to results that are in conflict with those norms.

Current English law reflects these tensions. Spouses and civil partners may enter into a contract setting out who owns what, but on divorce or dissolution,

---

[20] See, for example, *Jones v Padvatton* [1969] 1 W.L.R. 328; *Gould v Gould* [1970] 1 Q.B. 275.

[21] For discussion, see C. Barton, "Contract—a justifiable taboo?", in R. Probert, *Family Life and the Law: Under One Roof* (Aldershot: Ashgate, 2007).

[22] Law of Property (Miscellaneous Provisions) Act 1989 s.2. See the preceding Law Com. No.164, *Formalities and Contracts for the Sale of Land*, and earlier, Working Paper 92.

[23] This rule replaces the much more flexible rule formerly contained in the Law of Property Act 1925, which merely required such a contract to be evidenced in writing, and permitted contracts not so evidenced to be enforced if the plaintiff could show an act of part performance on his part such as would render it inequitable for the defendant to rely on the lack of formality.

[24] Law of Property (Miscellaneous Provisions) Act 1989 s.2(5).

[25] See, for example, *Yaxley v Gotts* [2000] Ch. 162 and see further below, para.5–020.

[26] See below, para.5–032.

assets are not divided in accordance with strict property rights. They may also enter into a pre-nuptial agreement as to how their assets will be divided in the event of breakdown, and if both parties are happy to stand by that agreement upon breakdown, there will be no occasion for the court to intervene. In addition, current policy is to promote a "settlement culture" in the resolution of financial disputes, and parties are discouraged from proceeding to full litigation and trial.[27] However, it is still the law that the parties cannot by contract preclude the court from exercising its jurisdiction or make financial provision and property adjustment orders,[28] and less weight will be attached to a pre-nuptial agreement than to one reached after the relationship has broken down.

Contracts between those who have not formalised their relationship raise rather different questions, since in this context there is no general regime for the parties to opt out of.[29] In the past it has been questioned whether such contracts might be unenforceable on the basis that they are deemed to be "founded on an immoral consideration" or likely to prejudice the status of marriage.[30] However, the authorities on which this proposition was based largely derived from the eighteenth century and involved agreements for sexual relations outside marriage, the usual arrangement being that the man would provide the woman with financial support if she agreed to cohabit[31] with him.[32] They were thus very different from modern cohabitation contracts, and in *Sutton v Mishcon de Reya*,[33] Hart J. drew a distinction between a contract *for* sexual relations outside marriage and a contract entered into by a cohabiting couple to deal with financial matters. The former would be void, while the latter—assuming that the general requirements of the law of contract had been met—would be valid.[34] While this part of the judgment was technically obiter (since the case involved an agreement between the parties to enter into a master–slave arrangement that was therefore void as a contract for sexual relations outside marriage), it does reflect the consensus among modern commentators that agreements which simply regulate the financial rights and duties of a cohabiting couple are valid. Indeed, books of legal precedents are available[35] to guide those who wish to enter into them and

---

[27] Discussed further in Ch.13.

[28] See *Hyman v Hyman* [1929] A.C. 601; *Sutton v Sutton* [1984] Ch. 184.

[29] This will change if the Law Commission's proposals for reform are enacted. In its proposals, considered at para.8–006, the Commission addressed the issue of whether a couple should be able to opt out of its proposed scheme.

[30] See the assertion by Lord Wright in *Fender v St John Mildmay* [1938] A.C. 1 at 42, and see, generally, J.L. Dwyer, "Immoral contracts" (1977) 93 L.Q.R. 386.

[31] In the eighteenth-century sense of engaging in sexual relations, rather than the modern sense of living together under the same roof: S. Johnson, *A Dictionary of the English Language* (London, 1756).

[32] See R. Probert, "Cohabitation contracts and Swedish sex slaves" (2004) 16 C.F.L.Q. 453.

[33] [2003] EWHC 3166 (Ch).

[34] For discussion see C. Barton, *Cohabitation Contracts* (Aldershot: Gower, 1985). Note also the recommendation of the Committee of Ministers of the Council of Europe that "contracts relating to property between persons living together as an unmarried couple, or which regulated matters concerning their property either during their relationship or when their relationship has ceased, should not be considered invalid solely because they have been concluded under these conditions": R(88)3.

[35] H. Wood, D. Lush, and D. Bishop, *Cohabitation: Law, Practice and Precedents*, 3rd edn (Bristol: Family Law, 2005).

their legal representatives (although the extent to which such agreements are made in practice is unclear[36]), while the Government's *Living Together* campaign actively encouraged cohabiting couples to enter into contracts,[37] which suggests confidence that such contracts would be upheld by the courts in case of dispute.[38]

B. Legal ownership of the family home

A deed is necessary to convey or create any legal estate in land.[39] If the conveyance of the family home is taken in the name of one partner it follows that the other cannot successfully claim to be entitled to the legal estate. If legal title is conveyed to two or more persons, then they will hold the legal title as joint tenants.[40]

5–008

It is now accepted that different principles apply to homes that are jointly owned and homes that are in sole ownership.[41] Among married couples, the family home is usually in joint ownership.[42] Among cohabiting couples, by contrast, this is less common, with fewer than half of such couples being joint owners.[43] The rules outlined below will therefore affect some types of families to a greater extent than others.[44]

C. Ownership of the beneficial interest

The fact that one person is the sole legal owner does not mean that he or she is solely entitled to the property; more important is the position in equity, since it is the beneficial owners who are entitled to the proceeds of sale if the property

5–009

---

[36] See, for example, A. Barlow et al., *Cohabitation, Marriage and the Law: Social Change and Legal Reform in the 21st Century* (Oxford: Hart Publishing, 2005), pp.78–80; C. Barton, "Cohabitants, contracts and commissioners" [2007] Fam. Law. 407.

[37] The *Living Together* campaign was launched by the Department of Constitutional Affairs in July 2004 and was intended to make cohabitants aware of their lack of legal rights. The website that was funded by the campaign included a template for a "living together agreement".

[38] Although this was not shared by a number of cohabiting couples who accessed the website, who felt that it was not worth entering into an agreement that might not be legally binding: see A. Barlow, C. Burgoyne and J. Smithson, *The Living Together Campaign—An Investigation of Its Impact on Legally Aware Cohabitants* (Ministry of Justice Research Series 5/07, 2007), p.33.

[39] Law of Property Act 1925 s.52.

[40] Law of Property Act 1925 s.36(2).

[41] *Kai Ltd v Chawla* [2007] EWHC 2357 (Ch).

[42] E. Cooke, A. Barlow and T. Callus, *Community of Property: A Regime for England and Wales?* (London: The Nuffield Foundation, 2006), p.22. Note also the somewhat rough-and-ready calculation by the Department of Constitutional Affairs to the effect that 16% of all households are owned by one spouse alone: *Administration of Estates—Review of the Statutory Legacy* (CP 11/05, 2005), fn.36.

[43] J. Haskey, "Cohabiting couples in Great Britain: accommodation sharing, tenure and property ownership" (2001) 103 *Population Trends* 26, p.33; S. Arthur et al., *Settling Up: Making Financial Arrangements after Separation* (National Centre for Social Research, 2002), p.13; G. Douglas, J. Pearce and H. Woodward, 'Dealing with property issues on cohabitation breakdown' [2007] Fam. Law 36, p.38.

[44] R. Probert, "Cohabitants and joint ownership: the implications of Stack v Dowden" [2007] Fam. Law 924.

is sold, and also who have the right[45] to occupy the property. Two situations need to be considered: first, where there is an express declaration as to the interests of the parties, and secondly, where no such information is forthcoming.

i. Express declaration

5–010 When a property is conveyed to two or more persons jointly, and where there is an express and explicit[46] declaration[47] of the beneficial interests, such a declaration will normally be conclusive of the parties' beneficial interests in the absence of fraud or common mistake.[48] For example:

> In *Goodman v Gallant*[49] the marriage between Mr and Mrs Goodman broke down, and Mrs Goodman and her new partner, Mr Gallant, negotiated to buy out Mr Goodman's interest in the former matrimonial home (which had been vested in him alone). Mr Goodman conveyed the property to Mrs Goodman and Mr Gallant as beneficial joint tenants. The conveyance also incorporated a declaration by Mr Gallant and Mrs Goodman that they were to hold the net proceeds of sale "upon trust for themselves as beneficial joint tenants." Five years later the relationship between Mrs Goodman and Mr Gallant broke down, and she claimed that she and Mr Goodman had once each had a 50 per cent beneficial interest in the property, and that the effect of the conveyance of Mr Goodman's interest to Mr Gallant and herself was simply to deal with Mr Goodman's half share, with the result that she had become beneficially entitled to a three-quarter interest in the house, whilst Mr Gallant had one-quarter. The Court of Appeal rejected this argument; the declaration of trust, explicitly stating that they were beneficial joint tenants, concluded the question of the respective beneficial interests of the two parties.

---

[45] Trusts of Land and Appointment of Trustees Act 1996 s.12. For discussion of the criteria set out in the Act, see J.G. Ross Martyn, "Co-owners and their entitlement to occupy their land before and after the Trusts of Land and Appointment of Trustees Act 1996: theoretical doubts are replaced by practical difficulties" [1997] 61 Conv. 254; D.G. Barnsley, "Co-owners' rights to occupy trust land" (1998) 57 C.L.J. 123.

[46] If the conveyance contains a provision dealing with the parties' beneficial interests, it is simply a question of construction as to what those words mean: see *Huntingford v Hobbs* [1993] 1 F.L.R. 736 at 742, *per* Sir Christopher Slade.

[47] A declaration of trust relating to land or an interest in land must be evidenced in writing that is signed by the person(s) declaring such trusts: Law of Property Act 1925 s.53(1)(b). However, it appears that it is unnecessary that a declaration in the conveyance should have been signed by the parties: *Roy v Roy* [1996] 1 F.L.R. 541.

[48] But note that there may—apart from cases of fraud and common mistake—be circumstances in which a court will be prepared to rectify a conveyance that does not give effect to the parties' true intentions: see, for example *Wilson v Wilson* [1969] 1 W.L.R. 1470, *per* Buckley J., and *Pink v Lawrence* (1978) 38 P. & C.R. 98 (both referred to without adverse comment in *Goodman v Gallant* [1986] 1 F.L.R. 513 at 524, *per* Slade L.J.); *Roy v Roy* [1996] 1 F.L.R. 541; and see also the other cases referred to in fn.5 on p.656 of the fourth edition of this work.

[49] [1986] 1 F.L.R. 513. This decision resolved a long-standing conflict of opinion between Lord Denning and others: note the discussion of this in *Stack v Dowden* [2007] UKHL 17, para.49.

Similarly, in *Clarke v Harlowe*,[50] the fact that the male partner had paid all the mortgage instalments, as well as for extensive refurbishments, could not affect the shares of the parties in light of the explicit declaration at the time of transfer that they held the property on trust for themselves as joint tenants.

It should, however, be noted that there is nothing to prevent those who have made a declaration as to their beneficial interests in the property from *formally* agreeing to vary those interests at a later stage. A new declaration of trust may be made by both parties, or one party may declare a trust of his or her beneficial interest in favour of another, or otherwise dispose of that interest.[51] Thus, in *Wallbank and Wallbank v Price*,[52] in which a husband and wife initially owned the family home as beneficial joint tenants, it was held that the wife had relinquished her interest when she signed a document stating that she forfeited her rights in the property.

In addition, even if there is a formal agreement as to the parties' beneficial **5–011** interests in the property, such an agreement is not conclusive as to their respective obligations. There may, for example, have been a separate agreement that one of the parties is to pay the other a sum of money; such an agreement, since it does not relate to an interest in land, need not comply with the formalities set out in the Law of Property Act.[53] Similarly, the amount of money to which each party is entitled when the property is sold will depend not only on their respective beneficial interests, but on whether one party is liable to account to the other for expenditure on the property.[54]

In any case, how likely is it that there will be written evidence of the parties' intentions regarding their beneficial interests? Since 1998 those purchasing a home together have been presented with a form that explicitly asks them whether they intend to hold the property as joint tenants, tenants in common in equal shares, or on other trusts.[55] If such evidence existed for all family homes, this chapter would be considerably shorter.[56] Unfortunately, the forms used prior to

---

[50] [2005] EWHC 3062 (Ch).

[51] A disposition of a subsisting equitable interest must be made in writing and signed by the person disposing of the interest: Law of Property Act 1925 s.53(1)(c). However, an informal agreement to dispose of such an interest will be enforceable if the intended beneficiary of the agreement has relied upon it to his or her detriment: see Law of Property Act 1925 s.53(2) and *Neville v Wilson* [1997] Ch. 14; *Slater v Simm* [2007] EWHC 951 (Ch). In *Stack v Dowden* [2007] UKHL 17, para.49, Baroness Hale also confirmed that a declaration of trust might be varied by proprietary estoppel. It would appear, however, that there must be some express discussion between the parties in order for their interests to be varied: the fact that one party has made greater contributions than the other will not displace an express beneficial joint tenancy (see, for example, *Clarke v Harlowe* [2005] EWHC 3062 (Ch)).

[52] [2007] EWHC 3001 (Ch).

[53] See, for example, *Young v Lauretani* [2007] EWHC 1244 (Ch), para.50.

[54] See, for example, *Clarke v Harlowe* [2005] EWHC 3062 (Ch), and below, para.5–048.

[55] The relevant forms are prescribed by the Land Registration Act 2002 s.25(1), and the Land Registration Rules 2003, rr.23 and 58.

[56] Solicitors have been judicially reminded on a regular basis that it is highly desirable that the conveyance should set out expressly the parties' beneficial interests, whether as beneficial joint tenants or as tenants in common: *Cowcher v Cowcher* [1972] 1 W.L.R. 425; *Bernard v Josephs* [1982] Ch. 391; *Walker v Hall* [1984] F.L.R. 126; *Goodman v Gallant* [1986] 1 F.L.R. 513; *Huntingford v Hobbs* [1993] 1 F.L.R. 736; *Carlton v Goodman* [2002] EWCA Civ. 545; [2002] 2 F.L.R. 259. Solicitors who fail to take steps to find out and declare the beneficial interests are failing in their professional duty: *Walker v Hall* [1984] F.L.R. 126; *Springette v Defoe* [1992] 2 F.L.R. 388.

1998 were less explicit,[57] and even today there is no legal requirement to complete the form.[58] It is therefore all too likely that cases in which there is no express declaration by the parties will continue to come before the courts.[59]

If one person is the sole legal owner of the family home, he or she may declare that all or part of the beneficial interest is held for another; such a declaration of trust must be evidenced in writing[60] and will be conclusive in the absence of fraud.

ii. No express declaration

5–012   If there is no declaration by the legal owners as to their beneficial interests in the property, then, at least in domestic cases,[61] "the starting point where there is joint legal ownership is joint beneficial ownership".[62] Thus, a legal joint tenancy is taken to indicate a beneficial joint tenancy.[63] The reasoning behind this, as Baroness Hale explained in *Stack v Dowden*,[64] is that if the parties had intended their beneficial interests to be different from their legal interests, they would have made this explicit. The burden of showing that the beneficial interests of the parties are different from their legal interests lies on the person making this claim, who is almost inevitably the person who is claiming a larger beneficial interest.

But how easily may a court depart from this starting point? In *Stack v Dowden*, Lord Neuberger took the view that the rule applied only "[i]n the absence of any relevant evidence",[65] but the majority of the House of Lords, by contrast, held that it would be very difficult to show that the parties intended their beneficial interests to be different from their legal interests.[66] If this approach was applied

---

[57] The common declaration was that the survivor of two or more registered proprietors could give a valid receipt for capital monies. It has been decided that this form of words does not amount to a declaration that the parties hold the equitable title as joint tenants: *Harwood v Harwood* [1991] 2 F.L.R. 274; *Huntingford v Hobbs* [1993] 1 F.L.R. 736; *Stack v Dowden* [2007] UKHL 17, paras 50–51.

[58] See *Stack v Dowden* [2007] UKHL 17, para.52, in which Baroness Hale suggested that completion of the form was not mandatory and that many couples failed to do so. Her analysis of the relevant forms has been challenged, but it appears that the land registry will not reject a form that fails to complete the declaration: "Anything to declare? Express declaration on Land Registry form TR1: the doubts raised in Stack v Dowden" [2007] Conv. 364; see also Law Commission, *Cohabitation: The Financial Consequences of Relationship Breakdown* (Law Com. No.307), para.2.19.

[59] See, for example, *Tackaberry v Hollis* [2007] EWHC 2633 (Ch), in which the property in dispute had been purchased in 1930.

[60] Law of Property Act 1925 s.53(1)(b).

[61] *Stack v Dowden* [2007] UKHL 17, paras 42 and 57.

[62] *Stack v Dowden* [2007] UKHL 17, para.56, *per* Baroness Hale. All four of her fellow judges agreed with her on this point: see Lord Hope (para.4); Lord Walker (para.14); and Lord Neuberger (para.109). Lord Hoffmann did not give a separate judgment but expressed his general agreement with Baroness Hale.

[63] *Stack v Dowden* [2007] UKHL 17, *per* Baroness Hale at para.58. It may, however, be questioned whether a decision that the property should be conveyed into joint names should be taken as evidence of an intention to hold the property as joint tenants in equity, rather than as tenants in common in equal shares, given that legal co-owners are obliged to hold the legal title as joint tenants.

[64] [2007] UKHL 17, at para.54.

[65] At para109.

[66] See, for example, Lord Walker at para.33 and Baroness Hale at para.69. Cf. the earlier view, as expressed in *McKenzie v McKenzie* [2003] 2 P. & C.R. DG6, at para.65, that the starting point could be "easily displaced".

rigorously, it would offer some certainty in this complex area, even if such certainty might on occasion be at odds with the true intentions of the parties.[67] But in *Stack v Dowden* itself, Ms Dowden received 65 per cent of the proceeds of sale, and it is difficult to identify what made this an unusual case. The only reason given by Lord Hope was that Ms Dowden had contributed significantly more to the purchase price than had Mr Stack, but this is hardly unusual, especially where one partner earns more than the other. For Baroness Hale, the clinching factor appears to have been the fact that the couple did not pool their resources, but, again, it is not unusual for cohabiting couples to operate separate bank accounts,[68] nor can the attitudes and intentions of the parties always be inferred from their choice of banking arrangements.[69]

Indeed, if one examines the cases that have been decided by the courts in the wake of *Stack v Dowden*, it is difficult to discern any in which the new approach has made any difference. In *Ritchie v Ritchie*,[70] for example, the home in question was jointly owned by Mrs Ritchie and her youngest son, Richard. The judge held that since this was a domestic case it was to be decided "in accordance with the new approach", but modified this by noting that:

"[I]t may well be, however, that where one is not dealing with the situation of a couple living together it will be easier to find that the facts are unusual in the sense that they are not to be taken to have intended a beneficial joint tenancy."[71]

He then decided that "this, too, is a very unusual case"[72] and awarded the son a one-third beneficial interest (although the basis of this was rather obscure). It has also been held that the presumption of joint ownership does not apply to assets that are purchased by family members by way of investment.[73] To date, the only post-*Stack* cases in which joint legal ownership has been reflected in joint beneficial ownership have all involved spouses, and would have been decided no differently before.[74]

---

[67] As Lord Neuberger noted, a property "may be bought in joint names for reasons which cast no light on the parties' intentions with regard to beneficial ownership": *Stack v Dowden* [2007] UKHL 17, para.113. Indeed, couples do not always appreciate the significance of even an express declaration of trust: see G. Douglas, J. Pearce and H. Woodward, *A Failure of Trust: Resolving Property Disputes on Cohabitation Breakdown* (Cardiff Law School Research Papers No.1, 2007), p.56. For a review of the evidence of attitudes towards equal division, see R. Probert, "Equality in the family home?: Stack v Dowden" (2007) 15 *Feminist Legal Studies* 341.

[68] See, for example, C. Vogler, M. Brockmann and R. Wiggins, "Intimate relationships and changing patterns of money management at the beginning of the twenty-first century" (2006) 57(3) *The British Journal of Sociology* 455.

[69] K.J. Ashby and C.B. Burgoyne, "Separate financial entities? Beyond categories of money management" (2008) 37 *The Journal of Socio-Economics* 458.

[70] Leeds County Court, August 17, 2007, Case No.7LS70535.

[71] At para.65.

[72] At para.67.

[73] In *Kai Ltd v Chawla* [2007] EWHC 2357 (Ch), para.17 it was suggested that such a factor "made it easier to rebut the presumption of equality", but in *Laskar v Laskar* [2008] EWCA Civ 347, the Court of Appeal held that the presumption was simply not appropriate in this context.

[74] See, for example, *Abbott v Abbott* [2007] UKPC 53; *Shah v Baverstock* [2008] 1 P. & C.R. DG3.

We will now turn to the way in which the court will determine the beneficial interests of the parties once the starting point of a beneficial joint tenancy has been displaced, or where the property is vested in a sole legal owner and there is no declaration of trust.

III. INFORMAL TRUSTS

5–013 The legal system recognises that absolute insistence on compliance with the formal requirements would produce injustice, particularly if the parties have in fact agreed to create proprietary rights. The absence of written evidence does not affect the "creation or operation of resulting, implied or constructive trusts"[75] and thus a person who cannot show any entitlement to the legal estate may nonetheless be able to establish a claim to a beneficial interest under these equitable doctrines.

It should be noted at the outset that the terms "implied, resulting and constructive trust" are not used consistently, either by the courts or by academic commentators, and there has been considerable controversy[76] as to the correct usage of these terms and the relationship between them.[77] In recent cases, however, the distinctions between the resulting trust and the constructive trust appear to have been sharpened,[78] and these are considered in more detail below. By contrast, it is generally thought that the term "implied trust" is simply a generic term for resulting and constructive trusts, and does not constitute an independent category.[79]

Intention[80] plays an important role in both resulting[81] and constructive trusts, but intention alone cannot be sufficient, else the formal requirements would be rendered nugatory. There has to be some justification for finding that property rights have been created in spite of the failure to comply with the prescribed formalities. The reluctance of the courts to impute intentions to the parties indicates that the "fairness" of a particular outcome is not deemed sufficient

---

[75] Law of Property Act 1925 s.53(2).
[76] N. Glover and P. Todd, "The myth of common intention" (1996) 16 L.S. 324, especially at 335–338, 339–341.
[77] Contrast, for example, the bold statement of Lord Diplock in *Gissing v Gissing* [1971] A.C. 886 at 905 that it may for certain purposes be unnecessary to distinguish between them (described by Lord Walker in *Stack v Dowden* [2007] UKHL 17, para.23, as an "insouciant approach to legal taxonomy"), with the suggestion by Peter Gibson L.J. in *Drake v Whipp* [1996] 1 F.L.R. 826 at p.827 to the effect that "[a] potent source of confusion, to my mind, has been suggestions that it matters not whether the terminology used is that of constructive trust . . . or that of resulting trust."
[78] See, for example, *Curley v Parkes* [2004] EWCA Civ 1515; *Stack v Dowden* [2007] UKHL 17.
[79] See, for example, *McKenzie v McKenzie* [2003] 2 P. & C.R. DG6, para.89.
[80] The concept of the remedial constructive trust imposed on the parties by the court irrespective of their intentions has no current role in English law. Such an approach was advocated by Lord Denning in the 1970s (see, for example, *Williams & Glyn's Bank Ltd v Boland* [1979] Ch. 312 at 329; and *Hussey v Palmer* [1972] 1 W.L.R. 1286), and is currently utilised in some overseas jurisdictions (for a discussion see J. Mee, *The Property Rights of Cohabitees* (Oxford: Hart Publishing, 1999); Law Commission, *Sharing Homes* (2002), Pt IV).
[81] Although the precise role played by intention in the resulting trust has been a matter of debate: see, for example, W. Swadling, "Explaining resulting trusts" (2008) 124 L.Q.R. 72.

reason either. Although the doctrines of resulting and constructive trusts are both based on the underlying principle that it would, in the circumstances, be unconscionable to allow the legal owner to assert the absolute ownership that appears on the title documents, the element of unconscionability is a necessary[82] but not a sufficient condition for the establishment of an equitable interest. Instead, the law has adopted an approach whereby expressed intentions combined with certain actions, or certain actions from which intentions will be inferred, may give rise to a trust. The fact that only a limited range of actions are sufficient for this purpose reflects the inevitable tension between certainty and fairness: accepting only a narrow range of actions as giving rise to a trust promotes certainty; widening the range increases fairness, but at the risk of certainty.

As a broad generalisation, property lawyers favour certainty while family lawyers favour a more flexible approach. The general principles of law and equity do not, in the main, operate as a means of resource redistribution (i.e. they do not transfer entitlement from one party to another in order to achieve a just result). Thus, their very nature and origins render these doctrines imperfect vehicles for achieving social justice in the context in which they are now commonly invoked: namely, the resolution of property disputes on the breakdown of unmarried relationships, an issue that will be discussed further in Ch.8.

What, then, are the circumstances in which a person will be able successfully to assert an equitable interest by way of informal trust?

A. Resulting trusts

The traditional presumption of resulting trust operates where one person makes a direct financial contribution to the purchase of property[83] conveyed into the name of the other.[84] The contributor will, in the absence of admissible evidence that some other result[85] was intended, be entitled in equity to a share in the property proportionate to the amount of the contribution.[86] The presumption may operate to impose a trust on a sole legal owner in favour of another; equally, it may impose a trust on co-owners in favour of the one who has been solely responsible for paying the purchase price.

5–014

The key question for current purposes is whether this presumption remains relevant in the family context. In *Stack v Dowden*, the majority of the House of

---

[82] See, for example, *Ledger-Beadell v Peach* [2006] EWHC 2940 (Ch), para.132.
[83] The presumption applies to transfers of money or other personal property: *Tinsley v Milligan* [1994] 1 A.C. 340 at 371, *per* Lord Browne-Wilkinson. No such presumption applies to the voluntary transfer of land (Law of Property Act 1925 s.60(3), and see *Lohia v Lohia* [2001] EWCA Civ 1691, para.39, but it may still be shown that the transferor did not intend to lose the beneficial interest: *Hodgson v Marks* [1971] Ch. 892.
[84] *Dyer v Dyer* (1788) 2 Cox Eq. Cas. 92; 30 E.R. 42.
[85] For example, that the contribution was intended as a gift or a loan: see, for example, *Sekhon v Alissa* [1989] 2 F.L.R. 94; *Tackaberry v Hollis* [2007] EWHC 2633 (Ch) (loans from family members precluded a finding of resulting trust); *Loosemore v McDonell* [2007] EWCA 1531 (money had been a gift to son and daughter-in-law).
[86] See generally *Cowcher v Cowcher* [1972] 1 W.L.R. 425; [1972] 1 All E.R. 943; *Re Vandervell's Trusts (No. 2)* [1974] Ch. 269.

Lords held that it did not, at least where the dispute concerned the matrimonial or "quasi-matrimonial" home.[87] As Baroness Hale pointed out, the presumption "is not a rule of law"[88] but merely, as Lord Diplock had pointed out in *Pettitt v Pettitt*:

> "[A] consensus of judicial opinion disclosed by reported cases as to the most likely inference of fact to be drawn in the absence of any evidence to the contrary."[89]

This being the case, in Baroness Hale's view it could and should move with the times: it could no longer be presumed that couples would intend their beneficial interests to be coterminous with their financial contributions.[90]

Yet the resulting trust will remain relevant in other family cases (e.g. where the dispute concerns wider family members[91] or a property that has been purchased for investment purposes), and so a brief consideration of its scope is appropriate.

i. Relevant contributions

5–015 Part of the problem of identifying what contributions will give rise to a resulting trust is the fact that the courts have not always distinguished clearly between resulting and constructive trusts. It is clear that direct financial contributions to the initial purchase price[92] of the property—such as paying the deposit—will suffice.[93] It is equally clear that non-financial contributions will not. More difficult questions are posed by the use of mortgage finance. Is the relevant contribution the assumption of liability under the mortgage or the payment of mortgage instalments? The orthodox view, as restated by Peter Gibson L.J. in *Curley v Parkes*,[94] is that a resulting trust "arises once and for all at the date on which the property is acquired",[95] and therefore the payment of mortgage instalments at a later date will not give rise to a resulting trust.[96] However, although assuming liability for the mortgage may give rise to a resulting trust, it

---

[87] [2007] UKHL 17, para.31, *per* Lord Walker, although cf. the cogently-argued opinion of Lord Neuberger, paras 110–122, and note too the criticisms of W. Swadling, "The common intention constructive trust in the House of Lords: an opportunity missed" (2007) 123 L.Q.R. 511.

[88] [2007] UKHL 17, para.60.

[89] [1970] A.C. 777, at 823.

[90] Although note that in the event the shares of the parties in *Stack v Dowden* did reflect their financial contributions, and see para.5–032 below for other examples of the result being at odds with the rhetoric.

[91] See, for example, *Laskar v Laskar* [2008] EWCA Civ 347.

[92] But not to general expenses of the purchase: *Curley v Parkes* [2004] EWCA Civ 1515.

[93] Similarly, any discount to which one party is entitled under the right-to-buy legislation will be regarded as a contribution to the purchase price: see, for example, *Springette v Defoe* [1992] 2 F.L.R. 388.

[94] [2004] EWCA Civ 1515.

[95] At para.14.

[96] See, for example, *McKenzie v McKenzie* [2003] 2 P. & C.R. DG6, para.81 (son's contributions towards the repayment of the re-mortgage did "not have the requisite direct nexus with the purchase"; see also *Buggs v Buggs* [2003] EWHC 1538, para.49, in which the fact that the wife contributed to the common pool out of which the mortgage was paid did "not show the intention that she was to acquire a beneficial interest in the property".

will not automatically have this result. The presumption that joint legal owners who have assumed joint and several liability under a mortgage have each made a relevant contribution giving rise to a resulting trust may be rebutted on the facts.[97] There have been a number of cases in which the intending purchaser has not been able to obtain a mortgage personally and has asked another to lend his or her name to the transaction simply for the purpose of securing the necessary finance. It has been decided that this form of assistance, by itself,[98] does not give rise to an interest under a resulting trust.[99]

ii. *Improper motive*

If it was the intention of the parties at the time of the purchase that each should **5–016** have an interest in the property, one might well wonder why they did not take steps to put this intention on a formal basis. One possible reason for failing to do so is that the parties had an ulterior motive whereby it was necessary for it to appear that only one of the parties owned the property. Does this affect the presumption of resulting trust? In most cases the answer will be no: if an individual is entitled to an interest under a resulting trust by virtue of contributions made, it will not be necessary to disclose the improper motive to the court. For example:

> A and B plan to live together. Both contribute equally to the purchase of the property, but the legal title is conveyed into the name of A alone in order to enable B to claim means-tested state benefits. The relationship then breaks down, and B claims an interest in the property. Since the initial financial contribution to the purchase price will give rise to a presumption of resulting trust, there is no need for B to disclose the illegal reason for putting the property in A's name alone.[100]

However, there is one context in which a person who has transferred property for an illegal or improper purpose may not be entitled to rely on the presumption of a resulting trust. As noted in the introduction, in certain situations equity traditionally presumed that the transferor intended to make a gift of the property.

---

[97] *Carlton v Goodman* [2002] EWCA Civ 545, para.38, *per* Ward L.J.
[98] Contrast *Ritchie v Ritchie* Leeds County Court, August 17, 2007, Case No.7LS70535, in which financial contributions were made by both parties.
[99] *Carlton v Goodman* [2002] EWCA Civ 545, para.22, in which Mummery L.J. described the defendant's involvement in the purchase as "so circumscribed and temporary that it cannot fairly be described as a contribution to the purchase price". See also *McKenzie v McKenzie* [2003] 2 P. & C.R. DG6; *Abbey National v Stringer* [2006] EWCA Civ 338.
[100] The facts are those of *Tinsley v Milligan* [1995] 1 A.C. 340, although such a stratagem is no longer open to same-sex couples after the Civil Partnership Act 2004. *Tinsley* was followed in *Lowson v Coombes* [1999] 1 F.L.R. 799 (property in name of woman to defeat any potential claims by the man's wife for financial relief under the Matrimonial Causes Act 1973); *Slater v Simm* [2007] EWHC 951 (Ch). One might ask what has become of the principle that he who seeks an equitable remedy must come with clean hands: see *Winkworth v Edward Baron Development Co Ltd* [1987] 1 F.L.R. 825 (not referred to in *Tinsley v Milligan*, and see the discussion by M. Halliwell, "Equitable property rights, discretionary remedies and unclean hands" (2004) Conv. 439.

The presumption of advancement applied when a husband purchased property in his wife's name,[101] or a fiancé in the name of his fiancée, or a father in the name of his child.[102] The presumption of resulting trust would yield to the (itself rebuttable) presumption of advancement. Obviously outmoded in a contemporary social context, the presumption of advancement now rarely holds sway,[103] and will yield to slight evidence suggesting a contrary intention.[104] Nevertheless, such evidence must be adduced, which means that where property is transferred for an illegal purpose, the transferor may not be able to avoid disclosing the illegal purpose in order to rebut the presumption of advancement. If so, the claim will fail[105] unless the illegal purpose has not yet been carried out[106] or there are other factors to show that a gift was not intended.[107] This result may seem curious and little more than an accident of history.[108]

iii. The quantum of the claimant's interest

5–017   According to the traditional concept of resulting trust, both the existence and the extent of the equitable interest are determined by direct financial contributions to the purchase price. Equating assumption of liability under a mortgage with a cash

---

[101] *Mercier v Mercier* [1903] 2 Ch. 98; *Silver v Silver* [1958] 1 W.L.R. 259.

[102] It also applies to a transfer to a person to whom the donor stands in loco parentis. However, it does not apply to transfers by mothers (see, for example, A. Dowling, "The presumption of advancement between mother and child" [1996] Conv. 274).

[103] Reliance on it came under attack as long ago as *Pettitt v Pettitt* [1970] A.C. 777, *per* Lord Reid at 793, *per* Lord Hodson at 811, *per* Lord Diplock at 824; see also *Harwood v Harwood* [1991] 2 F.L.R. 274, *per* Sir Christopher Slade at 294; *McGrath v Wallis* [1995] 2 F.L.R. 114. The sex-specific nature of the presumption is a bar to the UK's ratification of art.5 of Protocol 7 of the European Convention on Human Rights, and in 2005 an (unsuccessful) attempt to repeal it was made in the Family Law (Property and Maintenance) Bill: for discussion, see G. Andrews, "The presumption of advancement: equity, equality and human rights" [2007] Conv. 340.

[104] *Loades-Carter v Loades-Carter* (1966) 110 S.J. 51; *McGrath v Wallis* [1995] 2 F.L.R. 114; *Ali v Khan* [2002] EWCA Civ 974; *Lavelle v Lavelle* [2004] EWCA Civ 223, para.19, *per* Lord Phillips M.R. ("not satisfactory to apply rigid rules of law to the evidence that is admissible to rebut the presumption of advancement"); *Ledger-Beadell v Peach* [2006] EWHC 2940 (Ch), para.99; *Green v Green* [2006] EWHC 2010 (Fam).

[105] *Gascoigne v Gascoigne* [1918] 1 K.B. 223; *Chettiar v Chettiar* [1962] A.C. 294; *Tinker v Tinker* [1970] P. 136.

[106] See *Tribe v Tribe* [1995] 2 F.L.R. 966 *per* Nourse L.J. at 977 and *per* Millett L.J. at 984. In *Collier v Collier* [2002] EWCA Civ 1095, by contrast, the Court of Appeal held that the illegal purpose had already been carried out, and that the father was therefore prevented from adducing evidence of the trust in his favour.

[107] In *Ledger-Beadell v Peach* [2006] EWHC 2940 (Ch), for example, the presumption of advancement in favour of the donor's fiancée had been rebutted by evidence that the money was not intended as a gift. The judge noted (at para.151) that where there were "two or more genuine reasons why the gift was not intended, of which only one involves disclosing an illegality . . . it seems to me that one is left with a case which the court will entertain because the claimant does not have to rely on the underlying illegality". See also *Silverwood v Silverwood* (1997) 74 P. & C.R. 453.

[108] *Tribe v Tribe* [1995] 2 F.L.R. 966 at 974. Note the criticisms made by the Law Commission, *Illegal Transactions: The Effect of Illegality on Contracts and Trusts* Consultation Paper No.154 (1999), para.3.23; *The Illegality Defence in Tort*, Consultation Paper No.160 (2001), para.5.35. The Law Commission proposed that a "structured discretion" should replace the current arbitrary approach, but this has proved controversial, and, to date, no final recommendations have been made.

contribution has given rise to some difficulties[109] in the authorities. If the property has been purchased for investment purposes and is being rented out, then the court may well regard it as appropriate to treat the parties' assumption of joint liability under the mortgage as a joint contribution.[110] On the other hand, cases such as *Carlton v Goodman* show that the respective payments of the parties may be considered where one party has made *no* contributions. More difficult is the situation where the parties have made unequal contributions. In the light of *Stack v Dowden*, however, it seems likely that cases of this kind will be resolved by applying constructive trust principles, to which we shall now turn.

B. Constructive trusts

The question of whether or not a constructive trust has arisen might need to be asked whether the parties are joint legal owners or where one is claiming an interest in a property of which the other is the sole legal owner. In each case the burden of showing that such a trust has arisen is on the party claiming that the beneficial interests of the parties differ from the legal title,[111] but how onerous a task will this be? In *Stack v Dowden*, it was suggested that where the legal title to the family home was conveyed into joint names, it would be difficult to displace the presumption of a beneficial joint tenancy,[112] but there was nothing in their Lordships' opinions to suggest that it would be equally difficult to show that an individual has established an interest in a home solely owned by the other.

    In determining the beneficial interests in the property, there are two stages to the inquiry: (1) the claimant must establish an interest; and (2) the court must ascertain the extent of that interest. In cases where the parties are the legal co-owners of the disputed property, the first hurdle will usually have been surmounted[113]; where one is the sole legal owner, the claimant will be required to show that it was the common intention of the parties that each should have a beneficial interest in the property, and that the claimant has relied upon that common intention to his or her detriment.[114] These requirements will be considered in turn, and the principles applied when quantifying the interests of the parties will then be discussed.

5–018

---

[109] The principal issue being whether the *quantum* of the contribution is the entire mortgage debt or the payments made; the authorities are not easy to reconcile. See, for example, *Walker v Hall* [1984] F.L.R. 126; *Young v Young* [1984] F.L.R. 375; *Marsh v Sternberg* [1986] 1 F.L.R. 526; *Stokes v Anderson* [1991] 1 F.L.R. 391; *Huntingford v Hobbs* [1993] 1 F.L.R. 736; *Irvin v Blake* [1995] 1 F.L.R. 70; *The Mortgage Company v Shaire* [2000] 1 F.L.R. 973.

[110] See, for example, *Laskar v Laskar* [2008] EWCA Civ 347.

[111] *Stack v Dowden* [2007] UKHL 17, para.4, *per* Lord Hope, and para.56, *per* Baroness Hale.

[112] See above, para.5–012.

[113] *Stack v Dowden* [2007] UKHL 17, para.63, *per* Baroness Hale. The exceptions to this rule are presumably cases such as *Carlton v Goodman* [2002] EWCA Civ. 545, discussed above at para.5–016, in which there was a common intention that the beneficial interest should belong to only one of the legal owners.

[114] It has been suggested that the Privy Council dispensed with these specific requirements in *Abbott v Abbott* [2007] UKPC 53 (M. Dixon, "The never-ending story—co-ownership after Stack v Dowden" [2007] Conv. 456), but as yet it does not appear that the courts have abandoned the structured approach required to establish an interest in favour of the "holistic" approach employed when quantifying its extent (see, for example, *Tackaberry v Hollis* [2007] EWHC 2633 (Ch); *James v Thomas* [2007] EWCA Civ 1212).

i. Establishing a common intention

5–019   There are two ways in which it is possible to establish that it was the common intention of the parties to share the beneficial interest: (1) by evidence of express discussions to this effect; and (2) by evidence of conduct from which a common intention may be inferred.

(1) Express common intention

5–020   According to Lord Bridge of Harwich in *Lloyds Bank plc v Rosset*,[115] the first and fundamental question that must always be resolved is whether there have:

> "[A]t any time prior to the acquisition of the disputed property, or exceptionally at some later date,[116] been discussions between the parties leading to any agreement, arrangement or understanding reached between them that the property is to be shared beneficially."

This underlines the fact that "common intention" means a shared intention, not an intention that each party happened to have in his or her own mind but never communicated to the other.[117] It must also be an understanding that relates to the ownership of the property, not to its use or occupation.[118] Evidence that the legal owner intended to make a gift of the property to the claimant in the future is likewise irrelevant,[119] although an express promise may give rise to a claim in proprietary estoppel.[120]

Occasionally there may be clear evidence that the parties had made an agreement about beneficial entitlement. Thus, in *Barclays Bank v Khaira*,[121] a husband and wife, in the presence of a witness, signed a Land Registry form that purported to transfer their house to the wife. Although the document was stamped, it was never presented to the Land Registry for registration and was thus ineffective to transfer the legal estate to the wife. However, the trial judge held that the transfer was "the best evidence a court could reasonably expect of an express domestic arrangement as to the sharing of a beneficial interest", and that, accordingly, it was capable of being effective to give the wife an equitable interest in the property.

5–021   However, in most of the cases that have come before the courts, the matter has been much less clear-cut. The question of whether there has been an agreement

---

[115] [1991] A.C. 107 at 132.

[116] More recent cases have indicated that the relevant discussions may have occurred at any time: see, for example, *Clough v Killey* (1996) 72 P. & C.R. D22; *James v Thomas* [2007] EWCA Civ 1212, para.24.

[117] *Springette v Defoe* [1992] 2 F.L.R. 388 at 393, 395, *per* Dillon and Steyn L.JJ. See also *Evans v Hayward* [1995] 2 F.L.R. 511.

[118] See, for example, *Mollo v Mollo* (1999) EGCS 117, in which it was held that a common intention that the property be used to provide accommodation for the owner's adult sons was a long way from a common intention that they were to own it beneficially; and *James v Thomas* [2007] EWCA Civ 1212, para.33, in which comments such as "this will benefit us both" were held not to relate to the ownership of the property.

[119] See, for example, *Tackaberry v Hollis* [2007] EWHC 2633 (Ch).

[120] See below, para.5–033.

[121] [1993] 1 F.L.R. 343.

or understanding is essentially one of fact for the trial judge[122]; and it has been said[123] that the primary emphasis accorded by the law to actual discussions between the parties (however imperfectly remembered and however imprecise their terms):

> "[M]eans that the tenderest exchanges . . . may assume an unforseen significance many years later when they are brought under equity's microscope and subjected to an analysis under which many thousands of pounds of value may be liable to turn on fine questions as to whether the relevant words were spoken in earnest or in dalliance and with or without representational intent. This requires that the express discussions to which the court's initial inquiries will be addressed should be pleaded in the greatest detail, both as to language and to circumstance."[124]

Sometimes the problem is merely one of reconciling conflicting accounts of the discussions between the parties and thereby ascertaining their intentions. In *Ungurian v Lesnoff,*[125] a Polish woman came to England to live with the plaintiff, and he bought a house in which they lived. The judge rejected her claim that the plaintiff had promised that if she burnt her boats (by giving up her career and housing in Poland) and threw in her lot with him, he would buy a house that would be her absolute property; however, the judge was satisfied on the evidence that it had been understood that the plaintiff would provide her with a home in which she would be entitled to live for her life. The court may take the background circumstances of the case in assessing the likelihood that the alleged discussions actually took place; thus, in *Cox v Jones*, for example, the judge took the view that it would be natural for there to be conversations about joint ownership in the context of the relationship, which was one with "long-term commitments potentially close at hand".[126] In contrast, in *Barton v Wray,*[127] it was thought unlikely that the legal owner of the property would have agreed to confer a half-share on her cohabitant, given that she had two young children to provide for and there had been no discussion of marriage.

The more common question is whether any sufficient understanding can be found on which the parties have relied. In *Lloyds Bank plc v Rosset,*[128] Lord Bridge cited two cases as "outstanding" examples of common intention: *Eves v Eves,*[129] in which a man told the woman with whom he was living that the house

---

[122] Thus, if the parties provide different versions of events, it is for the judge to decide whose evidence is more convincing: see, for example, *Cox v Jones* [2004] EWHC 1486 (Ch). If the dispute concerns a third party the court may be chary of accepting at face value statements by the parties regarding their intentions: see, for example, *Midland Bank Plc v Dobson* [1986] 1 F.L.R. 171 at 174; *The Mortgage Company v Shaire* [2000] 1 F.L.R. 973; *Supperstone v Hurst* [2005] EWHC 1309.

[123] *H v M (Property: Beneficial Interest)* [1992] 1 F.L.R. 229 at 242–243, *per* Waite J.

[124] At p.243. See also *Midland Bank v Cooke* [1995] 2 F.L.R. 915, p.919, in which Waite L.J. referred to "the barrenness of the terrain in which the judges . . . who try [these cases] are required to search for the small evidential nuggets on which issues as to existence . . . of beneficial interests are liable to depend".

[125] [1990] Ch. 206.

[126] [2004] EWHC 1486 (Ch), para.67, *per* Mann J.

[127] Cambridge County Court, May 10, 2002, Case No.WD105051.

[128] [1991] A.C. 107.

[129] [1975] 1 W.L.R. 1338.

was to be their joint home, but that the conveyance would be taken in his sole name because she was under 21 (then the legal age of majority); and *Grant v Edwards*,[130] in which the woman was told by the man that the only reason for not acquiring the property in joint names was her involvement in divorce proceedings and the potential of joint ownership to operate to her detriment in those proceedings. In both of these cases a common intention was inferred, on the basis that no excuse would have been necessary if it had not been the intention of the parties that the woman should have an interest in the property. It might appear that there was no agreement between the parties in these two cases, and that it was not the man's intention that the woman should have an interest in the property but rather the reverse,[131] but the excuses related only to the *legal* title,[132] and, as Lord Bridge pointed out:

> "[T]he female partner had been clearly led by the male partner to believe, when they set up home together, that the property would belong to them jointly".[133]

Had the excuse proffered by the man in these two cases focused on why the other party was not to have an interest in the property at all, no such inference would have been possible.

The two cases also highlight the importance (and perils) of communication: a shared common intention that both parties are to have an interest is of no avail if it is never communicated,[134] but words that give one person the impression that he or she is to have an interest will be construed against the person uttering them even if they do not reflect the latter's true intentions.[135] In recent years, however, this means of evidencing intention that a property be jointly owned has been less commonly invoked in the reported case law than the alternative of drawing inferences from conduct.

(2) Inferred common intention

5–022   Since informal trusts, by definition, only arise where there has been no formal declaration of trust, it is often the case that the intentions of the parties have not been articulated. In the absence of express discussions to support a finding of an agreement or arrangement to share, the court will consider whether a common intention may be inferred from the parties' conduct.

The crucial question is the nature of the conduct that will be held sufficient. Here the case law has adopted a restrictive approach in relation to the existence (as opposed to the *quantum*) of an equitable interest. Where one partner has made a direct contribution to the acquisition costs, the court will readily[136] infer an

---

[130] [1987] 1 F.L.R. 87.
[131] P. Clarke, "The family home: intention and agreement" [1992] Fam. Law 72.
[132] See J. Mee, *The Property Rights of Cohabitees* (Oxford: Hart Publishing, 1999), p.123.
[133] *Lloyds Bank v Rosset* [1991] A.C. 107 at 133.
[134] See *Springette v Defoe* [1992] 2 F.L.R. 388.
[135] See also *H v M (Property: Beneficial Interest)* [1992] 1 F.L.R. 229.
[136] *Lloyds Bank plc v Rosset* [1991] 1 A.C. 107 at 133, *per* Lord Bridge of Harwich. See also *Re Densham* [1975] 1 W.L.R. 1519.

intention[137] that both parties should have a proprietary interest in the family home.[138] Thus, a cash contribution to the overall purchase price,[139] or to the initial deposit, will give rise to the necessary inference of intention.[140] It may be that the parties have received a gift from a third party to assist them in the purchase of their home; if the gift is made to them jointly, then each will be deemed to have contributed half of it towards the purchase price.[141]

If, as is likely, the home is being acquired with the assistance of a mortgage, both the assumption of liability under the mortgage[142] and regular and substantial direct[143] contributions to the mortgage instalments will also suffice.[144] The making of occasional payments seems less likely to lead the court to draw the necessary inference about the parties' intentions,[145] and in certain situations it is clear that financial payments should be regarded as rent rather than contributions to the mortgage.[146]

But what of the wide range of other contributions to family life, some at least **5–023** of which can be said to be indirectly related to the acquisition of property? In *Lloyds Bank plc v Rosset*, Lord Bridge of Harwich (with whom all the other Law Lords expressed agreement) went so far as to say that he thought it to be "extremely doubtful" whether contributions other than direct contributions to the purchase price would justify the inference necessary to the creation of a

---

[137] It should be emphasised that the issue is whether the contribution constitutes evidence of the parties' intentions at the time of the purchase (see, for example, *Re Gorman* [1990] 2 F.L.R. 184) rather than the bare question of whether such a contribution has been made. If a financial contribution is made by one party without the other's knowledge, no common intention can be inferred: see, for example, *Lightfoot v Lightfoot Brown* [2005] EWCA Civ 201, in which the claimant had paid £41,000 towards the repayment of the mortgage without his ex-wife's knowledge and was held to have gained no interest in the property thereby.

[138] In most cases the claimant's share in the property will arise at the time that the relevant contribution is made, but in *Ledger-Beadell v Peach* [2006] EWHC 2940 (Ch), para.132 it was suggested that a court could find a constructive trust "if satisfied on the evidence that it is to be inferred that at the time of the purchase the parties intended that the party contributing towards the purchase . . . .although not entitled to a share initially, would be entitled to a share in the circumstances as they stand when the matter is before the court".

[139] As in *Drake v Whipp* [1996] 1 F.L.R. 826.

[140] Contributions of this kind would also be capable of giving rise to a resulting trust, and the overlap between the two has been a matter of no little difficulty. In the wake of *Stack v Dowden* [2007] UKHL 17, however, it would appear that the resulting trust has no role to play in the case of disputes between those sharing a home (see para.5–017 above). The issues are discussed further in the context of quantification, see below at para.5–028.

[141] See, for example, *Midland Bank v Cooke* [1995] 2 F.L.R. 915; *Supperstone v Hurst* [2005] EWHC 1309, and note also *Abbott v Abbott* [2007] UKPC 53, in which the trial judge had decided that the plot of land conveyed to the husband by his mother was intended as a joint gift to husband and wife.

[142] *The Mortgage Co v Shaire* [2000] 1 F.L.R. 973; but see *Carlton v Goodman* [2002] EWCA Civ. 545; *Abbey National v Stringer* [2006] EWCA Civ 338, above para.5–015.

[143] However, if the mortgage is paid out of a fund to which the claimant contributes, this may not be sufficient: see, for example, *Buggs v Buggs* [2003] EWHC 1538. Similarly, in *James v Thomas* [2007] EWCA Civ 1212 it was held that the use of the receipts of the parties' business to pay instalments due under the mortgage did not give rise to an inference that the claimant was to have a share.

[144] *Gissing v Gissing* [1971] A.C. 886 at 908 *per* Lord Diplock, and note *Re Gorman (A Bankrupt)* [1990] 2 F.L.R. 284.

[145] *Kowalczuk v Kowalczuk* [1973] 1 W.L.R. 930 at 935, *per* Buckley L.J. See also *Lebens v Lebens* [2003] W.T.L.R. 251.

[146] See, for example, *Savage v Dunningham* [1974] 1 Ch. 181.

constructive trust. This dictum has been criticised as both unduly restrictive[147] and at odds with earlier authorities[148] accepting indirect financial contributions that were referable[149] to the purchase price. In *Le Foe v Le Foe*,[150] the judge drew on these earlier authorities and held that indirect contributions could give rise to the inference of a common intention that the contributor should have a share in the property. As he pointed out, "the family economy depended for its function on W's earnings. It was an arbitrary allocation of responsibility that H paid the mortgage, service charge and outgoings, while W paid for day-to-day domestic expenditure."[151] In *Stack v Dowden*, Lord Walker seemed to endorse this approach, noting that "the law has moved on [since Rosset], and your Lordships should move it a little more in the same direction".[152] There are clear indications, therefore, that this aspect of Lord Bridge's speech in *Rosset* is regarded as no longer representing the law.

What about non-financial contributions? Until recently, it has been clear that making improvements to the property will not raise the inference[153] that the parties intended to share the beneficial interest.[154] However, in *Stack v Dowden*, a majority of the House of Lords suggested that making improvements that added significant value to the property should be sufficient to generate an interest.[155] While any broadening of the range of contributions that may give rise to an interest in the home is to be welcomed, it should be noted that the emphasis on improvements—as opposed to day-to-day maintenance and domestic work— means that a development of this kind is likely to benefit male rather than female

---

[147] See, for example, A. Lawson, "Direct and indirect contributions to the purchase price of a home" [1996] Conv. 462; M.P. Thompson, "A holistic approach to home ownership" [2002] Conv. 273; M. Pawlowski, "Beneficial entitlement—no longer doing justice?" [2007] Conv. 354.

[148] *Gissing v Gissing* [1971] A.C. 886; *Burns v Burns* [1984] F.L.R. 216.

[149] An indirect financial contribution would be referable to the purchase price where the legal owner could not have afforded to pay the mortgage instalments had it not been for the claimant's payment of other household expenses.

[150] [2001] 2 F.L.R. 97.

[151] At p.973. For commentary, see M. Pawlowski, "Beneficial entitlement: do indirect contributions suffice?" [2002] Fam. Law 190.

[152] [2007] UKHL at para.26. Similarly Lord Hope opined that "a complete pooling of resources in both time and money so that it did not matter who paid for what during their relationship . . . ought to be taken into account as well as financial contributions made directly towards the purchase of the property". (para.12). See also *Abbott v Abbott* [2007] UKPC 53, para.3.

[153] Although if the parties are married or in a civil partnership (or have agreed to formalise their relationship), it is provided by statute that any such contributions give rise to a share (or enhanced share) in the property: see para.3–008.

[154] See, for example, *Thomas v Fuller-Brown* [1988] 1 F.L.R. 237, in which the plaintiff had designed and built a two-storey extension to the defendant's house, constructed a through-lounge, done some electrical and plumbing work, replastered and redecorated the property throughout, landscaped and reorganised the garden, laid a driveway, carried out repairs to the chimney and roof and repointed the gable end, constructed an internal entry hall and created a newly rebuilt kitchen. He was held to have acquired no beneficial interest in the property. Similarly, in *Lloyds Bank v Rosset* the House of Lords rejected as "quite untenable" the trial judge's view that the contributions of the wife (who was a skilled decorator and painter and had spent all her time over a period of seven weeks trying to make a newly acquired but semi-derelict farmhouse ready for occupation as the family home by Christmas) were sufficient evidence of a common intention that she should have a beneficial interest in the property.

[155] See, for example, Lord Hope (para.12); Lord Walker (para.36); Baroness Hale (para.70). However, in the subsequent case of *James v Thomas* [2007] EWCA Civ 1212, no account appears to have been taken of the renovation work carried out by the woman.

claimants.[156] As yet, there have been no developments that would enable a constructive trust to be established solely on the basis of the parties' domestic contributions.[157] Were a case such as *Burns v Burns*[158]—in which the woman took her partner's name, lived with him for 19 years, looked after their children for 17 years, put her earnings into the housekeeping, and bought fixtures and fittings for the house—to come before the courts again, the result would be no different.

(3) Imputed intentions?

It is one thing to infer a common intention from the conduct of the parties where there is no evidence as to their actual intentions. But what if the parties admit that they had no such intention?[159] This raises the question of whether it is legitimate for the court to impute[160] an intention to the parties in the light of evidence to the contrary.

In the event of the parties providing credible[161] evidence that they never intended to own the property jointly, then it would not be legitimate for the court to hold that they did. If, by contrast, there is simply no evidence as to the parties' intentions, then the authorities are clear that it is legitimate to infer their intentions from their conduct.[162] The case that appears to have caused confusion is *Midland Bank v Cooke*, in particular the statement by Waite L.J. to the effect that:

> "[I]t would be anomalous to create a range of home-buyers who were beyond the pale of equity's assistance in formulating a fair presumed basis for the sharing of beneficial title, simply because they had been honest enough to admit that they never gave ownership a thought or reached any agreement about it."

But if one reads the evidence given by Mr Cooke in that case, there *was* evidence from which a common intention could be inferred. While he freely admitted that

5–024

---

[156] It remains the case that men are more likely to carry out the DIY tasks that improve the property, while women are more likely to undertake the day-to-day domestic work: see *Social Trends 33* (London: TSO, 2003), Table 13.3.

[157] For criticism see J. Miles, "Property law v family law: resolving the problems of family property" (2003) 23 L.S. 624, p.641.

[158] [1984] Ch. 317.

[159] For discussion of the role of intention in the common intention constructive trust, see J. Mee, "Joint ownership, subjective intention and the common intention constructive trust" [2007] Conv. 14.

[160] The narrowness of the distinction between "inferring" and "imputing" an intention was considered by Lord Walker in *Stack v Dowden* [2007] UKHL 17, paras 17–23. The two can, however, be distinguished: "imputation" implies that there is no intention; "inference" that there may have been an unexpressed intention.

[161] If there is a dispute with a third party, such as a trustee in bankruptcy, then the non-bankrupt spouse may attempt to claim that he or she is the sole owner of the disputed property. However, the court is likely to treat such claims with suspicion: see, for example, *Shah v Baverstock* [2008] 1 P. & C.R. DG3.

[162] As Lord Walker noted in *Stack v Dowden*, para.25, in *Lloyds Bank v Rosset* the House of Lords was "unanimously, if unostentatiously, agreeing that a 'common intention' trust could be inferred even when there was no evidence of an actual agreement".

there had been no discussions relating to the ownership of the house ("We were just happy, I suppose"[163]), the absence of express discussions does not prevent the court from inferring an agreement. And when asked "whose house did you think this was to be once the transaction was completed", he responded "[t]o be truthful, I can't actually remember, but I always thought of it as 'our house' ",[164] explaining that his name alone appeared on the title deeds because at the time of the purchase his wife was a student at teacher-training college and had no income.[165] Rather than being a case in which a trust was imposed in the face of evidence that the parties had not given their shares a thought, *Cooke* should instead be regarded as a case in which there was a common, if unarticulated,[166] intention that each should have a share in the property.

If this interpretation is adopted, there is no authority for the proposition that the court may impute an intention to parties who expressly refute any such intention.

ii. Establishing detrimental reliance

5–025　A common intention that a property be jointly owned is necessary to the establishment of a beneficial interest by way of constructive trust, but it is not sufficient per se; equity will not assist a volunteer. It must also be shown that the claimant acted to his or her detriment or in some other way significantly altered his or her position in reliance thereon.[167]

In cases in which the parties' common intention has been inferred from their conduct, such conduct also establishes that the claimant relied to his or her detriment on that common intention.[168] If the claimant is relying on an express common intention, then detrimental reliance must be established as a separate element. At this stage a wider range of contributions may be taken into account than those from which a common intention may be inferred, the key question being whether the conduct of the claimant is "referable" to the common intention. This does not mean that the conduct in question must be related to the acquisition of the property[169] but rather that it must consist of something that the person claiming an interest would not have done but for the expectation of an interest in the property.[170]

---

[163] At p.920.

[164] At p.919. The fact that the parties refer to the family home as "our" home would not usually be regarded as sufficient to show a common intention that the beneficial interest was to be shared, but in this case Mr Cooke's answer should be read in the context of the question asked.

[165] At p.919. It was clear from his evidence that it was the decision of the building society, rather than the parties themselves, that Mrs Cooke should not appear on the legal title: "I told them that Jane was a student and they said they didn't want that on the form . . . because she had no income."

[166] The comment of Steyn L.J. in *Springette v Defoe* [1992] 2 F.L.R. 388 at 392–393, to the effect that "our trust law does not allow property rights to be affected by telepathy" therefore does not prevent a trust from arising if there is relevant conduct from which a common intention may be inferred.

[167] *Gissing v Gissing* [1991] A.C. 886; *Lloyds Bank v Rosset* [1991] A.C. 107.

[168] *Lloyds Bank v Rosset* [1991] A.C. 107 at 133.

[169] *Lloyds Bank v Rosset* [1991] A.C. 107 at 132, *per* Lord Bridge; *Grant v Edwards* [1987] 1 F.L.R. 87 at 100, *per* Nourse L.J.

[170] *Grant v Edwards* [1987] 1 F.L.R. 87.

This means that the contribution, whatever its nature, must be substantial. It also raises the question of what types of contribution can be expected as part of everyday family life. The courts have held that carrying out domestic work does not establish detrimental reliance[171]; nor, indeed, will decorating work be sufficient.[172] In *Lloyds Bank plc v Rosset*, for example, Lord Bridge opined that it was:

> "[T]he most natural thing in the world for any wife . . . to spend all the time she could spare and to employ any skills she might have . . . in doing all she could to accelerate progress of the work".[173]

However, making financial contributions (whether direct or indirect), performing tasks that would usually be remunerated[174] and embarking on renovation projects perceived to be out of the ordinary[175] have all been held to constitute detrimental reliance for these purposes.

iii. Quantifying the beneficial interests

The approach to be applied by the court in quantifying the interests of the parties **5–026** under a constructive trust has been the topic of much debate[176] and has recently been reviewed by the House of Lords in *Stack v Dowden*. Consideration was given to the suggestion of Chadwick L.J. in *Oxley v Hiscock* to the effect that each party would be:

> "[E]ntitled to that share which the court considers fair having regard to the whole course of dealing between them in relation to the property."[177]

However, a preference was expressed for the way in which the Law Commission had formulated the issue in its discussion paper *Sharing Homes*[178]:

---

[171] For criticism see A. Lawson, "The things we do for love: detrimental reliance in the family home" (1996) 16 L.S. 218, 224–226; L. Flynn and A. Lawson, [1995] 3 *Feminist Legal Studies* 105.

[172] See, for example, *Midland Bank plc v Dobson and Dobson* [1986] 1 F.L.R. 171.

[173] [1991] 1 A.C. 107 at 131.

[174] See, for example, *H v M (Property: Beneficial Interest)* [1992] 2 F.L.R. 229 (unpaid work in partner's business); *Cox v Jones* [2004] EWHC 1486 (Ch), para.73 (assistance in refurbishing the property held to be of value because the owner would either have to have done the work himself "or it would have had to have been done by a professional (who would have charged for it)". It could of course be argued that the same is true of domestic work, but the very ubiquity of such work is perhaps a barrier to a true realisation of its value).

[175] See, for example, *Eves v Eves* [1975] 1 W.L.R. 1338, in which Brightman J. commented that "I find it difficult to suppose that she would have been wielding the 14lb sledgehammer, breaking up the large area of concrete . . . except in pursuance of some express or implied agreement." Cf. *James v Thomas* [2007] EWCA Civ 1212, para.36, in which it was held that the claimant had "contributed her labour to the improvements to the property because she and Mr Thomas were making their life together as husband and wife".

[176] Contrast, for example, the views expressed in *Midland Bank v Cooke* [1995] 2 F.L.R. 915 and *Springette v Defoe* [1992] 2 F.L.R. 736.

[177] [2004] EWCA Civ 546, at para.69.

[178] Law Commission, *Sharing Homes: A Discussion Paper* (Law Com. No.278), para.4.27.

"If the question really is one of the parties' 'common intention', we believe that there is much to be said for adopting what has been called a 'holistic approach' to quantification, undertaking a survey of the whole course of dealing between the parties and taking account of all conduct which throws light on the question what shares were intended."[179]

The difference between the two formulations is subtle but important; the task of the court is to determine, in the light of all the evidence, what shares the parties intended, rather than to determine what shares are fair.[180] Of course, the court may well be influenced by perceptions of what would be fair in inferring what the parties intended, but it is not entitled to override evidence as to what the parties actually intended in favour of its own view as to what the shares of the parties should be.[181] Its task, according to Baroness Hale:

"[I]s to ascertain the parties' shared intentions, actual inferred or imputed, with respect to the property in the light of their whole course of conduct in relation to it."[182]

(1) Expressed intentions

5–027 The emphasis on what the parties intended means that any discussions between the parties must be taken into account when quantifying their shares, and will normally be conclusive.[183] In *Clough v Killey*,[184] for example, the male owner had assured his cohabitant that the farm and its contents would be shared 50:50, and the court decided that there was no justification for departing from this. However the court may find that there is an express intention as to the parties' shares even when no precise figure has been mentioned. In *Savill v Goodall*,[185] there was evidence that there had been discussions about joint ownership, and Nourse L.J. took the view that if:

"[A]n ordinary, sensible couple, without more, declare an intention to own their home jointly, they can only be taken to intend that they should own it equally."[186]

---

[179] And note the earlier formulation in similar terms in *Midland Bank v Cooke* [1995] 2 F.L.R. 915 at 926, *per* Waite L.J.

[180] See, for example, *Holman v Howes* [2007] EWCA Civ 877, para.32, in which it was noted that to take certain factors into account "would be to go back to the impermissible question of what the court considers fair".

[181] Conceptually, therefore, the holistic approach to quantification is distinct from imposing a trust to give effect to what would be fair and reasonable under the so-called remedial constructive trust doctrine.

[182] At para.60, and note the endorsement of this approach by Lord Hope (para.11); Lord Walker (para.35) and Lord Neuberger (para.145).

[183] *Lloyds Bank plc v Rosset* [1991] 1 A.C. 107 at 132F and 163F. See also *The Mortgage Company v Shaire* [2000] 1 F.L.R. 973; *Crossley v Crossley* [2005] EWCA Civ 1581.

[184] (1996) 72 P. & C.R. D22.

[185] [1993] 1 F.L.R. 755.

[186] At p.760.

In some cases there may even be written evidence of the parties' intentions, as in *Supperstone v Hurst*,[187] in which the spouses had made a statement as to their respective beneficial interests in the context of the husband's bankruptcy. Although this was deemed not to be a declaration of trust[188] (which would have been binding on the parties), it was still regarded as a "compelling factor" in ascertaining their beneficial interests.[189]

(2) Inferred intentions

Although the same approach is applicable to homes in joint ownership and those where the legal title is vested in one party alone, the starting point will be different in each case. In joint ownership cases the presumption is that the beneficial interest is held under a joint tenancy, and the questions for the court are therefore "did the parties intend their beneficial interests to be different from their legal interests?" and "if they did, in what way and to what extent?"[190] In cases of sole ownership, by contrast, there is no assumption that the claimant is to have a 50 per cent share in the property.

The key issue in this area of the law has been the extent to which beneficial interests under a constructive trust should be dictated by the parties' respective financial contributions. Under a resulting trust, as we have seen, the shares of the parties are fixed at the time that the property is acquired, and are proportionate to their direct financial contributions to the purchase price. However, a contribution to the purchase price may also give rise to the inference that the parties intended to share the beneficial interest—the basis for a constructive trust.[191] In such cases, should the shares of the parties be proportionate to their

5–028

---

[187] [2005] EWHC 1309.

[188] On the basis that it did not purport to create a trust "where either no trust or some different trust had existed before" (para.50). It should, however, be noted that s.53(1)(b) of the Law of Property Act 1925 only requires written evidence of a declaration of trust, not that the trust itself be constituted by writing, and there is nothing in the section to require that such written evidence should be contemporaneous with the declaration of trust.

[189] The case was decided on the basis that it would be unfair to the husband's creditors to disregard the statement made by the wife in earlier discussions, but it is equally applicable to the issue of the parties' intentions.

[190] *Stack v Dowden* [2007] UKHL 17, para.66, *per* Baroness Hale.

[191] This problem arose out of the suggestion of Lord Bridge in *Lloyds Bank v Rosset* [1991] 1 A.C. 107 that a constructive trust could arise, in the absence of any express discussions between the parties, where there had been a direct financial contribution to the purchase price. Prior to *Rosset*, the trust created by such a contribution would have been classified as a resulting trust, and the shares of the parties would have been proportionate to their contributions (see, for example, *Walker v Hall* [1984] F.L.R. 126 at 133; *March v Von Sternberg* [1986] 1 F.L.R. 526). The cases decided immediately after *Rosset* operated on the assumption that the same method of quantification would be applicable to what was now termed a constructive trust (see, for example, *Springette v Defoe* [1992] 2 F.L.R. 736; *Huntingford v Hobbs* [1993] 1 F.L.R. 736), but in 1995 a different approach was taken in *Midland Bank v Cooke* [1995] 2 F.L.R. 915, thereby making the distinction between the resulting and constructive trust a matter of substance rather than simply terminology. The decision in *Cooke* received a mixed reception from commentators, some criticising it as doctrinally heterodox and productive of anomalies, others welcoming it as liberalisation of the law: see, for example, G. Battersby, "How not to judge the quantum (and priority) of a share in the family home" (1996) 8 C.F.L.Q. 261; D. Wragg, "Constructive trusts and the unmarried couple" [1996] Fam. Law 298; M. Pawlowski, "Midland Bank v Cooke—a new heresy?" [1996] Fam. Law 484; N. Glover and P Todd, "The myth of common intention" (1996) 16 L.S. 325 at 340.

initial financial contributions, or should a wider range of factors be taken into account? The result may be very different depending on the approach adopted, as *Midland Bank v Cooke*,[192] illustrates:

> In this case the couple married in 1971 and moved into a house purchased in the husband's name. The purchase price of £8,500 was raised by a mortgage of £6,450 with the balance made up by the husband's own savings and £1,000 in the form of a wedding gift from the husband's parents. The wife, a teacher, made considerable financial contributions to the upkeep of the home and to household expenses. In 1978 the mortgage was replaced with a bank loan granted to the husband to secure a business guarantee. A year later the wife agreed to the mortgage having priority over any interest she might have in the home. In 1981 the couple executed a further charge in joint names. The property was subsequently transferred into their joint names as tenants in common. In 1987 the couple defaulted on payments and the bank sought possession. The county court judge found that the wife's equitable interest took priority over the bank's claim, but he held that her interest was 6.7 per cent of the house's value, being the proportion of the purchase price represented by her half-share of the wedding gift from her parents-in-law. The Court of Appeal, however, applying a broad-brush approach to quantification, held that she was entitled to half the beneficial interest.

The apparent overlap between the resulting and constructive trust in the context of direct contributions to the purchase price can, however, be resolved quite simply: if the only evidence of the parties' intentions is that they have made unequal contributions to the purchase price, then this should be treated as a resulting trust case, and the shares of the parties should be determined in accordance with their unequal contributions. But if there is other evidence as to the parties' intentions (as there was in *Midland Bank v Cooke*), a constructive trust is more appropriate, and the shares of the parties will be quantified in accordance with their intentions.[193]

5–029   Indeed, if one looks at the list of factors that are suggested to be relevant in "divining the parties' true intentions", it is clear that it will be a very unusual case indeed[194] where there is no other evidence as to the parties' intentions. Such factors include:

> "[A]ny advice or discussions at the time of the transfer which cast light upon their intentions then; the reasons why the home was acquired in their joint names; the reasons why (if it be the case) the survivor was authorised to give a receipt for the capital moneys; the purpose for which the home was acquired; the nature of the parties' relationship; whether they had children

---

[192] [1995] 2 F.L.R. 915.
[193] See, for example, *Drake v Whipp* [1996] 1 F.L.R. 826.
[194] At least where the parties are sharing a home, in contrast to the situation where the parties have bought the property as an investment, or where one party makes a contribution to the purchase of a property not intended for joint occupation.

for whom they both had responsibility to provide a home; how the purchase was financed, both initially and subsequently; how the parties arranged their finances, whether separately or together or a bit of both; how they discharged the outgoings on the property and their other household expenses." [195]

Even more personal factors may be relevant:

"The parties' individual characters and personalities may also be a factor in deciding where their true intentions lay. In the cohabitation context, mercenary considerations may be more to the fore than they would be in marriage, but it should not be assumed that they always take pride of place over natural love and affection." [196]

Not only is this list not exhaustive,[197] but it is recognised that the parties' intentions may change over time. Thus, in contrast to the resulting trust, where the shares of the parties are fixed at the time that the property is acquired, the shares of the parties under a constructive trust remain fluid until determined by the court.[198] Rather than looking at the conduct of the parties to cast light on what they intended at the time the property was purchased, the court must now consider the *present* intentions of the parties in light of their past conduct.[199]

As yet, there are only a handful of cases in which the approach in *Stack v Dowden* has been applied to the quantification of an interest under a constructive trust, and the results are, to say the least, somewhat mixed. In *Abbott v Abbott*,[200] which involved facts rather similar to those in *Midland Bank v Cooke*, it was held that the spouses enjoyed equal beneficial interests in the property, taking into account the fact that the land on which the home was built was given to them as a joint gift, and that they had organised their finances jointly throughout their marriage.[201] By contrast, in *Ritchie v Ritchie*,[202] a case in which the property in question was co-owned by a mother and her son, the latter was held to be entitled to a one-third beneficial interest, rather than the 50 per cent that might be

---

[195] *Stack v Dowden* [2007] UKHL 17, para.69, *per* Baroness Hale
[196] *Stack v Dowden* [2007] UKHL 17, para.69, *per* Baroness Hale.
[197] It has been described as "the property lawyers' equivalent of Pandora's Box—everything included with only a small Hope that this will not lead to endemic uncertainty": M. Dixon [2007] Conv. 352 at p.353.
[198] Although, as Baroness Hale pointed out, at any given point in time the parties' intentions, and therefore their interests, must be the same for all purposes: thus, "[t]hey cannot at one and the same time intend, for example, a joint tenancy with survivorship should one of them die while they are still together, a tenancy in common in equal shares should they separate on amicable terms after the children have grown up, and a tenancy in common in unequal shares should they separate on acrimonious terms while the children are still with them" (para.62).
[199] See, for example, *Kai Ltd v Chawla* [2007] EWHC 2357 (Ch). In that case it was held that the shared intention of the parties was that Mrs Chawla should no longer have any beneficial interest in the property. However, it does not appear that the court addressed the question of whether this constituted a disposition of a subsisting equitable interest that should have been made in writing as required by s.53(1)(c) (see above, para.5–010).
[200] [2007] UKPC 53.
[201] It would therefore appear that the courts are still more willing to draw the inference of intention to share beneficial ownership in the case of a married than an unmarried couple.
[202] Leeds County Court, August 17, 2007, Case No.7LS70535.

suggested by the legal joint tenancy or the 25 per cent that would reflect his actual financial contribution. The justification for this was not spelt out by the judge.

(3) Potential problems

5–030 Although the decision in *Stack v Dowden* would appear to take a more holistic approach to the quantification of interests in the family home (and therefore one that is more attuned to domestic contributions and the realities of family life), there are a number of problems with the approach advocated.

From a family law perspective, one problem is that this holistic approach applies only to the quantification of interests, and not to the question of whether an interest has arisen. It may seem a little unfair that the domestic contributions of an individual who has made a modest financial contribution to the purchase price should be taken into account, while the domestic contributions made by someone who has not made a financial contribution should be ignored.[203] If a wide range of contributions are deemed relevant in determining the extent of the parties' shares, perhaps an equally wide range of contributions should be relevant in determining whether each party should have an interest?

From a property-law perspective, an alternative objection may be made: namely, that the wider the list of relevant factors, the greater the uncertainty as to what the parties shares actually are. The list of factors set out by Baroness Hale is wide-ranging and includes matters of which objective evidence may be lacking. After all, it is often difficult enough to establish who contributed what, let alone the reasons behind the division of responsibilities. Nor does the way in which the parties manage their money always cast much light upon the way in which they regard their finances.[204] It may even have been the case that the parties had *different* intentions: one may have been motivated by love and affection while the other was motivated by the desire to preserve his or her own interests.

5–031   It is true that the majority of the House of Lords in *Stack v Dowden* indicated that it would be difficult to rebut the presumption of a beneficial joint tenancy in cases where the legal title was held jointly, and that a full examination of the circumstances would only be appropriate in unusual cases,[205] but this itself poses problems: how will the court know whether the case before it is an unusual one unless it has heard all the evidence?

Finally, it would seem that the courts continue to attach considerable weight to the basic issue of who paid for what. Financial contributions have always been regarded as relevant in "illuminating the common intention as to the extent of the

---

[203] Contrast the outcome in *Midland Bank v Cooke* [1995] 2 F.L.R. 915 with that in *Burns v Burns* [1984] Ch. 317.

[204] K.J. Ashby and C.B. Burgoyne, "Separate financial entities? Beyond categories of money management" (2008) 37 *The Journal of Socio-Economics* 458.

[205] Thus Lord Walker suggested that in joint ownership cases "there will be a heavy burden in establishing . . . that an intention to keep a sort of balance-sheet of contributions actually existed, or should be inferred, or imputed to the parties" and that "the court should not readily embark on [a] detailed examination of the parties' relationship and finances". (para.33). See also Baroness Hale at para.68.

beneficial interest".[206] Despite the references to the "whole course of conduct" of the parties, the actual shares of the parties in *Stack v Dowden* closely reflected their unequal financial contributions to the purchase price. Indeed, the same is true of the earlier case of *Oxley v Hiscock*[207]; even though the court in that case held that the beneficial interests of the parties should be quantified in accordance with what was fair, "fairness" was interpreted in light of their respective financial contributions. The new approach of the court may, in practice, produce results very similar to the old.

IV. PROPRIETARY ESTOPPEL

An alternative remedy may be found in the doctrine of proprietary estoppel, **5–032** which has for many years[208] prevented a person from asserting strict legal rights when it would be unconscionable or unjust to do so.[209] As with the constructive trust, the reference to "unconscionability" does not mean that the court has an untrammeled discretion to disregard the legal entitlements of the parties: what is necessary is some assurance, promise or representation by one party on which the other has relied to his or her detriment. As Oliver J. put it in *Taylor Fashions Ltd v Liverpool Victoria Trustee*[210]:

> "If A, under an expectation created or encouraged by B that A shall have a certain interest in land thereafter, on the faith of such expectation and with the knowledge of B and without objection from him, acts to his detriment in connection with such land, a Court of Equity will compel B to give effect to such expectation."

For ease of exposition, the discussion examines each of these elements in turn, but it should be borne in mind that, in practice, each may influence the others. As Robert Walker L.J. observed in *Gillett v Holt*[211]:

> "[T]he doctrine of proprietary estoppel cannot be treated as subdivided into three or four watertight compartments . . . the quality of the relevant assurances may influence the issue of reliance . . . reliance and detriment are often intertwined, and . . . whether there is a distinct need for a 'mutual understanding' may depend on how the other elements are formulated and

[206] *Stokes v Anderson* [1991] 1 F.L.R. 391 at 400B *per* Nourse L.J.; cited by Neuberger J. in *The Mortgage Co v Shaire* [2000] 1 F.L.R. 973 at 980.
[207] [2004] EWCA Civ 546.
[208] See the (dissenting) speech of Lord Kingsdown in *Ramsden v Dyson* (1866) L.R. 1, 129 at 170, and, generally, on the evolution of the doctrine *Taylors Fashions Ltd v Liverpool Victoria Trustee Co Ltd* [1982] Q.B. 133.
[209] *Crabb v Arun RDC* [1976] Ch. 179, *per* Scarman L.J.; *Gillett v Holt* [2000] 2 F.L.R. 266, *per* Robert Walker L.J. For discussion see P. Milne, "Proprietary estoppel and the element of unconscionability" (1997) 56 M.L.R. 34; E. Cooke, *The Modern Law of Estoppel* (Oxford: Oxford University Press, 2000).
[210] [1982] Q.B. 133, at pp.151–152.
[211] [2000] 2 F.L.R. 266 at 279.

understood. Moreover, the fundamental principle that equity is concerned to prevent unconscionable conduct permeates all elements of the doctrine. In the end the court must look at the matter in the round."

Once the elements of an estoppel have been made out, the court will award "the minimum equity to do justice" by way of remedy. There are obvious similarities between proprietary estoppel and the constructive trust; there are also some profound differences, which will be highlighted once the key elements of proprietary estoppel have been considered.

One final preliminary point relates to the application of the doctrine. It is obviously of broad scope and applies to many different kinds of disputes, non-familial as well as familial. The discussion in this section will focus on its application in the context of the family home,[212] but even within this specific context the reader will note that the cases in which estoppel has been invoked have tended to involve a broader range of family relationships[213] and more varied factual backgrounds than those in which a constructive trust was claimed. This may be attributed to the broader scope of the doctrine and to the greater remedial flexibility available in estoppel cases.

A. Assurance, promise or representation

5–033 The foundation of a claim in proprietary estoppel is that one party has encouraged the other to believe that he or she already owns or would be given some proprietary interest. Mere hopes of acquiring an interest are insufficient in the absence of any encouragement.[214]

It is usually necessary for there to be some specific assurance or representation, although less explicit words and conduct that is tantamount to an assurance may also suffice. Thus, in *Thorner v Curtis*,[215] the deceased—a Somerset farmer of few words who was not given to direct speaking—had made a number of rather elliptical comments about the future of the farm and what was to happen on his death[216]; in the circumstances, they were held to be tantamount to an assurance that he would leave the farm to his nephew. An estoppel may also arise where one party knew of the other's mistaken belief and failed to take steps to correct it.

---

[212] For a full discussion, see K. Gray and S.F. Gray, *Elements of Land Law*, 4th edn (Oxford: Oxford University Press, 2005), pp.947–1015.

[213] Indeed, a number of the cases have involved situations in which an initially commercial relationship—employer and employee or landlord and lodger—assumed a familial nature when promises were made and payment ceased. Thus, in *Gillett v Holt* [2000] 2 F.L.R. 266 at 289, it was accepted that counsel "was not putting it too high when he said that for 30 years Mr and Mrs Gillett and their sons provided Mr Holt with a surrogate family".

[214] See, for example, *Parker v Parker* [2003] EWHC 1846 (Ch), in which the claimant, the ninth Earl of Macclesfield, was held to have no more than a hope that he might acquire the right to live in the ancestral castle, rather than the expectation that he would be able to do so.

[215] [2007] EWHC 2422 (Ch).

[216] These included handing over a bonus notice relating to policies on his life with the statement that they were to pay the death duties and "little things about the farm" that would only matter to someone with a long-term involvement with the farm.

It is not necessary that the assurances be irrevocable in nature, a matter of considerable importance in the context of testamentary promises[217]; indeed, estoppel claims by their nature concern promises that are initially revocable,[218] and only become irrevocable once the claimant has relied on them to his or her detriment.[219] Nor is a mutual understanding or bargain essential to the operation of the doctrine of estoppel,[220] which is one important distinction between estoppel and the constructive trust.

It is not even necessary that the assurance relate to a specific item of property.[221] In *Wayling v Jones*,[222] for example, a promise to the effect that "[i]t'll all be yours one day" was held to suffice. The court will need to determine what "it" actually is,[223] but at least such promises "can be found in context to relate to an objectively ascertainable asset".[224] By contrast, general assurances of financial support will not be sufficient to establish an estoppel.[225] Thus, in *Lissimore v Downing*,[226] statements to the effect that the claimant would never want for anything and "did not need to worry her pretty little head about money" were insufficient; as, in *Negus v Bahouse*,[227] were the assurances that the claimant would always have a roof over her head.

B. Detrimental reliance

There must be a sufficient link between the promise relied upon and the conduct that constitutes the detriment. However, the promise relied upon does not have to be the sole inducement for the conduct,[228] and if there is conduct from which inducement can be inferred, the burden of disproving reliance shifts to the defendant.[229] Thus, in *Campbell v Griffin*,[230] a man who cared for the elderly

5–034

---

[217] *Gillett v Holt* [2000] 2 F.L.R. 266, disapproving *Taylor v Dickens* [1998] 2 F.L.R. 806.
[218] W. Swadling [1998] *Restitution Law Review* 220.
[219] Although note *Hunt v Soady* [2007] EWCA Civ 366, in which the offer was withdrawn before the relevant acts occurred. It may also be held that the promise was conditional on other events: see, for example, *Uglow v Uglow* [2004] EWCA Civ 987, in which the promise by the deceased to leave the claimant the farm was held to be conditional on their partnership not breaking down, and *James v Thomas* [2007] EWCA Civ 1212, para.35, in which the representation by Mr Thomas that Miss James would be "well provided for" on his death was held to have been made "on the basis of a common assumption that the parties would still be living together when that eventuality occurred".
[220] *Gillett v Holt* [2000] 2 F.L.R. 266 at 285, *per* Robert Walker L.J. (with whom Waller and Beldam L.JJ. agreed). For this reason the "excuse" cases that have been held to give rise to a constructive trust might better be classified as cases of proprietary estoppel: see, for example, *Laethem v Brooker* [2005] EWHC 1478 (Ch).
[221] *Re Basham (Deceased)* [1987] 2 F.L.R. 264.
[222] [1995] 2 F.L.R. 1029.
[223] Thus, in *Jennings v Rice* [2002] EWCA Civ 159, in which a similar promise was made, it was held that it did not relate to the deceased's entire estate, valued at £1.285m (especially since the claimant was unaware of its extent) but simply to the house and contents, worth a more modest £420,000.
[224] Gray and Gray, *Elements of Land Law*, p.980.
[225] See, for example, *Layton v Martin* [1986] 2 F.L.R. 227.
[226] [2003] 2 F.L.R. 308.
[227] [2007] EWHC 2628 (Ch).
[228] *Amalgamated Investment & Property Co. (In Liquidation) v Texas Comerce International Bank* [1982] Q.B. 84 at 104–105; *Wayling v Jones* [1995] 2 F.L.R. 1029.
[229] *Greasley v Cooke* [1980] 1 W.L.R. 1036; *Grant v Edwards and Edwards* [1986] Ch. 638 at 657.
[230] [2001] EWCA Civ 990.

couple with whom he lodged was held to have relied to his detriment on their promise that he would have a home for life, despite his admission that he did so out of "friendship and a sense of responsibility", while in *Wayling v Jones*,[231] the plaintiff succeeded in establishing the element of reliance even though he had stated that he would have remained with the deceased even if he had made no promises regarding the property.

Reliance and detriment are intertwined: the more substantial the contribution made, the more likely the court is to find that it was made in reliance upon a promise. As the Court of Appeal in *Gillett v Holt*,[232] pointed out:

> "[D]etriment need not consist of the expenditure of money or other quantifiable financial detriment, so long as it is something substantial. The requirement must be approached as part of a broad enquiry as to whether repudiation of an assurance is or is not unconscionable in all the circumstances."

In that case, the appellant became from the age of 12 the protegé of the respondent, a rich farmer with a large farming business. The appellant worked for the respondent, eventually as his business partner, for 40 years. The respondent made assurances that he would leave his estate to the appellant, but eventually made a will in favour of another person. Although the judge at first instance[233] dismissed the claim, the Court of Appeal held that detrimental reliance had been established. The appellant and his wife had in reliance on repeated assurances of testamentary provision, and because they trusted the respondent, devoted the best years of their life to working for him. The cumulative effect of the evidence was that the appellant had an exceptionally strong claim on the respondent's conscience.

In the wake of *Gillett v Holt* there have been a number of cases in which non-financial conduct has been held to constitute detrimental reliance.[234] However, it is still open to question whether domestic activities carried out in the course of a cohabiting relationship will constitute detrimental reliance, or whether they will be seen as "what anyone in such a relationship would do".[235] In *Coombes v Smith*,[236] the woman's actions in leaving her husband, becoming pregnant, looking after the child and failing to seek employment was held not to constitute detrimental reliance, and despite the subsequent liberalisation of the requirements needed to establish an estoppel, a similar result was reached more recently

---

[231] [1995] 2 F.L.R. 1029.

[232] [2000] 2 F.L.R. 266.

[233] [1998] 2 F.L.R. 470 (Carnwath J.).

[234] See, for example, *Campbell v Griffin* [2001] EWCA Civ 990; *Jennings v Rice* [2002] EWCA Civ 159 (working without pay and looking after former employer); *Thorner v Curtis* [2007] EWHC 2422 (Ch) (working on the farm of the deceased for 15 years and not pursuing other opportunities). See also *S v S (now M)* [2006] EWHC 2892, in which the wife was held to have relied to her detriment upon informal agreement that her husband would relinquish his interest in the family home to her by entering into an agreement with her mother that the latter would have an interest.

[235] *Lissimore v Downing* [2003] 2 F.L.R. 308, para.48.

[236] [1986] 1 W.L.R. 808.

in *Lissimore v Downing*.[237] In *Ottey v Grundy*,[238] by contrast, a cohabitant did succeed in establishing detrimental reliance on the basis that she had cared for her alcoholic partner and given up her career, but this was as the result of a specific finding that she was as much a carer as a girlfriend, and that "[c]oping with this situation cannot be characterised as part and parcel of an ordinary relationship".[239]

C. The remedy

At the third stage of determining the relief appropriate to satisfy the equity,[240] the restrictions on the doctrine of estoppel as currently applied, as well as its flexibility, become apparent. On the one hand, a wide range of possible relief is available. The court may order a transfer of the entire legal estate,[241] or that the claimant is entitled to a proportion of the beneficial interest or of the proceeds or sale,[242] or the right to occupy the property.[243] It may decide that monetary compensation is all that is required,[244] and, if the claimant has already received substantial benefit from the agreement or transaction, it may decide that the equity has already been satisfied and therefore make no award at all.[245]

5-035

Nevertheless, the modern[246] authorities predicate a cautious approach; the task of the court is to seek the minimum required to do justice between the parties.[247] This:

> "[D]oes not require the court to be constitutionally parsimonious, but it does implicitly recognise that the court must also do justice to the defendant."[248]

---

[237] [2003] 2 F.L.R. 308: giving up her job held not to constitute a detriment as she did so without reluctance and "there was no sense in which she was giving up a career" (para.36).

[238] [2003] EWCA Civ 1176.

[239] Quoted at para.25.

[240] M. Pawlowski, "Proprietary estoppel—satisfying the equity" (1997) 113 L.Q.R. 232; S. Gardener, "The remedial discretion in proprietary estoppel" (1999) 115 L.Q.R. 438.

[241] See, for example, *Pascoe v Turner* [1979] 1 W.L.R. 431; *Matharu v Matharu* [1994] 2 F.L.R. 597. In *Gillett v Holt* [2000] 2 F.L.R. 266, the minimum required to satisfy the equity was the transfer to the appellant of the freehold of the farmhouse and surrounding acreage plus a sum to compensate for his exclusion from the rest of the farming business.

[242] *Wayling v Jones* [1995] 2 F.L.R. 1029.

[243] *Greasley v Cooke* [1980] 1 W.L.R. 1036.

[244] See, for example, *Baker v Baker* [1993] 2 F.L.R. 247, in which the sum to be paid was calculated in terms of what the elderly father had lost (the right to rent-free accommodation) rather than the contributions he had made towards the purchase price, on the basis that his contribution had included an element of gift to the appellants.

[245] See, for example, *Sledmore v Dalby* (1996) 72 P. & C.R. 196.

[246] Compare the broader formulation of Sir Arthur Hobhouse in *Plimmer v Wellington Corporation* (1884) 9 App. Cas. 699 at 714: to look at the circumstances of each case to decide in what way the equity can be satisfied.

[247] *Crabb v Arun District Council* [1976] Ch. 179 at 198, *per* Scarman L.J.; *Pascoe v Turner* [1979] 1 W.L.R. 431 at 438, *per* Cumming-Bruce L.J.; *Gillett v Holt* [2000] 2 F.L.R. 266 at 290, *per* Robert Walker L.J.

[248] *Jennings v Rice* [2002] EWCA Civ 159 at para.48, *per* Robert Walker L.J.

For example, it will be necessary to take benefits received by the claimant into account,[249] as well as the impact that the award of the court will have on the other party.[250]

In cases where there has been an explicit bargain (where the claimant's expectations and what is expected of the claimant in return have been defined with reasonable clarity[251]), then it may well be appropriate to fulfil the expectations of the claimant by carrying out the bargain. If, however:

> "[T]he claimant's expectations are uncertain, or extravagant, or out of all proportion to the detriment which the claimant has suffered, the court can and should recognise that the claimant's equity should be satisfied in another (and generally more limited) way."[252]

This does not mean that the extent of the claim should be limited to any detriment suffered, especially as it may be difficult to quantify such detriment with any precision.[253] Nor does it mean that the expectations of the claimant are irrelevant. Rather, both elements should be taken into account; as Gardner has pointed out, the aim of the court's jurisdiction is to rectify unconscionability, and:

> "[T]he outcome must therefore reflect *both* the claimant's expectation and reliance, *and* the degree to which these can be ascribed to the defendant, given his encouragement or acquiescence."[254]

Another way of putting this is to say that the remedy should be proportionate to both the claimant's expectations and detriment[255]; after all, a remedy that is disproportionate would hardly achieve the aim of avoiding an unconscionable result.

5–036   The inter-relationship of these different factors may be illustrated by two cases with contrasting outcomes. In *Thorner v Curtis*, the claimant had expected to inherit the farm from his uncle and had worked on it for many years without pay. An earlier will did indeed leave the farm to him, but was revoked when the uncle had a disagreement with another intended beneficiary, and no new will was ever made. In the circumstances, it was deemed proportionate that the claimant should

---

[249] See, for example, *Sledmore v Dalby* (1996) 72 P & C.R. 196; *Powell v Benney* [2007] EWCA Civ 1283.

[250] See, for example, *Baker v Baker* (1993) 25 H.L.R. 408 (initial award deemed oppressive as it would have required the sale of the family home).

[251] *Jennings v Rice* [2002] EWCA Civ 159 at para.45.

[252] *Jennings v Rice* [2002] EWCA Civ 159 at para.50.

[253] Thus Robert Walker L.J. in *Jennings v Rice* [2002] EWCA Civ 159 at para.51 noted the unquantifiable detriment of "an ever-increasing burden of care for an elderly person, and of having to be subservient to his or her moods and wishes"; similarly, in *Thorner v Curtis* [2007] EWHC 2422 (Ch), para.142, the judge referred to the "virtually impossible task" of assessing the claimant's contribution, since this "would involve going far beyond a calculation of the hours [he] put in . . . multiplied by some sort of open market remuneration rates for the same, and looking at the other opportunities in life, both financial and social, that he has given up and can never get back".

[254] S. Gardner, "The remedial discretion in proprietary estoppel—again" (2006) 122 L.Q.R. 492, at p.500.

[255] See, for example, *Sledmore v Dalby* (1996) 72 P. & C.R. 196; *Jennings v Rice* [2002] EWCA Civ 159.

be entitled to the farm (worth £2.4m) and its assets (worth a further £650,000); however, it was thought to be disproportionate for him also to receive a further £620,000-worth of bank deposits, of which he knew nothing and in relation to which no assurances had been made. By contrast, in *Jennings v Rice*, the claimant had continued to hold down a full-time job while doing unpaid gardening work, running errands and providing ever-increasing amounts of care for the deceased, in the belief that he would receive all or part of her property. It was held that the value of the estate—£1.285m—was out of all proportion to what he might have charged for his services, and he was awarded £200,000, a sum that reflected what it would have cost to have provided full-time nursing care for the deceased during the relevant period. The cases may perhaps be distinguished on the basis that the expectations of the claimant in the first case were more precise—since he was well-acquainted with the value of the farm—and the extent of his detrimental reliance greater, since he devoted what the judge described as "an extraordinary amount of time and effort"[256] to the farm.

Finally, the mode of relief will also be influenced by the nature of the dispute. If, for example, the dispute concerned a once-shared home, and the relationship between the parties has broken down, then the court will award a remedy that enables them to go their separate ways rather than continue to live under the same roof.[257] In other cases the remedy awarded may reflect the degree of security needed by the claimant.[258]

D. The relationship between estoppel and the constructive trust

The doctrine of estoppel and of constructive trusts have developed separately, but **5–037** it is well recognised that there is a substantial degree of overlap between the two.[259] There have on occasion been suggestions to the effect that the two should be assimilated,[260] but at least one proponent of this view has recently resiled from such an approach:

> "I have to say that I am now rather less enthusiastic about the notion that proprietary estoppel and 'common intention' constructive trusts can or should be completely assimilated. Proprietary estoppel typically consists of asserting an equitable claim against the conscience of the 'true' owner. The

---

[256] [2007] EWHC 2422 at para.134.
[257] See, for example, *Burrows v Sharp* (1991) 23 H.L.R. 82; *Baker v Baker* (1993) 25 H.L.R. 408.
[258] See, for example, *Pascoe v Turner* [1979] 1 W.L.R. 431 (grant of freehold was required to ensure her security of tenure, given that the other party's conduct showed that he was determined to evict her from the house).
[259] *Grant v Edwards* [1986] Ch. 638 at 656; *Lloyds Bank plc v Rosset* [1991] 1 A.C. 107 at 132, *per* Lord Bridge; *Austin v Keele* [1987] A.L.J.R. 605 at 609, *per* Lord Oliver of Aylmerton; *Yaxley v Gotts* [2000] Ch. 162 at 951, *per* Robert Walker L.J. The Law Commission's Discussion Paper *Sharing Homes* (July 2002) discusses both the similarities and differences between the two doctrines: see paras 2.101–2.104 and 2.110.
[260] *Grant v Edwards* [1986] Ch. 638 at 656; *Yaxley v Gotts* [2000] Ch. 162 at 177, *per* Robert Walker L.J.

claim is a 'mere equity'. It is to be satisfied by the minimum award necessary to do justice . . . which may sometimes lead to no more than a monetary award. A 'common intention' constructive trust, by contrast, is identifying the true beneficial owner or owners, and the size of their beneficial interests."[261]

Moreover, at every stage in the process there are small but significant differences between the two doctrines: the common intention on which a constructive trust is based may be inferred from the conduct of the parties, but this would not suffice for an estoppel; contrarily, a promise capable of giving rise to an estoppel might relate to the occupation, rather than the ownership, of a home, whereas a constructive trust by definition entails an interest in the property. In estoppel, it is sufficient if the promise was "a" reason for the claimant's subsequent actions; to establish detrimental reliance in the context of a constructive trust, however, the claimant must show that he or she would not have acted in that way "but for" the expectation of an interest. Although there is a measure of flexibility in determining the quantum of the interest of the claimant under a constructive trust, the court does not have the option—as it does in estoppel cases—of awarding a remedy other than an interest in the property. Finally, estoppel is a remedial concept centred on the intervention of the court,[262] whereas the constructive trust is a means of creating a proprietary right that operates entirely independently of the court. There are, therefore, fundamental distinctions between the two.[263]

E. Reform?

5–038 The doctrine of estoppel enables the court to go some way in giving effect to a party's reasonable assumptions (even if they are not shared by the other partner) if to do otherwise would be unfair or unjust, without going so far as to introduce a general doctrine of remedial constructive trust whereby the courts would have discretion to do whatever they might consider to be just or reasonable in the circumstances of every individual case. This is not to say that the present law is wholly satisfactory. As the Law Commission noted in *Sharing Homes*, the very flexibility of proprietary estoppel means that "certain elements of the doctrine remain unclear and . . . it is difficult to predict when it will operate".[264] In the absence of any proposals for legislative reform, however, any development of the law will have to occur through the courts.

---

[261] *Stack v Dowden* [2007] UKHL 17, para.37, *per* Lord Walker.
[262] The grant of a property right is therefore not retrospective: see, for example, *Williams v Staite* [1979] Ch. 291.
[263] See, for a persuasive analysis, P. Ferguson, "Constructive trusts—a note of caution" (1993) 109 L.Q.R. 114; and compare the reply by D.J. Hayton, "Constructive trusts of homes—a bold approach" (1993) 109 L.Q.R. 485; see also I. Moore, "Proprietary estoppel, constructive trusts and s.2 of the Law of Property (Miscellaneous Provisions) Act 1989" (2000) 63 M.L.R. 912.
[264] Law Commission, *Sharing Homes*, para.2.110.

V. RESOLVING DISPUTES BETWEEN CO-OWNERS

Depending on the way in which the property is held, a number of different issues   **5–039**
may need to be resolved in the case of a dispute between co-owners. If the parties
are joint tenants, they might wish to take steps to sever the joint tenancy. If the
relationship has broken down, then one party might ask for the property to be
sold against the wishes of the other who wishes to remain in occupation. This
may require the payment of a sum of money to the excluded beneficiary by way
of compensation. Questions may also arise regarding the sums to which each is
entitled out of the proceeds of sale; this is not merely a matter of ascertaining the
shares of the parties but may be affected by the question of whether either is
liable to account to the other for sums expended on the property.

A. Severing the joint tenancy

If the parties are beneficial joint tenants, the interest of the one will, on death,   **5–040**
accrue automatically, by operation of law, to the survivor.[265] But either may sever
the joint tenancy, thus converting it into a beneficial tenancy in common[266] (i.e.
co-ownership in distinct although undivided shares).[267] The interest of a tenant in
common may be left to another by will, and in default will pass under the
intestacy rules upon death. Converting a joint tenancy into a tenancy in common
will thus be important if either party wishes to control the devolution of the
property after death.[268] Severance cannot prejudice the client's interests in
ancillary relief proceedings,[269] and it will effectively prevent what is often the
whole of the family capital passing to the other if death occurs before the final
ancillary order.[270]

There are four ways of severing a beneficial joint interest in land.

i. Written notice

The legislation provides that severance may be achieved by simply sending a   **5–041**
written notice of one's intention to sever to the other joint tenants.[271] Such a
notice need not be in any particular form, but it must be intended to take effect
forthwith, and must show an intention that the property be thenceforth held under

---

[265] Where two or more persons die in circumstances rendering it uncertain which of them survived
the other, the younger is deemed to have survived the elder: Law of Property Act 1925 s.184; and
accordingly the younger of two beneficial joint tenants killed in a common accident will (in the
absence of evidence to the contrary) succeed to the severable share. For an example of the difficulties
to which this presumption may give rise, see *Re McBroom (dec'd)* [1992] 2 F.L.R. 49.
[266] See *Re Draper's Conveyance* [1969] 1 Ch. 486; *Harris v Goddard* [1983] 1 W.L.R. 203.
[267] Law of Property Act 1925 ss.1(6) and 36(2).
[268] For example, if either wishes to leave their share to children from a previous relationship. See also
Dingmar v Dingmar [2006] EWCA Civ 942, in which the home was held by the husband and his son
from a previous marriage as joint tenants.
[269] The court can make whatever order is appropriate, whether the spouses' interests be as beneficial
joint tenants or beneficial tenants in common.
[270] *Re Palmer (dec'd) (Insolvent Estate)* [1994] Ch. 316.
[271] Law of Property Act 1925 s.36(2).

a tenancy in common. Hence in *Harris v Goddard*[272] it was held that a wife's application that the court make a property adjustment order over the former matrimonial home did not suffice to sever the joint tenancy, since it merely invited the court to consider exercising its powers in one of a number of different ways at some time in the future.[273] Severance is effective if the notice is left at the "last-known place of abode" of the other joint tenant(s),[274] even if it is never read or received.[275] This method of effecting a severance is extremely simple, and it should be standard practice for solicitors to discuss the desirability of severance with any joint tenant who is contemplating divorce.[276]

ii. By mutual agreement

5–042   The law "has been willing to mitigate the hazards of survivorship by allowing severance to occur relatively easily",[277] and mutual agreement exemplifies the law's readiness to allow severance to occur.[278] For example, an agreement will be effective notwithstanding the fact that it is not in writing,[279] and the fact that the agreement would not be specifically enforceable is irrelevant. Even an unimplemented and unenforceable agreement in the course of divorce negotiations may constitute a sufficient "agreement" for this purpose.[280]

iii. By an act operating on the joint tenant's "share"

5–043   The fact that one joint tenant sells or mortgages a "share" in the property will sever that share.[281] Even a concealed or dishonest act suffices. For example:

In *Ahmed v Kendrick*,[282] H and W were held to be joint tenants of the matrimonial home in law and equity. H agreed to sell the house to A, but did

---

[272] [1983] 1 W.L.R. 1203.

[273] An application to the court may constitute a sufficient notice in writing provided that the relevant documents clearly indicate a desire to sever: see, for example, *Re Draper's Conveyance* [1969] 1 Ch. 486 (application under Married Women's Property Act 1882 for sale and division of proceeds effective to sever; approved in *Burgess v Rawnsley* [1975] Ch. 429).

[274] Law of Property Act 1925 s.196(3). Notice will also be deemed to be served if it is sent in a registered letter and is not returned: s.196(4).

[275] See, for example, *Kinch v Bullard* [1999] 1 F.L.R. 66, in which the wife who had sent the letter changed her mind and destroyed it when it arrived at the property.

[276] And a fortiori if the parties are not married to one another, since in that case the court will have no power to vary their beneficial interests.

[277] Gray and Gray, *Elements of Land Law*, p.1053.

[278] *Williams v Hensman* (1861) 1 John and H. 546; *Burgess v Rawnsley* [1975] Ch. 429. See also *Wallbank and Wallbank v Price* [2007] EWHC 3001 (Ch).

[279] In contrast to the usual requirement of writing for any dealing in interests in land.

[280] See, for example, *Hunter v Babbage* [1994] 2 F.L.R. 806, in which the wife's solicitors agreed to the sale of the former matrimonial home on terms that she would have a lump sum from the proceeds, but the husband died before all the financial negotiations had been completed. It was held that the joint tenancy had been severed by agreement. The fact that the negotiations were originally on a "without prejudice" basis was not material, since both husband and wife had subsequently accepted the proposals; and the court rejected an argument that the fact the agreement was to be (but had not yet been) incorporated in a consent order prevented the agreement from severing from the tenancy.

[281] There is, of course, a conceptual difficulty in this mode of severance, since a joint tenant has no "share".

[282] [1988] 2 F.L.R. 22; distinguished on the facts in *Penn v Bristol and West Building Society* [1995] 2 F.L.R. 938.

not tell W. H subsequently forged W's signature on the land registry transfer. It was held that the effect of H's actions was to sever the beneficial joint tenancy and to transfer to A the beneficial tenancy in common to which he thereby became entitled. Accordingly the property was held on trust for W and A.[283]

The separate dealing may be involuntary, and in a number of cases it has been accepted that a joint tenant's bankruptcy severs the joint tenancy, the bankrupt's severable share vesting in his or her trustee in bankruptcy.[284] However, making a will does not have the effect of severing a joint tenancy: by the time the will has taken effect, the deceased's share will have accrued to the other joint tenant(s) by virtue of the right of survivorship.

iv. By a "course of dealing"

Severance by mutual conduct—a "course of dealing sufficient to intimate that the interests of all were mutually treated as constituting a tenancy in common"[285]—is difficult to distinguish from severance by mutual agreement.[286] It seems that the distinction between the two is that for severance by a "course of dealing" it is not necessary to show a concluded agreement provided a sufficient common intention is shown to treat the tenancy as severed (e.g., severance will occur in the absence of agreement if the parties have over a long period of time acted on the assumption that each owns a severed share rather than an interest liable to accrue to the other tenant on death).[287]

5–044

B. Disputes as to whether the property should be sold

Upon divorce or dissolution the court has the power to order the sale or transfer of any property owned by either party, but in other contexts if co-owners disagree about the sale of the property then it is necessary for them to resort to the general law. The Trusts of Land and Appointment of Trustees Act 1996 created a new regime governing all forms of co-ownership, whether commercial or familial: the legal owners are classified as trustees, holding the property on trust[288] for the beneficial owners.

5–045

In the family context, of course, the legal and beneficial owners are often the same persons, and much of the regulatory structure established by the Act seems rather artificial when applied to the context of the home. For example, the Act declares that any beneficiary who is beneficially entitled to an interest in

---

[283] See also *First National Securities Ltd v Hegerty* [1985] F.L.R. 850.
[284] See, for example, *Re Gorman (A Bankrupt)* [1990] 2 F.L.R. 284. A bankrupt is only divested of his estate when a trustee is appointed (s.306) and this will normally be some time after the making of the bankruptcy order. As to when severance takes place, see *Re Dennis (A Bankrupt)* [1996] Ch. 80 and *Re Palmer (Insolvent estate)* [1994] Ch. 316.
[285] *Williams v Hensman* (1861) 1 John & H 546 at 557.
[286] *Burgess v Rawnsley* [1975] Ch. 429.
[287] See *Gore and Snell v Carpenter* (1990) 60 P. & C.R. 456 at 462.
[288] Under the Act the "trust of land" replaced the previous "trust for sale".

possession has the right to occupy the land.[289] It also provides that the trustees may exclude one or more (but not all) beneficiaries.[290] Where the trustees and beneficiaries are identical, such powers obviously cannot be exercised, and it will be necessary to apply to the court for resolution of the matter.[291] Even if the trustees and beneficiaries are different persons, the protection afforded to a beneficiary in occupation of the property[292] may be overridden by a court order.[293]

Upon an application under s.14 of the 1996 Act, the court can make such order as it thinks fit[294] relating to the exercise of trustees' functions or declaring the nature or extent of the beneficiaries' interests in the land or its proceeds.[295] The court is directed to have regard to a number of factors in determining an application for a s.14 order: namely, the intentions of the person or persons (if any) who created the trust; the purposes for which the property subject to the trust is held; the welfare of any minor who occupies or may reasonably be expected to occupy the land subject to the trust as his or her home; and the interests of any secured creditor of any beneficiary.[296] If the application relates to the exercise of the trustees' powers regarding the right of any beneficiary to occupy the property, then the court is, in addition, required to have regard to "the circumstances and wishes of each of the beneficiaries . . . entitled to occupy the land",[297] while in other applications the court must take into account:

> "[T]he circumstances and wishes of any beneficiaries of full age and entitled to an interest in possession in property subject to the trust or (in case of dispute) of the majority (according to the value of their combined interests)."[298]

i. Deciding whether to order sale

5–046 How far do cases decided under the old law remain relevant, given that the very nature of the trust for sale presumed that the primary duty of the trustees was to sell the property? It is clear that there is no longer a presumption in favour of

---

[289] Trusts of Land and Appointment of Trustees Act 1996 s.12(1). This is subject to certain exceptions that do not apply to the family home.

[290] Trusts of Land and Appointment of Trustees Act 1996 s.13.

[291] Any trustee or any person with an interest in property subject to a trust of land may apply to court for an order: Trusts of Land and Appointment of Trustees Act 1996 s.14(1).

[292] The Act protects the position of those already in occupation by providing that in such cases the beneficiary cannot be excluded, in the absence of that beneficiary's consent or a court order: Trusts of Land and Appointment of Trustees Act 1996 s.13(7).

[293] Disputes regarding the occupation of the family home may also be dealt with by means of an occupation order under Pt IV of the Family Law Act 1996, considered in Ch.9. The two jurisdictions may, on occasion, overlap: in *Chan Pui Chun v Leung Kam Ho* [2003] 1 F.L.R. 23, this was resolved by incorporating the factors sets out in the Trusts of Land and Appointment of Trustees Act as part of "all the circumstances of the case" under s.33 of the Family Law Act 1996.

[294] This form of words does not, however, confer upon the court the discretion to vary the parties' property rights: see, for example, *Pettitt v Pettitt* [1970] A.C. 777 on the construction of s.17 of the Married Women's Property Act 1882.

[295] Trusts of Land and Appointment of Trustees Act 1996 ss.14(2) and 17(2).

[296] Trusts of Land and Appointment of Trustees Act 1996 s.15(1).

[297] Trusts of Land and Appointment of Trustees Act 1996 s.15(2).

[298] Trusts of Land and Appointment of Trustees Act 1996 s.15(3).

sale,[299] which means that the focus of the debate in the modern cases has shifted away from finding a reason to refuse sale to a broader examination of all the circumstances. However, the explicit reference to the purpose for which the property is held may be seen as an express endorsement of the collateral purpose doctrine developed in earlier case law, which held that sale could be postponed where the property was being used to provide a home for the children of the relationship,[300] but not where one party simply wished to remain in the property after the relationship had broken down.[301]

As yet there is relatively little case law on the interpretation of these factors in the family context. There have been two cases in which it was held that the purpose of the trust was to provide a home for one of the adult parties even in the event of relationship breakdown; both, however, were rather unusual in that the parties had specifically agreed that this was to be the case. In *Chan Pui Chun v Leung Kam Ho*,[302] the parties had specifically agreed that the property would not be sold unless both of them agreed[303]; it had also been agreed that Miss Chan was to have a 51 per cent share, which meant that the court was required to have regard to her wishes when deciding whether to order sale. Similarly, in *Holman v Howes*,[304] the property had been purchased after the parties had divorced, in the hope that a reconciliation might be possible, but the husband explicitly promised that his ex-wife could occupy the property for as long as she wanted. It was therefore held that the wife had the right to remain there.[305]

On the other hand, there is little evidence that the express reference to the welfare of minor children occupying the home has resulted in a more child-focused approach. In *W v W (Joinder of Trusts of Land Act and Children Act Applications)*,[306] a mother applied for the sale of the family home that she had shared with her cohabitant and their two children.[307] Sale was ordered: for the court, it was a matter of balancing:

> "[T]he two most important competing considerations, namely the mother's need for realisation of her only capital in order to acquire a home, and the

---

[299] *The Mortgage Company v Shaire* [2000] 1 F.L.R. 973; *Chan Pui Chun v Leung Kam Ho* [2003] 1 F.L.R. 23.

[300] See, for example, *Williams (JW) v Williams (MA)* [1976] Ch. 278; *Re Evers Trust* [1980] 1 W.L.R. 1327 at 1330, *per* Ormrod L.J.; *Dennis v McDonald* [1981] 1 W.L.R. 810; although cf. *Burke v Burke* [1974] 1 W.L.R. 1063.

[301] *Jones v Challenger* [1961] 1 Q.B. 176; *Rawlings v Rawlings* [1964] P. 398 at 419, *per* Salmon L.J.

[302] [2003] 1 F.L.R. 23.

[303] As the judge noted, such an agreement had "more of the flavour of a commercial negotiation than one normally finds between parties setting up home together in anticipation of married bliss", the reason being that Miss Chan's confidence in her paramour had been somewhat dented by his previous conduct, and she wanted the security of knowing that she would be able to remain in the property whatever happened.

[304] [2005] All E.R. (D) 169.

[305] This was confirmed on appeal (*Holman v Howes* [2007] EWCA Civ 877), although the Court of Appeal determined the wife's right to occupation on the basis of proprietary estoppel.

[306] [2003] EWCA Civ 924.

[307] It should be noted that this was the reverse of her original claim that sale should be deferred until the youngest child reached the age of 18 (her initial assumption having been that she would be the one to remain in the family home with them).

competing interests of the girls who, as the father has throughout emphasised, have known no other home."[308]

No weight was given to the father's wishes, and consideration of the intentions of the parties and the purpose for which the property was held was excluded on the basis that the provision of a family home was neither the intention of the parties (because the children were born after the acquisition of the property) nor the purpose for which the property was held (because the parties had not specifically agreed this[309]). Such an interpretation appears unduly restrictive and an unrealistic approach to the dynamics of family life.[310]

ii. Occupation rent

5–047   If the trustees decide that one of the beneficiaries should be able to occupy the property to the exclusion of the others, then they may require that beneficiary to pay the outgoings on, or other expenses associated with, the property[311]; it may also require payments to be made to the excluded beneficiaries by way of compensation.[312] Similar conditions may be imposed by the court upon an order that one party is entitled to remain in occupation of the property. The House of Lords in *Stack v Dowden* has confirmed that the court's statutory powers under the 1996 Act replace the old doctrine of equitable accounting whereby a beneficiary who remained in occupation might be required to pay an occupation rent to a beneficiary who had been excluded from the property.[313] This means that the factors set out in s.15 must be taken into account in determining whether such compensation is payable. There is no need for the beneficiary who was not in occupation of the property to prove that he or she was ousted by the one who remained in occupation.[314]

In *Stack v Dowden* itself, both Baroness Hale and Lord Neuberger agreed that it was likely that the same result would be achieved when applying the statutory rules as under the old equitable doctrine.[315] Somewhat ironically, however, they differed in their conclusions on the case before them. Baroness Hale confirmed

---

[308] At para.18, *per* Thorpe LJ.

[309] At para.24

[310] It should be noted that the father had applied for an alternative order under the Children Act 1989, and that Thorpe L.J. explicitly stated that "whatever case the father wishes to advance under Sch.1 should receive a determination which is not substantially prejudiced by the prior determination of the mother's application" (para.15). Even so, the reasoning of the court in this case is still to be deprecated because it may set an unfortunate precedent for the down-grading of children's interests in cases where the dispute concerns a creditor.

[311] Trusts of Land and Appointment of Trustees Act 1996 s.13(5).

[312] Trusts of Land and Appointment of Trustees Act 1996 s.13(6).

[313] [2007] UKHL, paras 94 and 150.

[314] *Murphy v Gooch* [2007] EWCA Civ 603, para.18; note too the earlier cases of *Re Pavlou* [1993] 1 W.L.R. 1046 and *Byford v Butler* [2003] EWHC 1267 (Ch). It is true that in *Stack v Dowden* [2007] UKHL 17, Baroness Hale seemed to attach weight to the fact that Mr Stack had agreed to leave the house in holding that he was not entitled to compensation for exclusion (see para.94), but the view of Lord Neuberger that this should not have counted against him is to be preferred. As the latter noted, "[t]o hold that a reasonable acceptance of exclusion would make it more difficult to claim compensation would put a premium on unreasonableness and encourage litigation" (para.156).

[315] [2007] UKHL, para.94 (Baroness Hale) and para.150.

the view of the Court of Appeal that no payment was due to Mr Stack, while Lord Neuberger argued that he should have been paid (or rather retrospectively credited with) £900 per month to reflect his exclusion from the home. Applying the factors set out in s.15, it could be argued that some compensatory payment was appropriate: the property had been purchased as a home for both parties, and there was no evidence that the payment of such a sum to Mr Stack would have been detrimental to the welfare of the parties' minor children.[316] It is, of course, possible to envisage cases in which the party caring for the children cannot afford to pay the outgoings on the property, let alone a sum to compensate the other, but in view of Ms Dowden's considerably higher earnings, this was not such a case.

C. Dividing the proceeds

If the property is sold some time after the parties have separated, a further issue   **5–048** may arise regarding the division of the proceeds of sale between the parties. If one party has remained in occupation, paying the mortgage instalments and other outgoings, can he or she then argue that such contributions increased the value of the other's share and seek an enhanced share of the proceeds of sale? Alternatively, can the excluded party claim a sum from the other in respect of the other's enjoyment of the property?

This question is separate to that of the extent of the beneficial interest that each party owns,[317] and may therefore arise even where there is an explicit declaration as to the parties' shares.[318] Indeed, this may be the situation most likely to give rise to a claim by the party that has made the greater financial contribution, since there is no other mechanism for recognising that contribution. There is no hard-and-fast rule that contributions made during the relationship cannot be taken into account, but it is not usual practice to do so. As Jonathan Parker L.J. noted in *Wilcox v Tait*:

> "in the ordinary cohabitation case it is open to the court to infer from the fact of cohabitation that during the period of cohabitation it was the common intention of the parties that neither should therefore have to account to the other in respect of expenditure incurred by the other on the property during that period for their joint benefit."[319]

Equally, it is open for the parties to show that it was their intention that each should account to the other for expenditure during the relationship; or, conversely, that it was not their intention that either should account to the other for payments made after the relationship has come to an end.[320]

---

[316] As Lord Neuberger pointed out, the fact that Ms Dowden had been paying Mr Stack the sum of £900 *per* month under a time limited order suggested that she was able to afford this sum.

[317] *Wilcox v Tait* [2006] EWCA Civ 1867, para.64, *per* Jonathan Parker L.J.

[318] See, for example, *Clarke v Harlowe* [2005] EWHC 3062 (Ch); *Wilcox v Tait* [2006] EWCA Civ 1867.

[319] [2006] EWCA Civ 1867, at para.66. See also *Clarke v Harlowe* [2005] EWHC 3062 (Ch), para.38, and *Young v Lauretani* [2007] EWHC 1244 (Ch), para.61.

[320] See, for example, *Wright v Johnson* [2001] EWCA Civ 1667, para.28 (Lord Neuberger).

The question of whether credit will be given for payments made, like that of the payment of compensation to an excluded beneficiary, is now governed by the provisions of the Trusts of Land and Appointment of Trustees Act 1996.[321] The court may, as was often done under the old law, take the view that the payments made by the beneficiary in occupation should be offset against the occupation rent payable to the excluded beneficiary, allowing the two to cancel each other out.[322] It may, of course, be the case that the excluded party has continued to make payments under the mortgage, in which case liability for such sums must be added to the occupation rent payable.[323]

VI. Disputes with Third Parties

5–049   As noted in the introduction, one of the key areas in which it is important to ascertain the property rights of family members is where there is a dispute with a third party, such as the bank or building society that provided the wherewithal to purchase the family home, or a business creditor. The precise nature of the issues to be considered will depend on the way in which the property is owned and the identity of the third party, but there are, broadly, three fundamental questions: (1) is the interest of the family member binding on the third party; (2) should the family member be able to escape liability under a transaction with the third party; and (3) should the property be sold to realise the debt owed to the third party? These are all separate issues; the fact, therefore, that a family member successfully establishes that his or her interest is binding on the third party, or that he or she is not liable under a transaction that was entered into as the result of undue influence, does not mean that sale cannot be ordered.[324] In each context the law must strike a balance between the interests of family members and the interests of commercial entities[325]; whether that balance is currently struck in the right place is perhaps open to question.

A. Is the beneficial interest binding on the third party?

5–050   The standard situation in which this question will need to be asked is where money has been borrowed from a bank or building society on the security of the home, the borrower later defaults on the mortgage, and another family member

---

[321] See, for example, *Murphy v Gooch* [2007] EWCA Civ 603, para.13, in which it was suggested that the relevant provision of the Act "must be" s.14(2)(b), which provides that the court may make an order "declaring the nature or extent of a person's interest in property subject to the trust".

[322] *Murphy v Gooch* [2007] EWCA Civ 603, para.22. In that case the beneficiary in occupation had made payments by way of interest instalments under the mortgage and by way of rent to the housing association that held a 75% share in the property. It was further held that his former cohabitant should pay him a sum equivalent to half of the premiums he had paid under the endowment policy, since the policy was to be divided between them, although the actual figures of the Court of Appeal have been challenged (see E. Cooke, "Accounting payments: Please can we get the maths right?" [2007] Fam. Law 1024.

[323] See, for example, *Young v Lauretani* [2007] EWHC 1244 (Ch), para.62.

[324] See, for example, *Bank of Baroda v Dhillon* [1998] 1 F.L.R. 524; *Alliance and Leicester plc v Slayford* [2004] EWHC 1908 (Ch).

[325] For a full discussion of the relevant interests, see L. Fox, *Conceptualising Home: Theories, Laws and Policies* (Oxford: Hart Publishing, 2007).

has an interest in the home.[326] The question is relevant to the amount of money that the family will be able to retain, and is particularly important in cases where the value of the debt exceeds the value of the equity in the property. If it can be established that a member of the family has an interest in the property that is binding on the third party, then that interest will have priority—and thus the first call on the proceeds of sale when the property is sold.

However, it is only in a fairly limited range of circumstances that this question will need to be asked. The legal owners who have entered into the transaction are obviously bound by the mortgage. It is also standard practice for a lender to ask the legal owner whether there are any other occupants of the family home, and, if so, to ask them to sign a document agreeing that any interest they might have is subject to the mortgage. In addition, if the beneficiary knew of the mortgage, then he or she will be held to have consented to it, and to the mortgage having priority.[327] The issue as to whether any individual has a beneficial interest that is binding on a mortgagee will thus only arise where that individual and the mortgagee were unaware of each other's existence.

Moreover, the circumstances in which a beneficial interest will be held to bind a third party have been progressively narrowed over the years. If the mortgage was taken out to fund the purchase of the family home, it automatically has priority over any beneficial interest[328]; the reasoning here is that the property could not have been purchased in the first place without the assistance of the mortgage. The same principle applies to replacement mortgages (i.e. where a subsequent mortgage is taken out to pay off the first),[329] so it is only if a second mortgage is taken out other than to pay off the first—as may be done where, for example, the legal owner wishes to raise a sum of money against the increased value of the house to fund improvements, a holiday, or to supply a cash injection to the family business—that the issue of priority even arises. Furthermore, where the legal title is held by two or more persons, the interests of any beneficiaries will be overreached when the property is mortgaged or sold,[330] with the result that there is no interest capable of binding a third party.

It is therefore only if the property is in sole legal ownership, and the **5–051** transaction involved a second mortgage of which the beneficiary was unaware, that the court will actually consider whether the mortgagee's interest is subject to that of the beneficiary. At this point the rules differ according to whether title to the land is registered or unregistered. In unregistered land, an equitable interest

---

[326] The rules discussed in this section are relevant to any third party who falls within the legal definition of a "purchaser", and it is not unknown for them to be invoked where the legal owner has sold the property to another (see, for example, *Chhokar v Chhokar* [1984] F.L.R. 313). However, problems are unlikely to arise if the purchaser has paid the full price for the property, since the beneficiaries will be entitled to a share of the proceeds proportionate to their shares.

[327] *Bristol and West Building Society v Henning* [1985] 1 W.L.R. 778; *Paddington Building Society v Mendelsohn* (1985) 50 P. & C.R. 244. Under this rule the beneficial owner is only bound to the extent that he or she consented. Thus, if the legal owner misrepresents that the mortgage will be for £10,000 and borrows £20,000, the beneficial owner is only bound by the first £10,000 of the mortgage.

[328] *Abbey National Building Society v Cann* [1991] A.C. 56.

[329] *Equity & Law Home Loans v Prestidge* [1992] 1 W.L.R. 137.

[330] *City of London BS v Flegg* [1988] A.C. 54; *Birmingham Midshires Mortgage Services v Sabherwal* (1999) 80 P. & C.R. 256.

under a trust will bind the mortgagee only if the latter has actual or con-structive[331] notice of that interest, and a mortgagee will be held to have constructive notice of any interest of which it should have been aware.[332] This boils down to the question of whether the mortgagee has made such inspections of the property as ought reasonably to have been made.[333] In registered land (which now accounts for the majority of titles in England and Wales), the general principle is that a registered proprietor takes free of any interest not disclosed on the register,[334] but there is an important exception to this in that a beneficial interest will bind a purchaser if the person who owns the interest was in "actual occupation" at the time of registration.[335] A third party will not, however, be bound by an interest: (i) that belongs to a person whose occupation would not have been obvious on a reasonably careful inspection of the land at the time of the disposition; and (ii) of which the person to whom the disposition, is made does not have actual knowledge at the time. In addition, the interest of a person in actual occupation will not override that of the mortgagee if inquiry was made of such a person before the disposition, and he unreasonably failed to disclose the right; this reproduces the old law. Thus, in both unregistered and registered land, the focus is on the discoverability of the interest.[336]

It will therefore be apparent that the circumstances in which a beneficial interest will be found to be binding on a third party are extremely narrow in scope. The rules are likely to differ in their impact on different types of family members. The interests of the elderly parents who move into a home in the joint names of their son and daughter-in-law will be overreached, while the parent who helps their adult son or daughter get a foot on the property ladder by contributing to the purchase of their home will not be in actual occupation of the property. In addition, minors who enjoy an interest under a trust are not regarded as being in "actual occupation" as they are not deemed capable of giving an informed answer to inquiries about their rights in the property.[337]

---

[331] "Constructive" notice is now in effect defined by s.199(1) of the Law of Property Act 1925.

[332] On the extent of inquiries necessary to avoid constructive notice, see *Williams & Glyn's Bank Ltd v Boland* [1981] A.C. 487 (although note that this case was exclusively concerned with registered land and references to the position in unregistered conveyancing are therefore obiter).

[333] Law of Property Act 1925 s.199. This was applied in *Kingsnorth Finance Co Ltd v Tizard* [1986] 1 W.L.R. 783, in which the finance company was held to be bound by an interest under a constructive trust belonging to the owner's wife, notwithstanding the fact that a surveyor had inspected the property and seen no evidence of occupation by her or any other female. The court held that while the owner had hidden his wife's belongings, his inconsistent statements to the surveyor should have alerted the company to the need for further inquiries.

[334] See Land Registration Act 2002 ss.11, 12.

[335] Land Registration Act 2002 Sch.3 para.2.

[336] In registered land, this confirms the shift away from treating occupation as a "plain factual situation" connoting simply physical presence (as in *Williams and Glyn's Bank v Boland* [1981] A.C. 487) to requiring that the occupation of the individual in question be apparent (*Abbey National Building Society v Cann* [1991] A.C. 56; *Stockholm Finance Ltd v Garden Holdings Inc* [1995] N.P.C. 162). It has been noted that "this rules out the old conundrum about undiscovered occupation, whereby a purchaser's protection could be weaker in registered land": E. Cooke, "The Land Registration Bill 2001" [2002] 66 Conv. 11 at 28.

[337] *Hypo-Mortgage Services Ltd v Robinson* [1997] 2 F.L.R. 71. This case also suggested that children were in occupation of the family home as "shadows" of their parents, echoing the approach once taken to wives vis-à-vis their husbands (see *Caunce v Caunce* [1969] 1 W.L.R. 286 and *Bird v Syme-Thompson* [1979] 1 W.L.R. 440) but rejected in *Williams & Glyn's Bank Ltd v Boland* [1981] A.C. 487.

B. Can the transaction be set aside?

The fact that the home is often the family's only substantial asset, and that it has almost invariably come to be owned jointly, has meant that it has become increasingly common for one partner to be asked to join in a mortgage or other transaction necessary to secure credit for the other's business (which may, of course, be the main source of the family's income).[338] Against this social and economic background, a series of cases have addressed the question of whether such a transaction should be set aside if the former was subject to pressure by the latter to enter into it, or agreed to it because of some misrepresentation. On the one hand, it may be argued that a vulnerable party has been unfairly taken advantage of by a person with whom they have a close relationship. On the other hand, it would not be in the interests of either family or commercial life if banks and other lenders were over-reluctant to advance money on the family home. There is therefore a need to strike a balance between the competing interests.[339] The risk of misrepresentation and undue influence in personal relationships cannot be wholly eliminated without making lenders' business practices unworkable.[340]

5–052

The origin of the current law is *Barclays Bank plc v O'Brien*,[341] in which the wife of an accountant executed a charge over the jointly owned matrimonial home securing to the bank her husband's liabilities as guarantor of a company's overdraft to the bank. She claimed that she had succumbed to undue pressure on her husband's part, that he had misrepresented to her the effects of the charge and that, accordingly, it was not enforceable against her. The House of Lords agreed that the husband had misrepresented the extent of the liabilities assumed by the wife, and the bank should, on the facts, have been put on inquiry. Accordingly, the bank was fixed with constructive notice of the husband's misrepresentation, and Mrs O'Brien was entitled to set aside the charge.[342]

There are therefore two questions to be asked in this type of case: first, does the party seeking to escape from liability have an equity as against the other owner to set the transaction aside; and secondly, if so, does the lender or other person seeking to enforce the transaction have actual or constructive notice of that equity?

i. The equity to set aside

In most cases, the basis on which the defendant will seek to escape liability is that the transaction had been induced by a misrepresentation or by the exercise of undue influence.

5–053

---

[338] See, for example, *Niersmans v Pesticcio* [2004] EWCA Civ 372, para.4.

[339] For analysis of the different policies pursued in the case law see S.M. Cretney, "Mere puppets, folly and imprudence: undue influence for the twenty-first century" [1994] R.L.R. 3. See also B. Fehlberg, *Sexually Transmitted Debt* (Oxford: Oxford University Press, 1997).

[340] *Royal Bank of Scotland plc v Etridge (No.2); Barclays Bank plc v Harris; Midland Bank plc v Wallace; National Westminster Bank plc v Gill; Barclays Bank plc v Coleman; UCB Home Loans Corporation Ltd v Moore; Bank of Scotland v Bennett; Kenyon-Brown v Desmond Banks and Co* [2001] UKHL 44; at para.2, *per* Lord Bingham and para.98, *per* Lord Hobhouse.

[341] [1994] 1 A.C. 180.

[342] Mr O'Brian, of course, remained liable to the bank.

(1) Misrepresentation

5–054   There is little conceptual difficulty in understanding the concept of a mis-representation that renders the transaction voidable. The case law provides numerous examples of knowing misrepresentation,[343] but a charge may equally be set aside where the misrepresentation was innocent. In *TSB Bank plc v Camfield*,[344] a wife joined with her husband in a charge over the matrimonial home, the effect of which was to impose on her beneficial interest an unlimited liability to meet the debts of a business in which the husband was a partner. The husband had innocently misrepresented to her that her liability would be limited to £15,000, and if a higher figure had been contemplated she would not have executed the charge. It was held that she was entitled as against her husband to set aside the charge.[345]

(2) Undue influence

5–055   There is more difficulty in defining what is meant by "undue" influence, but it is now well established[346] that the cases fall into two classes: Class 1 encompasses those cases where there is proof of actual undue influence,[347] while in Class 2 cases there is a rebuttable presumption of undue influence arising from the relationship between two persons. This is further subdivided into cases where the *type* of relationship[348] gives rise to a presumption of undue influence (Class 2A), and cases where the *actual* relationship gives rise to such a presumption (Class 2B).

The latter class is very broad; the presumption arises from the existence of a relationship where one party has acquired over the other a measure of influence or ascendancy of which unfair advantage is taken.[349] The *O'Brien* principle is not confined to cases of abuse of trust and confidence but extends to reliance, dependency and vulnerability; there is no single touchstone for determining its applicability.[350] It is not possible to list exhaustively the relationships in which it

---

[343] *Midland Bank plc v Massey* [1994] 2 F.L.R. 342; *Allied Irish Bank plc v Byrne* [1995] 2 F.L.R. 238; *Bank Melli Ian v Samadi-Rad* [1995] 2 F.L.R. 367; *Bank of Cyprus (London) v Markon* [1999] 2 F.L.R. 17. In *Barclays Bank plc v O'Brien* [1993] 1 F.L.R. 124, the husband had deliberately misrepresented to the wife both the extent of the security and the duration of the borrowing period.

[344] [1995] 1 F.L.R. 751.

[345] And, on the second stage of the *O'Brien* test, that her equity to do so bound the Bank.

[346] *BCCI SA v Aboody* [1990] 1 Q.B. 923; *Barclays Bank plc v O'Brien* [1993] 1 F.L.R. 124; *Credit Lyonnais Bank Nederland NV v Burch* [1997] 1 F.L.R. 11.

[347] According to *BCCI SA v Aboody* [1990] 1 Q.B. 923 at 967, a person relying on a plea of actual undue influence must show: "(a) that the other party to the transaction . . . had the capacity to influence the complainant; (b) that the influence was exercised; (c) that its exercise was undue; (d) that its exercise brought about the transaction." The court rejected suggestions that the complainant had to show that the influence exercised was accompanied by some "malign intent" or that it was necessary to show some positive action whether by way of coercion or otherwise and would (on the facts of that case) have been prepared to find that the elements set out above were present. For examples of findings of actual undue influence, see *CIBC Mortgages plc v Pitt* [1994] 1 A.C. 200; *Langton v Langton* [1995] 2 F.L.R. 890; *Bank of Scotland v Bennett* [1999] 1 F.L.R. 115 (although no constructive notice).

[348] Principally, these are solicitor and client, and medical practitioner and patient.

[349] *Royal Bank of Scotland v Etridge (No.2)* [2001] UKHL 44 at para.8. *per* Lord Nicholls.

[350] At para.11.

applies, since, as Lord Nicholls observed in *Royal Bank of Scotland plc v Etridge (No.2)*, "the reality of life is that relationships are infinitely various" and "[h]uman relationships do not lend themselves to categorisations of this sort".[351] The cases that have come before the courts have mostly involved spouses,[352] but there are also examples of a relationship of trust and confidence being found between cohabitants, parent and child(ren),[353] wider kin[354] and even employer and employee.[355]

In cases of presumed undue influence, the complainant has traditionally been required to show that the transaction was to his or her "manifest disadvantage"; the burden then shifts to the alleged wrongdoer to rebut the presumption by showing that the transaction was freely entered into.[356] In *Royal Bank of Scotland v Etridge (No.2)*[357] the House of Lords stopped short of holding that the requirement was not necessary, but urged that the label "manifest disadvantage" be discarded and that the doctrine return to the substantive approach articulated in *Allcard v Skinner*[358] and *National Westminster Bank v Morgan*[359]: namely, asking whether the transaction was readily explicable by the relationship of the parties. This approach better captures what is in issue; after all, making a substantial gift to another might, from one perspective, be regarded as disadvantageous, but:

> "[G]enerosity repaying past acts of kindness may be a perfectly intelligible reason why someone wishes to confer a benefit on another or his or her own free will."[360]

ii. Is the equity binding on the third party?

If a lender has notice, actual or constructive, of the right to impugn a transaction, **5–056** then the equity binds[361] the lender as well as the wrongdoer.[362] Cases of actual notice are rare, but there has been a considerable amount of case law on the circumstances in which a lender will be held to have constructive notice. First, the lender must be put on inquiry; this will occur when the transaction is not on

---

[351] At para.86.

[352] In most of the cases it is a wife who asserts the equity, but this is not invariably so: see *Barclays Bank plc v Rivett* [1999] 2 F.L.R. 731.

[353] *Bainbridge v Browne* (1881) 18 Ch. D. 188 (father and children); *Chater v Mortgage Agency Services Number Two Ltd* [2003] EWCA Civ 490 (mother and son); *Abbey National v Stringer* [2006] EWCA Civ 338 (mother and son).

[354] *Mahoney v Purnell* [1996] 3 All E.R. 61 (elderly man and son-in-law); *Randall v Randall* [2004] EWHC 2258 (Ch) (aunt and nephew); *Niersmans v Pesticcio* [2004] EWCA Civ 372 (siblings).

[355] *Re Craig (Dec'd)* [1971] Ch. 95; *Credit Lyonnais Bank Nederland plc v Burch* [1997] 1 F.L.R. 11; *Staples v Lee* [1998] 1 F.L.R. 138.

[356] *Langton v Langton* [1995] 2 F.L.R. 890.

[357] [2001] UKHL 44.

[358] (1887) 36 Ch.D. 145 at 185, *per* Lindley L.J.

[359] [1985] A.C. 686 at 704 *per* Lord Scarman.

[360] *Papouis v Gibson-West* [2004] EWHC 396 (Ch), para.26, *per* Lewison J.

[361] Partial enforcement is not appropriate, although terms may be imposed when a charge is set aside: *TSB Bank v Camfield* [1995] 1 F.L.R. 751; *Bank Melli Iran v Samadi-Rad* [1995] 2 F.L.R. 367; *Dunbar Bank plc v Nedeem* [1997] 1 F.L.R. 318.

[362] The claim against the lender is secondary to and parasitic upon the existence of the claim by one debtor against the other: *First National Bank plc v Walker* [2001] 1 F.L.R. 505.

its face explicable by the relationship of the parties,[363] and where (through the existence of a personal relationship of which the lender is aware) there is a substantial risk that the other party has committed a legal or equitable wrong entitling the transaction to be set aside.[364] The second question is whether the creditor had taken reasonable steps to satisfy him- or herself that the surety had entered into the obligation freely and in knowledge of the true facts. What constitutes reasonable steps was initially set out in *O'Brien* but more comprehensively articulated by the House of Lords in *Royal Bank of Scotland plc v Etridge*.[365] As the House of Lords emphasised in the latter case, the procedures henceforth to be followed are intended to be the minimum necessary to reduce the risk of pressure in a personal relationship to an acceptable level, not to eliminate it completely (which would be commercially unrealistic). Since the circumstances in which banks are put on inquiry are very wide:

> "The furthest a bank can be expected to go is to take reasonable steps to satisfy itself that the wife has had brought home to her, in a meaningful way, the practical implications of the proposed transaction."[366]

The lender who follows the procedures outlined by the House of Lords in *Etridge* will be entitled (save in exceptional cases) to assume that the security is enforceable.[367] The lender must insist that the surety attends a private meeting with its representative to warn her of the extent of liability and risks and to advise her to take independent legal advice and receive written certification[368] that she has done so. It is not unreasonable for a lender to prefer that the advice and information be given by an independent adviser. A solicitor is obliged to give

---

[363] This will not be the case where a loan is jointly granted for joint purposes and joint benefit: *CIBC Mortgages v Pitt* [1984] 1 A.C. 200; *Brittania Building Society v Pugh* [1997] 2 F.L.R. 7; *Dunbar Bank v Nadeem* [1998] 2 F.L.R. 457; this may be so notwithstanding that some risk is involved: *Society of Lloyds v Khan* [1999] 1 F.L.R. 246. For these purposes the bank need not go beyond the face of the loan: thus, in *Chater v Mortgage Agency Services Number Two Ltd* [2003] EWCA Civ 490, it was held that the lender was not put on inquiry where a mother and son obtained a joint loan charged against the home owned by the mother, since there was nothing on the face of the loan to indicate that the money was in fact to be used for the son's business venture. As Scott Baker L.J. pointed out, there was "nothing to set the alarm bells ringing" (para.63) and the lender was "not a detective" (para.67).

[364] *Barclays Bank Plc v O'Brien* [1994] 1 A.C. 180 at 196; *Royal Bank of Scotland v Etridge (No.2)* [2001] UKHL 44.

[365] [2001] UKHL 44.

[366] *Bank of Scotland Plc v Etridge* [2001] UKHL 44, *per* Lord Nichols at para.54.

[367] Cases where a bank has been fixed with constructive notice have, prior to *Etridge*, been comparatively rare. Examples are: *Allied Irish Bank Plc v Byrne* [1995] 2 F.L.R. 238; *Bank Melli Iran v Samadi-Rad* [1995] 2 F.L.R. 367; *Credit Lyonnais Bank Nederland NV v Burch* [1997] 1 F.L.R. 11; *Dunbar Bank Plc v Nadeen* [1997] 1 F.L.R. 318; *Bank of Scotland v Bennett* [1997] 1 F.L.R. 801; *Bank of Cyprus (London) v Markon* [1999] 2 F.L.R. 17. Note that in *Etridge* itself the House of Lords on the old guidelines allowed the appeals of four wives and dismissed those of three. An action may lie against the solicitor, the success of which will of course be dependent on satisfying the usual elements of liability in negligence, including breach of duty and causation: *Mahoney v Purnell* [1997] 1 F.L.R. 612; *Royal Bank of Scotland v Etridge (No.2)* [1998] 2 F.L.R. 843; *Mercantile Credit Co Ltd v Fenwick* [1999] 2 F.L.R. 110. It is difficult to envisage how a solicitor who complies with the obligations set out by the House of Lords in *Royal Bank of Scotland Plc v Etridge (No.2)* could be held to be in breach of duty.

[368] This may be signed by a legal executive acting within the authority of his principal: *Barclays Bank plc v Coleman* [2000] 1 F.L.R. 343.

advice covering at least the nature and consequences of documents to be signed, extent of liability and risks and the essential choice whether to sign or to refuse to sign. A solicitor may also act for the bank, absent any conflict of duty, but in advising the surety the solicitor is acting for her alone and in no way as the bank's agent. The bank itself has various obligations as to the provision of information.

The leading cases have undoubtedly had an influence on banking practice,[369] but, of course, there is only so much that the law can do to protect individuals from exploitation, and those who are the most susceptible to the undue influence of another might for that reason never even seek legal redress.

C. Should sale be ordered?

As noted above, even if the court decides that the beneficial interest of a family   **5–057** member is binding on the third party, or even if the transaction is set aside, it is still possible for the third party to make an application for the property to be sold.

i. Applications by a trustee in bankruptcy

Special statutory provisions apply when a dispute over property involves a   **5–058** trustee in bankruptcy of a family member. On bankruptcy, the whole of the bankrupt's property[370] vests by operation of law in a trustee in bankruptcy,[371] and the trustee comes under an obligation to realise the bankrupt's assets (including any interest in the matrimonial home) for the benefit of the creditors. Where the family home is jointly owned, bankruptcy severs the joint tenancy,[372] and the bankrupt's severed share vests in the trustee. The result will therefore be that the family home is owned by the trustee and the bankrupt's spouse or partner as tenants in common.

Obviously, the trustee will not usually wish to take up residence in the property, and the question of how the trustees will realise the bankrupt's interest for the benefit of the creditors arises. In practice, it appears,[373] that in many cases the trustee will often first negotiate with the bankrupt's spouse or partner, and that in some cases the spouse or relatives are able to buy out the bankrupt's

---

[369] See, for example, the requirements of *The Banking Code* (March 2005), para.13.4.

[370] For the definition of the bankrupt's "estate", see Insolvency Act 1986 s.283. Note that the definition excludes things that are necessary to the bankrupt for personal use in a employment, business or vocation (s.283(2)(a))—a definition wide enough in appropriate circumstances to extend to cars, computer equipment, etc.—and also clothes, bedding, furniture, household equipment and provisions "necessary for satisfying the basic domestic needs of the bankrupt and his family" (s.283(2)(b)). After three years the bankrupt's home will cease to form part of the estate: s.283A, as inserted by the Enterprise Act s.261(1) (in force from April 1, 2004).

[371] Insolvency Act 1986. In addition to the rules relating to the vesting of the bankrupt's property in the trustee, it should be noted that any disposition of property by the bankrupt is void, except to the extent that it was made with the consent of the court or was subsequently ratified by the court: Insolvency Act 1986, s.284.

[372] See, for example, *Re Gorman (A Bankrupt)* [1990] 2 F.L.R. 284.

[373] From research funded by the E.S.R.C. and carried out at Bristol by Cretney, Clark, Davis, Furey, Wadsley and others.

interest thereby preserving the family home intact. But in many cases such a buy-out is not practicable, and the trustee will apply to the court under the Trusts of Land and Appointment of Trustees Act 1996 for an order for sale.[374]

The exercise of the court's discretion on such an application is governed not by s.15 of the 1996 Act but instead by the relevant provisions of the Insolvency Act 1986.[375] The court is to make such order as it thinks just and reasonable having regard to: the interests of the bankrupt's creditors; the conduct of the spouse or former spouse[376] "so far as contributing to the bankruptcy"; the needs and financial resources of the spouse or civil partner (or former spouse or civil partner); the needs of any children; and all the circumstances of the case other than the needs of the bankrupt.[377] After one year from the bankruptcy the court is obliged to "assume, unless the circumstances of the case are exceptional, that the interests of the bankrupt's creditors outweigh all other circumstances".[378]

5–059 In practice, very few applications for sale are made within a year from the bankruptcy.[379] In one recent case, however, the application was made just 5 days short of the 12-month period, and the question arose as to which provision the court should apply. The judge took the pragmatic view that although the case had to be decided on the basis of the factors appropriate to an application within the initial year of bankruptcy, greater weight would be given to the interests of the creditors than would be usual upon such an application, and:

> "[T]hose interests would need to be outweighed by a more important consideration or considerations in order to avoid an immediate order for sale of the property."[380]

Although the Insolvency Act 1986 was intended to give greater weight to the interests of family members,[381] the courts have rarely been able to find that "exceptional" circumstances exist. All too often the adverse consequences that ordering a sale will have for the family—such as difficulties in finding suitable accommodation or the disruption of the children's schooling—have been regarded as simply the "melancholy consequences of debt and improvidence with which every civilised society has been familiar".[382]

Weighing the competing interests of families and creditors necessarily involves a value judgment; the effect of the case law continues to give weight to

---

[374] The ability to make such an application is not constrained by any order made in matrimonial proceedings that the property should not be sold: *Avis v Turner* [2007] EWCA Civ 748.

[375] See the Trusts of Land and Appointment of Trustees Act 1996 s.15(4). Which provision is applicable will depend upon the nature of the family in occupation of the home and the property rights of family members. S.335A of the Insolvency Act applies where the property is co-owned, s.336 where a spouse or civil partner has home rights, and s.337 where children under the age of 18 are residing with the bankrupt.

[376] Or civil partner or former civil partner.

[377] Insolvency Act 1986 s.335A(2).

[378] Insolvency Act 1986 s.335A(3). Similar provisions are contained in ss.336 and 337.

[379] From the Bristol Research referred to at fn.373 above.

[380] *Martin-Sklan v White* [2006] EWHC 3313 (Ch), quoted at para.11.

[381] See S.M. Cretney (1991) 107 L.Q.R. 177 where the legislative history is summarised; note also *Gotham v Doodes* [2006] EWCA Civ 1080, para.6.

[382] *Re Citro (A Bankrupt)* [1991] Ch. 142, *per* Nourse L.J. at 157. See also *Dean v Stout* [2004] EWHC 3315 (Ch).

the view that the policy of the law is that "a man has an obligation to pay his debts and to pay them promptly, even if discharging this duty affects his liability to maintain his wife and family".[383] The effect of the legislation is that the bankrupt's family will, in practice, be given one year's grace, but in the absence of truly exceptional circumstances, no more. The fact that the bankrupt's spouse[384] or, perhaps, child[385] suffers from a serious illness has been regarded as an exceptional circumstance, although depending on the facts of the case this may justify a delay to[386]—rather than outright refusal of[387]—sale. Rarer still are cases where the needs of the bankrupt's children have been held to justify a postponement of sale.[388] The only case to have succeeded on this basis in recent times is that of *Martin-Sklan v White*[389]: here the court took into account that the mother of the two young girls was an alcoholic (and that they were heavily dependent on the support of their neighbours)[390] in ordering that sale be delayed for six years.

There have been a number of suggestions that the current law is incompatible with art.8 and art.1 of Protocol 1 of the European Convention on Human Rights,[391] but so far no such challenge has been successful. Indeed, in *Nicholls v Lan*, it was suggested that the balancing exercise that the court was required to carry out "precisely captures what is required by art.8 and art.1 of the First

[383] *Re Bailey* [1977] 1 W.L.R. 278 at 284, *per* Walton J.
[384] The needs of the bankrupt are not a factor to be taken into account in carrying out the balancing exercise, although in *Re Bremner (A Bankrupt)* [1999] 1 F.L.R. 912 it was held that the wife of a bankrupt man who had been diagnosed with inoperable cancer and was expected to die within six months had an independent need to care for him in his final months that justified a delay. The court made it clear, however, that it would not have delayed sale had the bankrupt been less ill or had a longer life expectancy.
[385] In *Re Bailey (A Bankrupt)* [1977] 1 W.L.R. 278, Walton J. seemed prepared to accept that the fact that a house that had been specially converted to meet the needs of a disabled child might justify sale being refused.
[386] See, for example, *Re Raval (A Bankrupt)* [1998] 2 F.L.R. 719 (risk that relapse of the wife's paranoid schizophrenia might be triggered by move: possession order postponed for one year); *Hosking v Michaelides* [2004] All E.R. (D) 147 (impact that move would have on mental and physical health of wife justified short delay); *Nicholls v Lan* [2006] EWHC 1255 (Ch) (wife's schizophrenia justified a delay of 18 months).
[387] For cases in which no order for sale was made, see *Judd v Brown, Re Bankrupts (Nos 9587 and 9588 of 1994)* [1998] 2 F.L.R. 360 (wife suffering from ovarian cancer; outcome (i.e. recovery or death) would be known within a relatively short period); *Claughton v Charalambous* [1999] 1 F.L.R. 740 (wife suffering from renal failure and chronic osteoarthritis; property had been adopted to her needs, and creditors would in any case receive nothing from the sale of the house).
[388] Sale was postponed for five years in *Re Holliday (A Bankrupt) Ex p. the Trustee of the Property of the Bankrupt v Holiday* [1981] Ch. 405, but this case predated the Insolvency Act 1986, when arguably a more liberal test applied (as to which see R. Probert, "The security of the home and the home as security", in Probert (ed.), *Family Life and the Law*, and note too the views expressed in *Donohue v Ingram (Trustee in Bankruptcy of Kirkup)* [2006] EWHC 282 (Ch)).
[389] [2006] EWHC 3313 (Ch). Technically this was a case under s.337(5), and the "exceptional circumstances" test did not apply, but, as noted above, the court approved an approach that accorded significant weight to the interests of the creditors and used the language of "exceptionality" in describing the circumstances of the case (at para.22).
[390] The district judge described the support provided by their neighbours as "priceless and almost impossible to replicate" (quoted at para.15).
[391] *Jackson v Bell* [2001] EWCA Civ. 387. In this case leave was given to appeal to the Court of Appeal, but the matter apparently did not proceed to a hearing: see *Nicholls v Lan* [2006] EWHC 1255 (Ch), para.42.

Protocol".[392] There have, however, been some judicial suggestions that a different approach to the process of deciding whether there are "exceptional circumstances" might be appropriate. In *Barca v Mears* it was suggested that rather than requiring a bankrupt to show that the circumstances were of an exceptional kind, it would be possible to adopt an interpretation that included cases "in which the consequences of the bankruptcy are of the usual kind, but exceptionally severe".[393] That difference of emphasis made no difference on the facts of that particular case, however, and does not appear to have led to any difference in practice.

ii. Applications by a secured creditor where the home is co-owned

5–060 If a mortgagee or other creditor with a charge over the family home[394] wishes to apply for its sale, they must make an application under s.14 of the Trusts of Land and Appointment of Trustees Act 1996, and the factors to be applied are those set out in s.15.[395] Despite the fact that there is no indication that any of these are to be given greater weight than the others, the courts have continued to attach considerable weight to the interests of creditors.[396] At the same time, the other factors listed in s.15—the intentions of those who set up the trust, the purpose for which the property is held and the welfare of any children occupying the property—have been given a rather restricted interpretation.[397]

Three points deserve special mention as of particular relevance to the family home.[398] First, while it has been recognised that one purpose for which the property may be held is to provide a home for the children of the family,[399] both the terminology and the approach of the courts display some inconsistencies.[400] Secondly, it has been suggested that the purpose of providing a family home may come to an end if one of the adult members of the family uses the home as security for a debt[401]; it is submitted, however, that the better view is that, in such

---

[392] [2006] EWHC 1255 (Ch), para.43.

[393] [2005] 2 F.L.R. 1, para.40.

[394] Such a charge may have been explicitly created by the legal or beneficial owners of the property, or an unsecured creditor may have applied for a charging order under the Charging Orders Act 1979.

[395] See above, para.5–045.

[396] See, for example, *Bank of Ireland v Bell* [2001] 2 F.L.R. 809; *First National Bank v Achampong* [2003] EWCA Civ 487; *Pritchard Englefield (a firm) v Steinberg* [2004] EWHC 1908 (Ch); and note the views expressed in *Edwards v Lloyds TSB Bank Plc* [2004] EWHC 1745 (Ch), at para.30

[397] *Telecom Plus plc v Hatch* [2005] EWHC 1523 (Ch); *Bank of Ireland v Bell* [2001] 2 F.L.R. 809.

[398] For a more detailed analysis, see R. Probert, "(Mis)interpreting the Trusts of Land and Appointment of Trustees Act 1996", in M. Dixon and G. Griffiths, *Contemporary Perspectives on Property, Equity and Trusts Law* (Oxford: Oxford University Press, 2007).

[399] Or at least the minor children of the debtor: in *First National Bank v Achampong* [2003] EWCA Civ 487, the purpose of providing a family home was apparently thought not to extend to the grandchildren of the debtor, who lived there with their mentally disabled mother.

[400] Contrast *Bank of Ireland v Bell* [2001] 2 F.L.R. 809 (provision of "family home" came to an end when the husband departed) with *Edwards v Lloyds TSB Bank Plc* [2004] EWHC 1745 (Ch) (provision of "matrimonial home" held to have continued despite the departure of the husband). Note too the restrictive interpretation in the intra-family case of *W v W (Joinder of Trusts of Land Act and Children Act Applications)* [2003] EWCA Civ 924, considered above at para.5–046.

[401] *Barclays Bank v Hendricks* [1996] 1 F.L.R. 258; *Bankers Trust v Namdar* [1997] EGCS 20.

cases, the purpose of using the home as security for a debt is *additional* to that of providing the family with a home. To hold otherwise means that it will always—and perversely—be decided that the purpose of providing a family home has been extinguished in the very cases where it is most important to show that the property is still being used for this purpose: namely, where the property has been mortgaged to a third party who is now claiming sale. The idea that there can be only one purpose for which the property is held, and that a new purpose drives out an earlier purpose, is consistent with neither the spirit nor the terms of the 1996 Act. Thirdly, too little attention has been paid to the interests of minor children in occupation of the home, particularly where the "child" in question is on the verge of adulthood.[402] The courts have shown themselves more willing to imagine the hardships that may be caused to the creditors kept out of their money than how the welfare of children might be affected by the loss of the family home.[403]

As Miller has noted:

"[T]he task of tilting the balance in favour of the occupier will not be easy, but it must have been the intention that the balance would be tilted more in favour of the debtor's co-owner and family than is the case on an application for an order for sale by a trustee in bankruptcy where exceptional circumstances must be shown to avoid an order for sale."[404]

On the basis of the case law to date, it would seem that the courts have a long way to go before the balance is redressed.

iii. Applications by a creditor where the home is in single ownership
In some cases even the limited protection offered by the Trusts of Land and   **5–061**
Appointment of Trustees Act is not available: namely, where the property is held by a single owner. Since the legislation applies only where there is a trust of land, it cannot, by definition, apply where one person is the sole legal and beneficial owner of the land. In such cases the court has no discretion to postpone the sale of the home, whatever the impact this will have on the family that occupies it.[405]

---

[402] See, for example, *Bank of Ireland v Bell* [2001] 2 F.L.R. 809 (son almost 18, interests "should only have been a very slight consideration"); *Telecom Plus plc v Hatch* [2005] EWHC 1523 (Ch) (son almost 18, suffering from clinical depression, 4-week extension granted). It can be argued, however, that this confuses two separate factors: the interests of the minor, and the length of time for which the welfare of the minor will be a relevant consideration.

[403] See, for example, *First National Bank v Achampong* [2003] EWCA Civ 487.

[404] G. Miller, *The Family, Creditors and Insolvency* (Oxford: Oxford University Press, 2004), p.89. Note, by contrast, the argument of O. Radley-Gardner, "Section 15 of TLATA, or the importance of being earners" (2003) 5 Web J.C.L.I. that a more generous approach would merely result in more applications being made to bankrupt the mortgagor. This does not by itself justify the pro-creditor stance adopted by the courts under the Trusts of Land and Appointment of Trustees Act, since: (i) the creditor's assets may exceed any debts; and (ii) it should not be overlooked that the family of a bankrupt will usually have a year's grace before an application for sale is made.

[405] See *Pickering v Wells* [2002] 2 F.L.R. 798. In *Owo-Samson v Barclays Bank plc* [2003] EWCA Civ 714, para.64, it was held that this approach was not inconsistent with the European Convention on Human Rights.

VII. Personal Property

5–062   The family home will often be the only substantial asset at issue between the parties to a relationship, but there may also be disputes about the ownership of items of personal property and entitlement to funds in a bank account.

In general, items belong to the person who paid for them, whether or not they were intended for joint use,[406] but no formalities are required for a declaration of trust over personal property, and so a mere oral statement—such as "the money is as much yours as mine"[407]—might well be sufficient to create an express trust. A gift may also be made of an item of personal property, although it will be necessary to show that there was an effective delivery of it to the intended recipient.[408]

In the case of land or chattels, the claim that the courts often have to decide is whether the beneficial interest belongs to both husband and wife, even though the legal title is only in one. In the case of bank accounts, the claim is often the converse (i.e. that although the parties have had a joint account, the balance in it and any investments made out of it belong only to one of them).[409]

5–063   The courts have established a number of guidelines applicable to such cases. First, it seems that if the parties pool their resources in a common fund, then each will have an interest as beneficial joint tenant in the whole of the fund.[410] Thus, if both husband and wife pay their incomes into a joint bank account, each party is to be treated as equally entitled. On the death of one, the survivor will normally be entitled to the whole balance by operation of the right of survivorship generally applicable to joint ownership. However, if funds are withdrawn from a common pool account, property that is purchased with the proceeds will prima facie belong to the person who acquires the title: thus, if a wife buys shares in her own name, paying for them by drawing on a joint bank account, they will prima facie belong to her absolutely.[411] This will not be so if there is evidence that the assets acquired were intended to be held in the same way as the fund,[412] but this would be unusual.

These principles of the common fund will only apply in cases where there has been a pooling of resources. If, in contrast, virtually all the funds are provided by one party, the presumptions of advancement and resulting trust will (in the

---

[406] Thus in *Abrahams v Trustee in Bankruptcy of Abrahams, The Times*, July 26, 1999, a wife who had paid £1 per week into a lottery syndicate in the name of her husband, from whom she was separated, was entitled to his share of the winnings when the syndicate won over £3.6m.

[407] See, for example, *Paul v Constance* [1991] A.C. 103 (repeated statements to that effect); *Rowe v Prance* [1999] 2 F.L.R. 787 (boat registered in the man's sole name on the excuse that the woman did not have an Ocean Master's Certificate, but he frequently referred to it as "ours" and indicated that it was her security).

[408] *Re Cole* [1964] Ch. 175.

[409] The bank account may be in joint names simply for convenience: see, for example, *Stoeckert v Geddes* [2004] UKPC 54; *Papouis v Gibson-West* [2004] EWHC 396 (Ch); *Sillett v Meek* [2007] EWHC 1169 (Ch).

[410] *Jones v Maynard* [1951] Ch. 572; cf. *Gage v King* [1961] 1 Q.B. 188.

[411] *Re Bishop (dec'd)* [1965] Ch. 450.

[412] *Jones v Maynard* [1951] Ch. 572.

absence of other evidence) be applied to determine ownership.[413] It is for this reason that, if a husband has his salary paid into a joint bank account, prima facie the presumption of advancement will apply, with the result that the account will belong to the spouses as joint tenants, whereas if such an account were fed solely by a wife's earnings, the presumption would not apply and the account would belong to the wife alone.[414] However, the fact that the presumption of advancement is now much weaker means that it may be more easily rebutted (e.g. by evidence that the account was in joint names for reasons of convenience or for some limited purpose only).[415]

VIII. CONCLUSION

As Lord Hope noted in *Stack v Dowden*, a different approach should apply to the family home: **5–064**

> "A more practical, down-to-earth, fact-based approach is called for . . . The framework which the law provides should be simple, and it should be accessible."[416]

The reader may well feel that the current law fails on all points, and may echo the view of Carnwath L.J. (expressed when that case was before the Court of Appeal) that:

> "To the detached observer, the result may seem like a witch's brew, into which various esoteric ingredients have been stirred over the years, and in which different ideas bubble to the surface at different times. They include implied trust, constructive trust, resulting trust, presumption of advancement, proprietary estoppel . . . and so on. These ideas are likely to mean nothing to laymen, and often little more to the lawyers who use them."[417]

A more coherent concept of "family assets" might assist in the resolution of disputes between those whose relationship has broken down. It might also be

---

[413] See, for example, *Stoeckert v Geddes* [2004] UKPC 54, in which it was held that the funds in the bank account belonged solely to the male partner. However, it was accepted that the woman would have a beneficial interest in any funds that she actually withdrew from it.

[414] *Re Figgis (dec'd)* [1969] 1 Ch. 123; cf. *Heseltine v Heseltine* [1971] 1 W.L.R. 342, where a joint account was fed largely with the wife's capital; assets bought out of it were held to belong exclusively to her.

[415] *Marshall v Crutwell* (1875) L.R. 20 Eq. 328; *Harrods Ltd v Tester* [1937] 2 All E.R. 236; *Hoddinott v Hoddinott* [1949] 2 K.B. 406; *Re Figgis (dec'd)* [1969] 1 Ch. 123; *Heseltine v Heseltine* [1971] 1 W.L.R. 342; *Simpson v Simpson* [1992] 1 F.L.R. 601. However, although an account may originally have been put into joint names for convenience only, the intention may change so that a beneficial joint interest arises: *Re Figgis* (dec'd) [1969] 1 Ch. 123. Such a new intention will only affect monies subsequently paid into the account: cf. Law of Property Act 1925 s.53(1)(c).

[416] [2007] UKHL, para.3.

[417] [2005] EWCA Civ 857, para.75.

argued that the lack of any real analysis of the concept of "home" has undermined the protection afforded to the family home in disputes with third parties,[418] but a whole generation has passed since the Court of Appeal in *Burns v Burns* expressed the view that reform was a matter for Parliament rather than for the courts.[419] The proposals for reform that have been advanced—in relation to both matrimonial property, the co-owned home and the rights of cohabiting couples—are considered in Ch.8. In the meantime, however, we must turn our attention to another important source of family finances: the social security system.

---

[418] See, for example, L. Fox, *Conceptualising Home: Theories, Laws and Policies* (Oxford: Hart Publishing, 2007).
[419] [1984] F.L.R. 216, *per* Fox L.J. at p.230 and May L.J. at p.242.

CHAPTER SIX

STATE SUPPORT FOR FAMILIES

I.   STATE FINANCIAL SUPPORT: THE
WELFARE BENEFIT SYSTEM AND
FAMILY BREAKDOWN 6–002
   A. Historical introduction 6–003
   B. Tax credits 6–005
   C. Social security benefits 6–008
   D. The child trust fund 6–026
II. WORK–LIFE BALANCE 6–027
   A. Introduction 6–027

   B. Childcare 6–028
   C. Rights at work 6–029
III. HOUSING   DUTIES   AND
HOMELESSNESS 6–035
   A. Introduction 6–035
   B. Homelessness 6–036
IV. CONCLUSION 6–040

This chapter contains a short account[1] of key aspects of state support for families;   **6–001** financial support for bringing up children through tax credits and welfare benefits; employment rights, including maternity and paternity pay, parental leave and rights to request working hours that fit with caring responsibilities (so-called "flexible working"); rights to childcare for children below school age and childcare outside school hours for older children; and housing, particularly in cases of homelessness. With the exception of tax credits and benefits, much of this state support is not provided directly by the government; rather, it creates the legislative framework, which requires others to take account of families, and provides subsidies or incentives. Although there is some evidence of the promotion of policies to support families over the two last decades,[2] many of the developments have, at their roots, economic imperatives to increase labour supply or meet requirements set out in European directives to ensure a free market by equalising employment rights in all Member States. Government policies do not support all families equally, or even according to objective notions of need; rather, specific family practices are targeted for support, for reasons that are not necessarily connected with the wellbeing of the family or of individual family members. One of the best examples of this is the policy of supporting, or not supporting, the provision of childcare that enables parents with caring responsibilities (most commonly mothers) to work.[3]

---

[1] To which reference is made where appropriate in footnotes in this chapter.
[2] Home Office, *Supporting Families* (1998); L. Hantrais, *Family Policy Matters* (Bristol: Policy Press, 2004).
[3] See below, para.6–028.

I. State Financial Support: The Welfare Benefit System and Family
Breakdown

6–002   It would be impossible to give a comprehensive account of state financial
provision[4] in a book of this kind, but this part of the chapter attempts to outline
the main features likely to be relevant in situations of family breakdown.

A. Historical introduction

6–003   Family breakdown has always involved the risk of poverty, and for many years
the Poor Law provided a measure of relief to victims—sometimes by the
provision of subsistence level support in "outdoor" relief to those (e.g. widowed
mothers and their children[5]) considered "deserving", but otherwise by committal
to the workhouse[6] in an attempt to ensure that the pauper's condition was less
eligible than that of the poorest labourer, and that the poor law did not provide
a "bounty on indolence and vice".[7] In the first half of the twentieth century,
further provision was made by the creation of state-provided insurance-based
pensions for the widows and families of those who had made sufficient
contributions in their working lives,[8] but proposals to bring other unsupported
mothers and their families into the scheme were rejected.[9]

The *Beveridge Report*, published in 1942,[10] was the origin of the modern
social-security system. It comprehensively explored the possibility of extending
insurance-based contributory benefits to cover the risk of family breakdown
brought about by events other than the death of a husband,[11] but in the event, no
progress was made. The result was that widows whose husbands had made the
necessary contributions over the years became entitled to pensions, but no
comparable provision was available for divorced, deserted or separated wives or
for unmarried mothers. However, the creation of the Welfare State aimed to

---

[4] See *Social Security Legislation*, Vols 1–3 (Sweet and Maxwell, 2007); Child Poverty Action Group,
Welfare Benefits Handbook 2008 (London: CPAG, 2008).
[5] The single mother and her children were generally treated unfavourably—notably by being denied
outdoor relief and being required to enter the workhouse—in comparison with the widow and her
children: see M. Finer and O.R. McGregor, "The history of the obligation to maintain", App.5, in
Report of the Committee on One Parent Families (1974, Cmnd.5629) Vol.2, pp.121 *et seq.*
[6] Which imposed "severely deterrent conditions upon its inmates, as well as subjecting them to loss
of civic rights, separation from their spouses, and a deliberately imposed stigma of pauperism": Finer
and McGregor, "The history of the obligation to maintain", para.55.
[7] *Report of the Poor Law Commissioners* (1834) as cited in Finer and McGregor, "The history of the
obligation to maintain", para.54.
[8] Widows', Orphans' and Old Age Contributory Pensions Act 1925; and provision for widows'
pensions was extended by statute in 1929, 1937 and 1940.
[9] Finer and McGregor, "The history of the obligation to maintain", para.84.
[10] Social Insurance and Allied Services (1942, Cmnd.6404).
[11] See, generally, J. Harris, *William Beveridge: A Biography* (Oxford: Clarendon Press, 1997); and,
for the place of the *Beveridge Report* in the context of the welfare state, R. Lowe, *The Welfare State
in Britain since 1945* (Basingstoke: Palgrave, Macmillan, 2005). An account of the reactions of
officials and others can be found in Finer and McGregor, "The history of the obligation to maintain",
pp.136–14.

ensure that adequate support would be available for all who were truly poor. In 1948, the Poor Law was repealed[12] and replaced by the National Assistance Act 1948. The legislation provided that every person in Great Britain whose resources (as defined) were insufficient to meet his or her requirements (also as defined) became entitled to receive a supplementary allowance.[13] It was the policy of the law[14] to eradicate the stigma attached to the Poor Law by insisting that supplementary benefits were the subject of rights and entitlement, and that no shame was attached to the receipt of them. However, the supplementary benefit system preserved one important principle derived from the Poor Law: although the state might provide financial support for a claimant, it was also entitled to recover the amounts paid from any person legally bound to support the claimant (the so-called "liable relative"[15]). In practice, therefore, supplementary benefit law came to constitute a third system of family law, at least as important as the codes of family law administered in the divorce court and in the magistrates' domestic jurisdiction.

Changing political philosophies—in particular the commitment of successive governments to the values of economic self-reliance and personal responsibility—coupled with economic conditions have led to many changes in the social security system. For many years, lawyers and the courts developed schemes that maximised the availability of welfare benefits on divorce, particularly in the context of the so-called "clean break" settlement.[16] Dependence on welfare assistance—and government disapproval thereof—appeared to reach its height in the late 1980s and early 1990s. The number of single-parent families apparently grew at an unprecedented rate—from 8 per cent of all families in 1971 to 21 per cent in 1992[17]—and the proportion of lone parents in work declined to 40 per cent.[18] Almost a million lone parents came to depend on Income Support; government expenditure on welfare benefits rose substantially, as did the number of children living in poverty.[19] Less than a third of lone parents on Income Support received any child maintenance from the child's other parent. In light of these matters, the Conservative Government made significant changes in the social security system, some intended to increase the effectiveness of the liable relative procedure and some intended to improve the employment prospects of parents. The most far-reaching change was the enactment of the Child Support Act 1991 and the creation of the Child Support Agency, which intended to create an efficient system whereby absent parents would be required to support their

---

[12] National Assistance Act 1948 s.1.

[13] Supplementary Benefits Act 1976 s.1(1).

[14] *Per* Finer J., *Reiterbund v Reiterbund* [1974] 1 W.L.R. 788 at 797; see also *Reform of the Supplementary Benefits Scheme* (1979, Cmnd.773), para.4.

[15] See below, para.7.024; for an excellent account of the law and practice relating to liable relatives, see N. Wikeley, *Child Support: Law and Policy* (Oxford: Hart, 2006).

[16] See para.15–001, below.

[17] See *General Household Survey 1992*; and for a survey commissioned by the Government and heavily influential in the policy changes culminating in the enactment of the Child Support Act 1991, see J. Bradshaw and J. Millar, *Lone Parent Families in the UK* (London: HMSO 1991).

[18] *Working for Children* (2007, Cm.7067) p.3.

[19] *Children Come First* (1990, Cm.1263).

children at a realistic level. The Agency's failings and the subsequent attempt to secure maintenance for children are examined in Ch.15.

6–004   The Labour Government elected in 1997 has continued to promote a philosophy of economic self-reliance.[20] In 1999 the Prime Minister committed the Government to eradicating child poverty, which had risen to 1 in 3 children, a higher rate than almost every industrialised nation.[21] "Employment is the best route out of poverty and disadvantage"[22]: employment, childcare and benefits policies have all been revised with the aim of increasing employment and reducing the number of children in poverty. Parents and carers have been given new employment rights with the aim of making work wore flexible and securing more "family friendly" employment practices.[23] Childcare has been made more available through new obligations on local authorities to secure provision for working parents, and made more affordable through subsidies in the form of a childcare tax credit.[24] Financial support has been reconfigured with more generous provision being made through the Working Tax Credit, described below. Conditions for entitlement to benefits have been made more rigorous, but some practical support has been available to assist claimants into employment. Amounts available to help with housing costs (especially mortgage interest) have been curtailed.

In addition to compulsory measures, the Labour Government introduced a number of *New Deal* programmes,[25] which provide additional assistance to find and retain work for specific groups of people not in work. Personal advisors explain the financial advantages of employment by examining the applicant's rights to tax credits, and assist with finding employment, advice and childcare. New Deal programmes are the soft side of workfare, operated on the basis that, with adequate support and incentives, many of those not in work would prefer to be employed.

The principal statutes relating to welfare benefits are the Social Security Contributions and Benefits Act 1992 and the Social Security Administration Act 1992. The Jobseekers Act 1995 introduced the Jobseekers Allowance, replacing unemployment benefit and Income Support for the unemployed, and imposed demanding eligibility criteria based on availability for work, particularly in the case of young people. The Social Security Act 1998 reformed the system of decisions and appeals. Some further changes of substance were made by the

---

[20] DSS, *New Ambitions for our Country: A New Contract for Welfare* (1998, Cm.3805); DWP, *Working for Children* (2007, Cm.7067); D. Freud, *Reducing Dependency, Increasing Opportunity: Options for the Future of Welfare to Work* (DWP, 2007).
[21] Select Committee on Work and Pensions, *Second Report 2003–4, Child Poverty* (2002–3 HC 85); H.M. Treasury, *Child Poverty Review* (2004), para.2.4 and Annex B.
[22] Home Office, *Supporting Families* (1998), p.68; DWP, *Working for Children* (2007, Cm.7067) p.3.
[23] DTI, *Fairness at Work* (1998, Cm.3968), para.5.4; Employment Act 2002; Work and Families Act 2006.
[24] HM Treasury, *Pre-Budget Statement: Choice for Parents, the Best Start for Children: a 10 Year Strategy for Child Care* (2004); Childcare Act 2006.
[25] *New Deal* programmes are available for lone parents; partners of benefit claimants; young people aged 18–24; people over 25 who are long-term claimants of Jobseekers' Allowance and those over 50 who have been claiming benefits for at least six months; disabled people and musicians: see *http://www.jobcentreplus.gov.uk/JCP/index.html* [Accessed May 29, 2008].

Welfare Reform and Pensions Act 1999 and the Child Support, Pensions and Social Security Act 2000.[26] The rest of this section of the chapter provides a brief outline of the range of tax credits and benefits most relevant to family breakdown.

B. Tax credits[27]

In theory, a tax credit system integrates state support with income tax so that those who qualify for credits have the requisite amount added to their pay, just as they would have it deducted if they were liable for tax. In this way it is possible to improve work incentives by minimising the effects of the "poverty trap" and the "unemployment trap", which leave those who can only earn low pay losing income if they increase their earnings, or being better off unemployed.[28] In practice, the principles on which tax and benefits have been devised (individual taxation and means-tested benefits for households) are incompatible, and the practicalities of ensuring the correct payments where incomes (and therefore rights to credits) fluctuate have challenged Her Majesty's Revenue and Customs (HMRC).[29]

6–005

Tax credits were introduced in 1999 to create a "family-friendly tax and benefit system"[30] that would provide an incentive to families to take up even low-paid work rather than remaining dependent on welfare benefits, and help families without stigmatising them. Working Families Tax Credit was based on Family Credit, which it replaced, and provided support for 26 weeks, irrespective of changes in income during that period. The system was revised and developed with the aim of creating work incentives for families without children, and more clearly separating support for adults and for children.[31] In 2002 two new tax credits were announced: Child Tax Credit, to replace the couple's tax allowance, and targeted on lower- and middle-income families; and Working Tax Credit, to extend support to the low paid aged over 25 who are in work. The new system replaced the idea of a means test with a "modern income test" based on annual earnings, allowing those with modest savings to claim. The new system was more generous, was fairer because it was based on annual income and not income at the point of claim and allowed continuity of support despite significant changes in circumstances. Only changes in the adults in the household, the

---

[26] A comprehensive list of statutes and SIs and the text of all the legislation can be found at *http://www.dwp.gov.uk/advisers/#lawvols* [Accessed May 29, 2008].

[27] For details of the current Tax Credit system, see CPAG, *Welfare Benefits and Tax Credits Handbook* (London: CPAG 2008); basic information can be obtained from the guides available on the HMRC website: *http://www.hmrc.gov.uk/leaflets/* [Accessed May 29, 2008].

[28] HM Treasury, *The Modernisation of Britain's Tax and Benefit System: Number Two; Work Incentives: A Report by Martin Taylor*, March 17, 1998.

[29] Treasury Select Committee, *Sixth Report 2005–6, The Administration of Tax Credits* (2005–6 HC 811), pp.3, 50.

[30] N. Lee, "The new tax credits" (2003) 10 J.S.S.L. 7; H.M Treasury, *Work Incentive* (1998), para.3.19.

[31] (2005–6 HC 811), Annex.

circumstances directly relating to the claim (such as the number of children or the use of childcare) or certain changes in income would affect the level of award.[32] Unfortunately, for many families the complexity of tax credits and the obligation to provide information during the year led to substantial over payments that were then clawed back from subsequent payments, leaving families to struggle on lower income than they had expected. Further changes were introduced in 2006 in an attempt to reduce the problem of overpayments: changes of income below £25,000 no longer lead to the reduction of credit, and the amount of payment which can be withheld due to overpayment is reduced.[33] Whether or not the system as originally designed was adequate, it appears that reform has been necessary to make it function. There have also been substantial problems with fraud, error and organised crime.[34] Nevertheless, the introduction of tax credits has had a major impact on family income. Tax credits are paid to 6 million families and contribute to the support of 10 million children, far more than obtained support for low pay through the benefits system.[35]

Unlike tax allowances which relate to individual circumstances, tax credits must be claimed by couples if they are married, in civil partnership or cohabiting as if married or in partnership.[36] The value of the credit depends on the couple's financial and other circumstances; only single or permanently separated people can claim alone.[37] Claimants have substantial obligations to report various changes in circumstances to HMRC, and must complete end-of-year returns.[38]

i. Working Tax Credit

6–006   Working Tax Credit[39] is paid to working people on low pay. Additional amounts are provided if a member of the household is disabled, and also to cover the costs of childcare. In effect, childcare costs are only payable for approved childcare (at a nursery or after school club or by a registered childminder or registered carer in the child's home (nanny) and not where children are cared for by relatives).[40] The current maximum amount for childcare for 2 children is £240 per week (80p for every pound up to £300). Working Tax Credit is an important support for lone parents, who can claim so long as they are working at least 16 hours a week; higher payments are available to those working over 30 hours, including couples, so long as each works at least 16 hours. Payment is made direct to the employee;

---

[32] HM Treasury and Inland Revenue, *The Child and Working Tax Credits: The Modernisation of Britain's Tax and Benefit System* (2002), paras 2.29, 4.17.

[33] HM Treasury, *Pre-Budget Report 2005* (2005, Cm.6701).

[34] (2005–6 HC 811), p.34.

[35] (2005–6 HC 811), p.3.

[36] D. Salter, "Income tax and family life" in R. Probert (ed.) *Family Life and the Law* (2007) pp.115, 125.

[37] Tax Credits Act 2002 s.3.

[38] Tax Credits Act 2002 ss.6 and 22; Tax Credits (Claims and Notifications) Regulations 2002 (SI 2002/2014) and amendments thereto.

[39] Tax Credits Act 2002 ss.10–12; Working Tax Credit (Entitlement and Maximum Rate) Regulations (SI 2002/2005).

[40] Tax Credits Act 2002 s.12 and regulations. Different schemes for childcare approval exist for the separate parts of the UK.

any childcare element is paid to the child's main carer along with the Child Tax Credit.

ii. Child Tax Credit

Child Tax Credit[41] has replaced the additional amounts paid for dependent children in various benefits, both means-tested and non-means-tested, including Income Support. Child Tax Credit can be paid to anyone[42] aged 16 or over who is responsible for a child, or to a young person aged 16 but under 20 years and in full-time education or unwaged training. Where the child is the subject of a shared care arrangement, only one family may claim; the choice of claimant can be made by the families—if they cannot agree, HMRC will determine who is the main carer.[43] Claims may only be made by families below a (stated) level of income. A higher figure is set where the youngest child is under the age of one year or is disabled, to take account of the higher costs incurred. The amount paid depends on the number of children (up to three) and the couple's income. Claimants who also receive Income Support or Jobseeker's Allowance are paid the maximum level of credit. Child Tax Credit is paid either weekly or monthly through their bank account; couples can decide which of them receives the payment.

6–007

C. Social security benefits

Social security benefits can be classified as means-tested or non-means-tested (although the term "income-related" is often preferred to "means-tested" in official circles). Means-tested benefits are paid to those below thresholds of income and capital, and require a detailed investigation of the claimant's financial circumstances. Benefits may also be classified as contributory or non-contributory, entitlement to the former depending on contributions to the National Insurance Scheme paid by the individual or a spouse or dependant. The following brief discussion adopts the first classification. The means test is described separately.

6–008

i. Means-tested benefits

(1) Income Support

Income Support[44] is the main benefit for those who are not required to seek employment; it is therefore important for lone parents with young children.

6–009

---

[41] Tax Credits Act 2002 ss.8 and 9; Child Tax Credit Regulations 2002 (SI 2002/2007) and the numerous amendments thereto.

[42] A person subject to immigration control (Immigration and Asylum Act 1999 s.115(9)) cannot obtain tax credits, nor can a person who has given a maintenance undertaking as a condition of immigration: s.115(10).

[43] (SI 2002/2007) reg.3 rr.2–4.

[44] For qualifications, see Social Security Contributions and Benefits Act 1992 s.124; Income Support (General) Regulations 1987 (SI 1987/1967) as amended, especially reg.21.

Under the present rules, lone parents can claim Income Support so long as their youngest child is not over 16 years old. Many countries require that lone parents of younger children work,[45] and the Government proposes to reduce the age limit to 12 years from October 2008, and 7 years from October 2010.[46] Lone parents with older children will be able to claim Jobseekers' Allowance and will be required to satisfy its conditions relating to seeking employment, etc. Parents whose circumstances preclude work (e.g. those with disabilities) will transfer to other benefits. The claimant for Income Support must be over 16, must not be in "remunerative work" (defined as not less than 16 hours *per* week of paid work)[47] and must not be entitled to a Jobseekers' Allowance. This means that some part-time work can be undertaken without removing eligibility, but earnings affect the amount payable. The claim is made not simply for an individual but for a family unit, including a spouse or partner, but payments for children are now provided through Child Tax Credit. Income Support supplements income by an "applicable amount"[48] set by regulation. Only one member of a family can claim income support.[49] The "cohabitation rule" is discussed below.

A claimant's eligible housing costs are included in the "applicable amount"; this has been of particular significance in the context of marital breakdown since those costs include mortgage interest payments[50] on a loan used to "acquire an interest in the dwelling occupied as the home". However, because of the high cost of this subsidy to the Exchequer and the disincentive it created to self-sufficiency, the circumstances in which mortgage interest can be claimed and the amounts allowed have been severely restricted.[51] The same restrictions apply to the Jobseekers' Allowance. No mortgage interest has been payable during the first 39 weeks on benefit on new housing loans contracted from October 1, 1995.[52] Since April 10, 1995 the maximum loan has been £100,000,[53] and there is also a ceiling on the interest rate paid.[54] Although a person may be able to obtain benefits to cover mortgage interest costs, and may even be able to remortgage and move house, they cannot increase the size of their mortgage or cover capital payments. Also, arrangements will need to be made with the mortgage provider to avoid default proceedings where benefit is not available. Assistance with this is provided through the housing benefit scheme.[55]

---

[45] See D. Freud, *Reducing Dependency, Increasing Opportunity: Options for the Future of Welfare to Work* (DWP, 2007).
[46] *In Work, Better Off* (2007, Cm.7130), paras 17 and 18.
[47] Income Support (General) Regulations 1987 (SI 1987/1967) regs 2, 4, 6.
[48] Social Security Contributions and Benefits Act 1992 s.124(4).
[49] Social Security Contributions and Benefits Act 1992 s.134(2).
[50] A "qualifying home loan" is defined in the Income Support (General) Regulations 1987 (SI 1987/1967) Sch.3 para.15.
[51] "The generosity of the scheme for those out of work can create huge disincentives to move back into work—but to extend help with mortgages to people in work would be immensely costly": Mr Peter Lilley, *Hansard*, HC Vol.246, col.1207.
[52] Income Support (General) Regulations 1987 (SI 1987/1967) Sch.3 para.1(2).
[53] Income Support (General) Regulations 1987 (SI 1987/1967) Sch.3 para.11(4) and (5). Despite substantial increases in the cost of housing this figure has not been uprated.
[54] Income Support (General) Regulations 1987 (SI 1987/1967) Sch.3 paras 1, 6, 8–12.
[55] See below para.6–020.

(2) Jobseekers' Allowance

Jobseekers' Allowance[56] is the main benefit for the unemployed and for those employed for less than 16 hours a week who are seeking full-time employment. If the family unit comprises two adults (who are unemployed) or a lone parent, whose youngest child is over the maximum age to allow for an Income Support claim, Jobseekers' Allowance will be the principal benefit. The qualifications[57] are that a person is not in full-time work but is capable of work, is actively seeking it and otherwise satisfies labour market conditions. Where a couple has dependent children, the Jobseeker's partner is not currently required to seek work. However, as part of the programme to reduce child poverty by increasing levels of employment, mandatory work-focused interviews have been introduced for partners.[58] Thus, the Government is moving towards a system where two-earner families will be the norm, except for those with young children.[59] The "applicable amount" payable is the same as under Income Support. The system[60] requires a claimant to attend a new Jobseeker's Interview, to sign a Jobseeker's Agreement and thereafter to attend fortnightly interviews to ensure continued compliance with the labour market requirements, (e.g. of availability for work). Eligible housing costs are available—and restricted—in the same way for the Jobseekers' Allowance as for Income Support.[61]

6–010

(3) The means test

Both Income Support and income-based Jobseekers' Allowance are means-tested.[62] If the total of a claimant's capital assets exceeds a specified amount (currently £16,000), the claimant is not entitled to the benefit. If it exceeds £6,000, the capital is deemed to give rise to a so-called "tariff income" of £1 *per* week for each £250. The regulations lay down a general rule that the whole of the claimant's capital shall be taken into account and assessed at its current market value, save insofar as certain specified assets are disregarded. Disregards that are particularly relevant in the context of relationship breakdown include the dwelling occupied as the home, personal chattels and the surrender value of life policies.

6–011

As to income, the general principle is that the whole of the earnings and other income of members of the family is calculated on a weekly basis, and goes to reduce the amount of benefit entitlement. "Earnings" is widely defined, but

---

[56] Jobseekers' Allowance may also be contributory where National Insurance payments have been made.

[57] Jobseekers' Act 1995 s.1.

[58] Social Security (Jobcentre Plus Interviews for Partners) Regulations 2003 (SI 2003/1886); there are plans to extend this: *In Work, Better Off* (2007, Cm.7130), para.29.

[59] This is in marked contrast to the approach by the Conservative Party, which supports tax allowances for non-working partners see: Social Justice Policy Group, *Breakthrough Britain* (2007) paras 4.3–4.5.

[60] For details, see the Jobseekers' Allowance Regulations 1996 (SI 1996/207).

[61] See, for example, the Jobseekers' Allowance Regulations 1996 (SI 1996/207) Sch.2 paras 1(2), 10(3) and (4), 12 and 14.

[62] The details are beyond the scope of the present discussion. See Income Support (General) Regulations 1987 (SI 1987/1967) regs 35, 36, 45, 47, 53 Schs 9, 10; Jobseekers' Allowance Regulations 1996 (SI 1996/207) regs 98, 107, 116 Schs 6, 7.

certain income is disregarded; the amount of disregard (there are three levels) depends on the circumstances.[63]

(4) The cohabitation rule

6–012   The capital and income of both married and unmarried couples are aggregated for the purpose of Income Support and Jobseekers' Allowance. The legislation provides[64] that "married couple" means a man and woman who are married to each other and are members of the same household. It follows from this that when a couple separate they cease to be within this definition, and, in practice, a wife whose husband leaves will often have recourse to Income Support. The expression "unmarried couple" is defined[65] to mean a man and a woman who are not married to each other "but are living together as husband and wife otherwise than in prescribed circumstances". These notions have been extended to civil partners and same-sex couples living as if they were civil partners.[66] The underlying policy is clear: where a couple live together as if they were married or in a civil partnership, the fact that they have not formalised their relationship should not make their position either better or worse than a couple who has.[67]

The need to make investigations (often in secret) into a couple's private life in an attempt to ascertain whether they are cohabiting, is commonly seen as offensive by those concerned. It is not surprising that the application of the rule has given rise to much controversy, but case law has accepted a number of criteria.

It is clear that in order to establish that a couple are living together as husband and wife, etc. it is not sufficient to show that they are living in the same household. The fact that they are doing so may well be strong evidence, but it has been said to be necessary to ascertain, insofar as this is possible, the manner in which—and the reason why—the couple are living together in the same household.[68] Thus, for example, a person who lives in a household simply as a housekeeper, or to look after a sick or incapable person, would not fall within the definition.[69] It is clear that the intention of the parties is a highly relevant factor,[70] but, contrarily, it has been doubted whether a person's intention can be ascertained otherwise than by what he or she does and says at the relevant time.[71] On that view, conduct is the decisive factor.

---

[63] Income Support (General) Regulations 1987 (SI 1987/1967) Sch.8 paras 5, 6, 9; Jobseekers' Allowance Regulations 1996 (SI 1996/207) Sch.6 paras 6, 11–12. Earnings disregards are £5, £10 for couples and £20 for lone parents. Some maintenance or child support payments may also be disregarded: see Ch.15.
[64] Social Security Contributions and Benefits Act 1992 s.134; Jobseekers' Act 1995 s.35.
[65] Social Security Contributions and Benefits Act 1992 s.137; Jobseekers' Act 1995 s.35.
[66] Civil Partnership Act 2004 s.254 and Sch.24, paras 46 and 124.
[67] See *Crake v Supplementary Benefits Commission* [1982] 1 All E.R. 498 at 501, 502, *per* Woolf J.; see also *Paterson v Ritchie* 1934 S.C. (J.) 42, *per* Lord Anderson.
[68] at p.502.
[69] at p.504.
[70] R(G) 3/81; see also *Kaur v Secretary of State for Social Services* [1981] 3 F.L.R. 237; *Robson v Secretary of State for Social Services* [1981] 3 F.L.R. 232; *Kimber v Kimber* [2000] 1 F.L.R. 383.
[71] *Crake v Supplementary Benefits Commission* [1982] 1 All E.R. 498 at 505, *per* Woolf J.

It is for the authority that is seeking to establish that aggregation of the means of the two people concerned is justified to prove that cohabitation is occurring. Guidance is given in the *Decision Maker's Guide*,[72] as amended from time to time. The main criteria to be taken into consideration are as follows, although the list is not exhaustive.

(a) Members of the same household. The parties must be living in the same household, apart from periodical absences due to illness, holidays or work.[73]   **6–013**

(b) Sharing daily life. This means "mutuality in the daily round" of tasks and duties.[74]   **6–014**

(c) Stability. Living together as husband and wife clearly implies more than an occasional or very brief association. When a couple first live together, it may be clear from the start that the relationship is similar to that of husband and wife (e.g. if the woman has taken the man's name and has borne his child), but in cases where, at the outset, the nature of the relationship is less clear, it may be right not to regard the couple as living together as husband and wife until it is apparent that a stable relationship has been formed.   **6–015**

(d) Financial support. In most husband-and-wife relationships, one would expect to find financial support of one party by the other, or sharing of household expenses, but the absence of any such arrangement does not of itself prove that a couple are not living together.   **6–016**

(e) Sexual relationship. A sexual relationship is a normal part of a marriage and therefore of living together as husband and wife, but its absence at any particular time does not necessarily prove that a couple are not living as husband and wife, nor does its presence prove that they are. If a couple have never had such a relationship, it may be wrong to regard them as living together as husband and wife.[75]   **6–017**

(f) Children. When a couple are caring for a child or children of their union, there is a strong presumption that they are living as husband and wife.

(g) Public acknowledgment. Whether the couple have represented themselves to other parties as husband and wife is relevant. However, many couples living together do not wish to pretend that they are actually married. The fact that they retain their identity publicly as unmarried people does not mean that they cannot   **6–018**

---

[72] Available at *http://www.dwp.gov.uk/publications/dwp/dmg/* [Accessed May 29, 2008].
[73] *Kimber v Kimber* [2000] 1 F.L.R. 383 (a case on cessation of maintenance under the Matrimonial Causes Act 1973 but nevertheless arguably useful guidance in the social security context).
[74] *ibid.*
[75] *Re J (Income Support: Cohabitation)* [1995] 1 F.L.R. 660 at 666, *per* Social Security Commissioner M. Rowland.

be regarded as living together as husband and wife. What is important is the
public acknowledgement of their common life.

Finally, it should be noted that once the necessary relationship has been shown
to exist, it may be difficult to rebut the presumption that it is continuing.[76]

(5) Maintenance obligations of liable relatives

6–019　The Social Security Administration Act 1992 provides[77]:

> "[A] man shall be liable to maintain his wife or civil partner and any
> children of whom he is the father, and (b) a woman shall be liable to
> maintain her husband or civil partner and any children of whom she is the
> mother."

It is also provided that it is a criminal offence for a person to persistently refuse
or neglect to maintain themselves or a person whom they are liable to maintain
if, as a result, that person is paid various means-tested benefits.[78] Liability to
maintain, for these purposes, is not directly affected by any financial order made
in matrimonial proceedings. In *Hulley v Thompson*,[79] a consent order in divorce
proceedings provided that the husband transfer the matrimonial home to the wife,
but that he pay no maintenance to the wife or children. It was held that this did
not exclude his liability to maintain. However, claims for failure to support
children fell into disuse after the introduction of the Child Support Act 1991
because that Act treated parents claiming mean-tested benefits as having made a
claim for child support, and thus allowed the Child Support Agency to pursue the
liable relative/other parent directly.[80] The Child Maintenance and Other Payments Bill, when enacted will allow parents with care the freedom as to whether
to seek child support and repeal those aspects of the definition of "liable relative"
that relate to supporting children.[81] The procedure will therefore have little
relevance to family law.[82]

(6) Housing benefit[83]

6–020　The importance of housing to the welfare of families has long been reflected in
government policy.[84] Housing benefit is non-contributory and is available to
those on low incomes who pay rent. It is currently paid to about 4 million tenants,

---

[76] *Crake v Supplementary Benefits Commission* [1982] 1 All E.R. 498–502, *per* Woolf J.
[77] Social Security Administration Act 1992 ss.78(6) and 105(3).
[78] Social Security Administration Act 1992 s.105.
[79] [1981] 1 W.L.R. 159; and see *Crozier v Crozier* [1994] 1 F.L.R. 126.
[80] Child Support Act 1991 s.6; Child Maintenance and Other Payments Bill 2007, EN 360.
[81] Child Maintenance and Other Payments Bill 2007 cl.40 EN 357–362.
[82] For an account of its operation, see the seventh edition of this book, para.7.024, and Wikeley, *Child Support: Law and Policy*.
[83] For a detailed guide, see J. Zebedee et al., *Guide to Housing Benefit and Council Tax Benefit 2008–9* (London: Shelter, 2008).
[84] Financial assistance for rent was provided by central government from 1915. Responsibility was transferred to local government by the Social Security and Housing Benefit Act 1982, with support to them from central government.

80 per cent of whom rent from social landlords.[85] Most people who qualify for housing benefit are also in receipt of other benefits or tax credits. The current scheme is set out in the Social Security Contributions and Benefits Act 1992 and regulations made under it.[86]

Under the 1986 Act a person on Income Support was originally entitled to a maximum of 100 per cent of the eligible rent. In the changed political climate of the 1990s the housing benefit scheme was seen to be excessively generous. The Secretary of State[87] regarded the cost as being unacceptable, and pointed out that a scheme that gave full indemnity for tenants' rents meant that they had no incentive to choose the more economical of two dwellings or to negotiate over their rent level, while landlords were tempted to increase rents accordingly. It was said that taxpayers meeting their own rents resented subsidising higher rents than they could themselves afford, and that people on housing benefit should have similar incentives to those paying their own rents when deciding what they can afford. A series of changes to the scheme have reduced the maximum benefit payable; the "appropriate maximum housing benefit" is linked to local circumstances.[88] Further changes have been introduced by the Labour Government as part of its programme to simplify the benefits system and reduce poverty by encouraging employment.[89] Entitlement to housing benefit is conditional upon attending a work-focused interview,[90] and the legislation contains a power to reduce or withdraw it where a claimant has been evicted because of antisocial behaviour.[91]

(7) The Social Fund[92]

At one time, the social security system contained elaborate provisions giving   **6–021**
entitlement to single payments to meet exceptional needs. These provisions have now been repealed; the legislation instead provides that payments may be made out of the Social Fund in certain circumstances.[93] The legislation deals separately, on the one hand, with payments for maternity expenses, funeral expenses and payments made in cold weather to the elderly, the disabled and to persons caring for young children,[94] and on the other hand, payments in respect of other needs (such as to ease a domestic crisis or to visit a child who is with

---

[85] Welfare Reform Act 2007 EN, para.15.
[86] See the Housing Benefit Regulations 2006 (SI 2006/213). On both primary and delegated legislation, see *CPAG's Housing Benefit and Council Tax Benefit Legislation*, 20th edn (2008).
[87] Mr Peter Lilley, *Hansard*, HC Vol.246, col.1206.
[88] Social Security Contributions and Benefits Act 1992 s.130A, added by Welfare Reform Act 2007.
[89] DWP, *Building Choice and Responsibility: a Radical Agenda for Housing Benefit* (2002); Welfare Reform Act 2007.
[90] Welfare Reform and Pensions Act 1999 s.52, inserting new ss.2A–2C into Social Security Administration Act 1992.
[91] Social Security Contributions and Benefits Act 1992 s.130B added by Welfare Reform Act 2007.
[92] T. Buck, *The Social Fund: Law and Practice*, 3rd edn (Sweet & Maxwell, 2009).
[93] Social Security Contributions and Benefits Act 1992 s.138.
[94] Social Fund Maternity and Funeral Expenses (General) Regulations 2005 (SI 2005/3061); Social Fund Cold Weather Payments (General) Regulations 1988 (SI 1988/1724); Social Fund Winter Fuel Payment Regulations 2000 (SI 2000/729).

the other parent pending a court decision).[95] Such payments are to be made in accordance with Social Fund Directions issued by the Secretary of State. Social Fund Officers have a wide discretion in respect of decisions as to whether or not to make payments under the Directions, and it is provided that needs must be prioritised and payments kept within a stipulated overall, local budget.[96]

ii. Non means-tested benefits

6–022　Child benefit and Guardian's Allowance are non-contributory benefits that are not means-tested.[97] Unlike most non-means-tested benefits, they do not depend on any contributions to the National Insurance scheme.

(1) Child benefit

6–023　The Child Benefit Act 1975 made provision for the payment of benefit in respect of all children in a family, replacing the Family Allowance introduced in 1945. The legislation was consolidated in the Social Security and Contributions Act 1992 and was further amended in relation to claims in respect of those over the age of 16 years by the Child Benefit Act 2005. A person "who is responsible for one or more children or qualifying young persons in any week" is entitled to child benefit for that week in respect of each of them for whom he or she is responsible.[98] A "qualifying young person" must satisfy additional conditions, such as being in full-time non-advanced education or in specific unpaid vocational work-based training. The provisions of the Act are supplemented by detailed regulations.[99] A person is "responsible for a child"[100] if either: (i) he or she has the child living with them[101]; or (ii) is contributing to the cost of providing for the child at a weekly rate not less than the child benefit rate. It will often be the case, particularly after a relationship breakdown, that several people qualify for benefit under that test. The Act therefore lays down a code of priorities.[102] For example, a person who has the child living with them is entitled as against one who contributes to the child's maintenance, and where husband and wife reside together, the wife is entitled.[103] As between two unmarried parents, the mother is entitled.[104] Where the priorities do not determine the matter, the possible recipients can jointly elect which of them should receive the

---

[95] Social Fund Direction No.4, para.(b). No payment can be made to help with contact arrangements for children after the court has made its definitive decision.

[96] Social Fund Direction Nos 40, 41.

[97] This aspect of the scheme has been somewhat controversial: see the discussion of policy in Ogus, Barendt and Wikeley, *The Law of Social Security*, 4th edn (N.J. Wikeley et al. (ed.), 1995).

[98] Social Security Contributions and Benefits Act 1992 s.141.

[99] Principally the Child Benefit (General) Regulations 2006 (SI 2006/223).

[100] Social Security Contributions and Benefits Act 1992 s.143.

[101] This expression is a broad one: a child may be "living with" a parent even if he or she is in care and only returns home at weekends: see *England v Supplementary Benefits Commission* [1981] 3 F.L.R. 222; a child may also be regarded as "living with" a parent who enjoys staying contact: R(F) 2/79.

[102] Social Security Contributions and Benefits Act 1992 s.144 Sch.10.

[103] Social Security Contributions and Benefits Act 1992 Sch.10 paras 2 and 3.

[104] Social Security Contributions and Benefits Act 1992 Sch.10 para.4(2).

benefit; the Secretary of State decides if they do not agree.[105] Children cease to qualify for child benefit eight weeks after they become looked after by a local authority.[106] Consequently, foster carers cannot claim child benefit for their foster child unless the child ceased to be looked after (e.g. where they obtain a residence or special guardianship order).

(2) Guardian's allowance

This long-standing[107] non-contributory benefit is available to a person responsi- **6–024** ble for a child or "a qualifying young person" who is either an orphan or whose links with a surviving parent can for practical purposes be treated as non-existent. For example, benefit will be payable where the parents were unmarried, paternity has not been established and the mother has died.[108] Eligibility is not limited to legal guardianship, nor will a Special Guardian[109] necessarily qualify for the benefit. The claimant must qualify for child benefit in relation to the child. Consequently, those who foster a child on behalf of the local authority cannot receive the allowance.

(3) Contributory benefits[110]

There is a large number of benefits, entitlement to which depends on contribu- **6–025** tions made by the "insured person" or their spouse or civil partner. The legislation is consolidated in the Social Security Contributions and Benefits Act 1992, including substantial changes made by the Welfare Reform Act 2007. Contributory benefits include Employment and Support Allowance (which replaces incapacity benefit), maternity allowance, bereavement payment, widowed parent's allowance and retirement pensions. The legislation is daunting in its complexity; details may be found in the comprehensive specialist texts.[111]

D. The Child Trust Fund[112]

Child Trust Funds are long-term investment accounts introduced by the govern- **6–026** ment to encourage saving and widen opportunities for young adults in the future

---

[105] Social Security Contributions and Benefits Act 1992 Sch.10 para.5. Unlike most aspects of Child Benefit Administration that have been transferred to the Treasury, this decision remains the responsibility of the Secretary of State for Work and Pensions: Tax Credits Act 2002 s.49(1)(b).

[106] Social Security Contributions and Benefits Act 1992 Sch.9 para.1; SI 2006/223 reg.16.

[107] The allowance was introduced in 1946 to replace the orphan's pension payable since the enactment of the Widows', Orphans' and Old Age Contributory Pensions Act 1925. Eligibility is now governed by Social Security Contributions and Benefits Act 1992 s.77 and the Guardian's Allowance (General) Regulations 2003 (SI 2003/495), amended by SI 2006/204.

[108] Social Security Contributions and Benefits Act 1992 s.77(2); SI 2003/495 reg.5.

[109] For an explanation of Special Guardianship, see para.22–064, below.

[110] For a discussion of the historical background, see Ogus, Barendt and Wilkeley, *The Law of Social Security*, Ch.5; *Report of the Committee on One Parent Families* (1974, Cmnd.5629), App.5 (particularly pp.126–147).

[111] See *Social Security Legislation* (Sweet and Maxwell, 2007), Vol.1; Child Poverty Action Group, *Welfare Benefits Handbook 2008*.

[112] Child Trust Funds Act 2004 and Child Trust Funds Regulations 2004; SI 2004/1450; see also N. Wikeley, "Child trust funds—asset-based welfare or a recipe for increased inequality?" [2004] 11 *Journal of Social Security Law* 189; [2005] Fam Law 285 and *http://www.childtrustfund.gov.uk/* [Accessed May 29, 2008].

by providing them with "immediate access to a stock of assets" when they reach the age of 18.[113] All eligible children are provided with a voucher for an initial endowment from the Treasury of £250; a supplementary contribution of £250 is made for children from low income families (defined by reference to receipt of benefits or maximum-level tax credits) and those in local authority care.[114] In the 2006 and 2007 Budgets, further payments at the same level were announced for eligible children at the age of 7 years, and of £100 a year for each child in public care.[115] Individuals may make contributions up to £1,200 in any year.[116] All investments must be placed in an approved account[117] and no withdrawals may be made before the child is 18, except where the child is terminally ill or dies.[118] There are no restrictions on how the money is used by the eligible child in adulthood.

Children are "eligible" if they were born after August 31, 2002 and either someone is entitled to child benefit for them or they are excluded from child benefit because they are looked after by a local authority.[119] Accounts are normally opened by the "responsible" person, who is a person with parental responsibility for the child.[120] The voucher is sent to the child benefit recipient, but where both parents have parental responsibility, either may open the account; there is no provision for joint accounts. Local authorities may not open accounts for children in care; in most circumstances a parent of a child in care will qualify to open the account—in specific circumstances where this would be inappropriate (e.g. where there is a care plan for adoption), the Official Solicitor has this responsibility.[121] If no account is opened within 12 months, or the parent is under 16 years an account is opened by HMRC.[122]

By the end of November 2005, over 2 million vouchers had been issued, but less than half of them had been used.[123] Rather than selecting and opening accounts, many parents had left this to HMRC, suggesting that they had not engaged with the government's plan. The proportion of parents using the vouchers has increased, but a quarter of children do not have accounts.[124] Although the scheme has been welcomed as an "ambitious, pioneering programme" that involves a "significant long term investment by the Government",[125] it is less clear that it will be of particular benefit to low income

---

[113] Policy was originally set out in the consultation HM Treasury, *Savings and Assets for All* (2001) and *Delivering Saving and Assets* (2001). Detailed proposals, including financial projections, were published by HM Treasury in 2003.

[114] Child Trust Funds Act 2004 ss.8, 9. There is provision for further government contributions: s.10; Child Trust Funds Regulations 2004 (SI 2004/1450).

[115] HM Treasury, *Budget 2006* (2005–6 HC 968), para.1.13; HM Treasury, *Budget 2007* (2006–7 HC 342), para 5.39.

[116] Child Trust Funds Act 2004 s.12.

[117] SI 2004/1450 Pt 2.

[118] Child Trust Funds Act 2004 s.19 and SI 2004/1450 reg.18A added by SI 2004/2676.

[119] Child Trust Funds Act 2004 s.2(1), (2).

[120] Child Trust Funds Act 2004 ss.3(8), 5; SI 2004/1450 reg.5.

[121] SI 2004/1450 reg.33A, added by SI 2004/3382.

[122] Child Trust Funds Act 2004 s.6.

[123] Ivan Lewis M.P., Economic Secretary to the Treasury, evidence to the Treasury Select Committee, *Update of Child Trust Funds* (2005–6 HC 738), Q3.

[124] HM Treasury, *Budget 2007* (2006–7 HC 342), para.5.39.

[125] Treasury Select Committee, *Second Report 2003–4, Child Trust Funds* (2003–4 HC 86), p.20.

families. Without additional contributions, the value of a child's fund will be relatively modest on maturity[126]; children may obtain greater advantage by families providing for children's immediate needs than by diverting their resources for future savings. Where parents choose an equity-based fund, its value will necessarily reflect the state of the market and the investments chosen, which will mean different values for different children despite the same sums having been invested. Such equity-based accounts can go up or down. Perhaps the greatest danger is that future governments will neglect or abandon the scheme, or worse still seek to claw back their investment" by removing support for post-18 education or imposing charges for identity cards! The track record of successive governments in relation to maintaining support for pensions is not encouraging.

II. Work–Life Balance

A. Introduction

Combining employment and responsibility for young children necessitates access to reliable and affordable childcare together with employment laws and practices that recognise that employees have family responsibilities. Parents and carers may be unable to leave their children at times of illness; parents want to be involved in their child's upbringing, attending special events at school, etc. Although there is now greater recognition that men may be carers, and that fathers may be their children's main carer whilst the mother is the breadwinner, social attitudes and government policies have long been gendered. Expectations that women would stay at home to care for young children contributed to discrimination in employment, which reduced women's employment opportunities, particularly in relation to promotion, and depressed their pay.[127] The view that a mother's decision to work was a private matter negated the case for support in terms of nursery provision or financial assistance with childcare costs. The lack of childcare undermined choice and precluded employment for many mothers, as did fathers' limited involvement in caring. However, a series of economic, social and policy changes in the 1990s created a new climate for mother's employment, and for government support to encourage this. First, an impending labour shortage meant that employers became interested in the employment potential of women with young children. Also, the growth in the proportion of women in many professions and skilled occupations meant that employers were increasingly dependent on their female staff to maintain services. Secondly, the government's desire to reduce benefit dependency and end child poverty meant that it looked for ways to encourage parents to take employment.

6–027

---

[126] HM Treasury, *Detailed Proposals for the Child Trust Fund* (2003) p.11. An initial endowment of £500 will be worth less than £1,000 at age 18 if there are no further investments, but £14,000 if additional payments of £40 *per* month (i.e. half the maximum allowed) are made.

[127] I. Breugal, "Women's employment, legislation and the labour market" in J. Lewis (ed.) *Women's Welfare; Women's Rights* (London: Croom Helm, 1983); W. Creighton, *Working Women and the Law* (London: Hansell, 1979) Ch.1; J. Conaghan et al. (eds), *Labour Law in an Era of Globalization* (Oxford: Oxford University Press, 2002).

These included subsidies for low pay and childcare costs,[128] the development of a strategy to encourage more and better provision of childcare and improved working conditions. Thirdly, EU policies promoted improved rights for workers through various directives relating to equal pay, part-time work, parental leave and discrimination that the UK Government was obliged to implement, as well as through various non-binding measures.[129] Women increasingly expected to work outside the home even when their children were young, and families' expectations about living standards came to depend on both parents working. As a larger proportion of mothers remained in or returned to work whilst their children were young, this came to be seen as normal behaviour not one for negative comment.

B. Childcare[130]

6–028 State support for childcare in the United Kingdom has been closely tied to the need for women in the workforce. This was most notable during and immediately after the Second World War. State nurseries established to enable women to contribute to the war effort were quickly closed in 1945 so that jobs would be available for returning servicemen. Local authorities, which had provided nurseries, were informed by the government that "the right policy to pursue would be positively to discourage mothers with children under 2 from going out to work".[131] State nursery provision dwindled; facilities were largely focused on children in need whose circumstances necessitated substitute care because they were considered at risk of harm or their mother needed support because of health or social problems. Although the Education Act 1944 included a framework for establishing nursery schools, resources were not allocated by central government, and many education authorities provided for "rising fives" only.[132] Many of the childcare services that were developed were for part-time "play-groups" designed to ensure social interaction for children but not to support parents' employment. Women who worked relied largely on care from family members, and took part-time work (generally low paid) that they could fit round this informal childcare and the children's schooling.[133] During the 1980s government policy made explicit that responsibility for day-care services was "primarily a matter for private arrangements".[134] Indeed, in the 1991 Budget, employer subsidy for childcare was a taxable benefit. The Children Act 1989 included a new duty on local authorities to provide day care for children under school age, "as appropriate"[135] but this did not lead to any great increase in state provision.

---

[128] See above paras 6–005–6–007.
[129] See A. Idil Aybars, "Work-life balance in the EU and leave arrangements across welfare regimes" (2007) *Industrial Relations Journal* 38, 560–90 and C. McGlynn, "Work, family and parenthood: the European Union agenda" in J. Conghan and K. Rittich, *Labour Law, Work and Family* (Oxford: Oxford University Press, 2005), p.217.
[130] See P. Moss, "Day care in the UK" in E. Melhuish and P. Moss (eds), *Day Care for Young Children: International Perspectives* (London: Routledge, 1990); OECD, *Babies and bosses* (2005), Vol.2.
[131] Ministry of Health *Circular 221/45* (1945).
[132] Moss "Day care in the UK" in Melhuish and Moss, *Day Care for Young Children.*
[133] J. Martin and C. Roberts, *Women and Employment: a Lifetime Perspective* (HMSO 1984).
[134] Minister for Health, John Patten M.P., *Hansard Commons*, February 18, 1985, col.397.
[135] Children Act 1989 s.18.

Furthermore, the extension of regulation to services for under 8s, whilst ensuring minimum standards, may have inhibited the development of out-of-school care, which is essential if parents are not to be restricted to employment during school hours.

In 1998 the Labour Government adopted a childcare strategy.[136] In contrast to earlier views that childcare could be damaging to young children, it positively promoted the advantages of high quality childcare both in terms of children's development and their general well-being through assisting parents into employment.[137] The strategy aims to raise the quality of childcare by improving the standards of education and training for those providing care, and requiring higher levels of qualification from those in charge of services; to ensure that quality care remains affordable by providing subsidies for those in work who use childcare and providing some childcare free of charge; and to make childcare available by imposing duties on local authorities to ensure that there is "sufficient" childcare to meet the requirements of working parents and parents making the transition to work.[138] Local authorities are not expected to provide facilities but to support the development of services by others.[139] They are intended to become strategic leaders raising standards in childcare and making services more accessible for parents.

Childcare has been developed through the creation of more than 3,500 Children's Centres established under the *Sure Start* programme. A network of "extended schools" will make provision for school-age children. These will support children by providing breakfast clubs, homework assistance and social activities before and after school, and will enable parents more easily to combine family responsibilities with their work obligations.[140] In the future, extended schools will offer other services to support parents (e.g. to help them with their children's learning or behaviour).

Childcare services have long been regulated—registration and inspection provide some reassurance for parents and protection for children. In England, Ofsted is now responsible for maintaining a register of providers and inspection.[141] Local authorities have duties to advise parents about services[142]; help with locating childcare is also provided though government-sponsored websites, and for parents on the *New Deal* programme, through personal advisers in Jobcentres. The use of registered provision is also a condition for the receipt

---

[136] See HM Treasury, DES, DWP, *Choice for Parents, the Best Start for Children: a 10 Year Strategy for Childcare* (2004), para.1.7.
[137] *Choice for Parents, the Best Start for Children: a 10 Year Strategy for Childcare*, App.A, "Child development".
[138] Childcare Act 2006 s.6(1). Childcare matters are devolved, so separate provision is made in the 2006 Act for Wales, which also retains a separate regulatory regime based on the Children Act 1989.
[139] Childcare Act 2006 s.8. Local authorities may provide where no one else is willing to do so: s.8(3).
[140] DfES, *Extended Schools: Access to Opportunities and Services for All* (2005); *Extended Schools: Building on Experience* (2007). The development of extended schools is part of the government's *Every Child Matters* programme.
[141] Childcare Act 2006 ss.31, 32. In Wales this is a matter for local authorities subject to the supervision of the Welsh Assembly: ss.28 and 29.
[142] Childcare Act 2006 s.12(2); for Wales, s.27.

of childcare element in working tax credit, creating an incentive for parents to use such provision.[143]

C. Rights at work

6–029 In *Supporting Families*,[144] the Labour Government identified work as offering "the surest way" for families to provide for themselves, signalling a change in welfare policy with far higher expectations on benefit recipients to obtain employment. Rather than supporting individuals and families through benefits, it stressed government's role in supporting parental employment through rights to fair employment and the promotion of "family-friendly" working practices. Combining work with family responsibilities was no longer to depend on contracts of employment or the generosity of employers but to be based on statutory rights.[145] A series of EU directives increasing employee's rights in respect of parental leave, working time and part-time employment[146] necessitated changes to the law. In addition, the Government committed itself to reforms to "help parents devote more time to their children early in life"[147] through extending maternity and paternity rights, including rights for adoptive parents.[148]

i. Maternity rights

6–030 Employment rights for pregnant women developed slowly, starting with the exclusion of mothers from factories in the month following childbirth in the 1890s, and only included any form of financial support with the introduction of the Welfare State in 1946.[149] Rights were subsequently added in a piece meal way; rights to leave were not matched with pay, limiting the ability of those dependent on their wages to take all their leave. Nor were they generous: statutory maternity pay was capped so that those without additional contractual rights experienced a substantial fall in income after the first six weeks of paid leave.[150] Where some employers have been willing to meet their statutory obligations and provide further benefits in contracts of employment, others have viewed employees who become pregnant as a nuisance, have provided only rights required by law and have even sought to escape any duties to them.[151]

---

[143] See above, para.6–006.
[144] Home Office (1998), para.3.1.
[145] DTI, *Fairness at Work* (1998, Cm.3968), para.5.5.
[146] Parental leave: Directive 96/34/EC; Working time: Directive 93/104/EEC implemented by SI 1998/1833; Part-time work: Directive 97/81/EC implemented by SI 2000/1551.
[147] *Labour Party Manifesto* (2001).
[148] See M. Kilkey, "New Labour and reconciling work and family life: making It fathers' business?" (2006) *Social Policy and Society* 5, 167, Table 1.
[149] For an account of the history of maternity protection and the British government's resistance to it, see W. Creighton, *Working Women and the Law* (1979), pp.37–39; see also G. James, *The Legal Regulation of Pregnancy and Parenting in the Labour Market* (Abingdon: Routledge Cavendish, 2008).
[150] SMP is paid at 90% of earnings for the first six weeks and then at a fixed rate—£112.75 from April 2007 (uprated annually).
[151] There are frequently reports of women, some highly paid bank executives or lawyers, treated poorly during pregnancy or after their return to work. A few have gained very large sums of compensation, although the details are usually subject to confidentiality agreements.

However, sex discrimination laws provide women with some protection against dismissal or redundancy related to pregnancy.[152]

The package of maternity rights now includes: rights to paid time-off for antenatal appointments[153]; maternity leave; maternity pay; and the right to return to employment.[154] Statutory maternity pay is dependent on employment by the same employer for a minimum period of 26 weeks. Maternity Allowance, which is paid to women who cannot satisfy this condition, remains in effect a contributory benefit with both an employment and an earnings condition.[155] Although the Government has announced its commitment to securing 52 weeks' maternity leave with pay by enacting the Work and Families Act 2006 s.1, the current regulations provide 39 weeks' paid maternity leave for those whose baby was due on or after April, 1 2007.[156] Leave beyond the first 26 weeks can be effectively transferred to the mother's partner, and, subject to conditions about length of employment and earnings, the partner will be able to claim Statutory Paternity Pay or Paternity Allowance.[157]

ii. Paternity rights

The working father's role in caring for children has long been ignored in government policy.[158] Paternity leave and pay were proposed in a Green Paper in 2000 so that fathers could "do even more" (for their families).[159] The Employment Act 2002 introduced both paternity leave and paternity pay,[160] but the latter was restricted to two weeks at a flat rate (currently £106 per week), limiting its accessibility to those who could afford to forgo pay. Additional paternity leave will be available for up to 26 weeks where a mother who is entitled to maternity leave has returned to work when the Work and Families Act 2006 is fully implemented.

6–031

All those who seek paternity leave must satisfy requirements about the length of employment and must notify their employer.[161] A person need not be the child's father to qualify for paternity leave. A father qualifies if he has (or is likely to have) "responsibility for the upbringing of the child". A person who is not the father but is the mother's husband or partner (of either sex) qualifies if they have (or expect to have) "the main responsibility (apart from any

---

[152] Sex Discrimination Act 1975; Employment Rights Act 1996 ss.84, 96.

[153] Employment Rights Act 1996 ss.55 and 56.

[154] A detailed account of these can be found in the Selwyn's *Employment Law*, 14th edn (2006), Ch.6. Simplified accounts for employers and employees are available at *http://www.berr.gov.uk/employ ment/workandfamilies/index.html* [Accessed May 29, 2008].

[155] Social Security Contributions and Benefits Act 1992 ss.35(2) and 165(1); Social Security (Maternity Allowance) Regulations 1987 (SI 1987/416) and Statutory Maternity Pay (General) Regulations 1986 (SI 1986/1960), as amended.

[156] SI 2006/2379.

[157] Work and Families Act ss.3 and 6 adding Employment Rights Act s.80AA and Social Security Contributions and Benefits Act 1992 s.171EZA.

[158] See Kilkey (2006) *Social Policy and Society* 5, 167; McGlynn, "Work, family and parenthood" in Conaghan and Rittich, *Labour Law, Work, and Family*.

[159] DTI, *Work and Parents: Competitiveness and Choice* (2000, Cm.5005), para.1.4.

[160] By adding Employment Rights Act 1996 s.80A and Social Security Contributions and Benefits Act 1992 s.171ZA.

[161] Social Security (Paternity and Adoption Leave) Regulations 2002 (SI 2002/2788) regs 4(2), 6.

responsibility of the mother)" for this.[162] No proof is required of the person's relationship to the child, to the mother, or of their intentions in relation to the child's upbringing, but an employer can require a declaration by the employee in relation to these matters.[163]

Where a person claims paternity leave or additional paternity leave (when it is introduced), it is intended that their rights to return to their employment will be protected as a mother's rights are.[164]

iii. Rights for adopters

6–032 Adoption leave and pay, which is comparable to maternity leave, is provided (on similar terms) to a person adopting a child either from the United Kingdom or in an inter-country adoption arrangement.[165] Similarly their partner may qualify for paternity leave. Couples can choose which of them takes the more substantial leave.[166] Leave is not available where the adoption is by a parent and stepparent, nor for foster carers adopting a child originally placed for fostering, unless this child has subsequently been matched and placed by an adoption agency. There are no comparable provisions for those who obtain special guardianship orders, a policy which appears discriminatory and difficult to justify when the order is selected to meet the child's needs to retain their original legal identity, and does not relate to the adjustments carers may need to make when taking on such a responsibility.

iv. Parental leave

6–033 Parental leave is an essential component of support for working parents. It allows time off to cope with the common crises of parenthood, such as the child's illness or a breakdown of childcare arrangements. Without rights, leave depends on the employer's discretion; parents cannot be sure that it will be agreed or that they will be able to regain their job, a situation the Labour Government regarded as unfair.[167] Parental leave can thus be seen as one of the incentives to encourage lone parents into employment. Whilst obliged to implement the EU Directive, the Government sought to promote agreed arrangements for parental leave. The regulations provide a fallback where provision is not made in the contract of employment.[168]

---

[162] SI 2002/2788 reg.4(2).
[163] SI 2002/2788 reg.6(2). Knowingly giving a false declaration could amount to an offence of deception.
[164] Work and Families Act 2006 s.6.
[165] Employment Rights Act 1996 s.75A; Social Security Contributions and Benefits Act 1992 s.171ZL.
[166] SI 2002/2788 regs 17 and 18; reg.8 for paternity leave: adoption.
[167] DTI, *Fairness at Work* (1998, Cm.3968) para.5.28.
[168] The Maternity and Parental Leave etc. Regulations 1999 (SI 1999/3312), implementing Directive 96/34/EC.

A parent with parental responsibility who has been continuously employed for a year[169] may take parental leave for up to 13 weeks whilst their child is under the age of 5 years.[170] Leave may be taken in periods of one week, and no more than four weeks can be taken in any year. Parents of disabled children have additional rights to leave.[171] Notice must be given to the employer, who may postpone the leave for up to six months where he or she considers the leave would "unduly disrupt the business".[172] Under this fallback scheme, parents have quite limited assistance; leave remains unpaid and the employer retains considerable discretion, but parents exercising rights to leave are protected against detriment and dismissal.[173]

v. Right to request flexible working

The Employment Act 2002[174] introduced a right for "qualifying employees" to apply for a change in their terms and conditions to facilitate childcare. Employees who have been continuously employed qualify if they are mother, father, guardian, special guardian, carer with a residence order or foster parent of the child, or are married to or are the partner of such a person and they have or expect to have responsibility for the upbringing of a child under the age of six years.[175] There is no right to a change in working conditions, but the employer must consider applications made according to the set procedure, and can only refuse it for business reasons.[176] There are rights of appeal, but only one application for flexible working can be made in any 12-month period.[177] The Work and Families Act 2006 extended these rights for carers of disabled children and disabled adults.

6–034

Although it is now easier for parents to combine work with family responsibilities than it was a decade ago, because of the combination of tax credits, the wider availability of nurseries and improved employment rights, juggling the work–life balance remains a challenge, especially for lower paid workers whose employers are only willing to do the minimum, and for lone parents. In balancing concerns for the family and those of employers, the Government has relied on employers to adopt good employment practices rather than creating substantial social rights. This facilitates the creation of the flexible workforce, which supports economic development but not the individual flexibility that parents need.

---

[169] SI 1999/3312 reg.13.

[170] Where the child has been adopted, the five years runs from the date of placement: reg.15(c).

[171] Up to 18 weeks leave, leave may be taken up to the child's 18th birthday and can be taken a day at a time.

[172] SI 1999/3312 Sch.2.

[173] SI 1999/3312 regs 19 and 20.

[174] Employment Act 2002 s.47 adding Employment Rights Act 1996 ss.80F–80I.

[175] The qualification conditions are set out in regulations: Flexible Working (Eligibility, Complaints and Remedies) Regulations 2002 (SI 2002/3236) reg.5 as amended by SI 2006/3014 and SI 2007/1184.

[176] Employment Rights Act 1996 s.80G; Flexible Working (Procedural Requirements) Regulations 2002 (SI 2002/3207).

[177] Employment Rights Act 1996, ss.80F(4), 80H.

III. HOUSING DUTIES AND HOMELESSNESS

A. Introduction

6–035 The state's responsibility in relation to housing focuses on securing the economic climate, including the building of sufficient homes, so that individuals (and couples) can buy their own home; providing a legal framework that protects both landlords and tenants of rented accommodation, and assisting homeless people through advice and, for specific groups in specific circumstances, by providing housing.[178] Local authorities have responsibilities to develop a homelessness strategy including for the prevention of homelessness[179]; provide rented accommodation; and, using funds provided by central government, pay rent subsidies in the form of housing benefit to those on low income in rented accommodation.[180]

There is a major shortage of housing in the United Kingdom, particularly in the southeast of England. Seventy per cent of households live in owner-occupied accommodation, 18 per cent are "social renters" (that is, they rent from a local authority or a registered social landlord (a housing association)) and 12 per cent rent privately.[181] The pattern of occupation has changed substantially over the last three decades, with a reduction in local authority properties through the right to buy and through transfers to registered social landlords. Home ownership has increased in part because of the value of homes as investments, but house-price inflation means that property is no longer affordable for many young couples. The supply of private rented accommodation has begun to increase with the development of buy-to-let investments, the growth of which has contributed to house-price inflation. As a consequence, it is likely in the future that an increasing proportion of families will live in privately rented accommodation. High housing costs and the lack of available housing contribute to homelessness, as does family breakdown, both for parents and young people.

This section provides a brief account of the support for families and the casualties of family breakdown through housing law.[182]

B. Homelessness

6–036 The Housing Act 1996 Pt 6[183] requires local authorities to maintain an allocation scheme, setting out their priorities and procedures for allocating housing or nominating tenants for housing by other registered social landlords, but re-housing from the waiting list is rarely speedy. This being so, Pt 7 of the Act requires

---

[178] For an account of the developments in housing policy, see D. Cowan, *Housing Law and Policy* (Basingstoke: Macmillan, 1999).
[179] Homelessness Act 2002 s.1,3; Department of Communities and Local Government, *Homelessness Code of Guidance for Local Authorities* (2006).
[180] See above, para.6–020.
[181] Department of Communities and Local Government, *Housing Statistics Summary* (2007).
[182] For a substantial and lucid explanation of the law, see A. Arden et al., *Manual of Housing Law* (London: Sweet and Maxwell, 2007).
[183] Housing Act 1996 ss.159, 167.

a local authority to provide immediate assistance to certain eligible[184] persons who are homeless or threatened with homelessness. Homelessness may result from parents no longer being willing to have their (adult) children live with them,[185] particularly where relationships have been strained by parental separation or time spent in local authority care. Another common situation is the violent breakdown of a relationship where one partner, usually the woman (and often with young children) is restricted to short-term relief under the domestic violence legislation[186] and seeks help from the local authority.[187]

i. The local authority's duty

The Housing Act 1996 prescribes in detail the duties[188] that local authorities owe **6–037** to the homeless, the most significant being the "main homelessness duty"—the duty to secure that accommodation is available for the applicant's occupation.[189] "Homeless or threatened homelessness" is defined in the statute. The Act provides[190] that a person is homeless if he or she has no accommodation available for their occupation, which he or she is entitled to occupy by virtue of an interest in it or by court order, or by licence or statutory right. A person is not to be treated as having accommodation unless it is accommodation that it would be reasonable for that person to continue to occupy.[191] The Act further provides that it is not reasonable for a person to continue to occupy accommodation if it is probable that this will lead to violence[192] against him or her or a member of his or her family residing or expected to reside with that person. Violence is now defined so as to include threats of violence that are likely to be carried out[193] from another person. In the case of domestic violence, the persons must be "associated", which is defined in the same way as in the Family Law Act 1996.[194]

---

[184] Housing Act 1996 s.185. In general, applicants are not eligible for assistance if they are subject to immigration control; some British citizens (e.g. those not habitually resident in the Comon Travel Area) are also ineligible: Allocation of Housing and Homelessness (Eligibility) (England) Regulations 2006 (SI 2006/1294). For an illustration of ineligibility, see *R. (G) v Barnet LBC* [2004] 1 F.L.R. 454 H.L or the *Climbié Inquiry* (2005, Cm.5730). On the local authority's duty to provide suitable interim accommodation for asylum-seekers under s.188 of the Housing Act 1996, see the *Homelessness Code of Guidance* (2006) and *M v LB Islington and SS for the Home Department* [2004] 1 F.L.R. 867.

[185] A young adult excluded from the family home for not obeying "house rules" may be intentionally homeless: *Denton v LB Southwark* [2007] EWCA Civ 623 (20 year old with learning difficulties).

[186] See Ch.9, below.

[187] Research has indicated that 15% of those statutorily homeless are victims of domestic violence: Morley and Pascal, "Women and homelessness" [1996] J.S.W.F.L. 327.

[188] Including the duty to provide advice and information: Housing Act 1996 s.179. There is a duty to provide interim accommodation for an applicant considered to be eligible pending investigation: Housing Act 1996 s.188; *Homelessness Code of Guidance* (2006), Ch.7.

[189] Housing Act 1996 s.193(2).

[190] Housing Act 1996 s.175(1); *Homelessness Code of Guidance* (2006), Ch.8.

[191] Housing Act 1996 s.175(3). A restrictive interpretation was given in *Harouki v Royal LB of Kensington and Chelsea* [2007] EWCA Civ 1000. In *R. v Brent LBC Ex p. Awua* [1996] A.C. 55, it was held that the accommodation need not be settled or permanent.

[192] Housing Act s.177(1); extended from domestic violence to "other violence" by the Homelessness Act 2002 s.10(1). In *R. v Ealing LBC Ex p. Sidhu* (1983) 3 F.L.R. 438, it was held that a woman who has fled to a refuge may be classified as homeless; but see *per* Lord Hoffmann in *R. v Brent LBC Ex p. Awua* [1996] A.C. 55.

[193] Housing Act 1996 s.177(1A), as substituted by s.10(1) of the Homelessness Act 2002.

[194] Housing Act 1996 s.178; Family Law Act s.62(3); see Ch.9.

The duty to secure that accommodation is available for occupation[195] is owed only to those with priority need who are not homeless intentionally.[196] Priority need is defined; the statutory criteria most likely to be relevant on relationship breakdown are that the applicant is: (i) a person with whom dependent children reside or might reasonably be expected to reside[197]; (ii) vulnerable as a result of old age, mental illness, handicap, etc.[198]; (iii) a pregnant woman or a person with whom she resides[199]; and (iv) young people who are vulnerable because of their age or institutional background.[200] The commonest priority qualification is that the household has dependent children. It has been held that it is wrong for a local authority to require that a parent obtains a residence order as a means of proving that he or she satisfies the requirement of the Act.[201]

An authority has only limited duties[202] to a person who has become homeless intentionally.[203] The Act provides[204] that a person becomes homeless intentionally if he or she deliberately does or fails to do anything in consequence of which he or she ceases to occupy accommodation that is available for their occupation, and which it would have been reasonable for them to occupy. There is a vast amount of case law on the interpretation of the statutory provisions, but in practice, non-payment of rent or mortgage interest is often the crucial factor.[205] In the context of relationship breakdown, it has been claimed that many authorities require women who have been subjected to harassment by their former partners to use all available matrimonial remedies—notably to apply to exclude the partner from the home—if the woman is to avoid being classified as intentionally homeless. However, the *Homelessness Code of Guidance* specifically states that there is no obligation on those seeking provision from the local

---

[195] Lesser duties are owed to persons becoming homeless intentionally (s.190) and to those not in priority need who are not homeless intentionally (s.192); these mainly concern the provision of advice and assistance in obtaining accommodation.

[196] Housing Act 1996 s.193. The duty ceases where housing is provided in specified ways or if the person, having been fully informed, refuses a final offer of accommodation.

[197] Housing Act 1996 s.189(1)(b); The Homelessness (Priority need for accommodation)(England) Order 2002 (SI 2002/2051) and *Homelessness Code of Guidance* (2006), paras 10.6–10.11. Where joint residence results from a consent order, the housing authority may make its own determination about the priority need of each homeless parent because the court will have approved the arrangement without reference to the availability of housing: *Holmes-Moore v LB Richmond* [2007] EWCA Civ 970.

[198] Housing Act 1996 s.189 (1)(c); this also encompasses vulnerable persons residing with the applicant.

[199] Housing Act 1996 s.189(1)(a).

[200] SI 2002/2051 paras 3–6, but not those under 18 to whom Children Act 1989 ss.20 or 23A duties are owed; *Homelessness Code of Guidance* (2006), Chs 10 and 13.

[201] *R. v Ealing London Borough Ex p. Sidhu* (1982) 80 L.G.R. 534, DC.

[202] Housing Act 1996 s.190. Difficult questions can arise where intentional homelessness could be made out against one partner only: contrast *Lewis v North Devon DC* [1981] 1 W.L.R. 328 and *R. v Mole Valley DC, Ex p. Burton* [1989] Fam. Law 64 and see *Homelessness Code of Guidance* (2006), para.11.9 and *R. (Coinville) v LB Richmond* [2006] EWCA Civ 718.

[203] And to persons who are not homeless intentionally but are not in priority need: Housing Act 1996 s.192.

[204] Housing Act 1996 s.191(1).

[205] See *R. v Salford City Council Ex p. Devonport* (1983) 8 H.L.R. 54, CA; *R v Eastleigh Borough Council Ex p. Beattie (No.2)* (1984) 17 H.L.R. 168, Q.B.D; cf. *R. v Wandsworth LBC Ex p. Hawthorne* [1995] 2 All E.R. 331.

authority to do so, and that local authorities should recognise that injunctions may not be effective in deterring further violence.[206]

ii. To whom is the duty under the housing legislation owed?
The duty to secure that accommodation is available[207] is owed only to the person   **6–038**
who is homeless and in priority need:

> In *R v Oldham Metropolitan Borough Council Ex p. Garlick*,[208] the local
> authority found that an applicant was in priority need, but that he had—by
> deliberately omitting to make mortgage payments—become homeless
> intentionally. The applicant did not challenge that decision, but made a fresh
> application under the Act in the name of his four-year-old son. The House
> of Lords held that this application had been properly rejected: a healthy
> four-year-old child living with his or her parents[209] was owed no duty under
> the Act because dependent children were not amongst those classified as in
> priority need, and it was the intention of the Act that the child's
> accommodation be provided by the parents or those looking after the child.
> If the application were successful, the "intentional homelessness" provi-
> sions could rarely, if ever, be applied to a family with dependent chil-
> dren.

Accommodation is not available to a person unless it is available for occupation by the homeless person "together with (a) any other person who normally resides with him as a member of him family, or (b) any other person who might be expected to reside with him"; so a homeless spouse or (adult) child may require the local authority to house their intentionally homelesss spouse or parent with them.

iii. Relationship with other local authority duties
If a housing authority makes a finding of intentional homelessness under the   **6–039**
homelessness legislation, it is not obliged[210] to comply with a request[211] from a
social services department to help a child in need by providing housing for a
child in need, if to do so would not be compatible with the housing authority's
duties and obligations. For example:

---

[206] (2006) para.8.23. In *Bond v Leicester City Council* [2001] EWCA Civ 1544, the local authority can no more require a victim of domestic violence to seek an injunction than to take self-defence classes or buy a big dog!
[207] Housing Act 1996 s.193.
[208] [1993] 2 F.L.R. 194, HL.
[209] It was accepted that a child under 16 who left home might be vulnerable and able to establish a priority need: see *per* Lord Griffiths at 197.
[210] Under the Housing Act 1996: see *The Queen on the Application of G v Barnet LBC* [2001] EWCA Civ. 540; [2001] 2 F.L.R. 877.
[211] Made under Children Act 1989 s.27.

In *R. v Northavon District Council Ex p. Smith*,[212] Mr Smith applied to the housing authority (Northavon) for housing for himself and his five dependent children, but Northavon determined that he had become homeless intentionally. Mr Smith then approached Avon as the relevant social services authority with a view to their performing their duty to safeguard the welfare of the children by making cash payments to cover rent and deposits.[213] Avon refused to do so, but instead invoked the power to ask the Housing Authority (Northavon) to help with the provision of housing. Northavon said they had performed their duties under the Housing Act 1985, and that it would be a "contradiction" to offer the Smiths a tenancy in light of the intentional homelessness decision. Mr Smith's application to quash Northavon's decision failed. There was a duty for the authorities to co-operate with each other, but an action for judicial review was not the way to obtain that co-operation. The authorities[214] "must together do the best they can".

The relationship between local authorities' duties under the Housing Act 1996 and those under the Children Act 1989 has been examined by the House of Lords. In *The Queen on the Application of G v Barnet London Borough Council*,[215] the mother of a young child was ineligible for assistance with accommodation under the Housing Act 1996 as a homeless person because she did not satisfy the habitual residence requirement. After providing her with temporary accommodation, the local authority gave her notice that she would not be given further accommodation but offered to accommodate the child (who was assessed as being in need). Similarly, in *The Queen on the Application of W v Lambeth London Borough Council*,[216] the local authority applied its policy of refusing housing to an intentionally homeless mother, offering only to accommodate her children, expecting that she would reject this and arrange accommodation for her family.[217] The House of Lords, by a majority, upheld these decisions. Housing was primarily a responsibility of the local housing authority, not the children's services department. Although there could be occasions where separating parent and child amounted to a breach of Art.8 rights,[218] the Children Act 1989 s.17 did not require the local authority to meet all needs of children in need. It had a power to accommodate children with their parents but could not be required to exercise it.[219]

In reaction to this decision, Parliament enacted s.12 of the Homelessness Act 2002, requiring housing authorities to provide social services departments with advice and assistance in respect of families otherwise ineligible for housing assistance.

---

[212] [1994] 2 A.C. 402, HL.
[213] See Children Act s.17(6).
[214] *Per* Lord Templeman at 410.
[215] [2004] 1 F.L.R. 454 HL; [2003] UKHL 57.
[216] [2004] 1 F.L.R. 454 HL; [2003] UKHL 57.
[217] Lambeth gave evidence that since adopting this policy it had not been asked to accommodate any children because of parental homelessness: at para.50.
[218] *Per* Lord Nicholls, dissenting, at paras 52–53; *per* Lord Hope at para.69.
[219] There was conflict about this point in the Court of Appeal, but an amendment to the Children Act 1989 s.17(6) added by Adoption and Children Act 2002 s.116 removed all doubt about the power to accommodate families.

IV. CONCLUSION

Over the last decade, government policy has given considerable attention to **6–040** supporting families, but expenditure has largely been directed at facilitating employment so as to meet labour-market demands and reduce benefit dependency and child poverty. State supports are no longer limited to health services, state education, pensions and providing a safety net for those without work. Considerable sums have been directed at assisting parents of young children to remain in the workforce. In contrast, young adults have been required to take on debt to further their education. One effect of these policies has been to reduce the proportion of children in poverty, but the circumstances of the poorest are no better. Social exclusion remains a problem, and it has proved difficult to change the lives of the hardest to reach families. Substantial numbers of children have continued to live in poverty despite generally improved living standards and a buoyant economy. New policies will be required to secure improved wellbeing for those families who have not been able to benefit from the existing supports. Maintaining existing levels of support and providing the different (and greater) services excluded families require will challenge the will and resources of future governments operating in a less favourable economic climate.

CHAPTER SEVEN

DEVOLUTION OF FAMILY PROPERTY ON DEATH[1]

I.   WILLS... 7–001
     A. Effects of marriage, civil partner-
     ship, divorce and dissolution on wills   7–002
II. INTESTACY.................................... 7–003
     A. Where the intestate leaves a spouse
     or civil partner and issue................... 7–004
     B. Where the intestate leaves a spouse
     but no issue 7–005

     C. Where the intestate leaves no
     surviving spouse or civil partner........   7–006
III. THE INHERITANCE (PROVISION
     FOR FAMILY AND DEPENDANTS) ACT
     1975... 7–009
     A. Not a remedy for unfairness or
     unjust enrichment.............................   7–010
     B. Reform proposals   7–032

I. WILLS

Any adult person of sound mind may dispose of all his or her property on death   **7–001**
by making a will complying with the formalities prescribed by the Wills Act
1837.[2] Until 1938 this power to disinherit the testator's family members was
absolute. The Inheritance (Family Provision) Act 1938[3] gave the court a limited
power to override the deceased's testamentary provisions by ordering provision
to be made out of a deceased's estate for the maintenance of a surviving spouse
and a limited category of other dependants; the Inheritance (Provision for Family
and Dependants) Act 1975 gave the court more extensive powers. However, it
remains the case that in principle a testator is free to dispose of property by will
in whatever way he or she chooses.[4]

The statutory provisions in respect of devolution of property and claims arising
on death were comprehensively amended by the Civil Partnership Act 2004[5] in

---

[1] For fuller accounts, see Parry and Clark, *The Law of Succession*, 11th edn, (2002 by R. Kerridge);
A. Borkowski, *Textbook on Succession* (1997); and see J. Finch et al., *Wills, Inheritance, Families*
(1996).
[2] As amended by Administration of Justice Act 1982 Pt IV.
[3] For the historical background, see S.M. Cretney, *Law, Law Reform and the Family* (1998),
Ch.10.
[4] *Re Coventry (dec'd)* [1980] Ch. 461 at 474.
[5] Civil Partnership Act 2004 Sch.4. The Act came into force on December 5, 2005.

209

order to equate the position of surviving civil partners with that of surviving spouses.

A. Effects of marriage, civil partnership, divorce and dissolution on wills

7–002   A will is revoked by the testator's marriage or civil partnership.[6] Until January 1, 1983[7] the testator's divorce had no direct effect on his or her will.[8] However, statute now provides[9] that unless a testator has shown a different intention, any property given to the former spouse or civil partner will pass as if he or she had died on the date on which the marriage or civil partnership is dissolved or annulled[10] (and accordingly legacies and other gifts will lapse). It is, however, provided[11] that the former spouse or civil partner may make a claim for reasonable financial provision under the Inheritance (Provision for Family and Dependants) Act 1975.

The Law Commission in its Report *Cohabitation: The Financial Consequences of Relationship Breakdown*,[12] made no recommendations for reform of the Wills Act 1837 in respect of cohabitants.

II. INTESTACY[13]

7–003   Under the system of intestate succession introduced by the Administration of Estates Act 1925, the whole of the deceased's property (after payment of debts, etc.) is distributed in accordance with the following rules (the Administration of Estates Act 1925 and the Intestates' Estate Act 1925 were amended by the Civil Partnership Act 2004[14] in order to treat surviving civil partners in the same way as surviving spouses).

---

[6] Wills Act 1837 ss.18, 18B; Administration of Justice Act 1982 ss.18, 18B. Ss.18B and 18C were inserted into the Wills Act 1927 by the Civil Partnership Act 2004 Sch.4 paras 1–5.
[7] The date on which the relevant provision of the Administration of Justice Act 1982 came into force: ss.18(2), 76(11).
[8] Nor did the fact that the marriage had been annulled.
[9] See Law Reform (Succession) Act 1995 ss.3 and 4; Wills Act s.18C; and for the background, see the Law Commission's Report, *The Effect of Divorce on Wills* (Law Com. No.217 (1993)).
[10] Law Reform (Succession) Act 1995, s.4.
[11] Wills Act 1837 ss.18A(2), 18C(3). For a critique of the legislation, see R. Kerridge [1995] Conv. 12.
[12] Law Com. No.307 (2007), paras 6.59–6.64.
[13] C.H. Sherrin and R.C. Bonehill's *The Law and Practice of Intestate Succession*, 2nd edn (1994) is a comprehensive text; while the main principles of the law are fully analysed in *Distribution on Intestacy* (Law Com. PWP No.108 (1988)). The evolution of the law is considered in Cretney, *Law, Law Reform and the Family*, Ch.10.
[14] Civil Partnership Act 2004 Sch.4 paras 7–14.

A. Where the intestate leaves a spouse or civil partner[15] and issue[16]

Intestate succession is governed by the Administration of Estates Act 1925. The **7–004**
surviving spouse or civil partner takes[17]:

- the personal chattels absolutely[18];

- a "statutory legacy", currently amounting to £125,000[19];

- a life interest in one-half of the balance of the estate.

Subject to the spouse's or civil partner's rights, the estate is held on the
"statutory trusts" for the issue of the intestate. These trusts are defined in the
Act.[20] The intestate's children may receive maintenance out of income until they
are 18, and will then receive the capital; if any child of the intestate predeceases
the intestate leaving issue, the issue will take the child's presumptive share.

B. Where the intestate leaves a spouse but no issue

- If the deceased also leaves a parent, or a brother or sister,[21] the surviving **7–005**
  spouse or surviving civil partner takes:

  — the personal chattels absolutely;
  — a "statutory legacy" of £200,000[22];
  — one-half of any balance absolutely. The other half is held for the
    intestate's surviving parent or parents (in equal shares) absolutely, but
    if the intestate leaves no parent, the property is held on the statutory
    trusts for the brothers and sisters (or the issue of any predeceased
    brother or sister).

---

[15] "Spouse" does not include a former spouse, but spouses remain married until decree *absolute* of divorce: see *Re Seaford* [1968] P. 53 (where the husband was found dead, apparently as a result of a drug overdose, on the day on which the wife applied for the decree to be made absolute, and it was held that his death brought the marriage to an end, that the court had no jurisdiction to make the decree absolute and that the wife was entitled to succeed as his widow); *Re Collins (dec'd)* [1990] Fam. 56 (where the husband was entitled on the wife's intestacy, notwithstanding the fact that she had been granted a decree nisi of divorce founded on his violent behaviour to her during a short marriage).

[16] However remote. Broadly speaking, illegitimacy is no longer relevant in determining intestate succession rights: Family Law Reform Act 1987 s.18.

[17] Subject to the rule of public policy that debars a wrongdoer from benefiting from his own wrong: *Re Giles (dec'd)* [1972] Ch. 544; *Jones v Roberts* [1995] 2 F.L.R. 422 (H.H. Judge Kolbert) but the application of this rule may be affected by the Forfeiture Act 1982, which gives the court a discretionary power to relieve against forfeiture: see *Re H (dec'd)* [1990] 1 F.L.R. 441.

[18] Defined in s.55(1)(x).

[19] See Family Provision (Intestate Succession) Order 1993 (SI 1993/2906). Interest is payable on the legacy from the date of death until payment at such rate as the Lord Chancellor fixes from time to time by order: Administration of Justice Act 1997 s.28(1); Intestate Succession (Interest and Capitalisation) Order 1983 (SI 1983/1374).

[20] Administration of Estates Act 1925 s.47, as amended.

[21] Or issue of such. Only brothers and sisters of the whole-blood are eligible to take under these rules; half brothers and sisters become entitled only if the intestate left no spouse or civil partner.

[22] Family Provision (Intestate Succession) Order 1993 (SI 1993/2906).

- If the deceased leaves no relatives within these categories, the whole estate goes to the surviving spouse or civil partner.

C. Where the intestate leaves no surviving spouse or civil partner

7–006
- If the deceased leaves issue, the whole estate is held on the statutory trusts for their benefit.

- If the deceased leaves no issue but is survived by one or both parents, then they take (in equal shares if both survive) absolutely.

- If the deceased leaves neither issue nor parent, the following relatives take in order:

  — brothers and sisters of the whole-blood (the issue of any predeceased brother or sister taking their share);
  — brothers and sisters of the half-blood (and their issue, as above);
  — grandparents, equally;
  — uncles and aunts (i.e. brothers and sisters of the whole-blood of a parent of the intestate). The issue of a predeceased uncle and aunt take his or her share on the statutory trusts.

- In default, the estate passes as bona vacantia to the Crown.[23] In this event, the Crown may as a matter of grace make provision for "dependants" (whether kindred or not) of the intestate and for other persons for whom the intestate might reasonably have been expected to make provision.[24] This power may be used to provide some part of the estate for the deceased's cohabitant who has no entitlement on the deceased partner's intestacy. Although the Inheritance (Provision for Family and Dependants) Act 1975 would sometimes enable a cohabitant to obtain an order for financial provision out of the estate, it appears that ex gratia payments are still often made thus avoiding the expense of an application to the court.[25]

i. Rights in respect of the family home

7–007 The surviving spouse or civil partner has the right to require the intestate's interest in the matrimonial or civil partnership home in which the surviving spouse or civil partner was resident at the time of the intestate's death to be appropriated in or towards satisfaction of his or her share.[26]

---

[23] See, for example, *Cameron v Treasury Solicitor* [1996] 2 F.L.R. 716.
[24] Administrations of Estates Act 1925 s.46(1)(vi).
[25] See *Distribution on Intestacy* (Law Com. PWP No.108 (1988)), p.8, fn.15.
[26] Intestates' Estates Act 1952 Sch.2, as amended by the Civil Partnership Act 2004 Sch.4 para.13. The surviving spouse (and now civil partner) may require the personal representatives to exercise this power of appropriation partly in satisfaction of his or her interest in the estate and partly in return for a payment of money: *Re Phelps (dec'd)* [1980] Ch. 275.

ii. English intestacy law generous to surviving spouse or civil partner

The salient feature of this code of distribution is the generosity with which it **7–008** treats the surviving spouse or surviving civil partner[27]: it is only in the case of comparatively large estates that the survivor will not inherit the whole of the intestate's property.[28] There may be cases where this generosity causes injustice (i.e. where a parent with dependent children has married more than once), as the person married to the deceased at the date of death will take the estate, perhaps to the prejudice of children of an earlier marriage or other dependants.[29] Moreover, it will be noted that sibling relationships of the whole-blood are given substantial priority over those of the half-blood. The intestate's half-brother will not be entitled to any share of the property if the intestate left a surviving spouse, a surviving brother or sister of the whole-blood or any issue of such a brother or sister.

A cohabitant currently has no entitlement to any share of a deceased partner's estate on intestacy. The Law Commission in its Report,[30] *Cohabitation: The Financial Consequences of Marriage Breakdown*, addressed the question whether the intestacy rules should be changed in this respect. The Commission had little doubt that there would be wide pubic support for the introduction of some intestacy provision for cohabitants. However, as the Commission had concluded in 1989 in its Intestacy Report,[31] attempting to include cohabitants in the intestacy rules is very difficult. This is principally because the range of relationships encompassed by cohabitation is too diverse to be appropriately accommodated within the intestacy rules; further, any change in favour of cohabitants would require an appreciation of the overall effect on the entitlements of other family members.[32] The Commissions's provisional conclusion was that reform of the intestacy rules in respect of cohabitants should be rejected for the present; the preferable route was to reform the Inheritance (Provision for Family and Dependants) Act 1975, which is discussed below.

---

[27] The Law Commission recommended that a surviving spouse should be entitled to the whole of the intestate's estate: *Distribution on Intestacy* (Law Com. No.187 (1989)), but the Government (see *Hansard*, HL, Vol.547, col.WA 38) rejected this much criticised proposal: see R. Kerridge, "Distribution on intestacy, the Law Commission's report" (1990) 54 Conv. 358; Sherrin and Bonehill, *The Law of Intestate Succession*, 2nd edn (1994), p.24 (proposals "naive and simplistic") and the debates in *Hansard*, HL Vol.538, cols 170–178 and in *Hansard* HL Vol.561, col.502. It appears that the Law Commission continued to believe that the Government should have accepted their proposal or at least raised the amount of the statutory legacies to "a figure which resolves the serious injustices of the present law in modern times": Law Commission, *28th Annual Report 1993* (Law Com. No.223 (1993)), para.3.8; and, for a discussion of the policy issues, see Cretney, *Law, Law Reform and the Family*, p.273 *et seq.* Note that pursuant to the provisions of Sch.4 to the Civil Partnership Act 2004, the position of a surviving civil partner is now equated with that of a surviving spouse.

[28] See, for a particularly striking case, *Re Collins (dec'd)* [1990] Fam. 56; *Sivyer v Sivyer* [1967] 1 W.L.R. 1482.

[29] *Distribution on Intestacy* (Law Com. No.187 (1990)). The Law Commission's proposal is all the more surprising in the light of a Public Attitude Survey which showed little support for treating a second spouse so generously: see para.41.

[30] Law Com. No.307 (2007) paras 6.5–6.10.

[31] *Distribution on Intestacy* (Law Com. No.187)(1989).

[32] *Cohabitation: The Financial Consequences of Relationship Breakdown* (Law Com. No.307 (2007)), para.6.9.

III. The Inheritance (Provision for Family and Dependants) Act 1975[33]

7–009 The Inheritance (Family Provision) Act 1938, which first gave the court a discretion to award reasonable provision out of a deceased's estate for the maintenance of certain dependants if the will or intestacy failed to make such provision for them, was a controversial measure enacted only after prolonged campaigning. For this reason, it was limited in scope.[34] Experience of the operation of the law (and perhaps changes in public attitudes) suggested that much of the opposition to the legislation was not well-founded. Proposals made by the Law Commission[35] for substantial changes and extensions to the scope of the law were implemented by the Inheritance (Provision for Family and Dependants) Act 1975.[36] The 1975 Act was amended by the Civil Partnership Act 2004[37] in order to equate the position of surviving civil partners or former civil partners with that of surviving spouses or former spouses.

A. Not a remedy for unfairness or unjust enrichment

7–010 The Act does not confer rights to a particular share of the deceased's estate on any of his or her dependants.[38] The objective of the statute is not to remedy unjust enrichment, nor is it the function of the court to decide how the available assets should be fairly divided.[39] Rather, the legislation is concerned with dependency, and in particular (it has been said)[40] to remedy:

> "[W]herever reasonably possible, the injustice of one, who has been put by a deceased person in a position of dependency upon him, being deprived of any financial support, either by accident or by design of the deceased, after his death."

Accordingly, certain specified "dependants" may apply to the court,[41] which has

---

[33] See R.D. Oughton, *Tyler's Family Provision*, 3rd edn (1997) for an excellent and important account, drawing on departmental records, of the genesis and legislative history of the legislation.
[34] See Cretney, *Law, Law Reform and the Family* (1998), pp.250–252 and the sources there cited.
[35] See Law Com. No.61 (1974): *Family Provision on Death*.
[36] The Act largely follows the draft Bill annexed to Law Com. No.61 (1974). The draft is copiously and helpfully annotated. It has been said that the 1975 Act forms part of a continuum, and that the legislature did not intend to put on one side and ignore the body of case law on the 1938 Act insofar as it gives guidance on the exercise of the discretion to award reasonable provision: *Re Coventry (dec'd)* [1980] Ch. 461 at 487, CA, but the Court of Appeal has subsequently held that the earlier authorities should be approached with caution because of the substantial changes that have been made in the legislation itself, and that this is particularly true of claims where a surviving spouse is concerned: *Moody v Stevenson* [1992] Ch. 486, CA.
[37] Sch.4 paras 15–27.
[38] The Law Commission considered a system under which a surviving spouse would have fixed rights of inheritance: see (Law Com. PWP No.42), pp.215–259 and fn.26, above.
[39] *Re Coventry (dec'd)* [1980] Ch. 461 at 486, *per* Goff L.J.
[40] *Jelley v Iliffe* [1981] Fam. 128–138, Stephenson L.J; *Bishop v Plumley* [1991] 1 F.L.R. 121 at 123, CA.
[41] The Family Division and Chancery Division of the High Court both have jurisdiction. The Law Commission had recommended that the Family Division alone should have jurisdiction, and the decision to preserve the role of the Chancery Division seems to have reflected the need to compensate the Chancery Division for the loss of the wardship jurisdiction: see the Parliamentary Debates on the Administration of Justice Act 1970, *Hansard*, HC Vol.801, cols 109–117.

a discretion to order financial provision for the applicant if it is satisfied that the disposition of the deceased's estate[42] effected by the deceased's will or the law relating to intestacy, or a combination of his or her will and the intestacy, is not such as to make reasonable provision for the dependant. It is not sufficient to show that it would have been reasonable for the deceased to have provided for the claimant; the court must be satisfied that, looked at objectively, the disposition of the estate is unreasonable.[43]

i. Who may apply
The fact that a person is of full age, in good health and economically self-   **7–011**
sufficient is not a bar to a claim under the 1975 Act.[44] The Act provides[45] that any
of the following persons who survive the deceased may apply.[46]

(1) The spouse or civil partner of the deceased[47]
This category of applicant does not include persons whose marriage or civil   **7–012**
partnership has been terminated by decree absolute[48] of divorce or nullity, or final
order for dissolution or nullity. However, it does include persons whose
"marriage" or "civil partnership" was void, provided that they: entered into the
marriage or civil partnership in good faith; did not obtain a divorce, dissolution
or annulment; and did not enter into a subsequent marriage or civil partnership
during the deceased's lifetime.[49]

---

[42] It has been said that litigation in respect of small estates should be discouraged as far as justly possible: *Re Coventry* [1980] Ch. 461; *Jelley v Iliffe* [1981] Fam. 128 (where, however, the court refused to strike out a claim), settlements are to be encouraged (see, e.g. *Bouette v Rose* [2000] 1 F.L.R. 363) and that appeals concerning modest estates should not be dissipated by pursuing an appeal against a sensible judgment at first instance: see *Re Goodchild (dec'd)* [1997] 2 F.L.R. 644. In order to discourage unmeritorious litigation it has been suggested that judges should reconsider the conventional practice of ordering that the costs of all parties be paid out of the estate: *Re Fullard (dec'd)* [1982] Fam. 42, *per* Ormrod L.J.
[43] *Re Coventry (dec'd)* [1980] Ch. 461 at 488–489.
[44] See *Re Jennings (dec'd)* [1994] Chap. 286 at 299, *per* Henry L.J.
[45] Inheritance (Provision for Family and Dependants) Act 1975 s.1(1).
[46] No application may be made without leave of the court more than six months after the grant of administration. For a full consideration of the factors to be taken into account in deciding whether or not to grant such leave, see *Re Salmon (dec'd)* [1981] Ch. 167 (which should be read in the light of *Re Dennis (dec'd)* [1981] 2 All E.R. 140); and (on the factors governing applications made under this provision on behalf of a minor) see *Re C (dec'd) (Leave to Apply for Provision)* [1995] 2 F.L.R. 24, Wilson J. For a remarkable case in which leave was given six years after the grant of probate, see *Stock v Brown* [1994] 1 F.L.R. 840, Thorpe J. It should be noted that the grant of administration may not be made until long after the death: see for example, *Re Collins (dec'd)* [1990] Fam. 56. (death in 1980; letters of administration taken out in 1987); and no application under the 1975 Act can be made unless and until a grant has been taken out: see *Re McBroom (dec'd)* [1992] 2 F.L.R. 49, Eastham J.
[47] Inheritance (Provision for Family and Dependants) Act 1975 s.1(1)(a).
[48] *Re Collins (dec'd)* [1990] Fam. 56.
[49] Inheritance (Provision for Family and Dependants) Act 1975 s.25(4), as amended by the Civil Partnership Act 2004 Sch.4 para.27.

(2) A former spouse or civil partner of the deceased who has not formed a subsequent marriage or civil partnership[50]

7–013   In light of the court's extensive powers exercisable on divorce (and now dissolution of civil partnership), it has been suggested that there will now be comparatively few cases (perhaps, e.g., where periodical payments had continued for some time and on the payor's death it was discovered that capital was available, or where capital—e.g. from an insurance policy—was produced as a result of the death) in which it would be appropriate for a claim by a former spouse or civil partner to succeed.[51]

The court has power, on divorce or dissolution of a civil partnership, if it considers it just to do so, to order that a former spouse or civil partner shall not be entitled to apply, on the other's death, for provision under the Inheritance (Provision for Family and Dependants) Act 1975. This power can be used, in appropriate cases, and whether or not the parties agree, to secure a "clean break" between the parties to a marriage on their divorce or dissolution of civil partnership.[52] The same power is exercisable under the Matrimonial and Family Proceedings Act 1984.[53]

(3) A child of the deceased

7–014   This class extends to illegitimate,[54] adopted[55] and posthumous children of the deceased,[56] and there are no restrictions of age or status in respect of marriage or civil partnership An adult child may apply, but it has been said[57] that claims for maintenance by able-bodied and comparatively young persons in employment and who are able to maintain themselves should be "relatively rare", and are to be "approached with a degree of circumspection". This does not mean that a claim by a son (or daughter[58]) is viewed with disfavour; it simply means that, faced with a claim by a person who is physically able to earn his or her own

---

[50] Inheritance (Provision for Family and Dependants) Act 1975 s.1(b). For these purposes a person has formed a subsequent marriage or civil partnership even if it is void or voidable: s.25(5).

[51] *Re Fullard (dec'd)* [1982] Fam. 42; *Cameron v Treasury Solicitor* [1996] 2 F.L.R. 716; but cf. *Re Farrow* [1987] 1 F.L.R. 205 (lump sum awarded in divorce dissipated; further provision held appropriate).

[52] Inheritance (Provision for Family and Dependants) Act 1975 ss.15, 15A, 15ZA, 15B. payments are made from the other's pension fund: *H. v H. (Financial Provision)* [1988] 2 F.L.R. 114.

[53] Inheritance (Provision for Family and Dependants) Act 1975 ss.15A and 15B.

[54] Inheritance (Provision for Family and Dependants) Act 1975 s.15(1); and note *In the estate of McC* (1978) 9 Fam. Law 26; *CA v CC* (1979) 123 S.J. 35.

[55] See *Williams v Johns* [1988] 2 F.L.R. 475.

[56] Inheritance (Provision for Family and Dependants) Act 1975 s.25(1)(b). A child of the deceased who is adopted after the deceased's death is to be treated in law as the child of the adopters, and is not entitled to make a claim as the deceased's child: *Re Collins (dec'd)* [1990] Fam. 56.

[57] *Re Coventry (dec'd)* [1980] Ch. 461 at 495; and see *Re Jennings (dec'd)* [1994] Ch. 286 at 301, *per* Henry L.J. (where this approach is taken to apply to all those of full age, in good health and who are economically self-sufficient); *Re Goodchild (dec'd)* [1996] 1 F.L.R. 591 at 608–613, *per* Carnwath J. (exceptional case where some provision should be made).

[58] The principle of the earlier decisions expressed in relation to a son is "applicable no less to the case of a daughter and, with developments in the structure of society, instances of its application in such cases may become more common": *Re Jennings (dec'd)* [1994] Ch. 286 at 295, *per* Nourse L.J. In *Espinosa v Bourke* [1999] 1 F.L.R. 747, the Court of Appeal held that, on the facts, the deceased's 55-year-old married daughter had shown the existence of factors sufficiently weighty to justify a substantial award in her favour.

living, the court will be inclined to ask "why should anybody else make provision for you if you are capable of maintaining yourself?"[59]

(4) Any person (not being a child of the deceased) who, in the case of any marriage or civil partnership to which the deceased was at any time a party, was treated by the deceased as a child of the family in relation to that marriage or civil partnership

This provision enables children who have, in fact, formed part of a deceased's **7–015** family to apply, even though they are not biologically related to and have not been adopted by the deceased.

The definition is in one important respect restricted: it requires that the child should have been treated as a child of the family *in relation to a marriage or civil partnership* to which the deceased was a party; and it follows, for example, that a child cannot make a claim as a child of the family for provision out of the estate of the mother's cohabitant, notwithstanding the fact that the cohabitant may have been the only father-figure in the child's life.[60] The Law Commission in its Report, *Cohabitation: The Financial Consequences of Relationship Breakdown,*[61] considered that this was a "difficult area", was not convinced that the case for reform had been made out and, therefore, did not recommend that the definition of "child of the family" in the 1975 Act be amended to include those treated as children of the family of a cohabiting couple.

In considering applications by children and children of the family, the court is given additional[62] guidelines[63] that (in the case of children of the family) are similar to those applied in proceedings on divorce or dissolution of a civil partnership.

(5) Any person (not being a person included in the foregoing paragraphs of this subsection) who immediately before the death of the deceased was being maintained, either wholly or partly, by the deceased

This category extends to all those who were in fact dependent on the deceased at **7–016** the date of death, whether relatives or not. An elderly but impoverished relative

[59] *Re Dennis (dec'd)* [1981] 2 All E.R. 140 at 145, *per* Browne-Wilkinson J; and note *Re Jennings (dec'd)* [1994] Ch. 286 at 295, *per* Nourse L.J.: on an application by an adult son there must be some special circumstance, "typically a moral obligation", if a claim is to succeed but the Court of Appeal has subsequently held that these are not threshold requirements but are merely circumstances indicating that the deceased was under a weighty obligation to provide for the person concerned: see *Re Hancock (dec'd)* [1998] 2 F.L.R. 346; *Re Pearce (dec'd)* [1998] 2 F.L.R. 705; and *Espinosa v Bourke* [1999] 1 F.L.R. 747. See also *Re Goodchild (dec'd)* [1997] 2 F.L.R. 644 (parent's promise to make provision a weighty factor); and note the decision in *Re Abram (dec'd)* [1996] 2 F.L.R. 379 (where the fact that a son had worked without reward in the family business was held to be one of the factors establishing an "overwhelming" obligation to provide for him). See generally Borkowski, "Re Hancock (deceased) and Espinoza and Bourke: moral obligations and family provision" (1999) 11 C. & F.L.Q. 305; N. Peart and A. Borkowski, "Provision for adult children on death—the lesson from New Zealand" [2000] C. & F.L.Q. 333; J. Wilson and R. Bailey-Harris, "Family provision and the adult child" [2005] Fam. Law 555.
[60] See *J v J (Property Transfer)* [1993] 2 F.L.R. 56, Eastham J.
[61] Law Com No.307 (2007), paras 6.50–6.58.
[62] i.e. to those applied to all applications: see s.3, below.
[63] s.3(3); see below.

or friend taken into the deceased's household and given free board and lodging and treated as a member of the family would qualify,[64] as would a man who had been supported by the woman with whom he had lived.[65] In one case,[66] the Court of Appeal accepted that a woman who had cared for her brain-damaged child, using the damages the daughter had been awarded to provide housing and other facilities for the two of them, was entitled to make an application for provision out of the daughter's estate as someone being maintained by the deceased child.

The qualifying condition is economic dependence: the applicant must be a person who was "being maintained".[67] The courts at one time took the view that in those cases in which there had been some mutual provision of support (e.g. where the deceased had provided rent-free housing,[68] and the applicant had done the cooking and domestic chores), the court had to weigh up the value of the respective contributions, strike a balance and then say whether the balance of contributions (if any) was substantial. In short, the courts would ask the question, "has the deceased contributed more than the applicant?"[69] In effect, the more deserving the applicant, the less chance he or she appeared to have of establishing a claim to a share in the deceased's estate. However, more recently the Court of Appeal came to urge the value of common sense and to criticise the use of "fine balancing computations involving the normal exchanges of support in the domestic sense".[70] In *Bishop v Plumley*[71] the Court accordingly allowed an appeal against a decision that the services provided by the woman who had lived with the deceased for many years and provided exceptional care for him in his last illness equalled the benefits of secure housing that he had provided for her so as to disqualify her from putting forward a claim under this head. In *Churchill v Roach*[72] it was held that the fact that the claimant could have survived without the support of the deceased did not negate dependency.

Finally, it should be noted that the relevant time for ascertaining whether the condition is satisfied is immediately before the death of the deceased; if this provision had been given a literal interpretation it would have created absurd

---

[64] *Jelley v Iliffe* [1981] Fam. 128 at 135.

[65] *Re Beaumont (dec'd)* [1980] Ch. 444; *Jelley v Iliffe* [1981] Fam. 128.

[66] *Bouette v Rose* [2000] 1 F.L.R. 363. The mother was entitled to half the child's estate under the rules of intestate succession: see above. It appears, however, that she spent the whole of the assets received as her daughter's administrator notwithstanding the fact that she knew the child's father was legally entitled to a half share.

[67] Inheritance (Provision for Family and Dependants) Act 1975 s.1(3) contains a definition of that concept—for "the purposes of subsection (1)(e), above, a person shall be treated as being maintained by the deceased either wholly or partly, as the case may be, if the deceased, otherwise than for full valuable consideration, was making a substantial contribution in money or money's worth towards the reasonable needs of that person"—to which the court gave a restrictive interpretation: *Re Wilkinson (dec'd)* [1978] Fam. 22; *Re Beaumont (dec'd)* [1980] Ch. 444; *Jelley v Iliffe* [1981] Fam. 128; *Re Kirby* [1981] 3 F.L.R. 249.

[68] *Jelley v Iliffe* [1981] Fam. 128 at 138; see also *Harrington v Gill* [1981] 4 F.L.R. 265.

[69] See, for example, *Re Kirby (dec'd)* [1981] 3 F.L.R. 249 (couple pooled earnings; deceased said to have contributed 50% more than applicant).

[70] *Bishop v Plumley* [1991] 1 F.L.R. 121 at 126, *per* Butler-Sloss L.J., CA.

[71] [1991] 1 F.L.R. 121, CA.

[72] [2004] 2 F.L.R. 989.

anomalies. For example, suppose that the deceased had been supporting an aged parent in a nursing home, but the parent had been admitted to a national health hospital for urgent treatment a week before the deceased's death. In such circumstances, it might seem quite wrong to deny the parent a claim for provision, and the courts have taken the view that what is in question is the settled basis or general arrangement between the parties rather than the actual, perhaps fluctuating, variation of it which exists immediately before the death.[73] A relationship of dependence that has existed for years will not be treated as no longer subsisting, for example, during a few weeks of mortal sickness.[74] Contrarily, if it can be clearly shown that the deceased had divested himself of financial responsibility for the applicant before his death, the application must fail.[75]

(6) A person living with the deceased as a spouse or civil partner
The Law Commission, in its review of the law governing distribution on intestacy,[76] rejected suggestions that the intestacy rules should automatically provide for cohabitants[77] because of the complexity, cost and delay that would inevitably be involved. However, the Commission accepted that cohabitants should be able to apply for discretionary provision without the need to show dependence. It is currently[78] provided that a person who: **7–017**

- was living with the deceased in the same household immediately before the date of the death; and

- had been living with the deceased in the same household for at least two years before that date[79]; and

- was living during the whole of that period as the husband or wife or civil partner of the deceased

---

[73] See also, in the context of cohabitation, *Gully v Dix* [2004] 1 W.L.R. 1399.
[74] *Re Beaumont (dec'd)* [1980] Ch. 444; *Jelley v Iliffe* [1981] Fam. 128; *Re Kirby (dec'd)* [1981] 3 F.L.R. 249.
[75] See, for example, *Kourkgy v Lusher* [1981] 4 F.L.R. 65, where the applicant had been the deceased's mistress intermittently for more than 10 years; applicant established general arrangement by deceased for her maintenance up to July 14, 1979; deceased held to have abandoned responsibility on return from holiday with wife on July 29; deceased died on August 7; claim failed.
[76] Law Com. No.187 (1989).
[77] Law Com. No.187 (1989), para.58.
[78] Inheritance (Provision for Family and Dependants) Act 1975 ss.1(b)(a), 1(1A) and 1(1B), as amended by the Civil Partnership Act 2004 Sch.4 para.15.
[79] A period of three months interruption of cohabitation prior to death does not necessarily negate entitlement; what was to be looked at was "the settled state of affairs during the relationship . . . and not the immediate de facto situation prevailing before the deceased's death": *Gully v Dix* [2004] 1 F.L.R. 918. In *Churchill v Roach* [2004] 2 F.L.R. 989, the cohabitation had lasted less than two years, and so the claim under this category was dismissed. For consideration of whether cohabitation had ever commenced, see (in the context of the Fatal Accidents Act 1976) *Kotke v Saffarini* [2005] 2 F.L.R. 517.

may apply to the court for an order.[80] Although, as we shall see, such an applicant must show that provision is required for maintenance,[81] it has been said[82] that the express recognition of cohabitation as a qualification may reduce the problems faced by elderly couples in demonstrating a qualification based solely on their having been maintained by the deceased.

ii. What has to be established

7–018 The court, if it is to have discretion to make an order, must first be satisfied, as a threshold or condition precedent to the exercise of the jurisdiction[83]:

> "[T]hat the disposition of the deceased's estate effected by his will or the law relating to intestacy, or the combination of his will and that law is not such as to make reasonable financial provision for the applicant."[84]

This is essentially a question of fact (albeit one involving a value judgment), and the Court of Appeal will thus be reluctant to interfere with a decision on this point unless satisfied that it is plainly wrong.[85]

A number of points require further comment.

(1) Disposition effected by will or intestacy

7–019 It is usually assumed that the family provision legislation is most commonly invoked where the deceased has made a will excluding (or making only small provision for) the applicant, in favour of more extensive provision for others. However, the legislation is not limited to such cases, and would equally be available where a testator has tried by his or her will to make provision for the claimant but failed. For example, the testator may (miscalculating the size of his or her estate) have given large legacies to strangers and a residuary gift to his surviving spouse or civil partner. Under the general law, the legacies are paid in full before the surviving spouse or civil partner is entitled to anything. The test is easy to state: what testamentary provision would a reasonable person in the position of the deceased have made for the claimant in all the circumstances, including those specified in s.3 of the Act?[86]

---

[80] Additional guidelines for the exercise of the courts discretion on such applications are provided by Inheritance (Provision for Family and Dependants) Act 1975 s.3(2A). For an illustration of a finding of cohabitation made "with enormous hesitation" on the facts but upheld on appeal, see *Witkowska v Kaminski* [2007] 1 F.L.R. 1547.

[81] See *Re Jennings (dec'd)* [1994] Ch. 286, CA. On the meaning of "reasonable maintenance" in the context of where the deceased intended the claimant to live, see *Witkowska v Kaminski* [2007] 1 F.L.R. 1547.

[82] *Bouette v Rose* [2000] 1 F.L.R. 363 at 372.

[83] *Re Fullard (dec'd)* [1982] Fam. 42.

[84] Inheritance (Provision for Family and Dependants) Act 1975 s.2(1). In *Churchill v Roach* [2004], it was held that the deceased had failed to make reasonable provision for the claimant, whose income needs but not housing needs had been met.

[85] *Re Coventry (dec'd)* [1980] Ch. 461 at 487, *per* Goff L.J.; see *Espinosa v Bourke* [1999] 1 F.L.R. 747 and *Fielden v Cunliffe* [2006] 1 F.L.R. 745; [2006] 3 F.C.R. 593 for instances where an appeal was allowed.

[86] *Harrington v Gill* [1981] 4 F.L.R. 265 at 271, *per* Dunn L.J. For the matters specified in s.3 of the Act, see below.

The fact that the deceased died intestate is no bar to an application.[87] It seems, at first sight, strange that a court should ever hold that the rules laid down by law to govern the devolution of estates are capable of operating so as to produce an unjust result. However, the inflexibility of the general rules inevitably means that there will be such. For example, a cohabitant or other dependant without legal links with the deceased can never, as such, benefit on intestacy; as we have seen, the law treats an intestate's surviving spouse or civil partner with generosity so that the whole of all but the largest estates will go to the surviving spouse or civil partner to the exclusion of any dependent children. Thus:

> *In Re Sivyer*[88] the intestate left a widow and a 13-year-old daughter by his previous marriage. Under the intestacy laws the widow was entitled to the whole of his estate. It was held that the daughter should receive provision.[89]

The question of whether reasonable provision has been made is wholly objective.[90] The court is not to ask whether the deceased knew all the material facts; the issue is not whether the deceased has been reasonable or unreasonable but whether the provision in fact made is reasonable or not.[91] It follows that the question whether the operative dispositions make or fail to make reasonable provision must be approached in exactly the same way whether the court is dealing with a will or an intestacy or with a combination of the two.[92]

(2) What is "reasonable financial provision"?
The Act draws a crucial distinction between two categories of applicant.[93]   **7–020**

**(a) Criterion to be applied in the case of applications by the surviving spouse   7–021
or surviving civil partner.** The question is whether such financial provision has been made as it would be reasonable in all the circumstances of the case for a spouse or civil partner to receive, whether or not that provision is required for his or her maintenance.[94]

(b) Criterion to be applied in the case of all other applicants. The question is   7–022
whether the provision is such as it would be reasonable for the applicant to receive for his or her maintenance.[95] Maintenance may, for this purpose, be defined as:

---

[87] See, for example, *Re Cook* (1956) 106 L.J. 466; *Re Sivyer* [1967] 1 W.L.R. 1482; *Re Coventry* [1980] Ch. 461; *Re Kirby (dec'd)* [1981] 3 F.L.R. 249; *Harrington v Gill* [1981] 4 F.L.R. 265; *Bouette v Rose* [2000] 1 F.L.R. 36.
[88] [1967] 1 W.L.R. 1482.
[89] For an even more striking example, see *Re Collins (dec'd)* [1990] Fam. 56.
[90] *Moody v Stevenson* [1992] Ch. 486 at 494, *per* Waite J., CA.
[91] *Re Coventry (dec'd)* [1980] Ch. 461 at 474–475, 488–489.
[92] *Re Coventry (dec'd)* [1980] Ch. 461 at 488, *per* Goff L.J.
[93] See *Malone v Harrison* [1979] 1 W.L.R. 1353; *Re Coventry (dec'd)* [1980] Ch. 461.
[94] Inheritance (Provision for Family and Dependants) Act 1975 s.1(2)(a), (aa).
[95] Inheritance (Provision for Family and Dependants) Act 1975 s.1(2)(b).

"[S]uch financial provision as could be reasonable in all the circumstances of the case to enable the applicant to maintain himself in a manner suitable to those circumstances."[96]

Maintenance does not extend to cover all provision for the well-being or benefit of the applicant,[97] but rather what is needed to meet the recurring expenses of living[98] (such as housing, food, clothing and entertainment). Thus:

In *Re Jennings (deceased)*[99] the applicant was a 50-year-old who had been brought up from the age of four by his mother and stepfather. There was no contact between father and son after the divorce, and the only thing the father did for his son was to send him 10 shillings in a birthday card on his second birthday. The father left the residue of his estate (which amounted to some £300,000 after payment of inheritance tax) to charities. The son had been successful in business and the Court of Appeal held that because the son was in reasonably comfortable financial circumstances, and there was no evidence that he was likely to encounter financial difficulties in the future, it was impossible to show that he required "maintenance".[100]

However, the fact that the provision is intended to provide maintenance does not mean that the provision ordered must be restricted to income; the simplest method of providing housing, for example, may be to provide a lump sum with which the applicant can buy him- or herself a house. Moreover, if the estate is very small, the only sensible way of making provision for the applicant may be to award a lump sum[101] or to direct that the deceased's house be transferred to the applicant.[102]

iii. Circumstances to be taken into consideration

7–023　The Act provides[103] that the court shall, in considering whether the disposition of the deceased's estate makes reasonable financial provision for the applicant and

---

[96] *Re Coventry (dec'd)* [1980] Ch. 461 at 494, *per* Buckley L.J.

[97] For example, payment of the applicant's debts solely to remove the threat of bankruptcy proceedings: *Re Dennis (dec'd)* [1981] 2 All E.R. 140; and see *Re Abram (dec'd)* [1996] 2 F.L.R. 379. Payment of business debts, thereby enabling the applicant to carry on remunerative activity, may be regarded as provision for maintenance: see *Re Goodchild (dec'd)* [1997] 2 F.L.R. 644.

[98] *Re Dennis (dec'd)* [1981] 2 All E.R. 140 at 145, *per* Browne-Wilkinson J.

[99] [1994] Ch. 256, CA. Compare *Re Callaghan (dec'd)* [1985] Fam. 1, Booth J., where the applicant could show that he needed money to exercise the right to buy his council house without the burden of a substantial mortgage that he could not easily support.

[100] In *Re Jennings (dec'd)* [1994] Ch. 286, CA, both Nourse and Henry L.JJ. state that the provision must be "required" for the applicant's maintenance, following in this respect a dictum in *Re Coventry (dec'd)* [1980] Ch. 461 at 472, *per* Olivier J. But the word "required" does not appear in this provision of the Act, and it seems questionable whether Oliver J. was correct in thinking that it should be read into it.

[101] cf. *Kusminow v Barclays Bank Trust Co Ltd* [1989] Fam. Law 66, where expenses of administering a trust pointed to provision by outright payment rather than settlement; and see also *Harrington v Gill* [1981] 4 F.L.R. 265, where the contents were also transferred to the applicant absolutely; *Millward v Shenton* [1972] 1 W.L.R. 711.

[102] As in *Rajaballly v Rajaballly* [1987] 2 F.L.R. 390, CA (where the matrimonial home was vested in the deceased's widow subject to a charge for a lump sum legacy for a mentally disabled son).

[103] Inheritance (Provision for Family and Dependants) Act 1975 s.3(1).

in determining whether and in what manner to exercise its powers to make orders, to "have regard" to a series of matters, on the basis of the facts as they are known at the date of the hearing.[104]

Some matters are to be considered in all cases, and additional considerations have to be taken into account in the case of certain applicants.[105]

(1) Matters to be considered in all cases

The first group (to be considered whatever the head of dependency upon which the application is based) is as follows[106]:   **7–024**

"(a) [T]he financial resources and financial needs which the applicant has or is likely to have in the foreseeable future;

(b) the financial resources and financial needs which any other applicant for an order . . . has or is likely to have in the foreseeable future;

(c) the financial resources and financial needs which any beneficiary of the estate of the deceased has or is likely to have in the foreseeable future[107];

(d) any obligations and responsibilities[108] which the deceased had towards any applicant for an order . . . or towards any beneficiary of the estate of the deceased;

---

[104] Inheritance (Provision for Family and Dependants) Act 1975 s.3(5); and note *Re Hancock (dec'd)* [1998] 2 F.L.R. 346 (six-fold increase in value of land between testator's death and date of hearing; held, court to determine application on basis of values as known at date of hearing).

[105] Statements made by the deceased are admissible under the Civil Evidence Act 1968 as evidence of any fact stated therein: Inheritance (Provision for Family and Dependants) Act 1975 s.21; and see *Kourkgy v Lusher* (1983) 4 F.L.R. 65; cf. *Williams v Johns* [1988] 2 F.L.R. 475, where the court emphasised the objective nature of the test to be applied, and in consequence seemed to discount the importance to be attached to the deceased's statement of reasons.

[106] Inheritance (Provision for Family and Dependants) Act 1975 s.3(1); and *Espinosa v Bourke* [1999] 1 F.L.R. 747 (where the deceased's will included a statement that he made no provision for his daughter because she had been adequately provided for and had shown "a degree of irresponsibility"; the Court of Appeal held these matters were appropriate to be considered, but that they did not outweigh the obligation on the deceased to give effect to a promise to let the daughter have shares he had inherited from his wife).

[107] This will include payments under the deceased's pension scheme, for example, even though such payments are not part of his "net estate" for the purposes of the Act: see *Re Cairnes (dec'd)* [1982] 4 F.L.R. 225.

[108] In *Re Jennings* [1994] Ch. 286, CA, the Court of Appeal held that this referred to obligations and responsibilities subsisting at the date of the deceased's death; and accordingly held that the failure of a father to retain contact with, or support, his son during infancy was not relevant to a claim by the son on the father's death many years later. The mere existence of the relationship of father and son is insufficient to constitute such an obligation. The Court of Appeal seems to have treated the statutory list of specified "circumstances" as an exhaustive enumeration of conditions, at least one of which must be satisfied if the court is to be able to find that the deceased's provision was not reasonable, but this approach seems questionable, and more recent decisions have taken a flexible approach: see, notably, *Re Hancock (dec'd)* [1998] 2 F.L.R. 346; *Espinosa v Bourke* [1999] 1 F.L.R. 747.

(e) the size and nature of the net estate[109] of the deceased;

(f) any physical or mental disability of any applicant for an order . . . or any beneficiary of the estate of the deceased;

(g) any other matter, including the conduct of the applicant or any other person, which in the circumstances of the case the court may consider relevant."[110]

The "conduct" that the court is required to consider is not limited to misconduct. The court will wish to consider such matters as whether any of those affected had, for example, been generous in providing the deceased with financial support,[111] whether the applicant has given up his or her own house to live with the deceased, how far two competing parties had helped the deceased in his or her business, and so on.[112]

Inevitably, however, there will be cases in which the allegation is of morally culpable conduct, either by the claimant (in which case the suggestion will be that the applicant should get less than might otherwise be the case), by the deceased in relation to the applicant (in which case the applicant might expect to get more) or by other beneficiaries under the deceased's will or intestacy (in which case it may be argued that the claimant should be allotted some or all of the benefits to which the beneficiary would otherwise be entitled). How far are such matters relevant?

The conduct that the court takes into account may extend to a daughter's neglect to care for her father in his last years, and indeed her lifestyle.[113] The reference to conduct in the 1975 Act is in much wider and general terms than that in the ancillary relief provisions of the Matrimonial Causes Act 1973.[114]

---

[109] See, for example, *Re Rowlands dec'd* [1984] F.L.R. 813 (estate consisted largely of Welsh hill farm). "Net estate" is defined in s.25 of the Act; and s.8 provides that *donationes mortis causa* and nominated property are to be treated as part of the net estate. (However, the definition of nominated property relates to nominations under statutory powers; and the deceased's right to nominate a beneficiary under a private pension scheme has been held not to fall within the definition: *Re Cairnes dec'd* [1982] 4 F.L.R. 225.) If the deceased was a joint tenant of property, the court may treat his severable share as forming part of the net estate: s.9; and see *Kourkgy v Lusher* [1981] 4 F.L.R. 65; *Jessop v Jessop* [1992] 1 F.L.R. 591, CA; *Powell v Osbourne* [1993] 1 F.L.R. 1001; *Re McBroom dec'd* [1992] 2 F.L.R. 49, Eastham J. (this power cannot be exercised unless and until a grant of administration has been taken out to the deceased's estate).

[110] This will extend to divorce and its financial consequences: *Re Fullard dec'd* [1982] Fam. 42.

[111] See *Jelley v Iliffe* [1981] Fam. 128 at 140.

[112] *Re Thornley* [1969] 1 W.L.R. 1037.

[113] *Espinosa v Bourke* [1999] 1 F.L.R. 747 at 757.

[114] See Matrimonial Causes Act 1973 s.25(2)(g); the s.1 provision is applied on the dissolution of civil partnerships by the Civil Partnership Act 2004 s.72 and Sch.5. On the difference in legislative formulation, see *Malone v Harrison* [1979] 1 W.L.R. 1353 at 1364, *per* Hollings J.; cf. *Re Snoeck dec'd* [1982] 13 Fam. Law 18, where Wood J. refused to interpret the reference to conduct in a sense different from that of the divorce legislation. Accordingly, with some hesitation, it was held that the wife's conduct, at a time when the deceased was terminally ill, in throwing water over him on three occasions, driving a car at him, striking him over the head with a rolling-pin, milk bottle and umbrella, puncturing the tyres of his car, and writing abusive and offensive letters to his business colleagues did not justify a failure to make any provision at all for her, since it did not cancel out her contributions in the early part of the 20-year marriage and her contributions in managing the home and bringing up the children.

(2) Matters to be considered in relation to particular categories of applicant
There are further statutory guidelines applicable to particular categories of   **7–025**
applicant.

(a) Spouses, civil partners, former spouses and former civil partners. *(i) The*   **7–026**
divorce/dissolution expectation. In the case of an application by the deceased's
spouse or civil partner, the court must have regard to the provision that the
applicant might reasonably have expected to receive if the marriage or civil
partnership had been ended by divorce or dissolution on the day of the deceased's
death[115]; this "divorce/dissolution expectation" is a very important consideration.[116] It has been said that the minimum posthumous provision for a surviving
spouse (and now a surviving civil partner) should correspond as closely as
possible to the inchoate rights enjoyed by that spouse or civil partner in the
deceased's lifetime by virtue of his or her prospective entitlement under
matrimonial or civil partnership law.[117] However, this is not to say that the
divorce/dissolution expectation will determine the outcome—even although it
may be the "logical starting point".[118] For example, in divorce or dissolution
cases, the parties' respective needs are often of overriding importance, and the
fact there is only one person's need to be considered when the marriage is ended
by death may justify a larger award than could have been expected on divorce or
dissolution, whilst the considerations which point to the clean break on divorce
or dissolution are not all present when a marriage is ended by death.[119] Thus:

> In *Moody v Stevenson*[120] the deceased's 81-year-old husband continued to
> live in the former matrimonial home, which had been given to the deceased
> by her mother. The deceased's will gave her entire estate to her daughter by
> a previous marriage, and stated that she considered her husband had
> adequate resources of his own. The daughter sought possession of the house,
> and the husband applied for reasonable provision out of the estate. The
> Court of Appeal held that the starting point should have been to look at the
> provision a divorce court would have made for the husband, and this would
> undoubtedly have included provision for his housing. Accordingly he
> should be given the right to occupy the house for so long as he was able and
> willing to do so.
>
> In *Davis v Davis*[121] the applicant's husband had given his wife of seven
> years £15,000 shortly before his death, and in his will gave her a life interest
> in the residue of his estate (amounting to something in the region of a

---

[115] Inheritance (Provision for Family and Dependants) Act 1975 s.3(2), as amended by the Civil Partnership Act 2004 Sch.4 para.17.
[116] *Re Besterman (dec'd)* [1984] F.L.R. 503, CA; and see *Kusminow v Barclays Bank Trust Co Ltd* [1989] Fam. Law 66; *Moody v Stevenson* [1992] 1 F.L.R. 494; *Davis v Davis* [1993] 1 F.L.R. 54, CA: *Powell v Osbourne* [1993] 1 F.L.R. 1001, CA.
[117] *Moody v Stevenson* [1992] 1 F.L.R. 494 at 505, CA *per* Waite J.
[118] *Moody v Stevenson* [1992] 1 F.L.R. 494 at 505, CA *per* Waite J.
[119] *Re Krubert (dec'd)* [1996] 3 W.L.R. 959; *Re Bunning (dec'd)* [1985] F.L.R. 1; *cf. Smith v Smith (Smith and Others Intervening)* [1991] 2 F.L.R. 432, CA; see further *Fielden v Cunliffe* [2006] Ch. 361; [2006] 1 F.L.R. 745; [2005] 3 F.C.R. 593.
[120] [1992] Ch. 486, CA.
[121] [1993] 1 F.L.R. 54, CA.

£250,000). The trustees (who were directed by the will to have regard to his widow's expressed wishes) arranged for the purchase of a house for the widow's occupation, but she applied to the court for the house to be transferred to her absolutely. Although it was clear that, if the marriage had been ended by divorce the court would have ordered an outright clean break capital payment, the Court of Appeal considered that a life interest was a perfectly reasonable provision in all the circumstances.

In *Fielden v Cunliffe*[122] the estate was valued at approximately £1.4 million. The executors appealed against an order to pay £800,000 to the deceased's widow. The widow had originally been the deceased's house-keeper, and married him six months later. They had been married only 12 months at the time of the deceased's death. The widow had few assets and no independent income, although £226,000 was accrued to her by survivor-ship. The Court of Appeal allowed the appeal and substituted a lump sum of £600,000. It held that, with appropriate adjustments based on the different statutory provisions, the principles in *White v White*[123] applied in ancillary relief claims could also be applied to a widow's claim under the 1975 Act. The objective was to achieve a result that was fair and non-discriminatory; a balancing exercise between the various considerations had to be conducted—the brevity of the marriage was an important factor, as was the widow's future housing needs. She was entitled to a reasonable expectation of lifestyle, although not of the standard enjoyed during the marriage.

7–027   *(ii) Other factors in relation to spouse, civil partners, former spouses and former civil partners.* The court must also have regard to[124]:

> "(i) [T]he age of the applicant and the duration of the marriage or civil partnership;
>
> (ii) the contribution made by the applicant to the welfare of the family of the deceased, including any contribution made by looking after the home or caring for the family."[125]

7–028   **(b) Children and children of family.** The court must have regard to the manner in which the applicant was being—or in which the applicant might expect to be—educated or trained.[126] In the case where the applicant is a child of the family,[127] the court is also directed[128] to have regard:

---

[122] [2006] Ch. 361; [2006] 1 F.L.R. 745; [2005] 3 F.C.R. 593.

[123] [2001] 1 A.C. 596.

[124] Inheritance (Provision for Family and Dependants) Act 1975 s.3(2).

[125] cf. Matrimonal Causes Act 1973 s.25(1)(d), (f).

[126] Matrimonial Causes Act s.3(3). Cf. Matrimonial Causes Act 1973 s.25(3)(4). There are special provisions for children of the family: Inheritance (Provision for Family and Dependants) Act 1975 s.3(3)(a), (b), (c), as to which see *Re Leach* [1986] Ch. 226, CA.

[127] See *Re Leach* [1986] Ch. 226, CA; *Re Callaghan* [1985] Fam. 1, Booth J.; and *Re Debenham* [1986] 1 F.L.R. 404, Ewbank J.

[128] Inheritance (Provision for Family and Dependants) Act 1975 s.3(3); see *Re Leach* [1986] Ch. 226, CA. In *Gors v Treasury Solicitor* [2003] Fam. Law 93, the deceased had assumed responsibility for a step-daughter exactly as if she had been his own child; she received the entirety of the modest estate, net of costs of the Treasury Solicitor.

- to whether the deceased had assumed any responsibility for the applicant's maintenance, and, if so, to the extent to which and the basis upon which the deceased assumed that responsibility, and to the length of time for which the deceased discharged that responsibility;

- to whether, in assuming and discharging that responsibility, the deceased did so knowing that the applicant was not his/her own child;

- to the liability of any other person to maintain the applicant.

(c) Persons being maintained by the deceased. Where the applicant's claim is   **7–029** based on the fact that the applicant was being maintained by the deceased at the time of the death, the court is to "have regard" not only to the factors set out above but also:

"[T]o the extent to which and the basis upon which the deceased assumed responsibility for the maintenance of the applicant and to the length of time for which the deceased discharged that responsibility."[129]

(d) Cohabitants. Where an application is made under this head, the court, in   **7–030** addition to the matters specifically mentioned,[130] is directed to have regard to:

- the age of the applicant and the duration of the cohabitation;

- the contribution made by the applicant to the welfare of the family of the deceased, including any contribution made by looking after the home or caring for the family.[131]

iv. Orders that can be made
The court has extensive powers. In addition to periodical payments and lump   **7–031** sums,[132] the court may make orders:

- for the transfer or settlement of property[133];

- that property (e.g. a house) be bought and transferred to the applicant or settled for his or her benefit[134];

- varying ante-nuptial or post-nuptial settlements or settlements made during a civil partnership or in anticipation of the formation thereof (subject to certain restrictions).[135]

---

[129] Inheritance (Provision for Family and Dependants) Act 1975 s.3(4); and note *Harrington v Gill* [1983] 4 F.L.R. 265, CA: the court will, under this head, consider the standard of living enjoyed by the applicant during the deceased's lifetime, and the extent to which the deceased contributed to that standard of living.
[130] See s.3(1)(a)–(f).
[131] Inheritance (Provision for Family and Dependants) Act 1975 s.3(2A), as inserted by Law Reform (Succession) Act 1995 s.2(4); compare Matrimonial Causes Act 1973 s.25(2)(f); Ch.13, below.
[132] Inheritance (Provision for Family and Dependants) Act 1975 s.2(1)(a), (b). A lump sum may be payable by instalments: s.7.
[133] Inheritance (Provision for Family and Dependants) Act 1975 s.2(1)(c), (d).
[134] Inheritance (Provision for Family and Dependants) Act 1975 s.2(1)(e).
[135] Inheritance (Provision for Family and Dependants) Act 1975 s.2(1)(f), (g).

In deciding whether to exercise these powers, and, if so, in what manner the court is directed to have regard to the "guidelines" referred to above.[136] The objective is to ensure that the claimant will receive the reasonable financial provision that the deceased has failed to make; the powers are sufficiently flexible to ensure, for example, that the claimant is enabled to live in the deceased's house for the rest of his or her life.[137]

Orders for periodical payments in favour of a former spouse or former civil partner must determine on the formation of a subsequent marriage or civil partnership. Orders in favour of a spouse or civil partner need not do so.[138]

Orders for periodical payments (but not for lump sums or transfer of property) can be varied.[139]

There is a wide range of ancillary powers,[140] including a power to order interim payments,[141] powers to vary maintenance agreements made by the deceased and also maintenance orders.[142]

The Act also contains provisions giving the court extensive powers where the deceased has made dispositions[143] or contracts[144] intended to defeat applications under the Act.

B. Reform proposals

7–032   The Law Commission in its Report, *Cohabitation: The Financial Consequences of Divorce*,[145] made a number of reform proposals in respect of cohabitants' claims under the Inheritance (Provision for Family and Dependants) Act 1975. The Commission considered it important to ensure consistency between the remedies it proposed on separation and those contained in the 1975 Act, and hence, if a new scheme for financial relief on separation were to be enacted, there should be reform of the 1975 Act. The Commission's main provisional proposals in this respect were:

- amendment of the definition of "cohabitant"[146] so as to move away from the marriage/civil partnership analogy and to be consistent with the definition in the proposed new separation scheme;

---

[136] Inheritance (Provision for Family and Dependants) Act 1975 s.3(1).
[137] *Re Abram (dec'd)* [1996] 2 F.L.R. 379 (where the applicant had made an Individual Voluntary Arrangement with his creditors under the provisions of Insolvency Act 1986; and the court directed that provision be made for the applicant by protective trusts that would benefit him and his family rather than the creditors).
[138] Inheritance (Provision for Family and Dependants) Act 1975 s.19(2).
[139] Inheritance (Provision for Family and Dependants) Act 1975 s.6 This provision is narrowly drawn: see *Fricker v Personal Representatives of Fricker* [1981] 3 F.L.R. 228.
[140] See, for example, ss.2(4), 19, 20.
[141] See Re *Besterman (dec'd)* [1981] 3 F.L.R. 255.
[142] See ss.16–18.
[143] Inheritance (Provision for Family and Dependants) Act 1975 s.10.
[144] Inheritance (Provision for Family and Dependants) Act 1975 s.11.
[145] Law Com. No.309 (2007), paras 6.11–6.49.
[146] See ss.1(ba) and 1(1A).

- review of the definition of "reasonable financial provision" as applied to cohabitants' claims[147] under the 1975 Act, to ensure consistency with the proposed new separation scheme;

- in determining a cohabitant's claim under the 1975 Act, the court should have regard to the provision that he or she might have reasonably expected to receive in proceedings for financial relief on separation; thus, a "separation expectation" would be relevant, analogous to the "divorce/dissolution expectation" under the current law[148];

- on granting financial relief on separation, the court should be entitled to direct that neither cohabitant should thereafter be entitled to make a claim under the 1975 Act; this would mirror the power available on making an order for financial relief on divorce or dissolution of a civil partnership.[149]

These proposals[150] were contingent on the enactment of a statutory scheme for financial relief on separation. On March 8, 2008, the Justice Minister Bridget Prentice announced that the Government would take no immediate action on the Law Commission's proposals; it wished to await research findings on the costs of similar provisions contained in the Family Law (Scotland) Act 2006.

---

[147] See ss.3(1) and 3(2A).
[148] See para.7–026, above.
[149] See para.7–013, above.
[150] See further, S. Bridge, "Financial relief for cohabitants: eligibilty, opt out and provision on death" [2007] Fam. Law 1076.

CHAPTER EIGHT

REFORM OF FAMILY PROPERTY LAW: THE FUTURE

I.   INTRODUCTION.............................. 8–001
II. THE CASE FOR A SPECIAL
SCHEME FOR FORMAL RELATION-
SHIPS.. 8–002
III. REFORM OF PROPERTY RIGHTS

IN OTHER RELATIONSHIPS 8–005
IV. THE CASE FOR A SPECIAL
SCHEME FOR UNFORMALISED
RELATIONSHIPS 8–006

I. INTRODUCTION

It can be forcefully argued that family law—including the rules governing **8–001**
property rights—is an instrument to secure and safeguard the values that society
upholds in the family.[1] In modern society, however, there is an increasing degree
of plurality in those values.[2] Furthermore, the socio-economic context in which
the legal rules operate has become increasingly complex, as the roles assumed by
men and women in the family and in society have progressively become less
distinct. It may seem uncontroversial that the law should endeavour to give fair
recognition to the varied contributions that partners make to their common life.
Nevertheless, the means by which that goal is best achieved, and the precise
content of fairness,[3] continue to generate much debate. For instance, should the
parties' rights in relation to family assets be defined during the currency of a
relationship, or only realised at the time of breakdown? Should the law aim to

---

[1] J. Eekelaar, "Family law and social control", in *Oxford Essays in Jurisprudence* 3rd Series (Oxford:
Oxford University Press, 1987), Ch.6. Houlgate, "Must the personal be political?: family law and the
concept of family" (1998) 12 I.J.L.P.F. 107; J. Dewar, "The normal chaos of family law" (1998) 61
M.L.R. 467; J. Dewar, "Family law and its discontents" (2000) 12 I.J.L.P.F. 59.
[2] See the comments of Lord Hoffmann in *Piglowski v Piglowski* [1999] 2 F.L.R. 763 at 785; R.
Bailey-Harris, "Lesbian and gay family values and the law" [1999] Fam. Law 560; A. Diduck, *Law's
Families* (London: Butterworths, 2003).
[3] R. Bailey-Harris, "Dividing the assets on family breakdown: the content of fairness", in Freeman
(ed.), *Current Legal Problems* (Oxford: Oxford University Press, 2001), p.533. Contrast, too, judicial
views of fairness in the context of ancillary relief—as articulated in *White v White* [2000] 2 F.L.R.
981 and discussed in Ch.13—and in the context of property law, discussed in Ch.5.

achieve formal equality between the parties, or substantive equality?[4] Should its task be to dictate how assets acquired during the relationship should be divided, or to provide a solution that recognises the impact of the relationship on the parties? How far should the legal rules differ according to whether the parties have formalised their relationship or not? These complex issues inevitably underpin any discussion of future reform of family property law.

As noted in Chapter 4, individuals in many different types of relationships may need to rely on the general law of property at some stage in their lives—where there is a dispute with a third party who has an interest in the property, where relationships other than marriage or civil partnership break down, and where one party dies. If the general law of property is deemed inappropriate as a tool for dealing with family life, then two questions fall to be considered: (1) what rules are appropriate for intact families?; (2) and what approach should be taken where a relationship ends?

Proposals for reform have therefore tended to fall into one of three categories: (1) those recommending a special regime for those who have formalised their relationship; (2) those suggesting changes to the general law of property in order to make it better fitted to the realities of family life; and (3) those arguing that special remedies should be available to those whose relationship breaks down. The proposals that have been advanced in each of these three categories will be considered in turn.

II. The Case for a Special Scheme for Formal Relationships

8–002　　The possibility of creating a special scheme for those who have formalised their relationship is one that has received detailed consideration and, despite the lack of legislative action, deserves examination. From its foundation in 1965 to 1988, the Law Commission published a number of extensive and careful discussions of various reform issues in the context of matrimonial property.[5] The case for reform was summarised in its 1988 report on the subject,[6] the three principal reasons identified being: (1) the unfairness and lack of clarity in the existing rules; (2) the need for justice between spouses not only on divorce but also during

---

[4] For a discussion of these issues see, for example, M. Fineman, "Implementing equality: ideology, contradiction and social change. A study of rhetoric and results in the regulation of the consequences of divorce" [1983] *Wisconsin Law Review* 789; J. Scutt, "Equal marital property rights" (1983) 18 *Australian Journal of Social Issues* 128; E. Cox, "Beyond community of property: a plea for equity" (1983) 18 *Australian Journal of Social Sciences* 142; A. Diduck and H. Orton, "Equality and support for spouses" (1994) 57 M.L.R. 681; R. Bailey-Harris, "The role of maintenance and property orders in redressing equality" (1998) 12 *Australian Journal of Family Law* 3.

[5] Law Commission, *First Report on Matrimonial Property: A New Approach* (Law Com. No.52 (1973)); *Third Report on Family Property: The Matrimonial Home* (Law Com. No.86 (1978)); *Property Law: The Implications of Williams and Glyn's Bank v. Boland* (Law Com. No.115 (1982)); *Family Law: Matrimonial Property* (Law Com. No.175 (1988)).

[6] *Family Law: Matrimonial Property* (Law Com. No.175 (1988)), para.1.4. For another cogent account of the case for reform, see the *Report of the Australian Law Reform Commission Matrimonial Property* (1987), extracted in H.A. Finlay, A. Bradbrook and R.J. Bailey-Harris, *Family Law, Cases Materials and Commentary*, 2nd edn (Sydney: Butterworths, 1993), pp.669–675.

the existence of the marriage; and (3) the effect on negotiation of settlements[7] of a backdrop of defined property rights.[8] In the 20 years that have elapsed since the publication of that report, the relevance of those reasons has by no means diminished; indeed, the current method of reallocating assets on divorce has arguably created a need for greater certainty regarding the ownership of those assets during the marriage.

Three main kinds of matrimonial property regime have been proposed in an attempt to meet criticisms of the current law.[9] The first is a community of property regime. The essence of a community system is that, by virtue of the marriage, the parties' property is at some stage subjected to joint ownership. As one recent report notes:

> "In its most traditional form, community of property provides for the automatic sharing of property and liabilities during the relationship; and all forms of community of property provide for a rule-based sharing of property when the community is dissolved by divorce or death."[10]

Community of property is particularly widespread in the civil-law world, and is not unknown within common law jurisdictions. However, there is considerable variation between different jurisdictions.[11] Some systems operate a "community of acquests" whereby only property that is acquired during the relationship is subjected to joint ownership; others operate a more extensive system whereby property acquired before the relationship began is also included. In some systems, property is owned in common from the moment that the relationship is formalised, but others adopt the model of "deferred community" whereby the parties' proprietary rights are unaffected until something (commonly, divorce) occurs requiring a dissolution of the community.[12] Some jurisdictions offer a range of options, allowing couples to choose which model best fits their particular circumstances or to opt out of community of property altogether.

The possibility of immediate community of property during marriage was rejected by the Morton Commission when it considered the issue in the 1950s,[13]

8–003

---

[7] For the operation of the current ancillary relief jurisdiction, see further Ch.13, below; on unpredictability of outcomes, see G. Davis, S. Cretney and J. Collins, *Simple Quarrels* (Oxford: Clarendon Press, 1994).

[8] See the fifth edition of this book at pp.221–223 for a full account of the Law Commission's reasoning.

[9] Discussed in greater detail in the sixth edition of this book, pp.223–230.

[10] E. Cooke, A. Barlow and T. Callus, *Community of Property: A Regime for England and Wales?* (The Nuffield Foundation, 2006), p.1. For a review of the philosophical underpinnings of such schemes, see L.-A. Buckley, "Matrimonial property and Irish law: a case for community?" (2002) 53 N.I.L.Q. 39.

[11] For a review of the variety of schemes that exist, see Cooke et al., *Community of Property*, pp.2–10; for information on individual jurisdictions, see C. Hamilton and A. Perry, *Family Law in Europe* (London: Butterworths, 2002).

[12] See, for example, the scheme in New Zealand, discussed by J. Miles, "Principle or pragmatism in ancillary relief: the virtues of flirting with academic theories and other jurisdictions" (2005) I.J.L.P.F. 242.

[13] *Royal Commission on Marriage and Divorce* (Cmnd.9678 (1956)), paras 650–653. A minority, however, did take the view that the principle had much to commend it: see para.652.

become law, and the government bill that became the Civil Partnership Act 2004 simply applied the rules applicable to spouses to civil partners.

The aim of equal treatment also underpinned the most recent bill dealing with matrimonial property to come before Parliament. The Family Law (Property and Maintenance) Bill 2005 was motivated by the desire to eliminate some of the special rules that currently apply to married couples—namely, the housekeeping allowance[34] and the presumption in favour of advancement[35]—largely because their sex-specific nature prevents the ratification of art.5 of Protocol 7 of the European Convention on Human Rights.[36] Although the Bill failed to secure a second reading, the Government had previously committed itself to the repeal of these rules, and so reform along these lines cannot be ruled out.

III. Reform of Property Rights in other Relationships

8–005 In 1993 the Law Commission embarked on a project examining the property rights of home-sharers. This was a broad term that encompassed not only married and cohabiting couples who shared a home but also relatives and friends who lived under the same roof. Such breadth of scope was perhaps necessary in order to achieve a holistic reform of property law as it applied to the family home, but it was to be the project's undoing. In 2002 the Commission published a discussion paper, *Sharing Homes*,[37] admitting that it had experienced insuperable difficulties in trying to devise a solution that would be appropriate in the context of all home-sharing relationships. It discussed whether a contribution-based approach would provide a sound basis for reform, but ultimately decided that:

> "[T]he infinitely variable circumstances affecting those who share homes have rendered it impossible to propose the scheme as a viable and practicable reform of the law."[38]

It therefore advocated that property law should be developed through judicial decisions rather than legislative reform. Yet legislative reform was not ruled out as inappropriate; the Commission identified "a wider need for the law to recognise and to respond to the increasing diversity of living arrangements in this country".[39]

IV. The Case for a Special Scheme for Unformalised Relationships

8–006 In the course of the debates occasioned by the creation of the new institution of civil partnerships, it was pointed out that the law provided no redress for couples

---

[34] See para.3–007.
[35] See para.5–016.
[36] See para.5–016.
[37] Law Commission, *Sharing Homes: A Discussion Paper* (Law Com. No.278 (2002)).
[38] At para.1.27.
[39] Pt IV, para.7.

who had not formalised their relationship, and the Law Commission was accordingly asked to undertake a review of the law relating to cohabitants. The project undertaken by the Commission was not a review of all the laws encompassing cohabitants (which would include tax law, social security and many other areas), but focused instead on "the financial hardship suffered by cohabitants or their children on the termination of the relationship by breakdown or death".[40] Work began in 2005, and two substantial papers—a consultation paper in 2006[41] and a report in 2007[42]—were produced with impressive swiftness and thoroughness.

In these, the Commission reviewed the demographic evidence indicating that cohabitation was increasing, and identified the deficiencies of the current law. It concluded that in light of such evidence, reform was necessary,[43] that there would be public support for such reform[44] and that it was unlikely that any amelioration in the position of cohabiting couples would have an impact on the number of couples choosing to formalise their relationship.[45]

Given the fact that many cohabitants are unaware of their legal rights,[46] it was thought appropriate that the application of the scheme should not depend on couples taking any positive action to opt into it, although those who did not want it to apply to them would be able to opt out.[47] Under the Commission's proposed scheme, eligible cohabitants would be able to apply to a court for financial relief upon separation. In order to be eligible to apply, couples would have to be "living together as a couple in a joint household"[48] without being parties to a legally recognised marriage or civil partnership,[49] and either have had a child together or have lived together for a minimum number of years.[50]

---

[40] Law Commission, *Ninth Programme of Law Reform* (Law Com. No.293 (2005)), para.3.6.
[41] Law Commission, *Cohabitation: The Financial Consequences of Relationship Breakdown: A Consultation Paper*, Consultation Paper No.179 (HMSO, 2006).
[42] Law Commission, *Cohabitation: The Financial Consequences of Relationship Breakdown* (Law Com. No.307 (2007)).
[43] See also S. Bridge, "Cohabitation: why legislative reform is necessary" [2007] Fam. Law 911.
[44] See, for example, A. Barlow et al., "Just a piece of paper? Marriage and commitment", in A. Park et al. (eds), *British Social Attitudes: The 18th Report—Public Policy, Social Ties* (London: Sage, 2001).
[45] At para.2.43, citing K. Kiernan et al., "Cohabitation law reform and its impact on marriage" [2006] Fam. Law 1074.
[46] See paras 2.49–2.51; A. Barlow et al., *Cohabitation, Marriage and the Law; Social Change and Reform in the 21st Century* (Oxford: Hart Publishing, 2005); G. Douglas, J. Pearce and H. Woodward, *A Failure of Trust: Resolving Property Disputes on Cohabitation Breakdown*, Cardiff Law School Research Papers No.1 (2007).
[47] Any opt-out agreement would have to be in writing and signed by both parties; it would also have to be clear that it was intended to disapply the statutory scheme. The court would retain a residual discretion to set aside an agreement "if its enforcement would cause manifest unfairness having regard to (1) the circumstances at the time when the agreement was made; or (2) circumstances at the time the agreement comes to be enforced which were unforeseen when the agreement was made" (para.5.61). Factors such as independent legal advice and full mutual disclosure of assets would be taken into account in deciding whether an agreement should be set aside.
[48] Fleeting relationships and those who are "living apart together" are therefore excluded from the Commission's scheme.
[49] At para.3.13.
[50] At para.3.63. The Commission suggested that the appropriate period would be between two and five years but left the precise duration for the government to decide.

8–007   Eligibility would not, however, guarantee any award. The second hurdle for
the applicant would be to show that there was some ground for relief: either that
the respondent had "a retained benefit . . . as a result of qualifying contributions
the applicant has made"[51] or that the applicant would suffer economic disadvantage as a result of the relationship. The former is intended to cover financial
contributions and improvements to the property, while the aim of redressing
economic disadvantage is an attempt to ensure that the relationship does not
leave one party economically worse off because of the non-financial contributions that they have made.[52]

In quantifying what award would be appropriate, the basic principle is that a
retained benefit is to be reversed while economic disadvantage is to be shared.
However, the court would be directed to achieve this only insofar as this would
be "reasonable and practicable", having regard to a list of discretionary factors[53]
and, in the case of claims based on economic disadvantage, "an economic
equality ceiling". The primary consideration would be the welfare, while a
minor, of any child of both parties who has not attained the age of 18, the welfare
of other children living with either party being a separate factor for consideration.
The financial needs, obligations and resources of both parties would also be taken
into account, together with their conduct.[54]

The scheme has the potential to redress some of the deficiencies of the current
law, which has, to date, taken little account of the impact of caring responsibilities in informal relationships, but is not without its flaws.[55] Early in 2008 it was
announced that the Government intends to await the outcome of research to be
conducted by the Scottish Executive on the operation of the similar (but not
identical) provisions of the Family Law (Scotland) Act 2006.[56] From this
research the Government will:

> "[E]xtrapolate . . . the likely cost to this jurisdiction of bringing into effect
> the scheme proposed by the Law Commission and the likely benefits it will
> bring."[57]

It is therefore highly unlikely that any reforms will be enacted in the near
future.

---

[51] At para.4.33.
[52] See further, S. Bridge, "Financial relief for cohabitants: how the Law Commission's scheme would
work" [2007] Fam. Law 998.
[53] At para.4.37.
[54] This would bear the same restrictive definition as is used by the courts when deciding how to
allocate assets on divorce, although it is suggested that the fact that a contribution is made against the
express wishes of the other party might be taken into account.
[55] For discussion, see R.J. Probert, "A Review of Cohabitation: The Financial Consequences of
Relationship Breakdown", Law Com. No.307 (HMSO, 2007)" (2007) 41 F.L.Q. 521.
[56] See Family Law (Scotland) Act 2006 s.28.
[57] *Hansard*, HC, col.122WS (March 6, 2008).

PART III

FAMILY BREAKDOWN

CHAPTER NINE

PROTECTION FROM VIOLENCE AND HARASSMENT

I.	INTRODUCTION	9–001	III.	THE ROLE OF THE CIVIL LAW	9–007
II.	THE ROLE OF THE CRIMINAL			A. Occupation orders	9–009
LAW		9–003		B. Orders for personal protection	9–025
	A. Offences under the general law	9–004	IV.	CONCLUSION	9–043
	B. Specific protection against harassment	9–005			

I. INTRODUCTION

It is a sad but undeniable fact that the home is not always a safe haven, and that **9–001** once-loving relationships may turn violent. Studies show that violence may occur in any type of relationship, between couples of the same or opposite sex or between wider kin.[1] In some cases the violence is triggered by the breakdown of the relationship, but it is also a feature of many ongoing relationships.[2] Many factors may keep the victim of violence from leaving, including the fear that separation may provoke more extreme violence.[3]

Nor is the harm that one party may inflict on the other limited to physical violence: domestic violence may include:

> "[A]ny incident of threatening behaviour, violence or abuse (psychological, physical, sexual, financial or emotional) between adults who are or have

---

[1] See, for example, A. Finney, *Domestic Violence, Sexual Assault and Stalking: Findings from the 2004/05 British Crime Survey* (Home Office, Online Report 12/06, 2006), Table 3.1; CPS, "Domestic violence monitoring snapshot" (*http://www.cps.gov.uk/publications/prosecution/domestic/snapshot_2006_12.html* [Accessed May 29, 2008]); L. Henderson, *Prevalence of Domestic Violence among Lesbians and Gay Men* (London: Sigma Research, 2003).

[2] Finney, *Domestic Violence*; A. Robinson and D. Cook, "Understanding victim retraction in cases of domestic violence: specialist courts, government policy, and victim-centred justice" (2006) 9 *Contemporary Justice Review* 189.

[3] See, for example, C. Humphreys and R. Thiara, "Neither justice nor protection: women's experiences of post-separation violence" (2003) 25 J.S.W.F.L. 195.

been intimate partners or family members, regardless of gender or sexuality."[4]

This definition encompasses a wide range of behaviour and relationships but is not uncontroversial: some commentators, for example, argue that only violence between partners should be classified as "domestic" violence.[5]

Indeed, the very terminology used in this area is riddled with controversy. The term "victim" has been criticised on the ground of its negative stereotyping, much feminist literature preferring that of "survivor" with its connotations of empowerment.[6] In the past it has been argued that the term "domestic violence" downgrades the seriousness of the violence in question, an effect reinforced by the notion that the family is sacrosanct and that the home is a private place to be guarded against outside intervention.[7] In recent years, however, the increasing awareness of the nature and seriousness of domestic violence has perhaps led to a change in attitudes, to the point that the fact that the incident has occurred within a domestic context is seen as an aggravating rather than a mitigating factor.[8]

9–002   One further element of controversy relates to the extent to which domestic violence consists of violence perpetrated by men against women. While there are examples of women inflicting violence upon men, the evidence suggests that women are more likely to be the victims of domestic violence,[9] that they are more likely to suffer repeated attacks and that the violence they suffer tends to be more serious than that inflicted upon men.[10]

The issue of domestic violence has implications for a number of topics considered elsewhere in this book—for example, the appropriateness of some methods of dispute resolution (such as mediation) if the relationship between the parties has been characterised by violence[11]; the availability of alternative housing[12]; whether contact between a violent parent and a child should be

---

[4] This is the definition proposed by the Inter-Ministerial Domestic Violence Group, which was subsequently adopted by other agencies: see Home Office, HM Court Service and CPS, *Specialist Domestic Violence Court Programme: Guidance* (London: 2005), App.1, p.17.

[5] See, for example, H. Reece, "The end of domestic violence" (2006) 69 M.L.R. 770.

[6] See, for example, L. Kelly, *Surviving Sexual Violence* (Cambridge: Polity, 1988).

[7] See K. O'Donovan, *Sexual Divisions in Law* (1985); S. Edwards, *Sex and Gender in the Legal Process* (1996), Ch.5; J. Bridgeman and S. Millns, *Feminist Perspectives on Law* (London: Sweet & Maxwell, 1998), Ch.1; A. Diduck and F. Kaganas, *Family Law, Gender and the State: Text, Cases and Materials*, 2nd edn (Oxford: Hart Publishing, 2006), Ch.10.

[8] CPS, *Policy for Prosecuting Cases of Domestic Violence* (2005), para.1.2. See also *H v O (Contempt of Court: Sentencing)* [2004] EWCA Civ 1691; and *Hammerton v Hammerton* [2007] EWCA Civ 248, para.37.

[9] S. Nicholas, C. Kershaw and A. Walker (eds), *Crime in England and Wales 2006/07* (Home Office, 2007), found that 77% of the victims of domestic violence were women (see Table 3.03).

[10] See, for example, R. Dobash and R. Dobash, "Violence against women in the family", in S. Katz, J. Eekelaar and M. Maclean (eds), *Cross Currents; Family Law and Policy in the US and England* (Oxford: Oxford University Press, 2000).

[11] See para.13–010, and note also Diduck and Kaganas, *Family Law, Gender and the State*, Ch.11; F. Kaganas and C. Piper, "Domestic violence and divorce mediation" (1994) 16 J.S.W.F.L. 265; F. Raitt, "Domestic violence and divorce mediation" (1996) 18 J.S.W.F.L. 11; M. Richards, "Domestic violence and mediation" [1997] Fam. Law 127.

[12] See para.6–035.

ordered[13]; and the point at which the harm caused to children witnessing domestic violence requires state intervention.[14] It also has ramifications that extend beyond the scope of this work: there is, for example, a vast literature on the causes of domestic violence[15]; the strategies that should be put in place to discourage such abuse from occurring[16]; the steps that should be taken to support the victims; and the cost of domestic violence to society as a whole.[17] The Government has set out a strategy of "prevention, protection and justice and support"[18] that addresses many of these issues, but it is the civil remedies available to protect the victim of domestic violence that fall within the province of family law, and on which this chapter will focus. First, however, a brief outline of the role of the criminal law is necessary in order partly to show the range of ways in which domestic violence may be dealt with by the law, and partly because this is an area in which the civil and criminal law intertwine.

II. The Role of the Criminal Law

The role of the criminal law in the context of domestic violence is not without controversy. Some commentators argue that prosecution of offences, and the creation of a specific offence of domestic violence, is necessary to send the message that domestic violence will not be tolerated.[19] Others note that the imprisonment of the aggressor may well lead to unemployment and consequent financial hardship for the victim and the children, and may exacerbate the problem by provoking further violence.[20] The objectives of punishing the offender and deterring future offences can, on the one hand, be justified in the interests of the community as a whole, but, on the other hand, the victim may not want the perpetrator to be prosecuted, and the likelihood of such prosecution may be a deterrent to seeking help in the first place.[21] Linked to this is the argument that the criminal process marginalises the victims of domestic violence,

9–003

---

[13] See para.8–019.

[14] See para.21–032.

[15] See, for example, J. Miles, "Domestic violence", in J. Herring (ed.), *Family Law: Issues, Debates, Policy* (Willan Publishing, 2001); E. Gilchrist et al., "Domestic violence offenders: characteristics and offending related needs" (Home Office, 2003).

[16] See, for example, Home Office, *Domestic Violence: A National Report* (2005).

[17] See, for example, S. Walby, *The Cost of Domestic Violence* (Women and Equality Unit, 2004), estimating the financial cost of domestic violence to be around £23 billion per year.

[18] *Safety and Justice: The Government's Proposals on Domestic Violence* (Cm.5487 (2003)), para.19.

[19] See the discussion by J. Hodgson and S. Cowan, "Violence in a family context: the criminal law's response to domestic violence", Ch.4, in R. Probert (ed.) *Family Life and the Law: Under One Roof* (Aldershot: Ashgate, 2007), pp.49–52.

[20] See the Law Commission's *Report on Domestic Violence and Occupation of the Family Home* (Law Com. No.207, 1992), paras 2.8 *et seq.* for a sensitive and perceptive account of the relationship between the criminal and civil law procedures in the context of domestic violence.

[21] See, for example, M. Burton, "Criminalising breaches of civil orders for protection from domestic violence" (2003) Crim. L.R. 301, although note the views expressed by S. Choudhry and J. Herring, "Righting domestic violence" (2006) 20 I.J.L.P.F. 95.

although in recent years a number of initiatives have been put in place to try to address this.[22]

In short, the criminal law may well provide a solution where the relationship between the parties has broken down,[23] but may be less able to do so where the relationship is ongoing.[24] This section will look first at the offences under the general law that may have been committed by the perpetrator, and will then examine legislation dealing specifically with the problem of harassment.

A. Offences under the general law

9–004   An incident of domestic violence may involve the commission of a criminal offence. It is now well settled that marriage does not constitute a licence to assault a spouse against his or her will,[25] and the supposed common law doctrine that would allow a husband to beat his wife provided he used a stick no thicker than his thumb[26] has long since been consigned to the museum of legal folklore.[27] The criminal law may accordingly be invoked for offences[28] ranging from murder and manslaughter,[29] through unlawful wounding,[30] grievous bodily harm,[31] assault occasioning actual bodily harm[32] and aggravated assault,[33] to

---

[22] These are succinctly summarised by S. Cammiss, "The management of domestic violence cases in the mode of trial hearing: prosecutorial control and marginalising victims" (2006) 46 *British Journal of Criminology* 704 at 706, as "the Criminal Injuries Compensation Scheme, compensation and reparation orders, Victim Impact Statements, special measures to protect the victim in the courtroom, specialist teams to respond to sensitive crimes, Victim Support and Witness Support, rape crisis centres and women's refuges, the reinforcement of needs through the Victim's Charter and restorative justice processes". The Domestic Violence, Crime and Victims Act 2004 s.32 made provision for a code of practice as to the services to be provided to a victim of criminal conduct, and this code states that victims of domestic abuse are eligible for an "enhanced service": Home Office, *The Code of Practice for Victims of Crime* (2005), para.4.9.

[23] Note, for example, the conditions on the payment of compensation to the victims of domestic violence. The Criminal Injuries Compensation Authority understandably adopts the general principle that the person who causes the injury should not benefit from an award paid to the victim. This means that if the parties were living in the same household at the time of the injury, compensation will not be awarded unless the perpetrator has been prosecuted "or there are good reasons why this has not happened", and the parties stopped living together before the victim applied for compensation "and are unlikely to do so again": Criminal Injuries Compensation Authority, *Guide to the 2001 Compensation Scheme*, p.30.

[24] See, for example, A. Robinson and D. Cook, "Understanding victim retraction in cases of domestic violence: specialist courts, government policy, and victim-centred justice" (2006) 9 *Contemporary Justice Review* 189 on the prevalence of retractions in the context of ongoing relationships.

[25] See *R. v Jackson* [1891] 1 Q.B. 671 at 679, 682; *R. v Reid* [1973] Q.B. 299. The extent to which consent is capable of being a defence to a charge of sexual assault presents considerable difficulties: see *R. v Brown* [1994] 1 A.C. 212; and the Law Commission's Consultation Paper, *Consent in the Criminal Law* (Law Com. CP No.139 (1995)).

[26] See *per* Lord Denning M.R., *Davis v Johnson* [1979] A.C. 264 at 270.

[27] See, generally, M. Doggett, *Marriage, Wife Beating and the Law in Victorian England* (London: Weidenfeld & Nicolson, 1992).

[28] And note that the police now have the power to arrest for any offence: Police and Criminal Evidence Act 1984 s.24, as amended by the Serious Organised Crime and Police Act 2005 s.110.

[29] The Domestic Violence, Crime and Victims Act s.9 makes provision for domestic homicide reviews to be held, but at the time of writing this provision has not been brought into force.

[30] Offences against the Person Act 1861 s.20.

[31] Offences against the Person Act 1861 s.18.

[32] Offences against the Person Act 1861 s.47.

[33] Offences against the Person Act 1861 s.43

common assault.[34] Similarly, it was long thought that a man could not be convicted of raping his wife,[35] but in 1991 the House of Lords held[36] that this rule no longer formed part of English law. Statute has subsequently confirmed and clarified this position,[37] whilst the courts have laid down that the fact that a rapist is married to his victim does not justify a lenient sentence.[38] More generally, the Court of Appeal has stated that marital disharmony does not of itself excuse, let alone justify, the commission of acts of violence.[39]

In the past, the criminal law has been criticised for its apparent failure to afford real protection from intra-family violence.[40] Whether the perpetrator of the violence is ultimately convicted of a criminal offence will depend not only on the willingness of the victim to report the violence, but also on the actions taken by the police, on the decision of the Crown Prosecution Service whether or not to proceed with prosecution, and on the evidence available to the court.[41] In addition, even if the perpetrator is convicted, it may be for a more minor offence,[42] or may be dealt with by a lower level of court[43] than would be the case in respect of equivalent violence in a non-domestic context.

Recent years have, however, witnessed concerted efforts to deal with the problem of domestic violence.[44] More perpetrators have been charged with a criminal offence, and a higher proportion of those charged have been convicted.[45] A number of initiatives intended to improve the process by which information is

[34] Offences against the Person Act 1861 s.42.
[35] See J.L. Barton, "The story of marital rape" (1992) 108 L.Q.R. 260 for a provocative historical account.
[36] *R. v R* [1992] 1 A.C. 599.
[37] Criminal Justice and Public Order Act 1994 s.142; see now Sexual Offences Act 2003 s.1.
[38] *R. v W* (1993) 14 Cr. App. R. (S.) 256.
[39] *R. v Rossiter* [1994] 2 All E.R. 752 at 753, *per* Russell L.J. In addition, the fact that an assault is repeated is regarded as an aggravating factor: Sentencing Guidelines Council, *Assault and Other Offences against the Person* (2008), para.13.
[40] See, for example, S. Edwards and A. Halpern, "Protection for the victim of domestic violence: time for radical revision?" [1991] J.S.W.F.L. 94; S. Edwards, *Sex and Gender in the Legal Process* (1996), pp.192–213; S. Wright, "Policing domestic violence: A Nottingham case study" (1998) 20 J.S.W.F.L. 397; HM Inspectorate of Constabularies and HM Inspectorate of the CPS, *Violence at Home: A Joint Inspection of the Investigation and Prosecution of Cases Involving Domestic Violence* (HMIC/HMCPSI, 2004).
[41] Although a spouse is now a competent and compellable witness against the other in proceedings involving an assault on the witness or on a person under 16 (Police and Criminal Evidence Act 1984 s.80), research indicates that many domestic violence prosecutions fail because the complainant withdraws or fails to give evidence: see A. Cretney and G. Davis, "Prosecuting 'domestic' assault" [1996] Crim. L.R. 162; Robinson and Cook, "Understanding victim retraction in cases of domestic violence". On the steps that could be taken to provide other evidence, see, for example, L. Ellison, "Prosecuting domestic violence without victim participation" (2002) 65 M.L.R. 834.
[42] Cretney and Davis, "Prosecuting 'domestic' assault".
[43] See Cammiss, "The management of domestic violence cases in the mode of trial hearing".
[44] Hodgson and Cowan, "Violence in a family context", Ch.4 in Probert (ed.), *Family Life and the Law*, p.49 note recent initiatives, including "widespread publicity campaigns; the establishment of specialist domestic violence courts; specialist offender programmes within probation . . . policy and guidance on investigation and prosecution for police and prosecutors linked to national training; the introduction of Area Domestic Violence Co-ordinators in the CPS . . . and the development of a Key Diagnostic Indicator by the Crown Prosecution Service in order to track domestic violence cases" (references omitted).
[45] In 2006, 66% of those charged were convicted: CPS, *Domestic Violence Monitoring Snapshot*.

gathered have been developed by the police,[46] and specialist domestic violence courts have been introduced.[47] The past decades have also seen an increase in the percentage of incidents of domestic violence that are reported to the police, from under 20 per cent in 1981 to almost 35 per cent in 2001, and just over 44 per cent in 2006/7.[48]

B. Specific protection against harassment

9-005   Recent years have witnessed some innovative legislation addressing the issue of molestation.[49] There are specific offences in respect of communications[50] and intentional harassment,[51] but of most significance in this field is the Protection from Harassment Act 1997. The genesis of the Act was widespread public concern over "stalking",[52] a phenomenon generally perceived as involving:

> "[T]he obsessive harassment of a victim, normally female, by someone who pursues her by following her movements, telephoning and so on. Any relationship between the parties has ended, if, indeed, it ever existed outside the imagination of the perpetrator."[53]

At first sight, therefore, such legislation might appear to have little relevance in a domestic context, but studies have shown that the "stalker" is in fact usually a person that the victim knows, often an ex-partner.[54] The legislation, thus has a role to play in the context of relationship breakdown,[55] and the following discussion will focus on its application in that context.[56]

---

[46] See Police and Crime Standards Directorate, *Lessons Learned from the Domestic Violence Enforcement Campaign 2006* (2006).

[47] D. Cook et al., *Evaluation of Specialist Domestic Violence Courts/Fast Track Systems* (London: CPS/DCA, 2004); HM Court Service, Home Office and CPS, *Specialist Domestic Violence Courts Review 2007–8: Justice with Safety* (2008).

[48] *Crime in England and Wales 2006/07*, Table 2.10.

[49] Note, for example, Representation of the People Act 1983 s.9B, inserted by the Electoral Administration Act 2006 s.10, which allows for anonymous registration where this is necessary for the safety of those resident in the household.

[50] Malicious Communications Act 1988 (as amended by the Communications Act 2003 Sch.17 para.90).

[51] Public Order Act 1986 s.4A, inserted by the Criminal Justice and Public Order Act 1994 s.154, and amended by the Serious Organised Crime and Police Act 2005 Sch.17(2) para.1.

[52] For the history of the legislation, see [1996] Fam. Law 527; T. Lawson-Cruttenden, "The government's proposed stalking law—a discussion paper" [1996] Fam. Law 755; [1997] Fam. Law 4; T. Lawson-Cruttenden and N. Addison, "Harassment and domestic violence" [1997] Fam. Law 429; H. Conway, "Protection from Harassment Act 1997" [1997] Fam. Law 714.

[53] R. Bird, *Domestic Violence and Protection from Harassment: The New Law*, 2nd edn (Bristol: Family Law, 1997), p.109. The Act protects only individual human beings and not a limited company: *DPP v Dziuezynski* [2002] EWHC (Admin) (2002) 166 JP 545.

[54] J. Harris, *The Protection from Harassment Act 1997—An Evaluation of its Use and Effectiveness* (Home Office Research, Development and Statistics Directorate, Research Findings No.130, 2000) examined a sample of cases brought under the 1997 Act and found that only 2% involved strangers, while 41% involved partners, ex-partners or relatives.

[55] See, for example, *R. v Molyneux* [2007] EWCA Crim. 3417.

[56] For examples of its use in other areas, see, for example, *Thomas v News Group Newspapers Ltd* [2001] EWCA Civ. 1233 (publication of press articles likely to incite racial hatred of another); *Howlett v Holding* [2006] EWHC 41 (secret surveillance); *Oxford University v Broughton* [2008] EWHC 75 (QB) (protection from animal rights' protesters of those working on a new laboratory). For full discussion of the criminal aspects of the Act, see Bird, *Domestic Violence and Protection from Harassment*, Ch.10; T. Lawson-Cruttenden, *The Protection From Harassment Act* (Blackstone Press, 1997). See also T. Lawson-Cruttenden, "DIY, harassment law" [2007] 157 N.L.J. 19.

The 1997 Act created a number of criminal[57] offences relating to "harassment", a term it left undefined. Section 1(1) provides that:

"A person must not pursue a course of conduct[58]—

(a) which amounts to harassment of another, and
(b) which he knows or ought to know[59] amounts to harassment of the other."

There are two levels of offence. Section 2(1) provides that a person who breaches s.1 commits an arrestable offence, with a maximum term of imprisonment of six months or a fine, or both.[60] Section 4 is directed to the more serious offence of putting people in fear of violence; thus, a person whose course of conduct causes another to fear, on at least two occasions, that violence will be used against him is guilty of an offence if he knows, or ought[61] to know, that this will be the effect; the penalty for an offence under this section is, if convicted on indictment, a maximum term of five years' imprisonment or a fine or both, or, on summary conviction, a maximum term of six months' imprisonment or a fine or both.[62]

The availability of the two levels of offence is useful both in terms of the **9–006** punishment and deterrence of harassment, but there are nevertheless certain (clearly unintended) weaknesses in the drafting of the relevant provisions.[63] The maximum penalty under the first-level offence might be inadequate to deal with persistent offenders who cause serious psychiatric injury to victims, whilst there may be difficulty in securing convictions under s.4 in respect of repeated silent telephone calls; the victim in such cases may have cause to fear that violence *may* be used against him or her but no more.

More generally, the operation of the Act in relation to both offences is limited by the need to establish a "course of conduct".[64] In *Lau v DPP*[65] (where a conviction for the lower level offence based on two incidents separated by four months was quashed), it was held that the fewer the incidents and the wider they are spread, the less likely it will be that a finding of harassment will be made. A

[57] It also created new civil remedies, which are considered below, para.9–038.
[58] Defined to include speech: s.7(4).
[59] According to the objective test of the reasonable person: s.1(2). As the Court of Appeal noted in *R. v Colohan* [2001] EWCA Crim 1251, the legislation was designed to protect persons from conduct likely to be pursued by those of an obsessive or unusual psychological disposition, and so a subjective test would be inappropriate.
[60] Protection from Harassment Act 1997 s.2(2).
[61] The same objective test of the reasonable person applies: Protection from Harassment Act 1997 s.4(2).
[62] Protection from Harassment Act 1997 s.4(4). For guidance on sentencing under ss.2 and 4, see *R. v Liddle; R. v Hayes* [1999] 3 All E.R. 816, and for examples of sentencing in cases involving ex-partners and spouses, see *R v Molyneux* [2007] EWCA Crim 3417; *R. v Watling* [2007] EWCA Crim 2307; *R. v Miller* [2007] EWCA Crim 2852; *R. v Alass* [2007] EWCA Crim 2504; *R. v Maher* [2007] EWCA Crim 3296; *R. v Norwood* [2007] EWCA Crim 2669; *R. v Richards* [2007] EWCA Crim 2516.
[63] As noted by Lord Steyn in obiter dicta in *R. v Ireland; R. v Burstow* [1998] 1 F.L.R. 105 at 107–108; comment by S. Cretney in [1997] Fam. Law 137.
[64] Protection from Harassment Act 1997 ss.4(1) and 7(3).
[65] [2000] 1 F.L.R. 799; comment by G. Douglas in [2000] Fam. Law 799.

nexus is required to link the acts complained of,[66] which was absent in that case, as it was in *R. v Hills*[67] (two assaults some six months apart).

III. THE ROLE OF THE CIVIL LAW

9–007   The conviction of the perpetrator does not guarantee the future safety of the victim. The need for the law to protect the victim of domestic violence is underlined by the fact that repeated victimisation is often a feature of domestic violence.[68] Violence or other psychological pressures of a collapsing relationship may necessitate remedies directed both to the future behaviour of the parties and to the future use of the home that they have shared. These have been identified as:

> "[T]wo distinct but inseparable problems: providing protection for one member of the family against molestation or violence by another and regulating the occupation of the family home when the relationship has broken down either temporarily or permanently."[69]

These matters are generally regarded as the province of the civil rather than the criminal law, since what is primarily at issue is the relationship between the individuals involved rather than the relationship between a particular individual and the community as a whole. Moreover, it is generally agreed that[70] the main aim of the civil law (in contrast with the criminal law) in this context is to regulate and improve matters for the future rather than making judgments upon or punishing past behaviour. Nevertheless, a number of not uncontroversial policy issues arise in relation to the degree to which the civil law remedies should depend on the parties' status and proprietary rights. Should the nature of the remedies available differ according to whether the parties had ever formalised their relationship? To what extent should orders regulating the home reflect existing legal and equitable rights in the property concerned? Should a distinction be drawn in this respect between personal protection orders and those which confer—and interfere with—occupation rights? As will be seen, the current law adopts some uneasy compromises on these issues, having been driven in part by political pressures. In order to understand the complexities of the current law, a brief review of the history of the current legislation is necessary.

---

[66] See also *R. v Patel* [2004] EWCA Crim 3284, in which the necessity of the link was emphasised.
[67] [2001] 1 F.L.R. 580. In *Hipgrave and Hipgrave v Jones* [2005] 2 F.L.R. 174, the Divisional Court emphasised that whether two acts eight months apart constituted a course of conduct was a question of fact for the trial judge. The acts were held to constitute a course of conduct.
[68] See, for example, *Crime in England and Wales 2006/07*, p.21.
[69] Law Commission, *Report on Domestic Violence and Occupation of the Family Home* (Law Com. No.207 (1992)), para.1.1.
[70] *Report on Domestic Violence and Occupation of the Family Home* (Law Com. No.207 (1992)), para.2.11.

By the middle of the 1990s a hotchpotch of remedies had developed piecemeal over the years, and the resulting law was complex, confusing and riddled with anomalies both substantive and jurisdictional. Protection was provided both by the so-called "inherent jurisdiction"[71] inherited from the Court of Chancery, and by various statutes[72] of limited scope that had been enacted "to meet specific situations or to strengthen the powers of specified courts".[73] The matter was referred to the Law Commission, upon whose report[74] the reforming legislation was based. The Commission identified three objectives[75] in reforming the civil law[76] in this field: first, to remove gaps, anomalies and inconsistencies with a view to synthesising the available remedies so far as possible into a clear, simple and comprehensive code; secondly, to provide adequate protection; and thirdly, to avoid exacerbating hostilities between the adults involved, so far as this would be compatible with providing proper and effective protection both for adults and for children. The report's major proposal was for a single consistent set of civil law remedies to be contained in one statute and to be available to family members in all family courts. As a matter of policy, the Commission drew a distinction[77] between orders for personal protection on the one hand, and ouster orders on the other, on the basis that the former in no way prejudice the respondent's legitimate interests, whereas the latter (albeit temporarily) will, where the respondent has proprietary or other legal rights over the property in question. The report therefore recommended that the new statute embody two distinct types of remedy—the non-molestation order and the occupation order—which could, of course, be combined in appropriate circumstances.

In 1995 the Government introduced the Family Homes and Domestic Violence **9–008** Bill, which closely followed the Law Commission's recommendations and was initially thought to be non-controversial. However, just as the Bill was about to complete the final stages of its passage through Parliament,[78] an angry campaign was mounted by some MPs[79] and others,[80] who believed the Bill would erode the

---

[71] See the discussion in *Richards v Richards* [1984] A.C. 175 and para.9–042 below.

[72] The most important statutes empowering the court to grant orders were: (i) Matrimonial Homes Act 1983 (consolidating the provisions of the Matrimonial Homes Act 1967 and subsequent amendments); (ii) Domestic Violence and Matrimonial Proceedings Act 1976; and (iii) Domestic Proceedings and Magistrates' Courts Act 1978. The Introduction to the Law Commission's Report, *Domestic Violence and Occupation of the Family Home* (Law Com. No.207 (1992)) provides a useful succinct explanation of the inter-relationship between the different statutory provisions.

[73] *Richards v Richards* [1984] A.C. 174 at 206–207, *per* Lord Scarman.

[74] *Domestic Violence and Occupation of the Family Home* (Law Com. No.207 (1992)).

[75] Law Com. No.207, para.1.2.

[76] The report did not address the criminal law.

[77] Law Com. No.207 para.2.48.

[78] It had received a most thorough examination by a House of Lords Special Public Bill Committee, had been passed by the House of Lords, and had virtually completed its passage through the House of Commons. For a full account of the history, see the speech by Lord Brightman (who had chaired the committee): *Hansard*, HL Vol.570, col.618 (March 11, 1996).

[79] According to the Labour Party's shadow Lord Chancellor, Lord Irvine of Lairg, the Government had allowed itself to be "blown off course by an irrational reaction on the part of a tiny unrepresentative minority... trying to claim a spurious moral high ground for party political reasons": *Hansard*, HL Vol.568, col.1397 (January 30, 1996).

[80] The *Daily Mail* conducted an outspoken and evidently effective campaign against the Bill (and the Law Commission), but as the Law Commission pointed out, the broadsheet press "saw the benefits that the changes would bring": Law Commission, *Thirtieth Annual Report* (Law Com. No.239 (1996)), para.1.20.

distinction between the legal rights of married and unmarried couples and thereby undermine the institution of marriage. The Government therefore decided to withdraw the Bill for further consideration. Modified provisions were subsequently re-introduced into Parliament as part of the Family Law Bill 1995. These modifications were largely motivated by political expediency (namely, the Government's desire to secure the passage of the Bill in the Commons), and, as will be seen, their genesis is, in terms of substance, all too evident.

The relevant provisions are now found in Pt IV of the Family Law Act 1996. This gave effect to the Commission's proposal that all remedies against domestic violence should be available in all courts[81] having jurisdiction in family matters.[82] However, the Law Commission's aspiration of this legislation providing a *single* set of remedies available to family members was swiftly overtaken by events when the Protection from Harassment Act 1997 was passed, which, in addition to the criminal offences already discussed, created a new civil remedy for harassment in the form of injunctive relief and damages. In addition, the High Court may still issue injunctions under the general law, although there will rarely be any need to invoke this procedure due to the existence of specialised legislation.

The following sections will first discuss the making and enforcement of occupation orders, and will then move on to the orders that are designed for personal protection: namely, non-molestation orders under the Family Law Act and injunctions under the Protection from Harassment Act.

A. Occupation orders

9–009 Part IV of the Family Law Act 1996 empowers the court[83] to make orders regulating the occupation of a home.[84] The statutory provisions are complex, both as regards who is entitled to seek the orders and the criteria governing the exercise of the court's discretion.

The sophisticated drafting of the legislation makes the precise extent of the court's powers depend in part on the nature of the applicant's interest (if any) in the property.[85] To this end, the Act draws an important distinction between an

---

[81] The general principle embodied in the Act is that remedies are available in the High Court, the County Court and magistrates' courts: s.57(1). However, it is provided (s.59(1)) that a magistrates' court is not competent to entertain any application, or make any order, involving any disputed question as to a party's entitlement to occupy any property by virtue of a beneficial estate or interest or by virtue of an enactment giving him the right to remain in occupation, unless it is unnecessary to determine the question in order to deal with the application or make the order; and rules provide for the transfer of cases between different courts and different levels of court.

[82] Applications constitute "family proceedings" for the purpose of the Children Act 1989. An application for an order under Pt IV may also be made in the course of other family proceedings: s.39(2).

[83] The High Court, county court, or magistrates's court: Family Law Act 1996 s.57(1).

[84] There was comparatively little debate on the provisions of this part of the Act, but a great deal of useful material is to be found in the parliamentary proceedings on the Family Homes and Domestic Violence Bill in 1995, especially the House of Lords Special Public Bill Committee (1995, HL 55). Where the provisions of the 1996 Act are identical to those of the 1995 Bill, these proceedings are referred to without further explanation.

[85] For a succinct summary of the complex differences, see M. Horton, "The Family Law Bill—domestic violence" [1996] Fam. Law 49, especially at 51.

applicant who is "entitled" and one who is "non-entitled". The underlying policy is that the court's powers should be more extensive in the case of an applicant who can point to some recognised legal, equitable or statutory right than in the case of a person who merely has the use of a family home; in addition, those who have formalised their relationship have more extensive rights than those who have not. These policies—not wholly uncontroversial from the point of view of the victim of violence[86] or in the opinion of all commentators[87]—stem both from the distinction drawn by the Law Commission between occupation and non-molestation orders as regards prejudice to legitimate interests,[88] and from amendments with a political motivation made following the withdrawal of the original Family Homes and Domestic Violence Bill 1995.

One distinctive feature of this area of the law is that most applications are made ex parte (i.e. without notice being given to the respondent). When the legislation was passed, it was recognised that the court needs power to intervene immediately and without notice in some cases,[89] and provision was made for orders to be made ex parte where it was just and convenient to do so.[90] While case law had emphasised that such orders should be made "with great caution and only in circumstances in which it is really necessary to act immediately",[91] ex parte applications have far outnumbered those of which notice is given to the respondent.[92]

i. The scope of an occupation order

An occupation order can be made in relation to a dwelling house that is, was or **9–010** was intended to be[93] the home of the applicant and of another person with whom he or she is "associated".[94] The following discussion will focus on the provisions relating to homes that are owned by at least one of the parties.[95]

---

[86] Not all comparable legal systems observe such distinctions as to status and ownership in the context of intra-family violence: see Pt XV of the Family Law Act 1975 (Cth) in Australia.

[87] See J. Eekelaar and M. Maclean, *The Parental Obligation* (Oxford: Hart Publishing, 1997), p.144.

[88] Law Commission, *Report on Domestic Violence and the Family Home* (Law Com. No.207 (1992)), para.2.48.

[89] Discussed by the Law Commission in its *Report on Domestic Violence and Occupation of the Family Home* (Law Com. No.207 (1992)), paras 5.5–5.10.

[90] Family Law Act 1996 s.45(1). The court is required to have regard to all the circumstances (s.45(2)), and if it does decide to make an ex parte order, it must afford the respondent an opportunity to make representations relating to the order, as soon as just and convenient, at a hearing of which proper notice has been given to all parties (s.45(3)).

[91] *Ansah v Ansah* [1977] Fam. 138 at 142–143, *per* Ormrod L.J.

[92] Ministry of Justice, *Judicial and Court Statistics 2006* (2007), Table 5.8. In 2006, 6,565 applications for occupation orders were heard ex parte, compared to 2,838 on notice.

[93] Family Law Act 1996 s.33(1)(b)(i) and (ii), as amended by the Civil Partnership Act 2004 Sch.9 para.1. Compare the Matrimonial Homes Act 1983, which only extended to a property that had at some time actually been the matrimonial home. Provided the dwelling house is or at some time has been the parties' home, protection is available notwithstanding a shift in the nature of the qualifying tenancy: *Moore v Moore* [2004] EWCA Civ 1243.

[94] For the definition of this term (which bears a wide meaning), see below, para.9–028.

[95] The Act also makes provision for applications to be made in respect of homes (such as accommodation provided by an employer, or by a relative or as a squat) that neither party is entitled to occupy: see ss.37, 38.

The Act gives courts jurisdiction to make two main types of order: declaratory and regulatory orders.[96] A declaratory order is an order declaring that the applicant is entitled to occupy a dwelling house[97]; as such, it merely declares the nature of the interest claimed. The court may also enforce the applicant's entitlement to remain in occupation against the respondent[98] by making an order for possession.

In practice, however, regulatory orders are much more commonly sought. Such an order may "prohibit, suspend or restrict" the exercise of rights of occupation by a person who would otherwise be entitled to occupy the dwelling house.[99] It may require the respondent to allow the applicant to enter and remain in the house, or that the respondent should leave the house.[100] The order may regulate the occupation of the house by requiring the respondent to allow the applicant to live in part of the property (or at specific times) and by excluding the respondent from that part (or at those times)[101]; it may also exclude the respondent from a defined area around the house.[102]

ii. Who may apply for an occupation order?

9–011 There are two categories of persons who may apply for an occupation order: "entitled" and "non-entitled" applicants. This presupposes a third, unmentioned category of persons who are not able to apply for an occupation order at all.[103]

(1) Entitled applicants

9–012 There are two main categories of person who come within the definition of "person entitled"[104]: those who have a right under the general law to occupy the property and those who have "home rights" in the property.

---

[96] Family Law Act 1996 s.33(4) (declaratory orders); s.33(3) (regulatory orders). See *Domestic Violence and Occupation of the Family Home* (Law Com. No.207 (1992)), para.4.2.

[97] The court may also declare that the applicant is entitled to "home rights", and may also, where it considers that it is in all the circumstances just and reasonable to do so, make an order that those rights should not be brought to an end by the ending of the marriage or civil partnership: s.30(5), (8), as amended by the Civil Partnership Act 2004 Sch.9 paras 1(6) and (9).

[98] Family Law Act 1996 s.33(3).

[99] i.e. under s.30(1)(a)(i). This power can be exercised by ordering one joint tenant to leave the house altogether, or to leave it for 48 hours, or only to exercise the rights to which the respondent is entitled if someone else is present (e.g. whilst a child is living in the house).

[100] Family Law Act 1996 s.33(3).

[101] See, for example, *Panchal v Panchal* (2000), unreported, in which the husband, an artist, was excluded from the house but entitled to use the studio in the garden.

[102] For example, excluding the respondent from the block of flats in which the home is situated or from the street or neighbourhood in which the home is situated (see, e.g. *Pluck v Pluck* [2007] EWCA Civ 1250, in which the man was prevented from entering the housing estate where the woman's house was situated). In the earlier case of *Vaughan v Vaughan* [1973] 1 W.L.R. 1159, the court ordered a husband not to go within 50 miles of the home, but it is open to question whether this would be a "defined area".

[103] For example, a relative who is living in the same home as the perpetrator but who does not have any interest in the property. It should also be noted that the Act provides that a child under the age of 16 may not apply for a non-molestation order or an occupation order except with the leave of the court, and that the court may grant leave only if it is satisfied that the child has sufficient understanding to make the proposed application: s.43.

[104] Family Law Act 1996 s.33(1)(a).

(a) A person entitled to occupy a dwelling house by virtue of a beneficial 9–013
estate or interest or contract or by virtue of any enactment giving him or her
the right to remain in occupation. The crucial element of this definition is that
the applicant should have the right to occupy the dwelling in question.[105]
Examples include a person who owns the fee simple absolute in possession, a
person who has a legal tenancy or a person entitled to be in occupation of a house
under the Rent Acts. It is clear that a person entitled to a beneficial interest in the
property is thereby "entitled to occupy" the land[106]; however, if the applicant is
claiming that he or she is entitled to an interest under an informal trust, there may
be some uncertainty as to his or her entitlement.[107] In such cases, the applicant
may choose to assert and prove that he or she is entitled to such an interest, but
may prefer to apply under one of the other categories, and the legislation makes
provision for such a choice.[108]

(b) A person with home rights. Spouses and civil partners who have no 9–014
ownership rights in respect of the shared home are entitled to "home rights".[109]
There may, of course, be uncertainty as to whether a spouse or civil partner does
have ownership rights. The legislation addresses this by providing that those who
have no legal estate in the home may be treated, for the purpose of determining
entitlement to home rights, as not being entitled to occupy the home by virtue of
an equitable interest. This somewhat opaque phrasing means that such a person
will be entitled to home rights in this situation, and the result is that a spouse or
civil partner is always an entitled applicant when applying for an occupation
order.

(1) Non-entitled persons
The Act[110] allows certain categories of person—former spouses or civil partners, 9–015
and cohabitants or former cohabitants[111]—to apply for an occupation order
notwithstanding that they have no existing right to be in occupation of the
property. The rationale is the:

> "[O]verriding need for short term protection in cases of domestic violence
> or for short term accommodation for themselves and their children when a
> relationship breaks down."[112]

---

[105] As defined, s.63(1).
[106] Trusts of Land and Appointment of Trustees Act 1996 s.12.
[107] See Ch.5 on the means by which such a trust may be established.
[108] Family Law Act 1996 ss.30(9), 35(11) and (12), and 36(11) and (12), and see the evidence of Hale
J. to the Special Public Bill Committee on the Family Homes and Domestic Violence Bill (1995, HL
55), March 15, 1995, questions 68–72.
[109] See para.3–010.
[110] Family Law Act 1996 ss.35, 36.
[111] As defined in Family Law Act 1996 s.62(1)(a). The original definition of the 1996 Act limited the
application of this provision to heterosexual cohabitants, but the Civil Partnership Act 2004 amended
it to include same-sex cohabitants: Civil Partnership Act 2004 Sch.9 para.13(2).
[112] Law Commission, *Report on Domestic Violence and Occupation of the Family Home* (Law Com.
No.207 (1992)), para.4.10.

However, as we shall see, the protection afforded to non-entitled applicants is less extensive than that enjoyed by their entitled counterparts.

It would obviously be to the advantage of such persons if they were able to establish a proprietary right in the property in question. The Act provides that a person who has an equitable interest, but not a legal estate in a dwelling house, "is to be treated only for the purpose of determining whether he [or she] is to be eligible to apply" under the Act "as not being so entitled".[113] The effect of this is simply to make it clear that an equitable owner will be able to apply for a short-term occupation order as a non-entitled person, but the Act also preserves the applicant's right to apply for a longer term order as an "entitled person" by establishing a beneficial interest in the property.[114] The difficulty of choosing which section to make a claim under is mitigated by the fact that the court may still make an order under the appropriate provision even if the claim was brought under one that turns out to be inapplicable.[115] In addition, the fact that an application is made on the basis that the applicant is a non-entitled person does not stop the applicant from subsequently asserting a beneficial interest.[116]

iii. Exercise of the discretion whether to make an occupation order

9–016 The factors to be considered by the court, and the extent to which it has a discretion whether or not to make an occupation order, will depend on the status of the applicant.

(1) Applications by entitled applicants

9–017 The first question to ask when considering an application by an entitled applicant is whether there is any evidence that the applicant or any relevant child is likely to suffer significant harm if the order is not made. Under the Act, the court is *required* to make an order in such a case, unless the respondent (or a relevant child) would suffer harm as a result of the making of an order and it appears that the harm likely to be suffered by the child or respondent in that event "is as great as or greater than the harm attributable to conduct of the respondent likely to be suffered by the applicant or child if the order is not made".[117]

The concept of "significant harm"—borrowed from the Children Act 1989[118]—is therefore of crucial importance. In relation to children, the Family Law Act embodies the same test as that used in the initial version of the 1989 Act, in which harm is defined to mean ill-treatment[119] or the impairment of health

---

[113] Family Law Act 1996 ss.35(11), 36(11). It is apparent that this clause is modeled on the Matrimonial Homes Act 1983 s.1(11), as to which see the Law Commission, *Report on Financial Provision* (Law Com. No.25 (1969)), para.5.

[114] Family Law Act 1996 ss.35(12), 36(12).

[115] Family Law Act 1996 s.39(3).

[116] Family Law Act 1996 s.39(4).

[117] Family Law Act 1996 s.33(7).

[118] Children Act 1989 ss.31(9), 31(10) and 105. See further para.21–032.

[119] Family Law Act 1996 s.63(1). This is further defined to include sexual abuse and forms of ill-treatment that are not physical.

(whether physical or mental) or development.[120] If the issue is one of a child's health or development, the test is that which could reasonably be expected of a similar child.[121] In relation to adults, by contrast, the definition of "significant harm" contains no statutory reference to "development",[122] and there is no requirement of comparison with a similar person. The main question in relation to adults will be whether the harm is "considerable, noteworthy or important".[123] In *Chalmers v Johns*[124] the Court of Appeal held that the "slight" nature of the domestic violence involved (minor violence on occasions in the course of a tempestuous relationship) meant that neither party was at risk of significant harm. As to the requirement that the harm be "attributable" to the respondent, it has been made clear that the conduct in question need not necessarily be intentional; rather, it is its effect that the court must assess, although lack of intention to cause harm may be a relevant consideration.[125]

If the "significant harm" criterion is met, and the "balance of harm" test applies, what is the likely outcome? According to the Law Commission:

> "It is highly likely that a respondent threatened with ouster on account of his violence would be able to establish a degree of hardship (perhaps in terms of difficulty in finding or unsuitability of alternative accommodation or problems in getting to work). But he is unlikely to suffer significant harm, whereas his wife and children who are being subjected to his violence or abuse may very easily suffer harm if he remains in the house."[126]

The "balance of harm" test thus tends prima facie to favour the applicant[127] **9–018** but will not necessarily do so. It requires a comparison of the harm that would be suffered by the applicant and any relevant child if the order were not made, with that which would be suffered by the respondent and any relevant child if the order were made; it is erroneous to compare the two situations from the

---

[120] The 1996 Act has not, however, been amended to reflect the changes made to the definition of "harm" by the Adoption and Children Act 2002 s.120, which included "impairment suffered from seeing or hearing the ill-treatment of another". It seems odd that the harm suffered by a child witnessing domestic violence is not within the definition of harm in a statute concerned with domestic violence.

[121] Family Law Act 1996 s.63(3).

[122] As Hale J. noted, "one hopes that adults have done their developing": Evidence given to the Special Public Bill Committee on the Family Homes and Domestic Violence Bill (1995, HL 55), March 15, 1995, question 47.

[123] Such is the interpretation of "significant" under the Children Act 1989 (see *Humberside CC v B* [1993] F.L.R. 357, *per* Booth J.) that has been adopted for cases under the 1996 Act (see *Chalmers v Johns* [1999] 1 F.L.R. 392 at 399, *per* Otton L.J.).

[124] [1999] 1 F.L.R. 392; comment in [1999] Fam. Law 16; F. Kaganas (1999) 11 C.F.L.Q. 193. See also *Banks v Banks* [1999] 1 F.L.R. 726; comment in [1999] Fam. Law 209.

[125] *G v G (Occupation Order: Conduct)* [2000] 2 F.L.R. 36; *Banks v Banks* [1999] 1 F.L.R. 726 (respondent suffering from dementia).

[126] *Domestic Violence and Occupation of the Family Home* (Law Com. No.207 (1992)), para.4.34.

[127] It appears that the Family Law Bar Association and the Society of Conservative Lawyers were opposed to the balance of harm test because they considered that it would lean too far in the favour of applicants and could lead to occupation orders almost on demand: see *Domestic Violence and Occupation of the Family Home* (Law Com. No.207 (1992)), para.4.23; and see, in particular, the Evidence of East London Families Need Fathers to the Special Public Bill Committee on the Family Homes and Domestic Violence Bill (1995, HL 55).

applicant's perspective.[128] A graphic illustration of the comparative exercise is *B v B (Occupation Order)*.[129]

> After suffering serious violence from the husband, the wife moved out of their council house with their two-year-old daughter, and they were provided with unsatisfactory bed-and-breakfast accommodation. The husband remained in the home with his six-year-old son from an earlier relationship. The husband appealed an order under s.33 that he vacate the home. The Court of Appeal set aside the order: weighing the respective likelihoods of harm to each of the children, the balance came down clearly in favour of the husband's child—if an exclusion order were made, he would have to change schools, and separating him from his father was not an option.[130]

If there is no question of any party suffering significant harm, then the court has a discretion whether or not to make an order. Section 33(6) of the Act provides that, in deciding whether to exercise its powers to make regulatory orders and, if so, in what manner, the court shall "have regard to all the circumstances[131] including:

> "(a) [T]he housing needs and housing resources of each of the parties and of any relevant child[132];
>
> (b) the financial resources of each of the parties;
>
> (c) the likely effect of any order, or any decision by the court not to exercise its powers to make regulatory orders, on the health, safety or wellbeing of the parties and of any relevant child; and
>
> (d) the conduct of the parties in relation to each other and otherwise."

9–019   The criteria in s.33 include—contrary to the recommendations of the Law Commission—references to "conduct".[133] The case law on the 1996 Act continues the trend of authorities decided under the repealed legislation[134] by

---

[128] *G v G (Occupation Order: Conduct)* [2000] 2 F.L.R. 36.

[129] [1999] 1 F.L.R. 715; comments in [1999] Fam. Law 208 and [1999] C.F.L.Q. 193. See also *Banks v Banks* [1999] 1 F.L.R. 726.

[130] Note, however, that the Court of Appeal observed obiter that Pt IV of the Family Law Act 1996 is designed to protect family members from domestic violence, and that nothing in its judgment in this case, which turned on its particular facts, should be read as weakening that objective.

[131] Adequate reference to the factors listed must be made in the judgment: *G v G (Occupation Order: Conduct)* [2000] 2 F.L.R. 36.

[132] Defined by s.62(2) as: (a) any child who is living with or might reasonably be expected to live with either party to the proceedings, (b) any child in relation to whom an order under the Adoption Act 1976, the Adoption and Children Act 2002 or the Children Act 1989 is in question in the proceedings, and (c) any other child whose interests the court considers relevant.

[133] The reference to conduct did not appear in the Family Homes and Domestic Violence Bill 1995 or in the original draft of the Family Law Bill.

[134] Which apparently may remain of some relevance: see S.M. Cretney, "Family law—a bit of a racket" (1996) 146 N.L.J. 191.

emphasising that an exclusion order is draconian in nature[135] because it affects proprietary rights and should not be made lightly—even going so far as to suggest that it should be restricted to exceptional cases, at least where the final determination of ancillary relief matters is only a matter of weeks away.[136] The absence of actual (or substantial) violence may justify the refusal of an order,[137] although, conversely, its presence will satisfy the criterion in s.33(7). Overall, however, the force of the criticism that the Law Commission's proposals made it likely that men would be more likely to be ousted from their homes under the new law than under the law it replaced has been somewhat weakened by the experience of case law on the 1996 Act.

(2) Application by non-entitled former spouse or civil partner

Consistent with the legislation's policy of privileging the institution of marriage **9–020** (and now civil partnership), former spouses[138] and former civil partners are given the most favourable treatment amongst non-entitled applicants, but they are nevertheless not treated identically with those who are in a subsisting marriage or civil partnership.

The first question is whether the court should make an order allowing the applicant to return to, or remain in, the home.[139] The exercise of the court's discretion in relation to non-entitled former spouses and former civil partners is structured by s.35(6). The court must have regard to "all the circumstances", which are defined to include a number of specific considerations. The first four of these are identical to those found in s.33(a)–(d) in relation to entitled applicants,[140] but, in addition, the court must consider:

> "(e) [T]he length of time that has elapsed since the parties ceased to live together;
>
> (f) the length of time which has elapsed since the marriage or civil partnership was dissolved or annulled;

---

[135] See, for example, *Chalmers v Johns* [1999] 1 F.L.R. 392; *Re Y (Children)* [2000] 2 F.C.R. 470. For a critical perspective, see M. Humphries, "Occupation orders revisited" [2001] Fam. Law 542.

[136] *Chalmers v Johns* [1999] 1 F.L.R. 392; *G v G (Occupation Order: Conduct)* [2000] 2 F.L.R. 36.

[137] *Chalmers v Johns* [1999] 1 F.L.R. 392; *G v G (Occupation Order: Conduct)* [2000] 2 F.L.R. 36.

[138] Parties to a marriage that is actually or potentially polygamous are within the meaning of the word "spouse" for the purposes of this Act: s.63(5).

[139] If the applicant is already in occupation, the order must contain provision giving the applicant the right not to be evicted or excluded from the home or any part of it by the respondent for the period specified in the order: Family Law Act 1996 s.35(3). If, however, the applicant is not in occupation, the order must give the applicant the right to enter into and occupy the home for the period specified in the order, and require the respondent to permit the applicant to do so: Family Law Act 1996 s.35(4).

[140] See para.9–018 above.

(g) the existence of any pending proceedings[141] between the parties."

These additional considerations are sensible and realistic, since they address the essentially factual questions of when the marriage or civil partnership broke down, and of how imminent is a final resolution of disputes in relation to property and finances.[142]

If, on consideration of the above matters, the court decides to make an order that the applicant is not to be evicted or excluded by the respondent, it will then proceed to consider whether the order should, in addition, require the respondent to leave part or all of the property.[143] In reaching its decision, the court must consider all the circumstances including those specified in subs.(6). The "balance of harm" test then applies,[144] but with a subtle difference when compared with entitled applicants: in relation to non-entitled former spouses and former civil partners, it comes into play as an overriding requirement only when the court has decided to make an order.[145]

(3) Applications by non-entitled cohabitants and former cohabitants

9–021 The questions to be posed when considering an application by a non-entitled cohabitant or former cohabitant are subtly different again. In this context, the "balance of harm" test, as such, does not apply to the making of occupation orders in favour of non-entitled cohabitants and former cohabitants. The court is instead required by s.36(8) to have regard to the "harm questions"[146]: that is, to the two components of the test, namely: (1) whether the applicant or a relevant child is likely to suffer significant harm attributable to conduct of the respondent if no such provision is included; and (2) whether the harm likely to be suffered if such a provision is included is as great or greater than the harm attributable to conduct of the respondent that is likely to be suffered if it is not. The fact that the balance tilts in favour of the applicant does not, however, require the court to make an order in this context; the court is instead required to have regard to a list of factors in deciding whether to make an order or not. These include,[147] in addition to those that apply to entitled applicants[148]:

> "(e) [T]he nature of the parties' relationship and in particular the level of commitment involved in it;

---

[141] Specified as applications for property adjustment in divorce or dissolution of a civil partnership, and applications for financial relief for a child against a parent, or proceedings relating to the ownership of the house: s.35(6)(g).

[142] Note the importance attached to the imminence of such proceedings in *Chalmers v Johns* [1999] 1 F.L.R. 392 and *G v G (Occupation Orders: Conduct)* [2000] 2 F.L.R. 36. For a case in which s.35 was applied, see *S v F (Occupation Order)* [2000] 1 F.L.R. 255.

[143] For the full range of orders that can be made see Family Law Act 1996 s.35(5).

[144] Family Law Act 1996 s.35(8).

[145] Bird, *Domestic Violence and Protection from Harassment*, pp.43–44.

[146] P. Pearson, "Domestic violence", Ch.4 in *The Family Lawyer's Handbook* (The Law Society, 1997), pp.120, 123.

[147] Family Law Act 1996 s.36(6)(e)–(i).

[148] See Family Law Act 1996 s.36(6)(a)–(d) and para.9–018 above.

(f) the length of time during which they have cohabited;

(g) whether there are or have been any children who are children of both parties or for whom both parties have or have had parental responsibility[149];

(h) the length of time that has elapsed since the parties ceased to live together;

(i) the existence of any pending proceedings between the parties."

In considering the nature of the parties' relationship, the court was initially required "to have regard to the fact that the parties have not given each other the commitment involved in marriage".[150] This was one of the modifications to the original Bill that was clearly intended to satisfy those MPs perturbed by the spectre of the erosion of the institution of marriage. The formulation was open to criticism (the underlying message being that cohabitants were intrinsically less committed than married couples), and it appeared to have little impact on the everyday practice of the courts. It was repealed by the Domestic Violence, Crime and Victims Act 2004[151] with effect from December 5, 2005,[152] and replaced by a direction to the courts to have regard to the level of commitment involved in the relationship under consideration.[153]

iv. Duration of occupation orders

Occupation orders in favour of entitled applicants may be made "for a specified **9–022** period, until the occurrence of a specified event or until further order".[154] Nevertheless, such orders are not intended to be permanent; disputes between the parties will most generally be resolved on a long-term basis by ancillary relief proceedings under Pt II of the Matrimonial Causes Act 1973 in the case of divorcing couples[155], by proceedings under Sch.5 to the Civil Partnership Act 2004 by civil partners seeking dissolution, or by proceedings for the realisation of equitable interests[156] or by transfer of tenancy for unmarried couples.[157]

---

[149] "Parental responsibility" has the same meaning as in the Children Act 1989: s.63(1), and see para.17–013.

[150] Family Law Act 1996 s.41.

[151] Domestic Violence, Crime and Victims Act 2004 s.2(1).

[152] Domestic Violence, Crime and Victims Act 2004 (Commencement Order No.5) Order 2005 (SI 2005/3196).

[153] Family Law Act 1996 s.36(6)(e), as amended by Domestic Violence, Crime and Victims Act 2004 s.2(1).

[154] Family Law Act 1996 s.33(10). Orders may not be made after the death of either of the parties; and (save in the case of home rights, which the court may extend: Family Law Act 1996 s.33(5)(a), (9)) will cease to have effect on the death of either party (s.33(9)(b)).

[155] Discussed in Ch.13.

[156] Discussed in Ch.5.

[157] Family Law Act 1996 s.53 and Sch.7. The power of the court to transfer a statutory, protected, secure or assured tenancy is also exercisable upon divorce or dissolution, but assumes more significance in relation to cohabitants because of the paucity of other remedies available to them. Where the court exercises the power of transfer, it may direct the transferee to make a compensation payment to the other (Sch.7, para.10). Guidelines are given for the exercise of the discretion to transfer, and on the question of whether a compensation order should be made (Sch.7 para.5). The court must consider all the circumstances, including the parties' (and children's) housing needs and

Occupation remedies for non-entitled applicants are intended to be a:

> "[R]elatively short term measure of protection, just to give sufficient time to find alternative accommodation or to await the outcome of property proceedings."[158]

An order in favour of a former spouse or former civil partner can have effect only for a specified period not exceeding six months, but may be extended on one or more occasions for further specified periods, each not exceeding six months.[159] Orders in favour of non-entitled cohabitants, by contrast, may be made for a maximum of six months, renewable only once for a further term of no more than six months.[160]

v. Ancillary provisions

9–023 Once an occupation order has been made in respect of a home, the Act contains additional powers that should, in principle, be very useful, such as the power to grant either party possession or use of the furniture or other contents.[161]

The court may also impose obligations as to repair, maintenance and the discharge of outgoings in respect of the house (including the mortgage[162]), and to pay what is in effect an occupation rent to someone excluded from property that he or she would otherwise have been entitled to occupy.[163] However, in practice, these statutory provisions are ineffective because of the absence of an enforcement mechanism,[164] and the issue merits urgent parliamentary attention.[165]

vi. Enforcing an occupation order

9–024 If the respondent breaches the occupation order (e.g. by entering the home from which he or she has been excluded), then proceedings for contempt of court may be brought. It is also possible for the court to attach a power of arrest to an occupation order,[166] and the legislation directs that this should be done if the

---

resources, financial resources, the effects of any order, their suitability as tenants and, in relation to cohabitants, the nature of their relationship and the duration of their cohabitation.

[158] *Domestic Violence and Occupation of the Family Home* (Law Com. No.207 (1992)), para.4.19.

[159] Family Law Act 1996 s.35(10).

[160] Family Law Act 1996 s.36(10). The same distinction is drawn in respect of applications relating to a home that neither party was entitled to occupy: see ss.37(5), 38(6).

[161] Family Law Act 1996 s.40(1)(c)–(e). The power is exercisable at any time after an occupation order has been made. There was no power under the Domestic Violence and Matrimonial Proceedings Act 1976 to make orders in respect of the household goods, and experience showed that the gap in the law enabled a vindictive person to inflict considerable hardship on his former partner—in *Davis v Johnson* [1979] A.C. 264, for example, it was reported that when the applicant returned to the home, she found it empty save for some plastic ornaments and plates.

[162] A. Grand, "Getting the mortgage paid" [1999] Fam. Law 833.

[163] Family Law Act 1996 s.40(1)(b). The Act contains guidelines for the exercise of these discretionary powers: s.40(2).

[164] *Nwgogbe v Nwgogbe* [2000] 2 F.L.R. 744.

[165] M. Humphries, "Occupation orders revisited" [2001] Fam. Law 542.

[166] Family Law Act 1996 s.47.

respondent has used or threatened violence against the applicant or a relevant child. In addition, an occupation order will often be accompanied by a non-molestation order, and a provision inserted by the Domestic Violence, Crime and Victims Act 2004 specifically requires the court to consider whether to make a non-molestation order when making an occupation order.[167] It is to non-molestation orders that we shall now turn.

B. Orders for personal protection

As noted above, there are two types of order available to a person seeking **9–025** protection from another by means of a civil remedy: the non-molestation order under the Family Law Act 1996 and an injunction under the Protection from Harassment Act 1997. Each will be considered in turn.

i. Non-Molestation orders under the Family Law Act 1996

The Family Law Act 1996 confers on the courts a wide power to make orders **9–026** prohibiting "molestation" in cases where the applicant is "associated" with the respondent in some defined way, and also provides the means by which such orders may be enforced in case of breach. The different elements of the scheme are examined in the following sections.

(1) The concept of "molestation"

The Act deliberately—in the interests of flexibility—leaves the concept of **9–027** "molestation" undefined.[168] Molestation is certainly wider than, but inclusive of, physical violence. According to the Law Commission,[169] it:

> "[E]ncompasses any form of serious pestering or harassment and applies to any conduct which could properly be regarded as such a degree of harassment as to call for the intervention of the court."

Conduct that has been held to constitute molestation includes verbal abuse[170]; constantly calling at a person's home and place of work[171]; persistent telephone

---

[167] Family Law Act 1996 s.42(4A), as inserted by Domestic Violence, Crime and Victims Act 2004 Sch.10 para.36; in force from July 1, 2007 (Domestic Violence, Crime and Victims Act 2004 (Commencement No.9 and Transitional Provisions) Order 2007 (SI 2007/1845).

[168] The Law Commission recommended that there should be no statutory definition, in part because the lack of a statutory definition had not given rise to difficulty in the past, and in part because of concern that a definition might become over-restrictive or could lead to borderline disputes: see *Domestic Violence and Occupation of the Family Home* (Law Com. No.207 (1992)), para.3.1; and see further the evidence of Hale J. to the Special Public Bill Committee on the Family Homes and Domestic Violence Bill (1995, HL 550), March 15, 1995, question 96.

[169] *Domestic Violence and Occupation of the Family Home* (Law Com. No.207 (1992)), para.3.1.

[170] *George v George* [1986] 2 F.L.R. 342.

[171] *Vaughan v Vaughan* [1973] 1 W.L.R. 1159.

calls[172]; and allegations or revelations designed to cause the victim distress.[173] By contrast, the behaviour in *C v C (Non-Molestation Order: Jurisdiction)*[174] was held to fall outside the scope of "molestation":

> In the course of an acrimonious divorce, the wife provided a tabloid newspaper with information about her husband's treatment of his former wives. Sir Stephen Brown P., discharging a restraining order obtained ex parte by the husband, held that "molestation" implies some quite deliberate conduct aimed at a high degree of harassment of the other partner so as to justify the intervention of the court. Here, the wife's revelations came nowhere near molestation as envisaged by s.42, which—significantly—was located in Pt IV of the Act concerned with the topic of domestic violence. The husband's real concern was not about molestation but about damage to his reputation, for which the remedy lay in an action for defamation.

This decision has been described as "a robust attempt to keep the concept of molestation within bounds"[175]; it can be reconciled with earlier authorities on the basis that the husband was not claiming that the threatened publication would cause him distress. A further limitation on the availability of a non-molestation order is that only a person who is "associated" with the respondent may apply for such an order.

(2) Applications by "associated persons"

9–028   The Family Law Act[176] provides that the court may make a non-molestation order if an application[177] has been made for the order by a person who is associated with the respondent.[178] The definition of "associated person" is therefore of crucial importance; the underlying policy is that people who have or have had a family or domestic relationship should, by virtue of that fact, be entitled to the special legal protection afforded by this legislation if they are in

---

[172] See, for example, *Horner v Horner* [1983] F.L.R. 50.
[173] See, for example, *Horner v Horner* [1983] F.L.R. 50, in which the husband hung on the school railings scurrilous posters about the wife addressed to the parents of the children she taught, and *Johnson v Walton* [1990] 1 F.L.R. 35, in which a man sent photographs of the partially nude plaintiff to a national newspaper with the intention of causing her distress.
[174] [1998] 1 F.L.R. 554.
[175] G. Douglas in [1998] Fam. Law 254.
[176] Family Law Act 1996 s.42(2)(a).
[177] The application may be "free-standing" (i.e. not associated with any application for other relief) or may be made in other family proceedings (e.g. in divorce proceedings: s.39(2)(a)). As with an occupation order, the application may be made ex parte (see Family Law Act 1996 s.45(1) and para.9–009 above), and, in practice, most are (Ministry of Justice, *Judicial and Court Statistics 2006* (2007), Table 5.8).
[178] The Act provided that an application could be made by a third party (s.60), but this provision has not been implemented. On the desirability of proceedings being brought by a third party, see, for example, C. Humphreys and R. Thiara, "Neither justice nor protection: women's experiences of post-separation violence" (2003) 25 J.S.W.F.L. 195 at 204.

need of it.[179] In short, the nexus of the relationship is the qualification for access to the swift emergency remedies.[180]

That nexus was very widely defined by the Act, and has been widened even further by the Domestic Violence, Crime and Victims Act 2004 and the Civil Partnership Act 2004. Section 62(3) of the 1996 Act now defines a person as being "associated" with another if:

"(a)   they are or have been married to each other;

(aa)   they are or have been civil partners of each other[181];

(b)   they are cohabitants or former cohabitants;

(c)   they live or have lived in the same household, otherwise than merely by reason of one of them being the other's employee, tenant, lodger or boarder;

(d)   they are relatives;

(e)   they have agreed to marry (whether or not the agreement has been terminated)[182];

(eza)   they have entered into a civil partnership agreement[183] (whether or not that agreement has been terminated)[184];

(ea)   they have had an intimate personal relationship with each other which is or was of significant duration[185];

(f)   in relation to any child, they are both persons falling within subsection (4)[186]); or

(g)   they are parties to the same family proceedings."[187]

---

[179] See the discussion in the Law Commission's *Report on Domestic Violence and Occupation of the Family Home*, paras 3.1–3.27.

[180] See the Second Reading speech of the Lord Chancellor: *Hansard*, HL (February 23, 1995), and the discussion in Bird, *Domestic Violence and Protection from Harassment*, pp.15–21.

[181] Inserted by the Civil Partnership Act 2004 Sch.9 para.13.

[182] There must be either evidence in writing of the existence of the agreement to marry (s.44(1)(2)) or the agreement must be evidenced by the gift of an engagement ring in contemplation of the marriage or by a ceremony entered into by the parties in the presence of one or more other persons assembled for the purpose of witnessing the ceremony (s.44(2)). The nature of the necessary "evidence in writing" was raised but not answered by Wall J. in *G v G (Non-Molestation Order: Jurisdiction)* [2000] 2 F.L.R. 533 at 544.

[183] As defined in s.73 of the Civil Partnership Act 2004.

[184] Inserted by the Civil Partnership Act Sch.9 para.13.

[185] Inserted by the Domestic Violence, Crime and Victims Act 2004 s.4.

[186] The Act provides that a person falls within the necessary relationship if he is a parent of the child or has or has had "parental responsibility" for the child (Family Law Act 1996 s.62(4)). Thus, the father of a child who has never had parental responsibility for that child is nevertheless associated with the child's mother (who could therefore seek an order against him). It is further provided that two persons are associated with each other if: (a) one is the child's natural parent or that parent's natural parent; and (b) the other is the child or any person who has applied for or been granted an adoption order or a person with whom the child has been placed for adoption: s.62(5), as amended by the Adoption and Children Act 2002.

[187] As defined: s.63(1), (2). However, a local authority cannot seek these remedies, a body incorporate being expressly excluded: s.62(6).

Some of these categories are self-explanatory; others are defined in a particular way for the purposes of the legislation and require further commentary.

9–029   Cohabitation is now defined[188] to include both heterosexual and same-sex couples. Case law in other fields has established useful (though non-exclusive) criteria indicating the existence of cohabitation,[189] but the particular context may require a more generous approach to be taken. As Wall J. pointed out in *G v G (Non-Molestation Order: Jurisdiction)*[190]:

> "[W]here domestic violence is concerned, [courts] should give the statute a purposive construction and not decline jurisdiction, unless the facts of the case before them are plainly incapable of being brought within the statute. Part IV of the 1996 Act is designed to provide swift and accessible protective remedies to persons of both sexes who are the victims of domestic violence, provided they fall within the criteria laid down in s 62. It would . . . be most unfortunate if s 62(3) was narrowly construed so as to exclude borderline cases where swift and effective protection for the victims of domestic violence is required."[191]

The changes to the definition of "cohabitant" effected by the Civil Partnership Act 2004 will remove the need for same-sex couples to classify themselves merely as persons living in the same household. This is a broad category in which a familial element is not necessary,[192] and was intended to include those who have lived in the same household other than on a purely commercial basis.[193] The crucial test is the degree of community of life that goes on; there must be an element of shared lifestyle.[194] Once that is satisfied, this category encompasses arrangements such as a group of students sharing the one flat or house.[195] On normal principles of statutory interpretation—*expressio unius exlusit alterius*—it must be taken as excluding familial relationships such as a nephew and aunt sharing the same home, since such an arrangement would fall under the category of "relatives".

---

[188] Family Law Act 1996 s.62(1)(a), as amended by Domestic Violence, Crime and Victims Act 2004 Sch.1 para.2(1) and Civil Partnership Act 2004 Sch.9 para.13(2).

[189] See, for example, *Crake v Supplementary Benefits Commission; Butterworth v Supplementary Commission* [1982] 1 All E.R. 498; *Atkinson v Atkinson* [1988] 2 F.L.R. 353; *Re J (Income Support: Cohabitation)* [1995] 1 F.L.R. 660; *Re Watson (dec'd)* [1999] 1 F.L.R. 878; *K v K (Enforcement)* [2000] 1 F.L.R. 383.

[190] [2000] 2 F.L.R. 533.

[191] [2000] 2 F.L.R. 553 at 543.

[192] The expression is wider than that of "member of the . . . family . . . residing in the same household" in para.3 of Sch.1 to the Rent Act 1977 discussed in *Fitzpatrick v Sterling Housing Association* [1999] 3 W.L.R. 1113.

[193] Law Commission, *Domestic Violence and Occupation of the Family Home* (Law Com. No.207 (1992)), para.3.21.

[194] Law Commission, *Domestic Violence and Occupation of the Family Home* (Law Com. No.207 (1992)), para.3.21.

[195] Persons who share a flat would be within this definition if they are all joint tenants of the property, but not if one of them has taken a lease and then agrees to allow others to share the flat: Law Commission, *Domestic Violence and Occupation of the Family Home* (Law Com. No.207 (1992)), para.3.22.

Indeed, many relationships will fall within the expansive definition of "relative" under the 1996 Act. The term includes not only an individual's own relatives (down to first cousins[196]) but also relationships derived from the connections of marriage, civil partnership and cohabitation.[197] The authors know of no more extensive statutory definition of a person's kin.

Wide though the definition may be, it is at least certain whether any given **9–030** person is associated with the applicant in such a way. More difficult is the provision that two persons are associated if they have had an "intimate personal relationship with each other which is or was of significant duration".[198] Those seeking enlightenment from the Explanatory Notes that accompanied this somewhat opaque provision are likely to be disappointed; they state, somewhat unhelpfully, that the relationship need not be sexual but that platonic friends are excluded, as are one-night stands.[199]

A person falling outside the wide definition of "associated person" is not without legal protection, but must seek it elsewhere, usually under the Protection from Harassment Act 1997, discussed below. However, the very breadth of the definition in the 1996 Act—broadened still further by the Domestic Violence, Crime and Victims Act 2004 and the Civil Partnership Act 2004—means that, in practice, a wide range of applicants will be able to apply for a non-molestation order, especially given the courts' purposive interpretation of the legislation.[200]

Of course, the fact that such persons are entitled to *apply* for a non-molestation order does not mean that such an order will automatically be granted. In particular, the court may take the view that the dispute between the parties is not one that calls for this particular remedy. This was considered in *Chechi v Basheer*:

> The case concerned a family quarrel originating in a land dispute. The appellant originally obtained non-molestation orders ex parte under the Family Law Act 1996 against his brother and six nephews, but these were

---

[196] As added by the Domestic Violence, Crime and Victims Act 2004 Sch.10 para.41, in force from December 5, 2005: Domestic Violence, Crime and Victims Act 2004 (Commencement Order No.5) Order 2005 (SI 2005/3196).

[197] Family Law Act 1996 s.63(1)(a) and (b), as amended by Domestic Violence, Crime and Victims Act 2004 and by the Civil Partnership Act 2004 Sch.9, para.14(4), as meaning: (a) the father, mother, stepfather, stepmother, son, daughter, stepson, stepdaughter, grandmother, grandfather, grandson or granddaughter of the person concerned or of that person's spouse or civil partner or former spouse or civil partner; or (b) the brother, sister, uncle, aunt, niece or nephew or first cousin (whether of the full blood or of the half blood or by affinity) of that person or of that person's spouse or civil partner or former spouse or civil partner, and includes, in relation to a person who is living or has lived with another person as husband and wife or as civil partner, any person who would fall within (a) or (b) if the parties were married to or in a civil partnership with each other.

[198] Family Law Act 1996 s.62(3)(ea), inserted by the Domestic Violence, Crime and Victims Act 2004 s.4, and brought into force with effect from July 1, 2007, by the Domestic Violence, Crime and Victims Act 2004 (Commencement No.9 and Transitional Provisions) Order 2007 (SI 2007/1845).

[199] Explanatory Notes, para.24.

[200] Indeed, it has been argued that the current definition of "associated persons" is too wide: see H. Reece, "The end of domestic violence" (2006) 69 M.L.R. 770. However, one study of criminal prosecutions found that 20% of victims of domestic violence are related by blood to the perpetrator, which would suggest that there is a sound empirical reason for including such persons: see CPS, "Domestic violence monitoring snapshot", *http://www.cps.gov.uk/publications/prosecution/domestic/snapshot_2006_12.html* [Accessed May 30, 2008].

discharged at the full hearing on the basis that the family relationship was incidental and that the case should therefore be dealt with as civil rather than family proceedings. The Court of Appeal disagreed on this point, holding that the dispute was genuinely within the ambit of Pt IV of the 1996 Act: although it was in origin about land, it was "patently overlaid and magnified by the family relationship".[201]

(3) Orders made by court of its own motion

9–031 The 1996 Act provides that the court may make a non-molestation order in any family proceedings against any party to those proceedings if it considers that the order should be made for the benefit of any other party to the proceedings or any relevant child,[202] whether or not any application has been made for the order.[203] The Children Act Sub-Committee of the Advisory Board on Family Law has recommended more robust use of this power in order to secure the safety of the residential parent and child in cases involving domestic violence where interim or longer contact is ordered under s.8 of the Children Act 1989.[204]

(4) Terms that may be included in a non-molestation order

9–032 The Act empowers the court to make orders prohibiting the respondent from molesting a person who is associated with the respondent or from molesting a relevant child.[205] A non-molestation order may[206] refer to molestation in general, to particular acts of molestation or to both. In practice, orders are commonly worded in terms of prohibitions on threatening, intimidating, harassing or pestering the applicant or named children.[207] Non-molestation orders may be made for a specified period or until further order.[208] The duration of a non-molestation order is a matter for the court's discretion; an order for an indefinite period may be appropriate in the circumstances, and courts are not obliged to regard such cases as exceptional or unusual.[209] The issue of the terms and duration of a non-molestation order is anterior to and distinct from that of a power of arrest; the latter cannot be used as a reason for limiting the former.[210]

---

[201] [1999] 2 F.L.R. 489 at 493; comment in [1999] Fam. Law 528. However, the appeal was dismissed on the basis that the (then) mandatory power of arrest under s.42 would have been inappropriate in the circumstances.

[202] Defined in s.62(2).

[203] Family Law Act 1996 s.42(2)(b).

[204] CASC, *Report to the Lord Chancellor on the Question of Parental Contact in Cases Where There is Domestic Violence* (1999), paras 5.4(d) and 5.7(c). See Ch.18.

[205] Family Law Act 1996 s.42(2)(b).

[206] Family Law Act 1996 s.42(6).

[207] See the pro forma suggested by D.J. Ashton at [1998] Fam. Law 4, 7.

[208] Family Law Act 1996 s.42(7).

[209] *Re B-J (Power of Arrest)* [2000] 2 F.L.R. 443, overruling *M v W (Non-Molestation Order: Duration)* [2000] 1 F.L.R. 107; comment in [2000] Fam. Law 107.

[210] *Re B-J (Power of Arrest)* [2000] 2 F.L.R. 443.

An order made in other family proceedings will cease to have effect if those proceedings are withdrawn or dismissed.[211]

(5) Matters relevant to the exercise of the court's discretion

The 1996 Act provides[212] that in deciding whether to exercise its powers to make **9–033** a non-molestation order (and if so in what manner), the court is to have regard to all the circumstances, including the need to secure the health, safety and wellbeing of the applicant[213] and of any relevant child.[214] The grant of a non-molestation order is obviously much less intrusive than the grant of an order excluding a person from his or her home; as the Law Commission noted, there is a distinction between non-molestation orders that can be obeyed without prejudice to the respondent's interests, and occupation orders that obviously prejudice those interests, however temporarily or justifiably.[215] Under the current law, as under the old,[216] courts experience little difficulty in exercising their discretion in cases where they have jurisdiction.

However, there may be circumstances in which it is not appropriate to make an order. For example, in *Banks v Banks*[217] the husband's application for a non-molestation order was dismissed. The respondent wife suffered from manic depression and dementia, and the abuse to which she subjected the husband was a symptom of her condition and something over which she had no control.[218] By contrast, in *Westcar v Westcar*[219] it was held that a non-molestation order should be terminated, as there had been no further difficulties between the parties since the husband had been committed for breach of an earlier order, the existence of the suspended order of committal being thought to provide adequate protection.

One alternative to the making of a non-molestation order is to accept an undertaking from the other party that he or she will not engage in the conduct complained of.[220] However, the Domestic Violence, Crime and Victims Act 2004 has made it more difficult for a court to accept an undertaking, since it is no longer able to do so if it appears either that the respondent "has used or threatened violence against the applicant or a relevant child" or that a non-molestation order is necessary for their protection in light of the means available to enforce such orders.[221]

---

[211] Family Law Act 1996 s.42(8).
[212] Family Law Act 1996 s.42(5).
[213] Or, where the court decides to make an order of its own motion, the person for whose benefit it considers the order should be made: s.42(5)(a).
[214] As defined s.63 and s.62(2).
[215] Report on *Domestic Violence and Occupation of the Matrimonial Home*, para.2.48.
[216] See the fifth edition of this book at p.217.
[217] [1999] 1 F.L.R. 726; comment in [1999] Fam. Law 209.
[218] Even assuming she had capacity to understand an order; see further, *P v P (Contempt of Court: Mental Capacity)* [1999] 2 F.L.R. 897, and G. Ashton, "Injunctions and mental disorder" [2000] Fam. Law 39.
[219] [2006] EWCA Civ 1414.
[220] Family Law Act 1996 s.46(2).
[221] Family Law Act 1996 s.46(3A), as inserted by Domestic Violence, Crime and Victims Act 2004 Sch.10 para.37 and in force from July 1, 2007 (Domestic Violence, Crime and Victims Act 2004 (Commencement No.9 and Transitional Provisions) Order 2007 (SI 2007/1845).

(6) The means of enforcing an order

9–034   An order for personal protection would be of little use if there were no means of enforcing it. The importance of providing adequate enforcement mechanisms was recognised by the Family Law Act (which introduced new mechanisms for this purpose), and was a key element in the passage of the Domestic Violence, Crime and Victims Act 2004. Two different enforcement mechanisms now exist.

9–035   **(a) Committal for contempt of court.** It is a contempt of court to disobey a court order. Whether or not there has been a breach of a non-molestation order must be proved to the criminal standard: as Wall L.J. emphasised in *Hammerton v Hammerton*, "[n]othing less will suffice".[222] A sentence of contempt serves a dual purpose: first, in the interests of the administration of justice, to signal the court's disapproval of disobedience of its orders and to secure future compliance; and secondly, to punish for the breach itself in light of its gravity.[223] The dilemma facing a judge in committal proceedings[224] involving family members is that discussed at the outset of this chapter: how to reconcile the objectives of the justice system in relation to seriously antisocial conduct[225] with sensitivity to the special character of family proceedings and the continuing relational and emotional ties of the parties commonly involved therein.[226]

The range of sentencing options available to the court in cases of contempt is more limited than under the general criminal law,[227] and the maximum sentence that can be imposed is two years' imprisonment.[228] The Court of Appeal in *Hale v Tanner*[229] provided valuable guidance on the mode of sentencing for contempt in family proceedings. It noted that the court has a discretion whether or not to commit to prison for the first breach of an order,[230] while pointing out that this is not common practice and that much will depend on the nature of the conduct

---

[222] [2007] EWCA Civ 248 para.43. See further, *Re JC (Committal Proceedings)* [2007] EWCA Civ 896.

[223] *Neil v Ryan* [1998] 1 F.L.R. 1068; *Wilson v Webber* [1998] 1 F.L.R. 1097; *Rafiq v Muse* [2000] 1 F.L.R. 820; *Hale v Tanner* [2000] 2 F.L.R. 879 at 884, *per* Hale L.J.; *Harris v Harris* [2001] 2 F.L.R. 955; *A-A v B-B* [2001] 2 F.L.R. 1; *Aquilina v Aquilina* [2004] EWCA Civ 504; *Greensill v Greensill* [2007] EWCA Civ 680.

[224] On the nature of committal and the distinction from prosecution, see *M v M (Committal: Contempt)* [1997] 1 F.L.R. 762 and *DPP v Tweddle* [2001] EWCA Admin. 188.

[225] *Wright v Jess* [1987] 2 F.L.R. 373; *Brewer v Brewer* [1989] 2 F.L.R. 251; *G v G (Contempt: Committal)* [1993] Fam. Law 335; *Jones v Jones* [1993] 2 F.L.R. 377; *Hudson v Hudson* [1995] 2 F.L.R. 72; *Delaney v Delaney* [1996] 1 F.L.R. 458; *Thorpe v Thorpe* [1998] 2 F.L.R. 127; *Neil v Ryan* [1998] 1 F.L.R. 1068; *Wilson v Webber* [1998] 1 F.L.R. 1098; *Rafiq v Muse* [2000] 1 F.L.R. 820.

[226] *Ansah v Ansah* [1977] Fam. 138 at 142–143, *per* Ormrod L.J.; *Hale v Tanner* [2000] 2 F.L.R. 879 at 884 and 885, *per* Hale L.J.

[227] The options open to the court include adjournment, imprisonment, fine and mental health orders (Contempt of Court Act 1981 s.14(1), (2)). Magistrates' courts have powers to punish for disobedience to their orders under the Magistrates' Courts Act 1980 s.63(1); and magistrates are given powers (comparable to those of the High Court and county courts) to pass suspended sentences, and to make orders under the Mental Health legislation: Family Law Act 1996 ss.50, 51.

[228] Sentences will be proportionate to this maximum: see, for example, *Loughran v Pandya* [2005] EWCA Civ 1720; *Legge v Legge* [2006] EWCA Civ 1484; *G v G* [2006] EWCA Civ 1670; *Patel v Patel* [2007] EWCA Civ 384.

[229] [2000] 2 F.L.R. 879.

[230] *Thorpe v Thorpe* [1998] 2 F.L.R. 127.

in question.[231] It also emphasised that the length of committal should be determined without reference to whether or not it is to be suspended.[232] Finally, it was noted that account should be taken of any concurrent proceedings in order to avoid double punishment, and that the court should endeavour to explain the nature and purpose of its orders to the contemnor. Further guidance on the duration of any sentence was provided in *H v O (Contempt of Court: Sentencing)*,[233] which emphasised that the courts should bear in mind the sentences that might be expected in the Crown Court for comparable offences.[234]

The serious nature of committal proceedings and their potential to deprive an individual of liberty necessitate procedural fairness to comply with art.6 of the European Convention for the Protection of Human Rights and Fundamental Freedoms.[235] It has been held that proceedings for committal are a criminal charge for the purposes of art.6.[236] As a consequence, the defendant has the right:

> "[T]o defend himself in person or through legal assistance of his own choosing or, if he has not sufficient means to pay for legal assistance, to be given it free when the interests of justice so require."[237]

A lack of legal representation has been a matter of concern for the courts in a **9–036** number of recent cases, with Wall L.J. commenting in *Hammerton v Hammerton* that:

> "[I]n the absence of exceptional circumstances, it is a breach of a party's ECHR Article 6 rights to be sent to prison for contempt of court without the benefit of legal representation."[238]

An individual who is committed to prison for contempt of court may apply to the court to purge his or her contempt—a process that usually "involves the

---

[231] See, for example, *Legge v Legge* [2006] EWCA Civ 1484 and *Gull v Gull* [2007] EWCA Civ 900 (breaches did not involve any violence or threat of violence).
[232] Suspension is a very useful power, and may be used in this context in a far wider range of circumstances than in criminal cases: for discussion, see *Griffin v Griffin* [2000] 2 F.L.R. 44. The duration for which a committal order should be suspended is a separate consideration from the duration of the sentence, although it will often be appropriate to link it to compliance with the underlying order.
[233] [2004] EWCA Civ 1691.
[234] See further, *Bramley v Bramley* [2007] EWCA Civ 1483, and see Sentencing Guidelines Council, *Assault and Other Offences Against the Person* (2008) on the sentences deemed appropriate in cases of violent offences.
[235] *Manchester City Council v Worthington* [2000] 2 F.L.R. 531; *Begum v Anam* [2004] EWCA Civ 578. See also President's Direction, *Committal Applications*, March 15, 2001 (see [2001] Fam. Law 333).
[236] *Re K (Contact: Committal Order)* [2002] EWCA Civ 1559, para.21, *per* Hale L.J.
[237] Art.6(3)(c). See also *Benham v United Kingdom* (1996) 22 E.H.R.R. 293.
[238] [2007] EWCA Civ 248, para.52.

contemnor apologizing to the court for his past behaviour and promising to comply in future with the court's orders".[239] Upon such an application, there are only three possible outcomes: immediate release, deferred release or refusal—or, as Thorpe L.J. put it in *Harris v Harris*, "yes, no, or not yet".[240] There is no jurisdiction to suspend the unserved part of the sentence.[241]

A contemnor is not required to understand the nature of the court's jurisdiction nor the concept of contempt, but must have sufficient mental capacity to understand that an order has been made forbidding him or her from doing certain things and that if the contemnor does them, he or she will be punished.[242]

9–037   **(b) Breach as a criminal offence**. The limitations of the committal procedure—in particular the fact that the maximum sentence available was two years' imprisonment—led to the courts encouraging applicants to bring proceedings under the Protection from Harassment Act 1997 for cases warranting a more severe sentence.[243] The need to do so has since been obviated by the Domestic Violence, Crime and Victims Act 2004, which provides that the breach of a non-molestation order is in itself a criminal offence,[244] for which the maximum sentence is five years' imprisonment.[245] It is still possible for a person in breach of a non-molestation order to be committed for contempt of court, but only as an alternative to prosecution under this new procedure.[246]

The fact that a breach of a non-molestation order is in itself a criminal offence means that the police automatically have the power to arrest the perpetrator in cases of breach, and the earlier requirement that, in cases where there has been actual or threatened violence, the court should attach a power of arrest to a non-molestation order is therefore abolished.[247]

While the rationale for providing that a breach of a non-molestation order constituted a criminal offence was to give both victims and the police the certainty that the perpetrator might be arrested in cases of breach, it has been questioned whether this new provision will have an effect on the way in which orders are drafted. Given the seriousness of committal proceedings, however, there may be little difference between the level of precision required of an order

---

[239] *Harris v Harris* [2001] 2 F.L.R. 955, para.28.

[240] *Harris v Harris* [2001] EWCA Civ 1645, para.21.

[241] *Harris v Harris* [2001] EWCA Civ 1645, allowing the appeal from Munby J. (*Harris v Harris* [2001] 2 F.L.R. 955).

[242] *P v P (Contempt of Court: Mental Capacity)* [1999] 2 F.L.R. 897; comment in [1999] Fam. Law 690.

[243] See, for example, *Robinson v Murray* [2005] EWCA Civ 935; *Carabott v Huxley* (2005) 102(34) L.S.G. 30.

[244] Family Law Act 1996 s.42A(1), as inserted by Domestic Violence, Crime and Victims Act 2004 s.1, and brought into force with effect from July 1, 2007 by the Domestic Violence, Crime and Victims Act 2004 (Commencement No.9 and Transitional Provisions) Order 2007 (SI 2007/1845).

[245] Family Law Act 1996 s.42A(5), as inserted by Domestic Violence, Crime and Victims Act 2004 s.1.

[246] Family Law Act 1996 s.42A(3) and (4), as inserted by Domestic Violence, Crime and Victims Act 2004 s.1.

[247] On the policy underpinning the introduction of the power of arrest, and its operation, see the seventh edition of this work at pp.262–264.

whose breach may result in a criminal offence.[248] Parallels may also be drawn with the Protection from Harassment Act, to which we shall now turn.

ii. Relief under the Protection from Harassment Act 1997

As with "molestation" under the Family Law Act 1996, the concept of **9–038** "harassment" is left undefined, but conduct such as frightening silent telephone calls made repeatedly,[249] threatening letters[250] and watching the family home[251] have all been held to constitute harassment. So, given the remedies available under the 1996 Act, when will it be necessary or appropriate to make use of the Protection from Harassment Act 1997 in the context of relationship breakdown or a family dispute?[252]

One obvious situation in which use will be made of the 1997 Act is where the parties are not "associated" with each other within the definition set out in the Family Law Act. The expansion of the categories of associated persons renders this less likely, but there may still be situations (e.g. where someone is being harassed by the former partner of their new partner[253]) that fall outside the scope of the 1996 Act.[254] Even if the victim is associated with the perpetrator, he or she may choose to rely on the 1997 Act if the harassment is not of the degree of seriousness[255] sufficient to satisfy the concept of "molestation" under the 1996 Act.[256] Also, until recently, there was an extra incentive to relying on the 1997 Act, namely, that the sanctions available to enforce an order of the court were more stringent[257]; in the wake of the changes effected by the Domestic Violence Crime and Victims Act, however, the sanctions available under the Family Law Act are equally tough.

It is clear that the fact that the harassment has occurred in a domestic context is not seen as rendering the 1997 Act inapplicable. As the judge pointed out in *Singh v Bhakar and Bhakar*[258]:

---

[248] See S. Gore, "The Domestic Violence, Crime and Victims Act 2004 and Family Law Act 1996 injunctions" [2007] Fam. Law. 738.
[249] *R. v Ireland; R. v Burstow* [1998] 1 F.L.R. 105; accepted obiter, although it was doubted whether such conduct would constitute the more serious s.4 offence of putting people in fear of violence: *per* Lord Steyn at 107H–108B.
[250] *R. v Colohan* [2001] EWCA Crim. 1251.
[251] *Crawford v CPS* [2008] EWHC 148 (Admin).
[252] For a comparison between the two, see T. Lawson-Cruttenden and N. Addison, "Domestic violence and harassment—a consideration of Part I of the Family Law Act 1996 and the Protection from Harassment Act 1996" [1998] Fam. Law. 543 and Bird, *Domestic Violence and Protection from Harassment*, pp.114–115.
[253] See, for example, *Hale v Tanner* [2000] 2 F.L.R. 879.
[254] See also *Khorosandjian v Bush* [1993] Q.B. 727, although note the impact of the decision in *Hunter v Canary Wharf Ltd* [1997] A.C. 655 on the availability of a remedy under the general law on the facts of that case.
[255] See, for example, *C v C (Non-Molestation Order: Jurisdiction)* [1998] 1 F.L.R. 554, above at para.9–027.
[256] And note that in *R. v Hills* [2001] 1 F.L.R. 185, the Court of Appeal observed obiter that the 1997 Act might, on appropriate facts, be used to prevent stalking of a former partner or estranged spouse.
[257] See *Robinson v Murray* [2005] 3 F.C.R. 504.
[258] [2007] 1 F.L.R. 880 at para.163.

"[I]n my view a judge should be very slow to refuse on policy grounds to grant a statutory remedy if the provisions of the statute apply to the facts of the case."

(1) The orders that may be made

9–039   As noted above, the 1997 Act created an unusual hybrid of criminal offences and civil remedies. Civil remedies are created by s.3, which provides that an actual or apprehended breach of s.1 (which states that an individual must not pursue a course of conduct that amounts to harassment of another) may be the subject of a civil claim by the actual or potential victim.[259] Thus, while more than one incident must have occurred in order for there to be a course of conduct that constitutes the criminal offence under s.2, the apprehension that the perpetrator is embarking on a course of conduct would be sufficient to establish the need for protection under s.3.

The civil remedy may take the form of an injunction or damages; the latter "may be awarded for (among other things) any anxiety caused by the harassment and any financial loss resulting from the harassment".[260] In considering such claims, the court is required to apply the civil standard of proof.[261] The principles on which damages are to be quantified under the Act were considered in *Singh v Bhakar & Bhakar*[262]:

> In this case, a young Sikh woman was subjected to a campaign of harassment by her mother-in-law, which led to the breakdown of the former's marriage and caused her to suffer from depression. The court awarded damages of £35,000. This figure was made up of two components: £27,500 for what she had suffered and a further £7,500 for the way in which the defence had been conducted. The former reflected what might be awarded for moderately severe psychiatric damage, according to the Judicial Studies Board's *Guidelines for the Assessment of General Damages*, 7th edn (2005), while taking into account the differences between a single traumatic event and a deliberate campaign lasting several months.

In addition, if the defendant is accused of an offence under s.2 or s.4, the court may issue an order restraining future conduct that amounts to harassment or that will cause fear of violence.[263] Under the original terms of the 1997 Act, such an order can only be made if the defendant is convicted of one of these offences, but the Domestic Violence, Crime and Victims Act 2004 provides that the court will be able to make an order if the defendant is convicted of any offence[264] or, if it

---

[259] Protection from Harassment Act 1997 s.3(1).
[260] Protection from Harassment Act 1997 s.3(2).
[261] *Hipgrave and Hipgrave v Jones* [2005] 2 F.L.R. 174.
[262] [2007] 1 F.L.R. 880.
[263] Protection from Harassment Act 1997 s.5(1) and (2).
[264] Protection from Harassment Act 1997 s.5(1), as amended by Domestic Violence, Crime and Victims Act 2004 s.12(1). At the time of writing, this provision has not been brought into force.

considers it necessary to do so in order to protect a person from harassment by the defendant,[265] even if the defendant has been acquitted.

The injunction or restraining order will usually be couched in broad terms. As the Court of Appeal pointed out in *R. v Evans*[266]: **9–040**

> "Harassment can and does take many forms. A determined defendant who has been found guilty of harassment and is prohibited from committing a particular kind of harassment is likely to find a different way of harassing the target of his or her conduct. In order to make this jurisdiction effective, it is necessary to give courts the power to prohibit conduct in reasonably general terms."

A restraining order may be made for a specified period[267] or until further order.[268] If an application is made to discharge a restraining order, it must be shown that "something has changed so that the continuance of the order is no longer necessary or appropriate."[269]

(2) The means of enforcing an order

Breach of an injunction made under the Act is itself a criminal offence,[270] **9–041** punishable by fine, imprisonment or both[271]; so too is the breach of a restraining order.[272] Conviction is intended to be an alternative to civil committal; these avenues of enforcement are mutually exclusive.[273] There is no jurisdiction under the Act to attach a power of arrest to an injunction, but where an injunction has been granted to prohibit harassment, and the plaintiff considers that prohibited conduct has occurred, he or she may apply to court for a warrant for the arrest of the defendant.[274]

iii. Injunctions under the general civil law

Part IV of the Family Law Act 1996 and the provisions of the Protection from **9–042** Harassment Act 1997 will provide remedies against molestation and harassment in the vast majority of cases involving any domestic element, but for the sake of completeness, brief mention must be made of the availability of injunctive relief under the general civil law.

---

[265] Protection from Harassment Act 1997 s.5A, as inserted by Domestic Violence, Crime and Victims Act 2004 s.12(5). At the time of writing, this provision has not been brought into force.
[266] [2005] 1 W.L.R. 1435, para.20.
[267] Which may be extended upon an application to vary the order under s.5(4): *DPP v Hall* [2005] EWHC 2612 (Admin).
[268] Protection from Harassment Act 1997 s.5(3).
[269] *Shaw v DPP* [2005] EWHC 1215, para.14, *per* Laws L.J.
[270] Protection from Harassment Act 1997 s.3(6).
[271] Protection from Harassment Act 1997 s.3(9).
[272] Protection from Harassment Act 1997 s.5(5) and (6). See, for example, *R. v Danny Michael Edwards* [2005] EWCA Crim 1738 (custodial sentence required in light of flagrant breaches of restraining order).
[273] Protection from Harassment Act 1997 s.3(7), (8).
[274] Protection from Harassment Act 1997 s.3(3).

Section 37 of the Supreme Court Act 1981 provides that the High Court[275] may grant an interlocutory or final injunction "in all cases in which it appears to the court to be just and convenient to do so". Obviously this power extends far beyond the context of violence and harassment that is the subject of the present discussion. In the context of personal relationships, the inherent jurisdiction can be invoked to restrain the defendant from, for example, communicating with the applicant's employers or disclosing confidential material to the press,[276] which would be beyond the powers conferred by the Family Law Act 1996[277] or (possibly) the Protection of Harassment Act 1997.[278] The jurisdiction may be used to oust a person from premises in order to protect a child.[279] Nevertheless, the extent of the courts' jurisdiction is restricted. The right to obtain an injunction is not itself a cause of action; it must support some pre-existing recognised legal or equitable right[280] or at least an arguable cause of action.[281]

IV. CONCLUSION

9–043   One key theme in this chapter has been that of achieving an appropriate balance—between punishment of the perpetrator and protection of the victim—when assessing the relative harm that would be caused by granting or not granting an occupation order, and in determining the appropriate sentence in cases of breach. One further balancing act that needs to be borne in mind relates to the human rights of those involved[282]: reference to art.6 of the European Convention has already been made, but also of relevance are art.3 (right to be

---

[275] County Courts Act 1984 s.38 (as substituted by the Courts and Legal Services Act 1990) provides that the country court may make an order that could be made by the High Court if the proceedings were in the High Court; it is often said that this provision enables the county court to exercise the so-called "inherent jurisdiction" of the High Court to grant injunctions: see, for example, *Pearson v Franklin (Parental Home: Ouster)* [1994] 1 F.L.R. 246. But on one view the Act merely gives the county court power to grant remedies and does not empower the county court to exercise the inherent jurisdiction of the High Court, see, for example, *D v D (County Court Jurisdiction: Injunctions)* [1993] 2 F.L.R. 802. But see *Tameside Borough Council v M (Injunctive Relief: County Courts: Jurisdiction)* [2002] 1 F.L.R. 318.

[276] For discussion of recent case law, see A. McLean and C. Mackay, "Is there a law of privacy in the UK? A consideration of recent legal developments" (2007) E.I.P.R. 389; A. McColgan, "Privacy, freedom of expression and the grant of interim injunctions" (2008) 27 C.J.Q. 23.

[277] See *C v C (Non-Molestation Order: Jurisdiction)* [1998] 1 F.L.R. 554, discussed above at para.9–027.

[278] Although see *Thomas v News Group Newspaper Ltd* [2001] EWCA Civ 1233.

[279] *C v K (Inherent Powers: Exclusion Order)* [1996] 2 F.L.R. 506; *Re P (Care Orders: Injunctive Relief)* [2000] 2 F.L.R. 385.

[280] See, for example, *Patel v Patel* [1988] 2 F.L.R. 179; *C v K (Inherent Power: Exclusion Order)* [1996] 2 F.L.R. 506; Fricker, "Inherent jurisdiction, ouster and exclusion" [1994] Fam. Law 629; K. Barnett, "Inherent jurisdiction, ouster orders and children" [1997] Fam. Law 96.

[281] *Burris v Adzani* [1996] 1 F.L.R. 266; Davey (1996) 8 C.F.L.Q. 269. The absence from the common law of a tort of harassment that underpinned the refusal of injunctive relief in some of the earlier authorities has in practice been remedied by the enactment of the Protection from Harassment Act 1997.

[282] See, from a civil liberties' perspective, the written evidence given to the Special Public Bill Committee on the Family Homes and Domestic Violence Bill (1995, HL 55) by S.M. Cretney, p.13.

free from inhuman or degrading treatment), art.5 (right to liberty and security), art.8 (respect for private and family life) and art.10 (freedom of expression). On the one hand, the law must ensure that its processes for dealing with domestic violence are compatible with the Convention rights of the perpetrator; relevant issues include the ambit of any order restraining certain forms of behaviour, the conduct of the hearing and the way in which any order is enforced.[283] On the other hand, it has been powerfully argued that the human rights of the victim may require state action to protect those involved.[284]

While the law can only do so much in this field, it can attempt to ensure that the legal system does not exacerbate the problems experienced by the victim of domestic violence. One aspect that has attracted criticism in recent years is the relationship between the criminal and civil law: as Thorpe L.J. noted in *Lomas v Parle*, the "the present interface between the criminal and family courts . . . is expensive, wasteful of resources and time consuming".[285] It has been suggested that the way forward might be to create "integrated domestic-violence courts" able to deal with both criminal and civil aspects of the same case.[286]

The legal response to domestic violence must be devised in such a way that it is applicable to ongoing relationships as well as those that have come to an end. For many victims, of course, violence may signal the end of the relationship, and the next chapter will consider the ways in which a marriage or civil partnership may be legally terminated.

---

[283] See, for example, J. Platt, "Human Rights and Part IV of the Family Law Act 1996" [2000] Fam. Law 905.
[284] S. Choudhry and J. Herring, "Righting domestic violence" (2006) 20 I.J.L.P.F. 95.
[285] [2003] EWCA Civ 1804 at para.52.
[286] See, for example, D. Cook et al., *Evaluation of Domestic Violence Pilot Sites at Gwent and Croydon 2004/05: Interim Report* (CPS, 2004); *Domestic Violence: A National Report* (March 2005), para.56.

Chapter Ten

DIVORCE AND DISSOLUTION

I.   INTRODUCTION............................... 10–001
II. TRENDS IN DIVORCE...................... 10–002
   A. The significance of divorce rates:
   cause for concern?............................ 10–003
III. THE   EVOLUTION   OF   THE
DIVORCE LAW 1857–1969...................... 10–004
   A. The doctrine of the matrimonial
   offence... 10–004
   B. The decline of the matrimonial
   offence doctrine 10–005
   C. The post Second World War
   campaign for reform.......................... 10–006
   D. Irretrievable   breakdown: the
   compromise.. 10–007
IV. DIVORCE: THE MODERN LAW 10–008
   A. The process of obtaining a divorce . 10–008
   B. The ground for divorce.................. 10–015

   C. Judicial interpretation of the five
   "facts".. 10–017
V. CRITICISMS   AND   REFORM
INITIATIVES 10–047
   A. Criticisms of the current law......... 10–047
   B. The recommended reform.............. 10–048
   C. The scheme of the Family Law Act
   1996.. 10–049
   D. Piloting the Family Law Act......... 10–050
   E. The decision not to implement the
   Act... 10–053
   F. A different approach: FAINs and
   FAInS 10–054
   G. Where next? 10–055
VI. DISSOLUTION   OF   CIVIL
PARTNERSHIPS 10–057
VII. CONCLUSION 10–058

I. Introduction

For the lawyer, a marriage or civil partnership creates a legal status from which   **10–001** legally enforceable rights and duties arise; from the same legalistic perspective, divorce or dissolution simply terminates[1] that legal status.[2] The court does have extensive powers to make financial and other orders on divorce or dissolution, but the rights of the parties thereafter flow from the order,[3] and not from the

---

[1] Divorce and dissolution are thus conceptually distinct from nullity, which (in theory) holds that there was some obstacle that prevented the legal relationship from ever coming into being (see Ch.2).

[2] The court must be satisfied that there is a valid marriage to dissolve, and the burden of proof is on the petitioner: see *R. v Nottingham County Court Ex p. Byers* [1985] 1 W.L.R. 403. For a case in which it became apparent in the course of divorce proceedings that the "marriage" had been bigamous (and was therefore void), see *Whiston v Whiston* [1995] 2 F.L.R. 268. Compare *W v W (Physical Inter-sex)* [2001] Fam. 111, where the court had previously granted the respondent to a nullity petition a decree absolute of divorce in respect of the marriage, and it was conceded that the divorce decree did not found any argument based on estoppel or laches.

[3] *De Lasala v De Lasala* [1980] A.C. 546: *Thwaite v Thwaite* [1981] 2 F.L.R. 280.

parties' agreement or from their previous relationship. However, an order of divorce or dissolution only operates prospectively: the parties may have acquired rights in the course of the marriage or civil partnership (e.g. in respect of property) that will not be lost merely because the formal relationship of the parties has been terminated.[4]

Although in emotional terms divorce and dissolution may often be what an American scholar has described as a "high impact experience",[5] as a matter of legal analysis they are simply processes that deal with legal status and with legal rights and duties; they bring to an end a legal relationship but have no necessary bearing on personal relationships. For example, a couple may have cohabited for only a few days after marriage and thereafter for years lived separate and apart, consumed with mutual hatred and bitterness, but so far as the law is concerned they remain a married couple entitled to the rights flowing from that legal relationship. Conversely, the ending of the legal relationship does not necessarily bring the parties' personal relationship to an end. It is not unknown for a couple to resume cohabitation after divorce[6]; more commonly, the fact that the couple have children requires them to continue to collaborate to a greater or lesser extent. On one view, therefore, the main consequence of divorce or dissolution in a monogamous society is not that it ends an existing relationship but that it constitutes a licence to formalise a new one.

This chapter focuses on the circumstances in which the law allows marriages and civil partnerships to be terminated. There are a few differences in terminology: a marriage is terminated by *divorce*, a civil partnership by *dissolution*; a spouse will *petition* for divorce, while a civil partner makes an *application*; and the terms *petitioner* and *applicant* are used accordingly. For this reason, it is convenient to discuss divorce and dissolution separately. A further justification for doing so is that divorce has generated a vast literature (legal, demographic and social), and the equivalent data relating to the dissolution of a civil partnership will take some time to accumulate. Finally, since the ground for dissolution was modelled on the ground for divorce, we need to know how divorce law arrived at its current state before considering its extension to civil partners.

In order to set the topic in context, Part II discusses the rise of divorce, a phenomenon that has caused much uneasiness in certain circles. Part III then explains how the law has developed, summarising the evolution of the law down to the enactment of the Divorce Reform Act 1969. The 1969 Act, as consolidated

---

[4] For example, a divorced woman is entitled to rely on her former husband's contribution record in establishing entitlement to the state retirement pension. However, a divorced woman does not become her husband's widow: see *Ward v Secretary of State for Social Services* [1989] 1 F.L.R. 119.

[5] F.E. Zimring, foreword to S.D. Sugarman and H.H. Kay (eds), *Divorce Reform at the Crossroads* (New Haven: Yale University Press, 1990).

[6] For a remarkable example, see *S v S (Financial Provision) (Post-Divorce Cohabitation)* [1994] 2 F.L.R. 228 (couple resumed living together after divorce and cohabited for 15 years) and note also *Hewitson v Hewitson* [1995] 1 F.L.R. 241 (relationship continued for four years after divorce). Cases in which one former partner provides a home when the other is incapacitated by illness are also not unknown; see, for example, *Fuller v Fuller* [1973] 1 W.L.R. 730.

in the Matrimonial Causes Act 1973, forms the current law and is analysed in Part IV. Part V considers criticisms of the current law, and the attempts that have been made over the past decade or more to address those criticisms. The final section, Part VI, is devoted to an examination of the ground on which a civil partnership may be dissolved.

II. TRENDS IN DIVORCE

For many years the conventional view was that the state has a vital interest in the **10–002** control of marriage and divorce, and that there must be some restriction on the availability of divorce in order to uphold respect for the sanctity of marriage. But since judicial divorce first became available in this country in 1858 there has been an almost constant—and at times meteoric—upward trend in the number of divorces granted. In 1858 there were only 244 divorce petitions, and it was not until 1914 that the number exceeded 1,000. Less than 30 years later, in 1942, it had risen above 10,000, and after a further 30 years it passed the 100,000 mark.[7] The number of petitions filed finally peaked at 184,471 in 1993.[8] Of course, the bare number of petitions filed, or even of divorces granted, is a rather crude measure of the likelihood that a marriage will end in divorce, since it takes no account of the number of couples marrying. A more meaningful measure is the divorce rate, which calculates the number of divorces per 1,000 married persons. This too has seen a significant rise, from 2.1 divorces per 1,000 married persons in 1961, 6.0 in 1971, 11.9 in 1981, and 13.5 in 1991, peaking at 14.4 in 1993.[9]

Since 1993, both the absolute number of divorces and the divorce rate has fallen slightly. The annual publication of official statistics showing that the number of divorces is either rising or falling tends to provoke a flurry of speculation in the media, but the prosaic truth is that the last decade has seen the number fluctuate within a fairly narrow band, neither rising above 160,000 nor falling below 130,000.[10] Such minor fluctuations should not alter the basic message that there has been an enormous increase in recourse to divorce over the past 40 years, that there has been a rapid growth in the number of persons

[7] In 1971 (the first year of the operation of the Divorce Reform Act 1969 permitting divorce on the basis of irretrievable breakdown) there were 110,017 petitions.
[8] *Judicial Statistics, Annual Report 1993*, Table 5.7. The number of decrees absolute is smaller than the number of petitions: in 1993 162,579 decrees absolute were granted.
[9] Law Commission, *Facing the Future. A Discussion Paper on the Ground for Divorce* (Law Com. No.170 (1988)), App.A; (1994) 24 *Social Trends*, Table 2.14; National Statistics, *Marriage, Divorce and Adoption Statistics*, Series FM2 No.29 (London: ONS, 2003), Table 4.1.
[10] Ministry of Justice, *Judicial and Court Statistics 2006*, Cm.7273 (London: HMSO, 2007), p.82. Similarly, the divorce rate has fluctuated between just over 12 *per* 1,000 married persons and 14 *per* 1,000: *Marriage, Divorce and Adoption Statistics*, Series FM2 No.32 (London: ONS, 2007), Table 4.1; Office for National Statistics, *News Release: Divorce Rates Lowest for 22 Years* (ONS, 2007); "Report: Divorces in England and Wales during 2006" (2007) 129 *Population Trends* 61.

divorcing for a second or third time[11] and that England and Wales has one of the highest divorce rates in Europe.[12]

B. The significance of divorce rates: cause for concern?

10–003 The question of whether the increased divorce rate is a matter for concern is one that has given rise to much discussion. In one respect it seems that there is no room for dispute: the increase has meant that an increasing number of children have been affected by their parents' divorce, with all the adverse consequences that may have for their wellbeing,[13] but there is evidently room for considerable dispute about such issues as whether a high divorce rate poses a threat to the institution of marriage, and whether an increasing divorce rate necessarily indicates an increase in the rate of marital breakdown. There is, of course, an important distinction between the *legal* act of divorce and the *social* fact of marital breakdown: the lower recourse to divorce in the nineteenth and early twentieth centuries should be set in the context of the restricted availability of divorce and the use of informal alternatives such as separation or desertion. Even so, the increase in recent decades is greater than can be accounted for by a simply shift from informal to formal means of terminating a marriage.[14]

A second issue of some controversy is the relevance of the law to these matters. Is the liberalisation of the divorce laws a factor in increasing the rate of marital breakdown, or is the increase attributable more to social (as distinct from legal) change? It is, of course, true (as a Government consultation paper on divorce reform[15] put it in 1993) that no statute, however "cleverly and carefully drafted, can make two people love each other, like and respect each other, help, understand and be tolerant of each other or force them to live together in peace and harmony"; and the days when the courts made orders requiring one spouse to return to the other and render conjugal services[16] have long since gone. And it is equally true—to quote the 1993 Consultation Paper[17] again—that:

> "It is pointless, and harmful, not to recognise that many marriages break down. The causes for this lie deep in the fabric of society. Even if it were thought desirable, the ability of the Government to influence family relationships at this level is limited. Certainly, changing the divorce law cannot save . . . marriages."

But this may be thought to confuse two issues. Whether or not it is thought that

---

[11] In 2006 10% of all divorces involved parties who had both previously been divorced; overall, 21% of divorcing men and 20% of divorcing women had previously been divorced: "Report: Divorces in England and Wales during 2006", Table 2. This proportion has doubled since 1981.

[12] (2004) 34 *Social Trends*, Table 2.1.

[13] In 2006, 125,030 children under 16 had parents who were divorcing: "Report: Divorces in England and Wales during 2006", Table 4.

[14] See, for example, C. Gibson, *Dissolving Wedlock* (London: Routledge, 1994).

[15] *Looking to the Future: Mediation and the Ground for Divorce* (Cm.2424, para.3.4).

[16] By means of the decree of Restitution of Conjugal Rights: see para.3–003.

[17] At para.1.3

the law can identify particular marriages that can be "saved",[18] it has been argued that the law does exercise a general influence on attitudes, and that the ready availability of divorce contributes to the growth of "a habit of mind in the people",[19] and thus[20] does play a part in weakening the security of marriage. In this view, the ready availability of divorce leads to an increasing disposition to regard divorce not as the last resort but as the obvious way out when things begin to go wrong,[21] and so (it is argued) the law does have some influence in establishing standards and modes of behaviour.[22] In particular, it has been claimed that for Parliament to *change* the law by statute inevitably conveys a certain message about what is and what is not acceptable.[23]

These considerations have all influenced the development of English law over the years,[24] and some knowledge of the evolution of the law is necessary both to understand the modern law and to be in a position to evaluate arguments of policy about the law's objectives and its success in attaining them.

III. THE EVOLUTION OF THE DIVORCE LAW 1857–1969[25]

A. The doctrine of the matrimonial offence

Until 1858 no English court had the power to grant a degree of divorce **10–004** terminating a valid marriage. The ecclesiastical courts had jurisdiction to annul

---

[18] The desirability of identifying marriages capable of being saved was a consistent theme in the debates on the Family Law Act 1996; see further below, para.10–049.

[19] See the dissenting report by the Archbishop of York, Sir William Anson, and Sir Lewis Dibdin to the Gorell Commission Report (Cd.6478 (1912)), p.185. A not dissimilar view is expressed by R. Deech (1990) 106 L.Q.R. 229 at 242: "Any increase in the divorce rate results in increased familiarity with divorce and its effects as a solution to marital problems and increased willingness to use it and to make legislative provision for its aftermath."

[20] An eloquent summary of arguments derived from Hume and Paley was given by Lord Stowell in a frequently quoted passage: "[T]he general happiness of the married life is secured by its indissolubility. When people understand that they must live together, except for a very few reasons known to the law, they learn to soften by mutual accommodation that yoke which they know they cannot shake off, they become good husbands and good wives from the necessity of remaining husbands and wives . . . If it were once understood that upon mutual disgust married persons might be legally separated, many couples who now pass through the world with mutual comfort, with attention to their common offspring, and to the moral order of civil society, might have been at this moment living in a state of mutual unkindness, in a state of estrangement from their common offspring, and in a state of the most licentious and unreserved immorality . . . The happiness of some individuals must be sacrificed to the greater and more general good": *Evans v Evans* (1790) 1 Hag. Con. 35 at 36–37.

[21] *Royal Commission on Marriage and Divorce* (Chairman: Lord Morton of Henryton) (Cmd.9678 (1956)), para.47.

[22] See A. Allott, *The Limits of Law* (London: Butterworths, 1980), particularly at pp.168–174, for the view that "the availability of a possibility which was previously unthinkable or not thought about transforms the psychology of the subjects as well as the legal possibilities. Their expectations and tolerances alter." (p.173).

[23] See *Hansard* HL, Vol.569 col.1638 (February 29, 1996), *per* Baroness Young: "Law influences behaviour and it sends out a very clear message. There would be no point in legislating at all if the law did not influence behaviour."

[24] On the competing views among policy-makers, see E. Hassan, "Setting a standard or reflecting reality? The "role" of divorce law and the case of the Family Law Act 1996" (2003) 17 I.J.L.P.F. 338.

[25] R. Phillips, *Putting Asunder, A History of Divorce in Western Society* (Cambridge: Cambridge University Press 1988) is a detailed, scholarly and comprehensive comparative study of marriage

marriages, and they also had jurisdiction to grant decrees of divorce *a mensa et thoro*, which relieved the parties of the duty to cohabit but did not permit either party to remarry. The only way in which a spouse could obtain the freedom to remarry was by obtaining a private Act of Parliament (having first obtained a divorce *a mensa et thoro* from the ecclesiastical court, and a judgment awarding damages for adultery from the common law courts or providing good reason for failing to do so).[26]

The Matrimonial Causes Act 1857, passed in part as a consequence of the rationalisation of the structure of the courts dealing with probate, and in part as a response to criticism of the cost and delay of the private Act procedure,[27] created[28] the Court for Divorce and Matrimonial Causes, and conferred on that court jurisdiction to grant decrees of dissolution of marriage, nullity, etc., but the 1857 Act did not change the underlying principles on which divorce had been granted under the Parliamentary procedure.[29] These were:

- that the only ground upon which divorce could be obtained was the respondent's adultery;

- that the petitioner had to show that he or she was free from guilt; and

- that the court had to be satisfied that there was no connivance or collusion between parties seeking to escape from the solemn obligations of matrimony.

Divorce was thus a legal remedy available to an injured and legally guiltless

---

breakdown; see also L. Stone, *Road to Divorce, England 1530–1987* (Oxford University Press, 1990) (and the same author's *Broken Lives, Separation and Divorce in England 1660–1857* (Oxford: Oxford University Press, 1993), which makes illuminating use of case studies to give a picture of divorce before the introduction of judicial divorce in 1857). O.R. McGregor's *Divorce in England, A Centenary Study* (London: Heinemann, 1957) is a work containing much statistical, demographic and historical material of great value by a deeply learned social historian who does not conceal his passionate commitment to reform of the law and his impatience with those taking a different view. S.M. Cretney, *Family Law in the Twentieth Century: A History* (Oxford: Oxford University Press, 2003), Pt II is a magisterial account of the process of law reform that makes extensive use of archival material and policy documents.

[26] A full historical account of the private bill procedure is given in the *First Report of the Commissioners into the Law of Divorce* (1853); and see Stone, *Road to Divorce*, Ch.10; and the case studies in Stone, *Broken Lives*. Historical research has cast fresh light on the realities of the divorce process and has undermined confidence in the accuracy of much previously accepted material: see S. Anderson, "Legislative divorce—law for the aristocracy" in G.R. Rubin and D. Sugarman, *Law, Economy and Society, Essays in the History of English Law 1750–1914* (Abingdon: Professional Books, 1984); and S. Wolfram, "Divorce in England 1700–1857" (1985) 5 O.J.L.S. 155.

[27] On the issue of cost, compare the discussion in Wolfram (1985) and Anderson (1984) with Stone, *Road to Divorce*, pp.326–327: it is noted that some persons following "fairly lowly occupations" were able to divorce, but it is suggested that they would need to have been in very comfortable circumstances to afford the costs involved.

[28] Matrimonial Causes Act 1857 s.6.

[29] See App.5, pp.102–104, of the *Report of Committee on One-Parent Families* (Cmnd.5629 (1974)).

petitioner who could establish that the respondent had committed the most serious of matrimonial offences: adultery.[30]

Exclusive reliance on adultery[31] as the ground for divorce was never universally accepted[32] and came under increasing attack over the years,[33] but reform was delayed until 1937. The Matrimonial Causes Act of that year (often known as A.P. Herbert's Act) extended the grounds for divorce and provided that either spouse could petition for divorce on the ground of the other's adultery, cruelty, desertion for a continuous period of three years or more or incurable insanity. However, the Act still conceptualised divorce as a remedy for a legal wrong: to allow divorce by consent would (so it was thought) destroy the institution of marriage and the sanctity of family life, and, accordingly, the posture of a petitioner for divorce still had to be that of an innocent party willing to perform his or her side of the contract, neither conniving at nor condoning the wickedness of the other party, and above all seeking no deal or understanding with him or her to let the divorce through.[34] In one respect, however, the 1937 Act marked the acceptance of an important change of principle: it permitted a petitioner to obtain a divorce on the ground that the respondent was incurably of unsound mind and had been continuously under care and treatment for a period of at least five years preceding the presentation of the petition.[35] Divorce was thus to be available because of misfortune, and a serious inroad[36] had thereby been made into the offence principle.

---

[30] Judicial separation was seen as the appropriate relief in cases of cruelty. Moreover, a wife petitioner for divorce could not rely solely on adultery, but had to show either: incestuous adultery; adultery and bigamy; rape, sodomy or bestiality; adultery with cruelty; or adultery and desertion for at least two years. After 1884, failure to comply with a decree of Restitution of Conjugal Rights was treated as statutory desertion, so that a wife who was able to establish adultery could obtain a divorce immediately, provided the husband failed to comply with a decree of Restitution: Matrimonial Causes Act 1884 s.5. It was not until the Matrimonial Causes Act 1923 that a wife was given the right to petition on the ground of adultery alone.

[31] The reasons for exclusive reliance on physical infidelity as the ground for divorce can be summarised as follows: (i) it followed the historical precedent of the private divorce Acts, the justification for which was originally to prevent illegitimate children being foisted on "the unhappy husband whose bed had been violated" (*Mr Lewkenor's Case*, 13 *State Trials* 1308); and (ii) scriptural justification for divorce was usually based on adultery. It was also thought by some, until well into the twentieth century, that adultery was regarded with particular opprobrium by public opinion.

[32] See J. Milton, *The Doctrine and Discipline of Divorce 1643* (London: Dent, 1927), p.276, who thought that the canon law should regard spiritual and civil companionship rather than carnal coupling as the true basis of marriage: "[H]e who affirms adultery to be the highest breach, affirms the bed to be the highest end of marriage, which is in truth a gross and boorish opinion, how common soever, so far from the countenance of scripture, as from the light of all clean philosophy or civil nature."

[33] Notably by the Gorell Commission (Cd.6478 (1912)), whose report was ultimately the basis of the Matrimonial Causes Act 1937, and in some ways foreshadowed the modern concept of breakdown. See also E. Waugh, *A Handful of Dust* (London: Chapman & Hall, 1934); A.P. Herbert, *The Ayes Have It* (London: Methven & Co, 1937).

[34] Sir Harold S. Kent, *In On The Act* (London: Macmillan, 1979), pp.78–84, which contains much interesting background.

[35] Matrimonial Causes Act 1937 s.2.

[36] Law Commission, *Reform of the Grounds of Divorce: The Field of Choice* (Law Com. No.6 (1966)), para.21.

B. The decline of the matrimonial offence doctrine

10–005   After 1937, the retention of the matrimonial offence as the basis of divorce law came under increasing attack. This was for three main reasons.

First, although it was a fundamental principle that divorce was so much a matter in which the community was vitally concerned that the parties' mutual agreement was not a basis upon which it could be allowed, and although divorce procedure was based on the assumption that the litigation was contentious, the facts were that over 90 per cent of petitions were undefended. It seemed quite clear that in many cases the parties had agreed on divorce.[37]

Secondly, as we have seen, the 1937 Act allowed divorce for misfortune; in 1964, decisions of the House of Lords[38] established that a respondent who was in no way morally blameworthy might nonetheless be divorced for the matrimonial offence of cruelty. Increasingly the crucial question seemed to be simply whether the petitioner could reasonably be expected to endure the marital situation.

Finally, although it usually remained necessary to prove that the respondent had committed a matrimonial offence, it ceased to be essential to establish that the petitioner was an aggrieved and innocent victim. This was because statute[39] made collusion into a discretionary[40] rather than an absolute bar, and restricted the scope of the bar of condonation.[41] Where the court did have a discretion to refuse a divorce because the petitioner had committed a matrimonial offence, it became increasingly accepted that no public interest was served by keeping legally in existence a marriage that had, in fact, broken down.[42] If full and frank disclosure were made,[43] the court's discretion would normally be exercised and a divorce granted.[44] Increasingly, in these circumstances, a decree was awarded to both parties and, in consequence, "the guilty/innocent dichotomy" became blurred.[45]

---

[37] And might even have agreed to provide false evidence of adultery for this purpose, as in the so-called "Hotel Cases", where the husband would arrange to provide evidence of adultery (possibly never committed) sometimes with the assistance of a professional companion: see A.P. Herbert, *Holy Deadlock* (London: Methven & Co, 1934).

[38] *Gollins v Gollins* [1964] A.C. 644; *Williams v Williams* [1964] A.C. 698.

[39] Matrimonial Causes Act 1963 s.4.

[40] This meant that the court was not obliged to grant a divorce, but might do so if on consideration of all the circumstances it considered it to be right to do so. In effect, the fact that both parties were agreed in wanting a divorce was no longer a sufficient reason for preventing their obtaining one (always provided that there was acceptable evidence of the commission of a matrimonial offence): see *Nash v Nash* [1965] P. 266; *M v M* [1967] P. 313; *Gosling v Gosling* [1968] P. 1.

[41] Matrimonial Causes Act 1963 ss.1 and 2, containing the so-called "kiss and make-up" provisions designed to facilitate reconciliation.

[42] *Blunt v Blunt* [1943] A.C. 517; *Masarati v Masarati* [1969] 1 W.L.R. 393; cf. *Bull v Bull* [1968] P. 618.

[43] A respondent seeking the exercise of discretion had to file a "discretion statement"; it was the duty of the petitioner's solicitor to make clear to his client the duty of full disclosure; see *Pearson v Pearson* [1971] P. 16. This rule sometimes led to absurd and embarrassing results: *Barnacle v Barnacle* [1948] P. 257, where the petitioner had not understood the meaning of adultery, and the trial judge gave examples of misunderstanding on other occasions: "it is not adultery if she is over 50". "I did not think it was adultery during the daytime"; "I thought it meant getting a girl into trouble"; "I thought it meant drinking with men in public houses" (at 261).

[44] *Masarati v Masarati* [1969] 1 W.L.R. 393 at 396, *per* Sachs L.J.

[45] *Field of Choice*, para.21.

C. The post Second World War campaign for reform

The Second World War inevitably imposed a great strain on many family   **10–006**
relationships. There were hasty weddings, enforced separations—sometimes
lasting for years—and all the tensions of life in an uncertain, dangerous and
deprived world. There was a divorce explosion. In 1939 there had been 8,517
divorces, but by 1947 the number had soared to an unprecedented 47,041.[46] Yet
there remained a large and increasingly vocal number of people who wanted to
escape from a relationship that had become meaningless to them but who were
unable to do so because their legal spouse refused to petition for divorce and
could not be shown to have committed a matrimonial offence. Particular hardship
was caused to people who had formed what came to be called "stable illicit
unions" and who wanted to marry, not least to legitimise their children. Not
surprisingly, there was mounting pressure to reform the divorce law so that
marriages that had ceased to exist in *fact* could be terminated in *law*.

The idea began to be articulated that the very existence of such broken
marriages was more damaging to the institution of marriage than their legal
termination would be,[47] and a number of bills were introduced with the aim of
making separation a ground for divorce.[48] It was during the debates on one such
unsuccessful bill that the Archbishop of Canterbury announced[49] that he had
decided to appoint a Committee to investigate the formulation of a principle of
breakdown of marriage. The report of this group, *Putting Asunder*, was published
in 1966, and was the catalyst for reform.[50]

D. Irretrievable breakdown: the compromise

Putting Asunder favoured, as the lesser of two evils,[51] the substitution of the   **10–007**
doctrine of breakdown for that of the matrimonial offence; the Archbishop's
Committee accepted that a divorce decree should be seen simply as a judicial
recognition of this state of affairs, with a consequent redefinition of status.[52] But
breakdown was not to be established on the mere say-so of the parties. Rather, the
court would in every case have to carry out a detailed inquest into the alleged fact
and causes of the "death" of a marriage relationship; to inquire effectively into
what attempts at reconciliation had been made, into the feasibility of further
attempts, into the acts, events and circumstances alleged to have destroyed the
marriage, into the truth of statements made (especially in uncontested cases) and
into all matters bearing upon the determination of the public interest.[53]

---

[46] *Royal Commission on Marriage and Divorce, Report 1951–1955* (Cmd.9678 (1956)) (the *Morton Report*), Table 1.
[47] See, for example, the views expressed by Lord Walker: *Morton Report*, pp.340–341. His views were not shared by the other 18 members of the Commission, who favoured the retention of the matrimonial offence principle: see Cretney, *Family Law in the Twentieth Century*, pp.338–339.
[48] Cretney, *Family Law in the Twentieth Century*, pp.324, 346–348.
[49] *Hansard* HL Vol.250, col.1547 (June 21, 1963).
[50] Cretney, *Family Law in the Twentieth Century*, pp.355–359 contains a full account.
[51] *Putting Asunder*, para.68.
[52] *Putting Asunder*, para.66.
[53] *Putting Asunder,* para.84.

The Lord Chancellor, Lord Gardiner, was able[54] to refer *Putting Asunder* to the recently established Law Commission (some of whose members had been active supporters of the move for reform[55]). The Law Commission's report, *The Field of Choice*, published in 1966, took as its starting point the view that a good divorce law should seek:

> "(i) To buttress, rather than to undermine, the stability of marriage; and
> (ii) When, regrettably, a marriage has irretrievably broken down, to enable the empty legal shell to be destroyed with the maximum fairness, and the minimum bitterness, distress and humiliation."[56]

The Commission concluded that the offence-based divorce law failed to satisfy these criteria,[57] but it did not accept the proposal made by the Archbishop's group that divorce should be available only after a full inquest into the alleged breakdown. The Law Commission thought that such an inquiry would be humiliating and distressing to the parties, and that it would be impracticable, in the absence of a vast increase in expenditure of money and human resources,[58] to have a full inquiry in every case.

The Law Commission therefore put forward various options which, it considered, provided a practicable basis for reform.[59] Discussions took place between representatives of the Law Commission and the Archbishop's group,[60] and agreement was reached on the principles ultimately embodied in the Divorce Reform Act 1969:

- the basic principle was to be that breakdown should be the sole ground for divorce; but

- breakdown should not be the subject of a detailed inquest by the court; instead it should be inferred, either from one of several specified facts akin to the traditional matrimonial offences or from the fact that the parties had lived apart for two years if the respondent consented or five years if there were no consent.

Like other reforms to divorce law, these proposals came before Parliament by virtue of a private member's bill, and eventually became law as the Divorce Reform Act 1969.[61]

---

[54] Under Law Commissions Act 1965 s.3(1)(e).
[55] See S.M. Cretney, *Law, Law Reform and the Family* (Oxford: Clarendon Press, 1998), p.57. The Commission had included matrimonial law in its *First Programme of Law Reform* (Law Com. No.1 (1965)), Item X.
[56] *Field of Choice*, para.15.
[57] *Field of Choice*, paras 23–28.
[58] *Field of Choice*, para.2.
[59] *Field of Choice*, paras 54–55.
[60] For a detailed account of the negotiations, see Cretney, *Law, Law Reform and the Family*, pp.63–69. See also *Third Annual Report of the Law Commission*, App., where the agreement between the two bodies is set out.
[61] The Parliamentary debates were protracted, and the organisational skills of Mr Leo Abse (who effectively managed the Bill's passage) made a significant contribution to the eventual success. Part of the price that opponents of the Bill exacted was that it should not be brought into force until

IV. DIVORCE: THE MODERN LAW

A. The process of obtaining a divorce

Before examining the substance of the law of divorce, it is important to have an **10–008** understanding of the framework within which the law operates; as we shall see, changes to the administrative framework have had a significant impact on the way in which the law operates in practice.

i. No divorce proceedings to be started in first year of marriage

Between 1937[62] and 1984, no petition for divorce could be presented before the **10–009** expiration of the period of three years from the date of marriage unless it was shown that the case was one of exceptional hardship suffered by the petitioner or one of exceptional depravity on the part of the respondent. In 1984[63] Parliament accepted the Law Commission's view[64] that this provision was unsatisfactory, not least because it involved the making of distressing and humiliating allegations in more than a thousand cases each year. But it was thought desirable to retain some restriction on the availability of divorce early in marriage so as to assert (symbolically at least) the state's interest in upholding the stability and dignity of marriage, and to prevent divorce being apparently available within days of the marriage ceremony.[65] The legislation was therefore amended to provide[66] that no petition for divorce shall be presented to the court before the expiration of the period of one year from the date of the marriage.

This rule prevents *divorce* proceedings being *started* within one year of the marriage, but it does not prevent the presentation of a petition based on matters that occurred before the expiration of the year,[67] nor does it prevent other proceedings[68] being started to provide legal remedies during the first year of the marriage. In addition, there is nothing to prevent the parties from de facto separating within that first year.

January 1, 1971, to enable the Government to introduce legislation intended to protect the financial position of divorced spouses: see further Ch.13, below.

[62] Matrimonial Causes Act 1937 s.1.

[63] Matrimonial and Family Proceedings Act 1984 s.1.

[64] *Time Restrictions on Presentation of Divorce and Nullity Petitions* (Law Com. No.116 (1982)).

[65] For the background to the 1984 legislation, see the fifth edition of this work at pp.95–97. It may, however, be argued that some of the reasons articulated by the Law Commission in the 1980s have little relevance over two decades on (see R. Probert, "England and Wales juxtaposed to the European principles of family law", in E. Örücü and J. Mair (eds), *Juxtaposing Legal Systems and The Principles of European Family Law: Divorce and Maintenance* (Antwerpen: Intersentia, 2007)): the "difficult early years" of marriage have largely been replaced by cohabitation, and there is little evidence that young couples are rushing into marriage.

[66] Matrimonial Causes Act 1973 s.3(1), as substituted by Matrimonial and Family Proceedings Act 1984 s.1.

[67] Matrimonial Causes Act 1973 s.3(2), as substituted.

[68] For example, a petition for a decree of judicial separation (see Ch.12, below); an application under Matrimonial Causes Act 1973 s.27 for a financial order based on failure to provide maintenance (see para.3–015); an application under the Children Act 1989 for orders relating to the upbringing of children (see Part V, below); or an application for a non-molestation or for an occupation order relating to the family home under Family Law Act 1996 Pt IV (see Ch.9).

ii. The court and the "special procedure"

10–010   Divorces may be granted by the High Court and by certain designated county courts. However, there is usually no need for the parties to attend court for their case to be heard. In 1973 a "special procedure" was introduced for undefended divorces based on the fact of two years' separation plus consent, although only where the couple did not have children. This new procedure allowed a divorce to be granted on the basis of affidavit evidence alone. In 1977 it was extended to all undefended divorces, and the "special" procedure became the norm.[69]

The procedure was summarised by Waite L.J. in *Pounds v Pounds*:

> "Following presentation of the petition, the petitioner's solicitor lodges an application for directions for trial together with a standard affidavit in the form required to verify the particular ground alleged in the petition. In routine cases . . . the [district judge] gives directions for trial by entering the cause in the special procedure list and thereafter considers the evidence filed by the petitioner. If he is satisfied that the petitioner has sufficiently proved the contents of the petition and is entitled to the decree sought and any costs prayed for, he will make and file a certificate to that effect. The court then sends notification to the parties of the date, time and place fixed for the pronouncement of the decree nisi. The parties are also told that their attendance at the pronouncement of decree is not necessary. The actual process of pronouncement of the decree has become reduced to a very brief ceremony of a purely formal character in which decrees are listed together in batches for a collective mention in open court before a judge who speaks (or nods) his assent. The right to a decree absolute six weeks thereafter is automatic . . . [T]he sole truly judicial function in the entire process is that of the [district judge] when granting his certificate. Everything that follows is automatic and administrative, and the open court pronouncement of the decree is pure formality, to which the pronouncing judge . . . has no option but to consent."[70]

iii. Investigation

10–011   This is not to say that the judge has no means of making further inquiries. If the court's suspicions as to the facts alleged in the petition are aroused, it may refer the matter to the Queen's Proctor (in effect, the office of the Treasury Solicitor), and detailed inquiries will be made in appropriate circumstances.[71] This may, of course, result in a divorce being refused even where both parties wish it, as occurred in *Bhaiji v Chauhan, Queen's Proctor Intervening (Divorce: Marriages Used for Immigration Purposes)*.[72] In this case the court's suspicions had been aroused by similarities in the phrasing of a number of petitions. Since these were

---

[69] See now the Family Proceedings Rules 1991 (SI 1991/1247) r.2.36.
[70] [1994] 1 F.L.R. 775 at 776.
[71] See Matrimonial Causes Act 1973 s.8; *Moynihan v Moynihan (Nos 1 and 2)* [1997] 1 F.L.R. 52 at 68.
[72] [2003] 2 F.L.R. 485.

marriages that had apparently been entered into for immigration purposes,[73] the parties' desire to divorce once the marriage had served its purpose was no doubt genuine, but (as Wilson J. pointed out in that case) in England and Wales, "divorce is not yet available simply upon joint demand immediately following separation".[74]

iv. Decree nisi and decree absolute

All decrees of divorce are in the first instance decrees *nisi* ("unless"). A decree **10–012** nisi does not legally terminate the marriage; it is only a decree absolute of divorce that ends the legal status of marriage previously existing between the parties. A decree nisi may be made absolute on the application of a party in whose favour it has been pronounced six weeks after the decree nisi has been pronounced, and the party against whom the decree has been granted may apply to the court for it to be made absolute three months later.[75] If the decree is not made absolute within 12 months, the court may require the applicant to file an affidavit or give evidence in open court accounting for the delay. The two-stage procedure was originally intended to give time for inquiries to be made into the circumstances surrounding the petition, and for the Queen's Proctor or anyone else who considered that the divorce should not be granted to intervene and "show cause" against the decree being made absolute. Now, however, the period between decree nisi and absolute is more often used to negotiate over the financial and other consequences of the ending of the marriage.[76]

v. Arrangements for children

If the divorcing parties have children under the age of 16, the court is required **10–013** to consider whether it should exercise its powers under the Children Act 1989 in relation to them.[77] In exceptional circumstances, if the court considers that it may need to make an order under the 1989 Act but is not in a position to do so without giving further consideration to the case, it may direct that the decree is not to be made absolute unless and until the court so orders.[78] In practice, however, this option is rarely exercised.[79]

---

[73] Each of the marriages involved a UK citizen and an Indian citizen who had recently come to the UK, and in each case the petition for divorce was presented after indefinite leave to remain had been granted to the latter. The period that had elapsed between the granting of indefinite leave and the date on which the marriage was alleged to have broken down varied between 5 days and 16 months.
[74] At para.20.
[75] These time restrictions are strict and may not be waived by the court. Thus, in *Dennis v Dennis* [2000] 3 W.L.R. 1443 (in which the court mistakenly granted the respondent husband a decree absolute within the three-month period), the court held that the divorce had not been properly granted and the husband's subsequent marriage to another woman was consequently void.
[76] Although the fact that such issues have not been resolved is not a reason for delaying the grant of the decree absolute: *Re G (Decree Absolute: Prejudice)* [2002] EWHC 2834 (Fam).
[77] Matrimonial Causes Act 1973 s.41(1).
[78] Matrimonial Causes Act 1973 s.41(2).
[79] See G. Douglas, et al., "Safeguarding children's welfare in non-contentious divorce: towards a new conception of the divorce process" (2000) 63 M.L.R. 177.

vi. Religious divorces

10–014   There is, in addition, one further context in which a court may refuse to make the decree absolute. Within certain religious groups, a civil divorce is not regarded as effective to dissolve a marriage. If, for example, a Jewish husband refuses to grant a *get*—a Jewish divorce—to his wife, the parties remain married under Jewish law even if they are no longer regarded as husband and wife under English law. The law now allows either party to apply for the divorce not to be made absolute until a declaration is made by both parties that they have taken the necessary steps to dissolve the marriage in accordance with their own religious usages.[80] The result is that a wife can prevent her husband from divorcing her in the eyes of English law but leaving her bound to him according to their own religious law. She cannot, however, force him to grant a religious divorce. The provision is thus of limited scope, and at present applies only to Jewish divorces.

B. The ground for divorce

10–015   The law[81] provides that "the sole ground on which a petition for divorce may be presented to the court . . . shall be that the marriage has broken down irretrievably".[82] As we have seen, the Act was presented to Parliament as if irretrievable breakdown were the basis on which divorce would be granted, but for three reasons the reality is very different.

First, the provision asserting that breakdown is to be the ground for divorce is immediately followed by a statement that the court should not hold the marriage to have broken down irretrievably unless the petitioner satisfies it of one or more of five "facts".[83] These facts are:

> "(a)   [T]hat the respondent has committed adultery and the petitioner finds it intolerable to live with the respondent;
>
> (b)   that the respondent has behaved in such a way that the petitioner cannot reasonably be expected to live with the respondent;
>
> (c)   that the respondent has deserted the petitioner for a continuous period of at least two years immediately preceding the presentation of the petition;
>
> (d)   that the parties to the marriage have lived apart for a continuous period of at least two years immediately preceding the presentation of the petition . . . and the respondent consents to a decree being granted;

---

[80] Matrimonial Causes Act 1973 s.10A (as inserted by the Divorce (Religious Marriages) Act 2002).
[81] The 1969 Act was consolidated in the Matrimonial Causes Act 1973 and subsequent references are to the latter, unless otherwise stated.
[82] Matrimonial Causes Act 1973 s.1.
[83] Matrimonial Causes Act 1973 s.1(2).

(e) that the parties to the marriage have lived apart for a continuous period of at least five years immediately preceding the presentation of the petition."

Almost inevitably, there is a tendency to see these facts (rather than the breakdown of the marriage) as the true grounds for divorce, since it is insufficient to establish simply that the marriage has broken down irretrievably. For example:

> In *Buffery v Buffery*[84] the parties had been married for more than 20 years. They had grown apart (although they had continued to live together), had nothing in common and could not communicate. The Court of Appeal accepted that the marriage had irretrievably broken down, and also accepted that the husband had been insensitive about money matters, but this was insufficient to establish the "behaviour" fact, and, accordingly, a decree could not be granted.

Secondly, the Act provides that if a "fact" is proved, the court is to grant a **10–016** divorce decree "unless it is satisfied on all the evidence that the marriage has not broken down irretrievably".[85] The petitioner does not have to show that the marriage had broken down *by reason* of the "fact" in question, and it is virtually impossible for one spouse to prove that the marriage has not broken down irretrievably if the other persists in the claim that it has.[86]

Thirdly, the so-called "special procedure" for undefended divorces—whereby a divorce may be granted on the basis of affidavit evidence without the parties needing to attend court—effectively precludes any real inquiry into whether a marriage has indeed broken down beyond repair,[87] or even into the genuineness of the "facts" alleged. For example, a petitioner relying on the first "fact"—that the respondent has committed adultery and the petitioner finds it intolerable to live with the respondent—does not need to identify with whom the adultery has been committed,[88] and merely has to write the word "yes" on the form that asked whether he or she finds it intolerable to live with the other spouse.

While the special procedure only applies to undefended divorces, it is difficult—and consequently rare—for a divorce to be defended. To defend a

---

[84] [1988] 2 F.L.R. 365; and see for another example, *Richards v Richards* [1972] 1 W.L.R. 1073.

[85] Matrimonial Causes Act 1973 s.1(4). In *Cotterell v Cotterell* (1998) 3 F.C.R. 199, the Court of Appeal held that the court should always first consider whether the marriage has irretrievably broken down and only then go on to consider what it regarded as the subsidiary question of whether one of the "facts" had been made out, but this decision stands on its own and is difficult to reconcile with the language of the statute.

[86] J. Burgoyne, R. Ormrod and M. Richards, *Divorce Matters* (Harmondsworth: Penguin, 1987), pp.57–58.

[87] The legislation gave the court power to adjourn the proceedings to enable reconciliation attempts to be made: Matrimonial Causes Act 1973 s.6(2).

[88] The prescribed form merely asks the respondent whether the adultery was admitted, and an affirmative answer constituted sufficient proof: *Report of the Matrimonial Causes Procedure Committee* (Chairman: the Hon. Mrs Justice Booth DBE) (1985), para.2.15. This contrasts sharply with law's traditional insistence that adultery is a serious matrimonial offence that requires a high standard or proof: see, for example, *Bastable v Bastable* [1968] 1 W.L.R. 1684.

divorce is always expensive[89] and sometimes counter-productive.[90] Moreover, there is little point in defending a divorce since the process is unlikely to bring about a reconciliation with the other spouse[91] or to prevent the eventual grant of a divorce, and the grant of a divorce to one spouse rather than another now has no impact on the determination of financial provision or the perceived suitability of either parent to care for any children of the marriage.[92] Most solicitors would therefore discourage a client from seeking to defend a petition.[93] As a result of such considerations, the special procedure is used by over 99 per cent of divorcing couples.

In this way, the special procedure transformed the whole basis of divorce almost without anyone noticing the fact. The decision as to whether a marriage should be ended is now essentially an administrative act, dependent solely on the filing of the appropriate forms correctly completed. In outward form, English law still attempts to emphasise the institutional solemnity of marriage by insisting that it can be ended only by a judicial pronouncement, but the reality is that most of the procedural steps on the path to the grant of a decree have become administrative and automatic, albeit complex.

C. Judicial interpretation of the five "facts"

10–017 Between 1971 (when the Divorce Reform Act 1969 came into force) and 1977 (when the "special procedure" was made available in virtually all undefended divorces), the courts gave a considerable amount of guidance on the interpretation of the statutory language describing the "facts" on the basis of which the inference of irretrievable breakdown would be drawn. As explained above, the use of the "special procedure" has, in practical terms, greatly reduced the value and relevance of this case law guidance. In the great majority of cases there will be no dispute between the parties,[94] and (although practice may to some extent differ from court to court) it seems that the courts do not usually seek to investigate statements made in a petition that is undefended. Nevertheless, no decree of divorce can be granted unless the court is satisfied that one of the "facts" has been established to its satisfaction,[95] and hence the practising lawyer still needs to have an understanding of the statutory provisions, if only so as to give appropriate advice to the client and to be able to ensure the relevant forms

---

[89] Public funding is not normally available simply to defend a divorce petition in cases in which the marriage appears to have broken down irretrievably.

[90] See, for example, *Hadjimilitis v Tsavliris* [2003] 1 F.L.R. 81.

[91] Indeed, the *Report of the Matrimonial Causes Procedure Committee* noted that the "court itself discourages defended divorce not only because of the futility of trying a contention by one party that the marriage has not broken down despite the other party's contention that it has, but also because of the emotional and financial demands that it makes upon the parties themselves and the possible harmful consequences for the children of the family" (para.2.16).

[92] See further Chs 13 and 18.

[93] G. Davis and M. Murch, *Grounds for Divorce* (Oxford: Clarendon Press, 1988), Ch.7.

[94] Indeed, the *Code of Practice* issued by Resolution (formerly the Solicitors' Family Law Association) suggests that it is good practice to consider whether the "facts" to be alleged should be agreed in advance in order to minimise any misunderstandings: A. Greensmith (ed.), *Resolution Family Law Handbook* (London: The Law Society, 2007); App.1, para.16.

[95] See, for example, *Buffery v Buffery* [1988] 2 F.L.R. 365.

have been completed correctly. Moreover, the law student may find that judicial interpretation of the "facts" remains important in the examination room. For these reasons, a brief[96] account follows.

i. Adultery and the intolerability of further cohabitation

The petitioner must show both: (i) that the respondent has in fact committed adultery; and (ii) that the petitioner finds it intolerable to live with the respondent.   **10–018**

(1) The fact of the respondent's adultery   **10–019**

Adultery involves voluntary or consensual sexual intercourse between a married person and a person (whether married or unmarried) of the opposite sex[97] not being the other's spouse. In reality, the court has no way of investigating whether uncontested allegations of adultery are true. Although the courts have emphasised the overriding importance of honesty and the fundamental seriousness of the divorce process, a petition based on the adultery "fact" will almost invariably, if undefended, lead to a speedy divorce by consent.[98]

(2) The petitioner finds it intolerable to live with the respondent   **10–020**

The policy of the Divorce Reform Act was that adultery should be relevant only insofar as it was a symptom of marital breakdown, and the Act was influenced by the philosophy that adultery should:

> "not in itself ... be regarded as demonstrating breakdown unless the petitioner can in addition satisfy the court that the act of adultery is so offensive and deeply wounding to him or her that any further married life with the respondent is unthinkable."[99]

However, the legislation does not require the petitioner to allege that he or she finds it intolerable to live with the respondent *because of* the latter's adultery, and it accordingly fails to achieve that objective:

> In *Cleary v Cleary and Hutton*[100] the Court of Appeal held that the adultery fact can be established provided the petitioner genuinely finds it intolerable

---

[96] For a fuller account, reference may be made to the fifth edition of this book at pp.101–129, whilst a full citation of authorities will be found in the standard practitioner work, M. Everall et al. (eds) *Rayden & Jackson's Law and Practice in Divorce and Family Matters*, 18th edn (London: Lexis Nexis Butterworths, 2005).

[97] A sexual relationship with a person of the same sex does not constitute adultery, although it may constitute a fact from which breakdown may be inferred under s.1(2)(b): see further para.10–057 below.

[98] In 2006, 21% of husbands and 18% of wives relied on this ground: "Report: Divorces in England and Wales during 2006", Table 5.

[99] Lord Stow Hill, *Hansard*, HL Vol.303, col.296 (June 30, 1969).

[100] [1974] 1 W.L.R. 73.

to live with the respondent, even if the adultery has not played any significant part in the breakdown of the marriage.

The fact that there need be no link of this kind could lead to apparently bizarre results,[101] but the Court of Appeal's interpretation gives effect to the plain words of the statute.

(3) Six months living together a bar

10–021 If one spouse knows that the other has committed adultery but has continued thereafter to live with him or her for six months or more, a divorce petition cannot be based on that act of adultery.[102] Conversely, if they have lived together for *less* than six months, that fact is to be disregarded "in determining . . . whether the petitioner finds it intolerable to live with the respondent".[103] This was intended to make it clear that a couple could seek a reconciliation without running the risk that by living together for a short period the innocent party would be held to have forgiven the adultery and could thus no longer be held to find living with the respondent intolerable.

ii. Behaviour rendering further cohabitation unreasonable

10–022 This is the fact that is most commonly relied upon in divorce petitions, perhaps because of the wide spectrum of conduct it is capable of encompassing. Allegations range from the uncontestably serious (e.g. domestic violence) to the apparently trivial,[104] but the greater subjectivity of what is reasonable in this context means that petitions based on this fact are the most likely to be defended; for this reason, the case law discussing the interpretation of the "behaviour" fact cannot be regarded as entirely academic.

The court needs to be satisfied: first, that the respondent has behaved in a certain way; and secondly, that on the basis of such facts as are proved about the respondent's behaviour, the petitioner cannot reasonably be expected to live with him or her.[105]

(1) "Behaviour"

10–023 The Act requires that the respondent should have "behaved" in such a way that the petitioner cannot reasonably be expected to live with him or her, and it has been said that:

---

[101] In *Roper v Roper* [1972] 1 W.L.R. 1314 at 1317, Faulks J. suggested that a wife might even divorce a husband who had committed a single act of adultery because he blew his nose more than she liked.

[102] Matrimonial Causes Act 1973 s.2(1).

[103] Matrimonial Causes Act 1973 s.2(2).

[104] See, for example, *Livingstone-Stallard v Livingstone-Stallard* [1974] Fam. 47, in which the court had to consider the parties' methods of washing their underwear.

[105] *Andrews v Andrews* [1974] 3 All E.R. 643 at 644.

"[B]ehaviour is something more than a mere state of affairs or a state of mind . . . [it] is action or conduct by the one which affects the other."[106]

Thus, if an accident or illness rendered a spouse comatose and totally passive (a "cabbage existence"), it could be that a petitioner would be unable to rely on the behaviour "fact".[107]

Yet negative or passive conduct can still constitute "behaviour". For example:

> In *Carter-Fea v Carter-Fea*[108] the husband was unable to manage his financial affairs. The wife suffered much stress and unhappiness and ultimately decided that she could not go on living in a world of fantasy with "unpaid bills, bailiffs at the door, and second mortgages". She was held to be entitled to a decree.

However, it should be noted that the abbreviation "unreasonable behaviour" (although convenient) is somewhat misleading: as Eekelaar has put it, it "is not the behaviour that needs to be unreasonable, but the expectation of cohabitation".[109]

(2) Test objective, but reasonableness judged through eyes of the parties

The test is objective insofar as the question to be answered is: "can the petitioner **10–024** 'reasonably be expected' to live with the respondent?", but the court must consider the particular parties to the suit before it, not "ordinary reasonable spouses". The question is whether this particular petitioner can live with this particular respondent, taking into account the faults and attributes of each.[110] It seems to follow that mere incompatibility is not sufficient,[111] and that if the parties share the same faults or foibles, it would not be unreasonable to expect them to continue living together.[112]

The test is therefore what could reasonably be expected of these parties, but the determination of what is "reasonable" in this context would seem to require the making of value judgments about the nature of marriage and about the obligations and standards of behaviour implicit in the marriage contract.[113] The

---

[106] *Katz v Katz* [1972] 1 W.L.R. 955 at p.960, *per* Sir George Baker P.
[107] So held in *Smith v Smith* (1973) 118 S.J. 184 (wife suffering from Alzheimer's disease), not followed in *Thurlow v Thurlow* [1976] Fam. 32 insofar as it decided that involuntary behaviour caused by disease of the mind could not constitute behaviour for the present purpose.
[108] [1987] Fam. Law 130.
[109] [1975] A.S.C.L. 188.
[110] *Ash v Ash* [1972] Fam. 135, *per* Bagnall J. at 140.
[111] *Pheasant v Pheasant* [1972] Fam. 202.
[112] *Ash v Ash* [1972] Fam. 135. It is unlikely, however, that a modern court would endorse the suggestion of the judge in that case that a violent petitioner could be expected to live with a violent respondent, given the wealth of evidence of the asymmetry of violence between men and women.
[113] The courts (e.g. in *O'Neill v O'Neill* [1975] 1 W.L.R. 1118) have deprecated reference to the wording of the marriage service in the Book of Common Prayer ("for better or for worse, in sickness and in health"), but it is not clear that the test of "reasonableness" can be applied without some view as to the nature of the mutual commitment implied in marriage.

Court of Appeal has favoured an approach that puts the issue in terms of a direction to a jury[114]:

> "Would any right-thinking person come to the conclusion that this husband has behaved in such a way that his wife cannot reasonably be expected to live with him, taking into account the whole of the circumstances and the characters and personalities of the parties?"

However, this is not always easy to answer, especially where the behaviour in question is attributable to mental or physical illness. On the one hand, there are certainly cases in which it is clear that, whatever the excuse, the petitioner cannot reasonably be expected to live with the other. For example:

> In *White v White*[115] the husband was, by his own account, intending to kill himself by jumping from a balcony. However, he then believed that he had heard a message from God telling him to kill his wife instead. He told the wife that he would obtain a shotgun, use it to blow her head off and then play football with the severed head. On such facts a decree would be granted, and it would be immaterial that the husband was affected by mental illness to such an extent as not to be responsible for his actions.

10–025 On the other hand, some cases may be more difficult. For example:

> In *Thurlow v Thurlow*[116] a husband was granted a decree against his epileptic and bed-ridden wife. The court declared that it would take full account of the obligations of the married life, including "the normal duty to accept and share the burdens imposed upon the family as a result of the mental or physical ill-health of one member", but the underlying question remains: "can the petitioner reasonably be expected to go on living with the respondent?"

In practice, the fact that the health of the petitioner or that of the family as a whole is likely to suffer is a powerful factor influencing the court in favour of granting a decree. Many of the most obvious difficulties arise in cases of mental illness, but similar considerations would presumably apply if the respondent's behaviour was attributable to physical illness or disability.

(3) Relevance of continued cohabitation
10–026 Does the fact that the petitioner has, in fact, gone on living in the same household as the respondent mean that the petitioner can be expected to continue to do so? The Act contains a provision[117] intended to facilitate reconciliation by enabling the parties to live together for a short period without losing the right to seek

[114] *O'Neill v O'Neill* [1975] 1 W.L.R. 1118.
[115] [1983] Fam. 54; and see also *Katz v Katz* [1972] 1 W.L.R. 955.
[116] [1976] Fam. 32.
[117] Matrimonial Causes Act 1973 s.2(3).

divorce if the attempt is unsuccessful: in deciding whether the petitioner can reasonably be expected to live with the respondent, the court must disregard cohabitation for up to six months after the last incident. Longer periods do not constitute an absolute bar,[118] but the longer the period the more likely it is that the court will draw the inference that the petitioner could reasonably be expected to put up with the respondent's behaviour. However, the petitioner is entitled to refute any such inference; in *Bradley v Bradley*[119] (where the wife was still living in a four-bedroomed council house with the husband and seven children) the Court of Appeal held that she should be allowed to prove that it would be unreasonable to expect her to go on doing so.

iii. Desertion

For many years, the courts, in administering a fault-based divorce law, adopted **10–027** a restrictive attitude to the concept of desertion for fear that too wide a definition would lead to divorce by consent after a period of separation. The effect of the courts' struggles with changing policy considerations over the years was to introduce what Lord Diplock called "metaphysical niceties"[120] into the law; it is virtually impossible to make clear statements of principle without over-simplification.[121]

Although the Divorce Reform Act retained desertion as one of the facts from which the court will infer the irretrievable breakdown of the marriage, it is rarely the basis for a divorce petition.[122] If a couple have lived apart for two years, and both consent to a divorce, this is sufficient to establish a "fact" evidencing breakdown; if they have lived apart for five years, that is of itself a "fact".[123] For these reasons desertion can only be relevant in exceptional cases, for example: where the couple have lived apart for at least two (but not five) years and the respondent is unwilling to agree to a divorce; and where they have lived apart for five years but the petitioner fears that the grant of a decree based on that fact might be opposed on one of the "hardship" grounds available in such cases.[124] Against this background it seems justifiable to give only the briefest explanation of the essence of desertion.

The main elements of desertion are: (i) the fact of separation; and (ii) the intention to desert.

---

[118] Cf. s.2(1) in relation to the adultery "fact": above, para.10–021.

[119] [1973] 1 W.L.R. 1291.

[120] *Hall v Hall* [1962] 1 W.L.R. 1246 at 1254.

[121] One complication that can now be ignored is the doctrine of constructive desertion (i.e. where one party drives the other out, it is that party who is guilty of "constructively" deserting the other). Where (as is usually the case) it is the behaviour of the party concerned that is said to have made continuance of the common life intolerable, the "behaviour" fact discussed above will almost always be available as the foundation for a divorce petition. In cases where one party simply orders the other to leave, it has been held that the case must be dealt with as one of desertion (see *Morgan v Morgan* (1973) 117 S.J. 223).

[122] In no year since 1973 for which a breakdown of the facts relied on is available has the proportion of desertion petitions exceeded 5% of the total. In 2006 only 499 of the 132,418 divorces granted were based on desertion: "Report: Divorces in England and Wales during 2006", Table 5.

[123] Matrimonial Causes Act 1973 s.1(2)(d) and s.1(2)(e).

[124] Matrimonial Causes Act 1973 s.10(2): see below, para.10–042.

(1) The fact of separation

10–028   The requisite factual separation can be established even if the couple remain under the same roof. The question is whether there is one household or two. If there is still any sharing (however minimal) of a common life (e.g. sharing a common living room or taking meals together), the parties are not, for this purpose, separated:

> In *Le Brocq v Le Brocq*[125] the wife excluded her husband from the matrimonial bedroom by putting a bolt on the inside of the door. There was no communication between them save that which was unavoidable, but the wife continued to cook the husband's meals and he paid her a weekly sum for housekeeping. The court held that the necessary factual separation had not been established: there was, as Harman L.J. put it, "separation of bedrooms, separation of hearts, separation of speaking: but one household was carried on."

(2) The mental element: the intention to desert

10–029   The greatest difficulty in deciding whether a person is in desertion lies in the mental element: the intention to desert. What is required is an intention (usually, of course, inferred from the words and conduct of the spouse alleged to be in desertion) to bring the matrimonial union permanently to an end. By no means will every separation constitute desertion, since: (i) the separation may be consensual; (ii) there may be good cause for the separation (e.g. where a mentally ill husband terrified the children or where the husband has behaved badly to the wife); or (iii) the respondent may lack the mental capacity necessary to form the intention to desert.

10–030   **(a) Separation consensual.** If and so long as[126] both parties consent to a separation, there can be no desertion. Whether or not there is such consent is a question of fact.[127] Consent may also be implied,[128] but the court makes allowance for the emotional realities of the situation: a wife who told her husband, "Go if you like, and when you are sick of her, come back to me", was not giving a consent to his living apart from her,[129] and the fact that one spouse is glad that the other has gone does not mean that he or she has consented to the separation.

10–031   **(b) Good cause for separation.** The respondent may be justified in leaving the petitioner against the latter's will, either by necessity or because of the petitioner's behaviour. Such cases could perhaps more sensibly be described as

---

[125] [1964] 1 W.L.R. 1085.
[126] *Nutley v Nutley* [1970] 1 W.L.R. 217.
[127] *Bosley v Bosley* [1958] 1 W.L.R. 645.
[128] As in *Joseph v Joseph* [1953] 1 W.L.R. 1182, where the wife obtained a *get* (a Jewish divorce). Although this was ineffective in English law to dissolve her marriage, the fact that she had done so showed that she had no objection to the husband living apart from her.
[129] *Haviland v Haviland* (1863) 32 L.J.P.M. & A. 65.

cases of "reasonable excuse" (e.g. the reason for the separation may be that one of the spouses is in prison, or separation may be justified in the interests of the children's mental health).[130] In other cases the other spouse's behaviour is the justification for leaving. The court held that only "grave and weighty" behaviour would suffice for this purpose.[131]

(c) Mental incapacity. Mental illness may prevent the formation of the intention   **10–032**
to desert.[132] If, by reason of insanity, one spouse has deluded beliefs about the conduct of the other, the rights of the parties in relation to the charge of desertion are to be adjudicated on as if that belief were true. For example:

> In *Perry v Perry*[133] the wife believed that her husband was trying to murder her. She left him. If the deluded belief had been true she would have been justified in doing so. Hence she was not in desertion.

(3) The requirement that desertion be for a continuous period of two years
Desertion only constitutes the "fact" from which the court may infer that the   **10–033**
marriage has irretrievably broken down if it has lasted for a continuous period of two years immediately preceding the presentation of the petition.[134] It is therefore an inchoate offence, and may be terminated if the parties resume cohabitation or if the necessary mental element is ended.[135] However, the law provides that the parties are allowed to resume living together for as long as six months without prejudicing their right to rely on this fact,[136] but the time they have spent together has to be deducted in calculating the overall period. For example, if H deserted W on January 1, 2006, W could not petition on January 1, 2008 if they had lived together from Christmas Eve 2006 until May 1, 2007, but would have to wait until May 2008.

---

[130] See, for example, *G v G* [1964] P. 133: the court held that where the husband's behaviour (a symptom of mental illness) terrified the children, the wife was justified in not allowing him into the matrimonial home, notwithstanding the fact that he was no longer morally responsible for his actions.
[131] A husband's conduct in taking a second wife has been held to justify his first wife in leaving him, notwithstanding the fact that he was legally entitled to contract such a marriage: *Quoraishi v Quoraishi* [1985] F.L.R. 780.
[132] At common law, the onset of mental illness would terminate desertion if the person concerned had ceased to be capable of forming the necessary intention. Statute now provides that the court may treat desertion as having continued if the evidence would have led it to infer that the desertion would in fact have continued: Matrimonial Causes Act 1973 ss.2(4), 17(1). But this provision does not affect the need to show that there was an intention to desert at the start of the period.
[133] [1964] 1 W.L.R. 91.
[134] Matrimonial Causes Act 1973 s.1(2)(c).
[135] In the days of the matrimonial offence of divorce, it was common for lawyers to draft "bona fide" offers to return, in an attempt to demonstrate that the client no longer had the necessary intention to desert. If the parties remained factually separated after such an offer had been unreasonably refused, the courts might well hold that the person refusing to live with his spouse had become guilty of desertion.
[136] Matrimonial Causes Act 1973 s.2(5).

iv. Living apart

10–034   The two remaining "facts" are similar and can best be dealt with together. The first[137] is that the parties to the marriage have lived apart for a continuous period of at least two years immediately preceding the presentation of the petition, and the respondent consents to a decree being granted. The second[138] is that the parties to the marriage have lived apart for a continuous period of at least five years immediately preceding the presentation of the petition.

These provisions permit divorce by consent after a period of separation, and divorce by repudiation after a longer period of separation; they best justify the claim that the law is now based on the irretrievable breakdown of marriage. "Separation", it has been said,[139] "is undoubtedly the best evidence of breakdown, and the passing of time, the most reliable indication that it is irretrievable".

(1) Computing the period

10–035   In relation to both "living apart" facts, the relevant period must have been completed when the petition is filed.[140] Moreover, the separation must have been for a period immediately preceding the presentation of the petition.

It is also necessary that the separation be "continuous", but by this the Act does not require an unbroken period of separation. To encourage reconciliation, no account is to be taken of any period or periods (not exceeding six months in all) during which the parties resumed living with each other. However, no period during which the parties lived with each other is to count as part of the period for which they lived apart. It has been pointed out[141] that in cases based on the two year period,[142] the spouses could spend up to 20 per cent of their time together (i.e. 6 months in a period of 30 months) without interrupting the continuity of separation.

(2) Meaning of "living apart"

10–036   It is the apparently simple requirement that the parties should have "lived apart" for the relevant period that requires most explanation. This is, partly at least, because the courts have held that living apart involves both: (i) a physical and (ii) a mental element.

10–037   **(a) physical separation—two households, not two houses.** In the typical case, the parties will have established separate households in different places, and there will be no doubt that they are physically "living apart", but even if they continue to live under the same roof it may still be possible to establish separation: the

---

[137] Matrimonial Causes Act 1973 s.1(2)(d).
[138] Matrimonial Causes Act 1973 s.1(2)(e).
[139] *Pheasant v Pheasant* [1972] Fam. 202 at 207, *per* Ormrod J.
[140] A petition filed on the second or fifth anniversary of the commencement of separation will fail; the period has not been completed until the end of that day: *Warr v Warr* [1975] Fam. 25.
[141] *Santos v Santos* [1972] Fam. 247 at 262.
[142] The same rule applies in petitions based on the five-year period; but the effect is less dramatic.

statute provides that the parties are living apart unless they are "living with each other in the same household",[143] and this is usually regarded as establishing for this "fact" the same test as was ultimately accepted for the "factum" of desertion under pre-1970 law.[144] The question therefore becomes: "was there still any kind of community of life between the parties?" The practical test applied in cases where the parties are still living under the same roof is usually whether there is any sharing of domestic life. Thus, if a husband shuts himself up in one or two rooms of the house and ceases to have anything to do with the wife, there will be a sufficient separation of households.[145] If, however, the estranged parties still share the same living room and eat at the same table[146] (or perhaps watch television together), they are not to be regarded as living apart. They are still living in the same household, even if "they are living what only the most determined pessimist could regard as a normal married life".[147] For example:

> In *Mouncer v Mouncer*[148] the parties had for some time been on bad terms—to the extent that the wife petitioned for divorce on the ground of cruelty in 1969. Although that divorce suit did not go ahead, and the parties continued to live under the same roof, relations between them were strained and they occupied separate bedrooms. However, they usually took their meals together, and the wife did most of the household cleaning. In 1971 the husband left the house and petitioned for divorce. Although the wife consented to divorce, the court held that the "fact" of living apart for two years had not been made out. There had been a single household between 1969 and 1971 and it made no difference to the result that the parties had acted "from the wholly admirable motive of caring properly for their children".

However, there may be exceptional cases in which the parties live under the same roof and the one provides services for the other in some capacity other than that of a spouse. For example:

> In *Fuller v Fuller*[149] husband and wife separated in 1964. The wife began to cohabit with another man. In 1968 the husband had a serious heart attack. The medical advice was that he could not live on his own again. He therefore moved into the house in which the wife was living with her partner. The husband lived as a lodger, sleeping in a back bedroom, and was provided with food and laundry by the wife in return for a weekly payment. The Court of Appeal held that the parties were not living with each other in the same household. "Living with each other" connoted something more

---

[143] Matrimonial Causes Act 1973 s.2(6).
[144] *Santos v Santos* [1972] Fam. 247 at 262; *Mouncer v Mouncer* [1972] 1 W.L.R. 321 at 323.
[145] *Hopes v Hopes* [1949] P. 227 at 235.
[146] *Hopes v Hopes* [1949] P. 227 at 235.
[147] J.L. Barton (1970) 86 L.Q.R. 348 at 350.
[148] [1972] 1 W.L.R. 321, approved in *Fuller v Fuller* [1973] 1 W.L.R. 730.
[149] [1973] 1 W.L.R. 730.

than living in the same household; the parties must also be living with each other as husband and wife, rather than as lodger and landlady.

10–038   **(b) the mental element.** In *Santos v Santos* the Court of Appeal[150] held that living apart only starts when at least one party recognises that the marriage is at an end:

> "[L]iving apart does not begin to exist until that day on which, if the spouse in question were compellingly asked to define his or her attitude to cohabitation, he (or she) would express an attitude averse to it. Until this state is reached, cohabitation is not . . . broken. When it is reached, living apart begins."[151]

However, strangely, the Court also held that it was not necessary for the one spouse to communicate the belief that the marriage was at an end to the other. If applied strictly, these rules would have curious consequences:

> H, with W's agreement, took up employment abroad in 2006. He has now met another woman whom he wishes to marry. W recognises that the marriage has irretrievably broken down, and is prepared to consent to a divorce, but she cannot petition under s.1(2)(d) until the end of two years from the date when H told her that he believed the marriage had broken down and that he wished to remarry. (Of course, if H admits adultery, she will be able to petition under s.1(2)(a).)

Or:

> H has been a patient in a mental hospital for over 10 years. W decided more than five years ago that she would never resume married life with H, but has not told him because she knew that to do so would upset him, and also because she did not wish to remarry. However, she has now met someone she does wish to marry, and there is no hope of H ever recovering sufficiently to leave hospital. W can immediately petition for divorce under s.1(2)(e) although H has had no ground to suspect that the marriage was in difficulties.

10–039   It is therefore not surprising that the *Santos* decision was controversial.[152] In practice, the adoption of the "special procedure"[153] has undermined the assumption (on which the Court of Appeal's reasoning was founded) that consensual divorces based on separation require, and will receive, close judicial scrutiny. It is true that the Rules[154] require a petitioner to state the date when petitioner and respondent separated, to give "briefly the reason or main reason

---

[150] [1972] Fam. 247; see 88 L.Q.R. 328 (P.M. Bromley).
[151] *Sullivan v Sullivan* [1958] N.Z.L.R. 912 at 924, *per* Turner J.
[152] The arguments are summarised in the fifth edition of this work at pp.126–127.
[153] See above, para.10–010.
[154] Family Proceedings Rules 1991 (SI 1991/1247), r.2.24(3), App.1, Form M7(e).

for the separation" and to state "the date when and the circumstances in which you came to the conclusion that the marriage was in fact at an end", and the District Judge will need to be satisfied that the documentation has been correctly completed. However, it is only in exceptional cases that there will be an opportunity for any probing of that evidence to take place; accordingly, in practice, the only result of the *Santos* decision seems to be to complicate the law. The worst consequence of the *Santos* decision may therefore be that petitioners without access to legal advice, not realising the importance of stating that they had come to the conclusion that the marriage was over more than two or five years ago, will be denied for a time the divorce that a law truly based on irretrievable breakdown would have allowed them.

(3) Differences between two- and five-year periods
There are two main differences between these two "facts". First, in two-year **10–040** cases the respondent must agree to the grant of the decree. Secondly, where the petition is founded solely on five years living apart, the court has a statutory power[155] to refuse a decree if to do so would cause grave financial or other hardship to the respondent.

(a) Respondent's consent to divorce. The Act requires a positive consent by the **10–041** respondent to the grant of a decree, and a mere failure to object is insufficient. Rules of Court seek to ensure that the respondent is given information necessary to understand the consequences (e.g. relating to possible loss of pension and succession rights) of consenting to the grant of a decree.[156] The respondent will usually consent by answering in the affirmative the appropriate question in the form of acknowledgment of service, but until the pronouncement of decree nisi, the respondent has an absolute right, for any or no reason, to withdraw any consent previously given.[157] Hence, consent may be given conditionally (e.g. on terms that the petitioner will not seek an order for costs against the respondent[158]), but even after decree nisi, the court may rescind the decree if it is satisfied that "the petitioner misled the respondent (whether intentionally or unintentionally) about any matter which the respondent took into account in deciding to give his consent".[159] The question appears to be entirely subjective: "did this particular respondent in fact take the matter into account (not, would a reasonable respondent have done so)?" However, the petitioner must have misled the respondent; the fact that the respondent was mistaken is not sufficient to justify recission.

(b) Refusal of decree in cases of grave financial or other hardship, etc. In the **10–042** discussions leading up to the enactment of the Divorce Reform Act 1969, a great

---

[155] Matrimonial Causes Act 1973 s.5.
[156] Matrimonial Causes Act 1973 s.2(7); Family Proceedings Rules 1991 (SI 1991/1247), App.1 (Notice of Proceedings; Notes on Questions).
[157] *Beales v Beales* [1972] Fam. 210 at 221–222.
[158] *Beales v Beales* [1972] Fam. 210 at 224.
[159] Matrimonial Causes Act 1973 s.10(1).

Divorce and Dissolution

deal of anxiety was expressed about the plight of the "innocent" wife (that is to say, a wife who could not have been divorced under the matrimonial offence doctrine), and it was thought necessary to provide special protection for spouses threatened with divorce against their will.

The negotiations between the Law Commission and the Archbishop's group resulted in a proposal that the court be required to refuse a decree if satisfied that, having regard to the conduct and interests of the parties, the interest of the children and other persons affected, it would be wrong to dissolve the marriage, notwithstanding the public interest in dissolving marriages that have irretrievably broken down. However, the corresponding provisions of the Act[160] are far more restrictively drafted than the terms of the agreement would suggest, and the legislation has in turn been given a restrictive interpretation by the courts. There are three elements that must be satisfied: first, the hardship (whether financial or otherwise) must be "grave"; secondly that hardship must result from the dissolution of the marriage (rather than from the fact that it has broken down); and thirdly, it must be "in all the circumstances . . . wrong" to dissolve the marriage.[161]

10–043 *(i) "Grave hardship".* The word "grave" has its ordinary meaning of "important or very serious". It is not sufficient to show that a spouse will lose something, and a spouse is not entitled to expect to be compensated pound-for-pound for everything that he or she will lose in consequence of the divorce. This can be illustrated from two cases with contrasting facts:

> In *Reiterbund v Reiterbund*[162] a 52-year-old wife would lose her entitlement to the state widow's pension if her 54-year-old husband died before she reached the age of 60, but the risk of her husband dying in the next eight years was not great, and even if he did, Mrs Reiterbund would receive exactly the same income from means-tested benefits as she would have done from a state widow's pension. The court therefore rejected the defence and granted a decree.
>
> In *Archer v Archer*[163] a 55-year-old consultant orthopaedic surgeon had a large income but few substantial capital assets. His 53-year-old wife claimed that she would suffer grave hardship because if (as was statistically probable) he pre-deceased her, the £18,000 maintenance order against him would come to an end. However, the wife had her own investments amounting to nearly £300,000, and she owned a house worth more than £200,000. The Court of Appeal agreed that the loss of the maintenance

---

[160] Matrimonial Causes Act 1973 s.5.

[161] There is an extensive body of case law on the interpretation of Matrimonial Causes Act 1973 s.5. Although the threat of invoking the defence may be used in negotiating favourable financial settlements with a petitioner anxious to remarry, applications to the court are now rare, and discussion has been abbreviated. For a full discussion, reference should be made to *Rayden & Jackson's Law and Practice in Divorce and Family Matters*, whilst much of the case law is cited in the fifth edition of this book at pp.129–138.

[162] [1975] Fam. 99.

[163] [1999] 1 F.L.R. 327.

payments could not, in the circumstances, be regarded as "grave" hardship.

Although it is, in theory, open to a respondent to establish grave hardship that is not financial hardship, there has been no reported case in which such a defence has succeeded. In particular, the courts have taken a robust approach to pleas based on religious belief. It is not enough for the respondent to show that divorce is contrary to his or her religion and that divorce will cause unhappiness and a sense of shame; there must be evidence of some specific hardship flowing from the divorce:

> In *Banik v Banik*[164] a Hindu wife's pleadings that she would be ostracised if divorced were held to establish a prima facie case of grave hardship, but the evidence was eventually held not to substantiate her claim, and a decree was granted.[165]

(ii) The hardship must result from the divorce, not from the breakdown. The **10–044** respondent must prove that her position as a divorced spouse is worse than it would be as a separated spouse. This is difficult to do. It is, for example, true that many divorced people suffer serious financial problems, but the court has wide powers to make financial orders on divorce, and the problems usually stem from the fact that the marriage has broken down and that there is insufficient money to keep two households, rather than from the fact that the marriage has been legally dissolved by divorce. Exceptionally, the "hardship" defence was sometimes successful where the wife could show that she would lose a substantial pension that would have been payable to her as the husband's widow,[166] but it seems that the powers which the court now has (to make pension sharing orders on divorce) will reduce the number of cases in which inability to deal with pension assets causes hardship.[167]

(iii) "Wrong in all the circumstances." If, but only if, the court is satisfied that **10–045** grave financial or other hardship would be caused by a divorce, it will proceed to the next stage and consider whether it would "in all the circumstances"[168] be wrong to dissolve the marriage. This requires the court to put the hardship that divorce would cause the respondent into the scales against the policy embodied in the modern divorce law (which "aims, in all other than exceptional circumstances, to crush the empty shells of dead marriages"[169]). Case law suggests the balance will often be in favour of termination. There have been very few cases in which a decree has been refused; *Julian v Julian*[170] is one such:

---

[164] [1973] 1 W.L.R. 860.
[165] *Banik v Banik (No.2)* (1973) 117 S.J. 874.
[166] See also *Le Marchant v Le Marchant* [1977] 1 W.L.R. 559.
[167] See para.13–119.
[168] The Act specifically directs attention to the "conduct of the parties to the marriage and the interests of those parties and of any children or other persons concerned".
[169] *Reiterbund v Reiterbund* [1974] 1 W.L.R. 788 at 798, *per* Finer J.
[170] (1972) 116 S.J. 763.

The husband was 61 and the wife 58. Neither was in good health. The wife was receiving periodical payments from the husband (which would cease if the husband predeceased her) and the result of a divorce would be that the wife would lose her right to a police widow's pension, leaving her with only a very small total income. The decision that it would be wrong to grant a divorce and thus (as the law then stood) deprive her of the pension was largely based on the belief that it was not particularly hard on the ailing husband to deprive him of the chance to remarry.

(4) Other protection for respondents in separation cases

10–046 The Act contains a complex provision[171] that is intended to secure the financial position of a spouse who is divorced on either of the two "living apart" facts. A respondent may apply to the court after the granting of a decree nisi for consideration of his or her financial position after the divorce. In such a case, the court must not make the decree absolute unless it is satisfied that the financial arrangements are "reasonable and fair" or "the best that can be made in the circumstances". This provision was originally enacted when the court had less extensive financial powers than it now enjoys, and it is today rarely invoked. However, there may be cases in which it is desirable for the court to ensure that all appropriate matters have been properly dealt with before the marriage is finally terminated. For example:

> In *Garcia v Garcia*[172] the wife alleged that her husband had failed to make the stipulated payments under a Spanish maintenance agreement. The court held that it had power to refuse to make absolute the decree nisi granted to the husband based on five years living apart.

V. CRITICISMS AND REFORM INITIATIVES

A. Criticisms of the current law

10–047 Although the reformed divorce law introduced by the Divorce Reform Act 1969 unquestionably allowed a large number of broken marriages to be legally terminated, it soon began to be questioned whether the Act had really achieved the objectives outlined by the Law Commission in 1966.[173] Some were concerned about the continued increase in the divorce rate, and suggested that the 1969 legislation (and the "special procedure" used for processing divorce petitions) had made divorce "too easy". Was the law doing all that could be done to identify savable marriages and to facilitate the making of attempts to reconcile those whose marriages were in difficulty? From a different perspective, there was concern that—in spite of the optimism expressed by reformers in the 1960s—

[171] Matrimonial Causes Act 1973 s.10(2).
[172] [1992] 1 F.L.R. 256.
[173] *Field of Choice*, para.15: see above.

bitterness, distress and humiliation refused to go away. Why should someone who did not want a divorce, and believed that the marriage had broken down because of the other spouse's behaviour, have to be told that there was no point in seeking to resist divorce, perhaps founded on a petition alleging that it was the respondent who had been guilty of behaviour such that the petitioner could not reasonably be expected to go on living with him? What was the point of effectively depriving the parties of the right to have issues of responsibility adjudicated by a court when it still remained possible to consume so much time, money and emotional energy in deciding on the financial and other consequences of the breakdown?

B. The recommended reform

Would-be reformers therefore faced a difficult challenge: to remove the fault **10–048** element from the law[174] while encouraging couples to take time to reflect on whether their marriage had truly broken down. In 1990 the Law Commission[175] proposed that divorce should no longer require proof of one of the "facts" specified in the 1969 Divorce Reform Act; instead, breakdown would be inferred from the fact that a period of one year had elapsed since either party had formally signified their wish to divorce. This period was intended for consideration of the practical consequences that would result from a divorce and for reflection upon whether the breakdown in the marital relationship was irreparable; the Commission believed that the law should concentrate on bringing parties to an understanding of the practical reality of divorce: what it would be like "to live apart, to break up the common home, to finance two households where before there was only one, and to have or to lose day to day responsibility for the children which was previously shared",[176] and so on. The Commission also endorsed an increased role for mediation and counselling, suggesting that:

> "[I]t is by the provision of these services, to the people who want and need them, that the most harmful emotional, social and psychological effects of marital breakdown can best be avoided or mitigated."[177]

After further consultation,[178] the then Conservative Government accepted the main thrust of the Law Commission's proposals for divorce.[179] The Government was particularly enthusiastic about the potential role of mediation, seeing it as a means by which couples could resolve ancillary matters for themselves "with the

---

[174] The *Report of the Matrimonial Causes Procedure Committee* (Chairman: Mrs Justice Booth, D.B.E.) had concluded that the bitterness and unhappiness of divorcing couples was frequently exacerbated and prolonged by the fault element in divorce, particularly where the fact relied upon was behaviour, whether or not the suit was defended (para.2.10). See also Law Commission, *Facing the Future, A Discussion Paper on the Ground for Divorce* (Law Com. No.170 (1988)), paras 3.48–3.50.

[175] *The Ground for Divorce* (Law Com. No.192 (1990)).

[176] *The Ground for Divorce* (Law Com. No.192 (1990)), para.2.17.

[177] *The Ground for Divorce* (Law Com. No.192 (1990)), para.3.38.

[178] *Looking to the Future, Mediation and the Ground for Divorce* (Cm.2424 (1993)).

[179] *Looking to the Future, Mediation and the Ground for Divorce, the Government's Proposals* (Cm.2799 (1995)).

minimum involvement of lawyers and courts".[180] It was thought that this would minimise both hostility and cost within the divorce process.

The Family Law Bill was introduced in November 1995. The Bill did not have an easy passage through Parliament, in part because of the lack of enthusiasm of many (and opposition on the part of some) of the Government's own support-ers.[181] In order to save the Bill from defeat, the Government had to accept many amendments.[182] The result was that what had been an essentially simple and elegant legislative scheme became exceedingly complex.[183] Questions also arose regarding the best means of delivering certain key features of the new legislative scheme. As a result, although the Bill passed on to the statute book as the Family Law Act 1996, implementation of the new scheme was delayed in order for certain aspects to be piloted.

C. The scheme of the Family Law Act 1996

10–049   In order to understand the subsequent course of events, a brief outline of the requirements of the 1996 Act is necessary. The Act retained the general principle that the irretrievable breakdown of the marriage should be the only ground for divorce,[184] but such breakdown was to be inferred exclusively[185] from: (i) the lodging of a statement of marital breakdown with the court (which could only be done after attendance at an information meeting[186]); (ii) the expiration of a period after the making of the statement for "reflection and consideration"[187]; and (iii) the making of an application for a divorce order.[188] Under this scheme the facts from which breakdown could be inferred were objective and required no judicial evaluation (although the court retained the power in some circumstances to make an order preventing divorce if it was satisfied that dissolution of the marriage

---

[180] *Looking to the Future, Mediation and the Ground for Divorce* (Cm.2424 (1993)), para.7.6.

[181] 112 Conservative members voted against the Government in the crucial free vote in the House of Commons on the retention of fault-based divorce: *Official Report* (HC) April 24, 1996 Vol.276 col.543.

[182] 137 amendments were made to the Bill in the course of its passage through the House of Commons; and many amendments had already been made in the House of Lords. Some of the amendments reflected concern about the need to uphold the institution of marriage, in practice by making it more difficult to obtain a divorce. Others were intended to ensure that the possibility of reconciliation be fully explored by increased use of counselling and marriage support services. Yet others reflected concern that the interests of children should be given greater protection.

[183] The Labour Party's spokesman on the Bill in the House of Commons, Mr Paul Boateng, is said to have described it as a "dog's breakfast": *Law Society Gazette*, May 30, 1996, p.10.

[184] Family Law Act 1996 s.3(1)(a).

[185] Family Law Act 1996 s.5(1).

[186] Family Law Act 1996 s.3(1)(a); s.8. The Law Commission had suggested that the aim of ensuring that the parties were fully informed about the divorce process could be achieved by providing the spouses with a "comprehensive information pack": *The Ground for Divorce* (Law Com. No.192 (1990)), para.5.15. The Government preferred the idea of "information meetings", the form of which was to be determined by pilot schemes to be conducted before the legislation came into force.

[187] Family Law Act 1996 s.7(1), (2).

[188] Such application would have to show that the parties had complied with the Act's requirements that the parties' arrangements for the future in respect of children and financial matters had been resolved (s.3(1)(c); s.9), and be accompanied by a declaration that the applicant believed the marriage could not be saved (s.5(1)(d)).

would result in substantial financial or other hardship to a spouse or to a child of the family[189]).

In requiring the applicant to attend information meetings, and making a period of "reflection and consideration" mandatory, the Act sought to promote a remarkable collaboration between the legal process necessary to terminate the legal status of marriage, and various applied social work measures intended to minimise the damage done to children and adults by marital breakdown and its consequences. The Act itself opened with a set of general principles stating that the institution of marriage was to be supported; that couples were to be encouraged to take "all practicable steps" to save a marriage that might have broken down; and that if a marriage was brought to an end, this should be done with minimum distress to the parties and to the children affected, in a way designed to promote as good a continuing relationship between all those affected as possible and without costs being unreasonably incurred.[190]

How were these principles to be promoted? Support for the institution of marriage and encouragement to "save" particular marriages was to be given by making marriage support available,[191] particularly in seeking to promote prospects of reconciliation. It was anticipated that information about such services could be provided at the information meeting that would, under the new scheme, have to precede any formal steps. At the same time, minimising distress, promoting continuing relationships and minimising cost was to be achieved by promoting mediation.

D. Piloting the Family Law Act
In order to ascertain whether information meetings and mediation would achieve these objectives, two sets of pilot schemes were established, and research into each was commissioned from independent researchers.[192] The Lord Chancellor also established an Advisory Board on Family Law to provide independent advice on the implementation and operation of the Act.

        10–050

i. Mediation pilot schemes
In March 1997 the Government brought into force the provisions of Pt III of the Act ("Legal Aid for Mediation in Family Matters").[193] This enabled the Legal Aid Board to secure the provision of mediation in disputes relating to family matters, and it was provided that a person should not be granted legal aid for representation unless he or she had first attended a meeting with a mediator to determine whether mediation was suitable to the dispute, and, if so, "to help the

        10–051

---

[189] Family Law Act 1996 s.10.
[190] Family Law Act 1996 s.1. A final general principle stated that any risk to one of the parties to a marriage, and to any children, of violence from the other party should, so far as reasonably practicable, be removed or diminished: however, the mechanisms for protecting family members against such violence fall outside the law of divorce.
[191] Family Law Act 1996 s.22.
[192] The research into Information Meetings was conducted by the Centre for Family Studies at the University of Newcastle upon Tyne under the direction of Professor Janet Walker. The Mediation research (intended to assess aspects of the effectiveness of publicly funded mediation) was directed by Professor Gwynn Davis.
[193] Family Law Act 1996 (Commencement No.1) Order 1997 (SI 1997/1077).

[applicant] to decide" whether to apply for funding of mediation rather than legal representation.[194]

The research into the operation of publicly-funded mediation[195] demonstrated that the experience of people participating in mediation was on the whole positive, but it appears that many of those required to attend an "intake" meeting under the provisions set out above "seemed to accept that mediation was a good idea in principle" but "they were less sure that it would work in their case".[196] Only around 30 per cent of those attending an intake meeting as a precondition of obtaining public funding actually went on to mediation.[197] The Lord Chancellor's Advisory Board noted that it was difficult to assess the impact of mediation so long as the substantive law of divorce relies heavily on "fault-based facts", and that while mediation had a valuable part to play in the divorce process,[198] the Family Law Act "perhaps embodied unrealistic expectations" as to the extent to which mediation could properly "replace" legal services.

ii. Information meeting pilot schemes

10–052 Fourteen pilot information meetings were established,[199] but these schemes could not and did not replicate the conditions that would be experienced if the relevant provisions of the Act were implemented. This is because, under the Act, attendance would be obligatory; under the "pilot schemes", it was necessarily optional. However, the research report (covering 957 pages of single-spaced typescript[200]) was based on a "thorough and detailed evaluation" of the pilots and (in the judgment of the Lord Chancellor's Advisory Board[201]) provided an "impressive analysis". The report discussed many aspects of information giving and made it clear that "information was valued and appreciated by those attending" the meetings.[202] The research indicated that it was "unlikely that a rigidly structured information meeting would suit all circumstances and that people required a flexible format tailored to their personal needs".[203] The Research Team produced a new model for the information meeting that the Lord

---

[194] Family Law Act 1996 s.29. The provisions of Pt III of the Act were repealed by the Access to Justice Act 1999, but its effect is continued in the provisions of the Funding Code adopted by the Legal Services Commission.

[195] The final research report by Professor Gwynn Davis, *Monitoring Publicly Funded Family Mediation*, was published by the Legal Services Commission in December 2000. A summary was printed as Annex D to the *Fourth Annual Report* of the Advisory Board on Family Law, 2000/2001. A number of articles by Professor Davis and others summarise the findings and comment on relevant issues: see [2001] Fam. Law 110, 186, 265, 378.

[196] *Fourth Annual Report* of the Advisory Board on Family Law, 2000/2001, Annex D, para.6.2.

[197] J. Walker et al., *The Family Advice and Information Service: A Changing Role for Family Lawyers in England and Wales? Final Evaluation Report* (Newcastle: Newcastle Centre for Family Studies, 2007), p.14.

[198] *Fourth Annual Report*, para.3.34.

[199] *Fourth Annual Report*, Annex C, p.38.

[200] *Information Meetings and Associated Provisions within the Family Law Act 1996* (Lord Chancellor's Department, 2001).

[201] *Fourth Annual Report*, para.2.6.

[202] *Fourth Annual Report*, para.2.1.

[203] *Fourth Annual Report*, para.2.2

Chancellor's Advisory Board believed could, within the terms of the Act, "cope with the diversity of people's situations".[204]

E. The decision not to implement the Act

On the basis of the emerging research findings, the Advisory Board formed the　**10–053** view that there were sufficient grounds for believing that full implementation of the Act could and should proceed.[205] However, the then Lord Chancellor, Lord Irvine, first (in 1999) announced that implementation would be deferred, and then (in 2001) that the Government had decided not to proceed to implementation, and that Parliament would be invited to repeal the relevant sections of the Family Law Act once a suitable legislative opportunity arose.[206] Remarkably, no full explanation of the Government's decision has ever been given, but it has been suggested that the failure of couples to opt for mediation in preference to legal representation[207] on the scale apparently expected was significant, whilst the fact that many of those attending pilot information meetings chose a solicitor as their main path through divorce was manifestly not what the Government wished to hear.[208]

F. A different approach: FAINs and FAInS

The divorcing public's continuing preference for lawyers led to a new approach　**10–054** being conceived "[that] would place family lawyers at the centre of a more holistic service".[209] Family Advice and Information Networks, or FAINs, were intended to:

> "[F]acilitate the dissolution of broken relationships in ways which minimise distress to parents and children and which promote ongoing family relationships and co-operative parenting [and] provide tailored information and access to services that may assist in resolving disputes and/or assist those who may wish to consider saving or reconciling their relation-ship."[210]

It was envisaged that solicitors would not only take a more holistic approach to their clients' problems, but would also refer them on to other agencies better suited to dealing with specific problems.

This time the pilot schemes were preceded by a *pre*-pilot. Research into the operation of the scheme found that, insofar as solicitor-client interactions were concerned, it was perceived as involving "little more than a 'tweaking' of

---

[204] *Fourth Annual Report*, para.3.15.
[205] *Third Annual Report* of the Advisory Board on Family Law, 1999/2000, para.2.2.
[206] *Fourth Annual Report*, para.2.13.
[207] *Fourth Annual Report*, para.3.19.
[208] *Fourth Annual Report*, Annex C, p.42.
[209] J. Walker et al., *The Family Advice and Information Service*, p.14.
[210] Legal Services Commission, *Developing Family Advice and Information Services* (2002), para.2.1.

existing practice".[211] By contrast, referring clients on to other services was hampered by a lack of knowledge about what services might be available. As a result of these findings, the Legal Services Commission changed the name of the scheme to the Family Advice and Information Service, or FAInS, thereby "taking the emphasis away from the notion of networks and focusing more on the interaction between solicitors and their clients".[212]

The final evaluation report on the operation of FAInS in a number of pilot areas was published in 2007, and its findings largely echoed the verdict on the earlier pre-pilot. Fewer solicitors than expected had participated in the pilot schemes,[213] and among those who did there had been little change in practice. Some solicitors did adopt a slightly more client-centred approach[214] that paid more attention to clients' practical and emotional needs,[215] but they were no more likely to uncover non-legal problems,[216] or to refer clients on to agencies able to deal with such problems,[217] than they had been before participating in the scheme. Although most regarded collaboration with other agencies as a good idea in theory, they did not see it as their role to develop the network of contacts to achieve such collaboration.[218] Nor was there any evidence that their clients expected or wanted to be referred to other agencies by their solicitor,[219] regarding the latter's role as the provision of legal advice.[220] Finally, the researchers concluded that "at best", FAInS might be cost-neutral".[221]

G. Where next?

10–055 The decision not to implement the Family Law Act 1996 means that the substantive law of divorce in England and Wales remains as set out in the Matrimonial Causes Act 1973, and that the "special procedure", with all its well-substantiated imperfections, continues to govern the divorce process. While s.1 of the 1996 Act remains in force as a statement of the general principles adopted by Parliament as appropriate guides to the courts and others administering the divorce law, it has no legal substance as a part of the code of law governing divorce as a legal process.[222] Section 22, which deals with funding for marriage support, also remains in force, but in recent years the emphasis has shifted from

---

[211] Walker et al., *The Family Advice and Information Service*, p.24.
[212] Walker et al., *The Family Advice and Information Service*, p.25.
[213] Walker et al., *The Family Advice and Information Service*, pp.27, 271.
[214] Walker et al., *The Family Advice and Information Service*, pp.140, 147, 152, 157, 255.
[215] However, this did not tend to lead to more time being spent with the client: "in reality, the first meeting between solicitors and clients lasted on average eight minutes longer after the introduction of FAInS than it had done beforehand" (Walker et al., *The Family Advice and Information Service*, p.37).
[216] Walker et al., *The Family Advice and Information Service*, pp.156, 257.
[217] Walker et al., *The Family Advice and Information Service*, pp.39–42, 200–201, 257–258.
[218] Walker et al., *The Family Advice and Information Service*, pp.252, 260.
[219] Walker et al., *The Family Advice and Information Service*, pp.70–71, 203, 259.
[220] Walker et al., *The Family Advice and Information Service*, pp.208, 253.
[221] Walker et al., *The Family Advice and Information Service*, p.264.
[222] This is because the section applies only to "the court and any person . . . exercising functions under or in consequence of Parts II and III" of the Act. Pt II contained the new substantive law governing divorce and separation, has never been brought into force and is to be repealed. Pt III applied to the provision of Legal Aid for mediation, which was also repealed and replaced by the Legal Services' Commission's funding code.

marriage support to relationship support, and in 2004 the Marriage and Relationship Support Grant was subsumed within the *Strengthening Families Grant Programme*.[223] As Walker has commented, "the shift in political discourse has been away from the preservation of marriage towards supporting parents".[224]

By contrast, attendance at a mediation meeting remains a prerequisite for certain forms of legal funding,[225] and the advantages of mediation have been extolled in recent official publications.[226] In the meantime, however, there have been changes in the practice of family-law solicitors. In the past, mediation was sometimes favourably contrasted with legal representation, mediation being portrayed as a civilised process in which a disinterested mediator facilitated the shared purpose of reaching agreement, whilst legal representation was depicted as involving hostile courtroom duels between partisan lawyers paid to ignore all but their own client's interests. In reality, this was a caricature that misrepresented the role played by lawyers in general and family-law solicitors in particular.[227] A number of solicitors have trained as mediators, while still more have "absorbed the ethos behind mediation".[228] And in recent years there have been initiatives intended to encourage family-law solicitors to take a more conciliatory approach[229] and to regard litigation as a last resort.[230]

Such initiatives are, of course, less about the actual process of obtaining a divorce and more about the resolution of the consequences of separation. As a result, the gap between the formal process of ending a marriage, and the way in which the consequences of separation and divorce are resolved, has widened still further:

> "[T]he divorce law of England and Wales continues to use fault-based facts as a means to an end, maintaining an essentially adversarial system within a framework which has become increasingly conciliatory."[231]

---

[223] For a critical discussion of this shift, and a calculation of the amount of support being provided for marriage support services, see the report published by the Social Policy Justice Group of the Conservative Party, *The State of the Nation Report: Fractured Families* (2006), pp.94–95.

[224] J. Walker, *Picking Up the Pieces: Marriage and Divorce Two Years After Information Provision* (London: DCA, 2004), p.10.

[225] See now Legal Services Commission, *Funding Code Criteria* (2007), paras 11.4.2, 11.11.2, 11.12.2. See also *Funding Code Decision Making Guidance—Family (Section 20)* (2007), and the comments by N. Robinson, "The LSC: Working in Partnership Update" [2007] Fam. Law 751.

[226] The National Audit Office, *Legal Services Commission: Legal Aid and Mediation for People Involved in Family Breakdown* (HC 256) (London: TSO, 2007); House of Commons Committee of Public Accounts, *Legal Services Commission: Legal Aid and Mediation for People Involved in Family Breakdown* (HC 396) (London, TSO, 2007).

[227] See G. Davis, *Partisans and Mediators* (1988); R. Ingleby, *Solicitors and Divorce* (1992).

[228] K. Wright, "The role of solicitors in divorce: a note of caution" [2007] 19 C.F.L.Q. 490.

[229] See, for example, Law Society, *Family Law Protocol*, 2nd edn (The Law Society, 2006); A. Greensmith (ed.), *Resolution Family Law Handbook* (The Law Society, 2007), App.1; *The Private Law Programme: Guidance Issued by the President of the Family Division* (2004).

[230] The idea that the parties will resolve matters without going to court is central to the new initiative of "collaborative law", which involves the parties agreeing that they will neither use nor threaten to use the court system: see, for example, P. Tesler, "Collaborative family law" [2004] I.F.L. 153; S. Lloyd, "The continuing growth of the collaborative process" [2007] Fam. Law 270.

[231] Walker et al., *The Family Advice and Information Service*, pp.4–5.

10–056　　Yet although this is a problem that exercises those with a professional interest in the divorce process, there seems to be no evidence of popular pressure for change. Practitioners and academics have continued to propose more substantial reforms to the law of divorce, whether the introduction of no-fault divorce[232] or a shift to a simple administrative procedure.[233] It could be argued that such changes would, in the light of the popularity of the "special procedure",[234] be changes in appearance rather than substance, but, as was noted at the start of the chapter, this is an area in which the *appearance* of change may send out unwelcome messages about the appropriateness of divorce. Given the lack of any popular enthusiasm for change, coupled with the fact that avowedly radical change would engender strong opposition not confined to any one political party, it seems unlikely that any government will introduce new primary legislation in this area in the foreseeable future.

VI. Dissolution of Civil Partnerships

10–057　For same-sex couples, the debate has, to date, focused on the right to enter into a legally recognised relationship. Yet it is inevitable that some civil partnerships will break down, and the question thus arises: in what circumstances can a civil partner seek dissolution of the partnership? The Civil Partnership Act 2004 provides that an application for a dissolution order may be made on the basis that the partnership has irretrievably broken down[235]; there are, however, only four facts from which such breakdown may be inferred.[236] Adultery was omitted on the basis that it:

> "[H]as a specific meaning within the context of heterosexual relationships and it would not be possible nor desirable to read this across to same-sex civil partnerships."[237]

This is, of course, identical to the reason given for the omission of the non-consummation grounds from the list of grounds that render a civil partnership voidable,[238] but it can be argued that there are differences between the two. A

---

[232] See, for example, K. Boele-Woelki et al., *Principles of European Family Law Regarding Divorce and Maintenance Between Former Spouses* (Antwerp: Intersentia, 2004); N. Shepherd, "Ending the blame game: getting no fault divorce back on the agenda" [2007] Fam. Law 1053.

[233] See, for example, S.M. Cretney, "Private ordering and divorce—how far can we go?" [2003] Fam. Law 399.

[234] As Wilson J. noted in *Bhaji v Chauhan* [2003] 2 F.L.R. 48, para.5, the continued use of the term "special" in this context "well illuminates the time-warp in which the law and practice governing the dissolution of marriage have become caught".

[235] Civil Partnership Act 2004 s.44(1).

[236] Civil Partnership Act 2004 s.44(5).

[237] Women and Equality Unit, *Response to Civil Partnership: A Framework for the Legal Regulation of Same-Sex Couples* (November 2003), p.35.

[238] See para.2–060.

civil partner may, of course, be unfaithful with a member of the opposite sex—just as the infidelity of some married persons may take the form of a sexual relationship with a person of the same sex.[239] The reason that a civil partner cannot commit adultery must therefore be because only a married person can commit adultery, rather than (as in the case of consummation) the nature of the sexual act involved.

Of course, this omission does not mean that a civil partner will be unable to apply for dissolution where his or her partner is unfaithful; such infidelity might well be considered to be behaviour of such a kind that the applicant could not reasonably be expected to live with the respondent.[240]

In all other respects, the law regulating the dissolution of a civil partnership is identical to that described above; thus there is a bar on any application before one year has elapsed from the formation of the civil partnership,[241] the facts from which breakdown may be inferred are identical to those listed in s.1(2)(b)–(e) of the Matrimonial Causes Act 1973,[242] and dissolution may be refused on the basis of grave financial or other hardship where the application is based on five years' separation.[243] Powers are even conferred upon the Queen's Proctor to intervene where appropriate.[244] Civil partners will also be able to take advantage of an equivalent "special procedure",[245] and a "conditional" order will be made "final" after the appropriate time period has elapsed.[246]

VII. Conclusion

The legal process of bringing a marriage or civil partnership to an end has been simplified with the hope that this will minimise the extent of hostility and bitterness between the parties. Yet perhaps all that a "good divorce law" can do is to ensure that the legal requirements do not add to existing hostility and bitterness. It is also possible that if such emotions are not allowed an outlet in one

10–058

---

[239] It is interesting to note that, under the legislation passed in 1857, 1923 and 1937, a wife could petition on the basis that her husband had committed sodomy, but until 1937 a husband had no legal form of redress if his wife embarked on a lesbian affair, since this would not be regarded as adulterous, and cruelty was not a ground for divorce until 1937. As the court noted in *Kerr v Kennedy* [1942] 1 All E.R. 412, lesbianism was not a matrimonial office nor were gross acts of indecency between men falling short of sodomy.

[240] Note, for example, *Coffer v Coffer* (1964) 108 S.J. 465, in which it was held that a spouse's homosexual relationship could constitute cruelty if it affected the mental or physical health of the other.

[241] Civil Partnership Act 2004 s.41.

[242] Civil Partnership Act 2004 s.44(5).

[243] Civil Partnership Act 2004 s.47. See also s.48 on the extra protection provided for the respondent in separation cases.

[244] Civil Partnership Act 2004 ss.39 and 40.

[245] Family Proceedings Rules 1991 (SI 1991/1247), r.2.36, as amended by Family Proceedings (Amendment) (No.5) Rules 2005 (SI 2005/2922), r.29.

[246] Civil Partnership Act 2004 s.38.

area of the law, they will find an outlet in another—as may be witnessed by the increasing prevalence of disputes over the allocation of property and issues concerning the children of the marriage. It is these areas—rather than the issue of the ground for divorce—that have become controversial in recent years,[247] and to which an increasing proportion of any family textbook must be devoted.[248]

[247] See, for example, S. Cretney, "Breaking the shackles of culture and religion in the field of divorce?", in K. Boele-Woelki (ed.), *Common Core and Better Law in European Family Law* (Antwerp: Intersentia, 2005), p.8
[248] See for example, Chs 13 and 18.

Chapter Eleven

JUDICIAL SEPARATION AND SEPARATION ORDERS

I.   INTRODUCTION.............................. 11–001
II.   JUDICIAL SEPARATION 11–002
      A. Grounds for judicial separation 11–002
      B. Effects of a decree of judicial
      separation 11–003

C. The use made of judicial separation 11–004
III. SEPARATION ORDERS..................... 11–005

I. Introduction

The ecclesiastical courts did not grant decrees of divorce dissolving marriage, but **11–001** they did grant decrees of *divorce a mensa et thoro*[1] relieving the parties of the duty—at one time enforceable by an order for restitution of conjugal rights—to cohabit. The Matrimonial Causes Act 1857 renamed such decrees "judicial separation",[2] and judicial separation remained available after the enactment of the Divorce Reform Act 1969.[3] The Civil Partnership Act 2004 introduced a similar order for civil partners, termed a "separation order". However, the term "judicial separation" is somewhat misleading (and "separation order" arguably even more so) since a decree does not in fact require a couple to separate, much less does it mean that the court will compel them to do so. This chapter examines, first, the decree of judicial separation, considering the grounds upon which the decree is granted, the effect of the decree and the purposes that a decree may serve, and then sets out the parallel (but not identical) provisions relating to separation orders.

---

[1] Which may be rather freely translated as "from bed and board".
[2] Such decrees—as equally their counterpart available from 1878 in magistrates' courts—were capable of causing great hardship since they denied the parties the possibility of remarriage.
[3] And was indeed frequently invoked, often apparently in order to give the parties the right to seek the financial orders (the court having powers similar to those exercisable in divorce).

II. Judicial Separation

A. Grounds for judicial separation

11–002　The Divorce Reform Act 1969 amended the law so as to be consistent with the code of divorce introduced by that Act. A petition for judicial separation may[4] be presented to the court by either party to a marriage on the ground that one or more of the "facts" on which a divorce petition may be founded exists.[5] It is specifically provided that in the case of petitions for judicial separation, the court is not to be concerned with the question of whether the marriage has broken down irretrievably.[6] Hence, the court is bound[7] to grant a decree provided that one of the relevant facts—adultery, behaviour, desertion or living apart—is proved.

B. Effects of a decree of judicial separation

11–003　A decree of judicial separation has two main legal consequences. First, the court may, on or after granting a decree of judicial separation, exercise extensive ancillary financial powers, and it has power to make orders relating to the upbringing of the children of the family. The court may also grant injunctions in the course of judicial separation proceedings, and it may well be that this fact at one time explained why many judicial separation petitions were filed. However, the courts now have power (under Pt IV of the Family Law Act 1996) to make occupation and non-molestation orders without it being necessary to apply for any other relief.

　　　　The second effect of a decree relates to the law of succession. For the purposes of intestate succession, a decree of judicial separation has the same effect as a divorce[8]: neither spouse has thereafter any right to succeed to the property on the other's intestacy,[9] but judicial separation has no effect on entitlement under a will.[10]

---

[4] Matrimonial Causes Act 1973 s.17(1).

[5] The "special procedure" applies to undefended judicial separation petitions in exactly the same way as to undefended divorce petitions: Family Proceedings Rules 1991 (SI 1991/1247) r.2.24(3). However, there is no provision for a decree nisi in judicial separation, and the decree takes effect as soon as it is pronounced.

[6] Matrimonial Causes Act 1973 s.17(2).

[7] The only exception to the rule that proof of a specified fact gives a right to a decree is that the court has power, in exceptional circumstances, to withhold the decree if it is concerned about arrangements for any children: Matrimonial Causes Act 1973 (as substituted by Children Act 1989 Sch.12 para.31). The defence (Matrimonial Causes Act 1973 s.5) to divorce based on grave financial or other hardship does not apply to judicial separation.

[8] Matrimonial Causes Act 1973 s.18(2).

[9] This rule does not prevent a spouse applying to the court for reasonable provision under the Inheritance (Provision for Family and Dependants) Act 1975; see Ch.7, above.

[10] Compare the effect of divorce: property given to a former spouse passes as if he or she had died at the date of divorce: see Wills Act 1837 s.18A(1), as inserted by Administration of Justice Act 1982 and amended by Law Reform (Succession) Act 1995.

C. The use made of judicial separation

Divorce can now be obtained on the basis of five years' separation. If either party **11–004** wants the marriage dissolved, he or she will, in time, be able to get a divorce.[11] It is only in the very rare case where a bar to the granting of a divorce exists that the empty legal shell of a marriage can now be preserved at the instance of one party against the will of the other.[12] In consequence, judicial separation would only seem to be appropriate in the following cases:

- where the parties have religious or other objections to divorce but nevertheless want the advantages of court orders regulating their affairs;

- where a decree of divorce cannot yet be obtained because one year has not elapsed since the celebration of the marriage, and the petitioner seeks the exercise of the court's ancillary powers to make financial orders and orders relating to the upbringing of the children of the family;

- where the petitioner does not wish to obtain a divorce but wants a formal recognition of the separation, and the respondent is not yet in a position to establish one of the "facts" necessary for a decree of divorce. For example, a wife may obtain a decree of judicial separation on the basis of her husband's adultery or behaviour; he may want a divorce, but may not be able to obtain one until he can establish the five-year living apart "fact".

In 2006, 613 judicial separation petitions were filed, and the court granted 353 decrees.[13]

III. Separation Orders

A separation order may be granted upon proof of one or more of the four "facts" **11–005** upon which a dissolution order may be founded.[14] As with the decree of judicial separation, there is no requirement that the court be satisfied that the civil partnership has broken down irretrievably. Unlike under the Matrimonial Causes Act 1973, however, the Civil Partnership Act 2004 does not state that where such

---

[11] In effect, a decree of judicial separation can in due course be converted into a divorce, but procedurally it is still necessary to file a petition for divorce in the usual way: see *Butler v Butler (The Queen's Proctor Intervening)* [1990] 1 F.L.R. 114.

[12] So long as divorce was only available on proof of a matrimonial offence, judicial separation allowed one party to a marriage to obtain financial orders against the other, whilst denying him the freedom to remarry: see, for example, *Sansom v Sansom* [1966] P. 52.

[13] Ministry of Justice, *Judicial and Court Statistics 2006* (HMSO, 2007), Table 5.5. This is significantly lower than the 7,480 petitions filed in 1982. The numbers fell sharply in the wake of the Matrimonial and Family Proceedings Act 1984 (which made it possible to petition for divorce after one year from the marriage, rather than three), and again after the Family Law Act 1996 Pt IV removed any advantage to obtaining a decree as a prelude to seeking injunctions.

[14] Civil Partnerships Act 2004 s.56(1).

an order is granted it shall no longer be obligatory for the parties to cohabit together,[15] implying that civil partners are not deemed to be under any such obligation in the first place. Apart from this, the legal consequences of a separation order are the same as those of a decree of judicial separation.[16] It remains to be seen whether any use is made of this alternative procedure.

[15] cf. Matrimonal Causes Act 1973 s.18(1).
[16] Civil Partnerships Act 2004 s.57.

CHAPTER TWELVE

TERMINATION OF MARRIAGE AND CIVIL PARTNERSHIP BY DEATH

I.   THE PRESUMPTION OF DEATH AT
COMMON LAW 12–002

II.   DECREE OF PRESUMPTION OF
DEATH AND DISSOLUTION.................... 12–003

In recent years, so much attention has been given to rates of divorce and the **12–001** consequences thereof that there is some danger of forgetting that the majority of marriages are ended by the death of one of the spouses. Equally, there is no reason to suppose other than that the majority of civil partnerships will be ended by death rather than dissolution. A surviving spouse or civil partner, as we have seen, has significant rights in relation to inheritance[1] and otherwise.[2] In order to establish entitlement to any of the rights to which a surviving spouse or civil partner potentially has, it is necessary to prove, first, that the applicant was married to or in a civil partnership with the deceased at the date of the death; and secondly, that the person said to be deceased is indeed dead. Normally these matters do not give rise to any difficulty: marriage, civil partnership and death can readily be proved by production of an official copy of the relevant entry in the appropriate register,[3] but this will not always be so. First, as we have seen, in some cases the validity of the survivor's marriage or civil partnership to the deceased will be put in issue.[4] Secondly, there may be cases in which there is no conclusive evidence that the spouse or civil partner concerned has in fact died.

What is the position if there is no positive proof that death has occurred? There are two possibilities. First (quite independently of any distinctive family law procedure), the court has jurisdiction to presume death for the purpose of

---

[1] See Ch.7, above.
[2] For instance, under the Fatal Accidents Act 1976.
[3] See, for example, Civil Partnership Act 2004, Pt 2, Ch.1; Births and Deaths Registration Act 1953 s.34.
[4] See Ch.2 above.

distributing property, and may presume it for other purposes.[5] Secondly, there is now a distinctive procedure that in some cases allows death to be presumed, but also dissolves the marriage or civil partnership if that presumption in fact turns out to be incorrect.

I. The Presumption of Death at Common Law

12–002 The court may presume death[6] if there is no affirmative evidence that, for a continuous period of seven years or more the person concerned was alive, provided that:

- that there are persons who would be likely to have heard from the missing person during that period;

- that those persons have not heard from him or her; and

- that all due inquiries have been made appropriate to the period

II. Decree of Presumption of Death and Dissolution

12–003 The shortcomings of the common law presumption can be seen by taking an example:

> Suppose that a man who has been married to W1 subsequently goes through a ceremony of marriage with W2. If the conditions governing the presumption of death set out above are satisfied, the marriage will be presumed to be valid, but if it subsequently transpires that W1 was alive at the date of the purported marriage to W2, that marriage will be void.

It was obviously unsatisfactory that a person whose spouse had disappeared should be unable to re-marry without the risk that the second marriage would be invalidated in this way by the reappearance of the absent party. The Matrimonial

---

[5] See J. Jackson, *Formation and Annulment of Marriage*, 2nd edn (1969), pp.150–155. For a modern exercise of this power, note that the death of the seventh Earl of Lucan who disappeared after the killing of his children's nurse has been presumed to have occurred "on or since November 8, 1974": see *The Times*. February 15, 1995 and, generally, Treitel (1954) 17 M.L.R. 530 and D. Stone, "The presumption of death: a redundant concept" (1981) 44 M.L.R. 516.

[6] *Chard v Chard* [1956] P. 259; see also *Tweney v Tweney* [1946] P. 180 (presumption applied: first spouse absent for 12 years and exhaustive inquiries made); *Re Watkins* [1953] I W.L.R. 1323 (presumption applied: 25 years' absence); *Taylor v Taylor* [1967] P. 25. It should be noted that there is no "magic" for this purpose in seven years' absence, and that the three additional requirements referred to in the text must also be satisfied: *per* Harman J., *Re Watkins* [1953] 1 W.L.R. 1323 at 1327. If, for instance, there exist reasons why the missing person might have wished to disappear, or if they were a solitary person, the court might well refuse to presume death; contrarily, death might more easily be presumed if the missing person had been a gregarious man and/or leading a public life, who had been in poor health or was following a dangerous occupation.

Causes Act 1937[7] accordingly made it possible to obtain a decree of presumption of death and dissolution of marriage. A decree absolute[8] under this procedure terminates the marriage even if the other party is in fact still alive,[9] and, accordingly, the petitioner can safely remarry.

The Matrimonial Causes Act now provides[10] that:

> "Any married person who alleges that reasonable grounds exist for supposing that the other party to the marriage is dead may present a petition to the court to have it presumed that the other party is dead and to have the marriage dissolved, and the court may, if satisfied that such reasonable grounds exist, grant a decree of presumption of death and dissolution of the marriage."

The task of a petitioner[11] in satisfying the court that reasonable grounds exist for supposing that the other party to the marriage is dead is facilitated by the provision[12] that:

> "[T]he fact that for a period of seven years or more the other party to the marriage has been continually absent from the petitioner and the petitioner has no reason to believe that the other party has been living within that time shall be evidence that the other party is dead until the contrary is proved."

Equivalent provisions are contained in the Civil Partnership Act 2004.   **12–004**
Thus:

> "The court may, on an application made by a civil partner, make a presumption of death order if it is satisfied that reasonable grounds exist for supposing that the other civil partner is dead".[13]

The evidentiary presumption as to absence for seven years applies.[14] A presumption of death order in respect of a civil partnership is in the first instance a conditional order,[15] which is not normally to be made final before the end of six weeks.[16] As is the case with a decree of presumption of death and dissolution in

---

[7] Matrimonial Causes Act 1937 s.8.
[8] A decree of presumption of death and dissolution must in the first instance, be a decree nisi, which is not normally to be made absolute before the end of six weeks. Matrimonial Causes Act 1973 s.19(4). If it is found—after the decree nisi but before the decree absolute—that the other party is still alive, the decree will be rescinded: *Manser v Manser* [1940] P. 224.
[9] If the respondent subsequently appears, the court could exercise its powers to make financial provision and property adjustment orders: *Deacock v Deacock* [1958] P. 230.
[10] Matrimonial Causes Act 1973 s.19(1). There are no absolute or discretionary bars to a decree on this ground: Matrimonial Causes Act 1973 s.19(6); see Law Com. No.33 (1970), p.55.
[11] On whom the onus lies: *Parkinson v Parkinson* [1939] P. 346.
[12] Matrimonial Causes Act 1973 s.19(3).
[13] Civil Partnership Act 2004 s.55(1); see also s.37(1).
[14] Civil Partnership Act 2004 s.55(2).
[15] Civil Partnership Act 2004 s.37(1).
[16] Civil Partnership Act 2004 s.38(1).

respect of a married person, a final presumption of death order terminates the civil partnership even if the other party is in fact still alive; thus the person who has obtained the order may lawfully enter into a subsequent civil partnership or marry, as the case may be.

It has been held[17] that the words "the petitioner has no reason to believe that the other party has been living within" the seven-year period should be read as: "if nothing has happened within that time to give the petitioner reason to believe that the other party was then living". The test of whether there is "reason to believe" relates to the standards of belief of a reasonable person: "pure speculation" is excluded.[18] If seven years' absence cannot be shown, the petitioner may still obtain a decree if reasonable grounds are shown for believing the missing person to be dead.[19]

---

[17] *Thompson v Thompson* [1956] P. 414.
[18] *Thompson v Thompson* [1956] P. 414.
[19] *MacDarmaid v Att-Gen* [1950] P. 218. For example, a decree or order could no doubt have been obtained in cases on which no trace was found of a person known to have been in the World Trade Center, New York, on September 11, 2001. The same may be the case in respect of major natural disasters such as the tsunami in South East Asia on December 26, 2004.

CHAPTER THIRTEEN

FINANCIAL CONSEQUENCES OF THE BREAKDOWN OF MARRIAGE AND CIVIL PARTNERSHIP

I.   INTRODUCTION............................ 13–001
II. THE SETTLEMENT CULTURE 13–003
     A. A conflict of principle: ouster of
     court's jurisdiction contrary to public
     policy.. 13–004
     B. Reconciling the conflict of
     principle: the consent order................. 13–005
     C. Procedure for obtaining a consent
     order: the court's role........................ 13–006
     D. Agreements not embodied in a
     court order... 13–008

     E. Facilitating settlement.................... 13–010
     F. Incentives to settle: costs?............. 13–011
III. FINANCIAL   RELIEF: THE
     LEGISLATIVE FRAMEWORK.................. 13–012
     A. The extent of the court's powers... 13–013
IV. WORKING OF THE LAW IN
     PRACTICE: HOUSING AND PENSIONS . 13–109
     A. Housing... 13–110
     B. Orders dealing with pensions 13–119

I. INTRODUCTION

This chapter deals with the court's extensive powers to make financial-relief **13–001** orders on the breakdown of marriage or civil partnership. The powers are found in Pt II of the Matrimonial Causes Act 1973 and Sch.5 to the Civil Partnership Act 2004. Section 72(1) of the Civil Partnership Act 2004 states that Sch.5 to the Act makes provision for financial relief in connection with civil partnership that "corresponds" to the provision made in respect of marriage in the Matrimonial Causes Act 1973. This has been described as "an important declaration" that:

> "[G]ives the clearest indication possible that the purpose of the civil partnership regime is to extend all of those rights and responsibilities invoked by marriage between opposite sex couples at least as regards ancillary relief to same sex couples who choose to register a civil partnership."[1]

It has been judicially observed[2] that the Civil Partnership Act 2004 effectively accords civil partnership all the rights, responsibilities and advantages of civil

---

[1] M. Harper et al., *Civil Partnership* (Family Law, 2005), p.67.
[2] *Wilkinson v Kitzinger* [2006] 2 F.C.R. 537; [2006] 2 F.L.R. 397.

marriage, save the name. Accordingly, it is to be expected that the approaches developed by case law and practice on financial relief consequential on the breakdown of marriage will be applied to civil partnership, although at the time of writing there is a dearth of case law in respect of civil partnerships. The court's powers in respect of financial relief are described[3] as its power to grant "ancillary relief" because the court's powers only arise[4] on or after the grant of a decree or order (whether of divorce, dissolution, nullity, judicial separation or separation in the case of financial provision and property adjustment orders, and of divorce, dissolution or nullity in the case of pension sharing orders).

Financial matters commonly prove to be contentious for the parties following the breakdown of a relationship, and the costs of protracted[5] proceedings can be very substantial; judicial criticism of disproportionate costs is not infrequently voiced.[6] We consider in this chapter the contemporary "settlement culture" and the various policies and procedures that have been developed in recent years in order to promote settlement and curtail the costs of litigation.[7] However, there is a certain tension between the policy of encouraging settlement (and promoting individual autonomy) and the traditional view that the state has a vital interest in ensuring that any settlement is fair and reasonable, in the interests both of the individuals concerned and of the community as a whole. As will be seen, this tension manifests itself in various aspects of the reported case law. The first part of this chapter discusses the extent to which so-called "private ordering" is permitted. The text then analyses the legislative framework within which negotiations are conducted (both by lawyers and mediators) and which is applied to determine the small minority of cases that proceed to adjudication.

The financial consequences of marital[8] breakdown have attracted considerable professional and public debate in recent years, due in no small part to a number of high-profile cases involving very substantial assets. One of the major issues is the difficulty of steering between the Scylla of too wide a discretion vested in the

---

[3] The term "ancillary relief" is defined and used in the procedural code governing financial matters: Family Proceedings Rules 1991 (SI 1991/1247) rr.1.2(1), 2.51A–2.70.

[4] Matrimonial Causes Act 1973 ss.23(1), 24(1), 24B(1); Civil Partnership Act 2004 Sch.5, paras 1(1), (2), 6(1), 15(1). Orders made under the powers to make financial provision, property adjustment and pension sharing orders in favour of the spouses cannot take effect unless the decree (order in the case of civil partnership) had been made absolute (final in the case of civil partnership): see *Dackham v Dackham* [1987] 2 F.L.R. 358, CA (where a decree was purportedly made absolute in defiance of the rules in order to allow the court to make a property adjustment order).

[5] For examples, see *F v F (Ancillary Relief: Substantial Assets)* [1995] 2 F.L.R. 45 at 70–71, *per* Thorpe J.; *Piglowska v Piglowski* [1999] 2 F.L.R. 763, HL.

[6] See, for example, per Munby J. in *A v A* [2007] 2 F.L.R. 467 and *A v A (No.2)* [2007] EWHC 1810 (Fam.).

[7] *Gojkovic v Gojkovic (No.2)* [1991] 2 F.L.R. 233 at 238, *per* Butler-Sloss L.J. Less than a quarter of the cases studied at three court centres in Davis, Cretney and Collins, *Simple Quarrels* (1994) resulted in formal adjudication by the court. The study by a team at Cardiff University of the pre-settlement process found that only a minority of parties obtained court orders for ancillary relief: A. Perry et al., *How Parents Cope Financially on Marriage Breakdown: Report to the Joseph Rowntree Foundation* (Cardiff Law School, November 1999). See also the reports of further research conducted at Bristol by Davis et al.: "Ancillary relief outcomes" (2000) C.F.L.Q. 43; D. Bird, "Ancillary relief outcomes" (2000) Fam. Law 831. The National Centre for Social Research has recently conducted a study into the financial arrangements after separation and divorce: see S. Arthur et al., *Settling Up: Making Financial Arrangements after Divorce or Separation* (National Centre for Social Research, 2002).

[8] At the time of writing, the dissolution of individual civil partnerships has not yet attracted media attention nor generated reported case law.

courts (inevitably involving a degree of diversity in judicial application, unpredictability of outcome[9] and high costs in cases involving protracted litigation, as well as difficulties for practitioners in offering advice to clients) and the Charybdis of too-rigid a statutory formulation of principle (potentially productive both of injustice in the individual case and of increased litigation in rebuttal or by way of exception). Even if agreement could be reached on the desirability of legislative articulation of clearer and universally applicable principles to govern ancillary relief, it would still be necessary to decide what the precise content of those principles should be.[10] This involves complex issues of social policy, on which there is no clear consensus within the community.[11] What (if anything) should replace the established system of justice fashioned to fit the circumstances of each individual case under the very general objective of achieving a fair outcome?[12] Needs, expectations, compensation for disadvantage and equalisation of the economic effects of the marriage, entitlements built up by incommensurable contributions to family welfare and equal division of the fruits of the marriage all merit consideration.[13] The implicit over-arching objective of legislation in seeking to achieve a *fair* outcome has been stated by the House of Lords in *Piglowska v Piglowski*,[14] *White v White*[15] and *Miller v Miller; McFarlane v McFarlane*.[16] However, to state the objective of a fair outcome in financial terms begs the question of what is the content of fairness[17] in the individual case, and whether there are agreed community values that can inform the judicial answer.[18]

Legislative consideration of these difficult policy questions has not been forthcoming in recent years. In 1998 the Lord Chancellor's Advisory Group on Ancillary Relief recommended[19] against introducing the principles of Scottish law[20] into the Matrimonial Causes Act 1973; the changes in social policy would have been far greater than perhaps contemplated by the Lord Chancellor when referring the question to the group. Some recommendations for further structuring the exercise of judicial discretion through clearer articulation of objectives were made in the Green Paper, *Supporting Families*,[21] but a White Paper was

13–002

---

[9] *Piglowska v Piglowski* [1999] 2 F.L.R. 767 at 783, *per* Lord Hoffmann.
[10] R. Bailey-Harris (ed.), *Dividing the Assets on Family Breakdown* (Family Law, 1998), Introduction.
[11] Bailey-Harris, *Dividing the Assets*, Introduction.
[12] *Piglowska v Piglowski* [1999] 2 F.L.R. 767, HL; *White v White* [2001] 1 A.C. 596; HL; [2000] 2 F.L.R. 981; *Cowan v Cowan* [2001] 2 F.L.R. 192, CA; *C v C* [2001] EWCA Civ. 1791; [2002] 1 F.L.R. 207.
[13] R. Bailey-Harris, "Dividing the assets on family breakdown: the content of fairness" [2001] *Current Legal Problems* 533 at 535.
[14] [1999] 2 F.L.R. 763.
[15] [2000] 2 F.L.R. 981.
[16] [2006] 1 F.L.R. 1186.
[17] Bailey-Harris, "Dividing the assets" 533.
[18] *Piglowska v Piglowski* [1999] 2 F.L.R. 763 at 785, *per* Lord Hoffmann; *White v White* [2000] 2 F.L.R. 981 at 984, *per* Lord Nicholls.
[19] Report of the Lord Chancellor's Advisory Group on Ancillary Relief (LCD, July 1998).
[20] For the law of Scotland, see the Family Law (Scotland) Act 1985 ss.9–10; E.M. Clive, *The Law of Husband and Wife in Scotland*, 3rd edn (1992), Ch.24.
[21] HMS (1998), paras 4.47–4.49.

never published[22] and the proposals (which in any event lacked rigour of analysis) have apparently now been dropped. The continuation of the status quo received both support[23] and criticism.[24]

In recent years, the House of Lords and the Court of Appeal have displayed increasing enthusiasm for a judicial role articulating fundamental policies and rationales to underpin the distribution of assets and income on marriage breakdown, such being absent from the face of the relevant statutory provisions. This recent trend contrasts sharply with the pragmatic approach to the width of judicial discretion voiced in 1999 in *Piglowska v Piglowski*,[25] The landmark judgments in *White v White*,[26] *Miller v Miller; McFarlane v McFarlane*[27] and *Charman v Charman (No.4)*,[28] each of which addresses issues both of social policy and the appellate court's role in the formulation of guidelines, will be discussed in this chapter. The recent trend of appellate-court activism has received a mixed response from commentators both academic and practitioner.[29] Furthermore, the marked contrast between the systems of England and Wales and other members of the European Community has arguably made London the "divorce capital" for very high-asset cases, leading in turn to the question as to whether a greater degree of harmonization would be desirable in future.[30]

II. The Settlement Culture

13–003   Reported cases may give the misleading impression that the majority of divorce financial settlements are achieved by a trial before a judge, leading to a formal adjudication. Indeed, for many years, "collusion" was a bar to divorce, and the fact that a divorcing couple had come to an agreement about the financial consequences of divorce might lead the court to suspect that they had done so as part of a collusive bargain,[31] but since the Divorce Reform Act 1969 introduced divorce based on irretrievable breakdown, it has been the policy of the law to

---

[22] The summary of responses to the Green Paper published in June 1999 reported at para.4.19 that relatively few had responded on the ancillary relief question but that the majority who did were in favour of the Government's proposals.

[23] S. Thorpe L.J., "The English system of ancillary relief", Ch.1 in Bailey-Harris *Dividing the Assets*; S. Cretney, "Trusting the judges: money after divorce" (1999) 52 *Current Legal Problems* 286.

[24] J. Eekelaar, "Should section 25 be reformed?" [1998] Fam. Law 46; Cleverley, "An opportunity missed?" [1999] Fam. Law 326.; Thorpe L.J. and Robert Walker L.J. in *Cowan v Cowan* [2001] 2 F.L.R. 192.

[25] [1999] 2 F.L.R. 785.

[26] [2001] 1 A.C. 596.

[27] [2006] 2 A.C. 618.

[28] [2007] 1 F.L.R. 1247.

[29] S. Cretney [2001] Fam. Law 3, R. Bailey-Harris [2001] Fam. Law 12; Bailey-Harris, "Dividing the assets" 533; J. Eekelaar, "Back to basics and forward into the unknown" [2001] Fam. Law 30; R. Bailey-Harris, "Fairness on financial settlement on divorce" [2001] L.Q.R. 199; E. Cooke, "White v White: a new yardstick for the marriage partnership" [2001] C.F.L.Q. 81; P. Duckworth and D. Hodson, "White v White: bringing s 25 back to the people" [2001] Fam. Law 24.

[30] D. Hodson, "Brussels III: financial provision: the next generation" [2002] Fam. Law 30; *Charman v Charman (No.4)* [2007] 2 F.C.R. 217; [2007] 1 F.L.R. 1247.

[31] At common law, any agreement made between the parties to divorce proceedings was invalid if made collusively: *Hope v Hope* (1856) 22 Beav. 35; (1857) 8 De GM and G 731.

encourage parties to settle their money and property affairs between them-selves,[32] and what has been described[33] as the "settlement culture" came to pervade the divorce process. The settlement ethos is now all-pervasive of lawyers' conduct of matrimonial proceedings,[34] and Resolution (formerly the Solicitors Family Law Association), the Family Law Bar Association and the Law Society have developed professional codes of conduct[35] that embody it.

A. A conflict of principle: ouster of court's jurisdiction contrary to public policy

The modern policy thus favours the making of private agreements, but tradition-ally the law has been reluctant to view the financial consequences of marriage (and now civil partnership) breakdown as a purely private concern. Thus the common law did not enforce, and statute-law[36] renders void, any provision in an agreement[37] purporting to restrict the right by a spouse or civil partner to apply to the court for an order for financial relief.[38] The result is that however clear it may be that the parties intended an agreement to be conclusive and final, it will be open to one of them, whether because of second thoughts or changed circumstances, to seek to reopen it if he or she becomes dissatisfied with the bargain[39]:

13–004

> In *Xydhias v Xydhias*[40] the Court of Appeal purported to state that, in principle, an agreement for the compromise of an ancillary relief application does not give rise to an agreement enforceable in law and is not governed by ordinary contractual principles; the purpose of negotiation between parties is not to determine financial liability (which can only be done by the court) but rather to reduce the length and expense of the legal process. However, the width of the principle as stated in *Xydhias* has been

---

[32] Divorce Reform Act 1969 s.1(2)(d); collusion no longer invalidates an agreement not to defend a petition: *Sutton v Sutton* [1984] Ch. 184.

[33] Davis, Cretney and Collins, *Simple Quarrels* (1994), p.211.

[34] Davis, Cretney and Collins found that some practitioners regard a contested hearing as tantamount to an admission of professional failure: *Simple Quarrels*, pp.211–212; but the preference for a negotiated (as distinct from an adjudicated) outcome has not been without controversy: pp.211–227 and Ch.11.

[35] See, for example, the *Resolution Code of Practice* (2007); Law Society, *Family Law Protocol* (2002, as updated).

[36] Matrimonial Causes Act 1973 s.34(1); see, for example, *Jessel v Jessel* [1979] 1 W.L.R. 1148 at 1152, CA; and see now Civil Partnership Act 2004 Sch.5, para.68.

[37] The status of pre-nuptial agreements had been discussed in Ch.4.

[38] *Pounds v Pounds* [1994] 1 F.L.R. 775 at 776, *per* Waite L.J.; and see for the policies involved in *Hyman v Hyman* [1929] A.C. 601, HL; *Sutton v Sutton* [1984] Ch. 184 (public policy consideration survived 1969 divorce reforms and abolition of collusion as bar to divorce). However, the precise scope of the principle is not clear: contrast *Sutton v Sutton* [1984] Ch. 184 with *Amey v Amey* [1992] 2 F.L.R. 89 and *Smallman v Smallman* [1972] Fam. 25, CA.

[39] *Pounds v Pounds* [1994] 1 F.L.R. 775 at 776, *per* Waite L.J. The procedure whereby such an attack can be made depends on the circumstances—sometimes, for example, there will be an application to the court under the provisions of the Matrimonial Causes Act 1973 s.35 or the Civil Partnership Act 2005 Sch.5, para.69; whilst in others it may be possible to pursue an application for financial relief in divorce proceedings: see, for example, *G v G (Financial Provision: Separation Agreement)* [2000] 2 F.L.R. 472, FD; *Re X and X (Y and Z Intervening)* [2002] 1 F.L.R. 508, FD.

[40] [1999] 1 F.L.R. 683.

doubted in obiter dicta by a differently constituted Court of Appeal in *Soulsbury v Soulsbury*.[41] Ward L.J. considered the proposition formulated by Thorpe L.J. in *Xydhias* to have been too broad, and in conflict with earlier authority[42]; even an agreement subject to the approval of the court is binding on the parties, to the extent that neither can resile from it. In *Soulsbury*, the Court of Appeal emphasised that an agreement in respect of ancillary relief that does not purport to oust the jurisdiction of the court does not fall foul of the principle in *Hyman v Hyman*,[43] and may be enforced on ordinary contractual principles.

B. Reconciling the conflict of principle: the consent order

13–005   The law has developed a technique whereby these conflicting principles may be resolved in many cases. What cannot be finalised by private agreement can be achieved by asking the court to embody the parties' agreement in a court order, and the parties' rights and duties and all other legal consequences would then flow from the order,[44] just as would be the case if the order had been made in hostile litigation in which both parties had set out all the material they considered relevant. Under the consent-order[45] procedure, the parties' agreement ceases to be a source of obligation or entitlement,[46] and in this way court approval to the parties' agreement enables them to enjoy relative security and peace of mind.[47] Bad legal advice is not a ground on which a consent order incorporating a clean break can be re-opened.[48]

C. Procedure for obtaining a consent order: the court's role

13–006   The involvement of the court in the process gives rise to a number of difficult questions of legal principle, most of which stem from the essential difference between family litigation and other civil litigation. As Waite L.J. has said[49]:

> "In most areas of our law, parties to litigation who are sui juris and independently advised can settle their differences on terms ... with the authority of a judge who may not be aware of the terms of the deal at all (for example when they are endorsed on counsel's brief), still less be concerned with any question as to their suitability or fairness. That is not so in financial

---

[41] [2007] EWCA 967; [2007] Fam Law 16.
[42] *Goodinson v Goodinson* [1954] 2 Q.B. 118; *Gould v Gould* [1970] 1 Q.B. 275 and *Smallman v Smallman* [1972] Fam 25.
[43] [1929] A.C. 601.
[44] *De Lasala v De Lasala* [1979] 2 All E.R. 1146.
[45] Defined in Matrimonial Causes Act 1973 s.33A(3); see also Civil Partnership Act 2004 s.43. On the stage at which a consent order comes into existence, see *Rose v Rose* [2002] EWCA Civ. 208; [2002] 1 F.L.R. 978. There, the court had approved the agreement, and it only remained for its detailed terms to be drafted by counsel. The court had made an unperfected order.
[46] *De Lasala v De Lasala* [1980] A.C. 546; *Thwaite v Thwaite* (1981) 2 F.L.R. 280, CA; *Xhydias v Xhydias* [1999] 1 F.L.R. 683, CA; *Rose v Rose* [2002] EWCA Civ. 208; [2002] 1 F.L.R. 978.
[47] *Pounds v Pounds* [1994] 1 F.L.R. 775 at 779, per Waite L.J.
[48] *Harris v Manahan* [1997] 1 F.L.R. 205; *L v L* [2006] EWHC 956 (Fam.).
[49] *Pounds v Pounds* [1994] 1 F.L.R. 775 at 776–777, CA.

proceedings between husband and wife, where the court does not act, it has been said, as a rubber stamp."

However, this raises the question of what precisely is the court's role when dealing with an application for a consent order, and some understanding of the evolution of the law is necessary to answer that question.

In 1984[50] the House of Lords held that the court could not lawfully exercise its discretion to make orders relating to financial provision or property adjustment—whether by consent or otherwise—unless the court had before it information about all the circumstances of the case that was not only correct but also complete and up to date. It was the duty of the court in every case, whether it was proceeding by consent of the parties or after a contested hearing, to be satisfied that the provision of the order fulfilled the criteria laid down[51] by the Matrimonial Causes Act.[52]

This ruling caused concern, since it had apparently been common practice for district judges not to investigate the case at all but to rely on the fact that the parties were represented by competent solicitors who (it could be assumed) would carry out such investigations as were necessary to protect their clients' opposed interests. The possibility that many consent orders might be vulnerable to subsequent attack on the ground that the failure to investigate all the relevant facts had deprived the court of jurisdiction led to the insertion into the Matrimonial and Family Proceedings Act 1984 (then before Parliament) of a provision designed to achieve a workable compromise by minimising the risk that consent orders would be made without jurisdiction whilst at the same time seeking to ensure that the court would have all relevant information before it to enable it to perform its statutory duty of considering all relevant circumstances. **13–007**

Legislation accordingly provides that the court may make a consent order for financial relief in agreed terms on the basis only of prescribed information furnished with the application,[53] and the rules[54] provide that every application for a consent order should be accompanied by two copies of the draft order sought and a statement of information, including such matters as the duration of the marriage, an estimate of the means of the parties, the arrangements to be made for the accommodation of the parties and any child, whether either party has any

---

[50] *Livesey (formerly Jenkins) v Livesey* [1985] A.C. 424.

[51] *Pounds v Pounds* [1994] 1 F.L.R. 775 at 779, CA, *per* Waite L.J.

[52] Matrimonial Causes Act s.25; see below. A further consequence of the approach taken to the nature of consent orders by the House of Lords is that only terms which the court has jurisdiction to embody in an order can be included. Provisions about such matters as liability for outgoings will not usually be within the court's powers, and should accordingly be dealt with by undertakings given to the court. Difficult questions may arise in relation to enforcement of undertakings: see P. Moor and N. Mostyn [1992] Fam. Law 233; District Judge Price [1992] Fam. Law 371; and District Judge Bird [1990] Fam. Law 420; but it appears that undertakings to discharge financial obligations may in some cases be enforced by the judgment summons procedure: see *Symmons v Symmons* [1993] 1 F.L.R. 317; *M v M (Enforcement: Judgment Summons)* [1993] Fam. Law 469. On judgment summons procedure generally, see Ch.16, below.

[53] Matrimonial Causes Act 1973 s.33A(1), as inserted by Matrimonial and Family Proceedings Act 1984 s.7; see also Civil Partnership Act 2004 s.43 and Sch.5, para.66.

[54] Family Proceedings Rules 1991 (SI 1991/1247) r.2.61.

present intention to marry or to cohabit with another person and also "any other especially significant matters".[55]

It has been said[56] that the effect of these provisions is:

> "[T]o confine the paternal function of the court when approving financial consent orders to a broad appraisal of the parties' financial circumstances as disclosed to it in summary form, without descent into the valley of detail."

Also, that it is:

> "[O]nly if that survey puts the court on inquiry as to whether there are other circumstances into which it ought to probe more deeply that any further investigation is required of the judge before approving the bargain that the spouses have made for themselves."

The extent to which a court can sensibly discharge such a function—striking a balance between the role of rubber stamp on the one hand and "forensic ferret" on the other[57]—is self-evidently difficult, and there may well be diversity in judicial practice.[58] According to one district judge with great experience in this field, the court's role is limited to satisfying itself that the proposed order is within the band of reasonable discretion and does not offend any obvious principle.[59] In reviewing the established case law in the role of a judge in considering the terms of a propose consent order, Munby J. recently observed in *L v L*[60] that:

> "[T]he judge is not a rubber stamp. He is entitled but not obliged to play the detective. He is a watchdog but is not a bloodhound or a ferret."

D. Agreements not embodied in a court order

13–008   What is the legal status of an agreement (in this context, commonly a separation agreement) that has not been embodied in a consent order? The existence of an

---

[55] The information is prescribed as Form M1 in the Appendix to Family Proceedings Rules 1991, and is limited. Information presented in Form M1 was considered in *X v X (Y and Z Intervening)* [2002] 1 F.L.R. 508, FD.

[56] *Pounds v Pounds* [1994] 1 F.L.R. 775 at 780, CA, *per* Waite L.J.

[57] *B-T v B-T (Divorce: Procedure)* [1990] 2 F.L.R. 1 at 17, *per* Waite L.J.

[58] For empirical studies, see R. Ingleby, "Rhetoric and reality: regulation of out of court activity in matrimonial proceedings" [1989] O.J.L.S. 230; G. Davis et al., "Ancillary relief outcomes" (2000) 12 C.F.L.Q. 43; R. Bird, "Ancillary relief outcomes" (2000) Fam. Law 831. For reported examples of courts expressing concern about the information provided in Form M31, see *B v Miller & Co* [1996] 2 F.L.R. 22, FD, and *X v X (Y and Z Intervening)* [2002] 1 F.L.R. 508, FD.

[59] R. Bird, *Ancillary Relief Handbook*, 5th edn (Family Law, 2005), p.98.

[60] [2006] EWHC 956 (Fam.).

agreement is an important factor for the court to consider in exercising its discretion to achieve a just and fair outcome under s.25[61] of the Matrimonial Causes Act 1925 or para.21(2) of Sch.5 to the Civil Partnership Act 2004 in ancillary relief proceedings.[62] Since the court retains its discretion, the agreement cannot per se be conclusive of outcome,[63] but in the end result may prove to be strongly persuasive.[64] According to Connell J. in *G v G (Financial Provision: Separation Agreement)*[65] the most relevant questions for the court to ask are: "How did the agreement come to be made?" "Did the parties attach importance to it?" "Have they acted upon it?" In *X v X (Y and Z Intervening)*[66] Munby J. emphasied[67] that the court must have regard to all the circumstances, judged in their totality; those surrounding the making of the agreement are important, but relevant circumstances also include social, personal, religious and cultural considerations.

That said, the court will not lightly permit parties who have made an agreement to depart from it.[68] Formal agreements, properly and fairly arrived at with competent legal advice, should not be displaced unless there are good and substantial grounds for concluding that an injustice will be done by holding the parties to the terms of the agreement.[69] A solemn and freely negotiated bargain by which a party with competent legal advice[70] defines his own requirements ought to be adhered to, unless there are clear and compelling grounds for concluding that an injustice will be done if the parties are held to it. A drastic and unforeseen (or overlooked) change of circumstances, or the presence of factors (such as undue pressure[71] by one side, exploitation of a dominant position to secure an unreasonable advantage, inadequate knowledge, as well it seems as

---

[61] Either as one of the "circumstances" referred to in Matromonial Causes Act s.25(1) or as "conduct" under s.25(2)(g): *Edgar v Edgar* [1980] 1 W.L.R. 1410 at 1419; *Camm v Camm* [1982] 4 F.L.R. 577; *G v G (Financial Provision: Separation Agreement)* [2000] 2 F.L.R. 472, FD; *X v X (Y and Z Intervening)* [2002] 1 F.L.R. 508; *A v B (Financial Relief: Agreements)* [2005] 2 F.L.R. 731. See also Civil Partnership Act 2004 Sch.5 para.21(1), (2)(g).

[62] See *Hyman v Hyman* [1929] A.C. 601 at 608–609, *per* Lord Hailsham; *X v X (Y and Z Intervening)* [2002] 1 F.L.R. 508, *per* Munby J. at para.[103].

[63] The separation agreement in *Beach v Beach* [1995] 2 F.L.R. 160 was not adhered to strictly but instead taken into account as part of the developing history.

[64] As in *G v G (Financial Provision: Separation Agreement)* [2000] 2 F.L.R. 18, FD.

[65] *G v G (Financial Provision: Separation Agreement)* [2000] 2 F.L.R. 18, FD ("starting point for the order").

[66] [2002] 1 F.L.R. 508, FD.

[67] [2002] 1 F.L.R. 508, FD at para.[103].

[68] *Edgar v Edgar* [1980] 1 W.L.R. 1410 at 1424, *per* Oliver L.J.; *Benson v Benson (dec'd)* [1996] 1 F.L.R. 692; *N v N (Consent Order: Variation)* [1993] 2 F.L.R. 868 at 876, *per* Butler-Sloss L.J.; *H v H (Financial Relief: Non-Disclosure)* [1994] 2 F.L.R. 94, *per* Thorpe J.; *Smith v McInerney* [1994] 2 F.L.R. 1077, *per* Thorpe J; *X v X (Y and Z Intervening)* [2002] 1 F.L.R. 508, *per* Munby J.

[69] *Edgar v Edgar* [1980] 1 W.L.R. 1410; *Camm v Camm* (1983) 4 F.L.R. 577; *X v X (Y and Z Intervening)* [2002] 1 F.L.R. 508; *A v B (Financial Relief: Agreements)* [2005] 2 F.L.R. 730.

[70] *Camm v Camm* (1983) 4 F.L.R. 577, CA (where the quality of legal advice offered to the wife was a factor in allowing her to resile from an agreement), but note that in *Smith v McInerney* [1994] 2 F.L.R. 1077, Thorpe J.—who had appeared as counsel for the unsuccessful husband in Camm—described it as a "truly exceptional case . . . the only case in the Court of Appeal post *Edgar v Edgar* in which an applicant has been allowed more than he or she contracted for; *B v B (Consent Order: Variation)* [1995] 1 F.L.R. 9; *B v Miller & Co* [1996] 2 F.L.R. 22.

[71] *NA v MA* [2006] EWHC 2900 (Fam.); [2007] Fam. Law 295; [2007] 1 F.L.R. 1760.

poor legal advice) that affected the conclusion of the agreement may be relevant.[72]

If one party seeks to resile from the agreement, the statutory exercise has to be undertaken, and the agreement is not per se determinative of the claim but is only one of the s.25(2) considerations.[73] The court enquires whether, in the light of the totality of the s.25(2) criteria, the agreement was fair at the time it was concluded and at the date of the hearing.[74]

13–009   The leading case is still[75] *Edgar v Edgar*[76]:

> The wife of a multi-millionaire entered into an agreement whereby she accepted property worth some £100,000 from her husband, and agreed not to seek any further capital or property provision from the husband whether by way of ancillary relief in divorce proceedings or otherwise. Three years later she petitioned for divorce, claimed a substantial capital sum and at first instance was awarded a lump sum of £760,000. The Court of Appeal held that the wife had shown insufficient grounds to justify going behind the original agreement. It was immaterial that there may have been a disparity of bargaining power between the husband and the wife, since on the facts he had not exploited it in a way that was unfair to the wife (who had had the benefit of proper professional advice and had deliberately chosen to ignore it).

> In *X v X (Y and Z Intervening)*[77] the parties were both Jewish and the wife's family very wealthy. The parties separated after five years of marriage, whereupon there was media gossip concerning the wife's alleged adultery. Following negotiations between the husband and the wife's family and between the parties' solicitors (who were highly experienced in the conduct of wealthy cosmopolitan divorces), minutes of a consent order for a clean break settlement were agreed between the parties, whereby inter alia the wife would petition for divorce on the ground of the husband's behaviour, the husband would receive £500,000 (to be paid by the wife's brother) and the husband would give a Get. The Get was duly given and a decree nisi subsequently granted. The district judge refused to approve the minutes of order; there were doubts about disclosure and an inadequate explanation of the basis of the husband's entitlement to receive the lump sum, given that the wife claimed she had no assets of her own and the husband admitted to £620,000 plus a £60,000 pension fund and £75,000 salary. The wife resiled from the agreement, on the basis that the essential condition of amicable, expeditious and discrete means of settling their affairs had not been met. The husband applied to require the wife to show cause as to why the minutes of order should not be made an order of the

---

[72] *Edgar v Edgar* [1980] 1 W.L.R. 1410; *Camm v Camm* (1983) 4 F.L.R. 577; *L v L* (2006) EWHC 956 (Fam.); [2008] 1 F.L.R. 26.

[73] *Edgar v Edgar* [1981] 2 F.L.R. 601; *Smith v Smith* [2000] 3 F.C.R 374; *A v B* [2005] 2 F.L.R. 730.

[74] *A v B (Financial Relief: Agreements)* [2005] 2 F.L.R. 730.

[75] *A v B (Financial Relief: Agreements)* [2005] 2 F.L.R. 730.

[76] [1980] 1 W.L.R. 1410, CA.

[77] [2002] 1 F.L.R. 508, FD.

court. The court granted the husband the summary order he sought. The wife should be held to the agreement, which she had willingly entered into with the benefit of expert advice. She had not established inequality of bargain power, or, even if it had existed, that it was the husband who had sought to exploit it. Far from the wife showing that she would suffer injustice if held to her agreement, it was the husband who would suffer serious injustice if she were not. He had faithfully performed his part of the bargain in circumstances where there could be no *restitutio in integrum*.

In contrast:

In *B v B (Consent Order: Variation)*[78] a wife in a depressed and highly confused state accepted a settlement under which she would receive a lump sum and diminishing periodical payments over a specified term, which was not to be capable of being extended. It was held that the wife had received such manifestly bad legal advice (given that it was most unlikely that she would be able to survive without lifetime periodical payments) that she should not be bound by the agreement; and an award of periodical payments at the rate of £25,000 for the parties' joint lives was made.

In *NA v MA*[79] the wife had signed a post-nuptial agreement allowing her £3.3 million plus £252,000 for joint lives or until her remarriage, plus provision for the children. The husband was worth about £40 million. The judge awarded the wife £9.176 million. On the particular facts, the wife had been placed under undue influence by the husband, who had used his dominant position, both emotional and financial, to ensure that the wife felt that she had no alternative but to sign the agreement. Further, the agreement had not been founded on fairness, and its terms had been non-negotiable. It would have been wholly unfair to have implemented the terms of the agreement, and unfair even to use its terms as a starting point by which to judge the fairness of any award.

There may be a dispute as to whether an agreement has been concluded and, if so, what its terms are:

In *Xydhias v Xydhias*[80] there were intensive negotiations prior to trial; a number of draft consent orders were produced by counsel and the wife's solicitors asked the court to vacate the hearing date and substitute a short appointment. At that appointment it was stated that all offers made by the husband were withdrawn. The wife sought an order in the terms of the agreement reached by the parties at the end of their negotiations, and succeeded. The Court of Appeal held inter alia that the court has a discretion in determining whether an accord was reached, although it is to be hoped that the occasions on which it is required to exercise it will be rare.

---

[78] [1995] 1 F.L.R. 9, *per* Thorpe J.
[79] [2007] 1 F.L.R. 1760.
[80] [1999] 1 F.L.R. 683, CA.

Ordinarily, heads of agreement (as distinct from a draft of the consent order) signed by the parties, or a clear exchange of solicitors' letters, will establish the necessary consensus:

> In *Rose v Rose*[81] the judge had approved the agreement and it only remained for its detailed terms to be drafted by counsel. In these circumstances the Court of Appeal held that there was an unperfected order of the court.[82]

The law governing the setting aside of out-of-court agreements has been criticised unsatisfactory[83]; In the words of Hoffmann L.J. (as he then was):

> "If one of them changed his or her mind, they would have to go back to the negotiating table or litigate the matter de novo. This may be tiresome, as in the case of a house purchase where one party changes his or her mind before contracts are exchanged. But the parties would at least know where they stood. The result of the decision . . . in *Edgar v Edgar* . . . is that we have . . . the worst of both worlds. The agreement may be held to be binding only after litigation, and may involve, as in this case, examining the quality of the advice which was given to the party who wishes to resile. It is then understandably a matter for surprise and resentment on the part of the other party that one should be able to repudiate an agreement on account of the inadequacy of one's own legal advisers, over whom the other party had no control and of whose advice he had no knowledge . . . We have created uncertainly and . . . added to the cost and pain of litigation."

E. Facilitating settlement

13–010   During the 1990s a number of developments contributed to reform of procedures with a view to facilitating settlement. Some of these originated from the courts themselves.[84] From 1992 a group of judges and practitioners met to consider procedural improvements, and this group later expanded into the Lord Chancellor's Advisory Group on Ancillary Relief.[85] The group devised a pilot scheme seeking to encourage early definition of the matters in issue between the parties, and envisaging that in most cases financial issues would be referred to a Financial Dispute Resolution appointment, at which the parties would use their best endeavours to reach agreement, with assistance from the court. This scheme was

---

[81] [2002] EWCA Civ. 208; [2002] Fam. Law 344; [2002] 1 F.L.R. 978; D.J. Davies, "FDRs and the unperfected order" [2002] Fam. Law. 613.

[82] It was suggested that the considerations identified in *Stewart v Engel* [2000] 1 W.L.R. 2268 were likely to be relevant where one party sought release between the making of an order in court and its subsequent perfection.

[83] See *Pounds v Pounds* [1994] 1 F.L.R. 775 at 790, *per* Waite L.J and at 791, *per* Hoffmann L.J.

[84] See Davis, Cretney and Collins, *Simple Quarrels*, pp.162–202 on the experience of the Bristol County Court, including mediation appointments.

[85] R. Bird, *Ancillary Relief Handbook*, 2nd edn (Family Law, 2000), p.166.

introduced in selected courts in 1996[86] and, after evaluation and amendment, was implemented nationwide as standard procedure in 2000.[87] The overriding objective is to enable the courts to deal with cases justly and proportionately[88] through active case-management, including identification of issues, limiting disclosure, setting timetables and providing opportunities for settlement.[89] The details of the scheme are beyond the scope of a text of this nature,[90] but key elements[91] include a standard form in which evidence is given by each party, a statement of issues, a first appointment before a district judge designed to define issues and save costs, and a Financial Dispute Resolution appointment. The latter (which is privileged) is squarely aimed at facilitating settlement; the parties are obliged to use their best endeavours to reach agreement on the matters in issue. At the Financial Dispute Resolution appointment, the judge may make a neutral evaluation of the likely outcome. An effective Financial Dispute Resolution hearing, conducted by an experienced judge who has sufficient time to read the papers and to engage with the parties, is essential to the settlement process.[92] The flexibility of judicial conduct of the Financial Dispute Resolution appointment was highlighted by the Court of Appeal in *Rose v Rose*,[93] where it was also emphasised that in a finely balanced case, the Financial Dispute Resolution (FDR) is no substitute for a trial, and should not be used as a discouragement to either party to go to trial in a case that can only properly be resolved by adjudication. If the case does proceed to a final hearing,[94] the district judge who has conducted the FDR appointment can have no further involvement.[95]

F. Incentives to settle: costs?

The starting point in civil litigation in England is that costs "follow the event". **13–011**
The Civil Proceedure Rules 1998 state that the court has a discretion as to costs,

---

[86] See [1996] Fam. Law 197 at 230.
[87] The new procedure was implemented by the Family Proceedings (Amendment No.2) Rules 1999 (SI 1991/3491), which govern all applications for ancillary relief filed after June 5, 2000.
[88] Family Proceedings Rules 1991 (SI 1991/1247) r.2.51B(1).
[89] Family Proceedings Rules 1991 (SI 1991/1247) r.2.51B(5), (6).
[90] For comprehensive accounts, see R. Bird, *Ancillary Relief Handbook*, 5th edn (Family Law, 2005), Ch.16; Thorpe L.J., "Procedural reform in ancillary relief" [1996] Fam. Law 376; Coleridge et al., "FDR—the pilot scheme" [1996] Fam. Law 746; on the consultation process, see [1999] Fam. Law 200; for a critical account, see D.J. Gerlis, "Ancillary relief—progress or decline?" [2001] Fam. Law 891; and for a response, see R. Bird, "Ancillary relief procedure—a reply" [2002] Fam. Law 167.
[91] Family Proceedings Rules 1991 (SI 1991/1247) rr.2.61A–2.69F. On procedure under the 1999 Rules, see *Practice Direction of 25 May 2000 (Ancillary Relief Procedure)* [2000] 1 F.L.R. 997.
[92] *S v S (Ancillary Relief: Importance of FDR)* [2007] EWHC 1975; [2008] 1 F.L.R. 944.
[93] [2002] EWCA Civ. 208; [2002] 1 F.L.R. 978.
[94] Note the comments by Wilson J. on the problems to which the limited evidence contained in Form E (Family Proceedings Rules 1991) (SI 1991/1247, Appendix 1A) may pose for the exercise of judicial discretion at a final hearing: *W v W (Ancillary Relief: Practice)* [2000] Fam. Law 473. On procedure at the final hearing, see *Practice Direction of 10 March 2000 (Family Proceedings: Court Bundles)* [2000] 1 F.L.R. 536.
[95] Save to make a consent order, give directions or hear a variation application: Family Proceedings Rules 1991 (SI 1991/1247) r.2.6(1)(e)(ii): *G v G (Role of FDR Judge)* [2007] 1 F.L.R. 237 (but note that the jurisdiction to vary was conceded in that case).

and then reiterates the general rule that the unsuccessful party will be ordered to pay the costs of the successful party.[96] In family proceedings, but the general principle of civil litigation, that costs follow the event, does not in terms apply.[97] It is nevertheless necessary to have some starting point for costs in family proceedings. For many years, this—according to judicial interpretation of the rules—was that costs prima facie follow the event, although that presumption is more easily displaced in family proceedings than in other civil proceedings.[98]

In family proceedings, courts for many years made use of the costs sanction in an attempt to encourage parties to settle financial matters by agreement, particularly in big-money cases.[99] This policy was manifested in the development of the *Calderbank*[100] offer (i.e. an offer to settle the case on specified terms "without prejudice save as to costs"). If the offer was accepted, the parties would seek a consent order[101] incorporating agreed terms about the allocation of liability for costs, but if the *Calderbank* offer was not accepted, the case proceeded to trial with no reference made at the trial to the offer until the court has announced its award. If that award was more than the amount of the *Calderbank* offer, the successful party would normally be awarded his or her costs[102]; if it was less (implying that the applicant has incurred the costs of the hearing unnecessarily), the court would usually[103] make an order that the person who has rejected the offer should pay all the costs incurred by both sides after the time when the offer was made. The influence of the *Calderbank* doctrine was often a powerful factor in persuading an applicant to accept an offer.[104] The *Calderbank* principles were codified in the Family Proceedings Rules 1991.[105]

However, the *Calderbank* procedure came in for increasing criticism.[106] Reported authority sought to remind courts of the extent of their discretion in respect of costs.[107] Recommendations for change to the Family Proceedings Rules were recommended by the Costs Sub-Committee of the President's

---

[96] Civil Proceedings Rules 1998 (SI 1998/) r.44.3(1), (2), (4), (5).
[97] Family Proceedings (Miscellaneous Amendments) Rules 1999 (SI 1999/1012) r.4; *Practice Direction: Costs: Civil Procedure Rules 1998* [2000] 2 F.L.R. 428.
[98] *Gojkioic v Gojkovic (No.2)* [1991] 2 F.L.R. 233, CA. Litigation misconduct in general sounds in costs and not in the substantive order: *Tavoulareas v Tavoulareas* [1998] 2 F.L.R. 418; *Young v Young* [1998] 2 F.L.R. 1131; but see *Clark v Clark* [1999] 2 F.L.R. 498 where such misconduct was reflected in the quantum of the substantive award.
[99] *F v F (Duxbury Calculation)* [1996] 1 F.L.R. 833; *White v White* [2000] 2 F.L.R. 981.
[100] *Calderbank v Calderbank* [1976] Fam. 93, CA.
[101] See above, paras 13–005 and 13–006.
[102] *Gojkovic v Gojkovic (No.2)* [1991] 2 F.L.R. 233, CA; *A v A (Costs Appeal)* [1996] 1 F.L.R. 14; *Thompson v Thompson* [1993] 2 F.L.R. 464, CA; *Butcher v Wolfe and Wolfe* [1999] 1 F.L.R. 334.
[103] Subject to there being sufficient assets available: [1991] 2 F.L.R. 233 at 237, *per* Butler-Sloss L.J.
[104] Davis, Cretney and Collins, *Simple Quarrels*, p.18; *Singer v Sharegin* [1984] F.L.R. 114 at 119, *per* Cumming-Bruce L.J.; but see S. Gerlis, "Don't bank on Calderbank" [1997] Fam. Law 624.
[105] Family Procedure Rules 1991 (SI 1991/1247) rr.2.69B, 2.69D; See Bird, *Ancillary Relief Handbook*, 5th edn, pp.191–196 for a detailed discussion.
[106] *H v H (Financial Relief: Costs)* [1997] 2 F.L.R. 57; *GW v RW (Financial Provision: Departure From Equality)* [2003] 2 F.L.R. 108; P. Watson-Lee, "Ancillary relief costs—time for regime change?" [2003] Fam. Law 487.
[107] *Norris v Norris; Haskins v Haskins* [2003] 2 F.L.R. 1124; *C v C (Costs: Ancillary Relief)* [2004] 1 F.L.R. 291.

Ancillary Relief Advisory Group, and were placed for public consultation by the Department for Constitutional Affairs in 2004.[108] New rules were enacted in 2006.[109] Family Proceedings Rules 1991 (SI 1991/1247) rr.2.69, 2.69B and 2.69D (on *Calderbank* offers) are repealed, and Civil Procedure Rules 1998 (SI 1998/3132) r.44.3(1) to (5) are disapplied to ancillary relief proceedings. The new r.2.71 provides that *Calderbank* offers are abolished and that only open offers will be admissible. The general rule now is that the court will not make an order requiring one party to pay the others costs. However, the court has a discretion to make a costs order in light of a party's litigation conduct (both before and during the proceedings). The court, in exercising its discretion, is to consider a checklist of matters, including open offers and whether it was reasonable to raise, pursue or contest an issue.[110] The intention is that costs will become part of the substantive judicial determination and will be treated as debts. Reported authorities on the operation of the new costs rules are, at the time of writing, still awaited. The costs of litigation in ancillary relief proceedings continues to be a matter of concern.[111]

III. FINANCIAL RELIEF: THE LEGISLATIVE FRAMEWORK

The fact that the vast majority of financial disputes are settled rather than adjudicated at a final hearing does not render the statutory provisions and their interpretation in the case law irrelevant. First, as we have just seen, final and conclusive agreements can only be made by means of a court order, and the court exercises a paternal jurisdiction (as we have seen, albeit now attenuated[112]) over the agreements submitted for its approval. The court can only assess the reasonableness of the parties' agreement by reference to what might have occurred had the case been fought out. Secondly, legal practitioners in negotiating inevitably have in mind what the outcome of a contest might be; the parties therefore negotiate (as it has been said[113]) in the shadow of the law. Even if the parties wish to reach an agreement by themselves, or with the aid solely of a mediator, they cannot rationally decide whether what emerges is fair unless they have some knowledge of the "going rate" for their situation. Inevitably, there are

13–012

---

[108] *Costs in Ancillary Relief Proceedings and Appeals in Ancillary Relief Proceedings* (CP(l) 29/04).

[109] Family Proceedings Rules 2006 (SI 2006/352), which apply to applications for ancillary relief contained in a petition or answer filed on or after April 3, 2006. See also *Practice Direction (Ancillary Relief: Costs)*, February 20, 2006.

[110] For an example of cost consequences under the "old" rules for unreasonable pursuit of an issue, see *A v A (No.2) (Ancillary Relief: Costs)* [2007] EWHC 1810 (Fam.); [2008] 1 F.L.R. 1423.

[111] See the comments of Munby J. in *A v A (No.2)* [2008] Fam. Law 206.

[112] See para.15–005; *Pounds v Pounds* [1994] 1 F.L.R. 775 at 780, CA, *per* Waite L.J; *L v L* [2006] EWHC 956 (Fam.); [2008] 1 F.L.R. 26 at [73], *per* Munby J.

[113] See R. Mnookin and L. Kornhauser, "Bargaining in the shadow of the law: the case of divorce" (1979) 88 Yale L.J. 950; an abbreviated version can be found in (1979) 32 C.L.P. 65.

cases where the parties' approach is one of mutual hostility, inevitably leading to litigation. Finally, there are cases in which the particular facts raise issues on which no clear guidance is given in reported case law, and parties may be advised to "take their chances" in litigation.

A. The extent of the court's powers

13–013   English law is remarkable for the extent of the court's statutory[114] powers to make financial orders in divorce (and now dissolution)[115] proceedings. The policy of the law is to put all economically valuable assets of the two spouses (and now civil partners) at the disposition of the court. As Waite L.J. observed in *Thomas v Thomas*[116]:

> "The discretionary powers conferred on the court by the amended sections 23–25A of the Matrimonial Causes Act 1973 to redistribute the assets are almost limitless."

The law reports are replete with illustrations of the court's willingness to exercise their ample powers.[117]

Almost as striking as the extent of the court's powers is the flexibility of the principles governing their exercise. The process has been graphically described by Lord Denning.[118] The court:

> "[T]akes the rights and obligations of the parties all together and puts the pieces into a mixed bag. Such pieces are the right to occupy the matrimonial home or have a share in it, the obligation to maintain the wife and children, and so forth. The court then takes out the pieces and hands them to the two parties—some to one party and some to the other—so that each can provide for the future with the pieces allotted to him or to her. The court hands them out without paying any too nice a regard to their legal or equitable rights but simply according to what is the fairest provision for the future, for mother and father and the children."

---

[114] The powers are conferred only by statute: *Livesey (formerly Jenkins) v Jenkins* [1985] F.L.R. 813 at 820, HL, *per* Lord Brandon of Oakbrook.

[115] Unless otherwise indicated, the powers are available in separation and nullity as well as in divorce proceedings.

[116] [1995] 2 F.L.R. 668 at 670D.

[117] Extensive as the court's powers are, they are not limitless. All the terms of the court's order must come within the statutory powers. Thus there is no power to include in an order (even an order made by consent of the parties) a provision that one party should be solely responsible for a mortgage and outgoings in respect of a house, and for servicing and repayment of other loans. Such matters should be dealt with by undertaking: *Livesey (formerly Jenkins) v Jenkins* [1985] F.L.R. 813, HL. It is, however, now common for the court to order one spouse to execute a charge for a proportion of the sale proceeds of the matrimonial home in favour of the other, notwithstanding the absence of any statutory provision clearly authorising such a provision.

[118] *Hanlon v The Law Society* [1981] A.C. 124 at 146, CA.

As Baroness Hale observed in *Miller v Miller; McFarlane v McFarlane*,[119] the flexible statutory powers that the court exercises once a marriage comes to an end exist against the background of separate property during marriage.[120]

The text of this chapter first discusses who can apply for orders; secondly, it analyses the powers of the court; thirdly, it outlines the statutory guidelines for the exercise of the court's discretion; and fourthly, it deals with the court's powers to vary orders if, for example, there has been a change of circumstances or if the original settlement was made under some misapprehension.

i. The applicants

(1) Spouses and civil partners
All orders can be made in favour of either party to a marriage or civil partnership. That ancillary relief orders have more commonly been made in favour of wives than husbands does no more than reflect economic and social realities in relation to income generation, asset acquisition and childcare.[121] **13–014**

(2) Other persons
There may be circumstances in which a third party wishes to seek a financial order—particularly an order in favour of a child for whom the applicant has assumed responsibility.[122] The rules make provision for such applications by persons with appropriate interests.[123] **13–015**

(3) Orders for children
The court has power to make orders in respect of children of the family. These powers—which are now, by reason of the enactment of the Child Support Act 1991, of restricted relevance in practice—are considered in the chapter dealing with Child Support.[124] **13–016**

---

[119] [2006] 1 F.L.R. 1186 at [123], [124].
[120] See Ch.4.
[121] For examples of the exercise of the court's powers in favour of a husband, see, for example, *Griffiths v Griffiths* [1973] 1 W.L.R. 1454 (£7,000 lump sum); *B v B (Financial Provision)* [1982] 3 F.L.R. 298, CA. (£50,000); *Browne v Browne* [1989] 1 F.L.R. 291, CA. (£175,000); *Beach v Beach* [1995] 2 F.L.R. 160 (£60,000); *A v A (Elderly Applicant: Lump Sum)* 2 F.L.R. 969 (£350,000); *Rampal v Rampal (No.2)* [2001] EWCA Civ. 989; [2001] 2 F.L.R. 1179, CA (husband's claim reinstated); *X v X (Y and Z Intervening)* [2002] 1 F.L.R. 508 (£500,000). In *Wills v Wills* [1984] F.L.R. 672 (a case under Domestic Proceedings and Magistrates' Courts Act 1978), it was accepted that an order for periodical payments might be made against a wife in favour of her disabled husband.
[122] Such a person may now apply for orders under the Children Act 1989 Sch.1: see further Ch.15, below.
[123] Family Proceedings Rules 1991 (SI 1991/1247) r.2.54. An adult child may intervene with leave in the parents' divorce suit—perhaps many years after the making of the decree absolute—in order to apply for financial orders: see *Downing v Downing (Downing Intervening)* [1976] Fam. 288, CA. See Ch.15.
[124] See Ch.15, below.

ii. Orders that can be made

13–017   The orders available can usefully be divided into three main categories: (1) those ordering periodical payments of an income nature; (2) those concerned with the transfer of capital assets[125]; and (3) pension sharing orders.[126]

(1) Income orders

13–018   The court may order one spouse or civil partner to make regular income payments to the other, and it may order that the payments be secured.[127] If the order is unsecured, it simply directs a spouse or civil partner to make payments (weekly, monthly or annually). In the event of default, the payee may bring enforcement proceedings (e.g. by seeking an order attaching the defaulter's wages, or a charging order which may lead to the defaulter's property being sold).[128] In practice, however, enforcement procedures are often unsatisfactory (e.g. because the defaulter has no employer and no property that can be found). If, however, the order is secured, a fund of capital (usually[129] stocks and shares, and usually vested in trustees) has to be set aside, and that fund can then be resorted to if the payments are not made as they fall due. The main advantage of a secured order is that it remains enforceable even if a spouse or civil partner disappears or ceases to earn.[130] A further advantage is that such orders may continue throughout the lifetime of the payee.

The court has an unfettered discretion as to whether to order security, and if it does so, discretion as to the proportion of the total payments that should be secured. Traditionally secured provision was regarded as a form of relief only suitable in cases in which a payor had substantial assets.[131] However, the courts have become increasingly prepared to order security if there is a special

---

[125] Matrimonial Causes Act 1973 s.21 and para.2 of Sch.5 to the Civil Partnership Act 2004 draw a distinction between "financial provision orders" (i.e. periodical payment orders and lump sum orders) on the one hand and "property adjustment orders" (i.e. transfers and settlements of property and variations of settlements) on the other. As Lord Diplock has said (see *De Lasala v De Lasala* [1980] A.C. 546 at 559), "the difference between a lump sum order . . . and a property transfer order . . . is the difference between providing money and money's worth"; and a lump sum award (unless of a very small amount) is as much an order for the transfer of capital as any of the other orders.

[126] Matrimonial Causes Act 1973 ss.21A and 24B, inserted by the Welfare Reform and Pensions Act 1999; Civil Partnership Act 2004 Sch.5, para.15–19 and 34.

[127] Matrimonial Causes Act 1973 ss.21(1)(a), (b), s.23(1)(a)(b); Civil Partnership Act 2004 Sch.5, paras 1, 2(1)(a)(b), 4.

[128] See Ch.14.

[129] But not always: see e.g. *F v F* [1976] 1 W.L.R. 793 (former matrimonial home).

[130] *Shearn v Shearn* [1931] P. 1 at 5, *per* Hill J.; and see *A v A (A Minor: Financial Provision)* [1994] 1 F.L.R. 657 (application under Children Act 1989 Sch.1: foreign resident, precarious lifestyle).

[131] *Shorthouse v Shorthouse* (1898) 78 L.T. 687; *Barker v Barker* [1952] P. 184 at 194–195; cf. *Hulton v Hulton* [1916] P. 57.

need for it.[132] In particular, there is no reason why the former family home should not be used as security in appropriate cases.[133]

(a) Duration of periodical payment orders. A periodical payment order in **13–019** favour of a spouse or civil partner will cease to have effect in certain circumstances.

(i) Death of either party. An unsecured order must terminate on the payer's **13–020** death; a secured order need not.[134]

(b) Remarriage, formation of a subsequent civil partnership or marriage of **13–021** *the payee.* The Matrimonial Causes Act 1973[135] gave effect to the recommendation of the Law Commission that periodical payment orders made in divorce or nullity proceedings should not extend beyond the remarriage of the party in whose favour the order was made. The Civil Partnership Act 2004 adopts the same policy: such an order terminates where the payee forms a subsequent civil partnership or marriage.[136]

Criticisms can be leveled against this rigid rule. First, the application of the rule may mean that a person whose marriage or civil partnership has been terminated loses substantially by the formation of a subsequent formal relationship. Secondly, the fact that formation of a subsequent relationship means the end of entitlement to periodical payments may act as a disincentive to the formation of such a marriage. Under the current law, cohabitation—even on a stable long-term basis—will only be taken into account to the extent that it has financial consequences, whereas the formation of a subsequent formal relationship of remarriage means automatic termination of the right to receive periodical payments.[137] Reported authorities continue to emphasise this distinction made in the legislation,[138] but some judicial criticism has been voiced in light of modern social conditions and other developments in the law.[139] Were the Law Commission's proposals for a statutory regime governing the

---

[132] See *Aggett v Aggett* [1962] 1 W.L.R. 183, where maintenance was secured on the husband's only valuable asset (a house) in view of the fact that the wife had set up a guest-house in it that was her only means of earning a living, and that the husband (who had shown himself irresponsible and unconcerned for her welfare) might well go abroad, leaving her without any other means of support.
[133] See Law Com. No.25, para.11; see *F v F* [1967] 1 W.L.R. 793; *Parker v Parker* [1972] Fam. 116 (second mortgage on husband's house).
[134] Matrimonial Causes Act 1973 s.28(1)(a), (b); Civil Partnership Act 2004 Sch.5 para.47(2)(a), (3).
[135] Matrimonial Causes Act 1973 s.28(1)(a).
[136] Civil Partnership Act 2004 Sch.5 para.47(2)(b).
[137] See *Duxbury v Duxbury* [1987] 1 F.L.R. 7, CA; *Atkinson v Atkinson* [1988] 7 F.L.R. 353, CA; *Hepburn v Hepburn* [1989] 1 F.L.R. 373, CA; *Clutton v Clutton* [1991] 1 F.L.R. 242; *Atkinson v Atkinson* [1995] 2 F.L.R. 356; *Jessel v Jessel* [1979] 1 W.L.R. 1148 at 1154, *per* Lord Denning M.R.; *Frary v Frary* [1993] 2 F.L.R. 696, CA.
[138] *Fleming v Fleming* [2004] 1 F.L.R. 667, CA.
[139] *K v K (Periodical Payments: Cohabitation)* [2004] 2 F.L.R. 468.

financial consequences of termination of cohabitation to be enacted,[140] consequential amendments to the periodical-payments provisions in the Matrimonial Causes Act 1973 and the Civil Partnership Act 2004 should be considered.

A lump sum or capital provision order, once made, cannot be varied or cancelled if the spouse remarries or the civil partner forms a subsequent civil partnership or remarriage.

13–022   *(iii) The expiry of a specified term.* The court is specifically required[141] to consider whether it would be appropriate to require periodical payments to be made:

> "[O]nly for such term as would ... be sufficient to enable the party in whose favour the order is made to adjust without undue hardship to the termination of his or her financial dependence on the other."

This provision is discussed later in this chapter in the context of the court's general obligation under s.25A to consider making such orders as will effect a "clean break" between the parties. The circumstances in which such a term may be extended are also dealt with there.

(2) Capital orders

13–023   The court has power, in the case of divorce, dissolution, separation and nullity proceedings to make lump sum orders, orders for the transfer or settlement of property and variation of settlement orders.[142] It also has power[143] in certain circumstances to order the sale of property.

13–024   **(a) Lump sum payments.** The court may order payment of a lump sum in cash.[144] A lump sum payment commonly represents the amount required to effect an overall adjustment of the parties' capital assets. The Act also provides that the court may order payment by instalments, in which case payment may be secured,[145] and the court may order that the sums in question should carry interest.[146] The power to make an instalment order may be of use in cases where the parties are of modest means and need time to pay, but it

---

[140] *Cohabitation: The Financial Consequences of Relationship Breakdown* (Law Com. No.307).
[141] Matrimonial Causes Act 1973 s.25A(2); Civil Partnership Act Sch.5 para.23.
[142] Matrimonial Causes Act 1973 s.24, Civil Partnership Act 2004 Sch.5 paras 6–9.
[143] Matrimonial Causes Act 1973 s.24A; Civil Partnership Act 1973 Sch.5 paras 10–14.
[144] Matrimonial Causes Act 1973 s.21(1)(c), 23(1)(c); Civil Partnership Act 2004 Sch.5 paras 2(1)(c), 3.
[145] Matrimonial Causes Act 1973 s.23(3)(c); Civil Partnership Act 2004 Sch.5 para.3(3).
[146] Matrimonial Causes Act 1973 s.23(6); Civil Partnership Act 2004 Sch.5 para.3(5). The power to order interest can only be exercised when the order is made: *L v L (Lump Sum: Interest)* [1994] 2 F.L.R. 324. Subject to that, interest attaches to lump sum orders as judgment debts from the date when the lump sum is due to be paid: Judgment Act 1838; but interest is only payable on lump sum orders made in the County Court of £5,000 or more: County Courts Act 1984 s.74; County Court (Interest on Judgment Debts) Order 1991 (SI 1991/1184).

may also be of use in cases where a spouse has substantial assets[147] (e.g. farming land or a shareholding in a company) that would be difficult, impracticable or undesirable to realise quickly.[148] In *R v R (Lump Sum Repayments)*[149] there were no liquid assets available for distribution; Wilson J. ordered the husband to pay the wife a lump sum of £30,000 immediately, and thereafter 240 monthly instalments in a sum equivalent to her obligations under a 20-year repayment mortgage for £225,000.

(b) Transfer of property. The court may[150] order that specified property be   **13–025** transferred to the other spouse. This power may be used, for example, to order the transfer by one spouse to the other of specific shares, or very commonly the matrimonial home or one spouse's interest in it. It may be used in addition to a lump sum order where there is a special case for the transfer of a particular asset, or as an alternative to such an order.

(c) Settlements of property. The court may[151] direct that property to which   **13–026** a party to the marriage is entitled be settled for the benefit of the other party and/or the children of the family.

Traditionally, this power[152] was seen as a flexible way of using a fund of shares or other property for the family over a period of time (e.g. by giving the other spouse a life interest and preserving the capital for the children and their issue). In recent years, however, the power has most frequently been used in connection with the family home—often in an attempt to ensure that the parent who has day-to-day control will have a secure home for the children whilst preserving the investment interest of both spouses. This topic is considered below.

(d) Variation of settlements. The court may make an order varying an ante-   **13–027** nuptial or post-nuptial settlement made on the parties to the marriage for the benefit of the parties and/or the children of the family and, in the case of civil partnership, varying a settlement made during the subsistence of, or in anticipation of the civil partnership; such orders may extinguish the interest of a

---

[147] See, for example, *Penrose v Penrose* [1994] 2 F.L.R. 621, CA (order for £500,000 by instalments).

[148] See, for example, *N v N (Financial Provision: Sale of Company)* [2001] 2 F.L.R. 69 (£1 million to be paid to the wife according to a detailed timetable). The court has power not only to re-timetable and adjust the amounts of individual instalments but also to vary, suspend or discharge the principal lump sum itself, although the last power is to be used very sparingly in exceptional circumstances: *Penrose v Penrose* [1994] 2 F.L.R. 621, CA; *Tilley v Tilley* (1980) Fam. Law 89; *Westbury v Sampson* [2001] EWCA Civ. 407; [2002] 1 F.L.R. 166.

[149] [2004] 1 F.L.R. 928.

[150] Matrimonial Causes Act 1973 ss.24(1)(a), 21(2)(a); Civil Partnership Act 2004 Sch.5 para.7(1)(a).

[151] Matrimonial Causes Act 1973 ss.21(2)(a), 24(1)(b); Civil Partnership Act 2004 Sch.5 para.7(1))(b).

[152] Which originated in the court's power to order a wife guilty of adultery, cruelty or desertion to settle property in order to compensate the innocent parties for the pecuniary loss so caused to them: see *March v March* (1867) L.R. 1 P. & D. 440; *Ulrich v Ulrich* [1968] 1 W.L.R. 180; Law Com. No.25, paras 50, 66.

party in the settlement.[153] The only restriction on the court's power to vary the settlement is that the variation must be "for the benefit" of the parties or children, and in an appropriate case the terms of the settlement may be completely re-written.[154]

The power to vary dates back to 1857 and was, for a long time, the only way in which the court could deal with capital on the breakdown of a marriage. The courts have a broad interpretation of the word "settlement," so that, for example, it has been held to extend to the case where a dwelling-house had been purchased in joint names[155] (or even in the name of one party, provided that both had beneficial interests). The only qualification is that[156] although the settlement did not have to be a marriage settlement in the strict sense, some "nuptial element" is required; the settlement must have been made on the parties as spouses,[157] and the effect of the transaction must have been to make some form of continuing provision[158] for both or either of the parties to the marriage. A settlement will not necessarily lose its nuptial character by removal of spouses from the class of beneficiaries if they retain control of decision-making.[159]

The power to vary a nuptial settlement was, however, given some impact (albeit short-lived) by the decision of the House of Lords in *Brooks v Brooks*,[160] which provided a limited solution to the problem of dealing with pensions on divorce, in the absence at that time of the extensive powers subsequently conferred by legislation. *Brooks v Brooks* laid down that in some circumstances a pension scheme fell within the definition of a nuptial settlement, and that, accordingly, the court could vary the terms of the settlement for the benefit of the wife or children. The decision in *Brooks v Brooks* was always of limited scope[161] and now is of historical interest only. The scheme in question was comparatively unusual in having been created by the sole proprietor of a business, in which the wife was also employed; and it seems

[153] Matrimonial Causes Act 1973 s.24(1)(c), 21(2)(c); Civil Partnership Act 2004 Sch.5 para.7(1)(c), (1)(d), (3).
[154] See *E v E (Financial Provision)* [1990] 2 F.L.R. 233. The powers extend to replacing trustees: *E v E (Financial Provision)*, not following *Compton v Compton and Hussey* [1960] P. 201. The court's powers are not confined to varying the interests of the parties to the marriage but extend to varying the interests of children and others under the settlement: *Brooks v Brooks* [1995] 2 F.L.R. 13 at 20, *per* Lord Nicholls of Birkenhead. Note also that Matrimonial Causes Act 1973 s.24(1)(d) empowers the court to reduce or extinguish the interest of either spouse under a nuptial settlement; and it seems that this power may be exercised, notwithstanding the fact that to do so would not benefit the other spouse or children: *Cartwright v Cartwright* [1982] 4 F.L.R. 463. Third parties such as trustees may be joined as parties: *T v Y (Joinder of Third Parties)* [1996] 2 F.L.R. 357, FD.
[155] *Brown v Brown* [1959] P. 86.
[156] *Cook v Cook* [1962] P. 235.
[157] *Young v Young* [1962] P. 27; and see Law Com. No.25, para.66.
[158] Even a covenant securing an annuity to a spouse: *Bosworthick v Bosworthick* [1927] P. 64. It was also held that a life policy effected under a trust for the wife's benefit fell within the definition of a settlement (see *Brown v Brown* [1949] P. 91; *Lort-Williams v Lort-Williams* [1951] P. 395). In contrast, an outright gift by one party to the other falls outside the statutory definition of a settlement (see *Prescott (formerly Fellowes) v Fellowes* [1958] P. 260).
[159] *Charalambous v Charalambous* [2004] 2 F.L.R. 1093.
[160] [1995] 2 F.L.R. 13, HL. The first judicial suggestion that pension schemes might be susceptible to the exercise of this power was made by Ewbank J. in *Griffiths v Dawson & Co* [1993] 2 F.L.R. 315.
[161] It was applied in *W v W (Periodic Payments)* [1996] 2 F.L.R. 480.

that the scheme could—without prejudicing the Inland Revenue's approval of the scheme—be converted into a multi-member scheme in which the wife could participate. Lord Nicholls of Birkenhead[162] observed that[163]:

> "[I]f the court is to be able to split pension rights on divorce in the more usual case of a multi-member scheme where the wife has no earnings of her own from the same employer, or to direct the taking out of life insurance, legislation will . . . be necessary".

That power was given to the courts by the Welfare Reform and Pensions Act 1999, which abolished[164] the remedy created by *Brooks v Brooks* in the context of pensions. The range of powers that the court now possesses is considered later in this chapter.

(e) Power to order sale. The court has power on making an order for   **13–028** financial relief in divorce, nullity and separation proceedings, or at any time thereafter, to order the sale of any property in which, or in the proceeds of sale of which, either or both of the parties has or have a beneficial interest, either in possession or reversion, and an order may be made notwithstanding that a third party is also interested in the property.[165] However, the court has no power under this provision to direct the payment of the proceeds of sale to third parties[166]; in effect, the power is ancillary to or consequential upon the making of the other orders mentioned.[167]

(3) Pension sharing orders
The Welfare Reform and Pensions Act 1999 gave the court power to make   **13–029** pension sharing orders in respect of petitions filed after December 1, 2000.[168] Equivalent powers are contained in the Civil Partnership Act 2004.[169] The full

[162] Delivering a speech in which all the other Law Lords concurred.
[163] [1995] 2 F.L.R. 13 at 23.
[164] Matrimonial Causes Act 1973 s.24(1)(c) and (d), as amended by the Welfare Reform and Pensions Act 1999 Sch.3, excluding a marriage settlement in the form of a pension arrangement from the categories of settlement that are variable. See also Civil Partnership Act 2004 Sch.5 para.7(3).
[165] Matrimonial Causes Act 1973 s.24A(1); Civil Partnership Act 2004 Sch.5 paras 10–14. Before making an order in such a case, the court must give the third party an opportunity to make representations, and must consider those representations: Matrimonial Causes Act 1973 s.25(6), as inserted by Matrimonial Homes and Property Act 1981 s.8(1). The provisions of s.24A were intended to give effect to the Law Commission's *Report on Orders for Sale of Property under the Matrimonial Causes Act 1973* (Law Com. No.99 (1980)). See also Civil Partnership Act 2004 Sch.5 para.14.
[166] See *Burton v Burton* [1986] 2 F.L.R. 419, following *Mullard v Mullard* [1982] F.L.R. 330, CA (no jurisdiction to make order that house be sold and part of proceeds paid to husband's creditors).
[167] See *Norman v Norman* [1983] 1 W.L.R. 295; *Thompson v Thompson* [1985] F.L.R. 863, CA; cf. *R. v Rushmoor BC* [1988] 2 F.L.R. 252, CA, *per* Sir Frederick Lawton. It is in any event clear that although there is a statutory power to vary orders for sale made under s.24A (see Matrimonial Causes Act 1973 s.31(2)(f)), this power is not to be used so as to subvert the policy of the legislation that property adjustment orders should not be liable to be varied; see *Omielan v Omielan* [1996] 2 F.L.R. 306, CA.
[168] Welfare Reform and Pensions Act 1999 s.19 Sch.3 paras 1, 2, inserting ss.21A and 24B into Matrimonial Causes Act 1973.
[169] Civil Partnership Act 2004 Sch.5 paras 15–19 and 34.

range of the court's powers in relation to pensions are discussed later in this chapter.[170]

(4) When orders can be made

13–030 An order for maintenance pending suit in the case of marriage—and maintenance pending the outcome of dissolution, nullity or separation proceedings in the case of civil partnership[171]—can be made at any time after a petition for principal relief has been filed. The courts' powers to make financial provision, property adjustment and pension attachment under ss.23–24D of the Matrimonial Causes Act 1973 and paras 1–37 of Sch.5 to the Civil Partnership Act 2004 may be exercised only on or after the making of a decree of nullity, divorce or judicial separation. Pension sharing orders may only be made on or after the making of a decree of divorce or dissolution order or a decree or order of nullity.[172]

iii. The principles governing the exercise of the court's discretion

13–031 The Matrimonial Proceedings and Property Act 1970[173] was a comprehensive codification of the law,[174] setting out detailed guidelines to assist the court in the exercise of the extremely wide powers conferred on the court (for the first time) by that Act. However, the assumptions on which these guidelines had been formulated soon began to be questioned. The Law Commission undertook an examination of the issues, and some changes—supposedly of an evolutionary rather than a revolutionary nature—were made to the law by the Matrimonial and Family Proceedings Act 1984. Since then, as we will show, the development of further guidelines (both as to policy and practice) has been undertaken by the judiciary rather than the legislature. It may be helpful in understanding the contemporary law to give a brief account of its historical development.

(1) Historical evolution of the law

13–032 **(a) Financial relief under the offence-based divorce law.** Until the coming into force of the Divorce Reform Act 1969,[175] a petitioner only had an

---

[170] At p.413.

[171] Matrimonial Causes Act 1973 s.22; Civil Partnership Act 2004 Sch.5 para.38, discussed at para.13–037.

[172] Matrimonial Causes Act s.24B(1), inserted by the Welfare Reform and Pensions Act 1999 Sch.3 para.4. See also Civil Partnership Act 2004 Sch.5 para.15(1).

[173] Which was subsequently consolidated in the Matrimonial Causes Act 1973. After some initial hesitation, the radical nature of the change in the law effected by the 1970 Act came to be generally recognised, and it was described as "revolutionary"; *per* Lord Denning M.R. in *Trippas v Trippas* [1973] Fam. 134 at 140, and at 144–145, *per* Scarman L.J.; see also *Griffiths v Griffiths* [1974] 1 All E.R. 932 at 940, *per* Roskill L.J.; "drastically reformed the law"; *Calderbank v Calderbank* [1976] Fam. 93 at 101.

[174] *Wachtel v Wachtel* [1973] Fam. 72; *Trippas v Trippas* [1973] Fam. 134; *Hunter v Hunter* [1973] 1 W.L.R. 958 at 962, *per* Edmund Davies L.J.

[175] Which came into force on January 1, 1971.

unqualified right to divorce if he or she was an aggrieved and innocent victim of the other spouse's wrongdoing.[176] Marriage created a status, with reciprocal rights and duties; so long as the parties remained married and the wife refrained from committing a matrimonial offence, she had, as one of the incidents of that status, a legal right at common law[177] to be supported by her husband. It therefore seemed reasonable that the court's powers should be exercised in such a way as to keep the injured wife in the position in which she would have been had her husband properly discharged his marital obligations towards her. The principle applied was (as the Law Commission put it[178]):

> "[V]ery similar to that governing liability for breach of contract: a man who breaks a contract is liable to compensate the other party who is entitled to be put into the same position as if the contract had been carried out."

In practice, this contractual analogy was tempered over the years, particularly in a concern to ensure that a "guilty" wife (that is to say, one who had committed a matrimonial offence) should not necessarily forfeit all right to maintenance. However, the underlying principle of the law was at least clear. An "innocent" divorced wife was entitled to be kept in the same financial position as she would have enjoyed had the marriage continued, but the right and duty of maintenance was related to the performance of reciprocal matrimonial obligations, and the concept of a life-long right to and duty of support was "inextricably linked with the concept of divorce as a relief for wrongdoing".[179]

(b) The implications for financial provision of a divorce law based on 13–033
breakdown. How was financial provision to be regulated under a reformed divorce law, which sought to minimise reliance on guilt and innocence? Opponents of the Divorce Reform Act claimed that it would prove to be a "Casanovas' Charter" whereby blameless wives would be repudiated by their husbands and left destitute,[180] and a powerful movement developed that was concerned with achieving financial protection for divorced women. In response to these pressures, the Lord Chancellor gave an undertaking that the Divorce Reform Act 1969 would not be brought into force until legislation had been brought in to deal comprehensively with the financial consequences of divorce.[181]

---

[176] The Law Commission's Discussion Paper, *The Financial Consequences of Divorce: The Basic Policy* (Law Com. No.103 (1980)), para.9.
[177] See Ch.3, above.
[178] Law Com. No.103 (1980), para.11.
[179] Law Com. No.103, para.16.
[180] Law Com. No.103, para.16.
[181] See *Hansard*, Vol.794, col.1560; and cols 1597–1598; see further Law Com. No.103, para.19.

Unfortunately, the Law Commission's 1969 report[182] on which the 1970 legislation was based[183] contained virtually no discussion[184] of the implications that the change in the basis of the ground for divorce might have for the determination of the financial consequences of divorce. Moreover, the Commission made assumptions—soon to be falsified—about other important matters (such as the effect of misconduct by one or both parties). The Matrimonial Proceedings and Property Act 1970 was brought into force on the same day as the Divorce Reform Act, and, from one view, was no more than the political price that had to be paid to secure the enactment of the reformed divorce law.[185]

13–034   **(c) Minimal loss: preservation of status quo, 1970–1984.** The 1970 Act greatly extended the court's powers, and firmly adopted what has been called[186] the "minimal loss" (or status quo) principle. This meant that although the court was entitled to regard particular circumstances—(e.g. the duration of the marriage) as being of such weight as to override the general direction to place the parties in the financial position in which they would have been had their marriage not broken down, nevertheless:

> "[T]he primary objective is that the financial position of the parties should so far as possible be unaffected by their divorce. In short, although divorce terminates the legal status of marriage it will usually not terminate the financial ties of marriage which may remain lifelong."[187]

In this respect it can be said that although the English legislation was not based on any profound analysis of principle, it was at least alive to the risk that a shift to irretrievable breakdown as the ground for divorce would be what an American scholar has described as the "systematic impoverishment of

---

[182] *Financial Provision in Matrimonial Proceedings* (Law Com. No.25 (1969)).

[183] There was comparatively little discussion of the Bill in Parliament, since debate in the House of Commons was much shortened by the decision to dissolve Parliament.

[184] Law Com. No.25 contains little more than a single paragraph (see para.81) on the question of principle: the paragraph states that it is desirable to introduce a "uniform and more detailed set of guidelines than under the old law" (when the only direction was to do what was thought reasonable, fit or just). It does not advert to the objective of seeking to put the parties in the position in which they would have been had the marriage not broken down. The explanatory notes on the draft Bill annexed to the report, however, made it clear that the Commission was apparently seeking to codify the principle enunciated by Lord Merrivale in *N v N* (1928) 44 T.L.R. 324 at 328 with "some elaboration . . . to cover the possibility that, for example, both parties may have failed to discharge their marital obligations": draft cl.5, fn.2.

[185] See *per* Mr Leo Abse M.P., *Hansard*, HC, Vol.54, col.416: "we had to pay a price for the 1969 Act . . . In order to take the House with us, we had to concede provisions relating to finance and conduct which were either inappropriate or which had a built-in obsolescence . . . Since, for the first time, it would be possible to divorce a wife without her consent even though the marriage might have broken down many years before, it was necessary to include in the Bill the provisions with which we are dealing today."

[186] See J. Eekelaar, *Family Law and Social Policy*, 2nd edn (1984), p.109.

[187] Law Com. No.103, para.22.

divorced women and their children".[188] Indeed, in England, criticism about the effect of the law came mostly from men who argued that it was they and their new families who were impoverished by the law.

(d) Opposition to minimal-loss principle: the law re-examined. This **13–035** assumption that the parties to the marriage remained bound to provide for one another even after the marriage had been dissolved became the object of much criticism; in 1980 the Law Commission undertook an examination of the underlying issues and of the options for reform.[189] In the course of this examination, the Commission received an "overwhelming body of evidence that to direct the courts to seek to place the parties in the financial position in which they would have been if the marriage had not broken down is to impose a fundamentally mistaken objective, widely thought to be capable of producing unjust and inequitable results",[190] and it accordingly recommended "evolutionary" legislation,[191] to give effect to the following proposals:

- Statute should no longer impose on the court the duty so to exercise its powers as to place the parties in the financial position in which they would have been if the marriage had not broken down.[192]

- The law should seek to emphasise "as a priority" the necessity to make such financial provision as would safeguard the maintenance and welfare of the children.[193]

- Greater weight should be given to the importance of each party doing everything possible to become self-sufficient, so far as this would be consistent with the interests of the children; statute should positively assert this principle.

- Technical problems[194] that prevented the court from finally terminating a spouse's right to seek further support from the other should be removed "so that in those comparatively few (and where there were infant children almost non-existent) cases" in which it would be appropriate to achieve a final once-for-all financial settlement at the

---

[188] See L. Weitzman, *The Divorce Revolution* (1985) on the impact of no-fault divorce in the United States. Dr Weitzman's views are not universally shared: see, for example, M. Garrison in S.D. Sugarman and H.H. Kay, *Divorce Reform at the Crossroads* (1991).

[189] The Law Commission's analysis of the principles underlying the law, and of various models for reform, was published as a report: *The Financial Consequences of Divorce: The Basic Policy.* A Discussion Paper (Law Com. No.103). This analysis (summarised in the fourth edition of this book at pp.760–767) still repays study. Reference may also be made to the discussion of the objectives of financial provision in the Scottish Law Commission's Report on *Aliment and Financial Provision* (Scot. Law Com. No.67, (1981)), Pt III.

[190] Law Com. No.112, para.6.

[191] The report reported the tenor of the response to the earlier Discussion Paper and contained proposals, in general terms, for reform. For reasons set out in Law Com. No.112, para.3 and subsequently amplified in evidence to the House of Commons Special Committee, March 20, 1984, col.63 (S.M. Cretney), it did not contain draft legislation.

[192] Matrimonial Causes Act 1973 s.25(1).

[193] Law Com. No.112, para.24.

[194] *Dipper v Dipper* [1981] Fam. 31.

time of the divorce, the court would not lack the powers to do so.[195]

(2) The statutory guidelines for the exercise of the court's discretion

13–036 The Matrimonial and Family Proceedings Act 1984 amended the law in accordance with the Law Commission's recommendations, and the statutory guidelines for the exercise of the court's discretion remain substantially unchanged. As has already been indicated[196] and will be further explained, the appellate courts have, within the broad discretionary framework and the implicit over-arching objective of achieving a fair outcome, shown increasing enthusiasm for formulating guidelines to structure the exercise of discretion.

13–037 **(a) Maintenance pending suit and maintenance pending outcome of dissolution, nullity and separation proceedings.** The only guideline for exercise of the power to order maintenance pending suit in the case of marriage—and maintenance pending outcome of dissolution, nullity or separation proceedings in the case of civil partnership—is that the court shall make such order as it considers reasonable.[197] The question is "what is reasonable to provide for interim needs". Reasonableness is self-evidently a relative concept to be considered in the context of the financial circumstances of the case.[198]

The general principles applicable to MPs were summarised by Nicholas Mostyn Q.C. sitting as a Deputy High Court Judge in *TL v ML (Ancillary Relief: Claim Against Assets of Extended Family)*.[199] In short:

- The sole criterion is reasonableness, which is synonymous with fairness.

- Marital standard of living is an important consideration, although not necessarily to be replicated.

- There should be a specific budget that excludes capital and long-term expenditure.

- The budget should be critically examined for forensic exaggeration.

This summary was endorsed by Munby J. in *Re G (Maintenance Pending Suit)*.[200]

An issue of increasing practical importance—and by no means only in big-money cases—is that of the award of a costs allowance in an order for maintenance pending suit/outcome. In *A v A (Maintenance Pending Suit):*

---

[195] Law Com. No.112, para.29.
[196] See para.13–001.
[197] Matrimonial Causes Act 1973 s.22, Civil Partnership Act 2004 Sch.5 para.38.
[198] Compare *Peacock v Peacock* [1984] 1 W.L.R. 532 (very modest means) with *F v F (Ancillary Relief: Substantial Assets)* [1995] 2 F.L.R. 45 (standards of the ultra-rich).
[199] [2006] 1 F.L.R. 1263.
[200] [2007] 1 F.L.R. 1674.

Provision of Legal Fees[201] the question was whether an order for maintenance pending suit made against the petitioner husband could include the petitioner wife's legal fees for her applications for nullity and ancillary relief; her legal-aid certificate had been discharged. Holman J. held that the words of s.22 of the Matrimonial Causes Act 1973 were wide enough to include an element of the payee's legal costs, provided it was reasonable to do so and provided that the court proceeded with caution. His Lordship's conclusion was fortified by art.6 of the European Convention for the Protection of Human Rights and Fundamental Freedoms and by the concept of equality of arms in relation to legal representation.[202] A similar approach was adopted by Charles J. in *G v G (Maintenance Pending Suit: Costs)*.[203]

In *Moses-Taiga v Moses-Taiga*,[204] the Court of Appeal appeared to say that a costs allowance should only be made in *exceptional* cases, when a party can prove that she cannot raise the funding in any other way. However, the supposed requirement of exceptional was "softened" by Hedley J. in *C v C (Maintenance Pending Suit: Legal Costs)*,[205] where the wife has an unencumbered half-share in the former matrimonial home worth more than £500,000. Hedley J. held that it would be "wholly unfair" for her to borrow against that to fund representation.

The current law is now found in the decision of the Court of Appeal in **13–038** *Currey v Currey (No.2)*.[206] The law, as restated, is, in essence:

- The suggestion that the power to include a costs allowance should only be exercised in *exceptional* cases obstructs the proper exercise of the jurisdiction.

- The initial overarching enquiry is whether the applicant for a costs allowance cannot *reasonably* procure legal advice and representation by any other means. To the extent that he or she has assets, the applicant has to demonstrate that they cannot reasonably be deployed, whether directly or as the means of raising a loan, in funding legal services. Furthermore, the applicant has also to demonstrate that they cannot reasonably procure legal services by the offer of a charge on ultimate capital recovery.

- It would not be reasonable for the court to exercise the discretion to make a costs allowance unless the applicant has thus duly demonstrated that they cannot reasonably procure legal advice and representation by any other means. That is a necessary but not a sufficient

---

[201] [2001] 1 F.L.R. 377; [2001] 1 W.L.R. 605, FD.
[202] In *Sears Tooth (A Firm) v Payne Hicks Beach (A Firm)* [1997] 2 F.L.R. 116 at 11H–119A, Wilson J. drew attention to "a grave and widespread problem encountered increasingly in the Family Division: namely, how can a spouse, usually a wife, who is ineligible for legal aid but who has negligible capital, secure legal advice and legal representation in order to pursue her rights against her husband, particularly one who is rich, litigious or obstructive . . . ?".
[203] [2003] 2 F.L.R. 71.
[204] [2006] 1 F.L.R. 1074.
[205] [2007] 1 F.L.R. 946. For a review of the recent case law, see D. Salter, "Maintenance pending suit and the costs allowance" [2007] Fam. Law 218.
[206] [2006] EWHC Civ. 1338; [2007] 1 F.L.R. 946; [2007] Fam. Law 12.

condition. Other factors may well come into play that will no doubt on occasions lead the court to decline to make it, notwithstanding the demonstration.

- Whenever a court decides to make a costs allowance, it ought to proceed with a judicious mixture of realism and caution as to both its *amount* and *duration*.

- There may be good sense in limiting the duration of a component for legal representation only up until the end of the FDR appointment.[207] The FDR is a watershed, and all reasonable inducements to both parties there to negotiate should be in place. The FDR judge cannot, at the conclusion of the FDR, determine the issue of whether a costs allowance should be continued up to trial. Where a costs allowance is expressed to continue only to FDR, any application for its extension to trial will have to be considered by a different judge. That fresh judge will have access to rival open offers to assist in the assessment of the reasonableness, or otherwise of the parties' positions in the ancillary relief proceedings overall.

(b) All other orders.

13–039 *(i) The legislative provisions.* The scheme of the legislation, on its face, is as follows:

- It is the duty of the court in deciding whether to exercise its powers and, if so, in what manner to have regard to all the circumstances of the case, first consideration being given to the welfare, while a minor, of any child of the family who has not attained the age of 18.[208]

- As regards the exercise of the powers to make orders, it is provided that the court shall "in particular have regard to" certain specified matters,[209] and the the court is further "in particular" to have regard to certain specified matters as regards the exercise of its powers to make such orders in relation to a child of the family.[210]

- Finally, the legislation contains a number of provisions designed to direct the court's attention to the principle of self-sufficiency, and to facilitate the making of a "clean break" between the parties to the marriage in appropriate cases.[211]

13–040 *(ii) Judicial guidelines to interpretation of the statutory provisions.* Section 25 of the Act since its amendment in 1984, expresses no objective, and the wide-ranging survey of "all the circumstances" that the court is required to

---

[207] See para.13–007.
[208] Matrimonial Causes Act 1973 s.25(1); Civil Partnership Act 2004 Sch.5 para.20.
[209] Matrimonial Causes Act 1973 s.25(2); Civil Partnership Act 2004 Sch.5 para.21(2).
[210] Matrimonial Causes Act 1973 s.25(3); Civil Partnership Act 2004 Sch.5 para.22.
[211] Matrimonial Causes Act 1973 s.25A; Civil Partnership Act 2004 Sch.5 para.23.

undertake does not of itself give any clear guidance as to the principles on which the court should act, nor of the underlying policies on which asset and income distribution are justified.[212] According to Lord Nicholls in *Miller v Millere; McFarlane v McFarlane*, achieving fairness in the division of matrimonial property following divorce is "that most intractable of problems".[213] The absence of declared objective is particularly apparent where there are no minor children of the family, and thus no "first" consideration, and in "big money cases" where there is a large surplus of assets after the satisfaction of needs. In the absence of principles, the width of discretion leads inevitably to diversity in judicial approach, reflecting in turn a diversity of community views.[214] As has already been indicated,[215] in recent years the House of Lords and the Court of Appeal have shown themselves increasingly ready to formulate guidelines, in large part motivated by the desire to increase certainty of outcome and thereby to promote settlement and reduce the costs involved in protracted litigation.[216] According to Lord Nicholls in *Miller v Miller; McFarlane v McFarlane*, legitimate—indeed necessary—for the highest court to "articulate, if only in the broadest fashion, what are the applicable if unspoken principles guiding the court's approach".[217] This, it is said, is "not to usurp the judicial function" but rather "to perform a necessary judicial function in the absence of parliamentary guidance".[218]

This recent activism by the highest judiciary in formulating principles based on social policy stands in marked contrast to the earlier approach evidenced in *Piglowska v Piglowski*.[219] There, the leading speech of Lord Hoffmann (which, given the particular fact, focused heavily on criticism of the appellate process and litigation costs), emphasised the width of judicial discretion conferred by s.25. It was stated that the factors listed in s.25(2) are not, as a matter of law, ranked in any hierarchy, and that the weight to be accorded to them depends entirely on the facts of the case. Further, pronouncements in appellate decisions on ancillary relief do not have the status of principles, and diversity in judicial application of the statutory provisions is inevitable.[220]

The following discussion examines the contributions that the landmark cases of *White v White*,[221] *Miller v Miller; McFarlane v McFarlane*[222] and *Charman v Charman (No.4)*[223] have made to the interpretation of the provisions contained in Pt II of the Matrimonial Causes Act 1973. Decisions on the equivalent provisions in Sch.5 to the Civil Partnership Act 2004 are at the

---

[212] *Miller v Miller; McFarlane v McFarlane* [2006] 1 F.L.R. 1186, paras [5], [124]–[134].
[213] *Miller v Miller; McFarlane v McFarlane* [2006] 1 F.L.R. 1186, para.[1].
[214] See *Piglowska v Piglowski* [1999] 2 F.L.R. 763 at 785, *per* Lord Hoffmann.
[215] para.13–001 above.
[216] See, for example, *Piglowska v Piglowski* [1999] 2 F.L.R. 763 at 785; *Miller v Miller; McFarlane v McFarlane* [2006] 1 F.L.R. 1186, paras [6], [122].
[217] [2006] 1 F.L.R. 1186, para.[6].
[218] [2006] 1 F.L.R. 1186, para.[7].
[219] [1999] 2 F.L.R. 763.
[220] R. Bailey-Harris and P. Coleridge, "Family assets, costs and avenues of appeal" [2001] 117 LQR 1571.
[221] [2000] 2 F.L.R. 981.
[222] [2006] 1 F.L.R. 1186.
[223] [2007] 1 F.L.R. 1246.

time of writing awaited, but it is predicted that the same principles will be applied, not least because to do otherwise would be discriminatory.

13–041 *(iii) The overriding objective implicit in section 25.* The objective to be implied in s.25 is that of achieving a fair outcome, with fairness involving non-discrimination between husband and wife in the evaluation of their contributions to family welfare in their respective roles.[224] However, fairness is a very general concept; as Lord Nicholls observed in *White v White*,[225] "fairness, like beauty, lies in the eye of the beholder". Subsequently, in *Miller v Miller; McFarlane v McFarlane*, Lord Nicholls declared that fairness is "an elusive concept" based on "social and moral values" that can be "stated" but not "justified, or refuted, by any objective process of logical reasoning" and which change over time.[226] The overriding objective of fairness was glossed by Baroness Hale as being "to give each party an equal start on the road of independent living".[227]

13–042 *(iv) Guidelines additional to the overriding objective.* In a recent series of landmark cases, the House of Lords and the Court of Appeal have developed guidelines—now arguably accorded the status of principles—that are more specific than the overriding general objective of the statutory provisions. These are best explained through an analysis of the cases.

13–043 *(v) White v White and its aftermath.* In *White v White*[228] the spouses had, throughout their 33-year marriage, operated in partnership a farming business on two farms. One farm belonged to the couple jointly, the other to the husband. The husband's father had provided an interest-free loan and some capital for the purchase of the first farm, and had purchased an estate from which the second farm, acquired on advantageous terms, was derived. On divorce, both parties claimed ancillary relief. The assets were worth £4.6 million, and all the surviving children were adults. Holman J., applying the then well-established "reasonable requirements" approach,[229] awarded the wife £800,000 in addition to retention of her sole assets. The lump sum reflected her housing and capitalised-income requirements, but her wish to farm in her own right (which would have required division of the enterprise) was rejected. The Court of Appeal increased the wife's award to £1.5 million. Thorpe L.J.[230] identified the farming partnership as the dominant feature of the case, with considerations of contributions and overall fairness also relevant

---

[224] *Piglowska v Piglowski* [1999] 2 F.L.R. 783, *per* Lord Nicholls in *White v White* [2000] 2 F.L.R. 981 at 992; *per* Munby J. in *X v X (Y and Z Intervening)* [2002] 1 F.L.R. 508 at para.[103].
[225] [2000] 2 F.L.R. 981 at 983.
[226] [2006] 1 A.C. para.[4].
[227] [2006] 1 A.C. para.[144].
[228] [2000] 3 W.L.R. 1571; [2000] 2 F.L.R. 98.
[229] *O'D v O'D* [1976] Fam. 83; *Page v Page* (1981) 2 F.L.R. 198; *Preston v Preston* [1982] Fam. 17; *Gojkovic v Gojkovic* [1990] L.R. 140; *R. v R (Financial Provision: Reasonable Needs)* [1994] 2 F.L.R. 1004; *F v F (Ancillary Relief: Substantial Assets)* [1995] 2 F.L.R. 45; *Dart v Dart* [1996] 2 F.L.R. 286. This approach is discussed below, at para.13–057.
[230] With whom Mantell L.J. agreed.

358

to
mo|
cont
husb|
in all
misdir
ceiling   **13–044**
ambit o
was no

The de
signalled
wife's awa
Dart[233] ha|
Parliament |
to criticism |
proper recog|
observed,[235] w
rial once the re
remain with the
tions,[236] needs (|
was derived) ca|
House of Lords
Piglowski) emphas|

However, in juri|
did not stop there. |
equal value in resp|
ily:

"[T]here is one p|
with confidence. I|
for discrimination |
roles . . . If, in thei|
family, then in princ|

and built up the assets. sources are limited, and the
earner and against the e children will continue to
[243] Hence most of the finer
id departure therefrom have

Yet this principle arguably
it is derived from a consid| factual situations emerged   **13–045**
welfare of the family". F One relevant consideration
recognition and equal val n a third party?" In *White*
effort ("[If], in their diffe contribution of which the
could invite evaluation of spouses was a "notable
different spheres. We sha hat the order of the Court
(most recently) "special" d to interfere gave Mrs
resulting in an (arguabl| justification appeared to
assets. er, highlighted by Lord
As a means of trans rtant "feature" than the
outcome in ancillary re Cooke expressed some
stick of equal division iage, which would tend
through consideration n.[245] was the financial
Another circumstance
"Sometimes, hav ial division is that of
clusion involves ade a "special" con-
More often, this flair, generating busi-
stances, the judg ealth. This issue is
share than the o H-J[246] Coleridge J.
judge would al ion in the "ordinary
the yardstick o driven right into the
be departed fro
doing so. The | as a consideration
equality would al division. In an
ensure the abs in instalments in
nancial Provision:

Equal division as
was rejected by
permissible boun up and/or realis-
judicial gloss on White objective
point or presum t which may not
the latter *a post* House of Lords
applied as a ch wers to achieve
unequal divisio ought down or
te detriment of

[231] [1999] 2 F.L.R. 763.
[232] S. Cretney [2001] Fam. Law 3;
Hodson, "White—bringing s.25 bacl
basics and forward into the unknown"
to orthodoxy?" [2001] Fam. Law 191;
Law 682; D. Burrows, "Reform of s.2
financial settlements on divorce" (200
marriage partnership" (2001) 13 C.F.L.Ç
[233] [1996] 2 F.L.R. 286 at 301, Thorpe L,
for the legislature and not the judges to ii
[234] See, for example, P. Singer, "Sexual di,
paper delivered in 1992).
[235] [2000] 2 F.L.R. 981 at 992.
[236] [1999] 2 F.L.R. 763.

[237] Lord Nicholls a 555, FD; *Cordle v*
fashioned flavour i
them.
[238] Lord Nicholls
[239] See para.13–0(
[240] See earlier, Bu
[241] Though Lord
different results: 2002] Fam. Law
[242] [2000] 2 F.L.

was reduced on appeal to £180,000 *per* annum. The Court of Appeal restored the quantum of £250,000 but imposed a five year term.[260] The House of Lords dismissed the husband's appeal in *Miller*, and in *McFarlane* allowed the wife's appeal and restored the order of the district judge.

The speeches (of which the most significant were those of Lord Nicholls, Baroness Hale and Lord Mance[261]) were complex and did not speak with one voice, and therefore gave rise to much academic and professional debate. However, it is reasonably clear that the policies underpinning the speeches are that: (i) there should be no discrimination between the different roles assumed by the parties to a marriage, and (ii) marriage—including a short marriage[262]—is a partnership (of equals?). As has already been noted, the overriding objective remains that of achieving a fair outcome (as it has been since *White*), glossed by Baroness Hale as being "to give each party an equal start on the road of independent living".[263]

The speeches articulated guiding principles implicit in (or to be read into) s.25. There was consensus that there are three "elements", "strands", "rationales" or (even) "principles" that determine what is the content of fairness in any given case and that justify the redistribution of assets on divorce, against the background of a system of separation of property during marriage and the silence of the legislature on basic policy. These are: (i) needs, (ii) compensation for economic disparity arising from the marriage; and (iii) entitlement to a sharing of the assets/fruits of the marriage partnership. There was ambiguity as to the *order* in which these three elements are to be considered,[264] much ultimately turning on the facts of the individual case.

13–048   Needs[265] was already a familiar consideration, and one appearing on the face of the statute.[266] According to Baroness Hale (not without controversy), what is relevant is needs arising from the relationship, and not other needs.[267] It was emphasised that in many cases needs will be the first and last port of call[268]: at para.[12]. Novel, however, was the identification[269] of compensation as an implicit "unspoken" element in the statutory provisions. The essential concept is compensation for a party who has suffered economic disparity arising from the role-division consensually assumed during marriage. The issue is whether there is a relationship-generated disadvantage that should be compensated. The concept had surfaced earlier in Hale J.'s decision in *SRJ v DWJ (Financial Provision)*.[270] According to Baroness Hale,[271] the "best

[260] *McFarlane v McFarlane; Parlour v Parlour* [2005] Fam. 171.
[261] Lord Hope dealt virtually exclusively with "how the problem raised by these cases is currently dealt with in Scots law"; Lord Hoffmann expressly agreed with Baroness Hale and added nothing.
[262] [2006] 1 F.L.R. 1186, *per* Lord Nicholls at [17].
[263] [2006] 1 F.L.R. 1186 at [144].
[264] [2006] 1 F.L.R. 1186 at [29], [170].
[265] [2006] 1 F.L.R. 1186 [11], [138]–[139].
[266] Matrimonial Causes Act 1973 s.25(2)(b); Civil Partnership Act 2004 Sch.5 para.21(2)(b).
[267] [2006] 1 F.L.R. 1186 at [138].
[268] [2006] 1 F.L.R. 1186 at [12].
[269] [2006] 1 F.L.R. 1186 at [13], [140].
[270] [1999] 2 F.L.R. 176.
[271] [2006] 1 F.L.R. 1186 at [140].

example" is a wife like Mrs McFarlane, who has given up "what would very probably have been a lucrative and successful. According to Lord Nicholls,[272] what must be addressed is a double loss: a diminution in earning capacity and the loss of a share (post-separation) in the other spouse's earning capacity.

A number of questions immediately arose. "Is compensation a free-standing element for consideration in the s.25 exercise?" "Does it depend on proof of an established or at least blossoming career that would have flourished (as in the case of Mrs McFarlane), or can it be argued speculatively/hypothetically in respect of any career/job that might have been?" Lord Nichols appeared to doubt the latter.[273] "What is the measure of compensation?" "How will judges approach the evidentiary issues in practice: will details of foregone opportunities be required, or a broad-brushed approach adopted?" "How is a claim, once established, to be met?" Capital provision is clearly desirable, but Lord Nicholls indicated[274] that where there is insufficient capital available, the compensation claim will have to be met in the form of periodical payments, and that the imposition of a term is not apt where a periodical payments order is designed to provide for compensation and is not needs-dependent.[275]

The element of sharing[276] focuses on entitlement to matrimonial assets on divorce. It is founded in the idea of division of the fruits of the matrimonial partnership arising from the parties contributions, recognised under the Matrimonial Causes Act s.25(2)(f) (and now the Civil Partnership Act 2004 Sch.5 para.21(2)(f)). Lord Nicholls was the most robust in stating that the sharing should be equal, unless there are good reasons to the contrary, and that the right to share in principle applies equally to a short marriage as to a long one, since a short marriage is no less a partnership of equals than a long marriage.[277] The speeches gave new emphasis, in the context of the sharing element, to the categorisation of property as *matrimonial* and *non-matrimonial*, and to the differing force with which the yardstick of equality applies to the various different categories.

However, there were differences of approach to classification, in particular between Lord Nicholls and Baroness Hale, usefully summarised by Lord Mance.[278]

According to Lord Nicholls, the yardstick of equality prima facie applied to all matrimonial property, whatever the length of the marriage.[279] Lord Nicholls classifies as matrimonial property all property acquired during the marriage (save for by gift to or inheritance by one party) and was resistant to drawing a distinction between "family" assets and "business/investment" assets.[280] Significantly, he classified the matrimonial home, howsoever and

13–049

---

[272] [2006] 1 F.L.R. 1186 at [13].
[273] [2006] 1 F.L.R. 1186 at [92].
[274] [2006] 1 F.L.R. 1186 at [30]–[34].
[275] [2006] 1 F.L.R. 1186 at [36]–[39].
[276] [2006] 1 F.L.R. 1186 at [16]–[17], [141]–[143].
[277] [2006] 1 F.L.R. 1186 at [16], [17].
[278] [2006] 1 F.L.R. 1186 at [167]–[169].
[279] The durational approach (see *GW v RW (Financial Provision: Departure From Equality)* [2003] 2 F.L.R. 108 and the writings of John Eekelaar) is discriminatory and therefore unacceptable.
[280] [2006] 1 F.L.R. 1186 at [18], [20].

whensoever acquired, as matrimonial property[281]—and therefore prima facie subject to the yardstick of equality. Non-matrimonial property is other property acquired before marriage, or acquired during marriage by one party from an outside source by gift or inheritance, which should be treated differently from matrimonial property.[282] According to Baroness Hale,[283] assets subject to the yardstick of equality are "family assets" (such as homes, caravans, furniture, joint savings) and business assets built up by joint effort, as in *Foster v Foster*.[284] Baroness Hale (Lord Mance adopting a similar approach) added to Lord Nicholls' category of non-matrimonial property "business or investment assets which have been generated solely or mainly by the efforts of one party" (i.e. "non-business-partnership, non-family assets"[285]). A departure from the yardstick of equality may be justified in relation to such assets, particularly in the case of short marriages.[286] Both Baroness Hale and Lord Mance indicated that it may be appropriate, in cases of dual-career marriages and those where spouses have kept finances separate, to respect the arrangements they have made.[287] As to the relevant period during which family assets are acquired, Baroness Hale cumulated prior cohabitation and engagement with marriage.[288] According to Lord Mance, the cut-off date for calculating the marital acquest is separation.[289]

The speeches are notable more for the statements of general principle than for their precise application to the two appeals before the House. In the case of *Miller*, Lord Nicholls refered to the substantial wealth brought into the marriage by the husband as being "non-matrimonial property", but also pointed to "the increase in the husband's wealth during the marriage". The matrimonial property was "of great value. The gain in the husband's earned wealth during the marriage was huge." Having regard to this, plus the high standard of living enjoyed during marriage, the sum awarded by Singer J. had appropriate.[290] Baroness Hale saw the wife as "entitled to some share in the considerable increase in the husband's wealth during the marriage", but there was "a reason to depart from the yardstick of equality because those were business assets generated solely by the husband during a short marriage", and it would not be right to disturb the award of a trial judge with the "unrivalled experience" of Singer J.[291] Lord Nicholls justified allowing the appeal in *McFarlane* on the grounds of principle that: (i) the husband's high earnings were the result of the parties' joint endeavours; and (ii) the wife had given up a professional career that was originally as successful and highly paid as the husband's. In fixing a term to periodical payments, the Court of Appeal had

---

281 [2006] 1 F.L.R. 1186 at [22].
282 [2006] 1 F.L.R. 1186 at [22].
283 [2006] 1 F.L.R. 1186 at [149], [152].
284 [2003] 2 F.L.R. 299.
285 [2006] 1 F.L.R. 1186 at [150], [151].
286 [2006] 1 F.L.R. 1186 at [152], [169].
287 [2006] 1 F.L.R. 1186 at [153], [170].
288 [2006] 1 F.L.R. 1186 at 149.
289 [2006] 1 F.L.R. 1186 at [74], [159]. See also Lord Mance at [169], [175]–[180].
290 [2006] 1 F.L.R. 1186 at [69]–[73].
291 [2006] 1 F.L.R. 1186 at [74], [159].

failed to appreciate the distinction between needs and compensation.[292] Baroness Hale[293] justified the award made by the district judge on the bases of: (i) sharing the fruits of the matrimonial partnership, the husband's substantial earning power being "the main family asset"; and (ii) compensation.

(vii) Developments following Miller v Miller; McFarlane v McFarlane. The **13–050** aim of the speeches in *Miller v Miller; McFarlane v McFarlane* was to formulate guidelines that would facilitate the settlement of ancillary cases generally. It is questionable whether the guidelines were formulated with sufficient clarity to enable this laudable objective to be achieved in practice, and many consider the law to be in a state of some confusion.[294] In this section we attempt to summarise developments in the case law since *Miller v Miller; McFarlane v McFarlane.*

In *Charman v Charman (No.46)*[295] the Court of Appeal made its own contribution to the interpretation of s.25 of the Matrimonial Causes Act 1973,[296] setting itself the task of being loyal to the "spirit as well as the letter" of the guidance already given in *White* and *Miller; McFarlane*, saying that: "there is no doubt that, under that guidance, the House of Lords has left much for the courts to develop".[297] The further aim was to "express ourselves as clearly and simply as possible".

The facts were as follows: the husband and wife married in 1976, aged 23 and 22, when they had no assets of any value. At separation 30 years later, the husband's accumulated wealth was some £150–160 million. Six million was in the wife's name, some 30 million in a trust for the two adult children and the remaining £125,000 was either owned by the husband or in the Dragon Holdings Trust. The wife sought capital provision of 45 per cent of the total assets pool—some £59 million. She relied upon her full role in a very long marriage, during which the wealth had been generated. The husband offered a sum to bring the wife's assets up to £20 million. He argued inter alia that the assets owned by the Dragon Trust should be left out of account in the s.25 exercise because he had intended to found a "dynastic trust" to benefit future members of the family, and that he had made a special contribution that should be recognised in division of assets. Coleridge J. awarded the wife £48 million (i.e. some 37 per cent of the total assets). The special contribution aspects of the case are discussed later in the chapter; the present analysis focuses on the general contribution of the Court of Appeal to the s.25 exercise.

The Court of Appeal spelt out[298] that the exercise to be undertaken by the **13–051** court in order to achieve a fair outcome under s.25 is in two stages: computation and distribution. At the first *computation* stage:

---

[292] [2006] 1 F.L.R. 1186 at [91]–[96].
[293] [2006] 1 F.L.R. 1186 at [154]–[155].
[294] See e.g. S. Davis "Equal Sharing: A Judicial Gloss Too Far?" [2008] Fam. Law 428.
[295] [2007] 1 F.L.R. 1246.
[296] See also Civil Partnership Act 2004 Sch.5 para.21.
[297] [2007] 1 F.L.R. 1246, para.[63].
[298] [2007] 1 F.L.R. 1246 at para.[67].

"[T]he court should first consider, with whatever degree of detail is apt to the case, the matters set out in section 25(2)(a), namely, the property, income (including earning capacity) and other financial resources which the parties have and are likely to have in the foreseeable future. Irrespective of whether the assets are substantial, likely future income must always be appraised, for, even in a clean break case, such appraisal may well be relevant to the division of property which best achieves the fair overall outcome."[299]

At the second *distribution* stage, the three "rationales" articulated in *Miller; McFarlane* have now accorded the status of principles by the Court of Appeal:

"In *Miller*, the House of Lords unanimously identified three main principles which together inform the second stage of the enquiry, namely that of distribution: 'need (generously interpreted), compensation and sharing' per Baroness Hale at [144]; and see, similarly, Lord Nicholls at [10] to [14]. These three principles must be applied in the light of the size and nature of all the computed resources, which are usually heavily circumscribing factors."[300]

A distinctive contribution of *Charman* to the analysis is that the Court of Appeal attempted to rationalise the three principles in relation to the express provisions of s.25:

"It is worthy of note that, although two of them are not expressly mentioned, each of the three distributive principles can be collected from section 25(2), or at any rate from section 25(1) and (2) of the Act.[301]

13–052 The development of each of the three principles subsequent to *Miller v Miller; McFarlane v McFarlane* will now be considered in turn. Recent judicial warnings against the juridical elevation of the three principles must, however, be noted. In *RP v RP*[302] Coleridge J. expressed the following caution in respect of the three elements:

"They are very helpful in ensuring the court achieves a fair result and does not become stuck or formulaic in its approach as it has done from time to time in the past ... However, care needs to be taken to ensure that those passages are not treated as some kind of quasi statutory amendment. They are the commentary of the House of Lords on a very well-trodden statute now in its fourth decade."

[299] [2007] 1 F.L.R. 1246 at para.[67].
[300] [2007] 1 F.L.R. 1246 at para.[68].
[301] [2007] 1 F.L.R. 1246 at para.[69].
[302] [2007] 1 F.L.R. 2105 at para.[58].

In *CR v CR*,[303] Bodey J. expressed the view that the three "strands" should not be elevated into separate heads of claim independent of the words of the statute; such an approach would run the real risk of double-counting.

(viii) Analysis of the judicial guidelines. As has been stated earlier, the **13–053** consideration of needs appears on the face of the statute, and is in no way novel. According to the Court of Appeal in *Charman*,[304] the principle of needs requires consideration of a number of the considerations specifically mentioned in s.25; namely, s.25(2)(b)—needs, obligations and responsibilities; s.25(2)(c)—standard of living during marriage; s.25(2)(d)—the parties' ages; and s.25(2)(e)—any physical or mental disability.

The Court of Appeal in *Charman* did not add greatly to the analysis of compensation:

> "The principle of compensation relates to prospective financial disadvantage which upon divorce some parties face as a result of decisions which they took for the benefit of the family during marriage, for example in sacrificing or not pursuing a career: per Lord Nicholls in *Miller* at [13], Lord Hope at [117] and Baroness Hale at [140]."[305]

The facts of *McFarlane* in respect of the wife's foregone career were particular. Since then, it appears that compensation is not infrequently argued as a component of a claim in practice, but examples of successful claims are absent from the reported case law. At the time of writing, there is a degree of judicial reluctance in admitting compensation as a free-standing claim independent of other considerations in s.25.[306] The wife's claim was unsuccessful in *S v S (Non-Matrimonial Property: Conduct)*.[307] In *RP v RP*[308] Coleridge J. warned against the potential for double-counting and artificiality in the pursuit of a compensation claim, when fairness can be achieved by a sharing of the fruits of the marital partnership to which parties have contributed fully. In *CR v CR*[309] Bodey J. found that the wife had not demonstrated any significant lost career prospects for which compensation should be factored into the outcome, and observed that a wife with ordinary career prospects that are forfeited is likely to be adequately compensated (at least in big-money cases) by the equal division of family resources. The element of compensation has also surfaced in the context of variation applications,[310] which are discussed later in the chapter. In *VB v JP*[311] Sir Mark Potter P. reviewed the authorities. The President shared and endorsed the warning sounded by Coleridge J. in *RP v*

---

[303] June 19, 2007.
[304] [2007] 1 F.L.R. 2105 at para.[70].
[305] [2007] 1 F.L.R. 2105 at para.[71].
[306] See also Civil Partnership Act 2004 Sch.5 para.21.
[307] [2007] 1 F.L.R. 1496.
[308] [2007] 1 F.L.R. 2015, paras [59]–[63].
[309] June 19, 2007.
[310] *Lauder v Lauder* [2007] 2 F.L.R. 802; *VB v JP* [2008] EWHC 112 (Fam.).
[311] [2008] EWHC 112.

RP, above, against the introduction of an approach that seeks to separate out and quantify the element of compensation:

> "[R]ather than treating it as one of the strands in the overall requirement of fairness in the assessment of the parties joint contributions to the marriage, where the wife as a result of a joint marital decision has sacrificed her own earning capacity in the interests of bringing up the family. Attempts under the rubric of compensation to isolate and quantify the level of income or earning capacity sacrificed by a wife years after the event for the purpose of calculating a premium element on the award constitutes a search for precision which is to be discouraged both on the grounds of policy and practicality, and which goes beyond what is required or generally appropriate in the exercise required of the court under section 25."[312]

Furthermore:

> "Where it is necessary to provide ongoing periodical payments for the wife after the division of capital assets insufficient to cover her future maintenance, any element of compensation is best dealt with by a generous assessment of her needs unrestricted by purely budgetary considerations."[313]

13–054   On the facts, the President found it unnecessary to attempt to quantify the element of compensation separately from that of her needs generously assessed. Thus, the status of the compensation "principle" or "element" remains unclear at the time of writing. The current tendency appears to be to assimilate it within either needs or compensation. Appellate clarification is needed.

As has already been demonstrated, the House of Lords in *Miller v Miller; McFarlane v McFarlane* placed considerable emphasis on the categorisation of property—matrimonial or non-matrimonial—in relation both to the element of sharing and the yardstick of equal division, albeit that Lord Nicholls warned against too strict an adherence to such categorisation of property, and stated that each case must ultimately be approached on its own "with the degree of particularity or generality appropriate to the case".[314] Nevertheless, in the immediate aftermath of *Miller v Miller; McFarlane v McFarlane*, there was a sharp focus in some of the reported case law on the classifying process. In *Rossi v Rossi*[315] Nicholas Mostyn Q.C., sitting as a deputy High Court judge, stated that it was now a primary function of the court in all ancillary-relief cases to identify the matrimonial and non-matrimonial property, and

---

[312] [2008] EWHC 112 at para.[52].
[313] [2008] EWHC 112 at para.[59].
[314] [2006] 1 F.L.R. 1186 at para.[27].
[315] [2007] 1 F.L.R. 790.

provide detailed guidelines provided on the classification process. Other examples include *S v S (Non-Matrimonial Property: Conduct)*[316] and *S v S (Ancillary Relief After Lengthy Separation)*,[317] and *H v H*.[318]

However, a somewhat different approach was taken by the Court of Appeal in *Charman v Charman (No.4)*.[319] The Court's view was that the sharing principle applies to all of the parties' property rather than only to that identified as matrimonial, although the character of the property may be a reason to depart from equal division. Such departure takes place within the sharing principle rather than outside or after it. It therefore appears that, according to *Charman,* non-matrimonial property is susceptible to a sharing claim in addition to (as had been established on the prior authorities[320]) a needs claim. However, the characterisation of property as non-matrimonial will be a reason to depart from equal division on application of the sharing principle, and so the forensic exercise of classification is likely to continue, at least in big money cases.[321]

In *Charman*, the Court of Appeal stated that the sharing principle is said to be "dictated by" a number of considerations expressed on the face of the statute: s.25(2)(f) (contributions), s.25(2)(d) (duration of the marriage) and, in an exceptional case, s.25(2)(g) (conduct which it would be inequitable to disregard).[322] Furthermore (and significantly), the Court of Appeal viewed *Miller v Miller; McFarlane v McFarlane* as a movement on from the law as expounded earlier in *White v White*. As will be recalled,[323] a "principle", "guideline", "starting-point" or even "presumption" of equal sharing had been rejected by the majority in *White*, and the yardstick of equal division had been formulated to be applied at the conclusion of the dispositive stage, as a cross-check on the quantum of a provisional award. However, Lord Cooke had seen little substantive difference as flowing from the differences in terminology.

13–055

In *Charman*, at para.[65], the Court of Appeal stated[324]:

> "In *Miller*, the House clearly moved towards the position of Lord Cooke . . . It is clear that the court's consideration of the sharing principle is no longer required to be postponed until the end of the statutory exercise. We should add that, since we understand 'the sharing principle' to mean that property should be shared in equal proportions unless there is good reason to depart from such proportions, departure is not *from* the principle but takes place *within* the principle."

---

[316] [2007] Fam. Law 106; [2007] 1 F.L.R. 1496.
[317] [2007] Fam. Law 482; [2007] 1 F.L.R. 2120 at para.[66].
[318] [2007] 2 F.L.R. 548.
[319] [2007] 1 F.L.R. 1246.
[320] *White v White* [2000] 2 F.L.R. 981; *S v S (Ancillary Relief: Importance of FDR)* [2007] EWHC 1975 (Fam.); [2008] 1 F.L.R. 944.
[321] This approach was followed in *L v L* [2008] 1 F.L.R. 142.
[322] See also the equivalent provisions of Civil Partnership Act 2004 Sch.5, para.21.
[323] See para.13–042, above.
[324] [2007] 1 F.L.R. 1246 para.[87].

Hence, according to the Court of Appeal, the yardstick of equality (applied at the end of the s.25 exercise) has now become the sharing principle (applied at the disposition stage, along with needs and compensation). This represents a juridical change of status and it may perhaps be questioned as to whether, as a matter of precedent, the Court of Appeal's approach should be followed if it does not accord with that of the highest appellate tribunal. It does, however, appear to be followed by some courts: an illustration is *L v L*,[325] discussed below.

13–056   As to the concept of "unilateral assets" (i.e. those suggested by Baroness Hale in *Miller v Miller; McFarlane v McFarlane* as being the fruits of a business in which only one party has substantially worked), the Court of Appeal's view in *Charman* was that these observations were intended (and by Lord Mance) to apply *only* to short or dual-career marriages. To apply that concept in a case of a long marriage would be deeply discriminatory and would gravely undermine the sharing principle; there was a need "to keep the room for application of the concept closely confined".[326] The issue of whether a party's earning capacity is an asset to which the other party has contributed and "which might to some extent be subject to the sharing principle"[327] was left open, the Court of Appeal observing that:

> "this seems to us an area of complexity and potential confusion which it is unnecessary for us to visit."[328] (para.[67]).

The Court of Appeal stated in *Charman*[329] that where there is conflict between the results suggested by the principles of need, compensation and sharing, the criterion of fairness must supply the answer. When the result suggested by the needs principle is an award of property greater than the result suggested by the sharing principle, the former should prevail. When the needs principle produces a lesser award than that suggested by the sharing principle, the latter should prevail. This approach was followed by Richard Anelay Q.C. (sitting as a Deputy High Court judge) in *L v L*[330] in which the assets totalled £6.1 million. Following the guidance provided in *Charman v Charman*, the duty of the court in approaching the s.25 exercise is to: (i) determine the assets and general financial position of the parties; (ii) decide how all the property of the parties should be shared between them, applying the principle that property should be shared equally unless there was good reason to the contrary; and (iii) decide whether the result produced by the

---

[325] [2008] 1 F.L.R. 136.
[326] [2008] 1 F.L.R. 136 at para.[86].
[327] See *H v H* [2007] 2 F.L.R. 548 on both earning capacity and bonuses paid subsequent to separation: Charles J. considered that the bonus was non-matrimonial but could be used to recognise the wife's contribution to the husband's earning capacity or to enable her to adjust to independence.
[328] [2008] 1 F.L.R. 136 at para.[67].
[329] [2008] 1 F.L.R. 136 at para.[73].
[330] [2008] 1 F.L.R. 136.

sharing principle met the needs (generously interpreted) of the parties. Only if the application of the sharing principle failed to meet the parties' needs would needs dictate a greater share. If the parties' needs were less than the sum produced by the application of the sharing principle, that would not lead to a reduction.

The learned Deputy Judge thus considered that the outcome of the application of the sharing principle should be determined first, and that outcome then be checked against needs. In essence, this approach prioritises the sharing principle; sed quaere whether it would be appropriate in the classic small-money case, which is determined primarily on needs. A further illustration of the sharing principle being applied first, with a departure from equal sharing being justified on the facts, is provided by the judgment of the Court of Appeal in *Vaughan v Vaughan*.[331]

(3) Consideration of all the circumstances

Despite attempts in recent years to formulate guidelines or principles under-   **13–057**
pinning the exercise of ancillary relief powers, the statutory provisions[332]
expressly require[333] the court to consider all the circumstances of the case,
first consideration being given to the welfare of minor children.

(4) The first consideration: children's welfare

The legislation requires the court—in deciding whether to exercise its powers   **13–058**
to make financial provision, property adjustment, or sale orders—to:

> "[H]ave regard to all the circumstances of the case, first consideration being given to the welfare while a minor of any child of the family who has not attained the age of 18."

This gives effect the view of the Law Commission that the law should "emphasise as a priority" the need to make the financial provision necessary to safeguard the maintenance and welfare of the children, and thus refute the once widespread impression that the making of provision for children was a matter of secondary importance to the making of provision for an adult.[334] As mentioned above, the courts have usually tried to ensure that the child has secure housing—for instance by ordering the transfer of the house to the parent with whom the child is to live, or division of proceeds of sale

---

[331] [2008] 1 F.L.R. 1108.
[332] Matrimonial Causes Act 1973 s.25(1), (2); Civil Partnership Act 2004 Sch.5 paras 20, 21.
[333] See the continuing emphasis on this statutory duty in *RP v RP* [2007] 1 F.L.R. 2105; *CR v CR* [2008] 1 F.L.R. 323 and *L v L* [2008] 1 F.L.R. 136.
[334] Law Com. No.112, para.24.

permitting the parent to purchase accommodation, or settling it on terms that it be not sold during the children's dependency.[335] As explained above, the authorities[336] appear to confirm that this practice in smaller-money cases is largely unaffected by other developments since *White v White*.[337] The particular accommodation needs of a child may justify a substantial capital award to the parent with care, even where the marriage has been short.[338] Again, the court may consider that the welfare of the children requires that the wife—notwithstanding the provisions encouraging self-sufficiency considered below—should have periodical payments at least until the children no longer need her full-time attention.[339]

Where resources permit, in recent years the courts have emphasised the desirability[340] of the parent with whom the children do not have their principal home receiving an award sufficient to permit them to purchase accommodation suitable for staying contact, as in *M v B (Ancillary Proceedings: Lump Sum)*.[341] However, it has equally been emphasised[342] that there is, as a matter of law, no entitlement, where means are limited, that both spouses are entitled to purchase accommodation; everything turns on the particular facts, in particular the resources available.

The court has power to make property adjustment and financial provision orders to or for the benefit of any children of the family, but as a result of the enactment of the Child Support Act 1991 it is only in unusual circumstances that it will be able to exercise its powers to order periodical payments for children.[343]

---

[335] The courts have come increasingly to accept that children will in reality remain dependent on their parents beyond the age of majority: *Richardson v Richardson (No.2)* [1944] 2 F.L.R. 1051; *J v C (Child: Financial Provision)* [1999] 1 F.L.R. 152.

[336] *B v B (Financial Provision: Welfare of Child and Conduct)* [2002] 1 F.L.R. 555, FD; *Cordle v Cordle* [2001] EWCA Civ. 1791; [2002] 2 F.L.R. 207. See also *Elliott v Elloitt* [2001] 2 F.C.R. 477, in which proceeds of sale were used to purchase a new home for the wife and children but were subject to a charge-back of 45% to the husband.

[337] [2001] 1 A.C. 596; [2000] 3 W.L.R. 1571; [2000] 2 F.L.R. 981.

[338] *C v C (Financial Relief: Short Marriage)* [1997] 2 F.L.R. 26 (marriage of some nine months; mother needed to purchase a house in a clean air area suitable for the asthmatic child); *M v M (Prenuptial Agreement)* [2002] 1 F.L.R. 654 (marriage of five years, lump sum of £575,000 to meet costs of a suitable home in London; in child's interests to reside there with mother and enjoy stability).

[339] *Waterman v Waterman* [1979] 1 F.L.R. 380, CA; *E v E (Financial Provision)* [1990] 2 F.L.R. 233 at 249 (not in children's interests that mother be in straitened circumstances); *C v C (Financial Relief: Short Marriage)* [1997] 2 F.L.R. 26.

[340] Although it is a "misuse of authority" to interpret such cases as laying down "some rule that both spouses invariably have a right to purchase accommodation": *Piglowska v Piglowski* [1999] 2 F.L.R. 763 at 783, *per* Lord Hoffmann.

[341] [1998] 1 F.L.R. 5; see also *H v H (Financial Provision: Conduct)* [1998] 1 F.L.R. 971 and *Cordle v Cordle* [2001] EWCA Civ. 1791; [2002] 1 F.L.R. 207, CA.

[342] *Piglowska v Piglowski* [1999] 2 F.L.R. 763 at 783, *per* Lord Hoffmann; *B v B (Financial Provision: Welfare of Child and Conduct)* [2002] 1 F.L.R. 555, *per* Connell J.; *Cordle v Cordle* [2001] EWCA Civ. 1791; [2002] 1 F.L.R. 207, *per* Thorpe L.J. at paras [33] and [34].

[343] These are discussed in Ch.15, below. Even in cases where the court retains jurisdiction, it increasingly has regard to the Child Support Act's formulae in determining quantum: *E v C (Child Maintenance)* [1996] 1 F.L.R. 472 at 476, *per* Douglas Brown J.; *GW v RW (Financial Provision: Departure From Equality)* [2003] 2 F.L.R. 108.

(a) Limitations on the welfare principle. There are limitations on the scope   **13–059**
of the direction to give first consideration to children's welfare.

(i) First but not paramount. In deciding questions about the upbringing of a   **13–060**
child, the court is directed[344] to regard the welfare of the child as the
"paramount" consideration, even if that means that the just claims of the
child's parents or others affected have to be overridden. However, in considering financial relief, the court is not required to go so far. It need only give
"first" consideration to the welfare of the child in question, so that (it has
been held[345]) the court must simply consider all the relevant circumstances,
always bearing in mind the important consideration of the welfare of the
children, and then try to attain a financial result that is just as between
spouses or civil partners.

(ii) Applies only to children of the family. The expression "child of the   **13–061**
family" is widely defined in the legislation[346] and extends to any child who
has been treated by both of the parties to the marriage or civil partnership as
a child of their family. However, although this definition is wide, it does not
extend to all those children who may, actually or prospectively, be affected by
the orders made in the proceedings in question. It does not extend to a child
brought up in a cohabitation relationship; there are no proposals to reform the
law in this respect.

(iii) Applies only during infancy of children. The court is only required to give   **13–062**
first consideration to the welfare, while a minor, of any child of the family
who has not attained the age of 18. This has two particular consequences.
First, the court is not obliged to give such consideration to the welfare of any
child of the family who has, at the date of the hearing, already attained the
age of 18, even if the child is undergoing advanced education or training, or
is disabled. Secondly, even in the case of children of the family who are, at
the date of the hearing, under 18, the court is only obliged by this provision
to give first consideration to their welfare whilst they remain minors. This
provision does not require the court to take account of the fact that children
in practice do often stay in their homes until a later age, whether because they
are undergoing education or training or because they are disabled or unemployed or simply because they prefer to do so, particularly during the early
stages of their career. However, the courts have in fact shown an increasing
readiness to recognise that children have needs that extend well beyond their
attaining the age of 18,[347] but these needs do not have any priority.

---

[344] Children Act 1989 s.1(1).
[345] *Suter v Suter* [1987] 2 F.L.R. 232 at 238, *per* Sir R. Cumming Bruce; *Akintola v Akintola* [2002] 1 F.L.R. 701.
[346] Matrimonial Causes Act 1973 s.52(1), Civil Partnership Act 2004 s.135.
[347] *Richardson v Richardson (No.2)* [1994] 2 F.L.R. 105; *J v C (Financial Provision)* [1999] 1 F.L.R. 152, FD.

(5) The court's duty to consider all the circumstances

13–063   The court is directed to have regard to "all the circumstances of the case", and "in particular" to have regard to an elaborate list of specific matters in s.25(2) of the Matrimonial Causes Act 1973 and para.21(2) of Sch.1 to the Civil Partnership Act 2004. The expression "all the circumstances" is a very wide one,[348] and the court need not confine its attention to the listed matters, but may also investigate other circumstances, "past, present, and . . . future",[349] that arise on the facts of any particular case.

The matters specified in the legislation are in the text hereafter discussed in the order in which they appear in the statute, although, as the House of Lords has emphasised in *Piglowska v Piglowska*[350] and in *White v White*,[351] there is no hierarchy in law, and the weight to be accorded to each will depend on the exercise of judicial discretion on the particular facts.

(i) "[T]he income, earning capacity, property and other financial resources which each of the parties to the marriage has or is likely to have in the foreseeable future, including in the case of earning capacity any increase in that capacity which it would in the opinion of the court be reasonable to expect a party to the marriage to take steps to acquire" (Matrimonial Causes Act 1973 section 25(2)(a))

Ascertaining the facts and the "computation stage";

13–064   As was shown earlier in the chapter[352] that the Court of Appeal in *Charman v Charman (No.4)*[353] explained that the first stage in the exercise of ancillary-relief powers is the "computation stage" (i.e. the court's duty to ascertain the parties resources); at the second "dispositive stage", the court decides what is a fair division thereof.

The parties are required to provide and exchange financial evidence in standard form at an early stage of the proceedings prior to the first appointment.[354] The standard form[355] (which is a sworn document) requires full details of inter alia the parties' resources and their needs and obligations, and (in accordance with the spirit of the procedural reforms in reducing documentation and costs in the resolution of financial disputes[356]) is intended to be comprehensive for the vast majority of cases. The parties are under an obligation to make a full, frank and clear disclosure of all relevant circumstances,[357] but, in practice, this is not always done. A range of powers is

---

[348] *Kokosinski v Kokosinski* [1980] Fam. 72 at 183, *per* Wood J.
[349] *Per* Scarman L.J., in *Trippas v Trippas* [1973] Fam. 134 at 144.
[350] [1999] 2 F.L.R. 763.
[351] [2000] 2 F.L.R. 981.
[352] See para.13–051.
[353] [2007] 1 F.L.R. 1246.
[354] Family Proceedings Rules 1991 (SI 1991/1247) r.2.6B(1) and (2).
[355] Form E, contained in Appendix 1A of the Rules. Where the parties apply for a consent order there is a different procedure prescribed by r.2.61 and the relevant form is Form M1.
[356] Discussed above at para.13–010.
[357] *Livesey (formerly Jenkins) v Jenkins* [1985] A.C. 424, HL. This obligation underpins the whole basis of the exercise of the court's discretion to make financial orders (which is a paternal, and in an appropriate case, an inquisitorial jurisdiction: see *Hildebrand v Hildebrand* [1992] 1 F.L.R. 244 at

available to compel an unwilling spouse to supply the information needed to assess his or her financial position, and a solicitor who fails to obtain proper evidence on these matters may be held to have been guilty of professional negligence.[358] Failure to disclose may result in a penalty by way of costs order[359] and the drawing of adverse inferences.[360] The rules provide[361] for an investigation by the district judge of allegations, for the ordering of attendance of any person, for the disclosure of any document, for further statements and for an inspection appointment. Ultimately, the duty to disclose can be enforced by committal proceedings.[362]

Common issues
A number of issues arise frequently.   **13–065**

(i) Reality, not appearance
The term "financial resources" has a meaning in s.25(2)(a) that must be   **13–066** interpreted as deliberately distinct from and wider than "income" or "property". The court is concerned with the realities of the parties' financial situation.[363] For example, if a spouse has an interest under a discretionary

247, *per* Waite J.). A striking consequence of the duty to disclose is that a party who has resorted to self-help (e.g. by secretly photocopying bank statements or other documents belonging to another party) is under a duty to disclose that he or she has those copies: see *T v T (Interception of Documents)* [1994] 2 F.L.R. 1083, *per* Wilson J., where the judge ruled that a wife had been entitled to take such copies and to examine the contents of the husband's dustbins but not to break the door and window of his office in order to get access to other documents. See, generally, N. Wilson, "Conduct of the big money case" [1994] Fam. Law 504.

[358] See, for example, *Dickinson v Jones Alexander & Co* [1993] 2 F.L.R. at 521 (where £330,238 in damages was awarded against a solicitor who had left the conduct of a case to an unsupervised articled clerk) and for a case in which a solicitor was held liable for failing to take action to protect the wife's pension expectancies, see *Griffiths v Dawson & Co* [1993] 2 F.L.R. 315. The argument that an action based on a solicitor's negligence in not securing adequate disclosure before seeking a consent order constituted a collateral challenge to the final order of a court of competent jurisdiction was rejected in *B. v Miller & Co* [1996] 2 F.L.R. 22. In contrast, solicitors who waste costs in excessive inquiry may be ordered to pay the costs involved: see, for example, *Re a Solicitor (Wasted Costs Order)* [1993] 2 F.L.R. 959 (costs totalling £130,000 run up in case in which assets only justified lump sum award of £20,000).

[359] *J v V (Disclosure: Offshore Corporations)* [2004] 1 F.L.R. 1042; the same will apply under the new costs rules: see para.13–011 above.

[360] *Al-KhatKhatib v Masry* [2002] 1 F.L.R. 1053.

[361] Family Proceedings Rules 1991 (SI 1991/1247) r.2.62.

[362] In appropriate (and exceptional) cases, the High Court may make an *Anton Piller* order, in effect giving one party's representative the right to enter the other's premises without prior warning to inspect documents: see *Emmanuel v Emmanuel* [1981] 3 F.L.R. 319; Practice Direction: *ex parte Mareva* and *Anton Piller* Orders [1994] 2 F.L.R. 704; *Burgess v Burgess* [1996] 2 F.L.R. 33, CA. Such an order will be granted only in exceptional circumstances: *Araghinchi v Araghinchi* [1997] 2 F.L.R. 142.

[363] This is well explained by Waite L.J. in a passage in *Thomas v Thomas* [1995] 2 F.L.R. 668 at 670–671, which merits extended citation: "if justice is to be achieved between spouses at divorce the court must be equipped . . . to penetrate outer forms and get to the heart of ownership . . . [C]ertain principles emerge from the authorities. One is that the court is not obliged to limit its orders exclusively to resources of capital or income which are shown actually to exist. The availability of unidentified resources may, for example, be inferred from a spouse's expenditure or style of living, or from his inability or unwillingness to allow the complexity of his affairs to be penetrated with the precision necessary to ascertain his actual wealth or the degree of liquidity of his assets. Another is

trust,[364] the court will not be deterred from making an order merely because a beneficiary under such trust has no legal right to claim any part of the fund. In *A v A and St George's Trustees Ltd*,[365] Munby J. summarised the authorities as indicating that the essential question is whether it could be demonstrated that the trustees, if asked, would be likely, immediately or in the foreseeable future, to exercise their powers in favour of, or otherwise for the benefit of, the spouse in question; the court had to be careful not to jump too readily to the conclusion that trustees would always accede to judicious encouragement. On the evidence in that case, it was not likely that the trustees would be prepared to make capital distributions to the husband to meet obligations under an ancillary relief order.[366] The court may equally have regard to the realities of funds provided to a spouse by family members.[367] Furthermore, the realities include the ability to raise money by borrowing (particularly if that is the method the parties have used in the past to finance a particular lifestyle).[368] Adverse inferences may be drawn from non-disclosure and an order that reflect the assumed realities of undisclosed assets.[369] Notwithstanding the broad interpretation of the statutory provision, it may not be appropriate to make an order that operates on assets other than those under the direct ownership or control of the respondent.[370]

One of the most striking examples in recent years of the court's approach to assets held in a trust was *Charman v Charman (No.4)*,[371] the facts of which have been given above.[372] £68 million was held in the Dragon Trust. It was held by the Court of Appeal that all the evidence supported the trial judge's (Colerdidge J.) view that the trust was not a dynastic one and that the trustees were likely to advance the assets to the husband. It is essential for the court

that where a spouse enjoys access to wealth but no absolute entitlement to it (as in the case . . . of a beneficiary under a discretionary trust or someone who is dependent on the generosity of a relative), the court will not act in direct invasion of the rights of, or usurp the discretion exercisable by, a third party. Nor will it put upon a third party undue pressure to act in a way which will enhance the means of the maintaining spouse. [But] . . . there will be occasions when it becomes permissible for a judge deliberately to frame his orders in a form which affords judicious encouragement to third parties to provide the maintaining spouse with the means to comply with the court's view of the justice of the case."

[364] As in *Browne v Browne* [1989] 1 F.L.R. 291, CA, where the judge, in making a lump sum order against a wife of £175,000, had taken into account the fact that she had interests under substantial Swiss and Jersey trusts, and on the evidence had been able to obtain funds from those sources. See also *Minwalla v Linwalla* [2005] 1 F.L.R. 771. But the court will not wish to exercise improper pressure on trustees of a discretionary trust: see *Howard v Howard* [1945] P. 1; *TL v ML (Ancillary Relief: Claim Against Extended Family)* [2006] 1 F.L.R. 1263.

[365] [2007] 2 F.L.R. 467.

[366] Munby J. also rejected the wife's alternative argument that the trusts in question were shams; the judgment contains a detailed analysis on the law relating to sham trusts.

[367] In *X v X (Y and Z Intervening)* [2002] 1 F.L.R. 508, Munby J. did not need to find that the wife had very substantial resources available to her from her wealthy family, but would have been prepared to hold that they were more than sufficient to justify an order of £500,000 in favour of the husband. See also *R v R (Lump Sum Payments)* [2004] 1 F.L.R. 928.

[368] *Newton v Newton* [1990] 1 F.L.R. 33; *J v J* [1955] P. 236.

[369] *Baker v Baker* [1995] 2 F.L.R. 829; *Al-Khatib v Masry* [2002] 1 F.L.R. 1053.

[370] See *TL v ML* [2006] 1 F.L.R. 1263.

[371] [2007] 1 F.L.R. 1246; A Meehan, "Charman in the Court of Appeal'; [2007] Fam. Law 601. The husband's petition to the House of Lords was dismissed.

[372] See para.13–050.

to combine a judicious mixture of worldly realism and respect for the legal effects of trusts, the legal duties of trustees and, in the case of off-shore trusts, the jurisdictions of off-shore courts. In the circumstances of the case, it would have been a shameful emasculation of the court's duty to be fair if the assets that the husband built up in Dragon Trust during the marriage had not been attributed to him.[373]

As Munby J. observed in *A v A and St George's Trustees Ltd*,[374] even though the court is concerned with the realities of the parties' financial situations, and will adopt a robust, skeptical and questioning approach to trust and company structures, this does not mean that the court can ride roughshod over established principles where third-party interests are concerned. The determination of a dispute as to ownership between a spouse and a third party is completely different from the familiar discretionary exercise between spouses, and has to be determined in the Family Division on exactly the same legal basis as if it were being determined in the Chancery Division.[375]

(ii) Earning capacity and earning potential

The court is concerned with what each spouse could reasonably have if the earning capacity were fully exploited. In appropriate circumstances, an earning capacity greater than actual earnings will be attributed.[376] However, the court should only act on evidence that there is better paid work available. [377]   **13–067**

The Matrimonial and Family Proceedings Act 1984 added a specific reference to direct the court's attention to "any increase in earning capacity which it would be reasonable to expect" a spouse to take steps to acquire. This requires proof of two separate matters: first, that a spouse could in fact increase his or her prospects of earning[378]; secondly, that it would be reasonable for him or her to be expected to do so. Even if the first hurdle is surmounted, the court must still be satisfied that it is reasonable to expect a party to acquire the increase. The evaluative exercise is illustrated by *Leadbeater v Leadbeater*,[379] *M v M (Prenuptial Agreement)*[380] and *A v A (Financial Provision)*.[381]

(iii) Resources of a new partner

The court has no power to order that a third party (e.g. the husband's second wife or cohabitant) should provide for the applicant or the children of the   **13–068**

---

[373] See the comment by Professor Douglas in [2007] Fam. Law 682.
[374] [2007] 2 F.L.R. 467.
[375] See also *G v G (Matrimonial Property: Rights of Extended Family)* [2006] 1 F.L.R. 62; *Tl v ML (Ancillary Relief: Claims Against Assets of Extended Family)* [2006] 1 F.L.R. 1263.
[376] *Hardy v Hardy* [1981] 1 F.L.R. 321; *K v K (Conduct)* [1990] 2 F.L.R. 225.
[377] In *Williams (LA) v Williams (EM)* [1974] Fam. 55.
[378] It appears that expert re-employment consultants may be called on for evidence: see, for example, *B v B (Consent Order: Variation)* [1995] 1 F.L.R. 9 (where, however, their evidence was not found helpful).
[379] [1985] F.L.R. 789.
[380] [2002] 1 F.L.R. 654, FD.
[381] [1998] 2 F.L.R. 180, FD.

family[382]; it must not make an order that can only be satisfied by dipping into a third party's resources.[383] However, the fact that such a person has means available may be relevant, because thereby a spouse can more readily make appropriate provision.[384] As the Law Commission put it,[385] the husband is not allowed in such cases to say that he needs all or most of his income in order to provide for the needs of his new family. In effect, the means of the cohabitant are taken into account at what is often the decisive stage of calculating the net effect of the proposed order. In *K v K (Periodical Payments: Cohabitation)*,[386] on cross-applications to vary the periodical payments in favour of the wife in an ancillary relief order made seven years earlier, Coleridge J. reduced the payments from £16,000 per annum to £12,000, and capitalised at £100,000, and stated that a lengthy and settled period of cohabitation could be given considerable weight. In the absence of statutory reform, the courts should address the issue in the light of changed social conditions:

> "If cohabitation is said to be a social norm, surely financial independence from a previous partner, whether married or not, should go with it?"

(v) Expectations

13–069   Financial resources may, in appropriate circumstances, include expectations. It has been held that the court may take account of financial expectations under a will or intestacy (e.g. to inherit a house acquired from a local authority under the "right to buy" legislation) of a relative who is terminally ill— although in the normal case the uncertainties both as to the fact of the inheritance and as to the time when the death will occur makes the court reluctant to do so.[387]

(vi) Pensions

13–070   In many cases,[388] entitlements under an occupational or personal pension scheme will be amongst the parties' most valuable assets. The range of the court's powers in relation to pension entitlements is discussed below.[389]

---

[382] *Macey v Macey* (1981) 3 F.L.R. 7; *B v B (Periodical Payments: Transitional Provisions)* [1995] 1 F.L.R. 459.
[383] *Re L (Minors) (Financial Provision)* (1979) 1 F.L.R. 39; *Macey v Macey* (1981) 3 F.L.R. 7; and see also *Fisher v Fisher* [1989] 1 F.L.R. 423 at 430, CA; *B v B (Periodical Payments: Transitional Provisions)* [1995] 1 F.L.R. 459. Nevertheless, funds in fact made available by a third party may legitimately be treated as the financial resource of a spouse: *X v X (Y and Z Intervening)* [2002] 1 F.L.R. 508, FD (moneys made available by wife's wealthy family).
[384] *Macey v Macey* (1981) 3 F.L.R. 7; *Suter v Suter* [1987] Fam. 111, CA; *Atkinson v Atkinson* [1995] 2 F.L.R. 356, FD.
[385] Law Com. No.112, para.4.
[386] [2006] 2 F.L.R. 468.
[387] *Michael v Michael* [1986] 2 F.L.R. 389; *MT v MT (Financial Provision: Lump Sum)* [1992] 1 F.L.R. 362; *S v S (Ancillary Relief: Importance of FDR)* [2007] EWHC 1975 (Fam.); [2008] 1 F.L.R. 944.
[388] A solicitor will be guilty of professional negligence if no adequate inquiry is made about a client's pension expectations: see *Griffiths v Dawson & Co* [1993] 2 F.L.R. 315; and this duty has been reinforced by the provisions of Matrimonial Causes Act 1973, which states that the matters to be taken into account include any benefits under a pension scheme—which in this context has a wholly unrestricted meaning.
[389] At pp.415–422.

(vii) Other

A spouse's statutory entitlement as primary carer to be rehoused by a housing **13–071** association may be considered as a resource under s.25(2)(a).[390]

(ii) "[T]he financial needs, obligations and responsibilities which each of the parties to the marriage has or is likely to have in the foreseeable future" (Matrimonial Causes Act 1973 section 25(2)(b))

(i) "Needs"

In practice, needs assume crucial importance in cases where resources are **13–072** limited.[391] In that context, the housing needs of the parent with care will often be decisive, since first consideration must be given to minor children's welfare.[392] Where assets permit, the court should attempt to meet the housing needs of the other parent, particularly if staying contact is envisaged.[393] Where there are no minor children, the needs of the spouses must be weighed in the balance.[394] Where resources are limited, it may not be possible to meet the needs of both spouses, and priority may have to be given to one of them.[395]

In big money cases, for many years "needs" in s.25(2)(b), in practice, assumed a dominance over the other considerations mentioned in the subsection, in the guise of the "reasonable requirements" ceiling that was imposed on the *quantum* of an award (usually to the wife).[396] In such cases, it was accepted that the concept was a relative one; the wife of a wealthy man was entitled to maintain the high standard of living previously enjoyed. A classic example is *Dart v Dart*.[397] The domination of "reasonable requirements" was not removed until the decision of the House of Lords in *White v White*.[398] As discussed above, Lord Nicholls highlighted the unfairness inherent in the "reasonable requirements" ceiling, which invariably left the surplus of assets in the hands of the entrepreneur.

In many cases, the parties' needs will be self-evident (e.g. the provision of housing and a modest income). In cases involving substantial assets, the court may decide that it should try to put the applicant in the position of having a certain spendable income each year; a computer programme—the so-called *Duxbury* programme—has been devised[399] to calculate the lump sum needed

---

[390] *Akintola v Akintola* [2001] EWCA Civ. 1989; [2002] 1 F.L.R. 701.
[391] See the discussion at pp.358–359, above.
[392] Matrimonial Causes Act s.25(1), discussed earlier in this chapter.
[393] *M v B (Ancillary Proceedings: Lump Sum)* [1998] 1 F.L.R. 53, CA; *Cordle v Cordle* [2001] EWCA Civ. 1791; [2002] 1 F.L.R. 207.
[394] *Scheeres v Scheeres* [1999] 1 F.L.R. 241.
[395] As in *Piglowska v Piglowski* [1999] 2 F.L.R.763.
[396] *O'D v O'D* [1976] Fam. 83; *Page v Page* (1981) 2 F.L.R. 198; *Preston v Preston* [1982] Fam. 17; *Gojkovic v Gojkovic* [1990] F.L.R. 140, CA; *R v R (Financial Provision: Reasonable Needs)* [1994] 2 F.L.R. 1044; *F v F (Ancillary Relief: Substantial Assets)* [1995] 2 F.L.R. 45; *Dart v Dart* [1996] 2 F.L.R. 286.
[397] [1996] 2 F.L.R. 286, CA.
[398] [2000] 2 F.L.R. 981.
[399] See T. Lawrence, "Duxbury disclosure and other matters" [1989] Fam. Law 12; for judicial comment see *Gojkovic v Gojkovic* [1990] F.L.R. 140; *B v B (Financial Provision)* [1990] 1 F.L.R. 20; *Vicary v Vicary* [1992] 2 F.L.R. 271; *F v F (Ancillary Relief: Substantial Assets)* [1995] 2 F.L.R. 45;

to produce a given level of spending power allowing for inflation and a number of variables[400] and hypotheses (e.g. the possibility that the applicant might obtain employment after a number of years' training). Such programmes provide a useful reference base but cannot be more than a guide to the court, and may be wholly inappropriate in particular circumstances, for instance where a spouse has a long life expectancy or, alternatively, a short one,[401] or where the marriage has been short.[402] The importance of the *Duxbury* calculation has diminished with the removal of the "reasonable requirements" ceiling on awards in big money cases; needs are now only one of the considerations in the s.25 exercise.[403] It nevertheless remains a useful tool in calculating the income component of a lump sum.[404]

(iii) Obligations and responsibilities

13–073   The court is directed to consider the parties' financial "obligations and responsibilities". The problem of supporting successive families raises difficult issues of policy. Where resources are limited, reality demands that account be taken of financial support of a second family,[405] but what of cases where there is surplus of assets after both parties needs have been satisfied, and the principle of equality and the yardstick of equal division formulated in *White v White*[406] apply? Should the amount needed by one of the former spouses to support the child of a new relationship be notionally deducted from the pool of assets on which the yardstick operates, or at least be a valid reason for departure from equal division? To date, the sparse case law appears to be divided on the issue. In *S v S (Financial Provision: Departing From Equality)*[407] a man's financial responsibility to his second family was one of the considerations justifying a departure from equal division of assets. However, in *WH-J v WH-J*[408] Coleridge J. considered such an approach to be wrong in principle in a case involving sufficient resources; a man's responsibilities to a

---

F v F (Duxbury Calculation: Rate of Return) [1996] 1 F.L.R. 833. The Family Law Bar Association publish a guide, *At a Glance*, which contains a table enabling a simplified calculation to be made; see also the computer programme *Capitalise* by Singer and Mostyn. For further discussion, see Lawrence, Mainz and Collinson [1996] Fam. Law 560; Posnansky [1998] Fam. Law 447; Singer *et al.* [1998] Fam. Law 741; Woelke [1999] Fam. Law 767; Woelke [1999] Fam. Law 52; Mostyn [2000] Fam. Law 52; Merron et al. [2001] Fam. Law 749; Marks [2002] Fam. Law 408.

[400] See *Gojkovic v Gojkovic* [1990] 1 F.L.R. 140; *B v B (Financial Provision)* [1990] 1 F.L.R. 20; *Vicary v Vicary* [1992] 2 F.L.R. 271; *Fournier v Fournier* [1998] 2 F.L.R. 662; *A v A (Elderly Applicant: Lump Sum)* [1999] 2 F.L.R. 662; *W v W (Ancillary Relief: Practice)* [2000] Fam. Law 493.

[401] See *Gojkovic v Gojkovic* [1990] 1 F.L.R. 140; *B v B (Financial Provision)* [1990] 1 F.L.R. 20; *Vicary v Vicary* [1992] 2 F.L.R. 271; *Fournier v Fournier* [1998] 2 F.L.R. 662; *A v A (Elderly Applicant: Lump Sum)* [1999] 2 F.L.R. 662; *W v W (Ancillary Relief: Practice)* [2000] Fam. Law 493.

[402] *M v M (Prenuptial Agreement)* [2002] 1 F.L.R. 654, FD.

[403] See the discussion at para.13–043, above.

[404] Marks [2002] Fam. Law 408. For a contrary view, see Merron et al., "Is Duxbury misleading? Yes it is" [2001] Fam. Law 747.

[405] *Barnes v Barnes* [1972] 2 W.L.R. 1381; *Delaney v Delaney* [1990] 2 F.L.R. 457.

[406] [2001] 1 A.C. 596; [2000] 2 F.L.R. 981, HL.

[407] [2001] 2 F.L.R. 246, FD.

[408] [2002] 1 F.L.R. 415.

new child were his choice and should be met from his own share of the assets after division with his wife. In Chapter 15 we discuss the recognition given by the Child Support Act 1991 to obligations towards children in second families.

It is recognised that moral obligations can be considered.[409]

(iii) "[T]he standard of living enjoyed by the family before the breakdown of the marriage" (Matrimonial Causes Act 1973 section 25(2)(c))

Under the "minimal loss" principle, standard of living was obviously an **13–074** important factor, since the court's objective was to ensure that the applicant's financial position remained unaltered.[410] As the law now stands after the amendments effected by the Matrimonial and Family Proceedings Act 1984, a spouse is no longer absolutely entitled to expect to keep the standard of living enjoyed by the parties during the marriage, but "standard of living" is a factor to be considered in the overall exercise.

Where resources permit, standard of living can be a highly relevant consideration in an award even after a short marriage, as was demonstrated in *Miller v Miller; McFarlane v McFarlane*.[411] This approach is discussed in the next section.

(iv) "[T]he age of each party to the marriage and the duration of the marriage" (Matrimonial Causes Act 1973 section 25(2)(d))

It is rarely necessary to consider the parties' ages as a matter distinct from the **13–075** court's assessment of their needs and resources.

The duration of the marriage is a matter of more importance in the exercise of the court's. In enacting the current legislation, Parliament decisively repudiated the notion that one spouse is entitled, solely by virtue of the status of marriage, to be maintained on a scale appropriate to the other spouse's standard of life, exemplified in *Brett v Brett*,[412] decided on the old law. There the wife was a childless 23-year-old solicitor whose marriage had lasted for less than six months. She was awarded (in 1996 values) yearly periodical payments of some £16,000 and a lump sum of some £200,000.

Under the current law, the significance attached to the duration of the marriage will depend on the facts; it is only one of the factors in the overall exercise.[413] After *White v White*[414] and *Miller v Miller; McFarlane v McFarlane*[415] it is tolerably clear that after a long marriage, at least, the matrimonial

---

[409] *Cowan v Cowan* [2001] 2 F.C.R. 331, *per* Mance L.J.
[410] See para.13–034, above.
[411] [2006] 1 F.L.R. 1186, discussed at para.13–047, above.
[412] [1969] 1 W.L.R. 487.
[413] *G v G (Financial Provision: Separation Agreement)* [2000] 2 F.L.R. 18, FD; on the facts, the most important consideration was the separation agreement.
[414] [2001] 1 A.C. 596; [2000] 2 F.L.R. 981.
[415] [2006] 1 F.L.R. 1186.

assets will prima facie be shared equally.[416] This approach is less apt in relation to a medium-length[417] or short marriage.

13–076   What is the current judicial approach to ancillary relief awards short marriages? In *Miller v Miller; McFarlane v McFarlane* the House of Lords did not deliver separate judgments on the two appeals, and the resolution of ancillary relief proceedings in relation to short marriages is not therefore addressed by means of self-contained principles in the speeches. Rather, the general principles articulated in the speeches are applied to short marriages, with appropriate adaptation to the facts. The House of Lords made clear as to what is no longer good law. The older pre-*White* cases on short, childless marriages are no longer good law, at least in big-money cases.[418] Those cases (often described as adopting a "rehabilitative" model) focused on need and compensation.[419] The court is now required also to consider entitlement to a fair share of the assets.[420] In a short marriage, the court will often be more ready to depart from equal sharing, and "unilateral assets" may be left in the hands of the party who generated them.[421] In assessing needs in big-money cases, the standard of living enjoyed during the marriage will be relevant, although legitimate expectation is not.[422] Conduct in the sense of responsibility for bringing a marriage to an end is not, as a matter of law, a relevant consideration, unless it passes the very high threshold discussed below in relation to ancillary cases generally.[423]

Everything turns on the particular facts. Where a short marriage has generated specific needs (particularly where there is a child), a substantial sum and continuing maintenance may be justified.[424]

(v) "[A]ny physical or mental disability of either of the parties to the marriage" (Matrimonial Causes Act 1973 section 25(2)(e))

13–077   This provision was not included in the draft Bill originally put forward by the Law Commission, but was added as a result of Parliamentary pressure during the passage of the original 1970 legislation. It adds little to the matters that are considered under other heads.[425]

---

[416] See the discussion at paras 13–054 and 13–055, above.
[417] *Smith v Smith* [2007] 2 F.L.R. 1103.
[418] [2006] 1 F.L.R. 1186 at [54]–[55], [158].
[419] For example, *S v S* [1977] Fam 127; *H v H (Financial Provision: Short Marriage)* (1981) 2 F.L.R. 392; *Robertson v Robertson* (1984) 4 F.L.R. 387; *Attar v Attar (No.2)* [1985] F.L.R. 653; *Hedges v Hedges* [1991] 1 F.L.R. 196.
[420] [2006] 1 F.L.R. 1186 at [55], [158].
[421] *Miller v Miller; McFarlane v McFarlane* [2006] 2 A.C. 618; *Charman v Charman (No.4)* [2007] 1 F.L.R. 1246.
[422] [2006] 1 F.L.R. 1186 at [57], [58], [72], [157], [158].
[423] See paras 13–082–13–084.
[424] *C v C (Financial Relief: Short Marriage)* [1997] 2 F.L.R. 27.
[425] Particularly the needs of the parties: see, for example, *C v C (Financial Provision: Personal Damages)* [1995] 2 F.L.R. 171; *C v C (Financial Relief: Short Marriage)* [1997] 2 F.L.R. 969.

(vi) "[T]he contributions made by each of the parties to the welfare of the family, including any contribution made by looking after the home or caring for the family"[426] (Matrimonial Causes Act 1973 section 25(2)(f))

The law governing beneficial entitlement to matrimonial property was, as we have seen, widely felt as to not to give adequate recognition to the contributions that wives in particular often made towards the acquisition of so-called "family assets"—"those things which are acquired . . . with the intention that there should be continuing provision for [the parties] and their children during their joint lives, and used for the benefit of the family as a whole", as Lord Denning put it in *Wachtel v Wachtel*.[427] That case made it quite clear that under the post-1969 divorce-law, such contributions would be taken fully into account. Nevertheless, over the last three decades, the courts, in applying s.25(2)(f) of the Matrimonial Causes Act 1973, have grappled with the respective and relative values to be accorded, in terms of ancillary relief outcome, to financial and non-financial contributions to family welfare.

13–078

Prior to the decision of the House of Lords in *White v White*,[428] there were signs of a growing recognition of a wife's indirect (as well as, self-evidently, direct[429]) contribution to the success of the business enterprise primarily generated by the husband. In *Vicary v Vicary*[430] the Court of Appeal accepted that the wife of a millionaire businessman who had "supplied the infrastructure and support in the context of which [he was] able to work hard, prosper and accumulate his wealth" could properly be allowed credit for such indirect contributions. The decision of Wilson J. in *Conran v Conran*[431] further liberalised the nexus between a range of different contributions and the creation of resources. In that case, the wife of a successful businessman had acted as primary homemaker and parent and was energetic in making business contacts for the husband and in entertaining, as well as having her own career as a journalist. The award, which brought her wealth up to £10.5 million (at the time reputedly the largest award ever made), recognised her outstanding contributions to the welfare of the family, in addition to her reasonable requirements.

We have already described the reasonable-requirements ceiling formerly imposed on awards in big money cases for several decades. While awards made on that basis may have appeared substantial, in fact they represented very small fractions of the total assets[432] and thus tended to undervalue non-

---

[426] Matrimonial Causes Act 1973 s.25(2)(f); Civil Partnership Act 2004 Sch.5 para.21(2)(f).

[427] [1973] Fam. 72, CA.

[428] [2000] 2 F.L.R. 981.

[429] *O'D v O'D* [1976] Fam. 83; *Page v Page* [1981] 2 F.L.R. 198. For another dramatic example of a husband and wife partnership, see *Gojkovic v Gojkovic* [1990] 1 F.L.R. 140, above.

[430] [1992] 2 F.L.R. 271, CA. But note that in *W v W (Judicial Separation: Ancillary Relief)* [1995] 2 F.L.R. 259, Ewbank J. expressed the view that in a case in which a wife had not made a direct contribution to the build-up of the family assets, the *Wachtel* principle should be limited to the division of the matrimonial home rather than the family assets as a whole.

[431] [1997] 2 F.L.R. 615.

[432] For example, 4.5% in *F v F (Ancillary Relief: Substantial Asset)* [1995] 2 F.L.R. 47; 2.25% in *Dart v Dart* [1996] 2 F.L.R. 286; 4.7% in *A v A (Financial Provision)* [1998] 2 F.L.R. 180.

financial contributions to family welfare.[433] We have shown that the reasonable-requirements approach was dominant but not wholly exclusive. Thus in *A v A (Elderly Applicant: Lump Sum)*[434] it was recognised that the *Duxbury* technique would not meet the justice of the case where the husband had made full contributions over a marriage of more than 40 years, and an entitlement approach was adopted.

13–079   The highest appellate interpretation of s.25(2)(f) had to await *White v White*,[435] which we have already discussed at some length.[436] The principle of non-discrimination between different roles assumed during a relationship goes a considerable way towards the recognition of marriage as an equal partnership. The ethos of marriage as a partnership was further articulated in *Miller v Miller; McFarlane v McFarlane*.[437]

Nevertheless, the case law recognises that unequal division of assets is appropriate where one spouse has made a "special" contribution. A in Lord Nicholls' speech in *White v White*[438] could be construed as suggesting that the principle of non-discrimination between different contributions is predicated on equality of contribution in the spouses' respective spheres of activity, and therefore—in appropriate case—as permitting an evaluation of their respective efforts and degrees of success. The Court of Appeal in *Cowan v Cowan*[439] endorsed the notion of exceptional contribution by one spouse, justifying departure from equal division of assets. In that case, the assets had been built up during the long marriage; the wife had made some initial contribution to the business, but the very substantial wealth had been generated by the husband's exceptional entrepreneurial skill in marketing plastic bin-liners. The Court of Appeal awarded the wife 38 per cent of the assets, and the House of Lords dismissed her petition for leave to appeal. In *WH-J v HH-J*[440] (where the assets totaled £2.7 million), Coleridge J., on the facts, found nothing special or exceptional about the husband's contributions, and was aware of the dangers of the thin end of the wedge being driven right into the heart of the principles underlying *White v White*; in the classic case of full contributions by each spouse over a long marriage, the courts should be slow to "start nibbling at the edges" of cases where all other factors were equal and 50 per cent being the natural and fair outcome. This was the first reported post-*White* instance of an equal division in a big money case. His Lordship further commented that even a small departure from equal division in a big-money case leaves one party feeling that her efforts have been undervalued, and warned against:

---

[433] P. Singer, "Sexual discrimination in ancillary relief" [2001] Fam. Law 115.
[434] [1999] 2 F.L.R. 969.
[435] [2000] 2 F.L.R. 981.
[436] See para.13–043.
[437] [2006] 1 F.L.R. 1186.
[438] [2000] 3 W.L.R. 1571 at 1598: "[i]f, in their different spheres, each contributed equally to the family."
[439] [2001] 2 F.L.R. 192; [2001] 3 W.L.R. 684; J. Eekelaar, "Asset distribution on divorce—the durational element" [2001] 117 L.Q.R. 552.
[440] [2002] 1 F.L.R. 415.

"[T]he broad and sweeping reform underlying the speeches in *White* . . . [becoming] bogged down in a welter of zealous, over sophisticated and costly forensic analysis, or watered down by judicial reticence."[441]

The husband's claim to special contribution (a fortune generated by the production of free newspapers financed by advertising) was rejected by the Court of Appeal in *Lambert v Lambert*[442] but accepted by Bennet J. and *Sorrell v Sorrell*.[443] In *Sorrell*, the assets available for division were some £75 million. Through a series of acquisitions, the husband had developed the second largest business of its type in the world. Bennett J. held that the judgment of the Court of Appeal in *Lambert* had confined the concept to the most exceptional and limited circumstances; nevertheless, special contribution remained a legitimate contribution, and the criteria were satisfied on the facts here, where the husband had exercised exceptional business talent amounting to genius. The husband was awarded 60 per cent of the assets.

Special contribution was not argued of the facts of either appeal in *Miller* **13–080**
v Miller; McFarlane v McFarlane, but, as part of the House's wide-ranging pronouncements on ancillary relief generally, was addressed in the speeches of Lord Nicholls and Baroness Hale.[444] Both accepted that special contribution is a "live" doctrine and remains a permissible reason for departing from equality of division, but only in very limited, exceptional circumstances. Both deprecated attempts to argue special contribution save in a very narrow category of case. The observations of Coleridge J. in *G v G (Financial Provision: Equal Division)* (discussed above), warning against the dangers of opening a "forensic Pandora's box", were cited with approval.[445] No reference was made in any of the speeches to the decision of Bennett J. in *Sorrell v Sorrell* (discussed above).

According to the speeches in *Miller v Miller; McFarlane v McFarlane,*[446] special contribution should be assessed by the same test as that for conduct *per Wachtel v Wachtel*[447] and s.25(2)(g) of the Matrimonial Causes Act 1973,[448] discussed below. That test poses the question of whether it would be inequitable to disregard such contribution. The focus has therefore now been placed on outcome: would disregard of the contribution lead to an inequitable result? As will be shown in the discussion below, case law on s.25(2)(g) illustrates that the threshold is very high in relation to conduct that would be inequitable to disregard. If this approach is to be carried over into special contribution, the threshold appears to be hard to cross. A further question raised by the use of the s.25(2)(g) analogy is "what is the measure of departure from equal division of assets?"

---

[441] [2002] 1 F.L.R. 415 at 430–431.
[442] [2003] Fam. 103.
[443] [2006] 1 F.L.R. 497.
[444] [2006] 1 F.L.R. 1186 at paras [66]–[68] and [145]–[146] respectively.
[445] [2006] 1 F.L.R. 1186 at [67] and [147].
[446] See the comment by Professor Douglas at [2006] Fam. Law 629.
[447] [1973] Fam. 72.
[448] See now Civil Partnership Act 2004 Sch.5 para.21(2)(g).

Special contribution was considered post-*Miller v Miller; McFarlane v McFarlane* in *Charman v Charman*.[449] The facts and outcome of this case have been given above. Coleridge J. awarded the wife some £48 million (i.e. just short of 37 per cent of the total) and the husband just over 63 per cent. His Lordship held that although the marriage was a long one in which both parties had played full parts, and all the wealth had been generated during the marriage, the case nevertheless fell into the very exceptional category where the created wealth was of extraordinary proportions and arose from one spouse's extraordinary talent and energy. In all the circumstances, unequal division of the assets was fair.

13–081   The husband's appeal was dismissed by the Court of Appeal. On special contribution, the judgment stated that:

- The size of the property in the present case should not compel departure from the usual conclusion that wealth generated by a party during a marriage is the product of a contribution on his or her part to the welfare of the family.

- It would be dangerous to identify any figure as a guideline threshold for the amount of a special contribution made by the generation of substantial wealth. However, as a guideline, and recognising that some cases might require departure from the range, it would be hard to conceive that, where a special contribution is established, the percentage of division of the matrimonial property should be nearer to equality than 55%–45%. Similarly, even in an extreme case, fair allowance for special contribution within the sharing principle would be most unlikely to give rise to percentages further from equality than 66.6%–33.3%. These are the perameters within which the concept should operate.

Nevertheless, the continued recognition of special contribution may be criticised[450] as inherently discriminatory and thus contrary to the spirit of *White v White* and *Miller v Miller; McFarlane v McFarlane* in the growing recognition accorded to marriage as a partnership to which spouses make different but equally valuable contributions. There has, to date, been no reported case in which special contribution had been recognised in the domestic, as opposed to the entrepreneurial, sphere.

Further, it now appears to be the size of the fortune, rather than an element of genius or originality in its generation, that attracts the recognition of the concept. This may indicate no more than that family-law reflects the current mores of a particular capitalist society.

---

[449] [2006] Fam. Law 1018; [2007] 1 F.C.R. 33; [2007] 1 F.L.R. 593 (Coleridge J.); [2007] 1 F.L.R. 1246 (Sir Mark Potter P, Thorpe, Wilson L.JJ.).
[450] R. Bailey-Harris [2001] Fam. Law 499; J. Eekelaar (2001) 117 L.Q.R. 552.

(vii) "[T]he conduct of each of the parties if that conduct is such that it would in the opinion of the court be inequitable to disregard it"[451]

The extent to which the conduct of the parties should be relevant in determin-   **13–082**
ing the financial outcome of divorce has been controversial, and a brief
account of the historical evolution of the law is necessary.

So long as divorce was based on the matrimonial-offence doctrine, the
parties' conduct was of crucial importance: an "innocent" wife was entitled to
full compensation for the loss of her status and the right to support flowing
from it at common law, but a "guilty" wife would not in principle be entitled
to maintenance at all. Over the years, the harshness of this rule was mitigated.
In the end it became accepted that a wife's misconduct would only be allowed
to affect her right to maintenance if it could be described as really serious,
disruptive, intolerable and unforgivable.[452]

The Divorce Reform Act 1969 was intended to allow the empty legal shell
of a broken marriage to be destroyed with the minimum of bitterness, distress
and humiliation, but the legislation dealing with the financial consequences of
divorce specifically required the court to have regard to the parties' conduct
in determining how far it was just to place them in the financial position they
would have been in had it not been for the breakdown. Did this mean—as
was suggested in some of the early cases—that the courts would have to carry
out an investigation into responsibility for the breakdown of the marriage?
Did it mean that the judge had to hear the parties' "mutual recriminations
and . . . go into their petty squabbles for days on end, as he used to do in the
old days"?[453]

In 1973, in the leading case of *Wachtel v Wachtel*,[454] the Court of Appeal   **13–083**
refused to allow the policy of the divorce-law to be subverted in this way. In
the vast majority of cases (said Lord Denning), both parties would have
contributed to the breakdown. In such cases, the court should not reduce its
order for financial provision merely because of what was formerly regarded as
guilt or blame. Nevertheless, there would remain a "residue of cases" where
the conduct of one of the parties had been (in the words of Ormrod J. at first
instance) "both obvious and gross", so much so that to order one party to
support another whose conduct fell into this category would be "repugnant to
anyone's sense of justice". It was only in such cases that the financial order
should be reduced.[455]

As a result of the acceptance of this decision, considerations of conduct
were held rarely to be relevant. It was evidently the intention of the draftsman
of the Matrimonial and Family Proceedings Act 1984 to codify the practice of
the Court of Appeal developed on the basis of *Wachtel*, whilst avoiding the
use of the expression "obvious and gross". Conduct is now, according to the

---

[451] Matrimonial Causes Act 1973 s.25(2)(g); Civil Partnership Act 2004 Sch.5, para.21(2)(g). Burles, "Conduct and ancillary relief" [1997] Fam. Law 804.
[452] *Ackerman v Ackerman* [1972] Fam. 1, *per* Sir G. Baker, P.
[453] *Wachtel v Wachtel* [1973] Fam. 72, CA.
[454] Above.
[455] [1973] Fam. 72 at 89–90.

statutes, was to be relevant only in those (exceptional) circumstances in which it would be "inequitable" to disregard it.[456] In *Miller v Miller; McFarlane v McFarlane* the House of Lords confirmed that no conduct other than that which passes the high threshold in s.25(2)(g) of the Matrimonial Causes Act 1973[457]; is not a permissible consideration in ancillary relief proceedings[458]; in the context of a short marriage, this means that responsibility for bringing a marriage to an early end is not, as a matter of law, a relevant consideration (unless it crosses the very high statutory threshold).[459] In *Sorrell v Sorrell*[460] Bennett J. observed that in the absence of any allegation of conduct under s.25(2)(g), sterile evidentiary disputes as to whether the husband had been a "good" husband assed nothing to the s.25 exercise.

There are a number of ways in which conduct is taken into account in the case law. "Conduct" is not a synonym for matrimonial misconduct, and may involve financial dealings. Thus, in *Martin v Martin*[461] the husband (who had been a millionaire dairy farmer) had:

> "[O]bstinately, unrealistically and selfishly trailed on to eventual disaster, dissipating in the process not only his money but his family's money, his friends' money, the money of commercial creditors unsecured and even-tually his wife's money."[462]

Accordingly, the husband should receive no more than was necessary to provide him with basic accommodation. In *Le Foe v Le Foe and Woolwich plc*[463] the husband's deceptive mortgaging of the home was reflected in the *quantum* of the award. In *M v M (Financial Misconduct: Subpoena Against Third Party)*[464] the husband's excessive gambling and failure to provide full disclosure justified the wife receiving more than half the assets (62.5 per cent). Furthermore, as we have seen in Chapters 4 and 5, the existence and terms of a separation agreement[465] or a pre-nuptial agreement[466] may be taken into account as conduct under s.25(2)(g).

13–084   In one very limited category of case, conduct bars a claim to ancillary relief *in limine* on public policy grounds derived from the maxim "*ex turpi causa non oritur actio*". In *Whiston v Whiston*[467] the husband obtained a decree of nullity on account of the wife's bigamy, of which she was well aware when she entered into her second "marriage". The Court of Appeal held that the

---

[456] For a fuller discussion, see the fourth edition of this work at pp.797–802 and, in particular, for a detailed summary of the case law, fn.13, p.800.
[457] See also Civil Partnership Act 2004 Sch.5 para.21(2)(g).
[458] [2006] 1 F.L.R. 1186 at paras [65], [69], [145], [161]–[165].
[459] [2006] 1 F.L.R. 1186 at paras [63]–[65], [145], [161]–[165]; disapproving *G v G (Financial Provision: Separation Agreement)* [2004] 1 F.L.R. 1011 (as applied in the courts below in *Miller*).
[460] [2006] 1 F.L.R. 497 at paras [86]–[92].
[461] [1995] 2 F.L.R. 160.
[462] *per* Thorpe J. at 169.
[463] [2001] 2 F.L.R. 970, FD.
[464] [2006] 2 F.L.R. 1253.
[465] *G v G (Financial Provision: Separation Agreement)* [2000] 2 F.L.R. 18, FD.
[466] *M v M (Pre-Nuptial Agreement)* [2002] 1 F.L.R. 654, FD.
[467] [1995] 2 F.L.R. 268.

crime of bigamy strikes at the heart of the institution of marriage, that her claim for ancillary relief derived from her crime, and that she should be prevented from proceeding further.[468] The Court of Appeal commented obiter that an innocent party to a bigamous marriage would be afforded relief and that a person entering a bigamous marriage in the genuine and reasonable belief that he or she was free to do so might also have an entitlement to ancillary relief. The narrow scope of the decision in *Whiston*—which has the drastic effect of barring the claim *in limine*—has been confirmed by subsequent case law. The Court of Appeal has confirmed that the principle is confined to cases of bigamy involving conscious deception, and does not apply in other cases of criminal conduct involving deception.[469] Furthermore, *Whiston* does not bar a claim by every culpable bigamist, whatever the circumstances. It is legitimate for the court to have regard to the nature of the crime in its factual context of the case. Thus in *Rampal v Rampal (No.2)*[470] the husband's ancillary relief claim was not barred, even though he knew the wife was married at the time he went through a ceremony with her; her culpability was greater than his, and the gravity of his offence was not such as to deny him his statutory rights on public policy grounds. Thus the *Whiston* principle will bar the claim of only the most culpable intentional bigamist.

The weight to be given to conduct under s.25(2)(g) is a matter for the court's discretion, of which the reported case law merely provides illustrations. At one extreme, in rare cases conduct may be regarded as so extreme as to result in a nil entitlement—for practical purposes, the same outcome as if the claim had been held to be barred *in limine*. Thus in *J v S-T (formerly J) (Transsexual: Ancillary Relief)*[471] the defendant, a female-to-male transsexual, went through a ceremony of marriage with the plaintiff, a wealthy woman; their relationship lasted more than 12 years and with AID treatment produced two children. At no stage during courtship nor after marriage did the defendant reveal his true sexual identity. The Court of Appeal held that the defendant had been guilty of perjury and had deceived the plaintiff. She was granted a nullity decree, and the Court of Appeal dismissed the defendant's claim for ancillary relief.[472] In *Evans v Evans*[473] a wife obtained a divorce from her husband, after a short marriage, in 1951. Over the next 35 years the husband meticulously complied with court orders for maintenance. However, in 1985 the wife was convicted of inciting others to murder the husband under a contract killing arrangement. She was sentenced to four years' imprisonment, and the husband then ceased to make the payments. In this case—so the

---

[468] See the comments by J. Dewar in [1995] Fam. Law 549 and S. Cretney in (1996) 112 L.Q.R. 33.
[469] *J v S-T (formerly J) (Transsexual: Ancillary Relief)* [1997] 1 F.L.R. 402 (CA *per* Sir Brian Neill and Potter L.J; Ward L.J. dissenting).
[470] [2001] EWCA Civ. 989; [2001] 3 W.L.R. 795; [2001] 2 F.L.R. 1179, CA.
[471] [1997] 1 F.L.R. 402.
[472] The majority (Sir Brian Neill and Potter L.J.) in the exercise of discretion having regard to s.25(2)(g); Ward L.J. regarded the claim as barred in limine in the application of *Whiston v Whiston* [1995] 2 F.L.R. 268.
[473] [1989] 1 F.L.R. 351, CA.

Court of Appeal held—it had been right to discharge the order since otherwise the public "might think we had taken leave of our senses".[474]

The following cases illustrate the exercise of the court's discretion in relation to conduct. In *K v K (Financial Provision: Conduct)*[475] the husband suffered from a depressive illness, which made his behaviour unpredictable and suicidal. The wife assisted the husband with suicide attempts not (so the judge found) from humanitarian principles but in order that she could set up home with her lover and get as much from the husband's estate as possible. In those circumstances (and also taking into account the wife's wholly deceitful conduct in relation to her association with her lover), it was held that it would be inequitable to disregard the wife's conduct as one of the relevant circumstances. In the result, the lump sum awarded to the wife was reduced from £14,000 to £5,000.[476] In *Clark v Clark*[477] a woman in straitened financial circumstances married a rich man some 36 years her senior. The marriage of five-years duration was never consummated. Despite the husband's generosity in purchasing assets for the wife, she reduced him to the status of a virtual prisoner in the luxurious matrimonial home from which he was eventually rescued by relatives. The judge condemned the wife for matrimonial misconduct but nevertheless awarded her a lump sum of £552,500. The Court of Appeal reduced this to £125,000, taking into account her retention of other assets worth £50,000. One party's conduct may be a consideration leading to a more substantial award in favour of the other than might otherwise have been the case. In *B v B (Financial Provision Welfare of Child and Conduct)*[478] the wife received the entire modest equity from the former matrimonial home; amongst several relevant considerations, it would have been inequitable to disregard the husband's conduct in respect of child abduction, non-disclosure and removal of assets and failure to support the child. At the other end of the resource scale, in *Al-Khatib v Masry*[479] Munby J., in awarding the wife £26.3 million, took account, inter alia of the husband's abduction of the children and the emotional effect on the wife and children. In *H v H (Attempted Murder as Conduct)*[480] the husband was convicted of the attempted murder of his wife and was sentenced to 12 years' imprisonment. This was conduct "at the very top of the scale", but the court should not be punitive for its own sake; rather, the correct approach was to see such conduct as magnifying the wife's needs, since the situation she found herself in was the husband's fault. In *S v S (Non-Matrimonial Property: Conduct)*[481] Burton J. did not find that the domestic violence in question left him with the requisite "gasp" factor to be taken into account under s.25(2)(g).

---

[474] *Per* Balcombe L.J. at 355.
[475] [1988] 1 F.L.R. 469.
[476] It should be noted that this was only a part of the provision ordered for the wife.
[477] [1999] 2 F.L.R. 498, CA.
[478] [2002] 1 F.L.R. 555, FD.
[479] [2002] EWHC Fam. 108; [2002] 1 F.L.R. 1053.
[480] [2006] 1 F.L.R. 990.
[481] [2007] 1 F.L.R. 1496.

Litigation misconduct is[482] normally[483] reflected by a penalty in costs rather than in the *quantum* of the substantive award in ancillary relief.[484]

(viii) "[T]he value to each of the parties to the marriage of any benefit which by reason of the dissolution or annulment of the marriage of that party will lose the chance of acquiring" (Matrimonial Causes Act 1973 section 25(2)(h))

This provision directs the court, in the exercise of its discretion, to consider **13–085** the loss of benefits that will result from divorce. Marriage creates a status, which automatically confers certain legal rights and privileges For example, a surviving spouse has rights to succeed on the other's intestacy and under a pension scheme connected with the deceased's employment. The court's extensive powers in relation to pension entitlements are discussed later in this chapter.

(6) The court's duty to consider terminating financial obligations: the "clean break"[485]

In 1984 the legislative guidelines contained in the Matrimonial Causes Act **13–086** 1973 were amended on the recommendation of the Law Commission[486] in order to give greater emphasis to the termination of financial obligations between former spouses (i.e. "to encourage and enable a clean break settlement"[487]). If the court decides to exercise its financial powers in favour of a party to the marriage, s.25A obliges it to consider "whether it would be appropriate so to exercise those powers that the financial obligations of each party towards the other will be terminated as soon after" the divorce as the court "considers just and reasonable". There is an identical provision in the Civil Partnership Act 2004.[488] The policy of the law thus encourages parties to go their separate ways wherever fairness and practicalities allow.[489] In

---

[482] On litigation misconduct under the new cost riles, see para.13–011, above.
[483] But the principle is not absolute, and litigation misconduct may occasionally be reflected in, for example, *Clark v Clark* [1999] 2 F.L.R. 498; *B v B (Financial Provision: Welfare of Child and Conduct)* [2002] 1 F.L.R. 555; *M v M* [2006] 2 F.L.R. 1253.
[484] *P v P (Financial Relief: Non-Disclosure)* [1994] 2 F.L.R. 381, FD. See the discussion at para.13–011, above.
[485] The term "clean break" originally referred to an arrangement whereby the wife abandoned her right to claim maintenance in return for a transfer by the husband of a capital asset, usually, though not always, the matrimonial home: see *Clutton v Clutton* [1991] 1 F.L.R. 242 at 245, *per* Lloyd L.J.
[486] Law Com. No.112, para.27. For the history of and background to the legislation, see *Whiting v Whiting* [1988] 2 F.L.R. 189 at 194–197, *per* Balcombe L.J. The section was formally amended by the Welfare Reform and Pensions Act 1999 s.19 Sch.3 paras 1 and 6.
[487] *Per* Baroness Hale in *Miller v Miller; McFarlane v McFarlane* [2006] 2 F.L.R. 1186 at para.[130].
[488] Civil Partnership Act Sch.5, para.23(2).
[489] For judicial comments in the policy, see, for example, *per* Waite J. in *Tandy v Tandy*, October 24, 1986 as cited in *Whiting v Whiting* [1988] 2 F.L.R. 189 at 199, *per* Balcombe L.J.; *S v S* [1986] Fam. 189 at 193, *per* Waite J. (referring to *Minton v Minton* [1979] A.C. 593, HL); *Morris v Morris* [1985] F.L.R. 1176 at 1179; *C v C (Financial Provision)* [1989] 1 F.L.R. 11 at 19, *per* Ewbank J.; *Mawson v Mawson* [1994] 2 F.L.R. 985 at 990–991, *per* Thorpe J.; *N v N (Consent Order: Variation)* [1993] 2 F.L.R. 868 at 875, *per* Butler-Sloss L.J.

Miller v Miller; McFarlane v McFarlane[490] Baroness Hale stated that the "ultimate objective" of the statutory provisions is "to give each party an equal start on the road to independent living" and that s.25A is:

> "[A] powerful encouragement towards securing the court's objective by way of lump sum and capital adjustment . . . rather than periodical payments. This is good practical sense."[491]

Nevertheless, the objective articulated in s.25A of the Matrimonial Causes Act 1973 and para.23(2) of Sch.5 to the Civil Partnership Act 2004 should not be elevated to the status of a principle,[492] nor is there a presumption in favour of a clean break.[493] The statute does not require courts to strive for a "clean break" regardless of all other considerations. Ultimately, the form of award remains a matter for the exercise of the court's discretion, which is very wide.[494]

Recent developments may appear to reduce the force of the clean break objective. It is now recognised that a party whose earning capacity has been impaired by the domestic and parenting role may be entitled to compensation from the other party, effectively to equalise the economic effects of marriage; where capital is unavailable, this may have to take the form of maintenance payments.[495] The element of compensation articulated in *Miller v Miller; McFarlane v McFarlane*,[496] and its reception in the ensuing case law, has been discussed in detail earlier in this chapter.[497]

13–087   Despite the public policy and private advantages of a clean break, such may not be possible or even desirable in cases involving private companies, where commercial and company-law solutions may be fairer.[498]

It is also important to bear in mind that the so-called "clean break philosophy" applies exclusively to the financial obligations of the adult parties to support one another; and the courts have consistently emphasised that neither the court nor the parties can bring about a "clean break" between parent and child.[499]

13–088   **(a) The general duty under section 25A(1).** The duty under s.25A(1) of the Matrimonial Causes Act 1973 and para.23 of Sch.5 to the Children Act 1973

---

[490] [2006] 2 F.L.R. 1186 at para.[144].

[491] [2006] 2 F.L.R. 1186 at para.[133].

[492] *Clutton v Clutton* [1991] 1 F.L.R. 242 at 245, *per* Lloyd L.J.

[493] *SRJ v DWJ (Financial Provision)* [1999] 2 F.L.R. 176 at 181, *per* Hale J.; *Phippen v Palmers (A Firm)* [2002] 2 F.L.R. 408.

[494] *Per* Slade L.J. in *Whiting v Whiting* [1988] 2 F.L.R. 189 at 202. That case illustrates the difficulty in the way of a successful appeal.

[495] A. Didduck and H. Orton, "Equality and support for spouses" 57 M.L.R. 681; R. Bailey-Harris, "The role of maintenance and property orders in redressing inequality" [1998] 12 *Australian Journal of Family Law* 3; *SRJ v DWJ (Financial Provision)* [1999] 2 F.L.R. 176, *per* Hale L.J.

[496] [2006] 2 F.L.R. 1186.

[497] See paras 13–047–13–053, above.

[498] *A v A (Ancillary Relief: Property Division)* [2006] 2 F.L.R. 115; *D v D and B Ltd* [2007] 2 F.L.R. 653.

[499] *Hulley v Thompson* [1981] 1 W.L.R. 159; *Preston v Preston* [1982] Fam. 17; *Crozier v Crozier* [1994] 1 F.L.R. 126.

arises when the court decides to exercise its property adjustment or financial-provision powers in favour of a party to the marriage on or after the grant of a decree of divorce or nullity of marriage or in favour of a civil partner after an order for dissolution or nullity. The duty imposed by these provisions is entirely general, and there are other statutory provisions relevant to its discharge.

(i) The duty to consider making a periodical payments order for a specified **13–089**
term. Where available funds permit, the court can discharge its duty to consider a termination of financial obligations by ordering a capital settlement, part of which may represent commutation of the right to be maintained on a periodic basis.[500] However, there will be many cases in which such a once-and-for-all settlement is not possible, and the court will feel it appropriate to make an order for periodical payments. If it does decide to make such an order in favour of a party to the marriage, the statutory provisions[501] then impose a mandatory duty "in particular" to:

> "[C]onsider whether it would be appropriate to require those payments to be made or secured only for such term as would in the opinion of the court be sufficient to enable the party in whose favour the order is made to adjust without undue hardship to the termination of his or her financial dependence on the other party."

It follows that in each case, the court must consider whether the order should be for a specified term and in making that decision the court must specifically ask[502] whether such a period would be sufficient for the applicant to adjust,[503] without undue hardship[504] to the changed circumstances. The issue of whether to fix a term is one for the exercise of discretion, and the reported cases are no more than illustrative.

Where a parent has care of young children, a term order may be inappropriate on the particular facts.[505] In *C v C (Financial Relief: Short Marriage)*[506] the short marriage had adversely affected the wife's health, and she had care of the child who also had health problems; no term was fixed to the order for substantial periodic maintenance in favour of the wife. The Court of

---

[500] Calculated according to the *Duxbury* formula, discussed earlier at pp.379–380.
[501] Matrimonial Causes Act 1973 s.25(A)(2); Civil Partnership Act Sch.5, para.23(3).
[502] *Boylan v Boylan* [1988] 1 F.L.R. 282, 290, *per* Booth J.
[503] *Suter v Suter* [1987] 2 F.L.R. 232 at 236, CA.
[504] The words "undue hardship" are not to be regarded as referring solely to the needs of the spouse concerned: *Boylan v Boylan* [1988] 1 F.L.R. 282 at 289, *per* Booth J.
[505] *N v N (Consent Order: Variation)* [1993] 2 F.L.R. 868, *per* Butler-Sloss L.J. at 875 ("it is impossible to predict what may happen after five years where a child is concerned"); but contrast *Richardson v Richardson (No.2)* [1994] 2 F.L.R. 1051, where the wife's periodical payment order was extended to the time when her youngest child would have finished tertiary education, and it could confidently be predicted that the wife would by then be free of the responsibility for upbringing that had restricted her ability to earn; and see *Mawson v Mawson* [1994] 2 F.L.R. 985, where the child's own maintenance was provided by a substantial child support assessment, and the wife's periodical payments were extended for a short period.
[506] [1997] 2 F.L.R. 26.

Appeal observed that it was not appropriate simply to presume the imposition of a term whenever there was a short marriage; it all depended on the particular circumstances, and here there was so much uncertainty in the wife's position that a term would have been inappropriate. In *Suter v Suter*[507] the court held that although it was likely that as the children grew up it would become progressively easier for the wife to organise and increase her earning capacity, and that she might expect to derive some financial support from her lover, there were too many uncertainties to predict the development of events over the next 10 years. The appropriate compromise was to make a nominal order, unrestricted as to time, which could be varied if the wife's financial position deteriorated. By contrast, in *Waterman v Waterman*[508] the 38-year-old wife had custody of the five-year-old child following breakdown of a short marriage. The judge made an order for periodical payments for the wife, and, on the basis that she had an earning capacity, that it was in her interests "to get her life on its feet, to obtain an occupation and some source of income for herself", and that the difficulty of caring for a child would interfere less with her obtaining employment when he was 10 years old, directed that the periodical payments should terminate in five years time. The Court of Appeal held that he had not been wrong to do so.

13–090   It may be unrealistic to expect older women who have assumed a primarily domestic and parenting role during marriage to achieve economic self-sufficiency after divorce. Thus in *M v M (Financial Provision)*[509] the court concluded that it would not be appropriate to terminate the wife's periodical payments order either in five years or at the end of any fixed period; nor would it be just and reasonable so to do. Such a termination would cause undue hardship to a 47-year-old woman with only limited earning capacity whose marriage to a £60,000-a-year chartered accountant had broken down after 20 years, the more so since it would be unrealistic to suppose that the wife could become self-sufficient before or at the end of five years or any other period that the court might specify. In *Flavell v Flavell*[510] the Court of Appeal observed obiter that it was not usually appropriate to provide for the termination of periodic payments in the case of a woman in her mid 50s; such orders would only be justified only where the wife had her own substantial capital or significant earning capacity.

In *Miller v Miller; McFarlane v McFarlane*,[511] which has been discussed at length above,[512] the House of Lords removed the term of five years that the Court of Appeal had imposed on Mrs McFarlane's award of £250,000 *per annum*. As has been explained, in that case there was insufficient capital to provide a clean break, and the periodical payments order contained an important element of compensation.

[507] [1987] 2 F.L.R. 232 at 236.
[508] [1989] 1 F.L.R. 380.
[509] [1987] 2 F.L.R. 1; and see *Boylan v Boylan* [1988] 1 F.L.R. 282.
[510] [1997] 1 F.L.R. 353; for an example of no clean break for a woman of 60, see *Phippen v Palmers (A Firm)* [2002] 2 F.L.R. 408.
[511] [2006] 2 F.L.R. 1186
[512] See paras 13–047–13–049.

The imposition of a term on an order for periodical payments implies that the court's intention (and the parties' expectations) is that the payer's obligations will terminate on that date; the exercise of the power to extend the term therefore requires some exceptional justification (i.e. the threshold is high: *Fleming v Fleming*[513]).

(ii) Power to direct that no application be made to extend specified term.[514]   **13–091**
Any periodical payments order may be varied at any time during the currency of the order,[515] and the court also has power at any time before the end of a specified term to extend that term. The only way in which the parties can know that the order will, under no circumstances, be extended is to obtain a direction from the court that application for an extension of the term will not be entertained.[516] It has been said[517] that such a direction is "draconian" and is inappropriate in cases where there is real uncertainty about the future, and particularly where young children are involved.[518] The absence of a s.28(1A) direction was considered to be significant in itself in *Flavell v Flavell*.[519] However, unless such a direction is made, the paying spouse is left, at risk, with what appears to be no more than an indication from the trial judge that it would be appropriate to terminate the payments at the end of the specified term.

(iii) The power to dismiss a claim for periodical payments and to impose a   **13–092**
clean break. The court has express power[520] to dismiss an application for periodical payments and to make a direction that the applicant be not entitled to make any further application for a periodical payments order. The court also has power to direct that no application be permitted by a spouse or civil partner for provision out of the other's estate under the provisions of the Inheritance (Provision for Family and Dependants) Act 1975.

iv. Changed circumstances: variation of orders, etc.
The court takes "all the circumstances" into account in deciding what orders   **13–093**
to make in ancillary relief proceedings, but what is to happen if those circumstances subsequently change or if one party failed to give proper disclosure of his or her finances at the time the order was made?
    The legal system provides three main procedures for dealing with such problems:

---

[513] [2004] 1 F.L.R. 667, CA; see also *D v D (Financial Provision)* [2004] 1 F.L.R. 988.
[514] Harcus, "Periodic payments—end of term?" [1997] Fam. Law 340.
[515] *Sandford v Sandford* [1986] 1 F.L.R. 412, CA; *Flavell v Flavell* [1997] 1 F.L.R. 353, CA.
[516] Matrimonial Causes Act 1973 s.28(1A); Civil Partnership Act 2004 Sch.5 para.47(5).
[517] *Waterman v Waterman* [1989] 1 F.L.R. 380, CA.
[518] "[O]nly in the most exceptional and unusual case" will such an order be made where a child under 18 remains in the care of the applicant: *N v N (Consent Order: Variation)* [1993] 2 F.L.R. 868 at 883, *per* Roch J.
[519] [1997] 1 F.L.R. 353.
[520] Matrimonial Causes Act 1973 s.25A(3), reversing the effect of *Dipper v Dipper* [1981] Fam. 31, CA; see now Civil Partnership Act 2004 Sch.5 para.23(4).

(1) The court has extensive powers to vary or discharge orders, or to suspend any provision of an order. However, in principle, these variation powers do not extend to property adjustment or lump sum orders,[521] save for lump sum attachment orders in respect of pensions.[522] A pension sharing order is variable if made before a decree or if an order is made absolute or final.[523]

(2) There is a right to appeal against the terms of an order, and where the basis or fundamental assumption on which the order has been made has been invalidated by a change of circumstances, the court has a discretion to give permission to appeal, notwithstanding the fact that the prescribed period within which appeals can be brought as of right[524] has expired.

(3) A party who alleges that an order has been obtained by fraud or non-disclosure may bring an action seeking to have the order set aside.

We consider these in turn.

(1) Variation of orders

13–094 There is a difference in the policy towards maintenance orders on the one hand, and lump sum and property adjustment orders on the other (except lump sum attachment orders made in respect of pensions).

13–095 **(a) Variation of maintenance orders.** Wherever a periodical payments order (or other order to which the section applies) has been made, the court has power to "vary or discharge the order or suspend any provision thereof temporarily and to revive the operation of any provision so suspended".[525]

13–096 *(i) When the power to vary arises.* The court's powers to vary arise whenever there is in force any order to which the legislation applies, even if the order is for a nominal amount such as five pence yearly.[526] However, if a spouse's application has been dismissed, there is no power to make a fresh order and there is no existing order that could be varied. The nominal order preserves a party's entitlement should the other party's fortunes subsequently improve.[527] However, a payor should not, in fairness, be expected to be the insurer against all hazards suffered by the payee, in particular those created by the payee's own financial mismanagement, etc.

---

[521] Except lump sum orders payable by instalments: *Tilley v Tilley* (1980) Fam. Law 89; *Penrose v Penrose* [1994] 2 F.L.R. 621; *Westbury v Sampson* [2002] 2 F.L.R. 166.
[522] Matrimonial Causes Act 1973 s.31(2)(dd); Civil Partnership Act 2004 Sch.5 para.50(1)(f).
[523] Matrimonial Causes Act 1973 s.31(2)(g); Civil Partnership Act 2004 Sch.5 para.50(2)(i).
[524] For time limits, see Family Proceedings Rules 1991 (SI 1991/1247) r.8.1; RSC O.58 r.1; Civil Procedure Rules 1998 (SI 1998/3132) r.52(4)(2).
[525] Matrimonial Causes Act 1973 s.31(1); Civil Partnership Act 2004 Sch.5 para.51(1).
[526] *Jessel v Jessel* [1979] 1 W.L.R. 1148; *North v North* [2007] 2 F.C.R. 601.
[527] *SRJ v DWJ (Financial Provision)* [1999] 2 F.L.R. 176.

(ii) Variation of specified-term orders.[528] The court has jurisdiction to vary an **13–097**
order originally made for a specified term, so that it could, for example,
extend an order made for three years for a further year, or for the joint lives
of the parties, or without a termination date.[529] Jurisdiction does not depend
on an exceptional change in circumstances.[530] However, it will have no such
power if the court, in making a periodical payments order (secured or unsecured), has directed that the party concerned shall not be entitled to apply for
an extension of the order.[531] Moreover, once the term has expired, there is
nothing to vary, but the court's jurisdiction is preserved provided the application for variation is issued during the life of the periodical payments order,
even if the hearing does not occur till after its expiry.[532]

There is also power[533] to direct that a variation or discharge shall not take
effect until the expiration of a specified period. This power could be exercised
in effect to give the person entitled to the payments some time to adjust to the
termination or reduction of the payment.

(iii) Exercise of the discretion to vary. In exercising the power to vary, the **13–098**
court is directed to have regard to all the circumstances of the case, first
consideration being given to the welfare, while a minor, of any child of the
family who has not attained the age of 18[534]; and it is provided that the
circumstances of the case shall include any change in any of the matters to
which the court was required to have regard when making the order to which
the application relates.[535] A change in circumstance is thus not a prerequisite
to the exercise of the jurisdiction to vary, but the absence of such change goes
to the exercise of the court's discretion.[536] The court's discretion on a
variation application is broad.[537] On hearing an application to vary, the court
is not required to proceed from the starting point of the original order but
considers the matter de novo, looking at all the relevant matters set out in s.25
of the Act afresh without being confined solely or essentially to matters of
change.[538] It has been observed that on an application to vary (at least on one
to increase payments), the applicant's needs are likely to be the dominant
factor, but a respondent will not invariably be held financially responsible for
all the applicant's needs (i.e. those created by financial mismanagement,

---

[528] See Harcus, "Periodical payments".
[529] *Flavell v Flavell* [1997] 1 F.L.R. 353.
[530] *Flavell v Flavell* [1997] 1 F.L.R. 353.
[531] *Flavell v Flavell* [1997] 1 F.L.R. 353; *Richardson v Richardson* [1994] 1 F.L.R. 286.
[532] *Jones v Jones* [2000] 2 F.L.R. 307, CA, disapproving obiter remarks of Ward L.J. in *G v G (Periodical Payments: Jurisdiction)* [1997] 1 F.L.R. 368.
[533] Matrimonial Causes Act 1973 s.31(10); Civil Partnership Act 2004 Sch.5 para.61(1). The variation may be retrospective: *Macdonald v Macdonald* [1964] P. 1; and as to the discretion to direct back-dating, see *S v S* (Note) [1987] 1 W.L.R. 382, CA.
[534] *Flavell v Flavell* [1997] 1 F.L.R. 353; *Jones v Jones* [2000] 2 F.L.R. 307.
[535] Matrimonial Causes Act 1973 s.31(7); Civil Partnership Act 2004 Sch.5 para.59(2).
[536] *L v L* [2006] EWHC 956 (Fam.); [2008] 1 F.L.R. 26.
[537] *Harris v Harris* [2001] 1 F.C.R. 68.
[538] *Lewis v Lewis* [1977] 1 W.L.R. 409, CA; *Garner v Garner* [1992] 1 F.L.R. 573; *Flavell v Flavell* [1997] 1 F.L.R. 353, CA.; *Cornick v Cornick (No.3)* [2001] 2 F.L.R. 1240, FD.

extravagance or irresponsibility).[539] The jurisdiction to vary is one of considerable amplitude.[540] The court must have regard to the circumstances existing at the date of the original order, the circumstances that exist now and those that will exist in the foreseeable future.[541] The overall objective is fairness.[542]

An issue that has not been without controversy is the extent to which an applicant for variation should be entitled to share in an increase in a former spouse's earnings years after the marriage partnership has been dissolved. Linked to this is the question of whether the consideration of compensation[543] is relevant on a variation application as well as at the exit point from marriage. It has been long established that after a long marriage where the husband's resources have increased substantially after divorce, an order on the former wife's variation application does not have to be limited to her budget but can reflect an enjoyment by her of some part of his success and an enhanced living standard.[544] More recently it has been held at first instance[545] that compensation is a legitimate consideration on a variation application.

The relevance of cohabitation will depend on the financial circumstances of that cohabitation; cohabitation per se has not yet been equated with marriage.[546] Coleridge J. has called for greater weight to be accorded to the fact of cohabitation, given modern social conditions and other developments in the law recognising cohabitation.[547]

13–099 *(iv) Imposing a clean break on a variation application.* In furtherance of the policy of making a clean break in appropriate cases, the court, in considering applications to vary periodical payment orders (secured or unsecured) made in divorce or nullity proceedings, is required[548] to:

> "[C]onsider whether in all the circumstances and after having regard to any such change it would be appropriate to vary the order so that payments under the order are required to be made or secured only for such further period as will in the opinion of the court be sufficient ... to enable the party in whose favour the order was made to adjust without undue hardship to the termination of those payments."

There must be evidence that the payee can adjust, without undue hardship, before an order terminating financial dependency is made; the legislation does

---

[539] *North v North* [2007] EWCA Civ 760; [2008] 1 F.L.R. 136.
[540] *B v B (Consent Order: Variation)* [1995] 1 F.L.R. 9.
[541] *K v K (Periodical Payments: Cohabitation)* [2006] 2 F.L.R. 468 at para.112.
[542] *McFarlane v McFarlane; Parlour v Parlour* [2004] 2 F.L.R. 1093.
[543] Discussed in detail above at para.13–048.
[544] *Cornick v Cornick (No.2)* [1996] 2 F.L.R. 490; *Primavera v Primavera* [1992] 1 F.L.R. 16.
[545] *Lauder v Lauder* [2007] 2 F.L.R. 802; *VB v JP* [2008] EWHC 112.
[546] *Atkinson v Atkinson* [1988] Fam 93; *Fleming v Fleming* [2004] 1 F.L.R. 667.
[547] *K v K (Periodical Payments: Cohabitation)* [2006] 2 F.L.R. 468.
[548] Matrimonial Causes Act 1973 s.31(7)(a). Civil Partnership Act 2004 Sch.5 para.59(4).

not "impose more than an aspiration that the parties should achieve self-sufficiency".[549]

(v) Power to order capital provision on variation application. Originally, the   **13–100**
court lacked power to require the making of a lump sum or property adjustment order in partial or total replacement for the periodical payments order
that would be terminated by a clean break order. However, this was felt to be
a gap in the legislation,[550] and the Family Law Act 1996[551] gave[552] the court
power on discharging[553] a periodical payments order[554] to order the payment
of a lump sum or to make a property adjustment order or one or more pension
sharing orders.[555] The court may also debar the person entitled under the
original order from making further applications for periodical payment orders
or for extensions of the term.[556] Identical provisions are contained in the Civil
Partnership Act 2004.[557]

In *Harris v Harris*[558] the Court of Appeal emphasised the width of discretion conferred by the new provisions. In *Pearce v Pearce*[559] the Court of
Appeal encouraged parties to use these capitalisation provisions if developments since the making of the periodical payments order permit a capital
substitution. In many cases the appropriate approach will be a capitalisation of
periodical payments on a joint-life basis. While the discretion conferred by the
statute is wide, there is no power to re-open or redistribute capital provision
made in the original order.[560]

(b) Variation of property adjustment and lump sum orders.

(i) General principle: no variation. Since one of the objects of property   **13–101**
adjustment and lump sum orders is to achieve finality, the general principle

---

[549] *Flavell v Flavell* [1997] 1 F.L.R. 535. However, the threshold for extending a term order is high: *Fleming v Fleming* [2004] 1 F.L.R. 5667 and *D v D (Financial Provision: Periodical Payments)* [2004] 1 F.L.R. 988.
[550] *Harris v Harris* [2001] 2 F.L.R. 955.
[551] Family Law Act 1996 Sch.8 paras 16(5)(a), (6)(b) and (7), inserting s.31(7A)–31(7G) into Matrimonial Causes Act 1973.
[552] The provision came into force on November 1, 1998.
[553] Or varying the order to provide for a fixed term: Matrimonial Causes Act 1973 s.31(7A)(b); Civil Partnership Act Sch.5 para.53(1)(b).
[554] Matrimonial Causes Act 1973 s.31(7B)(c), inserted by the Family Law Act 1996 Sch.10, para.6(2); Civil Partnership Act 2004 Sch.5 para.53.
[555] Matrimonial Causes Act 1973 s.31(7B) (a)–(c); Civil Partnership Act 2004 Sch.5 para.53(2).
[556] Matrimonial Causes Act 1973 s.31(7B)(c), as inserted by the Family Law Act 1996 Sch.8 para.16(7). On dismissal of an application, see Christy, "Dismissing the right to apply to capitalise" [2001] Fam. Law 457 and R. Spon-Smith, "The other side of the argument" [2001] Fam. Law 693.
[557] Civil Partnership Act 2004 Sch.5 para.53(2).
[558] [2001] 2 F.C.R. 68.
[559] [2003] 2 F.L.R. 1144.
[560] *Pearce v Pearce* [2003] 2 F.L.R. 1144, disapproving the approach taken by Charles J. in *Cornick v Cornick (No.3)* [2001] 2 F.L.R. 1240.

embodied in the legislation is that no variation of such orders should subsequently be possible.[561] To this principle there are three exceptions:

(1) If orders for settlement of property or variation of an existing nuptial settlement[562] are made in respect of a separation, the court may vary them if the marriage is subsequently dissolved; there are identical powers in respect of civil partnership.[563]

(2) Where a lump sum is ordered to be paid in instalments, the court may vary the number and timing of the instalments or security for such an order—(for example, if a husband is ordered to pay the wife £10,000 by 10 annual instalments of £1,000 secured on his shareholding in Abracadabra Ltd, the court could vary the order by providing that the money be paid in 15 instalments, and that the security be changed. Furthermore, it has been held that the court has power not only to discharge a particular instalment or even the whole outstanding balance[564] but also to vary the *quantum* of the principal lump sum, although that power should be exercised sparingly in exceptional circumstances.[565]

(3) Where the court has made an order under the powers described later in this chapter for a deferred lump sum to be paid by the trustees or managers of a pension arrangement.[566]

13–102 *(2) Appeals against orders: reopening clean break settlements.* The principle of finality of litigation is accorded great weight, particularly in cases in which the order has been made as part of a clean break arrangement. The essence of a clean break settlement is that once the couple's relationship is terminated and their capital divided, they cannot normally expect to profit from (any more than they would expect to lose by) later changes in the other's fortune[567]; each party (it has been said[568]) takes a clean break order for better or worse. Yet this principle must be made compatible with justice so that the law "exceptionally, allows appeals out of time: so the law still more exceptionally,

---

[561] Law Com. No.25, paras 87–88.

[562] Lump sum orders and transfer of property orders are not included: Matrimonial Causes Act 1973 s.31(2); Civil Partnership Act 2004 Sch.5 para.50(1); *Omielan v Omielan* [1996] 2 F.L.R. 306. If the separation is converted into a divorce, the court will be able to make further capital provision orders (under the general wording of ss.23 and 24, which s.31 does not cut down in this regard), and it was presumably thought undesirable that the court should be able to order repayment (although a new order could achieve this indirectly (i.e. by ordering payment of a compensating sum to the payer): Law Com. No.25, para.89).

[563] Matrimonial Causes Act 1973 s.31(4); Civil Partnership Act 2004 Sch.5 para.56.

[564] *Penrose v Penrose* [1994] 2 F.L.R. 621, CA; *Tilley v Tilley* (1979) 10 Fam. Law 89 (where the wife could not meet an instalment without selling the family home and making herself and the children homeless).

[565] *Westbury v Sampson* [2002] 1 F.L.R. 166.

[566] i.e. an order under Matrimonial Causes Act 1973 s.25B(4) or the Civil Partnership Act 2004 Sch.5 para.25(2).

[567] *Cornick v Cornick* [1994] 2 F.L.R. 530 at 537, *per* Hale J.

[568] *Barder v Barder* [1987] 1 F.L.R. 18 at 22, *per* Dillon L.J., CA.

allows judgments to be attacked on the ground of fraud"; or in some other circumstances.[569] The text deals first with applications for leave to appeal founded on a change of circumstances. In such cases, the crucial question is whether the court in the exercise of its discretion will grant such leave.[570] If the court does grant leave, it will have to decide how to resolve matters. The text deals with these issues. It then discusses the circumstances in which an order will be set aside because of non-disclosure or on any other ground.[571]

(a) Appeals out of time: the grant of permission. The circumstances in **13–103** which permission should be given to appeal out of time against a lump sum or property adjustment order in matrimonial proceedings were authoritatively stated by the House of Lords in the case of *Barder v Barder (Caluori intervening)*,[572] the facts of which were dramatic. The divorce court made a clean break order under which the husband was to transfer all his interest in the matrimonial home to the wife in full, and final settlement of all claims made or capable of being made. Some five weeks later the wife killed the two children of the family and committed suicide. She left a will giving her property to her mother.

According to the House of Lords, the court may give permission to appeal out of time in cases in which there has been an unforeseen change of circumstances,[573] provided that four conditions are satisfied:

(1) the basis or fundamental assumption underlying the order had been falsified by a change of circumstances;

(2) such change had occurred within a relatively short time[574] of the making of the original order;

---

[569] *Per* Lord Wilberforce, *The Ampthill Peerage* [1977] A.C. 547 at 569, HL.
[570] *Greig Middleton & Co Ltd v Denderowicz* [1998] 1 W.L.R. 1164.
[571] The various grounds of set-aside are summarised by Munby J. in *L v L* [2006] EWHC 956 (Fam.); [2008] Fam. Law.
[572] [1988] A.C. 20, HL.
[573] There is no right to appeal against a decision granting leave to appeal out of time, but there is a right of appeal against a refusal of such leave: *Rickards v Rickards* [1990] 1 F.L.R. 125, CA.
[574] In *Barder v Barder* [1988] A.C. 20, a maximum period of one year was suggested; and in *Cornick v Cornick* [1994] 2 F.L.R. 530 at 538, the short-term share price movements—the price had doubled within five months and trebled within eight—would have satisfied this test. On the other hand, in *Worlock v Worlock* [1994] 2 F.L.R. 689, CA, the relevant event—a transfer of shares to the husband, greatly increasing his wealth—had taken place two years after the original order (and four years before the hearing of the application for leave), and the Court of Appeal held that it was "far too late" for the *Barder* doctrine to apply: see *per* Stuart Smith L.J. at 696. See also *B v B (Financial Provision: Leave to Appeal)* [1994] 1 F.L.R. 219 (husband lost job as pilot nearly two years after order—not sufficiently close to order to justify reopening). However, there is no inflexible rule imposing a time bar—the matter may perhaps be seen as an aspect of the public policy favouring finality in litigation: *Penrose v Penrose* [1994] 2 F.L.R. 621 at 632, *per* Balcombe L.J.; and in *Hope-Smith v Hope-Smith* [1989] 2 F.L.R. 56, CA, leave was granted two years after the making of the original order. In *Benson v Benson* [1996] 1 F.L.R. 962, the wife died six months after the ancillary relief order; permission was refused.

(3) the application for leave was made reasonably promptly[575]; and

(4) that the granting of leave would not unfairly prejudice third parties who had acquired interests for value in the property affected.

In *Barder* itself, the court held that all these conditions had been satisfied, and that permission to appeal should be granted, and the appeal against the original order allowed.[576]

The case law gives some impression of the issues with which the courts have had to deal. For example, is the remarriage of one of the parties a sufficient change of circumstances in cases in which the family home has been transferred to that party? In such cases, the transferor—usually the husband—may have had a very bad bargain, since any liability under a periodical payments order would have ceased on remarriage.[577] The answer is that it is a question of fact and degree as to whether the change of circumstances is sufficiently fundamental. Thus, an appeal out of time was allowed in *Wells v Wells*[578] where the wife remarried[579] and began living with her second husband in his house six months after the divorce court had ordered the husband to transfer his interest in the matrimonial home (the parties' sole asset) to the wife in order to provide a home for her and the children. The Court of Appeal accepted that this was a fundamental change of circumstances, and that the basis on which the order had been made[580] had been destroyed.[581] By contrast, in *Hill v Hill*[582] the wife's post-divorce cohabitation

---

[575] See *Benson v Benson (dec'd)* [1996] 1 F.L.R. 692 (application more than one year after event—dismissed). In *S v S (Ancillary Relief: Consent Order)* [2002] EWHC 223; [2002] 1 F.L.R. 992, the wife's application more than eight months after the alleged supervening event was dismissed. The relevant date from which time begins to run is the date of the order (not the date when it had to be implemented): *B v B (Financial Provision: Leave to Appeal)* [1994] 1 F.L.R. 219. In *S v S (Financial Provision) (Post-Divorce Cohabitation)* [1994] 2 F.L.R. 228, leave was given to appeal 15 years after the order, but the facts of that case were (*per* Douglas Brown J.) unusual if not unique, in that the couple had resumed cohabitation after the decree; and note the critical comment of the Court of Appeal in *Hewitson v Hewitson* [1995] 1 F.L.R. 241. In *Den Heyer v Newby* [2006] 1 F.L.R. 1114, it was held that the wife's delay in applying to set aside the consent order was not fatal, as the husband had failed to provide information about a material change in a timely manner.

[576] And note to the same effect *Smith v Smith (Smith Intervening)* [1992] Fam. 69 (wife committed suicide six months after order—order based on her "needs" set aside). But the death of a party is not as such a sufficient change of circumstances to allow the matter to be re-opened: *Amey v Amey* [1992] 2 F.L.R. 89; but compare *Benson v Benson (dec'd)* [1996] 1 F.L.R. 692 (where a wife was thought to have a normal life expectancy but was subsequently diagnosed as suffering from terminal cancer).

[577] Compare *B v B (Financial Provision: Leave to Appeal)* [1994] 1 F.L.R. 219 (wife's remarriage to Q.C. not basis for reopening property adjustment order founded on recompensing wife for her contributions during the marriage).

[578] [1992] 2 F.L.R. 66, CA.

[579] Note that this was not a case in which non-disclosure by the wife was alleged; cf. *Livesey (formerly Jenkins) v Livesey* [1985] A.C. 424, HL.

[580] Contrast *Chaudhuri v Chaudhuri* [1992] 2 F.L.R. 73, CA, where the order against which it was sought to appeal expressly contemplated the wife's remarriage. Accordingly it could not be said that there had been a sufficient change of circumstances.

[581] Note also *S v S (Financial Provision) (Post-Divorce Cohabitation)* [1994] 2 F.L.R. 228, where the fact that the parties became reconciled and resumed cohabitation was held to destroy the fundamental assumption on which the order had been made.

[582] [1997] 1 F.L.R. 730. See also *Cook v Cook* [1988] 1 F.L.R. 51.

was held not to justify setting the order aside. In *Dixon v Marchant*[583] it was held by the majority[584] that the wife's remarriage six months after the consent order to the man with whom she had been in a long-term relationship had not invalidated any fundamental assumption on which the order had been based; the risk of her remarriage had been one the husband had had to accept.

Many applications have been based on misvaluation of assets at the time of **13–104** the order, or changes in the value of assets since the order was made. The essential question is always whether the fundamental assumption on which the order was made has been undermined. For example:

In *Cornick v Cornick*[585] an order was made giving the wife approximately half the couple's assets. The husband's investments subsequently rose dramatically in value—from £2.17 a share at the date of the hearing to a peak of £12.58 some 18 months later—and the wife's share of the assets was reduced to perhaps 20 per cent. However, Hale J. pointed out that the shares had been correctly valued at the hearing[586] and that what had happened was a natural, albeit dramatic, change in value.[587] The wife's case amounted in effect to no more than "saying that it is all terribly unfair"; the court refused to intervene.

In *B v B*[588] the former matrimonial home had been valued at £1.25 million and, following refurbishment by the husband, was sold for £1.6 million. Sir Matk Potter P. held that none of the *Barder* conditions were satisfied; valuation on a rising market was an inexact science, and improvements effected prior to sale could bring a disproportionate increase in the sale price. The rise in price was foreseeable.

---

[583] [2008] EWCA Civ. 11.

[584] See, however, the powerful dissenting judgment of Wall L.J.

[585] [1994] 2 F.L.R. 530. Subsequently, the wife obtained an upward variation in the periodical payment order: *Cornick v Cornick (No.2)* [1995] 2 F.L.R., CA, and eventually a lump sum order under Matrimonial Causes Act s.31(7A): *Cornick v Cornick (No.3)* [2001] 2 F.L.R. 1240, FD.

[586] It may be that the difficulty of valuing house property will lead the court to look more sympathetically on the claim that a substantial difference in the realised value justifies the inference that the valuation was incorrect and that, accordingly, the basis of the order has been falsified by subsequent events: see, for example, *Warren v Warren* (1983) 4 F.L.R. 529, CA (where the matrimonial home was sold for £92,000 five months after a hearing at which it had been valued at £52,000); *Heard v Heard* [1995] 1 F.L.R. 970, CA (house valued at £67,000; no purchase offer over £33,000 received); but contrast *Edmonds v Edmonds* [1990] 2 F.L.R. 202, CA (where the fact that the house—valued at some £70,000 at the hearing—was sold for £110,000 was held not to destroy the basis on which an order had been made, not least because the fact that the value was likely to increase had been known to all at the time of the hearing.) See also *Kean v Kean* [2002] 2 F.L.R. 28 (Fam. Div.).

[587] See also *Worlock v Worlock* [1994] 2 F.L.R. 689, CA, where the husband's family business had land which stood in its accounts at cost value (approximately £50,000). Subsequent to the hearing, the husband's mother transferred shares in the company to him; and the company obtained planning permission that increased the value of the land to some £3.5 million. The Court of Appeal refused the wife leave to appeal: it "is only the scale of events and the happening of those events which at the time of the order were unknown which have now come to pass" (*per* Stuart-Smith L.J. at 696). Similar considerations apply where property has fallen in value: see *B v B (Financial Provision: Leave to Appeal)* [1994] 1 F.L.R. 219 (fall in value of house from £340,000 to £250,000 not sufficient to undermine basis of order).

[588] [2007] EWHC 2472; [2008] 1 F.L.R. 1279; [2008] Fam. Law 111.

In *Ritchie v Ritchie*[589] the husband's receipt of a redundancy package subsequent to a clean break settlement was not considered to invalidate the fundamental assumptions on which the order had been based.

In *Maskell v Maskell*[590] the Court of Appeal held that the husband's redundancy was "a long way from a *Barder* situation".

In contrast:

In *Thompson v Thompson*[591] the parties had comparatively modest assets, amongst which was the former matrimonial home and the husband's, apparently failing, travel agency. The district judge was concerned to ensure that the wife and children had somewhere to live, and he made an order under which the wife took £52,500 of the assets, and the husband £6,500. This was a "stern order from the husband's point of view", but the district judge thought that it was the best that could be achieved in the circumstances. However, less than two weeks after the hearing the husband sold the business for £40,000 (twice the value placed on it at the hearing). The Court of Appeal held that all concerned acted reasonably on the probably mistaken assumption that the correct value was that taken at the hearing, and that the subsequent sale was thus a new event. Accordingly, there was a discretion to grant leave to appeal out of time; the interests of justice required that the matter be reopened.[592]

In *Middleton v Middleton*,[593] due to deliberate manipulation by the husband, the principal asset was worth not £69,000 but, after redemption of the mortgage, only £652; permission was granted and the wife's appeal allowed.

13–105 If one party's failure to comply with the terms of an order has frustrated the intention underlying the court order, the court will be more ready to allow the case to be reopened:

In *Hope-Smith v Hope-Smith*[594] the court ordered the husband to pay the wife £32,000 out of the proceeds of sale of the family home (the value of which was then estimated at £116,000). The assumption was that the

---

[589] [1996] 1 F.L.R. 898.
[590] [2001] EWCA Civ. 858; [2001] 3 F.C.R. 296.
[591] [1991] 2 F.L.R. 530, CA.
[592] It may be that the distinction between *Thompson* and *Cornick* is that the *Cornick* valuation was unquestionably correct; whereas it would seem that the *Thompson* valuation was not correct. (But note that in *Heard v Heard* [1995] 1 F.L.R. 970, CA, where a house sold for much less than had been estimated leave to appeal was granted although it is not clear that any valuation evidence was incorrect.) In any event, an application based on a mistaken valuation is likely to fail if the applicant has failed to probe material available at the trial: see *Edmonds v Edmonds* [1990] 2 F.L.R. 202, CA; *Worlock v Worlock* [1994] 2 F.L.R. 689. Similarly, the emergence of a substantial liability (e.g. for tax) will not be regarded as a sufficient supervening event if the person concerned could, with due diligence, have discovered the likely extent of the liability at the time of the hearing: *Penrose v Penrose* [1994] 2 F.L.R. 621.
[593] [1998] 2 F.L.R. 821.
[594] [1989] 2 F.L.R. 56, CA.

house would be sold very soon, but the sale was delayed for nearly three years "by the husband's quite disgraceful behaviour".[595] The wife was given leave to appeal out of time[596]; the house was worth £200,000 by the time of the setting-aside hearing, and the fundamental assumptions underlying the order (in terms both of the husband's share of the assets and the kind of house that the wife could buy with the funds to be released to her from the sale) had been falsified.

A further illustration is *Middleton v Middleton*,[597] in which the husband's unilateral actions in relation to a business rendered the consent order, in effect, a sham.

The courts have been confronted with the question as to whether a change in the law can constitute a *"Barder event"*.[598] The introduction of the child support scheme was regarded by many as a fundamental change to the basis upon which divorce settlements (usually involving the transfer of the matrimonial home to the wife, and only a nominal periodical payment order for the children) were made; however, in *Crozier v Crozier*[599] Booth J. held that the creation of the Child Support Agency did not alter the basic principle— recognised for many years—that a parent could not get rid of responsibility to support children. All that had changed was the mechanism for enforcing that responsibility.

Outside the family-law context, a change in the law was recognised by the Court of Appeal as capable of justifying permission to appeal out of time in *Greig Middleton & Co v Denderowicz*.[600] The question of whether the change in the law effected by *White v White*[601] is sufficient to undermine the basis on which consent orders in ancillary relief were made was first raised in the literature[602] and subsequently in litigation. In *S v S (Ancillary Relief: Consent Order)*[603] a consent order was made in September 2000, some six weeks before the delivery of the speeches of the House of Lords in *White v White*. More than eight months later the wife sought permission to appeal, arguing inter alia that had the reasonable-requirements ceiling not applied, she would have received considerably more. Bracewell J. dismissed the application. It was held that as a general proposition, a change in the law may constitute a supervening *Barder* event, and that *White v White* did constitute a new event, because although it involved an exercise of discretion, the effect in big-money cases was very significant, as demonstrated by the appeal in *Cowan v Cowan*.[604] However, Bracewell J. held further that the new event must be

---

[595] *Cornick v Cornick* [1994] 2 F.L.R. 530 at 534, *per* Hale J.
[596] Contrast *Rooker v Rooker* [1988] 1 F.L.R. 219, where leave was refused because the applicant had had it in her power to apply to the court for enforcement of the order in question but had failed to do so.
[597] [1998] 2 F.L.R. 821, CA.
[598] E. Hamilton, "Is White v White a 'Barder event'?" [2001] Fam. Law 135.
[599] [1994] 1 F.L.R. 126.
[600] [1998] 1 W.L.R. 1164.
[601] [2000] 2 F.L.R. 981.
[602] See fn.598 above.
[603] *S v S (Ancillary Relief: Consent Order)* [2002] EWHC Fam. 223; [2002] 1 F.L.R. 992.
[604] [2001] 2 F.L.R. 192.

unforseeable in the sense that it was not envisaged and could not reasonably have been envisaged at the time of making the order. Here, what happened in *White v White* was foreseeable and, in the words of Balcombe L.J. in *Chaudhuri v Chaudhuri*,[605] an "obvious possibility"; within the legal profession, *White v White* was anticipated to be a landmark decision, and the wife and her advisers knew or ought to have known that.[606]

13–106   **(b) Principles to be applied in reopened cases.** If the court does decide to grant leave to appeal,[607] it will decide what order should be made on the basis of all the facts as they are known at the time of the rehearing:

> Thus, in *Smith v Smith (Smith intervening)*[608] the judge made an order dividing the family assets between the parties equally, on the basis that the needs of the parties, and especially the wife's housing needs, were the predominant consideration. Five months later the wife committed suicide; under her will her estate would pass to her daughter. It was conceded that leave to appeal should be granted; the judge hearing the appeal made an order on the basis that he should only look at the factors that had been taken into account in making the original order. Since the wife no longer had any housing needs, the order should be reduced to the very small sum necessary to pay her debts. The Court of Appeal held that such an approach was wrong, and that the court should start again from the beginning. What would be the right order in a case in which the wife was known to have only six months to live?[609]

(3) Non-disclosure: setting aside orders, etc.

13–107   So far, we have been concerned largely with the effect of a change of circumstances after the making of the order, but what is the position if it is claimed that facts material to the making of the order (or to the giving of consent to the making of the order) were not disclosed or were perhaps even concealed from the court and the other party? As a result of the decision of the House of Lords in *Livesey (formerly Jenkins) v Livesey*,[610] it is clear that the parties have a duty[611] to provide the court with all information relevant to the making of an order and to ensure that such information is correct,

---

[605] [1992] 2 F.L.R. 73.

[606] Bracewell J. further held that there was no reasonable excuse for the wife's delay of over eight months in making her application.

[607] In many cases the application for leave and the hearing of the appeal will be combined: see, for example, *Middleton v Middleton* [1998] 2 F.L.R. 821. However, if an applicant makes out a clear prima facie case, the court will grant leave in order to allow the necessary detailed investigations to be carried out: see *Re C (Financial Provision: Leave to Appeal)* [1993] 2 F.L.R. 799 (and note the substantive hearing: *C v C (Financial Provision: Non-Disclosure)* [1994] 2 F.L.R. 272).

[608] [1992] Fam. 69, CA.

[609] An order to pay a lump sum of £25,000 to the wife was made; and the court stated that the question to whom this fund would pass under the wife's will was irrelevant.

[610] [1985] A.C. 424, HL.

[611] See the obligation to provide financial information in Form E (Family Proceedings Rules 1991 (SI 1991/1247) r.2.61B(1) and (2), discussed at para.13–010 above.

complete and up to date. If there is a failure in this respect, the matter may be reopened.[612] In that case:

> The wife agreed with the husband that she would accept a transfer of the husband's interest in the matrimonial home in place of any periodical payments and in settlement of all financial claims against him. On the day before application was made for a consent order embodying those terms she became engaged to be married; three weeks after the order was made she remarried. Had an order for periodical payments been made, it would have been terminated; the husband argued that he would not have agreed to the transfer of the family home to the wife had she disclosed her intentions.
>
> In *Vicary v Vicary*[613] a consent order was made on the basis that the husband had assets amounting to some £430,000, including the shares in his private company. The husband knew, but the wife did not, that negotiations were taking place for the sale of the company; shortly after the making of the consent, order the husband's shareholding was sold for £2.8 million. The judge found that the husband, a dishonest witness, had, by knowing non-disclosure of the true position about the value of his assets, led the wife to agree to the terms of the consent order; accordingly, it was set aside.
>
> In *T v T (Consent Order: Procedure to Set Aside)*[614] the husband had given his wife the impression that there was no free market in the shares of his company. A consent order was made on that basis. In fact he was negotiating a takeover by a public company, and soon after the date of the consent order he received £1.6 million for his holding. The consent order was set aside.
>
> In *Middleton v Middleton*[615] the husband failed to disclose his true plans with relation to a business and the consent order was set aside.

Not every failure of frank and full disclosure will justify the court in setting aside an order; it has been said[616] that it will only be in cases when the

---

[612] The basic principle was stated by the Privy Council in *De Lasala v De Lasala* [1980] A.C. 546 at 561: "where a party to an action seeks to challenge, on the ground that it was obtained by fraud or mistake, a judgment or order that finally disposes of the issues raised between the parties, the only ways of doing it . . . are by way of appeal from the judgment or order to a higher court or by bringing a fresh action to set it aside"; and a lump sum or property adjustment order is, for these purposes, a final order: *Thwaite v Thwaite* [1982] Fam. 1, CA. There is unresolved uncertainty about the appropriate procedure for bringing the matter before the court—appeal, rehearing, fresh action—and whether the choice of procedure has substantive consequences: see *B-T v B-T (Divorce: Procedure)* [1990] 2 F.L.R. 1 (Ward J.); *Re C (Financial Provision: Leave to Appeal)* [1993] 2 F.L.R. 799 (Thorpe J.); *Benson v Benson (dec'd)* [1996] 1 F.L.R. 692; *T v T* [1996] 2 F.L.R. 640 (Richard Anelay Q.C.); *Harris v Manahan* [1997] 1 F.L.R. 205, CA; *P v P (Consent Order: Appeal Out of Time)* [2002] 1 F.L.R. 743 (Bennett J.).

[613] [1992] 2 F.L.R. 271, CA. The leading case is *Livesey (formerly Jenkins) v Livesey* [1985] A.C. 424 (failure to disclose intention to remarry—order for transfer of matrimonial home set aside).

[614] [1996] 2 F.L.R. 640.

[615] [1998] 2 F.L.R. 821.

[616] *Livesey v Jenkins* [1985] A.C. 424 at 445, *per* Lord Brandon. See also *P v P (Consent Order: Appeal Out of Time)* [2002] 1 F.L.R. 743; *L v L* [2008] Fam Law.

absence of full and frank disclosure has led the court to make an order which is substantially different from the order that it would have made if disclosure had been made that a case for setting aside "can possibly be made good". Thus:

> In *Cook v Cook*[617] it was alleged that a spouse had failed to disclose the extent of her emotional commitment to a third party, but the Court of Appeal held that the original order should remain unaltered. Even if the true facts had been known, they would probably not have had any significant impact on the order made.

13–108   Are there any other grounds upon which an order may be set aside? The law is in a state of some uncertainty, but it would seem that orders obtained by fraud and possibly undue influence are vulnerable to attack.[618] An order made under a mistake of fact also appears vulnerable.[619] As to a mistake of law, in *S v S (Ancillary Relief: Consent Order)*[620] Bracewell J. declined to extend to the field of ancillary relief the retrospective mistake of law doctrine expounded by a majority in the House of Lords in the context of a restitutionary remedy in *Kleinwort Benson v Lincoln County Council*.[621] It was further held that there would be public policy considerations against setting aside a consent order on such a basis by reason of the floodgates opening.

The policy favouring finality in litigation requires that (possibly save in the most exceptional case of the cruellest injustice), bad legal advice should not be a ground for interfering with a consent order.[622] An aggrieved party may, however, wish to sue the legal adviser in negligence.[623]

IV. WORKING OF THE LAW IN PRACTICE: HOUSING AND PENSIONS

13–109   Settlements on divorce (now to include those on dissolution of civil partnership) often fall into one of three categories.[624] First, there is the case involving large capital, where a clean break can be imposed in accordance with the

---

[617] [1998] 1 F.L.R. 521, CA.

[618] *De Lasala v De Lasala* [1980] A.C. 546; *Thwaite v Thwaite* [1982] Fam. 1; cf. *Tommey v Tommey* [1983] Fam. 15. On the issue of mistake of law, see E. Hamilton, "White v White—a 'Barder event'?" [2001] Fam. Law 135. Mistake of law—as well as of fact—now gives rise to a restitutionary remedy on the principle of unjust enrichment: *Kleinwort Benson v Lincoln County Council* [1999] 2 A.C. 349.

[619] *Maskell v Maskell* [2001] 3 F.C.R. 296 (judge's mistake in valuation of pension).

[620] [2002] EHWC Fam. 223; [2002] 1 F.L.R. 992.

[621] [1999] 2 A.C. 349.

[622] *Harris v Manahan* [1997] 1 F.L.R. 205; *P v P (Consent Order: Appeal Out of Time)* [2002] 1 F.L.R. 743, FD; *S v S (Ancillary Relief: Consent Order)* [2002] EWHC Fam. 223; [2002] 1 F.L.R. 992; *L v L* [2006] EWHC 956.

[623] *Channon v Lindley Johnstone* [2000] 2 F.L.R. 734; Wagstaffe, "Bad legal advice in ancillary relief cases" [1999] Fam. Law 156; Denyer, "Professional negligence claims arising out of consent orders made in family proceedings" [1999] Fam. Law 773; *Hall and Co v Simms* [2000] 2 F.L.R. 545, HL; *Phippen v Palmers (A Firm)* [2002] 2 F.L.R. 415.

[624] See Davis et al., *Simple Quarrels*.

principles discussed above. The dominance of big-money cases in the law reports can give a misleading impression that this is the most common form of order. At the opposite extreme, there is the case in which one or both parties will inevitably depend on welfare benefits[625]; the court's role is effectively restricted to determining how far one party should be required to relieve the taxpayer of the burden that would otherwise fall on the community. However, in a large proportion of cases, the parties will have owned a house, and all the considerations referred to above—particularly the welfare of the children, the needs of the parties and the desirability of terminating financial obligations—make the allocation of the house the central issue. Section A below therefore examines the options available. However, in recent years, entitlements under pension arrangements have become an increasingly important component of family resources, and this has prompted legislation intended to facilitate the making of proper arrangements in that context. Section B seeks to explain those possibilities.

A. Housing

i. Types of housing orders often made by the court
As has been seen, the court's powers to make transfer of property and other property adjustment orders give it an almost total flexibility in the type of order it can make. In practice, however, the following seem to be the main types of order made.   **13–110**

(1) Outright transfer to one party: other compensated by reduction or extinction of periodical payments
This form of order can have the advantage of achieving a "clean break":   **13–111**

> In *Hanlon v Hanlon*,[626] both the husband (a policeman earning £4,200 *per* annum) and the wife (a nurse earning approximately the same amount) were in full-time work. The husband was living rent-free in a police flat. The wife, after the separation in 1971, continued to live in the former matrimonial home with the children of the marriage (the youngest of whom was aged 12). The house was worth approximately £14,000, subject to a mortgage of some £4,000. The Court of Appeal allowed the wife's appeal against the order of Rees J. under which the matrimonial home had been ordered to be transferred into the joint names of husband and wife upon trust for sale (the sale to be postponed until the youngest child attained 17), and substituted an order transferring the home to the wife outright whilst reducing the periodical payments for the children

---

[625] Welfare benefits are discussed in Ch.6, above.
[626] [1978] 1 W.L.R. 592. Note that the child support legislation would today make it impossible to fix the husband's maintenance obligation to the children at a nominal sum.

from £14 weekly to a nominal sum.[627] The reason for this order was that if the house were sold under the terms of the original order in five years' time (when the youngest child attained 17), the effect of the Legal Aid Charge would at that time have been that neither spouse would receive more than £2,500. The wife and children would then be homeless and unable to house themselves, with the result that the wife would have to be housed by the local authority (as would the husband when he left the police force). It was better that the parties should know where they stood, and the husband (with a larger income available than would otherwise be the case) enabled to make proper plans for his own future housing.

Outright transfer of the home or proceeds of sale thereof to the spouse with ongoing care of children of the marriage may be the only practicable solution where the equity is limited and there is no other capital available.[628]

(2) Outright transfer to one spouse: other compensated by immediate cash payment

13–112 This approach was again envisaged in *Wachtel v Wachtel*,[629] where Lord Denning M.R. said that if the husband remained in the house it should be transferred to him (subject to liability for the mortgage payments), the wife being compensated by a lump sum of an amount the husband could raise by further mortgage on the house without financially crippling him. This technique has been adopted in a number of cases and is particularly suitable when one party needs the house. For example:

In *Mortimer v Mortimer-Griffin*[630] the court had made a settlement order under which the husband would be entitled to 20 per cent of the value of the house when sold, but the husband had in fact acquired another house, and his mortgage liabilities were covered by welfare benefits. Moreover, the Court of Appeal considered that the wife—who had retrained and made herself self-supporting—had shouldered a wholly disproportionate burden since the breakdown of the marriage. It therefore substituted an order under which the husband would receive an immediate lump sum of £2,500—the most that could be paid to him without it attracting the statutory charge—and the house would be transferred to the wife outright. The court was particularly influenced by the possibility that the wife would find difficulty in rehousing herself when sale took place and by the fact that the husband was unlikely to benefit from any larger lump sum. Orders for a postponed sale (said Sir John Donaldson M.R.)

---

[627] It should be noted that a solution effectively exempting a parent from the liability to make a financial contribution to the child's welfare is, since the coming into force of the Child Support Act 1991, no longer available: see Ch.15, below.

[628] See, for example, *B v B (Financial Provision: Welfare of Child and Conduct)* [2002] 1 F.L.R. 555, FD.

[629] [1973] Fam. 72 at 96.

[630] [1986] 2 F.L.R. 315, CA.

suffered from the defect that "chickens come home to roost" at an unpredictable time and in unpredictable circumstances, and that percentage allocations often gave rise to difficulties.

In *Piglowska v Piglowski*,[631] discussed earlier in this chapter,[632] the house was transferred to the wife; the husband received a modest flat in Spain plus £10,000.

(3) Outright transfer to one spouse: other spouse compensated by deferred cash payment

Often it will be necessary to delay the payment of compensation to the party **13–113** who leaves the family home until it is eventually sold. In such cases, the courts will usually give the party affected a charge over the property for a share of the proceeds of sale. For example:

In *Knibb v Knibb*[633] it was ordered that the former matrimonial home be vested in the wife subject to her obtaining the husband's release from any liability under the mortgage and to her executing a charge in his favour for 40 per cent of the sale proceeds of the property. The charge provided that the statutory power of sale, and thus, in effect, the husband's right to enforce the charge,[634] should arise only on certain events (including the wife's death, her remarriage or cohabitation with another man for a period exceeding three months, or her voluntarily leaving the property) specified in the order.

(4) Order for immediate sale and division of proceeds

Such an order may be appropriate if the proceeds will suffice to rehouse both **13–114** parties, or if one or both of them is to be housed by a local authority.[635] It is unlikely to be satisfactory where the equity is limited and there are children whose needs have to be considered. The fact that children may be disadvantaged by a move (perhaps involving a change of school) is a factor that has influenced the court against ordering an immediate sale.

---

[631] [1999] 2 F.L.R. 763.
[632] At p.347.
[633] [1987] 2 F.L.R. 396.
[634] In *Knibb v Knibb*, the order provided that the charge could be redeemed within four months by the wife paying the husband £3,500. The Court of Appeal held that the date for redemption was a vital term of the order, and that there was no jurisdiction to extend this time (but note that it is a fundamental term that a mortgagor may redeem the mortgage; and it does not seem entirely clear whether the wife could redeem the mortgage at any time on tendering 40% of the sale proceeds, or only after the statutory powers of sale, etc. had arisen (i.e. on her remarriage, etc.)). See also *Kiely v Kiely* [1988] 1 F.L.R. 248, CA (wrong to allow husband to enforce charge (i.e. in effect requiring that the property be sold) before events stipulated in order because to do so would constitute variation of order); but cf. *Ross v Ross* [1989] 2 F.L.R. 257, CA, where leave to appeal against the terms of a charge was granted out of time (in part because the order as drawn up differed from the order pronounced by the judge); and *Masefield v Alexander (Lump Sum: Extension of Time)* [1995] 1 F.L.R. 100, CA (time for payment of lump sum—in effect purchase price of house—extended.
[635] See Ch.6, above.

In many cases it is agreed that the home shall be sold, and the only real issue is the proportions of division of the proceeds.[636]

(5) Settlement orders

13–115   Although the court's powers are extremely flexible, certain types of order have became common.

13–116   **(a) The Mesher order: order for sale and division postponed during dependence of children.** Such orders were at one time very popular, since they enabled the court to preserve each party's stake in what was then usually an appreciating capital asset, whilst at the same time preserving a home with their carer for the children:

> In *Mesher v Mesher*[637] the matrimonial home was in joint names and mortgaged (but there was a substantial equity). The husband intended to remarry and had already bought a new house; the wife intended to remarry but wished to stay in the former matrimonial home with the nine-year-old child of the family. The Court of Appeal held that it would be wrong to transfer the house outright to the wife since that would deprive the husband of the whole of his interest in the home, and that the right course was for the wife and child to have a home in which to live ("rather than that she should have a large sum of available capital"). Accordingly, it was ordered that the matrimonial home be held on trust for sale for the parties in equal shares, provided that the house be not sold so long as the child of the marriage was under the age of 17 (or until further order). The wife was to be at liberty to live there rent-free, paying and discharging all outgoings (except that repayments of the capital of the mortgage were to be borne equally).

After a time, the dangers inherent in such orders became apparent. In particular, such an order would often leave the parties in a state of complete uncertainty as to the future, since they would not be able to predict what would happen when the property came to be sold. Would the money available to each party suffice to rehouse him or her?[638] In some cases, it was clear that after the period of postponement the wife would inevitably be homeless and in a very weak position to rehouse herself, and unless the sum she received were large enough to buy another house outright, the wife might find great difficulty in obtaining a mortgage to finance the purchase.[639] Moreover, the use of a trust for sale might have the undesirable consequence that if the wife wished to move before the end of the period of postponement, she would not be entitled to have the husband's share of the proceeds applied towards the

---

[636] See, for example, *M v B (Ancillary Proceedings)* [1998] 1 F.L.R. 53; *Cordle v Cordle* [2001] EWCA Civ. 1791; [2002] 1 F.L.R. 207, CA.
[637] [1980] 1 All E.R. 126, CA.
[638] *Hanlon v Hanlon* [1978] 1 W.L.R. 592 at 599, above.
[639] *Carson v Carson* [1983] 1 W.L.R. 285, CA.

acquisition of a new house for herself and her family.[640] In the result, *Mesher* orders were no longer regarded as "the bible".[641]

A charge realisable on eventual sale may be the fair outcome.[642] However, authorities in small-money cases emphasise that *White v White*[643] did not create an in-principle entitlement of each spouse to some part of the equity, either immediately or on a deferred basis. The welfare of the child remains the first consideration, and thus in cases other than those involving big money, the housing needs of the parent with care will continue to dominate.[644]

The court has power to make a subsequent change to the terms of a *Mesher* order.[645]

(b) The Martin order: house settled on trust for one spouse for life. The **13–117** difference between such an order and a *Mesher* order is that a party's position is secured at least so long as she or he wishes to remain in occupation of the family home. For example:

> In *Martin (BH) v Martin (BW)*[646] the parties were childless. The court held that since the husband enjoyed secure council housing, and the wife would not get sufficient money from a sale to rehouse herself, the right solution would be for the house to be settled on trust for the wife during her life or until her remarriage or such earlier date as she should cease to live there. Subject thereto it was to be held on trust for the parties in equal shares.[647]
>
> In *Bateman v Bateman*[648] the court ordered that the home be held on trust for sale, but the sale was to be postponed until the wife ceased to use the home as her main place of residence, remarried or died, whichever should first occur. The wife was to receive one-quarter of the proceeds of sale if still alive at the time of sale; subject thereto, the proceeds were to be divided between the children.
>
> Finally, in *Clutton v Clutton*[649] the husband had a far greater earning capacity than the wife, and would have no difficulty in getting back "on the property ladder",[650] but the Court of Appeal felt that this was insufficient to justify depriving the husband forever of the sole capital asset of the marriage when a *Martin* order would be equally effective in protecting the wife's housing needs. The fact that the wife had a stable relationship with a man was also relevant to the court's decision to make

---

[640] See, for example, *Thompson v Thompson* [1985] F.L.R. 863, CA.

[641] *Mortimer v Mortimer-Griffin* [1986] 2 F.L.R. 315 at 319, *per* Parker L.J.

[642] *Elliott v Elliott* [2001] 1 F.C.R. 477.

[643] [2000] 2 F.L.R. 981.

[644] *B v B (Financial Provision: Welfare of Child and Conduct)* [2002] 1 F.L.R. 555, FD; *Cordle v Cordle* [2001] EWCA Civ. 1791; [2002] 1 F.L.R. 207, CA.

[645] *Swindale v Forder (Forder Intervening)* [2007] 1 F.L.R. 1905.

[646] [1978] Fam. 12, CA.

[647] It appears that there is power to require a spouse who is in occupation under a *Martin* order to pay an occupation rent: *Harvey v Harvey* (1982) 3 F.L.R. 141, CA.

[648] [1979] Fam. 25.

[649] [1991] 1 F.L.R. 242, CA.

[650] *Per* Lloyd L.J. at 247.

income of the employee, and the employee will not be charged income tax on any contributions made out of his or her earnings to the scheme, while the fund will be invested by the trustees with virtual immunity from taxation. The price to be paid for this favourable treatment is that, in order to comply with the Revenue's requirements, there will be severe restrictions on access to (and transfer of) the assets in the fund. The underlying policy of the Revenue rules is to restrict the conversion of income that had escaped tax into tax-free capital or other freely disposable resources, and accordingly, in principle, all except a lump sum not exceeding four times the final salary has to be taken from the fund in the form of income—effectively an annuity—that will itself be liable to tax.[668]

In recent years the powers of the courts to deal with pension entitlements and expectations in ancillary relief orders have been progressively and substantially increased by successive legislative enactments.[669] The text will outline[670] the range of powers available. However, some preliminary matters deserve mention. Before the court can decide whether to exercise its powers, and if so, how, it will require detailed information about pension entitlements. The parties' interests in pension funds must be valued. Valuation[671] is not an exact science, and the outcome depends on a number of assumptions, in part about economic factors—such as the anticipated yield on investments—and in part (at least in relation to some schemes, based on the employee's final salary) on personal matters—such as the employee's future earning pattern. However, regulations[672] stipulate that the so-called "cash equivalent transfer value" (CETV) be used for the purpose of calculating existing rights of members of pension schemes.[673] The value is to be determined on a date specified by the court between one year before the date of petition and the date of order.[674] Expert evidence is frequently sought on what percentage division of the CETV will produce a particular retirement income for the parties—most commonly, parity of retirement income.

It is important to appreciate that the court's powers to make orders in respect of pensions are not discrete or self-contained but merely part of the range of powers available in ancillary relief proceedings. Moreover, their exercise—as the exercise of other powers—is governed by s.25 of the Matrimonial Causes Act 1973 para.21 of Sch.5 to the Civil Partnership Act 2004

---

[668] However, pensions schemes are still an effective tax shelter, in part because the permissible lump sum is not insubstantial, while the entitlement to the periodical income payments will come at a time when the taxpayer is less likely to be subject to a high rate of income tax.

[669] Family Law Act 1996 s.16; Pensions Act 1995; Welfare Reform and Pensions Act 1999; Civil Partnership Act 2004; Pensions Act 2004.

[670] For detailed discussion, see R. Bird, *Pension Sharing: The New Law* (Family Law, 1999); R. Ellison and M. Rae, *Family Breakdown and Pensions*, 2nd edn (Butterworths, 2001).

[671] On the valuation of an occupational pension in payment, see *Martin-Dye v Martin-Dye* [2006] 2 F.L.R. 901.

[672] Made under Matrimonial Causes Act s.25D(2)(e): see Divorce etc. (Pensions) Regulations 2000 (SI 2000/1123) reg.3; Pensions on Divorce (Provision of Information) Regulations 2000 (SI 2000/1048) reg.3; Pension Sharing (Valuation) Regulations 2000 (SI 2000/1052).

[673] For judicial dicta on valuation in the context of ancillary relief, see *per* Thorpe L.J. in *Cowan v Cowan* [2001] 2 F.L.R. 192 at [69] and in *Maskell v Maskell* [2001] 3 F.C.R. 269 at para.[6].

[674] Divorce etc. (Pensions) Regulations 2000 (SI 2000/1048) reg.3(1)(a).

and the wide discretion thereby conferred. This was emphasised by Singer J. in *T v T (Financial Relief: Pensions)*.[675]

i. Methods of re-allocation

The following techniques are available to the court.   **13–120**

(1) Compensation from other assets: "offsetting"

As we have seen, pension entitlements are relevant considerations under   **13–121**
s.25(2)(a) and (h) of the Matrimonial Causes Act 1973 and para.21(2)(a) and
(h) of Sch.5 to the Civil Partnership Act 2004 when the court is exercising its
discretion in relation to ancillary relief. This is further spelt out in s.25B(1) of
the Matrimonial Causes Act 1973 and paras 24(1), (2) and 30 of Sch.5 to the
Civil Partnership Act 2004.

Under the approach now commonly known as "offsetting",[676] the pension-
scheme rights are left undisturbed, but their value is taken into account by the
court ordering that the other party receive on divorce as compensation an
appropriately enlarged share of the parties' other assets.[677] Notwithstanding
the availability of other statutory powers operating specifically upon pension
arrangements, this remains an attractive option because of its simplicity and
finality, and is likely to continue to be widely used. However, its crucial
limitation is that it is wholly dependent on the availability of other free
capital.[678]

(2) Attachment orders

Attachment (formerly known as "earmarking") was introduced by the Pen-   **13–122**
sions Act 1995[679] and elaborated by the Welfare Reform and Pensions Act
1999.[680] It is now governed by ss.25B–25D of the Matrimonial Causes Act
1973 and paras 25–29 and 31–37 of Sch.5 to the Civil Partnership Act 2004.
Attachment is an order made on divorce, dissolution or nullity, and takes the
form of an order for periodic payments (whether deferred or not) or a deferred
lump sum. It is not a separate power but rather a method of enforcing a

---

[675] [1998] 1 F.L.R. 1072.

[676] See *Brooks v Brooks* [1995] 2 F.L.R. 13 at 17, *per* Lord Nicholls of Birkenhead.

[677] "This compensatory approach suffers from the drawbacks that it is difficult to compare the value of pension rights, with their favourable tax treatment, and the value of non-pension rights subject to different tax treatment; unlike non-pension assets, pension values do not represent immediately available cash, so that typically a wife may finish up with the house and no pension, and the husband with a pension but no money for the time being; and this method cannot work if there are inadequate non-pension assets": *Brooks v Brooks* [1995] 2 F.L.R. 13 at 17, *per* Lord Nicholls of Birkenhead.

[678] For an illustration of the previous limitations on the court's powers in this context, see *K v K (Financial Relief: Widow's Pension)* [1997] 2 F.L.R. 35

[679] Pensions Act 1995 s.166.

[680] The power was made available where a petition for divorce or nullity was filed after July 1, 1996 and in respect of applications made on or after August 1, 1996.

periodic payments or lump sum order against the pension. In essence, an attachment order requires the persons responsible for the pension arrangement (i.e. the fund manager or trustee), once the pension becomes payable, to pay the sums involved direct to the spouse concerned. An attachment order must be specifically applied for.[681] Attachment and pension sharing orders (discussed below) cannot be made in respect of the same pension arrangement.[682] The amount to be attached is to be expressed in percentage terms.[683] An attachment order is variable, and this includes an order for a deferred lump sum.[684]

The disadvantages of attachment orders (inconsistency with the clean break objective and their highly speculative nature) had earlier been cogently summarised by Lord Nicholls of Birkenhead in *Brooks v Brooks*.[685] Since their introduction in 1996, attachment orders have not proved popular in practice (save where the spouse entitled to the pension is close to retirement or has already retired):

In *T v T (Financial Relief: Pensions)*[686] Singer J. declined to make an order in the wife's favour for deferred periodical payments from the husband's pension. Looking at all the s.25 considerations, she was immediately to receive, by way of ancillary relief, a substantial lump sum and periodic payments that would be capable of variation. Retirement was a long way off and there were, consequently, uncertainties. However, an attachment order relating to the husband's death-in-service benefits was used to protect the wife against the termination of her maintenance stream in the event of his dying prior to retirement.

In *Burrow v Burrow*[687] Cazalet J. drew a distinction between the lump sum and annuity components of an attachment order made by a district judge; the former (whereby the wife was entitled to 50 per cent), but not the latter, was upheld. Once again, the future uncertainties inherent in the making of an attachment order in respect of the annuity component were highlighted.

In *R. (Smith) v Secretary of State for Work and Pensions*[688] Wilson J. summarised the limitations of an attachment order as a vehicle for making provision for a wife out of a husband's pension rights. No part of the pension is payable to the wife until the husband chooses to retire,

---

[681] Family Proceedings (Amendment No.2) Rules 1996 (SI 1996/1674) r.3; Family Proceedings Rules 1991 (SI 1991/1247) r.2.6(1A)(3).
[682] Matrimonial Causes Act 1973 ss.24B(5), 25B(7B); Civil Partnership Act 2004 Sch.5 para.25(8).
[683] Matrimonial Causes Act 1973 s.25B(5); Civil Partnership Act 2004 Sch.5 para.25(3).
[684] Under Matrimonial Causes Act 1973 s.31(2)(dd) and Civil Partnership Act 2004 Sch.5 para.50(1)(f).
[685] [1995] 2 F.L.R. 13 at 17.
[686] [1998] 1 F.L.R. 1073.
[687] [1999] 1 F.L.R. 508.
[688] [2005] 1 F.L.R. 97 at para.[15].

whatever the wife's age or needs. No further payment will be made to her if following his retirement he predeceases her.

"In a sentence, the problem is that, notwithstanding divorce, the wife who has the benefit only of an attachment order remains hitched to the husband's wagon."

(3) Sharing the pension[689]

In many cases, the most equitable[690] method of dealing with a substantial **13–123** pension fund is to "share" it between the spouses by court order at the time of divorce, dissolution or nullity. Under the Conservative Government, the principle of pension sharing was (albeit reluctantly[691]) first expressed in s.16 of the Family Law Act 1996, but that particular statutory provision was widely recognised as unsatisfactory[692] and was never brought into force.[693] Both Green[694] and White[695] Papers further explored and endorsed the principle of pension sharing, and the Labour Government took up the consultation process in 1998.[696] The result was the Welfare Reform and Pensions Act 1999, the relevant provisions (amending Pt II of the Matrimonial Causes Act 1973) of which came into operation on December 1, 2000.[697] Identical powers are contained in the Civil Partnership Act 2004.[698] In addition, there is a substantial body of detailed regulations.[699] The courts no longer have power

---

[689] For detailed discussions, see Ellison and Rae, *Family Breakdown and Pensions*; R. Bird, "Pension Sharing" [2000] Fam. Law 455; R. Bird, *Pension Sharing: The New Law* (Family Law, 1999); National Association of Pension Funds *Pension, Sharing on Divorce* (2001); D. Salter, "A practitioner's guide to pension sharing: parts I, II and III" [2000] Fam. Law 489, 543 and 914; Brindley, "An actuary's view of pension sharing: parts I and II" [2000] Fam. Law 845, 918; R. Bird, *Ancillary Relief Handbook*, 3rd edn (Family Law, 2002), Ch.10; Salter, "The pitfalls of pension-sharing" [2002] Fam. Law 598; Smith, Brindley and Sanger, "The reality of pension sharing: parts I and II" [2003] Fam. Law 517, 679; *Rayden & Jackson on Divorce and Family Matters*, 18th edn (2005), para.16.197–16.204.

[690] For the administrative burdens involved, see *Brooks v Brooks* [1995] 2 F.L.R. 13 at 17, *per* Lord Nicholls of Birkenhead.

[691] *Official Report* (HL February 29, 1996).

[692] *Official Report* (HL June 27, 1996), col.1090.

[693] It was eventually repealed by Sch.13 of the Welfare Reform and Pensions Act 1999.

[694] *The Treatment of Pension Rights on Divorce* (Cm.3345 (1996)).

[695] *The Treatment of Pension Rights on Divorce* (Cm.3564 (1996)).

[696] *Pension Sharing on Divorce: Reforming Pensions for a Fairer Future* (1998).

[697] Welfare Reform and Pensions Act 1999 s.85(2)(a); Welfare Reform and Pensions Act 1999 (Commencement No.5) Order 2000 (SI 2000/1116). The pension sharing provisions were contained in Pts III and IV of and Schs 3 to 6 of the Welfare Reform and Pensions Act 1999. See Bird [2000] Fam. Law 455; Salter [2000] Fam. Law 489; Brindley [2000] Fam. Law 918.

[698] Civil Partnership Act 2004 Sch.5 paras 15–19 and 34.

[699] Divorce etc. (Pensions) Regulations 2000 (SI 2000/1123); Pensions on Divorce etc. (Provision of Information) Regulations 2000 (SI 2000/1048); Pension Sharing (Implementation and Discharge of Liability) Regulations 2000 (SI 2000/1053); Pensions on Divorce etc. (Charging) Regulations 2000 (SI 2000/1049); Pension Sharing (Valuation) Regulations 2000 (SI 2000/1052); Pension Sharing (Pension Credit Benefit) Regulations 2000 (SI 2000/1054); Pension Sharing (Consequential and Misc. Amendments) Regulations 2000 (SI 2000/2691); Welfare Reform and Pensions Act 1999 (Commencement Order No.12) Order 2001 (SI 2001/4049). The Occupational Pension Schemes (Transfer Values and Miscellaneous Amendment) Regulations 2003 amend the 200 Regulations.

to make a *Brooks v Brooks*[700] order under s.24(1)(c) of the Matrimonial Causes Act 1973.[701]

13–124   (a) Orders that can be made. A pension sharing order is defined in s.21A(1) of the Matrimonial Causes Act 1973 and para.16(1) of Sch.5 to the Civil Partnership Act 2004 as an order that:

> "(a) [P]rovides that one party's—
>
>> (i) shareable rights under the specified pension arrangement, or
>> (ii) shareable state scheme rights,
>
>> be subject to pension-sharing for the benefit of the other party, and
>
> (b)   specifies the percentages to be transferred."

"Pension arrangement" is widely defined[702] so as to cover most private pensions: an occupational pension scheme, a personal pension scheme, a retirement annuity contract, an annuity or insurance policy transferred to give effects to rights under the abovementioned schemes and an annuity to discharge liability under s.29 of the Welfare Reform and Pensions Reform Act 1999. The state-scheme rights that may be shared are more limited[703]: the earnings-related additional pension[704] and the shared additional pension.[705] The basic state pension cannot be shared. Pension sharing orders are available in respect of "shareable rights" in pension arrangements as defined[706] in s.27 of the 1999 Act. The public service pension entitlements of the Prime Minister, Treasurer and Speaker of the House of Commons are excepted.[707] In sum, most pension entitlements may be subject of an application for a pension-sharing order. The Pensions Act 2004 established the Pension Protection Fund to provide for the administration of certain occupational pension schemes where the employer is insolvent and the pension scheme assets are insufficient to meet payable benefits; consequential amendments have been made to the provisions of the Matrimonial Causes Act 1973 and the Civil Partnership Act 2004.

By virtue of the relevant rule,[708] most petitions will now, as a matter of course, include a claim for pension sharing. A pension sharing order can only

---

[700] [1995] 2 F.L.R. 13, discussed at para.13–026 above.
[701] See Matrimonial Causes Act 1973 s.24(1)(c) and (d), as amended by the Welfare Reform and Pensions Act 1999 s.19 and Sch.3. It is still possible to apply for a *Brooks* order where the petition was issued before December 1, 2000: Welfare Reform and Pensions Act 1999 s.85(4).
[702] Welfare Reform and Pensions Act 1999 s.26(1).
[703] Welfare Reform and Pensions Act 1999 s.47(2).
[704] Social Security Contributions and Benefits Act 1992 s.44(3).
[705] Welfare Reform and Pensions Act 1999 s.55A.
[706] All rights under a pension arrangement, save those excluded by the Pension Sharing (Valuation) Regulations 2000 (SI 2000/1052).
[707] Pension Sharing (Excepted Schemes) Order 2001 (SI 2001/358).
[708] Family Proceedings Rules 1991 (SI 1991/1247), as amended, r.2.53(1)(d), prescribing Form A.

(in the case of marriage) be made on or a decree of divorce[709] or nullity[710] (not on judicial separation[711]), and it does not take effect until the decree becomes absolute.[712] In the case of civil partnership, a pension sharing order may be made only on or after the making of an order for dissolution or nullity, and not separation; the pension sharing order takes effect only when the dissolution or nullity order becomes final.[713] If an attachment order has already been made in relation to a pension arrangement, no pension sharing order may be made.[714] If a pension sharing order has already been made in relation to a pension arrangement or state scheme, no further pension sharing order can be made in relation to that arrangement or scheme.[715]

The power to make a pension sharing order was made available only in respect of petitions filed after December 1, 2000.[716]

(b) The effect of a pension sharing order. The essence of pension sharing   **13–125** is the system of pension credit and pension debit.[717] The effect of a pension-sharing order is to credit the transferee with a percentage[718] of the transferor's pension arrangement, which is reduced accordingly.[719] For occupational and personal pensions, that percentage is a percentage of the CETV[720] of the transferor's benefit at the relevant date.[721] The transferee is thereby given not cash but an occupational or personal pension of their own. Putting the matter at its simplest,[722] the transferee normally has the choice as to whether to become a member of the original scheme or (subject to certain exceptions and

---

[709] Including an overseas divorce: Welfare Reform and Pensions Act 1999, s.22, amending the Matrimonial and Family Proceedings Act 1984.

[710] Where the petition was filed after December 1, 2000, see Glover, "Pension-sharing procedure" [2001] Fam. Law 691; *S v S (Recission of Decree Nisi: Pension-Sharing Provision)* [2002] 1 F.L.R. 457.

[711] Matrimonial Causes Act 1973 s.24B(1), as amended by the Welfare Reform and Pensions Act 1999 Sch.3 para.4.

[712] Matrimonial Causes Act 1973 s.24B(2), similarly amended.

[713] Civil Partnership Act 2004 Sch.5 paras 15(1), 19(1).

[714] Matrimonial Causes Act 1973 s.24B(5); Civil Partnership Act 2004 Sch.5 para.18(3).

[715] Matrimonial Causes Act 1973 s.24B(3) and (4); Civil Partnership Act 2004 Sch.5 para.18(1)(2).

[716] See *S v S (Recission of Decree Nisi: Pension-Sharing Provision)* [2002] 1 F.L.R. 457 (decree could be rescinded by consent to permit parties to take advantage of the pension sharing provisions; but not where the matter is contested: *H v H (Pension-Sharing: Recission of Decree Nisi)* [2002] 2 F.L.R. 116; *Rye v Rye* [2002] 2 F.L.R. 981. Where a cross-petition (but not the original petition) was issued after the relevant date, pension sharing provisions were not available: *W v W (Divorce Proceedings: Withdrawal of Consent After Perfection of Order)* [2002] 2 F.L.R. 1225.

[717] Welfare Reform and Pensions Act 1999 s.29.

[718] Matrimonial Causes Act 1973 s.21A(1)(b).

[719] Welfare Reform and Pensions Act 1999 s.29(1) (private pensions); s.49(1) (state pension).

[720] Welfare Reform and Pensions Act 1999 s.30; Pension Sharing (Valuation) Regulations 2000 (SI 2000/1052).

[721] Welfare Reform and Pensions Act 1999 s.29(2), (4), (5); to be determined by the court, but no more than one year prior to the petition and no later than the date on which the court makes the order: Divorce etc. (Pensions) Regulations 2000 (SI 2000/1123) reg.3(1)(a) and (b). Benefits must be calculated as set out in reg.3 of the Pensions on Divorce (Provision of Information) Regulations 2000 (SI 2000/1048).

[722] The details are contained in Welfare Reform and Pensions Act 1999 Sch.5.

modifications for unfunded public arrangements[723]) to have the fund transferred into a different arrangement[724] (which could be one in which she already has entitlements). There are Inland Revenue limitations on the extent to which the transferor can rebuild their pension fund. There is a four-month[725] implementation period, giving the trustees or fund managers time to make the necessary arrangements for transferring the funds. Where a state pension is shared, the effect of the pension credit is to give the transferee an additional pension.[726] The percentages of the parties' respective shares is entirely a matter for the court's discretion.

[723] Welfare Reform and Pensions Act 1999 Sch.5 paras 2, 3.
[724] Welfare Reform and Pensions Act 1999 Sch.5 para.1(3).
[725] Welfare Reform and Pensions Act 1999 s.34. It runs from the date when the order takes effect or that on which the prescribed information was received, whichever is later: Pensions on Divorce (Provision of Information) Regulations 2000 (SI 2000/1048) reg.5. On failure to discharge liability in time, see Welfare Reform and Pensions Act 1999 s.33 and the Pension Sharing (Implementation and Discharge of Liability) Regulations 2000 (SI 2000/1053).
[726] Welfare Reform and Pensions Act 1999 s.49(1) and Sch.6, inserting a new s.45B into the Social Security Contributions and Benefits Act 1992.

CHAPTER FOURTEEN

ENFORCEMENT OF FINANCIAL OBLIGATIONS[1]

I.   INTRODUCTION.............................. 14–001
II. RESTRICTIONS   ON   THE
ENFORCEMENT OF MAINTENANCE
ARREARS; REMITTING ARREARS......... 14–002
III. DIFFERENT COURTS; DIFFERENT
REMEDIES... 14–003
IV. THE SUPERIOR COURTS 14–004
     A. Enforcement in the superior courts. 14–004

V.   MAGISTRATES' COURT 14–015
     A. Enforcement in the magistrates'
     court.. 14–015
VI. RESTRICTING A CONTEMNOR'S
RIGHT TO PARTICIPATE IN PROCEED-
INGS 14–020

I. INTRODUCTION

It is one thing to obtain an order from a court; it is often quite another to make **14–001** the person to whom the order is addressed comply. Many reasons are offered for non-compliance with orders for financial provision.[2] It may be difficult or impossible to trace the debtor.[3] Many debtors assert that they lack the means to support their former partners.[4] Moreover, the payment obligation is connected with an intimate personal relationship that has broken down; even a debtor with

---

[1] See *Report of the Committee on Statutory Maintenance Limits* (Cmnd.3587 (1968)); *Report of the Committee on the Enforcement of Judgment Debts* (Cmnd.3909 (1969)); *Report of the Committee on One-Parent Families* (Cmnd.5629 (1974)); *Children Come First, The Government's Proposals for the Maintenance of Children* (Cm.1263 (1990)), Vols I and II; McGregor, Blom-Cooper and Gibson, *Separated Spouses* (1970); Gibson [1982] 12 Fam. Law 138; Gibson, "The future for maintenance" [1991] C.J.Q. 330; S. Oliver and P. Clements, *Enforcing Family Financial Orders* (Family Law, 1999); D. Levy, "Can't pay won't pay: enforcing financial orders in the UK" [2001] Fam. Law 48.

[2] See Ch.13, above.

[3] For means of obtaining information for tracing a debtor, see D. Levy [2001] Fam. Law 48 at 49 and 50–51.

[4] *Report of the Committee on the Enforcement of Judgment Debts* (Cmnd.3587 (1969)), saw the basic problem as "not a problem of enforcement but of economics . . . we cannot too strongly or too often invite attention to the simple fact that no improvement which we can suggest in the machinery of the courts will put more money into pockets of husbands and debtors or enable them to meet commitments beyond their capacity to pay" (para.1306).

ample means may not comply with an order.[5] This chapter seeks to give a brief outline of the current law and practice on enforcement.[6]

The Tribunals, Courts and Enforcement Act 2007 makes changes to the general law and procedure on enforcement, including seizure and sale of goods, attachment of earnings and charging orders. It is not yet clear to what extent the provisions contained in the 2007 Act will be applied to family proceedings. The 2007 Act has been progressively brought into operation from September 19, 2007 to June 1, 2008.[7]

II. Restrictions on the Enforcement of Maintenance Arrears; Remitting Arrears

14–002 Historically, periodical payment orders were regarded as fundamentally different from other legal obligations. Whereas in the case of a contract debt it was no business of the courts whether the creditor needed the money owed or not, a maintenance order was seen to be justified only as a means of providing support for a dependant[8]; the question of the parties' relative needs was therefore seen as highly relevant to the question of whether the obligation should be enforced or not, and, in particular, the court would exercise a discretion over the extent to which enforcement of accrued arrears under such orders should be allowed.[9] If the creditor waited for a year or more to seek enforcement, it might be thought that he/she did not in reality need the money or at least had managed well enough without it, and to allow arrears to be enforced without limit might cause serious

---

[5] See, for example, the long-running litigation in *Mubarak v Mubarak* [2001] 1 F.L.R. 673; [2001] 1 F.L.R. 698; [2003] 2 F.L.R. 553; and *Mubarak v Mubarik* [2004] 2 F.L.R. 932; [2007] 1 F.L.R. 722; [2007] 2 F.L.R. 364, discussed later in this chapter.

[6] The international enforcement of financial orders has become a highly complex and specialised field, and is therefore excluded from coverage in this edition, as it is inappropriate in a text of this nature.

[7] Tribunals, Courts and Enforcement Act 2007 (Commencement No.1) Order 2007 (SI 2007/2709 (C 104)); Tribunals, Courts and Enforcement Act 2007 (Commencement No.2) Order 2007 (SI 2007/3613 (C 158)); Tribunals, Courts and Enforcement Order (Commencement No.3) Order 2007 (SI 2008/749 (C 31)); Tribunals, Courts and Enforcement Act (Commencement No.4) Order 2008 (SI 2008/1158 (C 51)).

[8] *Re Robinson* (1884) 27 Ch.D. 160; *Linton v Linton* (1885) 15 Q.B.D. 239; *Watkins v Watkins* [1896] P. 222 at 226–227; *H v H (Financial Provision)* [1993] 2 F.L.R. 35; *B v C (Enforcement: Arrears)* [1995] 1 F.L.R. 467; *Re Bradley-Hole (A Bankrupt)* [1995] 1 W.L.R. 1097. It followed from this doctrine that the right to receive payments under such an order cannot be assigned: *Re Robinson* (1884) 27 Ch.D. 160. The doctrine was originally developed by the ecclesiastical court in the context of alimony for a judicially separated wife. It was subsequently applied to an order for maintenance made on divorce (*Watkins v Watkins*), and the same reasoning was held to be applicable to orders for maintenance made by magistrates: *Paquine v Snary* [1909] 1 K.B. 688. The convention that "stale" arrears are not to be enforced was based on the view that a creditor who did not act speedily was probably not in need of support but enforcement may now more readily be given if the order was part of a financial package and there is some reasonable explanation for the delay: *H v H (Financial Provision)* [1993] 2 F.L.R. 35.

[9] *Robins v Robins* [1907] 2 K.B. 13 at 17; *Campbell v Campbell* [1922] P. 187 at 193; *Re Hedderwick* [1933] 1 Ch. 669 at 675; *Luscombe v Luscombe (Westminster Bank Ltd Garnishee)* [1962] 1 All E.R. 668; *James v James* [1964] P. 303 at 306–307; and fn.17, below.

injustice to a debtor who might reasonably regard the liability as something he/she could forget about.[10]

For these reasons it became the practice not to allow the enforcement of more than one year's accumulation of arrears without leave of the court[11]; statute[12] now provides that arrears which became due more than 12 months before the institution of the enforcement proceedings[13] are not to be enforced through the High Court or any county court without the leave of the court.[14] If the court is asked to allow enforcement of arrears over one year old, the starting point is that the arrears should not be enforced unless there are special circumstances.[15]

The court also has a statutory power to remit the payment of the arrears or of any part thereof[16]; the exercise of this discretion is governed by a rule of practice (which is not, however, inflexible) that arrears accrued more than 12 months before the enforcement proceedings were started will be remitted.[17]

III. DIFFERENT COURTS; DIFFERENT REMEDIES

It is necessary to distinguish between enforcement of financial orders in the county court and the High Court ("the superior courts") on the one hand, and enforcement of maintenance orders in the magistrates' courts on the other. An important link between the two systems exists to the extent that a High Court or a county court maintenance order may be registered in a magistrates' court for enforcement and will be treated as a magistrates' court order for so long as the   **14–003**

---

[10] *Russell v Russell* [1986] 1 F.L.R. 465 at 473, *per* Lord Donaldson of Lymington.

[11] For the factors that were considered relevant to the exercise of the court's discretion, see *Pilcher v Pilcher (No.2)* [1956] 1 All E.R. 463; *Luscombe v Luscombe (Westminster Bank Ltd Garnishee)* [1962] 1 All E.R. 668; *Purba v Purba* [2001] 1 F.L.R. 444.

[12] Matrimonial Causes Act 1973 s.32 and Domestic Proceedings and Magistrates' Courts Act 1978 s.32(4) apply to enforcement in the High Court and county court and there is no statutory prohibition on the enforcement of arrears by proceedings in a magistrates' court: see *Pilcher v Pilcher (No.2)* [1956] 1 All E.R. 463; *Ross v Pearson* [1976] 1 W.L.R. 224; *Fowler v Fowler* (1981) 2 F.L.R. 141; *Dickens v Pattison* [1985] F.L.R. 610; *B v C (Enforcement of Arrears)* [1995] 1 F.L.R. 467 from which it appears that the usual practice is to refuse enforcement of arrears in accordance with the practice of the superior courts.

[13] The rule applies not only to arrears under unsecured periodical payment orders but also to arrears under other financial provision orders and interim orders for maintenance: Matrimonial Causes Act 1973 s.32(1).

[14] If an application for leave to enforce such an order is made, the court may refuse leave or grant leave subject to such restrictions and conditions (including conditions as to the allowing of time for payment or the making of payment by instalments) as the court thinks proper: Matrimonial Causes Act 1973 s.32.

[15] *Bernstein v O'Neill* [1989] 2 F.L.R. 1; *C v S (Maintenance Order: Enforcement)* [1997] 1 F.L.R. 298; *B v C (Enforcement: Arrears)* [1995] 1 F.L.R. 467; *King v Bunyon* [2008] Fam. Law 308.

[16] *B v C (Enforcement of Arrears)* [1995] 1 F.L.R. 467, *per* Johnson J. (relying on *Russell v Russell* [1986] 1 F.L.R. 465, CA). It may be more appropriate for the court to ask itself whether to exercise its discretion to enforce arrears rather than whether to make an order for remission of arrears: *King v Bunyon* [2008] Fam. Law 308.

[17] Magistrates' Courts Act 1980 s.95; Matrimonial Causes Act 1973 s.31(2A).

order is so registered.[18] In 1998 the Lord Chancellor's Advisory Group on Ancillary Relief submitted a *Report on Enforcement of Orders* in which it observed that one of the defects of the present system in the context of family proceedings is its fragmented nature and that there should be one originating process for enforcement.[19] The recommendations were not acted upon and it appears that the reform of enforcement remedies in family proceedings may have been subjugated to a wider review of enforcement procedures in civil justice.[20] The Tribunals, Courts and Enforcement Act 2007 has been referred to earlier in this chapter.[21]

IV. The Superior Courts

A. Enforcement in the superior courts

14–004 The following enforcement procedures may be relevant:

- bankruptcy;

- execution against goods;

- garnishee order;

- charging order;

- appointment of a receiver;

- sequestration;

- committal to prison: the judgment summons;

- attachment of earnings; and

- registration in the magistrates' court.

---

[18] *Russell v Russell* [1986] 1 F.L.R. 465, CA; *Bernstein v O'Neill* [1989] 2 F.L.R. 1; *R v Bristol Magistrates' Court Ex p. Hedge* [1997] 1 F.L.R. 88; *R. v Cardiff Magistrates Court Ex p. Czech* [1999] 1 F.L.R. 95. But the underlying principle is that the discretion is a discretion whether to enforce stale arrears, not whether there is a discretion to remit them: *B v C (Enforcement: Arrears)* [1995] 1 F.L.R. 467.
[19] LCD, *Report on Enforcement of Orders* (1998), para.5.1.
[20] *Per* Thorpe L.J. in *Mubarak v Mubarak* [2001] 1 F.L.R. 698 at para.[42]. Note that the new enforcement regime of the Civil Procedure Rules 1998 Pts 70–73 (in force March 25, 2002) does not currently apply to family proceedings, which continue to be governed by the "old" Rules of the Supreme Court and County Court Rules: Family Proceedings Rules 1991 (SI 1991/1247), r.1.3(1); Civil Procedure Rules 1998 r.2.1(2).
[21] See above, para.14–001.

i. Bankruptcy[22]

The making of a bankruptcy order[23] has a dramatic effect: in principle, the **14–005** bankrupt is debarred from dealing with his/her property,[24] and the bankrupt's estate will vest in a trustee[25] who is obliged to distribute the property amongst the creditors in respect of the "bankruptcy debts".[26] Bankruptcy also involves certain civic and other penalties.[27] In due course,[28] the debtor will usually be discharged from bankruptcy, and that discharge releases him/her from all bankruptcy debts.[29]

It has never been possible to found a bankruptcy petition on a failure to make periodical payments of maintenance[30]; although, at one time, a lump sum order was enforceable as a bankruptcy debt,[31] it is now provided[32] that obligations arising under an order made in family or domestic proceedings are not provable.[33] In *Levy v Legal Services Commission*[34] the Court of Appeal held that a costs order was not a provable debt. The Court went on to hold that it had jurisdiction[35] to make a bankruptcy order on the petition of a creditor with a non-provable debt,[36] but that it was difficult to envisage the exceptional circumstances in which the jurisdiction would be exercised.[37]

Hence bankruptcy is not generally available as a means of enforcing a lump sum or property transfer order made in ancillary relief proceedings. The trustee in bankruptcy cannot pay any of the bankrupt's estate to a wife seeking

---

[22] Miller, "The effect of insolvency on applications for financial provision" (1998) 10 C.F.L.Q. 29; Costley-White, "Bankruptcy—back to basics" [2000] Fam. Law 181.

[23] Under the Insolvency Act 1986.

[24] Insolvency Act 1986 s.284; see *Re Flint (A Bankrupt)* [1993] 1 F.L.R. 763 (divorce court consent order for transfer of bankrupt's interest in matrimonial home void). As to whether a court order constitutes a disposition for the purposes of this provision, cf. *Burton v Burton* [1986] 2 F.L.R. 419 at 425, *per* Butler-Sloss J.; and *Re Mordant, Mordant v Halls* [1996] 1 F.L.R. 334 at 343, *per* Sir D. Nicholls V.C. The court has power to give its consent to (or subsequently ratify) a disposition by the bankrupt, but the factors relevant to the exercise of that discretionary power are not discussed in *Re Mordant, Mordant v Halls*, notwithstanding the fact that it was an application by a wife to review the District Judge's refusal to consent to a payment made to her.

[25] Insolvency Act 1986 s.306.

[26] Insolvency Act 1986 s.324.

[27] A bankrupt may not sit as a Member of Parliament, nor may a bankrupt practise any of a large number of professions.

[28] Usually not more than three years after the commencement of the bankruptcy: Insolvency Act 1986 s.279.

[29] Insolvency Act 1986 s.281.

[30] *Linton v Linton* (1885) 15 Q.B.D. 239; *Re Henderson* (1888) 20 Q.B.D. 509; *Re Hawkins* [1894] 1 Q.B. 25; *Kerr v Kerr* [1897] 2 Q.B. 439.

[31] *Curtis v Curtis* [1969] 1 W.L.R. 422.

[32] Insolvency Rules 1986 (SI 1986/1925), r.12(3). The suggestion that this rule might have been ultra vires (see *Woodley v Woodley* [1992] 2 F.L.R. 417) was not accepted by the Court of Appeal: *Woodley v Woodley (No.2)* [1993] 2 F.L.R. 477. On the interpretation of r.12.3(3), see *Cartwright v Cartwright (No.2)* [2002] 2 F.L.R. 611 (CA).

[33] *Re A Debtor; JP v A Debtor* [1997] 1 F.L.R. 926.

[34] [2001] 1 F.L.R. 435. See also *Wehmeyer v Wehmeyer* [2001] 2 F.L.R. 84. See G. Miller, "Bankruptcy as a means of enforcement in family proceedings" [2002] Fam. Law 21.

[35] Under Insolvency Act 1986 s.264.

[36] *Russell v Russell* [1998] 1 F.L.R. 936, Ch.D. Note further that s.285(3)(b) renders void any proceedings against a bankrupt commenced without the required permission of a person who is a creditor in respect of a debt provable in bankruptcy: *Re Taylor (A Bankrupt)* [2007] 2 W.L.R. 148.

[37] [2001] 1 F.L.R. 435 at 445, *per* Jonathan Parker L.J.

enforcement of an ancillary relief order, who is left to pursue other methods of enforcement described below, after the other creditors have been satisfied.

ii. Execution against goods

14–006　In default of payment of any sum due, a creditor may[38] obtain a writ of *fieri facias*,[39] which authorises the sheriff or bailiff to seize sufficient of the defaulter's goods[40] to pay the debt and (unless the sum is paid off) to sell them to pay off the debt and costs. A substantial number of debtors pay under the threat of sale. However, although this process is relatively common in debt collecting, it now seems to be little used in family proceedings.

Part 3 of the Tribunals, Courts and Enforcement Act 2007[41] entitled "Enforcement by Taking Control of Goods" unifies the general law relating to enforcement by seizure and sale of goods.

iii. Garnishee orders

14–007　A garnishee order directs a person who owes money to the debtor to pay it to the creditor[42]—so that, for example, a spouse who has an unsatisfied order may obtain a garnishee order directed to the other spouse's bank, which must then (if the account is sufficiently in credit[43]) pay the sum due direct to the wife.[44] A garnishee order is a proprietary remedy.[45]

iv. Charging orders

14–008　The court has power[46] to make a charging order over certain specified interests

---

[38] Subject to compliance with the relevant Rules: RSC O.47; CCR O.26.

[39] The county court equivalent is called a warrant of execution: see Family Proceeding Rules 1991 (SI 1991/1247), Pt VII; and CCR O.25, 26. In the High Court the procedure is governed by RSC O.46.

[40] But certain items (notably "such clothing, bedding, furniture, household equipment and provisions as are necessary for satisfying the basic domestic needs" of the debtor and his family) are now exempt from seizure: Supreme Court Act 1981 s.138(3A) as inserted by Courts and Legal Services Act 1990 s.15(1).

[41] See para.14–001 above.

[42] The procedures are laid down by RSC O.49, and CCR O.30. In the Civil Procedure Rules 1998 (SI 1998/3132), Pt 72, the term "garnishee order" is replaced with "third-party debt order", but those Rules do not apply to family proceedings.

[43] See *Alawiye v Mahmood* [2007] 1 W.L.R. 79.

[44] For a case in which a wife successfully used garnishee proceedings against a bank account and solicitor's client account to enforce orders against her husband (who had left the country), see *Cohen v Cohen* [1982] 4 F.L.R. 451. In 2001 a total of 169 garnishee orders were made in the High Court and 4,139 in the county court: Judicial Statistics, *Annual Report* (2001), Tables 3.11 and 4.19.

[45] See, for example, *Kuwait Oil Tanker Co SAK v Qabazard* [2004] 1 A.C. 300.

[46] Under Charging Orders Act 1979 s.1. The Act is based on recommendations made by the Law Commission: see *Report on Charging Orders* (Law Com. No.74 (1976)) and the procedure (which involves a two-stage process of order nisi and order absolute) is governed by RSC O.50 and CCR O.31. The power to make an order is discretionary, and in deciding whether to make an order, the court is required to consider all the circumstances of the case, and, in particular, any evidence before it as to: (i) the personal circumstances of the debtor; and (ii) whether any other creditor of the debtor would be likely to be unduly prejudiced by the making of the order: s.1(5). Difficult questions have arisen where a commercial creditor of one spouse seeks a charging order in respect of that spouse's interest in property (often the former matrimonial home) that might be subject to a property adjustment order on the application of the other: see *First National Securities Ltd v Hegerty* [1985] Q.B. 850; [1985] F.L.R. 80, CA; *Harman v Glencross* [1986] Fam. 81, CA; *Austin-Fell v Austin-Fell* [1989] 2 F.L.R. 497, CA.

in property to which the debtor is entitled.[47] Such an order has the like effect,[48] and is enforceable in the same way as an equitable charge "created by the debtor by writing under his/her hand"[49]; the creditor accordingly gains a measure of priority and a right to resort to specific property of the debtor (for example, their house, or shares that they own). A creditor who has obtained a charging order over the debtor's interest in the family home or other property is a "person interested" in the property,[50] and may, in consequence, seek an order that the property be sold if the default continues.[51] It is understood that very few charging orders in fact result in a sale, and that creditors attach most importance to securing a degree of priority.

Amendments to the Charging Orders Act 1979 are contained in Pt 4 of the Tribunals, Courts and Enforcement Act 2007.[52]

v. Appointment of receiver

The court has power,[53] in all cases in which it appears just and convenient to do so, to appoint a receiver,[54] who is entitled to receive rents, profits and other proceeds of property belonging to the debtor,[55] or of a business carried on by him/her. The order may be supplemented by an injunction restraining the debtor from dealing with the property,[56] so that, in effect, the receiver intercepts the debtor's income before it reaches him/her, and accounts for it to the creditor. The remedy is, however, an exceptional one, and will only be granted in exceptional cases.[57] The Human Rights Act 1998 will normally require that a judgment

14–009

---

[47] A charging order may not be made against a pension fund under the trusts of which the judgment debtor has no beneficial interest and which contain an express provision that no benefit payable under the scheme is capable of being charged: *Field v Field* [2003] 1 F.L.R. 376.

[48] The property capable of being the subject matter of a charging order is specified in Charging Orders Act 1979 s.2, and includes the debtor's interest in land, most English stocks and shares and unit trusts and the debtor's beneficial interest under trusts, including, for example, the debtor's beneficial interest in the proceeds of sale of land held under a trust for sale: *National Westminster Bank Ltd v Stockman* [1981] 1 W.L.R. 67. In certain circumstances, the court also has power to make a charging order in respect of the land held under a trust for sale: Charging Orders Act 1979 s.2(1)(b); see *Clark v Chief Land Registrar* [1993] 2 F.L.R. 500. The charge may, in appropriate cases, be protected under the Land Charges Act 1972 and the Land Registration Act 2002: see *Parkash v Irani Finance* [1970] Ch. 101; *Barclays Bank Ltd v Taylor* [1974] Ch. 137, CA; *Clark v Chief Land Registrar* [1993] 2 F.L.R. 500.

[49] Charging Orders Act 1979 s.3(5).

[50] *Lloyds Bank plc v Byrne* [1993] 1 F.L.R. 369, CA.

[51] The court will normally order a sale unless there are exceptional circumstances: *Lloyds Bank plc v Byrne* [1993] 1 F.L.R. 369, CA; *Barclays Bank plc v Hendricks* [1996] 1 F.L.R. 258. The court also has power to appoint a receiver: see below.

[52] See above, para.14–001.

[53] The procedure is governed by RSC O.51; and CCR O.32.

[54] Supreme Court Act 1981 s.37; and see County Courts Act 1984 ss.38 and 107.

[55] Quaere whether in an appropriate case a receiver could be appointed to make elections in relation to a debtor's pension: *Field v Field* [2003] 1 F.L.R. 376.

[56] *Levermore v Levermore* [1979] 1 W.L.R. 1277.

[57] *S v S* (1973) 117 S.J. 649 (where the husband owed a substantial sum of money in respect of maintenance arrears and a receiver was appointed to receive the profits of a proprietary club in which the husband had an interest until the arrears were discharged); *Levermore v Levermore* [1979] 1 W.L.R. 1277 (where a receiver was appointed in respect of the husband's interest in a house that he owned jointly with his brother, the receiver being given liberty to take such proceedings in the name of the husband as were necessary to enforce a sale of the property. Note that since the coming into force of the Charging Orders Act 1979, the making of a charging order would have been the

debtor be provided with the opportunity of complying with an order before a receiver is appointed.[58]

vi. Sequestration

14–010　A writ of sequestration is a coercive measure primarily designed to prevent the defaulter from dealing with the property until he/she has made good their default.[59] The writ[60] is available when periodical payment[61] and other financial provision and property adjustment orders are not complied with, and is issued on the basis that the defaulter, by reason of failure to comply with the court order, is in contempt of court.[62] The procedure is very rarely invoked in financial cases,[63] but may be effective in coercing a debtor who is outside the jurisdiction but has property here.[64]

vii. Committal to prison—the judgment summons

14–011　The Debtors Act 1869[65] gave the court power to commit any person who made default in payment of a debt due in pursuance of any court order or judgment[66]

---

appropriate remedy). On the circumstances in which a receiver will be appointed, see further *Ranson v Ranson* [2002] 1 F.C.R. 261.

[58] *Ranson v Ranson* [2002] 1 F.C.R. 261.

[59] See *Romilly v Romilly* [1964] P. 22 at 23. The procedure in the High Court (which is normally considered the appropriate forum, notwithstanding the fact that the county court now also has jurisdiction: *Rose v Laskinkton Ltd* [1990] Q.B. 562) is governed by RSC O.46 r.5.

[60] Which takes the form of a command from the sovereign to not less than four commissioners chosen by the applicant, and authorises them "to enter upon the messuages, lands, tenements and real estate whatsoever of the [debtor] and to collect receive and sequester into [their] hands not only all the rents and profits of his said messuages, lands, tenements and real estate, but also all his goods, chattels and personal estate whatsoever". The sequestrators are commanded to "detain and keep the same under sequestration" in their hands until the defaulter pays the sums outstanding and thus clears his contempt: *Bucknell v Bucknell* [1969] 1 W.L.R. 1204 at 1206.

[61] *Capron v Capron* [1927] P. 243.

[62] *Pratt v Inman* (1889) 43 Ch.D. 175 at 179; *Coles v Coles* [1957] P. 68; *Bucknell v Bucknell* [1969] 1 W.L.R. 1204 at 1206.

[63] Sequestration may be used in an attempt to coerce a person who has removed a child from the jurisdiction: *Richardson v Richardson* [1989] Fam. 95; *Mir v Mir* [1992] 1 F.L.R. 624.

[64] As in *Romilly v Romilly* [1964] P. 22. It has been held that the court may authorise the sale of the property: *Mir v Mir* [1992] 1 F.L.R. 624; and see *Richardson v Richardson* [1990] 1 F.L.R. 186. However, sequestration is an expensive remedy (see *Clark v Clark* [1989] 1 F.L.R. 174; and *Clark v Clark (No.2)* [1991] 1 F.L.R. 179, where the sequestrator raised some £17,000 from the husband's assets, but all of this went to meet costs incurred).

[65] Now modified by the Civil Procedure (Modification of Enactments) Order 2002 from March 25, 2002.

[66] It has been held that an undertaking as to periodical payments to pay school fees was an integral and indivisible part of the court's order, and thus enforceable by way of judgment summons: *Symmons v Symmons* [1993] 1 F.L.R. 317; and in *M v M (Enforcement: Judgment Summons)* [1993] Fam. Law 469 a circuit judge held that an undertaking to pay an unquantified capital sum is enforceable in this way. Note also that in *Graham v Graham* [1992] 2 F.L.R. 406, CA, it was held that an order to bring a sum of money into court as security against the final determination of an ancillary application was an order for the payment of maintenance within the meaning of the 1970 Act. The question of whether an undertaking can be enforced by the judgment summons procedure is of great practical importance because *Livesey v Jenkins* [1985] A.C. 424, HL requires many financial matters (e.g. a requirement to make mortgage or insurance payments) to be dealt with by way of undertaking; and the law is not altogether clear: for a range of views, compare the views of P. Moor and N. Mostyn [1992] Fam. Law 371; District Judge Price [1989] Fam. Law 120; District Judge Bird [1990] Fam. Law 420; D. Burrows [1998] Fam. Law 158. An undertaking to the court

to prison for a term not exceeding six weeks, or until payment of the sum due; the Administration of Justice Act 1970 preserved this power in respect of orders for matrimonial, periodical or other payments.[67] However, the 1869 Act also provides[68] that the power to commit:

> "[S]hall only be exercised where it is proved to the satisfaction of the court that the person making default either has or has had since the date of the order . . . the means to pay the sum in respect of which he[/she] has made default, and has refused or neglected, or refuses or neglects, to pay the same."

The power is thus, in effect, a power to punish for dishonesty[69] or contempt of a court order, which should accordingly only be exercised if the court is satisfied beyond reasonable doubt that the debtor has or has had the means to pay.[70]

The judgment summons requires the debtor to appear and be orally examined on whether they have property or means of satisfying the judgment against them.[71] In practice, the making of a suspended committal order (in which the committal order is made but suspended on terms that the arrears be paid off by specified instalments) has traditionally proved the most effective, particularly the man or woman in business on his or her own account (against whom no attachment of earnings order can be made[72]) and generally against those of means and social status who refuse to comply with an ancillary relief order.[73]

The Human Rights Act 1998 has challenged the traditional use of the judgment summons as a means of enforcement of ancillary relief orders. For example:

> In *Mubarak v Mubarak*[74] the husband, a successful international jeweller, failed to comply with an order that he pay the wife £5 million. The wife sought enforcement by judgment summons in accordance with current procedural requirements.[75] In support of the judgment summons the wife relied—as had become usual practice—on the evidence adduced at the trial

recorded on a consent order may be enforced as a breach of contract: *Independiente v Music Trading On-Line (HK) Ltd* [2007] 4 All E.R. 736.

[67] See Administration of Justice Act 1970 s.11, and Sch.8 para.2A. The Act partially implemented the recommendations of the Payne Committee on the Enforcement of Judgment Debts (Cmnd.3909 (1969)).

[68] Debtors Act 1869 s.5(2).

[69] *Stonor v Fowle* (1887) 13 App. Cas. 20.

[70] See *Woodley v Woodley* [1992] 2 F.L.R. 417, CA. In that case it was held that the power to commit could be exercised notwithstanding the fact that the debtor had been made bankrupt (and all his assets had vested in his trustee because he had had the means to satisfy the court order for a period of two months between the date of the order and the bankruptcy. The legislation was both coercive and punitive in intention.

[71] RSC O.48 r.1(1); Family Proceedings Rules 1991 (SI 1991/1247) r.7.4. For civil proceedings, see now Civil Procedure Rules 1998 (SI 1998/3132) Pt 71.

[72] Because he is not in employment.

[73] Payne, *Committee on the Enforcement of Judgment Debts*: views of three members favouring retention of imprisonment for maintenance defaulters (Cmnd.3909 (1969)), para.1967. See, for example, *J v J* [1955] P. 215; *Ette v Ette* [1964] 1 W.L.R. 1433.

[74] [2001] 1 F.L.R. 698.

[75] Family Proceedings Rules 1991 (SI 1991/1247) r.7; Form M17 effectively reversed the burden of proof.

of her ancillary relief application, the judge's findings, the judgment of the Court of Appeal in refusing permission to appeal and affirmations by the husband. The husband was committed to prison for six weeks and the order suspended on condition that he made payments by specified dates.[76] The Court of Appeal set the committal order aside and formulated procedural requirements[77] necessary to make the judgment summons process compatible with art.6 of the European Convention for the Protection of Human Rights and Fundamental Freedoms, which is engaged because the judgment summons procedure, even when originating in family proceedings, is properly characterised as a criminal proceeding. Thus the respondent has a right to the presumption of innocence, precise articulation of the charge, adequate time to prepare a defence and examination of evidence. The procedures under the Debtors Act 1869 and the rules were not compatible with art.6, but the defect was capable of correction by practice direction.[78] In _Mubarak_, Thorpe L.J. predicted[79] that this re-evaluation of the judgment summons procedure, in the light of the Human Rights Act 1998, was likely to render it a largely obsolete method of enforcement, but there are contrary views.[80]

In judgment summons proceedings under the Debtors Act 1869, the essential issue to be determined is whether the neglect to pay was _willful_ on the part of the judgment debtor. In _Corbett v Corbett_[81] Thorpe L.J. opined that the court hearing a judgment should consider[82] whether the order of which enforcement is sought would have been varied or suspended if the debtor had made an application for variation. As a matter of pragmatic management, the court must ensure that the application for variation, including a full investigation not only of means but also of motivation and good faith, precedes the determination of the judgment summons.

viii. Attachment of earnings

14–012 An attachment of earnings order is an order directed to a person who appears to the court to have the debtor in their employment, which operates as an instruction to the employer to make periodical deductions from the debtor's earnings[83] and

---

[76] _Mubarak v Mubarak_ [2001] 1 F.L.R. 763, FD.

[77] Followed in _Corbett v Corbett_ [2003] 2 F.L.R. 385.

[78] _Practice Direction: Committal Proceedings_, May 28, 1999; expressly applied to family proceedings by _President's Direction: Committal Proceedings_, March 16, 2001; [2001] Fam. Law 333. See further the Civil Procedure (Modification of Enactments) Order 2002 (SI 2002/439); Family Proceedings (Amendment) Rules 2003 (SI 2003/184) r.11. The procedure is contained in Family Proceedings Rules 1991 (SI 1991/1247) as amended: r.7.2, 7.4–7.8.

[79] [2001] 1 F.L.R. 698 at para.[41]. See also P. Rutter, "Judgment summonses: the final nail in the coffin" [2003] Fam. Law 433.

[80] J Southgate, "Judgment summonses: still scope for a comeback?" [2003] Fam. Law 436.

[81] [2003] 2 F.L.R. 385.

[82] The power to consider variation is contained in Family Proceedings Rules 1991 (SI 1991/1247) r.7(4)(9)(b). Variation is discussed in Ch.13.

[83] In accordance with the provisions of Attachment of Earnings Act 1971 Sch.3, Pt I.

to pay over the sums deducted to the collecting officer of the court.[84] Restrictions on the availability of attachment (reflecting long-standing opposition on the part of organised labour to any interference with the sanctity of the wage packet[85]) have been gradually removed, and, as a result of a significant change of policy embodied in the Maintenance Enforcement Act 1991,[86] attachment is now freely available against those ordered to pay maintenance.

The legislation[87] is complex, but its main features are as follows:

- The court[88] may[89] make an attachment of earnings order[90]—either on the application of an interested party[91] or of its own motion—whenever it makes a qualifying periodical maintenance order.[92] This provision completely destroys the principle that attachment is an exceptional procedure, and that interference with the relationship between an employer and employee can only be justified in cases in which the employee is shown to be in default in respect of maintenance obligations.[93]

- The court may also make an order at any later time on an application by an interested party[94] or of its own motion in the course of any proceedings (e.g. a variation application) concerning the order.[95]

- Amount to be attached: the legislation seeks to ensure that the debtor is always left with an adequate level of income to support themselves and

---

[84] Attachment of Earnings Act 1971 s.6(1).

[85] Successfully reflected in the Wages Attachment (Abolition) Act 1870.

[86] Which abolished the principle that attachment could only be ordered against a spouse who had defaulted in making maintenance payments.

[87] Embodied in the Attachment of Earnings Act 1971, as amended (notably by the Maintenance Enforcement Act 1991). The relevant court rules are to be found in CCR O.27.

[88] i.e. the High Court and the county court: Maintenance Enforcement Act 1991 s.1(1). (As to attachment in the magistrates' court, see below.)

[89] In deciding whether to exercise its powers, the court must, if practicable, give every interested party an opportunity to make representations, and must have regard to any representations made by any such party: s.1(8).

[90] Maintenance Enforcement Act 1991 also empowers the court to make a means of payment order (e.g. to make payments by standing order): s.1(1), (4), (5).

[91] As defined: s.1(10).

[92] Maintenance order is widely defined by reference to the definition in Administration of Justice Act 1970 Sch.8 (see Maintenance Enforcement Act 1991 s.1(10)) and extends to most orders made in matrimonial proceedings and to financial orders made under Children Act 1989, Sch.1. An order is only a "qualifying" order if the debtor is ordinarily resident in England and Wales at the time the order is made: Maintenance Enforcement Act 1991 s.1(2).

[93] i.e. the principle of the sanctity of the wage packet. Until the coming into force of the Maintenance Enforcement Act 1991, an attachment order could only be made on a creditor's application if: (i) at least 15 days had elapsed since the making of the order; (ii) the debtor failed to make one or more of the payments due under the order; and (iii) the court was satisfied that the debtor's failure to make payments was due to the debtor's wilful refusal or culpable neglect: Attachment of Earnings Act 1971 s.3. The principle that default must first be established if an attachment order is to be made has been retained in respect of an order other than a maintenance order: Attachment of Earnings Act 1971 s.3, (3A).

[94] i.e. the person required to make the periodical payments, the person to whom those payments are to be made, and any other person who applied for the periodical payments order (e.g. the parent of a child): Maintenance Enforcement Act 1991 s.1(10), (2).

[95] Maintenance Enforcement Act 1991 s.1(3).

their family. To this end, it is provided[96] that the order shall specify two rates of deduction:

(1) The "normal deduction rate" is the rate at which the court thinks it reasonable for the debtor's earnings to be applied in meeting the liabilities under the order.[97] It is provided[98] that this is not to exceed the rate that appears to the court necessary for the purpose of meeting the payments under the order as they fall due, and payment within a reasonable period of any accrued arrears.

(2) The "protected earnings rate" is the rate below which, having regard to the debtor's resources and needs, the court thinks it reasonable that the earnings actually paid to them should not be reduced.[99] The expression "the debtor's needs" extends to the needs of any person for whom the debtor must, or reasonably may, provide.[100] The court will thus be able to consider the needs of the debtor's second spouse or of the debtor's cohabitant.

If, on any pay day, the debtor's attachable earnings[101] are equal to or less than the protected earnings, no deduction is to be made[102]; otherwise, the employer must[103] pay over a sum equal to the normal deduction[104] to the collecting officer of the court,[105] who must then pay the monies over to the creditor.[106]

---

[96] Attachment of Earnings Act 1971 s.6(5). In order that the court should be in possession of the information relevant to the exercise of these powers, the court may order the debtor to provide a signed statement giving: (i) the name and address of any person by whom earnings are paid; (ii) specified particulars as to the debtor's earnings and anticipated earnings, and resources and needs; (iii) specified particulars (such as a payroll number) for the purpose of enabling the debtor to be identified by an employer: s.14(1); and (iv) any person appearing to the court to have the debtor in their employment may be ordered to give a signed statement of the debtor's earnings and anticipated earnings: s.14(1)(b). If an attachment order has been made, the court may at any time order the debtor to provide the information set out above; it may also order the debtor to attend the court to give that information: s.14(2) as amended by Administration of Justice Act 1982 s.53.

[97] Attachment of Earnings Act 1971 s.6(5)(a).

[98] Attachment of Earnings Act 1971 s.6(6)(b), applied in *Billington v Billington* [1974] Fam. 24 (normal deduction rate fixed at £1.50, being £1 in respect of the weekly sum due under the order, and £0.50 in respect of outstanding arrears).

[99] Attachment of Earnings Act 1971 s.6(5)(b).

[100] Attachment of Earnings Act 1971 s.25(3).

[101] As defined in Sch.3, para.3, as amended.

[102] Attachment of Earnings Act 1971 Sch.3, para.6(4).

[103] The Act contains complex rules to cover the case where several attachment orders are in force against the same person: the basic principle is that orders rank for priority according to the date on which they were made, but maintenance orders and certain other orders (e.g. those made in respect of fines) are given priority as against simple judgment debts: Attachment of Earnings Act 1971 Sch.3 Pt II.

[104] Attachment of Earnings Act 1971 Sch.3 para.6(2). If the attachable earnings exceed the protected earnings but do not amount to the normal deduction, the employer will pay over the amount by which the protected earnings are exceeded, and the shortfall will in effect be carried forward and deducted from future attachable earnings: Attachment of Earnings Act 1971 Sch.3 para.6(3). The employer may also deduct and retain a prescribed sum (currently £1) towards the employer's administrative and clerical costs: s.7(4)(a); Attachment of Earnings (Employer's Deduction) Order 1991 (SI 1991/356).

[105] Attachment of Earnings Act 1971 s.6(1)(b). The term "collecting officer" is defined by s.6(7), and power has been taken (but not yet exercised) to remove this function from the courts in favour of other officers: s.6(9), as inserted by Courts and Legal Services Act 1990 s.125(2).

[106] Attachment of Earnings Act 1971 s.13.

The legislation leaves the fixing of the normal and protected earnings rates to the court's discretion[107]; it has been held that there is no rule of law under which the protected earnings rate must not be less than the appropriate income support scale rate,[108] and that there may be exceptional circumstances in which it would be appropriate to assess the debtor's needs at a lower figure.[109] However, the court may only take account of the debtor's actual earnings,[110] and it must not consider the potential earnings of the debtor in some other occupation.[111]

The attachment of earnings procedure is irrelevant in cases where the debtor **14-013** is either unemployed or self-employed.[112] The introduction of wage attachment had an immediate effect in reducing the number of persons imprisoned[113] for non-payment of maintenance orders.

Changes to existing legislation governing attachment of earnings orders are effected by Pt 4 of the Tribunals, Courts and Enforcement Act 2007.

ix. Registration in magistrates' court

The Maintenance Orders Act 1958 introduced a procedure whereby a periodical **14-014** payments order made by the county court or the High Court may[114] be registered in a magistrates' courts (and an order made by a magistrates' court may be registered in the High Court).[115] The main effects of registration are: first, that the order becomes enforceable in the court of registration as if it had originally been made by that court[116]; and secondly, that only the court of registration has power

---

[107] Compare the rigid formula for the assessment of support obligations under the Child Support Act 1991: see Ch.15, below.

[108] See Ch.6, above.

[109] For example, if the debtor is living with his parents: *Billington v Billington* [1974] Fam. 24.

[110] This expression is widely defined by Attachment of Earnings Act 1971, s.24(1) and extends to cover, for example, overtime pay and bonus payments (see *Billington v Billington* [1974] Fam. 24, at 30) as well as discretionary payments made by the trustees of a pension fund: *Edmonds v Edmonds* [1965] 1 W.L.R. 58. Certain categories of earnings (e.g. disablement pension and the pay of members of the Armed Forces) are not to be treated as earnings: s.24(2).

[111] *Pepper v Pepper* [1960] 1 W.L.R. 131 at 136.

[112] The court may, however, vary an order by redirecting it to any other person "who appears to have the debtor in his employment": Attachment of Earnings Act 1971 s.9(4) and the court can and should do this of its own motion if it has the necessary information: CCR, O.27 r.13; Lord Chancellor's Practice Direction (September 2, 1981), para.7. A debtor is required to notify the court whenever he or she changes their employment, and at the same time give particulars of their earnings, actual or anticipated; and a person who becomes the employer of the debtor, knowing that an attachment order has been made, and by what court, must notify the court that he or she is the employer, stating the debtor's actual and anticipated earnings: Attachment of Earnings Act 1971 s.15.

[113] In 1958 (before attachment was available), 4,910 maintenance defaulters were received in prison, and maintenance defaulters constituted 52% of all non-criminal prisoners; in 1961, 4,929 attachment orders were made, and the number of receptions into prison was only 2,867 (i.e. 30% of all non-criminal prisoners).

[114] The procedure is governed by Family Proceedings Rules 1991 (SI 1991/1247) rr.7.22–7.29. The court that made the order has a discretion whether to grant an application for registration: Maintenance Orders Act 1958 s.2(1); and it has been said that the general practice is that an interim order will not normally be registered and that even in the case of a final order it will usually be necessary to show some good reason for the application, for example, that there are arrears or that the benefit of the order has been diverted to the DSS under the procedure explained above: R. Bird, *Sweet & Maxwell's Family Law Manual*, p.439. Guidance has been issued: see *Notes for Guidance* (September 1985), issued by the Lord Chancellor's Department: para.11–022.

[115] Maintenance Orders Act 1958 s.1.

[116] Maintenance Orders Act 1958 s.1

to vary the order.[117] This is a popular enforcement route in cases of maintenance default. It appears that the efficient administrative procedure[118] available in the magistrates' courts for the collection of payments is the main factor influencing applications for registration since (as will be seen) the actual enforcement procedures available in respect of periodical payment orders[119] are not now notably different.

V. Magistrates' Court

A. Enforcement in the magistrates' court

14–015 A magistrates' court maintenance order[120] may be enforced by the following procedures[121]:

- distress;

- committal to prison;

- attachment of earnings; and

- fine for non-payment.

In addition, the Maintenance Enforcement Act 1991 empowered the court to make "means of payment" orders, under which payments are to be made by standing order or direct debit.[122]

i. Distress

14–016 A magistrates' court has power to issue[123] a warrant of distress for the purpose of levying a sum due under an order. Such a warrant[124] authorises the seizure[125]

---

[117] Maintenance Orders Act 1958 s.4(2); *Hackshaw v Hackshaw* [1999] 2 F.L.R. 876. It has been pointed out that the result of this provision is that the matrimonial jurisdiction of magistrates remains of greater significance than would appear from the number of financial applications originally made to magistrates under the Domestic Proceedings and Magistrates' Courts Act 1978 (see Ch.3, above): see C. Gibson [1982] Fam. Law 138–141.

[118] i.e. through the Clerk of the Court acting as Collecting Officer (see above).

[119] Procedures such as charging orders and garnishee orders have, of course, a part to play in the enforcement of capital orders.

[120] i.e. a maintenance order (as defined in Administration of Justice Act 1970, Sch.8) that has been made by or has been registered for enforcement in a magistrates' court: see Magistrates' Courts Act 1980 s.150.

[121] The court also has power to make a means of payment order under the Maintenance Enforcement Act 1991 in certain circumstances.

[122] Magistrates' Courts Act 1980 s.59(3)(c), as substituted by Maintenance Enforcement Act 1991 s.2. It appears that the magistrates lack the power given to the High Court and county courts by Maintenance Enforcement Act 1991 s.1(6) to order a maintenance debtor to open a bank account from which such payments may be made.

[123] There is power to postpone the issue of a warrant until such time and on such conditions as the court thinks just: Magistrates' Courts Act 1980 s.77(1) but once the warrant has been issued, the magistrates have no jurisdiction to suspend the operation of the warrant: *Crossland v Crossland* [1993] 1 F.L.R. 175.

[124] Issued under Magistrates' Courts Act 1980 s.76(1).

[125] The warrant is directed to the constables of the police area or others authorised: Magistrates' Courts Rules 1981 (SI 1981/1522) r.54(1)(b) and (c).

of money or goods[126] belonging to the debtor,[127] and goods seized are to be sold by public auction[128] if the sum due is not paid within six days. In 1974 the Finer Committee[129] said that the remedy had fallen into desuetude and recommended its abolition, but it is to be noted that distress continues to be the first option considered when a liability order is made in respect of a child support calculation.[130]

ii. Committal to prison[131]

It is provided[132] that where default is made in making payments due under an order,[133] the court may issue a warrant committing the defaulter to prison.[134] However, imprisonment is not to be ordered unless the court has inquired, in the presence of the defendant,[135] whether the default was due to the defendant's wilful refusal or culpable neglect,[136] and a committal order is not to be made in any case in which the court has power to make an attachment of earnings order or an order for payment by standing order, etc. if the court considers that it is appropriate to make such an order.[137] Even if the court has power to make a committal order, it has been said that the court will seek for methods of enforcing its orders that will avoid, where possible, the necessity to imprison a debtor

14–017

---

[126] The wearing apparel or bedding of the debtor or the debtor's family or the tools and implements of the debtor's trade up to a value of £150 are exempt from seizure: Magistrates' Court Rules 1981 (SI 1981/1522) r.54(4). Note that this exemption is considerably narrower in scope than that applicable when distress is levied under an order of the superior courts: see fn.41 above.

[127] Magistrates' Courts Rules 1981 (SI 1981/1552) r. 54(2). Subject to any direction to the contrary in the warrant, where the distress is levied on household goods, those goods are not without the written consent of the person concerned to be removed from the house until the day of sale, and in the meantime, the goods are marked and impounded: Magistrates' Courts Rules 1981 (SI 1981/1552) r.54(8).

[128] Or in such other manner as the debtor in writing allows.

[129] *Report of the Committee on One-Parent Families* (Cmnd.5629 (1974)), para.4.135.

[130] See Ch.15.

[131] For a historical survey, see the *Report of the Committee on One-Parent Families* (Cmnd.5629 (1974)), paras 4.135–4.139; see also O.R. McGregor, *Social History and Law Reform* (1981), Ch.5 ("The case of imprisonment for debt").

[132] Magistrates' Courts Act 1980 s.76.

[133] But proceedings cannot be started earlier than 15 days after the making of the order: Magistrates' Court Act 1980 s.93(2). Imprisonment cannot be ordered in respect of a failure to pay interest on arrears: Magistrates' Courts Act 1980 s.93(6)(c).

[134] Either when it has been established that the defaulter's money and goods are insufficient to satisfy a distress warrant, or instead of granting a distress warrant: Magistrates' Courts Act 1980 s.76(2). The term of imprisonment must be not less than five days, and the maximum (which depends on the amount of the arrears) must not exceed six weeks: Magistrates' Courts Act 1980 ss.76(3), 93(7), 132, and Sch.4 para.3. Imprisonment does not discharge the debtor from liability for the arrears (s.93(8)) but (unless the court otherwise directs) no arrears accrue whilst the defaulter is in custody, and he or she cannot be imprisoned twice for failure to pay the same sum: s.94.

[135] If the defendant fails to appear, a warrant for his or her arrest may be issued: Magistrates' Courts Act 1980 s.93(5).

[136] Magistrates' Courts Act 1980 s.93(6). These are words that "set the degree of blameworthiness . . . at a very high level. It is not just a matter of improvidence or dilatoriness. Something in the nature of a deliberate defiance or reckless disregard of the court's order is required": see *R. v Luton Magistrates' Court Ex p. Sullivan* [1992] 2 F.L.R. 196 at 197, *per* Waite J. But note also *R. v Cardiff Justices Ex p. Salter* [1986] 1 F.L.R. 162 (fact that debtor is on income support is not conclusive of the question of whether there is wilful default).

[137] Magistrates' Courts Act 1980 s.93(6)(b); and see *R v Birmingham Justices Ex p. Bennett* [1983] 1 W.L.R. 114 (distress should be resorted to in preference to imprisonment).

(particularly where there are children)[138]—the power to make a committal order is one of extreme severity that should be exercised sparingly and only as a last resort.[139] The court has power to fix a term of imprisonment but to postpone the issue of a warrant, subject to the defendant satisfying certain conditions[140] (e.g. that the arrears be paid off).[141] Although it is often claimed that the power to threaten imprisonment is effective in securing compliance with court orders, it can also be argued that the existence of a power to commit to prison for non-payment of maintenance in a society that long ago closed the Marshalsea prison and abandoned imprisonment as a primary remedy for the enforcement of civil debts is anomalous[142]; one view is that "imprisonment of maintenance defaulters ... is morally capricious, economically wasteful, socially harmful, administratively burdensome and juridically wrong".[143] For whatever reason, there has in recent years been a dramatic reduction in the number of persons serving sentences of imprisonment for non-payment of maintenance.

iii. Attachment of earnings

14–018 The procedure is similar to that already described in relation to the superior courts. It is not necessary that the debtor should be in default: as a result of amendments made by the Maintenance Enforcement Act 1991, a magistrates' court making a qualifying maintenance order[144] must exercise its powers relating to the method whereby payment is to be made, and these methods now include the making of an attachment of earnings order.[145] Moreover, the court may make an attachment order in proceedings for enforcement of a qualifying maintenance payment. It seems that the making of an attachment of earnings order is the most common outcome of enforcement action in the magistrates' court.

iv. Fine for non-payment

14–019 The Maintenance Enforcement Act 1991 provides that a debtor who fails to comply with a provision requiring payments to be made through the designated officer (formerly known as the "justices' clerk" and subsequently as the

---

[138] *Levermore v Levermore* [1979] 1 W.L.R. 1277 at 1278–1279, *per* Balcombe J.

[139] *R. v Luton Magistrates' Court Ex p. Sullivan* [1992] 2 F.L.R. 196; *R. v Slough Magistrates Court Ex p. Lindsay* [1997] 1 F.L.R. 695.

[140] Magistrates' Courts Act 1980 s.77(2); and see, for example, *Fowler v Fowler* (1981) F.L.R. 141.

[141] For example, £100 at the rate of £0.25 per week: *Pilcher v Pilcher (No.2)* [1965] 1 All E.R. 463.

[142] *per* Waite J.; *R. v Luton Magistrates' Court Ex p. Sullivan* [1992] 2 F.L.R. 196 at 201. The question whether the sanction should be retained divided the Committee on the Enforcement of Judgment Debts (The Payne Committee) (Cmnd.3909 (1969)), but the Finer Committee reached a strongly abolitionist conclusion.

[143] Views of the six members of the Committee on the Enforcement of Judgment Debts (The Payne Committee) (Cmnd.3909 (1969)) who favoured the abolition of imprisonment for maintenance defaulters: para.1099.

[144] As defined: Magistrates' Courts Act 1980 s.59(2).

[145] Magistrates' Courts Act 1980 s.59(1), (3)(d).

"justices' chief executive") or by standing order, etc., may be fined up to £1,000.[146]

VI. Restricting a Contemnor's Right to Participate in Proceedings

The court has a discretionary power of last resort where there is no other effective **14–020** method of compliance with a court order. It may restrict a party who is in contempt of an order from participating in proceedings (e.g. for variation) or may impose conditions upon their participation. The jurisdiction is to be exercised with proper consideration of the course of justice. The power is compliant with art.6 of the Convention for the Protection of Human Rights and Fundamental Freedoms 1950; under art.6(2), the conditions imposed must be proportionate to the legitimate aim of ensuring the proper course of justice. The power is not limited by arbitrary categorisations, such as the form of the original order that has not been complied with, or the size of the assets. These principles have been established in a line of authorities: namely, *Hadkinson v Hadkinson*,[147] *Mubarak v Mubarik*[148] and *Laing v Laing*.[149]

The jurisdiction is most commonly exercised in respect of an applicant, but may be exercised in respect of a respondent.[150]

[146] Magistrates' Courts Act 1980 s.59B.
[147] [1952] P. 285.
[148] [2004] 2 F.L.R. 932.
[149] [2007] 2 F.L.R. 199.
[150] *Mubarak v Mubarik* [2007] 1 F.L.R. 722.

PART IV

CHILD SUPPORT OBLIGATIONS

CHAPTER FIFTEEN

CHILD SUPPORT

I. INTRODUCTION.............................. 15–001
II. THE GENESIS, PASSAGE, CRITICISM AND SUBSEQUENT AMENDMENT OF THE CHILD SUPPORT ACT 1991 15–002
III. SUPPORT OBLIGATIONS: THE FORMULAIC APPROACH 15–005
    A. When does liability arise? 15–006
    B. Who is liable? 15–007
    C. Meeting the responsibility for maintaining a child 15–011
    D. Quantifying child support: the formulae 15–014
    E. Variations from the formula.......... 15–020
    F. Changes and appeals...................... 15–021
    G. Collection and enforcement........... 15–022

    H. Relevance of the child's welfare... 15–026
    I. The impact of child support payments 15–027
    J. Assessing the child support scheme 15–028
IV. CHILD MAINTENANCE: THE ROLE OF THE COURTS........................... 15–029
    A. Determining jurisdiction 15–030
    B. The courts' statutory powers 15–039
V. CAPITAL PROVISION FOR CHILDREN 15–042
    A. Orders for children in divorce or dissolution proceedings....................... 15–043
    B. Financial orders for children under the Children Act 1989 15–046
VI. CONCLUSION 15–053

I. INTRODUCTION

Child support raises "deeply complex issues of morality and social organisation".[1] Those issues include the respective responsibilities between individuals
and the state; which individuals (biological, legal or social parents) should be
held liable to provide for their children; and the priorities between first and
second families and between children and adult dependants.[2] Not surprisingly,
the law's response has varied over time according to the prevailing political,

15–001

---

[1] J. Eekelaar, *Regulating Divorce* (Oxford, Clarendon Press, 1986), p.91.
[2] For discussion of the ideological basis for imposing obligations on parents, see, for example, J.
Eekelaar, "Are parents morally obliged to support their children?" (1991) O.J.L.S. 340; S. Parker,
"Child support: rights and consequences" (1992) 6 I.J.L.F. 148; R. Bailey-Harris, "Child support: is
the right the wrong one?" (1992) 6 I.J.L.F 168; C. Barton and G. Douglas, *Law and Parenthood*
(London: Butterworths, 1995), pp.28–29; S. Altman, "A theory of child support" (2003) 17 I.J.L.P.F.
173; N. Wikeley, *Child Support: Law and Policy* (Oxford: Hart Publishing, 2006), Ch.1.

social and economic climate,[3] and different jurisdictions have devised different answers to these difficult issues.[4]

Historically the law did little to ensure that children were properly maintained by their parents, in part because of the reluctance to pierce the veil of privacy surrounding the family. It is true that the common law imposed on the father a duty to maintain his legitimate[5] children, but the duty was unenforceable.[6] The only effective[7] procedure for compelling fathers to provide for their children was through the agency of the poor law,[8] which required parents to reimburse the cost of providing relief for their offspring. However, financial orders were increasingly made available in divorce,[9] and legislation enacted in 1878[10] gave the magistrates' courts power to make separation orders and, in such cases, to grant custody to the mother and order maintenance for the child. As part of the divorce reform package of the early 1970s, the divorce courts'[11] powers were greatly extended, and orders could be made for financial provision and property adjustment in respect of children of the family.[12] Furthermore, the Matrimonial and Family Proceedings Act 1984[13] directed the court to give "first consideration" to the welfare, while a minor, of any child of the family who had not attained the age of 18 when considering whether and how to exercise those powers.

The way in which the courts have exercised those powers in relation to the adult parties has been reviewed in an earlier chapter. The key point for present purposes is that during the 1980s lawyers began to develop techniques to maximise the availability of welfare benefit support on divorce; the increasing

---

[3] J. Eekelaar and M. Maclean, *Maintenance After Divorce* (Oxford: Clarendon Press, 1986), pp.107 *et seq.*; J. Eekelaar, *Regulating Divorce* (Oxford, Clarendon Press, 1990), pp.103–111. For a comprehensive examination of the history of child support, see Wikeley, *Child Support: Law and Policy*, Chs 2–5.

[4] See, for example, L.J. Weitzman and M. Maclean (eds), *Economic Consequences of Divorce, The International Perspective* (Oxford: Clarendon Press, 1992), Pt IV; S. Parker, "Child support in Australia: children's rights or public interest?" (1991) 5 I.J.L.F. 24; J.T. Oldham, "Abating the feminization of poverty" (1994) 4 Brigham Young U.L.R. 841; Wikeley, *Child Support: Law and Policy*, Ch.6.

[5] There was no duty on a father at common law to maintain an illegitimate child, but the Poor Law Amendment Act 1844 gave the mother a right to obtain a maintenance order against the father that could remain in force until the child was 13.

[6] See, for example, N. Wikeley, "A duty but not a right: child support after R. (Kehoe) v Secretary of State for Work and Pensions" (2006) 18 C.F.L.Q. 287.

[7] At least in the sense of imposing a legal obligation accompanied by an enforcement mechanism, if not always in ensuring that maintenance was paid: see "History of the obligation to maintain" by M. Finer and O.R. McGregor, published as App.5 to the *Report of the Committee on One-Parent Families* (Cmnd.5629 (1974)), Table 2, p.104.

[8] The Statute of Elizabeth 1601 s.6 imposed penalties for failure to maintain, and the authorities would seek to reclaim expenditure incurred.

[9] Matrimonial Causes Act 1857 s.45 conferred a restricted power to order settlements for children of the marriage, and the courts' powers were extended over the years.

[10] Matrimonial Causes Act 1878.

[11] Under what is now the Matrimonial Causes Act 1973. The powers of magistrates' courts were extended by the Domestic Proceedings and Magistrates' Courts Act 1978 but remained comparatively restricted.

[12] The Family Law Reform Act 1987 gave comparable powers to make orders against parents and stepparents in proceedings instituted for that purpose, and those powers are now embodied in the Children Act 1989 Sch.1.

[13] See Matrimonial Causes Act 1973 s.25(1), as amended.

burden became difficult to sustain—particularly for the Thatcher Government in power at the time, committed as it was to reducing reliance on state provision. In addition, the system of court-ordered maintenance was seen to be slow, uncertain and inconsistent, with orders not being satisfactorily enforced. The position of children whose parents had never been married to each other was even worse, since the powers of the courts to award maintenance for such children was considerably more limited,[14] and the possibility of reallocating assets to the primary carer, irrespective of property rights, being non-existent.

At the start of the 1990s, therefore, a radical new approach to child support was mooted—one based on a universally applicable formula and administered by a dedicated government agency. Part II of this chapter will review how this new approach translated first into legislation and then into practice—and how it has proved necessary to revisit the issue on successive occasions. Part III outlines the key provisions of the current law, and how these are likely to change once the Child Maintenance and Other Payments Bill—currently being debated in Parliament—becomes law.[15] The focus then shifts to the residual jurisdiction of the court to make orders relating to maintenance and capital provision for children, in Parts IV and V respectively.

II. The Genesis, Passage, Criticism, and Subsequent Amendment of the Child Support Act 1991

The philosophy underpinning the changes advocated in the early 1990s[16] is easy **15–002** to state, even if it has proved difficult to bring into effect. The then Conservative Government[17] considered that parents had a clear moral duty to maintain their children until they were old enough to look after themselves; that although events might change the relationship between the parents, they could not change the parents' responsibilities towards their children.[18] The emphasis was thus on

---

[14] See R. Collins, "Upholding the nuclear family: a study of unmarried parents and domestic courts", in C. Marsh and S. Arber, *Families and Households* (London: Macmillan, 1992) on what were termed affiliation proceedings.

[15] The Bill is scheduled for its third and final reading in the House of Lords on June 2, 2008. References to the contents of the Bill are based on the latest version, HL Bill 57, as amended at the Report Stage.

[16] Described as the most far-reaching social reforms to be made for 40 years by the House of Commons Social Security Committee, *The Operation of the Child Support Act*, First Report, Session 1993–1994 HC 69.

[17] Under the forceful leadership of the Prime Minister, Margaret Thatcher, who subsequently wrote: "I was . . . appalled by the way in which men fathered a child and then absconded, leaving the single mother—and the taxpayer—to foot the bill for their irresponsibility and condemning the child to a lower standard of living. I thought it scandalous that only one in three children entitled to receive maintenance actually benefitted from regular payments. So—against considerable opposition from Tony Newton, the Social Security Secretary, and from the Lord Chancellor's department—I insisted that a new Child Support Agency be set up, and that maintenance be based not just on the cost of bringing up a child but on that child's right to share in its parents' rising living standards" (M. Thatcher, *The Downing Street Years* (London: HarperCollins, 1993), p.630).

[18] *Children Come First* (Cm.1263), foreword. See also the recent White Paper published by the DWP, *A New System of Child Maintenance* (Cm.6979 (2006)), para.1.7: "Relationships may end. Responsibilities do not."

individual responsibility wherever possible,[19] an approach that has persisted into the present century, a change of government notwithstanding.[20] And, despite the much-vaunted unpopularity of the scheme that was enacted, research suggests that this view of individual rather than collective responsibility has the approval of the wider public.[21] It is also consistent with international human rights instruments: the UN Convention on the Rights of the Child asserts the right of every child "to a standard of living adequate for the child's physical, mental, spiritual, moral and social development",[22] but goes on to attribute primary responsibility for providing this to "the parent(s) or others responsible for the child . . . within their abilities and financial capacities".[23]

The Child Support Act 1991 (which received all-party support[24]) was enacted in an attempt to give effect to the philosophy of individual responsibility. At one level, the objective was to change a culture "in which it had become common-place for maintenance to be regarded as optional and to ensure that regular and realistic maintenance was paid",[25] but there was also a second objective, which involved a major ideological shift. A corollary of the ideology of increased individual responsibility was a reduced role for the state in family matters. In the words of the House of Commons Social Security Committee,[26] the legislation "at long last challenged" what had become the common assumption (exemplified by the "welfare benefit divorce") that the state (or taxpayers) should assume financial responsibility for the first family when a marriage or partnership broke down. Henceforth, the obligation of the state was to be limited to providing assistance in genuine cases where the natural parents' resources were insufficient to support their children.

In addition, it was hoped that the new system would prove quicker, cheaper and more efficient, and that predictable and realistic levels of maintenance would be provided for all children.[27] To achieve these objectives, a fundamental change in technique was proposed. The case-by-case discretionary approach of the courts was to be supplanted by an administrative system that would assess all

---

[19] Contrast the ethos of collective responsibility that, some 15 years earlier, underpinned the *Report of the Committee on One-Parent Families* (Cmnd.5629 (1974)) (the "*Finer Report*"); see D. Burrows, "Anyone remember Finer?" [1998] Fam. Law 699. More recently it was proposed that further research be carried out into the possibility of guaranteed maintenance (Select Committee on Work and Pensions' Second Report, *The Performance of the Child Support Agency, 2004–5*, HC-44-I, para.152), but this did not find favour with the government at that time (*The Child Support Agency: Government Response to the Committee's 2nd Report of Session 2004–5*, HC 477, para.19).

[20] It should, however, be noted that state support for children has been increased since 1997: see Ch.6.

[21] See, for example, DWP, *A New System of Child Maintenance*, p.17; V. Peacey and L. Rainford, *Attitudes Towards Child Support and Knowledge of the Child Support Agency, 2004* (DWP Research Report No.226, 2004).

[22] UN Convention on the Rights of the Child art.27(1).

[23] UN Convention on the Rights of the Child art.27(2).

[24] And the approval of the House of Commons Social Security Committee: see HC 277–I (1990–1991) and HC 277–II.

[25] Mrs R. Hepplewhite, then Chief Executive of the Child Support Agency, introducing the Agency's 1993/4 Annual Report and 1994/5 Business Plan, *Child Support Agency, The First Two Years*, on July 4, 1994.

[26] House of Commons Social Security Committee, *The Operation of the Child Support Act*, First Report (Session 1993–4 HC 69), para.3.

[27] See *Children Come First* (Cm.1263), para.2.1.

maintenance according to uniform criteria. The Child Support Act 1991 therefore laid down a formula whereby the liability of parents in respect of their children's maintenance was to be met, and the Child Support Agency was established to calculate and enforce the appropriate level of maintenance according to that formula.

From the outset, the scheme proved deeply controversial and received **15–003** sustained criticism from the public,[28] the media[29] and professional[30] and official sources[31] alike. A comprehensive analysis of the criticisms lies beyond the scope of this chapter,[32] but they may be summarised as follows. First, the process of policy formation was deeply flawed: insufficient weight was given to the advice of those with knowledge of the working of the maintenance process on many of the problems inherent in the new system.[33] Secondly, the formula as originally conceived was over-complex and consequently difficult both to understand and to apply, with the result that there were long delays and inaccuracies in assessment. Moreover, the formula's rigidity was perceived as productive of injustice in individual cases, with lack of co-operation by parents and resulting damage to family relationships. Thirdly, the defects in the administration of the system led to the performance of the Child Support Agency being described as "a catastrophic administrative failure leading to the abandonment of many of the basic tenets of administrative justice".[34] The Government's confidence in improvements supposedly to be effected by managerial techniques and computer technology (as evidenced by the rhetoric of modern business management used

[28] R. Collier, "The campaign against the CSA" [1994] Fam. Law 384. Members of Parliament evidently received many complaints from constituents, and the Child Support Agency established a Parliamentary Business Unit expressly to deal with inquiries from Members of Parliament.
[29] The headline "Child agency blamed after man's suicide" was not untypical of the more restrained broadsheet coverage following the Act's implementation: *The Times*, December 7, 1993.
[30] Amongst the many commentaries, the following may be found particularly helpful: C.S. Gibson, "The future for maintenance" [1991] C.J.Q. 330; M. Maclean and J. Eekelaar, "Child support: the British solution" (1993) 7 I.J.L.F. 205; A. Garnham and E. Knights, *Putting the Treasury First* (London: CPAG, 1994); K Clarke, G. Craig and C. Glendinning, *Losing Support: Children and the Child Support Act* (London: The Children's Society, 1994); J. Millar, "Family obligations and social policy: the case of child support" (1996) 17 *Policy Studies* 181; G. Davis, N. Wikeley and R. Young, *Child Support in Action* (Oxford: Hart Publishing, 1998).
[31] For official reviews, see the Reports by House of Commons Social Security Committee: First Report Session 1993–4, *The Operation of the Child Support Act* (HC 69); Fifth Report Session 1993–4, *The Operation of the Child Support Act: Proposals for Change* (HC 470); and (on the administration of the scheme) Second Report from the House of Commons Social Security Committee Session 1995–6, *The Performance and Operation of the Child Support Agency* (HC 50); the Parliamentary Commissioner for Administration's Third Report Session 1994–5, *Investigation of Complaints Against the Child Support Agency* (HC 135) and the Parliamentary Commissioner for Administration's Third Report Session 1995–6, *Investigation of Complaints Against the Child Support Agency* (HC 20). See also M. Speed and J. Seddon *Child Support Agency: National Client Satisfaction Survey* (DSS Research Report No.39, HMSO 1994).
[32] For a detailed discussion, see Wikeley, *Child Support: Law and Policy*, pp.126–133.
[33] The Government promised consultation on the details of the scheme in its original form (much of which was left to delegated legislation), and around 100 organisations responded to a 158-page consultation document issued on November 1, 1991. However, neither the submissions nor even a summary was published, nor was any request made by the DSS for further details or clarification of the scheme (see Gamham and Knights, *Putting the Treasury First*, p.47); and there was little evidence that the Government had given serious consideration to the problems that the judiciary and practising lawyers had highlighted: see R. Bird, *Child Maintenance, The Child Support Act 1991*, 2nd edn (Bristol: Family Law, 1993), para.2.11.
[34] Davis et al., *Child Support in Action*, p.v.

in glossily produced successive Green and White Papers) proved to be sadly misplaced. The administrative machinery was wholly inadequate for the efficient introduction and sustaining of a scheme so ambitious in its original conception, and the Child Support Agency proved increasingly unable to cope with its intended caseload.

The result was that the aim of achieving universality for the new system was shelved, and its operation was increasingly confined to cases where the parent in care was in receipt of welfare benefits. Those who were not obliged to use the system sidestepped it[35]; non-benefit cases continued to use the courts to settle child maintenance, and the interface between the two jurisdictions accordingly proved complex. Amongst those on benefits, many single mothers refused to co-operate with the Agency; therefore, liable fathers were not identified and maintenance was not, in practice, collected, and many children in need failed to see increased levels of financial support. Where maintenance was collected by the Child Support Agency, families in receipt of means-tested benefits were no better off, due to the fact that any money received by way of child support resulted in a pound-for-pound deduction from such benefits.[36] This in turn removed the incentive to comply with the system. Hence the creation of the Child Support Agency had a claim to be regarded as the worst failure of public administration in this country in the twentieth century.

The response of successive governments to sustained criticisms of the child support system has been two-fold. On the one hand, there has been a continuing and consistent assertion that the basic principles underlying the child support system are right, and that a formulaic approach to the determination of child support is appropriate. On the other hand, changes of an increasingly substantial nature have been made to the details of the system's operation. As early as 1995 there were a series of climb-downs as embarrassing for the Government as they were confusing for professional advisers and for the public.[37] These not only resulted in additional elements being included in the already complex formula[38] but also led to an element of discretion being grafted on to the formula in the guise of the "departure system".[39] Following its election victory in May 1997, the Blair Government showed itself eager to make its mark on reform of the child support system, and embarked upon a process of consultation.[40] The resulting Child Support, Pensions and Social Security Act 2000 made more radical reforms to the system, simplifying the formula and introducing a "child maintenance premium" so that those in receipt of benefit would receive some tangible benefit from the payment of child support. It was envisaged that these

---

[35] S. Deas, "Family lawyers sidestep the CSA" [1998] Fam. Law 48.

[36] Davis et al., *Child Support in Action*, pp.220–201.

[37] See *Improving Child Support* (Cm.2745).

[38] Child Support and Income Support (Amendment) Regulations 1995 (SI 1995/1045).

[39] Child Support Act 1995. The grounds for departure were strictly confined, and in practice the system was little used: see J. Priest, "Departure directions under the child support scheme" (1998) 5 *Journal of Social Security Law* 104. On the discretionary element in the current scheme see the discussion of variations, para.15–020 below.

[40] *Children First: A New Approach to Child Support* (Cm.3992) (DSS, The Stationery Office, 1998); *A New Contract for Welfare: Children's Rights and Parents Responsibilities* (Cm.4349) (DSS, The Stationery Office, 1999).

changes would apply initially only to new cases but would gradually be extended to the entirety of the Agency's caseload. In the event, this proved too difficult to achieve,[41] and the old scheme continued to apply to all cases commencing before March 3, 2003.

At the time of writing, therefore, there are two child support schemes currently **15–004** in operation[42]: the old scheme, governed by the Child Support Act 1991 as amended by the Child Support Act 1995, and the revised scheme, governed by the Child Support Act 1991 as amended by the Child Support, Pensions and Social Security Act 2000; in the words of Wikeley, "in 2007 . . . the Government presided over not just one but two failing child support systems".[43] By the time of publication it is likely that a third variation (currently before Parliament as the Child Maintenance and Other Payments Bill) will also be on the statute book; this too makes amendments to the original 1991 Act. As with earlier reform initiatives, this was preceded by an analysis of what had gone wrong with previous attempts[44] and the publication of a number of papers with upbeat titles promising change.[45] The new Bill attempts to distance itself from previous initiatives by providing that a new body, the Child Maintenance and Enforcement Commission,[46] will assume responsibility for what is now to be termed "child maintenance".[47] A further fundamental change relates to the purpose of the system: ending child poverty, rather than recouping expenditure for the Treasury, takes centre stage.[48] Parents' responsibility to provide for their children is still asserted,[49] but in low income cases any maintenance paid by parents will be in addition to, rather than instead of, state provision.

However, despite the Government's insistence that its new proposals will represent a clean break with the past,[50] there are important continuities between

[41] A major reason for this was problems with the Agency's new IT system: see Wikeley, *Child Support: Law and Policy*, pp.140–143.

[42] Indeed, it is only as of March 2008 that the number of cases under the new scheme has equalled the number of cases on the old scheme: see DWP, *Child Support Agency Quarterly Statistics* (March 2008), Table 1.

[43] N. Wikeley, "Child support reform—throwing the baby out with the bathwater?" [2007] 19 C.F.L.Q. 434 at p.435.

[44] Sir David Henshaw's report to the Secretary of State for Welfare and Pensions, *Recovering Child Support: Routes to Responsibility* (Cm.6894 (2006)), identified policy problems, operational problems and legacy issues as contributing to the failure of the current system. See further N. Wikeley, "Child support—back to the drawing board" [2006] Fam. Law 312; C. Barton, "Child support and politicians" [2006] Fam. Law 701.

[45] DWP, *A Fresh Start: Child Support Redesign—The Government's Response to Sir David Henshaw* (Cm.6895 (2006)); *A new system of child maintenance* (Cm.6979 (2006)).

[46] This will take the form of a non-governmental public body rather than an executive agency. However, the transfer of property, rights and liabilities under the Bill may suggest that the change amounts to no more than, as one MP suggested, "unscrewing the CSA nameplate from the front of its building and replacing it with one saying 'Child Maintenance and Enforcement Commission'": *Hansard*, HC, Vol.462, col.997 (July 4, 2007) (Chris Grayling MP).

[47] Child Maintenance and Other Payments Bill 2007, HL Bill 57, cl.12. The reason for so doing, as the *Henshaw Report* made clear, was that the "Child Support Agency brand is severely damaged": *Recovering Child Support: Routes to Responsibility*, p.33.

[48] *A New System of Child Maintenance*, p.18. See also DCSF, DWP and HM Treasury, *Ending Child Poverty: everybody's business* (2008), para.5.13, and note the claim by the then Secretary of State for Work and Pensions, Peter Hain MP, that the Bill "makes tacking child poverty the No.1 priority for the child maintenance system": *Hansard*, HC Vol.462, col.981 (July 4, 2007).

[49] *A New System of Child Maintenance*, p.31.

[50] See, for example, *A New System of Child Maintenance*, p.17.

the 2007 Bill and earlier initiatives. Nor it is envisaged that the new scheme will immediately replace those already in place; according to the expected timetable, new applications will not be accepted until 2010–11, and it is not until 2012–13 that "all clients will be on a single set of rules managed by a single organization".[51] It would therefore be inappropriate to dismiss the existing law—whether the original rules or the revisions enacted in 2000—as irrelevant.

For this reason, rather than descending into the detail of the past, present and future systems of child support or maintenance, this chapter will focus on the policy and principles underlying the formulaic approach adopted since 1993 when the original Child Support Act came into force, identifying the key policy shifts that have occurred over the past 15 years.

III. Support Obligations: The Formulaic Approach

15–005   There are a number of key issues that pervade the system of child support in all its various incarnations: When does liability to pay child support arise?; Who is liable to provide such support?; How does the law envisage individuals meeting their responsibility to provide child support and how is the quantum of support calculated?; What scope is there for the circumstances of any individual case to be taken into account, and how is liability to be enforced if the person liable is reluctant to pay? The answers to some of these questions have remained more or less constant throughout the different versions of the formulaic approach first adopted by the Child Support Act 1991; others have seen more significant changes as policies have shifted.

A. When does liability arise?

15–006   The first point to note is that the legal duty of support is not an open-ended one. For the purposes of the statutory scheme, a "child" is a person under the age of 16,[52] although in certain prescribed circumstances those over that age may be regarded as children,[53] and the current trend of legal policy is to elongate the period for which those on the verge of adulthood may be so described.[54]

The second basic point to note is that the statutory scheme is concerned with the situation in which a family relationship has broken down (or has never come

---

[51] *A New System of Child Maintenance*, p.55.

[52] Child Support Act 1991 s.55(1)(a).

[53] See Child Support (Maintenance Assessment Procedure) Regulations 1992 (SI 1992/1813 Sch.1) on the conditions that had to be satisfied under the original scheme if persons aged 16 to 18 are to be regarded as children, and for discussion, see Wikeley, *Child Support: Law and Policy*, pp.217–223.

[54] See Child Maintenance and Other Payments Bill 2007, HL Bill 57, cl.42, amending C.S.A. 1991 s.55 and extending the definition of "child" to all those under the age of 20 who meet certain prescribed conditions and have neither married nor entered into a civil partnership. The extension is intended to bring the definition of a child in this area of law into line with that used in the context of child benefit, from which it has diverged since the passage of the Child Benefit Act 2005: see *A New System of Child Maintenance*, para.4.28.

into existence). This reflects the traditional pattern of English law, which is to refuse to interfere in determining how a functioning family unit should allocate its resources. The Act is not concerned in defining the level of support appropriate to a child living under the same roof with the parents; that is, when a family is intact.[55]

Thus a child will only be regarded as a "qualifying child" if he or she is living with "a person with care" in a different household from one or both parents; such parents are described as "non-resident".[56] Explication of the terms involved in this triangular relationship is not assisted by the fact that each depends to some extent on the others. A child is only a "qualifying child" if one or both parents is non-resident,[57] while a parent is only "non-resident" if he or she[58] is not living in the same household as the child and the child's home is with a "person with care".[59] The latter need not be a parent (raising the possibility that the child may have *two* non-resident parents), but institutional carers, such as a local authority, are excluded from the definition.[60] It should also be noted that the starkness of the distinction between "person with care" and "non-resident parent" will not always reflect the facts of the case: the person with care will always be the child's primary carer,[61] but the non-resident parent may well be a subsidiary carer. The language of "person with care" and "non-resident parent" is applied irrespective of whether the child was the product of a one-night stand who has never met the other parent, or whether care of the child is shared between the parents.[62]

B. Who is liable?

The underlying principle is that each parent of a qualifying child is responsible   **15–007**
for maintaining the child.[63] Parenthood for this purpose includes any person who is, in law, the mother or father of the child[64]; adoptive parents and any person

---

[55] Note too that the child has no right to apply for support, nor indeed any right to support: see *R. (Kehoe) v Secretary of State for Work and Pensions* [2005] UKHL 48, and note the commentary by N. Wikeley, "A duty but not a right: child support after R. (Kehoe) v Secretary of State for Work and Pensions" [2006] 18 C.F.L.Q. 287.

[56] The initial scheme used the terminology of the "absent parent", but this was criticised for its pejorative overtones (see, e.g. Second Report from the House of Commons Social Security Committee Session 1995–6, *The Performance and Operation of the Child Support Agency* (HC 50), para.54), and the Child Support, Pensions and Social Security Act 2000 accordingly introduced the terminology of the "non-resident parent".

[57] Child Support Act 1991 s.3(1).

[58] Usually he: within the caseload of the Child Support Agency, 94% of non-resident parents are male (DWP, *Child Support Agency Quarterly Statistics* (March 2008), Table 24).

[59] Child Support Act 1991 s.3(2).

[60] Child Support Act 1991 s.3(3)(c) excludes categories of person prescribed by delegated legislation (see the Child Support (Maintenance Calculation Procedure) Regulations 2001 (SI 2001/157) reg.21(1); Child Support (Maintenance Assessment Procedure) Regulations 1991 (SI 1992/1813) reg.51: these are local authorities and people (other than parents) with whom a child has been placed by a local authority. No child support maintenance is payable in such cases.

[61] A "person with care" is defined as the person "with whom the child has his home" and "who usually provides day to day care for the child (whether exclusively or in conjunction with any other person)": Child Support Act 1991 s.3(3).

[62] In cases of shared care, the non-resident parent will be the parent who provides less care for the child or, if care is shared equally, who is not in receipt of child benefit for that child: see Child Support (Maintenance Calculations and Special Cases) Regulations 2000 (SI 2001/155) r.8.

[63] Child Support Act 1991 s.1(1).

[64] Child Support Act 1991 s.54.

treated as a child's parent under the Human Fertilisation and Embryology Act 1990 are therefore within its scope.[65] The nature or even the existence of a relationship between the parents is irrelevant to the coming into existence of the child support obligation, as is that between the parent and child[66]; liability arises from procreation, not nurture.[67] Thus, liability under the Child Support Act 1991 arises even where the relationship between the parents was brief and the non-resident parent has no effective contact with the child.[68]

The scheme is therefore based on the principle that children should look primarily to their natural parents (actual or presumed) for support.[69] The question of who is under a duty to provide support for a particular child is distinct from the question as to who has parental responsibility for that child; it is not necessary for a parent to enjoy parental responsibility in order to be liable, and a non-parent may have parental responsibility without incurring liability under the scheme.[70] This is not to say that social parents have no financial obligations to children who have been in their care, but these are dealt with by the courts.[71]

Of course, the apparent simplicity of imposing liability on legal parents conceals some difficult questions, including the practical issue of proof. In addition, some legal parents may fall outside the jurisdiction of the scheme because they are not resident in the United Kingdom.

i. Proof of parentage

15–008 For obvious reasons, maternity is almost never in question, but disputes as to paternity are not uncommon. The Act provides that no maintenance calculation may be made against a person who denies that he is one of the child's parents, unless the case falls into certain defined categories.[72] Where it does so fall, the calculation will be made despite a denial of paternity: in other words, parentage is assumed, and child support can be calculated forthwith.[73] Some of the categories simply reflect the fact that legal parenthood does not always overlap with biological parentage (e.g. those relating to adoptive parents and those who

---

[65] Human Fertilisation and Embryology Act 1990 ss.27, 28, and see further Ch.17.

[66] Although it is likely to be highly relevant to whether payment is actually made: research has demonstrated a relationship in practice between contact and the payment of child maintenance: see, generally, M. Maclean and J. Eekelaar, *The Parental Obligation* (Oxford: Clarendon Press, 1997). In addition, disputes over contact are often linked to disputes over child support: see C. Smart et al., *Research and Contact Disputes in Court: Volume 1* (DCA Research Series No.6/03, 2003), pp.81–85.

[67] See S. Sheldon, "Unwilling fathers and abortion: terminating men's child support obligations" (2003) 66 M.L.R. 175 for a discussion of the justifications for imposing liability.

[68] However, staying contact will, above a certain threshold, affect the quantum of child support payable: see below, para.15–017.

[69] See *Children Come First* (Cm.1263), paras 3.16–3.17; Department for Work and Pensions, *A New System of Child Maintenance*, para.1.12.

[70] See further, N. Wikeley, "Financial support for children after parental separation: parental responsibility and responsible parenting", in R. Probert, S. Gilmore and J. Herring, *Responsible Parents and Parental Responsibility* (Oxford: Hart Publishing, 2009, forthcoming).

[71] For example, under the Matrimonial Causes Act 1973, the Domestic Proceedings and Magistrates' Courts Act 1978 Pt 1, and the Children Act 1989 Sch.1. See further below, at para.15–043.

[72] Child Support Act 1991 s.26(1).

[73] Child Support Act 1991 s.26(2). The categories were expanded by Child Support, Pensions and Social Security Act 2000. See N. Wikeley, "Child support, paternity and parentage" [2001] Fam. Law 125, and *Child Support: Law and Policy*, pp.226–233.

are regarded as parents by virtue of the Human Fertilisation and Embryology Act 1990).[74] Others reflect the presumptions that have long operated when determining parentage, assuming parentage where the man in question was married to the child's mother between conception and birth, was registered as the father on the birth certificate[75] or has been adjudged to be the child's father in earlier court proceedings.[76] Parentage will also be assumed where the alleged parent has refused to take a scientific test[77] or has taken such a test but refuses to accept its result, and where a formal declaration of parentage has been made by the courts.[78]

In cases involving disputed parentage that do not fall into any of the above categories, the Secretary of State or the person with care may apply to the court for a declaration under s.55A of the Family Law Act 1986 as to whether or not the alleged parent is one of the child's parents.[79] The court has power to direct (but not to order) that scientific tests be undertaken.[80] A refusal by the alleged parent to submit to such tests will almost inevitably give rise to the inference that he is in fact the child's father.[81] In the case of a child, either the person with care and control may consent to a sample being taken, or, where that parent objects, the court may do so if it considers that it is in the child's best interests.[82]

ii. Misattributed parentage

It is, of course, possible that a man who does not dispute parentage, and who pays child support in the belief that he is the father of the child in question, will discover at a later date that his belief was mistaken. Studies on the extent of misattributed paternity have suggested figures ranging from 0.8 per cent to 30 per cent; however, it has been pointed out that the higher rates derive from test groups who had actually undergone paternity testing, who presumably had some

15–009

---

[74] See Human Fertilisation and Embryology Act 1990 ss.27, 28 (definition of mother/father), 30 (parental orders).

[75] In the context of child support, this assumption dates only to the Child Support, Pensions and Social Security Act 2000. It was suggested that this might lead to a decrease in the number of men permitting their name to be registered on the birth certificate of children born outside marriage: Sharp, "Parental responsibility—where next?" [2001] Fam. Law 607. However, this has not proved to be the case.

[76] See further Ch.17

[77] As defined by Child Support Act 1991 s.27A(4).

[78] Under Family Law Act 1986 s.55A, replacing s.56 of that Act.

[79] Provision for this, and issues of standing, are dealt with by Child Support Act 1991 ss.27, 27(1A).

[80] Family Law Reform Act 1969 s.20. Provision is made for the recovery of the costs incurred by the Secretary of State in relation to scientific tests from the alleged parent if parentage is established: Child Support Act 1991 s.27A, as substituted by Child Support, Pensions and Social Security Act 2000 s.1(2) Sch.3 para.11(9).

[81] *Re A (A Minor) (Paternity: Refusal of Blood Test)* [1994] 2 F.L.R. 463; *Re H (Paternity: Blood Test)* [1996] 2 F.L.R. 65; *F v Child Support Agency* [1999] 2 F.L.R. 244; *Secretary of State for Work and Pensions v Jones* [2003] EWHC (Fam).

[82] Family Law Reform Act s.21(3), as amended by Child Support, Pensions and Social Security Act 2000 s.82(3): see Wikeley "Child support, paternity and parentage" [2001] Fam. Law 125 at 126–127. The power to order a blood test in a child's best interests was exercised in *Re T (Paternity: Ordering Blood Tests)* [2001] 2 F.L.R. 1190, in which Bodey J. weighed the child's interests against competing adult interests under art.8 of the ECHR.

suspicions as to their paternity.[83] The true figure is suggested, on a review of a number of studies, to be closer to 4 per cent.[84] Given that the caseload of the Child Support Agency is over one million, even this lower figure suggests that there may be a considerable number of cases in which non-fathers are paying child support.

Is there any provision for payments of child support to be reimbursed once the truth is discovered in such a case? The Child Support Act 1991 does give the Secretary of State the power to reimburse overpayments of child support to a non-resident parent, and there are examples of this being done,[85] but it has been questioned whether this encompasses the power to reimburse someone who is not a parent at all.[86] Should a court construe the statute narrowly to exclude this option, it is possible that the tort of deceit may offer an alternative remedy.[87]

iii. Lack of jurisdiction where parent is not habitually resident

15–010   Jurisdiction to make a maintenance calculation is confined to cases in which the non-resident parent[88] is habitually resident in the United Kingdom or is not so habitually resident but is a member of the British civil service, naval, military or air forces, or an employee of certain prescribed companies or bodies, working overseas.[89]

The Child Support Act 1991 does not itself define "habitual residence", but there is ample authority on its interpretation elsewhere in the family law context.[90] It has been held[91] (in the context of jurisdiction for divorce proceedings[92]) that a person may be habitually resident in two countries at the same time.

C. Meeting the responsibility for maintaining a child

15–011   Each parent of a qualifying child is responsible for maintaining the child.[93] It is assumed, however, that the parent with whom the child has their principal home

---

[83] M.A. Bellis et al., "Measuring paternal discrepancy and its public health consequence" (2005) 59 *Journal of Epidemiology and Community Health* 749.

[84] M.A. Bellis et al., "Measuring paternal discrepancy and its public health consequence" (2005) 59 *Journal of Epidemiology and Community Health* 749.

[85] Wikeley, *Child Support: Law and Policy*, p.236.

[86] N. Wikeley and L. Young, "Secrets and lies: no deceit down under for paternity fraud" [2008] 20 C.F.L.Q. 81 at p.90.

[87] See, for example, *P v B (Paternity: damages for Deceit)* [2001] 1 F.L.R. 1041; *A v B (Damages: Paternity)* [2007] 2 F.L.R. 1051. The cases concerned expenditure during the relationship, but the principle would apply with greater force to child support paid purely on the basis of assumed paternity.

[88] And the person with care and the qualifying child.

[89] Child Support Act 1991, as amended, s.44(1), (2A). For the prescribed bodies, see the Child Support (Maintenance Arrangements and Jurisdiction) Regulations 1992 (SI 1992/2645), as amended by the Child Support (Information, Evidence, Disclosure and Maintenance Arrangements and Jurisdiction) (Amendment) Regulations 2000 (SI 2000/161).

[90] *R. v Barnet LBC Ex p. Shah* [1983] 2 A.C. 309; *Re J (A Minor) (Abduction: Custody Rights)* [1990] 2 A.C. 562; *Cruse v Chittum* [1974] 2 All E.R. 940; *Re M (Minors) (Residence Order: Jurisdiction)* [1993] 1 F.L.R. 495; see S.M. Cretney (1993) 109 L.Q.R. 538.

[91] *Ikimi v Ikimi* [2001] 2 F.L.R. 1288.

[92] Domicile and Matrimonial Proceedings Act 1973.

[93] Child Support Act 1991 s.1(1).

is fulfiling that responsibility by dint of his or her care for the child; by contrast, non-resident parents fulfil their responsibility by making periodical payments of maintenance with respect to the child in accordance with the provisions of the scheme.[94] The legislation imposes a duty to make such payments on a non-resident parent in respect of whom a maintenance calculation has been made.[95]

It is important to understand that the obligation to make payments under the statutory scheme only arises on the making of a maintenance calculation, and such a calculation will only be made where an application is made.[96] Is it possible for parents to choose not to apply and to make their own arrangements? The answer is that some parents have always been able to opt out of the scheme, but that private ordering is far more central to the Child Maintenance and Other Payments Bill than to earlier versions of the scheme. In particular, the Bill eliminates the distinction—fundamental under the original scheme—between those who are in receipt of means-tested benefits and those who are not. The question also arises as to whether those who have made their own arrangements by means of a consent order will be able to make an application under the statutory scheme. These two issues will be considered in turn.

i. Parents in receipt of benefits

The original Child Support Act 1991 drew a sharp distinction between those **15–012** parents who were in receipt of benefits and those who were not. The former had little scope to make their own arrangements. A person with care of the qualifying child who was receiving, or had claimed,[97] certain means-tested benefits was required to apply for child support, and after March 2003[98] was treated as having so applied. Those who failed to provide the information necessary to trace the non-resident parent might face a reduced benefit direction, unless the Secretary of State was satisfied that there were reasonable grounds for believing that there would be a risk of the parent with care, or any child living with him or her, "suffering harm or undue distress" as a result of them taking such action.[99] Any existing arrangements between the parents, whether made by consent or with the assistance of the court, were overturned.

This, as the Government somewhat belatedly acknowledged, was "not what parents want from the child maintenance system".[100] Following the recommendations of the Henshaw Report, it was decided that there should be a greater

---

[94] Child Support Act 1991 s.1(2), as amended by Child Support, Pensons and Social Security Act 2000 s.1(2) Sch.3 para.11(2).
[95] Child Support Act 1991 s.1(3).
[96] Child Support Act 1991 s.4(1).
[97] The claim, not the calculation, brings s.6 into operation: *Secretary of State for Social Security v Harmon; Secretary of State for Social Security v Carter; Secretary of State for Social Security v Cocks* [1998] 2 F.L.R. 598.
[98] Following the amendments made by the Child Support, Pensions and Social Security Act 2000.
[99] Child Support Act s.46(3). See, for example, *Secretary of State for Work and Pensions v Roach* [2006] EWCA Civ 1746.
[100] Department for Work and Pensions, *A New System of Child Maintenance*, para.2.5.

emphasis on private ordering: those who did not wish to use the system would not be required to do so. The Child Maintenance and Other Payments Bill accordingly sets out to repeal s.6 of the Child Support Act.[101] This, as one commentator has noted, is a "virtual abandonment of one of the Child Support Agency's core rationales".[102]

In a further reversal of policy, the Child Maintenance and Other Payments Bill also removes the possibility for the state to recover expenditure on a child (e.g. in the form of Income Support) from a liable relative.[103] The result, as Wikeley has noted, is that:

"[I]f the parent with care elects for the quiet life, that will be the end of the matter. The taxpayer will be providing open-ended means-tested support."[104]

ii. Parents with a court order in place

15–013 The scheme, as initially enacted, provided that parents were entitled to enter into their own maintenance agreements, and the jurisdiction of the Child Support Agency could be excluded by the existence of a consent order. In 2003 this rule was modified so that the exclusive jurisdiction of the courts would end 12 months after the making of the consent order; after this period, either party could apply to the Child Support Agency for a child maintenance calculation.[105] The rationale for this change was that parents with court orders should be able to turn to the Agency if they so wished, in the shadow of which private child-maintenance arrangements should henceforth be made.[106] Despite criticism and recommendations for reform,[107] the 12-month rule has been retained in the new system on the ground that "it ensures maintenance is generally set at a substantial level that broadly reflects the child maintenance formula".[108]

---

[101] Child Maintenance and Other Payments Bill 2007, HL Bill 57, cl.15.

[102] See P. Parkinson, "Reengineering the child support system: an Australian perspective on the British government's proposals" (2007) 70 M.L.R. 812, at p.817.

[103] Child Maintenance and Other Payments Bill 2007, HL Bill 57, cl.45, amending s.105 of the Social Security Administration Act 1992.

[104] N. Wikeley, "The strange demise of the liable relative rule" [2008] Fam. Law 52 at p.55. However, just as this book was going to press, the Government announced that its Welfare Reform Bill, to be introduced in the 2008–2009 session, would include measures "to strengthen the requirements of non-resident parents to contribute to their children's upbringing, as part of a package which champions personal responsibility in the welfare system". This would appear to run counter to the changes contained in the 2007 Bill.

[105] Child Support Act 1991 s.4(1)(aa), as inserted by Child Support, Pensions and Social Security Act 2000 s.2(3).

[106] *Children's Rights and Parents' Responsibilities*, Ch.8, paras 23–25.

[107] *Recovering Child Support: Routes to Responsibility*, p.27; see also K. Fellowes, "The CSA—out with the old, in with the new?" [2006] Fam. Law 892.

[108] Department for Work and Pensions, *A New System of Child Maintenance*, para.2.36. See also DWP, *Report on the Child Maintenance White Paper* A new system of child maintenance: *Reply by the Government to the Fourth Report of the Work and Pensions Select Committee: Child Support Reform, Session 2006–07* (Cm.7062 (2007)), para.8.1.

D. Quantifying child support: the formulae

In principle, there are a number of possible theoretical models[109] available for **15–014** determining the *quantum* of parental child support, of which the two most straightforward are cost-sharing and resource-sharing. The cost-sharing model raises the question of whether the relevant cost is that of the hypothetical "average" child in the community, or is to be determined according to the income bracket of the family in question. The resource-sharing model looks to the standard of living the child could have expected had the family remained intact. The original formula of the Child Support Act 1991 appeared to adopt the cost-sharing model, albeit with child support costs calculated at a minimal basic level closely tied to benefit rates.[110] The revised formula introduced in 2003 followed, in part, a resource-sharing model, although certain details of the scheme seemed inconsistent with a pure version of that model. The new scheme, as proposed in the Child Maintenance and Other Payments Bill, adopts the same model, with some variations.

i. The original formula

The complexity of the original formula was designed to achieve universality of **15–015** application but was itself one of the major sources of criticism of the scheme.[111] A High Court judge described it as a "series of mathematically obtuse calculations in innumerable unintelligible Schedules to the Act".[112] The reader will no doubt be relieved that it is not proposed to deal in detail with the mode of calculating liability.[113] However, for the purposes of comparison it is useful to highlight certain key features of the scheme. First, the income of *each* parent was taken into account in calculating how much was payable as child support, a sum termed the "maintenance requirement".[114] Secondly, the amount needed for any given child's support was calculated by reference to the benefit rates payable to parents in respect of children in his care.[115] However, the scheme did also reflect the principle that children should share in the standard of living enjoyed by both parents: if the non-resident parent's available income exceeded the maintenance requirement, an additional element was payable.[116] Conversely, even the poorest of parents were expected to pay *something*: although some parents received a nil

---

[109] Discussed in Eekelaar and Maclean, *Maintenance after Divorce*, pp.37 *et seq.*; J. Eekelaar, *Regulating Divorce*, pp.104–111; Wikeley, *Child Support: Law and Policy*, pp.21–27.

[110] Eekelaar, *Regulating Divorce*, pp.116–117.

[111] See, in particular G. Davis et al., *Child Support in Action* (Oxford: Hart Publishing, 1998); *Children's Rights and Parents' Responsibilities*, Ch.1, paras 4–8.

[112] *Re C (A Minor) (Contribution Notice)* [1994] 1 F.L.R. 111, *per* Ward J. at 117.

[113] For a detailed account, see the sixth edition of this book at pp.512–520, and R. Bird, *Child Maintenance*, 3rd edn (Bristol: Family Law, 1996).

[114] The so-called "assessable income" was calculated by subtracting the parent's "exempt income" (which took account, inter alia, of a personal expenditure allowance at income support level, reasonable housing costs subject to a ceiling fixed by regulation, an allowance for any biological children in the household, significant travel-to-work costs and an allowance for property transfer made prior to April 1993) from his or her net income.

[115] This calculation took into account a number of elements, including the income support payable in respect of a child, the carer's personal allowance and family/lone parent premiums.

[116] Child Support Act 1991 prior to amendment by the Child Support, Pensions and Social Security Act 2000 Sch.1 para.2(3)(b).

assessment, parents who were themselves dependent on Income Support were required to pay a small sum. Finally, little account was taken of the parent's support for other children living in the same household.[117] The Government apparently believed that to make any such allowance would be to put step-children's interests before those of natural children.[118] This approach had the merit of logical consistency but was inconsistent with the recognition increasingly given to factual as distinct from status relationships, and created real difficulties in practice.[119] One commentator observed[120] that to demand that money should "follow blood rather than affective ties" was a considerable culture shock.

ii. The revised formula

15–016 The 1999 White Paper *A New Contract for Welfare: Children's Rights and Parents' Responsibilities*[121] was highly critical of the formula's complexity, and at the same time full of confidence in the capacity of a simplified formula both to restore public confidence and to improve its administration. Under the revised formula introduced by the Child Support, Pensions and Social Security Act 2000,[122] only the income of the non-resident parent was relevant, on the basis that the person with care already contributed financially by meeting housing and household costs. The principle that children should share in the standard of living enjoyed by both parents was asserted more strongly, with maintenance being calculated as a proportion of the non-resident parent's income, but, once again, even parents on low incomes were required to contribute towards their children's support; indeed, this principle was "more firmly embedded"[123] in the revised scheme, as the circumstances in which a non-resident parent would be exempt from making any payment were narrowed.

It is one thing to decide that parents should pay a proportion of their income to supporting their children; it is rather more difficult to decide what that proportion should be.[124] The Government started from the premise that the cost

---

[117] Stepchildren were ignored in determining an individual's "assessable income" but were taken into account in the assessment of "protected income", which was intended to provide a safety net slightly above income-support subsistence levels.

[118] House of Commons Social Security Committee's First Report, *The Operation of the Child Support Act*, Session 1993–4, HC 69, para.79.

[119] House of Commons Social Security Committee's First Report, *The Operation of the Child Support Act*, Session 1993–4, HC 69.

[120] G. Davis, "Comments on child support in the UK: making the move from court to agency" (1994) 31 Houston L. Rev. 539 at 541.

[121] (Cm.4349 (1999)), Ch.1.

[122] Child Support Act 1991 s.11(6) and Sch.1, as amended.

[123] N. Wikeley, "Financial support for children after parental separation: parental responsibility and responsible parenting", in Probert, Gilmore and Herring, *Responsible Parents and Parental Responsibility*.

[124] Or indeed what constitutes "income": see, for example, *Smith v Secretary of State for Department of Work and Pensions* [2006] UKHL 35 (although note that the decision in *Smith* has been reversed by regulations: see Child Support (Miscellaneous Amendments) Regulations 2007 (SI 2007/1979) regs 4 and 5) and *Chandler v Secretary of State for Work and Pensions* [2007] EWCA Civ 1211. For commentary, see N. Wikeley, "Child support, the self-employed and 'total taxable profits' " [2006] Fam. Law 872.

of supporting a child constitutes approximately 30 per cent of family income.[125] The basic rate of child support was therefore set at 15 per cent[126] of net weekly income[127] for one qualifying child, 20 per cent for two and 25 per cent for three or more.[128] It was originally envisaged that these percentages would be applied whatever the level of the non-resident parent's income,[129] but in the wake of widespread criticism it was provided that the legislation would only apply to weekly earnings of £2,000 per week or less, with the courts retaining the power to make top-up orders if the non-resident parent's income exceeded this amount.[130]

At the other end of the financial spectrum, three slightly different rates applied. The nil rate[131] applied where the non-resident parent's net weekly income was less than £5 or the parent fell into a prescribed category: namely, the parent was a full-time student, under 16, on income support if 16 or 17, in hospital for at least a year or in prison. The flat rate[132] operated where the nil rate was not applicable and where the non-resident parent's net weekly income was less than £100 or he or his partner were in receipt of a prescribed benefit, pension or allowance. Finally, the reduced rate[133] applied where the non-resident parent's net weekly income was between £100 and £200.

A further important change made by the 2000 Act was that an allowance for **15–017** children living with the non-resident parent was built into the calculation of maintenance.[134] This could be either the children of a new partner or the parent's own children. The allowance took the form of a deduction from the parent's net weekly income of 15 per cent for one such child, 20 per cent for two and 25 per cent for three or more.[135] The assessment of maintenance for that person's qualifying children was then based on the net weekly income minus the percentage deducted to take account of the support being provided for children in the household. The result is that the amount payable as child support for children from a previous relationship is slightly less than the amount hypothetically attributed to the support of children in the parent's household. An example may help to illustrate this:

---

[125] For criticism of this calculation, see P. Parkinson, "Reengineering the child support system", and on the assumption that the resulting figure should be divided equally, see J. Fortin, *Children's Rights and the Developing Law* (London: Butterworths, 2003), p.299.

[126] On the basis that the person with care was providing the other half of the 30%.

[127] To be determined "in such manner as is provided for in regulations".

[128] Child Support Act 1991 Sch.1 para.2(1), as substituted by Child Support, Pensions and Social Security Act 2000.

[129] *Children's Rights and Parents' Responsibilities*, Ch.2, para.36; *Official Report*, HL, cols 1251, 1252 (Baroness Hollis) (May 8, 2000).

[130] Child Support Act 1991 Sch.1 para.10.

[131] Child Support Act 1991 Sch.1 para.5; see the Child Support (Maintenance Calculation and Special Cases) Regulations 2000 (SI 2001/155) reg.5

[132] Child Support Act 1991 Sch.1 para.4; see the Child Support (Maintenance Calculations and Special Cases) Regulations 2000 (SI 2001/155) reg.4.

[133] Child Support Act 1991 Sch.1 para.3; see the Child Support (Maintenance Calculations and Special Cases) Regulations 2000 (SI 2001/155) reg.3.

[134] For discussion see *Children's Rights and Parents' Responsibilities*, p.10.

[135] Child Support Act 1991 Sch.1 para.2(2).

A has two children, C and D, from his previous relationship with B. The children both live with their mother, B. A now lives with E, who has two children, F and G. If A earns £1,250 per week, it is first necessary to deduct 20 per cent (or £250) from this on account of F and G, with the result that his liability for C and D would be £200 per week (20% of £1,250 = £250; 20% of (£1,250 − £250) = £200).

In other respects the 2000 Act modified the scheme as originally laid down. From the start of the scheme, rates of child support have been modified in cases of "shared care": under the original scheme the threshold for any reduction in child support was 104 nights per year,[136] but under the 2000 reforms this fell to 52 nights per year. Where the basic or reduced rate of child support was payable, a discount of one-seventh was applied if the child spent 52 to 103 nights per year with the non-resident parent, two-sevenths for 104 to 155 nights, three-sevenths for 156 to 174 nights and one-half for 175 nights or more.[137] Provision was also made for the flat rate to be reduced to nil in cases of shared care.[138]

15–018 The precise residence arrangements agreed by the parties, or ordered by the court, may therefore have a significant impact on liability for child support. In some cases the courts have had some regard to the financial consequences that a particular arrangement as to residence would have in making an order.[139] However, in the recent case of *Re B (Contact: Child Support)* it was maintained that, in determining the level of staying contact[140] to be ordered, no regard should be paid to the impact that this will have on the calculation of child support.[141] In the vivid metaphor of Wilson L.J.:

> "It would . . . put the cart before the horse. First breed your horse, namely the optimum arrangements for the child in terms of contact or shared residence, devised without reference to child support. Then, at the rear of the horse, let Parliament fit the appropriate cart, namely the amount of the liability for child support."[142]

Yet this approach is perhaps too stark. While arrangements relating to the residence of the child must be determined in accordance with the child's best interests and cannot be driven by considerations relating to child support, this does not mean that the court should not even consider such considerations. The absolute rule adopted by the Court of Appeal in this case may have been

---

[136] Child Support (Maintenance and Special Cases) Regulations 1992 (SI 1992/2645) reg.20.

[137] Child Support Act 1991 Sch.1 para.7; see Child Support (Maintenance Calculations and Special Cases) Regulations 2000 (SI 2000/155) reg.7A.

[138] Child Support Act 1991 Sch.1 para.8. However, this did not apply to those paying the flat rate who fell under para.4(1)(a).

[139] *Re R (Residence Order: Finance)* [1995] 2 F.L.R. 612, at p.613; *Re M (Children)* [2004] EWCA Civ 1413, para.20. See further S. Gilmore, "*Re B (Contact: Child Support)*—horses and carts: contact and child support" [2007] 19 C.F.L.Q. 357.

[140] On this, see further para.18–018.

[141] *Re B (Contact: Child Support)* [2006] EWCA Civ 1574.

[142] At para.19.

influenced by the fact that the case was couched in terms of contact (albeit staying contact) rather than residence.[143]

Finally, the legislation also makes provision for the parent who has children living in several different households. In this situation the amount payable will be divided between the qualifying children.[144]

iii. The new system

The system to be enacted by the Child Maintenance and Other Payments Bill bears many similarities to that introduced by the 2000 Act. Maintenance is to be calculated as a percentage of the non-resident parent's income, but the base from which calculations are to be made will be gross, rather than net, weekly income,[145] and the percentages to be deducted under the basic rate are correspondingly reduced to 12 per cent for one child, 16 per cent for two and 19 per cent for three.[146] The same percentages apply when making deductions to take account of other relevant children living in the same household as the non-resident parent.[147] However, one important difference is that the latter deductions apply to all of the non-resident parent's income, while the basic rate calculations only apply to income under £800 per week; above that level, the percentage to be paid by the non-resident parent on any income between £800 and £3,000[148] per week falls to 9 per cent for one child, 12 per cent for two and 15 per cent for three or more.[149] This will widen still further the difference between the amount notionally attributed to the support of children in the non-resident parent's household and the latter's liability towards qualifying children.

15–019

Again, an example may assist:

> A has two children, C and D, from his previous relationship with B. The children both live with their mother, B. A now lives with E, who has two children, F and G. If A earns £2,000 (gross) per week, it is first necessary to deduct 16 per cent (or £320) from this on account of F and G; by contrast,

---

[143] There is an interesting question as to the purpose of the reduction and whether it bears any relation to the cost of rearing a child: see N. Wikeley, "Contact and child support—putting the horse before the cart" [2007] Fam. Law. 343.

[144] Child Support Act 1991 Sch.1 para.6.

[145] Child Maintenance and Other Payments Bill 2007, HL Bill 57 Sch.4 para.2, amending Child Support Act 1991 Sch.1 Pt 1. As *A New System of Child Maintenance* explains, this has the consequence that "deductions of income tax and National Insurance contributions will no longer need to be made as part of a maintenance assessment" (para.4.15). In addition, the need to extract this information from reluctant non-resident parents will disappear, as liability will "be based on historical information from the latest tax year for which HM Revenue & Customs has full details" (para.4.9). There is, however, an exception to this if current income differs from that reported for the latest tax year by 25%: para.4.13.

[146] Child Maintenance and Other Payments Bill 2007, HL Bill 57 Sch.4 para.3(1), amending Child Support Act 1991 Sch.1 para.2. These percentages are, when applied to gross income, expected to produce a sum roughly equivalent to the previous percentages.

[147] Child Maintenance and Other Payments Bill 2007, HL Bill 57 Sch.4 para.3(3), amending Child Support Act 1991 Sch.1 para.2.

[148] Child Maintenance and Other Payments Bill 2007, HL Bill 57 Sch.4 para.10, amending Child Support Act 1991 Sch.1 para.10(3).

[149] Child Maintenance and Other Payments Bill 2007, HL Bill 57 Sch.4 para.3(3), amending Child Support Act 1991 Sch.1 para.2.

his liability for C and D would be considerably less, at £233.60 (16 per cent of £800 plus 12 per cent of £880 (£2000–£320 + £800).

This said, the overall liability of the non-resident parent is likely to be slightly higher under the new scheme.[150]

Maintenance assessments will also be more stable under the proposed reforms. The system will abandon the social security model, in which small changes in income had to be reported and child support recalculated,[151] and will move to awards that are fixed for the following year.[152] There is, however, to be an exception for significant changes in circumstances.[153]

The issue of shared care was considered by Sir David Henshaw in his report, and it was suggested that cases of shared care should be outside the child support scheme altogether.[154] The White Paper that followed this report dealt only with the issue of split care, proposing that a balancing payment would be appropriate in such a case. Similarly, the Bill itself only deals specifically with the situation in which each of the parents has at least one child from the relationship living with them.[155] In light of the increasing popularity of shared residence orders,[156] this is an issue that clearly requires further attention.

E. Variations from the formula

15–020 The original intention of the child support scheme was that the formula should be of universal application; its complexity was designed to achieve universality. However, this principle was compromised by the Child Support Act 1995 (and Regulations made under that Act[157]), which sought to give effect to the Government's view that there would always be a "small proportion of exceptional cases which cannot be fairly treated by any universal formula".[158] This was, in essence, an admission that the formula's rigidity could be productive of injustice. Under the system introduced by the Child Support Act 1995, either parent could apply for a "departure direction" (i.e. a variation of the formula) on the ground that the facts fell within one of three "cases" specified in the Act.[159]

---

[150] Note also that the flat rate is to be increased from £5 to £7: Child Maintenance and Other Payments Bill 2007 Sch.4 para.4, amending Child Support Act 1991 Sch.1 paras 3(3) and 4(1).
[151] *A New System of Child Maintenance*, para.4.12.
[152] *A New System of Child Maintenance*, para.4.14.
[153] *A New System of Child Maintenance*, para.4.13. Provision for this is to be made by means of Regulations rather than primary legislation.
[154] *Recovering Child Support: Routes to Responsibility*, p.49.
[155] Child Maintenance and Other Payments Bill 2007, HL Bill 57, amending Child Support Act 1991 s.42.
[156] See further, para.18–016.
[157] Child Support (Departure Directions and Consequential Amendments) Regulations 1996 (SI 1996/2907).
[158] *Improving Child Support* (Cm.2745 (1995)), para.2.1.
[159] Child Support Act 1995 Sch.2, the provisions of which were amplified by the Child Support (Departure Directions and Consequential Amendment) Regulations 1996 (SI 1996/2907). Briefly, these comprised, first, "special expenses" on costs incurred in travelling to work, in maintaining contact with a child, debts incurred for the benefit of the family before breakdown, pre-1993 financial commitments (provided that a court order or maintenance agreement was in force at April 5, 1993 and at the date the commitment was contracted), costs incurred in supporting stepchildren and certain

The unsatisfactory compromise of combining a formulaic approach with a limited discretion was continued when the scheme was revised by the Child Support, Pensions and Social Security Act 2000. Departures were renamed "variations", and were intended to be available only for "clearly exceptional" cases.[160] The circumstances in which a variation could be ordered were accordingly narrowed. The reasons for lowering the standard child support rates are strictly child-centred. Property and capital transfers effected prior to April 1993 to provide accommodation to help support a child were grounds for variations, as they were formerly grounds for departure.[161] The category of "special expenses"[162] of a non-resident parent was retained, and comprised costs incurred in maintaining contact, costs attributable to a relevant other child's long-term illness or disability, certain debts incurred prior to separation for the joint benefit of both parents or a child, boarding school fees and mortgage repayments on the former family home in which he/she no longer has an interest[163] but which is still the home of the qualifying child and parent with care. Finally, rates of child support could be raised in some exceptional circumstances. The revised scheme retained the category of "additional cases" in which a variation might be made (e.g. where the non-resident parent's weekly income was not an accurate reflection of their financial capacity), whether on account of capital assets or otherwise.[164]

An application for a variation may be made either before or after a maintenance calculation has been made.[165] As under the earlier scheme, variation is by no means automatic: an application will only succeed if it is judged to be "just and equitable" by the Secretary of State.[166] In considering whether it would be just and equitable, the Secretary of State must have regard, in particular, to the welfare of any child likely to be affected if he did agree to a variation[167]; to whether agreeing to a variation "would be likely to result in a relevant person ceasing paid employment"[168]; and, if the applicant is the non-resident parent:

---

costs incurred by reason of the long-term illness or disability of the applicant or a dependant; secondly, property or capital transfers made by court order or agreement before April 5, 1993 that effectively reduced the amount of the maintenance payable with respect to a child; thirdly, cases where the parent had income-producing assets, where income was diverted, a lifestyle inconsistent with declared income, unreasonably high housing costs, a partner's contribution to housing costs, and unreasonably high travel costs. If the case fell within one of the above categories, a departure direction was not automatic: there was a discretion whether to make one or not, and the ultimate question was whether it would be "just and equitable" to do so in light of a number of specified considerations. For a detailed discussion, see pp.533–536 of the sixth edition of this work, and note the decision in *R. (ota Qazi (Hamid) v Secretary of State for Work and Pensions* [2004] EWHC 1331.

[160] *Children's Rights and Parents' Responsibilities*, Ch.6 para.3.

[161] Child Support Act 1991 Sch.4B para.3.

[162] Child Support Act 1991 Sch.4B para.2(1). Special expenses are prescribed in the Child Support (Variation) Regulations 2001 (SI 2001/156).

[163] It would appear that this is confined to the situation where the non-resident parent has divested him/herself of their entire interest.

[164] For the details, see Child Support (Variation) Regulations 2001, (SI 2001/156) regs 18, 19, 20.

[165] Child Support Act 1991 as amended, s.28A(1), (3).

[166] Child Support Act 1991 s.28F(1), as amended by Child Support, Pensions and Social Security Act 2000 s.5(5).

[167] Child Support Act 1991 s.28F(2).

[168] Child Support (Variation) Regulations 2001 (SI 2001/156) reg.21(1)(a)(i).

"[T]he extent, if any, of his[/her] liability to pay child maintenance under a court order or agreement in the period prior to the effective date of the maintenance calculation."[169]

It should also be noted that, in contrast to the usual injunction to take "all the circumstances of the case" into account, the Secretary of State is specifically debarred from taking certain factors into account.[170]

Despite the need (identified in the latest round of proposals) to simplify the system, neither the Henshaw Report nor the White Paper that succeeded it made any reference to the system of variations, but it is implicit in the Bill that this aspect of the current system will remain largely unaltered.[171]

F. Changes and appeals

15–021 Given that the Child Support Agency has not been conspicuously successful in producing accurate assessments,[172] some mention should be made of the process by which its decisions may be challenged. The procedures have been described as being of "Kafkaesque complexity",[173] and what follows is an outline only.[174] There are two procedures whereby the Secretary of State may, either on application or on his own initiative, alter a decision: revision and supercession. As Wikeley has explained:

"[R]evision is a means of changing an initial decision which is wrong . . . whereas supercession is a means of substituting a new decision . . . for example because of a subsequent change in circumstances."[175]

The power to revise or supercede a decision is, however, only available in relation to a prescribed group of decisions.[176]

Should an aggrieved parent wish to appeal, there is a specific process to be followed.[177] The first level of appeal is to a Child Support Appeal Tribunal, which will usually consist of a single legally qualified member. The Tribunal may make a decision itself or remit the matter to the Secretary of State.[178] It is possible for either a person aggrieved or the Secretary of State to appeal on a question of law to a Child Support Commissioner[179]; there is then the possibility

---

[169] Child Support (Variation) Regulations 2001 (SI 2001/156) reg.21(1)(a)(ii).
[170] Child Support (Variation) Regulations 2001 (SI 2001/156) reg.21(2).
[171] Minor changes are made in the Bill: see Child Maintenance and Other Payments Bill 2007, HL Bill 57, cl.18.
[172] The latest figures indicate a 93% accuracy rate in relation to the old scheme, and a 85% accuracy rate in relation to the new scheme: DWP, *Child Support Agency Quarterly Statistics* (March 2008), Table 17a.
[173] G. Douglas [2007] Fam. Law 981, commenting on *R. (Howes) v Child Support Commissioners* [2007] EWHC 559 (Admin).
[174] For a detailed account, see Wikeley, *Child Support: Law and Policy*, Ch.13.
[175] Wikeley, *Child Support: Law and Policy*, p.410.
[176] See Child Support Act 1991 s.16 on revisions and s.17 on supercessions.
[177] See N. Wikeley, "Child support appeal rights and the fallout from Farley" [2006] Fam. Law 982 on the right to appeal.
[178] Child Support Act 1991 s.20(8).
[179] Child Support Act 1991 s.24.

of a further appeal on a question of law to the Court of Appeal.[180] At each stage, permission is needed for the appeal to proceed. Yet despite the criticisms of the complexity of the current process, the most recent round of reforms barely touch on such issues.[181]

The decisions of the Secretary of State are amenable to judicial review,[182] but it has been held that a parent has no action in negligence for the shortcomings of the agency.[183] This was justified in part on the basis that the existing remedies provided "substantial protection against incompetence on the part of the CSA",[184] an assertion which, as one commentator has noted, may meet with a "hollow laugh" from parents.[185]

G. Collection and enforcement

There had traditionally been a low level of compliance with court orders for periodical maintenance[186]; it was hoped that the Child Support Act 1991 would ensure that maintenance was paid regularly and on time, and that appropriate enforcement action would be taken if payments were not made.[187] Unfortunately the reality of the Agency's performance fell well short of expectations on both counts.[188] Nor did the reforms enacted in 2000 have the desired effect. The Child Maintenance and Other Payments Bill is no different from its predecessors in including provisions for the collection of maintenance and a range of sanctions to be used against those who refuse to pay. **15–022**

i. Arrangements for collection

From its inception, the Child Support Agency provided a collection service, involving either direct payments between parents or payments collected from the non-resident parent and passed on to the parent with care.[189] Parents with care who were on benefits were obliged to use the Agency's collection service; others could opt for private arrangements if they so wished. **15–023**

Under the scheme proposed by the Child Maintenance and Other Payments Bill, this element of compulsion will vanish; however, the Bill does involve a shift towards more direct forms of collection. Since the inception of the 1991 Act

---

[180] Child Support Act 1991 s.25.
[181] See D. Burrows, "Child support: what the white paper doesn't say" [2007] Fam. Law 242 for a discussion of options for reform.
[182] See, for example, *R (Sturton) v Social Security and Child Support Commissioners* [2007] EWHC 2957 (Admin); *R. (Davies) v Commissioners Office* [2008] EWHC 334 (Admin). For discussion, see D. Burrows, "The CSA: Judicial Review and compensation for maladministration" [2006] Fam. Law 44.
[183] *R. (Rowley) v Secretary of State for Work and Pensions* [2007] EWCA Civ 598.
[184] At para.72, *per* Dyson L.J.
[185] G. Douglas [2007] Fam. Law. 897, commenting on *R. (Rowley) v Secretary of State for Work and Pensions* [2007] EWCA Civ 598.
[186] See *Children Come First* (Cm.1263) para.5.1.
[187] *Children Come First*, para.5.3.
[188] *Children's Rights and Parents' Responsibilities*, Ch.1, paras 2, 18.
[189] Payment could be made by a variety of means: see Child Support (Collection and Enforcement and Miscellaneous Amendments) Regulations 2001 (SI 2001/157), as amended by Child Support (Miscellaneous Amendments) Regulations 2006 (SI 2006/1520) reg.6.

it has been possible for a deduction from earnings order to be made[190]; under the 2007 Bill, provision is made for such orders to be the basic method of payment except where there is good reason.[191] If such an order is in place, then the maintenance due may be deducted directly from the non-resident parent's earnings. It is recognised that such a move may prove controversial, and therefore it is to be tested on a pilot basis.

ii. Enforcement

15–024   A late payment penalty rate may be levied to encourage timely payment,[192] and a deduction from earnings order may be made to secure the payment of arrears. If such an order is not available (e.g. because the person concerned is not in employment) or has proved ineffective, then other enforcement methods may be used. A precondition for using such methods is the obtaining of a liability order from the magistrates court.[193] The magistrates must make the liability order if the court is satisfied that the payments in question have become payable and have not been paid[194]; it is not the role of the magistrates to question the assessment itself.[195] Once made,[196] it gives the authorities recourse to a wide range of enforcement powers, including distress (sale and seizure of goods by bailiffs to pay a debt)[197]; recovery through the county court[198]; disqualification from driving[199]; or imprisonment.[200] The more stringent sanctions are, however, only available in cases of wilful or culpable neglect.[201]

The Child Maintenance and Other Payments Bill proposes to add to this already considerable armoury of sanctions by making provision for regular or lump sum deduction orders,[202] a "disqualification for holding or obtaining travel

---

[190] For the traditional opposition to such measures, see the seventh edition of this work at p.147. Such methods of collection remain relatively rare, being used in only 21% of cases as of March 2008: DWP, *Child Support Agency Quarterly Statistics* (March 2008), Table 9. Contrast the position in Australia: see Parkinson, "Reengineering the child support system".

[191] Child Maintenance and Other Payments Bill, HL Bill 57, cl.20.

[192] See Wikeley, *Child Support: Law and Policy*, pp.446–447 on the use (or non-use) of this option.

[193] Child Support Act 1991 s.33(2). In *The Queen on the Application of Denson v CSA* [2002] EWHC Admin. 154; [2002] 1 F.L.R. 938, Munby J. held that a liability order was a necessary and proportionate part of the overall statutory scheme, and did not engage art.8 of the ECHR.

[194] Child Support Act 1991 s.33(3). On the number of such orders made, see DWP, *Child Support Agency Quarterly Statistics* (March 2008), Table 21.

[195] *Farley v Secretary of State for Work and Pensions* [2006] UKHL 31; see Wikeley, "Child support: liability orders after Farley" [2006] Fam. Law 675.

[196] Appeal is solely by way of case stated: see *T v Child Support Agency* [1998] 1 W.L.R. 144; *Re L (Family Proceedings Court) (Appeal: Jurisdiction)* [2003] EWHC 1682 (Fam); *Hickerton v Child Support Agency* [2006] EWHC 1683 (Fam); *Gilatane v Child Support Agency* [2006] EWHC 423 (Fam).

[197] Child Support Act 1991 s.35; Child Support (Collection and Enforcement) Regulations 1992 (SI 1992/1989), as amended, regs 30–32.

[198] Either by means of a third-party debt order (on funds in a bank or building society) or by means of a charging order (whereby property is sold to meet a debt): Child Support Act 1991 s.36.

[199] Child Support Act 1991 ss.39A and 40B, as inserted by s.16 of the Child Support, Pensions and Social Security Act 2000.

[200] Child Support Act 1991 s.39A.

[201] Child Support Act 1991 s.40(3). The maximum period of imprisonment is six weeks: s.40(6)(b).

[202] Child Maintenance and Other Payments Bill, HL Bill 57 cls 22 and 23.

authorisation"[203] and a curfew order.[204] It also provides that the new Commission will itself be able to make a liability order,[205] thus removing the need for court approval.[206] Provision is also made for the disclosure of information to credit reference agencies,[207] an innovation that may have rather more force in the current economic climate than when it was first mooted.

Yet the problem to date has not been the lack of enforcement methods but rather the under-use of such sanctions as do exist.[208] In the 12 months from February 2007, for example, only five non-resident parents were actually disqualified from driving on account of their failure to pay child support.[209] It seems that no government can resist the temptation of including eye-catching initiatives that appear to promise a tough stance; the purpose and utility of such measures must, however, be questioned.[210]

The enforcement scheme authorised by the Child Support Act 1991 is **15–025** comprehensive in that other remedies under the general law are not available in cases of non-payment.[211] Nor are parents with care entitled to enforce maintenance orders. This was challenged by one parent with care, Mrs Kehoe, who claimed that her inability to enforce maintenance payments constituted a breach of art.6 of the European Convention. However, the House of Lords, by a majority, dismissed her claim. Lord Bingham noted the theoretical advantages of the Child Support Agency:

> "It might well be thought that a single professional agency, with the resources of the state behind it and an array of powers at its command, would be more consistent in assessing and more effective in enforcing payment than individual parents acting in a random and uncoordinated way."[212]

The verdict of Mrs Kehoe perhaps reflects the operation of the Agency more accurately:

---

[203] Child Maintenance and Other Payments Bill, HL Bill 57 cl.27.
[204] Child Maintenance and Other Payments Bill, HL Bill 57 cl.26. Note, by contrast, that the inclusion of such orders in the Children and Adoption Act 2006—for residential parents who unreasonably frustrate contact between the child and the other parent—was rejected.
[205] Child Maintenance and Other Payments Bill, HL Bill 57 cl.28.
[206] See DWP, *A New System of Child Maintenance*, para.5.15, for the justifications underpinning this change, and for commentary see N. Wikeley, "Child support reform—throwing the baby out with the bathwater?" [2007] 19 C.F.L.Q. 434, pp.453–455.
[207] Child Maintenance and Other Payments Bill, HL Bill 57 cl.40.
[208] As Sir David Henshaw pointed out in his report, enforcement has been under-resourced: *Recovering Child Support: Routes to Responsibility*, p.31.
[209] DWP, *Child Support Agency Quarterly Statistics* (March 2008), Table 21. A further 20 received a suspended driving licence disqualification.
[210] See, for example, the short-lived attempt to "name and shame" non-resident parents who had been successfully prosecuted for information offences. The website featuring such parents was in operation for a mere four weeks, after which the Government announced that the practice would be discontinued.
[211] *Department of Social Security v Butler* [1996] 1 W.L.R. 1528; [1996] 1 F.L.R. 65, CA.
[212] *R. (Kehoe) v Secretary of State for Work and Pensions* [2005] UKHL 48 at para.6.

"My only remedy is to constantly pressurise the CSA which takes no real responsibility for ensuring maintenance is paid and for whom I am just a nuisance."

However, despite the well-documented flaws with the current system,[213] the new proposals do not include any facility for parents with care using the administrative system to enforce maintenance.[214]

H. Relevance of the child's welfare

15-026 Given the significance of the welfare of the child in other proceedings,[215] it may seem odd that considerations of child welfare have been left to such a late stage of the text. This, however, merely reflects the fact that within the rigidity of the child support scheme, the welfare of the individual child[216] is a subsidiary consideration. It does not, for example, apply so as to give any discretion to depart from the formula laid down by the Act for the calculation of child support maintenance.[217] Indeed, it is only when the Secretary of State is considering the exercise of any *discretionary* power conferred by the Child Support Act that he is required to "have regard to the welfare of any child likely to be affected by his decision".[218] The duty to have regard to welfare extends beyond the "qualifying children" in respect of whom a maintenance calculation is likely to be sought: so, for example, a child support officer is obliged to have regard to the effect of relevant decisions on the non-resident parent's other children, on a non-resident parent's stepchildren, and even, perhaps, on a parent who is a "child".[219]

While the duty to have regard to children's welfare does not arise in those cases in which the legislation imposes a mandatory duty on the Secretary of State or officer acting under his authority,[220] the range of discretionary powers to which the duty does apply is surprisingly wide: for example, the decision as to whether to arrange for the collection and enforcement of child support maintenance[221]; whether to revise or supersede an earlier decision[222]; whether to agree to a variation from the formula; and whether to take certain kinds of enforcement

---

[213] See, for example, T. Branigan, "Parents waiting five years for child support", *The Guardian*, October 15, 2007.

[214] For criticism of this omission, see Fellowes, "The CSA—out with the old, in with the new?".

[215] See, for example, Children Act 1989 s.1(1) (child's welfare paramount consideration in proceedings to determine upbringing or administration of property); Matrimonial Causes Act 1973 s.25(1) (child's welfare first consideration in ancillary relief proceedings).

[216] It should, of course, be noted that the scheme as a whole could be seen as promoting the welfare of children. This was an explicit factor within Sir David Henshaw's report, which noted that "the core principle behind child support arrangements is improving the welfare of children": *Recovering Child Support: Routes To Responsibility*, p.12.

[217] *R. v Secretary of State for Social Security Ex p. Biggin* [1995] 1 F.L.R. 851. Child Support Act 1991 s.11 imposes a mandatory requirement to fix the amount of child support maintenance in accordance with the provisions of the Act, but on the other hand, it would seem that the Secretary of State's extensive power to make regulations under the Act (see s.52) is a discretionary power in the exercise of which he is bound to take account of the welfare of all children likely to be affected.

[218] Child Support Act 1991 s.2.

[219] See the definition of "child" in Child Support Act 1991 s.55.

[220] Child Support Act 1991 s.11(1).

[221] Child Support Act 1991 s.4(2).

[222] Child Support Act 1991 ss.16, 17.

action. In general, the appropriate procedure will be to seek judicial review[223] of the decision on the ground that the decision was one that could not properly have been reached had the Secretary of State or officer acting under his authority properly directed themselves in accordance with this statutory requirement.

Finally, it should be noted that the duty to have regard to children's welfare is a real one: in *R. v Secretary of State for Social Security Ex p. Biggin*[224] the judge refused to accept a submission by counsel for the Secretary of State that the agency's decisions (in those situations where the principle did apply) could not be attacked if it were shown that the agency had merely taken note of the child's welfare in passing; the judge suggested that the statute required "considerable weight" to be given to the welfare principle.

I. The impact of child support payments

Whether or not the household in receipt of child support experiences any net **15-027** increase in income depends first on whether the person with care is on certain benefits; and, secondly, the scheme under which child support is paid. Under the scheme as originally enacted, any money received by way of child support operated to reduce the benefits[225] paid to the person with care, pound-for-pound. The payment of child support thus resulted in no net gain to the household.[226] The Child Support, Pensions and Social Security Act 2000 introduced the "child maintenance premium" whereby the first £10 of child support received would be disregarded in calculating entitlement to benefits. This change, however, only applied to cases under the revised scheme, whose applications to the Agency were made after March 3, 2003. As Sir David Henshaw pointed out in his review, as late as 2006, 42,000 parents with care received no net benefit from the payment of child support.[227]

The removal of the requirement for persons with care on benefits to apply for child support under the Child Maintenance and Other Payments Bill is to be accompanied by a higher maintenance disregard.[228] This is consistent with the new aim of ending child poverty.[229] It is intended that the disregard will initially

---

[223] As was (unsuccessfully) done in *R. v Secretary of State for Social Security Ex p. Lloyd* [1995] 1 F.L.R. 856; and see *R. v Secretary of State for Social Security Ex p. Biggin* [1995] 1 F.L.R. 851.
[224] [1995] 1 F.L.R. 851.
[225] The rule applies to Income Support and income-based Jobseeker's Allowance.
[226] Although note the limited child-maintenance bonus introduced under subsequent amendments: Child Support Act 1995 s.10; Social Security (Child Maintenance Bonus) Regulations 1996 (SI 1996/3195). This, however, was only payable if the parent with care ceased to be dependent on benefits and started work.
[227] *Recovering Child Support: Routes to Responsibility*, p.14.
[228] This does not appear in the Bill itself, and will be a matter for Regulations. It has already been provided that, with effect from October 27, 2008, there will be a full disregard of child maintenance received for the purpose of calculating entitlement to Housing Benefit or Council Tax Benefit: see Social Security (Miscellaneous Amendments) (No.2) Regulations 2008 (SI 2008/1042) regs 3 and 5.
[229] See, for example, *Recovering Child Support: Routes to Responsibility*, p.16, which noted that: "[T]he current system was originally designed primarily to reclaim money for the taxpayer when parents with care are on benefits. This may be difficult to achieve in a cost-effective way alongside tackling child poverty."

be increased to £20 per week and, from April 2010, to £40 per week,[230] initiatives that, it is suggested, will have the potential to lift 50,000 children out of poverty.[231] Given that the median amount of child support received per family was only £48 in 2006,[232] setting such a high level of maintenance disregard is tantamount to its abolition in a large number of cases.[233]

J. Assessing the child support scheme

15–028 Once again, the child support system is in a state of flux. This chapter has already highlighted the deficiencies of the original scheme and the failure of the reforms enacted in 2000 to produce the desired effect. It remains to be seen whether the Child Maintenance and Other Payments Bill will prove more successful than its predecessors in ensuring that maintenance is paid.[234] Somewhat ironically, the success of the new Child Maintenance and Enforcement Commission may depend on large numbers of parents choosing not to make use of it and thereby reducing its caseload. Whether the Government attains its target of eliminating child poverty will depend to a large extent on the choices made by those who do opt out of the administrative scheme; as has been pointed out, "the reason the CSA was established is precisely because so few people can arrive at voluntary agreements".[235] In a survey of parents with care in receipt of benefits (and therefore required to use the child support scheme), 44 per cent said that they would try to use the Agency, 32 per cent that they would try to make a private agreement and 24 per cent that they would probably not make any arrangement.[236] The last of these figures may simply reflect a realistic appreciation that the non-resident parent's financial situation may not be sufficient for any maintenance to be paid; as of May 2007, within the Child Support Agency's caseload, 25 per cent of non-resident parents were on benefits,[237] and 31 per cent of cases resulted in a nil maintenance liability.[238] There seems little point in

---

[230] HM Treasury, *Meeting the Aspirations of the British People: 2007 Pre-Budget Report and Comprehensive Spending Review* (Cm.7227 (2007)), p.78.

[231] DWP, *Information About Secondary Legislation Arising from the Child Maintenance and Other Payments Bill* (2008), p.2. A higher figure of 80,000–90,000 was suggested in the *Henshaw Report* on the basis of a full maintenance disregard: *Recovering Child Support: Routes to Responsibility*, p.19.

[232] A. Conolly and J. Kerr, *Families with Children in Britain: Findings from the 2006 Families and Children Study (FACS)* (DWP Research Report No.486, 2008), para.15.2.

[233] It has also been suggested that non-resident parents will only pay up to the level of the maintenance disregard: see, for example, Parkinson, "Reengineering the child support system".

[234] Including arrears incurred under the previous scheme: as of May 2007 there was £3.7bn of outstanding debt, of which £2.1bn was thought to be uncollectable: DWP, *Child Support Agency Quarterly Statistics* (March 2008), Table 22a. It was decided not to include a power to write off such debt: see *A New System of Child Maintenance*, para.5.36.

[235] "Resolution news" [2007] Fam. Law. 944. Resolution, the family lawyers' association, has further proposed that parents should be able to register and enforce such private agreements as are made, either through the courts or through the new administrative channels: [2007] Fam. Law 761.

[236] A. Kazimirski and E. Ireland, *Survey of Relationship Breakdown and Child Maintenance: Interim Report* DWP Research Report No.468 (2007), p.16.

[237] DWP, *Child Support Agency Quarterly Statistics* (March 2008), Table 13.2.

[238] DWP, *Child Support Agency Quarterly Statistics* (March 2008), Table 1.

processing cases of this kind. However, the number actually using the Agency is likely to depend on the cost of doing so.[239]

However, alongside the dual system of private and administrative arrangements, it is envisaged that there will be a third route: that of court-ordered maintenance.[240] We should now turn to the role that the courts play in the assessment of child maintenance.

IV. CHILD MAINTENANCE: THE ROLE OF THE COURTS

As noted at the start of this chapter, it was dissatisfaction with the court-based **15–029** system of child maintenance that led to the passage of the Child Support Act 1991.[241] The original intention of the reformers was that the Child Support Agency should assume full responsibility for assessing and reviewing child maintenance claims, and that the courts would lose that responsibility.[242] However, the courts retained the power to make orders for maintenance[243] in a number of different situations, and research suggests that court orders for child maintenance continue to play a significant role.[244] This section will first set out the situations in which such orders may be made, and then examine the principles governing the making of such orders under the relevant legislation.[245]

A. Determining jurisdiction

The Child Support Act provides that where a child support officer would have **15–030** jurisdiction to make a maintenance assessment with respect to a qualifying child and a non-resident parent, the court is debarred from exercising any power that it would otherwise have to make, vary or revive any maintenance order in relation to the child and non-resident parent concerned.[246] This is unambiguous, but there are, by definition, some cases where a child support officer does not have jurisdiction to make an order. In addition, the Act further sets out a number of cases in which the courts retain their powers.[247] These exceptions will be considered in turn.

---

[239] Charging parents for use of the system is justified as a further means of encouraging them to make their own arrangements: see *Recovering Child Support: Routes to Responsibility*, p.52. On the impact that different levels of charging may have on use of the system, see Kazimirski and Ireland, *Survey of Relationship Breakdown and Child Maintenance: Interim Report*, (DWP Research Report No.468, 2007), fig.3.1.

[240] *Recovering Child Support: Routes to Responsibility*, p.23.

[241] And see further N. Wikeley, "Child support—looking to the future" [2006] Fam. Law 360.

[242] *Children Come First* (Cm.1263 (1990)), para.4.1.

[243] The courts also retain the jurisdiction to make capital awards, which are dealt with in the next section.

[244] Around 8% of known maintenance arrangements derive from a court order, and a further 10% may involve a court order as part of a combination of orders: see C. Bullen, *Child Maintenance: The Eligible Population in Great Britain* (DWP Working Paper No.41, 2007), fig.3.1.

[245] Domestic Proceedings and Magistrates' Courts Act 1978, the Matrimonial Causes Act 1973 and the Children Act 1989 Sch.1.

[246] Child Support Act 1991 s.8(3). "Maintenance order" is defined in s.8(11).

[247] See, for discussion, A. Clift-Matthews, "The courts versus the CSA" [1996] Fam. Law 474; S. Deas, "Family lawyers sidestep the CSA" [1998] Fam. Law 48; G. Davis et al., "Child support and the residual role of lawyers" [1998] Fam. Law 304.

i. Child not a qualifying child: courts retain powers over children of the family

15–031   Since the Child Support Act only imposes liability on a legal parent, it follows that the Agency has no jurisdiction to make a maintenance assessment with respect to a social parent. By contrast, the Children Act 1989 and legislation dealing with divorce and dissolution empowers the court to make orders in respect of children of the family, and it follows that the court may still exercise its full range of powers to make financial orders against a child's stepparent.

ii. Older children and young persons

15–032   Some 17 and 18 year olds will not fall within the scope of the Child Support Act 1991 if they are not in full-time education or are in advanced education (i.e. a degree course).[248] The Child Maintenance and Other Payments Bill will extend the definition of "child" to those under the age of 20, but similar exceptions will apply. However, the fact that the Child Support Agency does not have jurisdiction over young persons above this age does not mean that the courts have the power to make orders for maintenance in their favour; the relevant legislation states that no such order shall be made in favour of a child who has reached the age of 18[249] unless there are special circumstances or the child is or will be in education or training.[250]

iii. Child support officer has no jurisdiction to make maintenance calculation

15–033   The child support officer has jurisdiction to make an assessment only if the parent with care and the qualifying child are both habitually resident in the United Kingdom, and the non-resident parent is either resident in the United Kingdom or is a British public servant working overseas.[251] Accordingly, in any other case the court will be entitled to exercise its full range of powers.[252]

iv. Topping-up orders

15–034   As noted above, there is an upper limit on child maintenance payable under the formula introduced by the 2000 reforms[253]; the non-resident parent's net weekly income in excess of £2,000 is disregarded for the purpose of calculating child support. However, above this "cap", if the maximum child maintenance assessment is in force,[254] the court has power to make an order for periodical

---

[248] See the definition of child in Child Support Act 1991 s.55(1), and above at para.15–006.
[249] Matrimonial Causes Act 1973 s.29(1); Children Act 1989 Sch.1 para.2(1); Civil Partnership Act 2004 Sch.5 para.49(1).
[250] Matrimonial Causes Act 1973 s.29(3); Children Act 1989 Sch.1 para.2(1) ; Civil Partnership Act 2004 Sch.5 para.49(5).
[251] Child Support Act 1991 s.44, as amended by Social Security Act 1998 s.86(1) Sch.7 para.41; Child Support, Pensions and Social Security Act 2000 ss.1(2), 22, Sch.3 para.11(2), and see para.15–010 above.
[252] Child Support Act 1991 s.8(1).
[253] See above, at para.15–016.
[254] Child Support Act 1991 s.8(6). The court cannot exercise its powers under this provision unless a maintenance calculation is actually in force.

payments, whether secured or unsecured, provided that the court is satisfied that the circumstances of the case make it appropriate for such additional payments to be made. The amount of a top-up order is determined in accordance with the relevant statutory criteria,[255] which require the court to have regard, inter alia, to the resources of both parents. Given the relatively high "cap", applications for top-up orders have been rare in practice, and this is likely to continue under the scheme to be established by the Child Maintenance and Other Payments Bill.[256]

v. Education expenses orders

The court may exercise its powers to make periodical payment orders in cases where the child[257] is, will be, or (if the order were to be made) would be receiving instruction at an educational establishment[258] or undergoing training for a trade, profession or vocation.[259] It is, in this case, not necessary that any child support calculation should have been made, but the court order must be "made solely for the purpose of requiring" provision of some or all of the expenses incurred in connection with the provision of the instruction or training. This provision covers, inter alia, school fees[260] and other school expenses, and the educational expenses at college or university of those under 18.

15–035

vi. Disabled children

The court may exercise its powers to make maintenance orders in respect of a child who is disabled,[261] whether or not a child support calculation is in force.[262] The order must be made solely to meet some or all of any expenses attributable to the child's disability, but a broad approach to the calculation of such expenses is adopted.[263]

15–036

---

[255] See below, at para.15–040.

[256] The Bill proposes that the upper limit be raised to £3,000 per week, but as this is gross rather than net income, the change is not as dramatic as might at first appear: see further, Child Maintenance and Other Payments Bill 2007, HL Bill 57 Sch.4 para.10, amending Child Support Act 1991 Sch.1 para.10(3).

[257] A person aged between 16 and 18 will only come within the definition of a "child" (Child Support Act 1991 s.55(1)) if he or she is attending a recognised educational establishment (see Child Support Act 1991 s.55(3)).

[258] This term is not defined: cf. Child Support Act 1991 s.55(3).

[259] Child Support Act 1991 s.8(7).

[260] *L v L (School Fees: Maintenance Enforcement)* [1997] 2 F.L.R. 252.

[261] Or in respect of whom a disability living allowance is paid. For the purpose of this provision a child is disabled if he or she is blind, deaf or dumb or is "substantially and permanently handicapped by illness, injury, mental disorder or congenital deformity" or any prescribed disability: Child Support Act 1991 s.8(9).

[262] Child Support Act 1991 s.8(8). In *C v F (Disabled Child: Maintenance Order)* [1998] 2 F.L.R. 1, the Court of Appeal held that s.8(8) of the Child Support Act 1991 granted jurisdiction to make a free-standing order under Sch.1 to the Children Act 1989, and therefore the age restriction in s.55 of the Child Support Act 1991 (to those under 19) did not apply.

[263] Thus, in practice, the approach under s.8(8) is unlikely to be very different from that under Sch.1 to the Children Act 1989, which permits consideration of all the circumstances: *C v F (Disabled Child: Maintenance Order)* [1998] 2 F.L.R. 1

vii. Orders against parent with care

15–037 The Child Support Act provides[264] that the rules restricting the court's powers shall not prevent a court from exercising any power that it has to make a maintenance order in relation to a child if the order is made against a person with care of the child. The policy underlying this provision is not altogether clear, but it may be that it was intended to fill the gap left by the inability of a child support officer to make a calculation against a parent with care, notwithstanding the fact that both parents are equally responsible for the child's support. However, there are no reported instances of this exception being relied upon.[265]

viii. Written agreements and court orders

15–038 Written maintenance agreements[266] entered into before April 5, 1993 (the date on which the Child Support Act 1991 came into operation) had the effect of ousting the Child Support Agency's jurisdiction, provided the parent with care did not become dependent on benefits.[267] While few such agreements will have continuing effect today, until 2003, parents had the option of achieving the same effect by asking the court to make a consent order in the same terms as a written agreement.[268] This too had the effect of permanently ousting the Agency's jurisdiction, assuming that the person with care was not in receipt of benefits, and the court had the power to vary and enforce the terms of such an order. Use of consent orders in private cases proved popular in practice,[269] but the 2000 Act reduced the period for which the Agency's jurisdiction was excluded to one year, and the Child Maintenance and Other Payments Bill adopts the same approach.

In addition, an order for maintenance for an ex-spouse or civil partner[270] may incorporate some of the costs of supporting children, subject to *pro tanto* reduction on a Child Support Agency calculation. It was held in *Dorney-Kingdom v Dorney-Kingdom*[271] that such a mechanism is legitimate, since it does not purport to oust the Agency's jurisdiction but is essentially a holding device until the Agency can carry out its proper function; a substantial element of spousal maintenance is essential to its operation.

---

[264] Child Support Act 1991 s.8(10).

[265] Wikeley, *Child Support: Law and Policy*, p.198.

[266] For the definition and effect of a maintenance agreement for these purposes, see Child Support Act 1991 s.9.

[267] Child Support Act 1991 s.4(10)(a); *B v B (Periodical Payments: Transitional Provisions)* [1995] 1 F.L.R. 459. Once the parent with care is in receipt of benefits and an assessment is made (even a nil assessment), the court order for maintenance ceases to have effect for all time: *Askew-Page v Page* [2001] Fam. Law 794.

[268] Child Support Act 1991 s.8(5); Child Maintenance (Written Agreements) Order 1993 (SI 1993/620). Where parties disagreed on the *quantum* of child maintenance, the Agency jurisdiction could nevertheless be avoided by the making of an nominal order at the start of proceedings, varied to an appropriate level at their conclusion: *per* Wilson J. in *V v V (Child Maintenance)* [2001] 2 F.L.R. 799 at para.[19]; comment by G. Douglas in [1996] Fam. Law 649.

[269] S. Deas, "Family lawyers sidestep the CSA" [1998] Fam. Law 48; J. Pirrie "Periodical payments by consent under the Children Act 1989" [1999] Fam. Law 680.

[270] Under s.23(1)(a) of the Matrimonial Causes Act 1973 or Sch.5 para.2 of the Civil Partnership Act 2004.

[271] [2000] 2 F.L.R. 855.

B. The courts' statutory powers

So far we have focused on the question as to when the courts retain the right to **15–039**
exercise their powers to make orders for maintenance in favour of children; we
can now turn to the question of what powers they have. Periodical payments for
children of the family may be ordered when the court is exercising its powers on
divorce or dissolution.[272] Such payments may be made directly to the child or to
another person on the child's behalf, and may be either secured or unsecured.[273]
Similar powers exist under the Children Act 1989.[274]

The concept of a "child of the family" is a broad one, encompassing both a
child who is the biological child of both spouses and a child who has been treated
by them both as a child of the family.[275] Foster children are, however, excluded,
and a cohabitant has no financial obligation to any children from the other party's
previous relationships.[276]

i. The exercise of the court's discretion

The welfare of any children of the family under the age of 18 will be the first **15–040**
consideration for the court considering how to exercise *any* of its powers on
divorce or dissolution,[277] and the way in which the courts exercise their
discretion in this context has been considered in an earlier chapter.[278] Our focus
in this section is on the specific issue of court-ordered maintenance for children:
how far, for example, has this issue been influenced by the Child Support Act
1991? The court is not specifically required to have regard to the formula
applicable under the Child Support Act, instead being referred to a wide range of
factors,[279] but, in practice, the formula exercises a powerful influence on the
quantum of child maintenance,[280] all the more so since there is now the facility

---

[272] Matrimonial Causes Act 1973 s.23(1)(d); Civil Partnership Act 2004 Sch.5 para.2(1)(d). The same
rules operate in the context of nullity proceedings. For its powers while the marriage or civil
partnership is intact, see para.3–015.
[273] Matrimonial Causes Act 1973 s.23(1)(e); Civil Partnership Act 2004 Sch.5 para.2(1)(e).
[274] Children Act 1989 Sch.1 para.1(2).
[275] Matrimonial Causes Act 1973 s.52(1); Civil Partnership Act 2004 Sch.5 para.80(2). The question
of whether the adult parties have treated the child as a child of their family is judged objectively: *Re
A (Child of the Family)* [1998] 1 F.L.R. 347. It should be noted that an unborn child cannot be treated
as a child of the family: if a man marries a woman who is pregnant by someone else, the baby will
be a child of their family if the husband treats it as such after birth (even if only for a very short time
and even if the wife has deceived him into thinking that he is the father), but if the relationship breaks
down before the birth, the child will be outside the definition, whatever the husband may have said
about his intentions to treat the baby as his own: *A v A (Family: Unborn Child)* [1974] Fam 6.
[276] *J v J (A Minor: Property Transfer)* [1993] 2 F.L.R. 56; *Morgan v Hill* [2006] EWCA Civ 1602 at
para.38.
[277] Matrimonial Causes Act 1973 s.25(1).
[278] See Ch.13. It should, of course, be borne in mind that in many ancillary relief cases the Child
Support Agency will have exclusive jurisdiction over the issue of child support, which renders the
task of the court in exercising its jurisdiction to make other orders (e.g. for spousal maintenance)
considerably more difficult. For criticism of the "unsatisfactory interface" between the jurisdictions,
see the comments of Wilson J. in *V v V (Child Maintenance)* [2001] 2 F.L.R. 799 at 800.
[279] Considered in more detail below, at para.15–044.
[280] *E v C (Child Maintenance)* [1996] 1 F.L.R. 472, *per* Douglas Brown J. See also *A v M* [2005]
EWHC 1721 (Fam) in which it was held that the rates under the child support regime "could be a
check on the level of orders made", *per* Sumner J. at para.88.

for consent orders to be reopened by either party after 12 months have elapsed.[281] As one judge has pointed out:

> "If a child maintenance order, whether made by consent or after a contest, is markedly at variance with the calculation under the [child support] regime then there will be a high temptation for one or other party after the order has been in force for a year, and after giving two-months notice, to approach the CSA for a calculation. Quite apart from the obvious acrimony that this would engender, a calculation in a different amount to the figure originally negotiated or awarded may cast doubt on the fairness of the original ancillary relief settlement between the parties, leading to further litigation. These spectres should be avoided at all costs."[282]

ii. Duration of orders and age limits

15–041 The basic rule is that periodical financial provision (whether secured or unsecured, and whether in nullity, divorce, separation or failure to maintain proceedings) will not, in the first instance, be ordered beyond the child's attaining the upper limit of compulsory school age.[283] However, the court may extend the obligation to make the payments to a later date (but not beyond the age of 18[284]) if it considers that, in the circumstances of the case, the welfare of the child so requires.[285]

Further, as noted above, the restrictions on making or continuing orders in favour of those who have attained the age of 18 do not apply if: (i) the "child is, or will be or [if provision extending beyond 18 were made] would be, receiving instruction at an educational establishment or undergoing training for a trade, profession or vocation, whether or not he[/or she] is also, or will also be in gainful employment"; or (ii) there are "special circumstances which justify" the making of a different order.[286]

Finally, it should be noted that a periodical payments order[287] in favour of a child will terminate on the death of the payer, whether or not the order so provides.[288]

---

[281] See *A New Contract for Welfare: Children's Rights and Parents' Responsibilities*, para.25, and above, para.15–013.

[282] *GW v RW* [2003] EWHC 611 (Fam).

[283] Matrimonial Causes Act 1973 s.29(2); Civil Partnership Act 2004 Sch.5 para.49(3)(a). Note that it is proposed to raise the age at which a child may leave education to 18: Education and Skills Bill 2007 cl.1.

[284] Matrimonial Causes Act 1973 s.29(2)(b); Civil Partnership Act 2004 Sch.5 para.49(3)(b).

[285] Matrimonial Causes Act 1973 s.29(2)(a); Civil Partnership Act 2004 Sch.5 para.49(3)(a).

[286] Matrimonial Causes Act 1973 s.29(3); Civil Partnership Act 2004 Sch.5 para.49(5). It is increasingly recognised that dependency may outlast majority: see, for example, *Richardson v Richardson (No.2)* [1994] 2 F.L.R. 1051, *per* Thorpe J.; *J v C (Child: Financial Provision)* [1999] 1 F.L.R. 152 (Hale J.). See, generally, M. Letts, "Children: the continuing duty to maintain" [2001] Fam. Law 839.

[287] But not a secured periodical payments order.

[288] Matrimonial Causes Act 1973 s.29(4); Civil Partnership Act 2004 Sch.5 para.49(6).

V. CAPITAL PROVISION FOR CHILDREN

The courts' powers to order capital provision for children have not been constrained by the Child Support Act 1991, although it is clear that this option cannot be used as a way to evade the restrictions imposed by that Act.[289]

15–042

A. Orders for children in divorce or dissolution proceedings

i. Orders that can be made

The court's powers to make financial orders on divorce in respect of a child of the family are wide (but not limitless).[290] In addition to periodical payments, considered above, the court may also order the payment of a lump sum or sums for the benefit of a child of the family to the child or to someone else on his or her behalf[291]; it may also order payment of a lump sum to meet liabilities or expenses incurred in maintaining or for the benefit of a child prior to the making of an application.[292] It may order the transfer of specified property to a child, or to a third party on a child's behalf[293]; it may order the settlement of property for the benefit of children of the family[294]; and it may make an order varying any "ante-nuptial or post-nuptial" settlement made on the parties to the marriage for the benefit of the parties to the marriage and/or of the children of the family.[295] If the court makes a secured periodical payments order, lump sum or property adjustment order, it may also order the sale of any property in which one or both of the parties has a beneficial interest.[296]

15–043

ii. Exercise of the court's discretion

The legislation provides that, as regards the exercise of its powers to make periodical payment orders, transfer of property orders or orders for the sale of property in relation to a child of the family, the court should have regard to all the circumstances of the case, and in particular to: the financial needs of the child; the income, earning capacity (if any), property and other financial resources of the child; any physical or mental disability of the child; the manner in which the child was being and in which the parties expected the child to be educated or trained; and the parties' financial resources and financial needs, the

15–044

---

[289] *Phillips v Peace* [1996] 2 F.L.R. 230.
[290] For a detailed consideration see the fifth edition of this work, pp.372–380.
[291] Matrimonial Causes Act 1973 s.23(1)(f); Civil Partnership Act 2004 Sch.5 para.2(f).
[292] Matrimonial Causes Act 1973 s.23(3)(a) and (b); Civil Partnership Act 2004 Sch.5 para.3(1) and (2). See *Askew-Page v Page* [2001] Fam. Law 794.
[293] Matrimonial Causes Act 1973 s.24(1)(a); Civil Partnership Act 2004 Sch.5 para.7(1)(a). See *Re B (Child: Property Transfer)* [1999] 2 F.L.R. 418; Webster [1999] Fam. Law 834.
[294] Matrimonial Causes Act 1973 s.24(1)(b); Civil Partnership Act 2004 Sch.5 para.7(1)(b). See L. Cooke, "Children and real property—trusts, interests and considerations" [1998] Fam. Law 349.
[295] Matrimonial Causes Act 1973 s.24(1)(c); Civil Partnership Act 2004 Sch.5 para.7(1)(c). The court may also make an order extinguishing or reducing the interest of either of the parties to the marriage under any such settlement: Matrimonial Causes Act 1973 s.23(1)(d); Civil Partnership Act 2004 Sch.5 para.7(1)(d).
[296] Matrimonial Causes Act 1973 s.24A; Civil Partnership Act 2004 Sch.5 para.10.

standard of living enjoyed by the family before the breakdown and any disability of either party.[297]

If the court is considering whether to exercise its financial powers against a spouse or civil partner who is not the legal parent of the child in question, the court is also to have regard to the following specified matters[298]:

"(a) to whether that party assumed any responsibility for the child's maintenance, and, if so, to the extent to which, and the basis upon which, that party assumed such responsibility and to the length of time for which that party discharged such responsibility;

(b) to whether in assuming and discharging such responsibility that party did so knowing that the child was not his or her own;

(c) to the liability of any other person to maintain the child."

It has been held that the court should not normally exercise the power to order a settlement of property so as to order life-long provision for a child who is under no disability and whose education is secured.[299] However, the housing needs of children during their minority will obviously be an important factor in any award.[300]

iii. Applications by children

15–045 The ancillary relief jurisdiction is primarily concerned with applications by one spouse or civil partner for an order against the other, but a child of the family who has attained the age of 18 may make an application for financial relief by intervening in the parents' divorce or dissolution proceedings.[301] Such a child may also intervene to seek a variation of an existing order.[302]

Therefore, a young person undertaking tertiary education may, where the parents are divorced or separated, bring an application against a parent for financial assistance with the expenses of that education. The court will consider all the circumstances in determining such an application, and the general statutory criteria apply.[303]

---

[297] Matrimonial Causes Act 1973 s.25(3); Civil Partnership Act 2004 Sch.5 para.22(2).

[298] Matrimonial Causes Act 1973 s.25(4); Civil Partnership Act 2004 Sch.5 para.22(3).

[299] *Lilford (Lord) v Glynn* [1979] 1 W.L.R. 78; *Chamberlain v Chamberlain* [1973] 1 W.L.R. 1557; *Kiely v Kiely* [1988] 1 F.L.R. 248; *Harnett v Harnett* [1973] Fam. 156.

[300] See, for example, *MB v KB* [2007] EWHC 789 (Fam).

[301] Family Proceeding Rules 1991 (SI 1999/1247) r.2.54; *Downing v Downing (Downing Intervening)* [1976] 3 W.L.R. 335 (even where the divorce was granted years earlier). The court can only make orders continuing after a child's eighteenth birthday if the child is receiving education or training or there are special circumstances: see below.

[302] Matrimonial Causes Act 1973 s.31; Civil Partnership Act 2004 Sch.5 para.51.

[303] *B v B (Adult Student: Liability to Support)* [1998] 1 F.L.R. 373; E. Harte, "University Students and financial provision" [1998] Fam. Law 103; R. Silcock, "University students and financial provision" [1998] Fam. Law 694; T. Costley-White, "Maintenance liability for students" [1999] Fam. Law 45; P. Snow, "Maintenance liability for students" [1999] Fam. Law 345.

B. Financial orders for children under the Children Act 1989

Before the coming into force of the Children Act 1989 there were a number of **15–046**
unco-ordinated procedures governing the making of financial provision orders
for children outside matrimonial proceedings—notably the provisions of the
Affiliation Proceedings Act 1957 under which the court could make an affiliation
order against the putative father of an illegitimate child, and provisions in the
Guardianship of Minors Acts that allowed married parents to seek orders about
the upbringing of their children without making any order about their marriage.
However, the Children Act 1989 reformed and assimilated the various private
law provisions relating to the courts' powers to order financial provisions in
proceedings that are not connected with the parents' relationship.[304] Although
parents who are or have been married to each other (or in a civil partnership) are
entitled to take advantage of the provisions of the Children Act, most choose to
resolve issues of this kind in divorce or dissolution proceedings. As a result, the
case law generated by the Children Act largely involves rich[305] fathers who were
not married to the mother.[306]

i. Who may apply for an order?

The following persons may apply[307] for a financial order under the Children Act **15–047**
1989 in respect of a child[308]:

- the child's legal parent: the ordinary meaning of the word is extended so
as to include any party to a marriage or civil partnership (whether or not
subsisting) "in relation to whom the child . . . is a child of the family"[309];
hence, it will be possible for a child's biological parent to initiate
proceedings claiming support for the child against the child's stepparent
or for the stepparent to seek an order against the biological parent;

- a guardian or special guardian;

- any person in whose favour a residence order[310] is in force with respect
to a child; hence, anyone given the right to care for a child by court order
can seek a financial order for the child's support.

---

[304] Law Com. No.172, para.4.63.

[305] See, for example, *A v A (A Minor: Financial Provision)* [1994] 1 F.L.R. 657; *Re P (Child: Financial Provision)* [2003] EWCA Civ 837, para.2 (father "fabulously rich"). For discussion see S. Gilmore, "Re P (Child: Financial Provision)—shoeboxes and comical shopping trips—child support from the affluent to fabulously rich" [2004] 16 C.F.L.Q. 103.

[306] Who would not, therefore, have any independent claim to maintenance or other financial provision from the father.

[307] The court may also make a financial order whenever it makes, varies, or discharges a residence order—and a residence order may be made in any family proceedings, whether or not applied for, if the court considers that the order should be made. The court can also make financial orders if the child is a ward of court, whether or not any application has been made for such an order.

[308] Children Act 1989 Sch.1 para.1.

[309] Children Act 1989 Sch.1 para.16(2).

[310] This is an order which settles the arrangements to be made about where a child is to live: see, further para.18–016.

In addition, an adult student or trainee or person who can show special circumstances may make an application for an order,[311] but in this case no order is to be made if the parents are living together in the same household.[312]

ii. Who may be required to make provision?

15–048   Only parents (as defined above) may be ordered to make provision for their children under the Children Act 1989. If children in the family have different parents, and it is envisaged that a claim will be brought against each, "the court should ensure that the applicant establishes their respective liabilities at a consolidated hearing or at consecutive hearings".[313]

iii. Orders that may be made

15–049   The range of orders available is now very wide, on the pattern of the range of orders available for children in divorce proceedings. On an application under the Children Act 1989, the court may, in addition to its powers to order periodical payments,[314] order the child's parent or parents:

- to pay a lump sum (and it is expressly provided[315] that such an order may be made to enable expenses in connection with the birth or maintenance of the child that were reasonably incurred before the making of the order to be met);

- to make a transfer or settlement of specified property to which the parent is entitled either in possession or reversion;

- to transfer a tenancy.[316]

The fact that the parents have previously entered into an agreement as to provision for the child does not automatically prevent the court from exercising its discretion; however, the agreement "must be either demonstrated to be unenforceable given the circumstances surrounding its creation or . . . inadequate in its extent".[317] However, the court is prohibited from making more than one

---

[311] But the court's powers on such an application are limited to making periodical payment or lump sum orders.

[312] The restriction thus gives effect to the settled policy of the law that a child cannot compel parents living together in a conventional relationship to provide support.

[313] *Morgan v Hill* [2006] EWCA Civ 1602, *per* Thorpe L.J. at para.54.

[314] Discussed above, at para.15–039.

[315] Children Act 1989 Sch.1 para.5(1).

[316] *K v K (Minors: Property Transfer)* [1992] 2 F.L.R. 220, CA (but note that the child's welfare is not the paramount consideration in determining such an application); *Pearson v Franklin (Parental Home: Ouster)* [1994] 1 F.L.R. 246, CA (application under Children Act 1989 Sch.1 is the appropriate procedure for dealing with occupation of family home). Under Family Law Act 1996 s.53 and Sch.7, the court has power to order the transfer of certain kinds of tenancy from one cohabitant to the other on the breakdown of their relationship. The use of this jurisdiction may have made applications for transfer of tenancies under the Children Act 1989 Sch.1 less frequent.

[317] *Morgan v Hill* [2006] EWCA Civ 1602, para.33. See Children Act 1989 Sch.1 para.10(3)(b).

settlement of property or transfer of property order against the same person for the same child.[318]

iv. Factors to be taken into account

The Children Act 1989 lays down guidelines for the exercise of the court's **15–050** powers which largely follow the precedent of matrimonial law.[319] It is provided that in deciding whether and how to exercise its powers, the court shall have regard to all the circumstances, including in particular[320]:

- the income, earning capacity, property and other financial resources that the applicant, parents[321] and the person in whose favour the order would be made has or is likely to have in the foreseeable future;

- the financial needs, obligations and responsibilities that each of those persons has or is likely to have in the foreseeable future;

- the financial needs of the child;

- the income, earning capacity (if any), property and other financial resources of the child;

- any physical or mental disability of the child;

- the manner in which the child was being, or was expected to be, educated or trained.[322]

There are minor differences between the guidelines for the exercise of the discretion in proceedings instituted under the Children Act and those laid down in relation to divorce and dissolution proceedings. The latter guidelines require the court to have regard to the contributions that each of the parties has made or is likely, in the foreseeable future, to make to the welfare of the family, to the age of each party and to the duration of the marriage or civil partnership; they also require the court to take into account the standard of living enjoyed by the family before the breakdown of the marriage. These omissions largely reflect the fact that the Children Act has the potential to apply to the briefest of relationships in which the parents may not have shared a home. The courts have held, however, that where the parties have lived together as a family, it is permissible to take the standard of living enjoyed into account, since:

---

[318] Children Act 1989 Sch.1 para.1(3). In *Phillips v Peace* [2004] EWHC 3180 (Fam), the court held that it would be inappropriate to make a further lump sum order to circumvent this prohibition.
[319] Law Com. No.172, para.4.64.
[320] Children Act 1989 Sch.1 para.4(1).
[321] This states the broad effect of the Children Act 1989 Sch.1 para.4(1)(b), but note the distinction drawn in the Act between applications for orders for persons over 18, and others.
[322] The legislation also contains a provision similar to that in the matrimonial legislation dealing with the factors to be taken into account where the "parent" against whom the order is sought is not the child's mother or father: Children Act 1989 Sch.1 para.4(2).

"[T]he extent to which the unit of primary carer and child have become accustomed to a particular level of lifestyle can impact legitimately on an evaluation of the child's needs."[323]

Similarly, the 1989 Act does not state that the child's welfare is to be the paramount or even the first consideration,[324] but it has been held that it is one of the circumstances to be taken into account.[325] Indeed, in *Re P (Child: Financial Provision)* it was stated that the child's welfare must be "a constant influence on the discretionary outcome".[326]

v. The exercise of the courts' discretion

15–051 As we have seen, the courts have the power to make capital orders in favour of children in divorce and dissolution proceedings as well as under the Children Act 1989.[327] In both contexts the courts have been insistent that the question is whether provision is required for the child's maintenance during dependency,[328] and that it is not appropriate to make provision by way of capital endowment to create a legacy to be enjoyed after dependency has ceased.[329] This policy is, however, perhaps more obvious in the context of applications under the Children Act, since here (unlike on divorce or dissolution) there is no basis on which property can be transferred to the primary carer for his or her own benefit.[330] Here, therefore, if the court deems it appropriate that a parent should provide a home for the child, the appropriate order would be for the settlement of property,[331] with a provision that the home should revert to the parent[332] once the child reaches the age of independence.[333]

It is clear, however, that the provision of a home for the child will benefit the child's primary carer as well as the child. In addition, it has been held that the child's needs may include an allowance for the parent caring for the child, for

---

[323] *F v G (Child: Financial Provision)* [2004] EWHC 1848 (Fam), *per* Singer J. at para.35.

[324] As noted by Wilson J. in *V v V (Child Maintenance)* [2001] 2 F.L.R. 799 at 807.

[325] *J v C (Child: Financial Provision)* [1999] 1 F.L.R. 152 *per* Hale J. at 156.

[326] [2003] EWCA Civ 837, *per* Thorpe L.J. at para.44.

[327] For commentaries, see R. Spon-Smith, "Provision of a home under the Children Act 1989: a suggested trust deed" [1999] Fam. Law 763; P. Cayford and J. Tod, "Schedule 1 to the Children Act 1989: consider the mother's future" [2007] Fam. Law 140.

[328] *Kiely v Kiely* [1988] F.L.R. 248.

[329] See, for example, *A v A (Minor) (Financial Provision)* [1994] 1 F.L.R. 657 in which Ward J. declined to order an outright transfer of the house in which the child was living even though the father was so rich that he could do so without even being aware of the fact.

[330] Unless he or she has an interest under property law: see Ch.5. The courts have noted that where there are potential applications under the Trusts of Land and Appointment of Trustees Act 1996 and Sch.1 to the Children Act 1989, they should be joined and determined together: *W v W (Joinder of Trusts of Land and Children Act Applications)* [2004] 2 F.L.R. 865.

[331] *Re P (Child: Financial Provision)* [2003] EWCA Civ 837, para.45. Note, however, the financial implications of the Finance Act 2006 Sch.20.

[332] Contrast *Francis v Manning* [1997] EWCA 1231 in which a transfer was ordered—although note that the transferee provided consideration for this. The alternative of paying for a rented property was considered in *Re C (Financial Provision)* [2007] 2 F.L.R. 13 but was rejected on the facts of that case.

[333] Now realistically seen as continuing beyond the legal age of majority: *J v C (Child: Financial Provision)* [1999] 1 F.L.R. 152 (age 21); *V v V (Child Maintenance)* [2001] 2 F.L.R. 799 (age 21).

example if the mother has had to give up work to care for the child.[334] This is a derivative rather than a personal entitlement,[335] but the special nature of the care provided by a parent, as opposed to a nanny, is taken into account in assessing the appropriate amount.[336]

To what extent is the presence of other children in the household, who are not the children of the parent being ordered to make provision, relevant? It is acceptable for them to receive an incidental benefit.[337] Indeed, it has been held that the needs of the child in question may include the provision of a property large enough to house any half-siblings,[338] but the courts have stressed that the court's jurisdiction is limited to making an order against a person "as a parent of a child",[339] and that such a person should not be fixed with responsibility for other children living in the household.[340]

In contrast to the settlement of property, lump sums: **15–052**

> "[A]re not designed to revert to the payer. It is of their essence that they are paid once and for all and are used to reimburse past expenditure or are spent on current or future needs."[341]

The provision of a lump sum should be used for the purpose of meeting specific expenditure, and not as means of capitalising periodic maintenance to circumvent the prohibition in s.8(3) of the Child Support Act 1991. In *Phillips v Peace*,[342] for example, the father's house was worth £2.6 million and he enjoyed a lavish lifestyle. He nevertheless obtained a nil child support assessment on the basis that he had no income. Johnson J. ordered him to pay £90,000 to provide a home and furniture,[343] holding that the court's powers under the Children Act should be exercised only to meet the child's needs for a particular item of capital expenditure, rather than a continuing future income. Lump sum orders may also be made for the specific purpose of meeting expenses or liabilities incurred in the past on the maintenance of children, or otherwise attributable to their benefit.[344] In this context the needs of the child may be widely construed.[345]

---

[334] *Haroutunian v Jennings* (1980) 1 F.L.R. 62; *A v A (A Minor) (Financial Provision)* [1994] 1 F.L.R. 657. Alternatively, a primary carer who is in paid employment may employ a nanny to provide some of the day-to-day care: *F v G (Child: Financial Provision)* [2004] EWHC 1848 (Fam).

[335] See, for example, *Re P (Child: Financial Provision)* [2003] EWCA Civ 837, para.48.

[336] *Re P (Child: Financial Provision)* [2003] EWCA Civ 837.

[337] See *Morgan v Hill* [2006] EWCA Civ 1602 at para.65.

[338] See, for example, *J v C (Child: Financial Provision)* [1999] 1 F.L.R. 152 at p.160.

[339] *Morgan v Hill* [2006] EWCA Civ 1602 at para.38.

[340] See, for example, *Phillips v Peace* [2004] EWHC 3180 (Fam), para.11.

[341] *Phillips v Peace* [2004] EWHC 3180 (Fam), para.27.

[342] [1996] 2 F.L.R. 230; J. Priest, "Child support and the non-standard earner" (1996) 9 C.F.L.Q. 63.

[343] Plus some items of past expenditure: expenses associated with the birth, baby clothing and equipment, and school registration.

[344] Children Act 1989 Sch.1 para.5. See, for example, *Phillips v Peace* [1996] 2 F.L.R. 230; *J v C (Child: Financial Provision)* [1999] 1 F.L.R. 152; *Askew-Page v Page* [2001] Fam. Law 794.

[345] See, for example, *M-T v T* [2006] EWHC 2494 (Fam), in which a payment in respect of the mother's legal costs was held to be a payment for the benefit of the children, given that she was acting in a representative capacity. This was the opposite conclusion to that reached in *W v J (Child: Variation of Financial Provision)* [2003] EWHC 2657, which was confined to its facts by the Court of Appeal in *Re S (Child: Financial Provision)* [2004] EWCA Civ 1685.

In deciding on the appropriate level of financial provision, the courts have consistently held in recent years that a child is entitled to be brought up in circumstances that bear some sort of relationship to the non-resident parent's own standard of living and resources.[346] One justification for so doing is to facilitate any ongoing relationship between parent and child,[347] but this principle is independent of the standard of living enjoyed while the family was intact, as is clear from *J v C (Child: Financial Provision)*.[348] In this case the child's father won £1.4 million on the national lottery some time after the parties had separated. Hale J. ordered that £70,000 should be settled to provide housing and £12,000 provided for furniture, noting that:

> "Parents are responsible for their children during their dependency. The fact that such riches as they have came after the breakup of the relationship cannot affect that."[349]

The courts have stressed, however, that there is no sliding scale of awards relative to wealth, and that the focus should be on the child's needs, viewed in the context of the resources available, rather than on the parent's wealth in relation to other parents who have been ordered to make provision.[350]

VI. Conclusion

15–053 Research suggests that at present, only a minority of those who are eligible to receive child maintenance actually do so: of the 2.5 million eligible parents with care, 49 per cent have no arrangement in place[351] and only 35 per cent actually receive maintenance.[352] Private arrangements are already the most common arrangement, and this looks set to continue in the future with the removal of any compulsion to use the administrative system and the likelihood of charges being introduced on the one hand, and the issue of access to the courts being exacerbated by cuts in legal funding on the other. Whether such private arrangements are likely to result in higher rates of compliance and satisfaction, as envisaged by Sir David Henshaw in his report, seems rather over-optimistic; those who have agreed on such matters are perhaps by definition those who are able to co-operate in the first place, and leaving other couples with no option other than private ordering might not result in the same benefits.

---

[346] See *H v P (Illegitimate Child: Capital Provision)* [1993] Fam. Law 515; *J v C (Child: Financial Provision)* [1999] 1 F.L.R. 152; *Re P (Child: Financial Provision)* [2003] EWCA Civ 837; *Re C (A Child: Financial Provision)* [2007] 2 F.L.R. 13; *SW v RC* [2008] EWHC 73 (Fam).
[347] See, for example, *Re P (Child: Financial Provision)* [2003] EWCA Civ 837, para.69.
[348] [1999] 1 F.L.R. 152.
[349] [1999] 1 F.L.R. 152 at p.160.
[350] See, for example, *Re S (Unmarried Parents: Financial Provisions)* [2006] EWCA Civ 479, in which the court stressed that it was erroneous simply to scale down the award in proportion to the father's wealth.
[351] C. Bullen, *Child Maintenance: The Eligible Population in Great Britain* (DWP Working Paper No.41, 2007), fig.3.1.
[352] Bullen, *Child Maintenance: The Eligible Population in Great Britain*, Table 3.5.

PART V

CHILDREN AND FAMILY LAW

Chapter Sixteen

CHILDREN

I.   INTRODUCTION................................ 16–001
II. CHILDREN'S RIGHTS 16–005
    A. Theoretical perspectives................. 16–005
    B. Children's rights in international
    law 16–007
III. CHILDREN'S   RIGHTS   AND
ENGLISH LAW.. 16–010
    A. The Gillick case 16–011
    B. The retreat from Gillick................. 16–015

C. Children's rights under the
European Convention of Human
Rights 16–017
D. Children's rights and the Children
Act 1989... 16–019
E. Children as parties in legal
proceedings 16–020
F. Rights in other legislation.............. 16–023
G. Children of unmarried parents....... 16–024

I. Introduction

"The modern tendency of the law is to recognise that children are indeed people."[1] The Children Act 1989 defines a child as "a person under the age of eighteen",[2] but neither all its provisions[3] nor other laws relating to children are linked to the age of majority.[4] Indeed, there is little consistency in the age below which legislation concerning children applies. Children under 18 may not be tattooed[5] or enter betting shops,[6] those under 17 may not buy crossbows,[7] and those under 16 may not buy National Lottery tickets[8] or obtain the "morning-

16–001

---

[1] *Kingston upon Thames BC v Prince* [1999] 1 F.L.R. 593, CA, *per* Hale J. at 603. For a discussion of earlier approaches, see below, para.16–002.

[2] Children Act 1989 s.105(1); similarly UN Convention on the Rights of the Child art.1 "unless . . . majority is attained earlier". The age of majority is 18 years: Family Law Reform Act 1969 s.1(1).

[3] Care and supervision orders may not be made in respect of children over the age of 17 years: s.31(3), but any existing order may last until age 18: s.91(10); s.8 orders may only be made in respect of children over the age of 16 in exceptional circumstances: s.9(7); for example, *Re M (Contact: Parental Responsibility)* [2001] 2 F.L.R. 342.

[4] C. Hamilton et al. *At What Age Can I?* (Children's Legal Centre, 2006).

[5] Tattooing of Minors Act 1969 s.1.

[6] Betting, Gaming and Lotteries Act 1963 s.21.

[7] Crossbows Act 1987 s.1.

[8] National Lottery Act 1993 s.12; National Lottery Regulations 1994 (SI 1994/189) r.3. Raising the age to 18 has been recommended: *Report of the Gaming Board for Great Britain* (1994–5 HC 587), and a third of pupils aged 13–15 have bought lottery tickets: National Lottery Commission, *Under 16s and the National Lottery* (2000).

after" pill without a prescription.[9] At common law[10] and by statute[11] a child's capacity to act may depend not on age[12] but maturity, so there is no simple way adults can know what adolescents may lawfully do.

Much of the law relating to children is based on paternalism or control.[13] Children are viewed as potential victims; Parliament has sought to protect the young from the exploitation of unscrupulous adults and from their presumed inability to make wise decisions.[14] There are many statutes that deny children access to substances and services[15] that may be equally damaging for adults, but it is unacceptable (or impracticable) to restrict the liberty of adults in a democratic society. In recognition of the investment children represent for society, paternalistic provisions have been enacted that are intended to help young people reach their full potential[16] and to protect them from the worst consequences of their own failings.[17] Young people are also seen as threats and are controlled for the good of society in the belief that they must be made to take responsibility[18] or because their labour might reduce adult wage rates or employment.

Most children[19] live for at least part of their childhood with their parents; parents are able to control the actions and determine the experiences at least of young children. The relationship between parents and the state, (i.e. the extent to which the law allows parents freedom to choose how their children grow up) is important. Originally, parents' control of young children was recognised by the

---

[9] Prescription Only Medicines (Human Use) Amendment (No.3) Order 2000, (SI 2000/3231); hormonal emergency contraception is available to under 16's on prescription.

[10] *Gillick v W Norfolk and Wisbech AHA* [1986] A.C. 112 discussed below para.16–009.

[11] e.g. Children Act 1989 s.10(8) (obtain leave to bring proceedings), ss.43(8), 44(7) (refuse a medical examination ordered by the court).

[12] But the Children (Scotland) Act 1995 provides that children aged 12 are presumed to be competent to form a view (s.6(1)).

[13] H. Hendrick, *Child Welfare, England 1872–1989* (London: Routledge, 1994); J. Eekelaar et al. "Victims or threats? Children in care proceedings" [1982] J.S.W.L. 68; L. Fox-Harding, *Perspectives in Child Care Policy* (London: Longman, 1991). Cretney (2003), Ch.20.

[14] There is considerable evidence that older children are not less capable, at least if they are able to obtain decision-making experience: see G. Melton, G. Koocher and M. Saks, *Children's Competence to Consent* (New York: Plenum, 1982), pp.14–16. Even young children can display considerable competence: P. Alderson, *Young Children's Rights* (London: SCF, 2000), pp.56–61. There are benefits for young people in developing their capacity towards autonomy through involving them in decision-making: J. Fortin, *Children's Rights and the Developing Law* (London: Butterworths, 2003), p.26.

[15] For example alcohol, tobacco, gambling and knives.

[16] Particularly compulsory education, although the intention may be merely to produce adults trained in the way society or the parents choose; see below. Also, local authority duties to children in need; see Children Act 1989 Pt III and Ch.21, below.

[17] For example the introduction of the juvenile court: see A. Platt, *The Child Savers: the Invention of Delinquency* (Chicago: University of Chicago Press, 1969); P. Parsloe, *Juvenile Justice in Britain and the United States* (London: Routledge and Kegan Paul, 1978). The Beijing rules (1985) set out internationally agreed standards for juvenile justice; see Van Bueren (1995) p.170.

[18] "Children above the age of criminal responsibility are generally mature enough to account for their actions and the law should recognise this": *No More Excuses—A New Approach to Tackling Youth Crime in England and Wales* (Cm.3809 (1997)), Introduction; C. Piper, "The Crime and Disorder Act 1998: child and community 'safety'" [1999] M.L.R. 397.

[19] For a statistical account of the child population, see B. Botting, "Children" (2002) 32 *Social Trends*; M. Willitts et al. *Families with Children in Britain 2004* (DWP Research Report No.340, (2006).

common law, subject only to criminal penalties for abuse.[20] However, exploitation of children in the harsh employment conditions of the nineteenth century led to the introduction of legislation that protected children and consequently limited parental action.[21] Later statutes enabled children to be removed from parents who ill-treated them.[22] The European Convention on Human Rights, particularly art.8, which imposes obligations to respect private and family life, has influenced state/family relationships for half a century.[23] The Children Act 1989 now provides that the state may intervene to protect children where they are suffering (or likely to suffer) significant harm.[24] The development of the welfare state improved access to health and social care,[25] but despite prosperity, the United Kingdom rates poorly in terms of children's wellbeing.[26] More children than ever before are now experiencing the consequences of the breakdown of their parents' relationship and the poverty and disruption this often brings.[27] The Government's attempts at ending child poverty have been focused on improving education and childcare, increasing employment (particularly amongst lone parents) and providing tax credits.[28] Changes in education have brought children into formal schooling earlier and have sought to raise the proportion continuing in education beyond age 18.[29] The Government has set a new reform agenda to develop and improve services so that every child has the chance to reach their potential.[30] The programme is focused on the five outcomes[31] that mattered most to children and young people. Children are also targeted and exploited as consumers.[32] Children's lives are thus shaped by their parents, by the state that controls and supports them and their parents, and by the commercial world. The law sets the balance

---

[20] See L. Pollock, *Forgotten Children: Parent Child Relations from 1500–1900* (Cambridge: Cambridge University Press, 1983), pp.92–95 for examples of newspaper reports of parents' trials.
[21] J. Eekelaar, "The emergence of children's rights" (1986) 6 Ox. J.L.S. 161 at 167.
[22] Prevention of Cruelty to Children Act 1889; see R. Cooter (ed.), *In The Name Of The Child: Health and Welfare 1880–1940* (London: Routledge, 1992).
[23] The UK ratified the Convention in 1951 and recognised the right of the Court of Human Rights to hear individual petitions in 1966. There were important decisions about child law from the late 1970s and the Children Act 1989 was drafted to comply with the obligations in the Convention; see below, para.16–013 and J. Fortin, *Children's Rights and the Developing Law*.
[24] Children Act 1989 s.31(2).
[25] See, generally, H. Hendrick, *Child Welfare in England 1872–1989* (1994); R. Rogers, *Crowther to Warnock* (London: Heinemann, 1984).
[26] UNICEF, *An Overview of Children's Well-being in Rich Countries* (2007).
[27] ONS, (2002) 32 *Social Trends* 18; ONS, *Focus on Families* (2005). For a discussion of the effect of family breakdown on children and their relationships, see B. Rodgers and J. Pryor, *Divorce and Separation: The Outcomes for Children* (York: Joseph Rowntree Foundation, 1998).
[28] E. Minoff, *The UK Commitment: Ending Child Poverty by 2020* (CLASP, 2006); M. Brewer and Paul Gregg, *Eradicating Child Poverty in Britain: Welfare Reform and Children Since 1997* (IFS, 2001).
[29] DFES, *Annual Report 2006* (Cm.6812 (2006)), Ch.2 sets out the Government's targets for education and skills.
[30] *Every Child Matters* (Cm.5860 (2003)); DfES, *Every Child Matters: Change for Children* (2004) outlines key changes.
[31] Children Act 2004 s.2(3) "physical and mental health and emotional well-being; protection from harm and neglect; education, training and recreation; the contribution made by them to society; social and economic well-being".
[32] D. Piachaud, "Child poverty, opportunities and the quality of life" [2001] *Political Quarterly* 446; M. John, *Children's Rights and Power: Charging Up for a New Century* (London: Jessica Kingsley, 2003), p.120.

between the state and the family, within the family between the parents and the child, and may regulate the markets in services aimed at children.[33]

16–002   The extent to which children have been recognised and treated as different from adults has varied over time and between social classes.[34] In medieval times, children beyond infancy worked and socialised alongside adults; childhood was less distinct and special than it is now.[35] Later, changes associated with the Renaissance and the Reformation led to children being placed in "a sort of quarantine"[36] for education and indoctrination before they were considered fit to join adult society. Industrialisation initially brought children into factories working alongside their parents, but the danger to their health and the threat they posed to adult employment lead to legislation[37] to exclude children from the workforce. Despite controls, many children worked.[38] The complexity of modern life and society's expectations of young people increased the period of education needed to prepare for it.[39] In recent years, the lack of employment opportunities for those without skills, the removal of social security benefits[40] and the shortage of affordable housing have together extended the period during which young people live with their families.[41]

Three separate but interwoven threads may be identified in the treatment of childhood by the law: minority, parental rights[42] and emancipation. In early English society, the age when a child reached his/her majority depended on the position of their family within the feudal system. Boys from the knightly class had to wait until they were 21; before that age they were considered physically

---

[33] For example, by restricting advertising during children's television programmes, as in Sweden, or controlling school lunches: School Standards and Framework Act 1998 s.114A, added by Education and Inspections Act 2006 s.86.

[34] P. Aries, *Centuries of Childhood* (London: Adam Philips, 1996); I. Pinchbeck and M. Hewitt, *Children in English Society, Vol. I* (1969); *Vol. II* (London: Routledge and Kegan Paul, 1973); F. Pollock and F. Maitland, *The History of English Law Before the Time of Edward I Vol. 2* (1923); L. Pollock, *A Lasting Relationship: Parents and Children over Three Centuries* (London: Fourth Estate, 1987); C. Heywood, *A History of Children and Childhood in the West Medieval to Modern Times* (Maklen, Mass.: Polity, 2001).

[35] Heywood, *A History of Children*, pp.18, 171; cf. Aries, *Centuries of Childhood*, p.125 who suggested that there was no concept of childhood.

[36] Aries, *Centuries of Childhood*, p.396.

[37] Children and Young Persons Act 1933 ss.18–21, as amended by the Children (Protection at Work) Regulations 1998 (SI 1998/276) to implement EC 94/33; Children (Protection at Work) (No.2) Regulations 2000 (SI 2000/2548). The UK has also ratified ILO Convention No.182 on the elimination of the most hazardous forms of child labour.

[38] TUC, *Dazed and Confused* (2004); Better Regulation Task Force, *The Regulation of Child Employment* (2004).

[39] Aries noted that childhood lengthened more rapidly for boys than girls who might be married and running a household in their early teens. This was reflected in Scots law: "pupils" (i.e. girls below 12 and boys below 14) had more limited capacity, but now the Age of Legal Capacity (Scotland) Act 1991 applies the same age to both boys and girls. The English common law took a contrary view; girls reached the age of discretion at 16 but boys at 14. This protective approach to girls is reflected in current attitudes to girls' sexuality.

[40] Social Security Act 1988 s.4(1); lower rates of benefit are also payable to single people under the age of 25 without children; see, generally, N. Harris, *Social Security for Young People* (1989) and G. Jones and C. Wallace, *Youth, Family and Citizenship* (1992).

[41] Nearly half those aged under 24 continue to live with a parent; the age of leaving home has risen since 1991: J. Matheson and C. Summerfield (eds), *Social Focus on Young People* (2000) p.12.

[42] Part of parental responsibility: see Children Act 1989 s.3, see paras 16–000 *et seq*.

too weak to take an adult role by wearing armour.[43] Gradually, the age of 21 came to be regarded as the age of majority for all children. However, the lack of clear or relevant reasons for that age encouraged the Latey Committee on the Age of Majority[44] to recommend the reduction to age 18.[45] This was enacted in the Family Law Reform Act 1969. The UN Convention on the Rights of the Child applies to all young people below the age of 18, unless they achieve full civil rights at an earlier age.[46] Below the age of majority, a person's participation in civic life is restricted. Under 18s may not vote,[47] sit on a jury[48] nor hold public office.[49] Minors cannot hold a legal estate in land,[50] nor can they make a valid will.[51] However, minority was never viewed as a time when a person lacked all legal capacity. Minors of any age can be liable in tort for their actions[52] and those beyond 10 under the criminal law.[53] At common law, contracts entered into by minors are enforceable by them but not against them, with the exception of contracts for necessaries or for certain lasting property rights and contracts of employment.[54] The position in Scotland is different. Children aged 16 have the capacity to enter into any transaction; any child may enter into transactions "of a kind commonly entered into by persons of the child's age and circumstances and on terms which are not unreasonable".[55]

The nature and extent of a parent's right to control a child's life has been the subject of considerable controversy.[56] In Victorian times, it appears that the father was viewed as having near absolute rights over his children, and could exercise

[43] Pollock and Maitland (1923), p.438.

[44] Cmnd.3342 (1967).

[45] "That most young people mature today earlier than in the past; at 18 most young people are ready for these responsibilities and would greatly profit by them as would . . . the community as a whole": para.134.

[46] UN Convention of the Rights of the Child art.1.

[47] Representation of the People Act 1949 s.1(1)(c) and Sch.2.

[48] Juries Act 1974 s.7(2)(a).

[49] This was used to justify the abolition of pupil governors for schools: Education (No.2) Act 1986 s.15(4); see *Hansard*, HC Vol.93, col.207 and D. Pannick (1986) 25 *Childright* 15.

[50] Law of Property Act 1925 s.1(6). They may hold an equitable estate under a trust: Trust in Land and Appointment of Trustees Act 1996 Sch.1; *Kingston upon Thames BC v Prince* [1999] 1 F.L.R. 593, CA.

[51] Wills Act 1837 ss.7, 11. The effect is that children die intestate: see *Bouette v Rose* [2000] 1 F.L.R. 363 CA.

[52] W. Rogers, *Winfield and Jolowicz on Tort*, 17th edn (2006), para.24.16; liability in negligence depends on the reasonable foresight of a child of the defendant's age: *Mullin v Richards* [1998] 1 All E.R. 920 CA.

[53] Children and Young Persons Act 1933 s.50, amended by Children and Young Persons Act 1963 s.16. The presumption of *doli incapax* that applied to those between ages 10 and 13 was abolished by Crime and Disorder Act 1998 s.34. The UN Committee on the Rights of the Child expressed concern at the low age of criminal responsibility: CRC/C/15/Add.188, para.59.

[54] The Infants Relief Act 1874 made minors' contracts for loans and non-necessaries "absolutely void", but following recommendations in Law Commission Report No.134 (1984 HCP 494), it was repealed by the Minors' Contracts Act 1987.

[55] Age of Legal Capacity (Scotland) Act 1991 s.2(1). Children of 12 may also make their will: s.2(2).

[56] The different views can be seen in views of the Court of Appeal and House of Lords in *Gillick v W Norfolk and Wisbech AHA* [1986] A.C. 112, HL, below 16–009. See also J. Hall, "The waning of parental rights" [1972B] C.L.J. 248; J. Eekelaar, "What are parental rights?" (1973) 89 L.Q.R. 210; S. Maidment, "The fragmentation of parental rights" [1981] C.L.J. 135; B. Dickens, "The modern function and limits of parental rights" (1981) 97 L.Q.R. 462; F. Zimring, *The Changing Legal World of Adolescence* (New York: Free Press, 1982).

these without consideration for their welfare. This approach to parental rights can be likened to treating the child as property.[57] However, there is authority for the propositions that parents had rights merely so that they could protect their children, that the proprietary right protected by the law was not the right to the child's custody but the right to determine the marriage of an heir,[58] and that parents' rights are not capable of founding an action in tort for the benefit of the parents.[59]

16–003   Where the law gave a parent control over the child's action, this did not make the child legally incapable nor the parent liable for the child's torts,[60] but put those who dealt with the child at risk of an action by the parent. Thus, a minor could contract a valid marriage, but the spouse might be liable to the parent for loss of the child's services.[61] A similar action could be brought by the parent when the child had been injured or killed. These actions were abolished by the Law Reform (Miscellaneous) Provisions Act 1970, and parents were left with no obvious way to enforce their control against third parties.

The modern conception of parental power is one of responsibilities rather than rights.[62] The Children Act 1989 defines "parental responsibility" in terms of "rights, duties and powers".[63] Parental responsibility is also seen as diminishing as the child grows in maturity—"it starts with a right of control and ends with little more than advice".[64] It therefore leaves older children with an ever increasing sphere within which to make their own decisions.

The concept of emancipation—which enables a child to gain the right to be free from parental control—has not yet been fully developed in English law. Children beyond the age of discretion (which was 14 for boys and 16 for girls)[65] were not subject to complete parental control; the courts would refuse a parent's action for habeas corpus in respect of a child who did not wish to return to the parents, and might apply the same rule to younger children who were mature.[66] There was, however, no general rule that minors acquired increased capacity at

---

[57] J. Montgomery, "Children as property?" (1988) 51 M.L.R. 323; Eekelaar suggests that children were viewed as agents for the devolution of property within the family: J. Eekelaar, "The emergence of children's rights" (1986) 6 Ox. J.L.S. 161 at 163.
[58] Pollock and Maitland (1923), p.444; W. Holdsworth, *A History of English Law*, 3rd edn (1923), Vol.III, p.512. Holdsworth refers to a conflict in the Middle Ages between the older view that guardianship was for the benefit of the guardian and the newer view that it was for the child, but notes that the common law had no machinery to enforce the guardian's responsibilities.
[59] *F v Wirral MBC* [1991] Fam. 69, CA; *D v E Berkshire Community Health NHS Trust* [2005] 2 F.L.R. 284 HL. But in *TP and KM v UK* [2001] 2 F.L.R. 549, both the mother and daughter obtained compensation for breach of their rights of respect for family life after the improper removal of the daughter by the local authority.
[60] Unless these were the result of the parent's negligent control of the child: *Winfield & Jolowicz* (2006), para.24.17.
[61] J. Fleming, *Law of Torts*, 9th edn (Sydney: LBC, 1998), p.721. Originally there was no action where a child had merely been abducted, because a parent had no proprietary right in their child: *Barham v Dennis* (1600) Cro. Eliz. 770, but a more general remedy was sanctioned probably in the seventeenth century.
[62] *Illegitimacy* (Law Com. No. 118 (1982)), para.4.19; *Guardianship & Custody* (Law Com. No.172 (1988)), para.2.4.
[63] Children Act 1989 s.3.
[64] *Per* Lord Denning M.R., *Hewer v Bryant* [1970] 1 Q.B. 357 at 369; see also *Gillick v W Norfolk and Wisbech AHA* [1986] A.C. 112, below para.16–009.
[65] *R. v Howes Ex p. Barford* (1860) 3 E. & E. 332; see also *Re Agar-Ellis* (1883) 24 Ch. D. 317.
[66] *R. v Gyngall* [1893] 2 Q.B. 232 at 245.

16.[67] Mature children under 16 may bring proceedings under the Children Act 1989 if they wish to live separately from their parents,[68] but the court does not remove the parents' parental responsibility. A residence order that determines where the child lives also confers parental responsibility on the person with the order.[69] Under Scots law, children acquire full legal capacity (but not civil rights) at age 16.[70] In the United States, the judiciary allowed the termination of obligations that arose from the parent/child relationship; emancipation statutes removed the disabilities of minors. Emancipation was intended to assist mature minors by recognising their independence, but is frequently sought by parents seeking to end their obligations.[71]

The inter-relation of these three concepts—minority, parental responsibilities **16–004** and emancipation—is not clear. The Latey Committee's confusion is evident from their acknowledgement that minors had legal capacity to act without parental consent but their acceptance that rigid disciplinary rules in colleges could be justified by reference to the concept of in loco parentis.[72] The law relating to contract developed separately from that relating to parental rights; whatever powers parents had, it appears that minors were able to enter into contracts of employment without parental consent.[73]

A fourth strand, social citizenship,[74] is beginning to influence public and private relationships with children, and the common law[75] but only has limited recognition in English law.[76] Social citizenship acknowledges children's capacity to influence[77] their own lives and their moral right to participate in decisions affecting them[78] by supporting children's consultation within and beyond the

---

[67] H. Bevan, *Child Law* (1989), para.1.12.

[68] The child must obtain leave: Children Act 1989 s.10(8), and may be permitted to bring proceedings without a guardian ad litem or next friend: Family Proceedings Rules 1991 (SI 1991/1247) r.9.2A; *Re S (A Minor) (Child Representation)* [1993] Fam. 263, CA; see also H. Houghton-James, "Children divorcing their parents" [1994] J.S.W.F.L 185, and below, para.16–020.

[69] Children Act 1989 ss.8(1), 12(2), and below, paras 17–044 and 18–016.

[70] Age of Legal Capacity Scotland Act 1991 s.1; see Scottish Law Commission, *Consultative Memo No.65, Legal Capacity and Responsibility of Minors and Pupils* (1985) for the background to this Act. Parental power is consequently limited in relation to over 16 year olds; Children (Scotland) Act 1995 ss.1, 2.

[71] R. Mnookin, *Child, Family & State* (Boston: Little Brown, 1978), Ch.6; C. Sanger and E. Willemsen, "Minor changes: emancipating children in modern times" (1992) 25 U. Mich. J. L. Ref 239.

[72] i.e. that college authorities were in the position of the parents.

[73] Eekelaar (1986) Ox.J.L.S. 161 citing *Doyle v White City Stadium Ltd* [1935] 1 K.B. 110 where a minor was held bound by his contract as a professional boxer.

[74] J. Roche, "Children's rights, participation and citizenship" (1999) 6(4) *Childhood* 475; B. Neale and C. Smart, *Good The Talk?* (2001).

[75] *Gillick v W Norfolk and Wisbech AHA* [1986] A.C. 112.

[76] The Children Act 1989 s.22(4)(5) requires local authorities to consult looked-after children in relation to their care, and s.1(3) requires the courts to consider the child's wishes and feelings when making decisions about upbringing. But there is no comparable obligation on parents: cf. Children (Scotland) Act 1995 s.6 where those exercising parental power to make major decisions are required to have regard to the child's views, and children aged 12 years are presumed to have sufficient maturity to form a view.

[77] Referred to by sociologists as their "agency": see A. James et al., *Theorizing childhood* (Cambridge: Polity, 1998); A. James and A. James, *Constructing Childhood: Theory, Policy and Social Practice* (Basingstoke: Palgrave Maxmillan, 2004).

[78] DH *Children Act Now* (2001), p.3. "Children's active participation is essential" for services responsive to their needs: DfES, *Children Act 1989 Report 2004 and 2005* (2006), p.48.

family. It reflects both the development of more democratic relationships within families[79] and the recognition by international law that children have rights.[80] Children's commissioners or ombudsmen have been established in many countries to promote children's rights and the implementation of the Children's Rights Convention.[81] There has been a major growth in advocacy and children's rights services in England and Wales, particularly for children in public care.[82] A Commissioner was established for Welsh children in 2001,[83] and the Children Act 2004 established the office "Children's Commissioner", with the function of promoting awareness of the views and interests of children in England, and in other parts of the United Kingdom in relation to matters that have not been devolved.[84] Individually and collaboratively these commissioners have begun to raise awareness of children's concerns.

II. CHILDREN'S RIGHTS

A. Theoretical perspectives

16–005 A discussion of children's rights requires a consideration of the nature of rights[85] and of the problems in applying theories of rights to children. It is necessary to determine which rights children should be recognised as holding, and whether rights provide an adequate framework for handling ethical issues relating to children. The phrase "children's rights" has been called a slogan in search of a definition, and has been used in many different ways.[86] "Rights" has been used in the Hohfeldian sense of something that another person has a duty to permit[87] (e.g. the right to express a view to a decision-maker, the right to education or the right to leave home). The word "right" has also been applied to indicate moral or social goals. Thus, the UN Declaration of the Rights of the Child, a forerunner of the 1989 Convention[88] set out the rights that were intended to produce a "happy childhood"[89] but established no enforcement mechanism.

---

[79] Neale and Smart, *Good The Talk?*, pp.6, 22.
[80] UN Convention on the Rights of the Child, art.12 sets out children's right to express views, and have them given due weight, in matters affecting them: see below, para.16–007.
[81] For a discussion of the role of such services, see: "Independent institutions protecting children's rights" (2001) 8 *Innocenti Digest*.
[82] Children Act 1989 s.26A, and below para.21–082. The Office for Standards in Education, Children's Services and Skills has a Children's Rights Director: Education and Inspections Act 2006 s.120.
[83] Care Standards Act 2000 ss.72A and 75A and Children's Commissioner for Wales Act 2001: see K. Hollingsworth and G. Douglas, "Creating a children's champion for Wales" [2002] M.L.R. 58.
[84] Children Act 2004 s.2(1); ss.6–8 include complex provisions for the division of responsibilities for the separate parts of the UK; and see J. Williams, "Effective government structures for children?: the UK's four Children's Commissioners" [2005] C.F.L.Q. 37.
[85] For a discussion of this issue, see W. Lucy, "Controversy about children's rights", in D. Freestone (ed.), *Children and the Law* (Hull University Press, 1990).
[86] See M.D.A. Freeman, "The rights of children in the International Year of the Child" [1980] C.L.P. 1, 16, and in *The Rights and Wrongs of Children* (London: Pinter, 1983), Chs 1, 2; M. Freeman and P. Veerman (eds), *Ideologies of Children's Rights* (Dordrecht: Nijhoff, 1992).
[87] W.N. Hohfeld, *Fundamental Legal Conceptions* (New Haven: Yale University Press, 1919).
[88] United Nations Convention on the Rights of the Child; see G. Van Bueren, *The International Law on the Rights of the Child* (Dordrecht: Nijhoff, 1995), Ch.1 and below.
[89] United National Declaration of the Rights of the Child 1959, Preamble.

There are two broadly competing theories of the nature of rights: the "will" and the "interest" theory. The "will" theory is based on the notion that to have a right involves being able to make a choice about the enforcement of duties imposed on others. It has been used to deny the possibility of young children having rights because they lack the physical and intellectual capacity to exercise choice over most aspects of their lives.[90] The "interest" theory does not require an autonomous claimant, only an identifiable interest and a corresponding duty. It allows the recognition of rights for children and has been relied on widely. Development of children's rights from this theory requires consideration of which of children's interests should give rise to rights.[91] Two approaches have been identified: the "Nurturance orientation" and the "Self-determination orientation".[92] Both have sought to improve children's lives; the former by protecting them, the latter by permitting them greater autonomy. Taking children's rights more seriously requires policies, practices, structures and laws that protect both children and their rights.[93] For this reason, Freeman, adapting Rawls' theory of justice,[94] has argued for "liberal paternalism",[95] a middle way that acknowledges both autonomy and protection. The first two of Freeman's categories—rights to welfare and rights to protection—are paternalistic—rights that the adult world would consider appropriate whether or not children claimed them for themselves. The third and fourth categories—the right to be treated like adults and rights against adults—belong to a more liberalist school.[96] Freeman recognises that these rights may conflict with each other and with parents' rights. He argues that children's rights to be treated like adults should depend on their capacity, assessed on a case-by-case basis.[97] Parents should be able to impose their decisions where these are consistent with an objective evaluation of Rawls' "primary social goods" (e.g. liberty, health and opportunity). In other cases, disputes between parents and children should be referred to the courts.[98] This approach largely reflects that taken under English law, but where a dispute about a child's upbringing is referred to the courts, the decision is made according to what is in the child's best interests. Thus, the court may refuse any order if this would enshrine a state of affairs that could be better resolved by discussion[99]; it may make orders that conflict with a child's wishes.[100]

---

[90] N. MacCormick "Children's rights: a test case for theories of right" (1976) 62 *Fur Rechts und Sozialphilosophie* 305 (reprinted in N. MacCormick, *Legal Right and Social Democracy* (1982), Ch.8); see also T. Campbell, "The rights of the minor" (1992) 6 Int. J. Law & Fam. 1, 2.

[91] Campbell, "The rights of the minor", p.7.

[92] C. Rogers and L. Wrightsman, "Attitudes towards children's rights—nurturance or self-determination" (1978) 34(2) *Journal of Social Issues* 59.

[93] M. Freeman, "Taking children's rights more seriously" (1992) 6. Int. J. Law & Fam. 52 at 69.

[94] J. Rawls, *Theory of Justice* (Oxford: Clarendon, 1972).

[95] M. Freeman, *The Rights and Wrongs of Children* (1983); M. Freeman, *The Moral Status of Children* (Hague: Nijhoff, 1997).

[96] Freeman, *The Rights and Wrongs of Children*, pp.45–49; A. Bainham, *Children the Modern Law* 2nd edn (Bristol: Family Law, 1998), p.87.

[97] Freeman, *The Rights and Wrongs of Children*, p.46.

[98] Freeman, *The Rights and Wrongs of Children*, pp.51–52.

[99] *Re C (A Minor) (Leave to Seek Section 8 Orders)* [1994] 1 F.L.R. 26.

[100] *Re C (A Minor) (Care: Child's Wishes)* [1993] 1 F.L.R. 832; *Re M (Minors) (Care Proceedings: Child's Wishes)* [1994] 1 F.L.R. 749; even refusing permission for a change of name for children aged 12, 14 and 16: *Re B (Change of Surname)* [1996] 1 F.L.R. 79.

John Eekelaar has examined the status of the concept of children's rights within English law.[101] Using Joseph Raz's definition of rights and interests,[102] he has identified three interests that merit protection as rights and which might plausibly be claimed by children. According to Eekelaar, children have a "basic interest" in receiving physical and emotional care within the social capabilities of their immediate care-givers, which is recognised by child protection legislation. They also have a "developmental interest" in having an equal opportunity to have their capacities developed to their best advantage.[103] The third interest, the "autonomy interest", which may only be a version of the developmental interest, is the child's interest in taking action freely without adult control. Since this interest might conflict with the basic interest and the developmental interest (without some protective control, a child might lose the opportunity to become a rational adult), Eekelaar ranks it as subordinate to the other two. He concludes that both the developmental interest and the autonomy interest have been recognised to some extent by English law,[104] and that the emphasis on decision-making capacity in the *Gillick* case[105] allows the conflicts between them to be reconciled.

16–006   Bainham notes that there is much common ground between these theories.[106] Although all the theories accept the legitimacy of some paternalistic interventions, there is disagreement about the basis of decisions that can be imposed on children.[107] Freeman and Eekelaar require adult decision-makers to follow what children would ideally want for themselves, but others suggest that they should form an objective view of what might be best for the child.[108]

Despite the predominance of rights talk, O'Neill has argued for the development of theories based on fundamental obligations because these can give a more complete view of the ethical aspects of children's lives.[109] Whereas rights theories were developed in relation to adults from the rejection of paternalism, O'Neill considers that paternalism may be what is required of those whose actions impact on children's lives.[110] She asserts that theories of rights are inadequate for dealing with "imperfect obligations", such as to help children or be kind and considerate to them, because they are neither owed to all children nor to identifiable individuals, so no one can claim or waive performance of the

---

[101] J. Eekelaar, "The emergence of children's rights" (1986) 6 Ox J.L.S. 161.
[102] J. Raz, "Legal rights" (1984) 4 Ox J.L.S. 1.
[103] J. Raz, "Legal rights", p.170.
[104] J. Raz, "Legal rights", p.176.
[105] See below, para.16–009.
[106] Bainham (1998), p.91.
[107] Bainham (1998), p.91.
[108] See R. Adler, *Taking Juvenile Justice Seriously* (Edinburgh: Scottish A. P., 1985), p.73 at 141. Children Act 1989 s.1 requires the court to give paramount consideration to the child's welfare, which includes wishes and needs. Bainham suggests that this accords more with allowing the decision-maker to impose a view than relying on the child's substituted judgement.
[109] O. O'Neill, "Children's rights and children's lives" (1992) 6. Int. J. Law & Fam. 24 (reprinted in P. Alston et al., *Children's Rights and the Law* (Oxford: Clarendon, 1992)).
[110] *ibid.* p.40. Archard also regards abandonment of parental authority as immoral: D. Archard, *Children, Rights and Childhood* (London: Routledge, 1993), p.11 . Other modern writers generally agree that paternalism should be kept to a minimum: J. Fortin (2003), p.26.

corresponding right.[111] These obligations are crucial to children's experience of childhood and their development[112]; focusing on the agent's perspective may deliver more for children,[113] but this view has been criticised by Freeman and others, who consider that O'Neill has not sufficiently considered the reality of childhood, the developing capacities of children and the similarities between children's and adults' needs.[114]

Even if rights theories do not adequately deal with all aspects of children's experience, Eekelaar argues that it remains important to recognise that children have rights. For Eekelaar, defining what should be included in the list of rights involves a consideration of what is, or might plausibly be, claimed by children. This is an empirical task that relies on what children say and demands that children are heard.[115] Recognising that children have rights places them in a central and powerful place where the value of being the subject and not merely the object of concern is acknowledged. Thus, although Eekelaar accepts that the UN Convention on the Rights of the Child could have been formulated as a list of duties owed by adults to children, he thinks that it would not have the same potential.[116]

B. Children's rights in international law

In 1989 the UN adopted the Convention on the Rights of the Child.[117] To date, **16–007** this Convention has been ratified[118] by 192 countries, including the United Kingdom,[119] making it the most successful international instrument.[120] This broad support for children's rights suggests that some of the Convention's

[111] O'Neill pp.26–27, but these might as easily be analysed in terms of rights: see C. Coady, (1992) 6. Int. J. Law & Fam. 43 at 45.

[112] O'Neill, "Children's rights and children's lives", p.37.

[113] O'Neill, "Children's rights and children's lives", p.34.

[114] C. Coady, "Theory, rights and children: a comment on O'Neill and Campbell" (1992) 6 Int. J. Law and Fam. 43 at 49; Freeman (1992) 6 Int. J. Law & Fam. 52 at 56–59. Eekelaar has also developed thinking about obligations: J. Eekelaar, "Are parents morally obliged to care for their children?" (1991) 11 Ox J.L.S. 340.

[115] J. Eekelaar, "The importance of thinking that children have rights" (1992) 6 Int. J. Law & Fam. 221 at 228–230. Children's right to be consulted is therefore crucial.

[116] J. Eekelaar, "The importance of thinking that children have rights", p.234.

[117] 28 I.L.M. 1448; see, generally, G. Van Bueren, *The International Law on the Rights of the Child* (1994); P. Newell, *The UN Convention and Children's Rights in the UK* (1991); S. Detrick (ed.), *The United Nations Convention on the Rights of the Child* (Dordrecht: Nijhoff, 1992); D. Hodgson, "The historical development and internationalisation of the children's rights movement" 6 Aust. J. *Fam. Law* 252; B. Walsh, "The United Nations Convention on the Rights of the Child: a British view" (1991) 5 Int. J. Law & Fam. 170; and for a more sceptical view, M. King, "Children's rights as communication: reflections on autopoietic theory and the United Nations Convention" [1994] M.L.R. 385 and L. LeBlanc, *The Convention on the Rights of the Child* (University of Nebraska Press, 1995).

[118] Ratifying states may enter reservations in relation to parts of the Convention so long as these are not incompatible with the principles of the Convention: art.51(2): see A. Bissett-Johnson, "Qualifications of signatories to the United Nations Convention on the Rights of the Child—what did States Parties really agree to?", in N. Lowe and G. Douglas (eds), *Families Across Frontiers* (1996), p.115.

[119] The Convention was ratified by the UK on December 16, 1991, and came into force in the UK on January 15, 1992.

[120] The United States of America, Somalia and Taiwan have not ratified. For an explanation of the USA's position, see S. Kilbourne, "The wayward Americans—why the USA has not ratified the UN Convention on the Rights of the Child" [1998] C.F.L.Q. 243.

provisions may acquire the status of customary international law and have universal application.

The idea for the Convention was suggested in 1979[121] by the Polish Government, who proposed that the principles in the UN Declaration of the Rights of the Child 1959 be translated into international law. The Polish draft was rejected, but work began to develop a new Convention on children's rights. The Convention brings a new approach to the rights of children; they are not to be seen as in opposition to the rights of adults or as an alternative to the rights of parents but as an integral part of human rights.[122] The general aims of the Convention have been referred to as the "four Ps" (prevention, protection, provision and participation[123]), each with equal importance in a holistic approach to the rights of the child.

The Convention applies to all persons below the age of 18 unless majority is achieved at an earlier age.[124] It avoids the conflict between states that accept contraception and abortion and those that do not by not defining the beginning of childhood.[125] The rights in the Convention are provided for all children without discrimination of any kind.[126] The Convention lists basic human rights: rights to name, nationality, identity, privacy and liberty[127]; civil and political rights: freedom of expression, thought, conscience, religion and of assembly[128]; economic and social rights: health care, standard of living and social security[129]; cultural rights: rights to education to develop the child's full potential, play and leisure[130]; and protective rights for children deprived of their families,[131] refugees,[132] those placed in care[133] and to protect all children from violence, drugs, abduction[134] and all forms of exploitation.[135] Two optional protocols adopted by the UN General Assembly in 2000 seek to provide further protection against sexual exploitation and for child soldiers.[136]

16–008   The Convention adopts the best interest standard as "a primary consideration" for all action concerning children by public and private institutions and

---

[121] The International Year of the Child.

[122] M. Santos Pais, "General introduction to the Convention on the Rights of the Child: from its origin to its implementation", in Defence for Children International, *Selected Essays on International Children's Rights* (1993), p.1.

[123] G. Van Bueren, "The UN Convention on the Rights of the Child" (1991) 3 J.C.L. 63.

[124] UN Convention on the Rights of the Child art.1.

[125] But States Parties recognise that every child has the inherent right to life: art.6(1).

[126] UN Convention on the Rights of the Child art.2(1). Perhaps the most important principle, given the divisions imposed on childhood within many countries based on gender, religion or ethnic background.

[127] UN Convention on the Rights of the Child arts 7, 8, 16 and 37.

[128] UN Convention on the Rights of the Child arts 13, 14 and 15.

[129] UN Convention on the Rights of the Child arts 24, 26 and 27.

[130] UN Convention on the Rights of the Child arts 28, 29, 30 and 31, and see General Comment No.1 (2001): The aims of education (CRC/GC/2001/1).

[131] UN Convention on the Rights of the Child art.20 and, see General Comments No.6 (2005) CRC/GC/2005/6.

[132] UN Convention on the Rights of the Child art.21.

[133] UN Convention on the Rights of the Child art.25.

[134] UN Convention on the Rights of the Child arts 19, 33 and 35.

[135] UN Convention on the Rights of the Child arts 32, 34 and 36.

[136] General Assembly Resolution A/RES/54/263. The UK ratified the protocol relating to child soldiers in 2003.

administrative bodies.[137] However, children who are capable of forming their own views are recognised as having the right to express those views freely in matters affecting them. Children's views should be given due weight in accordance with the child's age and maturity; children should have an opportunity to be heard in judicial and administrative proceedings affecting them.[138] Also, the fundamental importance to children of their parents is recognised.[139] Parents have the primary responsibility for their child's upbringing.[140] States must respect the responsibilities, rights and duties of parents and the wider family in a manner consistent with the child's evolving capacities[141] and should render appropriate assistance to parents.[142] Children should not be separated from parents against their will; where separation occurs, they should be enabled to maintain relationships.[143]

The correlative duties in the Convention are addressed to states, but the responsibility to ensure that children's rights are recognised lies with everyone. States are required to undertake all legislative, administrative and other measures for the implementation of the Convention. With regard to economic, social and cultural rights, they must undertake such measure to the maximum of their available resources.[144] They must publicise the Convention to adults and children.[145]

The Convention is not incorporated into English law; its provisions have been regarded as aspirational and unsuitable for legislation.[146] Individual children cannot rely directly on its provisions in the English courts[147]; enforcement in the international arena is by political, not legal, processes. The Convention establishes the Committee of the Rights of the Child; each state must report regularly to the Committee on its progress in implementing the Convention.[148] The Committee has issued guidance about how states compile their reports[149]; non-

---

[137] UN Convention on the Rights of the Child art.3. Note this is not the same as the duty in Children Act 1989 s.1; see below, para.20–001.

[138] UN Convention on the Rights of the Child art.12 and see below, para.16–015.

[139] As far as possible, the child should have a right to know and be cared for by his or her parents (art.7(1)).

[140] "States parties shall use their best effort to ensure recognition of the principle that both parents have common responsibilities for the upbringing and development of the child" (art.18(1)).

[141] UN Convention on the Rights of the Child art.5.

[142] UN Convention on the Rights of the Child art.18.

[143] UN Convention on the Rights of the Child art.9; art.10 provides for family reunification.

[144] UN Convention on the Rights of the Child art.4.

[145] UN Convention on the Rights of the Child art.42. The UK government was criticised for its failures in this respect: CRC/C/15/Add.188, para.20.

[146] Minister for Children, Evidence to the Joint Committee on Human Rights, *Tenth Report 2002–3*, para.21.

[147] This does not mean that the courts completely disregard it: see Joint Committee on Human Rights, *Tenth Report 2002–3* (HL117), para.20. Some jurisdictions, notably the Netherlands and Germany, have incorporated it into their constitutions.

[148] UN Convention on the Rights of the Child arts 43 and 44. Reports must be submitted within two years of the entry into force of the Convention, and then every five years (art.44(1)). For a discussion of the work of the Committee, see C. Price Cohen and S. Kilbourne, "Jurisprudence of the Committee on the Rights of the Child: a guide for research and analysis" (1998) Mich. J. Int. L. 633. It has been said that the Committee has a western bias in its approach: S. Harris-Short [2001] Melb. J. Int. Law 305.

[149] UN Doc.CRC/C/5 (1991).

governmental organisations may also submit reports.[150] The UK's reports have not been regarded positively by the Committee.[151] The Committee would like to see a "comprehensive and rights-based national strategy rooted in the Convention"[152] but it appears that much of government business has been conducted without any reference to these obligations.[153] However, the Convention has provided a focus for children's rights organisations to examine law and policy and to campaign for reform.[154] A consolidated 3rd and 4th Report was prepared in 2007.

16–009   The Convention is enormously influential.[155] It establishes that the signatories accept (or wish to be seen as accepting) that children are persons with the human rights. It is evidence that the international community has reached a consensus about the rights of children and the obligations of the family, the state and the international community.[156] Ratification by many countries and regular reporting promote and disseminate the idea of children's rights. It has the potential to transform adulthood as well as childhood, and lay the foundations for a better world,[157] not only because the rights in the Convention will enable children to reach their potential but because fulfilling these obligations to children will improve the lives of adults. However, converting social goals into law is a complex matter[158] that cannot automatically improve children's lives and may give a false impression that something is being done.[159] The Convention needs major world-wide changes to implement its principles fully. It remains to be seen how far it can improve children's lives.

The Convention has yet to have an impact on law reform in England and Wales. There is little acknowledgement of the Convention in government publications or the family courts on the basis that the Children Act 1989 encapsulates it.[160] The Children's Commissioner has no obligation to promote the Convention, only to "have regard to" it when considering the interests of

---

[150] Country reports are available on the UN website: *http://www.unhchr.ch* and those from NGOs on *http://www.crin.org.* [Both accessed June 1, 2008]

[151] CRC/C/11/Add.1 (1994); CRC/C/83/Add.3 (1999); concluding observations of the Committee: CRC/C/15/Add.63 (1996); CRC/C/15/Add.188 (2002).

[152] CRC/GC/2003/5, General Comment No.5 (2003), para.28.

[153] See Joint Committee on Human Rights, *Tenth Report 2002–3* (HL 117), paras 24–30 and *Nineteenth Report 2003–4* (HL 161), paras 14–22.

[154] Children's Rights Alliance for England, *The State of Children's Rights 2005* (2005); L. Lundy, "Mainstreaming children's rights to, in and through education in a society emerging from conflict", (2006) *International Journal of Children's Rights* 339, 341.

[155] J. Fortin *Children's Rights*, p.49.

[156] D. McGoldrick, "The United Nations Convention on the Rights of the child" (1991) Int. J. Law & Fam. 132 at 158.

[157] J. Eekelaar, "The importance of thinking that children have rights" (1992) 6 Int. J. Law & Fam. 221 at 234.

[158] See UNICEF, *Law Reform and the Implementation of the Convention on the Rights of the Child* (Florence, 2008).

[159] M. King, "Children's rights as communication: some reflections on Autopoetic Theory and the United Nations Convention" [1994] M.L.R. 385, 401.

[160] The Government regarded the Children Act 1989 as implementing many of the obligations under the Convention (Cm.2144, para.1.13) despite no mention of the Convention during Parliamentary debates. *Re C (HIV Test)* [1999] 2 F.L.R. 1004, 1021E: "Wilson J. set out various Articles of the UN Convention on the Rights of the Child 1989. We do not in a sense need that. It is all encapsulated in s.1 of the Children Act", *per* Butler-Sloss L.J.

children.[161] The Government seems more willing to promote the five outcomes identified in *Every Child Matters* and leave recognition of children's rights in relation to its aid programmes,[162] but in 2008 it consulted on withdrawing its reservation in relation to immigration law.[163] Although negative attitudes to the concept of children having rights remain,[164] there is growing awareness of the Convention's principles amongst those working with children in health and social services.

III. CHILDREN'S RIGHTS AND ENGLISH LAW

The extent to which children have rights as individuals that they can exercise without the permission of their parents depends on both case- and statute-law. During the 1980s there were two quite contradictory developments. The courts recognised the increased independence of young people by accepting that if they could establish their maturity they could make many decisions free from parental control. In contrast, Parliament, facing a weak economy and a reduction in employment opportunities for young people with few qualifications, legislated to remove social security rights so that young people's dependency on their families increased.[165] These contradictions are being repeated with the growing recognition of children's independence but concern to hold parents to account for children's anti-social behaviour, making them responsible for paying penalty notices for disorder.[166]

16–010

A. The Gillick[167] case

In December 1980 the DHSS issued a notice[168] that contained advice to doctors about the provision of contraceptive services to children under 16. It stated that

16–011

---

[161] Children Act 2004 s.2(11). The original drafting of the provision gave the Commissioner discretion whether to consider the Convention: Joint Committee on Human Rights, *Nineteenth Report 2003–4*, para.14. Regulations make similar provision for the Welsh Commissioner: SI 2001/2787.
[162] *UK's Second Report to the UN Committee on the Rights of the Child* (CRC/C/83/Add.3 (1999)), para.5.5.1. See also *UK's Consolidated Third and Fourth Reports* (2007).
[163] BIA, *Code of Practice for Keeping Children Safe From Harm—Consultation* (2008), Q.16.
[164] W. Utting, *People Like Us* (TSO, 1997), para.10.1.
[165] J. Masson, "The Children Act 1989 and young people: dependence and rights to independence", in D. Lockton, *Children and the Law* (London: Cavendish, 1993), pp.1, 10.
[166] HO, *Taking Anti-social Behaviour Seriously* (2006), para.3.7.
[167] [1986] A.C. 112; [1984] Q.B. 581; see Glanville Williams, "The Gillick Saga" (1985) New L.J. 1156 and 1179; J. Eekelaar, "The eclipse of parental rights" (1986) 102 L.Q.R. 4; S. Cretney, "Gillick and the concept of legal capacity" (1989) 105 L.Q.R. 356; A. Bainham, "The balance of power in family decisions" [1986] C.L.J. 262; J. Eekelaar, "The emergence of children's rights" (1986) 6 Ox. J.L.S. 161; J. Montgomery, "Children as property" (1988) 51 M.L.R. 323; P. Lewis, "The medical treatment of children", in J. Fionda (ed.), *Legal Concepts of Childhood* (Oxford: Hart Publishing, 2001), p.151.
[168] HN (80) 46 now replaced by DH, *Best Practice Guidance for Doctors and Other Health Professionals on the Provision of Advice and Treatment to Young People under 16 on Contraception, Sexual And Reproductive Health* (2004). This guidance was upheld in *R. (Axon) v SS for Health and the Family Planning Association* [2006] 2 F.L.R. 206; see below, para.16–014. See *http://www.dfes.gov.uk/teenagepregnancy/* [Accessed June 1, 2008] for the context for the new guidance.

it would be "most unusual" for a doctor to provide advice about contraception without parental consent, but acknowledged that in some circumstances, unless children were treated in confidence, they might not seek treatment and suffer in consequence. Doctors should seek to persuade children to involve parents, but the decision whether to treat was a matter for clinical judgment. Mrs Victoria Gillick, the mother of five girls under the age of 16, sought an assurance from the local health authority that the girls would not be given contraceptive treatment without her consent. When she did not receive a reply that she regarded as satisfactory, she sought a declaration that the DHSS notice had no authority in law and gave advice that adversely affected the welfare of the Gillick children, her rights as a parent and her ability to discharge her parental duties. At first instance, Woolf J. refused the application.[169] The Court of Appeal unanimously reversed the decision. The House of Lords, by a majority of three to two, allowed the appeal and provided the foundation for the development of a distinctive concept of children's rights.

Three separate arguments were put forward on behalf of Mrs Gillick: on criminal law, on the age of consent to treatment and on parental rights. These will now be considered.

First, the Sexual Offences Act 1956 makes it unlawful for anyone to have sexual intercourse with a girl under the age of 16[170] or to encourage anyone to do so.[171] It was therefore argued that a doctor who prescribed contraceptives for a girl without the parent's consent committed a crime, even though he or she only sought to act in her best interests. The DHSS notice was consequently unlawful because it amounted to advice to commit the offence of encouraging unlawful sexual intercourse or of being an accessory to unlawful sexual intercourse.[172] Woolf J. accepted that a doctor who provided contraceptives to a girl under 16, or her partner, with the intention of encouraging them to have sexual intercourse, would commit an offence, but rejected the view that a doctor could necessarily commit an offence by following DHSS guidelines.[173] This latter point was conceded by both sides.[174] In the Court of Appeal, Parker L.J. considered the protection against sexual intercourse provided to young girls by the criminal law, but based his reasoning on the fact that an internal examination would normally be carried out before contraceptives were prescribed,[175] and that this would amount to an indecent assault[176] by the doctor because the 1956 Act precluded a girl under 16 giving a valid consent to it. In the House of Lords, only Lord Brandon considered the criminal law in detail; and Woolf J.'s analysis was

---

[169] [1984] Q.B. 581.
[170] Sexual Offences Act 1956 ss.5, 6(1), replaced by Sexual Offences 2003 ss.9, 13: both parties commit offences under the 2003 Act.
[171] Sexual Offences Act 1956 s.28(1), replaced by Sexual Offences 2003 s.14, there is an exception in subs.2 for actions that protect the child and subs.3 lists protection from pregnancy or sexually transmitted infection.
[172] Contrary to ss.5, 6(1), 28(1).
[173] [1984] Q.B. 581 at 593–595, 599.
[174] [1986] A.C. 112 at 134.
[175] [1986] A.C. 112 at 136–137. Fox and Everleigh L.JJ. did not examine the criminal law.
[176] Contrary to Sexual Offences Act 1956 s.14, replaced by Sexual Offences Act 2003 s.9(1).

accepted by the other Law Lords. Lord Brandon concluded that to provide advice about contraception, to examine with a view to providing contraceptive services and their prescription promoted, encouraged or facilitated sexual intercourse and were contrary to public policy, whether or not they amounted to an offence.[177] The only answer the law should give to a girl who threatened to have unprotected intercourse was: "Wait till you are 16."[178] He rejected the view that the DHSS had a duty to provide contraceptive services to girls under 16 on the basis that either they were not "persons" within the meaning of the National Health Service Act 1977 or that their requirements were not reasonable.[179]

Although counsel for Mrs Gillick and Parker L.J. both linked criminal liability **16–012** with the absence of parental consent, Woolf J. clearly stated that if the doctor, or anyone else, commits an offence by or in the course of providing contraceptive services, the parent's consent is immaterial.[180] Indeed, if an offence were committed, a parent who consented might also be liable.[181] The arguments based on criminal law prompted an interesting discussion of public policy and adolescent sexual behaviour, but are not relevant to other areas. Had they been accepted, a further distinction between adolescent boys and girls would have been enshrined in law.

In relation to the second issue (the age of consent to treatment) the position is that if a valid consent[182] is not given, medical examination or treatment constitutes an assault, and the doctor is liable in tort. The Family Law Reform Act 1969 s.8(1) provides that a person of 16 may consent to medical treatment and that "nothing in this section shall be construed as making ineffective any consent which would have been effective" under the general law.[183] Thus, the courts had to consider in what circumstances, if any, a younger child could consent to treatment. Woolf J., relying on the decision in a Canadian case,[184] held that a child who was capable of making a reasonable assessment of the advantages and disadvantages of the treatment proposed could give a valid consent. This would depend on the child's age and intelligence and the nature and implications of the treatment.[185] Parker and Fox L.JJ., adopting a different view of parental power, interpreted the section as requiring parental consent for

---

[177] Williams criticised this reasoning: (1985) 135 New L.J. 1156 at 1159.

[178] [1986] A.C. 112 at 197F.

[179] There is a statutory duty on the Secretary of State to provide a service that meets all reasonable requirements for contraception in England and Wales: s.5(1)(b).

[180] [1984] Q.B. 581 at 594. Although a parent's consent may prevent treatment being an assault, if the doctor were behaving indecently, the agreement of the parent could not remove his or her liability.

[181] Sexual Offences Act 1956 s.14; a parent would commit an offence under Sexual Offences Act 2003 s.26.

[182] The doctrine of informed consent has no part in English Law: *Sidaway v Bethlem Royal Hospital Governors* [1985] A.C. 871 (Lord Scarman dissenting).

[183] Enacted following the recommendations of the Latey Committee, which was concerned that some minors would have to wait for treatment if parental consent was required. The Committee did not specifically consider children under 16, but acknowledged that it was customary to accept the consent of those over 16, Cmnd.3342 (1967), para.179.

[184] *Johnston v Wellesley Hospital* (1970) 17 D.L.R. (3d) 139.

[185] [1984] Q.B. 581 at 596.

any treatment of a child under 16.[186] The majority[187] of the House of Lords rejecting this view agreed with Woolf J.'s interpretation.

However, the importance of the case derives from their Lordship's opinions on the third issue: namely, the nature and extent of parental power and their acceptance that children could act independently. The Court of Appeal's view of parental rights and duties has been described as traditional and simplistic, and contrasted with the radical view of the House of Lords.[188] Parker and Fox L.JJ. concluded that the right to legal custody, which included the right to decide "the place and manner in which [the child's] time is spent",[189] gave parents complete control over the child's actions until he or she reached the age of discretion.[190] These rights could only be abridged by statute or by the courts in proceedings where the decision had to be based on the paramountcy of the child's welfare.[191] There was no discussion in the Court of Appeal of the purpose of parental rights but there was some indication that parents were in the best position to make judgments in the child's welfare.[192]

16–013   In the House of Lords, in contrast, Lord Fraser, relying on Blackstone, stated that parental rights "exist for the benefit of the child and are justified only in so far as they enable a parent to perform his duties towards the child".[193] Lord Scarman was also clear that they exist for the child's protection[194] and consequently:

> "[Y]ield to the child's right to make his own decisions when he reaches sufficient understanding and intelligence to be capable of making up his mind on the matter in question."[195]

Thus, there was no parental right to forbid an action within a mature minor's capacity unless this was specifically provided by statute:

> "[T]he right to determine whether or not their minor child below the age of 16 will have medical treatment terminates if and when the child achieves sufficient understanding."[196]

It is less clear that Lord Fraser accepted that parental rights were terminated in these circumstances. His speech may be interpreted as accepting the retention of

---

[186] [1986] A.C. 112 at 123, 138, 145; Everleigh L.J. did not consider the general issue.
[187] Lord Fraser, Lord Scarman, with whom Lord Bridge agreed. Lord Templeman agreed on this point, although he did not consider that girls under 16 had the maturity to consent to decisions about contraception.
[188] Cretney [1985] All E.R. Rev. 171 at 172.
[189] Children Act 1975 s.86 (repealed by Children Act 1989).
[190] [1986] A.C. 112 at 124, 143.
[191] [1986] A.C. 112 at 125–127, 140, a parent's decision could always be challenged in wardship: see below.
[192] [1986] A.C. 112 *per* Everleigh L.J. at 146–147.
[193] [1986] A.C. 112 at 170.
[194] "[P]arental rights are derived from parental duty and exist only so long as they are needed for the protection and property of the child", *per* Lord Scarman at 184.
[195] At 186.
[196] *Per* Lord Scarman at 188.

parental control that could only be disregarded if it were in the child's best interests so to do.[197] Alternatively, he may have intended that consultation with a mature minor's parents was relevant only to good professional practice. Lord Bridge agreed with both Lord Scarman and Lord Fraser. Lord Templeman appears to have agreed with Lord Scarman, although, on the issue of contraception, he viewed all girls under 16 as insufficiently mature to make a valid decision.[198]

Although a test based on maturity rather than age created difficulties for those dealing with young people and for young people themselves,[199] the majority of the House of Lords considered that age-related limits should not be imposed on the process of growing up. Whether a child was sufficiently mature was a question of fact. Both Lord Scarman and Lord Fraser gave guidance about what a child had to understand to establish that he or she had capacity, but there is, arguably, substantial difference between them. Lord Scarman stated that:

> "She must also have a sufficient maturity to understand what is involved. There are moral and family questions, especially her relationship with her parents; long term problems associated with the emotional impact of pregnancy and its termination; and there are risks to health of sexual intercourse at her age, risks which contraception cannot eliminate."[200]

Lord Fraser merely said that the girl must understand the doctor's advice. However, in the conclusion to his opinion he set out, without reasons, five points that would justify a doctor providing contraceptive treatment without parental consent:

> "(1) that the girl (although under 16 years of age) will understand his advice;
>
> (2) that he cannot persuade her to inform her parents or allow him to inform the parents that she is seeking contraceptive advice;
>
> (3) that she is likely to begin or continue having sexual intercourse without contraceptive treatment;

---

[197] Eekelaar (1986) 102 L.Q.R. 4 at 5–6; the parent may have a duty to act reasonably: see Bainham [1986] C.L.J. 262 at 280. This appears to have been accepted by Silber J. in *R. (Axon) v SS for Health* [2006] 2 F.L.R. 206, paras 87 and 91.

[198] "[A]ny decision on the part of a girl to practise sex and contraception requires not only knowledge of the facts of life and of the dangers of pregnancy and disease but also an understanding of the emotional consequences to her family, her male partner and to herself. I doubt whether a girl under the age of 16 is capable of [the necessary] balanced judgement . . . there are many things which a girl under 16 needs to practise but sex is not one of them" (at 201).

[199] See Bainham [1986] C.L.J. 262 at 277 and *R v D* [1984] 1 All E.R. 574 at 581, where the Court of Appeal decided that a child could not be kidnapped by a parent because of difficulties of establishing the child's consent. The House of Lords, reversing the decision, considered this could safely be left to the jury: [1984] 2 All E.R. 449 at 457; for criticism, see G. Williams, "Can babies be kidnapped?" [1989] Crim. L.R. 473.

[200] At 186.

(4) that unless she receives contraceptive advice or treatment her physical or mental health or both are likely to suffer;

(5) that her best interests require him to give her contraceptive advice, treatment or both without parental consent."[201]

16–014 This would seem to subject the child to professional control in place of parental authority. On either formulation, it may be possible for a person who disagrees with the child to conclude that the child's decision is an immature one and thus one that he or she has no right to take.[202] The issue of parental involvement and child confidentiality has been re-litigated. It was held that no special rules applied to abortion decisions, ECHR art.8 did not give parents rights to be consulted and, consequently, the 2004 Guidance was not unlawful.[203]

The House of Lords decision is rightly regarded as a milestone in the development of adolescent's rights. The concept of "*Gillick* competence" has been applied to decisions about medical treatment, requests for access to personal records[204] and children's participation in civil proceedings,[205] and is reflected in some of the provisions of the Children Act 1989.[206]

The concept of "*Gillick* competence" or maturity has advantages. It is flexible in recognising children's capacity to make simpler decisions at younger ages, and can protect children[207] by ensuring that they understand fully the implications of what they propose. The general test of capacity to make decisions applies; children must be able to comprehend and retain information relevant to the decision, believe it and weigh it in the balance to arrive at a choice.[208] However, it has been suggested that, in the case of children who may be influenced by their carers, understanding may not be a sufficient basis for accepting that a decision is autonomous.[209] It is also vague allowing professionals to deny children competence because of the complexity of the decision[210] by withholding

---

[201] At 174; Eekelaar (1986) 102 L.Q.R. 4 at 7; Montgomery (1988) 51 M.L.R. 323 at 339. The formulation has been incorporated into the guidance. For Silber J.'s version, see *R. (Axon) v SS for Health* [2006] 2 F.L.R. 206 at 154.

[202] Eekelaar (1986), p.9.

[203] *R. (Axon) v SS for Health and the Family Planning Association* [2006] 2 F.L.R. 206, *per* Silber J.; R. Taylor [2007] C.F.L.Q. 81.

[204] DH, *Data Protection Act (1998) Guidance for Local Authorities* (2000), para.5.8; the Data Protection Act 1998 makes no special reference to access by children except in relation to Scotland (s.67).

[205] *Re T (A Minor) (Child: Representation)* [1994] Fam. 49, CA; *Re S (A Minor) (Representation)* [1993] Fam. 263 CA; see below, para.16–020.

[206] See below, para.16–019.

[207] *Re R (A Minor) (Wardship: Consent to Treatment)* [1992] Fam. 11 at 26, *per* Lord Donaldson M.R.

[208] *Re C (Adult: Refusal of Medical Treatment)* [1994] 1 F.L.R. 31 at 33, *per* Thorpe J., applied by Wall J. to children in *Re C (Detention: Medical Treatment)* [1997] 2 F.L.R. 180.

[209] M. Brazier and C. Bridge, "Coercion or caring: analysing adolescent autonomy" (1996) L.S. 84 at 91.

[210] Lord Scarman set a high standard for understanding sexual activity and contraception in *Gillick* at 189. In *Re S (A Minor) (Representation)* [1993] Fam. 263, an 11-year-old boy was said to lack sufficient understanding to participate in an emotionally fraught residence dispute between his parents. The boy finally succeeded in establishing his maturity when he was 13.

information from them,[211] or if they appear childlike,[212] are mentally disturbed[213] or make unacceptable decisions.[214] Thus, in *Re E* a 15-year-old leukaemia patient's refusal of treatment was rejected because he did not have sufficient comprehension of the pain he would suffer or the distress to his family of watching him die.[215] Similarly, a 15-year-old girl with a potentially fatal condition was regarded as immature because she hoped for a miracle cure.[216] Also, it has been said that children who are mentally ill are not "*Gillick* competent", even at times when their symptoms are not apparent.[217]

B. The retreat from Gillick

If young people have the right to consent to medical treatment, logically they **16–015** should also have the right to refuse treatment.[218] However, the Court of Appeal, lead by Lord Donaldson M.R., has held that the court exercising its inherent jurisdiction, or a person with parental responsibility, may override the child's refusal and give the doctor the necessary consent to treatment[219]:

> In *Re R*[220] a 15-year-old girl in care[221] with florid psychotic behaviour was placed by the local authority in an adolescent psychiatric unit. When she refused treatment, the local authority made her a ward of court and sought the court's permission for treatment. The Court of Appeal held that her mental condition meant that she was not "*Gillick* competent",[222] but proceeded to discuss whether a valid refusal could veto all treatment.

Lord Donaldson interpreted Lord Scarman's dictum that "the parental right to determine whether their child will have medical treatment terminates if and when

---

[211] *Re L (Medical Treatment: Gillick Competency)* [1998] 2 F.L.R. 810 (a 14-year-old girl's refusal of a blood transfusion was overridden because she was unaware that she faced a painful death from gangrene if she did not have an operation); see Bridge [1999] M.L.R. 585.

[212] *Re S (A Minor) (Consent to Medical Treatment)* [1994] 2 F.L.R. 1065 at 1076, *per* Johnson J. (the child's growth was stunted because of her medical condition).

[213] *Re R (A Minor) (Wardship: Consent to Treatment)* [1992] Fam. 11; in *Re W (A Minor) (Medical Treatment: Court's Jurisdiction)* [1993] Fam. 64 at 80, Lord Donaldson, M.R. doubted the correctness of Thorpe, J.'s view that a 16-year-old anorexia nervosa patient was *Gillick* competent.

[214] *Re E (A Minor) (Wardship: Medical Treatment)* [1993] 1 F.L.R. 386.

[215] *Per* Ward J. at 391. The young man died after refusing further treatment when he reached age 18.

[216] *Re S (A Minor) (Consent to Medical Treatment)* [1994] 2 F.L.R. 1065 at 1076, *per* Johnson J. But irrationality has been said not to indicate incompetence: *per* Lord Donaldson, M.R. in *Re W (A Minor) (Medical Treatment: Court's Jurisdiction)* [1993] Fam. 64 at 76.

[217] *Re R (A Minor) (Wardship: Consent to Treatment)* [1992] Fam. 11 at 26, *per* Lord Donaldson M.R.

[218] Bainham (1992) 108 L.Q.R. 194, 198; M. Brazier, *Medicine patients and the law*, 2nd edn (Penguin, 1992), p.345; I. Kennedy and A. Grubb, *Medical Law*, 3rd edn (Butterworths, 2000), pp.971, 985.

[219] *Re R (A Minor) (Wardship: Consent to Treatment)* [1992] Fam. 11; *Re W (A Minor) (Medical Treatment: Court's Jurisdiction)* [1993] Fam. 64. But the discussion of the power of the court was obiter: see *S. Glamorgan CC v W and B* [1993] 1 F.L.R. 574 at 584, *per* Douglas Brown J.

[220] [1992] Fam. 11.

[221] i.e. the girl was subject to a care order: Children Act 1989 s.33. The local authority had parental responsibility as a result of the order: see para.21–041.

[222] [1992] Fam. 11 at 26.

the child achieves sufficient understanding" as only preventing a parental veto of treatment consented to by the child.[223] Each parent retained an independent right to consent, which was sufficient to enable the doctor to treat their child without incurring liability for trespass to the person.[224] Similarly, the court could override the decisions of "*Gillick* competent" children either by exercising its inherent jurisdiction[225] or by making an order under s.8 of the Children Act 1989.[226]

This decision was followed in *Re W*[227]:

> A 16-year-old orphan in the care of the local authority was suffering from anorexia nervosa. She had been treated for some time in a local hospital, but her condition had not improved. A place had been found for her at a specialist unit, but she refused to go there. The local authority applied for leave to seek an order under the inherent jurisdiction so that the girl could be moved without her consent.[228] The order was granted and the girl appealed unsuccessfully.

Lord Donaldson M.R. took the opportunity to apply his reasoning where the young person was "*Gillick* competent". He held that Family Law Reform Act 1969 s.8(3), which states that "Nothing in this section shall be construed as making ineffective any consent . . . ", preserved the parental right to consent to examination and treatment of children over 16. Those with parental responsibility therefore had a "flak jacket" that they could use to defend the doctor from a claim of assault by a child over 16 or any "*Gillick* competent" child.[229] Once a child had given a valid consent, only the court exercising its inherent jurisdiction could override the child's decision, but doctors could not be required to treat except in accordance with their clinical judgement.[230] Lord Donaldson also suggested that the court could make a prohibited steps or specific issue order.[231]

16–016   Although this allows the court and those with parental responsibility to disregard a child's refusal of treatment, the importance of giving young people progressively more responsibility whilst protecting them from unacceptable risks

---

[223] [1992] Fam. 11 at 23. Staughton L.J. clearly did not agree, and confined his decision to the powers of the High Court under the inherent jurisdiction (at 27), as did Farquharson L.J.

[224] [1992] Fam. 11 at 22. A person with parental responsibility is a "keyholder" who can unlock the legal door to treatment. Where the patient objects, the doctor may have ethical problems.

[225] For an explanation of this High Court jurisdiction, see below, para.18–049.

[226] [1992] Fam. 11 at 25. A specific issue order has been held to be sufficient to override the refusal of a parent to give consent: *Re R. (A Minor) (Blood Transfusion)* [1993] 2 F.L.R. 757. But a local authority may not apply for a specific issue order if the child is in care: s.9(1).

[227] [1993] Fam. 64.

[228] Such an order is only available to a local authority if there is no other way for it to proceed: s.100(4), (5). But if parental responsibility enables the child's decision to be overridden, leave cannot be given where there is a care order.

[229] [1993] Fam. 64 at 78.

[230] [1993] Fam. 64 at 83.

[231] [1993] Fam. 64 at 82. But these orders under the Children Act 1989 s.8 can only be available if parental responsibility continues. If a parent is unable to veto the child's decision, it would appear that the court cannot exercise its statutory powers in this way.

was affirmed.[232] The court must have regard to the child's wishes and feelings[233]; Nolan L.J. suggested that the question of whether major surgery or abortion should be carried out against a competent child's consent should always be referred to the court.[234] However, the recognition that some aspects of parental power endure when children have become competent means that children who refuse treatment are reliant on medical ethics or the court's exercise of its welfare jurisdiction rather than rights.[235] Given the deference to medical opinion, it is most unlikely that a request for authority to treat an objecting child will be refused by the courts.[236]

There are further reasons for criticising these decisions. They allowed young people to be treated for mental illness as voluntary patients with the consent of their parents or under care orders, and without the safeguards in the Mental Health Act 1983.[237] However, so far as 16 and 17 year olds with capacity to consent are concerned, amendments have clarified that those with parental responsibility cannot override a refusal of treatment.[238] The court's power to override the refusal of treatment conflicts with provisions in the Children Act 1989, which uphold the refusal of assessments ordered in child protection proceedings[239] and require consent for assessments and treatment where the child is subject to a supervision order.[240] Moreover, if the child is in care, there appears to be no way the local authority's decision to authorise treatment can be challenged except by applying for discharge of the care order.[241]

C. Children's rights under the European Convention of Human Rights[242]

This Convention was drafted in the immediate post-war period when protection **16–017** from oppression by fascist states was a major concern and the concept of children's rights remained undeveloped. Consequently, it is "adult oriented", focusing on protecting civil and political rights, does not explicitly recognise the

---

[232] "[G]ood parenting involves giving minors so much rope as they can handle without an unacceptable risk that they will hang themselves" *per* Lord Donaldson M.R. at 81. Best interests is not confined to medical issues: *Re P (Medical Treatment: Best Interests)* [2004] 2 F.L.R. 1117, *per* Johnson J.

[233] *Per* Balcombe at 88; *per* Nolan L.J. at 93.

[234] At 94.

[235] But the child's co-operation my be essential for successful treatment; see P. Alderson, *Children's Consent to Surgery* (Open University Press, 1993).

[236] Proceedings are unnecessary where a person with parental responsibility consents: *Re K, W and H (Minors) (Medical Treatment)* [1993] 1 F.L.R. 854 at 859, *per* Thorpe J. It is unlikely that compulsory medical treatment would breach ECHR, art.3 see Swindells et al. (1999), para.3.12 and *Herczegfalvy v Austria* (1992) 15 E.H.R.R. 437.

[237] For example, second opinions and review of the treatment; see Masson [1992] Fam. Law 528.

[238] Mental Health Act 2007 s.43, amending Mental Health Act 1983 s.131, Mental Capacity Act 2005 s.2(5).

[239] Children Act 1989 s.38(6) (interim care or supervision orders); s.43(8) (child assessment order); s.44(7) (emergency protection order).

[240] Children Act 1989 Sch.3, paras 4(4), 5(5).

[241] A prohibited steps order could not be made: s.9(1); the inherent jurisdiction is not available: *A v Liverpool CC* [1982] A.C. 363.

[242] See, generally, J. Fortin, *Children's Rights and the Developing Law*; U. Kilkelly, *The Child and the European Convention on Human Rights* (Aldershot: Ashgate, 1999); J. Fortin, "Rights brought home for children" [1999] M.L.R. 350; J. Fortin, "Accommodating children's rights in a post Human Rights Act Era" [2006] M.L.R. 299–326; H. Swindells et al. (1999).

specific requirements of children, and provides no clear guidance on reconciling parents' rights to freedom from state interference with children's rights to develop independence from their parents.[243] However, in balancing parents' and children's rights to family life, the European Court of Human Rights has attached particular importance to the best interests of the child.[244] Although there have been few applications to the European Court of Human Rights by children, the Convention has had considerable impact on children's rights throughout Europe. The incorporation of the Convention into UK domestic law has raised its importance by requiring public bodies to act in accordance with it[245] and facilitating enforcement of the rights it guarantees.[246]

Although the whole of the Convention can apply to children, it is art.8—the right to respect for private and family life—that has had the greatest influence on children's lives.[247] The state's responsibility is not limited to restricting interference with rights but includes taking positive action to promote family relationships.[248] In assessing state's decisions under art.8, the European Court of Human Rights allows a margin of appreciation, and the breadth of this margin depends on the nature of the issues at stake. Where there is no consensus amongst states, the margin is widest[249]; a wide margin is given to state's decision about protecting children, but restrictions of contact are subject to strict scrutiny.[250] The Convention led to major changes in childcare law, particularly restricting local authority discretion and requiring local authorities to consult parents and to promote contact between children and their families.[251] Corporal punishment was ended in all schools[252] following decisions that it could infringe a parent's rights in relation to their child's education[253] or a child's right to be protected

---

[243] J. Eekelaar and R. Dingwall, *Human Rights: Report on the Replies of Governments to the Enquiry under Art.57* (Council of Europe, 1987), p.21; Fortin [1999] M.L.R. 350, 354; Fortin (2003) *Children's Rights and the Developing Law*, p.54.

[244] "[A] fair balance must be struck between the interests of the child and those of the parent . . . the best interests of the child . . . depending on their nature and seriousness, may override those of the parent": *Sahin v Germany* [2002] 1 F.L.R. 119 at 42. Only in *Yousef v The Netherlands* [2003] 1 F.L.R. 210 at 73 have the child's rights been held the paramount consideration.

[245] Human Rights Act 1998 s.6(1).

[246] Human Rights Act 1998 s.7; *Re W and B, Re W* [2001] 2 F.L.R. 582 CA; *sub nom. Re S (minors) (care order: implementation of care plan)* [2000] 1 F.L.R. 815, HL. It will no longer be necessary to go to the European Court of Human Rights to obtain a remedy, although this will provide a last resort: see Masson [2002] C.F.L.Q. 77.

[247] See J. Fortin, "The HRA's impact on litigation involving children and their families" [1999] C.F.L.Q. 237 at 247.

[248] *Marckx v Belgium* (1979) 1 E.H.R.R. 330; *Hokkanen v Finland* [1996] 1 F.L.R. 289.

[249] *Evans v UK* [2006] 2 F.L.R.172 at 59–62.

[250] *P, C and S v UK* [2002] 2 F.L.R. 631 at 116; *Johansen v Norway* (1996) 23 E.H.R.R. 38 at 64.

[251] *TP and KM v UK* [2001] 2 F.L.R. 549; *W v UK* (1987) 10 E.H.R.R. 29. The parents' inability to challenge local authority decisions on contact breached their rights under arts 6 and 8, and was remedied by legislation: Health and Social Services and Social Security Adjudications Act 1983. Further obligations were imposed on local authorities by the Children Act 1989 ss.22(4)(5), 34 and Sch.2 para.15.

[252] See now Education Act 1996 ss.548, 549; in *R. (on the application of Williamson) v Secretary of State for Education and Employment* [2005] UKHL 15, parents and teachers unsuccessfully claimed the ban infringed their rights under art.9 or art.2 of Protocol 1.

[253] Contrary to Protocol 1, art.2; *Campbell and Cosans v UK* (1982) 4 E.H.R.R. 293.

from degrading treatment.[254] Failure to protect children from corporal punishment at home has also been held to breach children's rights.

In *A v UK*[255] a nine-year-old boy was beaten with a garden cane by his step-father on a number of occasions, leaving obvious bruises. The step-father was prosecuted for assault but was acquitted. From this it could be inferred that the jury regarded the beating as "reasonable chastisement".[256] In Strasbourg, the Government accepted there had been a violation of the boy's art.3 rights; the court unanimously found a violation because English law did not provide adequate protection against such punishment. Following the decision, the Government consulted on reform.[257] The Children Act 2004 s.58 limits the reasonable chastisement defence to common assault.

Article 3 has also provided the basis for a claim where a local authority social-services department failed to protect children from severe abuse and neglect.[258] This has allowed children to sue in tort where they have been harmed through negligence in the child protection system.[259] Changes have also been made to the way children are tried for serious offences.[260]

Not all decisions have promoted children's rights: **16–018**

In *Neilson v Denmark*[261] the European Court of Human Rights held that there had been no violation of the rights of a 12-year-old boy caught up in a residence dispute between his parents, who was committed to a psychiatric unit at the request of his mother. The placement did not amount to detention[262] but was a responsible exercise by his mother of her rights.

Since the implementation of the Human Rights Act 1998, the analysis of Convention Rights by the domestic courts in cases concerning children has been haphazard.[263] Where children have not been parties, their rights have been

---

[254] Contrary to art.3; *Tyrer v UK* (1978) 2 E.H.R.R. 175 (the Manx Birching case); *Costello-Roberts v UK* (1993) 19 E.H.R.R. 112 (seven year old slippered at prep school). The court, by a majority, found no breach of art.3 in *Costello-Roberts*, but regarded it as a borderline case. The Commission (but not the court) considered there was a breach of art.8.

[255] *A v UK* [1998] 2 F.L.R. 959.

[256] Children and Young Persons Act 1933 s.1(1)(e).

[257] Children Act 2004 s.58; see DH, *Protecting Children, Supporting Parents: a Consultation Document on the Physical Punishment of Children* (2000); J. Fortin, "Children's rights and the use of physical force" [2001] C.F.L.Q. 243.

[258] *Z v UK* [2001] 2 F.L.R. 612. The House of Lords in *X (Minors) v Bedfordshire CC* [1995] 2 A.C. 633 held that the local authority was immune from liability in negligence for failing to remove the children from their parents; see Ch.21, below.

[259] *D v E Berkshire Community NHS Trust* [2005] 2 F.L.R. 284, HL.

[260] *T v UK; V v UK* [2000] All E.R. 1024 (note).

[261] (1988) 11 E.H.R.R. 175.

[262] Contrary to art.5. In *Re K (Secure Accommodation Order: Right to Liberty)* [2001] 1 F.L.R. 526 CA, Thorpe L.J. (dissenting) applied this same reasoning to use of secure accommodation under Children Act 1989 s.25; see Masson [2002] C.F.L.Q. 77.

[263] Fortin (2006).

ignored,[264] and where the welfare principle applies, the courts have paid little attention to the child's Convention rights or have adopted the "controversial view" that a decision that is in the child's best interests automatically satisfies art.8(2).[265] Only where it has been accepted that the issue is not one about upbringing have the courts conscientiously balanced the child's rights with other rights and interests. For example, in *Re Roddy*[266] Munby J. gave detailed consideration balancing arts 8 and 10 when considering a 16-year-old girl's rights to sell her story of early pregnancy and her baby's adoption. However, where the issue is a decision taken by a public authority, it is the impact of the decision on the individual's rights and not the process through that the decision was reached that is at issue.[267] The incorporation of the Convention has potential to change the way children are viewed and treated by the law. Despite the many obstacles, it is far easier for children (and their parents) to assert their rights in the domestic courts. The judiciary are beginning to recognise that children have rights, and this is likely to lead to some change in approach. However, fewer cases will be brought against the United Kingdom in Strasbourg; applications of the Convention to practices elsewhere in Europe are likely to have only limited influence. A greater recognition of children's rights will depend on the practice of public authorities and the courts seeing children's welfare as an aspect of their rights, rather than distinct from, and in conflict with, their rights.

D. Children's rights and the Children Act 1989

16–019   It has been stated that the Children Act 1989 does nothing to change the underlying principle of the *Gillick* decision.[268] However, the Act neither recognises that mature children necessarily have legal capacity nor attempts the impossible task of defining how parental responsibility and children's rights inter-relate.[269] Where there is a dispute about a child's upbringing, the court's decision is to be made applying the welfare principle.[270] The child will not necessarily be a party to those proceedings.[271] The child's consent is not required for a parent to arrange the child's emigration or for a change of name,[272] nor for

---

[264] *R. (on the application of Williamson) v Secretary of State for Education and Employment* [2005] UKHL 15.

[265] Fortin (2006); see also J. Herring, "The Human Rights Act and the welfare principle in family law—conflicting or complementary?" [1999] C.F.L.Q. 223, 23, and below, para.19–004.

[266] *Re Roddy (a child) (identification: restrictions on publication)* [2004] 2 F.L.R. 949, *per* Munby J.; see Fortin (2006) and J. Munby, "Families old and new—the family and Article 8" [2005] C.F.L.Q. 487, 506.

[267] *R. (ota Begum) v Denbigh High School* [2006] UKHL 15, *per* Lord Bingham at 29–31; Lord Hoffman at 68.

[268] *Per* Lord Mackay, Lord Chancellor; Children Bill Committee stage, *Hansard*, HL Vol.502, col.1351.

[269] Law Com. No.172, para.2.2.

[270] Children Act 1989 s.1; the welfare checklist in s.1(3) includes: "(a) the ascertainable wishes and feelings of the child concerned (considered in the light of his age and understanding)": see Ch.19, below.

[271] Party status is discussed below, at para.16–020.

[272] Children Act 1989 s.13(1); *Practice Direction (Child) (Change of Surname)* [1995] 1 F.L.R. 548; for a discussion of children's participation in migration decisions see: Ackers [2000] C.F.L.Q. 167.

the imposition of a family assistance order.[273] A child who objects to a parent's decision may seek leave to apply for a prohibited steps order,[274] but leave will only be granted where the court is satisfied that the child has sufficient understanding,[275] and the court's decision on the substantive issue will be made applying the welfare principle. Children who were not parties to the original proceedings may not apply to have a contact order varied, and must rely on their carer or direct action to avoid contact.[276] Where provision of services is being considered or a child is looked after by the local authority or is the subject of child protection action, the Act recognises the child's right to be consulted,[277] but it removed the rights[278] of mature children under 16 to refer themselves to local authority accommodation or to remain there against their parents' wishes.[279] However, the consent of a mature child is required for a medical or psychiatric examination, even where this has been ordered in court proceedings,[280] for emigration arrangements[281] and for the provision of an independent visitor.[282] Also the power of the courts to make orders is curtailed; s.8 orders[283] will only be made, or will remain in force, in respect of children over the age of 16 in exceptional circumstances.[284] Thus, the Children Act 1989 takes a narrow view of *Gillick*; mature children may make some decisions that are essentially personal, but where others are involved, the decision is left to the carers, whose actions may be challenged in the courts.[285]

---

[273] Children Act 1989 s.16. The consent of all other people named in the order must be obtained: s.16(3).

[274] Children Act 1989 s.8. For details of court powers, see Ch.18 below.

[275] Children Act 1989 s.10(8); *Re T (A Minor) (Child: Representation)* [1994] Fam. 49, CA; *Re H (Residence Order)* [2000] 1 F.L.R. 780, FD.

[276] Despite the clear wording the child is not apparently "named in the order" for the purpose of s.10(6); *Re H (Residence Order)* [2000] 1 F.L.R. 780 at 784, *per* Johnson J.

[277] Children Act 1989 ss.17(4A), 20(6), 22(4)(b), (5)(a), 47(5A).

[278] The DHSS considered that children of 16 had such a right, and stated that it might be appropriate to grant this to younger children "provided that this did not interfere with the competing interest of the parents": *Review of the Child Care Law* (Discussion Paper 2), para.72. The discussion paper was written before the House of Lords decision in *Gillick*, which can be interpreted as providing this right for all mature children.

[279] Children Act 1989 s.20(8), (11).

[280] Children Act 1989 s.44 and Sch.3, para.4(4). But not under the inherent jurisdiction: *Re R. (A Minor) (Wardship: Consent to Treatment)* [1992] Fam. 11; *Re W (A Minor) (Medical Treatment: Court's Jurisdiction)* [1993] Fam. 64; *S Glamorgan CC v W and B* [1993] 1 F.L.R. 574; and para.16–014.

[281] Children Act 1989 Sch.2, para.19(3); this only applies where there is a care order.

[282] Children Act 1989 Sch.2, para.17; independent visitors are appointed to befriend children looked after by a local authority who have little or no contact with their families: see M. Winn Oakley and J. Masson, *Official Friends or Friendly Officials* (1999).

[283] For an explanation of these orders, see Ch.18 below.

[284] Children Act 1989 ss.9(6), 91(10), for example, if the child had limited intellectual capacity or is irresponsible: *Re M (Contact: Parental Responsibility)* [2001] 2 F.L.R. 342, FD. Residence orders in favour of people other than parents and guardians can last until the child is 18: s.12(5), added by Adoption of Children Act 2002 s.114(1).

[285] If a child under 16 wants to remain in local authority accommodation against the wishes of the parent, the court may not be able to intervene. Neither the inherent jurisdiction nor a s.8 order can be used to "achieve a result which could be achieved by a residence order" or to "require a child to be accommodated by the local authority": ss.9(5), 100(2). Residence orders may not be made in favour of the local authority: s.9(2). The child could complain about the failure to take care proceedings, but judicial review is likely to be refused: *R v E Sussex CC Ex p. W* [1998] 2 F.L.R. 1082.

E. Children as parties in legal proceedings[286]

16–020 Children have the same rights to bring or defend ordinary civil proceedings as do adults, but they are regarded as "legal incompetents" and are subject to procedural protections and controls like those applied to mental patients.[287] However, in family proceedings, three distinct systems have been devised to allow children to participate in proceedings where it is considered appropriate for them to do so.[288] The Family Proceedings Rules 1991 (SI 1991/1247) r.9.5 allows the court to make a child a party and to appoint a guardian ad litem where it is in their best interests to do so. Alternatively, with leave, a child who is competent may participate as a party without either a next friend or a guardian.[289] In "specified proceedings",[290] children are parties automatically, and usually have tandem representation by a children's guardian and a solicitor.[291] Children's access to the courts in private law family proceedings is restricted; a child who wishes to seek a s.8 order, (e.g. a contact order to require a parent to allow contact with a sibling,[292] or a residence order to enable the child to live with a relative)[293] must first obtain leave.[294] Originally applications were restricted to the High Court to discourage them but, in future, the county courts will hear them.[295] The court must find that the child has sufficient understanding to make the application[296] and that the issue could not properly be considered without this application.[297] The views of other potential parties may be heard.[298]

Courts have regarded children's involvement in family disputes negatively. There is a fear that it could "drive a wedge between parents and children" and

---

[286] See J. Masson, "Representations of children" [1996] C.L.P. 245. For a review of the nature and extent of litigation by children, see J. Masson and A. Orchard, *Children and Civil Litigation* (LCD Research Report No.10, 1999); A. O'Quigley, *Listening to Children's Views: The Findings and Recommendations of Recent Research* (2000). The Australian Law Reform Commission has conducted an extensive review of children's involvement in litigation: ALRC, Report No.84, *Seen and Heard: Priority for Children in the Legal Process* (1997).

[287] Civil Procedure Rules 1998 (SI 1998/3132) r.21; see below, para.17–021.

[288] Family Law Act 1996 s.64 which provides for children to be parties in some family proceedings, has not been implemented.

[289] Family Proceedings Rules 1991 r.9(2A).

[290] Children Act 1989 s.41 and Family Proceedings Rules 1991 (SI 1991/1247) r.4.2(2). Adoption of Children Act 2002 s.122 provides for rules to make some s.8 applications "specified proceedings".

[291] Children Act 1989 s.41; Family Proceedings Rules 1991 (SI 1991/1247) rr.4.10, 4.11, 4.11A and 4.12 and see below, para.21–058.

[292] *Re F (Contact Child in Care)* [1995] 1 F.L.R. 510, FD; *Re S (Contact: Application by a Sibling)* [1998] 2 F.L.R. 897, FD (application for contact with adopted sibling).

[293] *Re T (A Minor) (Child Representation)* [1994] Fam. 49.

[294] Children Act 1989 s.10(8)(9); s.10(9) applies to contact but not to residence applications: *Re S (Contact: Application by a Sibling)* [1998] 2 F.L.R. 897 at 904–907, *per* Charles J.

[295] Draft Allocation and Transfer of Proceedings Order 2008; DCA, *Focusing judicial resources appropriately* (2005) recommended complexity, public importance and precedent setting as the basis for use of the High Court, para.7.

[296] Children Act 1989 s.10(8) and where s.10(9) applies, *Re S (Contact: Application by a Sibling)* [1998] 2 F.L.R. 897, 906B, *per* Charles J.

[297] *Re H (Residence Order)* [2000] 1 F.L.R. 780 at 783, *per* Johnson J. A similar approach applies to making adults parties to proceedings: *Re W (Care Proceedings: Leave to Apply)* [2004] 2 F.L.R. 468, Sumner J.

[298] Family Proceedings Rules 1991 (SI 1991/1247) r.4.3. Leave may be granted without a hearing: r.4.3(2)(a).

make proceedings more acrimonious.[299] Judges have been haunted by the "spectre" of parents being cross-examined on behalf of their children,[300] and are also concerned to protect children from the stresses of litigation.[301] However, it is now recognised that the proper conduct and disposal of proceedings may require making the child a party,[302] that children can benefit from participation[303] and that it can be harmful to deny children knowledge of and participation in proceedings.[304] Article 6 of the European Convention on Human Rights is likely to encourage this trend.[305]

There are two rationales for allowing children to be parties in private law proceedings: (1) to achieve a better outcome by enabling the court to have a clearer picture of the child's welfare; or (2) to recognise children's rights, particularly under UN Convention on the Rights of the Child art.12[306] and give the child a voice in the proceedings. These may overlap; the court may acquire a better understanding of the child's interests by hearing the child's views. In practice, r.9.5 appointments have focused on children's welfare—the average age of children involved is only eight years.[307] The courts have found the involvement of a guardian ad litem helpful in resolving disputes,[308] and made appointments in private law cases where there are major child protection issues or in an attempt to resolve highly conflicted and intractable contact and residence applications.[309]

> In *Re A*[310] the mother made allegations of sexual abuse against the father when he applied for staying contact. The judge ordered psychiatric reports on both parents and made a contact order. The mother refused to allow contact and failed to attend any further hearings. She was at risk of imprisonment for disobeying the orders. The mother approached the National Youth Advocacy Service (a voluntary organisation) who sought

---

[299] Advisory Board on Family Law, *First Annual Report* (1998), para.4.12.

[300] *Re H (Residence Order)* [2000] 1 F.L.R. 780 at 783, *per* Johnson J.

[301] *Re C (A Minor) (Care: Child's wishes)* [1993] 1 F.L.R. 832, 841, *per* Waite J.; *Re W (Secure Accommodation Order: attendance at court)* [1994] 2 F.L.R. 1092 at 1096, *per* Ewbank J.

[302] *President's Direction: Representation of Children in Family Proceedings* [2004] 1 F.L.R. 1188, para.1. See also *Re S (unmarried parents: Financial Provision)* [2006] 2 F.L.R. 950 CA, para.17.

[303] *Re K (Secure Accommodation: Right to Liberty)* [2001] 2 F.L.R. 526 at 541, *per* Butler-Sloss P.

[304] *Mabon v Mabon* [2005] 2 F.L.R. 1011, *per* Thorpe L.J. at 29.

[305] The termination of contact between a child and a parent infringes both their civil rights and so hearing must satisfy art.6(1) in respect of the parent and the child; see Fortin [1999] C.F.L.Q. 237, 244 and *Sommerfield v Germany* [2002] 1 F.L.R. 119.

[306] Also, art.9(2) provides that in any proceedings concerning the separation of a child from his or her parents, "all interested parties shall be given the opportunity to participate in the proceedings and make their views known" and this could justify party status: A. Moylan, "Children's participation in proceedings—the view from Europe", in Thorpe and Cadbury (eds), *Hearing the Children* (2004).

[307] G. Douglas et al., *Research into the Operation of Rule 9.5 of the Family Proceedings Rules 1991 Report to DCA* (2006), para.6.7.

[308] There appears to be some variation in the use: C. Bellamy, "Rule 9.5: further reflections" [2006] Fam. Law 298.

[309] G. Douglas et al. (2006) para.2.3.

[310] [2001] 1 F.L.R. 715, CA.

leave for the child to be made a party to the proceedings and to act as her guardian ad litem. This application was refused but the Court of Appeal appointed the Official Solicitor[311] as the child's guardian ad litem so that there could be a proper investigation of the abuse allegations.

16–021   Concerns about the increase in the use of r.9.5 and particularly about the greater demands placed on CAFCASS in representing children compared with providing welfare reports led the Department of Constitutional Affairs to propose restrictions on its use to cases where there was a *legal need* for such representation.[312] Such an approach suggests that the Government is not interested in securing direct participation in proceedings for children, and is content to take a minimalist approach to art.12.[313]

As a general rule children may only bring or defend civil proceedings if they are represented by a litigation friend.[314] This person then serves and accepts service of any documents,[315] instructs the solicitor and determines how the proceedings should be conducted. However, a radical departure from long-established practice, introduced with apparently little consideration of its potential effects,[316] enables children who have "sufficient understanding" to bring or continue private law proceedings[317] under the Children Act 1989 or the inherent jurisdiction of the High Court[318] without a next friend or guardian ad litem.[319] A child who wishes to proceed independently must seek leave from the court.[320] Although the rules provide for a solicitor to accept the instructions of a child who has sufficient understanding,[321] and it has been held that in such cases the court has power to determine whether the child can proceed,[322] the Court of Appeal has signalled a more positive approach of direct participation by older children:

---

[311] Representation would now be provided through CAFCASS: *CAFCASS Practice Note* [2004] 1 F.L.R. 1190 and para.1–010, above.

[312] DCA, *Representation of Children* (2006). Prior to the consultation, appointments under r.9.5 had been restricted to Circuit Judges: see para.35.

[313] The UN Convention on the Rights of the Child criticised the Government for its inconsistent approach to art.12: *Concluding Observations*, CRC/C/15/Add.188, para.29.

[314] Civil Procedure Rules 1998 (SI 1998/3132) r.21.2(3) (the court has the power to make an order allowing a child to proceed without a litigation friend); Family Proceedings Rules 1991 (SI 1991/1247) r.9.2 (next friend or guardian ad litem); Johnston [2001] Fam. Law 515. Parents can act as the child's next friend unless they have interests that conflict with those of the child. A solicitor cannot be retained by a client incapable of giving instructions: Law Society, *Guide to Professional Conduct of Solicitors*, 8th edn (1999), para.24.04.

[315] Family Proceedings Rules 1991 (SI 1991/1247) r.9(2), (3).

[316] M. Thorpe, "Independent representation of minors" [1993] Fam. Law 20.

[317] i.e. proceedings that do not involve a local authority. A local authority may take action to protect the child in public law proceedings under the Act. The child's position in public law proceedings is discussed below.

[318] For an explanation of this jurisdiction, see Ch.18, below.

[319] Family Proceedings Rules 1991 (SI 1991/1247) r.9.2A added by Family Proceedings (Amendment) Rules 1992 (SI 1992/456) r.9.

[320] Family Proceedings Rules 1991 (SI 1991/1247) r.9.2A(1)(a).

[321] Family Proceedings Rules 1991 (SI 1991/1247) r.9.2A(1)(b).

[322] *Re T (A Minor) (Child: Representation)* [1994] Fam. 49, CA; *Re S (A Minor) (Independent Representation)* [1993] Fam. 263, CA.

In *Mabon v Mabon*[323] the parents had separated acrimoniously, the mother taking the three youngest children and leaving the three eldest with the father in the family home. The mother applied for residence; a welfare report was ordered and the children were subsequently made parties under r.9.5. The older children consulted solicitors with a view to being separately represented. The court rejected the application in relation to the fact-finding hearing that related to events on a specific day. After this had been completed, the boys applied again but were refused after a contested hearing. Their appeal was allowed. Both Thorpe and Wall L.JJ. made strong statements in favour of the children's participation. Although the tandem model serves children well and was appropriate in the overwhelming majority of cases, for "articulate teenagers . . . the right of freedom of expression and participation outweighs the paternalistic judgment of welfare".[324]

Once a child has become a party, the court cannot impose a guardian ad litem on a child who has sufficient understanding to participate without one.[325] There is no definition of "sufficient understanding" in relation to an application for leave to proceed independently, but this is a test of "*Gillick* competence" that must be "assessed relatively to the issues in the proceedings".[326] Although Lord Scarman in *Gillick* referred to the ability "to exercise a wise choice in one's own interests",[327] it has been accepted that a child with sufficient rationality to give consistent and coherent instructions could instruct their own solicitor.[328] Guidance has been prepared to help solicitors[329] assess whether children have sufficient understanding:

> "Maturity can be assessed on the child's ability to understand the nature of the proceedings and to have an appreciation of the possible consequences of the applications to the court both in the long and short term."[330]

Leave may be revoked and a guardian ad litem imposed if it becomes clear that the child lacks the necessary understanding.[331] It has also been said that the court is unlikely to permit a child who proposes not to be legally represented to proceed independently unless the guardian ad litem agrees.[332] Solicitors should

---

[323] [2005] 2 F.L.R. 1011, CA.
[324] *Per* Thorpe L.J. at para.28 and Wall L.J. at para.40.
[325] Family Proceedings Rules 1991 (SI 1991/1247) r.9.2A(6); *Re T (A Minor) (Wardship: Representation)* [1994] Fam. 49.
[326] *Re S (A Minor) (Independent Representation)* [1993] Fam. 263 at 276, *per* Sir Thomas Bingham M.R.
[327] [1986] A.C. 112 at 188.
[328] *Re H (A Minor) (Care Proceedings: Child's wishes)* [1993] 1 F.L.R. 440 at 449. Thorpe J. regarded the level of understanding required to participate in legal proceedings as less than that required to refuse a psychiatric examination.
[329] Resolution, *Guide to Good Practice for Solicitors Acting for Children*, 6th edn (2002). In the past, solicitors have approached this task in different ways: C. Sawyer, *The Rise and Fall of the Third Party* (1995).
[330] Resolution, *Guide to Good Practice*, para.F 1.
[331] Family Proceedings Rules 1991 (SI 1991/1247) r.9.2A(8), (10).
[332] *Re S (A Minor) (Independent Representation)* [1993] Fam. 263 at 276.

act scrupulously and conscientiously when assessing children's ability to give instructions, and risk withdrawal of legal aid if they do not.[333] Participating as a party requires more than instructing a solicitor about one's views; a party must be able to follow the evidence and given instructions on issues as the case proceeds.[334] Children who are parties may need to give instructions relating to psychiatric reports[335] or may want their lawyer to advocate that they should live with an abuser.[336]

16–022   The rules make very different provision for the representation of children in "specified proceedings".[337] The child is represented by a children's guardian from CAFCASS[338] and a solicitor.[339] The guardian's duties include investigating the case, explaining matters to the child and advising the court on the child's best interests and wishes.[340] The children's guardian instructs the solicitor unless the child is competent,[341] wants to do so and has instructions that conflict with those of the children's guardian.[342] In such a case the solicitor must follow the child's instructions, but the court still controls the proceedings and can refuse permission for the child to file evidence.[343] The solicitor may have to advocate that a child not receive professional help for disturbance that is ruining their educational prospects[344] or be allowed to live with a sibling the child is thought to have abused.[345] Where there is a conflict, the court should be informed, and it may

---

[333] *Re S (A Minor) (Independent Representation)* [1993] Fam. 263 at 276, *per* Sir Thomas Bingham M.R. But in borderline cases, solicitors should be given the benefit of the doubt: *Re T (A Minor) (Wardship: Representation)* [1994] Fam. 49 at 67, *per* Waite, L.J.

[334] *Re H (A Minor) (Guardian ad litem requirement)* [1994] Fam.11 at 13, *per* Booth J. The extent to which a child party may be protected by being excluded from proceedings is unclear: see below.

[335] *Re M (Minors) (Care proceedings: Child's wishes)* [1994] 1 F.L.R. 749 (psychiatric reports about parents); *Re H (A Minor) (Care proceedings: Child's wishes)* [1993] 1 F.L.R. 440 (psychiatric report on child).

[336] *Re H (A Minor) (Guardian ad litem requirement)* [1994] Fam.11.

[337] Children Act 1989 s.41; Family Proceedings Rules 1991 (SI 1991/1247) r.4.2(2). Specified proceedings include applications under Children Act 1989 ss.25 (secure accommodation applications), 31 (care and supervision applications), 34 (contact applications relating to a child in care), 39 (discharge applications and applications under Pt V). Adoption of Children Act 2002 s.122 makes provision for rules to include some s.8 applications in the list. For a detailed analysis of representation in public law proceedings, see J. Masson and M. Winn Oakley, *Out of Hearing* (Chichester: Wiley, 1999) and J. Masson, "Representation of children in England" [2000] F.L.Q. 467.

[338] Children Act 1989 s.41; Criminal Justice and Court Services Act 2000 s.12. The children's guardian is normally a qualified social worker with substantial childcare experience.

[339] Family Proceedings Rules 1991 (SI 1991/1247) rr.4.10–4.12. But it has been held that this does not entitle the child to public funding where the merits test applies: *W v Legal Services Commission* [2000] 2 F.L.R. 821, CA.

[340] Family Proceedings Rules 1991 (SI 1991/1247) rr.4.11, 4.11A.

[341] Disputes about the child's competence should be referred to the court: *Re H (A Minor) (Care proceedings: Child's wishes)* [1993] 1 F.L.R. 440. In practice, children's guardians and solicitors work to avoid conflict: Winn Oakley and Masson, *Out of Hearing*, pp.77–79.

[342] Family Proceedings Rules 1991 (SI 1991/1247) rr.4.11A(1)(b), 4.12(1)(a).

[343] *Re O (Care Proceedings: Evidence)* [2004] 1 F.L.R. 161, para.39 but evidence crucial to the outcome should not be excluded.

[344] *Re H (A Minor) (Care proceedings: Child's wishes)* [1993] 1 F.L.R. 440.

[345] *Re M (Minors) (Care proceedings: Child's wishes)* [1994] 1 F.L.R. 749. But if the child's instructions are wholly unreasonable the solicitor must report the matter to the Legal Services Commission and funding will be withdrawn: *Funding Code*, Part C, para.13.5 1a.

direct that the child's guardian is separately represented.[346] This procedure should enable the court to hear full arguments relating both to the child's wishes and the child's welfare.

Children do not have the right to attend proceedings brought under the Children Act 1989, even where they are parties, but a party may not be excluded unless they are represented by a children's guardian or a solicitor.[347] Attending court is considered by some to be damaging to children because it may make them feel responsible for the decisions and increase their anxiety.[348] It is not an experience that should be wished on a child as young as 13.[349] The trial judge should balance the rights of children to participate and be heard in litigation with the need to protect children from exposure to material that might be damaging.[350] Children subject to secure-accommodation proceedings must be afforded the protection the European Convention of Human Rights art.6(3), and should feel they have been treated fairly.[351] Children's limited involvement may mean that they are unclear about the proceedings or their outcome. There is provision for informing them of decisions in specified proceedings,[352] and the Department of Constitutional Affairs has sought views on how to meet adults' needs for objective information about proceedings that concerned them as children.[353]

Despite growing acceptance of children as individuals with rights, the courts remain most concerned to protect what they consider to be children's interests.[354] The ability of children to make an application and represent themselves does not lie easily with the adversarial procedures of the court.[355] Allowing children to appear without a next friend or guardian ad litem puts them at risk of being manipulated by parents or by solicitors.[356] However, rather than seeking change to legal proceedings to make it easier for children to participate, the judiciary has exercised its power to limit children's direct involvement.[357] Although there are signs[357a] that the courts are more willing to allow children some involvement,

---

[346] *Re M (Minors) (Care proceedings: Child's wishes)* [1994] 1 F.L.R. 749. The costs of the children's guardian's representation fall on CAFCASS.

[347] Family Proceedings Rules 1991 (SI 1991/1247) r.4. 16(2). But a child may be ordered to attend proceedings for an order under Pts IV and V of the Children Act 1989 (s.95(1)).

[348] The argument put by the Official Solicitor in *Re W (Secure Accommodation Order: Attendance at Court)* [1994] 2 F.L.R. 1092.

[349] *Re C (A Minor) (Care: Child's wishes)* [1993] 1 F.L.R. 832 at 841, *per* Waite J.

[350] *Re A (Care: Discharge Application by Child)* [1995] 1 F.L.R. 599 at 601, *per* Thorpe J.

[351] *Re C (Secure Accommodation Order: Representation)* [2001] 2 F.L.R. 169, paras 34 and 41, *per* Brooke L.J.

[352] Family Proceedings Rules 1991 (SI 1991/1247) r.4.11A(10).

[353] DCA, *Confidence and Confidentiality* (2006), p.49. Later-life letters are provided by Adoption Agencies for some adoptees.

[354] C. Sawyer, *Rules, Roles and Relationships: The Structure and Function of Child Representation and Welfare in Family Proceedings* (Centre for socio-legal studies, Oxford University, 1999); C. Sawyer, "Conflicting rights for children: implementing welfare autonomy and justice in family proceedings" [1999] J.S.W.F.L. 99.

[355] M. Booth, Address to Lawyers for Children Conference 1993: [1993] Fam. Law 652 at 653.

[356] M. Thorpe [1994] Fam. Law 20. The *Resolution Guide* (2002) recognises that solicitors may effectively take over the litigation, and reminds them to be prepared to allow the child to withdraw their action: para.H1.

[357] See J. Masson, "Representations of children" [1996] C.L.P. 245, and J. Roche, "Children's rights: in the name of the child" [1995] J.S.W.F.L. 281 at 285.

[357a] Family Justice Council, "Enhancing the participation of children and young people in family proceedings" [2008] Fam. Law 431.

proceedings about their upbringing are still constructed as disputes that concern them only indirectly.

F. Rights in other legislation

16–023   Education law takes even less notice of children's rights[358]; even international human-rights treaties promote rights in education from a largely adult perspective.[359] Choice of school is regarded as a parental right,[360] and children have no right to express preferences or make representations to the local education authority.[361] Only a parent may appeal a decision about a child's special educational needs.[362] The parent (not the child) may withdraw the child from religious education[363] or some sex education,[364] but children over compulsory school age have a right to withdraw from religious education and religious worship.[365] Only parents and pupils over the age of 18 have rights to appeal following a pupil's permanent exclusion,[366] but children can use judicial review or the Human Rights Act to challenge decisions by schools[367]:

> In *Ali v Lord Grey School*[368] a 13-year-old pupil was suspected of involvement in arson at the school and was excluded during a police investigation. The CPS decided not to prosecute but the boy was not immediately re-instated. The school offered a re-integration meeting, and when the parents failed to attend, arranged for a place at a pupil-referral unit. A subsequent request for re-instatement was refused. The boy sought judicial review of these decisions and argued that his rights under ECHR Protocol 1 art.2 had been breached. A majority of their Lordships rejected

---

[358] See: N. Harris, *Law and Education* (London: Sweet & Maxwell, 1993); D. Monk, "Children's rights in education—making sense of the contradictions" [2002] C.F.L.Q. 45 and Bainham (2005), Ch.16.

[359] J. Fortin (2003), p.345, citing the International Covenant on Economic, Social and Cultural Rights art.13(3), the ECHR Protocol 1 art.2 and UNCRC arts 14 and 29.

[360] Education Act 1996 s.9 imposes a qualified duty on the Secretary of State and Local Education Authorities to provide education which accords with the parents' wishes; School Standards and Framework Act 1998 s.86 obliges the LEA to make arrangements for parents to express a preference with which it may be bound to comply unless one of the exceptions applies: see Harris (*Law and Education*), pp.19–21 and Ch.5.

[361] School Standards and Framework Act 1998 s.94, as amended by Education and Inspections Act 2006 s.43.

[362] Education Act 1996 s.442; Disability Discrimination Act 1995 s.28K(2); *S v Special Educational Needs Tribunal and the City of Westminster* [1996] 1 F.L.R. 663, CA. This is the case even if the education concerns an adult: *per* Leggatt L.J. at 665.

[363] School Standards and Framework Act 1998 s.71(1).

[364] Education Act 1996 s.405, but not sex education that forms part of the National Curriculum in secondary schools. Parental control of sex education was criticised by the Committee on the Rights of the Child. Although the Government has set out a national programme to reduce the teenage conception rate, it has not removed parental control: *Second Report to the UN Committee on the Rights of the Child by the UK* (2002), paras 1.3.3e and 8.21.7.

[365] Education and Inspections Act 2006 s.55, amending School Standards and Framework Act 1998 s.71(1), (8).

[366] Education Act 2002 s.52 and Education (Pupil Referral Units) (Appeals against permanent exclusions) (England) Regulations 2002 (SI 2002/2550) and for Wales, (SI 2003/3227).

[367] *R. (ota Ali) v Lord Grey School* [2006] UKHL 14; *R. (ota Begum) v Denbigh High School* [2006] UKHL 15.

[368] [2006] UKHL 14.

the human rights claims because the ECHR only guaranteed access to education, and this had been provided. Lady Hale considered that Ali's exclusion without good reason or any procedural protections justified a declaration that the school had acted incompatibly with its rights.[369]

The emphasis on parental control, although it supports parenting, ignores the need to engage children and the disregard for education held by some parents. Such control may also be against the state's interest in achieving a healthy and well-qualified workforce.

Children's economic dependence on their families has not been reduced following *Gillick*. Reductions in social security provision have been made on the basis that they could (and should) reside with their parents.[370] State benefits are not generally available to enable children under 18 to live independently from their parents, and benefit for under 18s and those aged between 18 and 25 is set at lower rates.[371] Only limited recognition is given to the fact that there are children who have no family to live with or whose welfare demands that they live elsewhere.[372] Mature children who wish to leave their families must thus be more self-reliant than adults who can obtain state benefits when they are unemployed and seeking work. Children's economic dependence gives parents power that they could not claim as part of parental responsibility.

G. Children of unmarried parents[373]

Discrimination on the grounds of parents' status conflicts with both the UN **16–024** Convention on the Rights of the Child[374] and the European Convention on Human Rights.[375] At common law, children were only "legitimate" if the parents were married when they were born or conceived.[376] A child born to unmarried parents was a *filius nullius* or *filius populi*; no legal relationship was recognised with the mother or father nor with any other "relatives". Hence, the child had no

---

[369] At para.83. Ali has sought damages, and this claim was unanimously rejected because the school should not be made to pay for the parents' failure to respond to the various offers of education.

[370] N. Harris, *Social Security in Context* (Oxford: Oxford University Press, 2000), p.185.

[371] Social Security Contributions and Benefits Act 1992 s.124(1); Income Support (General) Regulations 1987 (SI 1987/1967) Sch.2 (as amended for annual uprating). See, generally, A. Ogus and E. Barendt, *The Law of Social Security*, 4th edn (1995), pp.461–466.

[372] Jobseekers Act 1995 s.16; Jobseekers Allowance Regulations (SI 1996/207) Pt IV (as amended). Local authorities remain financially responsible for young people under 18 who have left care: Children (Leaving Care) Act 2000 s.6.

[373] For a more detailed analysis of the history and social policy, see the fourth edition of this work, Ch.20.

[374] The anti-discrimination principle in art.2. Article 18 requires States Parties to use their best efforts to ensure the recognition of the principle that both parents have common responsibilities for the upbringing and development of the child.

[375] art.14. In *Marckx v Belgium* (1979) 2 E.H.R.R. 330 and *Inze v Austria* (1987) 10 E.H.R.R., the European Court of Human Rights held that discrimination against illegitimate children in relation to inheritance rights breached their art.14 rights. But the inheritance of a title is not protected: *Re Moynihan* [2000] 1 F.L.R. 113 HL and *X v UK* (1978) 2 E.H.R.R. 63.

[376] Blackstone, *Commentaries*, p.454. A child born after the husband's death or divorce was also legitimate: *Knowles v Knowles* [1962] P. 161.

legal right to succeed to their property, nor to receive maintenance[377] and other benefits deriving from the status of parent and child.

Legal intervention was originally primarily concerned to protect against the financial consequences of children becoming a charge on the community; thus, the Poor Law began the formal association between birth outside marriage and criminality, relics of which lingered on for many years. In the twentieth century, two separate developments mitigated the harshness of the common law. First, the definition of "illegitimate" was narrowed by allowing children whose parents married after their birth to be legitimated,[378] and by recognising as legitimate some children born of void marriages.[379] Secondly, rights accorded to children born within marriage were extended to all children. For example, the Fatal Accidents legislation[380] virtually eliminated the distinction for the purposes of "dependency" claims brought under it, and the law of inheritance was changed to enable a child born outside of marriage to claim under a will,[381] the father's intestacy,[382] and to seek family provision.[383] This process culminated in the Family Law Reform Act 1987, which, with two major exceptions,[384] ended the distinction between children based on their parent's marriage.

The Family Law Reform Act 1987 s.1(1) provides that for all legislation and instruments made after April 4, 1988[385]:

> "references (however expressed) to any relationship between two persons shall, unless the contrary intention appears, be construed without regard to whether or not the father and mother of either of them, or the father and mother of any person through whom the relationship is deduced, have or had been married to each other at any time."[386]

---

[377] Note, however, according to R.H. Helmholz, "Support orders, church courts and the rule of Filius Nullius. A reassessment of the common law" (1977) 63 Va L. Rev. 431, the church courts gave a right of support.

[378] The Legitimacy Act 1926 allowed legitimation if the father was domiciled in England at the date of the marriage and neither party was married to anyone else at the date of the child's birth. The Legitimacy Act 1959 allowed a child born of an adulterous relationship to be legitimated. The Children Act 1975 Sch.1 made changes to the status conferred by legitimation. These provisions were consolidated in the Legitimacy Act 1976 s.8, which provides that a legitimated person should have all the same rights as a legitimate one, but it did not affect titles nor dispositions made before January 1, 1976.

[379] The Legitimacy Act 1959 consolidated in the Legitimacy Act 1976 s.1 treated such children as legitimate, provided the father was domiciled in England at the time of birth and at least one parent believed at the time of marriage that the marriage was valid.

[380] See Fatal Accidents Act 1976 (as substituted by Administration of Justice Act 1982) s.1(5)(b).

[381] Family Law Reform Act 1969 s.16.

[382] Family Law Reform Act 1969 s.14; (the Legitimacy Act 1926 allowed succession under the mother's intestacy).

[383] Family Law Reform Act 1969 s.18; Inheritance (Provision for Family and Dependants) Act 1975 ss.1, 25(1).

[384] i.e. the status of the father and the child's citizenship (which affects the child's rights to enter and remain in the UK).

[385] For a full discussion see, *Current Law Annotated Statutes.*

[386] Family Law Reform Act 1987 s.1(3) defines a person "whose father and mother were married to each other at the time of his birth" to include all legitimate, legitimated and adopted children. See also, D. Pearl, "Recent changes in the law relating to children of unmarried parents" (1989) 1 J.C.L. 126 and N. Lowe, "The Family Law Reform Act 1987—useful reform but an unhappy compromise" [1988] Denning L.J. 77.

This rule of construction is also applied to some existing statutes.[387] Where the rule does not apply, it is still necessary to determine whether the child was or is legitimate; the provisions of the Legitimacy Act 1976 defining "legitimate", "legitimated children" and "children treated as legitimate" although their parents' marriage was void, are still relevant.[388] Thus, all children's inheritance rights[389] and rights of support are now the same.

The 1987 reforms left children born outside marriage without the automatic protection from birth of a father with automatic rights in relation to them.[390] Also, children born outside marriage to a British father and foreign mother did not acquire British citizenship in contrast to a child of married parents.[391] The Law Commission's terms of reference for the review that led to the 1987 Act precluded it, making definitive proposals about the citizenship,[392] but it accepted that differential treatment amounted to unjustified discrimination[393] and provisionally recommended reform.[394] The Government rejected this, apparently because there were at the time no adequate legal procedures for determining paternity.[395] When the United Kingdom acceded to the UN Convention on the Rights of the Child it made a wide-ranging reservation in respect of immigration and nationality laws. Despite the Committee's request and recommendations from both the Joint Committee on Human Rights and the Department of Education and Skills,[396] the Government has retained this reservation on the basis that it is necessary to ensure that those without connections to the United Kingdom do not make claims based on the Convention.[397] However, a major basis for the reservation (the differential treatment in relation to British citizenship of children born outside marriage) has now been removed.[398] The Nationality, Immigration and Asylum Act 2002 amends the definition of "parent" in the British Nationality Act 1981. Children may claim citizenship through either their mother or their father, and the definition of father is wide enough to include the mother's husband at the time of

16–025

---

[387] Family Law Reform Act 1987 s.2.

[388] Family Law Reform Act 1987 s.1(3) the definition of children treated as legitimate is amended by Family Law Reform Act 1987 s.28; see below.

[389] Family Law Reform Act 1987 ss.18–20; but inheritance of titles of honour and succession to the throne are generally not affected.

[390] See below, para.17–035.

[391] A child born overseas was also excluded if the mother was a British citizen by descent: British Nationality Act 1981 ss.1(1), 2(1) and 50(9)(b). For further details see seventh edition of this work at 17–019.

[392] Law Com. No.118, *Illegitimacy* (1982–3 HCP 98), paras 11.1, 11.20.

[393] Law Com. No.118, *Illegitimacy* (1982–3 HCP 98), para.11.6

[394] *Illegitimacy* (WP 74 (1979)), para.7.12.

[395] Law Com. No.118, para.11.8. It was not appropriate to devise such procedures just for citizenship claims.

[396] Joint Committee on Human Rights, *17th Report 2001–2* (HC 961); *18th Report 2002–3* (HL 187), para.7 and App.1.

[397] Joint Committee on Human Rights, *10th Report 2002–3* (HL 117), paras 81–84.

[398] Committee's Concluding observations to the UK's First Report (1995) CRC/C/15/Add.34, paras 7 and 12.

birth.[399] Paternity can be proved by being named on the birth certificate, by DNA test or a court order.[400] Henceforth the status of a child's parents will, for most children, be a matter without legal relevance.

---

[399] British Nationality Act 1981 s.50(9A) added by the Nationality, Immigration and Asylum Act 2002 s.9. The definition includes those with non genetic paternity under Human Fertilisation and Embryology Act 1990 s.28: see below, para.17–004.
[400] The British Nationality (Proof of Paternity) Regulations 2006 (SI 2006/1496) art.3 and see Sheldon [2007] C.F.L.Q. 1 for analysis of the broader trends this change reflects.

CHAPTER SEVENTEEN

PARENTS

I. INTRODUCTION—THE
CONCEPTS 17–001
II. WHO ARE THE CHILD'S
PARENTS? 17–003
  A. Mother 17–003
  B. Father 17–004
  C. Determination of parentage 17–006
III. WHAT IS PARENTAL
RESPONSIBILITY? 17–013
  A. Rights and powers 17–014
  B. Duties 17–027
IV. WHO HAS PARENTAL
RESPONSIBILITY? 17–030
  A. Married parents 17–030

  B. Unmarried parents 17–035
  C. Guardians 17–040
  D. Other persons 17–043
  E. Local authorities 17–047
V. WHERE PARENTAL
RESPONSIBILITY IS HELD BY MORE
THAN ONE PERSON 17–048
VI. REVOCATION OF PARENTAL
RESPONSIBILITY 17–049
VII. RIGHTS OF THOSE WITHOUT
PARENTAL RESPONSIBILITY 17–050
  A. Delegation 17–050
  B. De facto carers 17–051
  C. Unmarried fathers 17–052

I. INTRODUCTION—THE CONCEPTS

Modern child law has been shaped by a number of guiding principles, chief of which is that the primary responsibility for the upbringing of children rests with their parents.[1] The Children Act made parenthood, not guardianship, the primary concept; "parental responsibility" replaced parental rights and duties, and the courts now make decisions about a child's "residence", not "custody".[2] To some extent this may only be "cosmetic renaming"; those with parental responsibility have "rights",[3] but being a parent is increasingly portrayed as a matter of responsibilities.[4]

17–001

[1] See *The Law on Child Care and Family Services* (Cm.62 (1987)), para.5a and *Review of Child Law Guardianship and Custody* (Law Com. No.172 (1988)) HCP 594, para.2.1; C. Barton and G. Douglas, *Law and Parenthood* (1995).

[2] For the background to these reforms, see *Guardianship* (Law Com. WP 91 (1985)); *Custody* (WP 96 (1986)); *Care, supervision and interim orders in custody proceedings* (WP 100 (1987)); *Wards of Court* (WP 101 (1987)); J. Priest and J. Whybrow, *Custody Law in Practice in the Divorce and Domestic Courts* (supplement to WP 96) (1986); Report No.172, *Review of Child Law Guardianship and Custody*.

[3] *Re P (A Minor) (Parental Responsibility)* [1994] 1 F.L.R. 578 at 585, *per* Wilson J.

[4] DfES, *Parental Separation: Children's Needs and Parents' Responsibilities* (Cm.6273 (2004)); Education and Inspections Act 2006 s.103.

Guardianship was rooted in the feudal system: guardians were largely concerned with the property of the child heir.[5] The Court of Chancery developed the concept of the Crown as *parens patriae* for infants who needed protection. Guardians were also appointed by the ecclesiastical courts, by custom and under statute. Guardianship became the instrument for maintaining the father's authority over the children. Natural or parental guardianship was originally confined to the father of a legitimate child, but the Guardianship of Infants Act 1925[6] gave the mother[7] "like powers" to apply to the court. The Guardianship Act 1973[8] provided that the mother's rights and authority were the same as the father's, but neither Act expressly made her a guardian. The Law Commission considered that parenthood should be regarded as the primary concept and should be distinguished from guardianship to remove anomalies in the law and any doubts that mothers and fathers had equal status.[9] Their scheme also enabled the powers of guardians and others acting in the place of parents[10] to be defined by reference to the powers and responsibilities of parents.[11]

The Children Act 1975 used the phrase "the parental rights and duties" to describe all the rights and duties a mother and father had in relation to a legitimate child and the child's property.[12] This was "not only inaccurate as a matter of juristic analysis but also a misleading use of ordinary language".[13] The decision of the House of Lords in *Gillick v West Norfolk and Wisbech AHA*[14] underlined this by acknowledging that the powers parents have over their children exist only to enable them to perform their responsibilities.[15] Consequently, although it would make little difference in substance, the Law Commission recommended that "parental responsibility", a phrase that recognised the everyday reality of being a parent, should replace "parental rights and duties".[16]

17–002 The concept of parental responsibility performs two distinct but inter-related functions[17]: it describes the power of a parent in terms of responsibility, not rights, and locates the obligation to care for children with the parents, not with the state.[18] The change in terminology was intended to change perceptions about the parent–child relationship,[19] and its use appears to have made it easier to

---

[5] F. Pollock and F. Maitland, *The History of English Law* (1923), Vol.II, p.443.

[6] Guardianship of Infants Act 1925 s.2. The mother was not even the guardian of her illegitimate child, who thus had no guardian during her lifetime.

[7] See S. Cretney, "What will the women want next?" [1996] L.Q.R. 110.

[8] Guardianship Act 1973 s.1(1).

[9] Law Com. No.172, para.2.3; Law Com. Working Party 91, paras 3.2–3.4. The Commission rejected the notion that the Crown's power as *parens patriae* made guardianship the primary concept.

[10] *in loco parentis.*

[11] See Children Act 1989 ss.3(5), 5(6), 12(2).

[12] See Children Act 1975 s.85(1). Other phrases were used in other statutes: Childcare Act 1980 s.10(2), "powers and duties"; Guardianship Act 1973 s.1(1), "rights and authority".

[13] *Illegitimacy* (Law Com. No.118 (1982)), para.4.18.

[14] [1986] A.C. 112, see above.

[15] The Scottish Law Commission has proposed that this should be made clear by statute: Scottish Law Com. No.135, paras 2.14, 2.35; Children (Scotland) Act 1995 s.2(1).

[16] Law Com. No.172, para.2.4.

[17] J. Eekelaar, "Parental responsibility: state of nature or nature of the state" [1991] J.S.W.F.L. 37.

[18] Eekelaar, "Parental responsibility".

[19] Bainham, *Children, Parents and the State* (London: Sweet & Maxwell, 1993), p.63.

impose legal obligations on parents whose children commit offences or who fail to maintain their children adequately.[20]

The term "custody" was used variously to describe a state of fact—the child being under the adult's physical control (actual custody)[21]—and a state of law—the right to control the child physically or, in a wider sense (legal custody),[22] the "bundle of powers" relating to the child's person.[23] The courts had wide but inconsistent powers to reallocate legal custody, and could, in some circumstances, make orders in respect of actual custody, care and control[24] and access (contact).[25] The Law Commission considered that it was a:

> "[M]istake to see custody, care and control and access as differently sized bundles of powers and responsibilities in a descending hierarchy of importance."[26]

Rather, the law should recognise that a parent caring for a child needed to take responsibility for the duration of that care. The courts should determine the duration of care rather than the status of the person undertaking it. Under the Children Act 1989, the courts determine disputes about the child's residence, arrangements for child contact and any restrictions on the exercise of parental responsibility.[27] They can also make orders granting or removing parental responsibility from parents and others.[28]

II. WHO ARE THE CHILD'S PARENTS?

A. Mother

Motherhood has traditionally been established through birth,[29] although there is   **17–003**
evidence that any child could be considered the couple's child, and the father's

---

[20] S. Edwards and A. Halpern, "Parental responsibility an instrument of social policy" [1992] Fam. Law 113 discussing the Child Support Act 1991 and the Criminal Justice Act 1991; Gelsthorpe, "Youth crime and parental responsibility" in A. Bainham et al. (eds), *What is a Parent?* (Oxford: Hart, 1999), p.217.

[21] Children Act 1975 s.87(1).

[22] Children Act 1975 s.86(1); legal custody is now encompassed with "parental responsibility"; see Children Act 1989 s.3(1).

[23] Law Com. WP 96, para.2.34.

[24] Law Com. WP 96, paras 2.5, 2.34–2.51.

[25] Law Com. WP 96, paras 2.55–2.56, 4.27–4.34.

[26] Law Com. WP 96, para.4.31.

[27] Children Act 1989 s.8; private law disputes between persons with parental responsibility are dealt with applying the welfare principle: s.1. For details of the court's powers see Ch.18, below.

[28] Children Act 1989 ss.4, 4A, 12(1)(2) and 14C(1)(a); for revocation, see below, para.17–046. Parental responsibility can only be removed from married parents or mothers by adoption, although its exercise may be restricted by a court order: Children Act 1989 ss.2(8), 33(3)(4). Parental responsibility is retained even when another person acquires it.

[29] "Motherhood, although also a legal relationship is based on fact, being proved demonstrably by parturition", *per* Lord Simon, *Ampthill Peerage Case* [1977] A.C. 547 at 577. A procedure was established in Roman Law for the examination of women who claimed to be pregnant and the witnessing of births to prevent fraudulent claims and substitution of babies: Justinian XXV, iv i 10. Similar procedures existed in early England.

legitimate child if he accepted the child as such.[30] Modern developments in
assisted reproduction and the treatment of infertility[31] mean that the definition of
mother must be re-examined. If a child is born following the donation of an egg
or embryo and implantation, the law must decide whether the genetic mother or
the gestational/birth mother is the legal mother.[32] The Warnock Committee
recommended that the birth mother should be the legal mother.[33] They gave no
reasons for this view but considered it in the context of donation to an infertile
woman rather than the needs of a woman who could not carry a pregnancy for
someone to do this for her. However, the Family Law Reform Act 1987[34]
provided for parentage to be determined by scientific tests, indicating that the
genetic contribution determined motherhood. The Government subsequently
accepted the view of the Warnock Committee[35]; the Human Fertilisation and
Embryology Act 1990 provides that where a woman gives birth following egg or
embryo donation, she alone is to be treated as the child's mother.[36] Thus the law
discourages surrogacy by refusing automatic recognition to the commissioning
woman even if the child developed from her genetic material.[37] However, where
a woman or her husband provides genetic material for implantation in a
surrogate, and a child is born, the couple can apply to the court for a parental
order, which gives the woman the status of an adoptive mother.[38] The Human
Fertilisation and Embryology Bill 2008, if enacted, will apply this provision in
respect of civil partners and couples in an enduring family relationship.[39]

---

[30] Pollock and Maitland (1923), p.399. The willingness to accept this sort of informal adoption at the
instigation of the mother may reflect the very limited effect motherhood had on a woman's legal
rights.

[31] For a description of these, see *Report of the Committee of Inquiry into Human Fertilisation and
Embryology* (The *"Warnock Report"*) (Cmnd.9314 (1984)), Chs 5–7; *Human Fertilisation and
Embryology, A Framework for Legislation* (Cm.259 (1987)) and R. Deech, "The legal regulation of
infertility in Britain", in S. Katz et al. (eds), *Cross Currents* (2000) pp.165, 175.

[32] If the birth follows a surrogacy agreement, a third person, the requesting mother, who may be the
sperm donor's wife, may also have a claim, but English law does not consider surrogacy
arrangements enforceable, and any claim would seem to be defeated by the status provisions of the
Human Fertilisation and Embryology Act 1990 s.27; Human Fertilisation and Embryology Bill, cl.33;
see below.

[33] Cmnd.9314 (1984), para.6.8. The same view has generally been taken in the US; see D. Vetri,
"Reproduction technologies and US Law" (1988) 37 I.C.L.Q. 505 at 527.

[34] Family Law Reform Act 1987 s.23(1), amending Family Law Reform Act 1969 s.20(1), (2). This
may not have been intended but results from replacing references to "paternity" with "parentage".

[35] The effect of s.23 was not acknowledged in the *White Paper on Human Fertilisation* (Cm.259
(1987)) para.88.

[36] Human Fertilisation and Embryology Act 1990 s.27; Human Fertilisation and Embryology Bill
2008 cl.33; see, generally, G. Douglas, *Law, Fertility and Reproduction* (London: Sweet & Maxwell,
1991); S. McLean, *Law Reform and Human Reproduction* (Dartmouth, 1992).

[37] Douglas (1994) 57 M.L.R. 636 at 637. But in California the genetic mother has been accepted as
the legal mother because she intended to become a parent, whereas the gestational mother intended
to give birth and then hand over the child: *Johnson v Calvert* 5 Cal 4th 84 (1993); see G. Annas in
S. Katz et al. (eds), *Cross Currents*, p.153 and *Re W and B v H (Abduction surrogacy)* [2002] 1 F.L.R.
1008, FD.

[38] Human Fertilisation and Embryology Act 1990 s.30; Parental Orders (Human Fertilisation and
Embryology) Regulations 1994 (SI 1994/2767).

[39] Providing they are not within the prohibited degrees: Human Fertilisation and Embryology Bill
2008 cl.54(2). For further discussion see para.22–069.

B. Father

With four exceptions, the law recognises the child's biological father as his legal **17–004** father. First, if the parents are married,[40] any child born to the wife is presumed to be the child of the couple.[41] At common law the presumption could only be rebutted where evidence put the matter beyond reasonable doubt; now the matter is determined on the balance of probabilities using scientific tests that can clearly establish parentage.[42] However, where the mother's husband does not dispute paternity and no other man claims it, the husband will be the legal father, although his status could be overturned later in proceedings.[43] Secondly, following the recommendations of the Law Commission and the Warnock Committee,[44] a child born in England or Wales as a result of AID or embryo donation to the wife "shall be treated in law as the child of the parties to the marriage" and no one else, unless it is proved that the husband did not consent to the wife's treatment.[45] There is no formal means of establishing consent, and the civil standard of proof applies.[46] Where the couple is unmarried, there is a similar provision, but the woman must receive treatment services "provided for her and a man together" in a licensed clinic[47]:

In *U v W*[48] an unmarried woman sought to conceive using her partner's sperm. When treatment in England was unsuccessful they visited a clinic in Rome and were persuaded to use donated sperm. The man signed a document produced by the clinic accepting paternity, but, following the breakdown of the relationship, was unwilling to support the disabled twins who had been born as a result of the procedure. The woman sought a declaration that the man was the children's father so that she could obtain child support. The clinic in Rome was not licensed by the Human

---

[40] But not if they are judicially separated: *Ettenfield v Ettenfield* [1940] p.96.

[41] *Pater est quem nuptiae demonstrant*: see Bromley (1998), p.272. Child Support Act 1991 s.26(2), case A1, amended by Child Support and Pensions Act 2000 s.15.

[42] Family Law Reform Act 1969 s.26 following recommendations of the Law Commission: Law Com. No.16, *Blood Tests and the Proof of Paternity in Civil Proceedings*, para.15. Where tests are carried out, the point may be only academic, but s.23 allows the court to "draw such inferences, if any, as appear proper" from a person's failure to comply with a test direction: *Re A (A Minor) (Paternity: Refusal of Blood Test)* [1994] 2 F.L.R. 463 and cases discussed below. Also, paternity may be in dispute after the death of the "parents", as in the *Ampthill Peerage Case* [1977] A.C. 547.

[43] Family Law Act 1986 s.55A.

[44] *Warnock Report*, para.4.17; *Illegitimacy* (Law Com. No.118 (1982)), para.12.2.

[45] Human Fertilisation and Embryology Act 1990 s.28(2); Human Fertilisation and Embryology Bill 2008 cl.35(1). But not where the child was born before April 4, 1988 when the Family Law Reform 1987 was implemented: *Re M (Child Support: Parentage)* [1997] 2 F.L.R. 90. Where the father agreed to treatment for his wife using his sperm, he could not be taken to have consented to donor sperm and was therefore not the father of the child born after sperm samples were confused by the clinic: *Leeds Teaching hospitals NHS Trust v A* [2003] 1 F.L.R. 1091, FD.

[46] The Law Commission canvassed views on formal procedures for consent, but rejected them because of the disadvantages of complexity and the possibility of hardship to the child where the formalities were not met: Law Com. No.118, para.12.16. The Human Fertilisation and Embryology Authority *Code of Practice* (2007) states that centres should take "all practicable steps" to obtain the man's written consent (para.G.6.9.3).

[47] Human Fertilisation and Embryology Act 1990 s.28(3).

[48] [1997] 2 F.L.R. 282.

Fertilisation and Embryology Authority (HFEA); consequently, the declaration was refused.[49]

A test based on "treatment together" is problematic, since the male partner receives no treatment. This test will be replaced by a requirement for written consents from both the mother and the man if the Human Fertilisation and Embryology Bill 2008 is enacted[50]:

> In *Re R (IVF)*[51] the mother and her partner sought fertility treatment using donor sperm. The treatment was unsuccessful and the couple separated. The woman gave birth to a child after further IVF treatment. Her former partner claimed that he was the father and obtained a declaration of paternity. The woman's appeal was allowed; the man then appealed to the House of Lords. Adopting the analysis of Hale L.J., the Court held that treatment together required "a joint enterprise", and that the time for determining this was when the embryo was inserted. Consequently, the man was not the child's father.

Where a woman was treated with sperm her former partner had provided, he was not considered as only a sperm donor but was the father.[52] A female-to-male transsexual is not a man and therefore cannot be the father of a child born to his partner after donor insemination.[53] However, if the gender reassignment occurs after the child's birth, the biological father does not lose the right to be recognised as the child's father.[54] Thirdly, where treatment at a licensed clinic involves the use of donated sperm, the donor, despite being the genetic father, does not have this legal status.[55] This facilitates licensed infertility treatment by protecting sperm donors from the responsibilities of parenthood.[56] Fourthly, where a child is conceived using genetic material from a man who has already

[49] Wilson J. rejected arguments that this breached either Treaty of Rome art.59 or ECHR art.8. If the sperm donor gave consent for the donation, the child would legally be fatherless: Human Fertilisation and Embryology Act 1990 s.28(6)(a); Human Fertilisation and Embryology Bill 2008 cl.36(1).
[50] Human Fertilisation and Embryology Bill 2008 cl.37. There are comparable provisions where the mother agrees for her female partner to be a second parent: cl.44.
[51] [2005] 2 F.L.R. 843, HL. He may receive counselling; the clinic should record his attendance: *Code* (2007) para.G.6.9.5. Being the woman's partner is not sufficient to satisfy the test: *Re Q (Parental Order)* [1996] 1 F.L.R. 369 at 372, *per* Johnson J.
[52] *Re B (Parentage)* [1996] 2 F.L.R. 15.
[53] *X, Y and Z v UK* [1997] 2 F.L.R. 892. The Gender Recognition Act 2004 s.9 would now allow registration after a certificate has been obtained, and the Human Fertilisation and Embryology Bill 2008 cl.36 would allow the female-to-male transsexual partner to be the child's second parent if the consent requirements were satisfied: cll 37, 38.
[54] Gender Recognition Act 2004 s.12; in *Re L (Contact: Transsexual Applicant)* [1995] 2 F.L.R. 438, the father's application for parental responsibility was granted after he had changed sex.
[55] Human Fertilisation and Embryology Act 1990 s.28(6)(a); Human Fertilisation and Embryology Bill 2008 cl.41(1). But where sperm is used in error to treat a woman other than the man's wife, and the man has not consented to be a sperm donor, the exemption in s.28(6) does not apply: see *Leeds Teaching Hospitals v A* [2003] 1 F.L.R. 1091.
[56] Where sperm (or eggs) have been donated after March 31, 2004, any child born has a right to identifying information when they are an adult: Human Fertilisation and Embryology Authority (Disclosure of Donor Information) Regulations 2004 (SI 2004/1511) and see below, para.22–080.

died, that man is not recognised in law as the child's father.[57] The child is legally fatherless, but, following a campaign by Mrs Blood who wanted her deceased husband recognised on her children's birth certificates, the name of a man (who need not be genetically related to the child) can appear on the birth certificate.[58]

The provisions of the Human Fertilisation and Embryology Act 1990 have **17–005** been criticised as flawed, inconsistent and difficult to operate, and it has been suggested that parentage in cases involving infertility treatment should instead be based on assumption of responsibility for the child.[59] However, this would not allow the position of the partner to be clear before birth, and would allow a partner, even one who had consented, to disavow the arrangement before the birth. The Human Fertilisation and Embryology Bill 2008, if enacted, will provide a clear and consistent approach based on consent. It maintains the protection from the legal responsibilities of parenthood for those who are willing to donate gametes for fertility treatment and secures the status and responsibility of spouses and partners who are jointly engaged in the production of a child through fertility treatment.

As noted above,[60] modern developments in assisted reproduction necessitated a re-examination of the definitions of "mother" and "father". The provisions of the 1990 Act were not amended to reflect either the legal recognition of same-sex relationships[61] or the recent changes permitting same-sex and unmarried couples to adopt.[62] Also, definitions in the Act failed to recognise the wide range of people who seek such treatment.[63] Consequently, following a review of the Human Fertilisation and Embryology Act 1990, a White Paper[64] and a draft Bill[65] were produced, and the Human Fertilisation and Embryology Bill 2008 was introduced in the House of Lords. Part 2 of the Bill extends the definition of parenthood in cases involving assisted reproduction to include female same-sex couples. Mirroring the law on marriage,[66] the Bill provides that the civil partner of a woman who gives birth to a child conceived by artificial insemination is

[57] Human Fertilisation and Embryology Act 1990 s.28(6)(b), as in the case of the child born to Mrs Blood: *R. v Human Fertilisation and Embryology Authority Ex p. Blood* [1997] 2 F.L.R. 742, CA.
[58] Human Fertilisation and Embryology (Deceased Fathers) Act 2003, adding Human Fertilisation and Embryology Act 1990 s.28(5A)–(5I); Births, Marriages and Deaths Registration Act 1953 s.10ZA; Registration of Births Marriages and Deaths (Amendment) Regulations 2003 (SI 2003/3048). The Human Fertilisation and Embryology Bill 2008 cll 39 and 40 make comparable provisions for naming husbands and male partners; cl.46 similarly applies to female second parents.
[59] S. Bridge, "Assisted reproduction and the legal definition of parentage" in Bainham et al. (eds), *What is a parent?* (2000), p.87; cf. J. Masson, "Parenting by being: parenting by doing—in search of principles for founding families", in J. Spencer and A. Du Bois-Pedain (eds), *Freedom and Responsibility in Reproductive Choice* (Oxford: Hart, 2006), p.31.
[60] 17–003.
[61] Civil Partnership Act 2004; see above, para.17–004.
[62] Adoption and Children Act 2002; below, para.22–019.
[63] *Review of the Human Fertilisation and Embryology Act: Proposals for Revised Legislation (Including Establishment of the Regulatory Authority for Tissue and Embryos)* (Cm.6989 (2000)), para.2.67.
[64] Cm.6989, 2006.
[65] The Human Tissue and Embryos Bill (Cm.7087 (2007)).
[66] Human Fertilisation and Embryology Act 1990 s.28(2).

automatically the child's parent unless she did not consent to the treatment.[67] Similarly, cll 43 and 44 apply to female couples who are not civil partners.[68] As a result of the Bill, it will be possible for children born following fertility treatment to have a mother and a father, or a mother and a second female parent; no child can have more than two parents, but other people could obtain parental responsibility through court orders or agreements.[69]

C. Determination of parentage

17–006   There is a rebuttable presumption that the mother's husband is her child's father.[70] Registration of the birth also creates a presumption about the child's parentage so that the Child Support Agency (and others)[71] are entitled to regard a man named on the birth certificate as the father.[72] In practice, the development of genetic screening or DNA profiling has made it easier to resolve most disputes about parentage. Paternity is disputed in a wide range of situations, mostly those cases concerned with money (child support and inheritance) but also in cases about children's care. A man who was misled by the mother that he was her child's father has even succeeded in a claim for damages for deceit.[73]

We first of all give an outline of the part played by scientific test evidence in establishing parentage, then birth registration and, finally, the judicial procedures available for determining parentage.

i. Scientific tests

17–007   DNA profiling can establish parentage with virtual certainty.[74] DNA profiling compares the pattern produced by sequences of nucleotide bases known as mini satellites which can be obtained by subjecting body samples—blood, semen, saliva, hair-roots, etc.—to a series of complex processes that enable the pattern to be read like a bar code.[75] A child obtains half its genetic material from each parent, but is a unique individual. Thus, the child's DNA will include patterns identical to those found in each parent's DNA. DNA profiling where parentage

---

[67] Human Fertilisation and Embryology Bill cl.42.
[68] Human Fertilisation and Embryology Act 1990 s.28(3).
[69] Human Fertilisation and Embryology Bill cl.48(1), and below, paras 17–037–17–043.
[70] Child Support Act 1991 s.26(2), as amended by Child Support, Pensions and Social Security Act 2000 s.15; see Bromley (2006), pp.321–324.
[71] Child Support Act 1991 s.26(2) as amended by Child Support, Pensions and Social Security Act 2000 s.15; *Brierley v Brierley and Williams* [1918] p.257. Child Support Agency Leaflet CSL 304 (2007) describes the approach of the CSA.
[72] In some Commonwealth jurisdictions, cohabitation creates prima facie evidence of paternity, see: Law Com. WP 74, para.9.12. The Law Commission opposed such a presumption for English Law: see Law Com. No.118, para.10.54.
[73] *A v B (Damages: Paternity)* [2007] 2 F.L.R. 1051, QBD.
[74] K. Kelly, J. Rankin and R. Wink, "Method and application of DNA fingerprinting: a guide for the non-scientist" [1987] Crim. L.R. 105; R. White and J. Greenwood, "DNA fingerprinting and the law" (1988) 51 M.L.R. 145 and A. Hall, "DNA fingerprinting—black box or black hole" [1990] N.L.J. 203; A. Jefferys et al., "The efficiency of multilocus DNA finger print probes for individualisation and the establishment of family relationships" (1991) 48 *Am. J. Hum. Genet.* 824.
[75] Kelly et al. [1987] Crim. L.R. 1055. The chance of two non-related individuals having the same pattern is less than one in five thousand million million; see White and Greenwood at 147.

is disputed requires samples from the child and both alleged parents. However, sufficient information may be available from testing one parent and two siblings so long as the parentage of the second child is undisputed.[76] Although the validity of the test is not in doubt, its accuracy relies on the skill of the tester handling the samples and reading the results.

The testing of a child raises questions concerning welfare, rights of children and the rights of adults. A person with parental responsibility can arrange for a child's genetic parentage to be tested but will need access to genetic samples from at least one of the biological parents and the child. It is a criminal offence to have bodily samples with the intention of DNA testing without the qualifying consents.[77] Also, a Department of Health *Code of Practice* advises service providers not to undertake "motherless tests" (i.e. tests where no sample is provided by the mother) without her consent. Despite procedures for authentication, if the sample has been taken by the applicant, the tester cannot be sure it came from any named person.[78] Where unauthorised tests have been undertaken, the court may require further proof.

In any civil proceedings in which parentage is in question, the court may direct the use of scientific tests[79] with or without an application by any party.[80] There are no statutory guidelines as to when tests should be ordered. Where the case only concerns adults, a direction should be made if scientific evidence can promote a fairer trial[81]; the extent to which this may be so will depend on the availability of the relevant samples. In cases concerning children, the court conducts a balancing exercise. The child's welfare is not the paramount consideration,[82] but the court must see that "the interests of the child are not neglected".[83] Tests may be refused where one party is merely engaged in a "fishing exercise",[84] or where the outcome would be the same with or without blood tests.[85] Striking examples can be found in the law reports of the utility of blood testing.[86] More weight is given to scientific truth than to preserving legal

---

[76] White and Greenwood at 150. Testing the child and one alleged parent may establish the absence of a parental relationship.

[77] Human Tissue Act 2004 s.45; for details of who can consent, see Sch.4 Pt 1 para.2.

[78] DH *Code of Practice and Guidance on Genetic Paternity Testing* (2001), s.3 suggests the retention of signed photographs of applicants by the tester so that there is a reliable audit trail; see also [2001] Fam. Law 573.

[79] Originally, only blood tests could be used, but it is possible to use other "bodily samples", for example, saliva or cranial hair: Family Law Reform Act 1987 s.23; Blood tests (Evidence of Paternity) Amendment Regulations 2001 (SI 2001/773). These non-invasive samples avoid problems and objections to the use of blood samples.

[80] Family Law Reform Act 1969 s.20(1). This includes an application for contact: *Re E (Parental Responsibility: Blood Tests)* [1995] 1 F.L.R. 392. Anyone named in the application may be subject to tests in proceedings under Family Law Act 1986 ss.55A and 56 (s.20(2A)).

[81] A. Bradney, "Blood tests, paternity and the double helix" [1986] Fam. Law 378.

[82] Unless the child's upbringing is at issue, Children Act 1989 s.1.

[83] *S v McC, W v Official Solicitor* [1972] A.C. 24 at 44, *per* Lord Reid.

[84] *S v McC, W v Official Solicitor* [1972] A.C. 24 at 48, *per* Lord MacDemott. If paternity is not at issue, tests may not be ordered: see *Hodgkiss v Hodgkiss* [1985] Fam. Law 87. The husband had conceded the children were "children of the family", but wanted to satisfy his curiosity.

[85] *Re F (A Minor) (Blood Tests: Parental Rights)* [1993] Fam. 314. But where the right to respect for family life is in issue, the court would need to show that refusing a blood test was proportional: *MB v UK* App. No.22920/93 (the Commission found no violation of art.8 where blood test was refused to man who was not seeking custody).

[86] See, for example, *Re Moynihan* [2000] 1 F.L.R. 113, HL.

presumptions or the status quo.[87] It has been said that a child's long-term interests are better served by knowing the truth and securing that adults found their lives on fact rather than wish.[88] Current emphasis on rights[89] and the increasing emphasis on genetic heritage in health-care is likely to strengthen this trend:

> In *Re H and A (Paternity: Paternity: Blood Test)*,[90] following a quarrel that led to the mother refusing contact, her former lover sought a declaration of parentage and scientific tests in relation to twins. The mother had concealed both her affair and the litigation from her husband who cared for the twins whilst she was at work. The judge at first instance refused the tests on the basis that there was only a slight chance that the lover was the father, and establishing the lover's paternity could have a disastrous effect on the family. The Court of Appeal overturned this decision. As both the husband and the lover were having sexual relations with the mother around the time of conception, each had an equal chance of being the father. Paternity should be established by science and not by legal presumptions or inferences.

17–008   However, the contrary view has also been expressed by the Court of Appeal:

> In *O v L*[91] the child was conceived whilst the mother was having an extra-marital affair. She continued to live with her husband until the child was three years old, and only suggested that he was not the father when she separated to live with and marry her lover. She sought an order for blood tests in her former husband's proceedings for contact but this was denied. The court thought she would undermine the child's beneficial relationship with her first husband, and it was better to postpone establishing the truth of the child's paternity.

The choice between the alternative types of tests is for the applicant to make; the court directs tests by an accredited provider.[92] The court may not order that a

---

[87] In *Kroon v The Netherlands* (1994) 19 E.H.R.R. 263, para.40 the European Court of Human Rights noted "respect for family life requires that biological and social reality should prevail over legal presumption which flies in the face of both established fact and the wishes of those concerned".

[88] *Re G (A Minor) (Blood Test)* [1994] 1 F.L.R. 495 at 502, *per* M. Horowitz Q.C.; *Re H (Paternity: Blood Test)* [1996] 2 F.L.R. 65; cf. *Re CB (A Minor) (Blood Tests)* [1994] 2 F.L.R. 762; *Re F (A Minor) (Blood Tests: Paternity Rights)* [1993] Fam. 314.

[89] Compliance with the UN Convention on the Rights of the Child, arts 7(1) and 8(2) which require States' Parties to provide assistance to children deprived of elements of the identity, may justify requiring blood tests.

[90] [2002] 1 F.L.R. 1145, CA; see also *K v M* [1996] 1 F.L.R. 312, where the lover's application was unsuccessful.

[91] [1995] 2 F.L.R. 930, CA,

[92] Family Law Reform Act 1969 s.20(1A) amended by the Child Support, Pensions and Social Security Act 2000 s.82(2). Conditions for accreditation are set out in Blood Tests (Evidence of Paternity) (Amendment) Regulations 2001 (SI 2001/773), those accredited should also comply with the DH *Code of Practice and Guidance on Genetic Paternity Testing* (2001).

party provides a sample; consent must be obtained before samples are taken.[93] Where there is no consent to taking a sample from a child, a sample may be taken if the court considers it would be in the best interests of the child.[94] Those who decline to comply with orders must expect adverse inferences to be drawn against them.[95] Thus, where the presumption of legitimacy operates, and a party fails to follow a direction, the court may dismiss the claim even though there is no evidence to rebut the presumption. However, it might be considered preferable to avoid decisions based on inference rather than fact by providing for compulsory testing.[96]

ii. Birth registration

(1) The significance of entries in the register
Entry of the name of a particular man as the child's father in the register is prima facie evidence that he is the father[97]; the onus of proof is on anyone who wishes to dispute the matter. Thus, birth registration constitutes an important method of establishing parentage. A brief account of it is given here.   **17–009**

(2) Registration
The Births and Deaths Registration Act 1953 provides[98] that the mother and father of every child born in this country must, within 42 days of the birth, give the Registrar of Births the required information.[99] A father who is not married to the child's mother is not under this duty.[100]   **17–010**

Registration is an administrative process; thus, no inquiry is usually made into the truth of the informant's statements. The informant is asked to state the name of the child's father, and that name will be recorded without further evidence if he is the mother's husband. If the couple is not married, the father's name can

---

[93] Family Law Reform Act 1969 s.21. A child who is *Gillick competent* can consent; if a child is not competent or does not consent, a person with parental responsibility can consent: Human Tissue Act 2004 s.2.

[94] Family Law Reform Act 1969 s.21(3), as amended by Child Support, Pensions and Social Security Act 2000 s.82. Where the court has already exercised its discretion to order tests it is unlikely to find testing against the child's interests. In effect, this produces compulsory testing of the child, see Human Tissue Act 2004 s.45 and Sch.4 para.5(1)(g).

[95] Family Law Reform Act 1969 s.23(1); Child Support, Pensions and Social Security Act 2000 s.15, case A3; *Secretary of State for Work and Pensions v Jones* [2004] 21 F.L.R. 282, FD. "The court should only uphold an objection that is objectively valid": *Re G (Parentage: Blood Sample)* [1997] 1 F.L.R. 360, CA, *per* Thorpe L.J. at 366H.

[96] Bromley and Lowe (1992), p.276. A system that ensured that paternity was established for all children would be more in keeping with UN Convention on the Rights of the Child art.8(1); see also M-T. Meulders-Klein, "The position of the father in European legislation" (1990) 4 Int. J. Law & Fam. 131, 141.

[97] Births and Deaths Registration Act 1953 s.34(2); *Brierley v Brierley and Williams* [1918] p.257.

[98] Births and Deaths Registration Act 1953 s.2; where the parents are incapable, this may be done by a "qualified informant": ss.1(2) and 2(b). It is an offence not to do so: s.36.

[99] Registration of Births, and Deaths Regulations 1987 (SI 1987/2088), as amended by SI 2006/2827 and the regulations cited therein.

[100] Births and Deaths Registration Act 1953 s.10(1).

only appear on the register where the statute permits.[101] The circumstances were considerably extended following the recommendations of the Law Commission[102] but basically require either the agreement of both parties or a court order establishing that the man is the father. The father's name can be included where the parties jointly request registration either by personal attendance before the registrar or by providing statutory declarations of paternity and the mother's acknowledgement of it,[103] or if the parties have made a parental responsibility agreement, by providing evidence of that agreement[104]; alternatively, where the court has made a parental responsibility order or certain other orders that involve determining parentage, by providing evidence of that order.[105] The father need not be the child's biological father,[106] but before the introduction of the Gender Recognition Act 2004 the Registrar-General has refused to register a female-to-male transsexual as a father after his partner gave birth to a child following artificial insemination.[107] If the father's name is not known, a line is entered in the relevant space on the electronic form; this also occurs if he dies without making a declaration or agreement, even though paternity was acknowledged or proved.[108] However, where the father's name was not originally included on the register, or the wrong man was named, the birth may be re-registered later, subject to conditions about evidence[109] and also the agreement of the child if he or she is 16 or over.[110] Re-registration may also occur where a declaration of parentage has been made under the Family Law Act 1986[111] or the parents have married.[112]

The Government has proposed major changes in the registration system, designed to improved security of establishing identity and facilitating registration.[113] However, it failed to convince Parliament that reform could be achieved by a regulatory reform order,[114] and further legislation has yet to be introduced.

---

[101] Births and Deaths Registration Act 1953 s.10, as amended by Children Act 1989, Sch.12 para.6. Many fathers are not aware of this: R. Pickford, *Fathers Marriage and the Law* (Family Policy Study Centre, 1999), p.25.
[102] *Illegitimacy* (Law Com. No.118 (1982)), para.10.59.
[103] Births and Deaths Registration Act 1953 s.10(1)(a), (b), (c).
[104] Births and Deaths Registration Act 1953 s.10(1)(d), added by Children Act 1989 Sch.12, para.6(2).
[105] Births and Deaths Registration Act 1953 ss.10(1A), 10A(1A) added by Children Act 1989 Sch.12, para.6(3); or a maintenance order under Children Act 1989 Sch.1: ss.10(1)(f), 10A(1)(f).
[106] Human Fertilisation and Embryology Act 1990 s.28; Human Fertilisation and Embryology Bill cll.35–38; see above.
[107] *X, Y and Z v UK* [1997] 2 F.L.R. 892, the European Court of Human Rights accepted that this was an area where there was no consensus, and a wide margin of appreciation should be given (para.44). But see now *Goodwin v UK*, App. No.28957/75.
[108] DNA testing does not require fresh samples.
[109] The Deregulation (Correction of Birth or Death Entries in Registers or Other Records) Order 2002 (SI 2002/1419).
[110] Births and Deaths Registration Act 1953 s.10A(1).
[111] Family Law Act 1986 s.56; Births and Deaths Registration Act 1953 s.14A, added by Family Law Reform Act 1987 s.26. It could therefore occur after the death of a parent.
[112] Family Law Act 1986 s.14. It is an offence for parents not to provide the necessary information: Legitimacy Act 1976 s.9.
[113] *Civil Registration; Vital Change* (Cm.5355 (2002)).
[114] Delegated powers and Regulatory Reform Committee, *Third Report 2004–5, Proposal for the draft Regulatory Reform (Registration of Births and Deaths) (England and Wales) Order 2004* (HLP 14).

It has also proposed that there should be far more encouragement on unmarried parents to register the birth jointly, in the belief that this will make fathers who would not otherwise do so take responsibility, particularly by paying child support.[115]

(3) Birth certificates

A birth certificate is simply a certified copy of the entry made in the register, and **17–011** is thus evidence of the birth to which it relates.[116] Birth certificates can be used to establish the date and place of birth, as well as parentage. The fact that there will be joint registration of the father's name, or worse, no name at all means that it may often be possible to tell whether a child's parents were married from the full birth certificate. In 1947, when considerable stigma was attached to the child because of illegitimacy,[117] provision was made for a short form of birth certificate to be issued.[118] This does not contain any particulars of parentage or adoption but only the child's name, sex, date and place of birth. It is still possible to obtain a full birth certificate, but the short form is issued free on registration and will be provided unless the full form is specifically requested. However, the full form may be required, for example, in adoption proceedings.[119] Although its contents may be embarrassing, they may provide the only information recorded about the parents and may therefore assist a child tracing them and other relatives.[120]

iii. Judicial procedures for determining parentage

Findings of parentage may be required for many purposes. A person may need **17–012** to establish that they are a "child of A" to inherit property, or a "father of B" to have standing to seek a parental responsibility order under the Children Act 1989. In divorce proceedings the issue may arise because proof that the husband is not the father of his wife's child may be proof of her adultery.[121] In all these cases the court will adjudicate on parentage, and its findings will bind the

[115] *Joint Birth Registration: Promoting Parental Responsibility* (Cm.7160 (2007)) Ministerial Foreword—John Hutton. There is research that indicates the success of such schemes in the US but the proportion of unmarried parents jointly registering is far lower there. In England and Wales, only about 7% of births are solely registered; para.38.

[116] Births and Deaths Registration Act 1953 s.34(6). A birth certificate does not establish that an individual is the person named but has been used, most notoriously in F. Forsyth, *The Day of the Jackal,* to obtain passports, etc.

[117] Vivid illustrations of the embarrassment of this were given in the parliamentary debates on the Births and Deaths Registration Bill—see particularly, *Hansard*, HC, Vol.432, col.2107; *Hansard*, HL, Vol.145, col.851.

[118] See Births and Deaths Registration Act 1953 s.33; Birth Certificate (Shortened Form) Regulations 1968 (SI 1968/2050).

[119] Because it is essential to know whether the application concerns a child of married parents; see Ch.22.

[120] This is of particular relevance to children who have been adopted, but may apply in other cases of family estrangement; for an explanation of family searching using birth records, see A. Pavlovic, in J. Masson et al. (eds), *Lost and Found* (Aldershot: Ashgate, 1999), Ch.10.

[121] See above, paras 10–019 *et seq.*

parties.[122] A finding of paternity will provide prima facie evidence that would need to be rebutted in any subsequent proceedings.[123]

The law also provides procedures solely for the conclusive resolution of disputes about legitimacy or the validity of a marriage. In 1988, following recommendations of the Law Commission, a more consistent legislative code was introduced,[124] but the law still failed to provide a simple and coherent scheme for determining paternity disputes. Declarations of parentage had to be sought by the child,[125] but a person with care or the Secretary of State could obtain a declaration solely for the purposes of child support.[126] In 1998 the Lord Chancellor's Department reviewed these provisions to ensure that the law adequately reflected modern social attitudes[127]; the results of the review have now been incorporated in legislation.

The Family Law Act 1986 (as amended) enables the family courts[128] to grant declarations of parentage, marital status or legitimacy.[129] Any person may apply to the court for a declaration as to whether or not a named person is or was the parent of another named person.[130] The court only has jurisdiction if at least one of the named persons is or was domiciled or habitually resident in England and Wales at the time of the application or their death.[131] Unless the applicant is a parent or child of a named person, the court can only hear the application if it considers that he or she has sufficient personal interest in the issue[132]; a parent with care (who may wish to seek child support) is treated as having a sufficient interest.[133] This precludes vexatious applications and mud-raking by the media, but should not prevent family members who want to establish a right to

---

[122] Although the rights of non-parties would not be affected: *Re JS* [1981] Fam. 22. For this reason it has been argued as inappropriate for the child to be made a party: *Re O and J (Paternity: Blood Test)* [2000] 1 F.L.R. 418, FD at 433F. But a declaration under the Family Law Act 1986 binds everyone: s.58(2).

[123] Civil Evidence Act 1968 s.12, as amended. If there was no finding, the matter is not treated as *res judicata* and a further application could be made: *Hager v Osborne* [1992] Fam. 94, FD (where a mother sought financial provision and wanted DNA testing although she had failed to obtain an affiliation order after inconclusive blood testing).

[124] *Declarations in Family Matters* (Law Com. No.132 (1984)); Family Law Act 1986 Pt III. s.56, which concerns parentage and legitimacy, was replaced by Family Law Reform Act 1987 s.22 and came into force on April 22, 1988.

[125] Family Law Act 1986 s.56; the family proceedings court had no jurisdiction; but see below for the amended provision.

[126] Child Support Act 1991 s.27.

[127] Lord Chancellor's Department, *Procedures for the Determination of Paternity and the Law on Parental Responsibility for Unmarried Fathers* (1998), and Advisory Board on Family Law, *Second Annual Report* (1999), Annex C, para.2. The parental responsibility proposals are discussed below.

[128] Family Proceedings Courts (Family Law Act 1986) Rules 2001 (SI 2001/778). Proceedings for declarations of marital status or legitimacy must still be brought in the High Court or the county court.

[129] Family Law Act 1986 ss.55, 55A and 56, as added and amended by Child Support, Pensions and Social Security Act 2000 s.83.

[130] Family Law Act 1986 s.55A. Similarly a declaration can be sought about the validity of a marriage, divorce or annulment: s.55(1).

[131] Family Law Act 1986 s.55A(2), or s.55(2) for declarations of marital status.

[132] Family Law act 1986 s.55A(3)(4); s.55(3) makes similar provision for declarations of marital status.

[133] Child Support Act 1991 s.27, as amended by Child Support, Pensions and Social Security Act 2000 Sch.8 para.18.

inheritance from doing so.[134] Also, where one of the named persons is a child, the court may refuse to hear the case if the determination would not be in the best interests of the child.[135] Since a declaration will concern the private or even the family life of the applicant and those named, decisions to refuse a hearing must comply with the European Convention on Human Rights.[136] Declarations may also be made regarding legitimacy or legitimation, but only the person concerned may apply.[137] These declarations cannot put in question the status of anyone else, although the validity of the parents' marriage may be in issue. Where the truth of the proposition is proved to the satisfaction of the court,[138] it must make the declaration unless this would manifestly be contrary to public policy. The declaration granted is binding on everyone[139] unless it has been obtained by fraud.[140] Where a declaration of parentage, legitimacy or legitimation is made, the birth may be re-registered.[141]

III. WHAT IS PARENTAL RESPONSIBILITY?

The Children Act 1989 s.3(1) provides that: **17–013**

"In this Act parental responsibility means all the rights, duties, powers, responsibilities and authority which by law a parent of a child has in relation to the child and his property."

This non-definition has been linked to respect for family privacy—there is a reluctance to state what parental responsibilities are or should be.[142] However, the Law Commission considered that it was not possible to provide a statutory

---

[134] Advisory Board on Family Law, *Second Annual Report* para.C2iv.

[135] Family Law Act 1986 s.55A(5); the Advisory Board on Family Law suggested that it could be appropriate to refuse a hearing where the child was settled in an adoptive family or, where the child had been conceived as the result of rape, the mother opposed the application; *Second Annual report* para.C2vi. Where a hearing is refused, the court may impose a leave requirement on the applicant: s.55A(6).

[136] A declaration cannot be made about the status of a living child unless the child is a party to the proceedings: *Re AB (care proceedings: service on husband)* [2004] 1 F.L.R. 527, CA, para.13; *Re L (Family Proceedings Court) (Appeal: Jurisdiction)* [2005] 1 F.L.R. 210, FD.

[137] Family Law Act 1986 s.56(1), (2). The provision precluding declarations of illegitimacy has been repealed: Child Support, Pensions and Social Security Act 2000 s.83(3).

[138] Family Law Act 1986 s.58(1). "This formulation is intended to make it clear that the standard of proof is high and that the court should only grant the declaration when the evidence . . . is clear and convincing" (Law Com. No.132), p.37, fn.365. But the Advisory Board on Family law thought that a simple test of balance of probabilities should be adequate given the certainty provided by DNA evidence: *Second Annual Report* para.C2ix. The Attorney-General has power to protect third parties: s.59.

[139] Family Law Act 1986 s.58(2).

[140] "[T]here must be conscious and deliberate dishonesty and the declaration must be obtained by it", *per* Lord Wilberforce, *The Ampthill Peerage* [1977] A.C. 547 at 571.

[141] Family Law Act 1986 ss.55A(7), 56(4) and Births and Deaths Registration Act 1953 s.14A. The Registrar-General contacts the person named in the application for a declaration to establish whether the court's findings are in dispute, allowing 28 days for a reply before re-registering the birth: Lord Chancellor's Department, (1998) para.18.

[142] W. Utting, *People Like Us?* (London: TSO, 1997), para.6.1.

list of parental obligations because this would need to change to meet differing needs and circumstances, and would need to vary with the maturity of the child.[143] In contrast, the Children (Scotland) Act 1995, following recommendations of the Scottish Law Commission, provides clear statutory statements of both parental responsibilities and rights.[144] Without such assistance, some attempt must be made to define what actions can be taken on the basis of parental responsibility.[145] This would seem to include the following.

A. Rights and powers

i. *The right to physical possession*

17–014 At common law, a parent has the right to possession of their child.[146] In the past, this right was enforced by means of the writ of habeas corpus.[147] A person who had parental responsibility could require any other person who had possession of the child to hand him or her back.[148] Whilst the child remained in another's care, the parent could also rely on this right to control the child's movements.[149]

The parental right to possession is a good illustration of the significance of the concept of parental rights today. On the one hand, it can be argued for two reasons that the legal right to possession is of no importance. First, even at common law the courts would not enforce the right against the wishes of the child who had reached the age of discretion.[150] Secondly, if a dispute about the

[143] Law Com. No.172, para.2.6.

[144] Children (Scotland) Act 1995 ss.1(1), 2(1), following Scottish Law Com. No.135, paras 2.2, 2.26.

[145] See generally, for discussions of the common law, Bainham (1993), pp.9–20; Bromley (1998), pp.350–375; Bevan, *The Law Relating to Children* (London: Butterworths, 1973) Ch.1; Craffe, *La Puissance Paternelle en Droit Anglais* (1971); J. Hall, "The waning of parental rights" [1972B] C.L.J. 248; J. Eekelaar, "What are parental rights?" (1973) 89 L.Q.R. 210; S. Maidment, "The fragmentation of parental rights" (1981) 40 C.L.J. 135; B. Dickens, "The modern function and limits of parental rights" (1981) 97 L.Q.R. 462 and Ch.16.

[146] *Re Agar-Ellis* (1883) 24 Ch.D. 317. Lord Scarman described this decision as horrendous in *Gillick v West Norfolk AHA* [1986] A.C. 112 at 183. But a woman has no right to have an embryo implanted without the consent of the man whose sperm fertilised the eggs: *Evans v Amicus Healthcare Ltd* [2004] 2 F.L.R 766, CA; *Evans v UK* [2006] 2 F.L.R 172; *Evans v UK* (App. No. 6339/05) handed down on April 10, 2007.

[147] For example, *Barnardo v Ford* [1892] A.C. 326. For an illuminating account of the background to this litigation, see G. Wagner, *Barnardo* (London: Weidenfeld and Nicolson, 1979), Ch.13.

[148] See *R. v Barnardo* (1889) 23 Q.B.D. 305, particularly at 310–311, *per* Lord Esher M.R. habeas corpus is no longer regarded as an appropriate remedy in the Family Division: *Re K (A Minor)* (1978) 122 S.J. 626; *Re S (Habeas Corpus)* [2004] 1 F.L.R. 590 at para.22. Wardship proceedings, proceedings for a residence order or to enforce a residence order under Children Act 1989 ss.8, 14 should be started if possession of the child is in issue. Where the child is in care, a recovery order under Children Act 1989 s.50 may be made, or a parent or child may appeal the order: see para.21–046.

[149] *Flemming v Pratt* (1823) 1 L.J. (OS) K.B. 195 (guardians of child directed her governess not to permit her to visit a tavern kept by a relative; held: guardians justified in sending police officers to remove her).

[150] It is not clear that a mature child under the age of 16 has a right to choose not to live with a person with parental responsibility against their wishes. However, where one person has a residence order, another person who takes the child against the child's will may be guilty of the offence of kidnapping, even if he or she has parental responsibility, and may also commit offences under the Child Abduction Act 1984. Where the child seeks refuge in a "safe house", those assisting that child are exempt from prosecution, but a child in care may still be recovered: see Children Act 1989 ss.50, 51.

child's upbringing is brought to court, the matter will be decided by reference to the child's best interests, not necessarily by ordering the return of the child to those with parental responsibility.[151]

On the other hand, it should be noted that these arguments apply primarily to cases where a person with parental responsibility seeks to enforce it against another by legal process. In contrast, where those seeking to detain the child have no parental responsibility, the significance of entitlement to physical possession is very clear. They have no right to keep the child against parental demands.[152] They could commence wardship proceedings, apply to adopt[153] or (with leave, if necessary) seek a residence order, but if they do not do so, the parent may simply take the child back[154]:

> In *Re B (Adoption: Child's Welfare)*[155] the parents, who were African, arranged that their daughter should go to England and stay for a prolonged holiday with an English couple they had met. After 18 months the English couple applied to adopt the girl who had become very attached to them. The parents objected but made no application to the court, arguing that as parents they had the right to the child without having to establish that return was in her best interests. Wall, J. accepted their argument and the girl's return was ordered; however, the order was disobeyed.[156]

Those detaining the child may be criminally liable.[157] Although a parent may effectively lose the right to the child to an individual who cares for him or her for a prolonged period,[158] the parent will retain the right to reclaim the child from a local authority unless a care order is made on proof of significant harm or adoption is planned and an order sought.[159] Indeed, it is fundamental to the system for providing local authority accommodation for children that parents should retain the right to remove their child at any time.[160] The parent's right to

---

[151] Children Act 1989 s.1: see, for example, *J v C* [1970] A.C. 668.

[152] The police may keep children for short periods for their protection, despite parental objections: Children Act 1989 s.46 and J. Masson, "Police protection—protecting whom?" [2002] J.S.W.F.L. 157.

[153] But there are restrictions on adoption where the child is not placed by an adoption agency.

[154] *Re F (A Minor) (Wardship: Appeal)* [1976] Fam. 238. Although Children Act 1989, s.3(5) may, according to the Lord Chancellor, justify the child's retention if the parent is unfit: *Hansard*, HL Vol.505, cols 370–371 Children Bill, 3rd Reading.

[155] [1995] 1 F.L.R. 895.

[156] The prospective adoptive father was subsequently apprehended and committed to prison for contempt of court: *Re B (Contempt: Evidence)* [1996] 1 F.L.R. 239.

[157] Child Abduction Act 1984 s.2, but not if they provide a certificated refuge: Children Act 1989 s.50.

[158] A foster carer who has cared for the child for one year will not need to seek leave to commence proceedings for a residence order: Children Act 1989 s.10(5A); the period is three years for others, and may be discontinuous: s.10(5), (10). Where a residence order is sought, the court will apply the welfare checklist and may favour the person who has been caring for the child; see para.19–009.

[159] Children Act 1989 ss.20(8), (9), 31; Adoption of Children Act 2002 s.30.

[160] *Per* Lord Mackay, Lord Chancellor, *Hansard*, HL, Vol.512, col.737; *per* David Mellor, Secretary of State for Health, Standing Committee B, cols 146–152 (Children Bill Committee Stage, May 18, 1989). In practice, such removal is frequently prevented: J. Masson, "Emergency intervention to protect children: using and avoiding legal controls" [2005] C.F.L.Q. 75.

physical possession of their child is also reflected in the regime of the Hague Convention on International Child Abduction. Where a child has been taken in breach of "rights of custody" from their country of habitual residence, the court must order their return.[161]

ii. The right to control or direct the child's upbringing[162]

17–015 This right above all others depends on the child's stage of development. The recognition by the majority of the House of Lords in *Gillick*,[163] that children acquire the right to make decisions as they gain the capacity to do so,[164] clearly establishes that the parental right is a diminishing one.[165] Parents do not have a right to control mature children's access to information or advice[166]; their status gives them strong entitlement to information about their child but this does not override rights to confidentiality.[167] Parents are not legally obliged to consult children about their views[168] or, in most cases, the other parent.[169] Parental decision-making is always potentially subject to court review on welfare grounds,[170] and no one may exercise parental responsibility in a way that conflicts with a court order.[171] The state may not intervene unless the child is suffering or likely to suffer significant harm,[172] but in *F v Wirral MBC*[173] the Court of Appeal held that interference with a parent's right to take care of a child's welfare did not give rise to a cause of action.[174] There was therefore no

---

[161] For a detailed discussion of these provisions: see Ch.20, below.

[162] The Scottish Law Commission preferred the enactment of a statutory right in these general terms to more specific rights relating to education, medical treatment and religion: Scottish Law Com. No.135, para.2.21; Children (Scotland) Act 1995 s.2(1)(b).

[163] [1986] 1 A.C. 112.

[164] See above, para.16–013.

[165] The Scottish Law Commission used the phrase "control, direct or guide" for this reason; Scottish Law Com. No.135, para.2.30. The UN Convention on the Rights of the Child art.5 requires States' Parties to respect parental responsibilities "in a manner consistent with the evolving capacities of the child".

[166] Children have the right to use confidential services; see above, para.16–014. The Scottish Law Commission considered it would be contrary to childrens' interests to oblige doctors to pass on information to parents and that to require others to do so would be an excessive interference with their legitimate interests: Scottish Law Com. No.135, para.2.33.

[167] *Re C (Disclosure)* [1996] 1 F.L.R. 797 at 803, *per* Johnson J; *R. (Axon) v SS for Health and the Family Planning Association* [2006] 2 F.L.R. 206, *per* Silber J.; above, para.16–014.

[168] cf. Children (Scotland) Act 1995 s.6 following the recommendations of the Scottish Law Commission: Sottish Law Com. No.135, paras 2.60–2.66. The UN Convention the Rights of the Child art.12(1) requires States Parties to assure to the child who is capable of forming his or her own view the right to express a view and have it taken into account.

[169] S. Maidment, "Parental responsibility?—Is there a duty to consult" [2001] Fam. Law 518.

[170] Children Act 1989 s.1.

[171] Children Act 1989 s.2(8).

[172] Children Act 1989 Pt IV, especially s.31; see Ch.21 below.

[173] [1991] Fam. 69; Bainham (1993) 517. Cf. Children (Scotland) Act 1995 s.2(4) which confirms that parents and others have title to sue in any action for the infringement of parental responsibilities.

[174] The interference was a result of the local authority's exercise of its childcare functions. To recognise responsibilities to the parents could adversely affect the carrying out of these functions; there were public law remedies, *per* Ralph Gibson L.J.

redress for a mother whose relationship with her children was ended by the local authority placing the children with a couple who expected to be able to adopt them; but a mother whose children were abducted overseas has successfully claimed damages for breach of contract against the solicitor who failed to prevent the issue of a passport for them.[175] Also, the European Court of Human Rights has awarded compensation where a mother's right to respect for family life was breached by the local authority removing her daughter following a negligent investigation.[176]

Parents may publicise aspects of their children's lives by giving agreement for the making of a film or speaking to reporters,[177] but giving interviews will not always amount to an exercise of parental responsibility.[178] Young children cannot participate in media activities without parental consent.[179] Parental power is limited; parents are not entitled to surrender their child's right to confidentiality in respect of medical treatment unless this is in the interests of the child.[180] Parents' rights to publicise their own lives, children's rights to privacy and freedom of the press must be carefully balanced by the court dealing with a dispute.[181] Any profit obtained by selling the child's story should belong to the child.[182]

iii. Power to control education

At common law, the person with parental rights could determine what education **17–016** (if any) the child received. The old books contain striking cases where this right was enforced. In *Tremain*'s case[183] the child:

---

[175] *Hamilton-Jones v David and Snape (a firm)* [2004] 1 F.L.R. 774.

[176] *TP and KM v UK* [2001] 2 F.L.R. 549. The court also found breaches of arts 6 and 13 because the mother had been unable to challenge the local authority's evidence and could not obtain a remedy under English law.

[177] *Re Z (A Minor) (Freedom of Publication)* [1996] 1 F.L.R. 191 at 210, *per* Ward L.J.; *Clayton v Clayton* [2007] 1 F.L.R. 11, CA para.114 *per* Wall L.J. Undermining children's privacy may undermine the parental relationship: para.116. Where the information relates to legal proceedings, there are controls on publicity: see para.18–053.

[178] *Oxfordshire County Council v L and F* [1997] 1 F.L.R. 235 at 254, *per* Stuart-White J. Where it does not, the parent cannot be restrained by a prohibited steps order.

[179] But the suggestion by Stephen Brown P. in *Nottingham City Council v October Films* [1999] 2 F.L.R. 347 at 358 that any approach by the media requires parental consent may go too far.

[180] *Re Z (A Minor) (Freedom of Publication)* [1996] 1 F.L.R. 191 at 214, *per* Ward L.J. See also Palmer, *The Spectator*, October 21, 1995. When she reached 18, the young woman concerned (Flora Keyes) and her mother complained bitterly about the effect of the restrictions on normal childhood (e.g. not being photographed in a school play).

[181] *Norfolk County Council v Webster* [2006] EWHC 2733, *per* Munby J.; Ryden [2007] Fam. Law 331.

[182] *Douglas v Hello! Ltd* [2001] 1 F.L.R. 982, CA. Children have no lesser rights to privacy under ECHR, art.8 than adults. In this case, the money was put into a trust fund for Dylan Douglas: *Douglas v Hello! (No.3)* [2003] 3 All E.R. 996, para.40.

[183] (1719) 1 Strange 167. Parental disputes about education are determined applying the welfare principle: *Re A (Specific Issue Order: Parental Dispute)* [2001] 1 F.L.R. 121, CA (appeal against order that child attend Lycee Francaise rather than an English-language school refused); *Re P (A Minor) (Education)* [1992] 1 F.L.R. 316, CA (father's appeal against decision that child attend boarding school allowed because the child, age 14, did not want to board).

" . . . [B]eing [under 21] . . . went to Oxford, contrary to the orders of his
guardian, who would have him go to Cambridge. And the court sent a
messenger to carry him from Oxford to Cambridge. And upon his returning
to Oxford, there went another tam to carry him to Cambridge, quam to keep
him there. "

A parent's rights in relation to education is protected by the European
Convention on Human Rights,[184] but parental power is now very much affected
by legislation, and the parents' powers under the Education Act 1996 can be
exercised by anyone with care of the child.[185] A parent[186] is, by law, obliged to
ensure that his or her child, being of compulsory school age, receives efficient
full-time education suitable to age, ability and aptitude, either by regular
attendance at school or otherwise.[187] Education authorities must comply with
parental preferences where this does not prejudice efficient education or efficient
use of resources, and where it is not incompatible with the character of the
school.[188] Where their child is refused a place at the chosen school, parents may
appeal to a local appeals committee.[189] In order to enable parents to make a
choice, they must be given information about the schools available[190] and
specified information about their curricula, discipline, pastoral care, examination
policies and results.[191] The introduction of the National Curriculum in state
schools means that parents who object to its ethos or content must seek an
independent school[192] or arrange for their child to be educated at home.[193] A
person with parental responsibility or the care of a child who fails to ensure that
the child is educated may be guilty of a criminal offence,[194] and the child may be

---

[184] Protocol No.1, art.2: "[T]he State shall respect the right of parents to ensure such education and
teaching [is] in conformity with their religious and philosophical convictions." The Government
entered a reservation limiting its acceptance of the protocol in line with the duty in Education Act
1996 s.9. This reservation is preserved by the Human Rights Act 1998 s.15.
[185] Education Act 1996 s.576(1)(b); *Fairpo v Humberside CC* [1997] 1 F.L.R. 339. Parental
responsibility is not required.
[186] The definition of parent includes anyone with care of the child: Education Act 1996 s.576.
[187] Education Act 1996 s.7. For a discussion of the origins of parents' rights to home-school their
children, see Monk [2004] L.S. 568.
[188] Education Act 1996 s.9, School Standards and Framework Act 1998 s.86.
[189] School Standards and Framework Act 1998 s.94, as amended by the Education Act 2002. The
DfES, *Schools Admissions Appeals Code of Practice* (2003) provides general guidance. A new code
is planned for 2008. If a statement of special educational needs is maintained in respect of the child,
appeal is to the Special Educational Needs and Disability Tribunal: Education Act 1996 ss.325, 326
and Sch.27 para.8(3).
[190] School Standards and Framework Act 1998 s.92 (as amended).
[191] Education Act 1996 s.537 and the regulations made thereunder.
[192] The National Curriculum does not apply to independent schools although some adhere to it:
Education Act 1996 s.352. Parents may require their children to be excused from any religious
education and sex education that does not form part of the National Curriculum: School Standards
and Framework Act 1998 s.71; Education Act 1996 s.405.
[193] Such education must be "efficient full-time education": Education Act 1996 s.7. Where the
education authority is satisfied that the duty to educate the child is not being complied with, it must
serve a school attendance order: Education Act 1996 s.437.
[194] Education Act 1996 ss.443 and 444. Parents may no longer be imprisoned for breach of a school
attendance order but may be fined or made subject to a parenting order: Crime and Disorder Act 1998
s.8(1)(d). Imprisonment could follow breach of an injunction requiring the parents not to interfere
with the child's attendance: *Re P (Care Orders: Injunctive Relief)* [2000] 2 F.L.R. 385, FD.

subject to an education supervision order.[195] If the child is excluded from school, the parent must prevent them being in a public place during school time.[196] Parents are effectively deprived of their right not to educate their children[197] but may exercise such choice as their social and economic circumstances permit about the type of schooling.

iv. Discipline

A person with parental responsibility has the right to inflict moderate and **17–017** reasonable corporal punishment.[198] Nine out of ten children have experienced smacking,[199] and the majority of parents believe that parents should be allowed to smack (but not use canes, etc.) on naughty children over two years old.[200] In response to *A v UK*[201] the British Government undertook to remove the defence of reasonable chastisement where children suffered injuries. It consulted on reform but indicated that it did not intend to make physical punishment by parents illegal.[202] Subsequently, it concluded that the Human Rights Act 1998 ensured children were adequately protected, and made reform unnecessary.[203] However, the UN Committee on the Rights of the Child pressed for removal of the reasonable chastisement defence,[204] and the Scottish Parliament responded by legislating that specific actions such as blows to the head or shaking could not be justifiable on grounds of discipline.[205] Finally, following a vociferous campaign by children's rights organisations, a provision (a compromise between outlawing smacking and retaining the defence) was inserted during the debates on the Children Act 2004.[206] Section 58 provides that reasonable chastisement is now only a defence to the offence of common assault, and cannot be used where there is a civil claim for battery.[207] Corporal punishment may no longer be

---

[195] Children Act 1989 s.36; or a care order, but only if the "significant harm" test in s.31 is satisfied: see *Re O (Care Proceedings: Education)* [1992] 1 W.L.R. 912 and para.21–032, below.
[196] Education and Inspections Act 2006 s.103.
[197] B. Hoggett, *Parents & Children*, 4th edn (London: Sweet & Maxwell, 1993), p.21.
[198] *R v Hopley* (1860) 2 F. & F. 202; C.Y.P.A. 1933 s.1(7); *R. v H (Assault of Child: Reasonable Chastisement)* [2001] 2 F.L.R. 431, CA. The right does not extend to a person not *in loco parentis*; *R. v Woods* (1921) 85 S.J. 272. For a wider discussion, see P. Newell, *Children are People Too* (London: Beford Square, 1989) and J. Fortin, "Children's rights and the use of physical force" [2001] C.F.L.Q. 243.
[199] M. Smith et al., "Parental control within the family the nature & extent of parental violence to children", in DH, *Child Protection Messages from Research* (1995), pp.83–85.
[200] ONS Survey (1998) quoted in *Protecting Children Supporting Parents* (2000). Annex A. There were similar findings in Scotland in a survey for the Scottish Law Commission: Scottish Law Com. No.135, paras 2.72–2.105.
[201] [1998] 2 F.L.R. 959 (caning of a boy by his step-father was held to breach the boy's art.3 rights); see above, para.16–017.
[202] DH, *Protecting Children*, p.13.
[203] DH, *Analysis of the Responses to the Protecting Children Supporting Parents Consultation Document* (2001), para.74.
[204] CRC/C/15/Add.188, paras 35–38.
[205] Criminal Justice (Scotland) Act 2003 s.51. The court must consider other factors such as the child's age, but contrary to the original proposal, there is no minimum age for physical discipline.
[206] Lord Lester, *Hansard* Lords, Vol.663, col.533; Children Bill, Report Stage.
[207] Children Act 2004 s.58. This approach was condemned as "naive, totally impractical and frankly dangerous"; David Hinchcliffe M.P., *Hansard* Vol.424, col.1040.

administered, even if the parents support it,[208] in schools,[209] day-care[210] or community homes[211] or by foster parents.[212] The continued acceptance of a right to hit children is controversial; an increasing number of states including Sweden, Denmark and Austria have outlawed it.[213] Indeed, in June 2007 Beverley Hughes, the Minister for Children, announced a review of the effectiveness of s.58 in protecting children from physical abuse.

Parents may also restrict the liberty of their children and may permit others to do so,[214] but if the child is looked after by a local authority or is in hospital or a residential school, detention in secure accommodation must be authorised by the court.[215]

v. Choice of religion

17–018 A person with parental responsibility has a common law right to determine the child's religious education,[216] and, by statute, may require the child's exclusion from religious studies lessons and school assembly.[217] Freedom of religion is protected by the European Convention on Human Rights art.9, but religious freedom does not prevent proportionate restrictions on activities just because they are based on religious tenets.[218] Where there is a dispute about a child's religious upbringing the court balances competing rights by applying the welfare

---

[208] *R. (Williamson) v SS for Education and Employment* [2005] 2 F.L.R. 374, HL. Parental delegation of their right to chastise did not overcome the statutory ban; *per* Lord Nicholls at para.13. It was a proportionate infringement of parents' religious freedom to outlaw corporal punishment in all schools; *per* Baroness Hale at para.86.

[209] Education Act 1996 s.548, as substituted by School Standards and Framework Act 1998 s.131. There is a large body of opinion that supports the ban: see *R. (Williamson) v SS for Education and Employment* [2005] 2 F.L.R. 374, HL. *per* Baroness Hale at para.85. Teachers may use reasonable force to maintain order or prevent injuries: Education and Inspections Act 2006 s.93.

[210] Day Care and Child Minding (National Standards) (England) Regulations 2003 (SI 2003/1996) reg.5; DfES, *Full Day Care National Standards* (2003), standard 11.

[211] Corporal punishment is banned in community homes under the Children's Homes Regulations 2001 (SI 2001/3967) reg.17(5); for Wales (SI 2002/327).

[212] Fostering service providers must take all reasonable steps to ensure that no form of corporal punishment is used: Fostering Services Regulations 2002 (SI 2002/57) reg.13; for Wales (SI 2003/237).

[213] Sweden (1979), Denmark (1986), Austria (1989), Israel (2000) Netherlands (2007); see *http://www.endcorporalpunishment.org/pages/frame.html* [Accessed June 2, 2008].

[214] *Re K (Secure Accommodation: Right to Liberty)* [2001] 1 F.L.R. 526, CA, but the majority (Thorpe L.J. dissenting) held that the restrictions of secure accommodation could not be justified on the basis of parental authority. The European Court of Human Rights has accepted that parental power is limited, but held, by a majority of nine to seven, that a parent's decision to commit a 12-year-old son to a mental hospital did not breach the child's right to liberty under art.5(1), (4) of the European Convention of Human Rights because it was "a responsible exercise by the mother of her custodial rights in the interests of the child": see *Neilsen v Denmark* (1989) 11 E.C.H.R. 175 and Masson [2002] C.F.L.Q. 77.

[215] Children Act 1989 s.25; Children (Secure Accommodation) Regulations 1991 (SI 1991/1505); Children (Secure Accommodation) (No.2) Regulations 1991 (SI 1991/2034). Detention is also permitted under the Mental Health Act 1983 and even perhaps under the inherent jurisdiction: *Re C (Detention: Medical Treatment)* [1997] 2 F.L.R. 180, FD.

[216] *Andrews v Salt* (1873) 8 Ch. App. 622; Bevan, paras 11.02–11.16; St. J Robilliard, *Religion and the Law* (1984), Ch.12; C. Hamilton, *Family Law and Religion* (London: Sweet and Maxwell, 1995); A Bradney, *Religion, Rights and Laws* (Leicester University Press, 1993), p.46.

[217] School Standards and Framework Act 1998 s.71. Sixth-form pupils will have the right to decide these matters for themselves when the Education and Inspections Act 2006 s.55 comes into force.

[218] *R. (Williamson) v SS for Education and Employment* [2005] 2 F.L.R. 374, HL.

principle.[219] The practical impossibility of a carer bringing up a child in a faith other than their own is now recognised by the courts.[220] In relation to older children, sensitivity to traditional or religious influences is likely to give way to the integrity of the child concerned,[221] and it has been said that children of mixed heritage should be allowed to decide for themselves which faith (if any) to follow.[222] The power to determine the child's religion is not acquired by a local authority that has parental responsibility under a care order, and where a child is to be adopted, the adoption agency must give due consideration to the child's religious persuasion.[223]

vi. Right to services

At common law, the person with parental responsibility has the right to the domestic service of his or her unmarried minor children.[224] It is not possible to enforce this right directly, but it was of some indirect practical importance since it was an actionable tort to do an act[225] wrongfully depriving a parent of a child's services. Hence a parent could have an independent cause of action against someone who negligently injured the child. However, this cause of action was abolished by the Administration of Justice Act 1982.[226] The right to services does not appear to fit with the view that rights exist so that parents can perform their responsibilities.[227] It may alternatively be seen as part of a mutual moral obligation that is necessary for communal living.

17–019

What is the position if a child takes paid employment? Can the parents insist on having wages paid over to them? Can they at least insist on receiving some contribution to the child's upkeep?[228] There is almost no modern English

---

[219] *Re J (Specific Issue Orders: Muslim Upbringing and Circumcision)* [1999] 2 F.L.R. 678 at 685, *per* Wall J., approved by the Court of Appeal at [2000] 1 F.L.R. 571, 575; *Re S (Specific Issue Order: Religion: Circumcision)* [2005] 1 F.L.R. 236 (the children had been brought up in a mixed-heritage household; after the parents separated the mother was refused permission for the boy's circumcision because this would have excluded him from his father's religion); *Re P (s.91(14) Guidelines and Religious Heritage)* [1999] 2 F.L.R. 573, CA.

[220] *Re S (Change of Names: Cultural Factors)* [2001] 2 F.L.R. 1005, FD at 1015 (the Sikh father also accepted that the child should be brought up as a Muslim by his Muslim mother); *Re P (s.91(14) Guidelines and Religious Heritage)* [1999] 2 F.L.R. 573, CA (when the foster parents obtained a residence order they were permitted to determine all questions of education, religion and upbringing and were no longer expected to maintain Jewish dietary laws for the child).

[221] *Re KR (Abduction)* [1999] 2 F.L.R. 542 at 548, *per* Singer J.

[222] *Re S (Specific Issue Order: Religion: Circumcision)* [2005] 1 F.L.R. 236, *per* Baron J.

[223] Adoption and Children Act 2002 s.1(5).

[224] For an account of the varying importance of children as economic assets, see V. Zelizer, *Pricing the Priceless Child* (Princeton University Press, 1994); P. Mizen et al. (eds), *Hidden Hands* (London: Routledge Falmer, 2001), pp.24–36, 59–68.

[225] Provided the act was not rape, seduction or enticement: see Law Reform (Miscellaneous Provisions) Act 1970 s.5 (implementing the recommendations in Law Com. No.25, paras 101, 102). In *Lough v Ward* [1945] 2 All E.R. 338, the father obtained damages of £500 against a couple who ran a religious house where his daughter, aged 16, was living against his wishes. Such an action would seem to be precluded by the 1970 Act.

[226] Administration of Justice Act 1982 s.2(b). This was one of the reasons the court was unwilling to accept that parents had the broader right claimed in *F v Wirral MBC* [1991] Fam. 69: see Winfield and Jolowicz (1994), p.510.

[227] It is not mentioned by the Scottish Law Commission.

[228] See the discussion in the *International Encyclopaedia of Comparative Law*, Vol.IV, Ch.7 by S.J. Stoljar; and Jenk's *English Civil Law*, 4th edn (1947), para.1939 and the authorities there referred to.

authority on these issues,[229] but social security law has assumed that only reduced benefits are needed for a child whose parent is claiming Income Support on the basis that the child has an adequate income.[230]

vii. Administration of property

17–020 Parental responsibility includes the parent's right at common law over the child's property together with such rights as a guardian of the child's estate would have.[231] Since minors (unless they are on actual military service[232]) cannot make a valid will, parents (but not others with parental responsibility) also have the right to inherit their unmarried children's property.[233]

viii. Right to represent the child in legal proceedings

17–021 Except in the case of "family proceedings",[234] a child can generally only bring or defend legal proceedings by a "litigation friend".[235] A person with parental responsibility is prima facie entitled to act in this capacity[236] (unless he or she has an interest adverse to the child), but the court may remove a "litigation friend" if a proper case is made out.[237] There appears to be no right to continue proceedings that are not for the benefit of the particular child.[238] Nor may an action be settled without the court's approval.[239]

ix. Right to consent to medical treatment

17–022 A person with parental responsibility has some rights to consent to the treatment of his or her children.[240] Overriding the parents' objections without recourse to the court breaches art.8 of the ECHR,[241] but a court order may allow treatment

---

[229] See, however, *Hewer v Bryant* [1970] 1 Q.B. 357.

[230] Social Security Contributions and Benefits Act 1992, s.136(1); SI 1987/1967 regs 44(5), 47. Similar provision is made in regulations relating to other benefits; see N. Harris, *Social Security in Context* (2000), p.185. This provision was not taken over into Child Tax Credit.

[231] Children Act 1989 s.3(2); before the Act, the position was confused; see Law Com. WP 91, *Guardianship*, paras 2.32–2.34. The High Court may appoint a separate guardian of the child's estate: s.5(11).

[232] Wills (Soldiers and Sailors) Act 1918.

[233] Administration of Estates Act 1925 s.46(i), (iii); and Family Law Reform Act 1987 s.18(2). See Ch.7, above.

[234] Family Proceedings Rules 1991 (SI 1991/1247) r.9.2A. A child with sufficient understanding may "begin, prosecute or defend" any family proceedings (except "specified proceedings") with leave of the court; see above, para.16–020.

[235] Civil Procedure Rules 1998 (SI 1998/3132) r.21. The court has a discretion to allow a child to proceed alone: r.21.2(3).

[236] *Woolf v Pemberton* (1877) 6 Ch.D. 19. In practice, mothers take this role in the majority of cases: J. Masson and A. Orchard, *Children and Civil Litigation* (LCD research series No.10 1999).

[237] *Re Taylor's Application* [1972] 2 Q.B. 369 (successful application to remove parent who refused to accept compromise of thalidomide litigation, reversed on appeal); *Re A. (Conjoined Twins: Medical Treatment) (No.2)* [2001] 1 F.L.R. 267, CA (unsuccessful attempt by Pro-life Alliance to remove Official Solicitor and appeal against decision to allow separation of conjoined twins).

[238] *Kinnear v DHSS* (1989) 19 Fam. Law 146.

[239] Civil Procedure Rules 1998 (SI 1998/3132) r.21.10(1).

[240] *Gillick v W. Norfolk and Wisbech AHA* [1986] A.C. 112; *Re W (A Minor) (Medical Treatment: Court's Jurisdiction)* [1993] Fam. 64; see above, para.17–012.

[241] *Glass v UK* [2004] 1 F.L.R. 1019.

to be given or refused[242] against such a person's wishes where this in the child's best interests:

> *Charlotte Wyatt*[243] was born very prematurely with profound brain damage and many life-limiting conditions, which confined her to a special care baby unit. Her parents disagreed with the doctors' opinions as to her treatment; specifically, the parents wished her to be resuscitated should her condition worsen. Her treatment became the subject of litigation; Hedley J. was asked to make a series of declarations about medical intervention. The role of the court was to resolve the dispute between the doctors and the parents in the child's best interests, not to oversee the treatment plan. He refused to give the doctor a right to veto any further treatment but varied the declarations as her condition changed.

Although children over the age of 16 have a statutory right to consent to treatment,[244] a person with parental responsibility may give a valid consent overriding the child's refusal.[245] It has been said that parental responsibility is not sufficient to authorise sterilisation, and the matter should be referred to the court.[246] Also, it may not be ethical to treat where only one of three people holding parental responsibility consents.[247] Where a child is at risk of suffering significant harm because of lack of treatment, a care order or an emergency protection order can be made and the parent's refusal overridden.[248] In other cases a specific issue order may be obtained.[249] However, if a treatment such as a blood transfusion is essential in an emergency to save the child's life, doctors have been advised by the Department of Health that they are unlikely to be held liable for assault, and should treat without waiting for a court order.[250] Also, a

---

[242] *Re C (Welfare of Child: Immunisation)* [2003] 2 F.L.R. 1095 CA (MMR). A doctor cannot be required to treat against his clinical judgment: *Re C (A Minor) (Child in Care) (Medical Treatment)* [1993] Fam. 15; *Re C (A Minor) (Medical Treatment)* [1998] 1 F.L.R. 384, FD where the court accepted the Royal College of Paediatrics and Child Health, *Withholding or Withdrawing Lifesaving Treatment for Children* (1997).

[243] *Portsmouth NHS Trust v Wyatt* [2005] 1 F.L.R. 21; *Wyatt v Portsmouth NHS Trust (No.3)* [2005] 2 F.L.R. 480; *Portsmouth NHS Trust v Wyatt* [2006] 1 F.L.R. 652; *Re Wyatt* [2006] 2 F.L.R. 111; *Wyatt v Portsmouth NHS Trust* [2006] 1 F.L.R 554, CA.

[244] Family Law Reform Act 1969 s.8.

[245] *Re W (A Minor) (Medical Treatment: Court's Jurisdiction)* [1993] Fam. 64. Carers may incur criminal liability if they withhold consent: see A. Bainham (1993), p.252; M. Brazier and C. Bridge (1996) 16 L.S. 84.

[246] *Re D (Sterilisation)* [1976] Fam. 185; *Re B (A Minor) (Wardship Sterilisation)* [1988] A.C. 199. Cf. *Re H G (Specific Issue Order: Sterilisation)* [1993] 1 F.L.R. 587, it was held that sterilisation could be authorised by a specific issue order, indicating a decision within parental responsibility. In such cases, the child is represented by CAFCASS Legal Services: *CAFCASS Practice Note* [2001] 2 F.L.R. 151, para.5.

[247] *Re O (A Minor) (Medical Treatment)* [1993] 2 F.L.R. 149 at 154, *per* Johnson J.

[248] Children Act 1989 ss.31, 33, 44. If the child is subject to an interim care order or emergency protection order, the court may make directions about medical treatment: ss.38(6), 44(6).

[249] *Re R (A Minor) (Blood Transfusion)* [1993] 2 F.L.R. 757.

[250] Ministry of Health circular F/P9/1B, April 14, 1967. But it seems that it is more common to seek a court order: see *Re R (A Minor) (Blood Transfusion)* [1993] 2 F.L.R. 757 and *Re O (A Minor) (Medical Treatment)* [1993] 2 F.L.R. 149. In *Glass v UK* [2004] 1 F.L.R. 1019 the ECtHR considered that, where possible, court decisions should be obtained in emergencies.

decision about the child's treatment can always be over-turned by the court in exercise of its inherent jurisdiction.[251]

x. Right to consent to marriage or civil partnership

17–023 This right is governed by statute.[252] Parental refusal may be overridden by the court.[253]

xi. Right to contact with the child

17–024 It has been asserted that a parent has a common law right to contact,[254] but in the case of *Re KD* the House of Lords held that a parent has no fundamental right to contact with a child[255]; the parent's claim will always yield to the child's welfare.[256] Despite the very public campaigns of fathers' rights groups, and some support from the Conservative Party, the Government has refused to legislate for parental rights to contact or "parenting time".[257] The right to respect for family life in art.8 includes the right to maintain contact with children living separately.[258] Refusing contact between a parent and a child is an interference with art.8 rights, which must be justified by a public authority. The European Court of Human Rights applies strict scrutiny to such decisions[259]; the interests of the applicant and the child must be fairly balanced. Refusal of contact has been upheld where the child is resolutely against contact and there has been an extensive inquiry into the child's welfare.[260] The Children Act 1989 makes no specific reference to contact as a right, but where a child is in care, the local authority is under a duty to promote contact, and can only restrict it with permission of the court.[261] The courts are also empowered to make various orders

---

[251] *Re D (Sterilisation)* [1976] Fam. 185; *Re W (A Minor) (Medical Treatment: Court's Jurisdiction)* [1993] Fam. 64; *Re O (A Minor) (Medical Treatment)* [1993] 2 F.L.R. 149. Statutory powers in the Children Act 1989 may be sufficient; the court could make a specific issue or prohibited steps order on the application of any person who has obtained leave: ss.8, 10.

[252] Marriage Act 1949 Sch.2 as amended by Children Act 1989 Sch.12 para.5; Civil Partnership Act 2004 s.4 and Sch.2 Pt.1; above, 1–007.

[253] Marriage Act 1949 s.3(1)(b), (5); Civil Partnership Act 2004, Sch.2 Pts 2–4; above, para. 1–009.

[254] *Re C (Mental Patient: Contact)* [1993] 1 F.L.R. 940. Under the Children Act 1975 s.85(1), the right to legal custody included "a right of access" to the child.

[255] [1988] A.C. 806; J. Eekelaar (1988) 51 M.L.R. 629.

[256] Children Act 1989 s.1: see Ch.20; *Re L; Re V; Re M; Re H (Contact: Domestic Violence)* [2000] 2 F.L.R. 334, CA; *Re M (Contact: Welfare Test)* [1995] 1 F.L.R. 274, CA; *Re CH (Contact Parentage)* [1996] 1 F.L.R. 569.

[257] R. Collier, "The outlaw fathers fight back", in R. Collier and S. Sheldon, *Fathers' Rights Activism and Law Reform in a Comparative Perspective* (Oxford: Hart, 2006) p.60. An attempt to introduce a presumption of co-parenting after parental separation was rejected during the Report Stage of the Children and Adoption Bill, *Hansard*, Lords Vol.675, col.831.

[258] Failure by the state to enforce a parent's right of access was held to breach art.8; *Hokkanen v Finland* (1995) 19 E.H.R.R. 134. The court could not be expected to order contact where no application had been made: *C v Finland* [2006] 2 F.L.R. 597.

[259] *Johansen v Norway* (1996) 23 E.H.R.R. 33 at para.77; *Sahin v Germany* [2002] 1 F.L.R. 119, para.41.

[260] *Süss v Germany* [2006] 1 F.L.R. 522; it is not always necessary for the domestic court to hear from the child: *Sahin v Germany* [2003] 2 F.L.R 671 (Grand Chamber).

[261] Children Act 1989 Sch.2 para.15(1) and s.34; see below, para.21–074.

concerning contact between adults and the child,[262] and have interpreted these to establish a presumption of parental contact.[263] Quite extraordinary efforts have been made in an attempt to maintain contact where the non-resident parent seeks it.[264] In contrast, the Children (Scotland) Act 1995 specifically provides that parents have a right to maintain personal relations and direct contact with their children on a regular basis.[265] Contact relates to social relationships rather than the parental responsibility; consequently, the court need not establish the legal relationship before ordering contact.[266] However, only parents, stepparents and (former) long-term carers[267] can apply for contact without first seeking the leave of the court. Where leave is required, there is no presumption of contact.[268]

xii. Choice of name

The naming of a child used to be regarded as a matter of usage and custom, but **17–025** this is an area where rules have developed.[269] Surnames provide crucial recognition of the link between a child and the father, and in many communities with their culture.[270] The courts no longer regard even forenames as relatively unimportant:

> In *Re H (Child's Name: First Name)*[271] married parents separated when the mother was six weeks pregnant and had no contact until the father visited the hospital after the birth. Without the mother's agreement the father registered the child with his choice of names, precluding her from registering. The mother sought a specific issue order to allow her to rename the child. This was refused and she appealed. The Court of Appeal held that the mother could choose to call the child by any first name and use this for dealings with schools or doctors, but the registration was said to be immutable.

---

[262] Children Act 1989 ss.8, 34; Children and Adoption Act 2006. A child can also obtain an order to allow contact with another child: *Re F (Contact: Child in Care)* [1995] 1 F.L.R. 510, where the order was refused because siblings did not want to see the applicant.

[263] *Re O (Contact: Imposition of Conditions)* [1995] 2 F.L.R. 124, and see below, paras 18–016–18–020.

[264] In *Re A (Contact: Witness Protection Scheme)* [2006] 2 F.L.R. 551, contact via video link was arranged despite the child and mother being under a witness protection scheme because of violence and threats from the father's brother.

[265] Children (Scotland) Act 1995 s.2(1)(c) following Scottish Law Com. No.135, paras 2.31–2.35. But there is no presumption of contact under Scots Law: *S v M (Access Order)* [1997] 1 F.L.R. 980, HL(S).

[266] *O v L* [1995] 2 F.L.R. 930, CA (application by ex-husband granted); *K v M* [1996] 1 F.L.R. 312 (application by former lover refused).

[267] Children Act 1989 s.10(4), (5).

[268] *Re A (Section 8 Order: Grandparent's Application)* [1995] 2 F.L.R. 153, CA.

[269] See A. Bond, "Reconstructing families—changing children's surnames" [1998] C.F.L.Q. 17 and Hayes [1999] C.F.L.Q. 423, "What's in a name?".

[270] *Dawson v Wearmouth* [1999] 1 F.L.R. 1167 at 1174, *per* Lord Jauncey; *Re B (Change of Surname)* [1996] 1 F.L.R. 791 at 795, *per* Wilson J.; *Re S (Change of Name Cultural Factors)* [2001] 2 F.L.R. 1005, FD.

[271] [2002] 1 F.L.R. 973, CA.

Parents

Formally, a child is named when the birth is registered; only a parent with parental responsibility may effect the registration alone, although two unmarried parents may do this jointly. The name given at birth is not conclusive; forenames can be added and the birth re-registered in the first 12 months.[272] Any subsequent formal change[273] is a serious issue,[274] and will be permitted by the court only if it is in the interests of the child.[275] Where both parents have parental responsibility, neither may change the child's surname without the consent of the other.[276] A father without parental responsibility may use s.8 orders to prevent a name change or require a return to the former name.[277] Also, where the child is subject to a residence order, the consent of everyone with parental responsibility or leave of the court is required.[278] No one may change the name of a child who is in the care of the local authority, but the courts have permitted such changes in the child's interests.[279] A child' name may be changed on adoption, but before the order is made, written permission from the parents or court is required.[280]

xiii. Miscellaneous rights

17–026 A number of miscellaneous rights follow from those discussed above (e.g. a person with parental responsibility has certain powers to enter into contracts on the child's behalf[281]); as an incident to the parental right to have possession of a child, a parent may sometimes prohibit the child's emigration.[282] Consent of a person with parental responsibility is required before a child can obtain a

---

[272] Births and Deaths Registration 1953 s.10; Registration of Births and Death Regulations 1987 (SI 1097/2088). Re-registration can be effected by either parent using Form 14: see *http://www.gro. gov.uk/gro/content/births/* [Accessed June 2, 2008]. It is unclear why this approach was not taken in *Re H* (above).

[273] The Enrolment of Deeds (Change of Name) Regulations 1994 (SI 1994/604); *Practice Direction* [1995] 1 F.L.R. 46. It has been suggested that the court cannot control informal action: *Re B (Change of Surname)* [1996] 1 F.L.R. 791, CA, *per* Wilson J. at 795.

[274] *Re PC (Change of Surname)* [1997] 2 F.L.R. 730 FD. In *Dawson v Wearmouth* [1999] 1 F.L.R. 1167, the House of Lords rejected the suggestion that refusal to order that a child had the father's name breached the father's rights under ECHR, art.8.

[275] *Re W, Re A, Re B (Change of Name)* [1999] 2 F.L.R. 930 CA; *Re D, L and LA* [2003] 1 F.L.R. 339.

[276] *Re PC (Change of Surname)* [1997] 2 F.L.R. 730, FD. Despite the wording in Children Act 1989 s.13(1)(a), a residence order is not required. The Law Commission took the view that a parent should not be able to take unilateral action to change the name: Law Com.172, para.4.14. *Re T. (Change of Surname)* [1998] 2 F.L.R. 620, CA.

[277] But Hayes suggests that the courts should not interfere with the unmarried mother's statutory right to choose the child's name and that Children Act 1989 s.1 may not apply: Hayes, *op. cit.*, p.428.

[278] Children Act 1989 s.13.

[279] *Re M, T, P, K and B (Care: Change of Name)* [2000] 2 F.L.R. 645, FD (name changes required to protect children who had been abused and who required a witness protection programme); *Re S (Change of Name)* [1999] 2 F.L.R. 672, CA (name change allowed on appeal for 15 year old whose father was acquitted of abusing her).

[280] Adoption and Children Act 2002 s.28(2)(3); DfES, *Adoption Guidance* (2005), Annex A, para.70.

[281] See *Mills v IRC* [1973] Ch. 225.

[282] Children Act 1989 s.13 Sch.2, para.19. If the child is in care or subject to a residence order, the court may give approval, but a child who is accommodated by the local authority may not go to live outside England and Wales without the agreement of everyone with parental responsibility. In other cases, the court will determine an application to remove a child applying the welfare test: see below, para.18–026.

passport; a parent may also veto the issue of a passport.[283] The right to administer the child's estate carries with it duties to arrange the child's funeral.[284] Where the child was looked after by the local authority, it may arrange the funeral but must, so far as practicable, obtain the consent of everyone with parental responsibility.[285] In cases of dispute, the court may determine the matter.[286]

B. Duties

i. To care

It is clear that parents are expected to care for their children, but the standard of **17–027** that care is uncertain. Article 18 of the UN Convention refers to the parental responsibility "for the upbringing and development of the child". The Children (Scotland) Act 1995 requires parents to "safeguard and promote the child's health development and welfare".[287] A similar duty is imposed by the Children Act 1989 but only on local authorities in respect of the children they look after and those in need.[288] A parent's duties can be discerned from the consequence of their failure. Those who neglect their children may be liable to criminal prosecution under various statutes.[289] Failure to provide reasonable care or to protect the child from abuse by the other parent may justify a local authority bringing care proceedings if it leads or is likely to lead to "significant harm".[290] Thus, parents who refused to show affection might find their child subject to a care order,[291] but society must be prepared to tolerate very diverse standards of parenting.[292] Parents are not immune from liability in tort[293] for harm to their children, but expectations of parental care must make allowance for the rough

---

[283] There must be a court order preventing the child's removal or the request must come from the only person with parental responsibility see Passport Agency website: *http://www.ukpa.gov.uk* [Accessed June 2, 2008]. In *Hamilton-Jones v David and Snape* [2004] 1 F.L.R. 774, a solicitor who failed to review the notice was liable in breach of contract after the children's abduction.

[284] *Williams v Williams* (1881) 20 Ch.D. 659; the court may appoint another administrator: Supreme Court Act 1981 s.116; *Buchanan v Milton* [1999] 2 F.L.R. 846, FD. The position of a special guardian is unclear, but he or she has a duty to inform the parents of the child's death: Children Act 1989 s.14C(5).

[285] Children Act 1989 Sch.2 para.20.

[286] *Fessi v Whitmore* [1999] 1 F.L.R. 769, Ch.D.

[287] Children (Scotland) Act 1995 s.1(1)(a), following recommendations in Scottish Law Com. No.135, para.2.6.

[288] Children Act 1989 ss.17(1)(a), 22(3).

[289] Bainham *Children and the Law* (Family Law, 2005), pp.617–620. For a chilling example of neglect, see The Bridge Child Care Consultancy, *Paul, Death Through Neglect* (1995).

[290] Children Act 1989 s.31; see below, para.21–031.

[291] *M v Wigan MBC* [1980] Fam. 36, where parental rights were assumed under the Childcare Act 1980 s.3(1)(b)(v) because of the parents' failure to discharge the obligations of a parent.

[292] *Re L (Care: Threshold Criteria)* [2007] 1 F.L.R. 2050, at para.50 *per* Hedley J.

[293] *J Eastham v B Eastham and I Eastham* [1982] C.L.Y. 2141; *Pereira v Keleman* [1995] 1 F.L.R. 428; *S v W (Child Abuse Damages)* [1995] 1 F.L.R. 862; *Roller v Roller* 37 Wash. 242; 79 p.788 (1905). Parental immunity exists in most states of the US, and in England for pre-natal injury caused by the mother other than by driving: Congenital Disability (Civil Liability) Act 1976 ss.1(1), 2; see Wright (1994) 6 J.C.L. 104.

and tumble of family life.[294] The obligation to care for a child has been viewed as a trust,[295] and abuse of the child is a breach of trust.[296]

Although contact is termed "a right of the child", there does not appear to be a corresponding legal duty on parents to maintain personal relations and direct contact, but it has been suggested that the courts should have a role in encouraging contact by the non-resident parent.[297] The Children and Adoption Act 2006 contains a power to direct attendance at "contact acitivities" to assist establishing, maintaining or improving child contact.[298] Failure to exercise contact may lead to the conclusion that it would not be in the child's interests to re-establish it[299] or may justify an order for its termination. Rejection of a child may impair emotional development and mental health and may justify a care order.

Parents whose children commit offences are required to attend their child's court proceedings.[300] They are responsible for paying any financial penalties[301] and may be bound over or fined to ensure that their children do not commit further offences.[302] Parenting orders can be imposed where a child has engaged in anti-social or criminal conduct.[303]

Parental responsibility continues until the child is aged 18[304]; courts may grant residence (and parental responsibility) to a non-parent to last until then but only exceptionally make orders relating to parental responsibility for a child over the age of 16.[305] Under Scots law, parental duties end at different ages; the duties to maintain contact and administer the child's property end when the child reaches 16,[306] but other duties continue throughout childhood, although the way they are exercised varies with the child's age.[307]

---

[294] *Surtees v Kingston-upon-Thames RBC* [1991] 2 F.L.R. 559; liability of others *in loco parentis* rests on the standard of reasonable care: see *Carmarthenshire CC v Lewis* [1955] A.C. 549.

[295] L. Blom-Cooper, *A Child in Trust* (L.B. Brent, 1985); Blom-Cooper was particularly concerned with a child subject to a care order living at home: p.21; O'Donovan *Family Law Matters*, pp.102–104; Barton & Douglas *Law and Parenthood*, p.22.

[296] *M (K) v M (H)* (1992) 96 D.L.R. 596. The victim could sue her abusive father many years after the event because there was no limitation period for breach of trust: cf. *Stubbings v Webb* [1993] A.C. 498, but the decision of the House of Lords in *A v Hoare* [2008] UKHL 6 will enable the allegations to be brought for assaults beyond the six year limitation period.

[297] *Joint Committee on the Draft Children (Contact) and Adoption Bill* Session 2004–5 (HCP 400), para.38; cf. Children (Scotland) Act 1995, s.1(1)(c) and see Scottish Law Com. No.135, para.2.6.

[298] Children and Adoption Act 2006 s.1 adding Children Act 1989 ss.11A and 11B.

[299] *Re M (A Minor) (Access Application)* [1988] 1 F.L.R. 35. Cf. *Re P (A Minor) (Contact)* [1994] 2 F.L.R. 374.

[300] Children and Young Persons Act 1933 s.34A, but only if the child is under 16 years of age.

[301] Powers of Criminal Courts (Sentencing) Act 2000 s.137. Orders will not be made against parents (or local authorities) if it is unreasonable to do so, for example where they have done all that could be reasonably expected to control their child: *D v DPP* [1995] 2 F.L.R. 502, or if the offence is entirely outside their control: *TA v DPP* [1997] 2 F.L.R. 887, CA.

[302] Powers of Criminal Courts (Sentencing) Act 2000 s.150.

[303] Crime and Disorder Act 1998 ss.8 and 9; HO, *Parenting Contracts and Orders Guidance* (2004).

[304] Children Act 1989 ss.2, 3, 105(1).

[305] Children Act 1989 s.12(5)(6); and s.9(6), (7). Care orders cannot be made in relation to those over 17: s.31(3).

[306] Under Scots law, children have full legal capacity at 16 but the court may ratify or set aside transactions by those under 18: Age of Legal Capacity (Scotland) Act 1991 ss.1, 3, 4.

[307] Children (Scotland) Act 1995, ss.1(2)(b), 2(7) and see Scottish Law Com. No.135, paras 2.7–2.12.

ii. To maintain

The Child Support Act 1991 s.1 provides that for the purposes of the Act, each **17–028**
parent shall be responsible for maintaining a qualifying child. Where a
maintenance assessment has been made, the duty is satisfied by paying the sum
assessed.[308] A wide range of penalties may be imposed on those who do not pay,
including removal of a driving licence or imprisonment.[309] If Income Support is
paid in respect of the child, it can be recovered from a parent who may also be
liable to prosecution.[310] Increased emphasis is being placed on parents taking
responsibility and agreeing maintenance themselves.[311] However, the Child
Support Act 1991 suspended the jurisdiction of the courts to make or vary
maintenance orders against a parent who could be subject to a maintenance
assessment.[312] There are circumstances where a child (or young adult) can obtain
financial support from a parent[313] via the courts.[314] A child of any age may
intervene in the parents' divorce proceedings and seek a financial order[315]; with
leave, a child can apply for a residence order to be made or discharged, and the
court may make a financial order.[316] Where a young person is receiving
education or training, or there are special circumstances (e.g. disability) that
justify this,[317] maintenance orders may be made or extended beyond the age of
18.[318] However, there is no power to order a parent to maintain a child who is
looked after by the local authority after the age of 16.[319] There is no general
obligation to support adult children, nor to provide for them from the parent's
estate.

Parents can be required to pay financial support, but this does not depend on
their having parental responsibility; unmarried fathers without parental responsibility also have to pay. This is also the case for stepparents where the child is a
"child of the family".[320] In contrast, maintenance cannot be ordered from non-

---

[308] Child Support Act 1991 s.1(2)(3) and see Ch.15, above. The duty is owed to the Secretary of State,
not the other parent or the child: *R. (Kehoe) v SS for Work and Pensions* [2006] UKHL 48;
N. Wikeley, *Child Support* (2006), p.6.
[309] Child Support Act 1991 ss.39A, 40, 40B but only where there has been willful refusal or culpable
neglect.
[310] Social Security Administration Act 1992 ss.78, 105 and 106. This enforcement of the duty to
maintain is removed by the Child Maintenance and Other Payments Act 2008 s.45.
[311] Child Maintenance and Other Payments Act 2008 s.4; White Paper, *A New System for Child
Maintenance* (Cm.6979 (2002)) Ch.2.
[312] Child Support Act 1991 s.8(1).
[313] For these purposes, parent is defined in the Children Act 1989 Sch.1 para.16 to include "any party
to a marriage (whether or not subsisting) in relation to whom the child concerned is a child of the
family". It does not encompass all people with parental responsibility.
[314] A court may make an order against a parent to pay an additional amount or expenses relating to
education, training or a disabled child's disabilities; orders can also be made against a parent with
care: s.8. A former stepparent may also be requested to support a "child of the family": Matrimonial
Causes Act 1973 s.25 (3), (4).
[315] *Downing v Downing (Downing Intervening)* [1976] Fam. 288; but see above, para.15–045.
[316] Children Act 1989 Sch.1 paras 1, 6.
[317] *C v F (Disabled Child: Maintenance Orders)* [1998] 2 F.L.R. 1, CA.
[318] Children Act 1989 Sch.1 paras 2(1), 3(2). The policy of encouraging students to depend on loans
is not relevant to the court: *B v B (Adult Student: Liability to Support)* [1998] 1 F.L.R. 373.
[319] Children Act 1989 Sch.2 para.21(3).
[320] Matrimonial Causes Act 1973 ss.25(3),(4) and 52(1); S. Ramsey and J. Masson, "Stepparent
support of stepchildren: a comparative analysis of policies and problems in the American and English
experience" (1985) 36 Syracuse L.R. 659.

parents who have parental responsibility, but in the absence of other sources of financial support,[321] such people do have to support children living with them because they could be held liable for neglect if they failed to do so.

The importance of parental responsibility

17–029 Parental responsibility is not a unitary concept; the Children Act 1989 draws distinctions between the parental responsibility of parents and guardians and that of other people. Those who acquire parental responsibility by an agreement or court order can have it removed by the revocation or discharge of that order. Fathers (and second parents) without parental responsibility must maintain their children.[322] Also, despite the wording of Children Act 1989 s.3, parental responsibility does not provide all the important attributes of parenthood.[323] Only parents with parental responsibility and guardians can make decisions about adoption,[324] and non-parents can appoint a guardian to take responsibility for the child in the event of their death only if they are guardians or special guardians.[325] The absence of parental responsibility does not mean that a non-parent has no rights or responsibilities in relation to the child. A person whose parental responsibility was removed by the making of a care order must be allowed contact with the child.[326] Non-parents without parental responsibility can apply for s.8 orders without leave if they are married to a parent or have had care of the child for three years.[327] The above discussion of rights and duties makes clear that anyone with care of a child has some responsibility to ensure that the child attends school and is properly looked after. Also, where a person has a relationship that amounts to family life within art.8, public authorities must respect their rights.[328] Indeed having Convention rights may become more important than parental responsibility.

IV. WHO HAS PARENTAL RESPONSIBILITY?

A. Married parents

17–030 The Children Act 1989 provides that where a child's mother and father were married to each other at the time of the birth,[329] they shall each have parental

---

[321] Guardians, special guardians and those with residence orders may seek orders from the parent: Children Act 1989 Sch.1 para.1 and can receive support from the local authority (para.15). In some circumstances they will be entitled to state benefits.

[322] Above, para.17–028 and Human Fertilisation and Embryology Bill cl.53(1).

[323] J. Eekelaar, "Re-thinking parental responsibility" [2001] Fam. Law 426.

[324] Adoption and Children Act 2002 s.52(6); Children Act 1989 s.5 (as amended for special guardianship).

[325] Children Act 1989 s.5(3), (4), 14A.

[326] Children Act 1989 s.34(1), and see below, paras 21–074–21–076.

[327] Children Act 1989 s.10(5) (one year if they are a foster carer (subs.5A)) and see below, paras 18–036–18–039.

[328] Human Rights Act 1998 s.6; *K and T v Finland* [2001] 2 F.L.R. 707 and above, para.16–017.

[329] Children Act 1989 s.2(1). The phrase "married to each other at the time of [the child's] birth" is given a wide meaning by s.1(3) of the Family Law Reform Act 1987 and includes certain children born of void marriages, legitimated and adopted children and those treated as legitimate. Female civil partners will also acquire parental responsibility automatically under Human Fertilisation and Embryology Bill Sch.6, para.25 adding Children Act 1989 s.2(1A).

responsibility for their child, including a child born as a result of assisted reproduction.[330] An amendment to be added by the Human Fertilisation and Embryology Bill, if enacted, will make a similar provision in relation to a child born to female civil partners.[331]

The provision derives from the law relating to legitimacy that was modified by statute. At common law, the relationship between parent and child was only recognised if the child was "legitimate": that is, either born or conceived at a time when the parents were validly married. The ordinary case of birth to married parents involves both conception and birth during the parents' marriage, but under the common law, a child born after a marriage had been ended by death or divorce[332] is also legitimate. Despite the increase in births outside marriage, some couples marry during the pregnancy.[333] Originally, the father had the legal power over his legitimate child exclusively, but the father's power waned, and mothers were given greater legal recognition until equality was achieved.[334] The rigors of the common law were mitigated by allowing a child whose parents married later to be legitimated, and treating as legitimate some children of invalid marriages.[335] These notions were preserved when the Family Law Reform Act 1987 removed the remaining legal consequences of birth outside marriage so far as children are concerned,[336] and have been continued in relation to children conceived as a result of fertility treatment by female civil partners.[337]

In addition to the simple case of birth to married parents, both parents have parental responsibility in the following circumstances.

i. Void marriage

The Legitimacy Act 1976 provides that[338]:   **17–031**

> "The child of a void marriage, whenever born shall . . . be treated as the legitimate child of his parents if at the time of the insemination resulting in the birth or, if there was no such insemination, the child's conception (or at

---

[330] Human Fertilisation and Embryology Act 1990 s.29(1); Human Fertilisation and Embryology Bill 2008 cl.48(1).
[331] Children Act 1989 s.2(1A) to be added by Human Fertilisation and Embryology Bill 2008, Sch.6, para.25.
[332] *Knowles v Knowles* [1962] P. 161.
[333] The percentage of conceptions outside marriage that result in births within marriage has declined from 8.1% in 1971 to 3.2% in 1995; see C. Smart and P. Stevens, *Cohabitation Breakdown* (York: JRF, 2000) p.17 and K.E. Kiernan and V. Estough, *Cohabiting Extra-marital Child Bearing and Social Policy* (Family Policy Studies Centre, Occasional Paper 17, 1993), Ch.2.
[334] See S. Maidment, *Child Custody* (Croom Helm, 1984), Ch.5 and J. Brophy, "Parental rights and children's welfare. Some problems of feminist strategy in the 1920s" (1982) 10 Int. J. of Soc. L. 149, and S. Cretney, "What will the women want next?" (1996) L.Q.R. 110.
[335] For a historical account, see the fourth edition of this book at pp.581–584.
[336] Family Law Reform Act 1987 s.1.
[337] Human Fertilisation and Embryology Bill cl.42 and Sch.6 paras 15, 16.
[338] Legitimacy Act 1976 s.1 as amended by Family Law Reform Act 1987 s.28(1). Human Fertilisation and Embryology Bill 2008 cl.50 makes equivalent provision in respect of children born as a result of fertility treatment to a mother and a woman who is the child's other parent.

the time of the celebration of the marriage, if later) both or either of the parties reasonably believed that the marriage was valid."

The rule applies only if the child's father or second parent was domiciled in England or Wales at the time of birth.[339] It is only necessary for one party to have believed the marriage or civil partnership was valid. Thus, where the wife alone knows that she is under 16, or the husband that he is already legally married,[340] both parents will automatically gain parental responsibility. It is understandable that the law should be drafted generously to protect a child, but it is less clear as to why a father who knows that his marriage is invalid should nevertheless be able to rely on it to gain parental responsibility.[341] A belief may be reasonable, even though it was due to a mistake of law[342]; in relation to children born after April 4, 1988, and unless the contrary is shown, the Act presumes that one parent did have such a belief at the relevant time.[343] Where the father is claiming parental responsibility relying on a void marriage, his claim would only be defeated by establishing that neither parent reasonably believed in the validity of the marriage at the relevant time.[344] The belief must continue until the insemination, conception or, if later, the marriage, but a child may not apparently be treated as legitimate if he or she was born before the void marriage.[345] If the marriage or civil partnership is voidable rather than void, no problems arise relating to parental responsibility because decrees of nullity do not have retrospective effect.[346]

ii. Marriage after birth

17–032 The concept of legitimation by subsequent marriage was introduced into English law in 1926 and is now governed by the Legitimacy Act 1976. Providing that the father (or female parent) is domiciled in England or Wales at the date of their valid marriage (or civil partnership),[347] both parents will, from that date, have parental responsibility for any child of theirs born prior to the marriage.[348]

---

[339] Or if he died before the birth, was so domiciled immediately before his death: s.1(2). For this reason Daniel was not legitimate and could not succeed to his father's title: see *Re Moynihan* [2000] 1 F.L.R. 113 at 128, *per* Lord Slynn.

[340] See Matrimonial Causes Act 1973 s.11.

[341] The Law Commission's reasons for not extending parental responsibility to all fathers would seem to apply equally to the circumstance of a man who gets his wife pregnant knowing that their marriage is invalid: Law Com. No.118, paras 4.46 and 4.31–4.36.

[342] Legitimacy Act 1976 s.1(3) added by Family Law Reform Act 1987 s.28, following the recommendation of the Law Commission: *Illegitimacy* (Law Com. No.118 (1982)), paras 10.51–10.52.

[343] Legitimacy Act 1976 s.1(4).

[344] *Hawkins v Att-Gen* [1966] 1 W.L.R. 978 suggests that reasonableness should be assessed objectively.

[345] *Re Spence (dec'd)* [1990] Ch. 652, CA.

[346] Matrimonial Causes Act 1973 s.16 (for decrees granted after July 31, 1971); see above, para.2–053.

[347] *Re Spence (dec'd)* [1990] Ch. 652, where the marriage was void.

[348] Legitimacy Act 1976 s.2, and for female civil partners, s.2A, added by Human Fertilisation and Embryology Bill Sch.6 para.15. This includes a child of the parties who had been adopted by one of them as a single parent; see s.4. The child's birth can be re-registered to indicate this: General Register Office, Form LA1.

iii. Adoption

An adoption order gives parental responsibility to the adoptive parents. Except in **17–033** the case of adoption by a stepparent married to the natural parent, adoption ends parental responsibility held by the natural parents and anyone else under a court order.[349] Parental consent to placement and placement orders both give parental responsibility to the adoption agency and, if the child is placed for adoption, the prospective adopters.[350] The agency can determine how the prospective adopters exercise parental responsibility, and *Adoption Guidance* encourages agencies to give them increasing control over day-to-day matters.[351] Placement does not remove the parents' parental responsibility but prevents them from exercising it except in ways agreed by the adoption agency.[352]

iv. Surrogacy

A parental order[353] gives parental responsibility to the commissioning couple **17–034** through a process based on adoption.[354] It also destroys the parental responsibility held by anyone else by birth or a court order, but only for the period after the order was made.

B. Unmarried parents

Where the parents are unmarried at the time of the child's birth,[355] only the **17–035** mother has parental responsibility as of right; the father (or second parent) may obtain it by one of three ways: a court order, a formal agreement with the mother or registering the child's birth jointly with the mother.

Differential treatment for children dependent on their parent's marital status is contrary to the anti-discrimination principle of the UN Convention on the Rights of the Child.[356] The European Convention on Human Rights protects family life,[357] and this requires states to take positive steps to enable family life to develop normally.[358] The Convention protects family life, not bare rights, but very weighty reasons must be advanced before a difference in treatment between

---

[349] Adoption and Children Act 2002 ss.51(2), 67. Only from the date of the order: s.46(3)(a).
[350] Adoption and Children Act 2002 s.25.
[351] Adoption and Children Act 2002 s.25(4); DfES, *Adoption Guidance* (2005), Annex A, paras 40–41.
[352] Adoption and Children Act 2002 s.25(4).
[353] Human Fertilisation and Embryology Act 1990 s.30; Adoption and Children Act 2002, as modified by the Parental Orders Regulations 1994 (SI 1994/2767); see paras 22–076–22–077.
[354] Human Fertilisation and Embryology Act 1990 s.30 (for married couples only). The Human Fertilisation and Embryology Bill cll 54 and 55, if enacted, will also make parental orders available to civil partners and couples in enduring relationships.
[355] This phrase is given a wide meaning by Family Law Reform Act. 1987 s.1(3); see also A. Bainham, "When is a parent not a parent? Reflections on the unmarried father and his child in English Law" (1989) 3 Int. J. Law & Fam. 208.
[356] UN Convention on the Rigths of the Child art.2. States Parties are required to take all appropriate measures to ensure that the child is protected against "all forms of discrimination . . . on the basis of the status . . . of the child's parent" (art.2(2)).
[357] UN Convention on the Rigths of the Child art.8(1).
[358] *Marcx v Belgium* (1979) 2 E.H.R.R. 330; *Johnstone v Ireland* (1987) 9 E.H.R.R. 203. See J. Davidson, "The European Convention on Human Rights and the illegitimate child" in D. Freestone (ed.), *Children and the Law* (1990), p.75 at p.104 and C. Forder (1993) 7 Int. J. Law & Fam. 40.

children based on birth status can be justified.[359] In *B v UK*[360] a claim based on the treatment of unmarried fathers with regard to the acquisition of parental responsibility was declared inadmissible. Given that relationships between unmarried fathers and their children ranged from "indifference and ignorance to close stable relationships", it was reasonable for parental responsibility not to be automatic.[361] However, Irish legislation that precluded any involvement of an unmarried father in his child's adoption has been held to breach the Convention: the pregnancy had been planned and so the father had a right to family life with a child he had seen only once.[362]

Over the last 30 years there has been a substantial increase in the number of children born to unmarried parents,[363] repeated re-assessment of the position of unmarried fathers and a series of reforms that have reduced the scrutiny of individual claims and made it easier for fathers to acquire rights. Reforms have not had their origin in claims by the Fathers' Rights Movement[364] but from organisations supporting lone parents, the Law Commission and central government. Whereas ending discrimination on account of birth has been welcomed, attitudes to fathers' rights have been more equivocal.

17–036	In 1979 the Law Commission suggested the total abolition of illegitimacy so that unmarried fathers were in the same position as mothers and married fathers.[365] However, this caused serious anxiety to a significant body of commentators[366] and was therefore replaced by a more limited scheme whereby fathers could apply to the court to obtain parental rights and duties jointly with the mother. The infinite variety of relationships, the need to protect single mothers and children and the belief that court scrutiny was justified where rights were conferred outside marriage meant private agreements should not be allowed.[367] However, this view was criticised because it undervalued natural fathers, required unnecessary court proceedings in consensual cases and could discourage couples from legally sharing rights.[368] In 1985, in their Working Paper, *Guardianship,* the Law Commission noted that "[j]udicial proceedings, however, may be unduly elaborate, expensive and perhaps unnecessary, unless

---

[359] *Inze v Austria* (1987) 10 E.H.R.R. 394; *Sahin v Germany* [2002] 1 F.L.R. 119, para.57. But see the strong dissenting judgment by Judges Mifsud and Bonnici in *Kroon v Netherlands* [1995] 2 F.C.R. 28 at 44.

[360] [2000] 1 F.L.R. 1 (the father had been unable to obtain a declaration that the removal of his child by the mother was unlawful for the purposes of the Hague Convention on Child Abduction). But note following the decision in *Re H (Abduction: Rights of Custody)* [2000] 1 F.L.R. 374, HL, the father may have been able to get the child returned to the UK and see below, 20–016.

[361] *B v UK* [2000] 1 F.L.R. 1 at 5.

[362] *Keegan v Ireland* (1994) 18 E.H.R.R. 342. But in *Haas v The Netherlands* [2004] 1 F.L.R. 673 ECHR, the court held that "sporadic contacts and fatherly acts" did not amount to family life where the alleged father had never formally recognised the child under Dutch law.

[363] ONS, *Population Trends* (2006) 126, 43% of births were to unmarried parents in 2005.

[364] Collier makes no mention of the Family Law Reform Act 1987, which introduced the key reform relating to acquisition of parental responsibility: see R. Collier and S. Sheldon (eds), Fathers' *Rights Activism and Law Reform in a Comparative Perspective* (2006), p.55.

[365] *Illegitimacy* (Law Com. WP 74, (1979)), paras 3.17–3.22.

[366] *Illegitimacy* (Law Com. No.118, (1982)), para.4.46; M. Hayes (1980) 43 M.L.R. 299; R. Deech (1980) 10 Fam. Law 101.

[367] Law Com. No.118, para.4.39.

[368] J. Eekelaar, "Second thoughts on illegitimacy reform" (1985) 15 Fam. Law 261 at 262–263; R. Ingleby [1984] J.S.W.L. 170 at 172; A. Bainham [1985] J.S.W.L. 50 at 52.

the child's mother objects", and recommended a form of guardianship that would give the father parental responsibility alongside the mother.[369] It saw no inconsistency between extending guardianship and the earlier proposals, but acknowledged the resource implications of requiring proceedings.[370] Subsequently, the Law Commission issued a *Second Report on Illegitimacy*, reaffirming the need for court proceedings but expressing the hope that such orders would frequently be sought and granted.[371] The Family Law Reform Act 1987[372] gave the court power to grant parental responsibility to unmarried fathers; the proposal for agreements was widely supported[373] and was included in the Children Act 1989.[374] However, comparatively few fathers made use of these provisions.[375]

In 1998 the Lord Chancellor's Department sought views on reform to make obtaining parental responsibility easier for unmarried fathers.[376] It noted that over a third of all births were outside marriage,[377] and that ignorance of the law and assumptions about their rights meant that few fathers obtained parental responsibility.[378] The consultation paper considered three alternatives for acquisition of parental responsibility: (1) automatically for all fathers[379]; (2) for fathers who jointly register the birth; or (3) for fathers cohabiting with the mother at the time of birth.[380] None of these is without difficulty. Parental responsibility acquired automatically or via cohabitation would not necessarily be marked by any document identifying the father or showing his relationship to the child. This could cause difficulties where the father's consent is required; mothers and adoption agencies could be involved in further investigations to locate him, and paternity proceedings.[381] Cohabitation could not be taken to reflect commitment; housing difficulties might prevent couples establishing a common home.[382] Although joint registration could be a proxy for agreement, it takes place shortly after the birth when mothers might be easily pressured to agree.[383] If mothers

---

[369] *Guardianship* (Law Com. WP No.91, (1985)), para.4.21.
[370] *Guardianship*, para.4.24.
[371] *Illegitimacy* (Second Report) (Law Com. No.157 (1986)).
[372] Family Law Refrom Act s.4. This provision is now included in Children Act 1989 s.4(1)(a).
[373] Law Com. No.172, para.2.18.
[374] Children Act 1986 s.4(1)(b). The father's position is identical following an agreement or with an order.
[375] In 1996 the courts made 5,587 parental responsibility orders, and approximately 3,000 parental responsibility agreements were registered (Lord Chancellor's Department 1998).
[376] Lord Chancellor's Department, *The Procedures for the Determination of Paternity and on the Law on Parental Responsibility for Unmarried Fathers* (1998). The Scottish Executive has also consulted on this issue: *Improving Scottish Family Law* (1999); *Consultation Paper on Scottish Family Law* (2000).
[377] Lord Chancellor's Department para.52.
[378] Lord Chancellor's Department para.53, and see R. Pickford, *Fathers, Marriage and the Law* (1999).
[379] Scottish Law Com. No.135 *Report on Family Law* had proposed automatic parental responsibility in 1992, but this was not legislated.
[380] Lord Chancellor's Department paras 56–61.
[381] Lord Chancellor's Department para.57; R. Pickford, "Unmarried fathers and the law", in A. Bainham et al. (eds), *What is a Parent?* (1999), pp.143, 154–7; cf. J. Eekelaar [2001] Fam. Law 426, 430, who argues that parental responsibility makes very little difference to the position of unmarried fathers.
[382] Pickford, "Unmarried fathers and the law" (1999), p.154.
[383] SFLA evidence to Select Committee on the Adoption and Children Bill 2001 (2001 HC 431-iv), App.20.

registered the birth alone in order to preclude fathers obtaining parental responsibility,[384] there could be negative consequences for children who would be denied a record of their paternity, and for mothers because of the need to prove paternity for child support claims.[385] However, the expectations and beliefs of large numbers of unmarried parents provided the strongest reasons for extending parental responsibility to jointly registering fathers.[386] A provision was included in the Adoption and Children Act 2002.[387]

Further reform cannot be ruled out. In his report on the reform of Child Support, Sir David Henshaw recommended that unmarried parents should jointly be responsible for registering their child's birth in order to reduce the number of children whose paternity is unrecorded, and to facilitate the collection of child support. The Government has now proposed that father's should have the right to register the birth; mother's who object would have to apply to the courts.[388] This proposal, which runs counter to the previous understandings, is based on the belief that fathers who evade their responsibilities will become responsible if they are given these powers.

i. Court orders

17–037 An order under Children Act 1989 s.4 effectively places the father[389] in the same legal position as a married father, so that he holds parental responsibility alongside all others and can exercise it without consent.[390] If the court makes a residence order in favour of a father (or second parent) without parental responsibility, it must make such an order.[391] On an application for a s.4 order, the court considers the degree of commitment that the father has shown towards the child; the degree of attachment that exists between them; and the reasons the father has for applying for the order.[392] A parental responsibility order can not be suspended, but the court may adjourn to establish whether commitment is maintained.[393] The order can be revoked.[394] The welfare test applies to these

[384] Pickford, "Unmarried fathers and the law", p.153; approximately 194,000 (72% of births outside marriage were jointly registered, and of these, 77% of parents gave the same address: ONS, *Birth Statistics 1999*), (FM1 No.28), Table 3.10. See also J. Ashley [1999] Fam. Law 175.
[385] For this reason, Eekelaar argues that registration should merely be a recording exercise and all fathers should have parental responsibility: Eekelaar, [2001] Fam. Law 426, 430.
[386] Pickford, "Unmarried fathers and the law", p.157; C. Smart and P. Stevens, *Cohabitation Breakdown* (2000), p.48; Eekelaar, [2001] Fam. Law 426.
[387] Adoption and Children Act s.111, amending Children Act 1989 s.4. A comparable provision was included in the Family Law (Scotland) Act 2006 s.23.
[388] *Recovering Child Support; Routes to Responsibility* (Cm.6894 (2006)), para.109; A Fresh Start—The Government's response to Sir David Henshaw (Cm.6895 (2006)), paras 38–41; White Paper *Joint Birth Registration: Promoting Parental Responsibility* (Cm.7160 (2007)), para.62 and fig.3.
[389] The Human Fertilisation and Embryology Bill Sch.6, para.26 makes similar provision for second parents by adding s.4ZA.
[390] Children Act 1989 s.2(6)(7).
[391] Children Act 1989 s.12(4); Human Fertilisation and Embryology Bill Sch.6 para.22 adds s.12(1A). See below, 19–014.
[392] *Re H (Minors) (Local Authority: Parental Rights) (No.3)* [1991] Fam. 151 at 158, CA; *Re C (Minors) (Parental Rights)* [1992] 1 F.L.R. 1, CA. Other matters can also be considered such as the father's violence: *Re H (Parental Responsibility)* [1998] 1 F.L.R. 855, CA.
[393] *Re G (Parental Responsibility Order)* [2006] 2 F.L.R. 1092, CA.
[394] Children Act 1989 s.4(2A), (3).

proceedings.[395] It has been said that it is overwhelmingly in the child's interests for both parents to have parental responsibility.[396] Where the father has had regular contact and provided financial support, cogent evidence is required to establish that an order should not be made.[397] Abuse of power can be controlled by court orders,[398] but where the father could not exercise parental responsibility[399] or was highly likely to misuse it,[400] an order should not be made. Orders may be made even though the denial of contact[401] or adoption plans[402] makes it impractical for the father to exercise parental responsibility:

> In *Re H*[403] the mother left the father when the child was three months old, and married. The father continued to see his son until he was one year old, when the mother and step-father moved to Scotland. The step-father threatened to leave the mother if the father continued to see his son. The father's application for contact was rejected and he was banned from any contact until further order, but his appeal against refusal of a parental responsibility order was allowed. By maintaining contact and writing appreciatively to the mother about her care, the father had shown commitment and attachment to his son.

Parental responsibility has been granted despite the fact that the father has undergone an operation to acquire female characteristics[404]; where there is hostility and lack of respect between the parents[405]; and where the father's commitment to the children has not extended to providing regular maintenance.[406] However, the court has been prepared to refuse it where a father has not established commitment because of violence to the mother,[407] limited contact[408] or spending long periods in prison.[409]

---

[395] This appears to have been assumed rather than decided; see *Re F (A Minor) (Parental Responsibility Order)* [1994] 1 F.L.R. 504, CA; *Re J-S (Parental Responsibility Order)* [2003] 1 F.L.R. 399.

[396] *Re P (A Minor) (Parental Responsibility Order)* [1994] 1 F.L.R. 578 at 586, *per* Wilson J.

[397] *Re E (Parental Responsibility: Blood Tests)* [1995] 1 F.L.R. 392, CA.

[398] *Re S (Parental Responsibility)* [1995] 2 F.L.R. 648 at 657, *per* Ward L.J. It does not necessarily justify refusing the order.

[399] *M v M (Parental Responsibility)* [1999] 2 F.L.R. 737, FD (father had brain damage).

[400] *Re P (Parental Responsibility)* [1998] 2 F.L.R. 96, CA; *Re M (Contact: Parental Responsibility)* [2001] 2 F.L.R. 342, FD.

[401] *Re C and V (Contact and Parental Responsibility)* [1998] 1 F.L.R. 392; *Re H (A Minor) (Parental Responsibility)* [1993] 1 F.L.R. 484.

[402] *Re H (Minors) (Local Authority: Parental Rights) (No.3)* [1991] Fam. 151. Under the Adoption and Children Act 2002 s.52(9), (10), if the father acquires parental responsibility after the mother has consented to the child's placement, he is treated as having given consent but he can withdraw it: see para.22–026.

[403] *Re H (A Minor) (Parental Responsibility: Blood Tests)* [1993] 1 F.L.R. 484.

[404] *Re L (Contact: Transsexual Applicant)* [1995] 2 F.L.R. 438.

[405] *D v S* [1995] 3 F.C.R. 783; *Re J-S (Parental Responsibility Order)* [2003] 1 F.L.R. 399.

[406] *Re H (Parental Responsibility: Maintenance)* [1996] 1 F.L.R. 867, CA.

[407] *Re G (Domestic Violence)* [2000] 1 F.L.R. 865, FD.

[408] *Re D (Parental Responsibility: IVF baby)* [2001] F.L.R. 230 CA (consideration of application delayed so that father could show he maintained commitment); *Re J (Parental Responsibility)* [1999] 1 F.L.R. 784 (limited contact over 11 years inadequate).

[409] *S v P (Contact Application: Family Assistance)* [1997] 2 F.L.R. 277; *Re P (Parental Responsibility)* [1997] 2 F.L.R. 722, CA.

Court orders now provide a residual role where parental responsibility was not acquired through birth registration[410] and the mother refuses her agreement. Such cases may justify close scrutiny, particularly if the father has refused to co-operate with joint registration, or his behaviour undermines rather than supports the care of the children. The order confers status and should not be denied under s.1(5) because the parents agree about the child's care.[411]

ii. Formal agreements

17–038 Parents may make an agreement for the father (or second parent)[412] to have parental responsibility, but it is only effective if in the prescribed form[413] and registered with the court.[414] The court's role is administrative and not judicial; there is no investigation of the child's welfare when an agreement is registered,[415] nor can a local authority preclude parents agreeing to share parental responsibility for a child in care.[416] A court order is necessary to terminate an agreement. The limited use of this provision may indicate that the use of formal agreements is not an easy solution for extending rights or increasing protection within families.

iii. Registration of birth

17–039 Joint registration (or joint re-registration) of a child's birth on or after December 1, 2003[417] gives an unmarried father parental responsibility for his child.[418] This will be extended to second parents if the Human Fertilisation and Embryology Bill is enacted.[419] In effect, the act of registration is treated as an agreement between the parents. It follows that if the birth is re-registered by one parent following a court order that established paternity, the father will not gain parental

---

[410] For example, joint registration before December 1, 2003; *Re J-S (Parental Responsibility Order)* [2003] 1 F.L.R. 399.

[411] Applications are made as bargaining chips to secure agreements: I. Butler et al., "The Children Act 1989 and the unmarried father" (1993) 5 J.C.L. 157.

[412] Human Fertilisation and Embryology Bill Sch.6 para.26 adding Children Act 1989 s.4ZA(1)(b).

[413] Parental Responsibility Agreement (Amendment) Regulations 2001 (SI 2001/2261).

[414] Children Act 1989 s.4(2). Informal agreements may have limited effect: see ss.2(9) and 3(5), discussed below.

[415] S. Cretney [1989] Fam. Law 375. "The object is to ensure that, as far as possible, both parents understand the importance and effects of their agreement" (Law Com. No.172), para.2.19.

[416] *Re X (Parental Responsibility Agreement: Children in Care)* [2000] 1 F.L.R. 517, FD.

[417] Retrospective application was not discussed by the Lord Chancellor's Department, but the Scottish Executive, *Consultation Paper on Scottish Family Law*, considered that there was a need to avoid interference with the child's and the mother's life (para.2.16). This contradicts the main reason for the change: to align the law with current beliefs. Approximately 7% of registrations are sole registrations: Smallwood (2004) 117 *Population Trends* 20.

[418] Children Act 1989 s.4(1)(a), (1A), added by Adoption and Children Act 2002 s.111; similar provision is made for registrations of birth effected in Scotland and Northern Ireland. A short birth certificate does not include the names of parents and will not (unless redesigned) indicate whether the father has parental responsibility.

[419] Human Fertilisation and Embryology Bill Sch.6 para.26 adding Children Act 1989 s.4ZA(1)(a), (2).

responsibility. A short birth certificate does not indicate parentage, so a full certificate will be necessary to establish that the father's name was included by joint registration. As in other cases of unmarried fathers, parental responsibility can be removed by a court order.[420]

C. Guardians

The term "guardian of the child" has had a wide variety of meanings but in modern times has been limited in law to a parent or a person who takes over a parent's responsibilities after their death.[421]   **17–040**

Until 1991, parents and guardians had similar but not identical powers[422]; the Law Commission recommended that the distinctions should be abolished so that guardians could be brought fully within the scheme for parental responsibility,[423] and that the term "guardian" should be restricted to non-parents.[424] This was enacted in the Children Act 1989; under the Act guardians have parental responsibility.[425] Guardians can be appointed by parents and special guardians,[426] or, failing them, by the court.[427]

i. Appointments by parents, guardians and special guardians

A parent with parental responsibility, a guardian or special guardian[428] may appoint a person to be the child's guardian in the event of their death. The appointment takes effect immediately on death,[429] but where there is a surviving parent with parental responsibility, an appointment by the other parent only takes effect after the death of both parents.[430] A parent only has parental responsibility alongside a guardian if the deceased parent had a residence order and the surviving parent did not.[431]   **17–041**

---

[420] Children Act 1989 s.4(2A), (3) but this does not lead to an amendment of the birth certificate.
[421] *Guardianship* (Law Com. WP 91, (1985)), paras 2.4–2.6. A child may also have a guardian ad litem and a "children's guardian" whose powers are quite different; see above, para.16–020, and below, para.21–058. A special guardian is not a guardian in this sense: s.14C(1)(b) but can exercise parental responsibility to the exclusion of the parents.
[422] Law Com. WP 91, para.2.26.
[423] Law Com. No.172, paras 2.23–2.25.
[424] Law Com. No.172 para.2.3.
[425] Children Act 1989 s.5(6): a guardian is not liable to maintain the child: see Sch.1.
[426] Children Act 1989 s.5(1), (4) and (7).
[427] Children Act 1989 s.5(1)–(5). For the earlier law, see Guardianship of Minors Act 1971 (as amended) and the fourth edition of this book at pp.316–320.
[428] Children Act 1989 s.5(3), (4); two people may make an appointment jointly: s.5(10).
[429] Children Act 1989 s.5(7). Similarly, it will take effect on the death of the last surviving special guardian even if there is a parent with parental responsibility still living.
[430] Children Act 1989 s.5(8). An appointment by a guardian may take effect while the child has a guardian with a residence order, but a court may not make an appointment at such a time: s.5(1).
[431] Children Act 1989 s.5(1), (7), (8), or the child had a special guardian. The Law Commission thought that requiring a parent who was caring for a child to share parental responsibility with a guardian presented the parent with "individious choice", and that there was little reason to require such sharing.

The Law Commission wanted to simplify appointments.[432] Appointments only need be in writing and signed by the person making them, or signed and witnessed at his or her direction.[433] Appointments are revoked by written revocation, by intentional destruction of the document[434] or by making another appointment, unless it is clear that the intention is to add a guardian.[435] If the appointment is made by will, it is revoked if the will is revoked.[436] The appointment of a spouse is revoked by divorce or a decree of nullity unless a contrary intention appears.[437] A person appointed may disclaim the appointment but must do so within a reasonable time and in writing.[438] The court may also revoke an appointment.[439]

ii. Appointments by the court

17–042 The court's powers mirrored those of parents, and the Law Commission recommended that this should continue.[440] The court may appoint a person to be a child's guardian whether or not an application has been made.[441] A local authority may not be the child's guardian but may support an individual making an application.[442] A court may only appoint a guardian if the child has no parent with parental responsibility, or if a parent, guardian or special guardian with a residence order in their favour dies while the order is in force, or if the last surviving special guardian dies.[443] The court may exercise its power to appoint even though the deceased made a valid and effective appointment, and may do so either to add or to substitute a new guardian. Decisions about guardians are made applying the welfare test in s.1.

The Law Commission considered whether there should be a power to supervise or disqualify persons acting as guardians, but decided that it was difficult to justify the resources that this would require.[444] Guardians are exempt from the regulation of the Safeguarding Vulnerable Groups Act 2006 because they care for the child within a family relationship.[445] However, a court

---

[432] Law Com. WP 91, paras 1.31 and 3.43, so that more appointments would be made. Only a small minority of people make wills, but death rates for people with young children are low. Relatives and friends may care for children without formally being appointed guardians. Figures for court appointments are so low as not to be recorded separately in the *Judicial Statistics.*
[433] Children Act 1989 s.5(5).
[434] Children Act 1989 s.6(2), (3).
[435] Children Act 1989 s.6(1).
[436] Children Act 1989 s.6(4); if the testator marries see Wills Acts 1837 ss.18, 18A.
[437] Children Act 1989 s.5(3A), added by Law Reform (Succession) Act 1995 s.4(1) and amended by the Family Law Act 1996 Sch.8 para.41 and operative for deaths after January 1, 1996.
[438] Children Act 1989 s.6(5), (6). The power to make regulations has not been exercised.
[439] Children Act 1989 s.5(1), (2).
[440] Law Com. No.172, para.2.31.
[441] Children Act 1989 s.5(1),(2).
[442] DCSF, Children Act 1989 *Guidance and Regulations* (2008), Vol.1, paras 2.18–2.20; *Re SH (Care Order: Orphan)* [1995] 1 F.L.R. 746. Where the lack of any person with parental responsibility placed the child at risk of significant harm a care order could be obtained: *Re M (Care Order: Parental Responsibility)* [1996] 2 F.L.R. 84, FD.
[443] Children Act 1989 s.5(1) even if another person (who cannot be a parent) still has a residence order that is in force.
[444] Law Com. WP 91, paras 3.23 et seq.; Law Com. No.172, para.2.32.
[445] Safeguarding Vulnerable Groups Act 2006 s.58(1).

considering the appointment or discharge of a guardian may call for reports,[446] and a family assistance order may be made to provide short-term assistance for a guardian and the family.[447]

A guardian of the estate of any child may also be appointed under the inherent jurisdiction of the High Court in accordance with rules of court.[448]

D. Other persons

Other people, most frequently stepparents but also relatives[449] and foster carers, may take on the role of parent, but these "social parents" do not automatically acquire parental responsibility by marrying a parent or looking after the child. Some stepparents and relatives adopt,[450] but this use of adoption was criticised for disrupting or confusing relationships.[451] The Children Act 1975 restricted adoption by stepparents and made it possible for some carers to apply for custody or custodianship.[452] These orders never became popular, and few carers form-alised their relationships.[453] The Law Commission criticised the restrictive and inconsistent custody law, but their proposal for guardianship for carers whilst parents were alive received little support.[454] They also suggested that all non-parents should be able to apply for custody with leave of the court as a filter to prevent "unwarranted interference", and suggested further controls on foster carers to protect the local authority's plan for the child.[455] Orders in favour of non-parents should be very similar to those for parents[456]; non-parents caring for a children needed the same responsibilities as a parent and should not have a separate status.[457] The Children Act 1989 enacted the Law Commission's proposals with only minor changes, to create a simple and coherent scheme for

17–043

---

[446] Children Act 1989 s.7, discussed at para.18–010, below.
[447] Children Act 1989 s.16, discussed at 18–027, below.
[448] Children Act 1989 s.5(11), (12); Civil Procedure Rules 1998 (SI 1998/3132) r.20.12. Only the Official Solicitor may be appointed.
[449] J. Haskey, "Stepfamilies and stepchildren in Great Britain" (1994) 76 *Population Trends* 18; over a million children are estimated to live in step-families. In 2000, there were 6,300 children fostered by local authorities with friends or relatives: *Children Act Report 2000*, para.1.40. Many other children are cared for by relatives, privately.
[450] In 2005, 866 of the 4004 adoption orders were in favour of a parent and stepparent: *Judicial Statistics 2005*, Table 5.4, reflecting a continuation of the long-term decline of such orders in England and Wales: see J. Masson et al., *Mine, Yours or Ours?* (London: HMSO, 1983), fig.2.1a.
[451] *Report of the Departmental Committee on Adoption of Children* (Cmnd.5107 (1972)) (The "Houghton Report"), paras 105, 108, 111; see below, para.22–064.
[452] Children Act 1989 ss.10(3) and 11(4); Adoption Act 1976 ss.14(3) and 15(4); the restrictions were removed by the Children Act 1989. A form of custody; for details see the sixth edition of this book at p.645.
[453] E. Bullard and E. Malos, *Custodianship* (London: HMSO, 1991); 491 orders were made in 1991 (Cm.1990), Table 5.11.
[454] Law Com. WP 96, paras 5.21–5.25; *Inter-vivos* guardians (Law Com. WP 91), paras 4.9 *et seq.*; Law Com. No.172, para.2.2.
[455] Law Com. WP 96, paras 5.37–5.39; Law Com. No.172, paras 4.40–4.48. For a the law and practice relating to leave for residence order applications, see Ch.18, below.
[456] "Some of the statutory provisions which equate guardians with parents would not be appropriate, in particular the power to appoint a testamentary guardian or consent to adoption or to freeing the child for adoption. The child is not 'theirs' to dispose of in this way; indeed, they may wish to adopt him against the parent's will" (Law Com. No.172, para.4.27).
[457] Law Com. No.172, paras 4.26, 4.28.

the acquisition of parental responsibility. However, the desire to simplify acquisition of status by stepparents and to enhance the status of some permanent carers led to the introduction of stepparent responsibility agreements and special guardianship orders in the Adoption and Children Act 2002.[458]

i. Non-parents with residence orders

17–044 A *residence order* may be made in favour of anyone in any family proceedings.[459] Non-parents require leave of the court for an application unless they are a stepparent, have cared for the child for three years, are foster carers or have the relevant consents.[460] Foster parents, except those who are relatives of the child or have cared for the child for more than one year,[461] require the consent of the local authority before they can apply for leave.[462] A residence order confers parental responsibility for the child for the duration of the order, normally until the child is 16, but, at the request of a carer who is not a parent or guardian, the order may be extended to age 18.[463] A residence order discharges a care order and therefore enables a foster carer to end the involvement of the local authority. The local authority may continue to provide financial support[464] (but authorities are rarely generous in this respect); any other assistance would depend on the authority accepting that the child required services.[465]

Although the Children Act 1989 has introduced a coherent scheme for the acquisition of parental responsibility by court order, few stepparents or carers have made use of this.[466] Ignorance of the law, feelings that formal status is irrelevant to the practice of parenting or concerns about the cost and complexity of legal proceedings are all likely to be factors.[467]

ii. Stepparents

17–045 The Interdepartmental Review of Adoption Law proposed that stepparents should be able to obtain parental responsibility by agreement with both the

---

[458] Adoption and Children Act 2002 ss.112, 115 (adding Children Act 1989 ss.4A and 14A–G).

[459] Children Act 1989 s.10(1). A residence discharges a care order and may be used to secure the child lives with relatives who have not previously had care: see s.91(1).

[460] Children Act 1989 s.10(2), (5), see paras 18–031–18–39 and below.

[461] Children Act 1989 s10(5A), added by Adoption and Children Act 2002 s.113.

[462] Children Act 1989 s.9(3). This also applies to people who have fostered the child in the previous six months. This further restriction was not recommended by the Law Commission, but was thought necessary to avoid discouraging parents from placing their children in local authority accommodation. It also removes local authority decisions from court review in this respect.

[463] Children Act 1989 s.12(5), (6). This was originally recommended by the *Interdepartmental Review of Adoption Law* (1992), para.6.5. In other cases exceptional circumstances are required to make any s.8 order to extend beyond age 16; ss.9(6), 91(10); *Re M (Contact: Parental Responsibility)* [2001] 2 F.L.R. 342, FD.

[464] Children Act 1989 Sch.1 para.15.

[465] Children Act 1989 s.17 and see below, para.21–009.

[466] In a study in the south-west of England in 1996–1997, only 10% of applications for residence were made by non-parents and 8 out of 10 of these were grandparents: J. Pearce et al. [1999] Fam. Law 22, 23.

[467] All these views have been expressed by relatives caring for children and unmarried parents: see Bullard and Malos, *Custodianship* and J. Masson and B. Lindley, "Recognising carers for what they do—Legal problems and solutions for the kinship care of children", in E. Ebtehaj et al. (eds), *Kinship Matters* (Oxford: Hart 2006), p.135.

child's parents, or, if this was not forthcoming, a court order.[468] The Adoption and Children Act 2002 made provision for this.[469] The married partner[470] of each parent can acquire parental responsibility by an agreement or a court order. The requirement that both the parents consent to any agreement gives the parent who is not the stepparent's partner bargaining chips, an effect which the Law Commission sought to avoid in disputes between parents, and may make agreements unattractive. It is unclear why this parent's agreement is thought necessary; granting parental responsibility to a person does not involve the reduction of the power of others holding it, nor would it be possible to stop the other parent sharing responsibility informally, unless this placed the child at risk. Where the parent refuses agreement or cannot be found, a court order will be required. However, it remains possible for the parent (or anyone else with parental responsibility) to delegate this informally without any consent.[471]

iii. Special guardians

In 1993 the Government proposed a status termed "inter-vivos guardianship" or **17–046** "foster-plus" as an addition to a residence order and an alternative to adoption for relatives and foster parents.[472] Concern about the instability of arrangements, the lack of family life for children looked after by local authorities and the acceptability of adoption in the minority ethnic communities[473] led to the resurrection of these proposals, updated and renamed "special guardianship".[474] However, there has been no reconsideration of fundamental questions as to whether a new order is required, or whether carers want to formalise their relationships and, in the case of foster carers, whether they wish to take on more responsibility and exclude the local authority.

The Adoption and Children Act makes provision for special guardianship.[475] The order can be sought by anyone (except a parent or stepparent) over the age of 18 years who is a guardian, has a residence order, is entitled to apply for a residence without leave or has fostered the child for one year.[476] Others will be able to apply with leave or be granted the order without an application.[477] Two

---

[468] *Interdepartmental Review of Adoption Law* (1992), para.19.8. Stepparent adoption would also be available, but the existence of a simple alternative way of obtaining parental responsibility was intended to discourage unsuitable applications for adoption. The parental responsibility order would not effect inheritance rights: *Adoption: the Future* (Cm.2288 (1993)), para.5.21. The Scottish Executive has also considered such a scheme: *Consultation Paper on Scottish Family Law* paras 2.25–2.42.

[469] Adoption and Children Act 2002 s.112, adding Children Act 1989 s.4A. This extends to civil partners: Civil Partnership Act 2004 s.75.

[470] Or civil partner: Civil Partnership Act 2004 s.75; an unmarried partner could apply jointly with the parent for a residence order.

[471] Children Act 1989 s.2(9).

[472] *Adoption: The Future* (Cm.2288 (1993)), paras 5.24 *et seq.* No provision was made for this in the Draft Adoption Bill 1996. The history of the provision is reviewed in *Re S* [2007] EWCA Civ 54.

[473] Select Committee on Health, Second Report on Health, Session 1997–8, *Children Looked After by Local Authorities* (HC 247 (1998)); Performance and Innovation Unit, *Adoption Review* (2000).

[474] *Adoption—a new approach* (Cm.5017 (2000)) paras 5.8–5.11.

[475] Adoption and Children Act 2002 s.115, adding new ss.14A–14G to the Children Act 1989, and see below, para.22–064.

[476] Adoption and Children Act 2002 s.14A(2)–(5).

[477] Adoption and Children Act 2002 s.14A(3)(b) and (6)(b). But the court can only make the order if a report has been provided by the local authority.

(or more) people can apply together.[478] The statutory regime requires far more scrutiny than for residence order applications: applicants must give notice to the local authority three months before they apply; those who need leave cannot give notice until leave has been obtained.[479] The order can only be made if a report has been obtained; a judge who seeks to order special guardianship without an application must request the local authority to provide the required report.[480]

Despite the terminology, there is little that a special guardian can do which is not available to a person with a residence order; special guardians may appoint a guardian and can take the child abroad for up to three months without consulting others with parental responsibility.[481] A name change requires the consent of the court, and will only be granted in the child's best interests.[482] The court continues to have power over contact but may leave this to the discretion of the special guardians, or provide them with additional security by restricting further applications by the parents.[483] The order may be revoked.[484] There is provision for support for special guardians from the local authority; these are governed by regulations, and the Department for Education and Skills has produced very detailed guidance.[485] Where the child has been looked after by a local authority, children and their special guardians have rights to be assessed for support services.[486]

E. Local authorities

17–047 The Children Act 1989 provides that a care order gives the local authority parental responsibility for the child. The parent's parental responsibility is not removed, but the local authority has power to control the exercise of it to the extent necessary to safeguard and promote the child's welfare.[487] Local authority's powers are restricted; they cannot place the child outside England and Wales or restrict contact more than temporarily without a court order.[488] Whilst care proceedings are before the court, the court can direct certain matters relevant to

---

[478] There is no requirement, as there is for adoption, that couples are in a relationship (Adoption and Children Act 2002 s.144(4)), so two sisters could apply in relation to a niece or nephew, and elderly grandparents with a younger person who proposed to take over care in the future.
[479] Children Act 1989 s.14A(7); *Re R* [2006] EWCA Civ 1748, paras 95, 103.
[480] Children Act 1989 s.14A(9), (11); *Re R* [2006] EWCA Civ 1748, para.103.
[481] Adoption and Children Act 2002 s.14C. If the child is of school age, such a trip would exceed the permissible period of holiday absence. They cannot change the child's name or agree to adoption. For a comparison of the two arrangements, see the discussion regarding parental responsibility held by more than one person.
[482] *Re L* [2007] EWCA Civ 196.
[483] Children Act 1989 s.91(14); *Re S* [2007] EWCA Civ 54.
[484] Adoption and Children Act 2002 s.14D, and see below.
[485] Children Act 1989 ss.14F, 14G; Special Guardianship Regulations 2005 (SI 2005/1109); DfES, *Special Guardianship Guidance* (2005); Masson and Lindley, "Recognising Carers".
[486] Special Guardianship Regulations 2005 (SI 2005/1109) reg.11. Provision of services is a matter of local authority discretion.
[487] Children Act 1989 s.33(3)(b), (4); the local authority cannot prevent the parents making a parental responsibility agreement: *Re X (Parental Responsibility Agreement: Children in Care)* [2000] 1 F.L.R. 517, FD.
[488] Children Act 1989 Sch.2 para.19 ss.34, see below, paras 21–074, 21–076.

the proceedings.[489] Similarly, an Emergency Protection Order grants the applicant parental responsibility, although its exercise is restricted by statute and regulations.[490]

V. Where Parental Responsibility is Held by More Than One Person

None of the methods of acquiring parental responsibility outlined above, except **17-048** adoption and parental orders, automatically removes parental responsibility (but care orders discharge residence orders).[491] It therefore follows that parental responsibility may be held simultaneously by a number of people. Where this is so, the Act provides some guidance about what each may do, and permits any dispute—except some involving children in care or awaiting adoption[492]—to be determined by the court, applying the welfare principle.

The Law Commission thought that it was essential for individuals with parental responsibility to be able to act independently to prevent one person from making it more difficult for another to care for a child.[493] A legal duty to consult was undesirable and unworkable; the child could suffer if decisions were delayed or inhibited by the need to obtain consent. The Children Act 1989 provides that where more than one person has parental responsibility, each of them may act alone except where the consent of all is specifically required.[494] However, this approach was criticised for undermining the parental responsibility of parents who do not have care of the child.[495] It has been emphasised that parents should not be seeking to interfere while they do not have care of the child.[496] However, the courts have begun to identify a small group of important decisions that require the agreement of both parents or the court.[497] Also, it has been asserted that parental responsibility confers a right to be consulted or informed about important

---

[489] Children Act 1989 s.38(6), below, para.21–043.

[490] Children Act 1989 s.44(4)(c). The local authority may take over the order: Emergency Protection Order (Transfer of Responsibility) Regulations 1991 (SI 1991/1414). In practice, EPOs are only sought by local authorities.

[491] Children Act 1989 s.91(2); residence orders discharge care orders: s.91(1).

[492] The court may not make any s.8 order, other than a residence order in respect of a child who is in care. Contact can be dealt with under s.34, but other disputes must be brought within the complaints system under s.26. Similarly, under the Adoption and Children Act 2002, where an adoption agency is authorised to place a child for adoption, only disputes about contact can be referred to the court: ss.26, 29(3).

[493] See Law Com. No.172, para.2.10. The former law was unclear and inconsistent: the Guardianship Act 1973 s.1(1) allowed married parents to do so, but the Children Act 1975 s.85(3) only permitted one of "joint" holders of a parental right to act alone if the other had not signified disapproval.

[494] Children Act 1989 s.2(7).

[495] Bainham (1990) 53 M.L.R. 206 at 217–218.

[496] *D v D (Shared Residence Order)* [2001] 1 F.L.R. 495, CA, *per* Hale L.J. at para.23.

[497] *Re J (Specific Issue Orders: Child's Religious Upbringing and Circumcision)* [2000] 1 F.L.R. 571, CA, *per* Butler Sloss P. at 577; *Re C (welfare of child: immunisation)* [2003] 2 F.L.R. 1095 CA, *per* Thorpe L.J. at para.17, a view that appears to side with the discredited, unscientific approach to the dangers of MMR vaccine; and see Maidment [2001] Fam. Law 518.

steps such as sending a child to boarding school.[498] However, Eekelaar has asserted that the law should not require consultation on any matter[499] an approach that reflects the capacity of the law and the courts to regulate parenting.

In contrast, where the local authority looks after[500] a child, it has a duty to consult parents and people with parental responsibility about all decisions unless this is not reasonably practicable.[501] The local authority has power to determine how the parents may exercise their parental responsibility in relation to a child in care,[502] which it may use to avoid consultation that would be contrary to the child's welfare.[503] Given that the European Court of Human Rights applies strict scrutiny to restrictions on family life that go beyond the removal of the child from the parent's care,[504] such a decision must be exceptional.

Placement for adoption and adoption both require the agreement of all parents and guardians but not other people with parental responsibility or a local authority.[505] A special guardian will be entitled to exercise parental responsibility to the exclusion of all others (except the other special guardian) unless the decision requires the consent of more than one person with parental responsibility.[506] Children who wish to marry under the age of 18 require the consent of all parents and guardians, and the local authority if it has parental responsibility, but if there is a residence order, the consent required is that of the person with whom the child lives under the order.[507] Both changing a child's name and removing a child from the United Kingdom for more than four weeks require the consent of all persons with parental responsibility.[508] Where consent is not forthcoming, the court may approve the proposed action.[509] The Act also restricts decisions where there is a court order; no one may act incompatibly with an order, even though they have parental responsibility.[510] However, it is not clear whether limitations

---

[498] *Re G (Parental Responsibility: Education)* [1994] 2 F.L.R. 964, CA, *per* Glidewell L.J., but no authority or reasoning was given.
[499] Eekelaar [2001] Fam. Law 426, 430.
[500] Children Act 1989 s.22(1); the local authority duty applies both where it has a care order and where it only accommodates the child.
[501] Children Act 1989 s.22(4); see *Guidance* (2008), Vol.1, para.3.15–6 and below, Ch.21.
[502] Children Act 1989 s.33(3); Eekelaar was highly critical of the decision to allow parents to retain parental responsibility when there was a care order: [1989] New L.J. 217 at 760, and para.21–041, below.
[503] *Re P (Children Act 1989, ss.22 and 26: Local Authority Compliance)* [2000] 2 F.L.R. 910, FD.
[504] *Johansen v Norway* (1996) 23 E.H.R.R. 33, para.64. Where the child is disturbed by an abusive parent being consulted, it should be possible for the local authority to show that its actions are necessary.
[505] Adoption and Children Act 2002 ss.19 and 47; Children Act 1989 ss.12(3), 33(6). But where one parent has given consent for the child's placement for adoption, the other parent is treated as having also given consent if he or she only acquired parental responsibility at a later date: s.52(10).
[506] Children Act 1989 s.14C.
[507] Marriage Act 1949 s.3(1A) added by Children Act 1989 Sch.12. Even if the residence order expired when the child reached the age of 16: s.3(1A)(d). Special guardians will also be able to consent to marriage without reference to others unless there is a care order, residence order or placement order: s.3(1A)(b).
[508] Children Act 1989 s.13(1); (the period is three months if the removal is by a special guardian: s.14C(4)). This applies to name change even where there is no residence order: *Re PC (Change of Name)* [1997] 2 F.L.R. 730, FD.
[509] Children Act 1989 s.13(1), (3); the welfare test applies; see below, para.18–026 and Ch.19.
[510] Children Act 1989 s.2(8). There are penalties for breach of a residence order under the Magistrates' Courts Act 1980 s.63(3); Children Act 1989 s.14. See below, Ch.18.

on behaviour have to be explicit or can be inferred from the circumstances,[511] but there is a power to impose detailed conditions in s.8 orders on parents and persons with parental responsibility.[512] Where the residential parent dies and appoints a guardian, the Act gives no indication as to whether the guardian or the surviving parent is entitled to care for the child, presumably on the basis that this should be a welfare-based decision with any dispute referred to the court.[513] Despite the emphasis in the Children Act 1989 on private ordering, the fact that two or more estranged parties have parental responsibility for the child is likely to increase the opportunities for dispute and litigation rather than resolve problems.

VI. Revocation of Parental Responsibility

The parental responsibility of mothers, married fathers and second parents is only **17–049** terminated by adoption,[514] but in all other cases the court may remove parental responsibility on application of a person with parental responsibility or, with leave, the child.[515] To enhance their security, there are further restrictions on the revocation of special guardianship; parents and guardians need leave to apply for revocation and cannot seek leave within a year of the order, and leave can only be granted if there has been a significant change of circumstances.[516] The court may also terminate guardianship and special guardianship of its own motion.[517] Parental responsibility is only brought to an end in extreme cases:

In *Re P (Terminating Parental Responsibility)*[518] the parents made a s.4 agreement after the baby had been removed by the local authority because of severe injuries. Subsequently, it became clear that the father had caused the injuries. The mother successfully applied for the agreement to be ended.

---

[511] The Law Commission gave the example of a non-residential father arranging to have the child's hair done in a way that would lead to the child's exclusion from the school selected by the mother: Law Com. No.172, para.2.11. Unless there is a detailed order, the court may be unwilling to hold that there is a breach.

[512] Children Act 1989 s.11(7)(b); *Re O (A Minor) (Contact: Imposition of Conditions)* [1995] 2 F.L.R. 124; *Re T (A Minor) (Care Order: Conditions)* [1994] 2 F.L.R. 423, where a condition was included that the father should not share a bed with the child. There are further powers relating to contact orders: ss.11A–11G, added by Children and Adoption Act 2006.

[513] The Law Commission thought that the onus should be on "the person wishing to challenge existing arrangements": Law Com. No.172, para.2.28. Bainham argues that this does not make sense and is predicated on an assumption that the non-residential parent should not resume care: see [1990] Fam. Law 192, 195.

[514] Adoption Act 1976 s.12(3); Adoption and Children Act 2002 s.46(2); for second parents, see Human Fertilisation and Embryology Bill, cll 48, 49.

[515] Children Act 1989 ss.4(3), 4A(3), 91(1), (2). A power to revoke was recommended by the Law Commission, which thought that the ability to remove the father's powers might make the courts less reluctant to grant orders: Law Com. No.157, para.3.3.

[516] Children Act 1989 s.14D(5), (6).

[517] Children Act 1989 ss.5(1), (2), 14D(2). A local authority with a care order could seek the removal of the child's guardian: DCSF, *Guidance* (2008), Vol.1 para.2.26, or the court could do this when making a care order in relation to the child.

[518] [1995] 1 F.L.R. 1048.

The father had forfeited responsibility[519]; a court would not have granted a s.4 order had it been aware of the facts, and to allow the father to retain parental responsibility could be unsettling for the mother and foster carers.

VII. Rights of Those Without Parental Responsibility

A. Delegation

17–050 A parent cannot transfer or surrender parental responsibility by private agreement,[520] but it is common for parents to arrange with others, such as child minders or teachers, for some parental responsibilities to be exercised by them. The Law Commission thought that such arrangements should be recognised in order to encourage separated parents to make agreements and to assist those who looked after children during parental absence. Such agreements should not be irrevocable; no court would uphold an agreement that was contrary to the child's welfare, and the onus of bringing a case to court should not be with the parents.[521] The Children Act 1989 enacted these proposals. People with parental responsibility may arrange for all or some of their responsibilities to be met by others, but such agreements do not affect liability for failure to discharge parental responsibility.[522]

B. De facto carers

17–051 The Law Commission also sought to clarify the position of those without parental responsibility who were actually caring for a child.[523] The Children Act 1989 s.3(5) now provides that any person with care of the child but without parental responsibility may "do what is reasonable in all the circumstances of the case for the purpose of safeguarding or promoting the child's welfare". What is reasonable will depend on the circumstances. Where parents have indicated the course of action they approve (e.g. a haircut, dental treatment or participation in an adventure holiday), there should be little difficulty; this is also the case where the child needs immediate (and non-controversial) treatment because of an accident. Problems are likely to arise where the parents oppose action that, objectively, could be seen to be in the child's interests (e.g. a child accommodated by the local authority remaining with foster parents).[524] Even if it is

---

[519] At 1053, *per* Singer J.
[520] Originally a common law rule; see now Children Act 1989 s.2(9).
[521] Law Com. No.172, paras 2.13, 2.14.
[522] Children Act 1989 s.2(9), (10), (11).
[523] Law Com. No.172, para.2.16. Such a person could be liable under the general law of crime or tort, but their powers were unclear: Bevan, *The Law Relating to Children* paras 9.48–9.55, 10.25.
[524] The Children Act 1989 removed the former requirement to give notice, and the Government resisted all attempts of reintroduction because this would undermine the voluntary nature of local authority accommodation. However, the Lord Chancellor asserted that s.3(5) could justify the refusal to hand over a child late at night or to an incapable parent, *per* Lord Mackay, Lord Chancellor, *Hansard*, HL, Vol.502, col.1337.

unlawful for the foster parent to refuse to hand over the child until the following morning, it is not clear that the parents would have any redress.[525] Also, it may be difficult for carers to convince a doctor that they have sufficient authority to consent to medical treatment that may be desirable but is not essential, such as vaccination. Those caring for children may have art.8 rights even if they have no formal relationship with them,[526] and therefore must be consulted in plans that any public authority makes in relation to the child.[527]

C. Unmarried fathers[528]

Where an unmarried father does not have parental responsibility, the law does not **17–052** treat him as a stranger to his child; he is a parent within the meaning of any post-1987 statute. Thus, he does not require leave to seek an order giving him parental responsibility or any s.8 order.[529] Where his child is looked after by the local authority, he has some rights to be involved. There is a qualified duty to ascertain every father's wishes and feelings.[530] If there are care proceedings, he must be notified unless the court directs otherwise,[531] and where his child is subject to a care order the authority must allow him reasonable contact.[532] However, his consent is not required for adoption arrangements,[533] and he has no statutory right to be a party to placement order proceedings unless he was a party to related care proceedings.[534] Nevertheless, the adoption agency must record the father's wishes and feelings about the adoption unless this is not reasonably practicable,[535] and courts have ruled that fathers who might be able to claim art.8 rights[536] in respect of their child should be notified of the adoption[537]:

> In *Re C (Adoption: Disclosure to Father)*[538] the mother had a long relationship with the father who was currently in prison for burglary and

[525] The foster parent might commit an offence under the Child Abduction Act 1984 s.2 but the parent has apparently no cause of action in damages: see *F v Wirral MBC* [1991] Fam. 69. A limited interference to protect a child would probably not breach the parents' art.8 rights.
[526] *K and T v Finland* [2001] 2 F.L.R. 707 at para.150 (a man who was the unmarried partner of the mother and father of her younger child was held to have art.8 rights also in relation to her older child).
[527] Children Act 1989 s.22(4)(d) can be interpreted to allow this.
[528] Second parents who are not the civil partner of the mother and have not acquired parental responsibility in any other way will be treated in the same way if the Human Fertilisation and Embryology Bill 2008 is enacted.
[529] Children Act 1989 s.10(4)(a).
[530] Children Act 1989 s.22(4)(b); see below, para.21–072.
[531] Family Procedure (Adoption) Rules 2005 (SI 2005/2795) r.23; *Re P (Care Proceedings: Father's Application to be Joined as a Party)* [2001] 1 F.L.R. 781, FD.
[532] Children Act 1989 s.34(1) unless there is a court order limiting his contact; see Ch.21, below.
[533] Adoption and Children Act 2002 s.52(6).
[534] *Re C (Adoption: Parties)* [1995] 2 F.L.R. 483, CA.
[535] Adoption Agencies Regulations 2005 (SI 2005/389), reg.14(4); DfES, *Adoption Guidance* (2005), paras 7.36–7.40 and Annex. B.
[536] This requires more than a genetic link: *Keegan v Ireland* (1994) 18 E.H.R.R. 342 and above, para.16–017.
[537] *Re R (Adoption: Father's Involvement)* [2001] 1 F.L.R. 302, CA; *Re M. (Adoption: Rights of Natural Father)* [2001] 1 F.L.R. 745, FD (notification not required); *Re H; Re G (Adoption: Consultation of Unmarried Fathers)* [2001] 1 F.L.R. 646, FD (notification for H but not G);
[538] [2006] 2 F.L.R. 589, FD. The father was ignorant of the child, but his long relationship and birth of other children meant that he had art.8 rights.

drugs offences. She placed the child for adoption without informing the father, and told the local authority not to do so. She was concerned that he and his family would put pressure on her to keep the child. The local authority sought a direction that it should inform the father. This was granted and the local authority was invited to seek wardship, apparently so that adoption could be pursued on the basis that the mother consented to it.

Where fathers could claim that they had rights to family life, only the most compelling reasons will justify not informing them about plans for their child's adoption.

CHAPTER EIGHTEEN

COURT PROCEEDINGS

I.   INTRODUCTION.............................. 18–001
II. COURT   PROCEEDINGS—THE
PRINCIPLES 18–003
    A. The welfare principle.................... 18–004
    B. The "no order" principle.............. 18–005
    C. The principle of no delay 18–006
III. THE FAMILY COURT SYSTEM....... 18–007
IV. WELFARE SERVICES FOR THE
COURTS 18–009
    A. CAFCASS 18–010
    B. Local authorities............................ 18–011
V.   FAMILY PROCEEDINGS.................. 18–013
    A. The meaning of "family proceed-
ings" 18–014
    B. Orders that can be made............... 18–015
    C. Restrictions on making orders....... 18–029
    D. Children in respect of whom orders
can be made 18–030
    E. Who may apply for orders?.......... 18–031
    F. Procedure—the Private Law Pro-
gramme.. 18–040

VI. THE COURT AS A WELFARE
AGENCY....................................... 18–044
    A. Mediation services 18–045
    B. Contact centres............................. 18–046
    C. Arrangements for children on
divorce.. 18–047
    D. Court ordered investigation 18–048
VII. WARDSHIP AND THE INHERENT
JURISDICTION OF THE HIGH COURT... 18–049
    A. The rise and fall of wardship 18–050
    B. Proceedings under the inherent
jurisdiction.. 18–051
    C. Powers   under   the   inherent
jurisdiction.. 18–052
    D. Procedure under wardship and the
inherent jurisdiction 18–054
VIII. ENFORCEMENT OF ORDERS......... 18–055
    A. Powers of the court....................... 18–056

I. INTRODUCTION

The Children Act 1989 brought together the three separate levels of court **18–001**
(magistrates' courts, county courts and the High Court), enabling each to make
all orders under the Act. A single court could now make both orders in public-
law cases, those involving local authorities exercising their responsibilities to
protect children, and in private law cases, where family members disputed the
upbringing of a child. Orders had the same effect irrespective of the court that
made them. Similar procedures operated at each level, but separate rules applied
to family proceedings (magistrates') courts.[1] In other areas of family law
(divorce and remedies for domestic abuse[2]), courts' powers remained distinct.

---

[1] Family Proceedings Rules 1991 (SI 1991/1247), as amended, for the High Court and County Court;
Family Proceedings Courts (Children Act 1989) Rules 1991 (SI 1991/1395), as amended, for the
family proceedings court.
[2] Family Law Act 1996 s.59.

The Children Act 1989 reformed the magistrates' court, giving the "family proceedings court"[3] jurisdiction over all civil matters concerning the upbringing of children,[4] with the exception of matters such as sterilisation, which could only be determined under the inherent jurisdiction of the High Court.[5] It also established a system whereby cases could be transferred between courts to make better use of court resources, so that higher courts dealt with more complex disputes, and to allow all proceedings concerning a child to be heard together.[6] The Act created four orders relating to children. These are: the residence order, which states where the child should live; the contact order, which requires a carer to allow someone to have contact with the child; the prohibited steps order, which restricts the exercise of parental responsibility; and the specific issue order, which determines how parental responsibility is to be exercised.[7] Together, these are known as s.8 orders. It also provides for any of these orders to be made in any family proceedings.[8] Orders may be made with or without an application,[9] but the court should not impose the responsibility for children on individuals who have not sought it.[10] The power to make these orders can be exercised in the family proceedings courts, county courts or the High Court, either alongside other matters, such as domestic violence injunctions or divorce proceedings, or alone. The High Court's inherent jurisdiction (which includes wardship) now has a residual role.[11]

Although judges (and magistrates) with family jurisdiction have wide powers to direct the provision of evidence, hear witnesses and make detailed orders, in practice, the culture of the family courts is to seek to avoid adjudication. Only a small minority of either public or private law cases have contested final hearings.[12] Most cases are resolved through mediation and negotiation, with advocates, CAFCASS officers and the judge assisting, encouraging or cajoling agreements. Agreements are used to narrow the issues for court resolution and to determine final orders. Outcomes agreed by the parties are considered to be more satisfactory because they are "owned" by the parties (whose co-operation is necessary to make them work).

18–002   In nearly two decade since the enactment of the Children Act 1989 there have been further changes. There had long been calls for the creation of a unified

---

[3] Children Act 1989 s.92.
[4] Children (Allocation of Proceedings) Order 1991 (SI 1991/1677).
[5] Re B (A Minor) (Sterilisation) [1988] A.C. 199.
[6] Children Act 1989 s.92 and Sch.11; Children (Allocation of Proceedings) Order 1991 (SI 1991/1677), as amended. For a list of courts with jurisdiction in Children Act cases see Hershman and McFarlane, Handbook, (Bristol: Family Law).
[7] Children Act 1989 s.8, see below, paras 18–016 et seq.
[8] Children Act 1989 s.8(3), (4); see below, para.18–014.
[9] Children Act 1989 s.10(1), (2). In approximately half the cases where residence orders are granted to relatives in care proceedings, the relatives are not parties to the proceedings and no formal application has been made.
[10] Re K (Care Order or Residence Order) [1995] 1 F.L.R. 675.
[11] See below, paras 18–049 et seq. Wardship has a number of advantages: Re W (Wardship: Discharge: Publicity) [1995] 2 F.L.R. 466, CA; J. Mitchell [2001] Fam. Law 130–134, 212–216.
[12] Masson et al., Care Profiling Study (MoJ Research Report 04/08, 2008); J. Hunt and A. Macleod, Making Orders for Contact between Children and Parents with Whom They Do Not Share a Household Research for MoJ (forthcoming, 2008).

Family Court,[13] with jurisdiction over all matters concerning children. The Children Act Scheme provided a solution to the major problems of three separate jurisdictions without the need to tackle the fundamental structural difficulties arising from the separate administration arrangements for magistrates' courts. The Auld Report[14] (2001), which recommended the creation of a unified Criminal Court and a single agency for the administration of justice, gave a new impetus for reform. The Government accepted its proposals; the Courts Act 2003 made the Lord Chancellor responsible for ensuring "an efficient and effective" court system.[15] Her Majesty's Court Service (HMCS) administers all the courts and is now developing uniform administration for family courts. The Act also established the Family Procedure Rules Committee to advise on procedures for family courts.[16] Further reforms[17] have provided formally for leadership of Family Justice. The President of the Family Division is the Head of Family Justice, with power to give directions about court practice for all courts.[18] These changes are effectively creating a family court.

Although the Civil Procedure Rules (CPR) do not generally apply to family proceedings, the principles behind them—court control and reducing delay—were entrenched in the procedure, introduced by the Act and subsequently.[19] The President of the Family Division introduced the *Private Law Programme*[20] with the aim of achieving early settlement in private law disputes.[21] In April 2008, the *Public Law Outline*[22] was introduced to streamline the procedure in care proceedings. The Family Procedure Rule Committee has been working to produce a single set of Rules, harmonised with the CPR, which will cover all types of proceedings at all levels of court and remove antiquated terminology.[23] In April 2001, the Children and Family Court Advisory and Support Service (CAFCASS) was established by bringing together the staff and responsibilities of the three agencies that provided welfare services for the courts. CAFCASS undertakes the mediation and reporting work in private law matters previously undertaken by the probation service; representation of children and reporting in public law cases, which was formerly the responsibility of local Guardian ad litem and Reporting Officer panels; and the children work of the Official

---

[13] See below, para.18–006.

[14] *Review of the Criminal Courts in England and Wales* (2001). The report made no recommendations relating to family justice, but the Government's White Paper, *Justice for All* (Cm.5563 (2002)) para.9.27 recognised that it provided a "good opportunity to link" magistrates' family work more closely with that in the higher courts, and recommended changes relating to procedure and practice that were introduced in the Courts Act 2003.

[15] Courts Act 2003 s.1.

[16] Courts Act 2003 ss.75–81.

[17] Constitutional Reform Act 2005 s.9.

[18] Constitutional Reform Act 2005 Sch.2 Pt 1 and para.9, amending Courts Act 2003 s.81.

[19] Civil Procedure Rules 1998 (SI 1998/3132); they apply subject to modification to committal applications arising out of family proceedings: *President's Direction* [2001] 1 F.L.R. 949; *Practice Direction (Case Management)* [1995] 1 F.L.R. 456.

[20] See below, para.18–040.

[21] In 2004. Available at *http://www.dca.gov.uk/family/plpguide.pdf* [Accessed June 4, 2008].

[22] See *http://www.justice.gov.uk/guidance/careproceedings.htm* [Accessed June 4, 2008]. The PLO replaces the Protocol introduced in 2003, which largely failed to secure stronger judicial case management and reduce delay.

[23] Family Procedure Rules Committee, *A New Procedural Code for Family Proceedings* (HMCS Consultation Paper CP 19/06).

Solicitor's Department.[24] The Family Justice Council[25] was established in 2004, following proposals from the Lord Chancellor's Department,[26] to facilitate better and quicker outcomes for families and children who use the Family Justice System by promoting co-ordination between agencies. It effectively replaced earlier bodies[27] that were more narrowly focused on the implementation of specific legislation.

Despite these changes, significant problems remain with the family court system. Cases, particularly public law proceedings, take too long to resolve. Public confidence in the system has been undermined by fathers' rights organisations, which have asserted that the courts and CAFCASS are biased.[28] The media has complained that restrictions on access and reporting mean that the family courts operate unaccountable "secret justice".[29] Low income limits for legal aid, the costs of professional representation and government policy of paying for the court service through higher court fees[30] are making the family courts unaffordable for many middle-income families. In 2005, the Constitutional Affairs Committee concluded that the court system was not best suited to deal with many of the complex matters relating to the break up of families.[31] However, those who cannot resolve their disputes in other ways or require court orders to secure arrangements have no alternative than to use the courts.

II. COURT PROCEEDINGS—THE PRINCIPLES

18–003 Three guiding principles, introduced to make the operation of the law consistent and intelligible[32] apply to proceedings under the Children Act 1989.

A. The welfare principle
18–004 This is discussed in detail in the following chapter.

B. The "no order" principle
18–005 The Law Commission took the view that orders were not always necessary and should only be used where they were the most effective way of helping the child, not just as "part of the package". Orders could polarise parent's roles and

---

[24] See below, para.18–010.

[25] See *http://www.family-justice-council.org.uk* [Accessed June 4, 2008].

[26] Lord Chancellor's Department, *Promoting Inter-agency Working in the Family Justice System* (2002).

[27] The Children Act Advisory Committee and the Family Law Board.

[28] See S. Sheldon and R. Collier, *Fathers' Rights Activism and Law Reform in Comparative Perspective* (2006).

[29] See below, para.18–008.

[30] HMCS, *Civil Court Fees* (Consultation Paper 05/07), para.16; Family Proceedings Fees Order 2008 (SI 2008/1054).

[31] Constitutional Affairs Committee, *4th Report 2004–5, Family Justice: The Operation of the Family Courts* (HC 116 (2004–5)), para.149.

[32] *An Introduction to the Children Act 1989* (1990), paras 3.1, 3.13.

alienate them; "joint custody" arrangements appeared to provide the maximum opportunity for maintaining the child's relationship with both parents and could be achieved without an order.[33] Removing the need for an order could encourage the parties to reach agreement and make it clear that where they do so, the court is not free to impose its view on them.[34] It would also reflect the belief that compulsory intervention by local authorities should not be used where services would be accepted voluntarily.[35] The Government was also concerned to reduce the number of applications concerning children after divorce because of the cost to the public purse.[36]

The Children Act 1989 provides that the court "shall not make the order or any of the orders unless it considers that doing so would be better for the child than making no order at all".[37] There are three[38] elements to this: (1) it is wrong in principle to make unnecessary orders[39]; (2) no order is necessary if the parties can reach agreement[40]; and (3) the court should begin with a preference for the least interventionist response.[41] Where the parents are not disputing the arrangements for children at divorce, the court will almost certainly take the view that it should not make orders.[42] Guidance states that it is likely to be better to make an order where the court has had to resolve a dispute.[43] In practice, there is a strong preference in the courts for settlement over adjudication, but agreements are frequently ratified in orders, if this is what the parties want.[44]

---

[33] Law Com. No.172, para.3.2; Law Com. WP 96, paras 4.35–4.43.

[34] Law Com. No.172, paras 3.3–3.4. Where there are "family proceedings", the court may make orders relating to children even though no applications have been made; Children Act 1989 s.10.

[35] This approach has now been formalised by the pro-proceedings requirements for care proceedings: DCSF, *The Children Act Guidance and Regulations, Vol 1, Court Orders* (2008), paras 3.22–3.33 and Annex 1; cf. DH, *Children Act Report 1992*, paras 2.20–2.21.

[36] See J. Eekelaar, *Regulating Divorce* (Oxford: Clarendon Press, 1991); public funding is only available for litigation in most private law children cases where the matter cannot be resolved either through mediation or negotiation: see Legal Services Commission, *The Funding Code Decision Making Guidance* (2007), para.20.33.

[37] Children Act 1989 s.1(5). This does not apply to applications under Sch.1: *K v H (Child Maintenance)* [1993] 2 F.L.R. 61.

[38] A fourth—the burden lies on the person seeking the order—was stressed by Munby J. in *Re X and Y (leave to remove from the jurisdiction: no order principle)* [2001] 2 F.L.R. 118 but was rejected by the Court of Appeal in *Re H (Children: Residence Order: Condition)* [2001] 2 F.L.R. 1277, CA.

[39] A. Bainham, "Changing families and changing concepts—reforming the language of family law" [1998] C.F.L.Q. 1, stresses that the "no order" principle is about no unnecessary orders, but it has been reconfigured by commentators (including himself) as the basis for a policy of non-intervention. Whether an order is necessary is not purely a matter of its legal effect: in *Royal Wolverhampton Hospitals NHS Trust v B* [2000] 1 F.L.R. 953 (following a breakdown of trust with her parents, the clarity of an order relating to treatment was in the child's best interests).

[40] But where an agreement has been achieved after difficult negotiations, it may be counter productive for this not to be ratified by the court: see Phillimore and Drane [1999] Fam. Law 40.

[41] This fits with the notion of proportionality in ECHR art.8(2): see *Re O (Supervision Order)* [2001] 1 F.L.R. 923, 929, *per* Hale L.J.

[42] G. Douglas et al., "Safeguarding children's welfare in non-contentious divorce: towards a new conception of legal process?" [2000] 63 M.L.R. 177.

[43] *Guidance* (2008), Vol.1, para.2.73. Cf. *Re C (A Minor) (Leave to Seek Section 8 Orders)* [1994] 1 F.L.R. 26. The specific effects of orders may be required; see below.

[44] *Re G (Children)* [2006] 1 F.L.R. 771, CA (order justified because it would give mother peace of mind); R. Bailey-Harris et al., "Settlement culture and the use of the 'no order' principle" [1999] C.F.L.Q. 53.

Where there is no order but both parents have parental responsibility, the effect nearly equates to that under a shared-residence order; each parent can exercise parental responsibility without further restriction.[45] In practice, because the parents are now living apart they will need to agree on arrangements. If they can do so, an order may be unnecessary,[46] but in many cases the confirmation of arrangements for public authorities responsible for housing[47] or Income Support, and the clarification of the parties' respective roles, may make an order desirable in the interests of the children.[48] Where the carer is not a parent, a residence order is required to confer parental responsibility.[49]

There is a degree of tension between the "no order" principle and the welfare principle[50]; focusing on s.1(5) may mean that insufficient attention is paid to children's interests. Interpreted as a principle of "non-intervention", it is used to avoid adjudication by coercing disputing parties to achieve settlement on the basis that agreements promote parental autonomy. This is quite different from what was originally intended,[51] and fails to recognise the positive effect the authority of the court can have.[52] It is generally accepted that most children adjust best when they maintain contact with both their parents, but the "no order" principle may not help achieve this. Orders may be ineffective or counter-productive,[53] but the court's refusal to ratify agreements with orders precludes enforcement and may delay the re-introduction of contact.[54] Initially, the number of orders declined because the courts no longer routinely made orders on parental divorce. Whether or not s.1(5) discouraged use of the courts, there has been a steady rise in applications to court in private law disputes about children.[55]

---

[45] Even where there is no residence order, one parent may not change the child's name unilaterally: *Re PC (Change of Surname)* [1997] 2 F.L.R. 730, 739 *per* Holman J. It is an offence under the Child Abduction Act 1984 s.1(1)–(3) for a parent to remove the child from the UK without the permission of the other. The fact that there is no order will affect the right to remove the child from local authority accommodation: s.20(8), (9); the right to consent to applications for residence and contact orders: s.10(5)(c); the effect of an appointment as guardian: s.5(7)–(9); the right to consent to marriage: Marriage Act 1949 s.3(1A)(b); and will preclude action for enforcement.

[46] There is no general duty on one parent to consult the other: Children Act 1989 s.2(7); S. Maidment [2001] Fam. Law 518; A. Bainham, "The privatisation of the public interest in children" (1990) 53 M.L.R. 206 at 208–214. Cf. *Re G (Parental Responsibility: Education)* [1994] 2 F.L.R. 964, CA.

[47] See *Holmes-Moorhouse v London Borough of Richmond* [2007] EWCA Civ 970, above, para.6–037.

[48] Law Com. No.172, para.3.2.

[49] *B v B (A Minor) (Residence Order)* [1992] 2 F.L.R. 327. Johnson J. was prepared to overturn the magistrates' decision to refuse the order because the Education Authorities had been unwilling to accept the grandmother's signature, and if medical treatment were necessary, the grandmother could not give consent. Additionally, he referred to the child's concern about the lack of stability and the mother's impulsive nature.

[50] A. Bainham, "Welfare & non-interventionism" [1990] Fam. Law 143, 145.

[51] Bailey-Harris et al., "Settlement culture"; A. Bainham, "Changing families and changing concepts" [1998] C.F.L.Q. 1.

[52] Drane and Phillimore [1999] Fam. Law 40. Some courts continue to make consent orders: see Bailey-Harris et al., "Settlement culture".

[53] In *M v M (Defined Contact Application)* [1998] 2 F.L.R. 244, FD, the court made an order of no order but recorded in it the parents' joint expectations about contact.

[54] In *S v E (A Minor) (Contact)* [1993] Fam. Law 406, the magistrates refused a contact order because the parties had reached agreement but the mother failed to comply. It was 20 months before the father's appeal against the no order was heard.

[55] *Judicial Statistics 2006*, Table 5.1.

C. The principle of no delay

The paramountcy of the child's welfare and the speed with which young children **18–006** develop attachments mean that delay can determine the outcome of the dispute to the detriment of one of the parties[56]; protracted proceedings mean uncertainty for the child and can delay or even preclude permanent placement.[57] It had long been argued that decision-making processes should take account of the child's sense of time.[58] The damage the uncertainty of litigation could do to children[59] and the existence of a legal culture where delay was acceptable[60] led the Law Commission to propose that legislation should include a duty to minimise delay. The law acknowledges that any delay is likely to prejudice the welfare of the child,[61] and art.6(1) of the ECHR protects the right to "a fair hearing within a reasonable time". Public authorities must exercise "exceptional diligence"[62] where delay may lead to the loss of family relationships. Solicitors who fail to take prompt action may be liable in negligence:

> In *LR v Witherspoon, Sanders and Bostridge*,[63] when her baby was removed from her and placed with foster carers, the mother instructed her solicitors to "do anything to get my son back". The solicitors did nothing for a year, during which time the local authority placed the child with prospective adopters. When the court heard the mother's applications for residence and contact, it dismissed them because the child had spent 14 months (half his life) with prospective adopters. The judge described the solicitors' inaction as a "tragedy", and the mother brought an action in negligence.

Both the Private law Programme and the Public Law Outline are intended to ensure that cases are heard "expeditiously".[64] Timetables must be set for proceedings and cases completed within a set timescale.[65] Legal representatives have a duty to ensure that cases are resolved with the minimum of delay,[66] but hearing a case where a party is unprepared may breach their art.6 rights.[67] Purposeful delay, for example to allow the completion of an assessment, is to be encouraged,[68] but where a care order is inevitable, the court should not defer

---

[56] See, for example, *Stockport MBC v B & L* [1986] 1 F.L.R. 80, where the local authority took two years to bring the case to court by which time the child was settled with foster carers; *Re C (Change of Surname)* [1998] 2 F.L.R. 656, CA, where the father was unable to obtain a specific issue order to change the child's name back to that on her birth registration because she was used to the new name.

[57] H. Ward et al., *Babies and Young Children in Care* (London: Jessica Kingsley, 2006).

[58] J. Goldstein et al., *Beyond the Best Interests of the Child* (1973), p.40.

[59] Law Com. No.172, paras 4.54–4.58; see also Booth Committee Report (New York: Free Press, 1985), para.4.133.

[60] M. Murch and L. Mills, *The Length of Care Proceedings* (Bristol University Centre for Socio-legal and Family Studies, 1987), para.3.3.6.

[61] Children Act 1989 s.1(2).

[62] *H v UK* (1987) 10 E.H.R.R. 95, para.85.

[63] [2000] 1 F.L.R. 82, CA.

[64] The overriding objective: *PLP*, para.a; *PLO*, para.2.1(1).

[65] Family Proceedings Rules 1991 (SI 1991/1247) rr.4.14(2)(a), 4.15(2); Children Act 1989 s.32 and *Practice Direction: PLO* (2008), paras 3.2 and 4.1(2) for proceedings under Pt IV of the Act.

[66] CAAC, *Handbook of Best Practice in Children Act Cases* (1997), p.22–23.

[67] *P, C and S v UK* [2002] 2 F.L.R 631 E.Ct.H.R.

[68] *C v Solihull MBC* [1993] 1 F.L.R. 290 at 304, *per* Ward J.

making its decision in order to supervise the local authority.[69] Many factors contribute to delay[70]: the lack of court resources, particularly for long hearings[71]; the arrangements for transferring cases to higher courts[72]; resource constraints that lead to delays by CAFCASS[73]; the desire for certainty and thus the reliance on expert evidence; and poor management of proceedings.[74] On average, public-law cases take 41 weeks to complete in the family proceedings court and 50 weeks in the county court; in the *Care Profiling Study*, the average duration in the quickest county court was almost half that in the slowest court.[75] Firm judicial control and case management are required; there needs to be sufficient time allocated for the hearing and realistic timetabling; clear instructions should be given to experts; and late requests for assessments should not be allowed to derail the timetable.[76]

Although it is accepted that there may be grave disadvantages for parents if a full care order is made while they are awaiting criminal proceedings on substantially the same facts,[77] the fact that there are criminal proceedings is not a reason to adjourn care proceedings. The court dealing with the care proceedings must consider the particular circumstances, recognise the danger of delay for the child and treat the child's welfare as paramount.[78]

III. THE FAMILY COURT SYSTEM

18–007 Despite a powerful and prolonged campaign to create a unified Family Court,[79] the Children Act 1989[80] only established a system of concurrent jurisdiction in

---

[69] *Re S (Care Order: Implementation of Case Plan)* [2002] 1 F.L.R. 815, HL. The local authority's care plan must be appropriately specific to be tested by the parties, *per* Lord Nicholls at para.99.
[70] Booth J., *Avoiding Delay in Children Act Cases* (LCD, 1996); LCD, *Scoping Study on Delay* (2002); DCA/ DfES, *Review of the Care Proceedings System in England and Wales* (2006), paras 3.10–3.15; Masson et al., *Care Profiling Study* (MoJ Research Series 4/08, 2008), Table A2.50.
[71] Particularly judges and court accommodation: CAAC, *Report 1992/3*, pp.51–53, 83.
[72] Children (Allocation of Proceedings) Order 1991 (SI 1991/1677), as amended. Family proceedings courts in some areas transfer most of their public law cases, leaving the county court unable to hear cases within a reasonable time: Masson et al., *Care Profiling Study*.
[73] Committee on the Lord Chancellor's Department, *Third Report of 2002–3, CAFCASS* (HC 614 (2002–3)), para.62; CAFCASS, *Annual Report 2006–7*, pp.30–31.
[74] Judicial Review Team, *Thematic Review of the Protocol for Judicial Case Management* (2005), para.41.
[75] Masson et al., *Care Profiling Study*, Table A2.39.
[76] *Practice Direction: Experts in Family Proceedings relating to Children* (2008), para.1.9 gives guidance on when permission to instruct an expert should be sought.
[77] *Re S (Care Order: Criminal Proceedings)* [1995] 1 F.L.R. 151 at 153, *per* Butler-Sloss L.J., CA.
[78] *Re TB (Care Proceedings: Criminal Trial)* [1995] 2 F.L.R. 801, CA; *R v Exeter Juvenile Court Ex p. H and H* [1988] 2 F.L.R. 214 at 222B, *per* Stephen Brown P.
[79] See *Finer Report*, Chs 13 and 14; B. Hoggett, "Family courts and family law reform—which should come first" (1986) 6 *Legal Studies* 1. Such courts were introduced in Australia and New Zealand in the 1970s. Apart from the question of resources, the lack of agreement about the form of a family court inhibited its development: see M. Murch, *Justice and Welfare in Divorce* (London: Sweet and Maxwell, 1980), p.235.
[80] The Lord Chancellor stated that he hoped his speech introducing the Children Bill "redeemed his pledge to make a statement about the Family Court" but also that the Bill was not a "substitute for the Family Court . . . or . . . laying foundations for it", *per* Lord Mackay, *Hansard*, HL Vol.502, cols 495 and 537–538 (Children Bill, Second Reading).

the existing resources of the family proceedings court,[81] county courts and the High Court. Comparable procedures operate for all Children Act proceedings.[82] The courts have similar powers.[83] Also, the creation of HMCS, changes to the criminal courts and unified administration have brought a form of family court closer.[84]

There is not only a specialist division of the High Court (the Family Division); all family courts are specialist courts. Those who preside over them have been specially selected[85] and given training in matters such as child development and social work practice to ensure that they have "a firm commitment to the ideals and philosophy" of the Act.[86] County courts are divided into five categories: (1) "designated county courts", which can hear divorce and civil partnership cases; (2) family hearing centres; (3) care centres; (4) adoption centres; and (5) international adoption centres. Care centres that are also adoption centres can hear all types of case concerning children, except international adoptions. Family hearing centres can only hear private child-law cases.[87]

A system of allocating and transferring cases between the three tiers of court was devised to make full use of existing resources rather than reflect the gravity of the issue. It was originally expected that about 75 per cent of public-law cases would be heard in the family proceedings court.[88] However, a lack of specialist legal advisers in magistrates' courts, the time taken there to make decisions and loss of confidence in magistrates, exacerbated by their lack of experience, means few magistrates' courts now hear many care applications.[89] By 2005 there was considerable pressure on both the High Court and the county courts; large numbers of private law applications were being made to county courts, and many public law applications were transferred up. Lack of court and judge time in these courts was a factor in delay.[90] New rules for the allocation of cases between courts have been drafted to ensure more cases are started in, or transferred down

---

[81] A part of the magistrates' court; Children Act 1989 s.92(1).

[82] Currently there are separate rules governing Children Act 1989 proceedings in the family proceedings court (Family Proceedings Courts (Children Act 1989) Rules 1991 (SI 1991/1395), as amended) and in the higher courts (Family Proceedings Rules 1991 (SI 1991/1247), as amended). From 2010, it is intended that a single set of rules will apply to all courts. For the current wording of the rules, see Hershman and McFarlane, *Handbook*, Pt II.

[83] The President of the Family Division has indicated that certain matters cannot be dealt with in the FPC: *Practice Direction* [2003] 1 F.L.R. 1299 (HIV testing of children); *Practice Direction* [2004] 1 F.L.R. 1188 (appointment of a r.9.5 guardian) or must be heard in the High Court: *Practice Direction* [2000] 2 F.L.R. 429 (proceedings seeking a declaration of incompatibility under the Human Rights Act 1998). Applications by children may now be made to the county court: Allocation and Transfer of Proceedings Order 2008 art.6.

[84] See above, para.1–001.

[85] Under the Courts and Legal Services Act 1990 s.9, as amended by the Constitutional Reform Act 2005 Sch.17 para.213, the President of the Family Division in consultation with the Lord Chancellor has power to "nominate" judges for public and private family proceedings; see also *Practice Direction: Family Proceedings (Allocation to judiciary) (Amendment)* (2002 and 2003). The excessive complexity of the ticketing system impedes both training and listing.

[86] CAAC, *Report 1991/2*, pp.110–111. Training is the responsibility of the Judicial Studies Board.

[87] (draft) Allocation and Transfer of Proceedings Order 2008 art.2.

[88] CAAC, *Report 1992/3*, p.46.

[89] Masson et al., *Case Profiling Study*. Proportions of care cases heard in the FPC vary widely.

[90] Late transfers in individual cases caused delay: J. Brophy, C. Wale and P. Bates, *Myths and Practices* (London: BAAF, 1999).

to, the family proceedings court.[91] The rules require most public law applications to be made to the family proceedings court but allow the applicant to apply to the county court in private law cases. Transfers up to the county court are allowed to accelerate proceedings or for other good reasons such as where there are difficult points of law or conflicts of evidence. County courts are required to consider transfer to the family proceedings court. Cases can only be started in the High Court if they are exceptionally complex or involve matters of public importance.[92] Where family proceedings courts are presided over by magistrates rather than district judges, parties and their advocates may continue to prefer the county court. Cases can be consolidated; a mother's application to discharge a care order and a father's for a parental responsibility order can be heard at the same time as the local authority's application to terminate contact. If the court refuses the transfer, the applicant may appeal.[93]

The family courts are expected to play an active part in the proceedings and not merely act as umpires between the parties.[94] Judicial case management involves judges controlling proceedings by setting timetables, directing (or refusing) the appointment of experts[95] and the filing of witness statements. The court should identify key issues, narrow issues and resolve outstanding issues in the most proportionate way.[96] The process must be fair within the ECHR art.6(1). Judges may make orders without any application from a party.[97]

18–008   Proceedings under the Children Act 1989 are said not to be adversarial,[98] but it is less clear what this means. Parties and their representatives are encouraged to co-operate[99] but often treat proceedings as a contest, regarding cases and even children as won or lost.[100] In most[101] public law proceedings the child is represented by a children's guardian, appointed by the court, whose duty it is to investigate the case, to advise the court about the available options and to safeguard the child's welfare in the proceedings.[102] In private law proceedings the court may appoint a children and family reporter from CAFCASS to

---

[91] DCA, *Focusing Judicial Resources Appropriately* (CP 10/05 (2005)), especially paras 1–7 and 24–27; (draft) Allocation and Transfer of Proceedings Order 2008, replacing Children (Allocation of Proceedings) Order 1991 (SI 1991/1677).

[92] (draft) Allocation and Transfer of Proceedings Order 2008 arts 5–8 and 13–19.

[93] SI 1991/1677 art.9; (draft) Allocation and Transfer of Proceedings Order 2008 arts 24–26.

[94] *An Introduction to the Children Act 1989* (1990), para.1.51.

[95] Family Proceedings Rules (SI 1991/1247) r.4.14(2)(f); *Practice Direction: Experts in Family Proceedings relating to Children* (2008).

[96] *Practice Direction: PLO* (2008), paras 14.1, 15.1, 15.4.

[97] Children Act 1989 s.10(1) even if no application could be made; *Gloucestershire CC v P* [1999] 2 F.L.R. 61, CA; but not without proceedings: *Re C (Contact: Jurisdiction)* [1995] 1 F.L.R. 777 (children had been freed for adoption).

[98] *Oxfordshire CC v M* [1994] 1 F.L.R. 175 at 184, *per* Sir Stephen Brown P.; similar statements were made about care proceedings even in the 1970s: *Humberside CC v DPR* [1977] 1 W.L.R. 1251 at 1255, *per* Lord Widgery C.J.; see also *Re L (Police Investigation: Privilege)* [1996] F.L.R. 731, HL at 738 and 743.

[99] *Practice Direction: PLO* (2008), para.19.

[100] See R. Ingleby, *Solicitors and Divorce* (Oxford: Clarendon Press, 1992), p.99 and B. Lindley, *Families in Court* (Family Rights Group, 1994). The practical effects of orders may make this inevitable.

[101] A children's guardian should be appointed in "specified proceedings": Children Act 1989 s.41(6), as extended by Family Proceedings Rules 1991 (SI 1991/1247) r.4.2(2).

[102] Family Proceedings Rules 1991 (SI 1991/1247) r.4.11; and see para.21–058, below.

investigate the circumstances and make recommendations.[103] In cases of "significant difficulty", the child can be joined as a party under r.9.5 and be represented by a guardian ad litem.[104] The court may order the disclosure of reports commissioned by a party,[105] call evidence,[106] obtain reports on any matter relevant to the welfare of the child[107] and make orders of its own motion, but in practice, it remains essentially dependent on the parties.

Most family courts sit in private; only the parties, their representatives and those giving evidence can attend. The fact that there is a presumption that proceedings will be held in private does not conflict with art.6(1).[108] Certain types of case—contested divorce, judicial separation and nullity—are heard in open court.[109] In other types of case (e.g. ancillary relief or proceedings about children), judges have discretion to admit the public but do so only very rarely. Family cases in the Court of Appeal are invariably public.[110] The press may attend hearings (except adoption) in the family proceedings court but do not normally have access to cases concerning children in other courts. However, there are strict reporting restrictions imposed through the law of contempt and criminal statutes limiting what can be reported[111]; as a consequence, the press almost never attend. Children involved in proceedings under the Children Act may not be identified,[112] and it is contempt to disclose documents from these proceedings, except within narrow limits to advisers.[113] Concern of Ministers[114] to have equivalent rules in all the courts hearing children cases, of the judiciary[115] to counter accusations of "secret courts", of the Select Committee for greater transparency[116] and a media campaign resulted in proposals to allow

[103] Children Act 1989 s.7; Family Proceedings Rules 1991 (SI 1991/1247) r.4.13.
[104] *Practice Direction* [2004] 1 F.L.R. 1188; *Re N (Residence: Appointment of a Solicitor: Placement with Extended Family)* [2001] 1 F.L.R. 1028, CA; *Re A (Contact: Separate Representation)* [2001] 1 F.L.R. 715, CA; Douglas et al., *Research into the Operation of r.9.5* (2006).
[105] *Oxfordshire CC v M* [1994] 1 F.L.R. 175; *Re L (Police Investigation: Privilege)* [1996] 1 F.L.R. 731, HL. The court may also compel discovery of documents from the police or local authorities: *Re A & B (No.2)* [1995] 1 F.L.R. 351, *per* Wall J.
[106] *Re A & B (Minors) (No.2)* [1995] 1 F.L.R. 351; *Re DH (A Minor) (Child Abuse)* [1994] 1 F.L.R. 679, this process enables all parties to cross-examine the witness.
[107] Children Act 1989 s.7(1); RSC O.40; *Re K (Contact: Psychiatric Report)* [1995] 2 F.L.R. 432.
[108] *B v UK; P v UK* [2001] 2 F.L.R. 26; nothing must be done in secret: *Re CB and JB (Care Proceedings: Guidelines)* [1998] 2 F.L.R. 211 at 224, *per* Wall J.
[109] Family Proceedings Rules 1991 (SI 1991/1247) r.2.28.
[110] Department of Constitutional Affairs, *Confidence and Confidentiality Consultation Paper* (2006), pp.15–16.
[111] The Administration of Justice Act 1960 s.12 makes it contempt of court to publish details of proceedings brought under the inherent jurisdiction or the Children Act 1989, but other material can be published unless an injunction has been made and notified to the media: *Re G (Celebrities: Publicity)* [1999] 1 F.L.R. 409. There is a statutory bar on the identification of children involved in proceedings: Children Act 1989 s.97(2). For further details, see Department of Constitutional Affairs, *Confidence and Confidentiality Consultation Paper* (2006), Annex B.
[112] Children Act 1989 s.97(2).
[113] Family Proceedings Rules 1991 (SI 1991/1247) r.10.20A, added by SI 2005/1976; DCA, *Disclosure of Information in Family Proceedings Involving Children Consultation Paper* (2004).
[114] Harriet Harman had a particular interest; Sarah Harman, her sister, had been severely criticised disclosing papers: *Re B (a child) (Disclosure)* [2004] 2 F.L.R. 142, FD.
[115] Wall L.J., June 29, 2006; see also *Clayton v Clayton* [2007] 1 F.L.R. 11, CA; *Webster v Norfolk CC* [2007] 1 F.L.R. 1146, FD.
[116] Constitutional Affairs Committee, *4th Report of Session 2004–5*, para.148; *6th Report 2005–6*, para.18.

wider reporting.[117] However, these were heavily criticised by the Family Justice Council, children's organisations and children who thought that family privacy would be compromised and did not believe that reporting would improve public understanding.[118] The Ministry of Justice responded by issuing a second consultation paper that proposed to improve transparency by allowing more information out of the court rather than letting reporters in. It has suggested that in all children's cases there should be a judgment or a summary with reasons, and that these should be available in an anonymised form on a public website. In addition, more information should be available about the operation of the family justice system and those who have been involved in proceedings as children should be able to access information about these when they are adults.[119] Such changes will entail substantial resources, which have not properly been considered. Nor is it clear if formalised statements of reasons such as those that are currently produced will improve public confidence.

IV. WELFARE SERVICES FOR THE COURTS

18–009 There are a number of reasons why courts dealing with disputes about the care of children need access to welfare services. The inquisitorial nature of the jurisdiction, and particularly the duty to give paramount consideration to the welfare of children, may require a wider understanding of family functioning and independent assessments of the child's needs or the carers' capacities that the parties have not provided and which the court cannot obtain in the course of the hearing. The emphasis in the *Private Law Programme* on agreeing arrangements and thus diverting applicants from court necessitates services to assist the parties to negotiate and reduce conflict.[120] Also, the emotional, economic and social problems that family breakdown produces mean that those using the family courts may need advice and counselling.

Nevertheless, until the establishment of CAFCASS (the Children and Family Court Advisory and Support Service) in April 2001, there was no single body dedicated to providing welfare services for the courts. In private law cases, reports, mediation and advice were provided by court welfare officers, employed by the Probation Service and jointly funded by local authorities and the Home Office. In public law cases and adoption, reports and representation were the responsibility of specialist childcare social workers who were members of local GALRO panels, funded by local authorities and the Department of Health.[121] Advice for the court and representation for children in complex, public- or

---

[117] DCA, *Confidence and Confidentiality Consultation Paper* (2006).
[118] DCA, *Confidence and Confidentiality Response to Consultation Paper* (2007).
[119] MoJ, *Confidence and Confidentiality, Openness in Family Courts—A New Approach* (2007).
[120] *President's Private Law Programme* (2004); L. Trinder et al., *Making Contact Happen or Making Contact Work* (DCA Research Report 03/06, 2006); *The Longer-term Outcomes of In Court Conciliation* (MoJ Research Report 17/07, 2007).
[121] For details see J. Masson, "Representation of children in England" [2000] F.L.Q. 467 and the seventh edition of this work at para.19.007.

private law cases in the High Court or county courts was provided by the Official Solicitor's office under the Direction of the Lord Chancellor's Department.[122]

A. CAFCASS

In 1997, a joint review by the three government departments concluded that **18–010** integrating services could improve provision and efficiency in welfare services for the courts. A consultation paper was issued[123]; the Advisory Board on Family Law welcomed the introduction of a unified service with a clear vision beyond the administrative "tidying-up" of existing services.[124] However, the extent to which practices would be aligned and staff would work in both public and private law remained unclear. Legislation[125] was introduced and a project team was established to prepare for the operation of the Children and Family Court Advisory and Support Service as a non-departmental public body accountable to the Lord Chancellor. Delays in the parliamentary process left too little time to complete the arrangements for CAFCASS. Consequently, many of the tasks essential to the smooth running of the new services had not been completed by April 2001. The organisation's tribulations have been only too public.[126] Criticism by the Select Committee led to the resignation of the Board and a long period of reorganisation. Responsibility for CAFCASS was transferred to the Department of Children, Schools and Families; its work is now subject to inspection by Ofsted. There are still concerns about the adequacy of CAFCASS resources, the timely appointment of officers[127] and the quality of decision-making, particularly relating to their recognition of the impact of domestic violence on mothers and children.[128]

The functions of CAFCASS include: to safeguard and promote the welfare of children in family proceedings; to give advice to the court about applications; to provide representation for children; and to provide information, advice and other support services for children and their families.[129] In private law cases, CAFCASS officers (known as family court advisers) operate mediation services which form part of the *Private Law Programme*.[130] They carry out risk assessments[131] prior to the first appointment to assist the court to decide whether

---

[122] Supreme Court Act 1981 s.90; for a more detailed account of the work of the Official Solicitor, see the sixth edition of this work, at pp.667–668.

[123] DH, HO, LCD and WO, *Support Services in Family Proceedings—Future Organisation of Court Welfare Services—Consultation Paper* (1998).

[124] Advisory Board on Family Law, *Second Annual Report* (1999), para.3.6 and Annex D; *Third Annual Report* (2000), para.3.31.

[125] Criminal Justice and Court Services Act 2000 ss.11–17 and Sch.2.

[126] Select Committee on the Lord Chancellor's Department, *CAFCASS, Third Report 2002–3* (HC 614). There was also litigation by self-employed guardians challenging their contracts: *R. on application of Nagalro v CAFCASS* [2002] 1 F.L.R. 255, QBD.

[127] CAFCASS, *Annual Report 2006–7* (2007), pp.5–7 and 30–31.

[128] HMICA, *Domestic Violence, Safety and Family Proceedings* (2005), para.3.54; Ofsted, *CAFCASS E. Midlands Report* (2008), p.11 and paras 27–30.

[129] Criminal Justice and Court Services Act 2000 s.12(1).

[130] An outline of the process is provided in the CAFCASS Private Law Pathway available at *http://www.cafcass.gov.uk/publications/reports_and_strategies.aspx* [Accessed June 4, 2008].

[131] Children Act 1989 s.16A, added by Children and Adoption Act 2006 s.7; *Practice Direction* [2007] 2 F.L.R. 625.

the case should be referred for mediation or a finding-of-fact hearing. Where mediation is appropriate, they meet the parties for about an hour and assist them to resolve their dispute.[132] Where hearings are required, CAFCASS may be ordered to provide reports,[133] but it is directing more of its resources to dispute resolution and preparing fewer and shorter reports than in the past. If the court orders the child's separate representation under r.9.5, CAFCASS generally provides the child's guardian ad litem.[134] Where the court makes a Family Assistance Order, CAFCASS provides that assistance.[135] It will have further responsibilities for contact activities and enforcement under the reforms introduced by the Children and Adoption Act 2006.[136] In addition, CAFCASS commissions mediation, child contact and counselling services from local agencies.[137] The Act enables CAFCASS officers to conduct litigation, but only lawyers from CAFCASS Legal do so.[138] CAFCASS Legal undertakes cases in the High Court,[139] provides advice for CAFCASS officers in private law cases and provides training. The role and function of CAFCASS officers as children's guardians is discussed in Ch.21.

B. Local authorities

18–011 Although CAFCASS undertakes the majority of work in family proceedings, the courts may request reports and seek assistance from local authorities.[140] They do this where there are child protection concerns or the local social services department is known to be working with the family.[141] Local authority social workers who provide court reports are termed "welfare officers".[142] This work forms only a small part of the work of local authority children's social care departments, whose functions are discussed in Ch.21.

---

[132] Trinder et al., *Making Contact Happen or Making Contact Work* (DCA Research Report 03/06, 2006). CAFCASS participated in over 26,000 such meetings in 2006–7 and achieved at least partial resolution in 60%: *Annual Report* (2007) pp.6 and 32.

[133] Children Act 1989 s.7. CAFCASS responded to 24,000 requests for reports in private law cases in 2006–7: *Annual Report* (2007), p.4. Reports are undertaken by a different officer from the one who assisted with mediation.

[134] Douglas et al., "Safeguarding children's welfare"; over 1,200 appointments were made in 2006–7: *Annual Report* (2007).

[135] Children Act 1989 s.16.; and below, para.18–027. CAFCASS worked with 350 FAOs in 2006–7.

[136] Children Act 1989 ss.11A(5), 11G(2),11H(2), commissioning or providing contact activity services and monitoring compliance with orders: see below, para.18–058.

[137] *Annual Report* (2007), p.20.

[138] Criminal Justice and Court Services Act 2000 s.15; this provision was controversial; guardians and solicitors were concerned that it would end the tandem system of representation, but this has not occurred; see para.21–057, below.

[139] *CAFCASS Practice Note* [2001] 2 F.L.R. 151. CAFCASS legally only accepts cases that are "exceptionally difficult, unusual or sensitive".

[140] Children Act 1989 ss.7, 16 and 37.

[141] CAAC, *Handbook* (1997), App.AI, para.10; Judicial Studies Board, *Family Law Benchbook* (JSB 2007), paras 7.15–7.16.

[142] Family Proceedings Rules 1991 (SI 1991/1247) r.4.13. The duties are similar to those imposed on children and family reporters under r.4.11B but there is no duty to inform the child of the content of the report.

Welfare reports

The court has complete discretion as to whether or not to call for a welfare **18–012** report.[143] Approximately one-fifth of cases referred for dispute resolution proceed to reports.[144] The judge should establish how long a report will take and weigh the benefits of further information against the detriment of delaying the decision.[145] The decision to appoint a welfare officer should not be grounds for an appeal,[146] but refusal to make an appointment might preclude a fair hearing.[147] In practice, extensive use is made of the power.[148] When making the appointment, the court may specify particular matters to be covered,[149] but this does not preclude the inclusion of other issues.

The s.7 reporter is "the eyes and ears of the judge"[150] and is required to inquire professionally and impartially into the circumstances.[151] Work should be properly planned, taking account of the welfare checklist, and be properly recorded.[152] Their role is to help the judge decide what is best for the child.[153] Children and family reporters and welfare officers have the power to inspect the court file,[154] and will usually interview the parties and contact relevant agencies such as the school.[155] No confidentiality should be promised to anyone who provides information.[156] Although children's welfare is the focus of the inquiry, it has not been universal practice to see children alone. CAFCASS now states that "children will always be seen", and provides detailed guidance on working with children.[157] The report should be focused, concise and contain clear recommendations.[158]

---

[143] Children Act 1989 s.7; *Re W (Welfare Reports)* [1995] 2 F.L.R. 142, CA. Reports should only exceptionally be ordered following a request from the parties: CAAC, *Handbook* (1997), App.AVI, para.3.

[144] CAFCASS, *Annual Report* (2007), p.33.

[145] JSB, *Benchbook* (2007), para.7.14; *Re H (Minors) (Welfare Reports)* [1990] 2 F.L.R. 172; *Re C (Section 8 Order: Court Welfare Officer)* [1995] 1 F.L.R. 617, CA. A period of 16–20 weeks is usual.

[146] *Re W (Welfare Reports)* [1995] 2 F.L.R. 142, CA.

[147] *Elsholz v Germany* [2000] 2 F.L.R. 486 (a decision to dismiss an application for contact without seeking a report or holding a hearing has been held to breach ECHR arts 6(1) and 8).

[148] See above, para.19–010.

[149] Family Proceedings Rules 1991 (SI 1991/1247) r.4.14(3)(g); *Practice Direction* [1981] 2 All E.R. 1056. The judge may not specify how the inquiry is to be conducted: *Re A* (1979) 10 Fam. Law 114, nor require the local authority to refer the child to a psychiatrist: *Re K (Contact: Psychiatric Report)* [1995] 2 F.L.R. 432, CA.

[150] M. Wilkinson, *Children & Divorce* (Oxford: Blackwell, 1981), p.26; CAAC, *Handbook* (1997) App.AI, para.9.

[151] CAFCASS received over 600 complaints relating to its private law work in 2006–7: *Annual Report* (2007); CAFCASS has been criticised for failing to provide guidance for officer's assessments and failing to assure the quality of the work done: Ofsted, *CAFCASS E. Midlands Report* (2008).

[152] CAFCASS, *Organising for Quality* (2006), Standards 3 and 5.

[153] *Re C (Section 8 Order: Court Welfare Officer)* [1995] 1 F.L.R. 617 at 619, *per* Hale J.

[154] Family Proceedings Rules 1991 (SI 1991/1247) r.4.23(1).

[155] CAFCASS has been criticised for failing to provide adequate information, including failing to see the child: HMICA *Domestic Violence* (2005), para.3.51.

[156] *Re G (Minors) (Welfare Report)* [1993] 2 F.L.R. 293. The welfare officer may not provide other information to the judge in confidence.

[157] CAFCASS, *Organising for Quality* (2006), Standard 5.1; CAFCASS, *My Needs, Wishes and Feelings: Guidance for Practitioners* (2007).

[158] CAFCASS, *Organising for Quality* (2006), p.47.

The report is confidential[159]; it must be served on the parties before the hearing[160] and can only be disclosed to others in accordance with the rules.[161] Reports inevitably contain some hearsay, and have been excluded because of this.[162] Further information about the report or the way it was prepared can be obtained by cross-examining the person who prepared it.[163] A properly prepared report is invaluable,[164] but the court is not bound by any recommendation contained in it[165]; the decision should be made by the judge, not the report writer.[166] However, if the court wishes to depart from a firm conclusion in a welfare report, they should hear evidence from its author[167] and reasons should be given if the report is not followed.[168] Failure to give reasons or to consider the evidence in the welfare report is a ground for appeal.[169]

V. FAMILY PROCEEDINGS

18–013   In family proceedings the court may make any s.8 orders[170] and exercise its other powers under the Children Act 1989, for example order a report or an investigation into the child's circumstances[171] or make a family-assistance order.[172]

A. The meaning of "family proceedings"

18–014   "Family proceedings" are defined as proceedings under the inherent jurisdiction of the High Court (except an application by a local authority for leave to bring such proceedings) and any proceeding under the following provisions:

---

[159] Family Proceedings Rules 1991 (SI 1991/1247) r.4.23(1).This should be explained to the parties by the district judge or magistrates' legal adviser: CAAC, *Handbook* (1997), App.AVI, para.5.

[160] Family Proceedings Rules 1991 (SI 1991/1247) rr.4.11B(2), 4.13(1). Failure to disclose such reports breaches ECHR arts 6(1) and 8: *Kosmopoulou v Greece* [2004] 1 F.L.R. 800, ECtHR.

[161] Family Proceedings Rules 1991 (SI 1991/1247) r.10.20A; it can be used in connection with an application for legal aid or shown to an expert appointed by the court.

[162] Children Act 1989 s.7(4)(b); Children (Admissibility of Hearsay Evidence) Order 1993 (SI 1993/621). "Where a judge has to arrive at crucial findings of fact he should found them upon sworn evidence rather than unsworn report" *per* Buckley L.J. in *Thompson v Thompson* [1986] 1 F.L.R. 212 at 217.

[163] *Re I and H (Contact)* [1998] 1 F.L.R. 876, CA. But officers need only attend court if so directed: Family Proceedings Rules (SI 1991/1247) rr.4.11B(3), 4.13(3).

[164] *Per* Ewbank J., *Re H (Conciliation: Welfare Reports)* [1986] 1 F.L.R. 476.

[165] *Dimino v Dimino* [1989] 2 All E.R. 280, CA (the judge should not notify the parties of the order he intends to make on the basis of the report before he has heard the evidence).

[166] *Mnguni v Mnguni* (1979) 1 F.L.R. 184; *S v S* (1978) 1 F.L.R. 143.

[167] *Re A (Children: 1959 UN Declaration)* [1998] 1 F.L.R. 354, CA; *Re C (Section 8 Order: Court Welfare Officer)* [1995] 1 F.L.R. 617, CA; *Re CB (Access: Attendance of Court Welfare Officer)* [1995] 1 F.L.R. 622, CA.

[168] *Re M (Residence)* [2005] 1 F.L.R. 656, CA; *Re W (Residence)* [1999] 2 F.L.R. 390, CA.

[169] *Re CB (Access: Attendance of Court Welfare Officers)* [1995] 1 F.L.R. 622, CA.

[170] See below, paras 18–016–18–022.

[171] Children Act 1989 ss.7, 37; see above, para.18–012 and below, para.18–048.

[172] Children Act 1989 s.16, see below, para.18–027.

"(a) Parts I, II and IV of [the Children Act 1989];

(b) the Matrimonial Causes Act 1973;

(ba) Schedule 5 of the Civil Partnership Act 2005;

(d) the Adoption and Children Act 2002;

(e) the Domestic Proceedings and Magistrates' Courts Act 1978;

(ea) Schedule 6 of the Civil Partnership Act;

(g) Part III of the Matrimonial and Family Proceedings Act 1984;

(h) the Family Law Act 199;.

(i) sections 11 and 12 of the Crime and Disorder Act 1998."[173]

In addition, the Human Fertilisation and Embryology Act 1990 provides that proceedings for a parental order are "family proceedings".[174]

So long as there are family proceedings before the court, it can grant any private law orders under the Children Act.[175] The inclusion of the inherent jurisdiction of the High Court has facilitated the decline in that jurisdiction, which now only needs to be used if the statutory powers are inadequate.[176] The inclusion of the Matrimonial Causes Act 1973 and the Civil Partnership Act 2004 widens the court's powers in respect of children in proceedings for divorce, dissolution, nullity or separation or for financial relief. The court may make such orders where financial relief is sought after an overseas divorce. However, the restrictions on the court's jurisdiction over maintenance for children under the child support regime[177] means that the court cannot resolve all matters. Where there are adoption proceedings, the court can make additional or alternative orders.[178] In cases of domestic violence, the family proceedings court, the county court and the High Court can make orders relating to children when considering applications for occupation or non-molestation orders. It may be essential to determine who will be caring for the children and what contact the parents should have. Similarly, where a court makes or enforces a child-safety order under the Crime and Disorder Act 1998, it may be necessary to clarify the child's residence. Whether or not there is an application, the court must be clear that it

---

[173] Crime and Disorder Act 1998 s.8(4).

[174] Human Fertilisation and Embryology Act 1990 s.30(8)(a).

[175] Children Act 1989 ss.10(1), 16(1). But an order in favour of someone, for example, a foster carer who was precluded from applying under s.9(3), would be exceptional: *Gloucestershire CC v P* [1999] 2 F.L.R. 61, CA.

[176] Law Com. No.72, para.4.35. For a discussion of the use of the inherent jurisdiction, see below, paras 18–049–18–054.

[177] Child Support Act 1991 s.8(3) and above, Ch.15. The court jurisdiction remains ousted under the Child Maintenance and Other Payments Act 2008.

[178] For example, a residence or special guardianship order could be made instead of an adoption order: *Re S (Adoption Order or Special Guardianship Order)* [2007] 1 F.L.R 819, CA; see below, para.22–064.

has the necessary information about the child; orders for children should not be made in favour of those unwilling to accept this responsibility.[179] Not all proceedings brought under the Children Act 1989 are "family proceedings"; applications to place children in secure accommodation[180] and orders under Pt V are excluded.[181]

B. Orders that can be made

18–015   The Law Commission's scheme sought to focus the court's attention on issues that needed resolution.[182] Parents should retain their parental responsibility and power to act independently unless this is incompatible with a court order.[183] Since most parental responsibility can be exercised only while a parent is caring for a child, the court's powers should be directed to allocating the child's time between the parents rather than setting out differently sized bundles of powers and responsibilities.[184] This could help to "lower the stakes" in disputed cases because neither parent would lose their status nor responsibilities[185] and might also encourage co-operation between separated parents. Orders should normally be cast in general terms to leave the parties maximum flexibility when circumstances change, but there should be power to attach conditions to end or prevent further difficulties.[186] The same orders (with largely the same effects) should be available in disputes between parents and between parents and third parties.[187] Also, key powers under the inherent jurisdiction should be included in the statutory scheme to avoid resorting to that jurisdiction.[188]

The Children Act 1989 enacted the substance of the Law Commission's proposals. A person with parental responsibility may not act incompatibly with a court order[189]; no general duty was imposed on parents to consult one another.[190] Nevertheless, the courts have held that there are a few important and exceptional decisions that cannot be taken without the agreement of the other

---

[179] *Re K (Care Order or Residence Order)* [1995] 1 F.L.R. 675.
[180] Facilities where disturbed children may be locked up: Children Act 1989 s.25; see below, para.21–077.
[181] i.e. child assessment orders: s.43; emergency protection orders; s.44; recovery orders; s.50. No consideration to the making of private law orders in emergency proceedings was given by the *Review of Child Care Law* (para.19.10). In most cases, emergency proceedings would not provide the court with a sufficient basis for making a s.8 order, but an interim order for residence could secure care by a relative or friend and avoid the need for public law proceedings.
[182] Law Com. No.172, paras 4.2–4.5, 4.8.
[183] Law Com. No.172, para.4.6.
[184] Law Com. No.172, para.4.8. The Booth Committee took a very different view; see *Report of the Matrimonial Causes Procedure Committee* (1985), para.2.27.
[185] Law Com. No.172, paras 4.5, 4.9.
[186] Law Com. No.172, para.4.10.
[187] Law Com. No.172 paras 4.24–4.28.
[188] Law Com. No.172 para.4.1; Law Com. WP 101, *Wards of Court* (1987), paras 4.6, 4.21–4.25.
[189] Children Act 1989 s.2(8).
[190] Children Act 1989 s.2(7); cf. *Re G (Parental Responsibility: Education)* [1994] 2 F.L.R. 964 at 967, *per* Glidewell L.J. where it was suggested that the non-residential parent should be consulted over major decisions. See also Maidment [2001] Fam. Law 518. There is a duty on local authorities to consult: s.22(4)(5) and below, para.21–067.

parent.[191] Requiring consent places the burden on the parent wishing to take the decision to obtain the agreement of the other parent or apply to the court. Where communication between them is good, this should not cause difficulties, but there are cases where locating the other parent or getting agreement would make it oppressive. Where consent is not required, the objecting parent must apply for the court for the action to be prevented or over-turned.[192]

In family proceedings, the courts may make four types of private law order: a residence order, a contact order, a prohibited steps order and a specific issue order.[193] These are known collectively as s.8 orders and are often described as the "menu" of orders. In addition, the court has power to make directions or interim orders, to impose conditions in orders, to allow change of name or removal from the jurisdiction and to make family assistance orders. The use,[194] effects of and limitations on these orders will be considered in turn.

i. Residence order

A residence order is an order "settling the arrangements to be made as to the person with whom the child is to live".[195] It does not connote possession nor exclude the other parent.[196] Where a residence order is made in favour of the father without parental responsibility, the court must also make a parental responsibility order under s.4.[197] Non-parents obtain parental responsibility by virtue of a residence order, but they have no power to consent to the child's placement for adoption or an adoption order, or appoint a guardian for the child.[198] The residence order automatically debars anyone from changing the child's surname or removing the child from the United Kingdom for a period of more than one month without the written consent of everyone with parental responsibility or the court.[199] In addition, no one may act incompatibly with the order,[200] but this does not preclude the deportation of an adult with a residence

18–016

---

[191] *Re J (Specific Issue Orders: Child's Religious Upbringing and Circumcision)* [2000] 1 F.L.R. 571, CA; *Re C (Change of Surname)* [1998] 2 F.L.R. 656, CA. Permission would have been required for the change of name if there had been a residence order; s.13. But *Guidance* (2008) Vol.1, para.2.31 says consultation is only required where expressly provided by statute.

[192] See prohibited steps orders, below, para.18–021.

[193] Children Act 1989 s.8(1). The "public law" orders listed in Pt IV require an application by a local authority (or the NSPCC) and proof of the grounds in s.31.

[194] Details of the use of s.8 orders are found in studies by Davis and Peace [1999] Fam. Law 22; Smart et al. (DCA Research Series 6/03) and a forthcoming study for the MoJ by Joan Hunt.

[195] Children Act 1989 s.8(1).

[196] *Re W (Minors) (Residence Order)* [1992] 2 F.L.R. 332, CA.

[197] Children Act 1989 s.12(1)(4). A comparable provision (subs.(1A)) will be added by the Human Fertilisation and Embryology Bill 2008 for female parents who would not otherwise have parental responsibility.

[198] Adoption and Children Act 2002 ss.19, 52; Children Act 1989 s.5(3), (4). A special guardian may appoint a guardian: s.5(1)(b).

[199] Children Act 1989 s.13(1)(2); see below, para.18–026.

[200] Children Act 1989 ss.2(8), 3(5). Action that is forbidden by the order would prima facie not be reasonable. The Law Commission suggested that if the order resulted in the child going to a school with a strict dress code, the other parent could not arrange for the child to have their hair done in a way that led to exclusion from the school (Law Com. No.172, para.2.11). But unless the order were specific, enforcement action for breach would be problematic; see below, para.18–056.

order in respect of a child who has a right to remain in the United Kingdom.[201] The appointment of a guardian[202] by a parent with a residence order takes effect immediately on the death of the parent unless the residence order was made jointly with the surviving parent.[203]

In its simplest form, a residence order need do no more than name the person with whom the child will live, but the phrase "settling the arrangements" gives the court considerable scope to impose detailed directions or conditions on parents, people with parental responsibility and carers but not on others.[204] For example, the limited right of the person with a residence order to remove the child from the United Kingdom may be unacceptable to the non-residential parent who fears that the child may not be returned, will be taken overseas without proper arrangements for vaccination or medical insurance, or that travel may disrupt schooling. Orders may also prohibit a move to another town,[205] a change of school, allowing the child to meet a friend of the residential parent,[206] or even sharing a bed with the child.[207] Broader injunctions may be granted under the inherent jurisdiction.[208] Conditions may also be included to ensure that a child receives necessary medical treatment despite the objection of the carer[209]; to allow a child's move to a new carer to be phased over a period[210]; or to require the parents to co-operate over their assessment.[211] Unenforceable conditions should not be imposed.[212]

A residence order may be made in favour of two or more persons, even though they do not live together or in the same country,[213] and in cases of high

---

[201] *R v Secretary of State for Home Department Ex p. T* [1995] 1 F.L.R. 293; *R. v Secretary of State for the Home Department Ex p. Isiko* [2001] 1 F.L.R. 930, CA. Similarly, the court will not allow wardship to be used to fetter or influence the decision of the Secretary of State: *Re F (A Minor) (Immigration: Wardship)* [1990] Fam. 125.

[202] See above, para.17–041.

[203] Children Act 1989 s.5(7)(b), (9).

[204] Children Act 1989 s.11(7); *Leeds CC v C* [1993] 1 F.L.R. 269.

[205] Restrictions on the place where the carer lived should only be included in exceptional cases: *Re E (Minors) (Residence Orders)* [1997] 2 F.L.R. 638, CA; *Re H (Children) (Residence Order: Condition)* [2001] 2 F.L.R. 1277, CA (the test for relocation within the UK is less strict than for emigration); *Re G (Contact)* [2007] 1 F.L.R. 1663, CA. The adverse effect of similar orders on mothers in California has been noted; see C. Bruch, "And how are the children? The effects of ideology and mediation on child custody law and children's well-being in the United States" (1988) 2 Int. J. Law & Fam. 106 at 113.

[206] Restrictions preventing a parent from allowing a child contact with a third party were sometimes included in access orders: *G v G* (1981) 1 Fam. Law 148 (transsexual not to be accompanied by his male friend); and see *Plant v Plant* (1982) 4 F.L.R. 305 and D. Bradley, "Homosexuality and child custody in English law" (1987) 1 Int. J. of Law & Fam. 155. Such conditions reflect prejudice rather than understanding of child welfare.

[207] *Re T (A Minor) (Care Order: Conditions)* [1994] 2 F.L.R. 423.

[208] *D v N (Contact Order: Conditions)* [1997] 2 F.L.R. 797. An order could also be made under the Family Law Act 1996 or the Protection from Harassment Act 1997.

[209] But in *Re S (A Minor) (Blood Transfusion: Adoption Order Condition)* [1994] 2 F.L.R. 416, the Court of Appeal upheld the adopters' appeal against the requirement that they give an undertaking because the need for transfusion was speculative.

[210] For example, to allow a relationship to be built up between the child and the carer. Phased return could be arranged through wardship: *Re E (SA) (A Minor) (Wardship)* [1984] 1 All E.R. 289.

[211] *C v Solihull MBC* [1993] 1 F.L.R. 290.

[212] *Re H (Residence Order: Placement Out of the Jurisdiction)* [2006] 1 F.L.R. 1140, FD (no condition about contact in placement with relatives overseas).

[213] *M v H* [2008] EWHC 324 (Fam) (extremely conflicted parents, mother residing in Germany, father in England, child to attend school in England).

conflict.[214] There is no requirement for equal division of time; indeed, that will rarely be in the child's interests.[215] Where it reflects the reality of the parents' involvement, a shared residence order should be granted:

> In *Re P (Shared Residence Order)*[216] the couple separated when the child was aged three, and established separate homes for her. The father wanted joint residence, but conceded an order in favour of the mother alone. For two years the child divided her time, by rota, between the parents, spending slightly more time in the mother's home. The father then applied again for increased time with the child and joint residence. The judge refused both these applications and the father appealed. The Court of Appeal granted an order for shared residence.

However, this order appears to have become more common than originally intended.[217] It may be agreed to placate the contact parent and made even though one parent is effectively the child's carer.[218] Some children are expected to move routinely between the homes of warring parents so that their time is split fairly between them.[219] The order may specify the periods spent in each household or may leave this to the parties.[220] Although good communication between separated parents is important,[221] there is no duty on parents to consult with each other, but neither parent may take action that is incompatible with the order.[222] Consequently, the order may need to be specific on points such as schooling, which are fundamental to the success of the arrangement. A residence order made in favour of both parents ceases to have effect if they live together for a continuous period of more than six months.[223]

Residence orders were originally available only in respect of children over the age of 16 years in exceptional circumstances, in recognition of capacity for

18–017

---

[214] *D v D (Shared Residence Order)* [2001] 1 F.L.R. 495, CA; *Guidance* (2008), Vol.1, para.2.34. Such orders should not be made if they confuse the children: *Re WB (Residence Order)* [1995] 2 F.L.R. 1023.

[215] See *A v A (Shared Residence)* [2004] 1 F.L.R. 1195, FD, *per* Wall J. at paras 113–126.

[216] [2006] 2 F.L.R. 347, CA; cf. *Re R (Residence: Shared Care: Children's Views)* [2006] 1 F.L.R. 491, CA, where the judge's decision was unsupportable, but further litigation was contrary to the children's interests.

[217] *Guidance*, (1991) Vol.1 para.2.28, which is not reiterated in the 2008 edition; see para.2.34.

[218] *Re F (Shared Residence Order)* [2003] 2 F.L.R. 397, CA; *Clayton v Clayton* [2007] 1 F.L.R. 11 (where the mother agreed shared residence after the father's abduction); *Re H (Shared Residence: Parental Responsibility)* [1995] 2 F.L.R. 883, CA (order gave man who was step-father to one of the children parental responsibility).

[219] This does not necessarily avoid pressure on the children, as the courts believe: see C. Smart, "Children's narratives of post-divorce family life: from individual experience to an ethical disposition?" (2006) *Sociological Review* 54, 155.

[220] Children Act 1989 s.11(4); *D v D (Shared Residence Order)* [2001] 1 F.L.R. 495, CA. But if the court needs to set detailed schedules, joint residence will mean a childhood of litigation.

[221] The Children Act 1989 supports parallel, rather than co-operative, parenting after separation: see B. Hoggett "Joint parenting systems: the English experiment" (1994) J.C.L. 8; C. Smart and B. Neale, *Family Fragments?* (Cambridge: Polity, 1999).

[222] Children Act 1989 s.2(7); see above, para.17–048 and A. Bainham et al., *Children and Their Families: Contact Rights and Welfare* (Oxford: Hart, 2003).

[223] Children Act 1989 s.11(5); *Re P (Abduction Declaration)* [1995] 1 F.L.R. 831. The unmarried father will retain parental responsibility; cohabitation has no effect on the s.4 order made by virtue of s.12(1).

independence of older children and court practice.[224] Concern for the position of carers who were not parents resulted in an amendment to allow them to request that the order be continued until the child is 18.[225] A further amendment (if enacted) will extend all residence orders to age 18 "unless the court directs otherwise".[226] However, the effect of such an order on a young person who does not wish to comply with its terms is unclear.

Residence orders are frequently sought by and granted to mothers with care in order to confirm their position.[227] Approximately a quarter of orders made in care proceedings are residence orders,[228] but this is likely to decline as the number of special guardianship orders increases.

ii. Contact order

18–018 A contact order requires:

> "The person with whom the child lives or is to live to allow the child to visit or stay with the person named in the order or for that person and the child otherwise to have contact with each other."[229]

It imposes a duty on the carer to allow contact, but does not oblige the person with the order to make any visits.[230] An order is necessary where a satisfactory agreement cannot be reached and the carer is restricting or preventing contact, or where the child's welfare demands the control or termination of contact. It is government policy to promote "safe" contact.[231] Although it stated in the Green Paper, *Parental Separation: Children's Needs and Parent's Responsibilities* that it did not intend to legislate, the Children and Adoption Act 2006 was passed, giving the courts further powers aimed at facilitating and enforcing contact. These will enable the courts to impose "contact activity directions" when considering contact applications, and similar conditions when making orders.[232] These may be used to inform and advise parents about how to achieve successful

[224] Children Act 1989 s.9(6); Law Com. No.172, para.3.25. For example, where the child has major disabilities: *Re M (Contact: Parental Responsibility)* [2001] 2 F.L.R. 342, FD, or the parents want a framework for their agreement: *A v A (Shared Residence)* [2004] 1 F.L.R. 1195, FD.
[225] Children Act 1989 s.12(5), (6) added by Adoption and Children Act 2002 s.114.
[226] Children and Young Persons Bill 2008 cl.37; EN, para.153. The wording of the Bill appears to apply to all cases, but the Explanatory Notes are written as if it only applies where the order is made in favour of a non-parent.
[227] C. Smart et al., *Resident and Contact Disputes in Court* (DCA Research Report 06/03, 2003).
[228] J. Masson et al., *Care Profiling Study* (MoJ Research Report 04/08, 2008), Table A2.42.
[229] Children Act 1989 s.8(1).
[230] J. Masson, "Thinking about contact—a social or a legal problem" [2000] C.F.L.Q. 15; consequently there can be no legal right in the child to maintain contact; see also *Re KD (A Minor) (Ward: Termination of Access)* [1988] A.C. 806, 825, *per* Lord Oliver, and Advisory Board on Family Law: Children Act Sub-Committee, *Making Contact Work Report* (2002), paras 14.53–14.56.
[231] DCA, *Parental Separation: Children's Needs and Parents' Responsibilities* (Cm.6273 (2004)) Foreword.
[232] Children Act 1989 ss.11A and 11C. Implementation is planned for late 2008; what will be available remains unclear.

contact. Such schemes have been used elsewhere, although there is little evidence that they avoid disputes or improve children's contact.[233]

The language of judges explaining contact decisions has shifted over time; contact has been claimed as a parental right but has also been described as a right of the child.[234] These issues are both sidestepped by addressing the order to the carer.[235] The Law Commission considered that contact was generally beneficial to children, and sought to encourage it.[236] They saw positive attitudes to contact as more important than legally enforceable rights, and discussed ways of achieving these,[237] proposing guidance as to what constitutes "reasonable contact", and emphasised the continuing responsibility of parents that could be exercised during visits.[238] The Act took the second point on board, but set no standards for contact in the area of private law.[239] There is no statutory presumption of contact and no duty on the carer to permit it[240] unless there is a court order; the courts have repeatedly stated that maintaining contact with the non-residential parent is almost always in a child's interests.[241]

Contact orders may permit "reasonable" contact or may define the duration, frequency, times and location of visits.[242] In an unusual case it may be appropriate for a third party (e.g. a local authority or a child psychiatrist) to have the power to determine when contact occurs.[243] Contact may be supervised[244] or

---

[233] J. Hunt, "Intervening in litigated contact: ideas from other jurisdictions", in M. Maclean (ed.), *Parenting after Partnering* (2007), p.193.

[234] *Re L; Re V; Re M and Re H (Contact: Domestic Violence)* [2000] 2 F.L.R. 334 at 360, *per* Thorpe L.J., and see *Re KD* [1988] A.C. 806 (parent's right), where the House of Lords held that court decisions about access must nevertheless be subject to the welfare principle: *M v M* [1973] 2 All E.R. 81, *per* Wrangham J. (right of the child).

[235] This fits better with provisions that impose no limit on the individuals who could be named in the order.

[236] Law Com. WP No.96, paras 4.27–4.34.

[237] Law Com. WP No.96, paras 4.33–4.34. The Law Commission apparently dismissed the possibility that a non-residential parent might be required to maintain contact as they are to provide financial support.

[238] Law Com. WP No.96, para.4.34. Unfortunately the Law Commission had no empirical evidence against which it could test its theory.

[239] cf. in relation to public law: Children Act 1989 s.34(1) and Sch.2 para.15(1) which require the local authority to permit reasonable contact and to endeavour to promote contact between the child and his/her family and friends. Reasonable contact is contact that is agreed between the parties, or contact "which is objectively reasonable", *per* Ewbank J. in *Re P (Minors) (Contact with Children in Care)* [1993] 2 F.L.R. 156 at 161C.

[240] Although it could be argued that parental responsibility must be exercised for the child's benefit, and thus contact that is beneficial must be allowed: see *Gillick v W Norfolk and Wisbech AHA* [1986] A.C. 112, *per* Lord Scarman at 184. The Family Law Act 1996 s.11(4)(c) included a "general principle" that regular contact was in the child's interests.

[241] *Re O (Contact: Imposition of Conditions)* [1995] 2 F.L.R. 124 at 128, *per* Sir Thomas Bingham M.R.; *Re L: Re V; Re M; Re H; (Contact: Domestic Violence)* [2000] 2 F.L.R. 334 at 365, *per* Thorpe L.J; C. Sturge and D. Glaser [2000] Fam. Law 615. This amounts to "judge-made presumption": R. Bailey-Harris et al., "From utility to rights? The presumption of contact in practice" (1999) 13 Int. J. Law, Pol. and Fam. 111 at 114. For a critical view, see Smart and Neale [1997] Fam. Law 332.

[242] Children Act 1989 ss.8(1), 11(7). Orders may be very detailed, including, for example, the content of messages in cards and the cost of gifts: *A v L (Contact)* [1998] 1 F.L.R. 361, FD.

[243] *Re O (Transracial Adoption: Contact)* [1995] 2 F.L.R. 597.

[244] Children Act 1989 s.11(7); *Practice Direction (Access: Supervised Access)* [1980] 1 W.L.R. 334. Such contact will usually be at a supervised contact centre unless there is a third party able to supervise. If no relative is prepared to take a child to visit a parent in prison, only indirect contact can be ordered: *A v L (Contact)* [1998] 1 F.L.R. 361, FD. Supervision by the local authority cannot be required unless there are child protection issues: *Leeds CC v C* [1993] 1 F.L.R. 269.

ordered to take place at a contact centre.[245] A family-assistance order may be made to help establish contact.[246] Where direct contact is not allowed, the courts have gone to extreme lengths to ensure indirect contact:

> In *re F (Indirect Contact)*[247] the father had a history of serious and uncontrollable violence to the mother but was said to be loving and affectionate to the child. The mother had obtained injunctions against the father, which he had breached on 68 occasions, and had moved 10 times with the child to escape the father. The President concluded that the mother would be seriously at risk if the father discovered her whereabouts, revoked the father's parental responsibility and refused direct contact. Nevertheless, after the father approached CAFCASS to act as an intermediary for direct contact, he agreed to indirect contact via CAFCASS legal. The mother's appeal on the basis that the arrangement was not safe and would unsettle the child was refused.

When ordering indirect contact, the court may include conditions requiring the parent with care to read and keep letters and encourage a reply.[248]

18–019   The courts have taken the view that contact with the non-residential parent is crucial for the child's well-being,[249] and should be permitted unless there are cogent reasons for refusing it,[250] such as the child's refusal[251] or the risk of serious harm to the child.[252] The fact that a child has no relationship with a parent is not a reason for denying contact,[253] nor is the carer's implacable opposition, unless contact would have such an affect as to undermine the stability of the

[245] See para.18–046; most contact centres only provide supported contact: Aris et al., *DCA Research Report 10/02.* Courts must ensure that the centre will accept the referral before making an order: Protocol [2001] Fam. Law 616.

[246] Children Act 1989 s.16, and see below, para.18–027.

[247] [2007] 1 F.L.R. 1015, CA; see also *Re A (Contact: Witness Protection Scheme)* [2006] 2 F.L.R. 551, FD.

[248] *Re O (Contact: Imposition of Conditions)* [1995] 2 F.L.R. 124, CA (the mother was permitted to censor unsuitable material); In *Re S (Violent Parent: Indirect Contact)* [2000] 1 F.L.R. 481, FD (contact for a six-year-old who was frightened of the father and a three-year-old by pre-arranged phone call to the father).

[249] *Re M (Contact: Long-term Best Interests)* [2006] 1 F.L.R. 627, CA; cf. the views of Goldstein, Freud and Solnit (1973), p.38, and note the comments thereon of M. Richards and M. Dyson, *Separation, Divorce & the Development of Children* (Cambridge Child Care and Development Group, 1982), p.64.

[250] *Re H (Contact Principles)* [1994] 2 F.L.R. 969, CA; *Re W (A Minor) (Contact)* [1994] 2 F.L.R. 441, CA; *Re CH (Contact: Parentage)* [1996] 1 F.L.R. 569, FD (contact order granted in favour of a legal father who was not the biological father).

[251] *Re M (Contact: Welfare Test)* [1995] 1 F.L.R. 274; *Re F (Contact: Child in Care)* [1995] 1 F.L.R. 510; *Re F (Minors) (Denial of Contact)* [1993] 2 F.L.R. 677, CA.

[252] See the views expressed by the welfare officer in *Re CB (Access: Attendance of Court Welfare Officer)* [1995] 1 F.L.R. 622; *Re T (A Minor) (Parental Responsibility: Contact)* [1993] 2 F.L.R. 450, where the father behaved with callous cruelty detaining the child for nine days after a two-hour contact visit; *Re C and V (Contact and Parental Responsibility)* [1998] 1 F.L.R. 392 (where the father was unable to manage the child's serious health condition); *M v M (Parental Responsibility)* [1999] 2 F.L.R. 737, FD (father suffering brain damage, unpredictable and violent behaviour).

[253] *Re M (Contact: Supervision)* [1998] 1 F.L.R. 727, CA, and see C. Sturge and D. Glaser [2000] Fam. Law 615.

child's home.[254] The courts have been prepared to allow some contact between a sexually abused child and the abuser.[255] A parent who makes malicious allegations of abuse against another risks their own contact with the child being seen as potentially damaging.[256] Orders for direct contact are not made if (older) children strongly object to seeing a parent or are disturbed by the experience.[257] The courts have been prepared to determine contact without deciding questions of paternity.[258] The courts do not link the granting of contact with willingness to pay child support,[259] or consider the effect on child support when determining the quantum of contact.[260]

Increasing concern has been expressed about the court's failure to take account of the impact violence against the parent with care could have on children. Violence often continues despite parental separation; there are risks to the physical safety and emotional wellbeing of both parent and child.[261] The Advisory Board on Family Law's Children Act Sub-Committee consulted on the need for legislation and prepared good practice guidelines[262] but did not support statutory restrictions on contact orders.[263] Shortly after the report was published, the Court of Appeal decided *Re L; Re V; Re M; Re H (Contact: Domestic Violence).*[264] It upheld decisions refusing direct contact to all four fathers who

---

[254] *Re D (A Minor) (Contact: Mother's Hostility)* [1993] 2 F.L.R. 1, CA, where a violent father who separated from the mother before the child's birth was refused contact; cogent evidence will be required for the "draconian order" of no contact: *Re F (Minors) (Contact Mother's Anxiety)* [1993] 2 F.L.R. 830, CA; *Re W (A Minor) (Contact)* [1994] 2 F.L.R. 441, CA.

[255] *L v L (Child Abuse: Access)* [1989] 2 F.L.R. 16, CA (supervised access); *R v D (Sexual Offences Prevention Order)* [2006] 1 F.L.R. 1085, CA (variation of SOPO so contact order could be granted).

[256] *Re M (Contact: Welfare Test)* [1995] 1 F.L.R. 274; *Re F (Minors Denial of Contact)* [1993] 2 F.L.R. 677.

[257] *Re M (Contact: Welfare Test)* [1995] 1 F.L.R. 274; *Re C (Contact: Moratorium: Change of Gender)* [2007] 1 F.L.R. 1642, CA (moratorium in the father's direct contact until children understood about his sex change); cf. *Re W (Contact: Parent's Delusional Beliefs)* [1999] 1 F.L.R. 1263, CA (contact cut from fortnightly to short visits, monthly pending rehearing because children aged 10 and 11 found it boring and disturbing).

[258] *K v M (Paternity: Contact)* [1996] 1 F.L.R. 312; *O v L (Blood Tests)* [1995] 2 F.L.R. 930, CA, but courts are now more willing to order paternity testing, above, para.17–007.

[259] cf. A. Kitch, "Conditioning child support payments on visitation access: a proposal" (1991) 5 Int. J. Law & Fam. 318. In practice there are links between finance and contact—parents who see their children are more likely to support them: see Maclean and Eekelaar, *The Parental Obligation* (1997), p.127 and the child-support regime links contact with the amount of support; see above, para.15–018.

[260] *Re B (Contact: Child Support)* [2007] 1 F.L.R. 1949, CA.

[261] M. Hester and L. Radford, *Domestic Violence and Child Contact in England and Denmark* (Bristol: Policy Press, 1996); A. Mullender and R. Morley, *Children Living with Domestic Violence* (London: Whiting and Birch, 1994); R. Bailey-Harris et al., "From utility to rights? The presumption of contact in practice" (1999) 13 Int. J. Law Pol. and Fam. 111; Smart and Neale [1997] Fam. Law 332.

[262] Advisory Board on Family Law: Children Act Sub-Committee, *Consultation Paper on Contact Between Children and Violent Parents* (1999); Advisory Board on Family Law: Children Act Sub-Committee, *A Report to the Lord Chancellor on the Question of Parental Contact in Cases of Domestic Violence* (2000).

[263] Under New Zealand legislation, the court is required to refuse contact unless it is satisfied that the child will be safe during contact: Guardianship Act 1968 s.5(4)(b). The Family Homes and Domestic Violence (Northern Ireland) Order 1997 requires consideration of safety but only where an injunction has been granted: see Advisory Board on Family Law: Children Act Sub-Committee, *Consultation Paper on Contact Between Children and Violent Parents* (1999), Apps 2 and 4.

[264] [2000] 2 F.L.R. 334.

had attacked the children's mothers. The court relied heavily on an expert report, commissioned by the Official Solicitor, which explored the benefits and risks of contact where there was family violence.[265] This tentatively suggested the onus of establishing the value of contact should be on the violent parent—a view rejected by the court.[266] Butler-Sloss P. accepted that the courts had not previously regarded domestic violence as relevant to children, and that allegations should be adjudicated. She alluded to many aspects of the Sub-Committee's guidance, but stressed that these cases, like all others, required individual assessment. There was no presumption against contact; the court had to balance the seriousness of violence and risks to the child against any positive factors in favour of contact.[267] Thorpe L.J. agreed and doubted the need for specific guidelines.[268] Both judges denied that earlier decisions were inconsistent with the court's approach, and warned of a pendulum swing against contact where there has been domestic violence.[269]

This decision does not appear to have changed the court's approach to contact in cases where there has been violence. Women's Aid identified cases where children had been killed during contact, and the President referred their report to Wall L.J. for further investigation.[270] His report found that the courts had generally not been aware of the risks of violence, noted that information might not be available where orders were made by consent and suggested that the Family Justice Council be asked to examine the matter. The Family Justice Council advised that where there is domestic violence, professionals should not take agreements about contact at face value. It concluded that the culture of promotion of contact meant that insufficient attention was given to safety issues, and recommended a practice direction enshrining the original guidelines and focusing on safety and the court's responsibility to make findings of fact.[271] Her Majesty's Inspectorate of Court's Administration also issued a report critical of the CAFCASS's approach to issues of domestic violence and of safety arrangements in some courts.[272] Despite substantial training for CAFCASS's officers and the judiciary, the pro-contact approach continues to dominate, including where the parent with care has been abused. Although it has been said that an applicant who has been violent may need to make genuine efforts to change and

[265] C. Sturge and D. Glaser, "Contact and domestic violence—the experts' court report" [2000] Fam. Law 615. The experts agreed with the view in the Sub-Committee's report that more consideration should be given to the impact of domestic violence on children; *Re L (Contact Domestic Violence)* [2000] 2 F.L.R. 334, 337–338. Both Butler-Sloss P. and Thorpe L.J. drew extensively on the report.

[266] [2000] Fam. Law 615, 623, at 341 and 370.

[267] At 336, 341–344.

[268] At 370. Guidelines have not been formally issued.

[269] At 342 and 370. Amendments to formalise the consideration of domestic violence in contact proceedings were tabled during the Adoption and Children Bill (NC 10) but did not receive government support: *Hansard*, HC, Vol.385 col.948 (May 16, 2002); Lords Grand Committee col. CWH 331.

[270] Women's Aid, *29 Child Homicides* (2004); Lord Justice Wall's *Report into 29 Child Homicides* (2006) available at *http://www.judiciary.gov.uk/publications_media/judicial_views_responses/ index.htm* [Accessed June 5, 2008].

[271] Family Justice Council, *Everybody's Business* (FJC, 2006); The President agreed to issue a Practice Direction, in May 2008.

[272] HMICA, *Domestic Violence, Safety and Family Proceedings* (2005); HMICA, *CAFCASS Concerning Private Law Front Line Practice* (2006), p.1.

demonstrate that they are a fit person to exercise contact,[273] practice in the family justice system frequently ignores or minimises abuse by those seeking contact.[274] It is expected that contact will be normalised so that direct contact replaces indirect contact, supervision is ended and children having staying contact, not just visits.

Father' rights groups have been highly critical of the courts, alleging that **18–020** applications for contact are considered unfairly. Their case is not backed by empirical evidence, which generally indicates low levels of refusal of contact, particularly considering the high proportion of cases that involve allegations of domestic violence or other risks to children (e.g. from parental drug abuse).[275] The judiciary reject claims of bias; reported cases have identified that father's behaviour frequently leads to the failure of contact through pressuring children, constant litigation or ignoring them.[276] Indeed, the courts persevere to achieve contact.[277]

A child who wants to see siblings against the wishes of the children's parent or carer can, with leave, apply for a s.8 contact order.[278] This is the case even if the child applicant is in care, unless it is the local authority that is restricting contact.[279] A contact order may be sought to require foster parents or residential home staff to allow visits to a child accommodated by the local authority but not one who is in care.[280] The order cannot be directed to the local authority, and thus a separate application is necessary for each placement where difficulties arise. Grandparents, relatives and friends seeking contact orders must first apply for leave.[281] There is no presumption in favour of contact by grandparents who have obtained leave.[282]

---

[273] *Re L; Re V; Re M; Re H (Contact: Domestic Violence)* [2000] 2 F.L.R. 334 at 342, *per* Butler-Sloss P.; *Re M (Contact: Violent Parent)* [1999] 2 F.L.R. 221 at 333, *per* Wall J.

[274] *Hammerton v Hammerton* [2007] 2 F.L.R. 1133, CA at paras 18–19. The father's application for contact was viewed as more urgent than the application to commit him for breach of injunctions. See also, *Re H (Contact: Domestic Violence)* [2006] 1 F.L.R. 943.

[275] R. Aris and C. Harrison (MoJ Research Report 17/07) (60%); L. Trinder et al., *A Profile of Applicants and Respondents in Child Contact Cases in Essex* (DCA Research Report 1/05, 2005) (high: a third of cases involved risk to children); Smart et al. (DCA Research Report 6/03, 2003) (25%) and J. Hunt and A. Macleod, *Making Orders for Contact Between Children and Parents With Whom They Do Not Share a Household* (forthcoming, 2008).

[276] *Re Bradford, Re O'Connell* [2007] 1 F.L.R. 530, CA; *Re O (Contact: Withdrawal of Application)* [2004] 1 F.L.R. 1258, Wall J.

[277] *Re M (Contact: Long-term Best Interests)* [2006] 1 F.L.R. 627, CA; *A v A (Shared Residence)* [2004] 1 F.L.R. 1195.

[278] Children Act 1989 s.10(9); *Re S (Contact: Application by Sibling)* [1998] 2 F.L.R. 897, FD. The application does not have to be made to the High Court: (draft) Allocation and Transfer of Proceedings Order (2008) art.6(a).

[279] *Re F (Contact: Child in Care)* [1995] 1 F.L.R. 510. Disputes with local authorities about contact to children in care are governed by Children Act 1989 s.34, see para.21–074, below.

[280] Children Act 1989 s.9(1); orders under s.34 are available in such cases; see para.21–074. Contact should not be ordered at the foster carer's home without their informed consent: CAAC, *Final Report* (1997), p.31. A s.8 order may be made requiring a parent to let a child in care have contact with siblings living at home: *Re F (Contact: Child in Care)* [1995] 1 F.L.R. 510, FD.

[281] Children Act 1989 s.10(9); these criteria are also apposite if the child is in care: *Re M (Contact Care Grandmother's Application)* [1995] 2 F.L.R. 86. In disputed cases, evidence should be heard: *Re F & R (s.8 Orders: Grandparent's Application)* [1995] 1 F.L.R. 524.

[282] *Re A (A Minor) (Section 8 Order: Grandparent's Application)* [1995] 2 F.L.R. 153, CA; but this view may need to be revised following the Human Rights Act 1998: *Re W (Contact Application:*

A contact order that requires one parent to allow the other to visit or otherwise have contact with the child ceases to have effect if the parents live together for a continuous period of at least six months.[283] All contact orders cease to have effect if an adoption agency is authorised to place the child for adoption, or if a placement order is made.[284]

Only approximately 10 per cent of parents use the courts to formalise contact arrangements,[285] and those who do tend to be less satisfied than the others. In contrast with the picture given by father's groups and from law reports, mothers tend to want children to have more contact, whilst fathers are generally satisfied.[286] Most applications to court are made by non-resident parents seeking to obtain or increase their contact. Most cases are not decided through adjudication but because the parties reach agreement; consent orders are made to confirm agreements.[287] These agreements are generally made into orders by consent. In Trinder's study, 40 per cent of parents who used the courts re-litigated within two years of a mediated agreement.[288] The *Judicial Statistics* for 2006 record over 38,000 contact applications and 66,000 contact orders.[289] In a study of legally aided contact cases, 14 per cent resulted in supervised contact and 6 per cent in indirect contact.[290]

iii. Prohibited steps order

18–021 This order prevents any person taking "a step which could be taken by a parent in meeting his parental responsibility for a child" without the consent of the court.[291] It is commonly used to prevent any removal of the child from the jurisdiction, and may also be used to restrict the child's contact with a third party, to prevent a parent publicising aspects of the child's life[292] or, exceptionally, to control location within England and Wales.[293] The order cannot be used to control matters that do not relate to parental responsibility such as contact between the parents or the occupation of the matrimonial home,[294] but may be made against any person, even if they are not a party to the proceedings.[295] The

Procedure) [2000] 1 F.L.R. 263, FD; see also F. Kanagas and C. Piper, "Grandparents' contact: rights v welfare revisited" (2001) 15 Int. J. Law, Pol. and Fam. 250.

[283] Children Act 1989 s.11(6). This does not apply where anyone else is named in the contact order.

[284] Adoption and Children Act 2002 ss.26(1), 29(2). Contact orders will be available under s.26.

[285] Cm.6273 (2004), Foreword.

[286] A. Blackwell and F. Dawe, *Non-resident Parent Contact* (ONS, 2003).

[287] R. Bailey-Harris et al. (1999); Hunt and Macleod (forthcoming 2008).

[288] L. Trinder and J. Kellett (MoJ Research Report 15/07).

[289] *Judicial Statistics 2006*, Tables 5.3 and 5.4.

[290] S. Maclean, *Legal Aid and the Family Justice System, Research Paper 2* (1998); there were 178 cases in the sample.

[291] Children Act 1989 s.8(1). Thus it will not be effective to stop a child from making a decision that he or she is mature enough to make; see *Gillick v W Norfolk & Wisbech AHA* [1986] A.C. 112. The order can be used to prevent a parent publicising the child's activities; *Re Z (A Minor) (Freedom of Publication)* [1996] 1 F.L.R. 191, CA.

[292] *Clayton v Clayton* [2007] 1 F.L.R. 11, CA.

[293] *B v B (Residence: Condition Limiting Geographical Area)* [2004] 2 F.L.R. 979; *Re H (Children) (Residence Order)* [2001] 2 F.L.R. 1277.

[294] *Croydon LBC v A (No.1)* [1992] Fam. 169; *Nottinghamshire CC v P* [1993] 2 F.L.R. 134.

[295] *Re H (Prohibited Steps Order)* [1995] 1 F.L.R. 638, CA.

Law Commission proposed this order to incorporate the most valuable features of wardship into the statutory scheme, and because it was sometimes necessary for the court to play a continuing role.[296] When a child is warded, "no important step" may be taken without the leave of the court[297]; a prohibited steps order is narrower—the issues to be referred to the court must be specified. Where there is a residence or contact order, the bar on name change[298] and the power to impose conditions may avoid the need for this order.[299] If no order is made initially, it will still be open for a parent or guardian[300] to seek one when a particular problem arises. Neither this order nor the specific issue order is intended to substitute for residence, contact, care or supervision orders.[301] The *Judicial Statistics* record more than 11,500 prohibited steps applications and 9,500 orders in 2006.[302]

iv. Specific issue order

This order gives directions "for the purpose of determining a specific question which has arisen, or may arise, in connection with any aspect of parental responsibility for a child".[303] For example, the court may consent to medical examination or treatment,[304] determine where a child is educated,[305] approve a change of the child's name,[306] authorise the interview of a child for legal proceedings[307] or require the child is told of the father's identity.[308] Previously, such matters were dealt with in wardship.[309] The orders are limited to aspects of

18–022

[296] Law Com. No.172, para.4.20.
[297] See para.18–049, below for an explanation of the wardship jurisdiction.
[298] Children Act 1989 s.13(1); where there is no residence order, a prohibited steps order can be used: *Re B (Change of Surname)* [1996] 1 F.L.R. 791, CA.
[299] Children Act 1989 s.11(7); *Re WB (Residence Orders)* [1995] 2 F.L.R. 1023. A prohibited steps order may be valuable to assist proceedings overseas even after a child has been removed: see *Re D (A Minor) (Child: Removal from the Jurisdiction)* [1992] 1 F.L.R. 637.
[300] Children Act 1989 s.10(4); other people (except those with a residence order) need leave of the court. An order can be made to underline the refusal of a specific issue order: *Re J (Specific Issue Orders: Muslim Upbringing)* [1999] 2 F.L.R. 678, FD (order barring father arranging child's circumcision).
[301] Law Com. No.172, paras 4.19–4.20; Children Act 1989 s.9(5)(a); *Nottinghamshire CC v P* [1993] 2 F.L.R. 134.
[302] *Judicial Statistics 2006*, Tables 5.3, 5.4.
[303] Children Act 1989 s.8(1). Where the order sought goes beyond parental responsibility, the inherent jurisdiction can be used: *Re W (A Minor) (Medical Treatment: Court's Jurisdiction)* [1993] Fam. 64.
[304] *Re R (A Minor) (Blood Transfusion)* [1993] 2 F.L.R. 757; *Re C (HIV Test)* [1999] 2 F.L.R. 1004, CA; *Re C (Welfare of Child: Immunisation)* [2004] 1054 FD, 1095 CA. The availability of a specific issue order would seem to preclude the use of the inherent jurisdiction by a local authority: s.100(4): cf. *Re O (A Minor) (Medical Treatment)* [1993] 2 F.L.R. 149.
[305] *Re A (Specific Issue Order: Parental Dispute)* [2001] 1 F.L.R. 121, CA; *M v M (Specific Issue: Choice of School)* [2007] 1 F.L.R. 251, FD (taking voice test for Cathedral School).
[306] *Re W, Re A, Re B (Change of Name)* [1999] 2 F.L.R. 930, CA; *Dawson v Wearmouth* [1999] 1 F.L.R. 1167, HL. Where there is a residence order, the application is made for permission under Children Act 1989 s.13(1).
[307] *Re F (Specific Issue: Child Interview)* [1995] 1 F.L.R. 819, CA.
[308] *Re F (Paternity: Jurisdiction)* [2008] 1 F.L.R. 225, CA; *Re C (Contact: Moratorium: Change of Gender)* [2007] 1 F.L.R. 1642, CA (the children were made parties and NYAS appointed so work could be undertaken to prepare them to be told that the father had changed gender).
[309] Law Com. No.172, para.4.18.

parental responsibility; a determination that a child is "in need" and thus able to seek services from a local authority cannot be made,[310] nor may this order be used to exclude parents from the family home.[311] The court, applying the welfare principle, may impose its own view or can refer the issue to an appropriate third party such as a doctor,[312] but it has been said that it should not refer the matter back to one of the parties.[313] In 2006 almost 8,000 orders were sought and 4,300 were made.[314]

v. Order of "no order"

18–023 This order records a finding that it is not appropriate to make an order, for example where the threshold conditions for a care order are satisfied but an order is not required for the child's protection. In private law proceedings, this order allows the court to disengage from the dispute[315] and leaves the matter in the hands of the parties (or one of them).[316] Such orders are uncommon.

vi. "Interim orders"

18–024 There is no longer any distinction between interim and final s.8 orders.[317] All orders may be subject to specific time limits[318] and can be varied at any time before the child reaches the age of 16.[319] Where it is necessary to make an order on limited information (e.g. to ensure that the carer has parental responsibility), the court can set a timetable for a full hearing and specify the further material that it wants by that date.[320] However, the courts are advised to be cautious when making orders without a full understanding of the facts[321]; where the principle of

---

[310] Children Act 1989 s.17; *Re J (Specific Issue Order: Leave to Apply)* [1995] 1 F.L.R. 669.

[311] *Pearson v Franklin* [1994] 1 F.L.R. 246, at least if the parent has rights of occupation. The court may be able to order a transfer of the property under Sch.1 para.1(2)(e)(i) and exclude the non-owning parent under the Family Law Act 1996 Pt IV.

[312] The effect of the order in *Re C (A Minor) (Wardship Medical Treatment)* [1989] 3 W.L.R. 240, CA was to permit the medical staff to determine the treatment the child should have; cf. *Orford v Orford* (1979) 1 F.L.R. 260, CA, *per* Orr J., leaving a decision about contact to a welfare officer was said to be "wrong in principle".

[313] *Re P (Parental Dispute: Judicial Determination)* [2003] 1 F.L.R. 286, CA. This would be the effect of making no order, which could be in the child's interest where one parent repeatedly seeks to litigate.

[314] *Judicial Statistics 2006*, Tables 5.3, 5.4.

[315] Before the Children Act 1989, courts did this by adjourning sine die (without fixing any date for a further hearing).

[316] *M v M (Defined Contact Application)* [1998] 2 F.L.R. 244, FD, where the parents' joint wishes were recorded but a defined contact order was not made; *Re H (Contact Order) (No.2)* [2002] 1 F.L.R. 22 (appropriate to leave contact decisions to mother).

[317] *S v S (Custody: Jurisdiction)* [1995] 1 F.L.R. 153. Under some previous law, interim orders could only last for three months; the Law Commission saw no value in such rigid limits: Law Com. No.172, para.4.24.

[318] Children Act 1989 s.11(7)(c).

[319] Children Act 1989 s.9(7). A variation after age 16 is only permitted in exceptional circumstances unless s.12(5) applies.

[320] Children Act 1989 s.11(1), (7)(d); Family Proceedings Rules 1991 (SI 1991/1247). Without notice, residence orders should only be made for the shortest possible time: *Re G (Minors) (Ex p. Interim Residence Order)* [1993] 1 F.L.R. 910, CA; *Re P (A Minor) (Ex p. Interim Residence Order)* [1993] 1 F.L.R. 915, CA.

[321] *Re D (Contact: Interim Order)* [1995] 1 F.L.R. 495.

contact is genuinely in dispute, interim contact may be ordered so the potential for contact can be assessed, but not to establish a pattern of visits.[322]

vii. Permission to change the child's name
This is considered in Ch.17, above.

18–025

viii. Permission to remove the child from the jurisdiction[323]
The question of the child's removal from the jurisdiction may arise in connection **18–026** with visits with a parent[324] or permanent emigration. The court's control over visits allows it to impose mechanisms such as the requirement for "mirror orders"[325] or bonds[326] to secure the child's return. This is particularly important if the visit is to a country that has not ratified the Hague Convention on Abduction.[327] Emigration cases raise more complex issues; the court must balance the benefits to the child of living with the parent with care in a place they want to live and often has family support, against the detriment of attenuating the relationship with the other parent and their family:

> In *Payne v Payne*[328] the mother applied for leave so that she could return to New Zealand with her four-year-old daughter. She was isolated and unhappy, and this could impact on her child. The move would reduce the father's contact, but he could afford to visit three times a year. The father, who had regular staying contact amounting to about two-fifths of each month, cross-applied for residence. The mother was given permission to relocate; the father appealed. The court was satisfied that the judge had applied the welfare test appropriately and refused the appeal.

The courts in England and Wales are more willing to approve relocation than some others.[329] There is no presumption in favour of the applicant parent, but the

---

[322] *Re M (Interim Contact: Domestic Violence)* [2000] 2 F.L.R. 377, CA.
[323] See, generally, The Society for Advanced Legal Studies Family Law Working Group, *Report on the Cross Border Movement of Children* (1999) and J. Gilliat, *Family Law Week* (2007).
[324] Unless a prohibited steps order has been made, a residential parent may take the child out of the jurisdiction without permission for up to one month: Children Act 1989 s.13(2). Where the residential parent needs permission, the court should consider the application thoroughly: *Re K (Removal from Jurisdiction: Practice)* [1999] 2 F.L.R. 1084, CA.
[325] See para.20–006.
[326] *Re L (Removal from the Jurisdiction: Holiday)* [2001] 1 F.L.R. 241, FD. Bonds may also be used to ensure that contact continues after emigration: *Re S (Removal from Jurisdiction)* [1999] 1 F.L.R. 850, FD.
[327] See Ch.20, below for an explanation of the effects of this Convention.
[328] [2001] 1 F.L.R. 1052, CA. The couple separated, the mother had returned to New Zealand without permission, and the father obtained an order for the child's return under the Hague Convention prior to the relocation proceedings.
[329] See Family Law Council, *Relocation* (Att. Gen., Australia, 2006), which reviews practice in other jurisdictions.

reasonable proposals of a residential parent who wishes to live abroad carry great weight.[330] The conditions in the new country,[331] viability of life in this country[332] and the arrangements that will be made if permission is refused are relevant.[333] Although permission to take a child abroad impinges on the right to family life, it has been stated that a decision which gives primacy to the child's welfare does not conflict with art.8.[334] According to Resolution, there are approximately 1,200 applications to remove annually.

ix. Family assistance order[335]

18–027 The court may order the short-term involvement of a social worker[336] to assist a family in resolving problems and conflicts that arise from parental separation by making a family assistance order.[337] An order may be made whether or not s.8 orders are made.[338] The order cannot be imposed on any adult party; everyone named in the order (except the child) must consent to it.[339] The persons who may be named are the child, the parents or guardians, anyone with whom the child is living and anyone in whose favour a contact order has been made.[340] Named persons are required to keep the appointed officer informed of relevant addresses and to permit visits.[341] The officer is required to advise, assist and befriend any

[330] *Payne v Payne* [2001] 1 F.L.R. 1052 at 1079, *per* Butler-Sloss P.
[331] *Re K (Application to Remove from the Jurisdiction)* [1998] 2 F.L.R. 1006, FD. Despite the difficult conditions in Nigeria, the court granted permission for the mother to take the children there. Both parents were from Nigeria and had family there.
[332] *Re J (Leave to Remove: Urgent Case)* [2006] 1 F.L.R. 2033, CA (father dependent on parents who had decided to emigrate to Bulgaria); *Re M (Leave to Remove from Jurisdiction)* [1999] 2 F.L.R. 334, FD (mother given conditional leave so that she could apply to emigrate to Canada; both parents were asylum seekers and neither had permission to remain in the UK).
[333] *Re C (Leave to Remove from the Jurisdiction)* [2000] 2 F.L.R. 457, CA (appeal against refusal by mother who accepted that she would stay and not join new husband refused); *Re H (A Child)* [2007] 2 F.L.R. 317, CA.
[334] *Payne v Payne* [2001] 1 F.L.R. 1052 at 1064, *per* Thorpe L.J., referring to *Johansen v Norway* (1996) 23 E.H.R.R. 33. In *Zawadka v Poland* [2005] 2 F.L.R. 897, the Minority stated that the mother's right to travel abroad was fundamental.
[335] HMICA, *Assisting Families by Order* (2007); L. Sturgeon-Adams and A. James [1999] Fam. Law 471; L. Trinder and N. Stone, "Family assistance orders: professional aspiration and party frustration" [1998] C.F.L.Q. 291; J. Sedden, "Family assistance orders and promoting welfare" (2001) 15 Int J. Law, Pol. and Fam. 226.
[336] Usually a CAFCASS officer, but a local authority social worker (with the LA's consent unless the child lives in the area: s.16(7)); *Re C (Family Assistance Order)* [1996] 1 F.L.R. 424, FD (no enforcement proceedings against local authority that fails to allocate).
[337] *Guidance* (2008), Vol.1, para.2.67.
[338] Children Act 1989 s.16(1). The Law Commission intended that orders should not be available where the child was in care, but this is not expressly provided by the Act: see Law Com. No.172, para.5.15.
[339] Children Act 1989 s.16(3). HMICA *Assisting Families* (2007) found that parents did not think they had consented, or did not know what they were consenting to. In *Re M (Contact: Family Assistance: McKenzie friend)* [1999] 1 F.L.R. 75, CA, the court encouraged the mother to consent by preventing further applications by the father for six months if she did so.
[340] Children Act 1989 s.16(2).
[341] Children Act 1989 s.16(4). The obligations of the named persons are thus much more limited than those of the "responsible person" for a supervised child: see Sch.3, Pts I and II, and Ch.21, below.

person named in the order,[342] and can be directed to facilitate contact and to report to the court on matters such as the variation or discharge of a s.8 order.[343] Work under this order needs to be clearly focused if problems are to be resolved.[344] The court should make plain why family assistance is needed and what is hoped to be achieved by it.[345] Concerns over child abuse or neglect should be referred to the local authority for investigation.[346] Family assistance orders are mainly used in relation to difficulties over contact.[347] They provide the only specific mechanism for the professional supervision of contact[348] (e.g. to require the local authority to provide an escort so a child could visit her mother in a psychiatric hospital where this is the only way to ensure contact ordered in the child's best interests).[349] The order is not intended to provide long-term support; it lasts for up to 12 months but further orders can be made.[350]

Although family assistance orders were considered to have considerable potential for helping families, they have been little used. CAFCASS only responded to 351 orders in 2006–7, fewer than in previous year, possibly because the courts make appointments under r.9.5 instead.[351] There are wide variations in use between areas.[352] The low level of orders reflects the limited resources CAFCASS commits and also reflects judicial uncertainty about their value.[353] Some positive work is achieved, but there is a lack of clarity about why orders are sought and made.[354] The Advisory Board on Family Law proposed ending local authority responsibility for these orders, that CAFCASS develop specific programmes and the requirement for consent should be abolished.[355] However, the Adoption and Children Act 2006 focused on the provision of contact activities and made limited changes to these orders, extending their maximum length and allowing the court to direct a report.[356]

---

[342] Children Act 1989 s.16(1).
[343] Children Act 1989 s.16(4A), (6).
[344] HMICA *Assisting Families* (2007).
[345] *Guidance* (2008), Vol.1, para.2.69. The order is most likely to be successful where the CAFCASS officer has indicated to the court how a FAO will help, following discussion with the parties: HMICA *Assisting Families* (2007).
[346] CAFCASS, *Safeguarding Framework* (2007), para.2.63. The local authority has a duty to investigate by virtue of s.47(1)(b); if the case were still being heard, the court could order investigation under s.37 and make an order under s.38.
[347] HMICA (2007); L. Trinder and N. Stone, "Family assistance orders"; J. Sedden, "Family assistance orders".
[348] Lord Chancellor's Department, *Making Contact Work: Consultation Paper* (2001), p.23.
[349] *Re E (Family Assistance Order)* [1999] 1 F.L.R. 512, FD (the child had previously been in care but was now cared for under a residence order; cf. *S v P (Contact Application)* [1997] 2 F.L.R. 277, FD (family assistance order refused to escort children to prison to see violent father).
[350] Children Act 1989 s.16(5); *Re L (Contact: Transsexual Applicant)* [1995] 2 F.L.R. 438; *Re E (Family Assistance Order)* [1999] 1 F.L.R. 512, FD.
[351] CAFCASS, *Annual Report* (2007), p.4. For a discussion of r.9.5 see para.16–020.
[352] HMICA (2007); Sturgeon-Adams and James [1999] Fam. Law 471; Trinder and Stone, p.302.
[353] Their shortcomings were described by Thorpe L.J as "manifest": *Re L; Re V; Re M; Re H (Contact: Domestic Violence)* [2000] 2 F.L.R. 334 at 367B.
[354] Sturgeon-Adams and James, p.473 (in some areas similar work was undertaken as part of preparing a court report instead of under a FAO); Sedden, p.236; Trinder and Stone, pp.295–297.
[355] Advisory Board on Family Law: Children Act Sub-Committee, *Making Contact Work Report* (2002), paras 11.9 *et seq.*
[356] Children and Adoption Act 2006 s.6.

x. Orders restricting further applications, s.91(14)

18–028 The court has the power to preclude a party to proceedings making any further applications relating to the child without first obtaining the leave of the court.[357] The Act imposes no limits on the use of the power, and restrictions do not necessarily breach the ECHR.[358] The judge must decide whether the best interests of the child require interference with the right of access to the court.[359] The power is a useful weapon to control those who have harassed a family through litigation[360] or seek to pursue a hopeless case,[361] and to provide further security for special guardians.[362] The order may also be imposed where the parent's fragility or the child's need for stability mean that further proceedings are contrary to the child's welfare.[363] This is a draconian order that should be used sparingly where unreasonable applications have been made or proceedings have imposed unacceptable strain on the child.[364] The degree of restriction must be proportionate,[365] but restrictions lasting the rest of childhood may exceptionally be justified:

> In *Re J (A Child) (Restrictions on Applications)*[366] the parents had disputed residence, contact and other matters relating to their severely autistic son from his birth with at least 10 hearings. The mother obtained residence but she could not cope, and eventually a care order was made and he was placed with his father. The mother was allowed contact, but no contact order was made. She immediately applied; an order was refused and she made a further application. After this was refused she applied for discharge of the care order, making it clear that she would never accept these arrangements.

[357] Children Act 1989 s.91(14). Only the making of an adoption order provides carers against greater protection from litigation: *Re AJ (Adoption Order or Special Guardianship)* [2007] 1 F.L.R. 507, CA, at para.47, *per* Wall L.J.

[358] *Graeme v UK* [2000] I. Fam. Law 188, an application declared inadmissible; *Re P (Section 91(14) Guidelines) (Residence and Religious Heritage)* [1999] 2 F.L.R. 573, CA, *per* Butler-Sloss L.J. at pp.952–953.

[359] *B v B (Residence Order: Restricting Applications)* [1997] 1 F.L.R. 139, CA, *per* Waite L.J. at 146F–147A; s.91(14) should be read in conjunction with s.1(1); see Butler-Sloss L.J. in *Re P* [1999] 2 F.L.R. 573 at 592. The power to declare a person a vexatious litigant is more restrictive: Supreme Court Act 1981 s.42.

[360] *Re C (Contact: No Order for Contact)* [2000] 2 F.L.R. 723, CA (two applications in five years, appeal against s.91(14) order allowed); *Re R (Residence: Contact: Restricting Applications)* [1998] 1 F.L.R. 749, CA (three unsuccessful applications for residence in three years, appeal against order dismissed).

[361] *Re Y (Child Orders: Restricting Applications)* [1994] 2 F.L.R. 699, FD; *Re B (Section 91(14) order: duration)* [2004] 1 F.L.R. 871, CA, perpetual order should not be made where father had not used litigation abusively.

[362] *S v B and Newport City Council* [2007] 1 F.L.R. 116, FD at para.26; such an order may be perpetual.

[363] *Re M (Adoption or Residence Order)* [1998] 1 F.L.R. 570; *Re P (Section 91(14) Guidelines) (Residence and Religious Heritage)* [1999] 2 F.L.R. 573, CA.

[364] *Re P (Section 91(14) Guidelines) (Residence and Religious Heritage)* [1999] 2 F.L.R. 573, CA, *per* Butler-Sloss L.J. at 952–953; *Re C (Contact: No Order for Contact)* [2000] 2 F.L.R. 723.

[365] *Re P (Section 91(14): Residence and Religious Heritage)* [1999] 2 F.L.R. 573, CA, *per* Butler-Sloss L.J. at 593; *Re B (Section 91(14) order: duration)* [2004] 1 F.L.R. 871, CA (two-year bar substituted for perpetual order).

[366] [2008] 1 F.L.R. 369, CA.

She was restricted from making any further applications without leave, a decision that was upheld by the Court of Appeal.

Further conditions, for instance showing that the applicant has been treated for psychological problems, cannot be imposed.[367] It may be difficult to decide when a litigant is acting so unreasonably that access to the court should be restricted.[368] Public funding may be withdrawn from those with weak cases and unreasonable litigants, but this may only remove the moderating influence of the solicitor.[369] Where the restriction applies, leave applications can be considered without notice[370]; the applicant must persuade the judge that he or she has an arguable case with some chance of success.[371] Leave will be granted if the applicant demonstrates a need for further judicial investigation.[372]

C. Restrictions on making orders

Although both the Law Commission and the *Review of Child Care Law* **18–029** recommended that the effects of residence and care orders should be comparable, they also accepted that the boundaries between public and private law and the different roles of the courts and local authority social care departments should be clearly defined. Local authorities should not be able to intervene in family life without satisfying the "significant harm" test.[373] Only a local authority's major decisions about a child in care, such as contact or discharge of a care order, should be subject to scrutiny by the courts.[374] Consequently, the power to make s.8 orders is restricted in the Act.[375] A local authority's decision to place a child with foster parents or in another county is not subject to court review.[376] Residence and contact orders may not be made in favour of a local authority; nor may prohibited steps or specific issue orders be made to have a comparable effect.[377] Thus, the court may not restrict a parent's right to remove a child who

---

[367] *Re S (Permission to seek Relief)* [2007] 1 F.L.R. 482, CA; *Stringer v Stringer* [2007] 1 F.L.R. 1532, CA.

[368] CAAC, *Final Report* (1997), p.72: "Children who are the subject of repeated applications are almost always detrimentally affected."

[369] See M. Maclean and J. Eekelaar, *Family Lawyers* (Oxford: Hart, 2000), pp.103, 109, 185.

[370] *Re S (Permission to Seek Relief)* [2007] 1 F.L.R. 482, CA; cf. *Re A (Application for Leave)* [1998] 1 F.L.R. 1.

[371] *Re P (Section 91(14) Guidelines) (Residence and Religious Heritage)* [1999] 2 F.L.R. 573, CA, *per* Butler-Sloss L.J. at 953H.

[372] *Re A (Application for Leave)* [1998] 1 F.L.R. 1, CA.

[373] Law Com. No.172, paras 5.2–5.8; *Review of Child Care Law*, Ch.15. For a detailed discussion of this issue, see Ch.21, below.

[374] Law Com. No.172, paras 4.51–4.52; *Review of Child Care Law*, paras 2.20–2.21. The ways of challenging local authority decisions are discussed in para.21–081, below. Decisions about contact with children in care can be made by the courts; s.34 not s.8: see para.21–074.

[375] Children Act 1989 s.9(1)–(3). But the court could exceptionally make a residence order in favour of a foster carer who was not entitled to apply for leave to make an application: *Gloucestershire CC v P* [1999] 2 F.L.R. 61, CA.

[376] But where there is a departure from the care plan that threatens a parent's or child's human rights, a challenge may be made under the Human Rights Act 1998 ss.7, 8: *Re M (Care: Challenging Decisions by Local Authority)* [2001] 2 F.L.R. 1300, FD, approved in *Re S (Minors) (Care Order: Implementation of Care Plan)* [2002] 1 F.L.R. 815, HL, para.62.

[377] Children Act 1989 s.9(5)(a). This could confuse rather than clarify the position as to parental responsibility: see Law Com. No.172, para.4.19.

is accommodated by the local authority,[378] require a parent to allow a child to have contact with a social worker or give the local authority a right to exercise parental responsibility unless the "significant harm" test[379] is satisfied and a care or supervision order is made[380]:

> In *Nottinghamshire CC v P*[381] the local authority did not wish to take financial responsibility for the treatment of the father (a sexual abuser) in a specialist clinic for abusers. Therefore it chose not to apply for care orders in respect of his children, but chose to seek a prohibited steps order requiring the father not to reside with his children nor to have contact with them. The Court of Appeal rejected the local authority's appeal against the refusal of prohibited steps order and criticised the local authority for failing to use its powers under Pt IV of the Children Act 1989.[382]

However, a prohibited steps order may be used to end the contact of a non-parent who does not live with the child.[383] A local authority could therefore seek a prohibited steps order to keep an undesirable person away from a child who is not in care. Only residence orders may be made in respect of a child in care, and the making of such an order has the effect of discharging the care order.[384]

D. Children in respect of whom orders can be made

18–030   The court's powers can be exercised over "any child" about whose welfare a question arises in family proceedings.[385] The child need not be a "child of the family",[386] but this definition remains important for determining whether an adult who is not a parent or guardian may seek an order without first obtaining leave.[387] The phrase "any child" is wider and may permit the court to make orders in respect of children who are not treated by the parties as a child of their family, including children fostered with them by a local authority. Statutory limitations apply to certain individuals making applications[388] in respect of

---

[378] Children Act 1989 s.9(5)(b), 20(7)–(9), 100(2)(a), (b), (d). *Re S and D (Children: Powers of the Court)* [1995] 2 F.L.R. 456, CA. The existence of a residence order restricts removal, but not by a person with sole residence: s.20(9), (10).

[379] Children Act 1989 ss.31(2), 33, 35.

[380] Children Act 1989 ss.9(5)(b), 100(2)(a), (d).

[381] [1993] 1 F.L.R. 513, FD; [1993] 2 F.L.R. 134, CA.

[382] The part concerned with care proceedings, see below, Ch.21.

[383] *Re H (Prohibited Steps Order)* [1995] 1 F.L.R. 638, CA.

[384] Children Act 1989 ss.9(1), 91(1). An order for contact between a child in care and siblings not in care is made in respect of the siblings so it does not conflict with this provision: *Re F (Contact Child in Care)* [1995] 1 F.L.R. 510, FD.

[385] Children Act 1989 s.10(1). But the Adoption and Children Act 2002 ss.26(2) and 29(3)(4) preclude the making of s.8 orders in respect of children subject to placement orders.

[386] Children Act 1989 s.105(1); see para.18–034, below.

[387] Children Act 1989 s.10(5)(a).

[388] Children Act 1989 s.10(1)(b). Certain people may only apply for an order after obtaining the leave of the court: s.10(2)(b), (8), (9).

accommodated children,[389] and it has been held that orders in favour of those who could not apply for them would be most exceptional.[390]

There is, generally, no jurisdiction to make s.8 orders in respect of children who are not either habitually resident[391] in England and Wales or present there and not habitually resident in any other part of the United Kingdom.[392] Jurisdiction is also excluded under Brussels II Revised where there are family proceedings pending elsewhere in the EC.[393] It follows that s.8 orders cannot be made in preparation for a child's visit for contact in this country.[394] Even when a child resident overseas is in England, the court may refuse to make an order on the basis that the courts in the child's home country should make any decisions.[395]

Section 8 orders may only be made in exceptional circumstances in respect of children over the age of 16.[396] Custody orders endured until a child reached 18, but the Law Commission was concerned about the practicality and justice of enforcing orders against older children, and thus recommended the change.[397] However, concern for carers who only have parental responsibility under a residence order and their rights to financial support have led to proposals that such orders should last until age 18.[398] Orders may be necessary in respect of over 16s with disabilities[399] and others who are immature,[400] particularly if they are cared for by people who would not otherwise have parental responsibility for them. Where orders are made in respect of older children, they should be made parties to the proceedings.[401]

---

[389] Children Act 1989 s.22(1)(b), (2) and see para.21–012, below. These are children who are not in public care due to the making of a care order. There are restrictions on making orders in favour of local authorities and in respect of children in care: s.9(1), (2).

[390] *Gloucestershire CC v P* [1999] 2 F.L.R. 61, CA at 73, *per* Butler-Sloss L.J. (order in favour of foster carers who could not apply because they had not looked after the child for sufficient length of time; see s.9(3)).

[391] For an explanation of this concept, see 21–014, below; cf. *Re L (Residence: Jurisdiction)* [2007] 1 F.L.R. 1686 (residual jurisdiction where child had been resident in England but the court would rarely exercise it).

[392] Family Law Act 1986 ss.1(1)(a), 2(1), 2A, 3. These restrictions do not apply to s.4 orders that can be made in relation to children overseas; *Re S (Parental Responsibility: Jurisdiction)* [1998] 2 F.L.R. 921, CA.

[393] Council Regulation (EC) 2201/2003; SI 2005/265 and para.20–022 below.

[394] "Mirror" orders may be made under the inherent jurisdiction to support orders of courts in the state of habitual residence: *Re P (A Child: Mirror Orders)* [2000] 1 F.L.R. 435, FD.

[395] *Re F (Residence Order: Jurisdiction)* [1995] 2 F.L.R. 518. This is in keeping with the spirit of the Hague Convention on Abduction; see below, Ch.20.

[396] Children Act 1989 s.9(6); *Re M (Contact: Parental Responsibility)* [2001] 2 F.L.R. 342 (a severely disabled 17-year-old woman).

[397] Children over the age of 16 may apparently live away from their family home without parental consent: Law Com. No.172, para.3.25: "The older the child becomes, the less just it is even to attempt to enforce against him an order to which he has never been a party."

[398] *Care Matters* (Cm.7137 (2004)), paras 2.44–2.47; Children and Young Persons Bill 2008 cl.37(1).

[399] Major issues such as the child's sterilisation would still need to be referred to the court: *Re B (A Minor) (Sterilisation)* [1988] A.C. 199, *per* Lord Templeman at 205–206: see *Practice Note* [2001] 2 F.L.R. 158. Most other medical decisions will be able to be made by those with the residence order; Children Act 1989 s.2(7), and above para.17–022.

[400] *Re SW (A Minor)* [1986] 1 F.L.R. 24 was cited by the Law Commission as a case where the jurisdiction was required. But the label of immaturity may merely be used to justify control.

[401] But this is not mandated by the rules: see Family Proceedings Rules 1991 (SI 1991/1247) r.4.7.

E. Who may apply for orders?

18–031 The Law Commission sought to create a logical scheme to protect the family from unwarranted interference and reduce recourse to the inherent jurisdiction of the High Court. It therefore developed a three-tier scheme that allows direct access to some applicants whilst requiring others to obtain the leave of the court.[402] The Children Act 1989 enacts this scheme, which is modified by the Adoption and Children Act 2002 and the Children and Young Person's Bill 2008.[403] These most recent changes increase children's security by allowing relatives and foster carers to apply as of right for s.8 orders after caring for a child for one year, not three years.

i. All applications without leave

18–032 There are four categories of person who may apply for any s.8 order as of right[404]:

(1) parents (including fathers who do not have parental responsibility);

(2) guardians and special guardians;

(3) stepparents who have obtained parental responsibility under s.4A; and

(4) those in whose favour there is a residence order.

ii. Contact and residence applications without leave

18–033 A wide range of people can seek residence or contact orders without leave.[405] These are:

(5) any party to a marriage or civil partnership (whether or not subsisting) in relation to whom the child is a child of the family[406];

(6) any person with whom the child has lived for a period of at least three years within the previous five years;

(7) a local authority foster carer or a relative who has cared for the child for at least one year immediately proceedings the application[407]; and

---

[402] Law Com. No.172, para.4.41. For a detailed exposition of the old law, see the fourth edition of this work at pp.363–364, 377–379, 386, 410–412.

[403] The Adoption and Children Act 2002 ss.26(2)(a), 29(3) restricts applications for s.8 orders whilst a placement order is in force, requires leave for all residence order applications when there is a special guardianship order, adding subs.(7A), and reduces the restrictions on applications by local authority foster carers, adding subs.(5A). The Children and Young Persons Bill 2008 cl.36, if enacted, will reduce the restrictions of applications by relatives, adding subs.(5B).

[404] Children Act 1989 s.10(4).

[405] Children Act 1989 s.10(5).

[406] Children Act 1989 ss.10(5)(a), 105(1), and see para.18–034, below.

[407] Children Act 1989 ss.10(5A), (5B), 105(1) for definition of relative. These provisions make the waiting time for residence applications the same as that for adoption.

(8) any person who has obtained the relevant[408] consents.

Where such applicants are seeking to care for or have contact with the child (but not orders to restrict other's exercise of parental responsibility), their close relationship with the child or support from those with parental responsibility means that leave would be a meaningless formality.[409] Orders may be varied or discharged on the application of:

(9) any person who applied for the order or who is named in a contact order.[410]

The Act only removed the automatic right of application from some grand-parents[411]; there is power to restore this by rules, but it has not been exercised.[412]

Meaning of "child of the family"
A child of the family is now defined in relation to parties to a marriage or civil **18–034** partnership as:

"(a) a child of both those parties;

(b)   any other child, not being a child who is placed with those parties as foster parents by a local authority or voluntary organization, who has been treated by both those parties as a child of their family."[413]

All children of both parties are included, but the Act goes much further, reflecting the reality of family relationships[414] and making the existence of a biological or formal legal relationship (such as adoption) between the carers and child irrelevant so long as the child has been "treated as a child of the family" by both

---

[408] The following consents are required: "(i) where a residence order is in force . . . each of the persons in whose favour the order was made; (ii) where the child is in care . . . the local authority; (iii) in any other case the consent of each person with parental responsibility". Children Act 1989 s.10(5)(c).

[409] Law Com. No.172, para.4.48.

[410] Children Act 1989 s.10(6).

[411] Only some grandparents had an automatic right to apply: G.M.A. 1971 s.14A; Domestic Proceedings and Magistrates Court Act 1978 s.14; Children Act 1975 s.34(1)(a). Considerable concern was expressed about the treatment of grandparents in the debates on the Children Bill: *Hansard*, HL Vol.503, col.1342 (Report Stage); *Hansard*, HC Vol.158, cols 1288–1306. See also F. Kaganas and C. Piper, "Grandparents and the limits of the law" (1990) 4 Int. J. Law & Fam. 27; G. Douglas and N. Lowe, "Grandparents and the legal process" [1990] J.S.W.L. 89 and F. Kaganas and C. Piper, "Grandparents and contact: 'rights v welfare' revisited" (2001) 15 Int. J. Law & Fam. 250.

[412] Children Act 1989 s.10(7).

[413] Children Act 1989 s.105(1).

[414] A child who is a child of the family should be recognised as having a right to respect for their family life with the carers under ECHR art.8 and vice versa: see *K and T v Finland* [2001] 2 F.L.R. 707 (step-father held to have right to family life with stepchild). Note that if the Human Fertilisation and Embryology Bill 2008 cll 42(1), 43–45 are enacted, the partner of a parent who consented to reproductive treatment for the parent will be a parent.

parties.[415] A child who is being looked after long term by relatives[416] is likely to fall within the definition, as is a child who is being privately fostered.[417]

Indeed, it may be practically impossible for a stepparent with whom a child lives[418] to avoid treating the child as a child of the family. The test of "treatment" is objective, and it is immaterial that the wife has deceived her husband about the child's paternity,[419] but an unborn child cannot be treated by the husband as a member of his family.[420]

iii. Applications only with leave

18–035 All other applicants, including parents whose children are subject to placement or adoption orders,[421] require leave. Applications for leave can be considered without notice but only refused following a hearing.[422] The "welfare test" does not apply; instead the court must consider the criteria in the Act[423] and the likelihood of success of the substantive application.[424]

Restriction of access to the courts will not breach the ECHR art.6(1) unless the applicant can show that their civil rights (e.g. their right to family life) are at issue. Whether a relationship with a child amounts to "family life" is a question of fact,[425] and the state may impose a requirement of leave in order to pursue a legitimate aim such as family privacy.[426] Refusal of leave in accordance with the

---

[415] *W (RJ) v W (SJ)* [1972] Fam. 152. There must have been a family: *Re M (A Minor)* [1980] 2 F.L.R. 184, CA (child born after couple separated, not a child of the family even though husband visited and signed cards "Dad"); *Teeling v Teeling* [1984] F.L.R. 808, CA.

[416] *Re A (Child of the Family)* [1998] 1 F.L.R. 347, CA. A child whose grandparents had taken over her care and refused to allow the mother to reclaim her was a child of their family. Temporary helping out by relatives may not be sufficient, *per* Butler-Sloss L.J.

[417] Children placed by a local authority or voluntary organisation are specifically outside the definition, but only while the fostering arrangement lasts: see Law Com. No.172, para.4.46.

[418] See *D v D (Child of the Family)* (1980) 2 F.L.R. 93, *per* Templeman L.J. at 98. Unless, of course, the parties separate all responsibility for the child. Where the child merely has staying visits, he may not become a child of that family, *per* Orr L.J. at 96.

[419] *W (RJ) v W (SJ)* [1972] Fam. 152, although this would be relevant to the quantification of maintenance (see Matrimonial Causes Act 1973 s.25(3)) and might give rise to an action for deceit: *P v B (Paternity: Damages for Deceit)* [2001] 1 F.L.R. 1041.

[420] *A v A (Family: Unborn Child)* [1974] Fam. 6, approved in *W v W (Child of the Family)* [1984] F.L.R. 796 at 802, *per* Sheldon J.

[421] Adoption and Children Act 1989 ss.29, 46.

[422] Family Proceedings Act 1991 (SI 1991/1247) r.4.3; *Re S (Permission to seek Relief)* [2007] 1 F.L.R. 482, CA, *per* Wall L.J at para.95. All persons with parental responsibility should be notified of an application by the child concerned: see *Re SC (A Minor) (Leave to Seek Residence Order)* [1994] 1 F.L.R. 96. Where the applicant is a parent seeking contact with an adopted child, the Official Solicitor and the adoption agency should be notified: see *Re C (A Minor) (Adopted Child Contact)* [1993] 2 F.L.R. 431; cf. *Re T (Adopted Children: Contact)* [1995] 2 F.L.R. 792, CA.

[423] Children Act 1989 ss.10(8), (9); *Re J (Leave to Issue Application for a Residence Order)* [2003] 1 F.L.R. 114, CA. and below.

[424] *Re A and W (Minors) (Residence Order: Leave to Apply)* [1992] Fam. 182, CA; *Re J (Specific Issue Order: Leave to Apply)* [1995] 1 F.L.R. 669; cf. *Re C (A Minor) (Leave to Seek Section 8 Order)* [1994] 1 F.L.R. 26.

[425] Swindells et al., p.44 citing *X, Y and Z v UK* [1997] 2 F.L.R. 892; in *K and T v Finland* [2001] 2 F.L.R. 707, para.150 the court drew no distinction between the mother and the step-father because they jointly enjoyed "family life" with the children.

[426] See *Ashingdane v UK* (1985) 7 E.H.R.R. 528 at para.57; the restriction must be proportionate; a fair balance must be struck between the interests of parents and children: *C v Finland* [2006] 2 F.L.R. 597 at para.54.

Act may be a proportionate response even where the applicant has family life with the child (e.g. where further litigation would disrupt other relationships or harm the child).

Applicants who require leave can be divided into five categories:

(1) local authority foster parents and former foster parents;

(2) relatives with care of the child;

(3) children concerned in the proceedings;

(4) other persons with no right to apply; and

(5) persons on whom a leave requirement has been imposed under s.91(14).[427]

The need to seek leave can be avoided by an application to ward the child except where the child is being looked after by a local authority.[428]

(1) Criteria for leave—Local authority foster parents

Unless they are the child's relatives, local authority foster parents and those who **18–036** have fostered a child within the last six months require the permission of the authority before they may apply for leave for a s.8 order.[429] The Law Commission considered that such people should be in a special category to avoid undermining parents' confidence in the provision of accommodation[430] by local authorities. Parents should be no more "at risk of losing their children" than they would by making a private arrangement, and local authorities should feel confident of their responsibility to make plans for all the children they look after.[431] Originally, leave was required unless the foster carers had looked after the child for three years, but they could apply to adopt after one and so the period was reduced.[432] As a consequence, the protection of parents and local authority plans is much reduced:

> In *C v Salford City Council*[433] Jewish parents requested adoption for their child who suffered from Down's Syndrome. The child was placed with non-

---

[427] See above, para.18–028.

[428] *A v Liverpool CC* [1982] A.C. 363. In *C v Salford* [1994] 2 F.L.R. 926, Hale J. said (obiter) it would have been "a very bold decision" to permit an application in wardship where leave was refused.

[429] Children Act 1989 s.9(3). The local authority must consider this decision applying s.21(3)–(5); see below.

[430] For an explanation of local authority accommodation, see Children Act 1989 s.20 and 21–011, below.

[431] Law Com. No.172, para.4.43; Law Com. W.P. 96, paras 5.41–5.48.

[432] Adoption and Children Act 2002 s.42(4). But in *Re A* [2007] EWCA Civ 1383, the Court of Appeal granted leave to apply to adopt to a foster-mother who had only cared for the child for eight months and who could not have applied for leave for a residence order without the local authority's permission.

[433] [1994] 2 F.L.R. 926. The residence order was made. This case has been the subject of further litigation: *Re P (s.91(14)) (Residence and Religious Heritage)* [1999] 2 F.L.R. 573, CA, and see below, para.19–018.

Jewish carers while a suitable adoptive family was sought. The foster carers wanted to continue to look after the child and obtained permission from the local authority to seek leave for a residence order. Leave was granted despite the parents' objections and the fact that an adoptive family had been found. The child's life and the adoption plan would be disrupted if she had to move from the applicants, but the delay of a few months whilst the application for a residence order was considered would not cause any further harm.

Where the child is in care, the authority's permission enables a residence order to be obtained without leave.[434] If the child is only accommodated, leave of the court or of everyone with parental responsibility will also be required, but support from the local authority is likely to be influential[435]:

> In *Re A and W (Minors) (Residence Order: Leave to Apply)*[436] a foster carer used judicial review to challenge the decision of the local authority to remove four children placed with her. Before the hearing, the local authority agreed to the foster carer applying for leave to seek residence orders. However, leave was refused because it was unlikely that a court would make such orders against the wishes of the children who were aged between 13 and 9.

Foster carers who obtain residence orders may be supported financially by the local authority[437] but are not subject to regulatory controls.[438] Where the local authority refuses permission, a mature child could apply for a residence order in favour of the foster carers.

(2) Criteria for leave—relatives caring for the child

18–037 Relatives who are fostering a child for a local authority do not need the local authority's permission to seek leave for a s.8 order application. If reforms included in the Children and Young Persons Bill 2008 are enacted, they will be able to apply for a residence order without leave if they have cared for the child for one year.[439] These changes reflect a new policy of promoting fostering with

[434] Children Act 1989 s.10(c)(ii).
[435] The court must have regard to both the authority's plans and the parents' wishes and feelings: Children Act 1989 s.10(9)(d); see *C v Salford City Council* [1994] 2 F.L.R. 926 for an example of how these matters are considered.
[436] [1992] Fam. 182.
[437] Children Act 1989 Sch.1 para.15; payments are frequently lower than to foster carers, and there is no set scheme as applies for special guardians; see para.22–064, below.
[438] People who were disqualified from being foster carers following a change in the regulations could continue to look after a child under a residence order: *Re RJ (Fostering: Person Disqualified)* [1999] 1 F.L.R. 605, CA, at 610, *per* Butler-Sloss L.J. In the event, wardship was used: *Re RJ (Wardship)* [1999] 1 F.L.R. 619. The local authority supported the foster carers in their applications.
[439] Children Act 1989 s.9 (3)(b); Children and Young Persons Bill 2008 cl.36 adding Children Act 1989 s.10(5B).

friends and family[440] and the wish to secure permanent care for children who cannot be looked after by their parents in their extended family.

(3) Criteria for leave—the child concerned[441]

The requirement that children should obtain leave before initiating applications **18–038** is designed to ensure that the application is the child's, not that of any adult,[442] and the matter is serious enough to justify court proceedings. Children seeking leave will need to establish that they "have sufficient understanding" to participate as a party,[443] but competence does not qualify them for leave.[444] Unless the application relates only to the child, the court also considers the factors listed in s.10(9)—the nature of the application and the impact the child's presence may have on the proceedings (and vice versa)—and makes a broad assessment of its merits.[445] The application must be made in the High Court[446]; the child may appear without a next friend or guardian ad litem only if the court accepts that he or she is capable of instructing a solicitor[447]:

> In *Re C (Leave to Seek Section 8 Orders)*[448] a 14-year-old girl sought leave for a residence order and a specific issue order so that she could live with friends and go on holiday to Bulgaria with them. Leave was refused. Granting an order would formalise the arrangements, which would be better resolved by discussion within the family; granting leave might indicate a willingness in the court to side with children who disagree with their parents.
>
> In *Re SC (A Minor) (Leave to Seek a Residence Order)*[449] leave was granted to allow a 14-year-old girl living in a children's home and subject to a care order to apply for a residence order in favour of a friend who had agreed to care for her. Although the mother opposed the application and the local authority had previously rejected the friend as the girl's foster carer, the application had a reasonable prospect of success.

---

[440] Children and Young Persons Bill 2008 s.9 (adding Children Act 1989 s.22C(6)(a), (7)(a)); *Care Matters* (Cm.7137 (2004)), paras 2.34 *et seq.*

[441] Children Act 1989 s.10(8) applies where the person seeking leave is "the child concerned". Where a child wishes to obtain contact with another, the criteria in s.10(9) apply: *Re S (Contact: Application by Sibling)* [1998] 2 F.L.R. 897 at 905, *per* Charles J.

[442] Law Com. No.172, para.4.44; *Re H (Residence Order)* [2000] 1 F.L.R. 780, FD (leave refused because the child had no separate issue). The *Funding Code Decision Making Guidance* (2007), para.20.33.11 states: "Legal representation would be unlikely to be granted to a child to apply for a residence order as opposed [to] a contact order."

[443] Children Act 1989 s.10(8): *Re N (Contact: Minor Seeking Leave to Defend Removal of Guardian)* [2003] 1 F.L.R. 652, FD; see also paras 16–013 and 16–020, above.

[444] *Re SC (A Minor) (Leave to Seek Residence Order)* [1994] 1 F.L.R. 96; *Re C (A Minor) (Leave to Seek section 8 orders)* [1994] 1 F.L.R. 26.

[445] *Re C (Residence: Child's Application for Leave)* [1995] 1 F.L.R. 927 at 931. The test is not "no reasonable prospect of success": *Re S (Adoption: Contact)* [2006] 1 F.L.R. 373, CA.

[446] *Practice Direction* [1993] 1 F.L.R. 668.

[447] Family Proceedings Rules 1991 (SI 1991/1247) r.9.2A; *Re T (A Minor) (Wardship Representation)* [1994] Fam. 49; see also J. Masson, "Representations of children" [1996] C.L.P. 245.

[448] [1994] 1 F.L.R. 26. Johnson J. has now accepted that the child's welfare is not the paramount consideration in these cases: *Re H (Residence Order)* [2000] 1 F.L.R. 780, FD.

[449] [1994] 1 F.L.R. 96.

A child who objects to parental plans for their name change or emigration may seek leave to apply for a prohibited steps order.[450] A child who cannot seek leave may still be joined as a party to any proceedings,[451] but most children are dependent on the adult parties and the court to ensure that their interests are considered.

(4) Criteria for leave—other persons

18–039 In these cases and leave applications by local authority foster parents or relatives, the court must have regard to: the nature of the proposed application[452]; the applicant's connection with the child; and the risk that the child's life might be disrupted to a harmful extent by the proposed application.[453] The court must recognise that applicants have rights under ECHR art.6(1), and many also enjoy protection under art.8.[454] Leave should scarcely be a hurdle to close relatives such as grandparents, uncles and aunts or brothers and sisters who wish to care for or visit the child[455]:

> In *Re J (Leave to Issue Application for a Residence Order)* the mother was a psychiatric patient and was unable to care for her children. Her mother had brought up her older child and wanted to care for her baby grandchild. The local authority who had brought care proceedings considered the grandmother (aged 59) too old, and proposed adoption. The judge refused her application for leave but her appeal was allowed.[456]

However, parents whose children have been adopted,[457] adopted children[458] and a children's guardian[459] whose professional involvement in a case had ended have been unsuccessful in persuading the courts that an issue merited a judicial examination:

> In *Re E (Adopted Child: Contact Leave)*[460] the natural parents were promised photographs of their child by the adopters' social worker at a

---

[450] Alternatively the child could seek to enforce their rights by applying for an injunction or to be made a ward of court.

[451] Family Proceedings Rules 1991 (SI 1991/1247) r.9.5, above para.16–021; *Re N (Residence Appointment of Solicitor: Placement with Extended Family)* [2001] 1 F.L.R. 1028, CA.

[452] Children Act 1989 s.10(9)(a); successful applications for specific issue or prohibited steps orders by people who are not caring for the child are likely to be rare unless the child's welfare is seriously at risk: see Law Com. No.172, para.4.41.

[453] Children Act 1989 s.10(9)(c). The criteria are also relevant when leave is sought for a s.34 contact order: *Re M (Care: Contact: Grandmother's Application)* [1995] 2 F.L.R. 86, CA.

[454] *Re J (Leave to Issue Application for a Residence Order)* [2003] 1 F.L.R. 114, CA, *per* Thorpe L.J. at para.18.

[455] Law Com. No.172, para.4.41.

[456] [2003] 1 F.L.R. 114, CA.

[457] *Re C (A Minor) (Adopted Child: Contact)* [1993] 2 F.L.R. 431.

[458] *Re S (Contact: Application by Sibling)* [1998] 2 F.L.R. 898, FD.

[459] *Re M (Prohibited Steps Order: Application for Leave to Apply)* [1993] 1 F.L.R. 275.

[460] [1995] 1 F.L.R. 57. But in *Re T (Adopted Children: Contact)* [1995] 2 F.L.R. 792, CA, leave was given after the adopters had reneged on their agreement to provide the children's older sister her with annual reports.

hearing the adopters did not attend. No condition was put in the adoption order, and the adopters refused to provide the photographs. Although the court recognised the real injustice to the natural parents, it did not give them leave because contact was fundamentally inconsistent with an unconditional adoption order.

The applicant's rights must be protected through a careful inquiry, but the granting of leave does not create any presumption that the substantive application will succeed.[461]

F. Procedure—the Private Law Programme

In July 2004, the President of the Family Division announced the implementation **18–040** of a new framework for private law cases: the *Private Law Programme*. The aim was to divert cases from the courts, ensure the development of local schemes that would incorporate best practice in dispute resolution and resolve disputes without a fully contested hearing.[462] Three principles underlie the scheme: (1) provision for dispute resolution at a first hearing; (2) effective court control of proceedings, including judicial continuity; and (3) matching of resources to families.[463] The court seeks to handle cases according to the "overriding objective": that is, justly, expeditiously and with the minimum of delay; in ways that ensure the parties are on an equal footing, children's welfare is safeguarded, and distress to all parties is minimised; and in ways that are proportionate to the gravity and complexity of the issues and the intervention proposed.[464] In practice, applications are referred to CAFCASS for initial safety screening.[465] Suitable cases are then listed for a First Dispute Resolution Hearing Appointment (FDHRA), approximately four to six weeks after the application.[466] At this appointment the parties are expected to engage in dispute resolution, usually with the assistance of a CAFCASS officer.[467] At the Principal Registry, children over the age of nine are also seen.[468]

In contrast with the new arrangements for care proceedings,[469] there was little consultation about the introduction of this scheme. Rather, encouragement was given to develop in-court conciliation (which existed in some courts since the 1980s), and such arrangements were re-badged as part of the *Programme*. Issues such as the effectiveness of schemes and the best models for dispute resolution

---

[461] *G v F (Contact and Shared Residence)* [1998] 2 F.L.R. 799 at 802, *per* Bracewell J. (leave granted to a lesbian co-parent after separation from the child's mother).
[462] Potter P, speech to ALC [2006] Fam. Law 65. In-court conciliation schemes have existed in some courts since the 1980s.
[463] President of the Family Division, *Private Law Programme* (2004), p.5.
[464] President of the Family Division, *Private Law Programme*, p.5.
[465] Children Act 1989 s.16A; CAFCASS, *Private Law Pathway* (2007), Stage 1.
[466] *Private Law Programme*, p.7. The system was not originally available in family proceedings courts, but there are plans to extend it.
[467] For details of how schemes operate, see L. Trinder et al., *Making Contact Happen or Making Contact Work* (DCA Research Report 03/06, 2006) and *The Longer-term Outcomes of In-Court Conciliation* (MoJ Research Report 17/07, 2007).
[468] *Practice Direction* [2004] 1 F.L.R. 974; Kirby [2006] Fam. Law 970.
[469] See below, paras 21–030 and 21–053.

were apparently ignored in the desire to manage resources and avoid delays. Limited efforts were made to discourage applications[470]; resources were directed at reaching agreement at the FDHRA. Research by Trinder and colleagues indicated that approximately three-quarters of couples reached at least a partial agreement after a 45 minute conciliation meeting, and that these meetings led to increases in contact. However, parental communication and empathy (which provide a strong foundation for relationships after separation) were not improved. Many of these "quick fix" agreements failed; 60 per cent broke down within two years and 40 per cent of couples returned to court. Those who ceased to use the courts had generally done so because of dissatisfaction, not resolution of their disputes.[471] On this basis it is unclear as to what extent the *Private Law Programme* is cost effective.

Applications for orders under the Children Act 1989 are made by completing the appropriate application form and sending it to the court.[472] Where leave is required, a written request must be made.[473] The application must be served on all the parties; in private law proceedings this includes everyone with parental responsibility but not usually the child.[474] The parties and those caring for the child must generally be notified of the application, but the court may give leave and make orders without notice.[475] Thus, a specific issue order for medical treatment[476] or a prohibited steps order to prevent the child's removal from the country may be granted with great speed. Residence orders should only be granted without notice for the shortest time necessary.[477] There are systems for court decisions to be made out of hours in emergencies.[478]

18–041   If the case is not resolved at the FDHRA, the court gives directions. The judge should manage the case, consider transfer of the proceedings,[479] set the timetable, determine what evidence should be filed and, where necessary, order reports or agree the appointment of experts,[480] decide questions of party status and the form

---

[470] Parents could use the Parenting Plans devised originally for the Department of Constitutional Affairs or be advised about mediation and other services by their solicitors. Willingness to mediate is a requirement for legally aided applicants. A scheme for early intervention (the Family Resolutions Pilot project) was unsuccessful in attracting participants and was not extended: see L. Trinder et al., *Evaluation of the Family Resolutions Pilot Project* (2006); DCSF and Potter [2006] Fam. Law 65, 66.

[471] Trinder et al., *Family Resolutions Pilot*; DCA Research Reports 15/07.

[472] Family Proceedings Rules 1991 (SI 1991/1247) r.4.4. Form C1A includes questions to assist with screening for domestic violence, etc. but does not elicit the required information in a substantial proportion of cases: R. Aris and C. Harrison (MoJ Research Report 17/07).

[473] Family Proceedings Rules 1991 (SI 1991/1247) r.4.3; cf. *Re O (Minors) (Leave to Seek Residence Order)* [1994] 1 F.L.R. 172.

[474] Family Proceedings Rules 1991 (SI 1991/1247) rr.4.7, 4.8 and App.2. For a discussion of children as parties, see para.16–020, above.

[475] Family Proceedings Rules 1991 (SI 1991/1247) r.4.4(4), but not if this breached common law principles of fairness or ECHR art.6(1): *Re S (Ex p. orders)* [2001] 1 F.L.R. 308; *Re K (Procedure: Family Proceedings Rules)* [2005] 1 F.L.R. 764, CA.

[476] For example, *Re R (A Minor) (Blood Transfusion)* [1993] 2 F.L.R. 157.

[477] *Re G (Minors) (Ex p. Interim Residence Order)* [1993] 1 F.L.R. 910; *Re P (A Minor) (Ex p. Interim Residence Order)* [1993] 1 F.L.R. 915.

[478] CAAC, *Report 1992/3*, pp.50, 62; CAAC, *Report 1993/4*, pp.38, 51.

[479] Family Proceedings Rules 1991 (SI 1991/1247) r.4.6; *Practice Direction, Guide to Case Management I: Public Law Proceedings*, April 2008 (the PLO).

[480] *Practice Direction, Experts in Family Proceedings Relating to children*, April 2008.

of the hearing.[481] Although directions hearings enable the court to manage the litigation and should shorten final hearings, they require considerable resources and limit court time for substantive hearings.[482] Where directions are not complied with, a penalty of costs may be imposed.[483]

Advance disclosure of evidence is required; witnesses prepare signed statements for the lawyers and the court to read before the hearing.[484] Witness statements replace evidence-in-chief so that hearings are not prolonged. Justice precludes the court from relying on confidential material unless real harm would come to the children from disclosure.[485] In care proceedings, the positive obligation on the state to protect the interests of the family requires material to be given even though no request has been made.[486] Areas of conflict should be identified and focused on at the hearing. The parties must conduct the litigation reasonably.[487] Where one party acts oppressively, increasing costs by making unrealistic applications and false allegations, a penalty of costs can be imposed:

> In *M v H (Costs Residence Proceedings)*[488] the father agreed during mediation that shared residence was unrealistic. Later, during negotiations about contact arrangements, he applied for residence and refused to mediate unless the mother agreed to shared residence. He persisted with this application, knowing that it was causing the mother financial hardship, even after it was clear that he had no prospects of success. The judge ordered him to pay 75 per cent of the mother's costs: £42,628.

Costs can be ordered against lawyers who fail in their duties to the court.[489]

---

[481] Family Proceedings Rules 1991 (SI 1991/1247) r.4.7(2). Concern has been expressed about the proliferation of parties: CAAC, *Report 1992/3*, p.27. Additional parties should have interests distinct from those directly involved: *Re W (Care Proceedings: Leave to Apply)* [2005] 2 F.L.R. 468, FD.

[482] The increased emphasis on case management, in the Private Law Programme and the Public Law Outline are intended to improve the use of resources: *Practice Direction PLO*, April 2008, paras 2.1, 3.1(3); Ryder J., "Introduction", *Case Management the Public Law Outline, Training Pack for the Judiciary* (JSB, 2007) p.55.

[483] Family Proceedings (Costs) Rules 1991 (SI 1991/1832), r.15; *Practice Direction* [1999] 1 F.L.R. 1295. But it has been held that it would be wrong to exclude evidence where a direction is not complied with: *R v Nottinghamshire CC* [1993] Fam. Law 543.

[484] Family Proceedings Rules 1991 (SI 1991/1247) r.4.17. Sworn statements (affidavits) are used in proceedings under the inherent jurisdiction; see para.18–049. The advocates are expected to prepare a complete file of papers for the judge: *Practice Direction Bundles* [2006] 2 F.L.R.199. Judges note that the volume of papers precludes thorough preparation.

[485] *Official Solicitor v K* [1965] A.C. 201; *Re M (Disclosure)* [1998] 2 F.L.R. 1028, an opportunity should be given to the party affected to make representations. Lack of disclosure may amount to a breach of ECHR art.6(1): *McMichael v UK* (1995) 20 E.H.R.R. 205.

[486] *TP and KM v UK* [2001] 2 F.L.R. 549 at para.82. It may still be possible for the local authority to resist disclosure by claiming public interest immunity, leaving the question of disclosure to the court: *Re C (Expert Evidence: Disclosure Practice)* [1995] 1 F.L.R. 204.

[487] *Practice Direction PLO*, April 2008; the parties are required to help the court further the overriding objective and co-operate with case management; paras 2.3 and 5.4.

[488] [2000] 1 F.L.R. 52.

[489] Civil Procedure Rules 1998 (SI 1998/3132) r.48.7; *Re G, S and M (Wasted Costs)* [2000] 1 F.L.R. 52 (failure to ensure that expert witness had the necessary information).

Hearings take place in private; the privacy of the child and the parties, and the interests of justice justify this despite the general right to a public hearing.[490] The right to a fair trial demands that a person whose civil rights are at issue has an opportunity to be heard.[491] The interests of the children must also be considered.[492] The form of hearing is a matter for the judge; there is a spectrum of procedure from without-notice application on minimal evidence to full and detailed oral hearings.[493] There may be no need for further evidence where an issue has already been considered by the court,[494] but the practice of dismissing apparently weak cases without considering any evidence does not satisfy the Convention.[495]

18–042 The court also determines whether a child party can attend the proceedings. Child parties who are represented may be excluded if this is in their interests[496] and does not prevent effective representation.[497] Attending court has been considered potentially damaging for children and appropriate only in exceptional cases.[498] Consequently, arrangements have not been made to include children, and they have often not been asked whether they would like to attend.[499]

The child may be a witness for any of the parties, but the family courts are deeply reluctant to allow children to give evidence.[500] A child's statement may be given to the court by a third party; evidence given in connection with the upbringing, maintenance or welfare of a child is admissible despite the rules relating to hearsay. The admissibility of hearsay avoids the need for the child to repeat statements made to a teacher or other confidant (which would be impossible in the case of a young child) and protects children from court

---

[490] Family Proceedings Rules 1991 (SI 1991/1247) r.4.16(7); *B v UK; P v UK* [2001] 2 F.L.R. 261; *Pelling v Bruce-Williams* [2004] 2 F.L.R. 832, CA.

[491] art.6(1); *Re I and H (Contact: Right to Give Evidence)* [1998] 1 F.L.R. 876. The court may permit adoption proceedings without notification to the biological father who could not claim "family life" with his child: *Re H; Re G (Adoption: Consultation of Unmarried Fathers)* [2001] 1 F.L.R. 646, CA; cf. *Re AB (care proceedings: service on husband ignorant of child's existence)* [2004] 1 F.L.R. 527, CA.

[492] *Re B and T (Care Proceedings: Legal Representation)* [2001] 1 F.L.R. 485, *per* Buxton L.J. at para.21 (an adjournment would have delayed, unacceptably, providing security for the children).

[493] Family Proceedings Rules 1991 (SI 1991/1247) r.4.21; *Practice Direction* [1995] 1 F.L.R. 456; *Re B (Minors) (Contact)* [1994] 2 F.L.R. 1 at 5, *per* Butler-Sloss, L.J.

[494] *Re F (Contact: Enforcement: Representation of the Child)* [1998] 1 F.L.R. 691, CA.

[495] For example, in *Cheshire CC v M* [1993] 1 F.L.R. 463, and *Re B (Contact: Step-father's Opposition)* [1997] 2 F.L.R. 579, CA; see Swindells et al., *Family Law and the HRA 1998*, paras 8.118–8.119.

[496] Children Act 1989 s.95; Family Proceedings Rules 1991 (SI 1991/1247) r.4.16(2). The issue of attendance at appeals is uncertain: *Re C (A Minor) (Care: Child's Wishes)* [1993] 1 F.L.R. 832 at 841.

[497] A child party who is separately represented must have the opportunity to instruct their lawyer: *Re AS (Secure Accommodation Order)* [1999] 1 F.L.R. 103.

[498] *Re C (A Minor) (Care: Child's Wishes)* [1993] 1 F.L.R. 832 at 841; CAAC, *Handbook* (1997), p.21.

[499] Masson and Winn Oakley, *Out of Hearing* (Wiley, 1999), p.109. Young people involved in care proceedings are now informed that they can ask to attend: see NSPCC *Powerpack* (2001). There is some recognition of the benefits to children of participation: *Re K (Secure Accommodation Order: Right to Liberty)* [2001] 1 F.L.R. 526 at para. 44.

[500] Advisory Board on Family Law: Children Act Sub-Committee, *Making Contact Work* (2002), para.3.46; *Re M (family proceedings: affidavits)* [1995] 2 F.L.R. 100 (practice deprecated); *LM v Medway Council* [2007] 1 F.L.R. 1698, CA (decision to require child to give evidence upheld).

attendance and cross-examination.[501] Hearsay may not be allowed where the proceedings primarily affect the parents[502] and the need for the child's direct evidence may outweigh concerns for the child.[503] A welfare report is the usual way to obtain evidence of the child's views,[504] but some children write direct to the judge. Judges are being encouraged to be more creative about children's participation where a CAFCASS officer is not available or the child expresses a wish to meet the judge.[505] However, such meetings do not replace the need for skilled professionals who can work with children to be involved in proceedings.[506] Where the child is interviewed and the judge relies on something said without giving the parties the opportunity to question it, the order may be set aside.[507] Consequently, the child should not be offered confidentiality.[508]

Where matters are in dispute, the court should make findings of fact[509]; the case may be heard in two parts to establish the facts before consideration of proposals for the child's future.[510] The parties may give evidence or call witnesses on relevant matters.[511] The court has power to control access to court papers and assessments of the child[512]:

In *Re A (Family Proceedings: Expert Witnesses)*[513] the parents were involved in a very contentious contact dispute. During contact at a contact centre, the father made a secret video. His solicitors sent this to a psychologist with anonymised information about the family and instructions to prepare a report. The father then applied for residence attaching the report to his evidence. Although the rules about disclosure of papers and examination of children had not been broken, Wall J. strongly condemned the father, his solicitor and the expert who should not have accepted instructions anonymously.

---

[501] Children Act 1989 s.96(3) and Children (Admissibility of Hearsay Evidence) Order 1993 (SI 1993/621).
[502] *C v C (Contempt: Evidence)* [1993] 1 F.L.R. 220.
[503] *LM v Medway Council* [2007] 1 F.L.R. 1698, CA, where establishing the truth of allegations about domestic violence required the child's evidence because the mother had alleged she told the child to accuse the father.
[504] Children Act 1989 s.7. In specified proceedings the children's guardian provides a report: s.41.
[505] Family Justice Council, *Enhancing the Participation of Children and Young People in Family Proceedings* (2008).
[506] R. Hunter, "Close encounters of a judicial kind: 'hearing' children's 'voices' in family law proceedings" [2007] C.F.L.Q. 283.
[507] *Elder v Elder* [1986] 1 F.L.R. 610, CA.
[508] *Re D (Adoption Reports: Confidentiality)* [1995] 2 F.L.R. 687, HL; see also *Re C (Disclosure)* [1996] 1 F.L.R. 797.
[509] *Re L; Re V; Re M; Re H (Contact Domestic Violence)* [2000] 2 F.L.R. 334, CA at 341H, *per* Butler-Sloss P; *Re G (A Minor) (Care Proceedings)* [1995] Fam. 16, 20; *Re A (Contact: Risk of Violence)* [2007] 1 F.L.R. 283, FD; *Practice Direction* (2008). Researchers in the 1990s noted reluctance in the courts to adjudicate in private law matters: Pearce *et al.* [1999] Fam. Law 22.
[510] *Re G (Care Proceedings: Split Trials)* [2001] 1 F.L.R. 872, CA. The same judge should take both hearings: *Re B* [2008] UKHL 35.
[511] The parties may subpoena those who have relevant information: *D v M (A Minor) (Custody: Appeal)* [1983] Fam. 33 at 37 (health visitor).
[512] Family Proceedings Rules 1991 (SI 1991/1247) rr.4.18, 10.20A. Where permission is not obtained to seek an expert report, its cost will not be paid out of public funds.
[513] [2001] 1 F.L.R. 723.

18–043   The courts have become highly dependent on the use of experts in care proceedings, adding to the costs and delays in these proceedings. Expert opinions are sought on the cause of injuries, the child's future care needs and the parent's ability to meet them. Whilst it has been recognised that the evidential require-ments of the courts are different from those of treating physicians,[514] there are occasions where the courts have gone to extreme lengths to assess an issue:

> In *Haringey London BC v C, E and another Intervening*[515] Ryder J. considered the care plan for a two-and-a-half-year-old child who had been removed from his carers when he was a few weeks old. The carers had acquired the baby from Kenya and asserted that he was their biological child although there was evidence that the woman was infertile and had not been pregnant, and that both carers were members of a religious organisation involved in child trafficking. The court allowed extensive expert evidence, including the examination of the possibility that despite lacking common DNA the carers were indeed the child's parents. This contributed to the delay in providing a secure home for the child, during which he established bonds with a short-term foster carer who was not a potential adopter.

Expert witnesses must have the necessary knowledge and expertise and be able to complete their report within the court's timetable. They should be given full instructions so they are clear about the issues before the court and the questions on which their opinion is sought.[516] Their duty is to provide advice to the court on their area of expertise, not to assist one party.[517] Where there is more than one expert, they should meet to identify areas of agreement and the issues that need to be resolved[518]; where there is no arguable case, the proceedings should not continue.[519] Where leave has been given for expert evidence, the court can require its disclosure. Litigation privilege that would protect a party from having to disclose a report on which he or she chose not to rely does not apply[520]:

> In *Re L. (Police Investigation: Privilege)*[521] the House of Lords upheld a decision ordering the disclosure to the police of a pathologist's report commissioned by the mother for care proceedings. The parents were heroin addicts and their child had been poisoned by methadone accidentally,

---

[514] *Re M (Care Proceedings Best Evidence)* [2007] 1 F.L.R. 1006, CA.

[515] [2007] 1 F.L.R. 1035, High Court.

[516] *Practice Direction Experts in Family Proceedings Relating to Children* (2008).

[517] *Vernon v Bosley (No.2)* [1998] 1 F.L.R. 304, CA; Oldham. *MDC v GW and PW* [2007] 2 F.L.R. 597.

[518] *Practice Direction Experts* (2008), para.6.2; *Re R (Child Abuse Video Evidence)* [1995] 1 F.L.R. 451.

[519] *Re N (Contested Care Application)* [1994] 2 F.L.R. 992. Where all the experts concluded that the children should not be placed with the parents.

[520] *Oxfordshire CC v M* [1994] 1 F.L.R. 175, CA; *Re L (Police Investigation: Privilege)* [1996] 1 F.L.R. 731, HL; [1996] 1 F.L.R. 731, HL. But the court will not order a party to disclose details of experts instructed in criminal proceedings: *S CC v B* [2000] 2 F.L.R. 161.

[521] [1996] 1 F.L.R. 731, HL. Lord Nicholls delivered a strong dissenting opinion and expressly rejected the argument that there was a duty to disclose information (at p.747) but the ECHR declared inadmissible the art.6(1) complaint that requiring disclosure breached art.6(1): *L v UK* [2000] 2 F.L.R. 322.

according to the mother. The report indicated that the mother's story was improbable. Lord Jauncey, delivering the majority opinion, stated that litigation privilege had no place in Children Act proceedings. Communication between solicitor and client remains privileged.[522]

Before giving the decision, magistrates must record any findings of fact and the reasons for their decision.[523] Reasons should relate to the welfare checklist and other statutory criteria.[524] Judgments are not generally given in public; full written judgments are not usually transcribed, but anyone with an interest may be given leave to obtain a copy.[525] There are plans to make judgment summaries more widely available.[526]

VI. THE COURT AS A WELFARE AGENCY

The courts dealing with family matters are not primarily therapeutic agencies, **18–044** and those who use them seek justice, not welfare.[527] However, divorce proceedings and disputes about children have provided both the opportunity and the justification for entrusting the courts with welfare responsibilities, but facilities and resources have not reflected the level of concern expressed, nor even the needs of families.[528]

The court's role as a welfare agency developed from the recommendations of the Morton Commission.[529] They thought it essential that everything possible should be done to mitigate the effect on children of the disruption of family life.[530] Parents were not always the best judges of their children's interests. Therefore, the Commission suggested that the obligation to submit a "statement of arrangements" for the children with the divorce petition[531] should be strengthened and enforced by requiring the court's approval of arrangements

---

[522] This does not apply to criminal communication such as obscene and menacing statements: *C v C (Evidence Privilege)* [2001] 2 F.L.R. 184, CA.

[523] Family Proceedings Rules 1991 (SI 1991/1395); failure of magistrates to abide by r.21(5) has justified appeals; see, for example, *Re W (A Minor) (Contact)* [1994] 1 F.L.R. 843, but the rule also means waiting time for lawyers and the parties.

[524] Reasons should enable the parties to understand how the magistrates approached their task and their main findings: *Re L (Residence: Justices Reasons)* [1995] 2 F.L.R. 445 at 451.

[525] The ECtHR has accepted that this does not amount to a breach of art.6(1): see *B v UK; P v UK* [2001] 2 F.L.R. 261 at para.48.

[526] MoJ, *Confidence and Confidentiality, Openness in Family Courts—A New Approach* (2007), and above, para.18–008.

[527] S. Cretney, "Defining the limits of state intervention: the child and the courts", in D. Freestone (ed.), *Children and the Law* (1990), pp.59–60.

[528] See Murch and Hooper, *The Family Justice System* (1992), Ch.7. The establishment of CAFCASS provides the courts with an agency dedicated to advising and supporting the courts but its creation was marked by problems: Constitutional Affairs Committee, *CAFCASS, Third Report 2002–3* (HC 614).

[529] Royal Commission on Marriage and Divorce 1951–1955 (Cmd.9678 (1956)) (the *Morton Report*).

[530] *Morton Report*, para.362.

[531] This had been embodied in the Matrimonial Causes Rules 1947 following the recommendation in the *Final Report of the Committee on Procedure in Matrimonial Causes* (Cmd. 7024 (1947)), (the Denning Committee).

before a decree of divorce could be made absolute.[532] In addition, the Commission believed that there would be a few cases where the family could not make satisfactory arrangements; in these, the court should have the power to require the local authority to receive the children into care.[533] Both these recommendations were first enacted in the Matrimonial Proceedings (Children) Act 1958 and were incorporated, largely unaltered, in the Matrimonial Causes Act 1973.[534] However, both run counter to the fundamental principles of non-intervention in the Children Act 1989 and have consequently been reformed. Nevertheless, the courts retain some residual functions as a welfare agency.

A. Mediation services[535]

18–045 Mediation is a process whereby the parties are encouraged to reach agreement on some or all matters in dispute with the assistance a neutral person, the mediator. It can help the parties to re-establish a lasting co-operative relationship.[536] Family mediation involves discussions between adults, but, increasingly, mediators are including children in the process. Unlike in-court conciliation under the *Private Law Programme*, mediation is a consensual process; the mediator is not an officer of the court.[537] Although some lawyers act as mediators, legal representation is partisan and more narrowly focused.[538] Although it has been said that "there is no case however conflicted, which is not potentially open to successful mediation",[539] mediators may be unable to redress power imbalances between the parties[540]; consequently, mediation is not suitable where one party is so violent or oppressive that the other cannot function effectively.[541] Mediation is available free of charge or at reduced cost through schemes supported by CAFCASS or funded by the Legal Services Commission.[542] The Government also funds a family mediation helpline.

The Family Law Act 1996 contained a provision (never implemented) empowering the courts in divorce proceedings to direct the parties to attend a

[532] *Morton Report*, paras 366, 373.

[533] *Morton Report*, paras 395–396.

[534] Matrimonial Causes Act 1973 ss.41, 43. Children could also be committed to care or placed under supervision under the Domestic Proceedings and Magistrates' Courts Act 1978 s.10(1); Guardianship Act 1973 s.2(2)(b); the Children Act 1975 s.34(5); or the Adoption Act 1976 s.26(1).

[535] See, generally, R. Dingwall and J. Eekelaar (eds.), *Divorce Mediation and the Legal Process* (Oxford: Clarendon Press, 1988); G. Davis, *Partisans and Mediators* (Oxford: Clarendon Press, 1988); C. Piper, *The Responsible Parent* (New York: Harvester, 1993); J. Walker et al., *Mediation: The Making and Remaking of Co-operative Relationships* (Newcastle: Relate Centre, 1994).

[536] In Walker's study, over half the clients were satisfied with the outcome of comprehensive mediation; the figure for child-focused mediation was 38%, but settlement rates were higher: Walker et al. (1994), pp.71, 78.

[537] See above, para.18–040 for an explanation of the PLP, and below for a discussion of compulsion in mediation.

[538] Resolution, *Managing Difficult Divorce Relationships* (2006), p.100: "mediation . . . encompasses wider issues, including maintaining individual dignity."

[539] *Al-Khatib v Masry* [2005] 1 F.L.R. 381, *per* Thorpe L.J. at para.17.

[540] Davis, *Partisans*, p.51.

[541] Resolution *Managing Difficult Divorce Relationships*, p.101. Decisions about suitability for publicly funded mediation are made by mediators who screen for domestic violence: see LSC, *Funding Code* (2007), para.11.5.2.

[542] CAFCASS, *Annual Report 2007*, p.20; LSC, *Annual Report 2005–6*, Table CLS6 indicates that over 4,000 bills were paid for mediation, averaging £343 each.

meeting with a mediator.[543] In an attempt to encourage mediation and reduce litigation, those seeking public funding were required to co-operate with an assessment of the suitability of the dispute for mediation.[544] Mediation was seen as a better and cheaper alternative to lawyers who were suspected of aggravating family disputes.[545] Requiring attendance at mediation was controversial[546]; it changed what mediators were expected to do, demanded major development of mediation services and restricted access to legal advice, without evidence that mediation could deliver fair settlements in the interests of children. Compulsion can be inefficient; requiring one party to attend will only result in mediation if the other (non-legally aided party) is willing.[547] Compulsion is also contrary to the ethos of mediation that is based on co-operative working and agreement. Research commissioned to establish the cost-effectiveness of mediation compared with legal services found quite high levels of consumer satisfaction but higher levels of approval for solicitors.[548] Solicitors facilitated negotiation; there was no evidence that they inflamed disputes.[549] Mediation did not appear to reduce recourse to publicly funded legal services, or to reduce legal costs.[550]

In its Green Paper on *Parental Separation*, the Government stated that it intended to continue to promote mediation and review procedures so that "the strongest possible encouragement is given".[551] The Constitutional Affairs Committee supported the idea of diversion from litigation by mediation, and considered that a power such as that in the Family Law Act 1996 should be applied to all, not just those seeking legal aid.[552] When the Government introduced its draft Children and Adoption Bill, it made clear that litigants would not be forced to mediate.[553] However, it conceded that provision could be used to direct a meeting with a mediator.[554] Whether the courts will do this remains unclear; a meeting with a mediator before a court application could divert some cases; those who apply will be referred for in-court conciliation. In addition, consideration is being given to changing the rules of court so that those who are

[543] Family Law Act 1996 s.13(1).
[544] Introduced by Family Law Act 1996 s.29, now Access to Justice Act 1999 s.8 and LSC, *Funding Code* (2007) para.11.4.2, 11.5.
[545] Maclean and Eekelaar *Family Lawyers* (2000), Chs 1 and 9; G. Davis et al. [2001] Fam. Law 265.
[546] G. Davis et al. [2001] Fam. Law 265. Concern was expressed that victims of domestic violence would not be identified and would be required to mediate: C. Piper and F. Kanagas, "Family Law Act 1996, s.1(d): How will 'they' know there is a risk of violence?" [1997] C.F.L.Q. 279–289.
[547] Following the implementation of s.29, there were approximately four intake appointments for every mediation started: G. Davis et al. [2001] Fam. Law 265, 267.
[548] G. Davis et al. [2001] Fam. Law 110, 112–114; Cm.6273 (2004), para.23 shows slightly higher levels of satisfaction for mediation than court resolution, but draws on Blackwell and Dawe, Table 5.13, which did not distinguish between lawyers negotiation and mediation.
[549] G. Davis et al. [2001] Fam. Law 110, 112–114; J. Walker et al., *The Family Advice and Information Service: A Changing Role for Family Lawyers in England and Wales?* (2007), Summary 29.
[550] G. Davis et al. [2001] Fam. Law 186, 188. The authors acknowledge considerable limitations to this research, notably that it takes no account of whether mediated agreements last longer than court imposed ones. Davis et al.'s findings are the subject of critical comment by T. Fisher and D. Hodson [2001] Fam. Law 271.
[551] Cm.6273 (2004), para.65; *Next Steps* (Cm.6454 (2005)), paras 48–52.
[552] 2004–5 (HC 116), para.94; 2005–6 (HC 1086), para.28.
[553] Joint Committee on (draft) Children and Adoption Bill (2004–5 HC 400), paras 53 and 58.
[554] Children and Adoption Act 2006 s.1, adding Children Act 1989 s.11A(6); EN para.18.

not legally aided also have to consider mediation for making an application to court.[555]

Despite encouragement and coercion, only a minority of people resolve family disputes through mediation. There are approximately 13,000 publicly funded family mediations each year; approximately 5 per cent of disputes about children are resolved in this way.[556]

B. Contact centres

18–046 Contact centres provide a "neutral venue" (often a church hall) where children who would not otherwise have contact can meet their non-residential parent or other family members.[557] The development of contact centres was one of the most significant developments in the family justice system in the 1990s.[558] They are crucial for the management of contact disputes and are an integral part of court-based welfare services,[559] but most are run by voluntary organisations. Their aim is to provide a short-term venue for contact and thereby establish sufficient trust for contact to take place elsewhere. Most centres provide only "supported" contact, and do not monitor it, but a few provide supervised contact.[560] Centres may allow visits to be observed for court reports, but they will generally not provide reports themselves. Courts may refer families to contact centres but must first establish that resources are available and the referral is suitable.[561] Supported contact centres do not provide sufficient protection where the parent's behaviour poses risks to the child.[562] In 2007, approximately 15,000 children and nearly 10,000 fathers had contact through a centre affiliated to the National Association of Child Contact Centres.[563]

C. Arrangements for children on divorce

18–047 Before the introduction of the Children Act 1989, the procedure under Matrimonial Causes Act 1973 s.41 required the applicant for divorce to file "statement of arrangements" to be approved by a judge in chambers at a "children appointment"—a brief hearing usually attended only by the parent with care. If

---

[555] Government's response to the Constitutional Afffairs Select Committee Report (Cm.6971 (2006)), para.28.

[556] Cm.6273 (2004), para.64.

[557] E. Halliday, "The role and function of child contact centres" [1997] J.S.W.F.L. 53–60; B. Kroll, "Not intruding, not colluding: process and practice in a contact centre" (2000) 14 *Children and Society* 182J. Mitchell [2001] Fam. Law 613.

[558] Advisory Board on Family Law: Children Act Sub-Committee, *Making Contact Work* (2002), para.8.5.

[559] Advisory Board on Family Law, *Third Annual Report 1999/2000*, para.3.43. The Children Act Sub-Committee stressed the importance of CAFCASS developing close links with contact centres.

[560] For a detailed explanation of these terms, see National Association of Contact Centres, *Manual* (2000), para.8.1 reproduced in Advisory Board on Family Law: Children Act Sub-Committee, *Making Contact Work: Consultation Paper* (2001), para.3.18–3.19.

[561] Protocol for the referral of families by judges and magistrates to child contact centres: [2001] Fam. Law 616.

[562] Aris et al., *Safety and Child Contact* (DCA Research Report 1002, 2002); E. Butler-Sloss [2001] Fam. Law 355.

[563] NACCC, *Annual Review 2007*, p.9.

the judge was satisfied with the arrangements, he or she granted a "certificate of satisfaction" that allowed the divorce to be made absolute. Certificates were rarely refused.[564] This power and its operation were criticised on a number of grounds[565]: it failed to support families when they needed help; did not identify problems effectively; and took up scarce judicial and social work resources. Even if problems were identified, the power to withhold the decree was inappropriate where parents needed positive encouragement and assistance.

The Children Act 1989 amended s.41 in line with its philosophy of placing responsibility for children's interests primarily on their parents and reducing state intervention. Children's appointments were abolished and the statement of arrangements revised to require more information.[566] However, it is examined only after the district judge has determined that the petition is made out.[567] The court no longer has to approve arrangements, only "consider... whether it should exercise any of its powers under the Children Act 1989 with respect to" any children of the family.[568] Only if the court may need to exercise its powers, if it is unable to do so without giving further consideration to the case and if there are exceptional circumstances may it delay the divorce.[569] District judges consider statements of arrangements only briefly and rarely seek further information by requiring the parties to attend or ordering a welfare report.[570] The procedure remains largely ineffective for identifying cases where children's welfare may be at risk or making support available for parents at a stressful time; judges have neither the time nor the inclination to look at cases more closely.

Although the child's wishes and feelings are included in the welfare checklist that the court applies when making a decision about a child's upbringing,[571] the process for dealing with these undefended divorces makes no provision for involving children.[572] Consequently, it does not appear to satisfy the requirements of the UN Convention on the Rights of the Child art.12.[573] The Family Law Act 1996 emphasised children's welfare by requiring courts to treat this as

---

[564] For a discussion of the principle findings of the research into s.41, see G. Douglas et al., "Safeguarding children's welfare in non-contentious divorce: towards a new conception of the legal process?" (2000) 63 M.L.R. 177, 181.

[565] See, G. Davis, "Public issues and private troubles: the case of divorce" (1987) 17 Fam. Law 299; *Booth Committee Report* (1985) and Law Com. WP 96, paras 4.8–4.10.

[566] Form M4.

[567] Family Proceedings Rules 1991 (SI 1991/1247) r.2.39. There is no scrutiny where the parties are in dispute and an application has been made for a s.8 order; rr.2.39(1), 2.40. The Law Commission had recommended that scrutiny should take place early in the proceedings.

[568] Children Act 1989 s.41(1).

[569] Children Act 1989 s.41(2).

[570] Douglas et al., "Safeguarding Children's Welfare" pp.189–190. Out of 353 cases studied, the district judge sought additional information in 18; in only one was the divorce delayed. The fact that parents had not separated led district judges to exercise their powers, but the lack of contact did not.

[571] See Ch.19, below.

[572] Parents are not required to discuss arrangements with children, nor do children sign the statement of arrangements. The Children (Scotland) Act 1995 s.6 imposes a duty on parents to have regard to the children's views when making decisions. Lack of information about what is happening, and of involvement in arrangements, is a source of concern to children: B. Neale and C. Smart, *Good to Talk?* (London: Young Voice, 2001).

[573] Douglas et al. have suggested that this, taken with arts 6 and 8 of the ECHR, could possibly form the basis of a challenge that uncontentious divorce process fails to protect children's rights to respect for family life and for due process; p.195.

paramount, and to consider the checklist when handling undefended divorces, but did not include any process to involve children.[574] The Lord Chancellor commissioned a further review of s.41 which suggested that the parties should be encouraged to file a Parenting Plan[575]; the respondent should be required to comment on the arrangements; the court should obtain independent information from the child's school; and that district judges should be more proactive in referring parents to other agencies.[576] What and how children are told about parental divorce remains a matter for parents; the Department of Children Schools and Families encourages parents to tell their children and provides leaflets to assist them.[577]

D. Court ordered investigation

18–048 Before the introduction of the Children Act 1989, a court could commit a child into the care of the local authority in exceptional circumstances.[578] However, this conflicted fundamentally with the reform[579] because it allowed the court to intervene in the family without proof of significant harm, and to impose its standards on the local authority. The Law Commission recommended[580] that the courts should be able to order the local authority to investigate and, where the "significant harm" test is satisfied, to make an interim care or supervision order. In addition, the local authority should be able to intervene in any family proceedings and request a care order.[581] The Children Act 1989 implemented these proposals.[582] Also, if family proceedings are started whilst care proceedings are pending, the court has power to transfer so that cases can be heard together.[583]

The court may direct an investigation in any family proceedings relating to a child where it appears that it "may be appropriate for a care or supervision order to be made".[584] Where the court makes such a direction, it may also appoint a children's guardian.[585] The appointment is not automatic; if an interim care or

---

[574] Family Law Act 1996 s.11. The provision was never implemented.

[575] Parenting Plans (an Australian idea) are available to assist parental discussions about arrangements, but are not mandatory.

[576] Family Law Board, *Report 2000–2001*, paras 2.37–2.38.

[577] Parenting plans and a guidance leaflet are available on the DCSF website: *http://www.dcsf.gov.uk* [Accessed June 5, 2008].

[578] Matrimonial Causes Act 1973 s.43. Similar powers existed in guardianship and other proceedings relating to children. The effect of the order was similar to a care order. Few orders were made: see the sixth edition of this work at p.701.

[579] *Review of Child Care Law*, paras 2.23, 15.11, 15.35–15.37; Law Com. WP 100, paras 2.70–2.71, 2.52; *The Law on Child Care & Family Services* (Cm.62 (1987)), paras 5c, 59; Law Com. No.172, para.5.1. See also Ch.21, below.

[580] It provisionally proposed that the court should be able to treat a case as if a care order had been sought, but concluded that there were "obvious disadvantages" in making the local authority apply for an order it did not want: Law Com. WP 100, para.2.52(i); Law Com. No.172, para.5.4.

[581] Law Com. No.172 paras 5.3, 5.5–6.

[582] Children Act 1989 ss.31(4), 37, 38.

[583] Children (Allocation of Proceedings) Order 1991 (SI 1991/1677) art.7(1)(b).

[584] Children Act 1989 s.37(1); *Re H (A Minor) (Section 37 Direction)* [1993] 2 F.L.R. (application for a residence order for an unrelated child by a lesbian couple); *F v Cambridgeshire CC* [1995] 1 F.L.R. 516 (contact application where sexual abuse was an issue).

[585] Children Act 1989 s.41(6). The guardian's role is not to supervise the local authority's assessment: *Re M (Official Solicitor's Role)* [1998] 2 F.L.R. 815, CA.

supervision order is not being made, the court must be satisfied that an appointment is necessary and that the guardian will have a useful role.[586] The local authority must: investigate the case; consider whether to apply for a care or supervision order; provide services or to take any other action with respect to the child[587]; and report their decisions, reasons and actions to the court within eight weeks or such other period as the court directs.[588] Where the local authority decides not to apply for a care or supervision order, it must also decide whether and when to review its decision.[589] The court ordering an investigation may make an interim[590] care or supervision order.[591] If the local authority thinks this unnecessary, it may apply for the order to be discharged but cannot merely send the child home.[592]

Concern has been expressed about the misuse of s.37 in order to appoint children's guardians in private law proceedings.[593] Where a child is at risk of emotional or other abuse through the parents' dispute, involvement of the local authority through s.37 may be necessary, but unless removal of the children is envisaged, it may be more appropriate to involve CAFCASS through a r.9.5 appointment:

> In *Re M (Intractable Contact Dispute: Interim Care Order)*,[594] after contact was ordered, the mother persuaded the children that the father and grandparents had sexually abused them. The father applied to enforce contact; a s.7 report was ordered; the court found that the allegations of abuse were untrue and ordered contact. The mother disobeyed, and a suspended committal order was made. The older child applied for leave for a prohibited steps order to end all contact; a r.9.5 order was made and the children were joined as parties with a CAFCASS guardian ad litem. The court made a s.37 appointment and the local authority sought an interim care order because it was unable to make its assessment whilst the children were at home. However, in *Re F (Family Proceedings: s.37 Investigation)*[595] the court refused a s.37 direction so long as the father permitted the children, who were refusing contact with their mother, to be seen by a child psychiatrist.

---

[586] *Re CE (s.37 Direction)* [1995] 1 F.L.R. 26, *per* Wall J. at 41.
[587] Children Act 1989 s.37(2), for example the local authority could refer the case to the education department to consider an application for an education supervision order. There is no requirement to see the child: cf. Children Act 1989 s.47(4).
[588] Children Act 1989 s.37(3), (4). A letter from the local authority should normally be sufficient; there is no provision in the rules for attendance by the local authority, but it is unlikely that an invitation would be refused: *per* Wall J. in *Re CE (s.37 Direction)* [1995] 1 F.L.R. 26 at 48.
[589] Children Act 1989 s.37(5).
[590] A full order requires an application from the local authority or the NSPCC: s.31(1). The local authority thus retains control over the use of its resources.
[591] Children Act 1989 s.38(1)(b), (2).
[592] Children Act 1989 s.39(1)(c), (2)(c). The Placement with Parents etc. Regulations 1991 (SI 1991/893) apply.
[593] Directions should not be made unless it appeared that a public law order might be appropriate: see *Re CE (s.37 Direction)* [1995] 1 F.L.R. 26 at 41, *per* Wall J.; *Re L (Section 37 Direction)* [1999] 1 F.L.R. 984, CA.
[594] [2003] 2 F.L.R. 636, FD. See also *Re N (Sexual abuse allegations: Professionals not abiding by findings of fact)* [2005] 2 F.L.R. 340, FD.
[595] [2005] 1 F.L.R 1122, FD.

That the court has no power to compel the local authority to take action is a matter of deep concern,[596] as is the focusing of social work resources on investigations.[597]

VII. WARDSHIP AND THE INHERENT JURISDICTION OF THE HIGH COURT

18–049 Before the Children Act 1989, the inherent jurisdiction of the High Court was usually exercised through the machinery of wardship,[598] which gives the court a continuing responsibility for the child.[599] However, it is not necessary to make a child a "ward of court"[600]—the court's powers are equally exercisable outside wardship.[601] Proceedings under this jurisdiction are "family proceedings",[602] but the High Court, exercising its inherent jurisdiction, is not limited to making orders under the Act.[603] The main use is to supplement the statutory powers[604]; injunctions may be granted.[605] Where there are very serious concerns about a child's care, but the local authority is taking no action, the child may be warded and a s.37 direction sought.[606] Many of the circumstances where the jurisdiction was used are now dealt with by statute,[607] but it continues to have a role in

---

[596] *Nottinghamshire CC v P* [1993] 2 F.L.R. 134 at 148. Sir Stephen Brown P., regretting the absence of wardship, considered that the authority might lay itself open to judicial review.

[597] DH, *Child Protection Messages from Research* (London: TSO, 1995).

[598] *Re W (A Minor) (Medical Treatment: Court's Jurisdiction)* [1993] Fam. 64 at 85, *per* Balcombe L.J.

[599] Where the child is a ward, no important decision may be made without the leave of the court. For a list, see *Kelly v BBC* [2001] 1 F.L.R. 197 at 218. The court cannot control a ward's application to the ECtHR: *Re M (Petition to European Commission of Human Rights)* [1997] 1 F.L.R. 755 (a further step in the "Zulu boy" case: *Re M (Child's Upbringing)* [1996] 2 F.L.R. 441 and para.19–005, below).

[600] The law and practice is comprehensively discussed in N. Lowe and R. White, *Wards of Court*, 2nd edn (London: Kluwer, 1986). See also Law Com. WP No.101, *Wards of Court* (1987); J. Masson and S. Morton, "The use of wardship by local authorities" (1989) 52 M.L.R. 762.

[601] *Re W (A Minor) (Medical Treatment: Court's Jurisdiction)* [1993] Fam. 64 at 73, *per* Donaldson M.R. Cf. M. Parry, "The Children Act 1989: local authorities, wardship and the inherent jurisdiction" (1992) J.S.W.F.L. 212 at 214.

[602] Children Act 1989 s.8(3)(a).

[603] It may make s.8 orders but not care orders or residence orders in favour of local authorities: Children Act 1989 s.100(1), (2); *Re C (Contact Jurisdiction)* [1995] 1 F.L.R. 777, CA (variation of contact for child freed for adoption).

[604] See, for example, *Re M (Care: Leave to Interview Child)* [1995] 1 F.L.R. 825; *Re C (Contact: Jurisdiction)* [1995] 1 F.L.R. 777; *S Glamorgan CC v W and B* [1993] 1 F.L.R. 574; *Re X (A Minor) (Adoption Details: Disclosure)* [1994] 2 F.L.R. 450, CA.

[605] *Cambridge CC v D* [1999] 2 F.L.R. 42 (application by a local authority to prevent a boyfriend harassing a girl in care); *Re G (Celebrities: Publicity)* [1999] 1 F.L.R. 409, CA (to prevent parents speaking to the press about each other following their divorce); *Re O (Minors) (Adoption: Injunction)* [1993] 2 F.L.R. 737 (to prevent the birth parents approaching the children after adoption); *Re S (Minors) (Inherent Jurisdiction: Ouster)* [1994] 1 F.L.R. 623 (to exclude an alleged abuser, but the use of ouster by local authorities would appear to be against the spirit of *Nottinghamshire CC v P* [1993] 2 F.L.R. 134).

[606] *E v London Borough of X* [2006] 1 F.L.R. 730.

[607] Disclosure of the child's whereabouts, recovery and the surrender of a passport may all be achieved under the Family Law Act 1986 ss.33, 34 and 37. The Family Law Act 1996 Pt IV provides for injunctions to protect children, and the Adoption and Children Act 2002 ss.24, 26 gives the court power to revoke placement orders and regulate contact pending adoption.

complex cases, particularly relating to medical treatment.[608] The welfare principle applies.

A. The rise and fall of wardship

The inherent jurisdiction of which wardship is a part has its roots in the feudal **18–050** system and originates in the Crown's special duty, as *parens patriae*,[609] to protect minors against injury of any kind. Between 1875 and 1971 wardship was exercised in the Chancery Division, but the Administration of Justice Act 1970 transferred it to the Family Division,[610] and certain powers can now be exercised in the county courts.[611] The main function of the court was originally to protect the property[612] of a minor whose parents were dead or unable to act, and in practice it was only the concern of the wealthy.[613] In 1950 public funding (legal aid) was made available for wardship; transfer to the Family Division increased its availability[614] and its use. Wardship came to be seen by judges,[615] lawyers and particularly local authorities[616] as the appropriate forum for complex cases concerning children.[617]

Wardship increased dramatically in the 1980s; there were nearly 5,000 applications in 1991, over half by local authorities.[618] Not everyone favoured the development of wardship.[619] The *Review of Child Care Law* made no proposals for changes to wardship but thought reform would reduce the need to use it.[620] However, its scheme for compulsory intervention would have been severely

---

[608] *Re A (Conjoined Twins: Medical Treatment)* [2001] 1 F.L.R. 1; *Re M (Medical Treatment: Consent)* [1999] 2 F.L.R. 1097 (heart transplant for 15-year-old, parental consent given); *Royal Wolverhampton Hospital NHS Trust v B* [2000] 1 F.L.R. 953, FD (declaration that child should be treated in accordance with advice of paediatrician, i.e. not be ventilated if she collapsed). There may be advantages in bringing controversial medical decisions into the public domain, but a specific issue order could be used to order treatment. No order is required if there is consent for treatment; doctors cannot be required to treat against their medical judgement.

[609] "Father of the nation"; in *Re Gault* 387 U.S. 1 (1967) at 16, it was noted that the meaning of this expression is "murky and its historic credentials are of dubious relevance" to questions of the right of the state to intervene in a minor's life. See also, J. Seymour, "Parens patriae and wardship powers: their nature and origins" (1994) 14 Ox. J.L.S. 159.

[610] Administration of Justice Act 1970 s.1(2); see now Supreme Court Act 1981 s.61 and Sch.1.

[611] Matrimonial and Family Proceedings Act 1984 s.38(2)(b), (5).

[612] *Re F (Orse A) (A Minor) (Publication of Information)* [1977] Fam. 58 at 88, *per* Lord Denning M.R.

[613] The court could only act where it had property to use for the child's maintenance: see *Wellesley v Beaufort* (1827) 2 Russ 1 at [21]; *Wellesley v Wellesley* (1828) 2 Bligh (N.S.) 124 at [132]. If the ward was a girl the court considered (and if appropriate approved) the arrangements for her marriage: see *Latey Report* (Cmnd.2242 (1967)), para.200.

[614] Applications could be made to the district registries.

[615] *Re D (A Minor) (Justices' Decision: Review)* [1977] Fam. 158, *per* Dunn J. at 164; *Cleveland Report* (Butler-Sloss J.), p.253.

[616] See Masson and Morton [1989] M.L.R. 762 pp.769–773.

[617] But not before birth; *Re F (In Utero)* [1988] Fam. 122.

[618] The reasons for local authority use are discussed in Masson and Morton, and include difficulties in satisfying the statutory test, the lack of a right of appeal, dislike of magistrates' court procedure and party status for parents.

[619] R. Dingwall, J. Eekelaar and T. Murray, *The Protection of Children* (Oxford: Blackwell, 1983); *Care or Control?* (SSRC, 1981) were concerned about the extension of state intervention; *Second Report from the Social Services Committee 1983–84* (HC 360) (the *Short Report*) suggested that judges should exercise "self-denial" (para.82).

[620] *Review of Child Care Law* (1985), para.15.38.

undermined had local authorities continued to use wardship extensively. The Law Commission considered that the objective of a comprehensive code necessitated review of wardship. Wardship could operate as: an alternative jurisdiction to achieve results that could also be achieved under the code; an independent jurisdiction to fill any gaps left by the code; a supportive jurisdiction to achieve more effectively results that could be achieved under the code; and to review decisions taken under the code. It suggested that the alternative and review uses of wardship should be removed because they "made nonsense" of the careful consideration that had gone into framing the new statutory code. The independent use might also be inconsistent with the spirit of the code but would allow defects in the new scheme to be remedied as they arose. The supportive role merely pointed to ways in which the statutory scheme should be improved.[621] The Law Commission recommended incorporating elements of wardship into the statutory scheme[622]; the Children Act 1989 went further, restricting local authorities' use of wardship and the High Court's exercise of the inherent jurisdiction in respect of children in care.[623] The Court of Appeal also stressed that wardship should be restricted to cases that could not be resolved under the Act or where the child needed the court's protection.[624] Wardship now has a residual role; its importance lies not in the numbers of applications but the ways it can be used.[625]

B. Proceedings under the inherent jurisdiction[626]

18–051   Only unmarried[627] minors[628] may be warded; the child need not be a British subject nor be present in England and Wales.[629] Under the Family Law Act 1986 a court only has jurisdiction to make Pt I orders,[630] which include orders under the inherent jurisdiction for care, contact or education if: (i) the child is habitually resident in England and Wales; or (ii) is present in England and Wales and not

---

[621] Law Com. WP No.101, paras 3.53, 4.4–4.9.

[622] Law Com. No.172, para.1.4.

[623] Children Act 1989 s.100, a controversial measure: see N. Lowe [1989] New L.J. 87; Bainham (1990), paras 8.53–8.55; cf. J. Eekelaar and R. Dingwall [1989] New L.J. 217. Savings, through ending local authorities' use of wardship, were referred to in the Financial Memorandum attached to the Bill.

[624] *Re T (A Minor) (Wardship: Representation)* [1994] Fam. 49, *per* Waite L.J. at 60.

[625] J. Mitchell [2001] Fam. Law 130–134, 212–216.

[626] See N. Lowe, "The limits of the wardship jurisdiction: who can be made a ward?" (1988) 1 J.C.L. 6.

[627] There is no authority on this point: see Bevan, para.8.08, but wardship was held not to terminate on the ward's marriage: *Re Elwes (No.2), The Times*, July 30, 1958.

[628] *Re F (In Utero)* [1988] Fam. 122 (no jurisdiction over a foetus); *Re F* [1990] 2 A.C. 1 (no jurisdiction over mentally incapable adults). If the child has diplomatic immunity, there is immunity from suit: *Re C (An Infant)* [1959] Ch. 363; *Re P (Children Act: Diplomatic Immunity)* [1998] 1 F.L.R. 624, FD.

[629] *Re B-M (Wardship: Jurisdiction)* [1993] 1 F.L.R. 979. But a jurisdictional claim founded solely on nationality was "exorbitant": *Al Habtoor v Fotheringham* [2001] 1 F.L.R. 951 at 968, *per* Ward L.J. (mother unable to ward her child who she had taken to father in Dubai; the father had obtained orders there by fraud and would not return the child).

[630] Family Law Act 1986 s.1, as amended by Children Act 1989 Sch.13, para.62. Consequently a finding of habitual residence may be crucial if the court is to order the child's return from overseas: *B v H (Habitual Residence: Wardship)* [2000] 1 F.L.R. 388, FD (baby born overseas); *Re A (Habitual Residence: Wardship)* [2007] 1 F.L.R 1589, FD.

habitually resident elsewhere in the United Kingdom.[631] In addition, jurisdiction cannot be exercised if divorce, nullity or judicial separation proceedings are continuing in another part of the United Kingdom[632] or there are proceedings relating to parental responsibility elsewhere in the EC.[633] However, where the child is present in England and Wales when the proceedings are commenced, the inherent jurisdiction may be exercised if the court considers that this is immediately necessary for the child's protection.[634]

Any individual[635] who has a sufficient interest[636] may start proceedings. There is no requirement to obtain the court's leave. Although people with a professional interest[637] in a child's welfare may start proceedings, they do so in a personal capacity and are consequently unlikely to act unless their professional association or another organisation supports them. In practice, the availability of the s.8 orders to anyone with leave makes this aspect of wardship less important. Moreover, it has been said that it would be a "bold decision" to allow an application to proceed under the inherent jurisdiction after refusal of leave under the Children Act 1989.[638]

Unless it has the support of another party,[639] a local authority wishing to use the court's inherent jurisdiction must seek leave and satisfy the court that the result desired by the authority could not be achieved without these powers,[640] and that the child is likely to suffer significant harm if the jurisdiction is not exercised[641]:

> In *Re SA (Vulnerable Adult with Capacity)*[642] the local authority was concerned that the parents of a profoundly deaf British Pakistani girl who communicated only by British sign language would take her to Pakistan for

---

[631] Family Law Act 1986 s.3(1).

[632] Family Law Act 1986 ss.2A, 3(2).

[633] Council Regulation (EC) 2201/2003; SI 2005/265 (Brussels II Revised)—this instrument does not apply to Denmark.

[634] Family Law Act 1986 s.2(3)(b); Brussels IIR art.20 does not prevent a court taking provisional steps in urgent cases; and see European Judicial Network, *Practice Guide for the Operation of Brussels II Revised*, p.11; *A v L (Jurisdiction: Brussels II)* [2002] 1 F.L.R. 1042, FD (relating to the comparable provision, art.12 in Brussels II).

[635] Including the child, who may appear without a guardian ad litem; *Re T (A Minor) (Wardship: Representation)* [1994] Fam. 49; Family Proceedings Rules 1991 (SI 1991/1247) r.9.2A.

[636] cf. *Re Dunhill* (1967) 111 S.J. 113, where a night-club owner made a girl a ward largely for publicity purposes. Applicants must now state their relationship to the minor.

[637] *Re D (A Minor) (Wardship Sterilisation)* [1976] Fam. 185 (education psychologist); *Re B (A Minor) (Wardship: Medical Treatment)* [1981] 1 W.L.R. 1421 (doctor); *A v Berkshire CC* [1989] 1 F.L.R. 273, CA (guardian ad litem). Alternatively the court may recommend that a parent does so: *R v Portsmouth Hospitals NHS Trust Ex p. Glass* [1999] 2 F.L.R. 905, CA at 910 (following a recommendation by the Official Solicitor).

[638] *C v Salford CC* [1994] 2 F.L.R. 926, 933, *per* Hale J.

[639] Wilson J.'s pragmatic view: *Medway Council v BBC* [2002] 1 F.L.R. 104 at 107.

[640] Questions relating to medical treatment for children can be dealt with by s.8 orders: *Re R (A Minor) (Blood Transfusion)* [1993] 2 F.L.R. 757 at 760, *per* Booth J. Wardship has the advantage of independent representation, and family proceedings relating to siblings can be heard together: *Re F (Mental Health Act: Guardianship)* [2000] 1 F.L.R. 192, CA.

[641] Children Act 1989 s.100(3)–(5); Family Proceedings Rules 1991 (SI 1991/1247) r.4.3 applies; see r.5.1(2). If harm is not likely, leave must be refused: *Essex CC v Mirror Group Newspapers* [1996] 1 F.L.R. 585; *Medway Council v BBC* [2002] 1 F.L.R. 104, FD.

[642] [2006] 1 F.L.R. 867, FD.

marriage to an unknown person. They therefore applied under the inherent jurisdiction for injunction to prevent this. The court gave leave to bring the proceedings; it heard evidence that the girl wanted to live in England, marry when she was older and have a husband who spoke English. It made injunctions to prevent her removal to continue beyond age 18 because she would be a vulnerable adult.

C. Powers under the inherent jurisdiction

18–052   Although the court's powers have been described as "limitless",[643] this is clearly no longer true. Apart from restrictions in the Children Act 1989,[644] the courts have also recognised that it is inappropriate to make a wide range of orders.[645] The High Court will not exercise its jurisdiction where Parliament has provided a statutory code.[646] Consequently, in *A v Liverpool City Council*[647] the mother was unable to challenge the local authority's decision to refuse contact with her child. Where there are gaps in a code, wardship has sometimes been used to provide a solution, but this amounts to judicial legislation. Orders under the inherent jurisdiction are not limited to controlling the exercise of parental responsibility but may cover the actions of third parties for the child's protection.[648] Orders may be very detailed[649] and may bind the child as well as the adults.

There are other special features if the child is a ward of court. The court in effect becomes, in law, the ward's parent, and takes control of the child[650] and the

---

[643] *Re J (A Minor)* [1984] F.L.R. 535 at 539, *per* Wood J.; see also Fricker [1993] Fam. Law 226.
[644] Children Act 1989 s.100(1), (2); care orders discharge wardship: s.91(4).
[645] *Re JS (A Minor) (Declaration of Paternity)* [1981] Fam. 22 (bare declaration of paternity); *Re G (Wardship) (Jurisdiction: Power of Arrest)* (1983) 4 F.L.R. 538 (power of arrest attached to an injunction); *Re G (A Minor) (Witness Summons)* [1988] 2 F.L.R. 396 (to set aside a witness summons requiring a three-and-a-half-year-old to appear at a court martial conducted by the US Army); *Re Manda* [1993] Fam. 183 (to restrict access by a former ward to documents from the proceedings for use in a negligence action); *Re G, Re R (Wards) (Police Interviews)* [1990] 2 F.L.R. 347 (in ways that inhibit police investigations); *Medway Council v BBC* [2002] 1 F.L.R. 104 (to prevent the broadcast of an interview with the child obtained with consent); to prevent the Secretary of State using his powers to remove a person with no right to remain in the UK: *R (Anton) v SS for the Home Dept* [2005] 2 F.L.R. 818, FD.
[646] *Re Mohammed Arif* [1968] Ch. 643 (immigration decisions); but note in *Re F (A Minor) (Immigration: Wardship)* [1990] Fam. 125, the court continued the wardship to prevent the child being concealed pending the Secretary of State's decision; and in *Re K & S (Wardship: Immigration)* [1992] 1 F.L.R. 432, wardship was continued to ensure the children's care pending the carer's deportation.
[647] [1982] A.C. 363; the court accepted that Parliament had intended that local authorities should have complete discretion over contact. Where local authorities act improperly, judicial review can be used: *W v Hertfordshire CC* [1985] A.C. 791 at 793, *per* Lord Scarman.
[648] To prevent the Registrar General disclosing details of the child's adoption during her minority: *Re X (A Minor) (Adoption Details: Disclosure)* [1994] 3 All E.R. 372; to exclude a stepparent or son-in-law who poses a risk to the child from the home: *Re S (Minors) (Inherent Jurisdiction: Ouster)* [1994] 1 F.L.R. 623; *Devon CC v S* [1994] 1 F.L.R. 355 (restricting access to a family by a convicted sex abuser). See also N. Lowe, "The limits of the wardship jurisdiction the extent of the court's powers" (1989) 1 J.C.L. 44; Lowe and White *Words of Court*, Ch.6.
[649] *Re R (PM) (An Infant)* [1968] 1 W.L.R. 385 (the number of letters and the collection of luggage). Conditions in s.8 orders may achieve this: *Re O (Contact: Imposition of Conditions)* [1995] 2 F.L.R. 124, CA.
[650] *R. v Gyngall* [1893] 2 Q.B. 232 at 239, *per* Lord Esher M.R.; *Re E (SA) (A Minor)* [1984] 1 All E.R. 289 at 290, *per* Lord Scarman.

child's property. The court has the power to protect wards from decisions, even their own, that undermine their welfare,[651] but this does not place the ward above the law.[652] The court must exercise its powers in accordance with the Human Rights Act 1998; restrictions on parents or children must be proportionate, and those whose rights are restricted must have a fair hearing.[653] Orders do not have extra-territorial effect but have been known to encourage co-operation with authorities overseas:

> In *Re KR (Abduction)*[654] Sikh parents planned an arranged marriage for their daughter who had been born and brought up in England. They took her to India and left her with an aunt. Her elder sister made her a ward of court. The court made orders for her return to England, inviting the co-operation of judicial and administrative bodies in India to put her in contact with the British High Commission. KR managed to convince her family that she was willing to stay in India; they took her to the High Commission and she was returned to England.

The jurisdiction is a continuing one, and the court retains its overall responsibility to supervise the child's welfare. No major decision may be taken without the permission of the court[655]; action taken improperly without leave constitutes contempt of the court.[656] The person with care and control must look after the child in accordance with the court's directions[657]:

> In *Re W and X (Relatives Rejected as Foster Carers)*[658] care proceedings were brought after severe neglect by the parents. The children were placed temporarily with the maternal grandparents, who were considered the most suitable placement. However, a care order was required, and the local authority could not legally place the children with the grandparents who had been rejected as foster carers. Hedley J., emphasising the importance of the placement for the children's welfare, made residence and supervision orders and made the children wards so that the court could supervise their care.

---

[651] *Re R (A Minor) (Wardship: Consent to Treatment)* [1992] Fam. 11 at 25, *per* Donaldson M.R.

[652] *Re A (A Minor) (Wardship: Police Caution)* [1989] Fam. 103.

[653] On this basis, some injunctions granted in the past might breach art.8, for example, *Cambridge CC v D* [1999] 2 F.L.R. 42 (see above, p.620), and *Devon CC v B* [1997] 1 F.L.R. 591, where the judge at first instance had barred the mother from going within 10 miles of a named town until the child was 16. In *Re C (Detention: Medical Treatment)* [1997] 2 F.L.R. 180, the court provided the same protection as would have applied in secure accommodation proceedings.

[654] [1999] 2 F.L.R. 542, FD.

[655] See Lowe and White *Words of Court*, Ch.5.

[656] A party prejudiced may apply for a committal order under RSC O.52 and *Practice Direction* [2001] 1 F.L.R. 949 or sequestration of assets: *Re F (Orse A) (A Minor) (Publication of Information)* [1977] Fam. 58. The court may use the penalty of costs: *Havering LBC v S* [1986] 1 F.L.R. 489.

[657] They may be given discretion over some matters: see *Re RJ (Wardship)* [1999] 1 F.L.R. 618, FD, where the carers were allowed to arrange medical treatment and remove the children from the jurisdiction for up to 30 days. They would have had these powers if the court had made a residence order.

[658] [2004] 1 F.L.R. 415, FD; *Re K (Adoption and Wardship)* [1997] 2 F.L.R. 221, FD and CA (wardship after revocation of flawed adoption with former adoptive parents caring for child under control of the court).

Financial support for the relatives could be by a residence order allowance under Children Act 1989 Sch.1, para.16, but this was for the discretion of the local authority.

An officer of CAFCASS may be appointed to assist the court and act as a buffer between disputing parties.[659]

18–053   All these powers must be exercised applying s.1 of the Children Act 1989, but where the issue is the publication of articles about the child or their parents, other considerations apply, particularly ECHR arts 8 and 10.[660] The inherent jurisdiction cannot be used solely to protect a family's privacy; the court must strike a balance between protecting the child and freedom of speech[661]:

> In *Re S (Identification: Restriction on Publication)*[662] the child's mother was on trial for murdering her son by salt poisoning. Care proceedings were brought in respect of a surviving son, and the child's guardian sought injunctions under the inherent jurisdiction to prevent publication of news reports of the criminal trial. These were opposed by several newspapers. The injunctions were lifted; the child appealed unsuccessfully to the Court of Appeal and then to the House of Lords. Although the child's art.8 rights were engaged, so was art.10. These competing rights had to be balanced. The impact on the child was indirect, as he would not be the subject of reports in the media. Consequently, his rights did not outweigh the importance of open reporting of criminal trials, which was crucial for public confidence.

In most cases, the public interest in favour of publication can be satisfied without identification of the ward; for example, comment may be made about local authority action or medical decisions without identifying children, their parents or their current carers.[663] A convincing case of harm must be established before an injunction will be granted.[664] It is not contempt for the media to interview a ward[665]; only if the media activities are essentially bound up with the child's care

---

[659] *CAFCASS Practice Note* [2001] 2 F.L.R. 151 (this role was formerly undertaken by the Official Solicitor); *Re W (Wardship Discharge: Publicity)* [1995] 2 F.L.R. 466, CA, *per* Balcombe L.J., but the personal supervision envisaged can only be available to a small number of cases.

[660] For a succinct analysis of the case law, see *Kelly v BBC* [2001] 1 F.L.R. 197 at 216, *per* Munby J. For a discussion of the effect of the ECHR, see *Douglas, Zeta-Jones, Northern & Shell plc v Hello! Ltd* [2001] 1 F.L.R. 982 and *Thompson and Venables v News Group Newspapers et al.* [2001] 1 F.L.R. 791, FD.

[661] *Re W (Wardship: Publication of Information)* [1992] 1 F.L.R. 99 at 102, *per* Neill L.J.; *Re Local Authority (Inquiry: Restraint on Publication)* [2004] 1 F.L.R. 541.

[662] [2005] 1 F.L.R. 591.

[663] *Re Roddy (a child) (identification: restriction on publication)* [2004] 2 F.L.R. 949 (baby would be protected even though teenage mother told her story in the press).

[664] *Kelly v BBC* [2001] 1 F.L.R. 197 at 228–229 *per* Munby J.; *Thompson and Venables v News Group Newspapers et al.* [2001] 1 F.L.R. 791, FD, *per* Butler-Sloss P. at para.44. Injunctions against publication are inevitably granted without notice to all the media; those affected should be given a clear indication of the basis on which injunctions were made. Human Rights Act 1998 s.12(3), (4) must be satisfied. For proforma injunctions, see [2001] Fam. Law 644.

[665] *Kelly v BBC* [2001] 1 F.L.R. 197 at 212, 218; providing there is no injunction forbidding this. A media interview is not "a major step" requiring court permission.

has the court claimed the power to control them in exercise of its parental responsibility.[666]

D. Procedure under wardship and the inherent jurisdiction

The reforms introduced by the Children Act 1989[667] mean that there are few   **18–054** advantages in terms of procedure or evidence in using the inherent rather than the statutory jurisdiction of the High Court. Wardship is "instantly available".[668] As soon as the originating summons is issued, the child becomes a ward, but wardship lapses if the applicant fails to make an appointment for a hearing within 21 days.[669] Where immediate action is required, the court can give directions or grant injunctions without notice.[670] The first appointment is usually before a district judge, who may make agreed orders[671] and determine what should be referred to the judge. The main hearing takes place before a judge, but, outside London, this may be a Circuit judge, Deputy Circuit judge, Recorder or Assistant recorder, nominated to do family work.[672] The Matrimonial and Family Proceedings Act 1984[673] allows wardship proceedings but not orders warding or de-warding children to be transferred to the county court; however, more complex matters are kept in the High Court.[674] All proceedings take place in chambers, but judgment is occasionally given in open court. Children are not necessarily parties to these proceedings.[675] If they are, they may be represented by a CAFCASS officer or (rarely) by the Official Solicitor.[676]

VIII. Enforcement of Orders

It is pointless for the courts to make orders if those orders are not then enforced.   **18–055** Failure to enforce orders about contact is the basis for some of the claims that the

---

[666] *Re Z (A Minor) (Freedom of Publication)* [1996] 1 F.L.R. 191, where the court refused leave for a child to be filmed for a programme about her treatment at a therapeutic institute.

[667] Without notice, orders may be made under the Children Act 1989: see Family Law Proceedings Rules 1991 (SI 1991/1247) r.4.4(4); and above, para.18–040. Family Law Proceedings Rules 1991 (SI 1991/1247) r.9(2A) applies. Wardship does not provide a means of imposing a guardian ad litem on a competent but unwilling child: *Re T (A Minor) (Wardship: Representation)* [1994] Fam. 49. Evidence is given by affidavit, and oral testimony is required; cf. Family Law Proceedings Rules 1991 (SI 1991/1247) r.4.17; hearsay evidence is admissible under both jurisdictions: SI 1993/621.

[668] Law Com. WP 101, para.2.8. Supreme Court Act 1981 s.41(2).

[669] RSC O.90 rr.3, 4; see Lowe and White, *Words of Court*, paras 4.6–4.15.

[670] Duty judges are available to deal with emergency applications: see Lowe and White, *Words of Court*, paras 4.24 *et seq.; Re O (A Minor) (Medical Treatment)* [1993] 2 F.L.R. 149 at [154].

[671] RSC O.90 r.12 allows district judges to make orders on any matter that could be dealt with by a judge in chambers and has not been reserved by the judge; Lowe and White, *Words of Court*, paras 6.67–6.71.

[672] *Practice Direction* [1999] 2 F.L.R. 799.

[673] Matrimonial and Family Proceedings Act 1984 s.38(2)(b).

[674] *Practice Direction* [1992] 2 F.L.R. 87.

[675] Lowe and White, *Words of Court*, paras 3.4, 3.8; Masson and Morton [1989] M.L.R. 762 at pp.777–778.

[676] Family Law Proceedings Rules 1991 (SI 1991/1247) r.9.5(1); *CAFCASS Practice Note* [2001] 1 F.L.R. 151; *Practice Note (Official Solicitor appointment)* [2001] 1 F.L.R. 155.

family justice system is "biased against fathers".[677] This is not just a private
matter between the parties; the right to respect for family life means that the state
has a positive obligation to enable parents and children to maintain relationships,
and must provide effective remedies,[678] but enforcement is fraught with
difficulties: "What measures can be expected?" "How should conflicts between
adult's rights and children's interests be balanced?"[679]

In *Zawadaka v Poland*[680] the father claimed a breach of ECHR art.8 because
he had not been able to have his contact order enforced. Following a bitter
dispute, the parents agreed on residence to the mother and weekend contact
for the father. The mother refused to allow contact on at least one occasion
and the father sought to enforce the order. The court refused because the
order did not specify contact dates. The father then kidnapped the child and
went into hiding for 15 months, ignoring further court orders. After the child
was recovered, the court limited the father's parental rights and contact. The
mother did not allow contact and the court welfare officers refused to assist
the father. The mother relocated to England with the child; their whereabouts were unknown. The ECtHR by a majority of 4 to 3 found a violation
of the father's rights. The failure of the order to specify dates was not a good
reason to refuse to assist the father. Breach of the order did not justify
removing his rights without a finding that this was in the child's best
interests. In contrast, the minority considered that the domestic authorities
were justified in refusing to enforce contact. It was in the child's interests to
be protected from the bitter dispute of these parents who were completely
incapable of communicating in a rational manner. The removal of the
father's rights was justified because of his disregard of the child's wellbeing.

In cases concerning children, orders require personal actions and impact on
relationships. There are no easy answers. Some parents exhibit high levels of
emotion and obsessive behaviour,[681] and do not respond to judicial reasoning or
the powers of the court. Both attempts at enforcement and failure to enforce may
enrage disputes, undermine the welfare of children and breach human rights.

---

[677] Constitutional Affairs Committee, *Family Justice: The Operation of the Family Courts, 4th
Report 2004–5* (HC 116, (2005)), para.104.
[678] *Hokkanen v Finland* [1996] 1 F.L.R. 289; *Hansen v Turkey* [2004] 1 F.L.R. 142; cf. *Glaser v UK*
[2001] 1 F.L.R. 153, where initiating enforcement was seen as the responsibility of the applicant not
the State.
[679] See evidence of John Eekelaar to the Constitutional Affairs Committee (2004–5 HC 116),
para.109 and Ev 40–42.
[680] [2005] 2 F.L.R. 897.
[681] For example *Harris v Harris; A-G v Harris* [2001] 2 F.L.R. 895, FD, where the father, "a man
devoid of all moral scruple", harassed his family, the lawyers and the judges, and destroyed his
relationship with his children by his "obstinacy". There are cases where firm orders and the
intersession of a specialist can lead to resolution of apparently intractable disputes: *A v A (Shared
Residence)* [2004] 1 F.L.R. 1195, FD.

A. Powers of the court

Sanctions exist to secure compliance[682]; s.8 orders[683] made by a family **18–056** proceedings court can be enforced by fining[684] persons in default or committing them to custody until the default is remedied, but for no longer than two months.[685] The court may act on its own motion or by complaint,[686] but it has been said that courts should be inhibited by specific procedural safeguards from moving to committal without careful consideration of the consequences.[687] Considerable care must be taken that the correct procedures are followed; for example a residence order may only be enforced where a copy of the order has been served on the other person[688]; an order for contact must state the date and time of the handover.[689] Breach of the order must be willful; the act or omission must be carried out with knowledge of the terms of the order.[690]

In the county court and the High Court, breach of an order may be treated as contempt of court, but declaratory orders such as those for reasonable contact cannot be enforced.[691] Contemnors may be imprisoned for up to two years for breach of a High Court order, their property may be sequestered or they may be fined.[692] Sequestered property may be sold to raise money to pay for the enforcement of the order.[693] The court may act on its own motion or on application, but a judge should not both initiate and hear proceedings.[694] Considerable care must be taken that the correct procedures are followed before a person may be committed, and cumbersome procedural rules must be followed.[695] Committal proceedings are a criminal charge for the purposes of art.6 of the ECHR; provision must be made for legal assistance for the defendant;

---

[682] Many factors impact on compliance with child support: A. Atkinson and S. McKay, *Investigating Compliance of Child Support Agency Clients* (DWP, 2005); links between contact and child support are well established; pp.37, 45. Pressure to comply may from a party's solicitor: see C. Smart and B. Neale [1997] Fam. Law 332.

[683] Children Act 1989 s.14 mentions only residence orders, but it was held in *P v W* [1984] Fam. 32 that Magistrates' Courts Act 1980 s.63(3) applied to access orders because these were orders "to do anything other than the payment of money or to abstain from doing anything". This applies equally to all s.8 orders so long as they are made by a court, not a single justice. It may not apply to directions: see CAAC, *Report 1992/3*, p.42.

[684] £50 per day up to a maximum of £5,000; see also CAAC, *Report 1993/4*, p.52.

[685] Magistrates Courts' Act 1980 s.63(3); Contempt of Court Act 1981 s.17(2) and Sch.3.

[686] Contempt of Court Act 1981 s.17, Sch.3.

[687] CAAC, *Report 1993/4*, p.53.

[688] Children Act 1989 s.14(2).

[689] *Re H (Contact: Enforcement)* [1996] 1 F.L.R. 614.

[690] *P v W* [1984] Fam. 32 at 38, *per* Wood J.

[691] County Courts Act 1984 s.38; RSC O.52 r.5; *D v D (Access: Committal)* [1991] 2 F.L.R. 34. The order would need to specify when, where and by whom contact was to be allowed.

[692] Contempt of Court Act 1981 s.14. The duration of the committal must be fixed: *Re C (A Minor) (Contempt)* [1986] 1 F.L.R. 578. Credit should be given for admissions: *Re R (A Minor) (Contempt)* [1994] 2 F.L.R. 185. There is no power to suspended sentences for contempt: *Harris v Harris* [2002] 1 F.L.R. 248, CA.

[693] *Richardson v Richardson* [1990] 1 F.L.R. 186 (money raised by mortgaging the wife's house was used by the husband to bring proceedings in Eire for the return of the children). In *Mir v Mir* [1992] 1 F.L.R. 624, the husband's house was sold following a variation of the sequestration order; *Re S (Abduction: Sequestration)* [1995] 1 F.L.R. 858.

[694] *Re M (A Minor) (Contempt of Court: Committal of Court's Own Motion)* [1999] Fam. 263.

[695] *President's Direction* [2001] 1 F.L.R. 949, applying the Civil Procedure *Practice Direction* and modifying O.52 and CCR 1981 O.29. The requirements for information specified in the CPR *Direction* must be satisfied: *President's Direction* [2001] 1 F.L.R. 949, para.1.1(c).

the breach must be proved at the criminal standard; and the defendant cannot be required to give evidence.[696] A committal order is an order of last resort.[697] The courts need to bear in mind that the parties in family cases will probably have some continuing relationship. Breach of a court order may also give rise to criminal proceedings for offences such as child abduction[698]; contempt proceedings should be dealt with swiftly and not be delayed, pending the criminal trial.[699]

Where an order made in England or Wales that requires a child to be handed to another is disobeyed, the court may authorise an officer of the court (or in the case of a magistrates' court, a constable) to enter premises (with force if necessary), search, take charge of and deliver the child to the person concerned.[700] In practice, the courts appear reluctant to use these enforcement powers except to ensure that children are returned to their residential carer. Where a child is wrongfully kept following contact,[701] the court may order their return but may refuse to do so pending a hearing if the parent with care has a good relationship with the child, can provide adequately and has made serious allegations about the care of the residential parent.[702] There is no question that the courts disapprove of parents who "snatch" children and that this is a powerful factor in the consideration of the child's future care, but the welfare test applies.[703] Where a child is settled temporarily, a further move may be undesirable, but delay undermines the position of the other parent and may lead the court to sanction the arrangement.

18–057   Contact orders pose even more severe enforcement problems; courts go to considerable lengths in an attempt to get compliance—seeking reports, varying orders, making children parties, making family assistance orders or involving the local authority.[704] In some cases they use their enforcement powers. Courts can fine or imprison parents for breach of a contact order, or change the child's residence, but none of these powers may lead to co-operation, and any of them may be more detrimental to the child's welfare than lack of contact.[705] Moreover,

---

[696] *Hammerton v Hammerton* [2007] 2 F.L.R. 1133, CA; *Re G (Contempt: Committal)* [2003] 2 F.L.R. 58, CA.

[697] *A v N* [1997] 1 F.L.R. 533 at 542, *per* Beldam L.J.; *Re M (Contact Order)* [2005] 2 F.L.R. 1006 (suspended sentence not appropriate where defendant impecunious).

[698] Child Abduction Act 1984: see para.20–002, below.

[699] *Szczepanski v Szczepanski* [1985] F.L.R. 468; *Keeber v Keeber* [1995] 2 F.L.R. 748, CA.

[700] Family Law Act 1986 s.34, as amended. cf. *R. v Chief Constable of Cheshire Ex p. K* [1990] 1 F.L.R. 70. Unless there is an order directed at them, the police should not give the impression that they are enforcing civil court orders: *Re J (Children: Ex p. Orders)* [1992] 1 F.L.R. 606.

[701] *W v D* [1980] 1 F.L.R. 393; *Jenkins v Jenkins* (1978) 9 Fam. Law 215, CA.

[702] *Re J (A Minor) (Interim Custody)* [1989] 2 F.L.R. 304, CA.

[703] *Re J (A Minor) (Interim Custody)* [1989] 2 F.L.R. 304 at 307, *per* Butler-Sloss L.J. This is not generally the case in "International cases" where the child is moved from one country to another; see below, 20–014.

[704] See above paras 16–020, 18–012, 18–027 and 18–048.

[705] It is the quality of parental relationships that benefits children, not contact per se, and parental conflict is damaging: J. Hunt and C. Roberts, *Child Contact with Non-resident Parents* (Oxford University, Dept of Social Policy, 2004); B. Rogers and J. Pryor, *Divorce & Separation: the Outcomes for Children* (York: JRF, 1998). See also C. Smart and B. Neale [1997] Fam. Law 332, who view the emphasis on contact and enforcement as contrary to the welfare of carers and children.

contact orders are directed at the parent with care[706]; failure by the contact parent to meet their obligations by turning up for contact does not amount to a breach of the order. Consequently, it is parents with care (usually mothers) not contact parents (fathers) who are the focus of court enforcement.

Concerns about enforcement of contact led the Children Act Sub-Committee of the Advisory Board on Family Law to examine this area of law.[707] Its report, *Making Contact Work*,[708] favoured a structured approach to enforcing contact similar to that operating in Australia.[709] It proposed that the court should have much wider powers, and proposed a range of measures to advise and educate parents about the importance of contact, to make provision to support contact and to punish defaulters. The court would be able to direct resident parents to parenting programmes or require them to seek psychiatric advice—if they still disobeyed the contact order, they could be required to undertake community service or attend parenting classes; imprisonment would be a last resort.[710] Although these proposals are creative and well-meaning, it is difficult to ignore the illogicality of seeking to educate parents with care about their children's needs whilst large numbers of non-residential parents fail to maintain contact or pay child support, and some continue to abuse former partners.

The Government accepted the need for more diverse enforcement powers, and indicated that it would prepare a bill along the lines of the CASC proposals.[711] This approach was welcomed by the Constitutional Affairs Committee, which thought that emphasis should be placed on overcoming problems through CAFCASS intervention and education programmes rather than by traditional enforcement, because the court was not the best place to attempt to resolve complex family problems.[712] Although the Committee that examined the draft Children (Contact) and Adoption Bill agreed, it also suggested that resident parents should be able to enforce contact.[713] Such a change would have given the courts a large and even more futile role. A slightly amended[714] version of the Bill was introduced, and subsequently the Government agreed to a clause that required the CAFCASS officers to undertake risk assessments for proceedings.[715]

[706] Children Act 1989 s.8: "an order requiring the person with whom the child lives . . . to allow the child . . . to have contact with a named person".
[707] Advisory Board on Family Law, *Third Annual Report 1999–2000*, paras 3.54–3.57. This work followed on from its *Report to the Lord Chancellor on the Question of Parental Contact in Cases Where There is Domestic Violence* (2000).
[708] Advisory Board on Family Law: Children Act Sub-Committee, *Making Contact Work Report* (2002); *Consultation Paper* (2001). This work, and that on contact and domestic violence, was led by Wall J.
[709] *Making Contact Work* paras 14.23 and 14.55. The Australian regime has been strengthened by the Family Law Amendment (Shared Residence) Act 2006 Sch.2.
[710] *Making Contact Work* paras 14.50–14.57.
[711] Cm.6452 (2004), paras 84 and 85.
[712] 2005 (HC 116), paras 39, 111–114.
[713] Joint Committee on the Children (Contact) and Adoption Bill 2004–5 (HC 400), para.38.
[714] The draft bill contained a provision that would have allowed curfews and electronic tagging of parents in breach of contact orders.
[715] Children and Adoption Act 2006 s.7, adding Children Act 1989 s.16A. Throughout the debates, the Government resisted amendments from the opposition to include a presumption of contact. It was also reluctant to consider safety issues.

18–058   The Children and Adoption Act 2006 does not codify the enforcement of orders in family proceedings but merely adds to the powers of the court and the obligations of CAFCASS. Although there are 16 sections relating to enforcement, the additions to court powers are quite limited, and heavily circumscribed. The effectiveness of the Act will depend on the resources put at the disposal of CAFCASS and the courts.[716]

The Act gives the court powers to make directions when considering disputed applications for contact[717] and conditions in orders requiring either party to participate in contact activities. These can include meeting a mediator or attending a domestic-violence perpetrator programme; conditions could already be included, but a formal programme of contact activities has not existed.[718] A CAFCASS officer can be required to monitor contact for up to 12 months and report to the court on compliance.[719] Although such a report could lead to the court exercising its enforcement powers, such action is not encouraged.[720] In future, all contact orders will include a notice warning of the consequences of failure to comply. This amounts to a penal notice to make it easier to enforce the order by contempt proceedings.[721] Courts have been given new powers to make enforcement orders requiring the person in breach of the order to do unpaid work.[722] Before making this order the court must be satisfied that an unpaid work scheme accessible to the defaulter is available,[723] and must consider the welfare of the child subject to the contact order.[724]

The relationship between enforcement and child welfare is a contentious one. Prior to the 2006 Act, two different views had been expressed in the Court of Appeal. In *Churchard v Churchard*[725] the court, applying the welfare test, refused the father's applications for residence and refused to commit the mother for refusing contact. In contrast, in *A v N*[726] Ward L.J. doubted whether the child's welfare was paramount in proceedings for enforcement.[727] He refused an appeal against committal by a mother of a four-year-old for preventing the father's

---

[716] This issue was considered in detail by the Joint Committee, 2004–5 (HC 400), Ch.8. The Government asserted that the reforms would be cost neutral (RIA); see also 2004–5 (HC 400), para.150.

[717] Children Act 1989 s.11B(1), but not if it dismisses the application; s.11A(7).

[718] Children Act 1989 s.11A(5)(6). A wide range of conditions could be added under s.11(7).

[719] Children Act 1989 s.11H(2). Such monitoring can be of the carer, the person with contact or a parent: subs.3.

[720] *Re M (A Minor) (Contempt of Court: Committal of Court's Own Motion)* [1999] Fam. 263.

[721] Children Act 1989 s.11I. There is discretion whether to attach a penal notice: *Re F (Contact: Enforcement)* [1998] 1 F.L.R. 691, CA.

[722] Children Act 1989 s.11J. The power can only be exercised on application (subs.(5)); breach must be proved at the criminal standard (subs.(2)). The original suggestion of work with children was abandoned; defaulters will work alongside others doing community service: 2004–5 (HC 400), para.97. The maximum number of hours is 200: Children Act 1989 Sch.A1.

[723] Children Act 1989 s.11L(2) This may make enforcement more problematic because a harsher penalty should not be used where there is no such scheme: *Re M (Contact Order)* [2005] 2 F.L.R. 1006.

[724] Children Act 1989 s.11L(7).

[725] [1984] F.L.R. 635, CA.

[726] [1997] 1 F.L.R. 533, CA, and see *Making Contact Work Report* (2002), App.4.

[727] At 540; in *Re M (A Minor) (Contempt of Court: Committal of Court's Own Motion)* [1999] Fam. 263 at 281, he referred to "giving proper weight" to the interests of children even if their welfare was not strictly paramount.

contact, even though the mother's imprisonment would have "a grievous effect" on the child. The distress of separation is balanced against the long-term damage of not knowing the father. Courts should not tolerate the flouting of their orders.[728] Where the parent with care repeatedly fails to comply with contact orders, the Court of Appeal has accepted that the judge may have no realistic option other than committing them.[729] This more robust view appears to have gained ground. Welfare is paramount if the court's response to breach of a contact order is transfer of residence, but, again, the court appear to weigh the scales heavily in favour of contact:

> In *Re C (Residence Order)*[730] a girl, aged five, whose parents had separated when she was one year old, had lived all her life with her mother. Contact broke down when she was just over two; the father obtained contact orders but was only able to see his daughter on two occasions. The mother sabotaged contact by giving the child a negative impression of her father. The mother's reasons for refusing contact were discounted and an order for reasonable contact made. Six months later, the judge ordered immediate transfer of residence because the mother had continued in not complying with contact. She was given leave but her appeal was refused.

However, it has been said that a court that puts enforcement above harm to the child must be very clear about the correctness of the orders being enforced.[731] **18–059**

The 2006 Act gives the court a further power to compensate financial loss resulting from breach of a contact order. If a contact parent arranges a holiday for the child but the resident parent, in breach of the order and without reasonable excuse, refuses to allow the child to go, the court can award compensation.[732] This provision is also problematic and neither party may feel fairly treated. The order can only be enforced as a civil debt[733] and no account can be taken of arrears in child support payments because these are owed to the Secretary of State, not the parent with care.[734] Courts may also use their general powers to award costs against a parent whose intransigence leads to additional hearings.[735]

---

[728] At 540–541. The father had a history of violence, but Ward L.J. placed the blame firmly on the mother: "This little child suffers because the mother chooses to make her suffer".

[729] *Re S (Contact Dispute: Committal)* [2005] 1 F.L.R. 812, CA, *per* Thorpe L.J. at para.9. Before taking this stance, the court may adjourn to establish whether there will be compliance: *A v Y (Child's Surname)* [1999] 2 F.L.R. 5.

[730] [2008] 1 F.L.R. 211, CA; *V v V (Contact: Implacable Hostility)* [2004] 2 F.L.R. 851, FD; *Re P (Committal for Breach of Contact Order: Reasons)* [2007] 1 F.L.R. 1820, CA.

[731] *Re F (Contact: Enforcement)* [1998] 1 F.L.R. 691, CA at 696, *per* Hale J.

[732] Children Act 1989 s.110; theoretically a parent with care could obtain compensation if she suffered loss because the contact parent failed to collect the child from school or failed to care for the child at a specific time and she had to miss work.

[733] Children Act 1989 s.110(11). It was suggested to the Committee that it should be treated as a criminal debt: 2004–5 (HC 400), para.112.

[734] *R. (Kehoe) v Secretary of State for Work and Pensions* [2005] 2 F.L.R. 1249, HL.

[735] *Re T (Order for Costs)* [2005] 2 F.L.R. 681, CA.

CHAPTER NINETEEN

EXERCISE OF THE COURT'S DISCRETION: THE WELFARE PRINCIPLE

I.   CHILD'S WELFARE PARAMOUNT 19–001
A. Presumptions and assumptions 19–003
B. Welfare and the Human Rights Act
1998 19–004
C. The meaning of the principle 19–005
D. Application of the welfare
principle 19–009

E. Problems with the welfare
principle 19–011
F. The statutory checklist 19–014
G. Review of the court's decisions on
welfare 19–024

I. CHILD'S WELFARE PARAMOUNT

Section 1 of the Children Act 1989 provides: **19–001**

> "When a court determines any question with respect to—
>
> (a) the upbringing of a child; or
> (b) the administration of the child's property or the application of any
> income arising from it,
>
> the child's welfare shall be the court's paramount consideration."

The principle that the child's welfare should determine the outcome of disputes originates from the practice of the Chancery Court in wardship and guardianship cases in the late 18th and 19th centuries.[1] The Guardianship of Infants Act 1886 first prescribed the child's welfare as a relevant consideration, together with the conduct and wishes of the parents. Although there was growing concern for the welfare of children during the early part of the last century,[2] the Guardianship

---

[1] Law Com. WP 96; *Custody*, para.6.2.
[2] Concern for children developed the work of the great Victorian reformers, Barnardo, Shaftesbury, Carpenter et al.; see I. Pinchbeck and Hewitt, *Children in English Society* (1973), Vol.II; H. Hendrick, *Child Welfare England 1872–1989* (1994).

of Infants Act 1925 would not have been passed if feminists had not been claiming equality for mothers during marriage.[3] The 1925 Act made the child's welfare the "first and paramount consideration"[4] when a court determined a relevant issue and declared that neither parent had a superior claim.[5] It was subsequently held to be declaratory of the then-existing law and also to apply equally to disputes between the parents and other people.[6] The word "first" was thought by the Law Commission to suggest that the child's welfare should be balanced with other factors[7]; consequently, it was not retained in the Children Act 1989.

The welfare of the child who is the subject of the proceedings[8] has been said to be the "only" consideration in cases where s.1 applies,[9] but it has been argued that the "no-order" principle[10] undermines the paramountcy rule and the Human Rights Act overrides it.[11] Despite a recommendation from the Law Commission that the welfare of no one child in the family should prevail,[12] there is no statutory requirement to balance the interests of all children involved in the proceedings. Courts have avoided considering the conflicting interests of a parent below the age of 18 and her child,[13] and of siblings,[14] by focusing legalistically[15] on the application:

---

[3] For a full account drawing on unpublished official and other material, see S. Cretney, "What will the women want next? The struggle for power within the family 1925–1975" (1996) 112 L.Q.R. 110; Cretney *Family Law in the Twentieth Century*, p.569; S. Maidment, *Child Custody and Divorce* (1984), p.139; J. Brophy, "Parental rights and children's welfare: some problems of feminists strategy in the 1920s" (1982) 10 *International Journal of the Sociology of Law* 149–168.

[4] Guardianship of Infants Act 1925 s.1; the provision was re-enacted in the Guardianship of Minors Act 1971 s.1.

[5] Mothers did not have equality of parental rights: the child's father remained the sole legal guardian. Mothers only acquired guardianship rights by the Guardianship Act 1973 and even then were not described as the child's guardian; see the Guardianship Act 1973 s.1; Law Com. WP 91, *Guardianship*, para.2.8.

[6] *J v C* [1970] A.C. 668, *per* Lord Guest at 697. Both these claims seem at odds with the origins of the provision: see Cretney *Twentieth Century*, pp.570–573.

[7] Law Com. No.96, para.6.9; Law Com. No.172, *Review of Child Law Guardianship and Custody* (HC 594 (1988)), para.3.13.

[8] *Birmingham CC v H (No.3)* [1994] 1 F.L.R. 224, HL.

[9] *S (BD) v S (DJ)* [1977] Fam. 109; but Hall [1977] C.L.J. 252 considered there may still be room for considerations of justice in evenly balanced cases.

[10] A. Bainham, "The privatisation of the public interest in children" (1990) 53 M.L.R. 206. In *Re J (A Minor) (Contact)* [1994] 1 F.L.R. 729, CA, the Court of Appeal refused to overturn a decision to make no order even though they recognised this was unjust because it was clear that an order would be ineffective, but in *Re R (A Minor) (Contact)* [1994] 2 F.L.R. 441, the order was made despite threats of disobedience from the mother.

[11] See below, para.19–004.

[12] Law Com. No.172, para.3.13; Draft Bill cl.1(2).

[13] *Birmingham CC v H (No.3)* [1994] 1 F.L.R. 224, HL. The application was made under the Children Act 1989 s.34(4), but could as easily have been made under s.34(2) by the mother who was in care.

[14] *Re T and E (Proceedings: Conflicting Interests)* [1995] 1 F.L.R. 581; *Re S (Contact: Application by Sibling)* [1998] 2 F.L.R. 897.

[15] The approved approach involves considering which child is subject to the application: *F v Leeds CC* [1994] 2 F.L.R. 60 at 63, *per* Ward J.; in *Re F (Contact: Child in Care)* [1995] 1 F.L.R. 510, this was the child living with the parents, not the applicant child in care who would be named in the s.8 order; *Re S (Contact: Application by Sibling)* [1998] 2 F.L.R. 897 (leave refused despite the adverse effect on an applicant child).

In *Re T and E (Proceedings: Conflicting Interests)*[16] two children with the same mother were in care following sexual abuse of the older child, T, by her step-father who was also her uncle and father of the younger child, E. T's father applied to discharge her care order and for residence. No Children Act application was made in respect of E. The application was granted because it was in T's best interests, although it was in E's interests for T to be placed for adoption with her.

Where two or more children involved in the same proceedings have conflicting interests, it has been suggested that[17] the court should strike a balance between their interests and seek to find the least detrimental alternative.

All arguments must focus on the impact on the child of the behaviour or arrangements. Thus, parental conduct is relevant to the extent that it affects parenting capacity,[18] the child's relationship with the parent[19] or the child's safety[20] or development.[21] Violent behaviour may threaten the child's wellbeing by undermining the parent with care, damaging the child's emotional development and placing him or her at physical risk.[22] Doing justice between the parents, or the notion that parents have rights over their children,[23] has been said to play no part in the application of the welfare test. However, "the right to family life"[24] can only be restricted to the extent permitted by the European Convention on Human Rights.

The Children Act 1989 applies the "welfare principle" to cases concerning the upbringing of children, including care proceedings where the court must also be satisfied that the threshold conditions for an order exist.[25] Maintenance is

19–002

---

[16] [1995] 1 F.L.R. 581.

[17] *Re A (Conjoined Twins: Medical Treatment)* [2001] 1 F.L.R. 1 at 49, *per* Ward L.J.; at 102, *per* Robert Walker L.J.

[18] *Re R (Minors) (Custody)* [1986] 1 F.L.R. 6: the father had a criminal record and a drink problem.

[19] *Re M (Contact: Long-term Best Interests)* [2006] 1 F.L.R. 627, CA. There are dicta in *Richards v Richards* [1984] A.C. 174 that it is not good for a child to see one parent "get away" with behaving badly.

[20] *Re D* [1977] A.C. 602; the father's homosexuality (which the court appears to have confused with paedophilia) was said to endanger the child because of possible approaches from other men who visited the child's home; cf. *Re C (Residence Order: Lesbian Co-parents)* [1994] Fam. Law 468. If the issue is contact, the child may be protected by arranging for direct contact at a contact centre or be supervised, or for indirect contact; *Re A (Contact: Witness Protection Scheme)* [2006] 2 F.L.R. 551; *Re F (Indirect Contact)* [2007] 1 F.L.R. 1015, CA, but not if the child rejects the non-residential parent: *Re C (Contact: No Order for Contact)* [2000] 2 F.L.R. 723.

[21] In *Re C (Contact) (Moratorium: Change of Gender)* [2007] 1 F.L.R. 1642, CA, the expert advised that the children needed to be told of the father's change of gender. In *Re J (Paternity: Welfare of Child)* [2007] 1 F.L.R. 1064, the court made no order that the child's true paternity be established in the face of the child's dependency on the mother and her opposition to this.

[22] *Re L, Re V, Re M, Re H (Contact: Domestic Violence)* [2000] 2 F.L.R. 334, CA; Sturge and Glaser [2000] Fam. L. 615; H. Cleaver et al., *Children's Needs—Parenting Capacity* (London: TSO, 1999). Continued conflict can also undermine the carer: *Re M (Contact: Parental Responsibility)* [2001] 2 F.L.R. 342, FD.

[23] *Re KD (A Minor) (Ward: Termination of Access)* [1988] A.C. 806.

[24] ECHR art.8. and see below, para.19–004.

[25] Children Act 1989 s.31(2); the DHSS *Review of Child Care Law* (1985) rejected the welfare test as a basis for intervention in family life: para.15.10; see para.21–019, below.

specifically excluded[26]; decisions about the emigration of children in care require additional considerations.[27] Where the child has been abducted, the welfare test applies to cases not determined under the Hague Convention.[28] Also the decision to make a secure accommodation order is not one to which s.1 applies.[29] Other statutes, notably the Adoption and Children Act 2002 and the Child Support Act 1991, apply other welfare formulations.[30]

Where Parliament has provided a different standard, the courts may not apply the welfare test by considering the matter under the inherent jurisdiction.[31] Moreover, the rule of paramountcy does not apply where upbringing is only incidental to some other dispute.[32] The child's welfare is not paramount in a dispute concerning the occupation of the family home,[33] but where a decision about a child impinges upon a decision about the matrimonial home, and vice versa, it is desirable for them to be dealt with together so that the judge can look at matters as a whole.[34] Under the Family Law Act 1996[35] the court must consider whether the applicant or any "relevant child"[36] is likely to suffer "significant harm" attributable to the respondent's conduct, and balance this against the harm to the respondent or any relevant child. In the case of married or formerly married couples, the court must make the order unless the balance favours the respondent.[37] Welfare has been said to yield to considerations of public policy.[38] Freedom of speech is guaranteed in the ECHR; where a child's welfare is potentially at risk through publicity in the media, the court must conduct a balancing exercise weighing up the respective interests under arts 8

---

[26] Children Act 1989 s.105(1); in maintenance cases under that Act, the court must consider the matters in Sch.1 para.4; and see *K v K (Minors: Property Transfer)* [1992] 2 F.L.R. 220. Under the Matrimonial Causes Act 1973 s.25(1), the court must give "first consideration" to the child's welfare; see *Suter v Suter and Jones* [1987] Fam. 111, but note that this has become irrelevant in most cases because of the Child Support Act 1991.

[27] Children Act 1989 Sch.2 para.19; *Re G (Minors) (Care: Leave to Place Outside the Jurisdiction)* [1994] 2 F.L.R. 301; *MH v GP (Child: Emigration)* [1995] 2 F.L.R. 106, CA.

[28] *Re J (Child Returned Abroad: Convention Rights)* [2005] 2 F.L.R 802, HL; and see 21–013 and para.20–023, below.

[29] Children Act 1989 s.25; *M v Birmingham CC* [1994] 2 F.L.R. 141; *Re M (Secure Accommodation Order)* [1995] 1 F.L.R. 418, CA. cf. *Guidance*, Vol.4, para.8.9.

[30] Adoption and Children Act 2002 s.1(2) states that the child's welfare "throughout his life" must be the paramount consideration in adoption decisions. The Child Support Act 1991 s.2 only requires the Secretary of State and child support officers "to have regard" to welfare when exercising discretion. Children and Young Persons Act 1933 s.44: courts must "have regard" to the welfare of a child brought before them.

[31] *A v Liverpool CC* [1982] A.C. 363. cf. *Re N (A Minor) (Adoption)* [1990] 1 F.L.R. 58.

[32] See *Re X (A Minor) (Wardship Jurisdiction)* [1975] Fam. 47 at 62, *per* Pennycuick J., a case concerning the publication of a book about the ward's father. Or where the issue is the parent's deportation: *R v SS for Home Department, Ex p. Gangadeen* [1998] 1 F.L.R. 762, CA.

[33] *Richards v Richards* [1984] A.C. 174; the Children Act 1989 did not overrule this decision: *Gibson v Austin* [1992] 2 F.L.R. 437.

[34] *Re B (A Minor: Custody)* [1991] 2 F.L.R. 405, *per* Butler-Sloss L.J. at 409.

[35] Family Law Act 1996 Pt IV; see generally, Ch.9, above.

[36] Family Law Act 1996 s.62(2).

[37] Family Law Act 1996 ss.33(7), 35(8), 36(8); *B v B (Occupation Order)* [1999] 1 F.L.R. 715.

[38] See the fourth edition of this book at p.325 citing *Re Mohamed Arif* [1968] 1 Ch. 643, particularly *per* Russell L.J. at 662–663. However, this case is an early example of the ousting of wardship where the situation is within a statutory code (see *A v Liverpool CC* [1982] A.C. 363) and may be explained without this further rule.

and 10.[39] Where the publicity relates to a parent and involves no direct identification of the child by name or photograph, publication is likely to be allowed, even though it is distressing to the child, at least where the matter (such as the parent's trial) is of public interest.[40]

The welfare principle in s.1 applies to courts,[41] but parents, local authorities and children themselves must also have regard to children's welfare. Decisions by parents that conflict with welfare may be reviewed by the courts[42]; thus it has been said that parents must apply the welfare principle.[43] The same could be said of decisions by children.[44] Local authority decisions that do not require court approval are generally immune from review on the merits,[45] but children's services authorities and many other public bodies must have regard to the need to safeguard and promote the welfare of children when arranging to discharge their functions.[46]

A. Presumptions and assumptions

It is said that there are no presumptions in the Children Act 1989 that can displace the paramountcy of the welfare principle.[47] However, judges have suggested principles or assumptions[48] that should guide the application of the welfare test, and even used these to preclude the "balancing exercise" that

19–003

---

[39] *Re Roddy (A Child) (Identification: Restriction on Publication)* [2004] 2 F.L.R. 949; Fortin [2006] M.L.R 299, 319.

[40] *Re S (A Child) (Identification: Restrictions on Publication)* [2005] 1 F.L.R. 592, HL. The House of Lords doubted the relevance of pre-HRA 1998 case law on the restraint of publication, but noted that the reasoning in some inherent jurisdiction cases might assist in the ultimate balancing exercise (at para.23).

[41] CAFCASS officers must have regard to the welfare checklist in s.1(3): Family Proceedings Rules 1991 (SI 1991/1247) r.4.11(1); the welfare test in the Adoption and Children Act 2002 s.1 also applies to adoption agencies.

[42] Under the inherent jurisdiction or by seeking a s.8 order under the Children Act 1989. A child or third party who sought to bring proceedings would require leave: s.10(1)(a)(ii); and welfare is not paramount in proceedings for leave: see s.10(9): *Re A and W (Minors) (Residence Order: Leave to Apply)* [1992] Fam. 182.

[43] *Gillick v W Norfolk and Wisbech Health Authority* [1986] A.C. 112, *per* Lord Scarman at 184. However, parents' statutory duties require considerably less: see Children and Young Persons Act 1933 ss.1, 3, 4, 11 and Children Act 1989 s.31(2). Amendments to the Children Act 1989 which would have required local authorities to act "as a good parent" to children leaving care, were rejected because the notion was too vague; see Lord Mackay, Lord Chancellor, *Hansard*, HL Vol.503, col.144 (January 17, 1989, Children Bill, Lords, Committee Stage).

[44] *Re W (A Minor) (Medical Treatment: Court's Jurisdiction)* [1993] Fam. 64.

[45] *A v Liverpool City Council* [1982] A.C. 363 and see below, Ch.21. Decisions can be challenged under the Human Rights Act 1998: *Re M (Care: Challenging Decision by Local Authority)* [2001] 2 F.L.R. 1300, and Judicial Review is available for decisions that are ultra vires or irrational: *R v Harrow LBC Ex p. D* [1990] Fam. 133.

[46] Children Act 2004 ss.11, 28 (for Wales). Relevant functions include provision for children in need and looking after children: Children Act 1989 ss.17(1)(a), 22(3)(a); welfare may defer to the need to protect members of the public from serious injury: see s.22(6).

[47] *Re P (Section 91(14) Guidelines) (Residence and Religious Heritage)* [1999] 2 F.L.R. 573 at 585, *per* Butler-Sloss L.J.

[48] For a discussion, see C. Piper, "Assumptions about children's best interests" [2000] J.S.W.F.L. 261. Similarly, more prescriptive "rules of thumb" have been used, but "there are no rules of thumb": *per* Wood J.; *Edwards v Edwards* [1986] 1 F.L.R. 187 at 203.

welfare decisions normally require.[49] It has been assumed that being brought up by a parent,[50] maintaining current arrangements (the status quo) and contact with the non-residential parent are each in children's best interests.[51] These assumptions are derived from research into child development, the beliefs of child welfare professionals[52] and notions about how children should be brought up after parental separation.[53] Although assumptions cannot provide precedents for individual cases, they influence lawyers and their clients to settle on the basis of the court's likely approach. Where assumptions by professionals or courts replace the individual assessment of a case, they distort the balancing exercise required by s.1(1).

B. Welfare and the Human Rights Act 1998

19–004   The implementation of the Human Rights Act 1998 demands consideration of whether courts' approach to disputes about relationships with children complies with the ECHR. The welfare principle must be interpreted and applied in accordance with the Convention.[54] The right to respect for family life imposes positive obligations on the state, including to provide a framework for adjudication and enforcement for disputes between individuals[55]; the state can only interfere with private and family life to the extent permitted by art.8(2).[56]

It has been argued that art.8 and the welfare principle are not compatible because more evidence is necessary to show that interference with a right is "necessary" and the judgments required are qualitatively different.[57] Also, that the courts should use "parallel analysis" and examine the competing interests of

---

[49] See, for example, *Re K (A Minor) (Ward: Care and Control)* [1990] 2 F.L.R. 64, CA; *Re D (Care: Natural Parent Presumption)* [1999] 1 F.L.R. 135, CA.

[50] *Re D (Care: Natural Parent Presumption)* [1999] 1 F.L.R. 135, CA; J. Fortin [1999] C.F.L.Q. 435; cf. *Re G* [2006] UKHL 43 where Baroness Hale stated at para.44 that there was no presumption in favour of the natural mother.

[51] *Re O (Contact: Imposition of Conditions)* [1995] 2 F.L.R. 124 at 128, *per* Bingham M.R; R. Bailey-Harris et al., "From utility to rights? The presumption of contact in practice" [1999] Int. J Law, Pol. and Fam. 111. In *Re M (Contact: Parental Responsibility)* [2001] 2 F.L.R. 342, FD, the benefit of the contact for a severely disabled young woman amounted to maintaining the interest of the paternal family so they might remain involved if something happened to the mother.

[52] *Re L, Re V, Re M and Re H (Contact: Domestic Violence)* [2000] 2 F.L.R. 334 at 365, *per* Thorpe L.J.

[53] The (unimplemented) Family Law Act 1996 s.11(4)(c) included a rebuttable presumption that the child's welfare will be best served by regular contact with family members and those who have parental responsibility, and maintaining relationships with both parents. Similarly the Protection of Children Act 1999 operates on the presumption that those convicted of offences against children continue to pose a danger to children.

[54] Human Rights Act 1998 s.3; if this is not possible, the High Court should make a declaration of incompatibility: s.4.

[55] *X and Y v The Netherlands* (1986) 8 E.H.R.R. 235; *Glaser v UK* [2001] 1 F.L.R. 153, ECtHR. It creates a presumption of "normal contact": *Re C (Abduction: Residence and Contact)* [2006] 2 F.L.R. 277, at para.28.

[56] Decisions must be "in accordance with the law" and restrictions of rights must be "necessary" for the protection of the rights of others.

[57] J. Herring, "The Human Rights Act and the welfare principle in family law—conflicting or complementary?" [1999] C.F.L.Q. 223 at 231. Cf. J. Fortin, "The HRA's impact on litigation involving children and their families" [1999] C.F.L.Q. 237 at 251, who expressed concern that the welfare principle would be diluted after the Human Rights Act.

each party rather than assume that the child's welfare interest trumps all others.[58] The approach of the European Court of Human Rights is said to differ considerably from that of the domestic courts. It does not start from the assumption that the paramountcy principle will determine the issue, but it seeks to balance competing rights. It has frequently referred to its statement in *Johnssen v Norway*[59] that it attaches particular importance to the best interests of the child, which may override those of the parent "depending on their nature and seriousness" and only once asserted that the child's welfare is necessarily determinative.[60]

In 1988, in *Re KD (A Minor) (Ward: Termination of Access)*[61] Lord Oliver concluded that there was nothing in Convention case law that undermined the welfare principle. The approach of the domestic courts to the application of the welfare principle appears largely unchanged since the Human Rights Act 1998. In *Re B (Adoption Natural Parent)*[62] Lord Nicholls asserted that the balancing exercise required by art.8(2) did not differ in substance from the conventional approach of test in English law. Little mention is generally made of the Convention in judgments in welfare cases.[63] The courts appear to take the view that the child's welfare justifies the restrictions of other's rights in accordance with art.8(2) provided that decisions are proportionate.[64] The European Court of Human Rights has accepted this approach; it is for the national authorities to strike a fair balance between the competing rights of parents and children. Nevertheless, when determining disputes about children's upbringing, the courts should be mindful that they are also adjudicating on rights to family life, and must ensure that their decisions are based on facts and professional assessments[65] and not merely on presumptions or prejudice.[66]

C. The meaning of the principle

The leading case on the welfare principle is *J v C*[67] where the courts considered **19–005** whether a 10-year-old boy should be returned to his parents (Spanish nationals resident in Spain) or remain with English foster parents who had looked after him

---

[58] S. Choudury and H. Fenwick, "Taking the rights of parents and children seriously: confronting the welfare principle under the Human Rights Act" [2005] O.J.L.S. 453.

[59] [1997] 23 E.H.R.R. 134 at para.78. The parent is not entitled to measures from the state that would harm the child's health or development: para.72–73.

[60] *Yousef v Netherlands* [2003] 36 E.H.R.R. 20, para.73.

[61] [1988] A.C. 806 at 825, 828.

[62] [2002] 1 F.L.R 196, HL at para.31. A decision on the Adoption Act 1976 s.15(3)(b).

[63] Choudury and Fenwick, *op. cit.*; *Payne v Payne* [2001] F.L.R. 1052, CA; *Re C (A Child) (Immunisation: Parental Rights)* [2003] 2 F.L.R. 1054, FD.

[64] "Proportionality . . . is the key", *per* Hale L.J. *Re O (Supervision Order)* [2001] 1 F.L.R. 923, CA, at para.28; *Re S (Adoption Order or Special Guardianship Order)* [2007] 1 F.L.R 819, CA, para.49

[65] *Elsholz v Germany* [2000] 2 F.L.R. 486. The dismissal of the father's application for contact without a hearing or an independent psychological report breached the father's rights under arts 6 and 8.

[66] See *Hoffman v Austria* (1993) 17 E.H.R.R. 293, where the transfer of custody from the mother, who had become a Jehovah's Witness, to the father breached arts 8 and 14; *Salgueiro da Silva Mouta v Portugal* (1999) App.00033290/96, where transfer of legal custody from the father, a homosexual, to the mother breached arts 8 and 14.

[67] [1970] A.C. 668; Cretney *Family Law in the Twentieth Century* 572–573.

for all (except 18 months) of his life. The House of Lords upheld the decision of the trial judge and the Court of Appeal that he should stay in England. Lord MacDermott stated that paramountcy of welfare means:

> "[M]ore than that the child's welfare is to be treated as the top item in a list of items relevant to the matter in question. [The words] connote a process whereby, when all the relevant facts, relationships claims and wishes of parents, risks choices and other circumstances are taken into account and weighed the course to be followed will be that which is most in the interests of the child's welfare as that term is now understood . . . [It is] the paramount consideration because it rules upon or determines the course to be followed."[68]

The boy's welfare necessitated that he remain with the parent figures he was attached to, the more so since his natural parents would have been unable to cope with his consequent maladjustment. Against these considerations, the claims of "unimpeachable"[69] natural parents could not prevail. The court came to a different conclusion in a similar case in 1996:

> In *Re M*[70] a Zulu boy, aged six, was brought by an Afrikaner widow to England after her maid, the child's single mother, had signed papers (which she later claimed she thought related to insurance) agreeing to his adoption. He lived in London for four years, obtained a scholarship to attend public school and lost his ability to speak his mother tongue. Thorpe J. acknowledged that the child had "two psychological mothers" and favoured his return to South Africa after a series of visits to be paid for by the Afrikaner woman. The woman was unable to keep her undertaking to pay for visits and appealed. The Court of Appeal held, despite the boy's protests, that it was in his interests to return to live with his parents in South Africa immediately. However, after six months the boy had not settled, and was returned by his mother to live with the Afrikaner woman.

The current emphasis on genetic identity has been reflected in the House of Lord's most recent application of the principle:

> In *Re G*[71] a lesbian couple, C and W, decided to have children. C gave birth to two girls as a result of donor insemination, who were aged three and one when the couple's relationship failed. W obtained a contact order and looked after the children for two days a week and alternate weekends.

---

[68] [1970] A.C. 710–711.

[69] Before *J v C* conduct might determine the outcome of a dispute; see, for example, *Re L* [1962] 3 All E.R. 1, where the mother's adultery and the father's lack of bad behaviour or "unimpeachability" justified awarding custody to him. It has been said that the "umimpeachable parent" is in "forensic limbo". *Re R (Minors) (Wardship Jurisdiction)* (1981) 2 F.L.R. 416 at 425.

[70] [1996] 2 F.L.R. 441, CA. Despite the obvious similarities, *J v C* was not cited in the judgment, but considerable emphasis was placed on the child's right to be brought up in his homeland by his natural parents.

[71] [2006] UKHL 43.

Without telling W, C moved away, but W maintained her weekend contact. W sought shared residence and C indicated that she wanted to move to Cornwall with the children. The CAFCASS officer recommended continuation of the arrangements with the children spending equal time with C and W in the holidays. Shared residence was refused, but the Court of Appeal allowed W's appeal. C then moved with the children to Cornwall, concealing their whereabouts from W. W applied for orders for the children to live with her; this was granted and C's appeal to the Court of Appeal was refused. The House of Lords allowed the appeal and returned the girls to C. Baroness Hale, giving the main judgment, held that the judge had given too much weight to C's attempt to end W's relationship with the girls. Whilst both C and W were psychological parents, C was their biological mother, "which must count for something in the vast majority of cases". Its significance must be assessed.[72]

Applying the welfare test requires an individual assessment in each case. **19–006** Consequently, precedent has little value,[73] except perhaps to indicate the approaches that currently find favour with the judiciary. Indeterminancy (the lack of any precise meaning to the notion of welfare)[74] has enabled judges (and social workers) to use it to justify their own subjective decisions.[75] Thus, the Court of Appeal has upheld a decision that granted custody to a disciplinarian father rather than an easy going mother[76]; refused to disturb a decision that denied custody to an unemployed father because it was his duty to work and support the family[77]; refused custody to a mother who was a Jehovah's Witness because the children would not celebrate Christmas[78]; and favoured placement for adoption over custody to a teenage father who had yet to face the stresses of reaching maturity.[79]

The growth of child welfare professions and the desire to reach better and more justifiable decisions has shifted the reasoning in cases towards arguments based on child development theory.[80] The emphasis on evidence-based practice in medicine and social work has highlighted the importance of research, but this

---

[72] At para.38

[73] *Re K* [1977] Fam. 179 at 183, *per* Stamp L.J.; *Lonslow v Hennig* [1986] 2 F.L.R. 378 at 381.

[74] R. Mnookin, "Bargaining in the shadow of the law: the case of divorce" [1979] C.L.P. 65; D. Chambers, "Rethinking the substantive rules for custody disputes in divorce" [1984–85] Michigan Law Rev. 477.

[75] M. King, "Playing the symbols—custody and the law commission" (1987) 17 Fam. Law 186, 189; H. Reece, "The paramountcy principle consensus or contruct?" [1996] C.L.P. 267 at 272–275. For a discussion of different ideological approaches affecting social work decision-making, see L. Fox-Harding, *Perspectives in Child Care Policy*, 2nd edn (1997), and "The Children Act 1989 in context: four perspectives in child care law and policy" [1991] J.S.W.F.L. 179 at 285.

[76] *May v May* [1986] 1 F.L.R. 325; both parents were apparently equally capable of caring for the children. A decision against a parent and stepparent who had a liberal approach to nudity was overturned: *Re W (Residence Order)* [1999] 1 F.L.R. 869, CA.

[77] *B v B (Custody of Child)* [1985] F.L.R. 166.

[78] *T v T* (1974) 4 Fam. Law 190. They would be deprived of the "wholesome joys of life ... the charms of crackers and paper hats"; *per* Stamp L.J. at p.191. The mother's mental condition also gave rise to anxiety. Reasoning of this sort appears to breach ECHR arts 8 and 14: see *Hoffman v Austria* (1993) 17 E.H.R.R. 293 and *Salgueiro da Silva Mouta v Portugal* (1999), App.00033290/96.

[79] *Re M (A Minor: Custody Appeal)* [1990] 1 F.L.R. 291.

[80] See, generally, S. Maidment *Child Custody* (1984).

can only identify (and sometimes quantify) issues, risks and protective factors, not future outcomes for particular individuals. Research does not necessarily permit firm conclusions, but meta-analysis can provide a strong indication of the impact on children's wellbeing of family practices.[81] Welfare assessments need to be grounded in research, and reflect the realities of the care that can be provided for the child in the family or elsewhere.[82] They will also reflect the values of those undertaking the assessment.[83] Judges are hugely dependent on the assessments of CAFCASS officers[84] and expert witnesses[85] (whose views may conflict),[86] but it has been suggested that "child welfare knowledge" is captured and reconstructed by the legal process.[87]

Bowlby's work on attachment and separation[88] was for a long time the most influential, but re-assessments of it by Rutter[89] and others[90] mean, particularly in disputes between parents, that such theories may offer no solution. Attachment theory suggests that for healthy psychological (and physical) development, a child needs to have a close relationship with a limited number of adults who will relate closely to him or her, preferably in a warm and nurturing way. Bowlby, whose original work was done with institutionalised children, stressed the value of a single mother figure, but Rutter has shown that children can relate to more than one such figure and that gender is not important. Children become attached to these "psychological parents"[91]; separation from them produces anxiety, and prolonged separation leads to depression and disturbed behaviour. Younger children may regress, losing skills they had already mastered; older children may become aggressive or withdrawn. Attachment can occur at any age, although it develops more quickly with young children. Children who do not become attached, or whose attachments are disrupted, may successfully be attached to

---

[81] For example, indicating that there is no evidence that parental contact after separation per se benefits children: Hunt and Roberts, *Child Contact with Non Resident Parents* (2004).

[82] See DH, *Framework for the Assessment of Children in Need and Their Families* (London: TSO, 2000), para.1.57.

[83] These may be set out in service standards; see, for example, CAFCASS, *National Standards* (2007).

[84] *Re W (Residence)* [1999] 2 F.L.R. 390 at 395, *per* Thorpe L.J. The judge is not required to follow such a recommendation but must give reasons for not doing so: *Re CB (Access: Court Welfare Report)* [1995] 1 F.L.R. 622; *Re A (Children 1959 UN Declaration)* [1998] 1 F.L.R. 354, CA.

[85] Particularly from the Child and Adolescent Mental Health Service: J. Brophy et al., *Myths and Practices: A National Survey in the Use of Expert Evidence in Child Care Proceedings* (1999).

[86] Because they have made different observations or because they have made assessments from a different ideological standpoint; see Fox-Harding, *Perspectives on Child Care Policy.* Joint appointment of experts is used to limit the number of experts and avoid conflicts: CAAC, *Handbook of Best Practice in Children Act Cases* (1997), Ch.5 and see DH, *Bearing Good Witness* (2006).

[87] M. King and C. Piper, *How the Law Thinks About Children*, 2nd edn (Aldershot: Ashgate, 1995), p.43. King and Piper base their arguments on a development of Teubner's autopoietic theory. The model of family law that King and Piper use has been criticised for failing to reflect the discretionary and therapeutic mode for decisions about children: K. O'Donovan, *Family Law Matters* (London: Pluto, 1993), p.28.

[88] J. Bowlby, *Child Care and the Growth of Love*, 2nd edn (Penguin, 1953); J. Bowlby, *Attachment and Loss*, Vols I–III (Penguin, 1969, 1973 and 1980).

[89] M. Rutter, *Maternal Deprivation Reassessed*, 2nd edn (Penguin, 1981).

[90] W. Sluckin, M. Herbert and A. Sluckin, *Maternal Bonding* (Oxford: Blackwell, 1983).

[91] This phrase is used by J. Goldstein, A. Freud and A. Solnit in *Beyond the Best Interests of the Child* (1973). For a recent reassessment of this work, see M.D.A. Freeman, "The best interests of the child?" (1997) 11 Int J. Law, Pol. and Fam. 360.

others,[92] but adoption does not necessarily provide a better outcome for abused children.[93] Attachment is not the sole determinant; children may become attached to dangerous or disturbed parent figures[94] and may also be attached to both[95] or neither[96] of the parties involved in a dispute.

The term "resilience" is used to identify the capacity to function well despite **19–007** adversity.[97] Understanding what makes children resilient may help prevent harm and the development of programmes for those who have suffered trauma. Resilience is not innate, nor merely a product of development, but involves the interplay of psycho-social processes that support healthy development. There is considerable agreement about the attributes of resilient children, their psychological functioning and important protective factors but, as yet, far less understanding about the processes through which resilience is achieved. Resilient children are generally healthier, of higher socio-economic status and younger when they experience trauma but have not suffered early separations of losses. They have good self-esteem, self-control and a sense of humour. Resilient children have a warm relationship with at least one carer, receive competent parenting and have good friendship networks and educational experiences.

An awareness of individual's family, racial and cultural heritage is also important.[98] The courts are increasingly recognising importance of identity[99] and the need for children to be told the truth about their origins and family.[100] A well-developed sense of identity is important for children's adjustment. Identity has been said to be a sense of psycho-social wellbeing and a feeling of being at home in one's own body.[101] Although there are many theories about the development of identity, it is agreed that a child's identity is neither predetermined nor free

[92] B. Tizard, *Adoption, a Second Chance* (London: Open Books, 1977). A. Rushton and J. Treseder, "Developmental recovery" (1986) 10(3) *Adoption & Fostering* 54.

[93] DH, *Child Protection: Messages from Research* (1995), p.67, citing J. Gibbons et al., *Development after Physical Abuse in Early Childhood: A Follow-up Study of Children on Protection Registers* (London: HMSO, 1995).

[94] For example, where the child is abused, see D. Jones et al., *Understanding Child Abuse*, 2nd edn (Basingstoke: Macmillan, 1987).

[95] For example, *Re M (Child's Upbringing)* [1996] 2 F.L.R. 441, or in a dispute between parents at separation.

[96] For example, *Re D (Care: Natural Parent Presumption)* [1999] 1 F.L.R. 134, or where members of a child's family are seeking residence in care proceedings, but the local authority favours adoption.

[97] P. Fonagy et al., "The theory and practice of resilience" (1994) 35 J. Child Pyschol. Psychiat. 231; E. Hetherington and M. Stanley-Hagan, "The adjustment of children and divorced parents: a risk and resiliency perspective" (1999) 40 J. Child Pyschol. Psychiat. 129.

[98] DH Circular LAC (99)29; *Re M (Section 94 Appeals)* [1995] 1 F.L.R. 546; *Re O (Transracial Adoption: Contact)* [1995] 2 F.L.R. 597.

[99] *Re W (A Minor) (Contact)* [1994] 2 F.L.R. 441, CA; *Re P (A Minor) (Contact)* [1994] 2 F.L.R. 374 at 379; cf. *Re F (A Minor: Paternity Test)* [1993] 1 F.L.R. 598 at 604. The welfare test does not apply to the decision to order blood tests but is relevant to the application for a parental responsibility order. Indirect contact may be used to maintain links where direct contact is impracticable or inappropriate: *Re S (Violent Parent: Indirect Contact)* [2000] 1 F.L.R. 481; *Re K (Contact: Mother's Anxiety)* [1999] 2 F.L.R. 703.

[100] *Re G (Contact)* [2007] 1 F.L.R. 1663 CA (father's change of gender); *Re H and A (Paternity: Blood Tests)* [2002] 1 F.L.R. 1145, CA. Cf. *Re H (Paternity: Welfare of Child)* [2007] 1 F.L.R. 1064, FD, where the advantage of knowledge did not outweigh the negative impact on the mother of imposing the requirement to tell the child about his true paternty.

[101] E. Erikson, "The problem of ego identity" (1956) *Journal of the American Psychological Association* 74.

from outside influence. The most influencial theorist, Erikson, emphasised intra-psychic processes and the continual reworking of earlier life experiences.[102] Later writers have drawn attention to the ways that institutions, including the law, shape identity by permitting or restricting individual expression.[103]

Issues of identity and attachment are interlinked. A child with a poor sense of identity may not be able to make attachments.[104] Attachment may also affect the identity that develops. The identity of children of mixed parentage has been seen to be distinct, reflecting elements from each parent and culture,[105] and children placed transracially may not identify with either community.[106] Identity and attachment theories may lead to conflicting responses to maintaining links for children living away from their birth family. Contact may undermine security,[107] but if contact is terminated or a "closed" adoption arranged, this may have a damaging effect on the child's identity.

19–008   It is not clear that the court system ensures that the assessments necessary to make welfare decisions are available,[108] or that judges, magistrates, practising lawyers or social workers always understand child development sufficiently.[109] Decisions about welfare involve an element of prediction and can require fine judgments; experts' opinions cannot remove the responsibility of the judge to reach a conclusion on all the evidence. Neither experts nor judges are free from subjectivity. The approach taken can be inconsistent. Courts have been far more willing to recognise that contact may provide no benefit to a child, or is even damaging when the child is in state care[110] than when he or she is living with a separated parent,[111] and contact after adoption is rarely ordered. Also, insufficient

---

[102] E. Erikson, *Identity, Youth and Crisis* (London: Faber, 1968); *Identity and the Life Cycle* (New York: Norton, 1979).

[103] J. Shotter and K. J. Gergen, *Texts of Identity* (London: Newbury Park, 1989).

[104] H.R. Schaffer, *Making Decisions About Children* (Oxford: Blackwell, 1990).

[105] B. Tizard and A. Phoenix, *Black, White or Mixed Race?* (London: Routledge, 2002).

[106] O. Gill and B. Jackson, *Adoption and Race* (New York: St Martin's Press, 1983); D. Kirton, *Ethnicity and Adoption* (Buckingham: Open University Press, 2000); see also *Re B (Adoption Setting Aside)* [1995] 1 F.L.R. 1 for an account of the experience of the child of English Catholic and Kuwaiti Muslim parents adopted by Jewish parents.

[107] D. Quinton et al., "Contact between children placed away from home and their birth parents: research issues and evidence" (1997) *Clinical Child Psychol. and Psychiat.* 393. In *Re O (Transracial Adoption: Contact)* [1995] 2 F.L.R. 693, the court (unusually) accepted that adoption provided the security for contact that could develop the child's racial identity.

[108] Resource limitations and concerns about delay mean that welfare reports are only available in approximately half of contested cases. In the study by R. Bailey-Harris and colleagues, welfare reports were ordered in 49% of cases: [1999] C.F.L.Q. 53, 58. There is also concern about the quality of some CAFCASS reports: Ofsted, *Inspection of CAFCASS E. Midlands: Key Challenges and Opportunities* (2008).

[109] cf. Maidment *Child Custody*, p.205. Far greater efforts are now made to inform the judiciary. Understanding has certainly developed since the decision in *Re Thain* [1926] Ch. 676, where it was said that the effect of moving a seven-year-old child from an aunt and uncle to the father after six years would be "mercifully transient". But the legal system may reconstruct and misuse scientific knowledge about children; King and Piper *How the Law Thinks*, p.52; M. King and J. Trowell, *Children's Welfare and the Law* (London: Sage, 1992), Ch.6.

[110] The picture is quite mixed. For some children in permanent placement, birth-family contact is positive; for others it can be damaging: See E. Neil and D. Howe, *Contact in Adoption and Permanent Foster Care* (London: BAAF, 2004).

[111] Contact does not appear to benefit children per se; its benefits depend on the quality of relationships it supports: Hunt and Roberts, *Child Contact with Non-resident Parents* (2004); nevertheless, the courts have gone to extraordinary lengths to maintain separated father's contact: *Re*

attention has been given to the risks imposed and damage done by promoting contact with non-resident parents.[112]

D. Application of the welfare principle

Studies[113] of the outcomes of residence cases indicate that courts almost always make orders that confirm the current arrangements or status quo. In part, this reflects the use the parties make of the court; court orders are often sought to confirming arrangements agreed by the parties. Smart and colleagues found that most residence applications were made by mothers who sought an order to confirm their position. Where fathers were caring for children, the status quo also worked in favour of them.[114] There were only 33 cases out of a sample of 243 where the court did not confirm existing arrangements, and in 22 of these the father gained residence. In most of these cases the mother had serious mental health or substance abuse problems.[115] The court's preference for continuing existing arrangements is likely to lead to advice not to pursue applications for a change in residence, except where children's care is seriously deficient.[116] Eekelaar found that siblings were apparently rarely split.[117]

19–009

In the past, the view that the carer's new partner would substitute for the non-resident parent was accepted.[118] This approach has been replaced by preference for co-parenting, emphasising the durability of parenting relationships and the continued involvement of both biological parents.[119] Arrangements following separation are fluid so that agreements or court orders are varied or cease to reflect what is happening. Parents who continue to communicate can create flexible arrangements with co-operative parenting. In contrast, imposing co-parenting may create opportunities for parents to undermine each other and the welfare of the child.[120]

Research by Bailey-Harris and colleagues indicated that courts put considerable emphasis on the parents reaching their own agreement—even in contested cases—on the assumption that there is more likely to be compliance. Parents are

---

F (Indirect Contact) [2007] 1 F.L.R. 1015, CA; *Re A (Contact: Witness Protection Scheme)* [2006] 2 F.L.R. 551, FD.

[112] Sturge and Glaser [2000] Fam. Law 615; *Re L, Re V, Re M and Re H (Contact: Domestic Violence)* [2000] 2 F.L.R. 334; WAFE, *29 Child Homicides* (2004); Family Justice Council, *Everybody's Business* (2007).

[113] C. Smart et al., *Residence and Contact Disputes in Court Vol.1* (LCD Research Series 6/03, 2003); *Vol.II* (DCA Research Series 4/2005, 2005); Hunt and Macleod (forthcoming 2008). For previous practice, see J. Eekelaar et al., *Custody after Divorce* (SSRC, 1977); J. Eekelaar, "Children and divorce: some further data" [1982] Ox. J.L.S. 63; Priest and Whybrow (Law Com. WP Supplement (1986)).

[114] Smart et al. LCD Research 6/03, p.17.

[115] Smart et al. LCD Research 6/03, p.18. See also S. Maidment, *Child Custody: What Chance for Fathers* (National Council for One-parent Families, 1981).

[116] 20% of residence applications were withdrawn: Smart et al. LCD Research 6/03, p.15.

[117] Eekelaar and Clive (1977), para.5.2; Priest and Whybrow (1986) give no information about this, which perhaps calls into question the analysis in Table 7.

[118] The "clean break", the transfer of financial responsibility from fathers to the state, the acceptance of the end to contact and the practice of stepparent adoption re-inforced this approach.

[119] R. van Krieken, "The best interests of the child' and parental separation: on the civilizing of parents" [2005] M.L.R. 25.

[120] B. Neale and C. Smart, "In whose best interests? Theorising family life following parental separation", in S. Sclater and C. Piper (eds), *Undercurrents of Divorce* (Aldershot: Ashgate, 1999), pp.33, 37, 43–44; C. Smart and B. Neale, *Family Fragments?* (1999).

said to know their children best and have responsibility for working out arrangements. Where settlements are not reached quickly there are repeated directions appointments and delay.[121] The notion that the parents' agreed solution necessarily best serves the child's welfare does not sit easily with the court's responsibility to consider cases individually, nor with divorce legislation, which requires court oversight of arrangements. Also, agreements on contact achieved in the course of court proceedings appear unlikely to last.[122] Trinder and colleagues found that 60 per cent of agreements about contact reached through in-court conciliation had broken down within two years, with further court proceedings in 40 per cent of cases. Few parents had improved their relationship, and some relationships were worse.[123]

19–010   The Courts deal with around 70,000 contact applications each year[124]; approximately 10 per cent of separating couples use the courts to resolve issues of contact. Although around 30 per cent of cases result in consent orders, half as many lead to protracted disputes.[125] There is wide acceptance of the importance of maintaining contact between children and their parents after relationship breakdown,[126] but the courts are faced with disagreements about whether a particular parent should be permitted to have contact, whether contact needs to be supervised for the child's safety, where it should take place, for how long and how frequently it should occur. It is the quality of contact rather than the quantity that appears to be important,[127] a matter over which the court can have little influence. In determining disputes about contact, courts have tended to look to the future and avoid examining parents' past conduct. As part of the assessment of the welfare, they are expected to establish the truth of allegations.[128] However, the view that contact is almost always beneficial leads courts to focus on how it can be promoted in the face of opposition by parents with care of children.[129] The child's welfare may necessitate a transfer of residence to the other parent who will promote contact.[130] Other forms of enforcement do not involve applying the welfare test.[131] The fact that the courts are not able to change the intractable attitudes of parents is regarded by the courts as a failure.[132]

---

[121] R. Bailey-Harris et al. [1999] C.F.L.Q. 53, pp.57–59; 27% resulted in no order and 5% in an order of "no order".

[122] L. Trinder et al., *Making Contact Work or Making Contact Happen* (DCA Research Series 3/06, 2006).

[123] L. Trinder et al., *The Longer-term Outcomes of In-court Conciliation* (MoJ Research series 15/07, 2007).

[124] Many cases involve multiple applications.

[125] DfES et al., *Parental Separation: Children's Needs and Parents' Responsibilities* (Cm.6273, 2004), Ch.2; *Judicial Statistics 2006*, Table 5.3; Smart et al., (LCD 6/03, 2003); see also Hunt and Macleod (forthcoming 2008).

[126] A. Blackwell and F. Dawe, *Non-resident Parent Contact: ONS Report for DCA* (2003); (Cm.6273, 2004), Foreword: 'The Government believes . . . that both parents . . . should continue to have a meaningful relationship with their children after adult separation, so long as it is safe."

[127] Rodgers and Pryor *Divorce and Separation*, p.7.

[128] *Practice Direction 2008* (May, 8); CASC, *Contact and Domestic Violence* (1999); *Re F (Contact: Lack of Reasons)* [2007] 1 F.L.R. 65, CA.

[129] *Re M (Contact: Long-term Best Interests)* [2006] 1 F.L.R 627, CA; *Re S (Contact: Promoting Relationship with Absent Parent)* [2004] 1 F.L.R 1279, CA.

[130] *Re A (Residence Order)* [2007] Fam. Law 778, CA.

[131] See above, para.18–056.

[132] *Re D (Intractable Contact Dispute: Publicity)* [2004] 1 F.L.R 1226, FD.

Despite duties to promote contact, a third of children looked after by a local authority have no parental contact.[133] Any dispute about contact can be referred to the court, but judicial attitudes have been less favourable to contact where the child is likely to remain in care for the long term.[134]

E. Problems with the welfare principle

The welfare principle itself has been criticised on a number of grounds, and **19–011** alternative approaches have been suggested that involve balancing the interests of all concerned, or attempting to find a solution which maximises the wellbeing of all the parties to a dispute.[135] The move from easily applicable rules of thumb[136] to a broad, undefined approach to welfare demands sophisticated, individual assessments, which judges are unable to make alone.[137] Experts' assessments of the child's needs and parents' capacity to meet them lead to long and costly proceedings.[138] The lack of consensus on what children's welfare demands, and of adequate research evidence about what ensures healthy psychological development, enables those who take the decisions to impose subjective and value-laden views.[139] Without further rules or guidelines, the use of the welfare principle simply creates unexaminable discretion.[140] Such apparently arbitrary decisions undermine the authority of judges and the legal system, but indeterminacy may be reduced through the influence of community standards.[141] In addition, the lack of a comprehensible and predictable standard makes it more difficult for couples to reach settlements by negotiation. This may increase the number and intensity of disputed cases. It may also assist the stronger party to impose their preferred solution on the weaker one.[142] The effect

---

[133] H. Cleaver, *Fostering Family Contact* (London: TSO, 2000). There are a variety of barriers to contact in such circumstances: see S. Millham et al., *Access Disputes in Child-care* (Aldershot: Gower, 1989)—a study applying to pre-Children Act 1989 law; J. Masson, C. Harrison and A. Pavlovic, *Lost and Found* (1999). Contact arrangements in care plans often remain unimplemented: Health Select Committee, *2nd Report* (1997–8 HC 247), para.81 or are short term: J. Harwin et al., *Making Care Orders Work* (London: TSO, 2002).

[134] Children Act 1989 ss.8, 34; *Re B (A Minor) (Care Contact: Local Authority's Plans)* [1993] 1 F.L.R. 543; *Re T (Minors) (Termination of Contact)* [1997] 1 All E.R 65, CA and see para.21–074, below.

[135] J. Eekelaar, "Beyond the welfare principle" (2002) C.F.L.Q. 237; A. Bainham, "Non-intervention and judicial paternalism", in P. Birks (ed.), *Frontiers of Liability* (Oxford: Oxford University Press, 1994).

[136] For example, that girls and young children should live with their mother, and older boys with their father; see above, para.19–003.

[137] M. Fineman, "The politics of custody and gender", in C. Smart and S. Sevenhuijsen (eds), *Child Custody and the Politics of Gender* (London: Routledge, 1989), pp.27, 30, 32. The status quo approach may have replaced the old rules of thumb; see Maidment, *Child Custody*, p.212. But this can also be viewed as an honest response to the collapse of a hierarchy of values in the community; S. Parker, "The best interests of the child principle and problems" (1994) 8 Int. J. Law & Fam 36.

[138] DFES and DCA, *Care Proceedings System Review* (2006).

[139] H. Reece, "The paramountcy principle consensus or construct" [1996] C.L.P. 267, 272–273; Chambers, "Rethinking", p.481; King, "Playing" p.189; Law Com. WP 96, para.6.25: "There is always the danger that stereotyped, culturally conditioned judgments . . . will lead to decisions . . . which do not benefit children". J. Montgomery, "Children as property" (1988) 51 M.L.R. 323, 328.

[140] S. Parker, "The Best Interests".

[141] C. Schneider, "Discretion, rules & law: child custody decisions and the best interest standard", in K. Hawkins (ed.), *The Uses of Discretion* (Oxford: Clarendon, 1993).

[142] Mnookin [1979] C.L.P. 65, pp.86 *et seq.*

on private ordering is particularly important because of the influence existing arrangements have on court orders:

> In *Re V (Residence Order: Finance)*[143] the mother left the child, aged two, and the father in the matrimonial home and moved to a house nearby. Both parents worked full time, the paternal grandmother cared for the child during the day and he spent three out of four weekends and some holidays with his mother. Nine months later the mother applied for a residence order. The judge made an order confirming the existing arrangement and the mother's appeal seeking a transfer of the child's care to her was dismissed.

Despite this criticism, the welfare principle is widely supported because it represents an important social and moral value: that children who are necessarily vulnerable and dependent must be protected from harm and given every opportunity to become healthy and well adjusted adults.[144] Any change in the criteria could put children's welfare at risk because it would inevitably reduce the emphasis given to welfare.[145] Alternative rules may be no less indeterminate.[146] However, Goldstein, Freud and Solnit, while supporting the welfare principle, suggested that the phraseology be changed to "the least detrimental alternative", to remind decision-makers that they can only do their humble best.[147]

Various proposals have been made to improve the operation of the welfare principle by changing the decision-making process, removing the need to make certain decisions or assigning weight to particular factors.[148] It has been argued that decision-making would be improved if children had more opportunity to participate,[149] either by being represented[150] or by being able to speak to the judge. There appears to be less reluctance to allow children's involvement in proceedings.[151] Alternatively, people qualified in assessing children's welfare

---

[143] [1995] 2 F.L.R. 612, CA.

[144] King, "Playing" p.189; cf. Reece, "The Paramountcy Principle", pp.276–281 at 302, who argues that adults' rights should not be subordinated to children's needs. However, Neale and Smart, "In whose best interests", pp.46–49 argue that fathers who claim a right to a relationship with their child after separation do not work at maintaining their relationship and impose arrangements that may undermine the other parent.

[145] Law Com. WP 96, paras 6.17, 6.22; Law Com. No.172, para.3.13. The entrenchment of a best interest standard in the UN Convention on the Rights of the Child art.3(1) makes formal departures from the welfare principle unthinkable for countries that have ratified the Convention. See also P. Alston, "The best interests principle towards a reconciliation of culture and human rights" (1994) 8 Int. J. Law & Fam. 1.

[146] Parker, "The best interests" pp.29–36. Decisions may be indeterminate because the possibilities of all the alternative outcomes are unknown.

[147] Goldstein, Freud and Solnit, *Beyond*, p.62.

[148] For a theoretical analysis of the reasons for the failure of the Anglo-American system to make welfare based decisions, see King and Piper, *How the Law*.

[149] See above, para.16–020 *et seq.*

[150] R. Hansen, "The role and rights of children in divorce actions" (1966) 6 J. Fam. L. 1; Mnookin, p.95; C. Lyon et al., *Effective Support Systems for Children and Young People when Parental Relationships Break Down* (1998); B. Neale and C. Smart, *Good to Talk?* (2001); G. Douglas et al., *Research into the Operation of r.9.5* (2006). Inclusion of the child's views may be required: *Sahin v Germany* [2003] 2 F.L.R. 671.

[151] *Mabon v Mabon* [2005] 2 F.L.R. 1011, CA; N. Crichton, "Listening to children" [2006] Fam. Law 849; Ministry of Justice, *Separate Representation of Children Summary of Responses to Consultation Paper* (2007).

could replace lawyer judges and magistrates.[152] Again, this is likely to change biases in the system rather than remove them.

Lack of confidence in the welfare principle is one reason for the current **19–012** emphasis on settlement. Mediation[153] and negotiation are encouraged because judges, CAFCASS officers and lawyers recognise the problems of adjudication and wish to avoid them. Any solution chosen by the parties is considered more likely to be kept and is therefore better because it will reduce disputes and the uncertainties of litigation that are both thought to be contrary to children's welfare.[154] However, there appear to be differences between couples who agree arrangements without resort to the courts and those who agree during proceedings: parents using the courts for contact have more problems.[155] Court-based agreements are less durable and couples are less satisfied.[156] Not all agreed solutions produce good outcomes for children.[157]

The Law Commission sought to "lower the stakes" in disputes over children following divorce by removing the notion that "winner takes all". Its scheme for retention of parental responsibility after divorce was intended to reduce the opportunities for litigation.[158] Under the Children Act 1989, parental responsibility is unaffected by divorce.[159] The principal matters that concern the court are issues of the child's residence and continued contact. The retention of parental responsibility is intended to encourage involvement of the non-residential parent and thus promote the child's wellbeing.[160] However, this approach is not uncontroversial, and it is argued that it increases opportunities for dispute and for interference with decisions of the person caring for the child.[161] Indeed, disputes about children appear to have increased.[162]

Weighting of specific factors could clarify the likely outcome in most disputes over children, reducing the problem of indeterminacy and assisting the judges

---

[152] King and Piper, *How the Law*, p.158; Fineman has commented that "[t]he resort to non judicial decision-making in order to apply the best interests standard masks the severe problem with the substantive test". Fineman, "The Politics", p.31. The reformed Australian system combines both these ideas: R. Hunter, "Close encounters of a judicial kind: 'hearing' children's 'voices' in family law proceedings" [2007] C.F.L.Q. 283.

[153] L. Parkinson, *Conciliation in Separation and Divorce* (London: Croom Helm, 1986); M. Roberts, *Mediation in Family Disputes* (Aldershot: Wildwood, 1997). Just over half of the clients of mediation services in Walker's study thought that mediation had helped to protect the best interest of the children; J. Walker et al., *Mediation: The Making and Remaking of Co-operative Relationships* (1994), Table 5.4.

[154] Bailey-Harris et al. [1999] C.F.L.Q. 53, p.54.

[155] Trinder et al., *Making Contact* (2002); Trinder et al., *op. cit. A Profile Applicants and Respondents in Contact Cases in Essex* (DCA Research Series 01/05, 2005).

[156] Bailey-Harris et al. [1999] C.F.L.Q. 53, p.60; Trinder et al. DCA, 03/06; Trinder et al., DCA, 15/07; Blackwell and Dawe, ONS, DCA.

[157] Smart et al., DCA, 4/2005; Piper (1993), pp.186 *et seq.*; Walker et al., *Mediation*, Ch.5.

[158] Law Com. No.172, para.4.5.

[159] Children Act 1989 ss.2, 8, and above para.17–048.

[160] Neale and Smart, "In whose best interests", pp.37–39 consider that this reflects a new formulation of welfare that stresses the importance of fathers and the equality of their rights. See also Law Com. No.172, para.4.5.

[161] J. Brophy, "Custody law, child care and inequality in Britain", in C. Smart and S. Sevenhuijsen (eds), *Child Custody and the Politics of Gender* (1989), Ch.9; *Booth Report*, para.2.27.

[162] (Cm.6273, 2004), Ch.2. G. Davis and J. Pearce, "Privatising the family?" [1998] Fam. Law 614 at 616–617.

as well as parties who negotiate their own agreements.[163] Guidelines in the form of presumptions for maternal care (later replaced by the gender-neutral "primary carer" care) and for joint custody have operated in some American states[164] and elsewhere.[165] Chambers has argued that the effect of loss of care on the primary carer, combined with the advantages of an easily applicable test, justify a primary-carer preference for children under five years.[166] However, it has been argued that this standard fails to value a mother's special role and to recognise the interest a mother has in the care of children she gave birth to,[167] and that there should be a return to a maternal preference.[168] In contrast, it has also been suggested that preference should be given to arrangements where the care of the child is shared,[169] but this has been rejected on the basis that to replace the nuances of the welfare test with a standard approach would not take account of the wide variety of circumstances in which disputes arise.

19–013   The use of rules or guidelines was rejected by the Law Commission. It was difficult to frame guidelines that did not undermine the paramountcy rule.[170] The only guidelines that the Law Commission considered justified by current knowledge would not assist in the most typical disputes where the child was attached to both parents who could provide adequately.[171] Guidelines that could help in such a case were arbitrary because they could not be shown necessarily to promote the welfare of children.[172] Instead, the Law Commission favoured listing those matters that the court should consider without allocating weight to any of them.[173] This has been done by including a checklist in the Children Act 1989 s.1(3).[174]

F. The statutory checklist

19–014   In the Law Commission's view, a checklist could assist the courts to operate the welfare principle and make clear to all concerned the factors that the courts considered. It would thus help the parties to understand how judicial decisions are made and to focus their private discussions on relevant issues. It should

---

[163] Chambers, "Rethinking", p.48; Law Com. WP 96, para.6.29; Mnookin [1979] C.L.P. 65, pp.85 *et seq.*

[164] Law Com. WP 96, para.6.28; Chambers, "Rethinking", Fineman, "The Politics". But the effect of the two standards may be substantially the same: Maccoby and Mnookin, *Dividing the Child* (Harvard University Press, 1992), p.284. Presumptions of same-race placements have also been enacted for some care and adoption cases; see Indian Child Welfare Act 1978, US Public Law 95,608 and J. Hollinger, "Beyond the best interests of the tribe: the Indian Welfare Act and the Adoption of Indian Children" (1989) 66 U. Detroit L.R. 451.

[165] Law Com. WP 96, paras 6.28, 6.33.

[166] "Rethinking", p.561. Chambers argues for a presumption, not a rule, which would exclude demonstrably unfit parents, but this may shift the focus of the litigation to the caretaker's conduct.

[167] The nature of this interest in discussed by Chambers, "Rethinking", pp.499–503.

[168] Fineman, "The Politics", p.34; S. Boyd, "From gender specifity to gender neutrality", in Smart and Sevenhuijsen, "Child Custody", p.152.

[169] This has been sought by organisations such at the Equal Parenting Council. The Conservative Party proposed amendments to this effect in the Children and Adoption Bill: Grand Committee, October 11, 2005, Col.GC1.

[170] Law Com. WP 96, paras 6.30–6.34.

[171] Law Com. WP 96, para.6.31.

[172] Law Com. WP 96, para.6.32; see also Chambers, "Rethinking".

[173] Law Com. WP 96, paras 6.34–6.39; Law Com. No.172, paras 3.17–3.21.

[174] A similar checklist is applied to adoption cases: Adoption and Children Act 2002 s.1(4).

enable advisors to prepare relevant evidence and thus avoid prolonged hearings or delays caused by adjournments.[175] A checklist that does not ascribe weight to particular aspects of a case would be flexible. Its application can change as understanding of child welfare develops.[176] It is an *aide-memoire* designed to ensure that no relevant factors are forgotten.[177] However, it is not clear what assistance a checklist can provide if it merely lists the factors to be considered and does not indicate how they should be viewed. In children's cases, the courts perform a "balancing exercise" that is different from that undertaken for the re-allocation of resources. Cases reaching the appellate courts typically involve decisions by the lower courts that give inappropriate weight to relevant factors but rarely fail to consider them completely.

The Law Commission stated that a checklist would only be practicable if it were confined to major points.[178] A detailed list could not be applicable in all cases, and could increase opportunities for an appeal where the judge's reasons omitted an item from the list.[179] Working through the list is a useful and important discipline, but judges are not required to reflect on every item[180]; magistrates have pro formas for their reasons, which itemise the considerations in the checklist,[181] but nevertheless there continue to be cases where the reasons given are inadequate.[182]

Although the Law Commission thought that a checklist could provide a clear statement of "what society considers the most important factors in the welfare of children",[183] its own selection of factors appears to have been determined by the practice of the courts.[184] It did review the social-science evidence on the wellbeing of children after divorce when considering the objectives of custody law,[185] but based its list, with one exception, on the current approach of the English courts. Only the "wishes and feelings of the child" received any broader consideration.[186]

During the passage of the Children Bill through Parliament, some attempts **19–015** were made to change the content of the checklist, but these were rejected by the Government either on the basis that they would "upset the careful balance"[187] that had been achieved or because they were already implied by the general

---

[175] Law Com. No.172, paras 3.17 and 3.18.
[176] Law Com. No.172, para.3.19.
[177] *Southwark LBC v B* [1993] 2 F.L.R. 559 at 573, *per* Waite L.J.
[178] Law Com. No.172, para.3.19.
[179] Law Com. No.172, para.3.19. The rules relating to appeals are considered below.
[180] *H v H (Residence Order: Leave to Remove from the Jurisdiction)* [1995] 1 F.L.R. 529, CA; *Oldham MBC v E* [1994] 1 F.L.R. 568, CA; *B v B (Residence Order: Reason for Decision)* [1997] 2 F.L.R. 602 at 608, *per* Holman J.
[181] Magistrates must give written reasons before their decision: Family Proceeding Courts (Children Act 1989) Rules 1991 (SI 1991/1395) r.21(5); *Handbook of Best Practice in Children Act Cases* (1997) App.Ax, guidance prepared by Cazalet J.
[182] See, for example, *Croydon LBC v R.* [1997] 2 F.L.R. 675; *Re P (Contact: Supervision)* [1996] 2 F.L.R. 314; *R. v Oxfordshire CC (Secure Accommodation Order)* [1992] Fam. 150.
[183] Law Com. No.172, para.3.19.
[184] Law Com. WP 96, para.6.38. The only references in this paragraph are to decided cases.
[185] Law Com. WP 96, Pt III.
[186] Law Com. WP 96, paras 6.40–6.44; Law Com. No.172, paras 3.22–3.25.
[187] *Per* Sir Nicholas Lyell (Solicitor General) Children Bill, Committee Stage, *Hansard*, Standing Committee B, col.5, May 9, 1989.

words used. Thus, although there is no reference to keeping siblings together in this part of the Act,[188] this is one aspect of the child's emotional needs. The checklist also makes no reference to either short- or long-term needs, so both must be considered.[189] The order of the items has no special significance; factors should be weighted according to the circumstances.[190]

The Law Commission was concerned that the checklist should not lead to more intervention by the courts where the parties have reached their own agreement.[191] This approach was endorsed by Parliament and, consequently, the checklist only applies as a matter of strict law to contested applications to make, vary or discharge s.8 orders and any applications in relation to orders under Pt IV of the Children Act 1989.[192] Also, CAFCASS officers carrying out their functions representing children or preparing reports for the court are required to consider it when carrying out their duties.[193] However, the checklist need not be used in relation to other applications such as those for parental responsibility or guardianship orders, nor does it apply to emergency protection orders, but this does not mean that there are two potentially conflicting views of welfare.[194]

The provisions of the checklist will now be considered in turn.

a) *The ascertainable wishes and feelings of the child concerned (considered in light of the child's age and understanding)*

19–016   The right of mature children to express their views and of all children to be heard in legal proceedings concerning them is protected by the UN Convention on the Rights of the Child.[195] In the nineteenth century, children's wishes could be the determining factor in court decisions.[196] The Law Commission noted that welfare checklists from other jurisdictions included a consideration of children's views, and stated that these views should be taken into account not just as an aspect of welfare.[197] The checklist defines the child's views as an aspect of welfare[198] but

---

[188] It is mentioned in relation to placement of children in care: Children Act 1989 s.23(7)(b).

[189] *Re H (Minors) (Access)* [1992] 1 F.L.R. 148. Short-term interests may prevail on the basis that a variation can be made later; see *Thompson v Thompson* (1987) 17 Fam. Law 89, CA or because plans to meet long-term needs are speculative: *Berkshire CC v B* [1997] 1 F.L.R. 171. Long-term welfare may prevail if trauma is thought to be short lived: *Re B (Residence Order: Leave to Appeal)* [1998] 1 F.L.R. 520.

[190] *Re W (Minors) (Residence Order)* [1992] 2 F.C.R. 461.

[191] Law Com. No.172, para.3.19.

[192] Children Act 1989 s.1(4).

[193] Family Proceedings Rules 1991 (SI 1991/1247) r.4.11(1); F.P.C. 1991 r.11(1). For further explanations of these roles, see above, Ch.19 and below, Ch.22.

[194] *Southwark LBC v B* [1993] 2 F.L.R. 559 at 573, *per* Waite L.J.

[195] art.12; Fortin, *Children's Rights* (1998), Ch.8. The European Convention on the Exercise of Children's Rights (1997), which has not been ratified by the UK, grants children the right to receive information, to be consulted, to express their views and to be represented in family proceedings. The right is limited to those considered to have sufficient understanding: arts 3, 4.

[196] Custody of Children Act 1891 s.4; *R. v Clarke* (1857) 7 El. & Bl. 186; see J. Roche, "Children and divorce: a private affair", in Sclater and Piper, *Undercurrents*, pp.55, 70.

[197] Law Com. WP 96, paras 6.40 *et seq.*; Law Com. No.172, para.3.23; C. Piper, "The wishes and feelings of the child", in Sclater and Piper *Undercurrents*, pp.77, 79.

[198] J. Roche, "Children and divorce". Similarly, the Adoption and Children Act 2002 contains no provision other than s.1(4) through which the child's attitude to adoption is considered.

does not require a child to be *Gillick* competent[199] before his or her views are considered. In some cases the child's views are decisive[200]:

> In *Re M (Contact: Welfare Test)*[201] two children, aged seven and eight, had lived with their father for over five years following the separation of their parents. Contact with their mother broke down, but 18 months later she sought a contact order. Contact was refused and the decision upheld on appeal. The children did not wish to see their mother; ordering contact against their wishes would be harmful.[202]

In other cases the child's needs will be given more weight:

> In *Re V (Residence: Review)*[203] the father sought residence of one of his three children, a twin boy. Some years earlier the parents had witnessed the drowning of their other children. The father had suffered post-traumatic stress disorder. He was a damaged person, unemployable and vulnerable. The boy ran away to his father's home with his elder brother but was returned pending a full hearing. Although the child wanted to live with his father, and two of the three experts involved recommended this, the judge accepted that the mother was better able to deal with the boy's physical needs, and the judge also accepted the view of a child psychiatrist that the boy's emotional welfare would suffer if he lived with the father. The mother's residence was confirmed but with a review after six months.

The attitude of the courts to giving weight to children's views varies, in part reflecting the age of the child, the issue before the court and the views expressed. More weight is given to the views of adolescents, at least in relation to matters carrying little risk so that orders, except in relation to medical treatment,[204] which contradict "the wishes of normal children aged 16, 14 and 12 are virtually

---

[199] *Gillick v West Norfolk and Wisbech AHA* [1986] A.C. 112. The views of a *Gillick*-competent child should be given greater weight: *Re S (Change of Name)* [1999] 1 F.L.R. 672 at 674, *per* Thorpe L.J.

[200] For example, *Re P (A Minor) (Education)* [1992] 1 F.L.R. 316, where a 14-year-old boy's preference for a day school determined the dispute, although Butler-Sloss L.J. recognised there were undoubted advantages of boarding-school education, and would have imposed that choice on a younger child.

[201] [1995] 1 F.L.R. 274, CA.

[202] Children's hostility may be viewed as harmful and requiring intervention: *Re M (Contact: Long-term Best Interests)* [2006] 1 F.L.R 627, CA. There may be an obligation on the state to provide counselling to support the re-establishment of a parent-child relationship: *Ignaccolo-Zenide v Romania* (2001) 31 E.H.R.R. 7.

[203] [1995] 2 F.L.R. 1010, CA. The tort action arising out of the original tragedy is reported as *Vernon v Bosley (No.1)* [1997] 1 All E.R. 577. For subsequent litigation concerning the disclosure of evidence from family proceedings, see *Vernon v Bosley (No.2)* [1998] 1 F.L.R. 304.

[204] *Re E (A Minor) (Wardship: Medical Treatment)* [1993] 1 F.L.R. 386; *Re W (Medical Treatment: Court's Jurisdiction)* [1993] Fam. 64, where the court decided in favour of medically advised treatment.

unknown to family law".[205] But it is unusual for judges to find that the views of children under the age of 10 years are conclusive.[206] Judges have been hesitant to let children's antipathy dissuade them from the view that contact with a parent is in their best interests,[207] but where the child's wishes are rational and in accordance with views about their welfare, courts are more willing to comply with them.[208] The fervence and persistence of the child's views may also be influential.[209]

19–017   Many concerns have been expressed about stressing the importance of children's wishes. This places too great a burden on the child[210] and may enable them to manipulate the parents. It is unreliable because what children say may be inconsistent,[211] may not reflect what they really want or may be only a passing feeling.[212] Children are frequently seen as poor decision-makers, over influenced by material considerations or short-term gains.[213] Children may have been conditioned by the views of a carer,[214] bribery or the desire to care for their parents or live with them.[215] The circumstances in which the views were obtained may have influenced them.[216] Ultimately, what children want may not be accepted as in their best interests.[217]

However, ignoring children's views risks further endangering their welfare. Children may resort to self-help, conducting relationships secretly or running away.[218] Imposing decisions on unwilling children may be ineffective.[219] There

---

[205] *Re B (Change of Surname)* [1996] 1 F.L.R. 791 at 794, *per* Wilson J. The judge declined to hold that the refusal to allow the change of the children's surname was wrong.
[206] *Klentzeris v Klentzeris* [2007] EWCA Civ 533 is an example; see below, para.19–020.
[207] *Re K (Contact: Psychiatric Report)* [1995] 2 F.L.R. 432, CA, but where the child's objection is against a background of domestic violence, the court is becoming more sensitive: *Re L; Re V; Re M; Re H (Contact: Domestic Violence)* [2000] 2 F.L.R. 334, CA.
[208] *Re M, T, P, K and B (Change of Name)* [2000] 2 F.L.R. 645.
[209] *Re T (Abduction: Child's Objections to Return)* [2000] 2 F.L.R. 192, where the 11-year-old child ("mature beyond her years") wrote a series of letters objecting to return to her alcoholic mother.
[210] T. Campbell, "The rights of the minor" in P. Alston, S. Parker and J. Seymour, *Children's Rights and the Law* (Oxford: Clarendon, 1992), pp.21–22; *M v M* (1977) 7 Fam. Law 17; *Adams v Adams* [1984] F.L.R. 768.
[211] *Re M (Medical Treatment: Consent)* [1999] 2 F.L.R. 1097, where the girl did not want a heart transplant but did not want to die.
[212] B. Cantwell and S. Scott, "Children's wishes, children's burdens" (1995) J.S.W.F.L. 337.
[213] See comments of Lord Templeman in the *Gillick* case [1986] A.C. 112; Wallerstein and Kelly (1980), pp.314–315. *Re C (A Minor) (Care: Child's Wishes)* [1993] 1 F.L.R. 832.
[214] But "parental alienation syndrome" is not recognised condition: C. Sturge and D. Glaser, "Contact and domestic violence—the experts' court report" [2000] Fam. Law 615 at 622; *Re R (A Minor) (Residence: Religion)* [1993] 2 F.L.R. 163 where the views of a 10 year old who wanted to remain with members of the Exclusive Brethren after his mother's death were not decisive.
[215] B. Neale and A. Wade, *Parent Problems! Children's Views on Life when Parents Split Up* (Young Voice, 2000); *B v B (Minors) (Interviews and Listing Arrangements)* [1994] 2 F.L.R. 489, CA, at 495 (the children refused to state a preference).
[216] Younger and more dependent children are inevitably more prone to influence from their carers: C. Sturge and D. Glaser [2000] Fam. Law 615, 621.
[217] *Re C (A Minor) (Leave to Seek Section 8 Order)* [1994] 1 F.L.R. 26 where a 14 year old's wish for a residence order in favour of friends was overridden because it could prevent conciliation with her parents.
[218] *Re P (Abduction: Minor's Views)* [1998] 2 F.L.R. 825, CA.
[219] *Re B (Residence Order: Leave to Appeal)* [1998] 1 F.L.R. 520, where the boys' behaviour at contact with their mother made transfer of residence to her impracticable; *Re HB (Abduction: Child's Objections)* [1998] 1 F.L.R. 422, and see B. Hale [1999] C.F.L.Q. 377, 378 where a girl's refusal to take the plane prevented her return to Denmark under the Hague Abduction Convention.

is considerable evidence that some children do want to have a say in decisions that directly affect them, including with which of two disputing parties they should live,[220] and that parents do not always consult them.[221]

The phrase "wishes and feelings" encompasses not only what the child expresses directly but also information that may be obtained by a third party. There is no single procedure for ascertaining the child's views.[222] Judges and magistrates[223] may interview the child in private, but they should not seek to displace professionals nor offer children confidentiality.[224] In care proceedings there will normally be a children's guardian who has a duty to make the child's wishes known to the court[225]; in other cases this may be done by a children and family reporter appointed to provide a report, or more rarely, by making the child a party and appointing a guardian under r.9.5.[226] CAFCASS officers frequently consult very young children; some are very experienced in communicating with children and may seek to ascertain their feelings through play or by interpreting drawings, but children are not always given sufficient information about the options.[227] Also there are disputed cases where no one independent of the parties attempts to establish the child's views[228]; in such cases the court still has to consider them. The court's failure to hear the child's views conflicts with international obligations.[229]

---

[220] A Children's Legal Centre survey of 600 teenagers in 1989 indicated that 90% wanted to be consulted on this: see (1989) 60 *Childright* 6; Lyon et al., "In whose best interests"; Neale and Smart, *Effective Support*.

[221] M. Murch et al. *op. cit. Safeguarding Children's Welfare in Uncontentious Divorce: A Study of s.41 of the Matrimonial Causes Act 1973* (LCD, 1998), pp.156–158.

[222] For a review of the approaches, see Fortin, *Children's Rights* (2003), pp.210 *et seq.* and Crichton [2006] Fam. Law 849. Older children may seek party status and have their wishes advocated directly: *Mabon v Mabon* [2005] 2 F.L.R 1011, CA; above para.16–020, but this may not be allowed: *Re H (Residence Order: Application for Leave)* [2000] 1 F.L.R. 780.

[223] *Re W (A Minor) (Contact)* [1994] 1 F.L.R. 843; *Re M (A Minor) (Justices' Discretion)* [1993] 2 F.L.R. 706. But it is unnecessary or undesirable for magistrates to see the child if a CAFCASS officer is involved; *B v B (Minors) (Interviews and Listing Arrangements)* [1994] 2 F.L.R. 489, CA. The Family Justice Council is promoting increased engagement between the judiciary and children whose lives are the subject of litigation: see [2008] Fam. Law 431.

[224] *B v B (Minors) (Interviews and Listing Arrangements)* [1994] 2 F.L.R. 489 at 495, *per* Wall J.; those reporting about children's views should not promise confidentiality: *Re D (Adoption Reports: Confidentiality)* [1995] 2 F.L.R. 687, HL.

[225] Family Proceedings Rules 1991 (SI 1991/1247) r.4.11(4)(b); F.P.C. 1991 r.11(4)(b); J. Masson, "Representation of children in England" [2000] F.L.Q. 467.

[226] For a discussion of the practices of children's guardians, see J. Masson, "Representation". Information for s.7 welfare reports is not always obtained directly from the child or out of the presence of the parent: M. Hester and L. Radford, *Domestic Violence and Child Contact Arrangements in England and Denmark* (1996); and half the children in a recent study of private law proceedings felt that their voices had not been heard either by the court process or their parents: A. Buchanan et al., *Families in Conflict* (Bristol: Polity, 2001).

[227] Children have no specific rights to information in either private law or public law proceedings, nor are their parents required to inform them; cf. Children (Scotland) Act 1995 s.6(1).

[228] For solicitors' approaches to their role in ascertaining children's views (as required by the Legal Services Commission, *Family Transaction Criteria*), see Piper, "The wishes", pp.85–88.

[229] UN Convention on the Rights of the Child art.12; Council Regulation (EC) 2201/2003; SI 2005/265 (Brussels II (revised)).

b) *The child's physical, emotional and educational needs*

19–018   In the past, the concept of need relied heavily on subjective assessment, often informed by subjective views about what is good for children[230] and bias in favour of the dominant culture.[231] Far greater emphasis is now placed on formal assessments informed by research.[232] There is considerable research evidence on children's needs at various stages of their development.[233] Research also suggests that long-term problems occur when the parenting style is generally low on warmth and high on criticism.[234] Parental separation and divorce have been shown to affect children's life chances adversely,[235] but there is no clear understanding of what processes are occurring or the steps that should be taken to mitigate these. Considerable emphasis is placed on children's need to maintain a relationship with each parent and on the negative effects of conflict,[236] and for these reasons, permission to change a child's surname has been refused.[237] In disputes about medical treatment, courts place great weight on medical opinion about its likely outcome,[238] and there is a strong presumption in favour of action that will prolong life.[239] Where the child has special educational needs, there is provision for assessment (statementing) under the Education Act 1996.[240] Mothers may be favoured over fathers on the basis of a young child's physical[241] or emotional needs, particularly if the father is not going to care for the child himself.[242] In any particular case the child's various needs may conflict:

> In *Re R (A Minor) (Residence Order Religion)*[243] the court was faced with competing applications for residence and contact orders in respect of a 10-year-old boy whose mother had died, by an aunt, by some friends who were all members of the Exclusive Brethren sect and by the boy's father who had been excluded from the sect. The boy had been brought up within the sect and identified strongly with its teaching, but he also wanted to be with his father. These spiritual and emotional needs were incompatible;

---

[230] See *May v May* [1986] 1 F.L.R. 325 (judicial preference for firm discipline); *Re W (Residence Order)* [1999] 1 F.L.R. 869, CA (attitude of judges to nudity in the home).
[231] For example, bias against homosexual parents: see Reece [1996] C.L.P. 267, 286.
[232] HM Government, *The Common Assessment Framework for Children and Young People: Practitioner's Guide* (2006) (the *CAF* provides guidance on assessments under ss.17 and 47, and for other professionals.
[233] H. Cleaver et al., *Children's Needs—Parenting Capacity* (1999) Pt 4.
[234] DH, *Child Protection Messages from Research* (1995), p.19.
[235] B. Rodgers and J. Pryor, *Divorce and Separation: The Outcomes for Children* (1998).
[236] J. Pryor and F. Seymour, "Making decisions about children after parental separation" [1996] C.F.L.Q. 229; Rodgers and Pryor (1998), pp.16, 42; Sturge and Glaser [2000] Fam. Law 615.
[237] *Re B (Change of Surname)* [1996] 1 F.L.R. 791, CA. See also *Dawson v Wearmouth* [1999] 1 F.L.R. 1167 at 1175, *per* Lord Jauncey (dissenting).
[238] *Re C (HIV)* [1999] 2 F.L.R. 1004; *Royal Wolverhampton Hospitals NHS Trust v B* [2000] 1 F.L.R. 953; cf. *Re T (Wardship Medical Treatment)* [1997] 1 F.L.R. 502 (emphasis on the reasonable views of caring parents).
[239] *Wyatt v Portsmouth NHS Trust* [2006] 1 F.L.R 554, CA, *per* Wall L.J. at para.87.
[240] The poor levels of educational attainment for children looked after by local authorities is a matter of concern: Select Committee on Health, *Second Report* (1997–8) para.289.
[241] *Re W (A Minor) (Residence Order)* [1992] 2 F.L.R. 332 (breast feeding); cf. *Re D (Minors)* [1995] 1 F.C.R. 301, CA.
[242] *Re W (A Minor) (Residence Order)* [1993] 2 F.L.R. 625 at 635 (step-mother); *Plant v Plant* [1983] 4 F.L.R. 305 (child minder).
[243] [1993] 2 F.L.R. 163, CA.

there was no middle way. The Court of Appeal upheld a decision to grant a residence order to the father and to allow supervised contact with the aunt upon her undertaking not to speak to the child about religious matters.

Material factors, matters that have commonly been considered but are not specifically included in the checklist, may also be introduced under this heading.[244] Accommodation is clearly important, but its availability may depend on having care of a child.[245] There is evidence that poverty is linked with poor health, poor physical development and lower educational attainment.[246] However, emphasis on material standards is likely disproportionately to affect mothers because of women's lower wages.

c) *The likely effect of any change in circumstances*
The courts give close attention to the positive and negatives for the child of proposed changes.[247] Arrangements that are working satisfactorily are highly influential in applications for residence orders by relatives or foster parents who are caring for the child, and also in the variation applications: **19–019**

In *Re P (s.91(14)) (Residence and Religious Heritage)*[248] the parents, a rabbi and his wife, were unable to care for their daughter, who was born with Down's syndrome. At the age of 17 months the girl was placed by the local authority with a non-Jewish family where she thrived. A residence order was granted in favour of the foster carers when she was four years old. Four years later, her parents applied for variation of residence, arguing the crucial importance of her Jewish heritage. The court rejected the application and reduced their contact. Although her heritage was important, her welfare demanded that she remain with those she regarded as her parents; visits by parents who retained the hope that she would return to them might undermine the placement.

This factor is less helpful in disputes between parents at the time of separation. Research has highlighted the fluidity of arrangements at the time of breakdown

---

[244] Welfare is not to be equated with material advantages, but unwillingness to support one's children may indicate a failure to understand their needs: *Re S (Contact: Evidence)* [1998] 1 F.L.R. 798 at 802, *per* Hale J.; differences in resources should be dealt with by reallocating assets (Children Act 1989 Sch.1) and realistic levels of child support.
[245] A homeless person caring for a child has a priority need and some rights to rehousing: Housing Act 1996 s.193, as amended by the Homelessness Act 2002 ss.6–8.
[246] See the findings of the National Child Development Study, especially P. Wedge and H. Prosser, *Born to Fail?* (NCB, 1974) and E. Ferri, *Growing Up in a One-parent Family* (Windsor: NFER, 1976).
[247] *An NHS Trust v MB (A Child Represented by CAFCASS as Guardian as Litem)* [2006] 2 F.L.R. 319, FD.
[248] [1999] 2 F.L.R. 573, CA; the earlier history of this case is reported as *C v Salford* [1994] 2 F.L.R. 926; see also *Re M (care order: freeing application)* [2004] 1 F.L.R. 826, CA (where the Court of Appeal overturned a decision to adjourn care and freeing applications pending the assessment of relatives, favouring maintaining the current placement where the child had lived for 15 months. Placement with relatives did not provide greater respect for the father's art.8 rights).

and, has emphasised the importance of adjustment to new roles and relationships.[249] This factor is also relevant to disputes over contact where relationships have ended or never developed because of lack of contact. Re-introduction of a parent will help to meet the child's identity needs but needs careful planning.[250] The courts have sometimes justified refusing orders on the basis that it would be too disruptive to the child to re-introduce the parent,[251] although the research evidence on this is equivocal.[252] Adjustment to new roles is also crucial to a child's successful return after a period being looked after by a local authority.[253]

It is also recognised that emphasising the status quo may encourage one party to delay.[254] Delay in court proceedings can allow one party to establish a settled arrangement before the matter is considered by the court. The Children Act 1989 specifically draws the attention of the courts to the fact that any delay is "likely to prejudice the welfare of the child".[255] Delay prolongs the uncertainty for the child and carers, makes it more difficult for the court to reach a decision that is in the child's best interests[256] and may amount to a breach of human rights.[257]

d) *The child's age, sex, background and any characteristic of the child's that the court considers relevant*

19–020   There is some research evidence that parental separation affects children differently according to their age,[258] and also that new "parental" relationships may be established successfully for children beyond infancy.[259] Consideration of age is also linked with other factors, such as the child's needs,[260] wishes and education. The relevance of the child's sex was reflected in the old rules of thumb, but research does not appear to support the view that children do better living with a lone parent of the same gender.[261] There is no evidence that mothers

---

[249] Wallerstein and Kelly (1980); Maccoby and Mnookin, *Dividing the Child* (1992).
[250] Sturge and Glaser [2000] Fam. Law 615, pp.621–622, 625; *Re L (Contact: Transsexual Applicant)* [1995] 2 F.L.R. 438; *Re C (Contact: Change of Gender)* [2007] 1 F.L.R. 1642, CA; *Re K (Adoption and Wardship)* [1997] 2 F.L.R. 221.
[251] *Re M (A Minor) (Access Application)* [1988] F.L.R. 35, CA (child in local authority care); *Re W (A Minor: Access)* [1989] 1 F.L.R. 163.
[252] See J. Masson, "Contact between parents and children in the long-term care of others: the unresolved dispute" (1990) 3 Int. J. of Law & Fam. 97. A substantial proportion of children who return home from care have had little contact with their families whilst in care; see S. Millham et al., *Lost in Care* (Aldershot: Gower, 1986).
[253] R. Bullock et al., *Going Home* (Aldershot: Dartmouth, 1993), pp.177, 206.
[254] Law Com. WP 96, para.6.32.
[255] Children Act 1989 s.1(2); the Adoption and Children Act 2002 s.1(3); see para.18–006, above. The courts are required to set a timetable for the litigation: Children Act 1989 ss.11(1), 32; Family Proceedings Rules 1991 (SI 1991/1247) r.4.15.
[256] *R. v Bolton MBC, Ex p. B* [1985] F.L.R. 346, *per* Wood J. at 348; *Re R (No.1) (Intercountry Adoption)* [1999] 1 F.L.R. 1014.
[257] ECHR art.6(1); *H v UK* (1987) 10 E.H.R.R. 95.
[258] Rodgers and Pryor, *Divorce and Separation*, p.38.
[259] See B. Tizard, *Adoption: A Second Chance* (1977).
[260] See H. Cleaver et al., *Children's Needs—Parenting Capacity* (1999), Pt 4.
[261] Rodgers and Pryor, *Divorce and Separation*, p.39.

are necessarily better carers.[262] However, in a society where men and women engage in different activities on the basis of their gender, girls may prefer activities with mothers and boys with fathers. A parent of the same gender may also be better able to understand the problems experienced as the child grows up.

The Children Act 1989 lists four factors that must be considered by local authorities when making decisions about children, they are looking after, which may also be relevant to this paragraph. These are: religious persuasion, racial origin, cultural background and linguistic background.[263] Guidance for local authorities emphasises consultation with parents and children, and finding placements that fit with their views on religion and culture,[264] but all factors must be considered (e.g. half siblings with different ethnic origins may need to be placed together). A local authority's long-term plans should not exclude placement with a family who does not share the child's heritage.[265] The courts must not pass judgment on beliefs of parents but must only be concerned with the social or emotional effects of the parent's adherence to any particular sect.[266] It has been said that religious and cultural heritage cannot be an overwhelming factor[267]:

In *Re S (Specific Issue Order: Religion: Circumcision)*[268] the Muslim mother and Hindu father had brought up their children as Hindus with Islamic influences. After their separation, the mother sought a court order for the children to become practising Muslims, and for the boy to be circumcised. Baron J. regarded this change as meeting the mother's needs to portray herself as a good Muslim. The parents had agreed to bring the children up in both religions, and it was best for this to continue. The children should be able to make their own choice; circumcision would limit the boy's choice and was therefore contrary to his interests.

---

[262] See Chambers, "Rethinking", pp.515–524. Mothers are more likely to have experience of caring for children, but there is no presumption that they should have care: *Re W (A Minor) (Residence Order)* [1992] 2 F.L.R. 332, CA.

[263] Children Act 1989 s.22(5)(c).

[264] DfES, *Fostering Now Leaflets* (2004); DfES, *Adoption Guidance* (2005), Ch.2.

[265] LAC(98)20, pp.3–4. Private foster carers who did not recognise the child's racial and cultural needs were inappropriate carers: *H v Trafford BC* [1997] 3 F.C.R. 113.

[266] This would be discrimination contrary to ECHR art.14; see *Palau-Martinez v France* [2004] 2 F.L.R. 810. Concerns have been expressed about social isolation; see *Hewison v Hewison* (1977) 7 Fam. Law 207, CA (Exclusive Brethren); about psychological damage from indoctrination; *Wright v Wright* (1980) 2 F.L.R. 276 (Jehovah's Witness); about separation from the only surviving parent; *Re R (A Minor) (Residence: Religion)* [1993] 2 F.L.R. 163; and about health risks where the parent would not agree to a blood transfusion. However, health may be protected by making a specific issue order (Children Act 1989 s.8(1)) or accepting an undertaking from the parent: *Re S (A Minor) (Blood Transfusion: Adoption Order Condition)* [1994] 2 F.L.R. 416, CA. See, generally, A. Bradney, *Religion, Rights and Laws* (1993).

[267] *Re P (s.91(14)) (Residence and Religious Heritage)* [1999] 2 F.L.R. 573 at 586, *per* Butler-Sloss L.J. Issues of race must not be ignored for a child of mixed parentage: *Re M (Section 94 Appeals)* [1995] 1 F.L.R. 546.

[268] [2005 1 F.L.R. 236, FD; see also *Re J (Specific Issue Orders: Child's Religious Upbringing and Circumcision)* [1999] 2 F.L.R. 678; [2000] 1 F.L.R. 571, CA, where the court refused to sanction circumcision for a boy against the wishes of his non-practising Christian mother who was his main carer.

Issues of race are highly contentious and should not be ignored.[269] The courts recognise the special value of care by the natural parents that necessarily provides links with the child's culture and heritage.[270] There is some evidence that being brought up in a family that does not reflect racial, cultural and religious background negatively impacts on a child's identity and self-esteem; children from minority ethnic groups may not be equipped by carers to deal with the racism from the dominant community.[271] This has justified a decision to move a mixed-race child from a white family, where he had lived for 18 months from birth, to a black family,[272] but was insufficient to require a white surrogate mother to hand over twins to their Asian father when they were five months old.[273]

Where a child has lost or not acquired the language of their family, this is a factor that may prevent return to them, but carers may be required to ensure that a child receives appropriate instruction.[274] Cultural and linguistic factors are relevant in care proceedings where the risk to the child remaining in their family must be balanced with the risks of going into care and placement with strangers.[275] The only limit on considering something under this paragraph is that it must not be such that no reasonable judge would consider it.[276]

e) *Any harm that the child has suffered or is at risk of suffering*

19–021   A care order may only be made where the harm or likely harm is significant[277] and is proved on the balance of probabilities.[278] Similarly, in private law cases, the courts require evidence that the child is at risk of harm,[279] but the risk need not be attributable to the parent seeking the order.[280]

---

[269] *Re M (Section 94 Appeals)* [1995] 1 F.L.R. 546 at 550, CA.

[270] *Re M (Child's Upbringing)* [1996] 2 F.L.R. 441, CA (the Zulu-boy case); *Re B (Adoption: Child's Welfare)* [1995] 2 F.L.R. 895 (Gambian child).

[271] B. Prevatt Goldstein and M. Spencer, *"Race" and Ethnicity* (London: BAAF, 2000); see also Inter-departmental Review of Adoption Law, *Background Paper 2* (1990), pp.50–59. *Adoption, The Future* (Cm.2288, 1993) urged common-sense professional assessment and the avoidance of ideology (para.4.28). Contact may be beneficial in transracial adoptions: *Re O (Transracial Adoption: Contact)* [1995] 2 F.L.R. 597.

[272] *Re P (A Minor) (Adoption)* [1990] 1 F.L.R. 96; see also *Re N (A Minor) (Adoption)* [1990] 1 F.L.R. 58.

[273] *Re P (Minors) (Wardship: Surrogacy)* [1987] 2 F.L.R. 421.

[274] *Re K (Adoption and Wardship)* [1997] 2 F.L.R. 221.

[275] Special weight cannot be given to the child's culture if this would leave the child with unacceptably poor care; *Re H (Minors) (Wardship: Cultural Background)* [1987] 2 F.L.R. 12.

[276] *G v G (Minors: Custody Appeal)* [1985] 1 W.L.R. 647; see the discussion of appeals at para.19–024, below.

[277] Children Act 1989 s.31(2); "harm" is defined for the purposes of care proceedings as "ill-treatment or the impairment of health or development". s.31(9), and see below para.21–031.

[278] *Re H and R (Child Sexual Abuse: Standard of Proof)* [1996] 1 F.L.R. 80, HL.

[279] The courts have not specifically applied *Re H and R* [1996] 1 F.L.R. 80; see *Re N (Residence: Hopeless Appeals)* [1995] 2 F.L.R. 230 at 233, *per* Butler-Sloss L.J.; *Re P (Sexual Abuse: Standard of Proof)* [1996] 2 F.L.R. 333 at 342, *per* Wall J. Procedures have been devised to assess risks, and courts are expected to hold finding of fact hearings: see above, para.19–010.

[280] *Re K (Specific Issue Order)* [1999] 2 F.L.R. 280, where the mother had told the child that the father was dead and would undermine any attempt to tell the child the truth; *Re B (Contact: Stepfather's Opposition)* [1997] 1 F.L.R. 579, CA where the risk arose from the step-father's threat to reject the child and the mother if the proceedings continued.

Harm may arise from granting or denying contact. Witnessing a parent being abused is damaging to children.[281] There is no automatic assumption against contact where there has been domestic violence, but physical and emotional safety need proper consideration.[282] The ability of the violent parent to recognise the effects of their past conduct and the need to change are important considerations.[283] The seriousness of the parental problem (mental illness, domestic violence or substance abuse) is less relevant than the level to which the child is directly involved.[284]

The research evidence on the impact of abuse on children and their experiences in different forms of substitute care is complex.[285] Comparisons between children who have been abused and other children indicate more behaviour problems and greater difficulty with friendships amongst the abused group, but one in five abused children were said to have faired well at home.[286] Persistent abuse and a combination of abuse and neglect tended to make the outcome worse; a fifth[287] of children living at home were re-abused, but there was no link between this and the long-term outcome. Substitute care improved abused children's social status, physical growth and vocabulary but not their behaviour or mental wellbeing. Children who had been adopted had as many behaviour and friendship problems as those who remained with their parents after abuse, but children in foster care faired better.[288]

f) *How capable each of the child's parents and any other person in relation to whom the court considers the question to be relevant is of meeting the child's needs*

Capacity to parent should not be seen as predetermined[289]; carers may learn to parent, but the courts will not expect children to wait until deficient parents have gained the necessary skills.[290] Parental problems (mental illness, substance abuse **19–022**

---

[281] Children Act 1989 s.31(9), as amended; DH, *Child Protection Messages from Research* (1995), p.18.

[282] *Re L, Re V, Re M and Re H (Contact: Domestic Violence)* [2000] 2 F.L.R. 334, CA; Sturge and Glaser [2000] Fam. Law 615.

[283] *Re L, Re V, Re M and Re H (Contact: Domestic Violence)* [2000] 2 F.L.R. 334 at 344, *per* Butler-Sloss P.; *Re H (Contact: Domestic Violence)* [2006] 1 F.L.R. 943, CA.

[284] Cleaver et al., *Children's Needs*, p.42.

[285] DH, *Caring for Children Away from Home* (1998); DH, *Child Protection Messages from Research* (1995); DH, *Patterns and Outcomes in Child Placement* (1991); Cleaver et al., *Children's Needs*, (1999), Pt 3.

[286] J. Gibbons et al., "Development after physical abuse in early childhood", in DH, *Child Protection Messages from Research* (1995), p.66.

[287] This figure is comparable with those in other studies: see DH, *Child Protection Messages from Research* (1995).

[288] J. Gibbons et al., "Development after", p.67. But these findings are in contradiction to the weight of evidence in other studies where adopted children have faired well, and foster care has been associated with poor outcomes: see B. Tizard, *Adoption: A Second Chance* (1977) and DH, *Patterns and Outcomes in Child Placement* (1991). Gibbons suggests that poorer outcomes may relate to parenting styles.

[289] See Chambers, "Rethinking", pp.515–524. Research indicates that non-custodial fathers can acquire caring skills, but mothers are still seen as the natural carers for very young children: *Brixey v Lynas* [1995] 2 F.L.R. 499, HL (S), *per* Lord Jauncey at 504–505.

[290] *Re D (Grant of Care Order: Refusal of Freeing Order)* [2001] 1 F.L.R. 862, CA; *Scott v UK* [2000] 1 F.L.R. 958 at 970.

and domestic violence) impact on parenting capacity, particularly where they exist in combination.[291] A carer may simply demonstrate their ability to care; the potential of others will need to be assessed[292]:

> In *Re P*[293] the mother reneged on a surrogacy agreement and refused to hand over the child to the father and his wife. He applied for residence 10 days after the birth. Approximately 18 months later, at the hearing to determine the application, an expert gave evidence in favour of the father. The judge ordered residence for the father but suspended the handover. The mother's appeal was unsuccessful; the judge's approach was unimpeachable.

Capable parents need not care for their children full-time, but must show that they understand their children's needs when making alternative arrangements.[294] Parental remarriage is likely to improve the child's economic circumstances[295] but may impose greater emotional stress.[296] This paragraph is also relevant to consideration of the effect of an order on the parent caring for the child. Where contact will undermine the ability to care, the court may refuse an order, although this would not be done lightly[297]:

> In *Re H (Contact: Domestic Violence)*[298] the father had assaulted the mother and made threats to kill her, apparently because of her failure to conform strictly to the Muslim faith. The mother ran away with the children, changing her name and those of the children to avoid detection, and brought them up in a secular, westernised way. Three years later the father applied for contact. The judge accepted that the mother remained fearful that the father would abduct the children and that his influence would undermine her. Indirect contact was ordered and the father's appeal was dismissed.

g) *The range of powers available to the court under this Act in the proceedings in question*

19–023   There are wide powers in the Children Act 1989 to make orders, and the terms of the orders themselves provide considerable scope[299] to the court. Where there

---

[291] Cleaver et al., *Children's Needs*, Pt 2.

[292] A positive assessment from the local authority can be crucial: *B v P (Adoption by Unmarried Father)* [2000] 2 F.L.R. 717; *Re M-H (Assessment: Father of Half-Brother)* [2007] 2 F.L.R. 715, CA.

[293] [2007] EWCA Civ 1053.

[294] *Re K (Minors) (Children: Care and Control)* [1977] Fam. 179. The father's arrangements that involved a rota of childminders indicated that he did not or could not give sufficient attention to the children's needs for continuity and consistency.

[295] J. Eekelaar and M. Maclean, *Maintenance after Divorce* (Oxford: Clarendon, 1986), p.69.

[296] M. Maclean and M. Wadsworth, "The interests of children after parental divorce: a long-term perspective" (1988) 2 Int. J. Law & Fam. 155, 160–161; Rodgers and Pryor, *Divorce and Separation*, Ch.5.

[297] *Re L, Re V, Re M and Re H (Contact: Domestic Violence)* [2000] 2 F.L.R. 334; *Re K (Contact: Mother's Anxiety)* [1999] 2 F.L.R. 703; see also *Re F (Indirect Contact)* [2007] 1 F.L.R. 1015, CA.

[298] [2000] 2 F.L.R. 334, CA.

[299] Children Act 1989 ss.8, 11(7); above. For a discussion of special guardianship as an alternative to adoption, see para.22–064, below.

is no statutory power, the inherent jurisdiction may still be available.[300] The court has power to make orders other than those applied for,[301] but can only commit the child to local authority care when the grounds for a care order have been proved.[302] However, an individual who has not applied for a residence order and who does not want the responsibility conferred by it should not be required to accept it:

> In *Re K (Care Order or Residence Order)*[303] the local authority started care proceedings in respect of a child who had been injured by his schizophrenic mother. The child and his older brother were placed with their maternal grandparents. The grandparents were willing to care for the children but preferred to do this as foster carers so that they would have the financial and professional support of the social services department because both the children had muscular dystrophy, which would make them increasingly disabled as they grew up. The local authority wished to withdraw its application for care orders but the court made care orders.

Before making any order, the court must also be satisfied that "doing so would be better for the child than making no order at all".[304] The court may thus decide that it should make no order because it would only engender further conflict or, alternatively, because the parties are now able to make their own arrangements. It should be noted, however, that agreements do not have the same effect as orders, particularly when it comes to enforcement.[305]

G. Review of the court's decisions on welfare

The appellate courts have long been concerned as to not become involved in the reconsideration of the very many cases that have been determined applying the welfare test. These cases that involve the exercise of discretion have "no right answer", and there may be two possible decisions that are "both equally right".[306] Consequently, it would be wrong for the Appeal Court to substitute its view for that of the judge. Judges and magistrates hearing children cases are specifically trained to balance aspects of welfare; too-ready intervention by the Appeal Court judges (who are not necessarily specialists) risks robbing them of the discretion entrusted by law.[307] Where the judge has made findings of fact or

19–024

---

[300] *A v Liverpool CC* [1982] A.C. 363; but not where the limitations in Children Act 1989 s.100 apply.
[301] Children Act 1989 ss.10(1), 31(2); orders in favour of those who cannot apply for them are exceptional: *Gloucestershire CC v P* [1999] 2 F.L.R. 61, CA.
[302] Children Act 1989 ss.9(5) 31; see below, para.21–030.
[303] [1995] 1 F.L.R. 675.
[304] Children Act 1989 s.1(5); *Re G (Children)* [2006] 1 F.L.R 771, CA, and para.18–006, above.
[305] Children Act 1989 ss.2(8), 5(6), 12, 13; *Re W (A Minor) (Contact)* [1994] 2 F.L.R. 441 and above, para.18–055.
[306] *Per* Lord Fraser, *G v G* [1985] 1 W.L.R. 647 at 651. Cf. R. Ormrod [1978] C.L.P. 123 at 135–136, who states that he never had any difficulty distinguishing between right, plainly wrong and doubtful decisions; both disagreements and successful appeals were rare.
[307] *Per* Lady Hale, *Re J (Child Returned Abroad: Convention Rights)* [2005] 2 F.L.R. 802, HL, at para.12.

formed views of the parties, the appellate court is in a poor position to gainsay him or her, and would not be able to determine the case but only remit it for rehearing.[308] Moreover, the child's need for a final outcome without delay encourages policies that prevent prolonged litigation.[309] A requirement of leave for appeals is used to restrict appeals.[310] The court may hear the application for leave, grant it but dismiss the appeal in a single hearing. The more difficult the case, the more difficult it is said to be to mount an appeal.[311] Appeals can only be expedited if "extraordinary prejudice" to children is likely or if the case is brought under the Hague Abduction Convention.[312] Counsel should take care not to encourage hopeless appeals.[313] The Court of Appeal has warned that costs may be awarded against the appellant if it considers the appeal unjustified.[314]

In *G v G*[315] the House of Lords explained the role of the appellate court in welfare cases and set out the principles on which an appeal should be allowed:

> "[T]he appellate court should only interfere when it considers that the judge of first instance has not merely preferred an imperfect solution which is different from an alternative imperfect solution which the Court of Appeal might or would have adopted, but has exceeded the generous ambit within which a reasonable disagreement is possible."[316]

Thus, appeals should be allowed where the decision is "plainly wrong". For example, where the judge has preferred lay evidence to that of medical experts but has given no reasons[317]; or made no reference to the special position of the father in a dispute with relatives who were caring for the child[318]; or ordered staying contact pending an assessment of a child who was disturbed after contact[319]; or magistrates have dismissed a care application while an assessment is being carried out[320]; or decided only to make a supervision order despite

---

[308] *Re F (A Minor) (Wardship Appeal)* [1976] Fam. 238, *per* Bridge L.J at 266; see J. Eekelaar (1985) 48 M.L.R. 704 at 705.

[309] Eekelaar [1985] M.L.R. 704, *Re R (Residence : Shared Care: Children's Views)* [2006] 1 F.L.R. 491, CA, *per* Thorpe L.J. at para.15.

[310] Appeals to the Court of Appeal, except those in relation to habeas corpus or secure accommodation, require leave from the Court of Appeal: CPR Pt 52; *Practice Direction (Court of Appeal procedure)* [1999] 2 All E.R. 490; *Re Bradford; Re O'Connell* [2007] 1 F.L.R. 530. A survey for the Lord Chancellor's Department found that in 1997/8, 63% of appeals were successful where there was a leave filter, but only 29% where there was no filter.

[311] *Re D (Parental Responsibility: IVF baby)* [2001] 1 F.L.R. 972, CA, *per* Butler-Sloss P. at para.27.

[312] *Practice Direction (Court of Appeal procedure)* [1999] 2 All E.R. 490, para.6.7.3.

[313] *Re N (Residence: Hopeless Appeals)* [1995] 2 F.L.R. 230 at 231, *per* Butler-Sloss L.J.

[314] *Re G (A Minor) (Role of Appellate Court)* [1987] 1 F.L.R. 164; *R. v R. (Costs: Child Case)* [1997] 2 F.L.R. 92.

[315] [1985] 1 W.L.R. 647.

[316] *Per* Lord Fraser at 652.

[317] *Re B (Split Hearing: Jurisdiction)* [2000] 1 F.L.R. 334 (appeal allowed against finding).

[318] *Re N (Residence: Appointment of Solicitor: Placement with Extended Family)* [2001] 1 F.L.R. 1028.

[319] *Re W (Staying Contact)* [1998] 2 F.L.R. 450, CA.

[320] *C v Solihull MBC* [1993] 1 F.L.R. 290.

reasons indicating grave concern for a child's safety[321]; or where the judge has imposed a condition on adopters in the face of express opposition from their advocate.[322] However, quite comparable decisions have been held to be within the "generous ambit of the court's reasonable discretion". So a father whose application for contact was dismissed in the face of the mother's objections failed in his appeal[323]; and a mother's appeal against the imposition of shared residence was refused.[324] The Court of Appeal has also allowed appeals where subsequent events have indicated that the original decision was ill-founded[325] or inoperable,[326] and where the judge's reasons indicate he or she carried out the balancing exercise incorrectly[327] or "took a path which was not free from error and misdirection".[328] Indeed, the Court of Appeal sometimes appears unwilling to hold the *G v G* line. The court has complete discretion whether to admit new evidence but is in no position to evaluate conflicting testimony about the child's relationship with a parent.[329]

G v G does not preclude an appeal if the judge has applied the wrong test,[330] **19–025** nor if procedural requirements such as the giving of reasons have been ignored,[331] but an appeal may be denied where reasons are incomplete if the appellate court is satisfied that the same decision would have been reached.[332]

Lord Fraser, with whom the other members of the House agreed, expressly rejected the view that the court should approach these cases like judicial review of administrative action and only consider whether the judge had followed a course which "no reasonable judge having taken into account all the relevant

---

[321] *Leicestershire CC v G* [1994] 2 F.L.R. 329.
[322] *Re S (A Minor) (Blood Transfusion: Adoption Order Condition)* [1994] 2 F.L.R. 416.
[323] *Re J (A Minor) (Contact)* [1994] 1 F.L.R. 729.
[324] *A v A (Minors) (Shared Residence)* [1994] 1 F.L.R. 669.
[325] *Re W (A Minor) (Residence Order)* [1993] 2 F.L.R. 625. Similarly, decisions have been upheld when new evidence has justified them: *M v M (Minor: Custody Appeal)* [1987] 1 W.L.R. 404.
[326] *Re B (Residence Order: Leave to Appeal)* [1998] 1 F.L.R. 502; *Re HB (Abduction: Child's Objections)* [1998] 1 F.L.R. 422; both cases where children's behaviour made the implementation of the original order impossible.
[327] *W v P (Justices Reasons)* [1988] 1 F.L.R. 508, the magistrates described the child's welfare as the top item on their list; *Re M (Section 94 Appeals)* [1995] 1 F.L.R. 546, where the magistrates, amongst other errors, failed to refer to the issue of race; *Re L (Residence: Justices Reasons)* [1995] 2 F.L.R. 445, where the magistrates failed to make any finding on the central issue of the mother's alcohol problem; *Re P (Contact: Supervision)* [1996] 2 F.L.R. 314, where the court had given too much weight to the effect of contact on the mother's health; *Re T (Wardship: Medical Treatment)* [1997] 1 F.L.R. 502, where the judge emphasised the mother's unreasonableness and focused narrowly on the medical aspects of the transplant decision; *Re W (Residence Order)* [1999] 1 F.L.R. 869, where the judge allowed his aversion to nudity to override all other factors.
[328] *Re B (Leave to Remove: Impact of Refusal)* [2005] 239, CA, *per* Thorpe L.J at para.12.
[329] *Re M (A Minor) (Appeal) (No.2)* [1994] 1 F.L.R. 59 at 66, *per* Waite L.J. The appellate court is not a forum for testing fresh evidence: *Re V (Residence Review)* [1995] 2 F.L.R. 1010 at 1021, *per* Russell L.J.
[330] *Re H (Minors: Access)* [1992] 1 F.L.R. 148; *Re D (Natural Parent Presumption)* [1999] 1 F.L.R. 135, CA.
[331] F.P.C. 1991 r.21(5); *W v Hertfordshire CC* [1993] 1 F.L.R. 118. Also where a judge has failed to make clear the basis for the decision: *B v B (Residence Order: Reasons for Decision)* [1997] 2 F.L.R. 602
[332] *Re M (Section 94 Appeals)* [1995] 1 F.L.R. 546 at 550, *per* Butler-Sloss L.J. Additional reasons can be given when an appeal is sought for lack of reasons: *Re B (Appeal: Lack of Reasons)* [2003] 2 F.L.R. 1035, CA.

circumstances could have adopted".[333] However, the distinction between these two tests (if any) is a very fine one.[334] A judge who has exceeded the generous ambit has reached a decision that no reasonable judge would have reached. The same approach is also applied where a judge hears an appeal from the family proceedings court.[335] Where magistrates' reasons omit important factors, fail to explain a departure from a welfare officer's recommendation or are unclear on crucial matters, the appellate court is justified in looking to see that the magistrates have correctly carried out the balancing exercise.[336] This narrow approach to appeals has been criticised because it does not provide what litigants want[337] or what, in the interest of the child, a difficult case may require[338] (the opinion of a bench of senior judges); also because it may limit the guidance on matters of principle, which would improve decision making in the lower courts and remove the need for appeals.[339] It has been suggested that the appeal court should at least be able to direct a rehearing in other circumstances.[340]

---

[333] *Per* Stamp L.J. *Re F (A Minor) (Wardship Appeal)* [1976] Fam. 238 at 254, quoted by Lord Fraser at 653.
[334] See Lord Bridge [1985] 1 W.L.R. 647 at 656.
[335] Children Act 1989 s.94; *Re M (Section 94 Appeals)* [1995] 1 F.L.R. 546. Also where there is an appeal from a district judge at the Principal Registry: *Re S (Appeal from Principal Registry: Procedure)* [1998] 2 F.L.R. 856.
[336] *Re M (Section 94 Appeals)* [1995] 1 F.L.R. 546 at 549, *per* Butler-Sloss L.J.
[337] Maidment *Child Custody*, p.58 argued that appeals are being used to rectify the inadequacies of the decision-making process at trial level, and recommended a specialised panel of judges, which has now been provided; see above, Ch.18.
[338] H. Bevan, *Child Law* (1989), para.3.81.
[339] Eekelaar [1985] M.L.R. 704, 706–707. "[C]lear guidance from this court simplifies the task of the trial judge and helps to limit the volume of appeals." *Payne v Payne* [2001] 1 F.L.R. 1052 at 1061, *per* Thorpe L.J.
[340] Sir John Latey, letter to *The Times*, August 31, 1989.

CHAPTER TWENTY

CHILD ABDUCTION[1]

I.	INTRODUCTION	20–001	A. Role of the Central Authority	20–013
II.	PREVENTING ABDUCTION	20–002	B. Abduction to a country which has	
	A. Passport control	20–003	ratified or acceded to the Hague	
	B. All ports warning	20–004	Convention	20–014
	C. Security for the child's return	20–005	C. Abduction under the common law	
	D. "Mirror" orders	20–006	(from or to a country that has not	
III.	TRACING CHILDREN	20–007	ratified the Hague Convention)	20–023
IV.	RECOVERY OF THE CHILD	20–008	VI. ENFORCING CONTACT	
	A. Abduction within England and		DECISIONS	20–024
	Wales	20–009	VII. ABDUCTION AND HUMAN	
	B. Abduction from one part of the		RIGHTS	20–025
	United Kingdom to another	20–010	VIII. CONCLUSION	20–026
V.	INTERNATIONAL ABDUCTION	20–012		

I. INTRODUCTION

Children are taken by strangers for abuse or for ransom; by both parents for **20–001** forced marriage[2]; by non-residential parents from the parent with care; by the parent with care; and children are not returned after contact visits. All these are forms of child abduction. There are various reasons why parents abduct their children.[3] Some cannot bear to be parted from them or hope that abduction will force their former partner to return; others are motivated by a desire to hurt the

---

[1] P. Beaumont and P. McEleavy, *The Hague Convention on International Child Abduction* (Oxford: Oxford University Press, 1999); A. Hutchinson and H. Setright, *International Parental Child Abduction*, 2nd edn (Bristol: Family Law, 2007); A. Anton, "The Hague Convention on International Child Abduction" (1981) 30 I.C.L.Q. 537; C. Bruch, "International child abduction cases: experiences under the 1980 Hague Convention", in *Parenthood and Modern Society: Legal and Social Issues for the Twenty-first Century* (J. Eekelaar and P. Sarcevic (eds) (Dordrecht: Nijhoff, 1994); G. Van Bueren, *The Best Interests of the Child—International Co-operation in Child Abduction* (British Institute of Human Rights, 1993). Information is also available from Reunite at *http://www.reunite.org* [Accessed June 6, 2008].

[2] *Re KR (Abduction: Forcible Removal by Parents)* [1999] 2 F.L.R. 542; see Forced Marriage (Civil Protection) Act 2007 s.1, which adds new remedies under the Family Law Act 1996.

[3] See G.L. Grief and R.L. Hegar, *When Parents Kidnap* (NY, Free Press, 1993), p.8.

other parent or to protect the child from abuse.[4] After the breakdown of a relationship, parents who have previously emigrated may wish to return with their child to their former home country, for support from family and friends. Unless such a relocation is agreed,[5] it may amount to an abduction of the child.

Abduction can be used to gain advantage or avoid disadvantage in proceedings. Custody laws and court practices have encouraged parental abduction by exercising jurisdiction on the basis of mere presence in the country[6]; by giving great weight to the status quo without providing for speedy decisions; by favouring care by fathers rather than mothers (or vice versa); by making it difficult for a parent with care to relocate lawfully; and by failing to enforce decisions about contact. Although abduction has long-term adverse effects on children's welfare,[7] courts (applying the best-interests standard) have been willing to make orders in the abductor's favour, taking a nationalistic approach to welfare.[8]

Abduction potentially interferes with the right to family life of the left-behind parent and the child; where the law or the courts fail to protect these rights effectively, they breach the European Convention on Human Rights.[9] The legal system has been hard pressed to find a satisfactory solution to child abduction but is developing a range of strategies in criminal, civil, domestic and international law. These are based on the principle that the interests of children will be best served by preventing abduction. The aim is to make it more difficult for parents to succeed in abducting their children and to facilitate return so that disputes are heard in the courts of the child's home state. Ensuring that the abductor does not benefit from the abduction should deter others but will only do so if the rules relating to return are strictly adhered to.

II. Preventing Abduction

20–002   The Child Abduction Act 1984 was passed following the conclusion of the Criminal Law Revision Committee that the law on child stealing was inadequate.[10] Under this Act it is an offence for a person connected with the child[11] to

---

[4] J. Groner, *Hilary's Trial—The Elizabeth Morgan Case—A Child's Ordeal in the American Legal System* (New York: Simon and Schuster, 1991). Elizabeth Morgan spent two years in custody for refusing to disclose the whereabouts of her daughter whom she alleged had been sexually abused. The child's grandparents took her to New Zealand, which was not then a party to the Hague Convention.

[5] By the other parent and/or the court. For a discussion of the law and practice in relocation cases, see 18–026.

[6] As was the case under the inherent jurisdiction; see para.18–049.

[7] Greif and Hegar, *When Parents Kidnap*, p.209; M. Freeman, "Effects of international child abduction on children" [2006] I.F.L 129.

[8] A. Dyer, "The Hague Convention—towards global co-operation, its successes and failures" (1993) 1 Int. J. of Children's Rights 273.

[9] N. Mole, "The Hague Convention and art.8 of the European Convention on Human Rights" [2000] I.F.L. 121; Swindells *Family Law and the HRA*, para.7.46 *et seq.* and see para.20–025, below.

[10] Criminal Law Revision Committee, 14th Report, *Offences Against the Person* (Cmnd.7844 (1980)).

[11] Child Abduction Act 1984 s.1(2).

remove a child under 16 years from the United Kingdom without the appropriate consent.[12] Anyone who does not have parental responsibility also commits an offence if he or she removes or keeps a child under 16 from any person with lawful control.[13] In 1999 there were 111 prosecutions for offences under the Child Abduction Act 1984.[14] Moreover, the common law offence of kidnapping is committed by anyone, even a parent, who takes a child who does not consent,[15] but prosecution for this offence is rare.

The criminalisation of child abduction by a parent gives the police a role in what otherwise would be considered a civil matter, and enables enforcement action to be taken where there is no court order.[16] A constable can arrest anyone they reasonably suspect to be about to commit an offence, and can prevent the child's removal from the country.[17] It may even be possible for the abductor to be extradited from a country where civil action to reclaim the child would be difficult.[18] However, enforcement of the criminal law in this area requires sensitivity[19]; it has been argued that it may be counterproductive.[20] Although the possibility of conviction may deter some parents, it is also important to examine other ways of preventing abduction, and of securing the child's return if it occurs.

Where abduction is suspected, perhaps because of threats or because one parent has strong links with another country, s.8 orders should be sought and granted.[21] A residence order allows the residential parent to remove the child from the United Kingdom for up to one month[22]; further restrictions may be desirable[23] so that any removal without consent is prohibited.[24] The parent with care also needs to be vigilant in preventing opportunities for taking the child, and to ensure that those looking after the child (e.g. teachers or childminders) are aware of the risk. Any contact the suspect (or their family) has with the child may need to be supervised. A solicitor who is aware of plans to abduct a child is not

---

[12] The consent of all those listed in s.1(3) of the Child Abduction Act 1984 is required: the mother, the father if he has parental responsibility, any guardian or special guardian, any person in whose favour there is a residence order and any person with custody. Where there is a court order, leave of the court will be sufficient.

[13] Child Abduction Act 1984 s.2. The offence requires intentional removal from someone known to have lawful control: *O v Governor of Holloway Prison and Government of USA* [2000] 1 F.L.R. 147. A person who is or reasonably believes himself to be the child's (non-marital) father has a defence: s.2(3)(a).

[14] *Hansard*, HC Vol.373, col.82W (October 22, 2001).

[15] *R. v D* [1984] A.C. 778 and G. Williams, "Can babies be kidnapped?" [1989] Crim. L.R. 473.

[16] Home Office Circular 21/1986, para.3; where there is at risk of significant harm, the police may use their power under Children Act 1989 s.46 to take the child into police protection.

[17] Police and Criminal Evidence Act 1984 s.24 (as amended by Serious Organised Crime and Police Act 2005).

[18] *Re O (Child Abduction: Re-abduction)* [1997] 2 F.L.R. 712.

[19] Home Office Circular 75/1984, para.5.

[20] A. Dyer, "Childhood rights in international law" (1991) 5 Australia J. Fam. Law 103.

[21] Lord Mackay [1991] Fam. Law 457. A real risk of abduction is a reason for granting residence to the other parent: *Re K (Residence Order: Securing Contact)* [1999] 1 F.L.R. 583, CA (residence of the two-year-old child granted to father).

[22] Children Act 1989 s.13(2).

[23] Either by a prohibited steps order (*Re D (A Minor) (Child: Removal from the Jurisdiction)* [1992] 1 F.L.R. 637) or a condition under s.11(7)(b).

[24] Removal would then be an offence: Child Abduction Act 1984 s.1(4A); it would also be "wrongful" under the Hague Convention; see below.

required to maintain the confidentiality of a client seeking advice to plan a criminal offence[25]; the court may order a solicitor to disclose a client's whereabouts.[26] A solicitor who encourages the breach of a court order is in contempt of court and could also be liable for "wasted costs" incurred in proceedings.[27]

If the child is likely to be taken overseas, the following action should be considered.[28]

A. Passport control

20–003   Passports are normally granted to children on the application of a parent with parental responsibility; children can no longer be included in a parent's British passport.[29] Where there is a court order restricting the child's removal from the jurisdiction, a person who objects to the child travelling can ask the Identity and Passport Service not to issue a passport.[30] Where the child already has a British passport (or has been included on a parent's), the court may require its surrender if there is an order prohibiting or otherwise restricting the child's removal from the United Kingdom.[31] A parent who holds a foreign passport may be required to deposit it with solicitors as a precondition of contact,[32] but there is no way of preventing a foreign country from issuing a passport to one of its nationals.

B. All ports warning[33]

20–004   Since removal of a child from the United Kingdom may be an offence under the Child Abduction Act 1984, the police may be asked to assist by instituting a port-alert. The police must be satisfied that the danger of removal is "real and imminent" (i.e. that it is not merely sought for insurance and may occur within the next 48 hours).[34] No court order is required unless the child is over 16.[35] The request should provide as much relevant information as possible about the child, the suspected abductor, their likely travel plans and the grounds for seeking a

---

[25] Law Society, *Guide to Professional Conduct of Solicitors* 8th edn, (1999), para.16.02.

[26] *Re B (Abduction: Disclosure)* [1995] 1 F.L.R. 774, CA; *Re H (Abduction: Whereabouts Order to Solicitors)* [2000] 1 F.L.R. 766.

[27] *Re K (Minors) (Incitement to Breach of Contact Order)* [1992] 2 F.L.R. 108 (advice to parent to take children away to avoid contact); Supreme Court Act 1981 s.51.

[28] Further details of practical steps are set out in Reunite, *Child Abduction Prevention Pack*; see, fn.1, above.

[29] Guidance from the UK Passport Agency: see *http://www.ukpa.gov.uk* [Accessed June 5, 2008].

[30] The court will not do so: *Clarke Hall and Morrison on Children* Butterworths, Vol.2, para.5; *Practice Direction* [1986] 1 All E.R. 983. For information on what the UK Identity and Passport Service can do, see *http://www.passport.gov.uk/general_preventing.asp* [Accessed June 5, 2008]. Failure to prevent issue of a passport may amount to negligence: *Hamilton Jones v David & Snape (a firm)* [2004] 1 F.L.R. 774, ChD.

[31] Family Law Act 1986 s.37; for example, a residence order.

[32] See *Al Kandari v Brown* [1988] Q.B. 665. The solicitor owes a duty of care to the other parent, not merely to the client, and may be liable if the children are abducted after the client has obtained the passport; *Re A-K (Foreign Passport: Jurisdiction)* [1997] 2 F.L.R. 569, CA.

[33] See, generally, *Practice Direction* [1986] 1 All E.R. 983 and Home Office Circular 21/1986.

[34] See Home Office Circular 21/1986, para.9 for relevant factors.

[35] It is not an offence under the Act to remove a child over 16, although it could still amount to kidnap.

port-alert. Particulars of the child are circulated to all ports through the Police National Computer, and receiving forces are asked to make arrangements with the local Immigration Service. The child's name remains on the port-stop list for four weeks, but further applications may be made. An immigration officer has no right to detain the child or the abductor but could make a citizen's arrest.

C. Security for the child's return

A person permitted to remove a child for a visit may be required to give an undertaking,[36] to enter into a bond or to provide surety for the child's safe return,[37] but this may provide insufficient incentive where they are determined to abduct. However, such action should not be required routinely.[38] The property of someone who knows of a court order for return of the children and aids a parent to conceal them may also be sequestered.[39] The sale of sequestered property can be ordered to finance legal proceedings.[40]

20–005

D. "Mirror" orders

A parent who wishes to remove a child overseas for contact may sometimes be expected first to obtain orders in that jurisdiction, equivalent to the order of the UK court. Orders are preferable to undertakings given to the court here, which are likely to have no effect abroad. Where such "mirror" orders are obtained and the child is not returned, enforcement action can be taken in the country of contact.[41]

20–006

III. TRACING CHILDREN

In any proceedings relating to a s.8 order or an order under the inherent jurisdiction of the High Court, the court may order any person who has relevant information about the child's whereabouts to disclose it.[42] A person may not

20–007

---

[36] In *Re S (Leave to Remove from the Jurisdiction: Securing Return from Holiday)* [2001] 2 F.L.R. 507, FD, there was insufficient time to obtain mirror orders, but the court made the children wards and declared their state of habitual residence to be England.

[37] *Re L (Removal from the Jurisdiction: Holiday)* [2001] 1 F.L.R. 241 (£50,000 bond required where mother wished to take child to United Arab Emirates for a holiday).

[38] See *Practice Note* (1987) 17 Fam. Law 263; *Re H (Minors) (Wardship: Surety)* [1991] 1 F.L.R. 40.

[39] *Re S (Abduction: Sequestration)* [1995] 1 F.L.R. 858; *Re W (Ex parte Orders)* [2000] 2 F.L.R. 927. In *Al-Khatib v Masry* [2002] 1 F.L.R. 1053, FD, the court increased the wife's ancillary relief to enable her to bring proceedings.

[40] *Mir v Mir* [1992] Fam. 79; *Richardson v Richardson* [1989] Fam. 95.

[41] *Re T (Staying Contact in Non-Convention Country)* [1999] 1 F.L.R. 262 (Egypt); *Re A (Security for Return to Jurisdiction)* [1999] 2 F.L.R. 1 (Saudi Arabia). Mirror orders can also be obtained (exceptionally) in England to ensure a child returns home after staying contact here, even where the child is neither habitually resident nor present here: *Re P (A Child: Mirror Orders)* [2000] 1 F.L.R. 435.

[42] Family Law Act 1986 s.33(1) as amended. Such orders should only be made against the police in exceptional circumstances: *Chief Constable of W. Yorkshire Police v S* [1998] 2 F.L.R. 973, CA. There is a comparable power in relation to proceedings brought under the Child Abduction and Custody Act 1985 s.24A where a child has been abducted to the UK.

refuse to answer on the grounds of self-incrimination.[43] Assistance may be obtained via the court from various government departments in connection with proceedings under the Child Abduction and Custody Act 1985, or via the enforcement of a Pt I order (which includes any s.8 order or order for custody, access or care and control)[44] under the Family Law Act 1986.[45] The Department of Work and Pensions can trace people in employment (through their National Insurance number) and benefit claimants; the Office of National Statistics holds the National Health Service Central Register and can trace a person who registers with a GP; the Identity and Passport Service holds details of all applicants for passports; service personnel and those who have recently left the services may be traced through the Ministry of Defence. Liaison with the Home Office and its agencies is arranged through the Office of the President of the Family Division.[46] However, in some cases, particularly where the child has been taken abroad, it may be necessary to instruct a private investigator.

IV. RECOVERY OF THE CHILD

20–008 Recovery of children is never simple, but the difficulties posed, the procedures that must be used, and the principles that apply depend on the country to which the child has been taken. Within the United Kingdom, cases are dealt with under the Children Act 1989 and the Family Law Act 1986. The complexities of Brussels II Revised do to not apply to domestic cases.[47]

A. Abduction within England and Wales

20–009 Where a parent takes a child without consent of a person with parental responsibility, the courts may grant a residence order without notice[48] or on short notice[49] so that the child retains their settled home pending a decision about residence. However, there is no general rule that requires summary return.[50] A recovery order may be made by the court for the production, removal and return

---

[43] Family Law Act 1986 s.33(2). Orders may be made against solicitors overriding their duty of confidentiality to their client: *Re B (Abduction: Disclosure)* [1995] 1 F.L.R. 774, CA; *Re H (Abduction: Whereabouts Order to Solicitors)* [2000] 1 F.L.R. 766.

[44] Family Law Act 1986 s.1, as amended.

[45] *Practice Direction* [1989] 1 F.L.R. 307, amended by *Practice Direction* [1995] 2 F.L.R. 813.

[46] See Protocol from the President's Office [2004] 1 F.L.R. 638 (Home Office) and [2004] 1 F.L.R. 640 (Passport Service).

[47] The Regulation explained below at para.20–022 regulates matters between Member States, but see the discussion in Bromley (2007), pp.560–564 for an alternative interpretation importing the regulation.

[48] *Re B (A Minor) (Residence Order: Ex parte)* [1992] 2 F.L.R. 1, where a 20-month-old boy was returned to live with his father and sisters; *Re G (Minors) (Ex parte Interim Residence Order)* [1993] 1 F.L.R. 910, where return was not ordered because of "compelling reasons relating to drugs"— allegations relating to cannabis use.

[49] Family Proceedings Rules 1991 (SI 1991/1247) r.4.8(8) (b).

[50] Without notice (ex parte) orders should not be made without good reason: *Re J (Children: Ex parte Orders)* [1997] 1 F.L.R. 606, Hale J.

of any child in care, in police protection or subject to an emergency protection order who has been unlawfully removed, has run away or is missing.[51]

B. Abduction from one part of the United Kingdom to another

The Family Law Act 1986 is designed to ensure that jurisdiction relating to a **20–010** child's residence can generally be exercised only[52] by the courts in one part of the United Kingdom[53] at any one time, and that Pt 1 orders[54] relating to children are enforceable throughout the United Kingdom.[55] Consequently, abductors should not be able to strengthen their position by obtaining an order after taking the child, and those with court orders should be able to recover[56] abducted children.

However, the provisions do not always operate to achieve this:

> In *S v S (Custody: Jurisdiction)*[57] the father and mother both applied for custody in Scotland, and the father was successful. The mother failed to return the child at the end of the contact visit, went to England with the child and could not be found. Over a year later she applied for and obtained an interim order for residence. The father applied to have the English proceedings stayed and his Scottish order enforced. However, it was held that the Scottish order had ceased to have effect when the English order was made.[58]

A court in England and Wales can make a s.8 order only if it has jurisdiction under the Family Law Act 1986.[59] The courts for the country where the matrimonial proceedings are taking place has jurisdiction; if there are no such proceedings, jurisdiction can be exercised in that part of the United Kingdom

---

[51] Children Act 1989 s.50; *Re R (Recovery Orders)* [1998] 2 F.L.R. 401; DCSF, *Children Act 1989 Guidance and Regulation* (2008), Vol.1, paras 4, 85 *et seq.*

[52] Following recommendations by the English and Scottish Law Commissions: Law Com. No.138 and Scot Law Com. No.91.

[53] i.e. England and Wales, Scotland or Northern Ireland; Family Law Act 1986 s.42(1). The Act also applies to the Isle of Man: see Family Law Act 1986 (Dependent Territories) Order (SI 1991/1723).

[54] Family Law Act 1986 s.1.

[55] Family Law Act 1986 s.25.

[56] Family Law Act 1986 s.34. Orders for recovery are discretionary and should not be made without notice because of the risk of additional moves for children: *A v A (Forum Conveniens)* [1999] 1 F.L.R. 1.

[57] [1995] 1 F.L.R. 153; see also *D v D (Custody: Jurisdiction)* [1996] 1 F.L.R. 574, when courts in England and Scotland were seised of the same custody dispute because the parties failed to raise the jurisdictional issue.

[58] Family Law Act 1986 s.15. The new order had to be competently made. The child had presumably lost her habitual residence in Scotland and even possibly gained habitual residence in England after 18 months living there.

[59] Family Law Act 1986 ss.1(1)(a), 2(1), 2A(1), (2), 13 (Scotland), 21 (Northern Ireland); matrimonial proceedings are treated as continuing until the child reaches 18 (16 in Scotland): s.42(2)(3). The inherent jurisdiction of the High Court is restricted to cases where the child is present in England or Wales and needs immediate protection. The restrictions apply if the child is not habitually resident in England and Wales, is habitually resident in another part of the UK or there are matrimonial proceedings in Scotland or Northern Ireland: Family Law Act 1986 ss.2(3), 3.

where the child is habitually resident, and if the child has no habitual residence,[60] jurisdiction can be exercised in the country where the child is[61]:

> In *Re M (Minors) (Residence Order Jurisdiction)*[62] two children of unmarried parents were living with the mother's agreement with paternal grandparents in Scotland. The children visited their mother for a two-week holiday, and she decided that they should not return to Scotland. The grandparents obtained, ex parte, an order for custody in Scotland. On the day it was served on the mother, she applied for a residence order in England. The grandparents appealed against the decision that the English court had jurisdiction to decide the mother's applications. Whilst the children were in Scotland with the mother's agreement, they were habitually resident there. They had lost this habitual residence when they came to England but had not yet gained habitual residence there. Even though it might appear unfair that a two-week holiday visit should be decisive, the English court had jurisdiction because the children were present in England and not habitually resident elsewhere.[63]

20–011 Proceedings taken in conflict with these provisions are stayed.[64] Furthermore, a child who has been removed from the country of habitual residence without the necessary consents cannot acquire a new habitual residence for a year.[65]

Part I orders granted in one part of the United Kingdom are recognised and enforceable in any other part as if they had been made there.[66] The person in whose favour the order was made requests the court that made the order to send a certified copy of it to the appropriate court[67] for the country where the child has been taken.[68] The order is then registered in that country and an application to enforce it may be made.[69] Any person interested may apply to have the application stayed or dismissed but only on grounds that proceedings are being taken elsewhere or the order has ceased to have effect.[70]

V. INTERNATIONAL ABDUCTION

20–012 Article 11 of the UN Convention on the Rights of the Child requires States Parties to take measures to combat the illicit transfer and non-return of children, and to promote the conclusion of bilateral and multilateral agreements or

---

[60] This concept is discussed at para.20–015.
[61] Family Law Act 1986 ss.2, 2A and 3.
[62] [1993] 1 F.L.R. 495; Cretney (1993) 109 L.Q.R. 538.
[63] *Per* Balcombe L.J. at 502; Family Law Act 1986 s.3(1)(b).
[64] Family Law Act 1986 ss.5, 14, 22; *Re S (A Minor) (Stay of Proceedings)* [1993] 2 F.L.R. 912, CA.
[65] Family Law Act 1986 s.41.
[66] Family Law Act 1986 s.5.
[67] Family Law Act 1986 s.32(1)—the High Court in England and Wales or Northern Ireland, the Court of Session in Scotland.
[68] Family Law Act 1986 s.27.
[69] Family Law Act 1986 s.29.
[70] Family Law Act 1986 ss.30, 31.

accession to existing agreements.[71] It has been successful as a catalyst for such agreements; over 70 countries have joined the Hague Convention on the Civil Aspects of International Child Abduction.[72] The United Kingdom is a party to this Convention, the European Convention on the Recognition and Enforcement of Decisions Concerning the Custody of Children[73] and Brussels II Revised.[74] These treaties therefore determine the treatment of children abducted to (or from) the United Kingdom to other Convention countries. The United Kingdom has also concluded a bilateral agreement with Pakistan,[75] which follows the approach of the Hague Convention. Consequently, two distinct regimes are operated by the UK courts: the Hague scheme for Convention countries and the common law for everywhere else.

As the freedom of movement between countries increases, so does the number of international child-custody disputes. World travel is easy, and border controls have been reduced between many countries. Many abducted children have dual nationality and are nationals of the state to which they have been taken. The Foreign Office operates a policy of non-interference in such cases because of the general international-law principle of comity. This may create an insurmountable obstacle to securing the child's return from a non-Convention country.[76] International child abduction appears to be rising.[77] In 2003 there were approximately 1,250 cases for children's return under the Hague Convention[78]; in 2006, International Child Abduction and Contact Unit was notified about 290 children brought to England and Wales and 378 children removed from there.[79] Contrary to the expectations of those who drafted the Hague Convention, the majority of abductions are by parents with care who are seeking to relocate, rather than by non-residential parents attempting to obtain custody through removing the child.

A. Role of the central authority[80]

In every Convention country a designated central authority provides direct assistance to parties and their lawyers.[81] The central authority for England and

20–013

---

[71] UN Convention on Rights of the Child art.11(2).

[72] By ratification or accession. A current list of countries who are parties to this Convention can be found on the Hague Conference website: *http://www.hcch.net* [Accessed June 5, 2008].

[73] Child Abduction and Custody Act 1985.

[74] Council Regulation (EC) 2201/2003; SI 2005/265. Brussels II Revised takes precedence over the Hague Convention in Member States. For a guide to the relationship between the Regulation and the Hague Convention, see European Judicial Network, *Practice Guide for the Operation of Brussels II Revised*, p.40.

[75] Setright and Hutchinson (2003) I.F.L. 56. Details of the Protocol are available at *http://www.fco.gov.uk* [Accessed June 5, 2008].

[76] Van Bueren *The Hague Convention* (1993), p.6.

[77] Beaumont and McEleavy *The best interests* (1999), pp.14–15.

[78] N. Lowe, "Preparations for the Special Commission", in *Hague Convention Judges Newsletter* (2006) p.77.

[79] Official Solicitor and Public Trustee Office, *Annual Report 2006*, Annex 2.

[80] C. Bruch, "The central authority's role under the Hague Child Abduction Convention: a friend in deed" (1994) 28 Fam. L.Q. 35; Carter [1999] I.F.L. 102; see also Hague Conference, *Guide to Good Practice* (2003) vol.1.

[81] Hague Convention art.6; European Convention arts 4, 5; Child Custody and Abduction Act 1985 ss.3, 14.

Wales is the Lord Chancellor; the work is delegated to the International Child Abduction and Contact Unit.[82] Central authorities are required to co-operate with each other to achieve the objectives of the Convention and secure the return of the child. Their role includes discovering the whereabouts of the child, preventing further harm, securing voluntary return, initiating proceedings[83] and making the administrative arrangements for return.[84] The cost of the child's return falls on the parents. The central authority may refuse to handle a case that is manifestly not well founded.[85] Individuals whose children have been abducted are advised to contact any central authority.[86] The central authority in the home state deals directly with the central authority in the country where the child has been taken. It has been said that palpable advantages result from experience and the history of trustworthy professional relationships between staff in the various central authorities[87]; also that the successful operation depends on the mutual confidence of the parties, which may be difficult to maintain as the number of members increases.[88]

B. Abduction to a country that has ratified or acceded[89] to the Hague Convention

20–014   The Convention is based on the premise that children's best interests demand that they are not the subject of unilateral removals or retentions.[90] By strictly enforcing return, the Convention seeks to deter abduction, enable the courts in the child's home state to determine disputes and ensure that their orders are respected by other parties to the Convention.[91] Strict enforcement also encourages voluntary return. However, there is a danger that in any individual case the child's welfare will not be furthered by return.[92]

The Child Abduction and Custody Act 1985 Pt I implements the Hague Convention on Civil Aspects of Child Abduction, but the key concepts that determine the scope of the Convention are not dependent on their meaning in any

---

[82] This is part of the Official Solicitor and Public Trustee Office. Details of this work and links to related sites can be found at: *http://www.officialsolicitor.gov.uk/os/icacu.htm* [Accessed June 5, 2008].

[83] Approximately 20% of applications are resolved by agreement. The ICACU in London forwards applications to specialist solicitors within 24 hours: Lowe and Perry, "International abduction—the English experience" [1999] I.C.L.Q.138.

[84] Hague Convention art.7.

[85] Hague Convention art.27.

[86] Foreign and Commonwealth Office, *Child Abduction Leaflet* (2007), p.3.

[87] Bruch, "The central authority's role", p.48.

[88] *Re E (Abduction: Non-Convention Country)* [1999] 2 F.L.R. 642 at 646, *per* Thorpe L.J.

[89] In cases of accession, the Convention only operates between countries who have accepted the accession. An overview of the status of accessions can be found on the Hague Conference website: *http://www.hcch.net* [Accessed June 5, 2008].

[90] Beaumont and McEleavy *The Hague Convention* (1999), p.21.

[91] D. Harris, "Is the strength of the Hague Convention on child abduction being diluted by the courts? The English perspective." [1999] I.L.M. 35; Beaumont and McEleavy *The Hague Convention*, Ch.4.

[92] For example, if the home state court would agree to their relocation overseas, if the abducting parent is unable or unwilling to return or if the conditions there are adverse: see M. Kaye, "The Hague Convention and the flight from domestic violence: how women and children are being returned by coach and four" [1999] Int. J. Law Policy and Fam. 191 and para.20–020, below.

single legal system.[93] The Convention applies where a child under 16[94] who is habitually resident in one contracting state is wrongfully removed to, or retained in, another.[95]

i. Habitual residence[96]

Habitual residence requires voluntary presence in a country for some time,[97] with a settled purpose of remaining there[98]; it is a question of fact whether and when habitual residence is established.[99] A child's habitual residence follows that of the carers, but where both parents have parental responsibility, the child's habitual residence cannot be changed by one parent acting unilaterally,[100] but only in exceptional circumstances can a baby be habitually resident in a country to which they have never been.[101] Where the family divide their time between two homes, the child cannot be habitually resident in both places simultaneously but may be habitually resident in either, in accordance with the parents' arrangements.[102] Habitual residence may be ended by leaving with the intention

20–015

---

[93] Conclusion of the Second Meeting of the Special Commission to discuss the operation of the Convention (1994); *Re D* [2006] UKHL 51. The conclusions of the Third (1997), Fourth (2001) and Fifth Special Commissions (2006) are available at *http://www.hcch.net* [Accessed June 5, 2008]. A database of case law under the convention is available at *http://www.incadat.com* [Accessed June 5, 2008].

[94] *Re H (Abduction: Child of 16)* [2000] 2 F.L.R. 930.

[95] Child Abduction and Custody Act 1985 s.1; Hague Convention art.3; An order can be obtained even though children are not in England or Wales if there is good reason to think that they will be brought here: *A v A (Abduction: Jurisdiction)* [1995] 1 F.L.R. 341.

[96] For a detailed analysis of this concept, see Beaumont and McEleavy *The Hague Convention*, Ch.7 and R. Schuz, "Habitual residence under the Hague Abduction Convention—theory and practice" [2001] 1 C.F.L.Q. 1.

[97] *C v S (Minor: Abduction: Illegitimate Child)* [1990] A.C. 562 at 578, *per* Lord Brandon; the period required may be quite short: *Re F (A Minor) (Child Abduction)* [1992] 1 F.L.R. 548 (three months); a child may have little real connection with the jurisdiction where any dispute will be heard: see Beaumont and McEleavy *The Hague Convention*, p.108.

[98] Permanent residence is not required: *Re F (A Minor) (Child Abduction)* [1992] 1 F.L.R. 548, where the parents had shipped 19 packing cases to Australia; they had acquired habitual residence there even though they held return tickets. In *D v D (Custody: Jurisdiction)* [1996] 1 F.L.R. 574, renting a flat, acquiring furniture and buying school uniforms together suggested the parties were habitually resident. A young child, sent to live with relatives in Ghana, did not acquire habitual residence there because the mother had not established that she intended this residence to be long-term: *Re V (Jurisdiction: Habitual Residence)* [2001] 1 F.L.R. 253, FD.

[99] *Nessa v Chief Adjudication Officer* [1999] 2 F.L.R. 1116, HL.

[100] *D v D (Custody: Jurisdiction)* [1996] 1 F.L.R. 574 at 581, *per* Hale J. Where parents move abroad but only one becomes habitually resident, the children retain their original habitual residence: *Re N (Abduction: Habitual Residence)* [2000] 2 F.L.R. 899, FD. If the only parent with parental responsibility dies, the child retains their habitual residence: *Re S (Custody: Habitual Residence)* [1998] 1 F.L.R. 122, HL. A parent with a residence order who removes the child permanently in breach of the Children Act 1989 s.13(2) should not be able to end the child's habitual residence; see Bruch "International child abduction cases", p.66.

[101] *Re F (Abduction: Unborn Child)* [2007] 1 F.L.R. 627, FD; cf. *B v H (Habitual Residence: Wardship)* [2002] 1 F.L.R. 388, *per* Charles J., where the youngest child, who had not entered the UK was held to have habitual residence here because his mother had retained her UK habitual residence. In *W and B v H (Child Abduction: Surrogacy)* [2002] 1 F.L.R. 1008, FD, Hedley J. held that a baby had no habitual residence.

[102] *Re V (Abduction: Habitual Residence)* [1995] 2 F.L.R. 992. But a child who never lives in the parents' new state of habitual residence does not acquire habitual residence there: *Al Habtoor v Fotheringham* [2001] 1 F.L.R. 951.

not to return. Consequently, the unmarried father in *C v S (Minor) (Abduction: Illegitimate Child)*[103] could not rely on the Convention because the child was no longer habitually resident in Australia after her removal to England, but a Swedish mother whose absence from Sweden occurred whilst she studied could reclaim her child from the care of his father in England.[104] There is a fine balance to be struck between denying a child the protection of the Convention by failing to recognise that he or she has established habitual residence, and applying the Convention to return a child to a state with which there is little real connection. For this reason, Beaumont and McEleavy have suggested that six months should be treated as a guideline figure for establishing habitual residence.[105]

ii. Wrongful removal or retention

20–016 Removal or retention is wrongful where it is in breach of "rights of custody" attributed to a person, an institution or any other body[106] and actually exercised by them.[107] Thus, the unilateral removal of a child by one parent was wrongful because it precluded the other parent who had equal rights from exercising them.[108] Where a child has staying contact, his or her retention beyond an agreed period is wrongful.[109] Where there is doubt about the legality of the child's removal or retention, a declaration of wrongfulness may be sought from the state of habitual residence; such a declaration will almost invariably be conclusive.[110] A declaration of wrongfulness obtained in the state of habitual residence is more useful than any ex parte order for custody there[111]:

> In *Re D*[112] the parents divorced in Romania. The mother obtained custody of the child and the father had regular contact. Without informing the father, the mother brought the boy to England. The father started proceedings under the Hague Convention for the boy's return, but it was unclear whether he had rights of custody within the meaning of the Convention. Each parent obtained expert evidence about the effect of the Romanian order; the judge was unable to decide the matter and sought a declaration under art.15 from the Romanian Courts. Nearly three years later, the Romanian Court held that

---

[103] [1990] A.C. 562 at 578.

[104] *Re H (Abduction: Habitual Residence: Consent)* [2000] 2 F.L.R. 294.

[105] *The Hague Convention on International Child Abduction*, p.112.

[106] *The Hague Convention*, 3(a); *Re H (Abduction: Rights of Custody)* [2000] 1 F.L.R. 374, HL (rights of an Irish court seised of a guardianship application). Where a court has rights of custody, the application for return should be made by the person whose application gave rise to the court's rights, *per* Lord Mackay at 381H. *Re W, Re B (Abduction: Unmarried Father)* [1998] 2 F.L.R. 146, Hale J. (English court seised of parental responsibility application); *Re JS (Private International Adoption)* [2000] 2 F.L.R. 638 (overseas adoption agency).

[107] *The Hague Convention*, 3.

[108] *Re F (Child Abduction: Risk if Returned)* [1995] 2 F.L.R. 31 at 36, *per* Butler-Sloss L.J. Removal would be an offence under the Child Abduction Act 1984.

[109] Retention becomes wrongful when the decision not to return is made even though the period has not expired: *Re S (Minors) (Abduction: Wrongful Retention)* [1994] Fam. 70.

[110] art.15; *Re D* [2006] UKHL 51, *per* Lord Brown at para.80.

[111] Bruch "International child abduction cases", p.60; cf. Beaumont and McEleavy *The Hague Convention*, p.64 who are concerned about delay and suggest that proof of foreign law under arts 8f and 14 provides a better approach.

[112] [2006] UKHL 51.

the removal had not been wrongful, but the English judge ordered further expert evidence that disagreed with this finding. The child's return was ordered and the mother's appeal refused. On appeal to the House of Lords, it was unanimously held that the decision of the Romanian court should have been accepted and the father's application refused. The Romanian Court was better placed to understand the effects of Romanian orders; only if their interpretation did not accord with the international jurisprudence on the meaning of the Convention could it be disregarded.[113]

However, an art.15 declaration of wrongful removal obtained in the requesting state does not determine the matter because the requested state also had to consider whether the child was habitually resident at the time of removal[114] and whether any of the defences apply.

iii. Rights of custody

"Rights of custody" include rights relating to the care of a person and the right **20–017** to determine a child's place of residence.[115] The court must consider: (1) what rights the applicant has under the law of their home country; and (2) whether those rights are "rights of custody" within the meaning of the Convention.?[116] The rights held by the left-behind parents must be determined according to the law of the country of the child's habitual residence, but whether these rights are "rights of custody" is determined in the courts of the requested state, applying the autonomous interpretation of the Convention[117]:

> In *Re P (Abduction: Consent)*[118] the parents were unmarried US citizens living in New York. The mother had sole custody of the child and the father had visitation rights (contact). A court order precluded the mother from removing the child, except for temporary holidays, without a court order or the written permission of the father. The mother married and her husband moved to England. The mother planned to join him, leaving the child with the father. However, she changed her mind and brought the child with her to England, ostensibly having obtained the father's consent. The father objected and sought the girl's return. The Court of Appeal held that his rights to contact and to prevent removal from the US amounted to "rights of custody" under the Convention and ordered the child's return.

"Rights of custody" are distinct from contact (rights of access); a mere right to apply to prevent a child being removed from the jurisdiction will not amount to "rights of custody".[119] Under English law, removal of a child from England and

---

[113] *Per* Baroness Hale at para.44. The interpretation of the New Zealand court that equated right to contact with rights of custody was such an interpretation: see *Hunter v Murrow* [2005] 2 F.L.R. 1119, CA.

[114] *Re P (Abduction: Declaration)* [1995] 1 F.L.R. 831 at 838, *per* Millett L.J.

[115] *The Hague Convention*, 5.

[116] *Re D* [2006] UKHL 51, *per* Baroness Hale at para.39.

[117] Details of case law from other jurisdictions can be found at *http://www.incadat.com/index.cfm* [Accessed June 5, 2008].

[118] *Re P (Abduction: Consent)* [2004] 2 F.L.R. 1057, CA.

[119] *Hunter v Murrow (Abduction: Rights of Custody)* [2005] 2 F.L.R. 1119, CA.

Wales without permission of a person with parental responsibility or in contravention of a residence order[120] is wrongful. It might be thought that a mother who had not married the child's father would be able to move without constraint, and that a father without parental responsibility could not prevent his child being taken abroad.[121] This is not the case if the court has rights of custody because an application for parental responsibility or residence is pending.[122] The English court has taken an even broader view, recognising that a person without parental responsibility but caring for a child may have "inchoate rights" that amount to rights of custody.[123]

iv. Proceedings

20–018 A person whose rights have been breached may apply via the central authority in their country. The central authority will arrange for the necessary proceedings and will also seek to negotiate voluntary return.[124] In England and Wales, legal aid is provided,[125] but the Convention does not require states to provide legal aid unless it is available to nationals.[126] Proceedings are peremptory; the courts are forbidden to investigate the merits of the case[127] and are required to return the child unless one of the conditions in arts 12 or 13 applies.[128] The High Court has a good record in processing cases speedily.[129] Judges have been known to make arrangements with judges overseas to facilitate return.[130] Some children are interviewed by welfare officers at the Royal Courts of Justice.[131] There is no right

---

[120] Children Act 1989 s.13(1)(b)(2). Similarly, if the child is a ward or there is a prohibited steps order.

[121] This was the basis of the claim by the father in *B v UK* [2000] 1 F.L.R. 1 under ECHR art.14, which was held inadmissible.

[122] *Re H (Abduction: Rights of Custody)* [2000] 1 F.L.R. 374, HL. The court gains rights of custody when the relevant application is served; *per* Lord Mackay at 380F.

[123] *Re B (A Minor) (Abduction)* [1994] 2 F.L.R. 249, CA, *per* Waite L.J. Staunton L.J. held that an agreement between the parents for the child's care gave the father "rights of custody". Peter Gibson L.J. dissented. *Re O (Child Abduction: Custody Rights)* [1997] 2 F.L.R. 702 (grand parents); cf. *Re J (Abduction: Acquiring Custody Rights by Caring for Child)* [2005] 2 F.L.R. 791, FD. This development is criticised by Beaumont and McEleavy *The Hague Convention*, p.60, but it ensures that there is no discrimination against those without parental responsibility who have ECHR art.8 rights; see also K. Beevers, "Child abduction: inchoate rights of custody and the unmarried father" [2006] C.F.L.Q 499.

[124] As required by art.10; and see Reunite, *Mediation in International Parental Child Abduction* (2006).

[125] Non-means, non-merit-tested Legal Representation is available to the applicant for return under the Hague or European Conventions: see Legal Services Commission, *Funding Code Decision-making Guidance* (2007), 3C 217.6. Public funding is only available to defend proceedings subject to means and merit testing.

[126] Hague Convention, 26. In the US, no legal aid is available, but some inter bar agreements have been made for the provision of a pro bono counsel.

[127] Hague Convention, 19.

[128] The Convention is "draconian" in its adherence to summary return: *Re M (Abduction: Psychological Harm)* [1997] 2 F.L.R. 690 at 694, *per* Butler-Sloss L.J.

[129] See Lowe and Perry [1999] I.C.L.Q. 138, 138–139.

[130] *Re M and J (Abduction: International Judicial Co-operation)* [2000] 1 F.L.R. 803, Singer J. Hague Conference, *Best Practices* (2000), para.1e emphasises the value of direct communication between judges.

[131] *Re T (Abduction: Child's Objections to Return)* [2000] 2 F.L.R. 192, CA (the 11-year-old girl also wrote letters to the court).

to give oral evidence and it is rarely heard.[132] Strict limits on the use of oral evidence may make procedures more expeditious and fairer for the left-behind parent, but doubts have been expressed about the ability of English courts to assess claims under art.13b from affidavits alone.[133] Also, Brussels II Revised requires that children are heard; see para.20–020.

Return is mandatory if the child was taken less than 12 months before[134] unless, at the time of the removal, the applicant was not exercising custody rights; the applicant consented to it or subsequently acquiesced; there is grave risk of physical or psychological harm if the child is returned; or a mature child objects.[135] If the abduction has lasted for longer, the child must be returned unless settled in the new environment.[136] In other cases there is discretion to return; the court must balance the welfare of the child against the fundamental purpose of the Convention.[137] The normal expectation is that the court will order the child's return even where one of the exceptions applies,[138] unless the applicant was seeking a tactical advantage or return would lead to children yo-yoing between countries.[139] However, where the applicant fails to pursue the application for return, it may be struck out.[140] The English courts have been regarded as thoughtful and sophisticated in their interpretation of the Hague Convention,[141] but may have become over zealous in their disregard of children's views and risks to primary carers.

v. Article 13a—consent or acquiescence

A parent who has agreed to the relocation of a child cannot subsequently claim **20–019** their peremptory return. The concept of acquiescence is potentially broad, but the courts have been careful not to discourage amicable settlements by including negotiation within the definition. Except where the action is unequivocal, acquiescence depends on the subjective intentions of the wronged parent; it must be established by the parent resisting return.[142] The following have been held to amount to acquiescence: failing to object when the wife gave up her job and

---

[132] *Re E (A Minor) (Abduction)* [1989] 1 F.L.R. 135, CA; *Re F (A Minor) (Child Abduction)* [1992] 1 F.L.R. 548, CA.
[133] Harris "Is the strength of the Hague", p.44.
[134] Hague Convention, 12. Judicial refusals to return occurred in only about 5% of Lowe and Perry's sample; "International abduction", p.143.
[135] Hague Convention, 13. This provides a limited mechanism through which the courts can take a more traditional child-oriented approach: J. Caldwell, "Child welfare defences in child abduction cases—some recent developments" [2001] C.F.L.Q. 121.
[136] Hague Convention, 12; *Re N (Minors) (Abduction)* [1991] 1 F.L.R. 413, *per* Bracewell J. A parent who has concealed the child's whereabouts cannot rely on this to argue that the child is settled: *Re L (Abduction: Pending Criminal Proceedings)* [1999] 1 F.L.R. 433 at 441.
[137] *Re D (Abduction: Discretionary Return)* [2000] 1 F.L.R. 24 (return ordered); *Re D (Abduction: Acquiescence)* [1999] 1 F.L.R. 53 (return refused); *Canon v Canon* [2005] 1 F.L.R. 169, CA (return ordered despite settlement).
[138] Clarke Hall and Morrison, Vol.2, Division 2, para.61.
[139] *Re A (Minors) (Abduction: Acquiescence) (No.2)* [1993] Fam. 1; cf. C. Bruch, "International child abduction: the experience under the 1980 Hague Convention", in Eekelaar and Sarcevic (eds) (1994), pp.353, 356.
[140] *Re G (Abduction: Striking Out Application)* [1995] 2 F.L.R. 410.
[141] Bruch "The central authority's role", p.78.
[142] *Re H (Abduction: Acquiescence)* [1998] A.C. 72, *per* Lord Browne-Wilkinson at 88F.

cancelled the child's nursery place[143]; taking the wife and the children to the airport knowing they were making a one-way trip[144]; writing to the abductor that the father was not going to fight for custody[145]; and taking no action to oppose an application for residence.[146] Acquiescence requires some knowledge that action could be taken, but a full understanding of the position under the Convention was not necessary[147]:

> In *Re S (Minors) (Acquiescence)*[148] the mother removed three boys from Australia to England. The father immediately consulted solicitors who told him (incorrectly) that they required $5,000 before they could take any action. He consulted another firm and was told it would be difficult to obtain an order in respect of the older children because they were British. Subsequently, a law student who joined the firm advised him to apply to the central authority. He did so and began proceedings under the Convention. Despite the passage of eight months[149] (and fortunately for the firms' insurers), the father was held not to have acquiesced in the boys' removal.

vi. Article 13b—grave risk of harm or an intolerable situation

20–020 The court requires clear and compelling evidence of grave risk or harm or intolerability; this must be substantial and more severe than would necessarily result from an unwelcome return.[150] In *N v N (Abduction: Article 13 Defence)*[151] the father's mental illness, some evidence of sexual abuse and the children's disturbance were insufficient to justify refusal to return, but in *Re F (Child Abduction: Risk of Return)*[152] return was refused because the four year old who had been abused and observed violence by his father to his mother and grandmother exhibited fear and disturbance (bedwetting and aggression) at the suggestion of return to the place where the violence had occurred. Some harm is inevitable; the abductor cannot rely on harm that results from their behaviour.[153]

---

[143] *Re M (Abduction) (Consent: Acquiescence)* [1999] 1 F.L.R. 171.
[144] *Re R (Abduction: Acquiescence)* [1999] 2 F.L.R. 818.
[145] *Re A (Minors) (Abduction: Custody Rights)* [1992] Fam. 106, CA. But a statement that the father would not take "heroic action" did not amount to acquiescence: *Re R (Child Abduction: Acquiescence)* [1995] 1 F.L.R. 716, CA.
[146] *Re AZ (A Minor) (Abduction: Acquiescence)* [1993] 1 F.L.R. 682, CA.
[147] *Re A (A Minor) (Abduction: Custody Rights)* [1992] Fam. 106 at 119–120, *per* Stuart-Smith L.J.
[148] [1994] 1 F.L.R. 819, CA.
[149] But in *W v W (Child Abduction: Acquiescence)* [1993] 2 F.L.R. 211, the father's failure to take action for 10 months after hearing of his wife's refusal to return the children amounted to acquiescence.
[150] *Re C (Abduction: Grave Risk of Psychological Harm)* [1999] 1 F.L.R. 1145, *per* Ward L.J. at 1154.
[151] [1995] 1 F.L.R. 107. Similarly in *Re S (Abduction: Return into Care)* [1999] 1 F.L.R. 845, where the mother had separated from the abuser and there would be a social services assessment.
[152] [1995] 2 F.L.R. 31, CA. See also *Re D (Article 13b: Non Return)* [2006] 2 F.L.R. 305, where the mother had been shot.
[153] *Re L (Child Abduction) (Psychological Harm)* [1993] 2 F.L.R. 401 (return of the child alone); *Re C (Abduction: Grave Risk of Physical or Psychological Harm)* [1999] 2 F.L.R. 479 (separation of siblings).

However, where siblings have refused to return[154] or the caring abductor's mental health will seriously deteriorate on return,[155] the risk to the child may be sufficiently grave.

The power of the court in the state of return to grant injunctions,[156] and undertakings to provide a home and financial support for the abductor, are accepted by the English courts as mitigating the potential harm of return.[157] However, in some states these may be disregarded with impunity with dire consequences for the returning parent and children.[158] The narrow approach of the court to art.13a and its willingness to accept undertakings has been criticised, particularly for failing to recognise the impact of domestic violence.[159]

vii. The child's objections
A child's objection—the child's art.13 defence[160]—will only be sufficient where   **20–021**
it is strongly held and relates to the return to be ordered[161]:

> In *Klentzeris v Klentzeris*[162] a 10-year-old boy had panic attacks as he told the CAFCASS officer about his father's ill-treatment of his mother and objections to returning to Greece. The Court of Appeal refused to overturn the decision that the boy and his older sister who also objected, should not be returned. But in *Zaffino v Zaffino*[163] the appeal against refusal of return was allowed despite the objections of a mature 13 year old. The court had discretion to order return in the face of a child's objections. The practical consequences of a child being separated from the rest of her family who returned abroad could not be ignored.

Children are not usually separately represented in these proceedings[164] but must be heard in every case.[165] Although the court has respected the views of children as young as seven,[166] it has not accepted that the child's objections determine the

---

[154] *B v K (Child Abduction)* [1993] 1 F.C.R. 382.
[155] *Re G (Abduction: Psychological Harm)* [1995] 1 F.L.R. 64.
[156] *TB v JB (Abduction: Grave Risk of Harm)* [2001] 2 F.L.R. 515, CA; the majority of the Court of Appeal were satisfied that a woman who had been terrorised by her husband's violence would be protected by a court order.
[157] *Re O (Child Abduction: Undertakings)* [1994] 2 F.L.R. 349; *Re M (Abduction; Non-Convention Country)* [1995] 1 F.L.R. 89, CA.
[158] Kaye, "The Hague Convention and the flight from domestic violence" [1999] Int. J. Law Policy and Fam. 191. Undertakings may be regarded as undermining the exclusive jurisdiction of the court of habitual residence: Society for Advanced Legal Study, Family Law Working Group, *Report on the Cross Border Movement of Children* (London: SALS, 1999), p.75.
[159] Kaye [1999] Int. J. Law Policy and Fam. 191. In two-thirds of cases in a *Reunite* study, undertakings were breached: see *Returned Following an Abduction* (Reunite, 2003).
[160] *Vigreux v Michel* [2006] 2 F.L.R. 1180, *per* Wall L. J. at para.49.
[161] *Re S (Minors) (Abduction: Custody Rights)* [1993] Fam. 242; *Re R (A Minor: Abduction)* [1992] F.L.R. 105 at 107.
[162] [2007] EWCA Civ 533.
[163] [2006] 1 F.L.R. 410, CA.
[164] *Re H (Abduction)* [2007] 1 F.L.R. 242, CA, but see below, para.20–020.
[165] Baroness Hale regarded the obligation to hear the views of the child as applying in every Hague case because of the UK's ratification of the UNCRC art.12; *Re D* [2006] UKHL 51 at para.59.
[166] *Re M (Abduction)* [2007] EWCA Civ 260.

matter.[167] Rational objections from a child are more likely to be persuasive,[168] and where a mature child objects on their own behalf and for a younger sibling, the court has held that neither should be returned.[169] The court is "rightly sceptical of attempts by parents to invoke art.13 to try to stave off the almost inevitable requirement to return the child".[170] However, cases where return has been ordered, but children's behaviour has convinced airline staff not to take them, indicate that the courts cannot always assess the strength of children's feelings.[171]

In terms of numbers of ratifications and the operation of its provisions, the Hague Convention must be regarded as successful. In terms of promoting the welfare of children, it is unclear the extent to which it has deterred abduction. However, the narrow approach to art.13 and the lack of mechanisms to secure the wellbeing of those who have been returned means that it has adversely impacted on some children. There is a danger that, unless these concerns are addressed, the Convention will not retain the high regard that it has achieved.

viii. Abduction within Europe

20–022 Brussels II Revised,[172] which has been ratified by all the Member States of the European Union with the exception of Denmark, takes precedence over the Hague Convention in cases involving Member States. In furtherance of the EU principle of free movement, it seeks to ensure that decisions about parental responsibility, including contact orders, are recognised and enforceable in all Member States.[173] The Council Regulation aims to deter abduction and complements the Hague Convention, giving particular attention to speedy decision-making, hearing the views of the child and recognising court orders.[174]

Where a child has been abducted[175] from the state of habitual residence to another Member State, a request can be made for the child's return. The courts in the requested state must give the child and the requesting person the opportunity to be heard, unless it is inappropriate to hear the child because of their age or degree of maturity.[176] The child need not be made a party; it is

---

[167] *Re S (Minors) (Abduction: Custody Rights)* [1993] Fam. 242.

[168] See *Re B (Abduction: Children's Objections)* [1999] 1 F.L.R. 667.

[169] *Re T (Abduction: Child's Objections to Return)* [2000] 2 F.L.R. 192, CA.

[170] *Re P (Abduction: Minor's Views)* [1998] 2 F.L.R. 825, CA, *per* Butler-Sloss L.J. at 827. Here the 13-year-old boy had run away and lived rough after return had been ordered. The child's appeal was allowed and the case remitted.

[171] *TB v JB (Abduction: Grave Risk of Harm)* [2001] 2 F.L.R. 515, CA; *Re HB (Abduction: Children's Objection) (No.2)* [1998] 1 F.L.R. 654 (11-year-old girl), and for the subsequent outcome, see B. Hale, "The view from court 45" [1999] C.F.L.Q. 377 at 378.

[172] Council Regulation (EC) 2201/2003; SI 2005/265. See European Judicial Network, *Practice Guide* for the application of the New Brussels II Regulation (2005), and Bromley (2006), p.664.

[173] Brussels II Revised Preamble, paras 1, 5–8.

[174] Brussels II Revised arts 10, 11, 40, 42 and 55; European Judicial Network, *Practice Guide* (2005), pp.28–40.

[175] Unless domestic law gives a parent the right to relocate unilaterally in another jurisdiction, removal of the child from the state of habitual residence without the consent of the other parent amounts to abduction: *Practice Guide* (2005), para.2.1.

[176] Brussels II Revised, 11(2), (5). This exception should be applied restrictively: *Practice Guide* (2005), p.41. The emphasis on hearing the child may appear at odds with an approach that appears to require return regardless of the child's objections.

sufficient for the child to be interviewed by a CAFCASS officer or to speak to the judge directly.[177] The decision should be made within six weeks of the request, and for this reason it has been suggested that time limits should be restricted and a stringent approach be taken to requests for party status for the child.[178] Courts are required to order return even where a Hague Convention art.13b defence would be upheld if adequate measures are available to protect the child after return.[179] On this basis, it seems that only in the most extreme cases will it be possible to avoid return because of risk to the child. The courts in the original state retain their jurisdiction despite the abduction; an order made in this state is enforceable in the requested state.[180] Where return is refused, the court must send a copy of the order, transcripts and the judgment to the central authority in the requesting state. Either party may apply for orders in the state of habitual residence within the next three months. If this court then makes an order requiring the return of the child, it can be enforced directly, providing the child and the parties have been given an opportunity to be heard and the court has taken account of the decision to refuse return made by the court in the requested state.[181] In effect, the Regulation provides two means for the left-behind parent to secure the child's return. He or she can obtain a peremptory order for return from the refuge state or, if that is refused, obtain an order from the state of habitual residence and have that enforced in the refuge state.

C. Abduction under the common law (from or to a country that has not ratified the Hague Convention)

The welfare principle governs applications for return of children abducted from non-Convention countries.[182] A full investigation on the merits precludes the speedy return necessary to minimise disruption to the child's relationships with family and culture.[183] These cases may also be dealt with by peremptory return, where the child's welfare is best served by decisions being made in a court with direct knowledge and understanding of the conditions in the child's home state.[184] Underlying peremptory return is the principle of international comity, the assumption that judges in the state of habitual residence will provide a fair

20–023

---

[177] *Re D* [2006] UKHL 51, para.60.
[178] *Vigreux v Michel* [2006] 2 F.L.R 1180 CA, *per* Thorpe L.J. at paras 44–48; *Re H (Abduction)* [2007] 1 F.L.R. 242, *per* Thorpe L.J. at para.16.
[179] Brussels II Revised, 11(4). But this provision has no effect on the child's art.13 defence: *Vigreux v Michel* [2006] 2 F.L.R 1180, *per* Wall L.J. at para.78.
[180] *Practice Guide* (2005), pp.8, 40.
[181] Brussels II Revised, 42.
[182] *Re J (Child Returned Abroad: Convention Rights)* [2005] 2 F.L.R. 802 HL, (Saudi Arabia): return refused; *Re JA (Abduction: Non-Convention Country)* [1998] 1 F.L.R. 231, CA. (U.A.E.): return refused; *Re E (Abduction: Non-Convention Country)* [1999] 2 F.L.R. 642, CA (Sudan): return ordered.
[183] *Re L (Minors) (Wardship: Jurisdiction)* [1974] 1 All E.R. 913 at 926, *per* Buckley L.J.
[184] *Re J (Child Returned Abroad: Convention Rights)* [2005] 2 F.L.R. 802, HL. Matters such as the availability of legal aid to both parties may justify a merits hearing in England rather than overseas, at least if the child has a substantial connection here: *H v H (forum conveniens)* [1993] 1 F.L.R. 959.

hearing for the dispute.[185] However, peremptory return to a non-Convention country should not be ordered merely by analogy with the Hague Convention.[186] Nor is it appropriate to consider in an individual case the impact of the decision on another state's approach to abductions or future ratification of the Convention.[187] The courts in England and Wales will not reject an application for return merely because the requesting parent resides in a country that applies the very different notions of welfare of Muslim law.[188] However, differences between legal systems may be relevant; discrimination between the sexes or the lack of jurisdiction to permit relocation in the courts in the home state may mean that a decision to return the child is inappropriate.[189]

A parent wishing to use legal means to obtain the child's return from a non-contracting state may seek an order directing the child's return[190]; try to have the abductor extradited[191] for abduction and reclaim the child; or bring proceedings in the country where the child is now living. Limited help may be available through the Foreign and Commonwealth Office.[192] Despite the wide-scale ratification of the Convention on the Rights of the Child, many countries still do not recognise foreign orders, and action by a non-national is almost bound to fail.

VI. Enforcing Contact Decisions

20–024   The Hague Convention contains no mandatory provisions to enforce contact comparable with its provisions relating to custody.[193] It imposes no duties whatsoever on the courts, and creates no rights that parents can directly

---

[185] *Re M (Abduction: Peremptory Return Order)* [1996] 1 F.L.R. 478 at 480, *per* Waite L.J. Behind this is the hope that courts overseas will take the same approach if children are abducted from England: see Setright [2000] I.F.L. 125 at 127.

[186] *Re J (Child Returned Abroad: Convention Rights)* [2005] 2 F.L.R. 802, HL; *Re JA (Abduction: Non-Convention Country)* [1998] 1 F.L.R. 231 at 234, *per* Ward L.J.

[187] *Re J (Child Returned Abroad: Convention Rights)* [2005] 2 F.L.R. 802, HL, *per* Baroness Hale at para.29.

[188] *Re E (Abduction: Non-Convention Country)* [1999] 2 F.L.R. 642 at 650, *per* Thorpe L.J.

[189] *Re J (Child Returned Abroad: Convention Rights)* [2005] 2 F.L.R. 802, HL, *per* Baroness Hale at paras 39, 44 and 46.

[190] A residence order or an order in wardship: *Re V (Jurisdiction: Habitual Residence)* [2001] 1 F.L.R. 253, FD (the child must be habitually resident in the UK). But wardship cannot be exercised to punish a person unless they are in contempt of court: *Re B (Child Abduction: Wardship: Power to Detain)* [1994] 2 F.L.R. 479. The father who had abducted the children to Algeria could not be imprisoned to secure return of the children who had been warded by their mother. A bench warrant could be used to bring a person before the court.

[191] See Extradition Act 2003.

[192] See *Practice Direction* [1984] 3 All E.R. 640 and see Foreign and Commonwealth Office, *International Child Abduction Leaflet* (2006), pp.8–9. *Re KR (Abduction: Forcible removal by Parents)* [1999] 2 F.L.R. 542 is a striking example of co-operation (following proceedings instituted by her sister) to facilitate the return of a child abducted to India.

[193] A. Anton, "The Hague Convention on international child abduction" (1981) 30 I.C.L.Q. 537 at 554 and N. Lowe, "Problems relating to access disputes under the Hague Convention on international child abduction" (1994) 8 Int. J. Law and Fam. 374; Beaumont and McEleavy *The Hague Convention*, Ch.12. Abduction that interferes with access does not give rise to summary return if the wronged person does not have rights of custody: *S v H (Abduction: Access Rights)* [1997] 1 F.L.R. 971.

enforce.[194] However, central authorities are bound to promote the peaceful enjoyment of access rights and to remove obstacles to their enforcement.[195] Unless Brussels II Revised applies, those wishing to enforce contact in England and Wales must apply for a s.8 contact order.[196] The central authority arranges for a solicitor, but there is no special provision of legal aid.[197] It is accepted that satisfactory contact may reduce abduction, that the desire to enforce contact may lead to an application for the child's peremptory return and that the existing provisions are weak. The development of better mechanisms for the enforcement of contact is under active consideration[198]; indeed, a "treaty jungle"[199] appears to be developing.

Within the EU, Brussels II Revised[200] now provides a simple and speedy system for the recognition and enforcement of contact orders made in Member States. Certified[201] decisions on contact in favour of any person are directly enforceable, as they would be if made by the courts of the state where enforcement is sought.[202] Courts may make practical arrangements to make contact work but must respect the original order, unless it would be against public policy to do so.[203] The effect of this provision can be to enforce orders quite different from those that would be made had the matter been decided here:

> In *Re S (No.1)*[204] the parents who lived in Belgium separated before the child was one year old, and the mother obtained permission to relocate to England. The father started divorce proceedings in Belgium and obtained a contact order that gave him staying contact for two weeks at a time spread throughout the year. The father sought recognition and enforcement of the order in England, and the mother argued that the child who had never been separated from her was too young to spend such long periods away from her. Holman J. held that he was bound to recognise the order. In the

[194] *Per* Hoffman L.J. in *Re G (A Minor) (Enforcement of Access Abroad)* [1993] Fam. 216 at 229. Thorpe L.J. obiter has suggested that the courts should take a more positive approach to the enforcement of contact: *Hunter v Murrow* [2005] 2 F.L.R. 1119, CA at para.31.

[195] Hague Convention art.21. But this does not require the enforcement of a contact order against the wishes of a 13-year-old girl: *Re H (A Minor) (Foreign Custody Order)* [1994] Fam. 105, CA.

[196] *Re G (A Minor) (Enforcement of Access Abroad)* [1993] Fam. 216 at 229. A foreign order would be entitled to "grave consideration", but the child's welfare is the paramount consideration: *McKee v McKee* [1951] A.C. 352 at 365.

[197] *Re T (Minors) (Hague Convention: Access)* [1993] 2 F.L.R. 617 at 622–623.

[198] See Hague Conference International Child Protection, *Judges Newsletter* (2006), p.81; W. Duncan, *Transfrontier Access/Contact* (Hague Conference, 4th Special Commission Prel doc.4, 2001).

[199] *Re G (Foreign Contact Order: Enforcement)* [2004] 1 F.L.R. 394, CA, at para.32, *per* Thorpe L.J.

[200] Council Regulation (EC) 2201/2003; SI 2005/265; European Judicial Network, *Practice Guide for the New Brussels II Regulation* (2005).

[201] Brussels II Revised, arts 40, 41 and Annex III; see *Practice Guide* (2005), pp.24–25. The parties and the child must have had an opportunity to be heard.

[202] Brussels II Revised, arts 41, 47 and see above, para.18–055 for the difficulties that enforcing contact poses in England and Wales.

[203] Brussels II Revised, arts 23, 26; *Practice Guide* (2005), p.23.

[204] *Re S (Brussels II: Recognition: Best Interest of the Child) (No.1)* [2004] 1 F.L.R. 571. The case was decided under Brussels II EC 1347/2000, but the same principles apply in Brussels II Revised.

subsequent enforcement proceedings,[205] he made practical arrangements to phase the contact in to enable the child to get used to the father. Given the limits on the court's powers, the judge felt unable to restrict contact to France and Belgium as the mother wished, but did limit it to Hague states to give effect to the requirement for the father to return the child at the end of contact.

VII. ABDUCTION AND HUMAN RIGHTS

20–025 The European Court of Human Rights has consistently ruled that it should not be interpreted so as to undermine the objectives of the Hague Convention.[206] States must take active steps without delay to ensure that their decisions under the Hague Convention are implemented.[207] Although art.20 of the Hague Convention, which permits refusal of return where return would breach fundamental principles of human rights in the requested state was not included in the UK implementing legislation, it has been given effect by a different route.[208] The fact that unmarried fathers do not automatically have "rights of custody" does not necessarily amount to discrimination against them under the ECHR.[209] Parents' right to relocate are not absolute[210]; nor can the ECHR justify precluding relocation that is in the child's best interests. Peremptory return can be justified in terms of ECHR art.8(2) in order to protect the child's relationship with the other parent,[211] even where this impacts negatively on the family life of others:

> In *S v B (Abduction: Human Rights)*[212] the father sought return to New Zealand of his 20-month-old son. Return of the boy's 13-year-old half-brother (in respect of whom the father did not have rights of custody) was not sought. The older child was made a party to the proceedings and argued that return would infringe his right to family life with his mother. The court ordered return justifying it on the basis that it protected the rights of the father and younger child in accordance with ECHR art.8(2). The older child

---

[205] *Re S (Brussels II: Recognition: Best Interest of the Child) (No.2)* [2004] 1 F.L.R. 582.

[206] ECHR art.53; Mole [2000] I.F.L. 121, 123.

[207] Failure to do so is a breach of art.8; see *Ignaccolo-Zenide v Romania* ECHR App.31679/96; *Sylvester v Austria* [2003] 2 F.L.R. 210; *Gil and AUI v Spain* [2005] 1 F.L.R. 190.

[208] By the obligation in Human Rights Act 1998 s.6 to apply the law in compliance with rights under the ECHR: *Re D* [2006] UKHL 51, *per* Baroness Hale at para.65.

[209] art.14; *B v UK* [2000] 1 F.L.R. 1; the ECtHR declared the father's application inadmissible, but in *Sahin v Germany, Sommerfield v Germany* [2002] 1 F.L.R. 119, provisions in German law that made it more difficult for unmarried fathers to obtain contact were held to breach arts 6, 8 and 14.

[210] ECHR of the Fourth Protocol (which has not been ratified by the UK) guarantees freedom of movement but does not prevent a restrictive residence order being made in relation to children: see Beaumont and McEleavy *The Hague Convention*, p.175.

[211] *Payne v Payne* [2001] 1 F.L.R. 1052, CA.

[212] [2005] 2 F.L.R. 897.

was not prevented from returning to New Zealand but was merely reluctant to do so.[213]

Also, the emphasis on peremptory return and the absence of the wronged parent may justify a more limited hearing than of an ordinary residence dispute. Speed is of the essence; delay may mean that the trial is unfair.[214]

VIII. Conclusion

The number of countries that have ratified the Conventions continues to increase, but major parts of the world remain beyond its reach. Amongst Convention states, maintaining a consistent, international interpretation of the Convention is difficult.[215] Although implementation is considered generally to be good, there have been difficulties with some countries.[216] Despite provisions for mandatory return, return is ordered or agreed in only half the cases where applications are made.[217] In contrast, two-thirds of parents bringing proceedings in England and Wales were successful.[218] Courts may be expanding the use of the defences and refusing return more readily.[219] Ignorance of the Convention and low success rates undermine the Convention's deterrent effects. Also, the lack of provisions for repatriation and legal costs limit its effectiveness. Proceedings are slow[220]; few countries can make decisions within the six weeks demanded by Brussels II Revised, even applying procedures that rely on written statements rather than oral hearings. Moreover, the fact that the majority of abductions are by primary carers poses a major challenge. It calls into question the broad application of summary return, particularly to states where it is very difficult to obtain permission for relocation. Similarly, increased emphasis on the views of young people and their participation in decision-making challenges the notion that parents can decide to relocate, or can challenge a relocation undertaken without their permission through a process that relates to adult's rights rather than the rights or wishes of mature children.

20–026

---

[213] *Per* Potter P at paras 53–56. The President also indicated that the boy should not have been made a party to the proceedings. However, had the applicant also been able to claim this child's return, it appears that he might have had an art.13 defence, and had he done so, return of the younger child would also have been refused: *Re T (Abduction: Child's Objections to Return)* [2000] 2 F.L.R. 192, CA. To do otherwise would have left the older child without a carer.

[214] In *Larson v Sweden* App.33250/96, the Commission held that a delay of one year (six months of which was due to a request to delay from the applicant) was not excessive.

[215] L. Silberman, "Patching up the abduction convention: a call for a new international protocol and a suggestion for amendments to ICARA" (2003) 23 Texas L. J. 41.

[216] Beaumont and McEleavy *The Hague Convention*, p.241; *Gil and AUI v Spain* [2005] 1 F.L.R. 190.

[217] N. Lowe et al., *A Statistical Analysis of Applications Made in 2003* (Hague Prel Doc.3.1, 2006), p.31.

[218] Official Solicitor and Public Trustee Office, *Annual Report 2005* (2006) Annex B.

[219] L. Silberman, "The Hague children's conventions" in S. Katz et al. (eds), *Cross Currents* (2000), p.589 at 596; J. Caldwell [2001] C.F.L.Q. 121 at 136. The authors disagree as to whether this development is good or bad.

[220] A. Dyer, "The Hague Convention—towards global co-operation, its successes and failures" (1993) 1 Int. J. of Children's Rights 273, 275, 284. England and Wales have a good record for handling cases speedily: see N. Lowe and A. Perry, "International abduction—the English experience" [1999] I.C.L.Q. 127, 138–143.

CHAPTER TWENTY-ONE

LOCAL AUTHORITIES

I.   INTRODUCTION.............................. 21–001
     A. The development of children's
     social care services 21–002
     B. The reform of childcare law.......... 21–004
     C. The philosophy of the Children Act
     1989.. 21–005
     D. The role of central government..... 21–006
     E. The balance of power between
     court and social services departments. 21–007
II. MODERN   CHILDCARE   LAW—
SERVICES FOR CHILDREN IN NEED..... 21–008
     A. Family support and prevention...... 21–008
     B. Local authorities' duties to provide
     family support...................................... 21–009
     C. "Children in need" 21–010
     D. Duty to provide accommodation ... 21–011
     E. Voluntary agreement 21–013
     F. Co-operation between authorities .. 21–015
III. THE   CHILD   PROTECTION
SYSTEM... 21–016
     A. Child abuse and neglect................. 21–016
     B. Intervention in family life.............. 21–019

     C. The child protection system.......... 21–021
     D. Investigation of child abuse and
     neglect 21–022
     E. Compulsory measures of care 21–029
     F. Protection   of   children   in
     emergencies.. 21–047
     G. Child protection proceedings......... 21–053
     H. Child protection and the criminal
     law 21–061
IV. MODERN CHILDCARE LAW—THE
LOOKED-AFTER SYSTEM....................... 21–067
     A. Local   authorities'   powers   and
     duties 21–067
     B. The position of parents 21–072
     C. Rights of children........................... 21–073
V.   MODERN   CHILDCARE   LAW—
JUDICIAL   CONTROL   OVER   LOCAL
AUTHORITY DECISION-MAKING 21–074
     A. Decisions requiring court approval. 21–074
     B. Challenging   local   authority
     decisions... 21–081

I. INTRODUCTION

In this chapter we consider questions about the state's role in supporting children **21–001** and their carers, the proper limits of state interference in family life and the allocation of decision-making responsibility between the state (courts or local authorities) and individual members of the family. These are human rights issues; the state has obligations to protect children from abuse that may amount to inhuman treatment[1] and to respect family life. Action taken to safeguard children

---

[1] ECHR art.3; *Z v UK* [2001] 2 F.L.R. 612; *E v UK* [2003] 1 F.L.R. 348. The failure of the local authority to take action to protect children from abuse in their family amounted to a breach of arts 3 and 13. And see discussion of *X v Bedfordshire CC* [1995] 2 A.C. 633, HL, below, para.21–027.

(e.g. their removal from parents) disrupts family life, and must be limited to protect their art.8 rights and those of their parents.[2]

Despite "the most comprehensive and far reaching reform of child law in living memory",[3] intended to bring "clarity and consistency",[4] this remains an area of legal complexity but one where decisions are made by social workers,[5] sometimes without legal advice, and by (lay) magistrates rather than professional judges. Social workers are central, but legal agencies, play a crucial role in defining problems,[6] imposing procedures, determining disputes and ensuring the accountability of public authorities. The Children Act 1989 brought increased legalism; the Human Rights Act 1998 has added a further layer of domestic and European case law. Public child-law has become a specialist area of practice.

There has been further legislation: local authorities' responsibilities to those formerly in public care have been increased by the Children (Leaving Care) Act 2000, and new duties to those being looked after will be added if the Children and Young Persons Bill 2008 is enacted. The Children Act 2004, implementing the *Every Child Matters*[7] agenda, imposed additional obligations on local authorities and other agencies to co-operate to improve children's wellbeing, and created new institutional frameworks (including children's services departments, combining social care for children and families, and education) to achieve this. The state is taking on a greater role; monitoring children's lives and seeking to intervene to prevent problems in later life.[8]

A. The development of children's social care services

21–002   There was no comprehensive childcare service until the Welfare State was established in 1948. Parental poverty, ill-health or death and child abandonment, neglect and ill-treatment resulted in thousands of children being looked after outside their families.[9] They were cared for by voluntary organisations such as Dr Barnardo's Homes, by the Poor Law authorities and by local authorities acting as "fit persons" for children committed for their protection by the courts. The accommodation provided for children ranged from gloomy, unmodernised workhouses that also housed the elderly and disturbed, and spartan, barrack-type

---

[2] ECHR arts 6 and 8: *R v UK* [1988] 2 F.L.R. 445 (restriction on contact that could not be challenged violated arts 6 and 8); *K and T v Finland* [2001] 2 F.L.R. 707; *P, C and S v UK* [2002] 2 F.L.R. 631 (emergency removal of child for his protection violated art. 8); *Olsson v Sweden* (1988) 11 E.H.R.R. 259 (separate placement and distant placement of children violated art.8).
[3] *Per* Lord Mackay, Lord Chancellor Children Bill, Second Reading, *Hansard*, HL Vol.502, col.488.
[4] *The Law on Child Care and Family Services* (Cm.62 (1987)), para.4.
[5] Social care professionals who are required to register with the General Social Care Council (or its equivalent for Wales): Care Standards Act 2000 ss.58, 58 and 61.
[6] C. Grace, *Social Workers, Children and the Law* (Oxford: Clarendon, 1994); N. Parton, *Governing the Family* (London: Macmillan, 1991).
[7] (Cm.5860 (2003)). ECM was the government's response to Lord Laming's inquiry into the death of Victoria Climbié (Cm.5730 (2003)).
[8] N. Parton, "The 'Change for Children' Programme in England: towards the 'preventive-surveillance state' " [2008] J. Law & Society 166.
[9] See, generally, Cretney *Family Law in the Twentieth Century*; H. Hendrick, *Child Welfare England 1982–1989* (1994); R. Parker "The gestation of reform: the Children Act 1948", in P. Bean and S. MacPherson, *Approaches to Welfare* (London: RKP, 1983); J. Masson "From Curtis to Waterhouse: state care and child protection in the U.K. 1945–20" in, S. Katz et al. (eds), *Cross Currents*.

buildings, to bright purpose-built cottages[10]; children were also "boarded out" with families[11] and sent overseas.[12] There were few trained social workers, and welfare work in the community was largely provided by the clergy, family doctors, their wives and other volunteers.

The Children Act 1948 gave local authorities responsibility for orphans and children whose parents were unable to look after them, but voluntary organisations continued to play a major role. Local authorities were required to establish Children's Committees and to appoint a specialist Children's Officer.[13] In 1968 the policy of specialisation was rejected by the Seebohm Committee, which considered that integrated social services, staffed by generic social workers, would permit a more comprehensive response to problems.[14] This re-organisation was implemented in 1970. In consequence, childcare became one of the services provided by teams of social workers acting under a Director of Social Services, who was responsible to the Social Services Committee.[15] However, childcare work was increasingly seen as demanding specialists; local authorities re-introduced "children and families teams" and experienced difficulties in recognising children's needs and providing integrated services where parents have problems (mental ill-health or disability) that require support from adult services.[16] Local authority re-organisation, particularly the creation of unitary authorities, means that social services functions are now exercised around 150 authorities, some of which are too small to provide a range of specialist services.[17]

The Lord Laming's Inquiry into the death of Victoria Climbié identified widespread failures in services for children and families, and recommended structural changes including a National Agency to advise central government and stronger local management.[18] In response, the Government proposed children's services departments to combine local authority responsibilities for children's social care and education, and arrangements for pooled budgets or the creation of Children's Trusts to facilitate commissioning of children's services.[19] The Children Act 2004 now provides that each local authority with social services

[10] Katz et al., *Cross Currents*, paras 140, 234, 236. Those who believe in progress should read accounts of residential care in A. Levy and B. Kahan, *The Pindown Experience and the Protection of Children* (Staffordshire CC, 1991).

[11] This practice is now termed "fostering". The death of one such child, Dennis O'Neill, was the subject of an inquiry in 1945 (Cmd.6636 (1945)) *(Monckton Report)*.

[12] R. Parker, *Uprooted* (Bristol: Policy Press, 2008); P. Bean and J. Melville, *Lost Children of the Empire* (London: Unwin Hyman, 1989).

[13] Children Act 1948 ss.39, 41. On the important role of this official, see J. Packman, *The Child's Generation* (Oxford: Blackwell, 1981), pp.9–12.

[14] Committee on Local Authority and Allied Personal Services (Cmnd.3703 (1968)). For a discussion of the evolution of social policy over this period, see J. Cooper, *The Creation of the British Personal Social Services 1962–1974* (London: Heinemann, 1983).

[15] Local Authority Social Services Act 1970 ss.2, 3, 6.

[16] DH, *Children Act Now: Messages From Research* (2001), p.110; Cabinet Office, *Think Family: Improving the Life Chances of Families at Risk* (2007), and see *Re S (Minors) (Care Order: Implementation of Care Plan)* [2002] 1 F.L.R. 815, HL.

[17] G. Craig and J. Manthorpe, *Unfinished Business? Local Government Re-organisation and Social Services* (Bristol: Policy Press, 1999).

[18] (Cm.5730 (2003)), recommendations 1–9.

[19] HM Government, *Every Child Matters* (Cm.5860 (2003)); DfES, *Every Child Matters: Next Steps* (2004), and see *http://www.everychildmatters.gov.uk* [Accessed June 5, 2008].

responsibilities must appoint a Director of Children's Services and Lead Member with responsibilities under the Local Authority Social Services Act 1970, and for education, for care leavers and for co-operation with other agencies to improve the wellbeing of all children in their area.[20] Although this should make it easier to have a common approach to assessment,[21] to share information and to secure good education for children in care, the majority of children's social care departments are now directed by someone without a background in social work.

21–003　　　The Children Act 1989 gave local authorities responsibilities towards all children in need and those living away from home unless cared for by close relatives.[22] Children in hospital and those detained through the Criminal Justice System are included.[23] Despite the changes in the 2004 Act, children's services staff still need to work in conjunction with welfare workers in other organisations, particularly health visitors and Sure Start workers who have responsibilities for the under fives, Connexions with responsibilities for those between 14 and 18 years, and voluntary organisations, which still perform an important role providing specialist services. A mixed economy of care has developed,[24] with the private sector providing fostering and residential placements for local authorities. Moreover, the Children and Young Persons Bill allows a pilot scheme for the provision of some social work services by independent "social work practices".[25]

There have been major changes in the demands for children's social care. The re-discovery of child abuse in the 1960s led to increasing social work attention being given to child protection. Procedures were introduced to formalise response, and substantial amounts of staff time became devoted to child protection investigations.[26] "Abuse and neglect" is now the main reason for children entering the public care system, and almost a third of children receiving services in the community do so because of such concerns.[27] Poverty and substance abuse have also increased, undermining parents' abilities to care for children adequately. Children's departments initially focused on looking after children, and made considerable use of residential homes. From the early 1960s

---

[20] Children Act 2004 ss.10, 18 and 19.
[21] (Cm.5860 (2003)), para.4.13; DoH, *Assessment of Children in Need and Their Families* (2000); *Guidance* (2008), para.3.12.
[22] Children Act 1989 ss.17, 24, 62, 64, 67 and 85–87. Services for under 18s do not come within the National Health Service and Community Care Act 1990 s.42(1). Regulation and inspection of children's homes is now a matter for Ofsted under the Education and Inspections Act 2006.
[23] Children Act 1989 s.85; *R. (Howard League for Penal Reform) v Secretary of State for the Home Department* [2003] 1 F.L.R. 484, QBD.
[24] Cm.2584 (1994), para.2.16. Local authorities are required to facilitate the provision of services by voluntary or private organisations, and may subcontract service provision: Children Act 1989 s.17(5).
[25] *Care Matters: Transforming the Lives of Children and Young People in Care* (Cm.6932 (2006)), Ch.3; (Cm.7137 (2007)), para.7.19; Children and Young Persons Bill 2008 cll.1–6; DCSF, *Policy Statement on Children and Young Persons Bill* (2007). IROs and adoption services are excluded; cl.2(2), (3).
[26] N. Parton, *The Politics of Child Abuse* (1985). The DHSS first issued guidance on such matters in 1974; DH, *Child Protection: Messages from Research* (London: HMSO, 1995).
[27] DfES, *Children in Need in England Survey 2005* (2006), Table 5. Child protection concerns are a key gateway to services; DH, *Children Act Now* (London: TSO, 2001), p.44.

they were given powers to provide services to prevent the need to accommodate children. These powers were substantially extended in the Children Act 1989, with the aim of refocusing provision to support families. Each year children's social care departments receive over half a million referrals and look after 85,000 children away from home.[28] The size of the state care population has declined from over 100,000 in the 1980s to 61,000 in 2007.[29] The residential care service has shrunk; the high cost of provision and the recognition that many residents had been physically or sexually abused led to voluntary organisations and local authorities closing many children's homes.[30] Three-fifths of looked-after children live in (unrelated) foster families.

There is "striking variability" in services provided by local councils.[31] Despite changes in legislation, organisation and services, substantial problems with the quality of provision remain, and negative outcomes result for looked-after children.[32] Although there have been some improvements, and the care system is successful for many who enter as young children and are found permanent families, outcomes for those entering later remain poor.[33] Indeed, the gap between looked-after children and those in the community has widened.[34] In response, the Government has stated in *Care Matters* its determination to transform the working of the system and the quality of experience for those in it.[35] Legislation has been introduced to increase even further the responsibilities of local authorities, to strengthen accountability and to improve the quality of social workers.[36] In addition, responsibilities for regulation and inspection of children's social care (foster care, adoption and residential care), including services provided by voluntary and commercial organisations, have been removed from local authorities and placed in the hands of Ofsted.[37]

B. The reform of childcare law[38]

In the 41 years between the two great Children Acts,[39] Parliament did not neglect the welfare of children. A series of statutes, together with judicial decisions, produced a system that was complex, confusing and unsatisfactory, with far-

21–004

---

[28] DfES, *Children Act Report 2004 and 2005* (2006), paras 1.7 and 3.3.

[29] DCSF, *Children Looked After by Local Authorities* (published annually).

[30] W. Utting, *People Like Us* (London: TSO, 1997), p.21; *Lost In Care* (HC 201, 2000); C. Wolmar, *Forgotten Children* (London: Vision, 2000).

[31] SSI, *Developing Quality to Protect Children* (2001), para.1.7.

[32] DfES, *Outcome Indicators for Looked After Children* (London: JKP, 2007); Select Committee on Health, *Second Report of the Select Committee on Health Session 1997–8, Children Looked after by Local Authorities* (HC 247, 1998); W. Utting, *People Like Us*.

[33] I. Sinclair et al., *Pursuit of Permanence: A Study of the English Care System* (London: JKP, 2007).

[34] *Care Matters* (Cm.6932 (2006)), Ch.1.

[35] Alan Johnson, Secretary of State for Education, *Care Matters* (Cm.6932 (2006)), Foreword.

[36] *Care Matters: Time for Change* (Cm.7139 (2007)); Children and Young Persons Bill 2008. References is made to the changes throughout the text.

[37] Education and Inspections Act 2006 s.135. Inspection of childminding and day-care has also been transferred from local authorities to Ofsted so that that body now has responsibility for all early-years education.

[38] For a more wide-ranging discussion of the background to reform, see N. Parton and N. Martin, "Public inquiries, legislation and child care in England & Wales" (1989) 3 Int. J. Law & Fam. 21 and J. Eekelaar and R. Dingwall, *The Reform of Child Care Law* (London: Tavistock, 1990).

[39] 1948 and 1989.

reaching (and often adverse) consequences for the welfare of children.[40] There were more than a dozen ways in which children could enter local authority care, each one with different conditions and powers and giving rise to different rights of appeal.[41] The problems were exacerbated by overlapping and conflicting jurisdictions between courts, and the lack of a system that allowed all the issues relating to a child to be heard by a single court.[42] Many of the provisions now appear extraordinary; parents were not parties to care proceedings to remove their children; emergency powers allowed children to be removed from home for 28 days; and parents' rights could be removed without court proceedings.[43] The Children Act 1975 had weakened the position of parents in order to provide security for children in foster care. Pressure groups such as the Family Rights Group, the Children's Legal Centre and the National Association for Young People in Care were established in the late 1970s and early 1980s and began to campaign for improved services for children and their families and increased regulation of the social services. Cases were also taken to the European Court of Human Rights, challenging the removal of parental rights and the termination of parental contact without court proceedings[44] and highlighting the importance of making any new law compliant with the Convention.[45]

The House of Commons Select Committee on the Social Services began an inquiry into children in care in July 1982. It recommended a thorough review of the statute law,[46] and an inter-departmental working party was set up that issued discussion papers and a report: *The Review of Child Care Law*, in 1985.[47] The review adopted many of the ideas and recommendations of the Select Committee, with a view to the production of a clearer and more consistent body of law, comprehensible not only to those operating the system but also to those affected by it.[48] The Government generally endorsed the recommendations in its response, published in 1987.[49] Over the same period the deaths of a number of children about whose care a local authority had grave concern, including some under care orders, were the subject of detailed inquiries.[50] The reports of these

---

[40] *Second Report of the House of Commons Social Services Committee 1983–4, Children in Care* (HC 360) *(Short Report)*, para.118.
[41] *Children in Care*, paras 118–119. See also S. Maidment, "The fragmentation of parental rights of children in care" [1981] J.S.W.L. 21.
[42] This could occur in wardship cases, but the High Court was not able to handle a large number of cases, and the principle applied, "the welfare principle", was not appropriate; see below.
[43] Even in 1944 parental-rights resolutions were regarded as extraordinary; see Parker, *Uprooted*, p.243. The Short Committee recommended 25 changes to the law; see p.143, and see *Social Services Committee Second Report 1988–9, Children Bill* (HC 178), para.4.
[44] *R v UK* [1988] 2 F.L.R. 445.
[45] "The Children Act anticipated the introduction into English Law of the European Convention", *per* Scott Baker J. in *Re S (Sexual Abuse Allegations: Local Authority Response)* [2001] 2 F.L.R. 776 at 794; see also *Re F (Care Termination of Contact)* [2000] 2 F.C.R. 481.
[46] *Short Report*, para.119.
[47] DHSS, *Review of Child Care Law Discussion Papers 1–12* (1985); *Review of Child Care Law* (1985). Baroness Hale (then Professor Brenda Hoggett) was a member of the Review Team and the Law Commission.
[48] DHSS, *Review of Child Care Law Discussion Papers 1–12*, Foreword, para.2.
[49] *The Law on Child Care and Family Services* (Cm.62 (1987)).
[50] for example, Tyra Henry, Kimberley Carlile and Jasmine Beckford; see DH, *A Study of Inquiry Reports 1980–1989* (1991) and P. Reder et al., *Beyond Blame, Child Abuse Tragedies Revisited* (London: Routledge, 1993).

inquiries approved the Government's proposals. The publicity given to these cases and, particularly, that surrounding child sexual abuse in Cleveland[51] increased pressure for reform. The public lacked confidence in the child protection service—social workers seemed unable to protect children at risk or to respect the privacy and authority of innocent families. Greater control of social worker's power and increased recognition of parent's rights were seen as essential for the framework for childcare practice.[52]

The Children Bill was incomplete when it was introduced into the Lords in December 1988, and proceeded to the Commons before the Government had devised schemes for allocating cases between courts and appeals, and some other matters had been drafted. The Government tabled hundreds of amendments, most of which received little detailed consideration because of the timetabling and guillotining of debate. No amendments opposed by the Government were successful but some were taken into account.[53] Much was left to regulations and rules of court.

In last the 20 years, there have been many changes to local authorities and their responsibilities for children and families. In an attempt to set out in detail the action required by local authorities, the clarity of the original Children Act 1989 drafting has been obscured, and matters initially left to regulations or guidance have been grafted into the Act. Further guidance for local authorities has been issued, and a programme to update the original guidance has been started. New procedures for care proceedings have been introduced[54] so as to ensure that non-compulsory alternatives are ruled out before the local authority starts proceedings.

C. The philosophy of the Children Act 1989[55]

Childcare policy has operated like a pendulum, swinging between the various competing interests and favouring different approaches as social work styles changed and more became known of their effects on children in care and their families.[56] Concern for the plight of children in "voluntary care",[57] who had lost

21–005

---

[51] *The Report of the Inquiry into Child Abuse in Cleveland 1987* (Cm.412 (1988)).

[52] For a criticism of this legalism, see Parton *Governing the Family*; Parton and Martin, "Public inquiries", pp.26, 36.

[53] for example, the words "or complaints" were added to the provision dealing with procedures for making representations to the local authority; see now s.26(3). The definition of "specified proceedings" in s.41(6) was extended in the court rules, although an amendment with this aim was rejected.

[54] DCSF, *Children Act 1989 Guidance and Regulations. Vol.1: Court Orders* (2008), paras 3.22–3.33; the Welsh Assembly Government have produced a separate version of this document; MoJ, *The Public Law Outline* (2008), and see below, para.21–054.

[55] See B. Hoggett, "The Children Bill: the aim" (1989) 19 Fam. Law 217; M. Ryan, "The Children Bill 1989: the philosophy and the reality" [1989] 1 J.C.L. 102 (Cm.62 (1987)) and HMSO, *Guide to the Children Act 1989* (1989); B. Jordan, "Social work, justice and the common good", in *Social Work and Social Welfare Year Book(3)* (Open University Press, 1991), p.17; J. Roche, "The Children Act and children's rights: a critical reassessment", in B. Franklin (ed.), *The New Handbook of Children's Rights* (London: Routledge, 2001).

[56] See Grace *Social Workers*, pp.14, 32; Hendricks *Child Welfare in England*, Ch.11.

[57] i.e. children accommodated by local authorities in respect of whom the authorities did not have parental responsibility (Childcare Act 1980 s.2).

contact with their families but lacked a permanent substitute family led to emphasis being placed on obtaining control and on planning. The Children Act 1975 facilitated this by extending the grounds on which "parental rights" could be removed, strengthening the position of foster parents and introducing a procedure whereby children could be freed for adoption.[58] The phrase "permanency planning"[59] was coined to connote the work done to enable a child to return to his or her family or move to an adoptive home, but was most frequently associated with adoption rather than rehabilitation. Studies in the 1980s raised awareness of the damage that state care could do to family links, and also indicated that local policies and practices had an enormous impact on the numbers of children in care, their length of stay and the care provided for them. The emotional and financial costs of care encouraged local authorities to operate strong gate-keeping techniques to prevent children entering the system, but providing care only as a last resort left both families and social workers feeling that they had failed if a child came into care.[60] The repeated reports of child abuse and the need to satisfy the public that everything possible was being done for such children also focused social work attention on taking control and not taking risks. Social work thus became something that was done to clients rather than a way of helping families to help themselves.

Against this background, the changes in policy underlying the 1989 Act were quite dramatic. Central to the philosophy of the Act is the belief that children are best looked after within their family, with both parents playing a full part and without recourse to legal proceedings.[61] Services to families who need help should, where possible, be arranged in partnership with parents.[62] The care of children away from home should be a collaborative effort, with the local authority involving, consulting and valuing parents.[63] Supporting families and preventing the need for state care should be emphasised, but care is not to be viewed negatively. Local authorities should gain greater control of cases only following proof of risk of significant harm; an order must be sought in court proceedings where parents are represented. Even after a care order has been made, partnership should continue and links with family members be maintained. The Act repositioned the court; in some instances making it the key decision-making forum, in others withdrawing judicial scrutiny.[64] It is also a "charter for

[58] Children Act 1975 ss.14, 33, 57 (Childcare Act 1980 s.3); Adoption Act 1976 s.18. For a discussion of the 1980 Act, see the fourth edition of this work at pp.487–523; for freeing for adoption, see the sixth edition of this work at pp.908–911.
[59] See, especially, A.N. Maluccio, E. Fein and K.A. Olmstead, *Permanency Planning for Children: Concepts and Methods* (New York: Tavistock, 1986).
[60] See M. Fisher et al., *In and Out of Care* (London: Batsford, 1986).
[61] Children Act Report 1992 (Cm.2144 (1993)), para.1.8.
[62] "Partnership" is not a term in the legislation. *Guidance* (1991), Vol.3, para.2.10 states: "Partnership will only be achieved if parents are advised about and given explanations of the local authority's power and duties." Family Group Conferences that are arranged by some local authorities enable families to have greater influence on the services provided for their children: see Family Rights Group, *Family Group Conferences in the U.K.* (1995).
[63] Even if they have harmed their children: see DH, *The Challenge of Partnership in Child Protection: Practice Guide* (1995).
[64] J. Roche, "The Children Act and children's rights", p.63.

children",[65] allowing the child's views to be heard when decisions are taken about his or her care. The Act sought to strike a balance between the rights of children to express their views, the rights of parents to exercise their responsibilities and the duty of the state to intervene to protect children.[66] In so doing, the Act implemented many of the obligations in the UN Convention on the Rights of the Child.[67]

The Act did not merely provide the framework for practices that were already well-established. Rather, it required major changes in professional attitudes and service delivery[68] in order to establish a new balance between the family and the state,[69] and between child protection and family support services.[70] It drew on four distinct approaches to child welfare: laissez-faire, state paternalism, parents' rights and children's rights.[71] These approaches necessarily conflict; greater rights for social workers to protect children mean that parents lose some of their rights.[72] Emphasis on balance does not necessarily deny this conflict but recognises the need to take account of conflicting objectives in order to prevent both over- and under-reaction. The Children Act brought about major positive changes in the provision of social services for children and families but still left a system where there is wide variation in the availability of services and, too frequently, poor outcomes for children.[73]

D. The role of central government

The Department for Children Schools and Families deals centrally with issues **21–006** relating to care and adoption in England. There is a Minister for Children, Young People and Families, but this is not a cabinet post. These are devolved matters that are the responsibility of the Welsh Minister in Wales.[74] Other government departments, notably the Department of Health, the Ministry of Justice and the Department of Communities and Local Government, all have responsibilities that impinge on local authority care for children. The Children Act 1989 gave the Secretary of State considerable power to issue regulations that can extend or restrict the ambit of the Act or the way it is operated.[75] Under the Local Authority

---

[65] Cm.2144, para.1.6, although it removed some rights from children whilst recognising others; see above, Ch.17.
[66] Cm.2144, para.1.7.
[67] Cm.2144, para.1.13; for a less optimistic view, see Children's Rights Development Unit, *U.K. Agenda for Children* (1994).
[68] Cm.2144, para.1.15.
[69] DH, *Introduction to the Children Act 1989* (1989), p.iii; Cm.2144, para.1.7.
[70] DH, *Child Protection Messages from Research* (1995), Foreword.
[71] L. Fox-Harding, *Perspectives in Child Care Policy* (1991); L. Fox-Harding, "The Children Act 1989 in context: four perspectives in child care law and policy" [1991] J.S.W.F.L. 179 at 285.
[72] Fox-Harding *Perspectives*, p.230.
[73] *Children Act Now* (2001), pp.117, 124 and 145.
[74] These functions were undertaken by the Department of Health before 2003 and by the Welsh Office before devolution. The Department of Health commissioned a major programme for the implementation of the Children Act 1989: see J. Masson, "Implementing the Children Act 1989: action at the centre and local reaction" (1992) 19 J. Law & Society 320.
[75] Children Act 1989 s.104. For example, under s.17(4) the Secretary of State or the Welsh Minister may effectively rewrite Sch.2 to the Act.

Social Services Act 1970[76] the Secretary of State for Children, Schools and Families has power to issue guidance to local authorities; children's services authorities and their partners must exercise their functions with regard to such guidance.[77] The courts should have regard to such guidance.[78] Guidance may give rise to expectations about the way cases will be dealt with so that departure from it provides a basis for judicial review. It may be seen as a form of tertiary legislation. Ten volumes of guidance relating specifically to the Children Act 1989 were published in 1991; these are now being revised.[79] Guidance is also issued as Circulars.[80]

The Department of Children, Schools and Families also carries out other functions relating to childcare. The Department has responsibility for maintaining lists of people who are unsuitable to work with children or vulnerable adults.[81] It develops policy and standards[82] and advises Ministers. It has set minimum national rates payable to foster carers.[83] It publishes statistics and an annual report to Parliament on the Children Act 1989,[84] funds research and ensures the wide dissemination of its findings.[85] It jointly funds the Social Care Institute for Excellence (SCIE), which identifies and disseminates good practice and research. It is empowered to undertake inquiries.[86] Most services are financed by local authorities with the assistance of block grants from central government, but the Department of Children, Schools and Families also supports

---

[76] Local Authority Social Services Act 1970 ss.7, 7A; and see *R v Islington LBC, Ex p. Rixon* [1997] E.L.R. 66.

[77] Children Act 2004 s.10(8). Partners are defined in s.10(4) and include the district councils, police, youth offending teams, etc.

[78] *Oxfordshire CC v R.* [1992] 1 F.L.R. 648 at 654, *per* Douglas Brown J. The magistrates' failure to consider the guidance was a ground for appeal. But guidance is sometimes viewed as wrong in law: *R (Spink) v Wandsworth Borough Council* [2005] 1 F.L.R. 448 (local authority could take parents resources into account when providing services for disabled child).

[79] DH, *The Children Act 1989 Guidance and Regulations* (1991), referred to here as "*Guidance (1991)*"; DCSF, *Children Act 1989 Guidance and Regulations* (2008), referred to here as "*Guidance (2008)*". There is a separate edition for Wales.

[80] Details of many current circulars can be found in *Clarke, Hall and Morrison On Children* or on the Department of Health website.

[81] Under the Protection of Children Act 1999 and the Care Standards Act 2000 s.81; appeals against inclusion on the lists are to the Care Standards Tribunal. The Safeguarding Vulnerable Groups Act 2006 creates a new framework that will transfer responsibility from the Secretary of State to an Independent Barring Board; Safeguarding Vulnerable Groups Act 2006 s.1 and Schs 1 and 2.

[82] Standards must be published: Care Standards Act 2000 s.23. This work was undertaken by the Commission for Social Care Inspection, but responsibilities for the Inspection and regulation of children's services were transferred in 2007 to Ofsted.

[83] DfES, *National Minimum Fostering Allowance and Fostering Payment Systems* (2006). The minimum rate for 2007–8 for a baby is £100 *per* week. There is also a statutory scheme for special guardianship allowances, but minimum amounts are not fixed: Special Guardianship Regulations 2005 (SI 2005/1109), Ch.2.

[84] Children Act 1989 s.83(6); *Children Act Reports 2004 and 2005* (2006); for statistics: *http://www.dfes.gov.uk/rsgateway/* [Accessed June 5, 2008].

[85] The Department of Health funded major research programmes and published research reviews: see *Child Protection: Messages from Research* (1995) and *Children Act Now* (2001). The DCSF has recently supported research on Kinship care: J. Hunt et al., *Keeping Them In the Family* (London: BAAF, 2008); E. Farmer and S. Moyers, *Kinship Care: Fostering Effective Family and Friends Placements* (London: JKP, 2008).

[86] Inquiries Act 2005 s.1, replacing Children Act 1989 s.81. Most inquiries are undertaken by local authorities, but Lord Laming's inquiry into the death of Victoria Climbié was set up by the Secretary of State.

the work of some voluntary organisations and pays for specific training initiatives.[87] The Secretary of State has default powers that can be used where a local authority fails to carry out its functions.[88]

Throughout its period in office, the Labour Government has sought to transform children's services using initiatives that set local authorities targets, backed by specific grants and monitoring. The *Quality Protects* programme (1999–2004) set objectives relating to educational attainment, placement stability and health, and required local authorities to produce management action plans to show how they would develop services to meet these. *Choice protects*, launched in 2002, sought to improve outcomes by improving children's placements.[89] *Every Child Matters*[90] has focused on the development of universal services and improvements to joint working across all agencies that work with children and families. The most recent programme, *Care Matters*, is seeking to improve children's experiences in the care system through a range of measures, including new legal duties on local authorities, a "pledge" from each local authority to the children it looks after, additional resources, particularly for children's education, and better training for social workers.[91] The limited success of previous initiatives indicates that making the very substantial improvements necessary for all looked-after children will require more than legislation, guidance and examples of good practice.

E. The balance of power between court and social services departments

Before the Children Act 1989, the courts could commit children to care in 21–007 custody and wardship proceedings even without an application from a local authority, and could also direct the authority as to how the child should be cared for.[92] However, if the child was in care under other provisions, the courts had no power to review the care arrangements after making the care order. Both the *Short Report* and the *Review of Child Care Law* emphatically rejected the notion that the courts should have a role beyond determining whether an order should be made.[93] The *Review* sought to create a coherent scheme; the local authority should control day-to-day decisions about the care of children, including placement, so as to manage their resources but major decisions such as making or discharging care orders and adoption should be subject to court review.[94] This dichotomy is not without difficulty; placement decisions are crucial to the long-

---

[87] Children Act 1989 s.82.

[88] See below, para.21–084.

[89] See *Children Act 1989 Report 2002* (2003), Ch.1 and *Children Act 1989 Report 2003* (2004), paras 1.26–1.27 for a brief account of these. Some of the targets were unambitious, and others, particularly for the percentage of children placed for adoption, were highly controversial.

[90] (Cm.5860 (2003)); *Every Child Matters: Next Steps* (2004); Children Act 2004. Further details can be found at *http://www.everychildmatters.gov.uk* [Accessed June 5, 2008].

[91] Green Paper: Cm.6932 (2006); White Paper: Cm.7137 (2007); Children and Young Persons Bill 2008.

[92] In practice, the power to commit a child to care was rarely used without an application by the authority, and the courts had no system for monitoring compliance with directions.

[93] *Short Report*, para.71; *Review of Child Care Law*, paras 2.20 *et seq*. Where wardship was used, the court could consider and continue to oversee the arrangements for the child.

[94] *Review of Child Care Law*, para.2.21.

term outcome of care and also affect contact, which in turn affects rehabilitation and discharge from care.

The 1989 Act drew a clear line between the responsibility of the court and the local authority in line with the scheme in the *Review*.[95] Only a local authority can bring care proceedings; the court in private law proceedings can only require it to report on the child's circumstances.[96] The court's control is restricted to the period before the care order is made, and subsequently to matters of contact, emigration and adoption.[97] This was controversial; the courts were uneasy about trusting the local authority, and in some cases attempted to retain control by delaying final care orders or imposing conditions.[98] Nevertheless, in *Re S (Minors) (Care order: Implementation of Care Plan)*[99] the House of Lords refused to endorse a Court of Appeal decision that would have enabled closer supervision of local authority decisions once a care order had been made. Lord Nicholls noted that there was no effective machinery to allow a young child to challenge care decisions after the order had been made, but that this reflected the scheme of the Act.[100] The Children Act was not held to be incompatible with art.6(1), but the Act was amended to create a mechanism that would allow an application to court where failure to implement a care plan might infringe a child in care's Convention rights.[101] The Independent Reviewing Officer (IRO) has a duty to refer the issue to CAFCASS, who may bring proceedings.[102]

II. Modern Childcare Law—Services for Children in Need

A. Family support and prevention[103]

21–008   Children's services were originally focused on looking after children whose parents were prevented from doing so, but services were developed to support children in their families where this diminished the need for them to be received into or kept in state care.[104] In 1983 the Social Services Select Committee

---

[95] *Re S (Minors) (Care Order: Implementation of Care Plan)* [2002] 1 F.L.R.815, HL, *per* Lord Nicholls at para.25.

[96] See above, para.18–048. Judicial Review of a decision not to bring proceedings may be possible: *R. v E Sussex CC Ex p. W* [1998] 2 F.L.R. 1082, QBD.

[97] s.34 Sch.2, para.19; Adoption and Children Act 2002.

[98] See J. Dewar, "The courts and local authority autonomy" [1995] C.F.L.Q. 15; M. Hayes, "The proper role of the court in child care cases" [1996] C.F.L.Q. 20; M. Thorpe and E. Cooke, *Divided Duties* (Bristol: Family Law, 1998).

[99] [2002] 1 F.L.R. 815, overruling the decision in *Re W and B; Re W (Care Plan)* [2001] 2 F.L.R. 582, CA.

[100] At paras 86–88. Even if the scheme of the Act were incompatible a declaration would only be granted to a victim of an actual or proposed breach of a Convention right. The mother's art.6 rights had been met through her appeal; at para.88.

[101] Children Act 1989 s.26(2)(k), (2A), (2B), (2C), added by Adoption and Children Act 1 2002 s.118.

[102] See para.21–069 below for an explanation of the role of the IRO; and see CAFCASS (Reviewed Case Referral) Regulations 2004 (SI 2004/2187). Only one case was referred in the first three years.

[103] See D. Bedingfield, *The child in need*, 2nd edn (Bristol: Family Law, 2008).

[104] Childcare Act 1980 ss.1, 2, replacing the Children Act 1948. The original duty to provide preventative services was added by the Children and Young Persons Act 1963 following the recommendations of the Ingelby Committee (Cmnd.1191 (1960)).

acknowledged the importance of preventive work, but noted a lack of commitment to it within local authorities, and recommended that the power be extended.[105] The *Review of Child Care Law* considered that the emphasis on keeping children out of care placed insufficient stress on general family support and also undermined the role of short-term care as a positive means of helping families.[106] It wanted the duty to be a general one and not owed to individual families and children. There could therefore be no conflict between an authority's duty to take action to protect individual children and its duty to provide family support,[107] nor should it be possible for the courts to review a local authority's policy decisions on allocation of resources to preventive work. Emphasis on preventive work reinforced the notion that the family had the primary responsibility for the care of children, and portrayed the local authority positively as a resource for families in difficulty. The Government accepted this.[108] Part III of and Sch.2 to the Children Act 1989 now set out the duties of local authorities; these are more clearly targeted and owed only to "children in need" and their families.

B. Local authorities' duties to provide family support

The Children Act 1989 s.17(1) imposes general duties on local authorities to provide an appropriate range and level of services to: **21–009**

> "[S]afeguard and promote the welfare of children within their area who are in need; and so far as is consistent with that duty, to promote the upbringing of such children by their families."

Section 17(2) and Sch.2 imposes specific duties to: provide information about services; maintain a register of disabled children; assess children's needs; take reasonable steps to prevent neglect and abuse; and the need to bring children before the courts. These duties must be considered whenever local authorities exercise powers that affect children in need.[109] Local authorities must, in consultation with other agencies, prepare and publish plans for children's services.[110] Local authorities are required to take account of the needs of different racial groups (but only specifically in relation to day-care and fostering) and to make it easier for all separated children to live with or have contact with their

---

[105] *Short Report*, paras 30, 40.
[106] *Review of Child Care Law*, paras 5.7–5.17.
[107] General duties "cannot be tested on a child-by-child basis": *R. v Barnet LBC Ex p. B* [1994] 1 F.L.R. 592 at 611, *per* Auld J.
[108] *The Law on Child Care and Family Services* (Cm.62 (1987)), paras 15–17; *Review of Child Care Law* (1985), Ch.4.
[109] *R. v Wealden DC Ex. p. Wales* [1995] N.P.C. 145; a decision to direct removal of new-age travellers under the Criminal Justice and Public Order Act 1994 was quashed because of failure to consider the children's welfare.
[110] Children Act 1989 Sch.2 para.1A, added by Children Act 1989 (Amendment) (Children's Services Planning) Order 1996 (SI 1996/785).

families.[111] Social services departments are not expected to meet every need,[112] to provide services free of charge where families can pay[113] or to take over the responsibilities of housing authorities:

> In *The Queen on the Application of G v Barnet London Borough Council*,[114] G, a Dutch national of Somali origin with a young child, left the Netherlands, came to London and applied to Barnet for housing. This was refused because she was not habitually resident in the area, and she was referred to social services. Their assessment found that her child was "in need" and that these needs would best be met by returning with his mother to the Netherlands where she had rights to housing and benefits. Barnet offered to pay her travel costs. The mother refused to return and sought Judicial Review of the local authority's decision. The decision was quashed and the local authority appealed. The Court of Appeal reversed the decision and the mother appealed. In the House of Lords, the case was heard with two others[115]; the majority upheld the decisions of the Court of Appeal.[116] The local authority's responsibility under s.17 was to assess needs and to decide how to meet them. The assessment of an individual child did not crystallise the general duty to create an individual one; the local authority was not required to meet all identified needs. Where a parent was homeless, it was legitimate for the local authority to offer s.20 accommodation (fostering or residential care) to the child alone, although in some[117] cases separation of the parent and child might possibly amount to a breach of their art.8(1) rights.

Given finite resources and the infinite nature of need under the wide definition in s.17, it was inevitable that the courts would reject any responsibility for allocation. However, Lord Laming in his Report on the Climbié Inquiry, a case with remarkably similar facts to the *Barnet* case, was critical of the lack of services provided, and rejected the notion that local authorities could distinguish

---

[111] Children Act 1989 Sch.2 Pt I.
[112] *Guidance* (1991), Vol.2, para.2.11. The local authority can therefore take account of the cost of providing a service as in the case of community care: *R. v Gloucester CC Ex p. Barry* [1997] 2 All E.R. 1, HL, but must take account of the impact of its decisions on the child's needs: *R. v Hammersmith and Fulham LBC ex p. D* [1999] 1 F.L.R. 642.
[113] Children Act 1989 s.17(7)–(9); *Guidance* (1991), Vol.2, paras 2.38–2.41. Those on Income Support, Working Tax Credit or other means-tested benefits cannot be charged. There is a regime for levying and enforcing charges for looking after children: Children Act 1989 Sch.2 Pt 3. For a discussion of policy issues relating to charging, see K. Judge and J. Matthews, *Charging for Social Care* (London: Allen and Unwin, 1980).
[114] [2004] 1 F.L.R. 454 HL; [2003] UKHL 57.
[115] *R (A) v Lambeth LBC* [2001] 2 F.L.R 353, CA (social services failed to arrange rehousing for a mother with two severely disabled children); *R (W) v Lambeth LBC* [2002] 2 F.L.R.327, CA (accommodation of intentionally homeless mother and children refused).
[116] Lords Nicholls and Steyn dissented but proposed no relief for G or W. In A's case they suggested that the original judicial review that had been abandoned should be re-instated.
[117] If it were no more expensive to accommodate the parent and child together, and it is in the child's best interests to live with the parent; *per* Lord Nicholls at para.52. Lord Hope noted the wide margin of appreciation given by the Strasbourg Court; at para.69. In *R. ota A v Enfield LBC* [2002] 2 F.L.R. 1, QBD, the decision to refuse an HIV-positive mother accommodation with her child was quashed because of their art.8 rights.

between their support responsibilities and their duties to make child protection inquiries under s.47.[118] He proposed that new guidance be issued to improve consistency in the application of s.17.[119] Destitution amongst families who do not have rights to remain in the United Kingdom is a substantial problem, but one that is largely outside the powers of local authorities. Family support services cannot be provided for children living with such parents. Support is provided through the National Asylum Support Service; local authority responsibilities are limited to child protection and support for unaccompanied asylum-seeking children.[120]

In addition to accommodating children in foster or residential homes, a wide range of services is provided by local authorities. There are family centres offering advice to parents, practical training in childcare and budgeting, social activities for parents and play-groups for children. Some family centres also provide residential facilities to improve the parenting of parents who have had a child removed or are at risk of such action. Some provide play schemes or toy libraries to cater for the needs of children with disabilities.[121] Local authorities need not provide all these services themselves, and should liaise with voluntary organisations.[122] Local authorities may make payments to families in exceptional circumstances,[123] and may provide direct payments to parents of disabled children, or disabled children aged 16 years or over, so that they can purchase their own services.[124]

C. "Children in need"

A child who requires local authority services to maintain or achieve a reasonable standard of health or development or whose health or development will be significantly or further impaired without services, or who is disabled is a "child in need".[125] No indication is given in the statute as to what constitutes a "reasonable standard" of health and development, but it cannot mean merely freedom from significant harm. Whether or not a child is "in need" is a matter for the local authority alone, but a decision that a child is not "in need" is plainly

21–010

---

[118] Cm.5730 (2003), paras 17.99–17.111, and see J. Masson, "The Climbié Inquiry—context and critique"(2006) J. Law and Soc. 33, 221–243.

[119] DH, *What To Do If You're Worried a Child is Being Abused* (2003).

[120] Immigration and Asylum Act 1999 s.122(4); *R. (O) v Haringey LBC and SS for Home Dept* [2004] 2 F.L.R. 476, CA.

[121] For a discussion of the range of services, see *Guidance* (1991), Vol.2, Ch.3. Each local authority is required to publicise its services: Children Act 1989 Sch.2, para.1(2).

[122] Children Act 1989 s.17(5).

[123] Children Act 1989 s.17(6), but are under no duty to do so; *Re K and A (Local Authority: Child Maintenance)* [1995] 1 F.L.R. 688. The requirement for "exceptional circumstances" will be removed if Child and Young Persons Bill 2008 cl.24 is enacted. This provision is used to support children with relatives, instead of providing accommodation and paying fostering allowances.

[124] Children Act 1989 s.17A (the adult who receives payment for a child must have parental responsibility); similar provision is made for adults under the Community Care (Direct Payments) Act 1996.

[125] Children Act 1989 s.17(10). "Disabled" is defined in s.17(11) so the same groups are included as are within the National Assistance Act 1948 s.29.

susceptible to judicial review.[126] Services can be provided for the child's family
or any member of it if they are provided with a view to safeguarding or
promoting the child's welfare.[127] "Family" includes anyone who has parental
responsibility for the child or with whom the child has been living.[128] The
definition is "deliberately wide" to reinforce the emphasis on preventative
services for families,[129] and recognises the part played in caring for children by
significant others[130] but does not expressly include relatives who are willing to
look after a child in the future.[131] In contrast to the position relating to adults, the
duty to assess children's needs is implied rather than clearly expressed in the
Act.[132] Department of Health research indicated that assessment practices were
inadequate with clients matched to existing services, and little attention was
being paid to their particular needs.[133] Detailed guidance on conducting
assessments has now been produced.[134] The *Assessment Framework* is widely
referred to; children's services departments are expected to make an assessment
within a specific time to and complete core assessments before bringing care
proceedings.[135] Where families are dissatisfied because of services provided or
refused, they have a right to complain[136] and may even be able to obtain a review
by the courts, but there is no power in the courts to direct the provision of
services under Pt III.[137]

Most local authorities operate a priority system[138]; in practice this means that
services are focused on families where issues of child maltreatment are evident.
The Department of Health sought to re-orient social work away from child
protection investigations and towards family support by proposing a single
approach to assessment for all children, rather than separate systems for those in

[126] *Re J (Specific Issue Order: Leave to Apply)* [1995] 1 F.L.R. 669 at 673, *per* Wall J. (a specific issue
order could not be used to determine whether a child was "in need").
[127] Children Act 1989 s.17(3).
[128] Children Act 1989 s.17(10); *Re T (Accommodation by Local Authority)* [1995] 1 F.L.R. 159
(friends who were looking after the child were within the definition).
[129] *Guidance* (1991), Vol.2, para.2.7. A statement that conflicts with that in the Financial Statement
issued with the Children Bill, which estimated that the new responsibilities in Pt III would only cost
1.7 million and require 150 extra staff in England and Wales.
[130] *Children Act Now* (2001), p.64.
[131] Once the relative obtained a residence order, the child would form part of their family, but
relatives may prefer informal arrangements. It may be possible for the local authority to assist the
relative under s.17(3) if "family" is used there in the more usual sense of a group of related individuals.
[132] The duty to assess can be derived from Children Act 1989 Sch.2 para.3: *R (G) v Barnet LBC*
[2004] 1 F.L.R. 454 HL, at para.77, *per* Lord Hope; cf. NHS and Community Care Act 1990
s.47(1)(a).
[133] *Children Act Now* (2001), pp.118–122.
[134] DH et al., *Framework for the Assessment of Children in Need and Their Families* (2000) (a
comparable document has been published by the National Assembly for Wales). HM Government,
The Common Assessment Framework for Children and Young People: Practitioners' Guide (2006)
[135] *Guidance* (2008), para.3.18; *Public Law Outline* (2008), para.10.2 and Annex A. A core
assessment should be completed in 35 working days, para.3.16.
[136] Children Act 1989 s.26(3); the complaints service should be used before seeking judicial review:
R. v Kingston upon Thames RBC Ex p. T [1994] 1 F.L.R. 798; see below, para.21–082.
[137] *Re T (judicial review: local authority decisions concerning a child in need)* [2004] 1 F.L.R. 601,
QBD, *per* Wall J. at para.150 (decision on service provision found to be *Wednesbury* unreasonable);
R. (S) v Sutton LBC [2007] 2 F.L.R. 849, QBD (assessment inadequate); and see below,
para.21–082.
[138] Cm.2144, Ch.3; Audit Commission, *Seen But Not Heard* (1994), para.44.

need (s.17) and those requiring protection (s.47).[139] The Department's overview of research on the Children Act, *Children Act Now*, noted that s.17 has been poorly understood, resulting in many problems in its implementation.[140] Local authorities have focused on rationing rather than service development,[141] and used eligibility criteria based on risk to restrict services to cases of abuse and neglect.[142] It has been said that the inadequate implementation of the preventative provisions provides an object lesson in how a rational and humane policy can be undermined by a failure to provide adequate funding.[143]

In order to improve family support, the Government commissioned a census to establish levels of need.[144] In *Every Child Matters*, it recognised that there were significant constraints on increasing family support but noted that it was important that expenditure on public services was harnessed to support parents.[145] It has implemented this idea through a general duty on children's services authorities in the Children Act 2004 s.10 to co-operate with other agencies (partners) in order to improve the wellbeing of children, having regard to the importance to this of parents and carers. Partners are also under a duty to co-operate. Whilst this may break down barriers between agencies and allow them to justify particular expenditure, merely increasing local authority powers will not secure provision of services.

D. Duty to provide accommodation

Children who enter the care system come from the most disadvantaged sections **21–011** of society. This reflects not only the problems their parents face in caring for them, but also the fact that such families are subject to closer scrutiny and social-work practices.[146] Although their parents retain parental responsibility for looked-after children, the local authority has responsibility for their day-to-day care, and often for planning their futures. The local authority is their corporate parent.[147]

The Children Act 1948 imposed a duty on local authorities to receive into their care orphans and children whose parents were incapable of caring for them.[148] State care was used both for short-term needs (e.g. during a mother's illness or imprisonment) and cases of more intractable difficulty where parents were unable or unwilling to provide a home for their children because of their own problems,

[139] W. Rose, Deputy Chief, Social Services Inspector, *Children Act News* No.16, p.1 (1994); DH, *Child Protection: Messages From Research* (1995), p.55. These ideas have been taken forward in the *Framework for Assessment* (2000).
[140] *Children Act Now* (2001), p.22.
[141] Audit Commission, *Seen But Not Heard* (1994), p.19. The Department of Health recognised that lack of resources (staff and funding) contributed to this: *Children Act Now* (2001), p.127.
[142] *Children Act Now* (2001), pp.22 and 117.
[143] *Second Report of Select Committee on Health 1997–8* (HC 247), para.68.
[144] See *Children Act Report 2000* (2001), para.3.7; CiN data is now published annually.
[145] Cm.5860 (2003), para.3.13.
[146] Details of the childcare population can be found in the DCSF, *Children in Care Statistics* for the relevant year, and below. See also A. Bebbington and J. Miles, "The background of children who enter local authority care" (1989) 19 Brit. J. Soc. Wk. 349; H. Cleaver et al., *Children's Needs—Parenting Capacity* (1999) and Sinclair et al., *Pursuit of Permanence*.
[147] DfES, *If This Were My Child* (2003). "A good corporate parent must offer everything that a good parent would" (Cm.7137 (2007)), para.1.7.
[148] Children Act 1948 s.1, repeated in Childcare Act 1980 s.2.

the children's difficult behaviour or a combination of the two.[149] These children were not subject to court orders and could be removed by their parents at any time until the Children Act 1975 gave local authorities greater control over "voluntary care".[150] Changes in childcare policy affected the use made of reception into care. Social workers became more aware of the problems of rehabilitating children in care with their parents,[151] of the inadequacy of state care provided and of the high cost of residential care. The number of children received into voluntary care declined, but the use of compulsory measures of care increased.

The *Review of Child Care Law* considered that the existing framework for caring for children away from home was unsatisfactory for four reasons: (1) the respective powers of parents and local authorities were unclear, and this could lead to disputes; (2) some parents were reluctant to use care because they feared that they would not get their child back; (3) there was stigma associated with care; and (4) participation by parents, which was crucial to rehabilitation, was too low. The *Review* therefore recommended the replacement of voluntary care with "shared care", which provided more clearly for a genuine and voluntary partnership between parents and the local authority.[152] The Government accepted that care should be a service to families, provided so far as possible on a basis of partnership with parents.[153] Agreements should be made to cover such matters as the initial placement, schooling, access and notice prior to return home; changes in arrangements should also be settled by agreement.

21–012   The Children Act 1989 s.20(1) imposes a duty on local authorities to provide accommodation for children in need who require it as a result of:

"(a) [T]here being no person who has parental responsibility for him;

(b) [their] being lost or having been abandoned; or

(c) the person who has been caring for him being prevented (whether or not permanently, and for whatever reason) from providing him with suitable accommodation or care."

There are two distinct legal problems associated with this provision: (1) local authorities may seek to avoid their responsibilities; and (2) parents may be unwilling to agree to their child being accommodated.

If a child is accommodated, the local authority must provide maintenance; substantial further "leaving care" duties to provide support and assistance up to

---

[149] Such children were "victims, villains and the volunteered": see J. Packman, L. Randall and N. Jacques, *Who Needs Care?* (Oxford: Blackwell, 1986). This study has been repeated following the implementation of the Children Act: J. Packman and C. Hall, *From Care To Accommodation* (London: TSO, 1998).

[150] Children Act 1975 s.56 (Childcare Act 1980 s.13) parents could be required to give 28-days' notice before removing their child, and the local authority could pass a resolution or use wardship to prevent removal; see fifth edition of this work at p.597.

[151] In 1984, Millham and his colleagues concluded that the first six weeks of care were crucial to achieving rehabilitation. S. Millham et al., *Lost in Care* (Aldershot: Gower, 1986); and DH, *Patterns and Outcomes in Child Placement* (London: HMSO, 1991).

[152] *Review of Child Care Law*, paras 7.3–7.4.

[153] Cm.62 (1987), paras 21 *et seq.*

age 21 are owed to those who were accommodated for a period of at least 13 weeks, ending after the age of 16.[154] Consequently, a local authority may seek to limit their expenditure by refusing accommodation or making other arrangements that involve lesser duties.:

> In *R. (Berhe) v Hillingdon London Borough Council*[155] four unaccompanied asylum-seeking children were placed in a house by the local authority and provided with financial support. It subsequently refused them leaving-care support on the basis that they had never been accommodated under s.20, only assisted under s.17. Their claim for judicial review was accepted.
>
> In *Southwark London Borough Council v D*[156] a 14-year-old girl complained to her teacher that her father had attacked her. The teacher contacted the children's services department and a social worker came to the school and told her father that she could no longer stay with him. He accepted this. The social worker then contacted the father's former girlfriend who had cared for D before, and asked her to look after her. She agreed, but after the local authority refused to provide financial support she sought judicial review, claiming that she was fostering the child. The local authority argued that it had merely facilitated a private fostering arrangement for the father, but the Court of Appeal held that the girl had been accommodated. This was the most likely conclusion in a case where the local authority had taken a major role and the carer had not clearly consented to a private arrangement.[157]

Where possible, local authorities seek to secure that young people can remain with their families. Respite care, regular planned admissions for children with disabilities and some others has developed to be a major form of family support.[158] The Government has proposed that parents of some children with disabilities should have a right to such respite care, and that children supported in this way should not be treated as looked-after children.[159]

Although the s.20 duty applies to all children under age 18, it is further qualified in relation to those over the age of 16, limiting it to cases where the welfare of the child is likely to be "seriously prejudiced" if accommodation is not provided.[160] It is not clear that parents have a duty to maintain children over 16, and over 16s may apparently leave home, but their wish to do so does not

[154] Children Act 1989 ss.23A–24E and see below, para.21–071.
[155] [2004] 1 F.L.R. 439, QBD. The DfES subsequently introduced a scheme to support local authorities who found they were looking after substantial numbers of such young people: DCSF, *Unaccompanied Asylum-seeking Children Leaving Care Costs 2007–8 Guidance* (2007).
[156] [2007] 1 F.L.R. 2181, CA
[157] *Per* Smith L.J. at para.49.
[158] J. Aldgate and M. Bradley, *Supporting Families through Short-term Fostering* (London: TSO, 1999). There is a special regime for such placements: Arrangement for Placement of Children (General) Regulations 1991 (SI 1991/890) r.13; Fostering Services Regulations 2002 (SI 2002/57) r.37; for Wales; (SI 2003/237).
[159] Cm.7137 (2007), paras 2.31–2.33. A right to such breaks was added to the Children and Young Persons Bill 2008 cl.25.
[160] Children Act 1989 s.20(3). The possibility of support under s.17 is unlikely to justify refusal of accommodation for a child in need who is over 16 years of age: *Re T (Accommodation by Local Authority)* [1995] 1 F.L.R. 159 at 162.

entitle them to state provision.[161] Local authorities also have a power to provide any child with accommodation to safeguard or promote his or her welfare, and may provide accommodation in a community home for anyone aged between 16 and 21 in such circumstances.[162] However, few young people are provided for in this way.[163] Young homeless people have a priority need to housing, and may therefore be provided with accommodation by a housing authority. Where such provision is made, the leaving-care duties do not arise.[164] Young people aged 16 and 17 may request services on their own behalf.[165]

E. Voluntary agreement

21–013 The Children Act Pt III does not give local authorities any power to impose services; families have a right to receive sympathetic support and cannot be required to co-operate.[166] Children under 16[167] may not be provided with accommodation if a person with parental responsibility who is able or willing to accommodate them objects; nor can parents who have agreed to residential care be forced to accept foster care for their child:

> In *R. v Tameside MBC Ex p. J*[168] the local authority had accommodated a severely disabled girl in a residential home with her parents' agreement. The plan was for the girl to remain in residential care, with regular contact with her family who lived locally. The local authority then planned a move to a foster home; the parents, who objected, sought judicial review. The court held that the local authority's power to look after the child did not extend to making a placement[169] against parents' wishes, and endorsed the partnership approach set out in *Guidance*.[170]

Children who are accommodated may be removed by anyone with parental responsibility who will arrange for their care.[171] Court orders may not be made

---

[161] See *Homelessness Code of Guidance* (2006), paras 12.07–12.11.

[162] Children Act 1989 s.20(4), (5). Children over 16 may choose to leave at any time: s.20(11).

[163] See *Children in Care Statistics* (series A/F/12) and *Children Act Report 1995–1999* (2001), para.6.5.

[164] Housing Act 1996 s.188; *R. (M) v London Borough of Hammersmith and Fulham* [2007] 1 F.L.R. 256, CA (a local authority is entitled to consider a child's application for housing without referring the case to the children's services department); and see *Homelessness Code of Guidance* (2006), Ch.12.

[165] This is not explicitly stated in the Act, but the DHSS, *Review of Child Care Law* (Discussion paper No.2, 1985), paras 38–72 concluded that there was such a right, and the House of Lord's decision in *Gillick v W Norfolk and Wisbech AHA* [1986] A.C. 112 would seem to support this. It is clear that children over 16 cannot be removed from local authority accommodation by their parents against their will; see Children Act 1989 s.20(11).

[166] *Guidance* (1991), Vol.2, para.2.7.

[167] Children Act 1989 s.20(11); this apparently applies irrespective of the child's maturity.

[168] [2000] 1 F.L.R. 942, QBD.

[169] Counsel for the parents accepted that the local authority could substitute one residential home and another; at para.949D.

[170] *Guidance* (1991), Vol.2, paras 2.10–2.14, 2.50.

[171] Children Act 1989 s.20(7)–(10), unless another person with a residence order, special guardianship or care and control under the inherent jurisdiction agrees to accommodation; s.20(9). The objection of someone with parental responsibility who is unable or unwilling to care for the child may be discounted: s.20(7).

preventing removal of a child from local authority accommodation; nor may parents be required to give undertakings to this effect.[172] If there is a residence order, the child may enter or remain in local authority accommodation providing all of the people with the order agree to this.[173] Notice of removal is no longer required; nor can written agreements that impose it be enforced.[174] Several attempts were made during the passage of the Children Bill to add such a provision, but all were rejected by the Government because a notice requirement would undermine the voluntary nature of the arrangement and discourage those who needed the service from using it.[175] The Government accepted that it was good practice to prepare a child for any move, but this should not be forced on an unwilling parent. Nevertheless, the Lord Chancellor suggested that foster-parents were entitled by s.3(5) to refuse to hand over a child late at night or to a drunken parent, and that this provided adequate protection for the child.[176] This interpretation probably cannot be sustained. In *Lewisham London Borough v Lewisham Juvenile Court*[177] the House of Lords held that the comparable duty in the 1980 Act did not compel the child's return to an unfit parent because the local authority had a duty to keep the child so long as his or her welfare required.[178] Also, the Court of Appeal held that the 1948 Act imposed no absolute duty on the local authority to return the child,[179] and a mandatory injunction was refused because both the foster parents and the child (who was almost 18 at the hearing of the appeal) were unwilling for her to return home. In contrast, the Children Act 1989 appears to give a person with parental responsibility an unqualified right to remove the child,[180] and this must be interpreted as compatible with art.8 rights.

Despite these provisions, the right to remove a child from accommodation may be illusory. Where the local authority considers that removal would put a child at risk of significant harm, it can ask the police to use their emergency powers to detain him or her, or apply to the court for an emergency protection order.[181] These powers are frequently used, reflecting the use of accommodation for child protection. Alternatively, a foster carer may make the child a ward of court or

---

[172] Children Act 1989 ss.9(5), 100(2)(b): *Re S and D (Children: Powers of the Court)* [1995] 2 F.L.R. 456, CA; *Re B (Supervision Order: Parental Undertaking)* [1996] 1 F.L.R. 676, CA.

[173] Children Act 1989 s.20(9).

[174] This may not be understood by parents, particularly if they are informed that a court order will be sought if they attempt to remove the child.

[175] See *Hansard*, HL Vol.502, cols 1337, 1342–1344; Children Bill, Committee Stage; Vol.503, cols 1411–1413, Report Stage; Vol.512, cols 737–739, Consideration of Commons Amendments.

[176] *Hansard*, HL Vol.505, cols 370–371, Children Bill, Third Reading. *Guidance* (1991), Vol.3 is silent on this but advises of the use of emergency protection orders where removal could be harmful (para.2.66).

[177] [1980] A.C. 273.

[178] Childcare Act 1980 s.1(2). Lords Salmon and Keith suggested that the local authority had no right to retain the child, even though the parent demanding his return was incapable; at paras 290H, 301F.

[179] *Krishnan v Sutton LBC* [1970] Ch. 181.

[180] Foster parents are required to sign an undertaking to allow the local authority to remove the child; Fostering Services Regulations 2002 (SI 2002/57) r.36 and Sch.5 para.15. Where they breach their undertaking, the local authority may remove the child without permission or may take proceedings.

[181] In practice, local authorities resort to compulsory powers when parents seek to remove children inappropriately; J. Masson et al., *Protecting Powers* (2007), pp.90 and 151.

seek a residence order, but this could jeopardise their financial support from the local authority.[182]

21–014   Accommodation is used in a broad range of circumstances; almost half the children who enter public care do so because of abuse or neglect, and another third because of family dysfunction, acute family stress or lack of a carer.[183] When a child needs to be protected, social workers are expected to seek parental agreement for accommodation in preference to using emergency powers,[184] but must establish clearly that they have consent for the removal of a child:

> In *R. (G) v Nottingham City Council*[185] a troubled young woman who had been in the care of the local authority was shortly to give birth. The local authority prepared a birth plan for the baby to be immediately cared for in a separate ward, an arrangement that amounted to accommodation of the baby under s.20. They showed this to the mother and she made no objections. The plan was carried out and the mother sought judicial review. Munby J. held that the fact that the mother who had just given birth had raised no objection was not sufficient consent for her baby's accommodation; written consent was not required. The local authority should have sought an EPO.

Before bringing care proceedings, the local authority must explore whether a child can be cared for safely by a relative or friend.[186] This is intended to avoid unnecessary proceedings and ensure that cases are better prepared when applications are made.[187] Parents' rights are protected by the provision of legal aid for advice about care arrangements when a local authority plans such proceedings.[188]

Given that child protection concerns are the main trigger for local authorities offering services, questions arise about the extent to which parents are freely accepting services. Although there is evidence that agreements with parents have enabled local authorities to avoid lengthy court proceedings, research also raises

---

[182] There are restrictions on the use of wardship by local authorities and in relation to children subject to care orders: s.100, and above, para.18–049. A foster-carer may require leave to apply for a residence order: above, 19–034. Allowances may be paid to foster parents who obtain residence orders: Children Act 1989 Sch.1 para.15.

[183] DCSF, *Looked After Children Statistics year ending March 2007* (2007), Table C1 (but this includes children who first enter state care on court orders). Concerns about abuse and neglect were even higher in a sample of children who were accommodated: see J. Packman and C. Hall, *From Care to Accommodation* (1998), p.134.

[184] Children Act 1989 ss.44–46 and below, paras 21–041–21–050; J. Masson, "Emergency intervention to protect children: using and avoiding legal controls" [2005] C.F.L.Q. 75; Masson et al., *Protecting Powers*, p.141.

[185] [2008] EWHC 400 (Admin).

[186] *Guidance* (2008), paras 3.24 and 3.32. It is accepted that there will be cases where proceedings must be started without delay; para.3.30.

[187] DfES, *Review of the Care Proceedings System* (2006), paras 3.10 and 4.1: J. Masson, "Reforming care proceedings—time for a review" [2007] C.F.L.Q. 411, and below, para.21–054.

[188] *Guidance* (2008), para.3.26 and Annex 1, but only if a "letter before proceedings" has been issued.

concerns about pressure on parents to accept accommodation for their children,[189] the delay in bringing proceedings[190] and (conversely) inappropriate resort to court.[191] It is likely that changes to the care-proceedings system introduced in April 2008[192] will lead to greater use of voluntary arrangements. Although provision has been made for advice to parents, the protection of children's interests will be left to parents and social workers, rather than being overseen by the court as it is in care proceedings.[193]

F. Co-operation between authorities

Services for children in need cannot be met by one agency but demand the **21–015** pooling of skills and resources from many areas[194] such as housing, special education and health. The Children Act 1989 established a framework for co-operation by giving local authorities a power to request help from another local authority and from education, housing or NHS authorities.[195] Those agencies must comply with the request if it is compatible with their own statutory duties and obligations and does not unduly prejudice the discharge of any of their functions.[196] There has been wasteful litigation between local authorities in an attempt to avoid responsibility for children and families with connections elsewhere.[197] It has been stressed that the "game of pass the parcel" has no place in this field.[198] However, in *R. v Northavon District Council Ex p. Smith*[199] the House of Lords refused judicial review where a housing authority rejected a request from social services to rehouse an intentionally homeless family.[200] The court could not decide the form co-operation between authorities should take.[201]

In *Every Child Matters*, the Government proposed new organisations, Children's Trusts (including social care, education and some health services) and duties on a wide range of agencies to work in partnership with these Trusts to

---

[189] J. Hunt et al., *The Last Resort* (London: TSO, 1999); *Children Act Now* (2001), p.51.
[190] *Children Act Now* (2001), p.52; Hunt et al., *The Last Resort*; J. Packman and C. Hall, *From Care to Accommodation: Children Act Now* (2001), p.51.
[191] *Children Act Now* (2001), p.143. The Department of Health has expressed concern that proceedings should not be used indiscriminately.
[192] *Guidance* (2008) and the Public Law Outline; below, para.21–054.
[193] See below, para.21–055.
[194] *Children Act Now* (2001), p.96.
[195] Children Act 1989 s.27(3); help can also be requested from health authorities, NHS Trusts and the NSPCC.
[196] Children Act 1989 s.27(2), but it has been held that this does not require one department within a unitary authority to comply with a request from the social services department: *R. v Tower Hamlets LBC Ex p. Byas* (1992) 25 H.L.R. 109.
[197] *R. ota Stewart v London Borough of Wandsworth* [2001] EWHC Admin. 709 (s.17); *Northamptonshire CC v Islington LBC* [2000] 2 W.L.R. 193, CA (care order); *R. v Lambeth LBC, Ex p. Caddell* [1998] 1 F.L.R. 253, QBD (s.24).
[198] *Per* Lord Donaldson M.R., *R. v Tower Hamlets LBC Ex p. Begum* [1993] 1 All E.R. 447 at 456.
[199] [1994] 2 F.L.R. 671, HL.
[200] Housing authorities owe only limited duties to those who are intentionally homeless but have a priority need for housing: Housing Act 1996 s.190. They must secure temporary accommodation and provide assistance.
[201] *R. v Northavon DC Ex p. Smith* [1994] 2 F.L.R. 671 at 677, *per* Lord Templeman.

promote children's wellbeing.[202] The Children Act 2004 s.10 largely implements these proposals. Local authorities and their partners (which include the organisations responsible for local housing, the police, health, youth offending teams, probation and training for young people) are required to co-operate to improve children's wellbeing. They can operate pooled budgets, share resources and can therefore commission services jointly.[203] Substantial guidance on joint commissioning, generally and on specific types of service, has been prepared, but it is too early to see whether this is making a real difference in support for families.

III. The Child Protection System

A. Child abuse and neglect[204]

21–016 It is widely accepted that child maltreatment is a socially constructed phenomenon that reflects the values and opinions of a particular culture at a particular time.[205] Ill-treatment of children by their parents was recognised as a social problem in the nineteenth century. A number of voluntary organisations, including the National Society for the Prevention of Cruelty to Children (NSPCC), were established to improve the lot of abandoned, neglected and ill-treated children by rescuing them from the streets, by encouraging and cajoling their parents to act responsibly and by campaigning for legislation that would enable them to be protected.[206] However, it was not until the early 1960s that the extent and nature of the problem of child abuse began to be recognised in Britain.[207] American paediatricians had identified injuries commonly found together in young children—fractures of different ages to the long bones and subdural haematoma (a collection of blood immediately below the skull)—and suggested that these were caused by violent parents.[208] Henry Kempe, now recognised as a leading authority on child abuse, termed this the "battered child syndrome".[209]

---

[202] Cm.5860 (2003), Ch.5.

[203] Children Act 2004 s.10(6)(7).

[204] See B. Corby, *Child Abuse towards a Knowledge Base* (Maidenhead: Open University Press, 2006); NSPCC, *Child Maltreatment in the United Kingdom: A Study of the Prevalence of Child Abuse and Neglect* (2000); HM Government, *Working Together to Safeguard Children* (2006) (referred to below as *Working Together* (2006)), paras 1.29–1.33.

[205] See M. Brandon et al., *Safeguarding Children with the Children Act 1989* (London: TSO, 1999), p.2; DH, *Child Protection: Messages From Research* (1995); N. Parton, *The Politics of Child Abuse* (1985).

[206] See Pinchbeck and Hewitt, *Children in English Society*, p.622; Hendrick, *Child Welfare*, pp.49–67.

[207] For an account of developments up to 1969, see J. Eekelaar, R. Dingwall and T. Murray, "Victims or threats? Children in care proceedings" [1982] J.S.W.L. 67 and Hendrick, pp.242–246.

[208] J. Caffey, "Multiple fractures of the long bones of infants suffering chronic subdural haematoma" (1945) 55 *American Journal of Roentgenology* 1; Caffey did not identify parents as causing the injuries, but his work led to further investigations and articles that did; see Parton *The Politics of Child Abuse*, pp.49–54.

[209] See C.H. Kempe et al., "The battered child syndrome" (1962) 181 *Journal of the American Medical Association* 17; R. Kempe and C.H. Kempe, *Child Abuse* (Chicago University Press, 1978); R. Helfer and R. Kempe (eds), *The Battered Child*, 4th edn, (Fontana, 1987).

Child abuse is not limited to such injuries; indeed, such multiply-injured children are now rare amongst those identified as abused.[210] Burns, bruising (particularly as a result of shaking), squeezing or gripping and bite marks are frequently associated with child abuse, but what is abusive parenting cannot simply be determined from the occurrence of individual incidents. Most behaviour needs to be seen in context before it can be thought of as maltreatment.[211] An understanding of normal patterns of parenting,[212] children's needs and of the impact of styles of parenting on children is important for those making decisions about whether action should be taken to intervene in a family.[213] Children are still neglected: insufficient attention to physical care, hygiene and feeding leads to stunted growth and poor general development, a condition termed "failure to thrive". Children who receive adequate physical care may fail to develop normally where they are emotionally neglected or abused.[214] Parenting styles that are low on warmth and high on criticism are associated with poor outcomes for children.[215] A few parents fabricate symptoms so that their children are subject to repeated medical intervention.[216] Neglected children are sometimes also victims of physical or sexual abuse; some suffer injury because they are inadequately supervised. Sexual abuse has been defined as:

"[T]he involvement of dependent, developmentally immature children and adolescents in sexual activities that they do not fully comprehend and to which they are unable to give informed consent or that violate the social taboos of family roles."[217]

It includes molestation, sexual intercourse (oral, vaginal or anal), rape,[218] the involvement of children in prostitution and the creation of pornography.[219] It is sometimes perpetrated by organised groups who prey on children of members and others.

Child maltreatment is not confined to particular classes or family types. However, families whose children are dealt with by the child protection system

---

[210] D. Jones, et al., *Understanding Child Abuse*, 2nd edn, (1987), p.69 (for a description of the main physical manifestations of abuse and neglect, see pp.70–88).

[211] DH, *Child Protection: Messages From Research*, p.14.

[212] DH, *Child Protection: Messages From Research*, p.12; M. Smith and M. Grocke, *Normal Family Sexuality and Sexual Knowledge in Children* (1995); M. Smith et al., *Parental Control Within the Family: The Nature and Extent of Parental Violence to Children* (1995).

[213] DH, *Child Protection: Messages From Research*, p.15; H. Cleaver et al., *Children's Needs— Parenting Capacity* (1999), p.45.

[214] For examples of emotional abuse, see J. Furnell, P. Dutton and J. Harris, "Emotional abuse: references to a Scottish children's panel reporter over 5 years" (1988) 28 *Medicine, Science & Law* 219.

[215] DH, *Child Protection: Messages From Research*, p.19.

[216] The term "FII" (fabricated or induced illness) is now used for this condition; *Working Together* (2006), para.6.4

[217] M. Schechter and L. Roberge, "Sexual exploitation", in R. Helfer and C.H. Roberge (eds), *Child Abuse and Neglect: The Family and The Community* (Cambridge, Mass.: Ballinger, 1976). This definition was adopted in the *Cleveland Report* (1988), para.4.

[218] See, generally, J. La Fontaine, *Child Sexual Abuse* (Cambridge: Polity, 1990); *Cleveland Report* (1988), Ch.11 and Apps. F and L; *Working Together* (2006) paras 1.32, 6.2, 6.8 and 11.58.

[219] W. Utting, *People Like Us* (1997), pp.97–104; *Working Together* (2006), para.6.2. Young prostitutes should therefore be regarded as victims, not offenders.

differ from the population as a whole.[220] Over a third of them are headed by a lone parent, and in less than a third do both natural parents reside with the children. Nearly three-fifths lack a wage earner, and over half are dependent on Income Support. At least a quarter of the women are victims of domestic violence, and the lives of nearly a sixth of families are disrupted by mental illness. Many of the parents have been abused or were in care as children.[221]

21–017   The British public's awareness of child abuse was heightened following the death of Maria Colwell in 1971. Maria had been removed from her mother as a baby by a court order and fostered with an aunt and uncle. Her mother subsequently re-ordered her life, remarried and sought Maria's return. The care order was discharged, but Maria was neglected and finally died of multiple injuries aged seven and a half, despite the existence of a supervision order and a number of calls to the social services department and the NSPCC about her. The DHSS set up an inquiry that received wide publicity and set the tone for media coverage of child abuse.[222]

Hundreds of inquiries into child deaths have taken place since 1973[223]; most have identified failures by the agencies involved to co-operate with each other so as to identify signs of abuse, assess the quality of parental care and monitor the child's progress. Although frequently social workers have been blamed, prior to the Children Act 1989 the law was also seen as providing an inadequate framework for child protection because it was too difficult for social workers to understand, did not help to secure long-term placements and failed to ensure that the court had a complete picture of the child's situation.[224] The response of the Government has been to issue detailed guidance on the organisation of the child protection system and the handling of individual cases[225] and detailed guidance on assessment.[226]

Social work involvement with child sexual abuse began to increase in the mid 1980s following similar developments in the United States in the 1970s. Public consciousness was also raised by an inquiry.[227] In the spring of 1987, in Cleveland, there was a dramatic rise in the number of cases in which child sexual abuse was diagnosed. Over a hundred children were admitted to hospital

---

[220] DH, *Child Protection: Messages From Research*, p.25. Mental illness, substance abuse and domestic violence were even more frequent amongst parents whose children were the subject of care proceedings; see H. Cleaver et al. (1999), p.21

[221] J. Gibbons et al., *Operating the Child Protection System* (London: HMSO, 1995), Ch.4; drug and alcohol abuse is now a major factor: Advisory Council on Drug Misuse, *Hidden Harm* (2003).

[222] DHSS, *Report of the Committee of Inquiry Into the Care and Supervision Provided in Relation to Maria Colwell* (1974); see also Parton (1985), Ch.4.

[223] DHSS, *Child Abuse: A Study of Inquiry Reports* (1982); *1980–1989* (1991); R. Sinclair and R. Bullock, *Learning From Past Experience* (London: DoH, 2002), p.3 indicates about 90 serious case reviews each year.

[224] The Children Act 1975 remedied some of these defects, but piecemeal reform added to the problems caused by the complexity and volume of legislation.

[225] HM Government, *Working Together to Safeguard Children* (2006). The original circular on child protection was issued in 1974; see Parton *The Politics of Child Abuse*, pp.102–109.

[226] DH et al., *A Framework for the Assessment of Children in Need and Their Families* (2000).

[227] *Report of the Inquiry into Child Abuse in Cleveland 1987* (Cm.412 (1988)) (*Cleveland Report*); a brief account is contained in the short version of the report; Cm.413 (1988). For alternative accounts, see B. Campbell, *Unofficial Secrets* (London: Virago, 1988); S. Bell, *When Salem came to the Boro'* (London: Pan, 1988). For a Scottish parallel, see the *Report of the Inquiry Into the Removal of Children from Orkney February 1991* (HC 195 (1992)).

following such diagnosis, and their siblings were also removed for examination and protection under emergency court orders. The health service, the courts and the social services department could not deal adequately with the number of cases. Co-operation between the police and the social services department broke down so that it became difficult to investigate cases and prepare further action. There was widespread disbelief that child sexual abuse could have been identified in so many cases, and also considerable scepticism, particularly amongst the medical profession and the police, about one method of diagnosis (reflex anal dilatation)[228] that was given considerable prominence in the press. Aggrieved parents brought the matter to public attention, and a statutory inquiry[229] was held under the chairmanship of Dame Elizabeth Butler-Sloss, then a High Court Judge.

The *Cleveland Report* acknowledged that child sexual abuse was wide-spread[230] and that more information was needed about its incidence and identification, but gave the impression that the diagnosis had been incorrect in a large proportion of cases.[231] The report attributed the crisis to lack of communication and understanding amongst the agencies involved, but also criticised individuals and recommended changes to child protection law and practice.[232] Many of the changes in practice were accepted by the DHSS and incorporated in departmental guidance.[233] Legal changes that followed earlier government proposals were incorporated in the Children Act 1989.[234]

21–018

Inquiries in the 1990s alerted the public to the vulnerability of children who are looked after away from home. These have made local authorities aware of the need to vet staff and inspect homes,[235] and led to the establishment of stronger safeguards against unsuitable people working with or caring for children.[236] Lord

---

[228] C. Hobbs and J. Wynne, "Buggery in childhood—a common syndrome of child abuse" [1986] *The Lancet* 792; and see RCPCH, *Guidelines on Paediatric Forensic Examinations in Relation to Possible Child Sexual Abuse* (2007)

[229] Under National Health Service Act 1977 s.84 and Childcare Act 1980 s.76. Inquiries Act 2005 s.1 now makes provision for inquiries.

[230] *Cleveland Report*, p.243, para.1.

[231] The report was written in such a way that it was impossible to determine whether individual cases had been confirmed, but p.244, para.13 recorded that: "Most of the 121 children diagnosed by Drs Higgs and Wyatt as sexually abused, were separated from their parents and their home by place of safety orders. The majority have now returned home, some with all proceedings dismissed, others on conditions of medical examinations and supervision orders." The fact that children returned home does not necessarily mean that abuse did not occur.

[232] *ibid.* Pt 3, paras 2, 17; pp.245–253.

[233] DHSS, *Working Together* (1988); DH, *Diagnosis of Child Sexual Abuse: Guidance for Doctors* (1994).

[234] The report "strongly endorsed" the proposals in Cm.62 (1987) and recommended that courts should have more control over contact and medical examinations in child protection proceedings: pp.252–253. See now Children Act 1989 ss.38(1), (6) and 44(6). The report also recommended the continuation of wardship for care cases, and a Family Court but these proposals were not accepted.

[235] A. Levy and B. Kahan, *The Pindown Experience and the Protection of Children* (1991); A. Kirkwood, *The Leicestershire Inquiry* (Leicester CC, 1992) (into the management of children's homes following the conviction of Frank Beck for buggery); *Lost in Care* (HC 201 (2000) (the *Waterhouse Report*); W. Utting *op. cit.* and C. Wolmar, *Forgotten Children* (2000).

[236] DH, *Choosing With Care* (1992) (*Warner Report*); Protection of Children Act 1999; Care Standards Act 2000 s.22; Safeguarding Vulnerable Groups Act 2006.

Laming's inquiry into the death of Victoria Climbié[237] examined the operation of the child protection system more widely, including the work of police child protection units, communication between hospitals, police and social services departments and the management of safeguarding work. Lord Laming made over a hundred recommendations for improvement of practice and reform to the child protection system, including establishing new structures for children's services, a national database for children and new guidance. The Government responded by accepting some of the proposals, issuing *Every Child Matters*[238] and legislating its reforms in the Children Act 2004. Statutory Local Safeguarding Children Boards have been established to replace Area Child Protection Committees, and a wide range of agencies whose work includes services for children and families have been given statutory responsibilities for safeguarding children's welfare.[239] In addition, a series of joint inspections were carried out to assess the progress that agencies had made in improving practice.[240]

B. Intervention in family life

21–019 The limits of parental freedom to determine how their children should be raised and the role of the state in protecting children have been the subject of considerable debate.[241] The appropriate standard or threshold for state intervention in family life and how this should be determined are central to this debate. The placing of the threshold is influenced by moral and legal questions and pragmatic concerns, such as whether the local authority will be able to provide adequate care.[242] Evidence of outcomes and of parents' and children's concerns should contribute decisions about what is and what is not abusive.[243]

Before the implementation of the Children Act 1989 there were a large number of ways in which a child could be made the subject of local authority care compulsorily.[244] The DHSS noted that the statutory code had both strengths and weaknesses. The grounds were sufficiently widely drawn and had become familiar to those working with them, but there were variations in interpretation, some technical difficulties and a general problem of complexity.[245] Changes were

---

[237] Cm.5730 (2003); DFES et al., *Keeping Children Safe* (Cm.5861 (2003)) (the Government's response to the *Laming Report*); N. Parton, "From Maria Colwell to Victoria Climbié: reflections on public inquiries into child abuse a generation apart" (2004) *Child Abuse Review* 13, 80.

[238] Cm.5860 (2003).

[239] Children Act 2004 ss.11 and 13–16.

[240] See: *http://www.safeguardingchildren.org.uk* [Accessed June 5, 2008].

[241] M. Wald, "State intervention on behalf of 'neglected' children: a search for realistic standards" (1975) 27 *Standford Law Review* 985–1040; J. Goldstein, A. Freud and A. Solnit, *Before the Best Interests of the Child* (London: Burnett, 1979); and E. Szwed, "The best interests syndrome and the allocation of power in child care" in H. Geach and E. Szwed (eds), *Providing Civil Justice for Children* (London: Arnold, 1983); R. Dingwall, J. Eekelaar and T. Murray, *The Protection of Children*, Ch.10; DH, *Child Protection: Messages From Research*, p.15; R. Hetherington, *Protecting Children: Messages From Europe* (Lyme Regis: Russell House, 1997).

[242] DH, *Child Protection: Messages From Research*, p.15.

[243] DH, *Child Protection: Messages From Research*, p.17; H. Cleaver et al. *Children's Needs*.

[244] M.D.A. Freeman, "The legal battlefield of 'care' " (1982) 35 C.L.P. 117 at 118, and see the sixth edition of this work at p.790.

[245] *Review of Child Care Law* (Discussion paper 3), paras 19, 66–115; *Review of Child Care Law*, paras 15.6–15.9.

essential to simplify the law, to provide a coherent basis for intervention[246] and to restore faith in the system.[247]

The *Review of Child Care Law* examined proposals for committal to care based on a welfare test, but rejected them because this would lead to "widely varying and subjective interpretations . . . and [would] fail to offer (the family) the degree of statutory protection against unwarranted interference" that was essential.[248] For the same reason it rejected an "exceptional circumstances" criterion.[249] The court's power to commit a child to care in matrimonial, domestic and guardianship proceedings (but not in wardship) should be abolished[250]; changing the grounds for care proceedings and other improvements would reduce the need to resort to the High Court, but wardship should be retained as a safety net. The Law Commission disagreed; the existence of this broad jurisdiction "made nonsense" of carefully devised checks and balances in the statutory codes.[251] The *Review* proposed a standard for intervention based on actual or likely harm, where "harm" connoted a substantial deficit and rejected any grounds based on specific incidents or conditions. The court would be expressly required to find that parental care fell below an objectively acceptable level.[252]

The Government accepted the threshold for intervention proposed by the **21–020** *Review of Child Care Law* and agreed that exceptions should not be permitted. Although there was a danger that the new grounds might not cover all cases, other jurisdictions managed without a safety net like wardship. The Lord Chancellor reasoned that:

> "The integrity and independence of the family is a basic building block of a free and democratic society and the need to defend it should be clearly perceivable in law."[253]

Retaining wardship would give the courts, not local authorities, control over care. Also, the proposed system for concurrent jurisdiction required that all courts applied the same principles. The Lord Chancellor commented that the new test

---

[246] *Short Report*, para.117.
[247] *Review of Child Care Law* (Discussion paper 3), *op cit.* paras 19, 66–115; *Review of Child Care Law* supported by evidence: R. Dingwall et al. *The Protection of Children* (1983), p.225. There were wide variations between authorities in the extent that protection proceedings were used: see J. Packman et al. *Who needs care?* and Packman and Hall *From Care to Accommodation.*
[248] *Review of Child Care Law*, para.15.10. Judges of the Family Division were reported to have said that such a test, if applied literally, would lead to "a substantial proportion of the child population . . . [being] taken into care . . . [because] they would be better off with foster parents". However, it is now proposed that the child's welfare should be the main ground for dispensing with parental consent to adoption: see Adoption and Children Act 2002, s.52(1)(b).
[249] *Review of Child Care Law*, para.15.11.
[250] *Review of the Child Care Law*, para.15.35–15.38.
[251] Law Com. WP, *Wards of Court* (1987), paras 4.9–10. No proposals to abolish local authority use of wardship were included in the report; see Law Com. No.172, para.1.4.
[252] *Review of Child Care Law*, paras 15.23, 15.20.
[253] Lord Mackay, "Perceptions of the Children Bill and beyond" [1989] New L.J. 505 at 507.

for intervention in the Children Act should not be regarded as grounds for an order but as:

> "the minimum circumstances which the government considers should always be found to exist before . . . the state should be enabled to intervene compulsorily in family life."[254]

A single route for child protection proceedings does not mean that there is a uniform standard for intervention. Child protection is a process that involves a number of stages where social workers and other professionals have to decide whether they should take further action.[255] Thresholds vary over time and between authorities[256]; different professionals have different views.[257] It has been said that the state cannot spare children all the consequences of defective parenting[258]; also, that only the most extreme cases require adjudication by the courts.[259] Research indicates that the 1989 Act has achieved its purpose of raising thresholds for court intervention.[260] Where parents accept the need for support to improve childcare, the local authority can protect children by providing services, including accommodation, under the Children Act 1989 Pt III without court proceedings.

C. The child protection system

21–021   This is an interdisciplinary system, involving co-operation of many agencies. The Children Act 2004 s.11 requires specific agencies to safeguard children when carrying out their functions so that that they give greater priority to this and are encouraged to share early concerns about children's welfare.[261] The list includes organisations whose work impinges on children's lives even though their clients may be adults, such as district councils and probation services. They must all have regard to the government guidance, *Working Together to Safeguard Children*[262] and to local procedures. The primary responsibility for child protection, the prevention of abuse and neglect, its investigation, the bringing of care proceedings and the care of children who have been removed from their

---

[254] Lord Mackay, "Perceptions of the Children Bill and beyond" at 506.

[255] DH, *Child Protection: Messages From Research*, pp.15, 25.

[256] DH, *Child Protection: Messages From Research*, pp.15, 33. The overview concludes that thresholds have generally been lowered: see also J. Gibbons et al., *Operating the Child Protection System* (1995).

[257] J. Thoburn et al., *Paternalism or Partnership? Family Involvement in the Child Protection Process* (London: HMSO, 1995).

[258] *Re L (Care: Threshold Criteria)* [2007] 1 F.L.R. 2050, *per* Hedley J. at para.50.

[259] DH, *Child Protection: Messages From Research*, p.32.

[260] DH, *Children Act Now* (2001), p.55; cf. DfES and DCA, *Review of the Child Care Proceedings System for England and Wales* (2006), paras 1.5 and 4.1, which suggests that too many proceedings are brought.

[261] Children Act 2004 EN para.6.

[262] Children Act 2004 s.11; referred to here as *Working Together* (2006). Previous editions were published in 1988, 1991 and 1999.

families lies with local authority children's services departments.[263] The police play a major role, conducting joint investigations with social services in cases of suspected abuse and removing children in emergencies for their protection.[264] Agencies with responsibilities for health, who have contact with families and information about individual children, are also important for identifying concerns and making referrals. Local Safeguarding Children Boards (LSCB), with representation from relevant agencies, have been established to ensure a co-ordinated approach and the effectiveness of each of the agencies involved.[265] The LSCB has a senior representative from each agency and has responsibility for developing policies and procedures on such matters as thresholds for intervention and staff training, and raising awareness about safeguarding children.

D. Investigation of child abuse and neglect

i. Duty to investigate

Local authorities have a statutory duty to make inquiries in all cases where they **21–022** have reasonable cause to suspect that a child in their area is suffering or likely to suffer significant harm. The core assessment is the means for doing this.[266] They may start or continue inquiries after an alleged perpetrator has been acquitted.[267] Their inquiries must enable the authority to determine whether they should exercise any of their powers (e.g. to bring proceedings or provide services). They must ensure that access to the child is obtained unless they are satisfied that they already have sufficient information.[268]

Although local authorities monitor the care of children they have contact with, they rely on other agencies—health services,[269] the police, school teachers and members of the public[270]—to refer concerns about abused and neglected

---

[263] Local Authority Social Services Act 1970 Sch.1 as amended; Children Act 1989 ss.21, 23, Pts IV and V, and Sch.2 para.4. The NSPCC is authorised to bring proceedings under the Children Act 1989 s.31(9) but no longer does so.

[264] All forces has a dedicated unit handling child protection matters: see Her Majesty's Inspector of Constabulary, *Keeping Safe Staying Safe, Thematic Inspection* (2005) p.7 and below, para.21–024.

[265] Children Act 2004 ss.13 and 14; Local Safeguarding Children Boards Regulations 2006 (SI 2006/90); *Working Together* (2006) Ch.2. LSCBs replace Area Child Protection Committees.

[266] s.47(1); *Working Together* (2006), para.5.60; DH et al., *Framework for the Assessment of Children in Need and their Families* (2000).

[267] *Re S (Sexual Abuse Allegations: Local Authority Response)* [2001] 2 F.L.R. 776, QBD. Similarly it need only have reasonable cause to suspect that abuse has occurred.

[268] Children Act 1989 s.47(4). The statutory duty makes it plain to social workers what is expected of them, and provides a lever where families are reluctant to allow access. The social worker who investigated allegations of abuse to Kimberley Carlile told the inquiry into her death that he had only been allowed to see her through a glazed bedroom door: London Borough of Greenwich, *A Child In Mind* (1987), p.115.

[269] See J. Gibbons et al., *Operating the Child Protection System* (1995), p.41.

[270] Half of child protection referrals come via the child or a member of the family: see DH, *Child Protection: Messages From Research*, p.26 and H. Cleaver and P. Freeman, *Parental Perspectives in Cases of Suspected Child Abuse* (London: HMSO, 1995).

children.[271] The Government has issued advice about information sharing; the statutory obligation to safeguard children provides the legal basis for this.[272] Children, particularly those counselled through ChildLine,[273] may request help from teachers or other adults who then contact social services[274]; some parents seek help from social services because of fears that they or their partner will harm a child.

Doctors, general practitioners, casualty officers and paediatricians may all identify[275] child abuse in the course of examining or treating children. Although doctors have a legal and ethical duty to maintain confidentiality, the General Medical Council has advised that disclosures may be necessary to prevent risk of death or serious harm to the patient or others (e.g. to protect a child from abuse).[276] Children's health is also monitored by community-based nurses. Health visitors are primarily concerned with the healthy development of children under the age of five. They have no statutory powers but provide a service that typically involves visiting pre-school children at home and running clinics where babies are weighed, their development assessed and mothers are given advice about parenting.[277] Health visitors aim to maintain the confidence and co-operation of the families they visit so that they may continue to offer assistance and check children's progress.

21–023   School teachers' daily involvement with older children puts them in a position to identify cases and make referrals. They may see signs of ill-treatment when children prepare for PE lessons, observe disturbed behaviour or changes in behaviour that lead them to suspect abuse, or be told of incidents by a child. Educational authorities and institutions are required to exercise their functions with a view to safeguarding and promoting the welfare of children.[278] Each school should make a senior member of staff responsible for co-ordinating the

---

[271] See, generally, C. Wattam, *Making a Case in Child Protection* (Harlow: Longman, 1992). The need for referral should be discussed with the family unless this places the child at increased risk of significant harm: *Working Together* (2006), paras 5.4, 5.16.

[272] HM Government, *Information Sharing Practitioners' Guide* (2006); Data Protection Act 1998 Sch.3 para.7(1)(b).

[273] A confidential telephone counselling service.

[274] Solicitors may breach client confidentiality where there is a serious threat to a child's life or health: Law Society, *Guide to Professional Conduct of Solicitors* (8th edn), para.16.02.4; Solicitors Family Law Association, *Guide to good practice for solicitors acting for children*, 5th edn (2000), para.J.

[275] Identification, even in cases of physical abuse or neglect, may not be a simple matter. The doctor needs to examine the child for clinical signs and also needs to consider whether any explanation offered for the injuries is consistent with what has been found. In cases of failure to thrive, the doctor will also need to establish whether there is any organic reason for the child's condition. Diagnosis may be contested—*Re A (Non-accidental Injury: Medical Evidence)* [2001] 2 F.L.R. 657, FD—or missed—R. Dingwall, J. Eekelaar and T. Murray, *The Protection of Children* (1983), Ch.2.

[276] General Medical Council, *Protecting and Providing Information* (2004), paras 24 and 29. There is no statutory duty on doctors to report child abuse, only to co-operate with inquiries of the local authority: Children Act 1989 s.47(9)–(11). Cf. many states of the United States, where various professionals are legally required to report suspicions of abuse: see L. Bell and P. Tooman, "Mandatory reporting laws a critical overview" (1994) 8 Int. J Law & Fam. 337.

[277] The expectations of health visitors are clarified in *Working Together* (2006), paras 2.74 and 2.87.

[278] Education Act 2002 s.175.

school's response to child abuse and for referring cases to a named person in the children's services department.[279]

When the local authority receives a referral, it must make an initial assessment and determine whether to act immediately for the child's protection.[280] The children's services department, the police and other relevant agencies should hold a strategy discussion to share information, plan further inquiries and agree a course of action.[281] Typically, the initial investigation involves visiting the person making the allegation (unless it is anonymous) to verify details, and seeing the child,[282] the parents with care and other family members as appropriate and obtaining relevant information from professionals in contact with the family.[283] The NSPCC provides a specialist child protection service to investigate allegations where children have been abused in care.[284]

The local authority may call on the assistance of other local authorities, a local education authority, local housing authority, health authority and the NSPCC, who must comply unless it would be unreasonable in all the circumstances of the case.[285] It has been said that too many investigations are undertaken and resources expended with little apparent benefit.[286] However, the number of inquiries appears to have declined with the introduction of additional procedures.[287] Approximately 93,000 core assessments were completed in 2006–7, there were just over 40,000 children's cases considered at an initial child protection conference, and 33,000 children became the subject of a child protection plan, 13 per cent for at least the second time.[288] Care proceedings were brought in respect of 11,000 children. Over half of these were already the subject of a child protection plan and nearly a quarter had been protected by emergency measures before the care proceedings were started. Care proceedings resulted in a change of living arrangements for almost three-quarters of children involved.[289]

---

[279] *Working Together* (2006), paras 2.123–2.125.

[280] *Working Together* (2006), paras 5.49 *et seq.*; DH, *The Challenge of Partnership* (1995), paras 5.2, 5.10 *et seq.*

[281] *Working Together* (2006), paras 5.54 et seq. Each LSCB should have a protocol for joint police and social services investigations (para.3.19).

[282] s.47(4)(a), (5A). Research has identified common pitfalls in the conduct of initial child protection visits: see *Working Together* (2006), para.5.47 ("Ten pitfalls and how to avoid them").

[283] *Working Together* (2006), para.5.39; DH, *Framework for Assessment of Children In Need and Their Families* (2000); DH, *The Challenge of Partnership* (1995), paras 4.8, 6.15 *et seq.*

[284] B. Joel-Esam, "The NSPCC in the 1990s", in A. Levy (ed.), *Re-focus on Child Abuse* (London: Hawksmere, 1994), pp.157, 161 *et seq.*

[285] Children Act 1989 s.47(9)–(11).

[286] DH, *Child Protection: Messages From Research*, pp.54–5.

[287] The figures quoted in DH *Child Protection: Messages From Research*, p.28 are 160,000 referrals, of which 40,000 were closed without a home visit, 120,000 home visits and 40,000 child protection conferences, 3,000 children immediately separated and another 3,000 subject to care proceedings. 96% of children subject to child protection procedures were said to remain at home or with relatives.

[288] DCSF, *Referrals and Assessments and Children Who Are the Subject of a Child Protection Plan Etc* (2007). Core assessments are the method of completing s.47 inquiries, but they are also used to assess needs in some other cases.

[289] J. Masson et al., *The Care Profiling Study* (MoJ Research Report 4/08, 2008), pp.27, 41, Tables A2.1 and A2.43. The figures 200 and 2006 in the *Judicial Statistics* are markedly inaccurate (p.11).

The Department of Health noted that failure to follow through interventions with much needed services has prevented professionals from meeting the needs of children and families.[290] Families generally experience child protection inquiries negatively; they do not find the process helpful; nor do they feel involved in it.[291]

ii. The role of the police

21–024 Child protection policing is no more or less than the investigation of a crime.[292] The police have general responsibility for the protection of life and limb, the prevention and investigation of crime and the submission of cases for criminal proceedings.[293] In addition to their duty to investigate crimes, the police have emergency powers to enter premises and to ensure the immediate protection of children believed to be suffering from, or at risk of, significant harm.[294] The *Cleveland Report* identified failure of police co-operation as a contributory factor in the crisis, and recommended that police should recognise and develop their responsibility for child protection, but the Children Act 1989 imposed no obligation on the police to assist local authority inquiries.[295] Although specialist child-abuse investigation units were set up and close working relationships between the police and social services developed, child protection policing had low priority.[296] The *Climbié Report* was highly critical of police failure to investigate child abuse as other crimes, and the lack of training, resources and leadership for this work. It recommended strengthening the specialist units and giving child protection priority in policing plans.[297] Changes have occurred in police forces,[298] but a difficult balance remains between social work and police investigation. There are dangers that families may find the involvement of the police even more threatening, that their wider needs will be missed and that it will be difficult for social workers to establish co-operative relationships with them subsequently.

---

[290] DH, *Child Protection: Messages from Research*, p.55; *Children Act Now* (2001), pp.45–46.

[291] P. Freeman and J. Hunt, *Parental Perspectives on Care Proceedings* (London: HMSO, 1998); DH, *Child Protection: Messages From Research* (1995), p.43; J. Thoburn et al., *Paternalism or Partnership: Family Involvement in the Child Protection Process* (1995).

[292] Lord Laming, *The Climbié Report* (Cm.5730 (2003)), para.15.1.

[293] *Working Together* (2006), paras 2.97–2.105.

[294] *Working Together* (2006), para.2.105; Police and Criminal Evidence Act 1984 s.17(1)(e); Children Act 1989 s.46(1); J. Masson, "Police protection—protecting whom?" [2002] J.S.W.F.L. 157, and below, para.21–051.

[295] David Mellor, Secretary of State for Health, explained these omissions on the basis that "police refusal to co-operate on any matter would be indefensible": Children Bill, Committee Stage (Standing Committee B, col.342, June 6, 1989), see also *Cleveland Report* (1988), Ch.6.

[296] C. Hallett and E. Birchall, *Working Together in Child Protection* (London: HMSO, 1995); E. Farmer and M. Owen, *Child Protection Practice: Private Risks and Public Remedies* (London: HMSO, 1995), pp.123–127; HMIC, *Child Abuse, Thematic Inspection* (1998).

[297] Cm.5730 (2003), Ch.15 and recommendations 91–108.

[298] Her Majesty's Inspector of Constabulary, *Keeping Safe Staying Safe, Thematic Inspection* (2005), but less so nationally: J. Masson. "The Climbié Inquiry—context and critique" (2006) J. Law and Soc. 33, 221–243.

iii. Child protection conferences and family group conferences

Inquiring into child abuse involves more than receiving referrals and visiting the **21–025** child. All relevant information must be collated and considered; this is usually done by calling a child protection or case conference[299] and inviting the parents or carers and all professionals involved with the child to attend.[300] The purpose of the conference is to share and analyse information about the child and parents; to make judgments about the likelihood of significant harm in the future; and to decide what action should be taken to safeguard the child.[301] Conferences reduce professional anxiety by sharing the responsibility, and also develop an official view within agencies about a family.[302] Formally, the conference draws up an outline child protection plan where the child is at continuing risk of significant harm. Parents should be involved in the formulation of the plan and be given a copy of it.[303] The conference must also appoint a key worker.[304] The first review conference should be held within three months to review progress, consider changes or discontinue the plan.[305] The conference assesses the evidence of significant harm, but the decision of whether care proceedings should be brought is for the local authority. Where a child protection plan is not made or is ended, the conference should ensure, subject to parental agreement, that any needs for services are considered.[306]

Child protection conferences can lead to children being removed from the family. Parents must be involved in the decision-making process in order to protect their interests and to respect their right to family life.[307] *Working Together* advises that parents (including absent parents) and involved family members should normally be invited to conferences, but accepts that "exceptionally, it may be necessary to exclude one or more family members" (e.g. because of violence or intimidation).[308] Parents who are excluded or who are unwilling to attend should be given the opportunity to present their views. Parents may bring "an advocate, friend or supporter"[309] to the conference, and this could include a

---

[299] *Working Together* (2006), paras 5.80–5.114. It should occur within 15 days of the strategy discussion: para.5.81.

[300] The child may also be invited if this is appropriate: *Working Together* (2006) para.5.84. In practice, children attend where parents are unable to make babysitting arrangements: E. Farmer and M. Owen, *Children Protection Practice*, p.108. Where court permission is required for disclosure of material, there should be the utmost co-operation between the court and the conference: *Re M (Disclosure)* [1998] 1 F.L.R. 734, CA. (decision to preclude disclosure of material to health authority overturned).

[301] *Working Together* (2006), para.5.80; see also: DH, *Child Protection: Messages From Research* (1995), p.29.

[302] Farmer and Owen, *Child Protection Practice*, pp.90, 100.

[303] *Working Together* (2006), para.5.116. The parents' copy should be written in their first language.

[304] This person who must be employed by either the children's social care department or the NSPCC is responsible for developing the child protection plan, completing the core assessment and co-ordinating the implementation of the plan: *Working Together* (2006), paras 5.117–5.119.

[305] *Working Together* (2006), paras 5.128–5.136.

[306] *Working Together* (2006), paras 5.117 and 5.123. The conference can act as a gateway to services, but completion of the core assessment may still be necessary.

[307] *W v UK* (1988) 10 E.H.R.R. 29; *Scott v UK* [2000] 1 F.L.R. 958; and see S. Choudry [2001] Fam. Law 531.

[308] para.5.85. Criteria fo exclusion should be set by the LSCB, para.5.86.

[309] para.5.84, but suitable services may not be available: see B. Lindley et al., "Advice and advocacy for parent in child protection cases—what is happening in current practice" [2001] C.F.L.Q. 167.

lawyer,[310] but a case conference is a discussion, not a court hearing. Complaints about case conferences should be dealt with according to local authority procedures.[311] The courts have been reluctant to subject case-conference procedures and decisions to judicial review. It has been said that in balancing child protection against fairness to an adult, the interest of an adult may have to be placed second, and that the authorities should be allowed to perform this delicate task without constant supervision from the courts.[312] Moreover, failure to hold a conference, providing parents and others are properly consulted, will not amount to a breach of their art.8 rights.[313]

Family Group Conferences (FGCs) are based on an idea from New Zealand where (except in emergencies) compulsory measures of care can only be imposed after the family have been informed of the concerns about the child in a formal meeting with child protection services, and have had an opportunity for private discussion to formulate their own protection plan.[314] They can reduce the power imbalance between the family and the professionals and result in effective protection by care in the family without care proceedings. They do not replace the more formal procedures set out in *Working Together* but they may be useful to develop a protection plan, and where children need support.[315] The Child Care Proceedings System Review recommended greater use of FGCs and suggested that they could prevent children becoming looked after.[316] Local authorities are encouraged to hold a family group conference or other family meeting to explore options for care in the family before bringing care proceedings, but are advised that family members should not be contacted without the consent of the parents, and are required to inform only parents of their intentions.[317]

iv. The integrated children's system (ICS)

21–026 Central to many of the shortcomings in children's social services has been the failure to record, retrieve and understand the significance of information about children. The ICS aims to provide a system that uses information technology to overcome these. It supports the four key processes that underpin all work with children in need: assessment, planning, intervention and reviewing.[318] It supersedes the Child Protection Register; from April 2008 details of child protection plans will be kept on ICS. Those working with children who need to establish

---

[310] *R. v Cornwall CC Ex p. LH* [2000] 1 F.L.R. 236, QBD (policies to refuse permission for solicitors to attend case conferences and not to provide copies of the minutes to parents declared unlawful). Level 1 legal aid may be available.

[311] *Working Together* (2006), paras 5.101–5.104; Complaints Directions issued under Local Authority Social Services Act 1970 s.7B.

[312] *R. v Harrow LBC Ex p. D* [1990] Fam. 133 at 138, *per* Butler-Sloss L.J.; *R. v Hampshire CC Ex p. H* [1999] 2 F.L.R. 359, CA.

[313] But the lack of a conference does not make care proceedings ultra vires where parents were properly consulted: *Westminster City Council v RA, B and S* [2005] 1 F.L.R 1029, FD.

[314] Children, Young Persons and their Families Act 1989 (NZ) ss.31, 70. Care proceedings can only be started if the family have failed to agree a satisfactory plan.

[315] *Working Together* (2006), paras 10.1–10.4; see also K. Morris et al., *Family Group Conferences—A Training Pack* (London: FRG, 1998).

[316] DfES and DCA (2006), para.1.10 and p.21.

[317] *Guidance* (2008), paras 3.24, 3.33 and Annex 3; MoJ, *Statutory Guidance for Local Authorities and the Public Law Outline FAQs* (2008), p.7.

[318] DH, *Integrated Children's System Consultation* (2002).

whether they have identified needs will be able to access the required information through ICS. Harm to children will still be recorded under specific categories: physical, emotional, sexual abuse or neglect.[319] It has been held that a decision to record must be based on evidence of harm in the relevant category.[320] Almost 28,000 children were the subject of a child protection plan on March 31, 2007; each year the number of new plans approximately equals the number discontinued.[321] "Registration rates" differ widely between authorities and do not merely reflect differences in the incidence of abuse.[322]

A separate system, known as ContactPoint,[323] is being established with information about all children, including details of parents, school and the agencies working with the child. It will be updated with limited information from the ICS. This follows recommendations by Lord Laming for a feasibility study for a national children's database so that professionals and agencies could establish who was working with a child.[324] This is highly controversial; it has been likened to the introduction of identity cards, and there are concerns that family privacy will be undermined and children will be more at risk through breach of security in the system.

v. Negligent investigations

Incompetent investigation can lead to children being separated from their **21–027** families unnecessarily,[325] or sustaining long periods of abuse or neglect. The child protection system cannot be expected to prevent all deaths, but inquiries have identified numerous failures. However, child protection legislation is not treated as existing just for the benefit of abused children but for society in general. Thus, a local authority's failure to carry out its duties under the Children Act 1989 ss.17 and 47[326] does not give rise to an action for breach of statutory duty.[327] Also, the House of Lords has held in *D v E Berkshire NHS Trust*[328] that a duty of care is not owed to parents who are harmed by the negligence of agencies exercising child protection functions. The law had to balance two countervailing interests: (1) the protection of children, and (2) family privacy. The majority held (Lord Bingham dissenting) that imposing a duty to parents on health professionals needing to consider whether children had been harmed

---

[319] *Working Together* (2006), para.5.143.
[320] *R. v Hampshire CC Ex p. H* [1999] 2 F.L.R. 359, CA, but a psychologist's report is not necessary to establish emotional harm.
[321] *Children Act Report 2004 and 2005*, Ch.2; DCSF, *Referrals and Assessments and Children Who Are The Subject of a Child Protection Plan Etc* (2007).
[322] J. Gibbons et al., *Operating the Child Protection System* (1995), p.8.
[323] Children Act 2004 s.12 provides the statutory basis for the scheme.
[324] Cm.5730 (2003), paras 17.117–17.121 and recommendation 17.
[325] *M v Newham LBC* [1995] A.C. 648, HL, reported in the E.C.H.R. as *TP and KM v UK* [2001] 2 F.L.R. 549 (removal of child from mother's care); *L and P v Reading BC and the Chief Constable of Thames Valley Police* [2001] 2 F.L.R. 50, CA (exclusion of father).
[326] The same conclusion was reached in respect of the earlier legislation; Children and Young Persons Act 1969 s.2 and Childcare Act 1980 ss.1, 18.
[327] *X v Bedfordshire CC* [1995] 2 A.C. 633; see also R. Bailey-Harris and M. Harris, "The immunity of local authorities in child protection functions—is the door now ajar" [1998] C.F.L.Q. 227, 228.
[328] [2005] 2 F.L.R. 284, HL; the decision applies equally to other child protection workers: *Lawrence v Pembrokeshire County Council* [2007] 2 F.L.R. 705, CA. See also *M v Newham London Borough Council* [1995] 2 F.L.R. 276, HL and *B v A-G of New Zealand* [2003] UKPC 61.

would create a conflict of interest that could undermine the child's protection.[329] Nevertheless, where parents have not been sufficiently involved in the decision-making process, their art.8 rights have been infringed and they may be able to claim compensation under the Human Rights Act.[330]

Different considerations apply in the case of children. In *X v Bedfordshire County Council*[331] the House of Lords held that no duty of care was owed to five children whose gross neglect had been ignored by the local authority despite repeated referrals from professionals and neighbours. Although the local authority could foresee damage to the children if statutory duties were carried out negligently, and the relationship between the plaintiffs and the local authority was sufficiently proximate, it was not "fair, just and reasonable"[332] to impose a common law duty of care. First, such a duty would cut across the whole interagency system. It would be manifestly unfair to hold liable only one agency within a multidisciplinary group; imposing liability on all participant bodies would lead to impossible problems of determining the extent to which any one was negligent.[333] Secondly, these decisions are "extraordinarily delicate". Imposition of liability might make local authorities unwilling to take risks and could encourage further defensive investigations that would delay response and reduce the resources available for other social services activities. Thirdly, the nature of child protection work means the risk that local authorities would have to respond to many vexatious claims is too high to ignore.[334] Moreover, the development of a tort of in this area did not follow incrementally from any existing category of negligence[335]:

> In *Z v UK*[336] the Official Solicitor, acting for the children in the *Bedfordshire* case, sought redress under the European Convention of Human Rights, arguing breach of their rights under arts 3, 6, 8 and 13.[337] The Commission unanimously found that the children had been subject to inhuman and degrading treatment. The Government did not dispute this; the State had failed in its positive obligation under art.3 to protect the children.[338] Although there was no mechanism for redress, the Human Rights Act 1998

---

[329] See Lord Nicholls at paras 70–74 and 85–91.
[330] Human Rights Act 1998 s.6. Liability for breach of the procedural safeguards in art.8 was considered in *TP v KM v UK* [2001] 2 F.L.R. 549 at paras 57–83 (the *M v Newham* case). The ECtHR held that there was a positive duty to give the mother information about the child's interview with the child psychiatrist where she named her abuser. Had this been done, the mistake would have been discovered, the mother's partner would not have been considered a risk and the child would have been returned. Both mother and daughter were awarded compensation.
[331] [1995] 2 A.C. 633.
[332] *Per* Lord Browne-Wilkinson at 749, applying the test in *Caparo Industries Plc v Dickman* [1990] 2 A.C. 605.
[333] *Per* Lord Browne-Wilkinson at 750. Although this may be the effect of a Serious Case Review into a child's death; see *Working Together* (2006), Pt 8, or a Public Inquiry.
[334] *Per* Lord Browne-Wilkinson at 751.
[335] *Per* Lord Browne-Wilkinson at 751, as required by *Caparo Industries Plc v Dickman* [1990] 2 A.C. 605.
[336] [2000] 2 F.C.R. 245 (Commission Decision); [2001] 2 F.L.R. 612, ECtHR.
[337] The Court held that no separate issue arose in relation to art.8, paras 76, 77.
[338] [2001] 2 F.L.R. 612, paras 70–73.

now provides a remedy.[339] The children were awarded substantial compensation to cover psychotherapy, future loss of earnings and for their suffering.[340] However, the Grand Chamber accepted the Government's argument that, as a matter of law, the children had no case in negligence against the local authority. Consequently, there could be no breach of art.6 when the claims were struck out.[341]

Subsequently, the Court of Appeal refused to strike out a child's negligence claim where abuse was wrongly diagnosed,[342] but rejected the claim of another child, who was separated from his parents and fostered after a similar misdiagnosis, on the basis that there was no evidence that this had caused him sufficient harm to found an action in tort.[343] The House of Lord's reasons for rejecting the parents' claims in *D v E Berkshire NHS Trust* do not apply to claims by children. Where investigations have failed to match accepted standards, negligence actions by children who have suffered an identifiable psychiatric condition or other sufficient harm may succeed against social workers, doctors, police officers and their employers.[344] If, however, the negligence is by someone whose role is to provide an expert assessment for proceedings, that person may have witness immunity,[345] providing that they did not seek intentionally to mislead the court.[346]

In addition, a local authority may be liable in negligence in respect of actions in connection with childcare. The House of Lords has held that a local authority can be liable for negligently failing to safeguard the welfare of a child in care, and refused to strike out claims for negligently causing psychiatric injury to children and their parents resulting from sexual abuse to the children by a foster-child, placed without warnings about his behaviour.[347] Local authorities can also be held vicariously liable for the negligence of their staff.[348]

---

[339] [2001] 2 F.L.R. 612, paras 105–111; art.13 had been breached, but see Human Rights Act 1998 ss.7(1)(a), 8. The Government accepted that the Criminal Injuries Compensation Scheme, the Local Government Ombudsman and the Children Act 1989 complaints system did not satisfy art.13 in this case.

[340] But the awards may be low compared with damages in negligence; see R. Bailey-Harris [2001] Fam. Law 583, 585.

[341] [2001] 2 F.L.R. 612, paras 87–104. In doing so, the court accepted that it had misunderstood negligence law in *Osman v UK* [1999] 1 F.L.R. 193. The treatment of the claim did not amount to an exclusionary rule or an immunity, which prevented access to the courts, paras 96, 100.

[342] Case of *RK*; see [2005] 2 F.L.R. 284, HL, para.14.

[343] *D v Bury Metropolitan District Council* [2006] 2 F.L.R. 147, CA (failure to diagnose brittle-bone syndrome).

[344] Applying the test in *Bolam v Friern Hospital Management Committee* [1957] 1 W.L.R. 118.

[345] *M v Newham London Borough Council* [1995] 2 A.C. 633 at 755, *per* Lord Browne-Wilkinson.

[346] *L and P v Reading BC and the Chief Constable of Thames Valley Police* [2001] 2 F.L.R. 50 at 67, *per* Otton J. In this case, the applicant father's and child's claims, which remain to be considered at a full hearing, are based on misfeasance in public office and conspiracy to injure as well as negligence.

[347] *Barrett v London Borough of Enfield* [1999] 2 F.L.R. 426, HL; *W v Essex CC* [2000] 1 F.L.R. 657, HL, and see Bailey-Harris and Harris, "The immunity of local authorities".

[348] *Christmas v Hampshire CC* [1995] 2 A.C. 633; cf. *M v Newham London Borough Council* [1995] 2 A.C. 648, HL; *TP and KM v UK* [2001] 2 F.L.R 549, ECtHR; and see Bailey-Harris and Harris, "The immunity of local authorities", p.242.

vi. Registers of offenders and community notification[349]

21–028 Concern that those who have abused children may repeat their actions, and particularly seek positions with access to children, have led to the establishment of various registers. These are preventative, alerting prospective employers of the person's unsuitability, and can also assist the police investigating offences against children. Those who are convicted or cautioned for certain sexual offences are required to notify the police of their current address for a period related to the length of their sentence.[350] This information is stored in the police's national computer system and is accessible to all forces. The courts have powers to make disqualification orders when a person is convicted of certain offences against a child.[351] A separate register of individuals who are considered unsuitable to work with children has been created under the Protection of Children Act 1999.[352] Information may be included without a conviction (e.g. where there have been disciplinary proceedings by an employer, or a child protection investigation relating to a foster carer).[353] The Care Standards Tribunal hears disputes about an individual's inclusion. It is an offence for a person who is subject to a disqualification order or included (permanently) on the 1999 Act register to apply to work with children.[354] Childcare organisations are required to check this register and may not employ a person in a childcare position who is listed.[355] The information held in registers is used primarily by the police and childcare organisations but may be disclosed to others where there is a "pressing need" to protect children. Each case must be considered on its own facts[356]; disclosure is the exception, not the rule.

Multi-agency public protection arrangements (MAPPAs) provide a framework for the assessment and management of the risks posed by serious and violent offenders, including, for example, predatory paedophiles. The police, the probation and prison services are required to make these arrangements. Guidance is provided about sharing information between these agencies, and panels can recommend disclosure to others, including schools and voluntary groups.[357]

---

[349] For a more detailed discussion see: C. Cobley, *Sex Offenders* (Bristol: Jordans, 2000), Ch.7; *Exercising Constant Vigilance: The Role of the Probation Service in Protecting the Public from Sex Offenders* (1998); and *Working Together* (2006), Ch.12.

[350] Sexual Offences Act 2003 Pt 2 and Sch.3. It is an offence to fail to notify or provide false information: s.91.

[351] Criminal Justice and Court Services Act 2000 ss.28, 29 and Sch.4.

[352] This combines and puts on a statutory basis the "consultancy index" held by the Department of Health and "list 99" held by the Department for Education.

[353] Protection of Children Act 1999 ss.2–2C, 3.

[354] Criminal Justice and Court Services Act 2000 ss.35, 36; "regulated position" includes voluntary work, babysitting, being a school governor.

[355] Protection of Children Act 1999 s.7. These checks are made at the same time as criminal records checks under the Police Act 1997 ss.113A–113F. Poor practices in the employment of staff with access to children has been a continuing concern: see N. Warner, *Choosing with Care* (1992), the *Warner Report* and W. Utting, *People Like Us* (1997); *The Bichard Inquiry Report* (HC 653 (2004)).

[356] *R (J and P) v W Sussex CC and Wiltshire CC* [2002] 2 F.L.R. 1192, QBD; *R. v Chief Constable of North Wales Police Ex p. Thorpe* [1999] Q.B. 396, CA; Home Office Circular 39/1997.

[357] Criminal Justice and Court Services Act 2000 s.67, as amended; *Working Together* (2006) paras 12.12–12.21.

In contrast with many parts of the United States, where community notification statutes have been enacted, there is no provision for informing the public.[358] The risks of encouraging vigilante attacks and of offenders refusing to co-operate with registration are considered by professionals to make such provisions counter-productive; general notification also conflicts with the right to privacy.

E. Compulsory measures of care
In this section we consider the role of the court in child protection particularly, **21–029** the tests that must be satisfied if a child is to be committed to the care of the local authority, the orders the court can make, their discharge and appeal.

i. Care proceedings
Care proceedings are a last resort where there appears to be no other means of **21–030** protecting a child.[359] Only a local authority or the NSPCC may initiate care proceedings[360]; only a child under 17 can be made the subject of an application.[361] Proceedings involve the consideration of both a child's current circumstances and what arrangements should be made for their future care. These issues may be considered at separate hearings.[362] The court must first be satisfied that the threshold criteria in s.31 are met; then it must consider the local authority's care plan applying the welfare test, using the checklist[363] and the "no order" principle,[364] and decide whether to make an order.[365]

(1) Threshold criteria[366]
The Children Act 1989 s.31(2) provides that a care or supervision order may only **21–031** be made if the court is satisfied:

---

[358] U.S.C. 14071(d), known as Megan's law after Megan Kanka, who was murdered by her neighbour, a convicted sex offender; see B. Hebenton and T. Thomas, *Keeping Track? Observations on Sex Offender Registers in the U.S.* (Home Office Crime Detection and Prevention Series No.83, 1997); C. Cobley *Sex Offenders* paras 7.74 *et seq.*; ChildLine et al., *Protecting Children, Managing Sex Offenders in the Community* (1998).

[359] Bridget Prentice, Family Justice Minister, Public Law Outline Launch, April 1, 2008.

[360] Children Act 1989 ss.31(1), (7), (9), 92. The NSPCC now rarely brings proceedings: see Joel-Esam "NSPCC in the 1990s"

[361] No order may be obtained in respect of a married child over 16 or any child over 17: Children Act 1989 s.31(3); previously, such children could be warded: see *Re SW* [1986] 1 F.L.R. 24.

[362] *Re B (Split Hearing: Jurisdiction)* [2000] 1 F.L.R. 334, CA; *Re G (Care Proceedings: Split Trials)* [2001] 1 F.L.R. 872, CA. The two hearings should be before the same judge, *Re B* [2008] UKHL 35, but frequently they are not: Masson et al., *Care Profiling Study* (2008), p.54.

[363] Children Act 1989 s.1(3), (4).

[364] Children Act 1989 s.1(5); see above, 19–003.

[365] *Re J (Minors) (Care: Care Plan)* [1994] 1 F.L.R. 253 at 258, *per* Wall, J.; cross applications for residence orders do not have to be considered first; *Oldham MBC v E* [1994] 1 F.L.R. 568 at 576, *per* Waite L.J.

[366] See, generally, M. Freeman, "Care after 1991", in D. Freestone (ed.), *Children and the Law* (1990); A. Bainham, "Care after 1991—a reply" [1991] J.C.L. 99; M. Freeman, "Legislating for child abuse", in A. Levy (ed.), *Re-focus on Child Abuse* (1994), p.18 and M. Brandon et al., *Safeguarding Children with the Children Act 1989* (London: HMSO, 1999), Ch.1.

"(a) [T]hat the child is suffering or is likely to suffer significant harm; and

(b) that the harm or likelihood of harm is attributable to—

(i) the care given to the child or likely to be given to [the child] if the order were not made, not being what it would be reasonable to expect a parent to give to him; or
(ii) the child's being beyond parental control."

21–032   **(a) Significant harm.** "Harm" means "ill-treatment or the impairment of health or development".[367] This broad definition allows intervention both because of what carers do and where the care given to the child has a substantially deleterious effect on the child. It may allow intervention where the parents have adopted a lifestyle that has a damaging effect on their child's health or development (e.g. isolating their children from the community, continuously travelling or forcing a marriage[368] as well as more obvious cases of abuse or neglect).[369] The harm must be significant. There is no clear indication of what this means in cases of ill-treatment, but it has been said that s.31(2) contemplates "the exceptional rather than the commonplace".[370] It has been held that depriving a child of parental care by murdering the child's mother amounts to significant harm.[371] A minor injury may be significant because of the child's age[372] or disabilities already suffered; for example, minor burns to the hands could prevent a blind child learning to read Braille. Also minor injuries such as bruises may suggest that more serious harm is likely in the future. Where sexual abuse produces serious psychological disturbance or is likely to do so in the future, it clearly causes significant harm, but, arguably, any such ill-treatment is significant because of the way it is handled in the community.[373] Leading a child to believe that they have been sexually abused or constant parental conflict can cause emotional harm.[374] Harm may be significant because of the way it was caused; cigarette burns are usually deliberate. Behaviour that may not be recognised as serious, such as shaking a young baby, may produce serious brain

---

[367] Children Act 1989 s.31(9); "ill-treatment", "health" and "development" are all defined in s.31(9) and include physical, emotional and sexual abuse and neglect. An amendment added by the Adoption and Children Act 2002 s.120 recognises that seeing or hearing the ill-treatment of another can lead to impairment.

[368] *Re KR (Abduction)* [1999] 2 F.L.R. 542 at 548, *per* Singer J. (obiter).

[369] The *Review of Child Care Law*, para.15.16 stated that "the concept of substantial detriment will adequately distinguish between cases of real harm and cases of acceptable variation in parenting standards".

[370] *Re L (Care: Threshold Criteria)* [2007] 1 F.L.R. 2064, *per* Hedley J. at para.51.

[371] *Re M (A Minor) (Care Order: Threshold Conditions)* [1994] 3 W.L.R. 558 at 562, *per* Bracewell J. The House of Lords upheld the decision, but Whybrow [1994] J.C.L. 88, 89 notes that the ill-treatment was of the mother. The baby was present (possibly asleep); the impact on the child may thus have been from its consequences rather than the event itself.

[372] *Humberside CC v B* [1993] 1 F.L.R. 257.

[373] cf. *Review of Child Care Law*, para.15.16. The Review recommended the inclusion of the word "wellbeing" in the definition of harm, to cover cases of sexual abuse of older children.

[374] *Re M (Intractable Contact Dispute: Interim Care Order)* [2003] 2 F.L.R. 636, FD. See also *Re N (Sexual abuse allegations: Professionals not abiding by findings of fact)* [2005] 2 F.L.R. 340, FD.

damage.[375] Similarly, a bad diet can result in malnutrition or obesity and have significant consequences for the child's health and development. Over-protection may amount to harm.[376] Although it is possible for a local authority to bring proceedings on the basis of a single act of ill-treatment, this rarely occurs.[377] A few children who have been grossly abused need to be removed from the homes for that reason, but in the majority of cases the general family context is more important to the outcome for the child than an abusive event.[378]

In cases involving consideration of the child's health or development (but not ill-treatment), "significant" requires a comparison between the child and what "could reasonably be expected of a similar child".[379] This is intended to require comparison of children's attributes to take account of the fact that the child might ordinarily achieve more or less than an average child[380] but not to enable lower standards to be applied in respect of disadvantaged children.[381]

Truancy was the reason for approximately 10 per cent of the care orders under the 1969 Act.[382] However, the *Review of Child Care Law* considered that care proceedings were inappropriate for most cases of truancy.[383] Nevertheless, in *Re O (A Minor) (Care Proceedings: Education)*[384] the court recognised that failure to receive education can amount to significant harm, even to a child approaching the end of compulsory schooling. It is one of the factors causing concern in a quarter of care cases relating to school-aged children.[385] Local education authorities may enforce school attendance by prosecuting the parents or seeking an education supervision order.[386]

The commission of an offence is no longer a ground as such for a care order.[387] Criminal activity may indicate significant harm to a child's social development and can place a child who "joy rides" cars or couriers drugs at physical risk. Care proceedings could therefore be brought, and might be appropriate for offenders

[375] *Re A and D (Non-accidental Injury: Subdural Haematomas)* [2002] 1 F.L.R. 357.
[376] *Re V (Care or Supervision Order)* [1996] 1 F.L.R. 776, CA.
[377] DH, *Child Protection: Messages From Research*, p.18. For a discussion of the range of cases in which proceedings are used, see J. Hunt et al., *The last Resort* (1999); M. Brandon et al., *Safeguarding Children*, Ch.8; Masson et al. *Care Profiling Study.*
[378] DH, *Child Protection: Messages From Research*, p.54.
[379] s.31(10). In *Re O (A Minor) (Care Proceedings: Education)* [1992] 1 W.L.R. 912, the court compared a truanting child with "a child of equivalent intellectual and social development who had gone to school".
[380] B. Hoggett, "The Children Bill: the aim" (1989) 19 Fam. Law 217, 221.
[381] See Lord Mackay, Lord Chancellor, *Hansard*, HL Vol.503, cols 354–355, Children Bill, Committee Stage; Vol.503, col.1525, Report Stage.
[382] Children and Young Persons Act 1969 s.1(2)(e); DHSS, *Children in Care* (1986), para.A/F/12/86, Table 1.
[383] *Review of Child Care Law*, paras 12.22–12.23, 15.26.
[384] *Re O (A Minor) (Care Proceedings: Education)* [1992] 1 W.L.R. 912; for a more recent example, see *Re P (Care Orders: Injunctive Relief)* [2000] 2 F.L.R. 385, FD.
[385] See Masson et al. *Care Profiling Study* table A2.6; and see *Re K (Care: Threshold Criteria)* [20076] 2 F.L.R. 868.
[386] Education Act 1996 ss.443–444; Children Act 1989 s.36 and Sch.3 Pt III. An education supervision order lasts for one year but can be extended for up to three years. Successive orders may theoretically be made in respect of a child, but the court must be satisfied that the order will be effective (s.1(5)). The child's stated intention not to comply with the order is not determinative, but force would not be used: *Essex CC v B* [1993] 1 F.L.R. 866.
[387] cf. Children and Young Persons Act 1969 s.1(2)(f) but cautioning and prosecution had become the main ways of dealing with young offenders.

who need treatment, such as victims of sexual abuse who abuse others.[388] The fact that a member of the child's household had committed specified offences was also grounds for an order.[389] It is now necessary to establish that the previous incident makes it likely that the child will suffer significant harm.[390]

(b) "Is suffering".

21–033

In *Re M (A Minor) (Care Orders: Threshold Conditions)*[391] a baby was accommodated after his father murdered his mother. The local authority started care proceedings and, almost immediately, a relative, who was caring for the boy's half-siblings, applied for a residence order. The House of Lords held, reversing the decision of the Court of Appeal,[392] that the relevant time for applying the "is suffering" test is when the local authority "initiated protective arrangements", not the date of the hearing, provided that the arrangements had remained continuously in place.[393] Thus a care order could be made despite the relative's offer. However, because the child had been placed with her following the Court of Appeal's decision, he stayed with her.[394]

Arrangements the family makes for the child's protection after the initial local-authority intervention are not privileged and only have to be accepted where the child's welfare demands this.[395] Where the child suffered significant harm in the past, but this is no longer a matter of concern, the threshold criteria are not satisfied:

In *Re L. (Children) (Care Proceedings: Significant Harm)*[396] a girl aged 10 had been abused by a man the father allowed to stay in the family home, although he knew him to be a sex offender. Social services became involved, the man left and no further action was taken. Later an allegation of whipping was made against the parents, and the children were placed in foster care where they thrived. Care proceedings were brought on the basis of both allegations. The judge found that the threshold had been crossed, but

---

[388] See, generally, NCH, *The Report of the Committee of Enquiry into Children and Young People who Sexually Abuse Other Children* (1992); *Working Together* (2006), paras 11.32–11.38.

[389] Children and Young Persons Act 1933 Sch.1; Children and Young Persons Act 1969 s.1(2)(b), (bb).

[390] *Re S, S and A (Care Proceedings: Issue Estoppel)* [1995] 2 F.L.R. 244; a previous finding of abuse is relevant.

[391] [1994] 2 A.C. 424, approving *Northampton CC v S* [1993] Fam. 136.

[392] [1994] Fam. 95.

[393] [1994] 2 A.C. 424, *per* Lord Mackay at 433G. The local authority can rely on assessments that it obtained after this date if they indicate a state of affairs at the time of intervention: *Re G (Care Proceedings: Threshold Conditions)* [2001] 2 F.L.R. 1111, CA.

[394] The order was made on the understanding that he should do so, a rare example of the court imposing its view of a social services responsibility on the local authority.

[395] See Masson [1994] J.C.L. 170 and Whybrow [1994] J.C.L. 88, 177. Current practice favours placements with suitable relatives: *Children Act Report 2000*, para.1.41; Hunt et al. *Keeping Them Within the Family*; Farmer and Moyers *Kinship Care*, but relative placements are not without risk and require support.

[396] [2007] 1 F.L.R. 1068, CA, per Wall L.J. at para.42. The wording of the Bill was amended to replace the words "has suffered" with "is suffering": *Hansard*, Standing Committee B, col.221, May 23, 1989.

the Court of Appeal overturned the decision and remitted the case for rehearing. It was not sufficient that the children had thrived away from the care of their parents, who had learning difficulties. The court had to find the threshold proved by relevant facts, and the local authority could not advance its case on a different basis from that it had used to start the proceedings.

Specialist assessments can be an important part of identifying that a child is suffering significant harm.[397]

(c) "Attributable to the care given to the child". The significant harm must be attributable to care given to the child or the child being beyond parental control. This may not require the identification of the person who injured the child: 21–034

In *Lancashire County Council v B*[398] a baby sustained shaking injuries from two separate incidents whilst in the care of her parents or childminder. The local authority began care proceedings in respect of the girl and the childminder's baby. The judge dismissed both applications on the basis that the harm could not be attributed to any of the adults. The local authority appealed; the Court of Appeal granted the order in respect of the injured child but not the childminder's baby.[399] The parents appealed. The House of Lords, stressing the difficulties in establishing the facts in such cases and the need to protect children from abuse, dismissed the appeal. Where the care of the child was shared, the "care given to the child" covered the care from any of the carers. The threshold condition could therefore be satisfied even when there was only a possibility that a parent had caused the injuries.[400]

"Care" includes catering for a child's total needs.[401] It is judged objectively in relation to the particular child concerned. Thus, a parent is expected to take account of their child's particular needs (e.g. providing reasonable emotional care such as listening to and monitoring the behaviour of a child who has been abused).[402] Consequently, parents who fail to co-operate with assessments of children with serious problems may be failing to provide reasonable care. Concern was expressed that the drafting of the Bill would lead to impoverished parents and those from minority ethnic backgrounds being judged by the

---

[397] *Guidance* (2008), para.3.51, for example distinguishing between a a naturally small child and one who is malnourished: *R. (Plymouth City Council) v HM Coroner for Devon* [2005] 2 F.L.R. 1279, QBD.

[398] [2000] 1 F.L.R. 583, HL; and see Hayes [2004] C.F.L.Q. 63.

[399] This case concerned only risk of future harm; see below the discussion of *Re H and R (Minors) (Sexual Abuse Standard of Proof)* [1996] A.C. 563. The local authority did not appeal the decision about the childminder's baby.

[400] *Per* Lord Nicholls at 589D–589G. This did not mean that a care order would be made, but unless it is clear that a person was not responsible for the child's injuries, it may be difficult to assess their ability to provide care in the future.

[401] Freeman "Legislating for child abuse", p.27.

[402] *Re B (A Minor) (Interim Care Order: Criteria)* [1993] 1 F.L.R. 815.

standards of the white middle class.[403] The wording of the Act does not prevent this, but there is no evidence that cases are brought without good cause.[404]

There must be a direct connection between the harm and the care given by the parent, so if a third party injured the child, the test would only be satisfied if the parent could have been expected to intervene to prevent this.[405] An order may apparently be granted to prevent the removal of children whose relationship with their carers is such that removal would cause significant harm, even though the care offered by the parents would be adequate for other children.[406] This interpretation invites the conclusion that there is no care that would be reasonable for these parents to give this child. It also calls into question the need for sub.para.(ii); the parents of a child who is beyond control may similarly be seen as providing inappropriate care despite their best endeavours. Sub-paragraph (ii) refers to a state of affairs that may be in the past, present or future according to the context.[407] So, in *M v Birmingham City Council*[408] an order could be made in respect of a "wayward, uncontrollable, disturbed and periodically violent" teenage girl who was accommodated by the local authority despite the claim by her mother that she and her partner could control her.

21–035   **(d) Likelihood of harm.** An order may also be made where the child is likely to suffer significant harm. A risk of future harm may relate to the carers' inability to meet a child's needs because of their limitations or the child's condition. The fact that the parents have learning difficulties or are illicit drug users is not grounds for an order.[409] The Act does not indicate when the harm should occur, but it has been suggested that the test "would probably" be satisfied if carers were unable to meet the child's emotional needs years in the future.[410] Nor does the Act indicate how likely the harm should be; it has been said that a comparatively small risk of really serious harm can justify action, while even the virtual certainty of slight harm may not.[411] There must be a "real possibility" of

---

[403] *Per* Lord Banks, *Hansard*, HL Vol.503, col.1525, Children Bill, Report Stage.
[404] Masson et al. *Care Profiling Study*, p.34 but some BME parents do not feel understood in the system: J. Brophy et al., *Child Protection Litigation in a Multi-cultural Setting* (LCD Research series 1/03, 2003).
[405] *Guidance* (2008), para.3.40.
[406] The original wording: "standard of care"; but this was considered too narrow: see Children Bill, Committee Stage (*Hansard*, Standing Committee B, cols 222–226, May 23, 1989). An application by the carers for a residence or special guardianship order might be more appropriate. This was apparently the Government's original intention.
[407] *M.v Birmingham CC* [1994] 2 F.L.R. 141 at 147, *per* Stuart-White J.; see also *Re K (Secure Accommodation: Right to Liberty)* [2001] 1 F.L.R. 526, CA (care proceedings, because the parents were no longer willing for their son to remain in secure accommodation).
[408] [1994] 2. F.L.R. 141.
[409] *Guidance* (2008), para.3.9; *Re L (Children) (Care Proceedings: Significant Harm)* [2007] 1 F.L.R. 1068, *per* Wall L.J at para.49.
[410] *Re H (A Minor) (s.37 Direction)* [1993] 2 F.L.R. 541 at 548, *per* Scott Baker J. (the child had been placed in an arrangement akin to surrogacy with a lesbian couple, one of whom had a history of mental-health problems).
[411] *Re C and B (Care Order: Future Harm)* [2001] 1 F.L.R. 611, CA at para.28, *per* Hale L.J.

significant harm that cannot "sensibly be ignored" having regard to the nature and gravity of the feared harm[412]:

> In *Re C and B*[413] both parents had had a difficult childhood, and their relationship was marked by repeated separation; the mother had learning difficulties and had suffered from mental ill-health in the past. Care orders were imposed in relation to the oldest child, then aged nine, on the basis of emotional and intellectual impairment, and the second oldest because she was likely to suffer similarly. Two years later the local authority removed two children who had been born after the original proceedings, despite evidence that they were well cared for, on the basis that they were at risk. Care orders were granted by the county court and the parents appealed. The Court of Appeal accepted that there had been evidence that satisfied the threshold condition, but considered that a care order was not a proportionate response[414] and remitted the case for rehearing.

Where children have been orphaned, the local authority's powers to accommodate them may be sufficient, but if the local authority wishes to place the child for adoption, it will be necessary to obtain a placement order.[415]

(2) Evidence in care proceedings

The civil rules of evidence and standard of proof govern care proceedings[416]; the burden of proof lies on the applicant for the care order. In *Re H and R*[417] Lord Nicholls, expressing the opinion of the majority, rejected the notion that a higher standard had to be applied to more serious allegations.[418] Nevertheless, he asserted that the "inherent improbability of an event" should be taken into account, and "the more serious the event the less likely it is that the event occurred". Consequently, stronger, more cogent evidence should be required.[419] Where the matter to be proved is whether the child is at risk of harm, Lord Nicholls held that there must be proven facts from which the court can properly conclude that harm is likely. Thus, a care order could not be made for siblings

21–036

---

[412] *Re H and R (Child Sexual Abuse: Standard of Proof)* [1996] 1 F.L.R. 80, HL, *per* Lord Nicholls at 95; *Re B* [2008] UKHL 35.

[413] [2001] 1 F.L.R. 611, CA.

[414] See below, para.21–040; both considering the risks involved and ECHR art.8.

[415] Adoption and Children Act 2002 s.21(2). The threshold test need not be proved if the child has no parent or guardian. In *Re M (Care Order: Parental Responsibility)* [1996] 2 F.L.R. 84 (abandoned baby), a care order was made; cf. *Birmingham CC v D and M* [1994] 2 F.L.R. 502 where Thorpe J. considered that Pt III of the Act provided all the necessary safeguards; see also CAAC Report 1994/5, p.32.

[416] Evidence from covert video surveillance is admissible: *Re DH (A Minor) (Child Abuse)* [1994] 1 F.L.R. 679 at 709, *per* Wall J. But see now Regulation of Investigatory Powers Act 2000 and *Working Together* (2006), para.6.6.

[417] [1996] 1 F.L.R. 80, HL, and see Hayes [2004] C.F.L.Q. 63.

[418] [1996] 1 F.L.R. 80 at 96–97, disapproving *Re G (No.2) (A Minor) (Child Abuse: Evidence)* [1988] 1 F.L.R. 314 and *Re W (Sexual Abuse: Standard of Proof)* [1994] 1 F.L.R. 314. All the judges agreed on this point, although Lords Browne-Wilkinson and Lloyd dissented on other points; see below.

[419] [1996] 1 F.L.R. 80 at 96.

documents; the court could withhold information if its disclosure would breach the privacy right of a party.[439] Children's guardians have a statutory right of access to the children's services department's records concerning the child, and can therefore bring material to the court's attention without disclosure.[440]

The evidence of experts plays a major part in care proceedings.[441] Various medical experts may be able to determine how and when injuries were caused, and whether they were accidental; mental-health experts assess children's needs and development; psychologists assess parent's capacity to care.[442] Although social workers may know a family well, courts have relied very heavily on brief assessments by experts. The care-proceedings reforms aim to ensure that social worker's assessments are properly completed before proceedings are started so that fewer experts will be required.[443]

21–038 Expert evidence is costly and reporting by experts contributes to delay[444]; therefore, considerable attention is given to limiting the instruction of experts and focusing their work on key issues. It is crucial that experts of the right calibre and with appropriate experience are used, and that they are given clear instructions. Where possible, this should be agreed by the parties.[445] The court controls the use of experts and may refuse to admit evidence from assessments of the child undertaken without its permission.[446] However, parents' confidence in the fairness of proceedings may demand that they are able to obtain expert evidence, particularly where they face permanent separation from their children.[447]

The Children Act 1989 abolished the competency requirement in respect of children's evidence in all civil proceedings; a child's evidence may be heard if he or she understands the duty to speak the truth and has sufficient understanding of the events.[448] Particular justification is required for direct evidence from a child[449]; hearsay given in connection with the welfare of a child (e.g. a statement a child makes to a social worker or a video-recorded interview) is admissible.[450]

[439] *Re B (Disclosure to Other Parties)* [2001] 2 F.L.R. 1017, FD (disclosure refused to father of some information about mother and stepchildren on the basis that the harm would be disproportionate to any forensic purpose served by disclosure).

[440] Children Act 1989 s.42; *Re R (Care Proceedings; Disclosure)* [2000] 2 F.L.R. 751, FD and CA (disclosure of Pt 8 of report concerning death of child's sibling).

[441] J. Brophy et al., *Expert Evidence in Child Protection Litigation* (London: TSO, 1999); J. Brophy et al., *Myths and Practices* (1999).

[442] Child and adolescent psychiatrists provide the majority of expert evidence. A child and family psychiatric assessment appeared in 41% of cases: Brophy et al., *Expert Evidence*, p.12.

[443] DfES and DCA (2006) *op cit* para.5.15; *Guidance* (2008) paras 3.12.–3.18; *Public Law Outline*, Annex A.

[444] DfES and DCA (2006) *op cit.*, paras 3.5 and 3.14.

[445] *Practice Direction: Experts in Family Proceedings Relating to Children* (2008), replacing the *Public law Protocol* (2003).

[446] Family Proceedings Rules 1991 (SI 1991/1247) r.4.18; *Practice Direction* (2008), para.1.5.

[447] *Re B (Care Proceedings: Expert Witness)* [2007] 2 F.L.R. 979, CA; *Re K (Care Order)* [2007] 2 F.L.R. 1066, CA; see also J. Brophy and P. Bates [1998] J.S.W.F.L. 23.

[448] Children Act 1989 s.96(1), (2). See, generally, J. Spencer and R. Flin, *The Evidence of Children*, 2nd edn (1993).

[449] *LM (By her Guardian) v Medway Council* [2007] 1 F.L.R. 1698, CA.

[450] Children Act 1989 s.96(3); The Children (Admissibility of Hearsay Evidence) Order 1993 (SI 1993/621). See HO et al., *Achieving Best Evidence in Criminal Proceedings* (2002), Vol.3, and below para.21–064.

Similarly, the children's guardian's report and evidence given about matters in it is admissible.[451]

Concerns for the privacy of children and families involved in care proceedings, and the public interest in encouraging frankness in these proceedings, make it important to maintain confidentiality.[452] Family privacy is a major reason for restricting press access to court and reporting.[453] However, the rules have been relaxed; disclosure is now permitted for specific purposes, unless the court forbids this. For example, any information may be passed to a professional acting to protect children, so the local authority may pass information to other local authorities or to a police officer investigating crimes against children. A party can disclose any information to health-care professionals to facilitate treatment or counselling, and a judgment to the police or the GMC in connection with criminal investigations or complaints.[454] In addition, the courts have sometimes permitted the police to use documents that are confidential to care proceedings.[455] Despite concerns that fear of prosecution may inhibit a parent speaking frankly to a social worker, the importance of co-operation between agencies has shifted the balance in favour of permitting some disclosure.[456]

(3) Care plans

The local authority must prepare and file a care plan; the court may not make a **21–039** care order until it has considered the care plan.[457] The plan for care should be based on findings from the core assessment; informed by them, it should set out aims and intended outcomes for the child.[458] It follows that the parents, carers and child should all be involved in the work undertaken to develop the plan.[459] The plan should be explicit about the nature and frequency of the services provided by each agency involved with the child and give details of proposed placements[460] and the responsibility for implementing and reviewing the plan.[461] Plans should be sufficiently specific, make clear why a course of action has been

[451] Children Act 1989 s.41(11).

[452] *Re X (Disclosure of Information)* [2001] 2 F.L.R. 440 at 447, *per* Munby J.

[453] MoJ, *Confidence and Confidentiality* (2007), Foreword; and see above, para.18–008.

[454] Family Proceedings Rules 1991 (SI 1991/1247) r.10.20A(2); disclosure to protect vulnerable adults requires permission: *A Local Authority v K* [2007] 2 F.L.R 914, FD.

[455] *A Local Authority v D (Chief Constable of Thames Valley Police Intervening)* [2006] 2 F.L.R. 1053, FD; *Re C (A Minor) (Care Proceedings: Disclosure)* [1997] Fam. 76.

[456] But see Wells [1996] Fam Law 137; White [1995] N.L.J. 1649.

[457] Children Act 1989 ss.31(3A) and 31A; Circular LAC (99)29 provides further guidance. Planned placements will also need to comply with Children Act 1989 s.22C if the Children and Young Persons Bill 2008 is enacted.

[458] *Guidance* (2008), para.3.18.

[459] There is a duty to involve the parents and the child: s.22(4)(5) and ECHR art.8: *Scott v UK* [2000] 1 F.L.R. 958. Key elements of a plan cannot be abandoned during care proceedings without warning to the guardian: *Re X; Barnet LBC v X and Y* [2006] 2 F.L.R. 998, FD.

[460] *Guidance* (2008), para.3.18.The children's guardian may examine confidential reports on proposed placements and advise the court on their suitability: *Manchester CC v T* [1994] Fam. 181.

[461] Circular LAC (99)29, paras 12–13; Review of Children's Cases Regulations 1991 (SI 1991/1395).

chosen and give realistic time-scales for achieving key aspects[462] so the court can assess its suitability and viability.[463] The court must maintain a "proper balance" between satisfying itself about its appropriateness and "the avoidance of over zealous investigation" into matters that are for the local authority.[464] If the plan does not meet the child's needs, the court may adjourn and invite the local authority to reconsider[465] or refuse the order unless this represents the only practical course of action.[466] Where assessments are incomplete, the court may make an interim order, but this power must not be abused to prevent control passing to the local authority.[467]

Research[468] has found that in a substantial minority of cases, children were not placed according to the plan.[469] The shortage of specialist placements prevented adoptive, foster and residential placements; child protection concerns lead to the failure or non-implementation of plans to place children with their parents.[470] Non-implementation or change of care plans is a cause of concern. Although there is no evidence that local authorities intentionally mislead the courts, questions of justice to parents and children are raised where the court makes an order on the basis of a plan that is ignored or soon abandoned.[471] Nevertheless, in *Re S (FC)*[472] the House of Lords rejected an innovative scheme that would have required the court to identify essential milestones in the care plan and would have forced the local authority to inform the children's guardian if these were not met. A change made without full consultation may breach art.8 and can therefore be challenged, either by proceedings under the Human Rights Act 1998 or by seeking a discharge of the care order.[473] Action may be taken by CAFCASS on behalf of the child, following a referral from the Independent Reviewing Officer.[474]

---

[462] Circular LAC (99)29, para.14 for rehabilitation or the identification of a permanent placement.
[463] *Re S (FC)* [2002] 1 F.L.R. 815, HL, para.99.
[464] *Re S (FC) per* Lord Nicholls at para.102; Guidance (2008), para.3.42. The court does not oversee the local authority: *Re J (Minors) (Care: Care Plan)* [1994] 1 F.L.R. 253 at 265, *per* Wall J.
[465] *Re S and W (Care Proceedings)* [2007] 2 F.L.R. 275, CA.
[466] *Re B (Supervision Order: Parental Undertaking)* [1996] 1 F.L.R. 676, CA (decision to refuse a care order upheld); *Re S (Care or Supervision Order)* [1996] 1 F.L.R. 753, CA (decision to refuse a care order overturned).
[467] *Re S (FC)* [2002] 1 F.L.R. 815, HL, para.100; *C v Solihull MBC* [1993] 1 F.L.R. 290.
[468] J. Hunt and A. Macleod, *The Best-laid Plans* (1999); J. Harwin et al., *A Study to Investigate the Implementation of Care Orders under the Children Act 1989* (2002); both summarised in DH, *Children Act Now* (2001).
[469] Harwin, *The Implementation of Care Orders*: 58% for adoption, 68% for fostering, 60% for residential care, 78% for kinship care and only 41% for parental care (data relates to 21 months after the care order was made); Hunt and Macleod, Ch.7. There were considerable variations between areas in Hunt and Macleod's study: Table 7.9.
[470] Harwin, *Implementation*; Hunt and Macleod, *The Best Laid Plans* pp.196 *et seq.* and Table 8.7.
[471] *Re F, F v Lambeth LBC* [2002] 1 F.L.R. 217, FD.
[472] [2002] 1 F.L.R. 815, HL; on appeal from *Re W and B (Care Plan)* [2001] 2 F.L.R. 757, CA. The original idea of starred care plans was based on a paper to a judicial conference by A. Poysner: see M. Thorpe and E. Clarke, *Divided Duties* (1998).
[473] *Re M (Care Proceedings)* [2001] 2 F.L.R. 1300, FD; *Re C (Breach of Human Rights: Damages)* [2007] 1 F.L.R. 1957, CA (no damages awarded); and below, para.21–087.
[474] Children Act 1989 s.26(2)(k), (2A), (2B), (2C); see above, para.21–007 and below, para.21–069.

(4) Orders in care proceedings
The applicant indicates which type of order is being sought; the court, taking **21–040**
account of the children's guardian's analysis, decides what orders, if any, to
make. Where there are competing applications from the local authority for a care
order, and from relatives for a residence order, the court is not bound to consider
the residence application first.[475] The court may make a care or supervision order
only if it is satisfied that the significant-harm test is proved.[476] Alternatively, it
may make a s.8 order[477] or no order, whether or not there is proof of significant
harm. The choice between these depends on the best way of securing the child's
welfare but the court's response must be proportionate to the risk presented.[478]
The effects of the order[479] are relevant:

> In *Re C*[480] the mother had been repeatedly assaulted by the father. When the
> baby was two weeks old the mother left him in his father's care so that she
> could register the birth. Whilst she was out, the father attacked the child,
> causing serious brain damage. The local authority started care proceedings.
> The mother and child went to a residential unit; the mother showed a strong
> bond with her child, co-operated fully with all the professionals and was
> allowed to take him home. Nevertheless, the local authority, supported by
> the children's guardian, sought a care order because of the mother's lack of
> judgment in leaving the baby with his father and the risk that she might form
> a relationship with another violent man. The court granted a supervision
> order.
>
> In *Re M*[481] a girl, aged four, was admitted to hospital underweight,
> emaciated and severely dehydrated. She had bruises on many parts of her
> body and internal injuries caused either by a punch or a heavy fall. The local
> authority obtained an interim care order and the girl was placed in foster
> care. She made allegations of physical and sexual abuse by her mother and
> step-father. The local authority sought a care order; the mother and the
> maternal grandparents applied separately for a residence order. The allega-
> tions of abuse were not proved, but the judge found that the child had
> suffered significant harm because the mother had failed to seek medical
> assistance promptly. A residence order was granted to the mother on
> condition that she resided with the child at the step-father's parents' house.
> The local authority's appeal was refused.

---

[475] *Oldham MBC v E* [1994] 1 F.L.R. 568 at 576, *per* Waite L.J. This part of the decision was not
overruled by *Re M (A Minor) (Care Orders: Threshold Conditions)* [1994] 2 A.C. 424.
[476] Children Act 1989 s.31(1).
[477] ss.8(1), (3), (4) (a), 10(1). S.8 orders, except a residence order, may not be made in respect of
children in care: s.9(1); a residence order discharges a care order: s.91(1). A s.8 order may not require
a child to be accommodated: s.9(2), (5); *Re S and D (Children: Powers of Court)* [1995] 2 F.L.R.
456.
[478] *Re O (Supervision Order)* [2001] 1 F.L.R. 923, CA; *Re C and B (Care Order: Future Harm)*
[2001] 1 F.L.R. 611, CA; *Re C (Care Order or Supervision Order)* [2001] 2 F.L.R. 466, FD.
[479] *Re V (Care or Supervision Order)* [1996] 1 F.L.R. 776, CA; *Re O (Supervision Order)* [2001] 1
F.L.R. 923 at paras 24–28, *per* Hale L.J.
[480] [2001] 2 F.L.R. 466, FD.
[481] *Re M (A Minor) (Appeal) (No.2)* [1994] 1 F.L.R. 59; see also *Re M (Appeal: Interim Order) (No.1)*
[1994] 1 F.L.R. 54. The child later died from further injuries.

Care and supervision orders are fundamentally different. A care order gives the local authority parental responsibility, the power to control the parents' exercise of it and the right to remove the child without a further order.[482] Under a supervision order the child's safety depends on the parents.[483] Either order may be used where the child is placed with the parents at home or in a residential family centre.[484] A care order may be more appropriate if the parental care is declining[485] or there is a high risk of parents leaving the family centre, because it can be used to remove the child. In contrast, where the local authority's past decision-making has been flawed, leading to inappropriate removal of the children, only a supervision order should be made to prevent further removal without court approval.[486]

The effects of care orders and supervision orders will now be considered.

ii. Care order

21–041 A care order gives the local authority parental responsibility for the child and the power to determine the extent to which parents may exercise their parental responsibility. It does not remove the parents' parental responsibility.[487] This recognises the expectation that state care focuses on reunification, a process that is facilitated by parents remaining involved in their children's lives.[488] A care order discharges any s.8 order in respect of the child, thus ending the parental responsibility of non-parents.[489]

Although the local authority acquires parental responsibility, it lacks the power to take certain major decisions. It may not cause the child to be brought up in a different religion[490]; agree to the child's adoption[491]; or appoint a guardian (but it may apply to the court to have an existing guardian removed).[492] If it wishes

---

[482] *Re O (Supervision Order)* [2001] 1 F.L.R. 923 at paras 24–25 *per* Hale L.J. Removal must be a legitimate and proportionate response. Parents must be notified and consulted: *Re W (Removal into Care)* [2005] 2 F.L.R. 1022, CA.

[483] *Re S (J) (A Minor) (Care or Supervision Order)* [1993] 2 F.L.R. 919 at 950, *per* Judge Coningsby Q.C.

[484] *Re T (A Minor) (Care or Supervision Order)* [1994] 1 F.L.R. 103, CA; *Re R and G (Minors) (Interim Care or Supervision Orders)* [1994] 1 F.L.R. 793. If the child is at home under a care order, the Placement of Children with Parents etc. Regulations 1991 (SI 1991/893), must be complied with.

[485] *Re T (A Minor) (Care or Supervision Order)* [1994] 1 F.L.R. 103, CA.

[486] *Re O (Care: Discharge of Care Order)* [1999] 2 F.L.R. 119, FD.

[487] s.33(3)(4); *Guidance* (2008), paras 3.58–3.64. A mother retains the right to make a s.4 agreement with the father to share parental responsibility: *Re X (Parental Responsibility Agreement: Children in Care)* [2000] 1 F.L.R. 517, FD.

[488] *Johansen v Norway* (1996) 23 E.H.R.R. 22; R. Bullock et al., *Going Home* (1993); cf. J. Eekelaar and R. Dingwall [1989] New L.J. 217 at 238.

[489] ss.12(2), 91(2), but not the parental responsibility of a stepparent under s.4A.

[490] s.33(6)(a). But foster carers need not be of the same religious persuasion as the child nor give an undertaking to bring the children up in their own religion: the Fostering Services Regulations 2002 (SI 2002/57). Where the child is in residential care, the Children's Homes Regulations 1991 (SI 1991/1506) reg.11 apply; see also *Guidance* (1991), Vol.4, paras 1.121–1.124.

[491] s.33(6)(b)(i), (ii). The local authority must apply for a placement order: Adoption and Children Act 2002 s.21.

[492] ss.6(7)(a), 33(6)(b) (iii).

to change the child's surname[493] or arrange for the child to stay outside the United Kingdom for more than one month,[494] it must obtain the written consent of everyone with parental responsibility or permission from the court. If the local authority wishes to arrange the child's emigration (even to Scotland), it must obtain the court's approval.[495] The court also has control over contact between children in care and their parents.[496] No other conditions may be imposed by the court.[497] The local authority must also comply with any regulations made by the Secretary of State concerning the treatment of children in care.[498] Care orders last until the child is 18, unless they are discharged earlier.[499]

There have been increases in the number of applications for care orders since the introduction of the Children Act 1989,[500] but accurate figures for numbers of applications are not available.[501] Approximately 11,000 children were the subject of care proceedings in 2006; 5,000 children entered care under full care orders. In the *Care Profiling Study*, just under 60 per cent of applications resulted in care orders, 14 per cent in supervision orders and 23 per cent in residence orders. No order was made in 3 per cent of cases. In addition, 20 out of 386 cases were withdrawn before the final hearing. The figures for care and supervision orders were little different from those in a study two years after the implementation of the Act.[502] In 2007, there were just under 40,000 children looked after under care orders, a quarter of them on interim orders.[503]

iii. Supervision order

This order places the child under the supervision of a social worker[504] who is under a duty "to advise, assist and befriend" the child.[505] The local authority cannot be required to make facilities available, but there is no point making the

21–042

---

[493] s.33(7). An application can be made ex parte; a children's guardian may be appointed: *Re J (A Minor) (Change of Name)* [1993] 1 F.L.R. 699.

[494] Children Act 1989 s.33(8).

[495] Children Act 1989 Sch.2 para.19; court approval can only be given where the conditions in para.19(3) are satisfied. The consent of everyone with parental responsibility is required except where para.19(4) or (5) applies: *Re G (Minors) (Care: Leave to Place outside the Jurisdiction)* [1994] 2 F.L.R. 301.

[496] Children Act 1989 s.34; see below, paras 21–074 *et seq.*

[497] *Re T (A Minor) (Care Order: Conditions)* [1994] 2 F.L.R. 423, CA. But the court has been prepared to grant injunctions to stop parents preventing their child (those living at home under a care order) attending college: *Re P (Care Orders: Injunctive Relief)* [2000] 2 F.L.R. 385.

[498] See *Guidance* (1991), Vols 3 and 4 and the regulations included therein. Some of the controls on placements will be by statute if the Children and Young Persons Bill 2008 is enacted (adding Children Act 1989 ss.22A–22F).

[499] Children Act 1989 s.91(12). The local authority has aftercare responsibilities until the young person is 21: ss.23A–24D, as amended by the Children (Leaving Care) Act 2000; powers in relation to education will be extended to age 25: Children and Young Persons Bill cl.20.

[500] Before the 1989 Act, local authorities could also obtain control through wardship and matrimonial proceedings, or by parental rights resolutions under Childcare Act 1980 s.3.

[501] The only available figures are collected for the *Judicial Statistics*, but these are substantially flawed; see J. Masson et al. MoJ Research Series 04/08, p.11.

[502] J. Masson et al., MoJ Research Series 04/08; J. Hunt and A. Macleod, *The Best-laid Plans* (1999).

[503] *Children Looked After by Local Authorities 2007*, Table A2.

[504] Children Act 1989 Sch.3 para.9; *Guidance* (2008), paras 3.80–3.84.

[505] Children Act 1989 s.35(1)(a).

order unless the local authority will provide the services required. The order lasts for one year, or for any shorter period specified,[506] but may be extended for up to three years.[507]

The Short Committee noted that supervision orders were considered ineffective and infrequently made, and recommended that supervisors should have greater powers to impose conditions on children and parents.[508] The *Review of Child Care Law* agreed and proposed a list of conditions that have been incorporated in the Act.[509] Supervision orders are used in two different types of case: (1) where the child is at home, to support and monitor care by the parents; and (2) when a residence order has been made in care proceedings,[510] to support the child and carers, particularly with any difficulties they may have in building their relationship, or difficulties with the child's parents. The family can be required to accept services (e.g. to improve socialisation through the child's participation in activities, or care through the adults' attendance at courses).[511] Orders can be used to secure local authority supervision of parental contact with a child,[512] but the county court and the family proceedings court have no power to accept undertakings, so other conditions, such as medical treatment for a parent, cannot be required.[513] Directions are imposed by the supervisor, not the court.[514] The supervisor may enter into a written agreement with the child and any person who has parental responsibility or care of the child (responsible persons),[515] stating what they must achieve and what the supervisor will provide. The consent of responsible persons is required to any conditions,[516] but they may have little choice if the supervisor considers these essential for the working of the order.

The supervisor is required to take such steps as are reasonably necessary to give effect to the order.[517] The supervisor may require the responsible persons, with their consent, to take reasonable steps to ensure that the child complies with directions to participate in activities, and to keep the supervisor informed of their address.[518] The child may be required to submit to such medical or psychiatric examinations or treatment as the court thinks fit, but such conditions may not be

---

[506] *M v Warwickshire CC* [1994] 2 F.L.R. 593.

[507] Children Act 1989 Sch.3, para.6.

[508] *Short Report*, para.150.

[509] *Review of Child Care Law*, paras 18.6–18.12; Children Act 1989 Sch.3 paras 2–5.

[510] The court must make an interim supervision order if it makes a residence order in care proceedings unless the child's welfare is safeguarded without one; s.38(3); for example, *Re H (Residence Order: Placement Out of the Jurisdiction)* [2006] 1 F.L.R. 1140, FD.

[511] *Croydon LBC v A (No.3)* [1992] 2 F.L.R. 350; conditions should be apparent on the face of the order: *Re T (A Minor) (Care Order: Conditions)* [1994] 2 F.L.R. 423.

[512] *Re Z and A (Contact: Supervision Order)* [2000] 2 F.L.R. 406; *Re DH (A Minor) (Child Abuse)* [1994] 1 F.L.R. 679 at 700.

[513] *Re B (Supervision Order: Parental Undertaking)* [1996] 1 F.L.R. 676, CA; Neill L.J. did suggest that the mother's agreement to seek treatment could be recorded in the preamble to the order. Despite their unenforceability, undertakings are used.

[514] Children Act 1989 Sch.3 para.3; *Re H* (1994) 158 J.P.N. 211.

[515] Children Act 1989 Sch.3 para.1.

[516] Children Act 1989 para.3(1).

[517] Children Act 1989 s.35(1)(b).

[518] Children Act 1989 Sch.3 paras 1, 3, 7. The child must also keep the supervisor notified of his address: para.8.

imposed on a mature child who does not consent.[519] There is no direct way of enforcing a supervision order[520]; the supervisor has no right of entry to the child's home, and no right to remove the child. No penalties are prescribed for breach of a supervision order, but the supervisor may seek its variation and the magistrates could impose penalties.[521] In variation or extension proceedings, the court can only impose a care order if the significant harm test is re-proved.[522] In practice, lack of co-operation from parents or the failure of the local authority to provide resources, particularly to allocate a social worker, renders a supervision order ineffective. In Hunt and Macleod's study, only half of the families subject to supervision co-operated fully, and a third of these placements failed. None of the local authorities allocated a supervisor to all cases for the duration of the order. Overall, the researchers concluded that an unreservedly good outcome was only achieved for one in six of the children, and a more powerful order might have been helpful for half of them. Care orders were made subsequently in respect of a third of the children, and two were adopted.[523]

Despite the increase in powers, supervision orders have not become more widely used. The emphasis on voluntariness means that cases suitable for supervision orders are managed without any order.[524] Also, high thresholds for care proceedings may mean that cases that could be managed with a supervision order are not brought to court. Accurate figures are not available for the number of supervision orders, but it is likely that more than half are made to support residence orders.[525]

iv. Interim care and supervision orders

The *Review of Child Care Law* was concerned that care proceedings should be dealt with as quickly as possible, but recognised that it took time for the children's guardian to prepare the report. They recommended that interim orders should last eight weeks, with extensions only in exceptional circumstances for up to 14 days.[526] These proposals were accepted, but the Act is less restrictive; interim orders may be made for up to eight weeks, with extensions of four

21–043

---

[519] Children Act 1989 Sch.3 paras 4, 5; *Re W (A Minor) (Medical Treatment: Court's Jurisdiction)* [1992] Fam. 64.

[520] *Re R and G (Minors) (Interim Care or Supervision Order)* [1994] 1 F.L.R. 793. The supervisor can only refer it back to the court: s.35(1)(c). Consequently, it was inappropriate to make a supervision order in relation to a child just before his seventeenth birthday: *Re V (Care or Supervision Order)* [1996] 1 F.L.R. 776, CA.

[521] Magistrates' Courts Act 1980 s.63. However, the *Review of Child Care Law* considered that this would rarely be appropriate.

[522] Children Act 1989 s.39; *Re R and G (Minors) (Interim Care or Supervision Orders)* [1994] 1 F.L.R. 793; *Re A (Supervision Order: Extension)* [1995] 1 F.L.R. 335, CA. An extension beyond three years also necessitates re-proving the threshold conditions but this does not justify using a care order where long-term supervision is required: *Re O (Supervision Order)* [2001] 1 F.L.R. 923, CA.

[523] J. Hunt and A. Macleod, *The Best-laid Plans* (1999), pp.201–203 and Table 8.8. The study was based on 133 children involved in care proceedings in three local authorities. Supervision orders were made in 23 cases.

[524] *Children Act Now* (2001), p.62.

[525] J.Masson et al., MoJ research series 04/08, Table A2.42.

[526] *Review of Child Care Law*, paras 17.4, 17.16–17.18.

weeks.[527] The plan to complete cases within 12 weeks was wildly optimistic, but renewal is dealt with administratively where the parties consent.[528] On average, cases take 50 weeks in the county court and 42 weeks before magistrates. The making of interim care orders is contested in about 20 per cent of cases.

The Children Act 1989 permits the court to make an interim care or supervision order when proceedings are adjourned or a s.37(1) investigation is ordered, if it is satisfied that there are reasonable grounds for believing that the case passes the significant-harm test.[529] The child can be protected until the court is able to decide whether or not an order should be made.[530] If a residence order is made in care proceedings, the court must make an interim supervision order unless it is satisfied that the child's welfare does not require it.[531] Interim orders should not be used to keep a case under review by the court.[532] Care plans inevitably involve some uncertainties; it is for the judge to decide whether to approve the plan and make the final order or to allow a limited period of "purposeful delay" so that issues can be clarified.[533]

Concerns about repeated assessments of children led to a recommendation in the *Cleveland Report* that the courts should have powers to control assessments.[534] Where there is an interim order, the court can direct (or prohibit) assessments, but it cannot require mature children[535] or adults to participate.[536] Assessment during proceedings are intended to provide information to assist decision-making, not to allow the court to direct services or secure treatment.[537] No one has a right to be made a better parent at public expense,[538] but courts are reluctant to refuse assessments that might establish that parents are able to care for their children.[539] Assessments of a child's relationship with the parents may be undertaken in the safety of a residential centre, but the high cost of these facilities means that local authorities may be unwilling to pay for them. The Act is silent on funding assessments; courts stress the parents' and child's right under ECHR arts 6 and 8, and have required local authorities to provide detailed

---

[527] Children Act 1989 s.38(4), (5); Cm.62 (1987), para.61.

[528] CAAC, *Handbook of Best Practice* (1997), Ch.2.

[529] Children Act 1989 s.38(1), (2); *Re M (Interim Care Order: Removal)* [2006] 1 F.L.R. 1046, CA. The efficacy test in s.1(5) also applies.

[530] *Re S (FC)* [2002] 1 F.L.R. 815, HL at para.90; *Re B. (Care: Expert Witnesses)* [1996] 1 F.L.R. 667, CA.

[531] Children Act 1989 s.38(3).

[532] *Re S (FC)* [2002] 1 F.L.R. 815, HL at para.90; cf. *Buckingham CC v M* [1994] 2 F.L.R. 506 (full order not appropriate during rehabilitation); *C v Solihull MBC* (interim order pending parental assessment).

[533] *Re S (FC)* [2002] U.K.H.L. 10 at para.95.

[534] *Cleveland Report* (Cm.412 (1988)), pp.245, 252–253.

[535] The objection could be overridden by the High Court: *Re W (A Minor) (Medical Treatment: Court's Jurisdiction)* [1992] Fam. 64.

[536] Children Act 1989 s.38(6); *Re W (Assessment of Child)* [1998] 2 F.L.R. 130, CA. Co-operation will often provide parents with the only chance of rehabilitation.

[537] *Re G (Interim Care Order: Residential Assessment)* [2006] 1 F.L.R. 601, HL, *per* Baroness Hale at paras 64–66; *Guidance* (2008), para.3.49.

[538] *Re G (Interim Care Order: Residential Assessment)* [2006] 1 F.L.R. 601, HL *per* Lord Scott at para.24.

[539] *Re L and H (Residential Assessment)* [2007] 1 F.L.R. 1370, CA; *Re K (Care Order)* [2007] 2 F.L.R 1066.

information about implications for their budget to justify refusal to pay.[540] Assessment costs can be apportioned between the parties and partly funded by legal aid,[541] but the *Funding Code* now excludes all residential assessments.[542] The financial implications and the requirement, in the *Public Law Outline*, on local authorities to complete core assessments before bringing proceedings is also likely to make them less willing to agree to further assessments.

Figures are not available for the total number of interim orders made or the average number of interim orders *per* case. The average duration of proceedings suggests that repeated interim orders are necessary in most cases, unless children are protected by agreement with the parents.[543] In March 2007, 9,800 looked-after children were subject to interim care orders; approximately one-quarter of those who were subject to care orders.[544]

v. Domestic violence injunctions

The Law Commission proposed that the courts should have the additional power **21–044** to exclude a suspected abuser from the family home so that the child could remain at home and be protected there.[545] The Family Law Act 1996 amended the Children Act 1989 to enable a court making an interim care order[546] to include an exclusion requirement or accept undertakings.[547] This requirement can only be imposed where there is reasonable cause for believing that if a person is excluded from the child's home,[548] or prevented from entering it, the child will cease to suffer, or cease to be likely to suffer, significant harm.[549] In addition, another person living in the home must be able and willing to care for the child and consent to the requirement.[550] However, in contrast to exclusion injunctions,

---

[540] *Re G (Interim Care Order: Residential Assessment)* [2004 1 F.L.R. 876, CA; cf. *Re G* [2006] 1 F.L.R. 601, HL, *per* Baroness Hale at para.70.

[541] *Sheffield City Council v V (Legal Services Commission Intervening)* [2007] 1 F.L.R. 279, FD.

[542] LSC, *Funding Code* (2007), 1.3, from October, 1 2007.

[543] See CAAC, *Final Report 1997*, Tables 5A, 5B.

[544] *Children Looked After by Local Authorities* 2006/2007, Table A2. Some of these children were placed with a parent or relative.

[545] Law Com. No.207, *Domestic Violence and Occupation of the Family Home* (1992), paras 6.15 *et seq.*

[546] This provision was originally in the Family Homes and Domestic Violence Bill 1995. The Association of Directors of Social Services and the Family Rights Group both supported adding the power to interim supervision orders. Without such a power, there is a risk that the court would make an interim care order solely for this purpose: see Proceedings of the Special Public Committee on the Family Homes and Domestic Violence Bill, HL 55 (1994–5). A prohibited steps order could be made to prevent contact by an abuser without an interim care order: *Re H (Prohibited Steps Order)* [1995] 1 F.L.R. 638, CA.

[547] Children Act 1989 ss.38A, 38B; Family Proceedings Rules 1991 (SI 1991/1247) r.4.24A; *Guidance* (2008), paras 3.53–3.57. The local authority has a power to provide accommodation for an alleged perpetrator who leaves but no duty to do so: Children Act 1989 Sch.2 para.5.

[548] Children Act 1989 s.38A(3) or from a defined area where the home is, but not from the child's school, etc.

[549] Children Act 1989 s.38A(2)(a). By agreeing to the order, the local authority is accepting that the carer is not likely to cause significant harm, but in many cases there will be residual concerns: A. Pack [2001] Fam. Law 216, 219.

[550] Children Act 1989 s.38A(2)(b); Family Proceedings Rules 1991 (SI 1991/1247) r.4.24; F.P.C. 1991 r.24. DH Circular LAC (97)15 recognises that social workers undertaking a child protection investigation may feel a conflict of interest if they have to advise a carer about these provisions, and suggests that the carer should have access to independent advice: para.22.

the court is not required to balance potential hardship to the excluded parent and the child. The order cannot last longer than the interim care order; a power of arrest may be attached to allow a constable to arrest, without warrant, any person reasonably believed to be in breach.[551] Breach of an undertaking is enforced through proceedings for contempt of court.[552] Exclusion requirements and undertakings cease to be enforceable if the child is removed by the local authority for more than 24 hours.[553] It has been suggested that the wide powers to exclude a person without a full trial of the allegations are unfair and will encourage false allegations.[554] Few orders are made, probably because in cases where care proceedings are required due to domestic violence, the parents are unwilling to separate or unlikely to comply with orders.

These powers are additional to those under the Family Law Act 1996 to make occupation orders relating to the family home on application,[555] and non-molestation orders in any family proceedings where the respondent is a party.[556] The complex conditions that apply to occupation orders may make it impossible to continue the exclusion after the end of the interim order. The Law Commission found no support for long-term exclusion as an alternative to a care order.[557] This could be tantamount to imposing particular family relationships that might be unsustainable in the long term. Also, it was not appropriate to give the child's needs precedence without considering the balance of hardship between the adults.[558]

vi. Discharge of care and supervision orders

21–045   The child, any person with parental responsibility, the supervisor in the case of a supervision order and the local authority may apply for discharge of a care or supervision order.[559] Any other person who seeks discharge of a care order must apply for a residence order, which ends the care order and grants them parental responsibility.[560] The court may only discharge the order if it is in the child's best interests to do so[561]; it is not sufficient that the parents are fit and able to care for their child. Although the *Review* considered that state intervention in family life

---

[551] Children Act 1989 s.38A(5). Note this contrasts with the duty to include a power of arrest in certain circumstances under the Family Law Act 1996 s.47(2); see above. In relation to enforcement, see *President's Direction* [1998] 1 F.L.R. 495; *Re W (Exclusion Requirement: Statement of Evidence)* [2000] 2 F.L.R. 666.

[552] Children Act 1989 s.38B(3), and see below.

[553] Children Act 1989 s.38A(10), 38B(3), and see below.

[554] Proceedings of the Special Public Committee on the Family Homes and Domestic Violence Bill, HL 55 (1994–5), memorandum of Dr Susan Edwards and Ms Ann Halpern.

[555] Family Law Act 1996 ss.33–41. The provision for third-party applications for domestic-violence injunctions has not been implemented (s.60), and see sixth edition of this book at p.826.

[556] Family Law Act 1996 s.42(2).

[557] Law Com. No.207, para.17.

[558] Law Com. No.207, para.17.

[559] Children Act 1989 s.39. A child does not require the leave of the court: *Re A (Care Discharge Application by Child)* [1995] 1 F.L.R. 599.

[560] Children Act 1989 ss.8(1), 10, 91(1). Leave may be required; see above. A special guardianship order will have the same effect; s.91(5A), to be introduced by the Adoption and Children Bill 2002 Sch.3.

[561] Children Act 1989 s.1; the checklist applies: s.1(4)(b); the burden of proof rests with the person making the application: *Re MD and TD (Minors) (No.2)* [1994] Fam. Law 489.

should not be permitted by reference to a welfare test, this was the appropriate standard for discharge proceedings. It would be illogical to require parents to establish more than in private law proceedings; an alternative test could result in the court continuing an order that it knew was not in the child's best interests.[562] However, this approach may not accord with art.8. The Strasbourg Court has repeatedly emphasised that care should normally be seen as a temporary measure with the aim of family reunification. It has accepted that a child's interests in maintaining family relations with a foster carer may preclude return home,[563] but this argument would not prevent discharging an order in relation to a child who has lacked a stable home in care.

The local authority is required to review the case of a child regularly, and must consider whether the order should be discharged.[564] Reviews must be chaired by an Independent Reviewing Officer whose role is to ensure that the child's wishes and feelings are taken into account in the local authority's plan.[565] Most applications for discharge of care orders are made by local authorities,[566] usually after the child has returned home.[567] Parents may be reluctant to seek discharge because of the costs and memories of the order being made.[568] It is to the local authority's advantage to have the order discharged: a child who ceases to be looked after before age 16 is not owed after-care duties.[569] Where the child is not already at home, it is difficult for the parent or child to establish that this is in the child's best interests, particularly where they have little contact. The inability of the magistrates' court to order the child's phased return to the family was seen as a significant defect by the judiciary, but despite support in the *Review*, the Children Act 1989 made no specific provision for this.[570]

vii. Appeals

Before the introduction of the Children Act 1989, there was no coherent scheme **21–046** for appeals in childcare cases, and appeal rights were restricted.[571] The *Review*

---

[562] paras 20.11–20.21. See also *Review of Child Care Law Discussion Paper No.9* (1985).

[563] *Haase v Germany* [2004] 2 F.L.R. 39, ECtHR at para.93; *Johansen v Norway* (1996) 23 E.H.R.R. 33.

[564] Review of Children's Cases Regulations 1991 (SI 1991/895) reg.3 and Sch.2. There is a positive obligation to work for reunification of the family: *Eriksson v Sweden* (1989) 12 E.H.R.R. 183, para.71.

[565] SI 1991/895, reg.2A(6); *Guidance* (2008), para.3.67.

[566] See E. Farmer and R. Parker, *A Study of the Discharge of Care Orders* (University of Bristol, 1985), Table 4. Out of a sample of 186 applications for discharge, 144 were made by the local authority, 31 by parents and 9 by children. The success rate of LA applications was 88%; that of parents 32%.

[567] See, generally, R. Bullock et al., *Going Home* (London: HMSO, 1993); E. Farmer and R. Parker, *Trials and Tribulations* (Aldershot: Dartmouth, 1991).

[568] K. Broadhurst and T. Pendleton "Revisiting 'home on trial' in the context of the current concerns about cost and effectiveness of the looked after children system" (2007) *Child and Family Social Work* 380–389.

[569] Children Act 1989 ss.24–24D. It is government policy not to end care prematurely: see *Children Act Report 1995–99*, para.6.2.

[570] *Short Report*, Vol.III, Evidence, p.588. Parents could use wardship: *Re J (Wardship: Jurisdiction)* [1984] 1 W.L.R. 81; *Review of Child Care Law*, para.20.26. For possible mechanisms see the sixth edition of this work at p.819.

[571] See the fifth edition of this work at p.625.

recommended that parents and local authorities should be able to appeal; the Act gives all parties to the original decision a right to appeal,[572] but no appeal may be made against the making or refusal of an emergency protection order.[573] Appeals against decisions by a magistrates' court are heard in the High Court by a Family Division judge sitting in open court; other appeals go to the Court of Appeal.[574] The appeal is not a full re-hearing; the principles in *G v G* apply.[575]

The Act provides for the child's protection pending an appeal. If there is an interim care or supervision order, and a full order is refused, the court may nevertheless make an order for "the appeal period" subject to such conditions as it thinks fit.[576] This period expires with the time limit for appealing unless an appeal is made, and continues until the case is determined by court.[577] Similarly, where there is an appeal against the making of an order, the court may grant a stay so that the status quo is preserved pending an appeal. [578]

F. Protection of children in emergencies[579]

21–047   From the first introduction of child protection legislation, it was general practice to remove or "rescue" children before proving the case for their committal to care.[580] A magistrate could authorise a child's removal to a "place of safety" on the application of any person with reasonable cause to suspect that the child was being ill-treated.[581] The police also had the power to detain children on similar grounds.[582] "Place of safety" orders were the subject of considerable criticism: they lasted too long, were used too readily and were not subject to review; the grounds were not sufficiently focused on emergencies; the applicant had no clear

---

[572] *Review of Child Care Law*, Ch.19; Cm.62 (1987), para.66; Family Proceedings Rules 1991 (SI 1991/1247) r.4.22.

[573] Children Act 1989 s.46(10); *Essex CC v F* [1993] 1 F.L.R. 847; theoretically judicial review is available, alternatively, an application for an interim care order could be made: see *Re P (Emergency Protection Order)* [1996] 1 F.L.R. 482 at 484, *per* Johnson J.

[574] Children Act 1989 s.94(1); Family Proceedings Rules 1991 (SI 1991/1247) r.4.22; RSC Ords 55 and 59 (Civil Procedure Rules 1998 (SI 1998/3132) Sch.1); *Practice Direction* [1992] 1 W.L.R. 261.

[575] [1985] 1 W.L.R. 647; see above, para.19–024.

[576] Children Act 1989 s.40; *Re M (A Minor) (Appeal: Interim Order)* [1994] 1 F.L.R. 54. There are comparable provisions for cases of discharge. The appellate court cannot make an order under s.40(1) but may make an interim order under s.38: *Croydon LBC v A (No.2)* [1994] 2 F.L.R. 348.

[577] Children Act 1989 s.40(6); the magistrates may specify a different time (s.40(4)), but this may be extended by the appellate court: (s.40(5)).

[578] See, for example, *Re K and H* [2007] 1 F.L.R. 2043, CA.

[579] See J. Masson et al. *Protecting Powers* (2007); J. Masson, "Emergency protection to protect children: using and avoiding legal controls" [2005] C.F.L.Q. 75.

[580] H. Ferguson, "Cleveland in history: the abused child and child protection 1880–1914", in R. Cooter (ed.), *In the Name of the Child: Health and Welfare 1880–1940* (1992) and H. Ferguson, "Re-thinking child protection practice: a case for history", in Violence Against Children Study Group, *Taking Child Abuse Seriously* (London: Unwin Hyman, 1990).

[581] Prevention of Cruelty to Children Act 1894 s.10; Children and Young Persons Act 1969 s.28. See J. Masson et al., *Protecting Powers* Ch.2. Under the 1969 Act detention was limited to 28 days.

[582] Prevention of Cruelty to and Protection of Children Act 1889 s.4; Children and Young Persons Act 1933 s.40; Children and Young Persons Act 1969 s.28(2). Detention without warrant was limited to eight days by the 1933 Act, but the police could also obtain a warrant to search and detain a child for 28 days.

responsibility for the child's welfare; the powers to obtain medical examinations were unclear; and orders could result in long periods without contact with the family.[583] The Government accepted proposals from the Short Committee and the *Review of Child Care Law* to limit emergency powers.[584] Immediate separation of the child was not necessary and could be harmful to the child; compulsory separation could make it more difficult to work with the family for the child's rehabilitation.[585]

i. Emergency protection orders[586]

The purpose of the order is to enable a child to be provided with immediate short- **21–048**
term protection in a genuine emergency.[587] These orders are regarded as "draconian", so it is said that "extraordinary compelling reasons" are required for making them.[588] However, magistrates faced with a request from a local authority, backed by a credible statement from a social worker, do not want to take the risk of serious harm to a child, so they rarely refuse orders. Approximately one-fifth of care applications are preceded by an EPO.[589]

Anyone[590] may apply to the court for an emergency protection order, which empowers them to remove (or prevent the removal of) the child concerned. Although there is power for applications to be heard without notice by a single magistrate, a "compelling" case must be made for doing so.[591] Imminent harm to a vulnerable child or the need to act without alerting parents who may disappear with the child are common reasons for hearing applications without notice to the parents. Where the courts insist on notice of one day, local authorities often ask the police to use their powers.[592] There is provision for the appointment of a children's guardian, but only very limited inquiries are possible.[593]

The court may only grant the order if it is satisfied that there is reasonable cause to believe that the child is likely to suffer significant harm if he or she is

---

[583] *Short Report*, paras 122–130; *Review of Child Care Law*, Ch.13; *Cleveland Report*, pp.306–307; Cm.62, paras 45–47; T. Norris and N. Parton, "The administration of place of safety orders" [1987] J.S.W.L. 1. Approximately 5,000 place of safety orders (POSO's) were made in 1990: Cm.2584, para.3.10.

[584] Cm.62 (1987), para.46; *Short Report*, paras 122–130; *Review of Child Care Law*, Ch.13.

[585] Packman et al. (1986). Many of these points were re-iterated in the *Cleveland Report* (1988).

[586] Children Act 1989 ss.44–45B.

[587] *Guidance* (1991), Vol.1 para.4.28.

[588] *X County Council v B* [2005] 1 F.L.R. 341, FD, per Munby J. at para.57; *Re X. (Emergency Protection Order)* [2006] 2 F.L.R. 701, *per* MacFarlane J at para.64(1); *Guidance* (2008), para.4.25.

[589] Masson et al. *Protecting Powers*; Masson et al., *Care Profiling Study*.

[590] In practice, applications are only made by local authorities; Masson et al. (2007). Local authorities take over the cases brought otherwise: Emergency Protection Order (Transfer of Responsibilities) Regulations 1991 (SI 1991/1414).

[591] F.P.C. 1991 r.2(5)(a). Leave is required; rr.3, 4(4); *Re X (Emergency Protection Order)* [2006] 2 F.L.R. 701, *per* MacFarlane J. at para.64(viii). Alternatively, the court may allow the case to proceed with less than one days notice: *Essex CC v F* [1993] 1 F.L.R. 847.

[592] Masson et al. *Protecting Powers*, Table 7.3. Parents' rights are better protected in without-notice applications than if they attend having had little time to prepare: Children Act 1989 s.45(11).

[593] *Guidance* (1991), Vol.7, paras 2.69–2.71. A guardian was available in under half the cases in a recent study: see Masson et al. *Protecting Powers*, Table 7.2.

challenge. Children placed in foster care under an EPO are not detained, and so habeas corpus cannot be used to challenge the order.[617] Any person excluded may apply for the variation or discharge of an exclusion requirement.[618] There is no appeal.[619]

21–050   The very restrictive approach to emergency orders endorsed by the High Court is justified on the basis that sudden separation of a parent and child breaches the rights to family life of both, and by reference to decisions in the European Court of Human Rights. The Strasbourg Court has stated that "extraordinarily compelling reasons"[620] are needed to justify removal of a baby at birth, but has been less than clear in explaining the circumstances in which other emergency action is or is not justified:

> In *K and T v Finland*[621] the mother, K, who suffered from serious mental illness and was hospitalised from time to time, agreed to her son's accommodation by the welfare authorities. A few months later she gave birth to a daughter who was removed from her in the hospital delivery suite, under a court order. Shortly afterwards, her son was also made subject to an emergency order so that he could not be removed from the children's home. There was no prior discussion with the parents; the welfare authorities apparently rejected any possibility that T, the father, could care for his baby. The parents were allowed only supervised contact. Although the father demonstrated he could care for the baby, the authorities decided to place her in foster care with her brother. After unsuccessfully challenging the decisions, the parents applied to the European Court of Human Rights. The court found a breach of art.8. The State's action has been "arbitrary and unjustified". The mother did not appear ill or irrational when the baby was removed, no other measures of protection were tried, and despite pre-planning, no attempt was made to inform the parents.[622] Finland requested the case be referred to the Grand Chamber. There, the majority accepted that art.8 had been breached in removing the baby, but not in detaining the son. There were strong dissenting opinions from three judges who considered that there had been no violation in relation to the baby[623] and four judges who found a breach in the detention of the son. Underlying the reasoning was concern for the proper use of these extreme powers. The judges who found a breach of art.8 considered that intervention without notice should be

---

[617] *Re S (Habeas Corpus)* [2004] 1 F.L.R. 590, Munby J. This also applies to residential accommodation, except, possibly, secure accommodation, at para.28.

[618] Children Act 1989 s.45(8A), (8B) added by Family Law Act 1996 Sch.6.

[619] Children Act 1989 s.45(10); *Essex CC v F* [1993] 1 F.L.R. 847; judicial review is theoretically available. The lack of a mechanism for speedy review has been criticised: see *Re P (Emergency Protection Order)* [1996] 1 F.L.R. 482 at 485, *per* Johnson J.

[620] *K and T v Finland* [2001] 2 F.L.R. 707 at para.168.

[621] *K and T v Finland* [2000] 2 F.L.R. 79; [2001] 2 F.L.R. 707 (Grand Chamber); see also *PC and S v UK* [2002] 2 F.L.R. 631; *Haase v Germany* [2004] 2 F.L.R. 39.

[622] [2000] 2 F.L.R. 79 at paras 144–146.

[623] In addition, Pellonpaa J. and Sir Nicholas Bratza found a violation only because of the manner in which the order was implemented. They would apparently have accepted an order to prevent the removal of the baby from the hospital.

confined to unforeseen emergencies and imminent danger.[624] However, this conflicts with the decision of the majority in relation to the son, who was made subject to an order without any parental threat to remove him. The minority were more sympathetic to the dilemmas child protection emergencies create for the authorities.[625]

Although the majority of children are separated from their parents when care proceedings are started, this is more likely to be by agreement than by an emergency order.[626] Most local authorities have strong internal controls, including legal advice, before applications are made; this and magistrates' concerns for children's safety account for the high proportion of orders that are made. Approximately 90 per cent of EPO applications result in orders; arrangements for the child's protection are agreed in most of the rest.[627] Guidance issued with the *Public Law Outline* advises local authorities that they are not required to complete assessments before making a care application where this would place the child at risk. This includes both cases where emergency orders are required and other cases where proceedings cannot be delayed but temporary protection is agreed.[628]

ii. Police protection[629]

Little was known about how the police used their powers to detain children for **21–051** their protection when the Children Act was passed. The *Review of Child Care Law* accepted that the police needed power to act without a court order, but recommended that detention should be limited to 72 hours.[630] The Children Act 1989 s.46 implements this and imposes obligations on the police to safeguard children and their families when exercising this power.

A constable who has reasonable cause to believe that a child would otherwise be likely to suffer significant harm may remove a child or prevent their removal from hospital or elsewhere. The child is under police protection.[631] The constable must, as soon as practicable,[632] inform the local authority, the parents and the child; ensure an investigation by a designated officer; and secure suitable accommodation for the child.[633] The police do not acquire parental responsibility,

---

[624] paras 166–170 and the dissenting judgement of Rees, Fuhrmann, Pantiru and Kovler JJ. The majority appeared less concerned about the order relating to the son because he was already separated from his mother and step-father, but that made the risk of harm from their retaining rights far less.
[625] Bonnello J. favoured rescuing children over protecting the mother's rights.
[626] Masson et al. *Care Profiling Study*, pp.41–42.
[627] Masson et al. *Protecting Powers*, Figure 7.1 and pp.181–182.
[628] *Guidance* (2008), para.3.30, and below, para.21–054.
[629] Children Act 1989 s.46.
[630] paras 13.32–13.33.
[631] Children Act 1989 s.46(1), (2). Although officers and others refer to "police protection orders", the action requires no proceedings, nor the approval of a senior officer.
[632] Children Act 1989 s.46(3)(4). The constable must also take steps to discover the child's wishes and feelings but not specifically in relation to contact. If it were clear the child objected to seeing someone, arguably it would not be reasonable to allow it: s.46(10).
[633] Home Office Circular 44/2003 advises that police premises are not suitable except for a short period in exceptional circumstances: para.28.

but the designated officer has a duty to act reasonably to safeguard and promote the child's welfare. The family must be allowed reasonable contact with the child, provided it is in the child's best interests. The child must be released after 72 hours or sooner if there is no longer cause for concern. The designated officer has power to seek an EPO on behalf of the local authority, but this is never used.[634]

Police protection is used in two distinct ways.[635] Officers remove or detain children they find at risk following calls from parents, children and the public, or in the course of ordinary policing. In addition, they respond to requests from social services to take action where an EPO cannot conveniently be obtained.[636] Police protection should only be used in this way in exceptional circumstances, where there is insufficient time to seek an EPO or for reasons relating to the immediate safety of the child.[637] Where an EPO has been granted, police powers of removal should only be used if there are compelling reasons:

> In *Langley v Liverpool City Council*[638] the local authority obtained an EPO without notice because they knew that the father, who was blind, planned to drive his children to Derby. The social worker, finding the parents had already left home, asked for police assistance. A police officer visited after the parents had returned, and removed the child, who appeared fit and well, under police protection. Interim care orders were made, but the judge found that the local authority and the Chief Constable had acted unlawfully in removing the child, were liable for assault and false imprisonment and that the local authority had breached art.8. The Court of Appeal accepted that the police had acted unlawfully in removing the child. The police were not acting "in accordance with the law": there was no warrant attached to the EPO and the grounds for police protection were not satisfied. Although the local authority had acted proportionately in obtaining an EPO, it had played a major part in police decisions and was therefore also liable.

Child protection outside normal working hours is usually arranged through police protection, not by an application to court. Although it has been suggested that its use breaches art.5,[639] police protection appears permissible within art.5(1)(d).[640] There are no national statistics on the use of police protection, but it has been

---

[634] Children Act 1989 s.46(7), (8); Masson et al. *Protecting Powers.*
[635] Masson et al. *Protecting Powers*, pp.56–106; J. Masson, "Police protection—protecting whom" [2002] J.S.W.F.L. 157.
[636] Masson et al. *Protecting Powers*; Dame M. Booth, *Delay in Public Law Children Act Cases, Second Report* (1996), para.8.15.
[637] *Working Together* (2006), para 5.51; Home Office Circular 44/2003.
[638] [2006] 1 F.L.R. 342, CA.
[639] Aire Centre Quarterly Review, "Secure accommodation orders etc.", March 2001, p.4.
[640] Police protection is a preliminary to local authority investigation; the police are required to notify the local authority. Being looked after would amount to "educational supervision": *Bouamar v Belgium* (1988) 11 E.H.R.R. 1; *Re K (Secure Accommodation Order: Right to Liberty)* [2001] 1 F.L.R. 526, CA. It is also arguable that the child is not detained.

estimated that forces outside London use the power in respect of about 6,000 children each year, and that the Metropolitan Police uses it more frequently.[641]

iii. Child assessment orders

The idea for this order came from an inquiry into the death of an abused child.[642] **21–052**
The Government initially resisted its introduction on the basis that assessment could be achieved under an EPO, and the existence of two similar orders might confuse social workers and magistrates.[643] Pressure from voluntary organisations, notably the NSPCC, and support from the Association of Directors of Social Services led to a government amendment.[644] Concern then shifted to the grounds for the order and its duration. Originally, the Government proposed the child's removal for up to 28 days to allow for comprehensive assessment,[645] but following objections, and to fit with the more restrictive EPO, the order was limited to seven days.

The court may grant this evidence-seeking order[646] if the applicant[647] has reasonable cause to suspect that the child is suffering (or is likely to suffer) significant harm; an assessment of the child is necessary to determine this and is unlikely to be made without a court order. Orders are not appropriate merely because parents are reluctant to use child health services.[648] This order may not be made where there are grounds for an emergency protection order.[649] Notice of the application must be given[650]; the child should be represented by a children's guardian. The order requires the persons named to produce the child and comply with directions relating to assessment; it authorises the child's assessment and removal from home but only for the purposes of assessment.[651] A child assessment order lasts for seven days; it is clearly impossible to complete the assessment process[652] within such a period. Orders are rarely made.[653] It would

---

[641] J. Masson, "Police protection—protecting whom" [2002] J.S.W.F.L. 157, 159; Masson et al. *Protecting Powers*, p.63.

[642] London Borough of Greenwich, *A Child in Mind, Report of the Committee of Inquiry into the Circumstances Surrounding the Death of Kimberley Carlile* (1987), pp.153–156: see also (1989) 55 *Childright* 12.

[643] Lord Mackay, *Hansard*, HL Vol.503, cols 430–431, Children Bill Committee Stage; Vol.504, col.315, Report Stage.

[644] See *per* David Mellor, *Hansard*, HC Vol.158, col.593, Children Bill Report Stage; See also, N. Parton, *Governing the Family* ((1991), pp.177–192.

[645] See Standing Committee B, cols 276–329, May 25, 1989, especially *per* David Mellor, Secretary of State for Health at col.295.

[646] *Per* David Hinchcliffe M.P., *Hansard*, HC, Vol.158, col.604, Children Bill Report Stage; *Guidance* (2008), para.4.13.

[647] Only the local authority or an authorised person (NSPCC) may apply.

[648] *Guidance* (2008), para.4.24.

[649] Children Act 1989 s.43(1), (3), (4). Where a ground in s.45(1) is satisfied, an EPO may be made: s.43(3). This limitation is intended to prevent magistrates deciding in favour of the weaker order, but it does not require them to make an EPO.

[650] Children Act 1989 s.43(11); seven-days' notice: Family Proceedings Rules 1991 (SI 1991/1247) Sch.2.

[651] Children Act 1989 s.43(5)–(7)(9).

[652] See, generally, DH, *A Framework for Assessing Children and Families* (2000). In *Re B (A Minor) (Care Order: Criteria)* [1993] 1 F.L.R. 815, Douglas Brown J. granted an interim care order because the assessment would take three months.

[653] In 1993, less than 100 applications; a quarter of these were withdrawn and only 55 orders were made: Cm.2584 (1994), Table 3.1. Statistics are no longer published.

seem that the order provides a framework for negotiation and is only obtained where this fails.[654]

G. Child protection proceedings

i. The nature of care proceedings

21-053 Care proceedings developed from criminal proceedings; care cases were conceptualised as disputes between the local authority and the child; parents were not parties.[655] Concerns for justice for parents led some local authorities to use wardship instead of care proceedings.[656] Pressure for reform of care proceedings came from many quarters and favoured moves towards inquisitorial procedure.[657] Justice could not be done unless parents were full parties; the courts could only make the right decisions if cases were fully aired before them, and they had access to independent sources of information.[658]

Proceedings under the Children Act 1989 are not adversarial, although an adversarial approach is adopted by some parties; the court has a responsibility to investigate and to seek to achieve a result that promotes the child's welfare.[659] Substantial use is made of written statements rather than oral evidence; where there is a dispute about the source of harm to the child, the hearing can be split so that the facts are determined before any consideration of the care plan.[660] Such cases are unusual; in the *Care Profiling Study* less than a quarter of cases involved a contested final hearing.[661] Proceedings are confidential.[662]

ii. Care proceedings—the Public Law Outline

21-054 Concerns about the cost of care proceedings and the time individual cases take led the Government to establish a review of the care proceedings system in 2005.[663] The President of the Family Division also commissioned a review by

---

[654] See J. Dickens, "Assessment and control in social work: an analysis for the reasons for the non-use of the child assessment order" [1993] J.S.W.F.L. 88. It has been suggested that there should be a more general assessment order so that the court could control investigative assessments: see R. Lavery, "The child assessment order—a reassessment" [1996] C.F.L.Q. 41.

[655] Parents were only permitted to rebut allegations made against them; they could not obtain legal aid for representation before 1984. For further details see the fifth edition of this work at pp.626–674.

[656] J. Masson and S. Morton, "The use of wardship by local authorities" (1989) 52 M.L.R. 762. There was a major increase in wardship during the 1980s, and over half of cases were started by local authorities.

[657] See *Short Report*, paras 94–100; A. Morris *et al.*, *Justice for Children* (London: Macmillan, 1980), p.99, A. Macleod and E. Malos, *Representation of Children and Parents in Care Proceedings* (University of Bristol, 1984) and *R. v Hampshire CC Ex p. K* [1990] 1 F.L.R. 330.

[658] The lack of information to the court was a contributing factor in the deaths of Maria Colwell and Wayne Brewer; see A. Morris et al. *Justice*, p.100. Cf. Dingwall, Eekelaar and Murray (1983), pp.45, who thought that care proceedings "ought properly to be conceptualised as a dispute between parents and state agencies over the care of the child".

[659] *Oxfordshire CC v M* [1994] Fam. 151 at 161, *per* Sir Stephen Brown P.

[660] *Re B (Split Hearing: Jurisdiction)* [2000] 1 F.L.R. 334, CA; *Re G (Care Proceedings: Split Trials)* [2001] 1 F.L.R. 872, CA. The two hearings should be before the same judge.

[661] J. Masson et al. *Care Profiling Study*, p.55 (hearings in 33 out of 85 contested lasted less than 1 day); see also Hunt and Macleod (1999), p.39.

[662] See above, para.18–008.

[663] The Review was proposed in *A Fairer Deal for Legal Aid* (Cm.659 (2005)).

judges of the operation of the Protocol that sets out how these proceedings should be managed.[664] Despite a timetable in the Protocol designed to ensure cases were completed within 40 weeks, the average length of proceedings remained stubbornly above 50 weeks.[665] The Judicial Review Team suggested the introduction of a Children's Dispute Resolution Hearing, where a judge would provide "early neutral evaluation" of the case and set out a case plan, readily understandable by the parents for further decisions in the case.[666] It also noted that judicial case management needed to be strengthened so that cases were decided according to the timetable for the child.[667] The Child Care Proceedings System Review proposed a scheme for pre-proceedings legal advice for parents. Such advice would divert some cases from the courts by helping parents to realise the seriousness of concerns and address them, or help lead to agreed arrangements with the local authority for their child's care. It would ensure that applications to court were better prepared because local authorities would have clarified their concerns and explored alternatives with parents, (e.g. care by relatives). This would enable the courts to deal with cases more speedily and therefore reduce their cost. The Review also recommended the integration of all the guidance relating to care proceedings, and a new *Practice Direction* setting the minimum requirements for s.31 applications.[668] A new scheme for care proceedings called the *Public Law Outline (PLO)* was devised by the Judicial Review Team in consultation with the Ministry of Justice, combining elements of both reviews.[669] The Department for Children, Schools and Families developed the ideas for better preparation for proceedings, with focused attempts to engage parents by revising statutory guidance to local authorities on bringing proceedings.[670] The *Pubic Law Outline* was implemented on April 1, 2008.

Except where safeguarding concerns necessitate an immediate application to the court,[671] the local authority must issue a "letter before proceedings" setting out its concerns, and must meet with the parents and their lawyer to formulate a plan based on its assessments of the child's needs.[672] Where parents do not address these concerns adequately and will not agree arrangements for alternative care, the local authority remains responsible for making an application to court. However, immediately following the introduction of the PLO, the fees for s.31 applications were raised considerably; court fees for care proceedings now cost

---

[664] Judicial Review Team, *Thematic Review of the Protocol for Judicial Case Management in Public Law Children Act Cases* (MoJ, 2005). For a discussion of these reviews, see J. Masson, "Reforming care proceedings—time for a Review" [2007] C.F.L.Q. 411.

[665] President of the Family Division, *Protocol for Judicial Management of Public Law Children Act Cases* (2003); DfES and DCA, *Review of the Child Care Proceedings System in England and Wales* (2006), para.3.2.

[666] Judicial Review Team (2005), para.47.

[667] Judicial Review Team (2005), paras 33, 48–49.

[668] DfES and DCA, *Review of the Child Care Proceedings System*, paras 5.3–5.18.

[669] *Practice Direction: The Public Law Outline* (2008). The *PLO* was piloted in 2007–8, and its introduction was backed by training for judges, lawyers and children's guardians.

[670] DCSF, *The Children Act Guidance and Regulations, Volume 1: Court Orders* (2008), referred to here as *Guidance* (2008). There is separate guidance for Wales issued by the Welsh Assembly government.

[671] *Guidance* (2008), paras 3.27 and 3.30.

[672] *Guidance* (2008), paras 3.22–3.33. The s.47 inquiries are completed through undertaking a core assessment; see above, para.21–023.

local authorities up to £5,000 per family.[673] This is likely to act as a further disincentive to local authorities, lead to delays in making applications and may result in reliance on agreements in cases where children would be better protected by court orders.[674] Also, payments are staged, placing excessive pressure on the local authority to accept proposals from the parents or relatives, so as to avoid a final hearing.

Proceedings are started in the family proceedings court.[675] The local authority must file (and serve) the required documents, including the application form, its care plan and its proposals for the allocation of the case and the timetable for the child.[676] The respondents are the child and anyone with parental responsibility.[677] Other people must be notified[678] and can be made parties if they have a separate interest.[679] The court checks that the local authority has provided the required documents, determines whether the case needs immediate transfer, appoints a children's guardian and sets a first appointment, normally no later that six days from the issuing of proceedings.[680]

21–055   At the first appointment, the court makes directions for the filing of evidence and reports that will enable it to identify, at the Case Management Conference approximately eight weeks later, the key issues that have to be decided.[681] At this hearing, the court sets a date for the Issues Resolution Hearing (IRH) and makes directions that will enable it to resolve or narrow the key issues. Matters that remain undetermined are decided at a final hearing, but it is expected that many cases will be concluded at the IRH.[682] Before each of the major hearings, the legal representatives are required to discuss, prepare and file a draft order outlining the matters requiring decision by the judge or magistrates.[683] As in other child litigation, practice focuses on agreement. Although the court controls what evidence is brought into the proceedings, particularly the use of experts and

---

[673] The Family Proceedings Fees Order 2008 (SI 2008/1054). Before the change, the application fee was £150 and there were additional charges for renewing ICOs and certain hearings. Money was transferred to local authorities from HMCS, but the allocation formula was unrelated to the number of care applications made. Many organisations, including the Family Justice Council, strongly opposed the change.

[674] Inappropriate use of agreements has already been identified as an issue: DH, *Children Act Now* (2001), pp.51–53.

[675] The (draft) Allocation and Transfer of Proceedings Order 2008, art.5(2)(d). There are exceptions where other proceedings are pending: art.5(3), (4). Proceedings may be transferred to the higher courts: arts 15, 18.

[676] Family Proceedings Rules 1991 (SI 1991/1247) r.4.4; *Practice Direction: PLO* (2008), para.10 and Annex A.

[677] Family Proceedings Rules 1991 (SI 1991/1247) App.3.

[678] All parties in relevant pending proceedings and parents without parental responsibility: Family Proceedings Rules 1991 (SI 1991/1247) r.4.8(8) confers a general discretion allowing the court to dispense with notice; the child's welfare is not paramount for this decision: *Re X (Care: Notice of Proceedings)* [1996] 1 F.L.R. 186. Since the implementation of the Human Rights Act 1998, the courts have been less willing to dispense with notice: *Re AB (Care Proceedings Service on Husband Ignorant of Child's Existence)* [2004] 1 F.L.R. 527, CA.

[679] *Re W (Care Proceedings: Leave to Apply)* [2005] 2 F.L.R. 468, FD.

[680] *Practice Direction: PLO* (2008), para.11. The rules normally require three days' notice of the proceedings.

[681] *Practice Direction: PLO* (2008), para.12. Case management in the FPC can be done by the court, a single magistrate or a justices' clerk: para.22.1(3).

[682] *Practice Direction: PLO* (2008), para.15; Bridget Prentice, Justice Minister, April 21, 2008.

[683] *Practice Direction: PLO* (2008), para.13 and Annex C.

assessments, it will only adjudicate matters such as whether the local authority has satisfied the significant-harm test or the suitability of the care plan, where they are not conceded. Proceedings may only be withdrawn with the consent of the court.[684]

The *PLO* builds on existing practice, but it has formalised the advocates' negotiating role by requiring that discussions take place days before timetabled hearings, rather than at the court door. If cases are to be decided more quickly and without recourse to large numbers of costly experts, substantially stronger case management than that which occurred under the Protocol will be required.[685] It is unclear whether courts will accept that local authorities have done enough to support parents or find alternative family carers, or whether courts will agree to these matters being re-examined during lengthy proceedings. Recent decisions by the Court of Appeal do not support a restrictive approach to assessments.[686]

iii. Representation of the parties

In care and other "specified" proceedings, the child is represented by a children's guardian and a solicitor.[687] Children are represented so that the court has information about their welfare, their wishes and any relevant information, not so as to enable them to participate in the proceedings.[688] Children are rarely given access to documents, but the guardian's recommendations "should be shared with them".[689] Despite being a party, the child has no right to attend the proceedings; this is a matter for the court,[690] even where the order will result in the child's detention in secure accommodation.[691] Although guidance encourages the attendance of children at case conferences,[692] it has been said that there would need to be exceptional circumstances for a 15-year-old girl to attend her care proceedings because of the risk of emotional damage and the inhibition of submissions to the court[693]; also, that it is clearly undesirable for a child to hear

21–056

---

[684] Family Proceedings Rules 1991 (SI 1991/1247) r.4.5; cogent reasons should be provided for withdrawal: *Re N (Leave to Withdraw Care Proceedings)* [2000] 1 F.L.R. 134, FD.

[685] Substantial variations in case management were document in the *Care Profiling Study*. Some judges appeared more willing to allow (unarguable) points to be disputed or the timetable to be set aside to allow the late appointment of experts, p.50.

[686] *Re K (Care Order)* [2007] 2 F.L.R 1066; [2007] EWCA Civ 697; *Re B (Care Proceedings: Expert witness)* [2007] 2 F.L.R. 979; see also *Re L (A Child)* [2007] EWHC 3404.

[687] Children Act 1989 s.41; Family Proceedings Rules 1991 (SI 1991/1247) rr.4.10, 4.12; cf. *W v Legal Services Commission* [2000] 1 F.L.R. 821, CA. In cases of exceptional difficulty in the High Court or the county court, CAFCASS Legal (which has taken over this work from the Official Solicitor) may be appointed for the child: *CAFCASS Practice Note* [2001] 2 F.L.R. 151.

[688] J. Masson and M. Winn Oakley, *Out of Hearing* (1999), pp.21–26 and Ch.7; J. Masson, "Representation of children in England" [2000] F.L.Q. 467 at 488.

[689] Principles of good practice for working with children and young persons in CAFCASS, *My Needs, Wishes and Feelings: Guidance for Practitioners* (2007), para.10; Wilson [2007] Fam. Law 808.

[690] Children Act 1989 s.95; Family Proceedings Rules 1991 (SI 1991/1247) r.4.16(2); Masson and Winn Oakley, pp.109–116 and Crichton [2006] Fam. Law 170.

[691] *Re W (Secure Accommodation Order: Attendance at Court)* [1994] 2 F.L.R. 1092, but fairness requires that the child has a proper opportunity to give instructions: *Re C (Secure Accommodation Order: Representation)* [2001] 1 F.L.R. 857, FD.

[692] *Working Together* (2006), para.5.84.

[693] *J v Lancashire CC* (unreported), May 25, 1993; CAAC, *Report 1992/3*, p.72: see also *Re C (A Minor) (Care: Child's Wishes)* [1993] 1 F.L.R. 832 at 841.

The children's guardian has a statutory right of access to records held by the local authority, including confidential adoption reports.[719] If the local authority obtains disclosure of witness statements held by the police or the CPS, the guardian may also see them.[720] The court may give directions if the children's guardian wishes to observe meetings between the child and the parents or to have the child medically examined.[721] In addition, it has been held that while proceedings are pending, the local authority must consult the guardian before making a significant change in the child's placement.[722] Although the main focus of the guardian's work is providing an analysis for the court, in the past guardians have taken action to alleviate shortcomings in the representation of other parties,[723] and have even used judicial review to challenge local authority decisions.[724] CAFCASS is unlikely to support such independent action. The children's guardian's appointment continues for such time as is specified or until terminated by the court.[725] Where proceedings are continuing, the appointment can only be ended by a court order.[726]

(3) The practice of children's guardians

21–059 Before the creation of CAFCASS, there were considerable variations in the ways children's guardians approached their work and the time they spent on each case.[727] Their work is time limited and task-centred; they have to acquire enough knowledge and understanding to present the court with an analysis of the child's situation, the options available and a clear recommendation of the appropriate outcome for the child.[728] Direct work with the child occupies only a small proportion of the guardian's time; reading social services files, advising whether expert assessments are required and where they should be obtained, attending court appointments and hearings, analysing the various options in terms of the child's wishes and welfare and writing reports for the court take up most of the time. Before the *PLO*, cases were frequently quite fluid during the proceedings; now the guardian should ensure that key issues are identified and focused on. The

---

[719] Children Act 1989 s.42(1) (including NSPCC records); Adoption and Children Act 2002 s.103; *Manchester CC v T* [1994] Fam. 181.

[720] In *Nottingham CC v H* [1995] 1 F.L.R. 115, the order restricted disclosure to "those social workers or other members of [the director of social services] staff who are directly concerned in the care of [the children]".

[721] Children Act 1989 ss.38(6), 44(6); Family Proceedings Rules 1991 (SI 1991/1247) rr.4.14, 4.18.

[722] *R v N Yorkshire CC Ex p. M* [1989] 1 All E.R. 143, but the decision as to the form of representation to the adoption panel is for the panel: *R. v N. Yorkshire CC Ex p. M (No.2)* [1989] 2 F.L.R. 79.

[723] J. Brophy, *Expert Evidence*, p.77; J. Brophy and P. Bates, *The Guardian Ad Litem, Complex Cases and the Use of Experts Following the Children Act 1989* (1999).

[724] *R. ota L v Manchester CC* [2002] 1 F.L.R. 43.

[725] Family Proceedings Rules 1991 (SI 1991/1247) r.4.10(9); *Re M (Terminating Appointment of Guardian ad litem)* [1999] 2 F.L.R. 717, FD. Where there are fresh proceedings involving the same child it is usual to appoint the same guardian: *Re J (Adoption: Appointment of Guardian ad litem)* [1999] 2 F.L.R. 86, CA.

[726] *Re CE (s.37 Direction)* [1995] 1 F.L.R. 26 at 44, *per* Wall J.

[727] J. Hunt, *Understanding the Variation in the Hours Guardians Spend on Care Cases: Report to Department of Health* (2002); J. Masson, "Representation of children in England" [2000] F.L.Q. 467;

[728] DH, *Manual of Practice Guidance for Guardians ad litem and Reporting Officers* (1992), p.35.

guardian's analysis can influence the approach of the local authority and the attitudes of parents, facilitating agreement.[729] The children's guardian must file their analyses and final report in accordance with the court's directions, and serve them on the parties.[730] The court is free to reject any proposals but must give reasons for so doing.[731] The guardian's report is confidential to the proceedings; the court's permission is required for its disclosure.[732] The children's guardian has responsibility for ensuring that, where appropriate, the decision is explained to the child.[733]

(4) The child's solicitor

In 1983 the Law Society established a specialist panel of solicitors to act for **21–060** children in care proceedings; membership of the Children Panel is now open to solicitors with the necessary experience and training who act for any party in care proceedings.[734] Guidance is available to solicitors about acting for children; solicitors should always meet their child clients and assess their ability to give instructions.[735] Where a child has sufficient maturity to give instructions, and these differ from those of the children's guardian, the solicitor must follow the child's instructions.[736] In practice, these principles are not always applied; solicitors rely heavily on children's guardians and rarely involve child clients in the legal process.[737]

H. Child protection and the criminal law

i. Historical background

The earliest child protection laws in England and Wales required criminal **21–061** proceedings to be taken against the parent.[738] The NSPCC prosecuted thousands

---

[729] Masson, "Representation", p.478; DH, *Manual* (1992), p.88.

[730] Family Proceedings Rules 1991 (SI 1991/1247) r.4.11A(7), the period specified in the court rules is 14 days. The court may specify a different period. Information can be withheld where there are compelling reasons: *Re C (Disclosure)* [1996] 1 F.L.R. 797.

[731] *S v Oxfordshire CC* [1993] 1 F.L.R. 452 at 461, *per* Connell, J. Failure to do so is grounds for an appeal.

[732] *Re C (Guardian ad litem: Disclosure of Report)* [1996] 1 F.L.R. 61.

[733] Family Proceedings Rules 1991 (SI 1991/1247) r.4.11A(10).

[734] Law Society, *Children Panel Accreditation Scheme*, at *http://www.lawsociety.org.uk* [Accessed June 5, 2008]. Enhanced rates of remuneration are only paid by the Legal Services Commission for exceptional cases.

[735] Law Society, *Good Practice in Child Care Cases* (2007), paras 4.4 and 4.5.

[736] Family Proceedings Rules 1991 (SI 1991/1247) r.4.12(1)(a); Law Society (2007), paras 4.5.7 *et seq.*; *Re P (Representation)* [1996] 1 F.L.R. 486, CA.

[737] Masson and Winn Oakley, *Out of Hearing*, Ch.7; Masson "Representation", p.488.

[738] The Prevention of Cruelty of Children Act 1889 allowed the court to commit a child to the care of a fit person if the carer had been bound over, convicted or committed for trial for ill-treating the child. For a consideration of offences relating to sexual abuse, see V. Bailey and S. Blacktown, "The Punishment of Incest Act 1908: a case study in law creation" [1979] Crim. L.R. 708 and L. Zedner, "Regulating sexual offences within the home", in I. Loveland (ed.), *Frontiers of Criminality* (London: Sweet and Maxwell, 1995).

of parents in an attempt to coerce them and others to provide adequate care.[739]
The development of separate civil proceedings in 1952 and the difficulty of
proving cases at the criminal standard led to a decline in the use of prosecution.
Both the Cleveland and Climbié inquiries have highlighted problems in the
police approach to investigating child abuse, particularly treating offences
against children as crimes.[740] The inter-agency system now requires co-operation; police Child Abuse Investigation Unit officers work closely with social
workers.[741]

In recent years there have been a large number of investigations of "historic"
child abuse following allegations by former residents, now adults, of children's
homes and boarding schools. In some cases there has been evidence that earlier
complaints made by children were not believed.[742] These scandals indicate how
little regard was taken of children and their statements in the past, and how easy
it was for abusers to infiltrate child welfare services.[743] They also raise concerns
about the difficulties of testing evidence and providing a fair trial, long after
alleged offences took place.[744]

ii. The importance of prosecution

21–062 Although prosecution rates are low and have apparently declined since the
Cleveland crisis,[745] the prosecution of those who commit offences against
children plays an important role in the protection of all children, and may have
an enormous impact on individual children. A conviction for an offence against
a child[746] is no longer grounds for a care order, but is likely to prevent a person
working in any position with responsibility for children and preclude that person
and anyone they live with being registered as a childminder or foster carer.[747]
The conviction of an abuser may prevent the need for care proceedings; the
victim may also be helped by knowing that he or she has been believed.[748] There
is evidence that those who sexually abuse children frequently commit offences

---

[739] L. Housden, *The Prevention of Cruelty to Children* (London: Cape, 1955), Ch.4.

[740] Cm.412 (1988); Cm.5730 (2003), and above, para.21–024.

[741] See DH, *Working Together* (2006), p.11, paras 2.97 *et seq.*; HMIC, *Keeping Safe, Staying Safe* (2005).

[742] See C. Wolmar, *Forgotten Children* (2000); *Lost in Care* (HC 201 (2000)), Chs 50 and 51. Most police forces have been engaged in such inquiries: *Hansard* HC, col.856W (November 1, 2001).

[743] W. Utting *People Like Us*, p.1 and paras 1.40 *et seq.*

[744] Home Affairs Committee, *Conduct of Investigations into Past Cases of Abuse in Children's Homes: 4th Report 2001–2* (HC 836 (2002–2)).

[745] W. Utting (1997), paras 20.4–20.10; C. Wattam, *Making a Case in Child Protection* (1992); T. Frothingham et al., "Child sexual abuse in Leeds before and after Cleveland" (1993) 23 Child Abuse Rev. 23.

[746] Criminal Justice and Court Services Act 2000 s.26 and Sch.4 These were formerly known as "Sch.1 offences": Children and Young Persons Act 1933 Sch.1; see now *Working Together* (2006), para.12.4.

[747] Criminal Justice and Court Services Act 2000 s.28; Children Act 1989 s.68; *Working Together* (2006), Ch.2.

[748] L. Berliner, "Treating the effects of sexual assault" in K. Murray and D. Gough (eds), *Intervening in Sexual Abuse* (Scottish Academic Press, 1991); J. Fontaine, *Child Sexual Abuse*, pp.222 *et seq.*

against many children and target vulnerable children.[749] Those convicted of sexual offences are required to register with the police[750]; this information is used to prevent and detect offences, but labelling can have limited effect whilst conviction rates remain low.

The criminal justice system is ineffective in deterring offenders and in securing convictions of those who are guilty of offences. Its failings are most marked in relation to the most vulnerable: the very young and the disabled.[751] Conviction rates are low,[752] acquittals can undermine care proceedings[753] and a decision to appeal may also mean not co-operating with civil proceedings.[754] Criminal proceedings can have damaging effects on child victims of abuse. Prosecution of a parent may lead to children being blamed (or blaming themselves) for the imprisonment and the break-up of the family, rather than the child being supported.[755] Where the abuser is acquitted, the consequences may be very severe; the child suffers the abuse and the proceedings, the perpetrator's claim of innocence appears vindicated and the child goes into care. Despite a policy of ensuring their speedy progress, the prosecution of child-abuse cases takes a long time.[756] Conviction may enable the perpetrator to receive treatment so that he/she does not re-offend, but there is no guarantee that this will be available, and success rates are apparently low.[757] Many convicted abusers are detained in isolation[758] for their own protection so that they mix only with others with similar convictions. Sentences often seem short when the harm to the child is considered,[759] but it has been argued that the emphasis on custodial sentences discourages perpetrators from accepting responsibility.[760]

---

[749] C. Cobley, *Sex Offenders* (2000); J. La Fontaine, *Child Sexual Abuse*, Ch.5.

[750] Sex Offenders Act 2003 Pt 2; C. Cobley *op. cit.* pp.323–332.

[751] W. Utting, *People Like Us*, p.189; the Government rejected proposals to modify the standard of proof in these cases: *The Government's Response to the Children's Safeguards Review* (Cm.4105 (1998)), paras 10.8–10.9.

[752] Approximately half the defendants were acquitted in a study of cases involving child witnesses: see G. Davies et al., *Videotaping Children's Evidence and Evaluation* (Home Office, 1995), p.34; Utting cites figures of 14% for indecent assault against a female and 11% for rape, but these do not relate only to children, para.20.8.

[753] This appears to have been a major reason that the judge in *Re H and R (Sexual Abuse: Standard of Proof)* [1996] 1 F.L.R. 80 regarded the girl's evidence as inadequate.

[754] *Re U (Care Proceedings: Criminal Conviction)* [2006] 2 F.L.R. 690, FD (the court had no effective way of punishing the contempt of the father who refused to give evidence so as not to prejudice his appeal against conviction).

[755] J. La Fontaine (1990), p.230, cites a study of victims referred to Great Ormond Street Hospital for therapy; only 14% remained with both parents.

[756] J. Plotnikoff and R. Woolfson, *Prosecution of Child Abuse: An Evaluation of the Government's Speedy Progress Policy* (London: Blackstone, 1995).

[757] See A. Horton, *The Incest Perpetrator—The Family Member No One Wants to Treat* (Newbury Park: Sage, 1990) and C. Cobley, *Sex Offenders*, pp.254 *et seq.*

[758] Under Prison Rules 1964 (SI 1964/388) r.43. This may encourage more offending: K. Murray and D. Gough, "Implications and prospects", in K. Murray and D. Gough, *Intervening in Child Sexual Abuse*.

[759] For a discussion of the principles applied to sex offences, see, generally, C. Cobley, *Sex Offenders*, Ch.4; *Attorney General's Reference No.1 of 1989* (1989) 11 Cr. App. R. (S.) 409 (incest): *No.35 of 1994* (1995) 16 Cr. App. R. (S) 635 (indecent assault).

[760] D. Glaser and J. Spencer, "Sentencing, children's evidence and children's trauma" [1990] Crim. L.R. 371. Cf. S. Viinikka, "Child sexual abuse and the law", in E. Driver and A. Droisen, *Child Sexual Abuse: Feminist Perspectives* (Basingstoke: Macmillan, 1989), p.153.

iii. The decision to prosecute[761]

21–063   The decision to prosecute is made by the Crown Prosecution Service guided by the Code for Crown Prosecutors. There must be a "realistic prospect of conviction" and, therefore, sufficient, reliable evidence.[762] The strength of the complainant child's account and the existence of supporting evidence are crucial to the decision to prosecute.[763] The prosecution must be in the public interest. The interests of the victim are an important matter, but the Crown Prosecution Service acts in the public interest, not for individuals.[764] The Crown Prosecution Service appears concerned to protect children from court proceedings, but negotiation of charges and pleas operate to reduce the severity of sentences, delay proceedings and deny justice to children.[765]

iv. Children's evidence[766]

21–064   In many cases of child abuse, only the child's evidence links the incident to the perpetrator; unless the child can give credible evidence, there can be no prosecution. Rules of evidence applying to child witnesses and procedures that can help children to give evidence are therefore crucial. English culture and law have served children poorly in both respects. Children were not regarded as reliable informants; young children who could not understand the oath were not competent witnesses,[767] and children's evidence had to be corroborated.[768] The oral adversarial process required children to give evidence like adults in open court and face cross-examination,[769] which they often experienced as confusing and distressing[770]; this did not assist the court to establish the truth.[771]

A campaign for reform by academics, the NSPCC and others during the passage of the Criminal Justice Bill 1988 lead to the setting up of the Pigot Committee[772] and the introduction of a scheme whereby some children could give evidence by live-link video from an adjacent room. The Pigot Committee

---

[761] See C. Wattam, *Making a Case in Child Protection* (1992); C. Keenan and L. Maitland, "There ought to be a law against it—police evaluation of the efficacy of prosecution in a case of child abuse" [1999] C.F.L.Q. 379.

[762] Crown Prosecution Service, *Code of Practice for Crown Prosecutors* (2000), paras 5.1, 5.3.

[763] G. Davis et al., *An Assessment of the Admissibility and Sufficiency of Evidence in Child Abuse Prosecutions, Report to the Home Office* (1999).

[764] G. Davis et al., *An Assessment*, paras 4.2, 6, 6.7. The impact on the child and family are factors considered by the police when deciding whether to refer the case to the CPS: C. Keenan and L. Maitland (1999), "There ought to be a law", p.408.

[765] C. Wattam, *Making a Case*, p.146; CPS, *The Inspector's Report of Cases Involving Child Witnesses* (1998), para.2.1.

[766] For a detailed and authoritative account, see J. Spencer and R. Flin, *The Evidence of Children*, 2nd edn (1993); Home Office, *Speaking up for Justice* (1998), and for a discussion of recent reforms: P. Bates "The Youth Justice and Criminal Evidence Act—the evidence of children and vulnerable adults" [1999] C.F.L.Q. 289. For a comparative analysis, see J. Spencer et al. (eds), *Children's Evidence in Legal Proceedings* (1990).

[767] *R. v Wallwork* (1958) 42 Cr. App. R. 153; children were presumed incompetent.

[768] See J. Spencer and R. Flin *Evidence of Children*, pp.212 *et seq.*

[769] Children and Young Persons Act 1933 ss.42, 43 enabled evidence to be given on deposition but was almost never used: Spencer and Flin *Evidence of Children*, p.85.

[770] G. Davies and E. Noon, *An Evaluation of the Live Link for Child Witnesses* (Home Office, 1991). Utting considered it harmful: *People Like Us*, para.20.31.

[771] J. Spencer and R. Flin *Evidence of Children*.

[772] The Advisory Group on Video Evidence.

recommended a system that would have enabled children's evidence to be obtained at an early stage and avoided the need for them to attend the trial,[773] but this was rejected by the Government despite support from the judiciary.[774] Instead, the Criminal Justice Act 1991 introduced a package of measures that, although designed to facilitate prosecution by making it easier for children to give evidence, appears to have made the investigation of child-abuse cases more difficult. Pressure for further reform continued[775] and eventually led to the Youth Justice and Criminal Evidence Act 1999, which allows the court to apply "special measures" to assist and protect children and other vulnerable witnesses.[776]

Children, whatever their age, are competent to give evidence if they can understand questions put to them and give comprehensible answers.[777] Children's evidence does not have to be corroborated.[778] Competent child witnesses, like adults, can be compelled to give evidence. The child may give evidence in chief by pre-recorded video provided that this "is in the interests of justice",[779] and cross-examination may use the live link or a pre-recorded video.[780] Provision has also been made for children to be questioned by an intermediary rather than by counsel.[781] The accused may not cross-examine the child in person.[782]

The Home Office issued detailed guidance on how children should be **21–065** interviewed[783]; *Best Evidence* interviews are usually video-recorded; the recording is both the witness statement and the evidence for court. Police officers have been trained to undertake these interviews, and interview suites have been established. Although children are compellable witnesses, they cannot be required to provide a statement for the police, and their consent should be

---

[773] Home Office, *Report of the Advisory Group on Video Evidence* (1989), rec. 4.

[774] *Hansard*, HL Vol.527, col.127, Criminal Justice Bill (2nd Reading, May 21, 1991) reported by Lord Ackner.

[775] CAAC, *Report 1993/4*, p.40; W. Utting, *People Like Us*, para.20.19; Home Office, *Speaking Up for Justice* (1998); ChildLine conference (1999).

[776] Youth Justice and Criminal Evidence Act 1999 ss.18–30. Special measures include screening the witness box, giving evidence in private or by live link, using pre-recorded video evidence and questioning through an intermediary. These provisions replace those introduced by the Criminal Justice Act 1991, put on a statutory basis other practices to protect child witnesses, add to the protection for children and extend it to other vulnerable witnesses. See also Home Office, *Achieving Best Evidence in Criminal Proceedings* (2002).

[777] Youth Justice and Criminal Evidence Act 1999 s.53; children under 14 years cannot give evidence on oath; s.55.

[778] Criminal Justice Act 1988 s.34(2); Criminal Justice and Public Order Act 1994 s.32 abolished the requirement for a warning against convicting for sexual offences on uncorroborated evidence.

[779] Youth Justice and Criminal Evidence Act 1999 s.27(2); Home Office, *Achieving Best Evidence*.

[780] Youth Justice and Criminal Evidence Act 1999 ss.24; 28. Live link was originally introduced by the Criminal Justice Act 1988.

[781] Youth Justice and Criminal Evidence Act 1999 s.29; Home Office, *Guidance for the Use of an Intermediary under s.29 of the Youth Justice and Criminal Evidence Act 1999* (2002). Intermediaries should be used where children are very young, very traumatised or use idiosyncratic or specialised systems of communication: Home Office, *Achieving Best Evidence*, para.2.39.

[782] Youth Justice and Criminal Evidence Act 1999 s.35.

[783] Home Office, *Achieving Best Evidence*; this guidance replaces Home Office, *Memorandum of Good Practice on Video-recorded Interviews with Child Witnesses* (1992); and see G. Davies and H. Westcott, *Interviewing Children under the Memorandum of Good Practice* (Home Office Police Research Series No.115, 1999). The video provides the CPS with information about the child's demeanour at the time of interview, which is important to their decision to prosecute; Davis et al., *An Assessment*.

sought.[784] Parental consent is not required, but the guidance recognises that interviewing children without informing parents is exceptional and can create problems for any subsequent social services involvement.[785] Despite the submission of thousands of videos, prosecution rates have remained low.[786] Some children do not, apparently, find it easy to talk about their abuse with the constraints of a formal interview.[787] If children are required to attend court for cross-examination, they remain vulnerable to the most stressful part of the proceedings, without the preparation of giving evidence in chief.[788] Videoing interviews should ensure good practice by interviewers,[789] but there is no evidence that the availability of video-taped interviews increases either guilty pleas or convictions.[790] Practices necessary for working in partnership with parents and children may conflict with models of investigation developed to satisfy the requirements of a criminal trial.[791] Despite the rarity of prosecutions for abuse, the criminal model now dominates child-abuse investigations.

Attempts have been made to safeguard the welfare of child victims within the criminal justice process: courts have child liaison officers; the NSPCC has made a video explaining to children the process of being a witness; and the Witness Service arranges familiarisation visits to courts.[792] The CPS has issued guidance that states that the best interests of the child are the paramount consideration in deciding whether to provide therapy for a child witness before the trial.[793] Although the prosecution of parents should not delay care proceedings,[794] delay may be the inevitable consequence if the parents are involved in two sets of complex and contested proceedings. Where there are both civil and criminal

[784] Home Office, *Achieving Best Evidence*, paras 2.17–2.25, 2.68 *et seq.* Cf. if there is a direction for recorded cross-examination.
[785] Home Office, *Achieving Best Evidence* para.2.71; *Working Together* (2006), para.5.66; DH, *The Challenge of Partnership* (1995), para.5.19. If a parent refuses to consent to their child being interviewed, a specific issue order may be sought: *Re F (Specific Issue Order: Child Interview)* [1995] 1 F.L.R. 819, CA, or under the court's inherent jurisdiction if the child is in care: *Re M (Care Leave to Interview Child)* [1995] 1 F.L.R. 825.
[786] DH, *The Child, the Court and the Video* (1994), p.43; G. Davies et al., *Video Taping Children's Evidence: An Evaluation* (1995), p.17. There were 15,000 videos made in the first nine months; of these, 24% were submitted to be CPS, but up to June 1994, only 640 applications were made to show a video; of these, 470 were granted; p.26.
[787] This is unsurprising given what is known about the way children disclose sexual abuse: see Wattam *Making a Case*, pp.49 *et seq.* But Davies et al., *Video Taping*, p.22 found 70% to be articulate, *Video Taping*.
[788] The child may not give evidence in chief on matters included in the recording or without the permission of the court: Youth Justice and Criminal Evidence Act 1999 s.27(5)(b), (7).
[789] The same approach should be applied to interviews used in civil proceedings: *Re B (Sexual Abuse: Expert's Report)* [2000] 1 F.L.R. 871 at 873, *per* Thorpe L.J.
[790] Davies et al., *Video Taping*, p.42.
[791] H. Wescott, *One Year On: Professionals' Concerns about the Memorandum of Good Practice* (1994); Wattam, *Making a Case*, pp.187 *et seq.*; J. Masson, "Developing legal issues in child protection", in T. David (ed.), *Protecting Children from Abuse* (1994), pp.15, 23.
[792] NSPCC, *Being A Witness, What Its Really Like* (2000); NSPCC, *Child Witness Pack* (2000); Davies et al., *Video Taping*, p.29 found that 30% of children had no preparation for giving evidence.
[793] CPS, *The Provision of Therapy for Child Witnesses Prior to a Criminal Trial* (2001), para.4.4. The guidance expresses concerns that therapy may undermine the child's evidence and notes that records of therapy may be have to be disclosed: para.3.6 *et seq.*
[794] *Re TB (Care Proceedings: Criminal Trial)* [1995] 2 F.L.R. 801, CA; Home Office Circular 84/1982; cf. *Re S (Care Order: Criminal Proceedings)* [1995] 1 F.L.R. 151, CA, and see above.

proceedings, joint directions hearings may be held to cover such matters as timetables, medical examination of the child and the disclosure of evidence and unused material.[795] Guidance has been issued on the disclosure of police information for family proceedings[796] and on the disclosure of local authority records,[797] but disclosure of social services documents for criminal proceedings may undermine the trust between children and their carers. The CPS should instruct counsel with experience in these cases.[798]

v. Compensation for child abuse victims

In most cases child abuse amounts to a tort, so the victim should be able to claim **21–066** damages from the perpetrator.[799] However, the interpretation of the rules relating to the limitation of actions[800] meant that these were more restrictive for actions for intentional assault than for negligence. Consequently, in *S v W (Child Abuse: Damages)*[801] a young woman who had been sexually abused as a child could succeed in her claim against her mother, who had failed to protect her, but not against her father, who had abused her. Despite proposals from the Law Commission for a new limitation regime, these rules continued to apply.[802] Case-law enabled some adults who were victims of sexual abuse whilst they were children in boarding schools, residential care or detention centres to bring a successful claim. Although the House of Lords held that employers could be vicariously liable for abuse by care staff,[803] claimants had to show a systemic failure to prevent abuse so as to claim in negligence.[804] The House of Lords re-examined its earlier decision on the Limitation Act 1980 in six cases in 2008.[805] Overturning *Stubbings v Webb*,[806] their Lordships first held that the extendable three-year period applied to cases of deliberate harm as well as to negligence. Secondly, that the question of whether the injury was significant was an objective one, so the characteristics of the claimant were not relevant to determining this. Thirdly, the court had a wide discretion when considering whether to allow claims out of time; the claimant's reasons for delay, and any

---

[795] CAAC, *Final Report* (1997), p.35; see also *Re A and B (Minors) (No.2)* [1995] 1 F.L.R. 351.
[796] ACPO, *Code of Guidance for Disclosure of Police Information in Family Proceedings* (2006).
[797] CAAC, *Handbook of Best Practice* (1997), p.33.
[798] CPS, *The Inspector's Report of Cases Involving Child Witnesses* (1998): cases were frequently returned at the last moment and alternative counsel instructed.
[799] In *Pereira v Keleman* [1995] 1 F.L.R. 428, damages of between £16,500 and £10,500 were awarded to three sisters. Children abused by care staff have received compensation from local authorities (or their insurers); and see C. Wolmar, *Forgotten Children*, pp.189 *et seq.*
[800] *Stubbings v Webb* [1993] A.C. 498; the European Court of Human Rights held that this did not breach the Convention: *Stubbings v UK* (1997) 23 E.H.R.R. 213.
[801] [1995] 1 F.L.R. 862, CA.
[802] A three-year primary period would apply to all personal injury cases, but the court would have discretion to dis-apply the limitation period. There would be no special rules for sex-abuse cases, but where an adult was disabled, for example where abuse caused mental illness, the limitation period would be suspended for at least 10 years from the onset of the disability: Law Com. No.270, *Limitation of Actions* (HC 23 (2001)) paras 4.23–4.33.
[803] *Lister v Hesley Hall Ltd* [2001] 2 F.L.R. 307, HL.
[804] *KR v Bryn Alyn Community (Holdings) Ltd* [2003] Q.B. 1441.
[805] *A v Hoare* [2008] UKHL 6 (the lottery-winner rapist case). The five conjoined appeals all related to abuse in care homes, schools or detention centres.
[806] [1993] A.C. 498.

earlier recording of complaints, were relevant factors. Many compensation claims will now be simpler, based on intentional harm and vicarious liability. However, not everyone who brings a late claim can reasonably expect the court to exercise discretion in their favour. [807]

Child abuse is frequently an "offence of violence" so that a claim may be made to the Criminal Injuries Compensation Authority. It is not necessary that the offender be convicted,[808] but the victim should have informed an appropriate authority who could be a parent or a social worker.[809] Claims must be made within two years of the last incident, but in exceptional circumstances this requirement is waived.[810] An award will not be made if the perpetrator would benefit from it or if it is thought to be against a minor's interests.[811] Substantial awards should be placed in trust for the child. Where the child is in care, the application should be made by the local authority; in other cases it should be made by someone with parental responsibility.[812] Awards are low.[813] However, concerns have been expressed that compensation motivates those who make complaints, especially in cases of historic abuse.[814]

IV. Modern Childcare Law—The Looked-after System

A. Local authorities' powers and duties

21–067 The Children Act 1989 requires local authorities to safeguard and promote the welfare of each child they look after, promote their educational achievement, make reasonable use of services that are available to children cared for by their own parents and provide advice, assistance and friendship with a view to promoting the child's welfare afterwards.[815] The local authority is the child's "corporate parent" with responsibilities to promote his or her life chances.[816] In its White Paper, *Care Matters,*[817] the Government set out its plans to empower local authorities to be more effective corporate parents, with the aim of ensuring that children are cared about, not just cared for.[818] Key elements of this agenda were included in the Children and Young Persons Bill 2008. In addition, each local authority is expected to make a "pledge" to the children it looks after,

---

[807] *Per* Lord Brown at para.86; Limitation Act 1980 s.33; *Horton v Sadler* [2007] 1 A.C. 307.
[808] A full explanation of the reasons for the failure to prosecute is required: CICA, *The Criminal Injuries Compensation Scheme 2001*, para.10 ; CICA, *Guide to the Scheme* (2007), p.7.
[809] *Criminal Injuries Compensation Scheme 2001*, para.13(a); *Guide* (2007), p.25.
[810] *Criminal Injuries Compensation Scheme 2001*, para.18. The time limit is normally waived for claimants under 21.
[811] *Criminal Injuries Compensation Scheme 2001*, para.16.
[812] The Official Solicitor acts for children who cannot otherwise make a claim.
[813] Under the tariff scheme, the maximum payment for repeated rape or buggery over a period of more than three years is £22,000. Compare the awards from the CICA and the ECHR to the children in *Z v UK* [2001] 2 F.L.R. 612 at paras 49, 127 and 131.
[814] R. Webster, *The Great Children's Homes Panic* (1998) discussed in C. Wolmar, *Forgotten Children*, pp.161–166.
[815] Children Act 1989 ss.22(3), (3A), 24(1).
[816] DfES, *If This Were My Child* (2003), Foreword, Margaret Hodge, Minister for Children.
[817] Cm.7317 (2007).
[818] DCSF, *Children and Young Persons Bill Policy Paper: Improving Corporate Parenting and Strengthening the Voice of the Child* (2007).

listing the services and support they should expect to receive.[819] Although the pledge may not be enforceable, failure to provide a reasonable standard of care could possibly give rise to an action in negligence.[820]

In general, the local authority owes the same duties to all children it is looking after,[821] irrespective of their legal status, but has substantially more power over children in care for whom it has parental responsibility. Where a child is only accommodated, the local authority may take the same action as would be permitted if done by any other de facto carer. It may "do what is reasonable for the purpose of safeguarding and promoting the child's welfare".[822] It may therefore take day-to-day decisions and act in emergencies. If the parents will not agree to the local authority's proposals for the child's placement or education, the authority must obtain a care order.[823] Where the dispute relates to arrangements for contact, the parents may refer the matter to court by seeking a contact order.[824] However, it is unlikely that the courts would interfere with other aspects of local authority discretion unless there was a breach of the European Convention on Human Rights.[825]

A detailed consideration of the local authority's specific duties is beyond the scope of this work, but a brief indication of the main areas is given here because of their relevance to legal proceedings (e.g. the decision to grant a residence order rather than a care order, or to discharge a care order).

i. Maintenance and accommodation

The local authority must maintain all children they are looking after and provide accommodation for them.[826] The Children Act 1989 allows the local authority discretion about placement subject to an overriding welfare duty, obligations to consult and consider views and religion, race, culture and language, and a requirement "so far as is reasonably practicable and consistent with welfare" to secure accommodation near the child's family and with siblings, and which is not

21–068

---

[819] Cm.7317 (2007), para.1.25. Suggested items in the pledge include a place in a good school and a placement with carers who can meet needs. Many of the items in the pledge relate to service duties that are unlikely to found individual rights, see above, para.21–006.

[820] *Barrett v Enfield LBC* [1999] 2 F.L.R. 426, HL (the court refused to strike out a claim by a young man who had been brought up in the care system who alleged that his psychiatric condition resulted from the negligent way the local authority looked after him). The local authority may be liable for negligently placing or leaving the child with foster parents who harm him or her: *S v Gloucestershire CC* [2000] 1 F.L.R. 825, CA, and may be vicariously liable for abuse by care-home staff: *Lister v Hesley Hall Ltd* [2001] 2 F.L.R. 307, HL, above, para.21–066.

[821] Children Act 1989 s.22(1); this includes children accommodated under s.20.

[822] Children Act 1989 s.3(5).

[823] *R. v Tameside MBC Ex p. J* [2000] 1 F.L.R. 942, QBD, and above, para.21–013.

[824] Children Act 1989 s.8; see Ch.18 above.

[825] *A v Liverpool CC* [1982] A.C. 363; the House of Lords upheld the High Court's refusal to exercise its discretion in wardship to interfere with intra vires decisions of a local authority relating to children in compulsory care. There is no authority relating to accommodated children, but the basis for the decision—that Parliament had given discretion over a matter to the local authority and not to the courts—would seem to apply to prevent the courts making specific issue orders about the way a child is looked after.

[826] Children Act 1989 s.23(1); Children and Young Persons Bill 2008 cl.9, adding ss.22A and 22B and repealing s.23.

unsuitable for the child's disabilities.[827] The 2008 Bill creates a hierarchy of placements, with preference for placements with parents, relatives and friends over placements with strangers.[828] The local authority must place a child with their parent,[829] or a person who has (or had) parental responsibility, except where this is not consistent with the child's welfare or where this is impracticable. In such cases it must make the most appropriate placement and ensure that the placement meets similar criteria as required by the current law in relation to location, education, etc.[830] In practice, these criteria may well conflict; social workers will have to decide what they consider to be the most suitable placement, taking account of these criteria. Although research evidence suggests that placements with relatives are less likely to break down, they do not necessarily meet children's needs.[831] Relatives may prefer to care without the involvement of the local authority, informally or with a residence or special guardianship order. These children will not be looked after; their carers are unlikely to get support from the local authority.[832]

Where placements with kin cannot be made, children are frequently placed with foster carers who agree to provide a home indefinitely or for a specific period.[833] There are detailed regulations governing the selection of foster carers, medical examination of children and so on.[834] The regulations require foster carers to sign undertakings in specified form, to care for and bring, the child up as a member of their own family (but not administer corporal punishment), to look after the child's health and permit the child to be visited. Foster carers are required to allow children to be removed from their care.[835] Alternatively, children are placed in a residential establishment (a "community home" run by the authority, a "voluntary home" run by a voluntary organisation or a "registered children's home" run privately).[836] Subject to regulations, they may

---

[827] Children Act 1989 ss.22(3)(a)(4)(5) and 23(7), (8).

[828] Children and Young Persons Bill 2008 cl.9, adding s.22C; provision for the national authority: subs.(10). Relative foster carers should not be paid less than local authority carers: *R. ota L v Manchester CC* [2002] 1 F.L.R. 43, FD.

[829] Where a child in care is placed with a parent or someone who had parental responsibility before the care order was made, the placement must be authorised by the Director of Children's Service: Children Act 1989 s.23(5); Placement with Parents etc. Regulations 1991 (SI 1991/893); *Guidance* (1991), Vol.3, Ch.5; see, generally, E. Farmer and R. Parker, *Trials and Tribulations* (1991).

[830] Children and Young Persons Bill 2008 cl.9; Children Act 1989 s.22C(5)–(9).The weak approach to placement with siblings was criticised by the Joint Committee on Human Rights: *Legislative Scrutiny: 15th Report 2007–8* (HC 440 (2008)), para.1.27.

[831] J. Hunt et al., *Keeping Them in the Family* (2008); E. Farmer and S. Moyers, *Kinship Care: Fostering Effective Family and Friends Placements* (2008).

[832] See above, para.21–009 and below, para.22–064. The local authority cannot place with a relative and friend and assert that this is a private fostering arrangement: Children Act 1989 s.22C(6)(a); *Southwark LBC v D* [2007] 1 F.L.R. 2181, CA.

[833] I. Sinclair, *Fostering Now: Messages From Research* (London: Jessica Kingsley, 2005); *Guidance* (1991), Vol.3 and Arrangements for Placement of Children (General) Regulations 1991 (SI 1991/890); Fostering Services Regulations 2002 (SI 2002/57).

[834] Fostering Services Regulations 2002 (SI 2002/57). The power to make regulations is transferred to the appropriate national authority by Children and Young Persons Bill 2008 cl.9 and Sch.1, adding Children Act 1989 s.22C(11) and Sch.2 paras 12A–12F.

[835] Fostering Services Regulations 2002 (SI 2002/57) Sch.5.

[836] Children Act 1989 Pt VI–VIII; Children's Homes Regulations 1991 (SI 1991/1505); *Guidance* (1991), Vol.4; DH, *Caring for Children Away From Home: Messages From Research* (1998). All children's homes are now subject to inspection by Ofsted.

also be placed in lodgings or a flat, but where the children's services department provides such accommodation for a child, he or she is looked after.[837]

The emphasis on the provision of a substitute family, concerns about costs and abuse in residential homes has led to a reliance on foster care. There is a crisis in foster care[838] with a shortage of placements and a lack of placement choice. Private (for profit) agencies have been established to identify and support foster-carers for local authorities.[839] Many children experience a succession of unsatisfactory placements and repeated moves. Breakdown rates as high as 50 per cent occur.[840] Many factors contribute to the success or failure of fostering arrangements; the specific commitment of the carer to the child (and vice versa) underlies many positive arrangements. In contrast, failure by local authorities to provide adequate support undermines placements.[841] The government standard for placements is that no more than 16 per cent of looked-after children should have more than three placements in any year. This was achieved by over 90 per cent of councils in 2005.[842]

On March 31, 2007, 60 per cent of children looked after by local authorities in England were in foster placements with strangers, and another 11 per cent fostered with relatives. Only 11 per cent of looked-after children were in children's homes, 9 per cent were with their parents and the remainder lived in lodgings, hostels and boarding schools or were placed for adoption.[843]

ii. Reviews

Local authorities are required to review the care provided for all children they **21–069** look after in order to ensure effective provision through a continuous process of planning and monitoring progress.[844] The review is chaired by an Independent Reviewing Officer (IRO) who is responsible for monitoring the local authority's review of the child's care plan, to ensure that it is implemented and outcomes are monitored.[845] The Adoption and Children Act 2002 made provision for IROs, in response to the decision of the House of Lords in *Re S*,[846] so that a local authority's breach of a child's human rights by failing to implement the care plan

---

[837] *R (Behre) v Hillingdon London Borough Council* [2004] 1 F.L.R. 439, QBD; and above, 22–011.

[838] Select Committee on Health, *Second Report 1997–8: Children Looked After by Local Authorities* (HC 247), para.118.

[839] Approximately 20% of foster placements are arranged by agencies: DCSF, *Children Act 1989 Report 2004 and 2005* (2006), para.1.10. Agency carers receive more pay and support. Local authorities still have to approve the carers and visit children that are placed.

[840] J. Fratter et al., *Permanent Family Placement* (London: BAAF, 1991), Ch.3; Sinclair *Pursuit of Permanence*.

[841] I. Sinclair et al, *Foster Placements: Why They Succeed and Why They Fail* (London: Jessica Kingsley, 2004); I. Sinclair, *Fostering Now: Messages From Research* (2005). Fratter et al. (1991) shows comparable breakdown rates in adoption and fostering for children aged five or over at placement.

[842] DfES, *Children Act 1989 Report 2004/2005* (2006), para.1.14.

[843] DCSF, *Children Looked After in England 2006/2007*, Table A3.

[844] Children Act 1989 s.26; Review of Children's Cases Regulations 1991 (SI 1991/895); *Guidance* (1991), Vol.3, paras 8.1–8.3. Reviews should take place after four weeks, three months later and then every six months: reg.3.

[845] The Review of Children's Cases (Amendment) (England) Regulations 2004 (SI 2004/1419); DfES, *Independent Reviewing Officers Guidance* (2004).

[846] [2002] 1 F.L.R. 815, HL, and see above, para.21–039.

could be challenged. As a last resort, IROs have power to refer such cases to CAFCASS for legal action[847]; where the matter can be resolved through discussion, dealt with through the complaints process or the child is able to bring proceedings, the matter should not be referred to CAFCASS.[848] IROs have large caseloads and some may be too inexperienced or lack independence. Some have not challenged even obviously poor practice; almost no use has been made of the power to refer cases.

The Children and Young Persons Bill puts the framework for IROs into statute, ostensibly to enable the IRO to have a more effective independent oversight of the child's case.[849] The local authority will be under a duty to appoint an individual who will be the child's IRO, and provide the continuity of knowledge that was once expected from the child's social worker.[850] The Bill also provides a backstop power that will allow the Secretary of State (or Welsh Ministers) to transfer responsibilities for IROs from local authorities. Either CAFCASS or a newly created body have been mooted as recipients of the IRO service.[851] Despite the Minister's assurances that IROs have the independence necessary to secure plans that promote children's welfare, this provision gives the impression that the Government considers the current arrangements unsatisfactory.[852] If the quality of care for all looked-after children is to reach the high standards that *Care Matters* outlines, far more will be required than active oversight through independent reviews. Social workers have to be recruited, trained and supported to provide thorough assessments, and resources have to be made available to commission the services that children need, such as high quality carers, psychotherapy and special education.

iii. Permanency: rehabilitation and adoption

21-070   The European Court of Human Rights regards state care as a temporary measure; the right to family life requires states to work towards the reunification of families where children are in care.[853] It applies stricter scrutiny to further limitations on parent-child relationships but accepts that there are circumstances where children should not be returned to parents.[854] There has been concern to ensure that children in care have a secure family upbringing since at least the

---

[847] Review of Children's Cases Regulations 1991 (SI 1991/1895) reg.2A; *Guidance* (2004), para.5.4; CAFCASS, *Practice Note: CAFCASS and the work of Independent Reviewing Officers* (2007), para.3.1. An application could be made for Judicial Review or under the Human Rights Act 1998.

[848] *Guidance* (2004), paras 5.1 *et seq.*; CAFCASS, *Practice Note* (2007), para.4.1.

[849] Children and Young Persons Bill 2008 cl.11, adding Children Act 1989 ss.25A–25C; Children and Young Persons Bill 2008, EN para.67.

[850] Children and Young Persons Bill 2008 cl.11(1), adding s.25A(1); the IRO should get to know the child, meeting them before each review: Cm.7137 (2007), para.7.33; Children and Young Persons Bill 2008, EN, para.62.

[851] DCSF, *Policy Statement on Children and Young Persons Bill* (2007); Children and Young Persons Bill, cl.12–14. These powers expire if they are not exercised within seven years: cl.15.

[852] Joint Committee on Human Rights Legislative Scrutiny, 15th Report 2007–8 (HC 440 (2008)), para.1.35.

[853] *Andersson v Sweden* (1992) 14 E.H.R.R. 615; *Johansen v Norway* (1996) 23 E.H.R.R. 33; *Olsson v Sweden (No.2)* (1992) 17 E.H.R.R. 134 at para.81.

[854] *Olsson v Sweden (No.2)* (1992) 17 E.H.R.R. 134 at para.90; *L. v Finland* [2000] 2 F.L.R. 118 at paras 122–125.

1970s[855]; local authorities developed policies and practices designed to promote permanency, particularly through adoption, but it was also recognised that long-term fostering with family contact or returning children to their families fulfilled this aim.[856] The Children Act 1989 promoted partnership with families, but adoption continues to be regarded as the placement of choice for young children who cannot return to their parents or be cared for in their extended family; local authorities continue to seek adoptive placements for children whose families cannot provide adequate care.[857] *Care Matters* promotes two other approaches to permanence. It gives more attention to supporting children's return home by strengthening the local authority's duties to place children in their home area and by proposing that all children who return home should have a child-in-need plan to support them.[858] Also, it emphasises the potential benefit of securing care for children in their extended family by proposing a new framework for friends and family care, including encouraging such arrangements as an alternative to care proceedings, giving priority to such placements and making it easier for carers to obtain residence orders.[859]

In 2007, 24,700 children left the care system; many returned to their families, 3,300 were adopted, 1,000 made the subject of residence and 750 of special-guardianship orders. A third of those leaving care were over the age of 16.[860] A child who does not return home within six weeks is statistically likely to remain in care for at least two years; the longer the period of care, the less likely links with the family will be preserved.[861] Working with the parents and preparation for independence are crucial.

iv. Leaving care and aftercare

Following recommendations from the *Review of Child Care Law*, the Children **21–071**
Act 1989 extended the local authority's duty to make arrangements for children to live with their families to cover all children it looks after,[862] and imposed a new duty to prepare children for a life outside care.[863] Nevertheless, in 1998 the Select Committee on Health concluded that the current system did "deplorably little" for care leavers, and endorsed proposals to impose further duties on local authorities.[864] The Children (Leaving Care) Act 2000 removed the incentive on

---

[855] The extent of drift became clear in J. Rowe and L. Lambert, *Children Who Wait* (London: ABAA, 1972).
[856] J. Thoburn, "What kind of permanence?" (1985) 9 *Adoption and Fostering* 29.
[857] See below, para.22–040.
[858] Cm.7137 (2007), para.2.48; Children and Young Persons Bill 2008 cl.9 adding Children Act 1989 s.22C. CiN plans have been left to guidance; and see N. Biehal, *Patterns and Outcomes: Reuniting Looked After Children With Their Families* (London: NCB, 2006).
[859] Cm.7137 (2007), paras 2.34–2.47, and above paras 18–037, 21–054, 21–068 and below, para.22–064.
[860] DCSF, *Children Looked After in England 2006/2007*, Tables D1 and D2; nearly 60% of older care-leavers left at age 18: Table F1.
[861] S. Millham, *Lost in Care*, pp.196 *et seq.*; Sinclair, *Pursuit of Permanence*.
[862] *Review of Child Care Law*, paras 10.2–10.5; Children Act 1989 s.23(6). If the child is in care, the Placement of Children with Parents, etc. Regulations 1991 (SI1991/893), must be complied with unless the placement is a foster placement.
[863] Children Act 1989 s.24(1); *Guidance* (1991), Vol.3, Ch.9.
[864] Select Committee on Health, *Second Report 1997–8, Children Looked After by Local Authorities* (HC 247), para.313; W. Utting, *People Like Us* paras 8.54 *et seq.*

local authorities to discharge 16 year olds by removing access to Income Support for care leavers under age 18 and continuing their financial responsibilities.[865] It also strengthened the duties in relation to those leaving care over the age of 16 years, requiring local authorities to prepare pathway plans and provide personal advisers.[866] The personal adviser is the child's advocate in developing the pathway plan, and acts as a "go-between"; it is not their role to prepare the plan.[867] The Act also extended some of the leaving-care duties until the age of 24.[868]

Care Matters proposed further support for care leavers, including better preparation for independence, the right for those without families to remain with foster carers until age 21, bursaries for care leavers who attend university, and the provision of a personal adviser until age 25.[869] As part of the measures to improve educational support within the care system, the 2008 Bill requires local authorities to continue to provide a personal adviser to age 25, so long as the young person continues to follow agreed education or training, and enables regulations to be made to extend access to advisers in other circumstances.[870] Care leavers are required to be independent far earlier than most young people; successful transition to adulthood requires services that meet their needs. Currently, many young people; lose contact with their personal adviser, are lonely and struggle to keep accommodation, education or work without family support.[871]

B. The position of parents

21–072 The Children Act intended to encourage partnership between parents and the local authority so that arrangements to provide substitute care would equate with those made within the family. Parents retain parental responsibility; they have a right to be consulted before any decision is made about their child's care where this is reasonably practicable; and their views must be given due consideration.[872] Failure to consult parents amounts to a breach of their art.8 rights:

In *Re C (Breach of Human Rights)* [873] the mother had been in care since she

---

[865] Children (Leaving Care) Social Security Benefits Regulations 2001 (SI 2001/3074).
[866] Children Act 1989 ss.23A–23E and Sch.2 paras 19A–19C; Children (Leaving Care) (England) Regulations 2001 (SI 2001/2874); DH, *Children (Leaving Care) Guidance and Regulations* (2001).
[867] *R (J) v Caerphilly County Borough Council* [2005] 2 F.L.R. 860, QBD.
[868] Children Act 1989 s.24B.
[869] 2007 CM, 7137, Ch.6.
[870] Children and Young Persons Bill 2008 cl.22, adding s.23CA, and cl.23 amending s.23D.
[871] Children's Rights Director, *Young People's Views on Leaving Care* (2006).
[872] s.22(4)(b), (c), (5)(b); Arrangements for Placement of Children Regulations 1991 (SI 1991/893), reg.7; *Guidance* (1991), Vol.3, paras 2.45–2.53. Parents and people with parental responsibility are required to keep the authority informed of their address; Sch.2, para.15(2)(b).
[873] *Re C (Breach of Human Rights: Damages)* [2007] 1 F.L.R 1957, CA; *PC and S v UK* [2002] 1 F.L.R. 631.

was six years old, and gave birth at age 14. The local authority initially placed the mother and child together, but the baby was removed and care proceedings were started after he was bruised. The local authority planned rehabilitation, but proposed adoption if the mother did not succeed in demonstrating her ability to care. Mother and baby were placed together in a specialist foster home, but within days the mother had made threats to the foster carer. The local authority sent a written warning. The mother continued to make threats; the local authority decided to pursue adoption for the child. The mother was informed and another placement found for her alone. She challenged the change of plan under the Human Rights Act 1998, seeking injunctive relief that would require re-unification with her baby. The judge held that the local authority had been entitled to separate mother and baby, but that its change of plan, made without consulting her, was a breach of her art.8 rights. He refused to award damages and the mother's appeal was dismissed. The local authority's decision had breached the mother's rights, but this was only a procedural matter that had not been significant and had been mitigated by keeping her solicitor informed. The mother's aggressive behaviour indicated that she was not able to discuss her child's future.

If there is a care order, the local authority may determine how parental responsibility is exercised so far as this is necessary to safeguard the child's welfare.[874] In extreme cases, the court may sanction excluding a parent from discussions.[875]

Parents enter written agreements that set out the child's address, the services to be provided and the responsibilities of those concerned. Such agreements may delegate to the carer the right to consent to medical treatment, give permission for the child to participate in various activities and settle arrangements for the child's education.[876] Parents should be involved in the review of their child's case, be invited to meetings and be informed of decisions,[877] but unless parents have access to independent advice, they may be unaware of their rights. Parents may complain about the services provided,[878] but may have little alternative to accepting what is offered. Parents remain financially responsible for their children aged under 16 years, but cannot be required to pay if they are in receipt of means-tested benefits or tax credits.[879]

---

[874] Children Act 1989 s.33(3)(b), (4). The local authority may only control the parents' exercise of parental responsibility where the child's welfare demands this.
[875] *Re P (Children Act 1989, ss. 22 and 26: Local Authority Compliance)* [2000] 2 F.L.R. 910, FD; *Re C (Care: Consultation with Parents not in Child's Best Interests)* [2006] 2 F.L.R 787, FD.
[876] Arrangements for Placement of Children (General) Regulations 1991 (SI 1991/890), reg.3 and Sch.4; *Guidance* (1991), Vol.3, paras 2.30–2.39.
[877] Review of Children's Cases Regulations 1991 (SI 1991/895), reg.7. In practice, parents, particularly those who have no contact with their children, are not consulted: J. Masson et al. (eds), *Lost and Found* (Aldershot: Arena, 1999).
[878] s.26(3)(b). For a full discussion, see below, para.21–082.
[879] Children Act 1989 Sch.2 Pt III; where there is no agreement about contributions, the matter may be referred to the court: *Re C (Contribution Notice)* [1994] 1 F.L.R. 111.

C. Rights of children

21–073 A local authority with parental responsibility has no more authority over a child in care than parents have in respect of other children.[880] All children being looked after by the local authority have a right to be consulted about decisions that affect them, where this is reasonably practicable; children's views must be given due consideration, having regard to their age and understanding. Similarly, children must be involved in their reviews.[881] Many local authorities have established Children's Rights Services. Looked-after children have a statutory right to complain about the care provided for them,[882] and those who are refused contact may bring proceedings.[883] Unless they are subject to a court order, they may leave local authority accommodation once they are 16[884]; children in care may seek the discharge of a care order at any age.[885]

There is a "significant and widening gap" between the outcomes for those who are looked after and other young people in the community.[886] In order to improve children's prospects, the Department for Children, Schools and Families is focusing on placement stability and educational achievement. It has proposed a "pledge" to those in public care with specific entitlements, such as a minimum of four hours of sports and leisure activities each week, twice-yearly dental checks and an independent advocate.[887] More emphasis is also given to children's participation in decisions, but many remain poorly informed about plans for their care and their rights.[888] The Children's Rights Director in the Office for Standards in Education, Children's Services and Skills has responsibility for safeguarding the welfare of children in social care or boarding school, and for obtaining their views on services.[889] In Wales, this role is fulfilled by the Children's Commissioner for Wales, who has a broader remit that includes

---

[880] See above, 17–008 *et seq.* "The Bill does nothing to change the underlying principle of Gillick which has to be taken into account by all who exercise parental responsibility over a child mature and intelligent enough to make decisions for himself" *per* Lord Chancellor, *Hansard*, HL, Vol.502, col.1351, Children Bill Committee Stage.

[881] Children Act 1989 s.22(4)(a), (5)(a); *Guidance* (1991), Vol.3, paras 2.47–2.48, and above, para.21–069. In *R. v Devon CC Ex p. O* [1997] 2 F.L.R. 388, a decision to remove a child from prospective adopters was quashed because the child's wishes had not been ascertained.

[882] Children Act 1989 s.26(3)(a). For a full discussion, see below, para.21–082.

[883] Children Act 1989 ss.8 or 34; see below, para.21–074.

[884] Children Act 1989 s.20(11) gives children a right to remain against parental wishes after age 16. If they can do this, they may also leave.

[885] Children Act 1989 s.39(1)(b). In practice, they can only do this effectively if they have sufficient understanding to instruct a solicitor and have alternative accommodation, but they do not require leave from the court: *Re A (Care: Discharge Application by Child)* [1995] 1 F.L.R. 599.

[886] DfES, *Care Matters—Transforming the Lives of Children and Young People in Care* (Cm.6932 (2006)), Foreword; see also *Select Committee on Health 1997–8* (HC 247), para.3.

[887] Cm.6932 (2006), para.1.16. Some of the items in the list are already provided for in regulations; others such as social work support 24/7 exist in theory. Failure to provide items in the pledge could be the basis for a complaint; see below.

[888] *Children Act Now* (2001), pp.92–93, citing R. Grimshaw and R. Sinclair, *Planning to Care* (London: NCB, 1997); Children with sufficient understanding can exercise rights of access to their personal records held by social services: DH, *Data Protection Act 1998 Guidance for Local Authorities* (2001), para.5.8.

[889] Education and Inspections Act 2006 s.120; Office for Standards in Education, Children's Services and Skills (Children's Rights Director) Regulations 2007 (SI 2007/460). The Children's Commissioner has no specific role relating to looked-after children; see Children Act 2004 Pt I, but his remit extends to care leavers and young people with learning difficulties up to the age of 20: s.9.

reviewing the arrangements for complaints in any direct statutory service for children, and reviewing the effect of any actual or proposed legislation from the Welsh Assembly.[890]

V. MODERN CHILDCARE LAW—JUDICIAL CONTROL OVER LOCAL AUTHORITY DECISION-MAKING

A. Decisions requiring court approval

i. Contact with children in care

The mutual enjoyment by parent and child of each other's company is **21–074** fundamental to family life, and continues despite the child's entry to the care system. Unless the child's welfare demands otherwise, state care should be regarded as temporary and should be provided with a view to reuniting the family.[891] Interference with parental contact must be justified under art.8(2) and be proportionate to legitimate aims of safeguarding the child. The Strasbourg Court applies strict scrutiny to restrictions of contact.[892] Contact is not only a matter of rights but also of welfare. Contact is associated with return home for looked-after children, but there is no evidence that it causes it[893]; where there has been contact, rehabilitation is more likely to succeed.[894] It gives children the sense that their parents love them and helps to preserve children's sense of identity.[895] Contacts, however occasional, may continue to have value for the child even when there is no question of return to the family.[896] Contact is more likely to be maintained where the social worker sees the parents regularly.[897] However, visits to children in care by their parents can cause problems for carers, and supporting contact demands substantial social work resources.[898] Ending parental contact has been regarded as facilitating adoption, and consequently in the interests of looked-after children who cannot return home,[899] but there is no evidence that contact affects placement stability in early adoptions.[900]

---

[890] Care Standards Act 2000 Pt V, as amended by Children's Commissioner for Wales Act 2001; see K. Hollingsworth and G. Douglas, "Creating a children's champion for Wales?" [2002] M.L.R. 58–78.

[891] *Olsson v Sweden* (1988) 11 E.H.R.R. 259; *Andersson v Sweden* (1992) 14 E.H.R.R. 615; *Johansen v Norway* (1996) 23 E.H.R.R. 33; *Olsson v Sweden (No.2)* (1992) 17 E.H.R.R. 134, para.81.

[892] *Andersson v Sweden* (1992) 14 E.H.R.R. 615; *Johansen v Norway* (1996) 23 E.H.R.R. 33, para.64. Contact is a civil right, and a hearing that satisfies art.6(1) must be available: *W v UK* (1987) 10 E.H.R.R. 29.

[893] I. Sinclair et al., *Foster Children: Where They Go and How They Get On* (2005).

[894] S. Millham et al., *Lost in Care*; DH, *Patterns and Outcomes of Child Placement* (1991); R. Bullock et al., *Going Home*; DH, *Children Act Now* (2001), p.133.

[895] Berridge and Cleaver *Foster Home Breakdown*, a view endorsed by Simon Brown L.J. in *Re E (A Minor) (Care Order Contact)* [1994] 1 F.L.R. 146 at 155; H. Cleaver, *Fostering Family Contact* (2000).

[896] *Guidance* (1991), Vol.3, para.6.9.

[897] A. Bilson and R. Barker, "Parental contact with children fostered and in residential care after the 1989 Children Act" (1995) 25 Brit. J. Soc. Wk. 367; DH, *Children Act Now* (2001), p.133.

[898] H. Cleaver, *Fostering Family Contact* (London: TSO, 2000).

[899] S. Millham et al., *Lost in Care* (1986); J. Masson, "Contact between parents and children in the long-term care of others: the unresolved dispute" (1990) 4 Int. J. of Law & Fam. 97; S. Jolly, "Cutting the ties—the termination of contact in care" [1994] J.S.W.F.L. 229.

[900] D. Quinton and J. Selwyn, "Adoption: research, policy and practice" [2006] C.F.L.Q. 359, 473.

The Review of Child Care Law accepted that the courts should have a wider role in public law contact disputes.[901] Care orders should include a presumption of reasonable contact and that the court's permission should be required to vary or end arrangements under an order.[902] The Children Act 1989 largely adopted the *Review's* recommendations; new duties were imposed on local authorities and the court was given wider powers to determine contact issues.

Local authorities must endeavour to promote contact between children they are looking after and their families and friends, unless this is not reasonably practicable or consistent with the children's welfare.[903] Contributions may be made towards the cost of visits.[904] Before making a care order, s.34 requires the court to consider the local authority's arrangements for contact and invite the parties to comment on them.[905] Where the child is subject to a care order, the local authority must allow the child reasonable contact[906] with parents, guardians and anyone who had a residence order or care under the inherent jurisdiction immediately before the care order was made.[907] These people, the child and anyone else with leave of the court[908] may seek orders for contact. The local authority (and the child) may also apply to have contact ended but, without an order, it may only refuse contact for up to seven days where this is necessary (as a matter of urgency) for the child's welfare.[909] Such action is a serious step, and must be taken in accordance with regulations.[910] Contact orders may be made when a care order is made or in any family proceedings, with or without an application.[911] The welfare test in Children Act 1989 s.1 applies, and the court may impose such conditions as it thinks fit. Orders may define the frequency,[912] duration and location of meetings or may leave this for the parties to agree; any order may be varied by agreement.[913] Where reasonable contact is appropriate,

---

[901] For a discussion of the law prior to the introduction of the 1989 Act, see the fifth edition of this work at pp.645 *et seq.*

[902] paras 21.1, 21.12–21.16. In contrast, the Short Committee considered that Childcare Act 1980 ss.12A–12F had gone too far: paras 73, 324.

[903] Children Act 1989 Sch.2 para.15.

[904] Children Act 1989 Sch.2 para.16.

[905] Details of contact should be in the care plan: *F v Manchester CC* [1993] 1 F.L.R. 419; *Guidance* (1991), Vol.3, para.2.62; LAC 99(29) para.13, section 2.5.

[906] Contact is reasonable if the parties agree or it is "objectively reasonable": *Re P (Minors) (Contact: Children in Care)* [1993] 2 F.L.R. 156, *per* Ewbank J.

[907] Disputes about contact with children accommodated by the local authority can be dealt with by a contact order under Children Act 1989 s.8.

[908] The test for leave is not that in Children Act 1989 s.10(9), although those criteria are apposite. The applicant must satisfy the court that there is a good arguable case: *Re M (Care: Contact: Grandmother's Application for Leave)* [1995] 2 F.L.R. 86, CA.

[909] Children Act 1989 s.34(6); Contact with Children Regulations 1991 (SI 1991/891), reg.2.

[910] *Guidance* (2008), para.3.76. Contact also can be refused in exercise of the LA's parental responsibility if the visitor has no rights to contact.

[911] It was therefore immaterial whether a child in care who was also a parent was applying under s.34(2) or s.34(3): *Birmingham CC v H* [1994] 2 A.C. 212 at 223, *per* Lord Slynn.

[912] Very frequent contact may be appropriate during care proceedings relating to a baby but substantial daily contact is exceptional, and the financial cost to the local authority may be relevant: *Kirklees MBC v S* [32006] 1 F.L.R. 333, cf. *Re M (Care Proceedings: Judicial Review)* [2003] 2 F.L.R. 171.

[913] Contact with Children Regulations 1991 (SI 1991/891) reg.3. The child's agreement is required for any change if he or she has sufficient understanding, but there is no provision for representation of children.

there is no need to make an order.[914] If the local authority wants to terminate contact, an order may be made that there should be no contact, but this does not preclude re-introducing contact.[915] The local authority thus retains discretion over contact, subject only to the right of others to refer the matter to the court.

Contact orders are not routinely made in care proceedings; unless an order is made, it is assumed that the local authority will arrange the contact set out in the care plan.[916] The courts have been reluctant to challenge local authorities about contact. The Court of Appeal has stated that the local authority's proposals "command the greatest respect", that the presumption of contact should be considered against the long-term plan for the child, and that contact which endangers this will not be allowed.[917] Also, where the nature and extent of contact is an integral part of the local authority's care plan, review by the court would amount to straying into the forbidden territory of supervising the implementation of the authority's arrangements.[918] The local authority must justify the ending of contact,[919] and an order permitting the refusal of contact should not be made against the mere possibility that circumstances will change.[920] However, the courts have permitted termination on the basis that there is a plan for adoption, and have refused to reconsider such decisions without a change in circumstances:

21–075

> In *Re T. (Minors) (Termination of Contact)*[921] the court granted orders permitting the local authority to end contact on the basis that two seriously disturbed boys, S and B, would be adopted. Neither boy was adopted; S was with his third set of foster carers and B was in a therapeutic residential placement. The mother was allowed contact for one hour each month with the boys at a family centre. She applied to discharge the orders permitting termination of contact, and S requested increased contact. The mother's contact with B was suspended during the proceedings. The judge refused the application and the mother appealed. The Court of Appeal discharged the order in relation to S because the local authority had abandoned its plan for

---

[914] *Re S (A Minor) (Care: Contact Order)* [1994] 2 F.L.R. 222. "Contact at the local authority's discretion" also requires the authority to provide reasonable contact: *L v London Borough of Bromley* [1998] 1 F.L.R. 709, FD.
[915] *Re W (Section 34(2) Orders)* [2000] 1 F.L.R. 502, CA; *Kent CC v C* [1993] 1 F.L.R. 308, FD.
[916] Masson et al. (2008), *Care Profiling Study*, p.56 and Table A2.42.
[917] *Re B (Minors) (Termination of Contact: Paramount Consideration)* [1993] Fam. 301, *per* Butler-Sloss L.J. at 311.
[918] *Re S (A Minor) (Care: Contact Order)* [1994] 2 F.L.R. 222 at 226, *per* Simon Brown L.J.
[919] *Re B (Minors) (Termination of Contact: Paramount Consideration)* [1993] Fam. 301, *per* Butler-Sloss L.J. at 311; contact between a child and their family will be assumed to be beneficial and the local authority must justify their wish to terminate it; *Re M (Care: Contact: Grandmother's Application for Leave)* [1995] 2 F.L.R. 86, CA, *per* Ward L.J. at 95.
[920] *Re S (Care: Parental Contact)* [2004] 1 F.L.R. 469, CA. The convenience of the local authority is only an issue where impeding it would be contrary to the best interests of the child: *per* Sedley L.J. *Re H (Terminating Contact)* [2005] 2 F.L.R. 408, CA.
[921] [1997] 1 F.L.R. 517, CA. In *Re L (Sexual Abuse: Standard of Proof)* [1996] 1 F.L.R. 116 at 127, Butler-Sloss L.J. stated (obiter) that termination of contact was appropriate if there was no prospect of rehabilitation and the child was to be placed for adoption.

his adoption, but refused to do so in relation to B. It accepted that contact could be terminated where there was a probable need in the foreseeable future to end contact, and that such decisions could only be challenged by appeal or if there were a change in circumstances.[922]

Such decisions may not withstand a challenge under the Convention. This court-imposed restriction is not supported by the Act, which only precludes applications within six months of a refusal by the court.[923] Also, restricting contact is not a proportionate response to an adoption plan where no placement has been identified. Nor can it be necessary to terminate contact unless it can be shown to be damaging the child when the willingness of the adoptive carers to accept contact remains unknown.

The implementation of the Children Act 1989 has had a fundamental impact on contact. Four times as many children in foster care now see their parents weekly, but a third still have no parental contact.[924] However, where contact is in dispute, the courts remain more willing to accept arguments that contact disrupts placements or deters adopters than that it aids wellbeing and provides continuity.[925] The need to support fostering and the lack of a legal framework for open adoption[926] means that contact is seen as conflicting with the child's needs, despite evidence of the success of more inclusive, substitute care arrangements.[927] Where the plan is for the child's adoption, there are good reasons for continuing contact until the adoption order is made; adopters may not be found[928] or may be willing to continue contact.[929]

21–076   Although there is a duty to place siblings together,[930] there is no presumption of contact between siblings. For most people, relationships with their siblings are the most enduring; the loss of such relationships may be felt acutely by children in care. A child in care who wishes to see another child against the wishes of the

---

[922] Contact may be re-established if the child's social worker recognises the value of this, but may have no redress where the social worker opposes contact: see J. Masson "Thinking about contact—a social or a legal problem" [2000] C.F.L.Q. 15.

[923] Children Act 1989 s.91(17). There is nothing in the statute that justifies imposing a test of change of circumstance. If the court considers there should be no further applications, it has power to impose a condition under s.91(14); this should not be used routinely: *F v Kent CC* [1993] 1 F.L.R. 432, but it can be used in extreme circumstances: *Re Y (Child Orders: Restricting Applications)* [1994] 2 F.L.R. 699; or to provide stability: *Re P (s.91(14) Guidance)* [1999] 2 F.L.R. 573, CA.

[924] H. Cleaver *Fostering*; *Children Act Now* (2001), p.179. Two-thirds of looked-after children are in contact with mothers and half with siblings, but one-sixth have no family contact.

[925] J. Masson (1990) Int. J. of Law and Fam. 97 and see *Children Act Now* (2001), p.181.

[926] See Ch.22.

[927] J. Triseliotis, "Foster care outcomes" (1989) *Adoption & Fostering* 5. When allowance is made for the age of the child, permanent placements with contact are no less stable than those without: J. Fratter et al., *Permanent Family Placement*, p.50.

[928] Only 6 out of 10 children in Harwin and Owen's study of care plans were placed according to their plan: see *Children Act Now* (2001), p.125 and J. Harwin and M. Owen, "A study of care plans and their implementation", in M. Thorpe and C. Cowton (eds), *Delight and Dole* (2002), p.63.

[929] cf. *Re A (Adoption: Contact)* [1993] 2 F.L.R. 645 at 649–650, where Butler-Sloss L.J. noted that monthly contact was incompatible with adoption, and that "the view of open adoption embraced by experts does not seem to be shared by prospective adopters". Also, *Re S (Contact: Application by Sibling)* [1998] 2 F.L.R. 897, where the adoptive parents refused to allow contact with the child's sibling who had been placed separately.

[930] Children Act 1989 s.23(7)(b) (s.22C(8)(c) if the Children and Young Persons Bill is enacted), and see A. Mullender (ed.), *We are family* (London: BAAF, 1999).

local authority may make an application under s.34; the welfare of the child applicant is paramount,[931] but in other cases where a looked-after child wants to have contact with another child, leave must be obtained.[932] The application is made under s.8, and the welfare of the child named (not the applicant) is given paramount consideration.[933]

The Judicial Statistics for 2005 record almost 2,000 applications under s.34; more than three-quarters resulted in orders refusing contact.[934]

ii. Secure accommodation[935]

This is "accommodation provided for the purpose of restricting liberty"[936] where young people are looked after and receive education, etc. in a secure facility. Any accommodation used to restrict liberty is secure accommodation.[937] Confining a child to part of a building, or otherwise preventing free movement, is within the definition, but normal household security is allowed.[938] Regimes vary but have been likened to boarding school or a medium to high security prison.[939] Parental responsibility alone does not empower carers to impose this degree of restriction on children, except possibly for a very limited period.[940] Breach of the regulations amounts to false imprisonment.[941]

The basis for detention of children is obscure,[942] but detention for more than 72 hours within any 28-day period requires court approval. Applications for

21–077

---

[931] *Re F (Contact: Child in Care)* [1995] 1 F.L.R. 510 at 513–514, *per* Wilson J. The order does not oblige the other child to have contact: *Birmingham CC v H (No.3)* [1994] 2 A.C. 212.

[932] Children Act 1989 s.10(8) (9). The "child concerned" means the subject of the application, not the applicant: *Re S (Contact: Application by Sibling)* [1998] 1 F.L.R. 897, FD; therefore, a child applicant need not establish competence to make the application.

[933] *Re F (Contact with Child in Care)* [1995] 1 F.L.R. 510.

[934] *Judicial Statistics 2005*, Table 5.2.

[935] For a detailed discussion of the issues, see R. Harris and N. Timms, *Between Hospital & Prison or Thereabouts* (London: Routledge, 1993); R. Bullock et al., *Secure Treatment Outcomes—The Care Careers of Very Difficult Adolescents* (Aldershot: Ashgate, 1998); M. Parry, "Secure accommodation—the Cinderella of family law" [2000] C.F.L.Q. 101; *Guidance* (1991), Vol.4, Ch.8 and *Guidance* (2008), Ch.5.

[936] Children Act 1989 s.25(1).

[937] *A Metropolitan Borough Council v DB* [1997] 1 F.L.R. 767, FD (locked ward in a maternity hospital); cf. *Re C (Detention: Medical Treatment)* [1997] 2 F.L.R. 180, FD (special residential clinic treating anorexic girls); A. Downie [1998] C.F.L.Q. 101. Department of Health approval is required for the provision of secure accommodation in a community home; voluntary homes and registered children's homes are no longer prohibited from providing secure accommodation: Children (Secure Accommodation) Amendment Regulations 1995 (SI 1995/139).

[938] *Guidance* (1991), Vol.4, paras 1.91(vi), 8.10; DH, *Guidance on Permissible Forms of Control in Children's Residential Care* (1993), section IV.

[939] *Re K (Secure Accommodation: Right to Liberty)* [2001] 1 F.L.R. 526 at 542, *per* Thorpe L.J.; *Koniarska v UK* ECHR App. No.33670/96, hearing: December 10, 2000.

[940] *Re K (Secure Accommodation: Right to Liberty)* [2001] 1 F.L.R. 526, *per* Butler-Sloss P. at para.29 and *per* Judge L.J. at para.101. Thorpe L.J. disagreed: see paras 49–61; see also J. Fortin, "Children's rights and physical force" [2001] C.F.L.Q. 243.

[941] The pindown regime was considered to have breached the regulations: A. Levy and B. Kahan, *The Pindown Experience and the Protection of Children* (1991), para.12.60. Substantial compensation was paid to the children.

[942] In *Re M (Secure Accommodation Order)* [1995] 1 F.L.R. 418 at 425, Hoffmann L.J. said it derived from the local authority's parental responsibility or the parent's request for the child to be looked after, but this analysis was not accepted by the majority in *Re K (Secure Accommodation: Right to*

secure accommodation orders are made under the Children Act 1989 s.25; most of the detailed rules are found in regulations.[943]

Any child[944] over the age of 13[945] may only be placed or kept in secure accommodation if it appears:

"(a) [T]hat

    (i) he has a history of absconding and is likely[946] to abscond from any other description of accommodation; and

    (ii) if he absconds he is likely to suffer significant harm; or

(b) that if he is kept in any other description of accommodation he is likely to injure himself or other persons."[947]

21-078 This is a draconian order; children facing secure-accommodation proceedings should be afforded the same art.6(3) rights as those charged with criminal offences.[948] If the criteria are satisfied, the court must make the order; the child's welfare is not the paramount consideration.[949] The court's powers are limited to testing the evidence[950] and fixing the duration of the order[951]; orders may last for up to three months, with extensions of up to six months.[952] The court authorises the use of secure accommodation; the local authority must continually review

Liberty) [2001] 1 F.L.R. 526, paras 29, 97–101, who saw it as dependent on authorisation by the court.

[943] Children (Secure Accommodation) Regulations 1991 (SI 1991/1505), as amended; Children (Secure Accommodation) Wales Regulations 2006 (SI 2006/2986).

[944] Children may be detained under the Mental Health Act 1983, as amended, the Powers of Criminal Courts (Sentencing) Act 2000 (conviction for grave offences) or the Crime and Disorder Act 1998 without a secure accommodation order: SI 1991/1505, reg.5(1). The regulations apply, subject to modification, to children remanded to local authority accommodation: reg.6: *Re G (Secure Accommodation Order)* [2001] 1 F.L.R. 884. Children bailed with a condition that they reside in local-authority accommodation are subject to s.25: *Re C (Secure Accommodation: Bail)* [1994] 2 F.L.R. 922 but local authorities do not have an absolute duty to provide secure accommodation at the request of the police: *R. (M) v Gateshead Council* [2006] 2 F.L.R. 379, CA. Children accommodated under s.20(5) or s.43 may not be held in secure accommodation: reg.5(2).

[945] SI 1991/1505, reg.4; the Secretary of State's permission is required if the child is under 13: DCSF, *Revised Guidance*, September 20, 2007.

[946] A "real possibility which cannot be sensibly ignored" *per* Charles J. *S v Knowsley BC* [2004] 2 F.L.R. 716, para.37.

[947] Children Act 1989 s.25(1); there are two alternative conditions: *Re D (No.1)* (1996) J.P.N. 286.

[948] *Re C (Secure Accommodation Order: Representation)* [2001] 2 F.L.R. 169, CA at paras 25 and 34. These are "specified proceedings"; a children's guardian should be appointed: *Guidance* (2008), para.5.10.

[949] Children Act 1989 s.25(4); *Re M (Secure Accommodation Order)* [1995] 1 F.L.R. 418, CA. cf. *Guidance* (1991), Vol.4, para.8.9, which suggests that the court has a discretion. An interim order can be made even if full evidence has not been heard: s.25(5); *Re C (Secure Accommodation Order: Representation)* [2001] 2 F.L.R. 169, CA, *per* Thorpe L.J. at para.31.

[950] Hearsay evidence is admissible: *R. v Oxfordshire CC (Secure Accommodation Order)* [1992] Fam. 150.

[951] *Re W (A Minor) (Secure Accommodation Order)* [1993] 1 F.L.R. 692. The order should last no longer than necessary; overlong orders effectively delegate the court's responsibility to the local authority: *per* Booth J. at 679.

[952] SI 1991/1505, regs 11, 12. The time periods run from the date of authorisation; *Re B (A Minor) (Secure Accommodation)* [1994] 2 F.L.R. 707.

whether the child should be kept there.[953] Decisions to retain children in secure accommodation are appropriately challenged by judicial review.[954] Children who are only accommodated by the authority may be removed at any time by those with parental responsibility.[955]

Despite the restrictive nature of secure accommodation, the Court of Appeal held in *Re K (Secure Accommodation: Right to Liberty)*[956] that detention authorised under s.25 did not breach art.5. Under the Convention, detention "for the purpose of educational supervision" is lawful. Classroom teaching is not required, life-skills and social-skills training could be sufficient, but there must be "educational supervision", even where the child was over compulsory school age.[957] Even though the Act made no mention of education, s.25 was not incompatible with the Convention.[958]

Court proceedings have not operated as an effective check on the use of secure accommodation,[959] but (largely for reasons of cost) local authorities have developed procedures intended to limit its use. Secure accommodation should be seen as a "last resort" and not used merely because of lack of suitable alternatives, nor as a form of punishment.[960] Running away may indicate abuse or unhappiness that locking up will not remedy. Use of secure accommodation has increased because of the poor facilities (particularly the low level of staffing) in open units, the problems of caring for young sex abusers and children involved in prostitution and the desire to keep boys awaiting trial or convicted of grave crimes out of penal establishments.[961] There are 390 places available in secure children's homes, but over half are used by the Youth Justice Board for young people convicted or on remand[962]; fewer than half the residents were looked after by a local authority.[963] Some young people benefit from placements in secure units; for others it amounts to little more than prison.[964]

---

[953] *Re K (Secure Accommodation: Right to Liberty)* [2001] 1 F.L.R. 526 at paras 22 and 101; regs 15 and 16.

[954] *S v Knowsley BC* [2004] 2 F.L.R. 716 at para.72. Habeas corpus may be available: *Re S (Habeas Corpus)* [2004] 1 F.L.R. 590, QBD, at para.28, *per* Munby J.

[955] Children Act 1989 s.25(9). This is also relevant to children placed by health or education authorities. In *M v Birmingham CC* [1994] 2 F.L.R. 141, the local authority obtained a care order because of the mother's refusal to agree to a secure placement.

[956] [2001] 1 F.L.R. 526 ; J. Masson [2002] C.F.L.Q. 77; see also *S v Miller (No.2)* [2001] S.L.T. 34.

[957] ECHR art.5(1)(d); *Bouamar v Belgium* (1989) 11 E.H.R.R. 1; *Koniarska v UK* ECHR App. No.33670/96, hearing December 10, 2000.

[958] *Re K (Secure Accommodation: Right to Liberty)* [2001] 1 F.L.R. 526 at para.43 *per* Butler-Sloss P. and at para.116 *per* Judge L.J. The attention of the Court was not drawn to Education Act 1996 s.562, which disapplies the education duties to those detained under a court order.

[959] Timms and Harris, *Between Hospital and Prison*, p.49.

[960] *Guidance* (1991), Vol.4, para.8.6.

[961] The Department of Health rejected claims that use is determined by supply rather than need: *Children Act Report 1995–9*, para.9.35.

[962] DfES, *Children Accommodated in Secure Children's Homes 2006* Table A1.

[963] DfES, *Children Accommodated in Secure Children's Homes 2006*. On March 31, 2006, 16% of residents were accommodated under s.20; 12% under care orders; and 15% placed following remand with a security requirement by the court.

[964] See D. Simpson, "My experience in secure units" in *Evidence to Short Committee*, Vol.III, pp.364–365; W. Utting, *People Like Us*, paras 2.18–2.10.

iii. Placement outside England and Wales

21–079 Until the 1960s, arrangements were made by voluntary organisations and local authorities for thousands of children in their care to emigrate.[965] Children were placed overseas with families and in institutions to save costs and to populate the colonies, with the hope that they would have a better life. However, "child migration was bad and, in human terms, a costly mistake".[966] Changes in Britain and in the receiving countries—Australia, Canada and elsewhere—brought an end to this practice; children are now only placed overseas with relatives or if their foster carer emigrates.

Under the Children Act 1989, the agreement of all people with parental responsibility is required if an accommodated child is to leave England and Wales (e.g. to move to Scotland with foster carers).[967] If agreement is refused, there is no way of overriding this decision unless the foster carers obtain parental responsibility.[968] The emigration of children in care requires the court's permission.[969] The court may only give this where the move is in the child's best interests; suitable arrangements have been made for the child's welfare in the receiving country; and the child and every person with parental responsibility has consented. The court may act without the consent of an immature child or of a person with parental responsibility who cannot be found, is incapable of giving consent or is withholding it unreasonably.[970] Parents retain their parental responsibility; consequently, it is more difficult than in adoption to establish that refusal is reasonable, particularly where contact is to be maintained.[971] Where the child has no relationship with the parents or has no chance of living with them, the court will usually permit emigration.[972] Where permission has been granted, the child may also be adopted overseas.[973]

---

[965] See G. Wagner, *Children of the Empire* (London: Weidenfeld and Nicolson, 1981); P. Bean and J. Melville, *Lost Children of the Empire* (1989); R. Parker, *Uprooted* (2008).

[966] Select Committee on Health, *The Welfare of Former British Child Migrants*, Third Report Session 1997–8 (HC 755), paras 15–19 and 98.

[967] Children Act 1989 Sch.2 para.9(2); *Guidance* (1991), Vol.8, Ch.6; see below.

[968] By a residence or special guardianship order; Children Act 1989 ss.8, 13(1)(b), 14C(3); such a person could go to Scotland permanently without consent; the court's leave may be sought for the child's emigration outside the UK if permission is refused.

[969] Children Act 1989 Sch.2 para.19; permission is not needed for visits of one month or less: s.33(7)(b). In *Flintshire v K* [2001] 2 F.L.R 476, FD, the court approved a care plan so that the "internet twins" could be returned to the US and cared for permanently there.

[970] Children Act 1989 Sch.2, para.19(4)(5); *Re G (Minors) (Care: Leave to Place outside the Jurisdiction)* [1994] 2 F.L.R. 301. Children must give consent in writing; a deep level of understanding is therefore required: *Re J (Freeing For Adoption)* [2000] 2 F.L.R. 58 at 67, *per* Black J.

[971] *Re G (Minors) (Care: Leave to Place outside the Jurisdiction)* [1994] 2 F.L.R. 301 at 306, *per* Thorpe J. The children were placed with an aunt in the US with their parents' (reluctant) consent.

[972] *Payne v Payne* [2001] 1 F.L.R. 1052 (a private law case where the father was able to maintain good contact). Placement at a distance that undermined contact could breach art.8, particularly if there were viable alternatives: *Olsson v Sweden* (1988) 11 E.H.R.R. 259 (children placed in three separate foster homes far from parents' home).

[973] Children Act 1989 Sch.2, para.19(6), as amended, disapplies Adoption and Children Act 2002 s.85.

iv. Other decisions

Children in care sometimes want to change their names, either to identify with **21–080** foster carers or to cut links with abusive parents. It is provided that no person may cause a child in care to be known by a new surname without the written consent of all those with parental responsibility or leave of the court.[974] Children may apply[975]; foster carers without a residence order are unlikely to take proceedings or be granted permission.[976] These cases raise many of the same issues as other cases on name, but the objectives of the applicant, the motives and objections of parents and the views of the children's guardian are also relevant.[977] A child in care who wishes to marry must obtain the consent of the local authority and any parent with parental responsibility or their guardian, but may obtain consent from the court if this is refused.[978] The local authority's parental responsibility avoids the need for court permission and prevents review of other decisions.[979] For issues such as sterilisation,[980] which go beyond parental responsibility, the inherent jurisdiction of the High Court may be invoked, but only if the child would otherwise be at risk of significant harm.[981] Where the child is accommodated, the court may review relevant decisions in proceedings for a s.8 order.[982]

B. Challenging local authority decisions

Theoretically, services provided by children's services departments are the **21–081** responsibility of locally elected council members, who are accountable through the ballot box for the quality of services. However, political accountability is inadequate for minority concerns such as services for children in need that are rarely issues in local elections, and does not give a means of redress to individual complainants. The courts have taken a limited role in supervising local authorities through actions for judicial review, breach of statutory duty,[983] negligence or under the Human Rights Act 1998. The concentration of professional expertise and political, administrative and institutional authority in

---

[974] Children Act 1989 s.33(7)(a).
[975] These are specified proceedings but children's guardian may not be required: *Re J (A Minor) (Change of Name)* [1993] 1 F.L.R. 699.
[976] See para.17–025, but see *Re D, L and LA (Care Change of Forename)* [2003] 1 F.L.R. 339, FD (the court refused to require a foster carer to use the child's first name instead of the middle name).
[977] *Re M, T, P, K, and B (Care: Change of Name)* [2000] 2 F.L.R. 645, FD; cf. *Re S (Change of Surname)* [1998] 1 F.L.R. 672, CA.
[978] Marriage Act 1949 s.3(1)(b), (1A).
[979] *A v Liverpool CC* [1982] A.C. 363; but the court may determine disputes about the scope of parental responsibility: *Re M (Care: Leave to Interview Child)* [1995] 1 F.L.R. 825.
[980] *Re F (Wardship: Sterilisation)* [1990] 2 A.C. 1; *Re B (A Minor) (Wardship Sterilisation)* [1988] A.C. 199.
[981] Children Act 1989 s.100(4), (5); *Re X (A Minor) (Adoption)* [1994] 2 F.L.R. 450, where an order was granted restricting disclosure of details in the adoption register; see also above.
[982] Children Act 1989 s.9(2), (5); see the discussion of s.100 above.
[983] See Markesinis and Deakin's, *Tort Law*, 8th edn (2008); statutory duties relating to childcare will rarely give rise to a private law cause of action: *X v Bedfordshire CC* [1995] 2 A.C. 633; *O'Rouke v Camden LBC* [1998] A.C. 189.

the children's services department means that the power in relationships with clients rests with departments.[984] Partnership with parents requires the development of procedures and practices to shift that balance, empower clients, provide them with real opportunities to influence decisions made about them and to challenge those they disagree with. The complaints system makes children's services departments and social workers more accountable for their actions and responsive to clients' needs. An effective complaints procedure can ensure that the voices of young service users are heard and lead to improvements in services.[985] Individuals adversely affected by maladministration may be able to obtain financial or other redress.[986]

Procedures must be able to handle a wide range—and possibly a large number[987]—of different complaints. Clients may be dissatisfied with the professionalism of staff or the quality of the service they provide; the availability of a service (i.e. the resources committed by the authority to it and the criteria used for rationing); or the appropriateness of the services offered in their case. A disagreement with a local authority may contain all these elements, as well as disputes about the factual basis on which assessments were made, and disputes about the law. Different types of complaint may require different consideration and different action; the source of the problem may affect the chances of reaching a satisfactory solution. For example, where the lack of a local service results from a decision not to resource it, the matter is essentially a political one, unless there is a duty to provide it. Irrespective of the strength of complaint, provision can only be made if the service is available privately or from another authority, and money can be found to purchase it. In contrast, where the complaint concerns a professional issue such as the assessment of the client's needs and thus the priority of their claim for a service or its appropriateness, a review may reveal the justice of the complaint and lead to redress. In practice, it may be difficult for clients to distinguish between professional and political decisions and to know where their complaint should be directed. Most complaints about services will reflect, in some measure, the limitations of resources, but this should not justify poor quality or inappropriate provision.

The Children's Commissioner does not deal with individual complaints, but the Welsh Children's Commissioner can undertake this role.[988]

---

[984] National Consumer Council & National Institute for Social Work, *Open to Complaints* (1988), p.6; *Children Act Now* (2001), p.70; see also S. Braye and M. Preston-Shoot, "Accountability, administrative law and social work practice: redressing or re-inforcing the power imbalance?" [1999] J.S.W.F.L. 235.

[985] DfES, *Getting the Best from Complaints* (2006), Ministerial Foreword (*Guidance* (2006)). The complaints system must be monitored and any annual report provided: Representations Procedure (England) Regulations 2006 (SI 2006/1738), reg.13; *Guidance* (2006), para.5.6.

[986] Local Government Act 2000 s.92.

[987] The ability to attract and deal with complaints may be seen as a mark of success. Schemes that receive few complaints may be insufficiently accessible. A DH survey during the first nine months of the Children Act 1989 revealed under 4,000 complaints, 542 from children: Cm.2144, Table 3.12.

[988] Children Act 2004 s.2(7); Care Standards Act 2000 s.74 and Children's Commissioner for Wales Regulations 2001 (SI 2001/2787); K. Hollingsworth and G. Douglas, "Creating a children's champion for Wales?" [2002] M.L.R. 58.

i. Complaints procedures

Complaints procedures have an essential, protective function[989]; a lack of **21–082** complaints systems contributed to the failure to identify and stop the widespread abuse in children's homes in the 1970s and 1980s.[990] Both the *Short Report* and the *Review* recommended the introduction of a complaints system[991]; provision was made in the Children Act 1989, and this has now been substantially recast.

The Children Act 1989 s.26(3) makes provision for complaints about services for children and families, including child protection services.[992] Complaints may be made by children looked after by the local authority and other "children in need", their parents, those with parental responsibility for them, other people whom the authority considers have sufficient interest in the child's welfare to warrant their representations being considered,[993] local authority foster parents,[994] care leavers[995] and in connection with adoption services or special guardianship support services.[996] Complaints must be made within a year, but local authorities have discretion to consider older complaints if it would not be reasonable to expect a prompt complaint, and where it can still be considered effectively and fairly.[997] Where the matter of complaint is the subject of court proceedings, a disciplinary process or a criminal investigation, it cannot be dealt with as a complaint; once proceedings are started, the complaints process is frozen, but it should be continued when proceedings are completed.[998] Advocacy services must be provided for children and care leavers who complain.[999] Advocates should represent the views, wishes and needs of children, and help them to navigate the system.[1000] Securing the appropriate services for a looked-after child may involve their social worker, advocate, IRO and a complaint[1001];

---

[989] W. Utting, *People Like Us*, para.18.12. But the existence of a complaints system was one of the justifications for not imposing a duty of care on the local authority: *X v Bedfordshire CC* [1995] 2 A.C. 633.

[990] *Lost in Care* (HC 201 (2001)), pp.829 and 834. Sympathetic responses to residents' complaints about were also crucial to the discovery of abusive regimes in North Wales, Staffordshire and elsewhere.

[991] *Short Report*, paras 361 *et seq.*; *Review,* paras 9.10–9.12.

[992] Children Act 1989 s.26(3), (3A) added by the Adoption and Children Act 2002 s.117; Representations Procedure (England) Regulations 2006 (SI 2006/1738); Representations Procedure (Children) (Wales) Regulations 2005 (SI 2005/3365); DfES, *Guidance: Getting the Best from Complaints* (2006), para.2.2.2–3. The Children's Rights Director of the Office for Standards in Education, Children's Services and Skills should help ensure that young people's complaints about children's services are properly dealt with.

[993] Children Act 1989 s.26(3)(a)–(c), (e); *Guidance* (2006), para.2.6.1, including complaints on behalf of, or relating to, a child; paras 2.7 and 2.8.

[994] Children Act 1989 s.26(3)(d) including complaints about the number of children who may be fostered: Sch.7, para.5; (SI 2006/1738), reg.23.

[995] Children Act 1989 s.24D.

[996] Children Act 1989 s.26(3B), added by Adoption and Children Act 2002 s.117; (SI 2006/1738) regs 2–5.

[997] SI 2006/1738 reg.9; DfES, *Guidance* (2006), para.3.3.

[998] SI 2006/1738 reg.8.

[999] Children Act 1989 s.26A; Advocacy services and Representations Procedure (Children) (Amendment) Regulations 2004 (SI 2004/719); for Wales, SI 2004/1448; *Guidance* (2006), para.3.4.

[1000] DfES, *Independent Reviewing Officers Guidance* (2004), p.32.

[1001] For an explanation of the inter-relationship of these, see DfES, *IRO Guidance* (2004), paras 5.2–5.4, and above para.21–069.

Inquiries, particularly in the area of child protection, have had a major influence on children's social care policy, organisation and practice. There is a raft of intervention powers that allow the Secretary of State or the Welsh Assembly government to issue directions where a local authority is not meeting the government's "best value" requirements, failing to carry out its functions to an acceptable standard or not complying with its duties.[1021] Default powers in other legislation have rarely been used,[1022] but the Government has declared its willingness to intervene where councils are failing.[1023] In the past, local authorities whose standards were found unacceptable through inspection[1024] have been put under "special measures" involving target-setting and monitoring; and where a Director of Social Services resigned, the responsible central government department identified an experienced Director for appointment.

The existence of a default power has been held to preclude the use of other judicial remedies,[1025] but s.84 does not prevent the use of judicial review.[1026] However, the court, hearing an application by a person aggrieved may refuse to exercise its discretion where this might conflict with the minister's decision,[1027] thus the default power may be a hindrance to individuals as well as a lever against local authorities. Also, it has been said that where the minister has a default power, this will generally be a better remedy, particularly if the merits of the decision are at issue. The minister, unlike the court, has the department's expertise, can conduct an inquiry and can direct the solution to be applied.[1028] Where judicial review is refused, the minister may still be willing to investigate the case.[1029]

iv. Under the inherent jurisdiction of the High Court, by judicial review[1030] or under the Human Rights Act 1998 s.7

21–085 In 1981, in *A v Liverpool City Council*,[1031] the House of Lords confirmed the view that the High Court should not exercise its wardship jurisdiction to review decisions relating to children in care. Parliament had, by statute, entrusted the

---

[1021] Children Act 1989 s.84; Education Act 1996 s.497A, added by Children Act 2004 s.50. This could be in response to an inspection or a complaint.
[1022] J. Logie, "Enforcing statutory duties: the court and default powers" [1988] J.S.W.L. 185, 186, 196.
[1023] *Modernising Social Services* (Cm.4169 (1998)), para.7.21.
[1024] Inspection powers are now exercised by the Office for Standards in Education, Children's Services and Skills in relation to children's social care and the Commission for Social Care Inspection; in relation to adult social care, see Education and Inspections Act 2006 and Care Standards Act 2000, as amended by the Health and Social Care (Community Health and Standards) Act 2003 ss.42 and 44.
[1025] *Pasmore v Oswaldtwistle UDC* [1898] A.C. 387.
[1026] *R. v Brent LBC Ex p. S* [1994] 1 F.L.R. 203 at 214, *per* Peter Gibson L.J.
[1027] *R. v Secretary of State for the Environment Ex p. Ward* [1984] 1 W.L.R. 834; but see Logie, *op. cit.* at 194—the matter has only been considered by the High Court.
[1028] *R. v Devon CC Ex p. Baker and Johns* (1992) 11 B.M.L.R. 141, *per* Simon Brown L.J. at 160.
[1029] *R. v Brent LBC Ex p. S* [1994] 1 F.L.R. 203 at 214.
[1030] De Smith et al., *Judicial Review of Administrative Action*, 5th edn (London: Sweet and Maxwell, 1995) and M. Fordham, *Judicial Review Handbook*, 4th edn (Oxford: Hart, 2004).
[1031] [1982] A.C. 363; the approach dates back to the decision in *Re M* [1961] Ch. 328. Law Com. WP 101, *Wards of Court*, paras 3.39 *et seq.*

power and duty to make decisions to local authorities without reserving a power of review to the courts, and thus marked out an area where decisions about children are removed from both parents and the courts.[1032] The Children Act 1989 s.100 extended the restrictions; local authorities cannot refer any matter that could be dealt with under statutory powers to the High Court's inherent jurisdiction. Although the statutory restrictions do not apply to individuals, and the local authority may accept the jurisdiction, the High Court is unwilling to allow its powers to be used to circumvent the Children Act.[1033]

Where impropriety is alleged, the matter can be dealt with by judicial review[1034]; if the decision involves an infringement of human rights, the claim may alternatively be brought under the Human Rights Act.[1035] An application for judicial review may only be made with permission[1036] by someone with sufficient interest in the matter; this might preclude relatives initiating proceedings but not parents or children.[1037] The applicant must have exhausted other more-suitable remedies, including the complaints process.[1038] The grounds for judicial review have developed through case law; local authorities must not act unlawfully,[1039] unreasonably,[1040] in breach of reasonable expectations[1041] or without following the proper procedure, and they must comply with the rules of natural justice.[1042] The courts have been willing to review decisions taken where the authority has failed to consider issues required by statute or guidance,[1043] where it has fettered its discretion[1044] or acted without adequate inquiry.[1045] The courts have refused

---

[1032] *Per* Lord Wilberforce at 372.

[1033] *C v Salford CC* [1994] 2 F.L.R. 926, and see above para.18–036.

[1034] *Per* Lord Scarman in *W v Hertfordshire CC* [1985] A.C. 791 at 793; *Re DM (A Minor) (Wardship Jurisdiction)* [1986] 2 F.L.R. 122.

[1035] Human Rights Act 1998 s.7(1). *CF v Secretary of State for the Home Department* [2004] 2 F.L.R. 517, *per* Munby J. In either case, they should be heard by a Family Division Judge who also sits in the Administrative Court.

[1036] Civil Procedure Rules 1998 (SI 1998/3132) r.54; R. Spon-Smith [2001] Fam. Law 143.

[1037] D. Oliver [1989] J.C.L. 58. The test for locus standi is set out in *R. v IRC Ex p. National Federation of Self Employed and Small Businesses Ltd* [1982] A.C. 617.

[1038] *R. (Cowl) v Plymouth City Council* [2001] EWCA Civ 1935; *R. (BG) v Medway Council* [2006] 1 F.L.R. 663.

[1039] *R. v Cornwall CC Ex p. Cornwall Guardians ad litem Panel* [1992] 1 W.L.R. 427, where the director of social services' attempt to limit investigations by children's guardians was quashed.

[1040] The narrow approach to unreasonableness established in *Associated Provincial Picture Houses Ltd v Wednesbury Corporation* [1948] 1 K.B. 223 has been superseded in *R. v Secretary of State Ex p. Daly* [2001] 3 All E.R. 433, HL. A public authority must show that any decision which interferes with human rights is proportionate. A decision that conflicts with the recommendation of the complaints panel may be unreasonable: *R. v Kingston upon Thames RBC Ex p. T* [1994] 1 F.L.R. 798 at 815.

[1041] *R. on app Nagalro v CAFCASS* [2002] 1 F.L.R. 225; *R. v Cornwall County Council, Ex p. LH* [2000] 1 F.L.R. 236, QBD.

[1042] See *R. v Harrow LBC Ex p. D* [1990] 1 F.L.R. 70; the requirements of natural justice are not rigid: *R. v Avon CC Ex p. Crabtree* [1996] 1 F.L.R. 502, CA.

[1043] *R. v Wealden DC Ex p. Wales* [1995] N.P.C. 145, exercise of powers to remove campers without consideration of duties to children in need in the Children Act 1989; *R. v Devon CC, Ex p. O* [1997] 2 F.L.R. 388 (removal of child from long-term foster carers without consulting the carer or finding out child's wishes); *R. v Cornwall County Council Ex p. LH* [2000] 1 F.L.R. 236, QBD (disregard of the *Working Together* guidance on involvement of parents in case conferences).

[1044] *R. v Hammersmith and Fulham LBC Ex p. D* [1999] 1 F.L.R. 642, QBD (decision not to offer any alternative services if parent refused assistance to return to her own country).

[1045] *R. v Local Authority and Police Authority in the Midlands Ex p. LM* [2000] 1 F.L.R. 612, QBD (decision to disclose offences of bus operator to neighbouring local authority); *Re T (Accommodation*

to review decisions requiring a housing authority to co-operate with the social services department[1046] or a social services department to find a placement for a child in hospital.[1047] Where the local authority refuses to accept that a child is "in need" or is entitled to leaving-care services, redress is ultimately by judicial review.[1048] However, the duty in s.17 is a "general duty".[1049] The court considers financial constraints on the local authority and does not investigate its priorities[1050] or determine how they should be met:

> In *Re T (Judicial Review: Local Authority decision concerning child in need)*[1051] a 14-year-old boy who had sexually abused his sister was accommodated by the local authority. A local authority planning meeting considered that he needed a specialist residential assessment; the social services department agreed to provide one-third of the costs and approached the NHS and Education for the remainder. When invited to reconsider the matter in light of further reports, the authority decided that a specialist placement was not required. The child sought judicial review to quash the later decision and sought a mandatory order to require the local authority to fund the specialist placement. The court quashed the decision and ordered the local authority to refer the case and funding to its complex-cases panel. The court had no power to determine which services were provided for the boy.

Courts have stressed the value of the complaints system on the basis that they have no investigatory powers,[1052] and emphasised the importance of local authorities being able to exercise their child protection functions without fear of challenge by judicial review.[1053] The remedies for judicial review are discretionary; the court may make mandatory, prohibiting or quashing orders alongside other civil remedies including damages, and can issue declarations of incompatibility.[1054] Remedies may be illusory if the local authority reaches the same conclusion when it reconsiders the decision, but the granting of permission to seek judicial review may precipitate the necessary change of view.

21–086   Where a local authority acts (or proposes to act)[1055] in breach of the European Convention on Human Rights, a victim may bring proceedings against the

by Local Authority) [1995] 1 F.L.R. 159 (decision not to accommodate orphan under s.20(3) but only to make s.17 payment).
[1046] *R. v Northavon DC Ex p. Smith* [1994] 2 F.L.R. 671, HL; Children Act 1989 s.27(2).
[1047] *R. v Birmingham CC Ex p. A* [1997] 2 F.L.R. 841, QBD.
[1048] Sunkin (1992) 4 J.C.L. 109, 111; *R. (Behre) v Hillingdon LBC* [2004] 1 F.L.R. 439, QBD.
[1049] Children Act 1989 s.17(1); *R. (G) v Barnet LBC* [2004] 1 F.L.R. 454, HL. There is a duty to assess but no specific duty to meet needs.
[1050] *R. v Kingston upon Thames RBC Ex p. T* [1994] 1 F.L.R. 798 at 817.
[1051] [2004] 1 F.L.R. 601, *per* Wall J.; see also *R. (CD) v Isle of Anglesey CC* [2005] 1 F.L.R. 59.
[1052] *R. v Birmingham CC Ex p. A* [1997] 2 F.L.R. 841, QBD; *R. v East Sussex CC, Ex p. W* [1998] 2 F.L.R. 1082, QBD.
[1053] *R. v Somerset CC Ex p. Prospects Care Services* [2000] 1 F.L.R. 636, QBD, at 641, *per* Dyson J.; *R. v Hampshire CC Ex p. H* [1999] 2 F.L.R. 359, CA at 372, *per* Butler-Sloss L.J.
[1054] Human Rights Act 1998 s.4(2).
[1055] This can include a failure to act: *Re S (FC)* [2002] 1 F.L.R. 815, HL, 10 at para.49 *per* Lord Nicholls.

authority.[1056] Where there are current care proceedings, concerns should be raised in those proceedings, not separately.[1057] Leave is not required, but it has been said that applications should not be made under s.7 until other appropriate remedies have been explored.[1058] The court can grant such relief or order as it considers appropriate.[1059] Damages may be awarded, but where the breach does not have a substantial impact, a declaration that there was a breach may be just satisfaction.[1060] The High Court may also exercise its powers under the inherent jurisdiction to ensure compliance with Convention rights, but remains bound by the restrictions in the Children Act 1989 s.100. In *Re M*[1061] the court quashed a decision to abandon plans for a baby subject to a care order to live with either of his parents in favour of a placement with the maternal grandmother or adoption, because the parents' art.8 rights had been breached by failure to involve them in the decision-making. It also arranged for a further hearing to reconsider the new care plan. However, in *Re C (Breach of Human Rights Damages)*,[1062] the court was satisfied that despite the local authority's failure to consult before changing the care plan, the proceedings were substantially fair. In *R. ota L v Manchester City Council*[1063] (a judicial review application), the court struck down the local-authority policy of paying short-term relative carers less than local authority foster carers on the basis that this was unreasonable, failed to take account of the duty to safeguard the child's welfare and breached art.8 together with art.14 because it made it less likely that a child could be placed with relatives. The authority was ordered to pay damages under the 1998 Act. Human rights arguments have provided a new perspective on local authority practices. Whilst the courts are more open to the exposure of local authority failings, they remain unwilling for care proceedings to be derailed on the basis that decisions outside the proceedings have not involved the parents fully.[1064]

v. The European Court of Human Rights[1065]

Before the Human Rights Act 1998, this court provided the only means of **21–087** challenging decisions that, though lawful under domestic law, breached the European Convention on Human Rights. It has been highly influential in the

---

[1056] Human Rights Act 1998 s.7(1). Proceedings may be brought in either the country court that made the original care order or the High Court: *Re W and B; Re W* [2001] 2 F.L.R. 582, CA, *per* Hale L.J. at para.75. Alternatively, under s.7(1)(b) a party could raise the matter in any Children Act proceedings

[1057] *Re V (Care proceedings: Human Rights claims)* [2004] 1 F.L.R. 944, CA.

[1058] *Re S (FC)* [2002] 1 F.L.R. 815, HL, at para.62, *per* Lord Nicholls.

[1059] Human Rights Act 1998 s.8.

[1060] Human Rights Act 1998 s.8(4); Law Com. No.266, *Damages under the Human Rights Act* (Cm.4853 (2000)); *Re C (Breach of Human Rights Damages)* [2007] 1 F.L.R. 1957, and above, para.21–072.

[1061] *Re M (Care: Challenging Decisions by Local Authority)* [2001] 2 F.L.R. 1300, FD.

[1062] [2007] 1 F.L.R.1957, CA, and above, para.21–072.

[1063] [2002] 2 F.L.R. 43.

[1064] *Re J (care assessment: fair trial)* [2007] 1 F.L.R. 77, CA; Munby J.'s decision in *Re L (care assessment: fair trial)* [2002] 2 F.L.R. 730 was criticised.

[1065] H. Swindells et al., *Family Law and the Human Rights Act 1998* (1999); J. Fortin, *Children's Rights and the Developing Law* (2003); U. Kilkelly, *The Child and the European Convention on Human Rights* (1999) and above, para.16–017.

development of childcare law, but cost and delay of taking cases to Strasbourg meant that it could rarely remedy breaches of the right to family life.[1066] The incorporation of the European Convention on Human Rights into UK law has reduced the need to use this court, but it remains the last resort for those claiming a breach of Convention Rights. However, greater awareness of the Convention in the domestic courts may make it less likely that decisions made in the United Kingdom will be overturned in Strasbourg. Nevertheless, childcare practices in other jurisdictions continue to be considered there, and these decisions continue to have potential to shape domestic thinking about the limits of state action. In its examination of child protection intervention, the Strasbourg court allows domestic authorities "a wide margin of appreciation", but applies strict scrutiny to restrictions on contact or other decisions that interfere with rights to family life, such as restrictions on contact, requiring them to be fully justified.

[1066] Cases took at least five years and cost £30,000; see J. Fortin, "The Human Rights Act 1998: human rights for children too", in B. Franklin (ed.), *The New Handbook of Children's Rights* (2001), p.120. The Strasbourg court is unable to deal effectively with the number of cases brought before it: S. Greer, *The European Convention on Human Rights* (Cambridge: Cambridge University Press, 2006), Ch.7.

I.   INTRODUCTION.............................. 22–001
      A. The history and development of
      adoption.. 22–004
II.   EFFECTS OF ADOPTION ORDERS 22–005
      A. Adoption orders........................... 22–005
      B. Registration of adoption................ 22–010
      C. Access to birth and adoption
      records... 22–011
III. PROVISION OF ADOPTION
SERVICES... 22–014
      A. Organisation of adoption services . 22–015
      B. The role of the court..................... 22–017
      C. Eligibility and suitability of
      adopters 22–018
      D. Adoption support........................... 22–022
IV.   PRINCIPLES IN ADOPTION LAW .. 22–024
      A. Welfare... 22–024
      B. Consent... 22–025
      C. Human rights................................. 22–034
      D. Confidentiality 22–035
V.   MODERN ADOPTION PRACTICE.. 22–036
      A. The use of adoption 22–036

B. Relinquishment or baby placement. 22–037
C. Public law adoptions..................... 22–040
D. Intercountry adoptions 22–046
E. "In family" adoptions.................... 22–056
F. Open adoption 22–061
VI.   ORDERS   IN   ADOPTION
PROCEEDINGS 22–063
      A. Adoption, special guardianship or
      residence?.. 22–064
      B. Contact orders 22–066
      C. Other conditions........................... 22–067
      D. Interim orders 22–068
      E. Restrictions on making orders....... 22–069
VII. SURROGACY 22–070
      A. Introduction 22–070
      B. Surrogacy and adoption 22–072
      C. Enforceability of surrogacy
      contracts 22–073
      D. Regulation of surrogacy practice... 22–074
      E. Acquisition of the status of parent 22–076
      F. Knowledge of origins.................... 22–080

I. INTRODUCTION

Adoption is the legal process[1] whereby a court irrevocably extinguishes the legal **22–001** ties between a child[2] and the natural parents or guardians, and creates analogous ties between the child and the adopters.[3] "Simple adoptions", revocable or incomplete transfers of parental responsibility that exist in some countries, cannot be made; "special guardianship" is the nearest equivalent.[4] Some foreign

---

[1] This is more restrictive than the dictionary definition: see Shorter OED: "to take voluntarily into any relationship . . . especially that of a son".
[2] The courts will be able to grant orders on applications made before the child reached age 18 so long as he or she is under 19 years: Adoption and Children Act 2002 s.47(9), 49(4).
[3] Adoption and Children Act 2002 ss.46, 67 (Adoption Act 1976 ss.12, 39); see, generally, *per* Lord Simon of Glaisdale. *O'Connor v A & B* [1971] 1 W.L.R. 1227, 1235–1236 and *Re B (adoption: jurisdiction to set aside)* [1995] 2 F.L.R. 1, CA, *per* Swinton Thomas L.J at p.8.
[4] Children Act 1989 ss.14A–14G, added by Adoption and Children Act 2002 s.115.

"simple adoptions" are treated as full adoptions.[5] A court order is always required. So-called "de facto" adoptions, arrangements where the child lives permanently with people who have put themselves in loco parentis to the child, are not without legal effect,[6] but they do not give the carers parental responsibility, remove the parents' parental responsibility[7] or change the child's status.

Adoption in England and Wales[8] is entirely the creature of statute. It was introduced by the Adoption of Children Act 1926 and is now governed by the Adoption and Children Act 2002, which came into full effect on December 30, 2005.[9] This conception of adoption differs sharply from that in some civil law systems, which inherited the Roman Law concepts of *adoptio* and *adrogatio*. In the United Kingdom, adoption is associated with the desire to nurture a child as the natural child of the adopters. Hence, although adoption has important effects on citizenship, succession and other legal rights, these rights must be incidental to the factual relationship of dependence between the parent and child.[10] In contrast, in some foreign systems[11] adoption may be used to confer succession rights on the adopted person as in the striking case of *Bedinger v Graybill's trustee*[12] where the man adopted his wife so that she could succeed to settled property as his child and heir at law. This is particularly so in civil law systems under which certain relatives are entitled to a *legitima portio* or share of a deceased person's property.[13] Islamic systems do not recognise adoption in the sense of a complete transfer of a child to a new family, but they have developed the concept of *Kafalah* to provide substitute family care for children.[14]

Adoption may be seen as providing for children, for those who wish to be parents and even for parents who are unable or unwilling to care for their

---

[5] Simple adoptions are recognised under the Hague Convention on Intercountry Adoption art.26, but central authorities seek to ensure that the parents consent to a full adoption where the receiving state is England and Wales. The High Court has a power to treat a "simple adoption" as other than a full adoption where this would be more favourable to the child: Adoption and Children Act 2002 s.88.
[6] See, for example, *Brock v Wollams* [1949] 2 K.B. 388 (informally adopted child a "member of family of adopter" for purposes of the Rent Acts); cf. *Joram Developments Ltd v Sharratt* [1979] 1 W.L.R. 928, HL; *Re Callaghan (dec'd)* [1985] 1 F.L.R. 116 (adult child treated as a "child of the family" could apply under the Inheritance (Provision for Family and Dependants) Act 1975 s.1(1)(d)); informal adoption could give rise to "family life" but did not automatically do so: *Singh v Entry Clearance Officer* [2005] 1 F.L.R. 308, CA.
[7] Children Act 1989 ss.2(9), (11), 3(5). Such an agreement is not enforceable but would justify reasonable action by the carers "for the purposes of safeguarding or promoting the child's welfare".
[8] This is also the case in Scotland and Northern Ireland, where similar provisions apply: see Adoption and Children (Scotland) Act 2007; Adoption (Northern Ireland) Order 1987 (SI 1987/2203).
[9] The Adoption and Children Act 2002 (Commencement No.9) Order 2005 (SI 2005/2213).
[10] See: *Re B (Adoption Order: Nationality)* [1999] 1 F.L.R. 907, HL, where adoption was granted to enable grandparents to continue to care for their 16-year-old Jamaican grandchild whose mother lived in poverty and father had died; *Re W (Adoption: Non-patrial)* [1986] Fam. 54, where adoption was refused when it was sought in order to give a 17-year-old boy from Hong Kong British citizenship.
[11] For a full comparative analysis, see H.D. Krause, "Creation of relations of kinship", in *International Encyclopedia of Comparative Law*, The Hague, Monton (1973) Vol.IV, Ch.6.
[12] 302 S.W. (2nd) 594 (1957) (Court of Appeals, Kentucky).
[13] For example the attempt of Somerset Maugham (then aged 88) to adopt his male secretary in order to defeat the claim of his only daughter Lady John Hope.
[14] D. Pearl and W. Menski, *Muslim Family Law*, 3rd edn (London: Sweet & Maxwell, 1998), pp.410 *et seq.*; Van Bueren (1995), pp.94 *et seq.*; see also K. Beevers and S. Ebrahimi, "Iranian child protection law—towards a concept of adoption" [2002] I.F.L. 166.

children. Varying emphasis has been given to these three elements in the past and to the three sets of participants in the adoption triangle,[15] but now the fundamental purpose of adoption is as a service for children: to provide a new permanent family by severing the legal links with the birth family and creating new legal ties.[16] Adoption has become the placement of choice for some abused or neglected children, many of whom have disabilities[17] or behavioural problems, have been compulsorily removed from their families and for whom return home is considered contrary to their welfare. Indeed, through the introduction of new legislation, procedures and standards, the Government has promoted the wider use of adoption for looked after children who cannot return to their birth families.[18]

Increasingly, children who are placed for adoption have families with whom **22–002** they have emotional links, and so adoption has to be seen in terms of losses as well as gains.[19] A new form of adoption termed "open adoption"[20] has developed, where some links with the former family continue after adoption, and this brings into question the distinction between adoption, special guardianship and residence orders.

Adoption is still regarded by some as a service for childless families, but there are very few babies relinquished voluntarily for adoption in the United Kingdom. Placement, except with relatives, by those not registered as adoption agencies is illegal.[21] However, babies are available overseas, and the practice of intercountry adoption has developed to meet the needs of adults and to provide for destitute children. Intercountry adoption has only recently become significant in England but is the most common form of adoption in some western countries. A Convention to regulate intercountry adoption was drawn up by the Hague Conference on Private International Law in 1993. This has been implemented by the Adoption (Intercountry Aspects) Act 1999 and the Adoption and Children Act 2002.[22]

Alternative methods of relieving childlessness—artificial insemination by donor (AID), treatments for female infertility and surrogacy—raise similar issues to adoption such as whether children should have a right to know their origins,

---

[15] For example in 1975, concern for the rights and welfare of adopted adults justified breaching the confidentiality birth mothers had been given, providing a system of access to birth records; see below.

[16] DH and WO, *Interdepartmental Review of Adoption Law* (1992), para.3.1.

[17] H. Argent, *Find Me a Family* (London: Souvenir Press, 1984); Adoption agencies are arranging adoptive placements for babies born with AIDS; see D. Batty, *The Implications of AIDS for Children in Care* (BAAF, 1987).

[18] *Adoption: A New Approach* (Cm.5017 (2000)), para.1.13; PIU, *Prime Minister's Review: Adoption* (2000), p.5.

[19] J. Triseliotis, "Some moral and practical issues in adoption work" (1993) 13 (2) *Adoption and Fostering* 21, 23; and in relation to in family adoption: *Re B (Adoption by One Natural Parent to Exclusion of Other)* [2001] 1 F.L.R. 589 at para.14, *per* Hale L.J.

[20] See A. Mullender, *Open Adoption* (BAAF, 1991); M. Ryburn, *Open Adoption: Research Theory and Practice* (Aldershot: Avebury, 1994); SSI, *Moving Goal Posts: A Study of Post Adoption Contact in the North of England* (1995); R. Parker, *Adoption Now Messages From Research* (Chichester: Wiley 1999), Ch.5 and below, para.22–061.

[21] Adoption and Children Act 2002 ss.92, 93 (Adoption Act 1976 s.11). *Re Adoption Application (Non-patrial: Breach of Procedures)* [1993] 1 F.L.R. 947; *Gatehouse v Robinson and Robinson* [1986] 1 F.L.R. 504; *Re MW (Adoption: Surrogacy)* [1995] 2 F.L.R. 759.

[22] See below, para.22–051.

the obligation of the parents to tell the child and whether the birth parents (or donors) should have the right to secrecy.[23] Adoption law and practice have had some influence on these matters; this is another area where the European Convention on Human Rights can be expected to shape legal developments.[24]

22–003   Reform of adoption law was under discussion from 1989[25]; the partnership approach of the Children Act 1989 did not appear to fit with the adoption legislation drafted in the 1970s. A White Paper was published in 1993[26] and a draft bill in 1996,[27] but Parliamentary time was not made available. In 2000, the Prime Minister announced the Government's commitment to modernising adoption[28]; a new White Paper[29] was produced and a second Bill introduced to Parliament.[30] A third Bill, which drew heavily on the earlier two but took more account of complex human-rights issues, was introduced at the beginning of the 2001–2002 session. Following heated debate and considerable amendment, the Adoption of Children Act 2002 was enacted at the very end of the session and has been fully in force since December 30, 2005.[31] Much of the detail was left to regulations and court rules.[32] The Government also published detailed guidance[33] and established a register of children needing adoptive families and prospective adopters to facilitate placement.[34] The President of the Family Division issued and updated guidance designed to reduce delays and improve the service from the higher courts in adoption.[35]

---

[23] K. O'Donovan, "A right to know one's parentage?" (1988) 2 Int. J. of Law & Fam. 27; E. Haimes, "What can artificial reproduction learn from adoption" (1988) 2 Int. J. of Law & Fam. 46; Report of the Joint Committee on the Human Tissue and Embryos (Draft) Bill 2007 (HCP 630 (2006–7)), paras 268–272, and below, para.22–080.

[24] *Rose v Secretary of State for Health and the Human Fertility and Embryology Authority* [2002] 2 F.L.R. 962, FD.

[25] See Inter-departmental Review of Adoption Law Discussion Papers 1: *The Nature and Effect of Adoption* (1990); 2: *Agreement and Freeing* (1991); 3: *The Adoption Process* (1991); 4: *Intercountry Adoption* (1992); *Report to Ministers of an Inter-departmental Working Group* (1992); *Placement for Adoption* (1994); *The Future of Adoption Panels* (1994). Inter-departmental Review of Adoption Law Background Papers 1: *International Perspectives* (1990); 2: *Review of Research Relating to Adoption* (1990); 3: *Intercountry Adoption* (1992). Scottish law was also reviewed; see Scottish Office, *The Future of Adoption Law in Scotland* (1993); some amendments to Scottish law were included in the Children (Scotland) Act 1995.

[26] *Adoption: The Future* (Cm.2288 (1993)).

[27] DH and WO, *Adoption—A Service for Children* (1996).

[28] Performance and Innovation Unit, *Prime Minister's Review Adoption* (2000).

[29] *Adoption: A New Approach* (Cm.5017 (2000)).

[30] Bill 66 (2000–2001). This was largely to ensure wide consultation: see Select Committee on the Adoption and Children Bill (HC 431 (2001)); for a critique, see S. Harris-Short [2001] C.F.L.Q. 405 or C. Ball (2005) 29(2) *Adoption and Fostering* 6.

[31] The Adoption and Children Act 2002 (Commencement No.9) Order 2005 (SI 2005/2213).

[32] The Adoption Agencies Regulations 2005 (SI 2005/389); The Adoptions with a Foreign Element Regulations 2005 (SI 2005/392); The Restriction on the Preparation of Adoption Reports Regulations 2005 (SI 2005/1711); The Suitability of Adopters Regulations 2005 (SI 2005/1712); Family Procedure (Adoption) Rules 1991 (SI 2005/2795).

[33] Details of guidance can be found on the Department of Children Schools and Families website: *http://www.everychildmatters.gov.uk/adoption* [Accessed June 5, 2008].

[34] Adoption and Children Act 2002 s.125; The Adoption and Children Act Register is run by British Agencies for Adoption and Fostering (BAAF).

[35] The Family Procedure (Adoption) Rules 2005 (SI 2005/2795) were implemented to update adoption procedure. See *President's Guidance—Adoption: The New Law and Procedure* (March 2006). Available at *http://www.judiciary.gov.uk/docs/adoption_final.pdf (26/06/07)* [Accessed June 5, 2008].

A. The history and development of adoption

Adoption was reluctantly[36] introduced into English law following the recom- **22–004**
mendation of the *Tomlin Report*[37] in order to provide legal security for those
involved in de facto arrangements, which had become increasingly common.[38]
The Adoption of Children Act 1926 permitted adoption without parental consent,
and required independent scrutiny of all cases. It did not ensure the child's full
integration into the adoptive family; inheritance rights in the birth family were
not replaced.[39] Over the next half century, adoption law was repeatedly under
scrutiny, and a number of themes can be identified in three major reports on law
and practice.[40] Adoption was developed from a private or amateur activity to
form part of the childcare service offered by local authorities and professional
adoption agencies.[41] Increased emphasis was placed on protecting children:
advertising was controlled,[42] children were fully integrated into adoptive families
by the provision of inheritance rights[43] and placements were supervised by local
authorities.[44] The importance of identity was recognised, and adopted adults
were permitted access to their birth records and with it the possibility of tracing

---

[36] The Report of the Committee on Child Adoption (Cmd.1254 (1921)) (The *Hopkinson Report*) was
followed by six unsuccessful bills; see N. Lowe, "English adoption law: past, present and future", in
S. Katz et al., *Cross Currents* (2000), p.307; S. Cretney, "Adoption from contract to status", in S.
Cretney, *Law, Law Reform and the Family* (1998), p.184 and *Family Law in the Twentieth
Century—A History* (2003), Ch.17.

[37] The *Report of the Child Adoption Committee* (Cmd.2401 (1925), Cmd.2469 (1926)).

[38] I. Pinchbeck and M. Hewitt, *Children in English Society*, (1973) Vol.2, pp.605–607. The lack of a
legal framework that meant that children might be reclaimed when they reached working age, or that
birth parents might be forced to take them away, was thought to discourage adoption. The application
of the welfare principle should theoretically have provided security, but this was far from certain: see
Re Thain [1926] Ch. 676.

[39] Adoption of Children Act 1926 ss.2(3), 5(2); although there was a general power to dispense with
consent, it was interpreted narrowly; Cretney *Law, Law Reform*, p.194; attitudes to inheritance had
delayed the introduction of adoption in England; see J. Triseliotis (1995) 2 *Adoption & Fostering* 37,
39.

[40] (a) *Report of the Departmental Committee on Adoption Societies & Agencies* (Cmd.5499 (1937))
(*Horsburgh Report*) resulted in the Adoption of Children (Regulation) Act 1939; (b) *Report of the
Departmental Committee on the Adoption of Children* (Cmd.9240 (1954)) (*Hurst Report*) resulted in
the Adoption Act 1958; (c) *Report of the Departmental Committee on the Adoption of Children*
(Cmnd.5107 (1972)) (*Houghton Report*) resulted in the Children Act 1975 and the law was then
consolidated in the Adoption Act 1976, although parts of this were not implemented until the 1980s.
For a general account, see C. Walby and B. Symons, *Who am I?* (BAAF: 1990), Ch.1.

[41] Voluntary adoption societies pressed for the introduction of legal adoption, but substantial numbers
of placements were made directly by parents or by third parties, often doctors and vicars: see
Houghton Report, paras 81 *et seq*. Local authorities were permitted to arrange adoptions for children
by the Adoption Act 1949 s.7(2), and were required to provide an adoption service from 1988 by the
Adoption Act 1976 s.1. The Children Act 1975 outlawed third-party placements and required higher
standards, and some smaller agencies closed. Standards are now set for agencies: DfES, *National
Minimum Standards—Voluntary Adoption Agencies and Local Authority Adoption Service* (2003).

[42] Adoption Act 1976 s.58 (now Adoption and Children 2002 s.123); cf. advertisements by agencies
have become an important method of finding families for hard-to-place children: *Re K (Adoption:
Permission to Advertise)* [2007] 2 F.L.R. 326, paras 12–18.

[43] Adoption of Children Act 1949 ss.9, 10; Children Act 1975 Sch.1, para.5.

[44] Adoption of Children Act 1949 s.5; *Hurst Report*, para.67. Stepparent adoptions were exempted
from welfare supervision in the 1958 Act s.3 until the recommendations of the Houghton Committee
were implemented. Local authorities should supervise all non-agency cases; adoption agencies should
supervise their own placements: para.240.

birth relatives.[45] Stepparent adoption that could distort family relationships was discouraged.[46] Adoption came to be seen as a method of providing homes for children (not merely legalising existing arrangements), and changes were made to facilitate this. The grounds for dispensing with agreement were expanded by legislation; the "freeing for adoption" process was devised so that the giving of agreement could be separated from placement,[47] and provision was made for financial allowances for adopters.[48]

The character of adoption also changed markedly, particularly during the last quarter of the twentieth century.[49] Abortion, welfare benefits and the end of the stigma of single parenthood provided alternatives for birth parents so that very few babies were relinquished for adoption. Local authorities began to view adoption as an option for older children who could not return to their families after abuse, and increasingly these arrangements were made without the agreement of parents.[50] By the late 1980s, research and practice were showing the value of more open arrangements in adoption[51]; there was growing recognition of the need to involve birth parents in the adoption process,[52] and the Contact Register was established to facilitate contact between adopted adults and their birth relatives.[53] As the emphasis in the Children Act 1989 on local authorities working with families of looked-after children conflicted with the idea of non-consensual adoption, the proportion of children adopted from care declined. However, concern about the poor life chances of children brought up in care compared with those in secure families, and the belief that it was possible to find more adoptive families for looked-after children, encouraged the promotion of adoption and created the impetus for reform.[54] To ensure the opportunity of family life for as many children as possible, less restrictive attitudes were needed to select adopters; adoption orders could not be restricted to married couples and single people.[55] It was also recognised that caring for children adopted from care placed extra demands on parents, and that post-

---

[45] Houghton Committee, paras 303–306; J. Triseliotis, *In Search of Origins* (London: RKP, 1973); Adoption Act 1976 s.26. See now J. Triseliotis et al., *The Adoption Triangle Revisited* (BAAF: 2005).

[46] Houghton Committee, para.107; Children Act 1975 s.10(3); Adoption Act 1976 s.14(3), repealed by Children Act 1989; J. Masson et al., *Mine Yours or Ours?* (London: HMSO, 1983).

[47] Houghton Report, paras 173 *et seq.*; Children Act 1975 s.14; Adoption Act 1976 s.18.

[48] Houghton Report, para.93; Adoption Act 1976 ss.57(4), 57A; Adoption Allowance Regulations 1991 (SI 1991/2030).

[49] See N. Lowe in S. Katz et al. (eds), *Cross Currents*.

[50] Parker *Adoption Now*, Ch.1.

[51] Review of Adoption Law (1992), Foreword.

[52] Review of Adoption Law (1992), para.1.4.

[53] Children Act 1989 Sch.10, para.21; Adoption Act 1976 s.51A. See now Adoption and Children Act 2002 ss.80, 81.

[54] Prime Minister's Review (2000), pp.5–7 and Annex 4; *Adoption: A New Approach* (2000), Ch.2; J. Selwyn and W. Sturgess, *International Overview of Adoption* (2000) and the polemics published by the Institute of Economic Affairs: P. Morgan, *Adoption and the Care of Children* (1998) and P. Morgan (ed.) *Adoption: The Continuing Debate* (1999).

[55] Select Committee on Adoption and Children Bill (HC 431-ii (Bristol: Policy Press 2000–1)), evidence of BAAF para.9.1 and *Hansard, Commons*, Vol.385, col.976 *et seq.* (May 16, 2002), Report; *Lords*, Vol.639, col.865 (October, 18, 2002), Report; *Commons*, Vol.392, col.24 *et seq.* (November, 4, 2002) (Commons Consideration of Lords Amendments); *Lords*, Vol.641, col.569 *et seq.* (November 5, 2002) (Lords Consideration of Commons Amendments), and below para.22–019. The Equality Act (Sexual Orientation) Regulations 2007 (SI 2007/1263) reg.15 allows voluntary adoption

adoption services could enhance the wellbeing of adopters, adopted people and birth parents, and help maintain placements.[56]

II. EFFECTS OF ADOPTION ORDERS

A. Adoption orders

The Adoption and Children Act 2002 defines an adoption order as an order giving parental responsibility for a child to the adopters.[57] Adoptive parents may make any decision that other parents may make, including emigrating and appointing a testamentary guardian[58]; they are not subject to supervision by the courts or any other agency. With one exception (where a "step-parent" adopts their partner's child),[59] the making of an adoption order extinguishes the parental responsibility of any other person,[60] any order under the Children Act 1989 and any duty to pay maintenance except insofar as it relates to a period prior to the adoption.[61] The legislation states that an adopted child is to be treated as "the legitimate child of the adopter or adopters" and, where he or she is adopted by a couple,[62] "as the child of the relationship of the couple" and is not the child of any other person.[63] Unlike other orders relating to children, adoption does not cease to have effect when the child reaches age 18.

22–005

The consequences of adoption cannot be seen in purely legal terms. It is well recognised that adoption confers "an extra and psychologically and emotionally important sense of 'belonging'". It is said that there is a real benefit to the parent–child relationship in knowing that each is legally bound to the other and that the relationship is free from interference from outsiders.[64] This has justified allowing adoption without the agreement of the natural parents. However, adoption is not the only way of showing a child that a relationship is secure; special guardianship gives a carer parental responsibility and enhanced protection against interference without changing the status of the child or the parents.[65] However, there is no consensus about whether alternatives to adoption can

agencies to discriminate on the basis of sexual orientation when considering prospective adopters until December 31, 2008.

[56] N. Lowe et al., *Supporting Adoption* (BAAF: 1999); *Adoption: A New Approach* Cm.5017 (2000), Ch.6; Adoption and Children Act 2002 ss.3(3) and 4; The Adoption Support Services Regulations 2005 (SI 2005/691); DfES, *National Minimum Standards for Adoption Support Agencies* (2005).

[57] Adoption and Children Act 2002 s.46(1) re-enacting Adoption Act 1976 s.12(1) as amended by the Children Act 1989 Sch.10, para.3.

[58] Adoption and Children Act 2002 s.67; Children Act 1989 ss.3, 5.

[59] Adoption and Children Act 2002 ss.51(2), 67(3)(b). Partner is defined in s.144(4)–(7) and includes a spouse or another person (of either sex) living with the parent in an enduring family relationship.

[60] Adoption and Children Act 2002 s.46(3)(b).

[61] Adoption and Children Act 2002 s.46(2)(d) re-enacting Adoption Act 1976 s.12(2). A trust that expressly provides for continuance is unaffected: s.46(4), re-enacting s.12(4).

[62] Or by one of a couple who is the partner of the child's parent; Adoption and Children Act 2002 ss.51(2), 67(2)(b).

[63] Adoption and Children Act 2002 s.67(1)–(3) re-enacting Adoption Act 1976 s.39 (with amendments to take account of adoption by partners).

[64] *Re H (Adoption Non-patrial)* [1996] 1 F.L.R. 717 at 726, *per* Holman J. *Re AJ (Adoption Order or Special Guardianship)* [2007] 1 F.L.R. 507, CA *per* Wall L.J at para.45.

[65] Children Act 1989, ss.14A–G; *Re S (Adoption or Special Guardianship)* [2007] 1 F.L.R. 819, CA, paras 47–49 and below, para.22–004.

provide the security and commitment that children need.[66] Also, adoption will not necessarily ensure that a relationship is maintained with the adoptive parents.[67]

In three cases (succession rights, citizenship and the prohibited degrees of marriage), the general principles are modified by statutory rules.

i. Succession

22–006 Since 1950, an adopted child has lost any right to inherit on the intestacy of the birth parents but gained a corresponding right from the adoptive parents.[68] Adoption did not remove rights already vested in possession,[69] but wills and deeds were interpreted to exclude adopted children from general gifts made before the adoption. The Children Act 1975 removed the restrictions on the succession rights of adopted children where deeds were made or deaths occurred on or after January 1, 1976.[70] Special rules are, however, required for cases where a gift depends upon the date of birth of an adopted person or upon seniority as against other children in the adoptive family. It is provided that where a disposition "depends on the date of birth" of a child, it has to be constructed as if: (a) the adopted child had been born on the date of adoption; and (b) two or more children adopted on the same date had been born on that date in the order of their actual births.[71] Thus, if the will of a testator contains a gift "to the eldest son of X", and X had a natural child (A) born in 1990 and an adopted child (B) born in 1988 but adopted in 1991, A would be taken as the eldest child. However, these rules do not "affect any reference to the age of a child".[72] Thus, if the same testator gave his residuary estate "to the children of X at 25", B (the adopted child) would take in 2013 and not 25 years after the adoption. It also seems that B would benefit from a gift to "the first child of X to attain 25".[73]

ii. Citizenship

22–007 The British Nationality Act 1981[74] provides that where an adoption order is made by a court in the United Kingdom in respect of a child who is not a British citizen, he or she acquires British citizenship from the date of the adoption if the

---

[66] Triseliotis et al. *The Adoption Triangle* p.20.

[67] Comprehensive statistics on adoption disruptions are not available, but a study of 1,500 placements found that 9% broke down before the order was made, and another 8% subsequently: see Parker *Adoption Now* p.10.

[68] Adoption of Children Act 1949; Adoption and Children Act 2002 s.67(1)–(3), effectively re-enacting Adoption Act 1976 s.39(1).

[69] *Staffordshire County Council v B* [1998] 1 F.L.R. 261, Ch.D. (this includes an interest expectant on one vested in possession). Adoption and Children Act 2002 s.69(4) enacts this rule.

[70] Adoption Act 1976 ss.39, 42 introduced by the Children Act 1975 Sch.1. The Adoption and Children Act 2002 s.69 and Sch.4, para.17 maintains this regime. It does not apply to peerages: s.71, re-enacting s.44(1). Twenty-three peers and six baronets have adopted children: *Hansard Commons*, Special Standing Committee on Adoption and Children Bill, 11th session, December 6, 2001.

[71] Adoption and Children Act 2002 s.69(2), re-enacting Adoption Act 1976 s.42(2).

[72] Adoption and Children Act 2002 s.69(2), re-enacting Adoption Act 1976 s.42(2).

[73] There are special rules applying to children who are adopted by one of their own parents as a sole adoptive parent: Adoption and Children Act 2002 s.67(4), re-enacting Adoption Act 1976 s.43.

[74] British Nationality Act 1981 s.1(5).

adopter is a British citizen. British nationality is also conferred on Convention adoptions that take place overseas, provided that the adopters are habitually resident in the United Kingdom and at least one of them is a British citizen.[75] A child who has British nationality does not cease to be entitled to it because of adoption by a foreigner.[76] The Government and the courts have been concerned that adoption should not be used to evade immigration rules.

Children adopted overseas may enter for settlement if: the adoption was due to the parents' inability to care for them; there has been a genuine transfer of parental responsibility; and the adoption was not arranged to facilitate the child's entry to the United Kingdom.[77] Children are admitted *for* adoption at the discretion of the Home Secretary.[78] The Home Office must be notified of adoption applications where citizenship may be in issue.[79] Despite Home Office concerns, general considerations about maintaining effective immigration controls are unlikely to justify refusing any adoption order that will confer real benefits on a child during childhood.[80]

iii. Prohibited degrees

For the purposes of the prohibited degree of marriage, adoption does not destroy the prohibitions arising from birth to the child's natural parents.[81] If an adopted person (however innocently) marries a child of the natural parents, the marriage is void.[82] An adopted person and the adoptive parents are prohibited from marrying (even if the child is subsequently adopted by someone else),[83] but there are no further bars on marrying within the adoptive family. Hence an adopted child may legally marry a natural or adopted child of the adoptive family. This seems a curious exception to the principle that adoption integrates the child fully

22–008

---

[75] Adoption (Intercountry Aspects) Act 1999 s.7, amending British Nationality Act 1981 s.1(5). Under the Hague Convention on Intercountry Adoption art.5, Convention adoptions may only take place if the central authorities of the receiving state have determined that the child will be free to enter and reside permanently in that state. In the case of other overseas adoptions by a British adopter, application may be made for citizenship by registration under the Home Secretary's discretionary powers: British Nationality Act 1981 s.3(1).

[76] Adoption and Children Act 2002 s.74(2). The general principle in s.67 (Adoption Act 1976 s.39) does not apply for the purposes of the British Nationality Act 1981.

[77] Statement of changes in Immigration Rules (HC 395 (1994)), para.314; *RS v Entry Clearance Officer (New Dehli)* [2005] 2 F.L.R. 219, CA.

[78] Adoption applicants and those who have obtained a recognised adoption order overseas must apply for entry clearance before bringing the child to the UK; see DfES, *Adoption and Children Act Guidance* (2005), Annex C, paras 43–45.

[79] *Re H (A Minor) (Adoption: Non-Patrial)* [1982] Fam. 121; *Re W (A Minor) (Adoption: Non-patrial)* [1986] Fam. 54. Where a local authority discovers that the proper procedures have not been followed when bringing a child to the UK, it must notify the police: DfES, *Guidance* (2005), Annex C, para.10.

[80] *Re B (Adoption Order: Nationality)* [1999] 1 F.L.R. 907 at p.910, *per* Lord Hoffmann; benefits occurring after the age of 18 can be considered: *Re D (Adoption Order: Validity)* [1991] Fam. 137 but will not be sufficient: at p.911.

[81] Adoption and Children Act 2002 s.74(1), re-enacting Adoption Act 1976 s.47(1); a similar approach is taken to sexual activity with a family member, discussed in HO, *Setting the Boundaries* (2000), paras 5.6.1–5.6.4, see now Sexual Offences Act 2003 ss.25, 27(1).

[82] The Registrar-General can verify relationships for an adopted person intending to marry: Adoption and Children Act 2002 s.79(7), re-enacting Adoption Act 1976 s.51(2).

[83] Marriage Act 1949 Sch.1, Pt I, as amended by the Children Act 1975 Sch.3, para.8.

into the adoptive family. However, the approach to marriage between affines is now more liberal and it would be difficult to justify the imposition of the stricter rules which apply to consanguinity.[84]

iv. Revocation

22–009   Adoption orders are irrevocable. Where adoptive relationships break down,[85] the parents retain parental responsibility until a further adoption order is made.[86] It has been said that the edifice of adoption would be gravely shaken if adoption orders could be set aside.[87] This is clearly so if revocation could occur during childhood, but the continued imposition of a legal identity on an adult may appear unjust:

> In *Re B (Adoption: Setting Aside)*[88] a baby, whose mother was an English Roman Catholic and whose father was a Kuwaiti Muslim, was placed by the matron of a mother and baby home with a Jewish couple who were told that the baby's father was Jewish. When they discovered that the boy was not Jewish, they arranged to have him admitted to the Jewish faith. The boy was brought up as Jewish and later emigrated to Israel. There he was assumed, because of his appearance, to be an Arab; he was forced to leave. He made inquiries about his origin and wanted to have the adoption order revoked so that he could take on an Arab identity and be accepted in Kuwait. His application and his appeal were refused.

Exceptionally, an adoption order may be annulled on appeal: where a father agreed to a stepparent adoption in ignorance of his wife's fatal illness, the court was prepared to allow an appeal outside the time limit and return the children to his care.[89] Also where there was a "plethora of irregularities going to the heart of the adoption process", an intercountry adoption was set aside, but the child remained with the family under wardship.[90] Also, a child may be able to re-establish a legal link with a natural parent or other member of the birth family by applying for a residence order in their favour.[91]

---

[84] *Houghton Report*, paras 329–333; see also Marriage (Prohibited Degrees of Relationships) Act 1986; *B and L v UK* [2006] 1 F.L.R. 35 and above, para.2–011.

[85] The term "disruptions" is given to such breakdowns whether they occur before or after the order has been made. There are no accurate statistics, but see N. Lowe et al., *Supporting Adoption* (1999), Ch.12.

[86] Adoption and Children Act 2002 s.46(5). Charges may be levied on the adoptive parents if the child becomes looked after by a local authority: Children Act 1989 Sch.3, Pt III. Wardship may be used in an exceptional case: *Re O (Wardship: Adopted Child)* [1978] Fam. 196, CA, but this case should not be cited as a precedent, *per* Ormerod L.J. at p.205.

[87] *Re B (Adoption: Setting Aside)* [1995] 1 F.L.R. 1 at 7, *per* Sir Stephen Brown P.

[88] [1995] 1 F.L.R. 1, FD; [1995] 2 F.L.R. 1, CA.

[89] *Re M (Minors) (Adoption)* [1991] 1 F.L.R. 458. It was accepted that the father gave his agreement by mistake.

[90] *Re K (Adoption and Wardship)* [1997] 2 F.L.R. 221 CA.

[91] *Re T (A Minor) (Wardship: Representation)* [1994] Fam. 49 and above, para.20–020. In theory this option is also available to a parent and could be appropriate if the adoption failed.

B. Registration of adoption

The Registrar General maintains an Adopted Children Register and its index (like **22–010** the index to the Register of Births) is open to public search.[92] On adoption, the child's birth certificate is replaced with a certified copy of the entry in the Register[93]; this gives the child's names (normally with the adoptive parents' surname) and is sufficient evidence of date and place of birth.[94] A short form of birth certificate giving the child's name and date of birth may be issued. Where this is used, no one, including the child, can see that the child is adopted.[95] The small number of adoptions each year means that it might be possible for a parent to discover the child's new name by identifying the entry in the Adopted Children Register and thus be able to trace the child. The court may not prevent an adoption being included on the register but under its inherent jurisdiction could restrict the Registrar General from providing a copy of the adoption certificate whilst the child is under 18.[96]

C. Access to birth and adoption records[97]

The Registrar General is required to keep records so that it is possible to trace the **22–011** original birth registration of an adopted person,[98] but until November 26, 1976 a person adopted in England or Wales[99] had no right to this information. Following a recommendation of the Houghton Committee,[100] which recognised that some adopted people wished to know more about their background, provision was made for adopted adults to obtain access to the original birth certificate. Because of concerns for natural mothers who had been promised confidentiality when they relinquished their babies,[101] those adopted before the Children Act 1975 were required to undergo counselling before obtaining this.[102] The numbers of adoptees who have received their records has greatly exceeded expectations; it is

[92] The register itself is not open to public search: Adoption and Children Act 2002 ss.77(2), 79(2), re-enacting Adoption Act 1976 s.50(1), (3).
[93] Adoption and Children Act 2002 Sch.1, para.1 re-enacting Adoption Act 1976 Sch.1, para.1. Provision is also made for entries in relation to registrable foreign adoptions; para.3.
[94] Adoption and Children Act 2002 s.77(4)(5) re-enacting Adoption Act 1976 s.50(2).
[95] Births and Deaths Registration Act 1953 s.33; Registration of Births and Deaths Regulations 1987 (SI 1987/2088) reg.64 and Form 21.
[96] *Re X (A Minor) (Adoption)* [1994] 2 F.L.R. 450, CA; *President's Direction* [1999] 1 F.L.R. 315. For adoptions made after the implementation of the 2002 Act, access to birth records is via the adoption agency or local authority; ss.60, 79; any order preventing disclosure would in the future have to be against the agency.
[97] See, generally, J. Triseliotis et al., *The Adoption Triangle Revisited: A Study of Adoption Search and Reunion Experience* (2005). Details of how to search, where to find records of adopton agencies, the use of intermediary services and the experiences of those who have searched can be found at *http://www.adoptionsearchreunion.org.uk* [Accessed June 5, 2008].
[98] Adoption and Children Act 2002 s.79, re-enacting Adoption Act 1976 s.50(4).
[99] Children Act 1975 s.26; Scottish law permitted access to birth records at age 17. See now Adoption (Scotland) Act 1978 s.45(5). Research into the operation of the Scottish system convinced the Houghton Committee that access could be permitted: see J. Triseliotis, *In Search of Origins* (1973).
[100] *Houghton Report*, para.303 and recommendation 77.
[101] See E. Haimes and N. Timms, *Adoption, Identity & Social Policy* (Aldershot: Gower 1985), pp.17–18.
[102] Adoption Act 1976 s.51(7); but a person who knew their original name could obtain their birth certificate in the normal way. From 1991, provision was made for counselling overseas: s.51(8). DH leaflet ACR 114 lists organisations in Australia, Canada, New Zealand and South Africa that provide

estimated that a third of all adoptees will do so at some time in their lives.[103] The Act provided no absolute right to birth records information; the Registrar General may refuse access if there are public policy reasons[104]:

> In *R. v Registrar General, Ex p. Smith*,[105] Smith, the adopted person, was detained in Broadmoor following his convictions for murder of a stranger and manslaughter of a cell-mate. He was thought to suffer from psychiatric illness and had extreme hatred for his adoptive parents. He applied for a copy of his original birth certificate, but after receiving medical advice that his mother might be in danger if he were released, the Registrar-General refused to provide it. Smith sought judicial review of the decision but the refusal was upheld and his appeal refused.

The birth certificate provides little information, but the full names of the mother, and sometimes the father, often makes it possible to trace them. Detailed information about the adoption is held by the agency, the local authority that supervised the placement and the court. There was discretion to disclose this information to adopted adults, although some agencies took a restrictive approach.[106] Some birth relatives, particularly mothers, also sought assistance to find out how their (adult) children were faring. Intermediary services were established by some voluntary organisations, and via these it was possible for some birth relatives to obtain information and even initiate contact. Provision was also made for other people to apply to the court for an order permitting the disclosure of information from the register.[107] Orders were only granted if the applicant could establish truly exceptional circumstances,[108] for example to allow medical information to be passed to someone who might have inherited a genetic disorder or to allow a reunion between elderly siblings adopted separately.

22–012   The White Paper acknowledged the right of all adopted people to information about their family history and proposed that access to specific material in adoption records should be covered in the legislation.[109] However, when the Adoption and Children Bill was introduced, it provided a restrictive scheme for

---

counselling. Counselling was voluntary for other adopted people. The need for counselling was graphically portrayed in the film *Secrets and Lies* (1995).

[103] R. Rushbrooke, *Population Trends* (2001) 104, p.31. This does not include those adoptees who obtained records without using Adoption and Children Act 2002 s.51.

[104] *R. v Registrar-General, Ex p. Smith* [1991] 2 Q.B. 393, CA. The High Court has the power to order non-disclosure on the application of the adoption agency: s.60(2)(a), (3).

[105] [1991] 2 Q.B. 393, CA.

[106] *Gunn-Russo v Nugent Care Society* [2002] 1 F.L.R. 1, Q.B.D. This power was provided to enable adopted people to make inheritance claims where adoption did not end these rights in the natural family: Haimes and Timms, *Adoption, Identity and Social Policy*, p.13.

[107] Adoption Act 1976 s.50(5); applications were rare—only one or two a year: D. Howe and J. Feast, *Adoption, Search and Reunion* (Children's Society: 2000), p.9.

[108] *D v Registrar General* [1997] 1 F.L.R. 715, CA (birth mother's application refused because there was no benefit to the adopted person) overruling *Re H (Adoption: Disclosure of Information)* [1995] 1 F.L.R. 236 (information disclosed where sibling had genetic disorder).

[109] Cm.5017, paras 6.44 *et seq.; Prime Minister's Review* (2000), paras 3.136 *et seq.* and p.50.

access to information based on "data protection philosophy and human rights" that precluded the disclosure of identifying information (including the birth certificate) without consent.[110] These proposals caused consternation amongst adoption agencies who considered that adopted people had a right to know their birth identity, and they were not convinced that the existing scheme for access posed risks for birth parents, even in the context of adoption of abused children.[111] The Government put forward major amendments to meet their objections. There are now two distinct schemes covering access to adoption information: one relating to adoptions under the previous law[112] and one for adoptions under the 2002 Act. Adults who were adopted after December 30, 2005 can obtain a copy of their original birth certificate via the adoption agency, and details of their background from the report prepared for the prospective adopters.[113] In exceptional circumstances, where the agency wishes to withhold this information, it can seek an order from the High Court.[114] Adopted adults also have had the right to copies of specific documents from the court that made the order.[115] Concern about the impact of learning about one's background has resulted in duties on agencies to provide information about counselling, but there is no obligation to take counselling.[116]

Adoption agencies may pass on non-identifying information (e.g. about how a child is faring following adoption[117]), but disclosure of identifying "protected information" is closely regulated. The agency has discretion, but it must take reasonable steps to obtain the views of the person concerned; it must consider these, the welfare of the adopted person and the other circumstance.[118] Where the information concerns a child, the agency must consider the view of their parents, give paramount consideration to the welfare of an adopted child and consider the

---

[110] Adoption and Children Bill cll.53–60 and Ch.5, Special Standing Committee, 2nd Sitting; Memorandum of the Department of Health and oral evidence of James Paton, Department of Health.

[111] Memorandum and oral evidence of BAAF, 2nd sitting; Memorandum from NORCAP, 4th sitting; 18th sitting, cols 689 *et seq.*

[112] Adoption and Children Act 2002 s.98 and Sch.2; The Adoption Information and Intermediary Services (Pre-Commencement Adoptions) Regulations 2005 (SI 2005/890); DfES, *Guidance* (2005) Ch.10. The agency retains discretion to disclose under Adoption Agencies Regulations 1983 (SI 1983/1964) reg.15.

[113] Adoption and Children Act 2002 ss.54, 60(4); Disclosure of Adoption Information (Post-Commencement Adoptions) Regulations 2005 (SI 2005/888); DfES, *Guidance* (2005), Ch.11. The agency is required to obtain the birth certificate from the Registrar General for the adopted person, Adoption and Children Act 2002 r.19.

[114] Adoption and Children Act 2002 s.60(3). The adopted person will also be entitled to specific information that the agency was required to provide for the adopters; s.60(2)(b).

[115] Adoption and Children Act 2002 s.60(4); The Family Procedure (Adoption) Rules 2005 (SI 2005/2795) r.84. An adopted adult can obtain a copy of the adoption application and order from the court; this will provide details of the agency and local authority involved.

[116] SI 2005/888, rr.16 and 17.

[117] Adoption and Children Act 2002 s.58(2); SI 2005/888, r.8; DfES, *Guidance* (2005), Ch.11, para.10.

[118] Adoption and Children Act 2002 s.61; Disclosure of Adoption Information (Post-Commencement Adoptions) Regulations 2005 (SI 2005/888); DfES, *Guidance* (2005), Ch.11. Protected information is information that is or includes identifying information: s.57(1)–(3). Where disclosure is agreed at adoption, for example where a mother leaves a letter for an adopted child to receive at age 18 or in the event of her death, the agency will not need to carry out these checks; s.57(5).

welfare of any other children.[119] The discretion to withhold information or to disclose it against a person's wishes is subject to review.[120]

i. The adoption contact register

22–013 Until 1991 there was no official way for birth relatives to signal their interest in contact from those who had been adopted, although assistance was provided by NORCAP (the National Organisation for Counselling Adoptees and Parents). NORCAP established a register, an intermediary service to facilitate exchange of information or contact and support groups. It also campaigned for better services for birth relatives.[121] The Children Act 1989 required the Registrar General to maintain an Adoption Contact Register.[122] This provides a safe and confidential way for birth parents and other relations to assure an adopted person that contact would be welcome and gives a current address. The *Review of Adoption Law* recommended that the Register be extended to allow birth parents and relatives to indicate their wish not to be contacted[123]; this was not included in the Bill but is provided by the 2005 Regulations.[124]

A person adopted in England or Wales who has sufficient details about their birth may register their wishes relating to contact with relatives.[125] Relatives who know the details of an adopted person's birth may similarly register.[126] A fee is charged for this service.[127] Where there is a match, the Registrar General gives the adopted person the relative's name and address, but the relative is only told that a link has been made.[128] In the first 10 years of this service 20,000 adoptees and 8,500 relatives registered but only just over 500 matches were made.[129] Far more people establish contact in other ways, and most who do so, or who are contacted, are positive about the experience, although not all relationships are maintained.[130]

---

[119] Adoption and Children Act 2002 s.62.

[120] Adoption and Children Act 2002 s.12; The Disclosure of Adoption Information (Post-Commencement Adoptions) Regulations 2005 (SI 2005/888) r.15.

[121] The powerlessness of birth mothers and the sense of loss they experience is graphically described in D. Howe et al., *Half A Million Women* (London: Penguin, 1992).

[122] Adoption Act 1976 s.51A, added by the Children Act 1989 s.88 and Sch.10 para.21.

[123] *Review of Adoption Law* (1992), para.31.5; this was accepted in Cm.2288 (1993), para.4.22—see draft Adoption Bill 1996 cl.65(2). The original 2002 Bill, which prevented disclosure of information would have achieved this.

[124] Adopted Children and Adoption Contact Registers Regulations 2005 (SI 2005/924) reg.7.

[125] Adoption and Children Act 2002 s.80(2). Information is provided on the General Register Office website: *http://www.gro.gov.uk* [Accessed June 5, 2008]. See also A. Mullender and S. Kearn, *I'm Here Waiting* (BAAF: 1997); the researchers were critical of the impersonal service and the lack of publicity for the Adoption Contact Register.

[126] Adoption and Children Act 2002 s.80(5). Relatives need to know enough to obtain a birth certificate of the person who has been adopted.

[127] (2001) s.80(6) and SI 2005/924 reg.9.

[128] Adoption and Children Act 2002 ss.80(6)(a), 81(3). Where no contact has been specified, the parties are not informed if links are made.

[129] J. Haskey, *Population Trends* (2001) 106, 15, 16; see also J. Haskey and R. Errington, *Population Trends* (2001) 104, 18. By contrast, the NORCAP register contains 50,000 entries and has made 750 links in 19 years.

[130] Howe and Feast, *Adoption, Search and Reunion*; Trisliotis et al., *The Adoption Triangle*.

These provisions operate within a context where there is now considerable openness with exchange of information (usually via the adoption agency) and even contact between the birth family and the adopters before and after the adoption order has been made. The statutory regime thus represents the minimum access to information for those affected by domestic adoptions in England and Wales. Far less information may be available for those involved in adoption at earlier times, but special provision was made in the 2002 Act following a sustained campaign by NORCAP.[131] It criticised the limited assistance available to those who wished to make contact with adult relatives who had been adopted as children, and campaigned to place (licensed) intermediary services on a statutory footing with rights to access information to assist such people. The Government was unwilling to impose a duty on adoption agencies to provide intermediary services because this might draw resources from their main work of making placements. However, it finally accepted a scheme that will allow registered adoption support agencies to act as intermediaries and obtain information from the Registrar General, adoption agencies and the courts.[132] Those adopted before December 30, 2005 have the right to request assistance from an intermediary service to trace and contact birth relatives, but services have been advised to give priority to applications relating to adoptions before November 11, 1975 (when the original access to records provisions were implemented) because of the potentially greater need of elderly people and in relation to adoptions that were expected to remain closed.[133] Where a person was adopted through an adoption agency, the intermediary will be able to establish the name of the agency from the Registrar General and then approach the agency for further information; in non-agency cases, information may be available from the local authority or the court.[134] Under the relevant regulations, it is an offence for the intermediary to disclose information without the informed consent of the adopted adult.[135] However, direct discussion between the intermediary and the adopted person may facilitate the passing of information, even where he or she does not want contact.

Information is also limited in many international adoptions. Where children have been abandoned, their date of birth and parents' identities may be unknown; indeed, some countries protect mothers from identification because of the stigma of giving birth outside marriage. Even where identifying details are collected, records may be sealed, preventing any disclosure of, for example, the original birth certificate. The Hague Convention requires the competent authorities in each state to preserve any information they hold about the child's or parent's identity. Access to this is generally determined by the law of the state holding the

---

[131] NORCAP, Memorandum submitted to Select Committee on Adoption and Children Bill, paras 2.14 *et seq.*, Commons Committee, 4th Sitting, November 21, 2001; Lords Report, Vol.639, cols 935–938 (October, 18, 2002); Commons Consideration of Lords Amendments, Vol.392, cols 102–103.

[132] Adoption and Children Act 2002 s.98; Adoption Information and Intermediary Services (Pre-Commencement Adoptions) Regulations 2005 (SI 2005/890); DfES, *Guidance* (2005), Ch.10.

[133] SI 2005/890 reg.4; DfES, *Guidance* (2005), Ch.10, paras 9 and 14.

[134] Adoption and Children Act 2002 ss.64(4), 65(1), 98(2), (3); The Family Procedure (Adoption) Rules 2005 (SI 2005/2795) r.84.

[135] SI 2005/890 regs 7 and 17.

information, but there can be no disclosure of the identity of the birth parents unless this is permitted in the state of origin.[136]

III. PROVISION OF ADOPTION SERVICES

22–014 Adoption is strictly regulated in England and Wales; only local authorities and registered adoption societies can run adoption agencies,[137] and arrangements for adoption can only made by adoption agencies or by a person acting under a High Court order.[138] The provision of adoption support services is also regulated.[139] The formalisation of adoption always requires a court order.[140] There are restrictions on who may adopt, but the main responsibility for determining the suitability of prospective adopters falls on adoption agencies.

A. Organisation of adoption services

i. Local authority responsibilities

22–015 The Adoption and Children Act 2002 s.3 requires each local authority to maintain an adoption service, to make arrangements for adoption and to provide adoption support services in conjunction with their other services and local adoption societies. Local authorities must prepare and publish a plan for the provision of adoption services.[141] Although these services are under local control, they are subject to considerable direction by the Secretary of State, through regulations and guidance, including the *National Adoption Standards*. The Department for Children, Schools and Families monitors local authority adoption activity to ensure that targets are met, and provides training materials to assist local authorities to develop services. Ofsted has responsibility for inspecting local authority adoption services.[142] In Wales, adoption policy is a matter for the Welsh Assembly.

In relation to individual children it looks after, a local authority must consider whether to make an adoption plan, and if it does, obtain parental consent or apply

---

[136] Hague Adoption Convention arts 16(2), 30. Preserving information allows for access should the law be relaxed in future.

[137] Adoption and Children Act 2002 s.9; Adoption Agencies Regulations 2005 (SI 2005/389). Adoption societies are also known as voluntary adoption agencies.

[138] Adoption and Children Act 2002 s.92(1); *Re P; K and K v P and P* [2005] 1 F.L.R. 303; *Re A (Placement of Child in Contravention of Adoption Act 1976, s.11)* [2005] 2 F.L.R. 727. It is a criminal offence for other persons to undertake certain steps in connection with adoption: s.93(1).

[139] Adoption and Children Act 2002 s.8; Care Standards Act 2000 s.4(7A); Adoption Support Agencies (England) and Adoption Agencies (Miscellaneous Amendments) Regulations 2005 (SI 2005/2720).

[140] But adoptions made in specific overseas jurisdictions are valid without further proceedings in England and Wales; see below, paras 22–052 and 22–053.

[141] Adoption and Children Act 2002 s.5.

[142] Education and Inspections Act 2006 ss.147 and 148; The national minimum standards for adoption apply in the inspection of services.

for a placement order.[143] It must consider whether to approve prospective adopters and to make placements with them. It must also assess needs for adoption support services and decide whether to provide them.[144] Local authorities' responsibilities for adoption can give rise to actions in damages where children[145] or adopters[146] are harmed by decisions made negligently.

ii. Adoption societies

Voluntary organisations can operate as adoption agencies if they are registered   **22–016** under the Care Standards Act 2000.[147] They must comply with detailed regulations about their management, financial position, practice (including record keeping) and with national standards.[148] Adoption societies work alongside local authorities and may facilitate the adoption of looked-after children by undertaking assessments and identifying suitable adopters.

Adoption agencies are required to operate adoption panels, which include members independent of the agency to consider adoption plans, the approval of prospective adopters and the matching of children with them.[149] Agencies must consider the recommendation of the panel when making a decision about whether a child should be placed for adoption.[150]

B. The role of the court

The courts play a vital role in dealing with adoption.[151] They ensure that all the   **22–017** parties to an adoption are listened to and treated fairly before orders are made, consider whether plans for adoption are in the best interests of children, approve such plans in care or placement order proceedings[152] and make adoption orders. Officers from CAFCASS have a responsibility to ensure that those consenting to adoption understand the effects of their actions, to represent children where they are parties to the proceedings and to provide welfare reports.[153] Although the *Prime Minister's Review* questioned whether court proceedings were necessary

---

[143] Adoption and Children Act 2002 s.22; Adoption Agencies Regulations 2005 (SI 2005/389) regs 11–17; DfES, *Guidance* (2005), Ch.2 and see para.22–043, below.
[144] Adoption and Children Act 2002 s.4; The Adoption Support Services Regulations 2005 (SI 2005/691) and para.22–022, below.
[145] *B v A-G of New Zealand* [2003] UKPC 61.
[146] *B and B v A County Council* [2007] 1 F.L.R. 1189, CA (causation not established), and see below, para.22–021.
[147] Adoption and Children Act 2002 s.2. Ofsted is now responsible for regulating agencies in England. In Wales, the Care Standards Inspectorate for Wales undertakes this task. For-profit organisations may not be registered as adoption societies but can be registered as adoption support agencies: Adoption and Children Act 2002 s.8(1).
[148] Adoption and Children Act 2002 ss.9 and 10 and Adoption Agencies Regulations 2005 (SI 2005/389).
[149] The Adoption Agencies Regulations 2005 (SI 2005/389) Pt 2; DfES, *Guidance* (2005), Ch.1.
[150] SI 2005/389 Regs 19 and 33(1); *Guidance* (2005), Ch.4.
[151] Cm.5017 (2000), para.8.1.
[152] The plan must first be ratified through local authority procedures: *Re P-B (Placement Order)* [2007] 1 F.L.R 1106, CA, para.20.
[153] Family Procedure (Adoption) Rules 2005 (SI 2005/2795); "President's guidance (adoption: the new law and procedure)" [2006] 1 F.L.R. 1234. The overriding objective is "to enable the court to deal with cases justly, having regard to the welfare issues involved" (r.1).

for straightforward adoptions, the White Paper accepted that it was extremely difficult to identify such adoptions, and that the significance of adoption justified the involvement of the courts.[154] Adoption involves both judicial functions such as determining disputes about welfare, consent and contact, and the conferring of the new status on the adopters and child.[155]

All three levels of court have jurisdiction in adoption. Court rules require applications that discharge care orders to be made to the court that made that order,[156] but allow transfer to the level of court appropriate to the case. The majority of adoption orders are made in county courts. Concerns about delay and inefficiency led the President of the Family Division to issue guidance to increase specialism in the higher courts and to ensure active management of adoption cases.[157] Specific county courts have been designated as adoption centres[158]; only designated adoption judges can make county court adoption orders. However, the family proceedings court retains jurisdiction in adoption.

C. Eligibility and suitability of adopters

22–018   No one has the right to adopt[159]; adoption law sets out eligibility rules for adopters, and, where an adoption agency is involved,[160] the applicants must also satisfy it of their suitability. Adoption agencies are not permitted to discriminate against prospective adopters on the basis of sexual orientation, and for this reason some agencies linked to the Catholic Church have decided to close.[161] Guidance advises agencies against automatically excluding applicants on grounds of age, health or other factors, except certain criminal convictions that make them ineligible.[162]

i. Eligibility

22–019   The Adoption and Children Act 2002 lays down the following rules (and conditions about domicile or habitual residence that are beyond the scope of this book)[163]:

---

[154] PIU, *Review* (2000), paras 4.14 and 7.21; Cm.5017 (2000), para.8.32.
[155] The final hearing may end with "an adoption ceremony"; see Wilson J. [2007] Fam. Law 808 at 818.
[156] Children (Allocation of Proceedings) Order 1991 (SI 1991/1677) art.14.
[157] *President's Direction, Adoption Proceedings—A New Approach* (2001).
[158] County court adoption proceedings should be made in or transferred to such courts: *President's Direction* (2001), p.2.
[159] Jacqui Smith, Minister of State, Department of Health, *Hansard Commons*, Vol.392, col.96 (November 4, 2002) (Commons Consideration of Lords Amendments). The ECHR does not guarantee such a right: *Fretté v France* [2003] 2 F.L.R. 9.
[160] This includes all agency placements and intercountry adoptions where the official procedures are followed, but not "in family" adoptions; see below para.22–051.
[161] Equality Act (Sexual Orientation) Regulations 2007 (SI 2007/1253) reg.15 allows faith-based adoption agencies to continue to restrict provision on the grounds of sexual orientation until December 30, 2008, providing they refer applicants to other agencies.
[162] DfES, *Guidance* (2005), Ch.3, para.13.
[163] Adoption and Children Act s.49(2)(3). For an explanation, see Cheshire and North's *Private International Law*, 13th edn (London: Butterworths 1999), pp.134 *et seq.*

- An adoptive parent must be at least 21 years of age (a parent adopting his or her own child with their partner need only be 18 years of age).[164]

- If a couple wish to adopt jointly, they must either be married or "living as partners in an enduring family relationship".[165]

- Single people may adopt[166]; if a sole applicant is married, an order can only be made if the court is satisfied that his or her spouse cannot be found, or is incapable by reason of ill-health of applying, or that the spouses have separated and the separation is likely to be permanent.[167]

- In addition, regulations preclude an adoption agency placing any child for adoption or fostering in a household where any person over the age of 18 has been convicted or cautioned for a specified offence.[168]

Adoption has always been open to both married couples and single people. However, only one member of an unmarried couple could become an adoptive parent, but their partner could obtain a more limited legal relationship with the adopted child by a residence order.[169] When originally introduced to Parliament, the Adoption and Children Bill retained the requirement of marriage for adoption by couples, although it allowed for special guardianship orders in favour of unmarried couples.[170] Child welfare organisations expressed concerns that allowing adoption by one member of a couple was confusing for children, off-putting for prospective adopters and would make it more difficult to recruit the additional adopters needed.[171] Nevertheless, the Government took the view that unmarried couples should not be permitted to adopt until a status had been devised that would provide a formal legal relationship.[172] However, an amendment was accepted by the Commons to permit adoption by unmarried couples.[173] This proved very contentious, not least because it allowed adoption by same-sex couples. The supporters accepted that this was a natural development from adoption by single people living in relationships; that an adoptive family was

---

[164] Adoption and Children Act 2002 s.50.

[165] Adoption and Children Act 2002 s.144(4). A joint adoption order may be made in favour of a separated married couple: *Re WM (Adoption: Non-patrial)* [1997] 1 F.L.R. 132, FD, and where the unmarried partner of a parent applies to adopt alone, their relationship with the parent need not be "enduring".

[166] For a review of such adoptions, see M. Owen, *Novices, Old Hands and Professionals: Adoption by Single People* (BAAF: 1999).

[167] Adoption and Children Act 2002 s.51(3).

[168] The Adoption Agencies Regulations 2005 (SI 2005/389) reg.23 and Sch.3. Restrictions were originally introduced following the conviction of Roger Saint for serious offences against children. See C. Smith [2000] J.S.W.F.L. 367.

[169] Children Act 1989 s.8; *Re W (Adoption: Homosexual Adopter)* [1997] 2 F.L.R. 406, FD; *Re T, Petitioner* [1997] S.L.T. 724, Ct of Sess. (IH).

[170] Children Act 1989 ss.14A–14G, added by Adoption and Children Act 2002.

[171] See, for example, memorandum from BAAF, Special Standing Committee on Adoption and Children Bill, November 20, 2001. Only 1 of the 30 organisations submitting evidence supported retention of the marriage requirement.

[172] There were two Private Member's Bills before Parliament to establish such a relationship, but it was clear that neither would be enacted during the 2001–2 session.

[173] At Report Stage, *Hansard Commons*, Vol.385, cols 976–1007 (May 16, 2002), amendment tabled by David Hinchliffe, MP.

better for a child than growing up in state care; and that children should have a parental relationship with both parties. The objectors stressed the vulnerability of adopted children and the instability of relationships outside marriage, children's need for two parents of opposite sexes and the possibility of increasing the pool of prospective adopters in other ways. The Lords rejected this amendment and a further amendment that would have allowed adoption by unmarried, heterosexual couples was not moved.[174] The Joint Committee on Human Rights concluded that the Bill as amended by the Lords was not compatible with human rights.[175] The amendment was re-introduced in the Commons with Government support and passed again.[176] A further attempt in the Lords to restrict adoption was unsuccessful.[177] Under the Adoption and Children Act 2002, both members of an unmarried or same-sex couple may become joint adoptive parents.

ii. Suitability

22–020 Adopter assessment is designed to safeguard the children involved,[178] but prospective adopters have some rights: they must be given clear information about adoption and be treated fairly, openly and with respect.[179] Adoption agencies recruit prospective adopters, develop their understanding of adoption through individual and group activities and assess their suitability to adopt.[180] A detailed report must be prepared for the agency's adoption panel that makes recommendations about approval.[181] Where the agency considers that the applicants are unlikely to be suitable it need not continue to make a full report.[182] The agency decides whether to approve, but must take the panel's recommendation into account.[183] Approximately 95 per cent of applicants put to the panel are

[174] By Lord Jenkins of Roding; see *Hansard Lords*, Vol.639, col.910, Report Stage (October 18, 2002).

[175] Joint Committee on Human Rights, *24th Report* (2002). In its ninth Report (HC 475) the Committee had found that the original Bill was compatible, but the decisions of the European Court of Human Rights in *Fretté v France* App. No.36515/97 and of the South African Constitutional Court in *Du Toit and de Vos v Minister for Population Development*, judgment September 10, 2002, led the Committee to reconsider. Given the practice of permitting adoption by one member of a homosexual couple, restricting adoption by unmarried couples was likely to breach the art.8 rights of both children and prospective adopters when taken with art.14.

[176] Despite a three-line whip imposed on Conservative Members, *Hansard Commons*, Vol.392, cols 24–99 (Commons Consideration of Lords Amendments) (November 4, 2002).

[177] *Hansard, Lords*, Vol.641, cols 569–624 (Lords Consideration of Commons Amendments) (November 5, 2002).

[178] DH, *Adopter Preparation and Assessment and the Operation of Adoption Panels: A Fundamental Review* (October 2002), Foreword.

[179] DH *Adoption National Minumum Standards* (2003), Standard 3.

[180] This assessment is frequently referred to as "the home study" and covers details of the applicants' relationship, their health, lifestyle, etc. and personal references. The Department for Education and Skills has issued practice guidance to assist assessment of prospective adopters: DfES, *Preparing and Assessing Prospective Adopters: Practice Guidance* (2006).

[181] Adoption Agencies Regulations 2005 (SI 2005/389), regs 25, 26; DfES, *Guidance* (2005), Ch.3. The applicants should be given the report and allowed to comment on it (reg.25(8)) and be allowed to attend the panel meeting (reg.26(4)).

[182] The Suitability of Adopters Regulations 2005 (SI 2005/1712) reg.5.

[183] Adoption Agencies Regulations 2005 (SI 2005/389) regs 19 and 33

approved, but some others withdraw or are counselled out before a formal report is made.

Following a commitment in the White Paper intended to increase prospective adopters' confidence in agency decisions,[184] the 2002 Act established a new system of review. Decisions about the suitability of applicants are subject to independent review.[185] Complaints may be made to local authorities in respect of other decisions,[186] and judicial review remains an option only if these systems fail to correct untenable decisions or faulty procedure.[187]

iii. Matching

Once applicants have been approved, the agency considers whether there are **22–021** children waiting for adoption locally who might be a suitable match. The applicants are given brief details of such children. If the applicants wish to proceed, the adoption panel considers the match and makes a recommendation. After the agency decision-maker has approved the match, the placement can be made.[188] Prospective applicants should be provided with more information about the child at each stage of the process so that they can decide whether to proceed.[189] Before the child is placed, the applicants must be provided with the child's permanence report—information about the child's history, needs, health and other matters the agency considers relevant. A local authority that fails to disclose information may be liable to the adopters for losses suffered because of this:

> In *A. v Essex County Council*[190] the local authority placed a boy with the adopters without informing them that his experienced foster carers considered him to have an "enormous behaviour problem . . . an uncontrollable, vicious child" and that a child psychiatrist had recommended child guidance and 24-hour supervision. The court accepted that the adopters would not have proceeded with the placement had they known this. They boy damaged the adopters' home, caused them much distress and led to them suffering psychiatric illness. The Court of Appeal upheld the decision that the local authority was liable for the damage experienced before the order was finalised but not subsequently.[191] The damage suffered subsequently was not

---

[184] Cm.5107 (2000), para.6.23.
[185] Adoption and Children Act 2002 s.12; Adoption Agencies Regulations 2005 (SI 2005/389) regs 28 and 29; DfES, *Guidance* (2005), Ch.3 and Annex D.
[186] Children Act 1989 s.26(3B), and above, para.21–081.
[187] See above, paras 21–082–21–085.
[188] Adoption Agencies Regulations 2005 (SI 2005/389) regs 18–20; DfES, *Guidance* (2005), Ch.4.
[189] Jacqui Smith, Minister of State, Department of Health, Special Standing Committee, 14th Session, December 18, 2002, col.720 *et seq.* The Adoption Agencies Regulations 2005 (SI 2005/389) reg.31 requires information to be provided before placement; DfES, *Guidance* (2005), Ch.4, para.7.
[190] [2004] 1 F.L.R. 749, CA.
[191] The agency had negligently failed to provide the information it had decided the prospective adopters should have, and was therefore in breach of its duty to them, but agency staff did not owe a wider duty to prospectve adopters in compiling reports (paras 56–65).

caused by the local authority's failure to provide information—even if the adopters had been given further information after the placement, their commitment to the child was such that they would probably have proceeded with the placement. The boy was accommodated by the local authority.

D. Adoption support

22–022 Originally, adoption was viewed as creating relationships that could replace and mirror birth relationships. While placements largely concerned healthy babies, it was natural to expect adopters to take full responsibility and manage without further support. However, changes in understanding about adoption and in adoption practice led to a questioning of this approach and recognition of the importance of supporting adoption.[192] The task of adoptive parenting has become more complex with the placement of children with special needs and the maintenance of links with birth relations; support may be required by adopters and children after the adoption order has been made. Without support, carers may be unwilling to adopt; unsupported adopters may be unable to cope, putting placements at risk of breakdown. Support for adoption may be financial or practical, enabling the adopters to purchase additional services they think their family needs or providing assistance that the agency considers appropriate.

The Houghton Committee recommended the introduction of adoption allowances and the availability of social work support for those who sought access to their birth records.[193] The Adoption Act 1976 provided the legal framework for post-adoption services by including that the local authority adoption service should be designed to meet the needs of (amongst others) "children who have been adopted" and "persons who have adopted".[194] There was considerable opposition to providing adopters with allowances that were not available to birth parents, but pilot schemes were introduced, and the Children Act 1989 provided for a general scheme.[195] Agencies were permitted to pay an allowance where adoption was not otherwise practicable.[196] The system was inflexible; allowances could not be paid where difficulties arose only after the adoption. There were wide variations in the willingness of agencies to pay, the assessment of means and the amounts paid.[197]

Research on adoption in the 1990s highlighted the challenges faced by adopters and identified substantial unmet support needs during and after the adoption process. Despite government encouragement, many local authorities

---

[192] For a comprehensive discussion of this development, see N. Lowe et al., *Supporting Adoption Reframing the Approach* (1999) and N. Lowe, "The changing face of adoption—the gift/donation model versus the contract/services model" [1997] C.F.L.Q. 371.

[193] Cmnd.5107 (1972), paras 93–95 and recommendation 17, para.304.

[194] Adoption Act 1976 s.1; Lowe *et al. Supporting Adoption*, p.32.

[195] Adoption Act 1976 ss.57, 57A, added by Children Act 1989 s.88 and Sch.10, para.25 and Adoption Allowances Regulations 1991 (SI 1991/2030).

[196] For example so as to place a child with siblings, or the child needed special care that required greater expenditure; reg.2.

[197] N. Lowe et al., *Supporting adoption* (1999), Ch.14; PIU, *Report* (2000), para.3.121.

confined their post-adoption services to provision of allowances and counsel-ling.[198] Lowe and colleagues argued that agency mindset in providing services had failed to keep pace with the changes in adoption, and stressed that adoption should not be regarded as ending the state's obligations to looked-after children. There should be explicit duties to provide post-adoption support and agencies should make agreements with adopters and children about support.[199] The *Prime Minister's Review* considered that the lack of consistent support acted as a disincentive to local authorities placing children for adoption outside their area and also contributed to delay and drift. In order to improve the success of adoptive placements, the Government promised "to support a better deal for adopters" by giving all adoptive families a right to an assessment for post-adoption support services and by imposing a clear duty on local authority social services departments to provide post-adoption support.[200] The term "adoption support" is now used to include services concerned with adoption both before and after the adoption is finalised.

The Adoption and Children Act imposes a duty on local authorities to make **22–023** and participate in arrangements for the provision of adoption support services.[201] It gives specific persons[202] the right to request an assessment of their needs for adoption support[203] but does not require the local authority to ensure that needs are met.[204] Details of the required services are set out in regulations and supported by practice guidance. Provision of support should be planned and reviewed regularly; ongoing financial support is generally means-tested and subject to annual review. Local authorities can arrange for support to be provided by voluntary agencies.[205] Where there are needs for health or education services, the local authority must notify the relevant body; where another local authority could help, they may be requested to help and must comply if this is consistent with the exercise of their functions.[206]

The position of special guardians[207] and their children is even weaker. Although local authorities must make arrangements for support services, unless

---

[198] PIU, *Review* (2000), para.3.124 citing Cm.2288 (1993), paras 4.23, 4.25.

[199] Lowe et al. (1999), pp.429, 434; PIU, *Report* (2000), paras 3.118–3.122.

[200] Cm.5017 (2000), paras 6.26–6.27.

[201] Adoption and Children Act 2002 s.3(2). "The main financial implications of the Adoption and Children Bill lie in adoption support", Jacqui Smith, Minister of State, *Hansard Commons*, Vol.376, col.133w. There are national standards: DfES, *Adoption Support Agencies National Minimum Standards* (2005).

[202] "a) children who may be adopted, their parents and guardians, b) persons wishing to adopt a child, and c) adopted persons, their parents, natural parents and former guardians": s.3(1). This right may be extended to others by s.4(7)(a), and there is a discretion to assess others; s.4(3); Adoption Support Services Regulations 2005 (SI 2005/691) regs 4, 5 and 13; DfES, *Guidance* (2005), Ch.9.

[203] The specific obligation to assess contrast with Children Act 1989 s.17, see above, para.21–010.

[204] Adoption and Children Act 2002 s.4(1), (4). Where it decides to provide services, it must prepare a plan and keep this under review.

[205] Adoption and Children Act 2002 s.4(7). See: the Adoption Support Services Regulations 2005 (SI 2005/691); DfES, *Guidance* (2005), Ch.9.

[206] Adoption and Children Act 2002 s.4(9)–(11), but the House of Lords has refused to order co-operation from a housing authority under Children Act 1989 s.27: see *R v Northavon DC, Ex p. Smith* [1994] 2 F.L.R. 671 and above, para.21–014.

[207] See above, para.17–046 and below, para.22–065.

specific provision is made in regulations they have no duty to assess an individual's needs.[208]

There are many parallels between this scheme and Pt III of the Children Act 1989, which has failed to secure family support services for many children in need and which has been subject to considerable litigation.[209] Although committed to supporting adoption, the Government has been concerned not to provide greater rights than to family support services.[210] The Act does not impose a specific duty to provide a specific service even after an assessment of need has been made.[211] In deciding whether or not to meet a person's needs, the local authority must not act unreasonably and must comply with its human rights responsibilities. Where refusal of services undermines the art.8 right to respect for family life (e.g. because the adoption is at risk of breakdown or contact will cease), the local authority's decision can be challenged. Post-adoption services fall into two categories: services that relate to general needs (e.g. because of the child's behavioural problems) and services that relate specifically to adoption (e.g. birth records counselling). In relation to general services, local authorities must take care not to discriminate by providing easier or more difficult access to services for adoptive families than for other families of children in need. Those dissatisfied with services, or the lack of them, may use the complaints process.[212]

IV. PRINCIPLES IN ADOPTION LAW

A. Welfare

22-024 The Adoption and Children Act 2002 s.1 provides that:

> "[W]henever a court or adoption agency is coming to a decision relating to the adoption of a child the paramount consideration . . . must be the child's welfare, throughout [the child's] life."

This provision replaces a more limited test that only gave "first consideration to the need to safeguard and promote" welfare throughout childhood,[213] and did not apply a simple welfare test to determine whether a child could be adopted without parental consent. Parents were expected to give great weight to the welfare of their children, but their consent to adoption could only be dispensed

---

[208] Children Act 1989 s.14F(1), (2). There is a strong non-discrimination argument that similar provision should be made where looked-after children become subject to special guardianship rather than adoption; also, where relatives become special guardians where children would otherwise have to be looked after by a local authority.

[209] See above, paras 21–008–21–010 and 21–015.

[210] Lord Hunt, Parliamentary Under-Secretary, Department of Health, *Hansard Lords*, Vol.636, cols CWH76–CWH80 (Grand Committee) (June 27, 2002).

[211] *R. (G) v Barnet LBC; R. (W) v Lambeth LBC; R (A) v Lambeth LBC* [2004] 1 F.L.R. 454, HL, at para.93 *per* Lord Hope. The local authority is specifically permitted to determine whether to provide services; s.4(4).

[212] See above, para.21–082; s.26(3B) extends this to representations about adoption services.

[213] Adoption Act 1976 s.6.

with on specific grounds, including that they were withholding it unreasonably.[214] The 1993 White Paper recommended that the child's welfare in
adulthood should also be considered, and the 1996 Bill made welfare the basis
for dispensing with parental consent.[215] The 2000 proposals followed this
approach to ensure coherence with planning for the child's needs under the
Children Act 1989 and to promote permanence within the context of the belief,
set out in the *Prime Minister's Review*, that adoption delivers benefits to most
children and to society.[216] This welfare test applies to agency decisions about
placement, removal from placement, contact and post-adoption support and to
court decisions about placement and adoption orders, or alternative orders which
might be made in these proceedings such as special guardianship or residence
orders and some decisions about leave[217]:

> In *P v Serial No.52/2006*[218] a baby had been removed under an EPO at the
> age of one month because of serious and repeated violence by the father
> against the mother, fuelled by misuse of drugs and alcohol. The parents'
> request for an adjournment to allow a residential assessment was refused,
> and care and placement orders were made. When the child was 10 months
> old, she was placed with the prospective adopters where she thrived. Eight
> months later, the parents applied for leave to defend the adoption applica-
> tion, arguing that they had conquered their difficulties and were successfully
> caring for the child's sibling. The Court of Appeal upheld the judge's
> decision to refuse leave. The welfare of the child was paramount; the
> benefits of being brought up with her sibling did not outweigh the negative
> impact of the change of carers and the risks of care within a family where
> there would be three children under the age of three years were too high.

Despite the lack of a specific provision to this effect, the test applies to the court's
decision to dispense with a parent's consent to adoption.[219] The construction of
welfare in s.1 includes a broad consideration of the child's relationships in the
birth family and in adulthood, allowing some balancing of the different elements
that contribute to welfare. Consent may be dispensed with "where the child's
welfare requires" this.[220] Benefits largely experienced in adulthood, such as

---

[214] Adoption Act 1976 s.16(2). "[T]he fact that a reasonable parent does pay regard to the welfare of
his child must enter into the question of reasonableness as a relevant factor." *Re W (an infant)* [1971]
A.C. 682, 699, *per* Lord Hailsham. For this reason Stephen Cretney took the view that the non-
application of the welfare test made no difference to the decision to dispense with consent; see fourth
edition of this work at p.455.

[215] Cm.2288 (1993), para.4.2; *Adoption—A Service For Children* (1996) para.4.1.

[216] PIU, *Review*, paras 9, 2.81, 4.8 and 8.2–8.3. Concern was expressed that the courts gave "the
benefit of doubt to birth parents": para.3.62; Cm.5017 (2000), paras 1.20–1.21, 2.11, 4.14.

[217] Adoption and Children Act 2002 s.1(7), but not the decision to grant leave to apply for revocation
of a placement order: *M Warwickshire CC* [2007] EWCA Civ 1084, where welfare was only a
consideration.

[218] Including decisions whether to give parents leave to defend adoption proceedings: *P v Serial
No.52/2006* [2007] EWCA Civ 616, *per* Wall L.J. at paras 19–24.

[219] EN para.22 cl.1(8)(c), which specifically stated this was removed at Report Stage: *Hansard
Commons* Vol.385, col.959 (May 16, 2002).

[220] Adoption and Children Act 2002 s.52(1)(b).

citizenship, may now tip the balance in favour of adoption, and the fact that the child will soon be 18 should not weaken the case for adoption.[221]

Further guidance is provided in the form of a checklist similar to that in the Children Act 1989. This includes matters particularly relevant to adoption decisions such as the likely effect on the child of becoming an adopted person, the likelihood of relationships with relatives continuing, the willingness and ability of relatives to meet the child's needs and their wishes and feelings regarding the child.[222] In this context, "relatives" includes parents, who are thus recognised for their potential contribution to the child's welfare, not because parenthood gives them rights. Parents cannot prevent an adoption where this best meets their child's needs. The importance for welfare of protecting the child's identity is underlined by a duty on adoption agencies when placing a child to give due consideration to the child's religious persuasion, racial origin and cultural and linguistic background.[223] Adoption practice gives considerable emphasis to professional assessments of the child's needs, but the law recognises that the child's own views about arrangements are important to welfare decisions, and this is stressed in the adoption standards.[224]

B. Consent

22–025 Parental consent has been a mainstay of adoption law and is required under international law.[225] Adoption was conceived as a "court-sanctioned contract" that necessarily required the consent of the parties, but the 1926 Act allowed parental consent to be dispensed with.[226] Although widely drawn, these powers were narrowly interpreted until a decision in 1947[227] that was followed by legislation redefining the grounds for dispensing with consent. Apart from specific grounds that had their origin in the Poor Law, the 1949 Act allowed consent to be dispensed with where it was unreasonably withheld. This "piece of machinery", invented to determine whether the advantages of adoption were sufficient to override parental objections,[228] became the main ground and was

---

[221] *Re S and J (Adoption: Non-Patrials)* [2004] 2 F.L.R. 111, FD; cf. *Re B (Adoption Order: Nationality)* [1999] 1 F.L.R. 907 at p.911, *per* Lord Hoffmann: "Benefits which will accrue only after the end of childhood are not welfare benefits to which first consideration must be given."

[222] Adoption and Children Act 2002 s.1(4)(c), (f). Relationships in this context are not limited to legal relationships: s.1(8)(a). Therefore, where continuing contact is crucial to welfare, if arrangements have been agreed between the adopters and the agency to allow contact with birth relatives, or between siblings placed separately, adoption may nevertheless be in the child's interests.

[223] Adoption and Children Act 2002 s.1(5). A similar provision applies to all decisions by local authorities in relation to looked after children: Children Act 1989 s.22(5)(c), and see above, para.19–020.

[224] Adoption and Children Act 2002 s.1(4)(a); DH, *Adoption National Minimum Standards* (2003), Standard 2.

[225] *Review of Adoption Law* (1992), Discussion paper No.2, *Agreement and Freeing* (1991), para.80 (see also Background Paper No.1, *International perspectives* (1990)). The relevant treaties include The European Convention on Human Rights, the European Convention on Adoption and the Hague Convention on Intercountry adoption.

[226] Cretney *Law, Law Reform*, p.193; *Twentieth Century*, pp.613–614.

[227] Cretney *Law, Law Reform* citing *H v H* [1947] K.B 463, 466, DC.

[228] *Re C (a minor) (adoption: parental agreement: contact)* [1993] 2 F.L.R. 260, 272, *per* Steyn and Hoffman L.JJ.

used in more than half of all cases where orders were made without consent.[229]

The Adoption and Children Act 2002 provides a general power to dispense with consents,[230] but parental consent still has crucial importance in the adoption process. Where each parent has consented to the child's placement for adoption and have not withdrawn their consent, an adoption agency can place the child without obtaining a placement order from a court.[231] In such cases, withdrawal of consent necessitates the child's return to the parents (if he or she is not placed for adoption or the agency considers return to be in the child's interests) or a local authority application for a placement order.[232]

i. Whose consent?

Adoption requires the consent of all parents or guardians, but "parent" is defined **22–026** only to include parents with parental responsibility, so the consent of some fathers is not required. Where the father only obtains parental responsibility after the child has been placed for adoption with the mother's consent, he is treated as having given consent on the same terms as the mother.[233] Only guardians appointed under the Children Act 1989 are able to give consent, so where a child from overseas is adopted in England, the agreement of a person or institution who had rights under a foreign order is not required.[234] The child's consent is not required. Following the recommendation of the *Review of Adoption Law,*[235] the 1996 draft Bill included provisions requiring the agreement of children aged 12 years or over,[236] but this was criticised by adoption agencies who considered that having to "sign away" their birth families placed too great a burden on children.[237] Nevertheless, courts and agencies must have regard to the child's wishes and feelings as part of the welfare checklist; court rules will give children party status in placement order proceedings and will allow them to apply to be

---

[229] Parker *Adoption Now*, p.69; Review of Adoption Law, Discussion paper No.2, *Agreement and Freeing* (1991), para.37.

[230] Adoption and Children Act 2002 s.52(1), and see below, para.22–032.

[231] Adoption and Children Act 2002 s.19(1). But not if care proceedings are pending: s.19(3).

[232] Adoption and Children Act 2002 ss.22(1), 31, 32. But it is an offence for anyone other than the agency to remove the child: s.30(1), (3), (8). All agency decisions are subject to the welfare test in s.1, but an adoption society has no power to seek a placement order and continue with inchoate adoption plans if consent is withdrawn. In contrast, local authorities are under a duty to seek placement orders where they are satisfied that children ought to be placed for adoption, but they do not have the authority of parental consent to do so: s.22(1).

[233] Adoption and Children Act 2002 s.52(9)(10). The father may withdraw this consent, but this may not be effective if an application for adoption has already been made: s.52(4).

[234] Adoption and Children Act 2002 s.144(1); this is a different definition from that in the 1976 Act, which allowed the court to hold that the consent of the Director of the Romanian orphanage was required in *Re AGN (adoption: foreign adoption)* [2000] 2 F.L.R. 431, FD.

[235] *Review of Adoption Law* (1992), paras 9.5–9.6, 12.9. Also that children should be represented; paras 37.2 *et seq.*

[236] Draft Adoption Bill 1996 cll.41(7), 46(3). There is a similar provision in Scots law: Adoption and Children (Scotland) Act 2007 s.32. Only 17% of adoptions relate to children over the age of 10 years: ONS, *Marriage, Divorce and Adoption Statistics* (FM2, No.32, 2004) Table 6.2a.

[237] Select Committee on the Adoption and Children Bill 2001 (HCP 431 ii), evidence of BAAF, para.10.2.

parties in adoption,[238] but it is not clear that this ensures sufficient attention is given to children's views about whom they live with and the legal arrangements for this.[239] Particularly, issues of contact with siblings may not receive adequate attention[240] if children are not represented.

ii. Consent to what?

22–027 Until 1984, the consent required was to a specific adoption, but adoption agencies and adopters preferred not to let birth parents know who would be caring for the child, and from 1949 the identity of the adopters could be concealed.[241] The Houghton Committee recommended a new procedure "freeing for adoption", so that birth parents could finalise their consent before adopters had been found; this was included in the 1976 Act.[242] In practice, freeing did not work as intended, and seemed to contribute to delay.[243] By the time the freeing provisions were implemented, there were few consensual baby placements for which it was largely intended. When freeing applications were made, children were often already placed with prospective adopters so that, in contested cases, the process neither allowed parents to challenge the adoption plan nor protected the adopters from conflict. For these reasons, the 1992 review proposed its abolition and a new system whereby the court made "placement orders" to authorise the child's placement for adoption.[244]

(1) Consent and placement

22–028 A child can only be placed for adoption if each parent consents to the child's placement, either with identified prospective adopters or anyone chosen by the agency, or a placement order is obtained.[245] Placement orders also require

---

[238] 2002 Bill EN, para.279; Special Standing Committee 2001–2, 24th session, (January 17, 2002), col.905. "[The government] will need to ensure that children are not unnecessarily made party to proceedings, because involvement can be stressful for them" Jacqui Smith, Minister of State, Department of Health. If children are parties, they are likely to be represented by a children's guardian.

[239] For example, Cm.5017 (2000), para.5.11 gives a case example where a 13-year-old girl does not want to be adopted but wishes to remain with foster carers and her 9-year-old sister and see her birth family. It suggests special guardianship for both children without any reference to the views of the younger girl. There is some evidence that some children want more involvement: CSCI, *About Adoption—A Children's Views Report* (2006).

[240] The court must consider arrangements for contact before making placement or adoption orders: ss.27(4) and 46(6).

[241] Cretney *Law, Law Reform*, pp.190–192 and Cretney *Twentieth Century*, Ch.17, fn.101 and accompanying text. For this reason, de facto adoptions were not always formalised, although some birth parents were asked to sign consent forms in blank without the adopters' names being included.

[242] Houghton Committee, paras 173–183, 221–224. The process also protected adopters from disputes with parents, but this was given less emphasis: see J. Rowe, "Freeing and adoption from a historical perspective" (1984) 2 *Adoption and Fostering* 10.

[243] N. Lowe et al., *Report of the Research into the Law and Practice of Freeing for Adoption* (London: HMSO, 1993).

[244] *Review of Adoption Law* (1992), paras 14.6–14.9; Cm.2288 (1993), paras 4.8–4.9. The original proposals for placement orders were considered too cumbersome and were modified following further consultation: DH, *Placement for Adoption—A Consultation Document* (1994), and again for the 2002 Act.

[245] Adoption and Children Act 2002 ss.19(1), 21.

parental consent, but where this is refused or is withdrawn, the court may dispense with it and make the order.[246] Foster carers may apply to adopt without either the consent of the parents or the local authority obtaining a placement order if they have looked after the child for at least 12 months.[247] Further consent is required to the adoption order unless a placement order has been obtained.[248]

(2) Consent and adoption

Consent to the adoption order may also be specific or general, and may be given **22–029** at the same time as consent to placement or subsequently. Where advance consent is given, the parent need take no further part in the proceedings but can notify the agency that he or she wishes to be informed of any adoption application.[249] Consent given in advance may be withdrawn, but this is ineffective if an application for an adoption order has already been made.[250] Unless there is a placement order, an adoption order can only be made if the requisite consents are given, there is no opposition to adoption from someone who has given consent in advance or the court is satisfied that the consent should be dispensed with.[251] A person who has given consent to adoption cannot oppose the adoption without leave of the court; nor may a parent or guardian do so where a placement order has been obtained. Leave can only be given where there has been a change of circumstances.[252] These provisions are intended to ensure that most decisions about consent are taken earlier in the process, and are intended to reduce delay by excluding objections from those who initially consented to adoption or had their objections to placement overridden by a court.

Consents must be given "unconditionally and with full understanding of what it involves".[253] It follows that parents cannot bargain consent for contact; nor may adopters give inducements for consent.[254] Information about the effect of adoption is provided on the consent form, and consents must be witnessed by a CAFCASS officer, but this may not be adequate to protect a parent under

---

[246] Adoption and Children Act 2002 ss.21(3), 52.

[247] Adoption and Children Act 2002 s.42(4), but if the child were only accommodated, a person with parental responsibility could remove the child under Children Act 1989 ss.20(8)–(5)(a), and any person could remove the child with leave of the court: Adoption and Children Act 2002 s.38(5)(b). Foster carers who have cared for the child for five years have greater security: s.38(2), (3).

[248] Adoption and Children Act 2002 s.47. An order from Scotland or Northern Ireland freeing the child for adoption is also sufficient s.47(6).

[249] Adoption and Children Act 2002 s.20(4); EN para.68. Under the freeing procedures, a parent could make a declaration of no further involvement, and this also precluded an application for revocation of the order: Adoption Act 1976 ss.19, 20.

[250] Adoption and Children Act 2002 ss.20(3), 52(4).

[251] Adoption and Children Act 2002 ss.20(1)(2), 47(2).

[252] Adoption and Children Act 2002 s.47(2)(b), (3), (4)(b), (5); *P v Serial No.52/2006* [2007] EWCA 616 Civ, above, para.22–024. This is a two stage test: (1) whether there is a material change; and (2) whether it is in the child's interests for leave to be granted.

[253] Adoption and Children Act 2002 s.52(5).

[254] Adoption and Children Act 2002 ss.52(5), 92(1), (4). Making, offering or receiving such a payment is an offence: s.95(3). It does not necessarily preclude an adoption order; cf. Adoption Act 1976 s.24(2), but the High Court can retrospectively authorise an excepted payment: *Re MW (Adoption: Surrogacy)* [1995] 2 F.L.R. 759, FD.

stress.[255] The former provision and the consent form that required consent to be "freely" given were criticised on the basis that they discouraged parents from consenting by suggesting that they willingly gave up responsibility for their child rather than were resigned to doing so in the child's interests. The Government suggested that the form should be changed to encourage consent, reduce contested adoptions and speed up the process.[256] New forms have been introduced, but it seems unlikely that merely rewording the consent form can have such a substantial effect.

In cases of intercountry adoption, the child's state of origin may allow both simple and full adoption; the Hague Convention allows conversion of simple adoptions in the receiving state but only if the necessary consent has been given.[257] Where this is not the case, a Convention adoption is still treated as a full adoption, but the High Court has power to give it different effect where this would benefit the child.[258] In the case of simple adoptions from non-Convention countries, a further consent will be required for an adoption order in the United Kingdom.[259]

iii. When must consent be given?

22–030 The mother's consent to adoption is only valid if the child is at least six weeks old when it is given.[260] This ensures that she has had time to recover from the birth before making such an important decision. Where the law of the child's state of origin allows consent to be given earlier, this will not be valid for any adoption order made in England or Wales.[261] No such protection is given to fathers, nor in respect of a decision to consent to placement. Thus a mother could consent to her child's placement at birth and change her mind within a relatively short time but be unable to reclaim the child. She might be able to obtain leave to oppose the adoption, but the passage of time, the baby's relationship with the adopters and lack of relationship with the mother would be likely to encourage the court to dispense with her consent.[262]

---

[255] Adoption and Children Act 2002 ss.52(7), 102(1). In *Re A (Adoption: Agreement: Procedure)* [2001] 2 F.L.R. 455, CA, where the use of the same form for consent to adoption and freeing and the rapid pace of the process had confused the mother, a 15-year-old Kosovan rape victim. But in *Re D (Adoption: Freeing Order)* [2001] 1 F.L.R. 403, FD (not a freeing case), the court accepted the mother's agreement even though it had not been witnessed, because she refused to see the CAFCASS officer.
[256] Parker *Adoption Now*, p.68; PIU, *Review*, paras 3.64–3.65; Cm.5017 (2000), paras 8.27–8.28; *Special Select Committee Report 2001* (HCP 431ii), evidence of BAAF, para.10.1; no new form has been issued, but the word "freely" was removed at Report Stage.
[257] Hague Convention art.27. The central authority seeks to ensure that the parents consent to a full adoption where the receiving state is England and Wales.
[258] Adoption and Children Act 2002 s.88(2); EN para.230.
[259] *Re G (Foreign Adoption: Consent)* [1995] 2 F.L.R. 528, FD.
[260] Adoption and Children Act 2002 s.52(3). This protection was introduced by the Adoption Act 1949 s.3(4) and is reflected in the European Convention on Adoption 1967; see also DfES, *Guidance* (2005) Annex B.
[261] In *Re A (Adoption of Russian Child)* [2000] 1 F.L.R. 539, the court dispensed consent where the mother had signed the form shortly after the birth. A Convention adoption made in the state of origin would be valid providing the consent was given after birth and acceptable in that state: Hague Convention art.4(c)(iv).
[262] Adoption and Children Act 2002 ss.30(1), 47(5).

iv. Dispensing with consent

The changes relating to dispensing with consent sweep away most of the earlier **22–031** case law, replacing all but one of the previous grounds with a welfare test. The *Review of Adoption Law* expressed concern at the limited weight given to the parental views, and recommended that adoption should be permitted against the parents' wishes where the adoption plan had been approved by the court, and where the advantages to the child of becoming a member of a new family by adoption were "so significantly better" than any other option as to justify this, or the parent could not be found or was incapable of giving consent.[263] However, all the subsequent bills used a different formula.

Under the Adoption of Children Act 2002, the court can make placement or adoption orders without parental consent on two separate grounds.

(1) Section 52(1)(a): "the parent or guardian cannot be found or is incapable of giving consent"

This provision repeats one in earlier law[264] that was used in only a small **22–032** percentage of cases.[265] It may be used where the whereabouts of a person whose consent is required are unknown and cannot be discovered, or where he or she lacks the mental capacity to give agreement.[266] Notice of the proceedings must normally be served on each person whose consent is required[267]; if this is not done, the decision may be challenged.[268] Where there is no known address[269] for a person, very thorough inquiries should be made and assistance sought from appropriate government departments; it may be necessary to advertise in newspapers. However, if there are no practical means of communicating with a person whose consent is required, they "cannot be found" even if their whereabouts are actually known:

> In *Re A (Adoption of Russian Child)*[270] a child was brought to the United Kingdom after a Russian adoption order was made with the mother's consent given only two days after the birth. The adopters applied for adoption in England and needed a valid consent. The judge obtained advice that any contact with the mother would violate her rights, and that disclosure

[263] *Review of Adoption Law* (1992), paras 12.1, 12.6 and Ch.15; Cm.2288 (1993), paras 4.9 *et seq.* and 5.4–5.5. DH, *Placement for Adoption* (1994), para.3.3.
[264] Adoption Act 1926 s.2(3); Adoption Act 1976 s.16(2)(a).
[265] For 11% of non-agreeing mothers and 5% of non-agreeing fathers in Murch's study: see *Review of Adoption Law*, Discussion Paper No.2, *Agreement & Freeing* (1991), p.26.
[266] In *Re L (A Minor) (Adoption: Parental Agreement)* [1987] 1 F.L.R. 400, the court was unwilling to accept the mother's psychiatrist's certificate that she was so incapable; the fact that the parent is irrational is insufficient. Minority does not per se prevent a person having the capacity to consent.
[267] The requirements as to service are set out in the Family Procedure Adoption Rules (2005) (SI 2005/2795) Pt 6; the court has a power to dispense with service: r.39.
[268] Under the Human Rights Act 1998 or by granting leave out of time: In *Re F (R) (An Infant)* [1970] 1 Q.B. 385, the applicants made numerous attempts to contact the mother but did not ask her father, whose address they knew. Concern about a possible challenge to the adoption led the court to direct that a father whose consent was not required should be notified: *Re R (Adoption: Father's Involvement)* [2001] 1 F.L.R. 302, CA.
[269] If there is a known address, the parent can be found: *Re B* [1988] 1 Q.B. 12; but see below.
[270] [2000] 1 F.L.R. 539, FD. For an earlier example, see *Re R (Adoption)* [1967] 1 W.L.R. 34.

of the fact of adoption was a criminal offence. Considering the problems this might cause for the adopters who had business interests in Russia, he accepted that it was neither reasonable nor practical to contact the mother, and dispensed with her consent.

(2) Section 52(1)(b) "the welfare of the child requires the consent to be dispensed with"

22–033 The Department of Health noted in 1996 that because the welfare test has to be considered in all court adoption decisions, making welfare the principal ground for dispensing with consent added little.[271] However, it took the view that requiring the court to find that the advantages of adoption were "so significantly greater"[272] could create confusion but added nothing because the court had to apply the European Convention of Human Rights.[273] This approach was heavily criticised by adoption and social work professionals on the basis that fear of losing their children could deter families from seeking social services support and thus undermine the Children Act 1989. A simple welfare test gave insufficient weight to the families' views; there should be a clear limit to the state's right to intervene.[274] This formulation appears to remove any possibility of taking account of parents' rights or interests. Whereas parents could take a different view of their child's welfare and not be unreasonable,[275] the court now imposes an objective view of what the child's welfare requires. However, adoption without parental consent must be a proportionate response to the child's welfare needs,[276] and so it will be necessary to compare adoption plans within any proposals from the family.[277] At the placement order stage, the crucial issues will be the prospects for rehabilitation and the availability of suitable carers within the family. The application will only be sought because the local authority thinks the child ought to be placed for adoption; contesting parents will thus be challenging a professional assessment about their child's welfare and will need expert evidence.[278] The local authority will need a care order or will need to

---

[271] DH and WO, *Adoption: A Service for Children* (1996), para.4.1.

[272] Suggested in the *Adoption Review* (1992), para.12.6.

[273] Special Standing Committee, November 20, 2001, James Paton, Department of Health: "the test . . . would not be trivial or low".

[274] *Special Select Committee* (HCP 431), Memoranda of evidence from BAAF, para.11, BASW (British Association of Social Workers), paras 1–5, ADSS (Association of Directors of Social Services), cl.44, FRG (Family Rights Group), para.1. Particular concern was expressed because until it was amended in Committee, the bill allowed placement orders to be made without satisfaction of the "significant harm test" in Children Act 1989 s.31(2).

[275] Adoption Act 1989 s.16(2)(b); for a detailed discussion, see the sixth edition of this work at pp.923 *et seq.*

[276] ECHR art.8(2); *Re C and B (Care Order: Future Harm)* [2001] 1 F.L.R. 611, CA; *Re O (Supervision Order)* [2001] 1 F.L.R. 923, CA at para.28, *per* Hale L.J.

[277] One difficulty with this, noted by the Family Rights Group, is that members of the extended family may be unwilling to put themselves forward until it is clear that a care order will be made. By this time, plans for adoptive placements may be well advanced. However, local authorities are now expected to consider the possibilities of care within the family before bringing care proceedings: DCSF, *Children Act 1989 Guidance and Regulations* (2008), Vol.1, paras 3.7, 3.17.

[278] See J. Brophy et al., *Expert Evidence in Child Protection Litigation* (1999).

prove the significant-harm test; the parents' failure as carers will already have been established for the court. Considerable emphasis is placed on acting without delay[279]; to expedite matters, the placement order application may be made during the care proceedings, with the order made immediately following.[280] Offers of care from family members need to be considered before the court makes a care order approving a plan of adoption.[281] Where the issue is the legal arrangements for care, the court must be satisfied that adoption is a better arrangement than residence or special guardianship, which both allow the parents to retain their status and legal relationship with the child.[282] However, if the adopters have made their commitment to the child on the basis that adoption is intended and are unwilling to care for the child without an adoption order, the court is likely to dispense with parental consent. However, it may take a different view where a child objects to adoption.[283]

The Act restricts the circumstances when a parent can oppose an adoption if he or she has previously agreed to a placement or a placement order has been made.[284] The question of dispensing with parental consent to adoption rather than placement will generally be confined to cases where there is no placement order, for example: in agency cases where consent was given to placement; applications by foster carers or family members; and intercountry adoptions where the official procedures have not been complied with.[285] Where consent was originally given, the court may be easily satisfied that adoption is in the child's interests. There may be a case for arguing that the child's welfare does not require adoption, given the security that can be obtained through other arrangements, but this may be less persuasive where the parent initially agreed. In "in family" cases, it may be particularly difficult to establish that adoption is required for the child's welfare given that it involves losses rather than gains.[286]

---

[279] Adoption and Children Act 2002 s.1(3). Reduction of delay was a major reason for reducing opportunities to object to adoption: PIU, *Review*, paras 3.47 *et seq.*; Cm.5017 (2000) para.8.28.

[280] Where it is clear to the parents that adoption is the plan, it is not unfair to proceed with the placement order application with only a days notice: *Re P-B (Placement Order)* [2007] 1 F.L.R. 1106.

[281] *Re G and B (Children)* [2007] 2 F.L.R. 140, CA (where the court had objective evidence of a potential carer's unsuitability, it could reject a proposal that would delay the placement order).

[282] *Re AJ (Adoption Order of Special Guardianship)* [2007] 1 F.L.R. 507 CA, and below, para.22–064.

[283] See *Re M (Adoption or Residence Order)* [1998] 1 F.L.R. 570, CA, where the child's objections led to the local authority withdrawing support for adoption, and the court refused the order on the basis that the mother, who could not care for her daughter, was not unreasonable in refusing consent. If there is a placement order, the prospective adopters may have a legitimate expectation of adoption.

[284] Adoption and Children Act 2002 s.47(2)(c), (3), (4)(c), (5); leave of the court is required, which can only be given if there has been a change in circumstances: s.47(7): *P v Serial No.52/2006* [2007] EWCA Civ 616; above para.22–024.

[285] Where official procedures have been followed, a valid consent will have been given; this is required not only for adoption under the Hague Convention but for entry clearance where a child is to be adopted in the UK: DH, *Intercountry Adoption Guide—Practice and Procedures* (2001), paras 5.12–5.15.

[286] *Re B (Adoption by One Natural Parent to the Exclusion of Other)* [2001] 1 F.L.R. 5898, CA, *per* Hale L.J. at para.12 (reversed for other reasons, [2002] 1 F.L.R. 196, HL); cf. *Re M-J (Adoption Orders or Special Guardianship)* [2007] 1 F.L.R. 691, CA (no rule that special guardianship preferable in "in family" cases).

C. Human rights

22–034 Closed adoption effected in the face of parental opposition requires overriding justification if the European Convention on Human Rights art.8 is not to be breached.[287] However, the recognition of the crucial importance of de facto family ties with carers by adoption, even without the consent of the parents, may be justified in the interests of the child and the carers,[288] and adoption with the consent of a parent cannot breach his or her rights.[289] The requirement that adoption orders are only granted where they are in the child's interests is sufficient to ensure that adoption is proportionate to the child's needs.[290] Concerns to ensure compliance with the Convention were instrumental in shaping the Adoption and Children Act 2002, particularly in removing the discrimination between married, unmarried and same-sex couples.[291]

Parents must be sufficiently involved in decisions that lead to an adoption plan,[292] and their rights to a fair hearing demand competent representation by a lawyer instructed to protect their rights (e.g. by ensuring that issues of contact are fully considered).[293]

> In *P, C and S v UK*[294] the local authority became concerned about the welfare of the couple's unborn baby because the mother had been prosecuted in the United States for harming her older child. This boy had suffered repeated hospital admissions because of illness induced by being given laxatives. The local authority arranged a psychiatric assessment of the couple, but before it was received the mother gave birth following an emergency caesarean. The local authority obtained a without-notice emergency protection order and removed the baby shortly after birth. The baby was never returned to the couple although they were allowed contact. The parents' lawyers withdrew at the beginning of the four-week contested care hearing; the judge allowed only a short adjournment and the case proceeded without the parents being represented. A week after the care order was made, the judge heard the freeing proceedings, again without parental representation. The European Court of Human Rights found that the art.8 rights of the parents and the child had been breached and that the trials had

---

[287] H. Swindells et al., *Family Law and the Human Rights Act 1998* (1999), para.9.63; *P C and S v UK* [2002] 2 F.L.R. 631, ECtHR at para.118.

[288] *Soderback v Sweden* [1999] 1 F.L.R. 250; *Eski v Austria* [2007] 1 F.L.R 1650 (both stepparent adoptions).

[289] *Re B (Adoption by One Natural Parent to the Exclusion of Other)* [2002] 1 F.L.R. 196, HL, *per* Lord Nicholls at para.29.

[290] *Re B (Adoption by One Natural Parent to the Exclusion of Other)* [2002] 1 F.L.R. 196, HL, *per* Lord Nicholls at paras 30–32; for a critique of the House of Lord's approach to the Convention, see S. Harris-Short [2002] C.F.L.Q. 325, 336. The European Court of Human Rights has stated that relationships between parents and children should not be determined by the mere passage of time: *Görgülü v Germany* [2004] 1 F.L.R. 894 at para.45.

[291] Joint Committee on Human Rights, *24th Report* (2002); see para.22–019, above.

[292] *Scott v UK* [2000] 1 F.L.R. 958, ECtHR (application found inadmissible)

[293] *P, C and S v UK* [2002] 2 F.L.R. 631, ECtHR at paras 96–100. The court also found that the lack of representation in the care and freeing proceedings breached art.8, at paras 137–138. The parents were awarded compensation, but the court considered it inappropriate to award damages to the child, who was unaware of the proceedings and had no legal ties to the parents following the adoption.

[294] [2002] 2 F.L.R. 631, ECtHR.

been unfair. The need for speed in making arrangements for babies did not justify proceeding in this way. It was crucial for the parents to be able to put forward their case as favourably as possible.[295]

Although their consent may not be required, fathers must generally be involved in the adoption process. Adoption agencies are required to consult fathers about their views.[296] Where a father has "family life" in respect of the child, he must be sufficiently involved in decision-making, and his art.6 rights must be protected. Only in exceptional cases is it appropriate not to notify the father; the mother's desire for confidentiality is insufficient to justify non-disclosure.[297]

> In *Re M (adoption: rights of natural father)*[298] the local authority applied for and was granted a direction that the father need not be contacted about the adoption of a child he had been told was stillborn. The father had convictions for serious offences including rape, had assaulted the mother in front of their older child on his last visit, and the mother feared for her safety and the child's should the father learn of her deception.

Adoption also raises art.8 issues for those who are adopted:

> In *Odièvre v France*[299] an adopted person who was denied access to information about the identity of her birth parents so she could not establish her family history challenged the French system for allowing mothers to give up their children anonymously.[300] The European Court of Human Rights, in a controversial and poorly reasoned judgment, considered the competing interests of the adopted person to know her origins against her birth mother's interest in anonymity. Instead of examining the law on the basis that it was an interference with the applicant's rights to know her origins, which had to be "necessary" to satisfy art.8(2), the court considered the extent of the state's positive obligation to her. It did not, therefore, consider whether the interference was proportional but considered whether a fair balance had been set between the mother's and daughter's rights. Consequently, it held, by majority, that the adopted person's art.8 (and art.14) rights were not violated.

D. Confidentiality

Adoptions have been cloaked in secrecy in order to protect the parties from any stigma and to prevent interference in the child's upbringing. Information

22–035

---

[295] At para.136.

[296] Adoption Agencies Regulations 2005 (SI 2005/389), regs 14(1)(c), 14(4), 17(1)(d) and 46(3)(a).

[297] *Re H; Re G (Adoption: Consultation of Unmarried Fathers)* [2001] 1 F.L.R. 646, FD; *Re R (Adoption: Father's Involvement)* [2001] 1 F.L.R. 302, CA.

[298] [2001] 1 F.L.R. 745, FD *cf. Re C (A Child) v XYZ County Council* [2008] 1 F.L.R. 1294 CA.

[299] App. No.42326/98 (2003); Steiner [2003] C.F.L.Q. 425.

[300] Anonymous birth is not permitted in England and Wales, and the courts are assiduous to ensure that fathers and the wider family are aware that adoption is planned: *Birmingham City Council v S, R and A* [2007] 1 F.L.R. 1223, FD.

collected by adoption agencies[301] and for the courts is confidential,[302] and can be disclosed only as permitted by the legislation.[303] Court proceedings take place in private and may be arranged so that the parties do not see each other.[304] The applicants may apply for a serial number so that their identity cannot be discovered by the child's parents.[305] However, a birth parent cannot keep their identity secret from the adopters or the child.[306] Assessments of the applicants and the birth family are confidential. The court may exceptionally order that their contents are not disclosed where this is justified by the risk of significant harm to the child,[307] but in most cases the needs of a fair trial demand that there are no restrictions on disclosure to the parties.[308] A children's guardian cannot be refused copies of local authority adoption assessments in Children Act 1989 proceedings.[309]

V. MODERN ADOPTION PRACTICE

A. The use of adoption

22–036   Although adoption has a single meaning and its effects apply equally to all adoptions, there are distinct policies, laws and practices that apply to the different circumstances in which adoption is used: relinquishment or baby placement, public law adoptions, intercountry adoptions and "in family" adoptions. These will now be considered in turn.

B. Relinquishment or baby placement

22–037   Early adoption practice focused on the placement of babies, mostly born outside marriage, who had been handed over by their mothers. Adoption societies

---

[301] Adoption Agencies Regulations 2005 (SI 2005/389) reg.41; DH, *Adoption National Minimum Standards for England* (2003), Standard 26.
[302] Family Procedure Adoption Rules 2005 (SI 2005/2795) rr.20, 21, 28, 29 and Pt 8. Intermediary services must treat information as confidential: Adoption Information and Intermediary Services (Pre-Commencement Adoptions) Regulations 2005 (SI 2005/890) reg.16.
[303] Adoption and Children Act 2002 ss.54–65; see para.21–012, above. The Adoption Agencies Regulations 2005 (SI 2005/389) reg.24(2)(a) requires agencies to give prospective adopters information about the child's background.
[304] *Re F (Adoption: Natural Parents)* [2007] 1 F.L.R 363, CA, paras 28–32. Only those who have been given notice may attend the final hearing: SI 2005/2795 r.32.
[305] SI 2005/2795 r.20; *Re X (Adoption: Confidential Procedure)* [2002] 2 F.L.R. 476, CA. *The Review of Adoption Law*, Discussion Paper No.1, *The Nature and Effects of Adoption* (1990), para.102 suggested that the procedure might be being used too readily and that leave should be required.
[306] The Houghton Committee recommended this: para.298, recommendation 74.
[307] *Re D (Adoption Reports: Confidentiality)* [1995] 2 F.L.R. 687, HL at 700, *per* Lord Mustill; *Re K (Adoption: Disclosure of Information)* [1997] 2 F.L.R. 74, FD, but note placement with an applicant convicted of such offences is no longer permissible.
[308] *Re R (Care: Disclosure: Nature of Proceedings)* [2002] 1 F.L.R. 755, 776H, *per* Charles J.; and see *Re X (Adoption: Confidential Procedure)* [2002] 2 F.L.R. 476, CA.
[309] *Manchester CC v T* [1994] Fam. 181, CA.

accepted healthy white babies[310] and placed them with married couples, many of whom sought adoption because of infertility. Local authorities also arranged the adoption of children with the agreement of parents who could not care for them.[311] In 1968, the peak year for adoptions, baby adoptions accounted for three-quarters of all adoptions by non-parents, and approximately one in five illegitimate children were adopted.[312] Although placement was a voluntary act, harsh family and social pressures on women who became pregnant outside marriage and the lack of financial support for lone motherhood effectively forced women to hand over their babies for adoption.[313] The availability of effective contraception, the Abortion Act 1967 and changes in social attitudes to unmarried mothers led to a dramatic decline in this use of adoption. It is now unusual; each year about 50 mothers place their children with adoption agencies because of their own circumstances or the child's severe disabilities.[314]

i. Freeing for adoption

Until the child was adopted, parental responsibility continued and consent could **22–038** be withdrawn. The Houghton Committee thought this prevented mothers planning for their future, encouraged indecisiveness and caused anxiety for prospective adopters. They therefore recommended that parents should be able to choose to relinquish parental responsibility in favour of an adoption agency at an early stage in the adoption.[315] The court would decide whether or not to accept the mother's decision. The Children Act 1975 made provision for "freeing orders", but the system was not implemented until 1984.[316] By this time these voluntary placements had all but disappeared; freeing was largely used to protect prospective adopters from contests with birth parents.[317]

The 1992 review recommended that a "placement order" should be required before an adoption agency could place a child with prospective adopters.[318] However, the proposals for uncontested adoptions were revised and the need for a placement order removed because of concerns about delaying adoptions. Subsequent reviews did not consider these adoptions; the new provisions are

---

[310] For a brief account of the development of practice, see *Houghton Report*, paras 22–26.

[311] N. Lowe, "English adoption law: past present and future", in Katz et al., *Cross Currents* (2000), pp.306, 318.

[312] Lowe "English adoption law" p.316 and R. Leete, "Adoption trends and illegitimate births 1951–1977" (1978) 14 *Populations Trends* 9–16.

[313] D. Howe et al., *Half a Million Women* (1998). Lowe "English adoption law" fn.46 found that single mothers were subject to family pressure even in the late 1980s.

[314] Parker *Adoption Now*, p.4.

[315] *Houghton Report, op. cit.* paras 168–186; J. Rowe, "Freeing for adoption a historical perspective" (1984) 8 *Adoption and Fostering* 2, 10.

[316] Children Act 1975 s.14; Adoption Act 1976 s.18. For a detailed account of freeing, see the sixth edition of this work at pp.907–911.

[317] See, generally, N. Lowe et al., *Report of the Research into the Use and Practice of the Freeing for Adoption Provisions* (1993).

[318] *Review of Adoption Now* para.14.8. In uncontested cases it was proposed that the order could be made without a full hearing: para.15.1(d).

largely based on those in the 1996 Bill[319] but make special provision for the placement of children under the age of six weeks.[320]

ii. Relinquishment under the Adoption and Children Act 2002

22–039 The Act abolished freeing and allows agencies to place children for adoption with parental consent.[321] It seeks to protect both birth parents and prospective adopters and seeks to avoid delays by enabling final agreement to adoption to be given at an early stage removing the need for court proceedings to ratify this before the adoption order is made. Parents may agree to adoption when they agree to placement; they may withdraw their consent and reclaim the child but only where no application for a placement order or for an adoption order has been made.[322] Adoption societies may not press on with an adoption if parents withdraw their agreement at an earlier stage.[323] Consent to placement gives the agency parental responsibility for the child; it does not remove the parent's parental responsibility but allows the agency to restrict their exercise of it.[324] Also, where an adoption placement has been made, the agency is no longer under an obligation to seek the parents' views before making decisions about the child.[325] Authority to place[326] ends contact orders; the Government's preferred approach is for agreements to be made about contact at this stage, but there is a wide power to make contact orders.[327] Parents consenting to adoption may specify they do not wish to be informed about any application for adoption[328] and can thus choose to take no further part in the process.

Under this scheme, the protection of the parent's rights, and the child's right to be brought up by the parent rest on the skills of the agency to ensure that the parent fully understands and wants adoption for her child.[329] This is supplemented by the requirement that consent to placement and adoption are witnessed

---

[319] DH, *Placement for Adoption* (1994), paras 4.2 *et seq.*; Adoption Bill 1996 cl.19; Adoption and Children Act 2002 s.19.

[320] Adoption and Children Act 2002 s.18(1). The mother's consent is ineffective if given less than six weeks from the birth: s.52(3).

[321] Adoption and Children Act 2002 Sch.5 and s.19; under the Adoption Agencies Regulations 2005 (Si 2005/389); DfES, *Guidance* (2005), Ch.7. Under reg.35(4), adoption agencies may not place for adoption a baby less than six weeks old without parental consent in writing, unless a placement order has been made in respect of the child. If the mother then disappears, the adoption can proceed, but it will be necessary to dispense with the mother's consent: Baroness Andrews, *Hansard Lords*, Vol.640, col.211 (Third Reading) (October 30, 2002).

[322] Adoption and Children Act 2002 ss.20(1), (3), 32(1), 52(4). Parents who originally consented can only oppose the adoption with leave of the court on the basis of a change of circumstances after consent was given: s.47(2)–(7); *P v Serial No.52/2006* [2007] EWCA Civ 616.

[323] A local authority could seek a placement order: ss.22, 32(1).

[324] Adoption and Children Act 2002 s.25(1), (4). The effect of consenting to placement is analogous to that of a care order. Once the child is placed, the prospective adopters also acquire parental responsibility to the extent determined by the agency.

[325] Adoption Agencies Regulations 2005 (SI 2005/389); DfES, *Guidance* (2005), Ch.7, paras 1–5. Reg.45 modifies Children Act 1989 ss.22 and 61.

[326] i.e. consent to placement or a placement order.

[327] Adoption and Children Act 2002 s.26(3) sets out who may apply for contact; relatives will not need the leave of the court; the court may make orders without application: s.26(4).

[328] Adoption and Children Act 2002 s.20(4).

[329] The agency also has duties to counsel the child's father: Adoption Agencies Regulations 2005 (SI 2005/389), reg.14(1)(a); *Re R (Adoption: Father's Involvement)* [2001] 1 F.L.R. 302, CA.

by a CAFCASS officer.[330] Where adoption seems the obvious solution to immense difficulties, such safeguards may not prove adequate.[331]

C. Public law adoptions

The adoption of children from state care, with or without their parents'   **22–040**
agreement, has been the focus of the recent debates on adoption. Changes in law and practice have aimed to increase these adoptions and reduce the time taken to achieve them in order to provide new, permanent families quickly for children who cannot return home. This form of adoption is common in North America[332] but unusual in most of Europe, where public care is generally regarded as temporary and intended to restore children to their families.[333] The promotion of adoption for children in care reflects the view, backed by considerable research, that state care rarely provides the necessary security, and that even the wellbeing of older children can be improved through adoption.[334] It rests on the belief that children's needs can justify a complete and involuntary severance of parental ties.

The practice of arranging adoption for looked-after children developed in the 1970s. The Houghton Committee noted that there was a sizeable number of children accommodated by local authorities whose parents' unwillingness to agree to adoption deprived them of the security of a settled home life. It proposed that local authorities and adoption societies should be able to apply to the court for an order dispensing with parental consent with a view to a child's future adoption.[335] Rowe and Lambert's study *Children Who Wait*[336] emphasised the importance of planning for children in long-term care, and "permanency planning" became part of social work practice in some local authorities. The Children Act 1975 increased local authority powers over children they looked after, but the introduction of "freeing for adoption" was delayed until 1984, and only in 1988 were all local authorities required to run a comprehensive adoption service.[337] From this time there was a substantial increase in the number of adoptions from care.[338]

---

[330] Adoption and Children Act 2002 s.104.

[331] *Re A (Adoption: Agreement: Procedure)* [2001] 2 F.L.R. 455 (freeing order revoked on appeal; the mother, a 15-year-old Kosovan rape victim, had not understood what she was signing).

[332] Under the Adoption and Safe Families Act 1997, states are required to make reasonable efforts to secure a permanent placement, and strict time limits are set for permanency hearings; see: J. Selwyn and W. Sturgess, *International Overview of Adoption* (2001) and M. Guggenheim, "Child welfare policy and practice in the United States 1950–2000", in S. Katz et al., *Cross Currents*, pp.547, 559.

[333] See, for example, *Johansen v Norway* (1996) 23 E.H.R.R. 33 but "there are circumstances ... where a young baby might be adopted in conformity with Art.8 of the Convention", *P, C and S v UK* [2002] 2 F.L.R. 631 at para.122.

[334] Parker (1999), *Adoption Now* pp.10–18; B. Tizard, *Adoption—A Second Chance* (1977); J. Thoburn, *Success and Failure in Permanent Family Placement* (Aldershot, Avebury, 1990); J. Gibbons, *Development after Physical Abuse in Early Childhood* (1995); J. Triseliotis, "Long-term foster care or adoption? The evidence examined" [2002] Child and Family Soc. Wk. 22.

[335] *Houghton Report*, paras 221–225 and recommendation 53.

[336] J. Rowe and L. Lambert, *Children Who Wait* (ABAFA, 1973).

[337] Parker (1999), *Adoption Now*, pp.2–4; Lowe, "English adoption law", p.322.

[338] Parker (1999), *Adoption Now*, p.4; PIU, *Review* (2000), Fig.2.1.

Following the implementation of the Children Act 1989, these adoptions declined; the emphasis on working in partnership with families and on rehabilitation diverted attention from adoption. More prosaically, resources committed to implementing the Act or ensuring the compliance with child protection procedures were not available to develop adoption services.[339] There were wide variations between local authorities in the proportion of children leaving care for adoption and in the time taken to match children to adopters.[340]

22–041 The Department of Health began to focus local authority attention on the importance of adoption for children in public care, first by issuing a Circular on adoption,[341] by including "maximizing the contribution [of] adoption" as an objective in the *Quality Protects* programme[342] and by establishing a task force to improve services. In 2000 the *Prime Minister's Review* concluded that more use could be made of adoption to meet the needs of looked-after children. Targets, supported by central government funding, were set to increase by 40 per cent the number of looked-after children adopted by 2004–5.[343] In the year ending March 2005, approximately 6 per cent of the looked after population (3,700 children) were adopted, an increase of 65 per cent over the number in March 1999.[344] The increase has not been maintained; in 2006–7 only 3,300 children in care were adopted.[345] Nevertheless, a substantial proportion of children removed as babies become the subject of care and placement orders.[346]

The legal framework for adoptions from care remained unsatisfactory. The "freeing for adoption" procedure failed to secure speedy adoptions or to ensure that parental consent was given or dispensed with before the child's placement.[347] Freeing orders also left children in legal limbo without any individual who had parental responsibility for them.[348] The *Review of Adoption Law 1992* recommended the abolition of freeing and that the court's approval should be obtained by a placement order whenever adoption was planned.[349] The 1996 draft Bill on which the first 2001 Bill was based required adoption agencies to apply for a placement order if they were satisfied that the child should be adopted but did not have parental consent, or where the plan for a child in care proposed adoption.[350] However, no conditions were set for placement orders; unlike care

---

[339] The PIU *Review* identified barriers to adoption at all stages of the process (Ch.3) but did not find evidence of a conscious anti-adoption culture (para.6.6); Cm.5017 (2000), para.2.21 noted variation between councils in the quality of management of adoption.

[340] SSI, *For Children's Sake: An SSI Inspection of Local Authority Adoption Services—Part I* (1996); *Part II* (1997).

[341] LAC(98)20: *Adoption—Achieving the Right Balance* (1998).

[342] Published in September 1998: see DH, *The Government's Objectives for Children's Social Services* (1999).

[343] Cm.5017 (2000) p.5.

[344] DfES, *Children Looked-After by Local Authorities Statistics* (2006), Table AJ.

[345] ONS, *Looked After Children Statistics: First Release* (SFR 27, 2007), Table E1.

[346] J. Masson et al., *Care Profiling Study* (2008).

[347] N. Lowe et al., *Freeing for adoption* (1993).

[348] This was a particular problem if no adoption placement was found. A substantial, but unknown, number of children remained subject to freeing orders; the provisions for revocation of freeing were unsatisfactory: *Re C (Adoption: Freeing Order)* [1999] 1 F.L.R. 348, FD.

[349] *Review of Adoption Law* (1992), para.14.8; Cm.2288 (1993), para.4.8.

[350] Adoption Bill 1996 cl.23.

orders, they would be granted solely on the basis of the child's welfare. These provisions proved highly controversial; it was unfair to parents that they risked losing a child via adoption merely because they had sought help from a local authority. In order to meet objections, the second Bill restricted applications for placement orders to local authorities and made proof of the threshold conditions for a care order a precondition unless the child was an orphan.[351]

i. Planning adoption

A plan for adoption must be based on an assessment that the birth family is **22–042** unable to meet the child's needs within a reasonable time, and that adoption is likely to provide the best means for doing so.[352] Parents must be sufficiently involved in the planning process but need not be included in all meetings where adoption is considered.[353] There are wide variations in the use made of adoption by different local authorities, which are not explained by the differences in their care populations.[354] However, children under the age of four and those without direct contact with their parents or other family members are more likely to have a plan for adoption than for long-term fostering.[355] Plans must be realistic. Although it is said that no child is un-adoptable, it may be impossible to identify a family willing to adopt a particular child. A central register of children awaiting adoptive placement and approved adopters has been set up in order to maximise the chances of finding homes for children, but there remains a shortage of families and individuals willing and able to parent older children with disabilities or behavioural problems.

Focusing too long on rehabilitation can delay or deny a settled home,[356] but giving it too little attention undermines the child's and parents' rights to family life. The guidance sets out time scales for the various stages of the adoption process; children should be matched within six months of a decision that adoption is in their best interests.[357] Developments in practice are being made to improve permanency planning. Twin-tracking—simultaneous work with the family on rehabilitation whilst preparing for permanent placement elsewhere— aims to reduce the time taken to secure a home for the child.[358] Concurrent planning aims to minimise the number of placements prior to adoption by placing

---

[351] Adoption and Children Act 2002 s.21(2).

[352] Adoption and Children Act 2002 s.1(1), (2), (4). Where a child is looked after, a permanence plan must be drawn up by the second statutory review (i.e. four months after the child became looked after): Review of Children's Cases Regulations 1991 (SI1991/895) reg.3 and Sch.1; DfES, *Guidance* (2005), Ch.3, para.4.

[353] *Scott v UK* [2000] 1 F.L.R. 958, ECtHR (mother's application under art.8 declared inadmissible); *Re J (Care: Assessment: Fair Trial)* [2007] 1 F.L.R. 77, CA.

[354] N. Lowe and M. Murch, *The plan for the child* (BAAF, 2002), pp.141 *et seq.*

[355] Lowe and Murch, *The Plan for the Child*, Ch.3 (based on a study of 113 children aged under 12 who had been continuously looked after for the previous 12 months).

[356] J. Selwyn et al., *Costs and Outcomes of Non Infant Adoptions* (BAAF, 2006); H. Ward et al., *Babies and Young Children in Care* (2006).

[357] DfES, *Guidance* (2005), Ch.4, para.2; see also Ch.3. The average time from entry into care to adoption has reduced from 2 years 10 months in 2000 to 2 years 7 months in 2005: DfES, *Children Act 1989 Report 2004 and 2005* (2006).

[358] This approach has the approval of the courts: *Re D and K (Care Plan: Twin Track Planning)* [1999] 2 F.L.R. 872, FD; *Re R (Child of Teenage Mother)* [2000] 2 F.L.R. 660, FD.

the child with foster carers, approved as adopters, who have agreed to work with the agency and the parents for the child's rehabilitation. Only if this is unsuccessful will the placement become an adoptive placement. Such arrangements depend on the commitment and integrity of the carers and the supervision of the agency.[359]

ii. Adoption from care under the Adoption and Children Act 2002—placement orders

22–043 The placement order process seeks to protect the parents' rights by requiring court scrutiny of the local authority's adoption plan before the placement is made. A local authority must seek a placement order whenever it is satisfied that a looked-after child ought to be adopted but parental agreement has not been given.[360] An application for a placement order can only be made after the procedures—panel approval and a formal decision—have been completed.[361] Unless the child is already subject to a care order, the court can only make a placement order if the significant-harm test[362] is proved and parental agreement is given or dispensed with.[363] These proceedings provide an opportunity for parents and other family members to challenge the plan for adoption; the court must be satisfied that it is better for the child's welfare to make the placement order than not to do so.[364] The seriousness of the matter at stake demands that parents are given a fair hearing, including representation for these proceedings.[365]

The placement order facilitates the adoption plan by giving the local authority parental responsibility[366] and ending existing orders for contact.[367] Before making a placement order, the court must consider the agency's proposals for contact and may make orders for contact subject to any conditions.[368] It can

---

[359] Although pilot concurrent planning schemes were initiated in the UK in 1998, it is not a mainstream tool: see E. Monck, (2001) 25 *Adoption and Fostering* 1, 67; E. Monck et al., *The Role of Concurrent Planning* (BAAF, 2003). However, concurrent planning's ability to achieve rehabilitation to the birth family appears to be "very poor": in Wigfall et al, "Putting programme into practice: the introduction of concurrent planning into mainstream adoption and fostering services" (2006) Br. J. Soc. Wk. 36, 41–55. Only 2 out of 24 children returned to the birth parent (p.48).

[360] Adoption and Children Act 2002 s.22(1), (2). Placement order applications are not required for looked-after children who are orphans: s.21(2)(c), nor where the adoption is started by foster carers giving notice of intention to adopt: s.22(5).

[361] *Re P-B (Placement Order)* [2007] 1 F.L.R. 1106 CA.

[362] Children Act 1989 s.31(2); see above para.21–031 *et seq.*

[363] Adoption and Children Act 2002 s.21(2)(3). For the grounds for dispensing with agreement, see above, para.22–031.

[364] Adoption and Children Act 2002 s.1(6).

[365] *P, C and S v UK* [2002] 2 F.L.R. 631 (a case where a freeing order was made in respect of a child of unrepresented parents).

[366] Adoption and Children Act 2002 s.25(1). The agency has power to restrict the parental responsibility of the parents and the prospective adopters; s.25(4).

[367] Adoption and Children Act 2002 s.26(1), i.e. orders under Children Act 1989 ss.8 or 34; s.26(6).

[368] Adoption and Children Act 2002 s.27(4), (5). The provisions in ss.26 and 27 are modelled on Children Act 1989 s.34, but a wider group of relatives may apply for contact without obtaining the leave of the court.

therefore continue family contact pending the adoption.[369] The placement order also prohibits anyone other than the local authority removing the child from the adopters, and restricts further opportunities to prevent the adoption.[370] A parent or guardian can only apply to revoke the order or oppose the adoption with the leave of the court, and this can only be given where there has been a change of circumstances after the placement order was made.[371] Section 8, supervision and special guardianship orders may not generally be made in respect of a child subject to a placement order.[372] The existence of a placement order should reassure prospective adopters that the plan for adoption has been approved by the court, and that parental opposition will only exceptionally be able to undermine this.

iii. Revocation of placement orders

Where it is in the child's interest (e.g. because there is no longer a plan for adoption), the placement order may be revoked. Any person, including the adoption agency may apply for revocation but parents require the leave of the court.[373] Where the court refuses adoption it has discretion whether or not to revoke the placement order.[374] Where the child was in care, revocation of the placement order allows the care order to take effect so that the local authority retains control over the future plan for the child.[375]   **22–044**

iv. Adoption from care under the Adoption and Children Act 2002—by foster-carers

Foster carers may seek to adopt the child they are looking after whether or not a placement order has been made. Just under 15 per cent of children adopted from care are adopted by their foster carers.[376] Adoption by foster carers may proceed with the support of the agency.[377] Alternatively, foster carers can give notice to the local authority of their intention to adopt and apply for an adoption order, but only after the child has had his or her home with them for at least 12   **22–045**

---

[369] The arrangements for contact after adoption will largely depend on the attitude of the adopters; see below, para.22–066.

[370] Adoption and Children Act 2002 ss.34(1) and 47(4), (5).

[371] Adoption and Children Act 2002 ss.24(2), (3); *Warwickshire CC v M* [2007] EWCA Civ 1048. Leave will only be granted if there is a realistic prospect of success in overturning the order. The child's welfare is not paramount in these proceedings: s.1(7).

[372] Adoption and Children Act 2002 ss.26(2)(a), 29(3)–(5). There is no restriction on granting a residence or special guardianship order in favour of a person who has leave, or making orders after the placement order has been revoked; s.24(1)–(4); see below, para.22–069.

[373] Adoption and Children Act 2002 s.24(1), (2). Parents could only seek revocation of freeing after one year; there was no provision for a revocation application by the agency, but the inherent jurisdiction could be invoked: *Re C (Adoption: Freeing Order)* [1999] 1 F.L.R. 348, FD.

[374] Adoption and Children Act 2002 s.24(4).

[375] Adoption and Children Act 2002 s.29(1); cf. the position regarding revocation of freeing orders: *Re G (Adoption: Freeing Order)* [1997] 2 F.L.R. 202, HL.

[376] DfES, *Children Act 1989 Report 2004 and 2005* (2006), para.1.28.

[377] Some agencies did not encourage adoption by foster carers: Parker *Adoption now*, p.131, citing Lowe et al. *Supporting Adoption*.

months.[378] If the child is removed from the carers, the adoption plan would be undermined. Where the child is only accommodated, parents retain their right to remove the child from the foster carers, but once the foster carers have looked after the child for a year they can apply for a residence order and seek directions that the child should remain with them pending the full hearing.[379] In addition, where the child has lived with the applicants for five years and intention to adopt has been given, the child can only be removed with leave of the court or by the local authority exercising its statutory powers.[380] Any decision by the local authority to remove the child must be made in accordance with its responsibility to safeguard and promote the child's welfare.[381]

D. Intercountry adoptions[382]

22–046   Intercountry adoption began as an altruistic response towards orphans and the abandoned children of servicemen in World War II, the Korean War and the Vietnam War. It developed because of the decline in babies available for adoption in receiving countries, the abandonment and institutionalisation of children due to extreme poverty in countries of origin, increased awareness that children overseas could be adopted and the growth of intermediaries and agencies willing to arrange such adoptions.[383] Now, over 30,000 children from 50 countries are adopted outside their countries of origin each year. The United States is the main receiving country and the main countries of origin are China, Russia, Vietnam, Guatemala and Columbia.[384] Over a thousand children (almost all girls) have been adopted in the United Kingdom from China since 2000.[385]

Compared with the rest of western Europe, the number of these adoptions in the United Kingdom is low; only approximately 300 orders are made each year.[386] Intercountry adoption is also a recent development in the United Kingdom; there were few such adoptions before the revolution in Romania in December 1989 exposed the plight (and availability) of neglected children in

---

[378] Adoption and Children Act 2002 ss.42(4), 44.

[379] Children Act 1989 s.10(5A), added by Adoption and Children Act 2002 Sch.3 para.56.

[380] Adoption and Children Act 2002 s.38(2)(3), re-enacting Adoption Act 1976 s.28. For example, the local authority could remove the child where the placement was not suitable; Fostering Services Regulations 2002 (SI 2002/57) reg.36.

[381] Children Act 1989 s.22(3)–(5); *R. v Devon County Council, Ex p. O* [1997] 2 F.L.R. 388, Q.B.D., above, para.21–085.

[382] See P. Selman (ed.), *Intercountry Adoption* (BAAF, 2000); J. Rosenblatt, *International Adoption* (London: Sweet & Maxwell, 1995); Inter-departmental Review of Adoption Law, Background Paper No.3, *Intercountry Adoption* (1992) and Discussion Paper No.4, *Intercountry Adoption* (1992); UNICEF, *Intercountry Adoption*, (1998) *Innocenti Digest* 4.

[383] J. Masson, "Intercountry adoption: a global problem or a global solution" (2001) J. International Affairs 141, 143.

[384] P. Selman, "The demographic history of intercountry adoption", in P. Selman (ed.), *Intercountry adoption* (2000). Compared with their small populations, there is substantial resort to intercountry adoption in Scandanavian countries.

[385] DfES, *Adoption Statistics: Applications Received by Country from 2000 to 4 October 2006* (2006).

[386] DfES, *Adoption Statistics: Applications Received by Country from 2000 to 4 October 2006* (2006). See also statistics published by the Hague Conference at: *http://www.hcch.net/index_en.php?act =text.display&tid=45* [Accessed June 5, 2008].

orphanages.[387] In contrast to much of western Europe, official attitudes to intercountry adoption have been largely negative or neutral in the United Kingdom. There is no official programme bringing children here for adoption; and until 1998, some local authorities refused to assess would-be adopters.[388] Unlike other adoptions of unrelated children in the United Kingdom, intercountry adoptions are not arranged through adoption agencies regulated or registered here. United Kingdom adoption agencies have focused on developing adoption for older British children and are concerned about the welfare of children adopted transracially and transculturally.[389] The complexities of procedures for inter-country adoption and the lack of sources of information about them meant that in about one quarter of all cases, formal procedures were not followed.[390] This led to increasing concern about the suitability of the arrangements made and the welfare of the children involved.[391]

The adoption of children internationally has long raised legal concerns about the power of the courts to make orders in respect of adopters of children from other jurisdictions, the recognition of orders and the child's status for the purpose of immigration and inheritance rights.[392] Also, the Home Office has been concerned that adoption should not be used as a mechanism for avoiding immigration control; it has restricted entry for settlement to children whose (foreign) adoption is recognised and children who are to be adopted in the United Kingdom. Also, the adoption must be due to the inability of the birth parents to care for the child, and there must be a genuine transfer of responsibility to the adoptive parents.[393]

The growth of intercountry adoption has also raised ethical concerns.[394] **22–047**
Practices have tended to focus on the requirements of adults rather than the needs of children. Although adoption can provide individual children with a materially better life, it removes them from their culture and may expose them to racism. It also removes some impetus (and possibly financial assistance) for the provision

[387] P. Thurman, "Intercountry adoption—a view from the House of Commons", in M. Humphrey and H. Humphrey (eds), *Intercountry Adoption: Practical Experiences* (London: Tavistock, 1993), p.138; DCC and ISS, *The Adoption of Romanian Children by Foreigners* (1991), in Inter-departmental *Review of Adoption*, Discussion Paper No.4 (1992).

[388] See LAC(98)20, para.52. The obligations of local authorities in relation to intercountry adoptions were clarified by the Adoption (Intercountry Aspects) Act 1999 s.9; see now Adoption and Children Act 2002 s.2(8).

[389] J. Masson, "The 1999 reform of intercountry adoption in the United Kingdom: new solutions and old problems" [2000] F.L.Q. 221, 225–6; BAAF, *Policy Statement on Intercountry Adoption* (1998).

[390] Adoption (Intercountry Aspects) Act 1999 EN paras 4–5.

[391] There have been a series of international statements seeking to promote good practice in adoption, including the UN Declaration on Social and Legal Principles relating to the Protection and Welfare of Children (1986) para.A/41/898; UN Convention on the Rights of the Child (1989) art.21; Hague Convention on the Protection of Children and Co-operation in Respect of Intercountry Adoption (1993); European Parliament Resolution (1996), para.A4–0392 and Council of Europe Parliamentary Assembly Recommendation 1443 (2000).

[392] J. Van Loon, *Report on Intercountry Adoption* (Hague Conference on International Law, 1990).

[393] Immigration Rules (HC 395), para.310; for entry following adoption: para.316A for entry for the purpose of adoption in the UK, see Macdonald, *Immigration Law and Practice in the UK* 5th edn (Butterworths, 2001), paras 11.84 et seq. and *Singh v Entry Clearance Officer (New Delhi)* [2005] 1 F.L.R 308, CA.

[394] J. Triseliotis, "Intercountry adoption—global trade or global gift" (2000) *Adoption and Fostering* 24, 2, 45.

of better childcare services in the home country, and may encourage abandonment, child sale and kidnapping.[395] For these reasons the UN Convention on the Rights of the Child states that intercountry adoption may be considered as an "alternative means of care" if the child cannot be cared for "in any suitable manner" in the country of origin.[396] In the United Kingdom the lack of agency control has meant that adopters have not been subject to as rigorous assessment as those adopting domestically. Adopters have also been exploited by unscrupulous intermediaries who charge high fees to facilitate adoptions overseas.[397] The Government has sought to ensure that the same principles and safeguards apply as in domestic adoptions,[398] but, in practice, there has been a two-tier system with lower standards and ineffective controls against abuses in intercountry adoption.[399] The ratification of the Hague Convention and further legislative controls are intended to secure the welfare of internationally adopted children, and to prevent UK adopters avoiding controls.[400]

i. The Hague Convention[401]

22–048 In 1988, the Hague Conference on Private International Law decided to establish a Special Commission to attempt to develop a new[402] international convention on intercountry adoption. The Permanent Bureau was concerned about the dramatic increase in the number of international adoptions, the complex human and legal problems involved, the insufficiency of domestic laws and the need for a multilateral approach, particularly one that included the states from which children came for adoption. There was a need to establish legally binding standards and a system of supervision to ensure that these were observed. Good communication between the authorities in countries of origin and destination was essential to secure co-operation between them and confidence in the decisions made.[403] The meetings of the Special Commission involved 33 states that were members of the Hague Conference and 24 non-Member States, as well as a large number of NGOs concerned with adoption and child welfare. The Convention

---

[395] Abuses have led a number of countries to declare a moratorium on intercountry adoptions. DNA tests are used in some cases to ensure that the person giving consent to the adoption is the child's mother.

[396] UN Convention on the Rights of the Child art.21(b). See also Hague Convention, Preamble, paras 2 and 3. For a discussion of the subsidiarity principle in intercountry adoption, see J. Masson (2001) "Intercountry adoption", pp.157–160 and *Report of the Special Commission on the Practical Operation of the Hague Convention* (December 2000), paras 24 *et seq.*

[397] UNICEF, *Innocenti Digest 4* p.8.

[398] Cm.2288 (1993), para.6.10; DH *Intercountry Adoption Practice* (1997), para.2.4.

[399] *Re C (Adoption: Legality)* [1999] 1 F.L.R. 370, 362, *per* Johnson J.; and see J. Masson [2000] F.L.Q. 221, pp.232–233.

[400] See below, para.21–051.

[401] Copies of the Convention, Reports of the Special Commissions and details of ratifications can be found on the Hague Convention website: *http://www.hcch.net* [Accessed June 5, 2008].

[402] The Hague Convention on Jurisdiction, Applicable Law and Recognition of Decrees Relating to Adoption 1965 had been largely ineffective because it was ratified only by Austria, Switzerland and the UK. Almost no Convention adoptions were ever made.

[403] G. Parra-Aranguren, *Explanatory Report on the Convention on Protection of Children and Cooperation in Respect of Intercountry Adoption* (1993), paras 6–7.

was completed in 1993 and came into force in 1995. It has been ratified or acceded to by over 60 countries, including both sending and receiving countries: the United States, China and Russia, the three countries with the greatest use of intercountry adoption, are now members.

The Convention has three objectives: (1) to establish safeguards to ensure that intercountry adoptions take place in the best interests of the child; (2) to establish a system of co-operation between countries in order to prevent abduction, sale and trafficking in children; and (3) to secure the recognition of adoptions made under the Convention.[404] By establishing a system of international co-operation it is intended to raise standards and eliminate abuses. Adoptions following the Convention's procedures will be more child-centred, simpler for prospective adopters and of certain effect.[405] These advantages should make Convention adoptions more attractive and should discourage intending adopters from seeking children in jurisdictions where procedures remain unregulated.

The Convention applies where a child who is habitually resident in one contracting state is moved for or after adoption by a person who is habitually resident in another contracting state.[406] Adoptions can only take place after the competent authorities in the child's state have established that the child is "adoptable", and those in the prospective adopters' state have established that they are eligible and suitable to adopt.[407] A child is only "adoptable" if adoption overseas is in his or her best interests,[408] the required informed consents have been given freely and without inducements and consideration has been given to the child's wishes and opinions.[409] The receiving state must also have determined that the child will be able to enter and reside there.[410] Contracting states must designate a central authority to discharge the duties under the Convention. These include promoting co-operation over intercountry adoption internally, providing information to other central authorities and the Permanent Bureau about the law in their country and eliminating obstacles to the operation of the Convention.[411] Central authorities may delegate to other public authorities or accredited bodies duties in respect of individual adoptions such as the collection and exchange of information about the child and the applicants and measures to prevent abuses of adoption practice.[412]

Despite the fact that "private" adoptions arranged without the involvement of an accredited agency have been regarded as more at risk of abuse,[413] the Hague Convention allows individual intermediaries to undertake some of the functions **22–049**

---

[404] Hague Convention art.1.
[405] W. Duncan, "The Hague Convention on protection of children and co-operation in respect of intercountry adoption its birth and prospects", in P. Selman, *Intercountry Adoption* pp.40, 46.
[406] Hague Convention art.2.
[407] Hague Convention arts 4 and 5.
[408] It is therefore hard to see how the US can continue to allow agencies to place American babies overseas when there are very many prospective adopters seeking babies there.
[409] Hague Convention art.4.
[410] Hague Convention art.5(c).
[411] Hague Convention arts 6 and 7.
[412] Hague Convention arts 8 and 9.
[413] UNICEF *Intercountry Adoption* (1998), p.8.

of central authorities where the domestic law of the country allows this.[414] However, an individual state can declare that it will not allow children habitually resident there to be adopted through such arrangements, and the formal reports on eligibility and adoptability remain the responsibility of central authorities or other official bodies.[415] These provisions represent a compromise between the American free-market approach and the more regulated approach operating in Europe and in some Asian sending countries.[416] It was thought that the United States would be unlikely to ratify the Convention if individuals, often lawyers, could not continue to arrange adoptions, and that a Convention that excluded the major receiving state would be ineffective.[417]

Prospective adopters must apply for intercountry adoption via the central authority in their State of habitual residence. The Convention applies even if the child to be adopted is related to the applicant.[418] A "homestudy" report must be prepared on the applicants, their background, reasons for adopting and the children for whom they are qualified to care. This is transmitted to the child's state where a comparable report is prepared on the child. This is forwarded to the central authority in the applicants' state together, with proof of the required consents. The Convention forbids any contact between the applicants and the child's parents or carer until after their consent has been given, the child's adoptability has been established and the applicants have been found eligible and suitable to adopt. This is intended to prevent abuses such as direct approaches to parents or orphanages by people wanting to adopt, and the opportunity for money to be offered or requested to facilitate an adoption.[419] The adoption can only progress if the prospective adopters accept the selected child and both central authorities agree.[420] The adoption order can either be made in the child's or the applicants' state. However, if the child enters the applicants' state before the adoption order is made and the placement breaks down, the central authority there must protect the child, consult with the central authority child's state of origin about alternative placements and, as a last resort, return the child to it.[421] An adoption made under the Convention is recognised in all other Convention

---

[414] Hague Convention art.22 functions under arts 15 to 21 can be delegated.

[415] Hague Convention art.22(1)(5). If there is no declaration, the state accepts private arrangements.

[416] Parra-Aranguren, *Report* paras 242, 373 *et seq.* Euradopt, an organisation of European adoption agencies has agreed a set of ethical rules that should apply to all adoptions: *http://www.euradopt.org* [Accessed June 5, 2008].

[417] W. Duncan, "Regulating intercountry adoption—an international perspective", in A. Bainham and D. Pearl (eds), *Frontiers of Family Law* (London: Chancery Lane, 1993); W. Duncan, "The Hague Convention on the protection and co-operation in respect of intercountry adoption" (1993) 3 *Adoption and Fostering* 7.

[418] Hague Conference, *Report of the Second Special Commission on the Practical Operation of the Hague Convention on Intercountry Adoption* (2005), paras 138–140.

[419] Hague Convention art.29; and see Parra-Aranguren, *Report*, paras 495 *et seq.* Some US intermediaries arrange adoptions during a woman's pregnancy, with prospective adopters paying for maternity care and attending the birth—a clear breach of Hague principles.

[420] Hague Convention arts 14–17.

[421] Hague Convention art.21. If the placement breaks down after adoption, the domestic law of the receiving state determines what should occur. In England and Wales, the child would become looked after by a local authority, and the adopters would be responsible for making a contribution to the cost: see para.21–068 above, and Children Act 1989 Sch.2 Pt 3.

countries. Recognition may only be refused if the adoption is "manifestly contrary to public policy, taking into account the welfare of the child".[422]

The Convention forbids "improper financial or other gain" from intercountry adoption activities, but reasonable costs and expenses are permitted.[423] However, the Special Commission in December 2000 noted excessive legal fees, particularly in some South American countries and where the lawyer also identified a child for adoption. The Commission recommended that information about costs should be provided in advance, and that agency accreditation should ensure financial controls. Some orphanages also sought donations, and there were suggestions that the highest donors obtained children. The Special Commission was divided between those who thought that donations should not be condoned and those who accepted that support for childcare services could be an acceptable part of the cost of providing adoption services. The Second Special Commission affirmed that donations by prospective adopters should not be sought, offered or made.[424]

It is too soon to judge whether the Convention will successfully regulate **22–050** intercountry adoption and improve practice. There are currently wide variations in practice; some states have large numbers of accredited agencies and operate few controls on them; in others arrangements are closely supervised by the central authority or a well-established agency. A large number of children are adopted from non-Convention countries. The fact that applicants remain willing to adopt from countries with poor standards creates "a market for children" in those states[425] and undermines the work of the Convention. Concerns about abuses in Guatemala led UNICEF to propose that Convention countries should suspend all intercountry adoptions from there, but there is no power in the Convention to do this. It now appears that Guatemala is interested in acceding to the Convention, although concerns remain about its ability to control exploitation of children, parents and adopters.[426] The Special Commission agreed that states should seek to apply the same safeguards in arrangements with non-Convention countries and encourage such states to join the Convention.[427] It may be that suspension of adoption is the only effective way of dealing with abuses in non-Convention countries; following such a suspension, Cambodia acceded to the Convention, but it is unclear whether practice there is now free from corruption.[428]

---

[422] Hague Convention art.24. This should be interpreted very restrictively Parra-Aranguren, *Report*, para.426. The adoption of a refugee child where no attempts have been made to trace the family who are subsequently located could be contrary to public policy: see *Report of the Special Commission on the Implementation of the Intercountry Adoption Convention* (October 1994) and *Re K (Adoption and Wardship)* [1997] 2 F.L.R. 221, FD and CA.

[423] Hague Convention art.32. Central authorities have responsibilities for preventing this: art.8.

[424] *Report of the Special Commission on the Practical Operation of the Hague Convention* (December 2000), paras 37–41; *Report of the Second Special Commission* (2005), para.125.

[425] *Report of the Special Commission on the Practical Operation of the Hague Convention* (December 2000), para.52.

[426] *Report of the Second Special Commission* (2005), paras 179–183; and see the information provided by the US State Department at *http://travel.state.gov/family/adoption/country/country_369.html* [Accessed June 5, 2008].

[427] *Report of the Second Special Commission* (2005), para.48–57.

[428] See *R. (Charlton Thomson) v Secretary of State for Education and Skills* [2006] 1 F.L.R. 175. A statutory power of suspension has been introduced: Children and Adoption Act 2006 Pt 2.

ii. Intercountry Adoption in England and Wales[429]

22–051 The Adoption (Intercountry Aspects) Act 1999 was passed to give effect to the Hague Convention in England, Wales and Scotland[430]; most of its provisions were incorporated into the Adoption and Children Act 2002.[431] Depending on the country of origin of the child, one of three separate regimes[432] applies to intercountry adoptions in the United Kingdom. But in all cases the same process, based on that operated for many years,[433] is used for determining the eligibility and suitability of the applicants and regulating entry to the country for or after adoption. These controls are backed by criminal sanctions. Only adoption agencies may make arrangements for adoption; a person who undertakes an assessment or arranges a placement commits an offence.[434] A person who brings a child to the United Kingdom without previously obtaining notification of approval from the Department of Children, Schools and Families also commits an offence.[435]

Intending adopters must be assessed and approved by a local authority or a voluntary adoption agency; "home studies" provided by independent social workers cannot be used.[436] Applicants are approved to adopt from a specific country; if they wish to adopt from elsewhere they must demonstrate that they fully understand the cultural and other needs of a child from that country and must obtain a new approval from the agency.[437] The process of approval involves counselling and assessment, referral to the agency's adoption panel for a recommendation and notification of the applicants. Where the applicants are approved, the agency notifies the Secretary of State who decides whether to endorse the application. Adoption specialists in the Department for Children, Schools and Families review the reports provided by the agency; if they are satisfied, a Certificate of Eligibility is issued and forwarded to the relevant body

---

[429] Adoption (Intercountry) Aspects Act 1999; Adoption and Children Act 2002 Ch.6; Adoption with a Foreign Element Regulations 2005 (SI 2005/392); DfES, *Guidance* (2005), Annex C; Children and Adoption Act 2006 Pt 2; *President's Adoption Guidance: Intercountry Adoption Supplement* (2003).

[430] Adoption (Intercountry) Aspects Act 1999 ss.1, 4, 5. The Convention was implemented on June 1, 2003. See Intercountry Adoption (Hague Convention) Regulations 2003 (SI 2003/118). In Northern Ireland, the Convention is implemented by the Adoption (Intercountry Aspects) Act Northern Ireland 2001.

[431] Adoption (Intercountry) Aspects Act 1999 ss.1, 2, 7 and Sch.1 (the text of the Convention) remain in force. This was originally a Private Member's Bill promoted by Mark Oaten M.P. following failure by successive governments to provide Parliamentary time to implement the Convention having announced its intention to do so in 1993; Cm.2288 (1993), para.6.29.

[432] Convention adoptions, designated country adoptions and non-Convention adoptions, discussed below.

[433] See DCSF, *Intercountry Adoption Procedures Leaflet*. This and other information about intercountry adoption is available at: *http://www.dfes.gov.uk/intercountryadoption/index.shtml* [Accessed June 5, 2008].

[434] Adoption and Children Act 2002 ss.92–94.

[435] Adoption and Children Act 2002 ss.83(7), (8), re-enacting Adoption Act 1976 s.56A. Local authorities are required to notify the police where they identify that the procedures have not been followed: DfES, *Guidance* (2005), Annex C, para.10.

[436] Adoption and Children Act 2002 s.94; Restriction on the Preparation of Adoption Reports Regulations 2005 (SI 2005/1711).

[437] Adoption Agencies Regulations 2005 (SI 2005/389) reg.25(6); Adoptions with a Foreign Element Regulations 2005 (SI 2005/392) reg.15(4); DfES, *Guidance* (2005), Ch.3 para.97; Annex C, para.46.

in the applicant's chosen country.[438] Judicial review is not available where the applicants are rejected by the Department acting on professional advice.[439]

There is no single process for finding a suitable child. Applicants may use the services of an overseas agency or an intermediary, and in some countries it remains possible to identify a child directly through an orphanage.[440] When a child has been matched with the applicants, the applicants are informed and must decide whether or not to accept. If they do, they must arrange to travel to the child's country and continue the process there. They must obtain entry clearance to bring the child to the United Kingdom. Before granting this, the immigration officer checks with the Department for Children, Schools and Families that the required procedures have been followed and either a recognised adoption order has been obtained or that it is likely that a court in England will grant the order.[441] Where the applicants have not obtained an order overseas that is effective in the United Kingdom, they must complete the process by adopting here. Even where an order has been obtained, some countries require further reports on the child's welfare.[442]

(1) Adoptions under the Hague Convention

The central authority for England is the Secretary of State for Children, Schools **22–052** and Families; communications can be sent to the DCSF in relation to any part of Great Britain.[443] Adoption societies whose approval covers intercountry adoption are accredited bodies, but local authorities, as public authorities with responsibility to provide adoption services, deal with the majority of cases.[444] Detailed provisions defining "Convention adoption orders" and setting out the conditions thath must be satisfied before such an order can be made are provided by regulations.[445] Where at least one of the adopters is a British citizen, a "Convention adoption"[446] gives the child British citizenship; there are no restrictions on the adopters bringing the child to the United Kingdom.[447] Similarly, prospective adopters may bring a child from a Convention country to the United Kingdom for adoption, providing that they have followed the required procedures in the United Kingdom and completed the necessary stages in the

---

[438] DCSF, *Intercountry Adoption Procedures Leaflet*; Adoptions with a Foreign Element Regulations 2005 (SI 2005/392) reg.15(4); DfES, *Guidance* (2005), Annex C paras 21–24.

[439] *R v Secretary of State for Health, Ex p. Luff* [1992] 1 F.L.R. 59, FD.

[440] There are restrictions on advertising adoption: s.123; Electronic Commerce Directive (Adoption and Children Act 2002) Regulations 2005 (SI 2005/3222), but it remains possible to find advertisements for children from, for example, US agencies.

[441] DCSF, *Intercountry Adoption Procedures Leaflet*; DfES, *Guidance* (2005), Annex C, paras 42–45.

[442] DfES, *Guidance* (2005), Annex C, paras 64–66.

[443] Adoption (Intercountry Aspects) Act 1999 s.2(1), (2). In Wales, the National Assembly for Wales performs these functions, and in Scotland, the Secretary of State within the Scottish Executive.

[444] Adoption (Intercountry Aspects) Act 1999 s.2(3), (4); Adoption and Children Act 2002 ss.2(8), 3.

[445] Adoptions with a Foreign Element Regulations 2005 (SI 2005/392).

[446] i.e. an adoption made in a Convention country outside the British Islands.

[447] British Nationality Act 1981 s.1, as amended by Adoption (Intercountry Aspects) Act 1999 s.7.

child's home state. The High Court has power to annul adoptions made under the Convention that are contrary to public policy.[448]

(2) Designated country adoptions

22–053 Where a child is adopted overseas in a country listed in the Adoption (Designation of Overseas Adoptions) Order 1973,[449] the order is recognised as an adoption order in the United Kingdom.[450] so long as it is valid in the country where it was made.[451] The applicants do not need to re-adopt the child but must have complied with the formal procedures set out in regulations, unless the adoption was completed more than six months before entry to the United Kingdom.[452] The adoption can be included in the Adopted Children Register.[453]

(3) Other intercountry adoptions

22–054 Where the child has not been adopted in either a Convention or designated country, an adoption order must be obtained from a court in the United Kingdom. The applicants must notify their local authority of their intention to adopt within 14 days of entering the United Kingdom[454]; until the notification is made, the child is a private foster child.[455] The local authority must investigate and prepare a report for the court.[456] No application can be made until the child has had their home with the applicants for the required period,[457] and the order can only be made if the court is satisfied that the local authority has had sufficient opportunities to see the child with the applicants.[458] These provisions are intended to ensure local authorities are aware of children brought in for adoption.

[448] Adoption and Children Act 2002 s.89(1) implementing art.24, above. Similarly, a Convention adoption can be annulled by the state that made it: s.91.

[449] SI 1973/19. Designated countries include many but not all Commonwealth Countries, members of the EU and some other European countries, the US and China. Inclusion in the list does not indicate that the country applies similar standards to those in the UK or that there is a bilateral agreement with the UK relating to intercountry adoption. Although promises have been made to revise the list, action has not yet been taken: Adoption and Children Bill 2002 EN para.10. Countries will only appear in the new list if their adoption practices meet specific requirements; Jacqui Smith, *Hansard Commons*, Vol.386, col.25 (May 20, 2002) (Adoption and Children Bill, Report Stage).

[450] The adoption is an "overseas adoption": Adoption and Children Act 2002 s.87(1), (2)(b).

[451] In *Flintshire CC v K* [2001] 2 F.L.R. 476, FD, the order was defective because the parties did not satisfy the residence requirements to allow jurisdiction in Arkansas, a state chosen for the proceedings because of its lax adoption rules.

[452] Adoption and Children Act 2002 s.83(1)(b), (3).

[453] Children can then be provided with a UK adoption certificate so that he or she does not need to rely on foreign documents to establish their status: see Adopted Children and Adoption Contact Registers Regulations 2005 (SI 2005/924) and DfES, *Guidance* (2005), Ch.12.

[454] Adoptions with a Foreign Element Regulations 2005 (SI 2005/392) reg.4(4). It is an offence to fail to do so: s.83(7).

[455] Children Act 1989 Pt IX.

[456] Adoption and Children Act 2002 s.44(5).

[457] Adoption and Children Act 2002 s.42(5); s.81(6) provides that requirements in Ch.3 of the Act may be modified for overseas adoptions. Where s.83(4) and (5) have been complied with, the probationary period is reduced to six months; in other cases it is 12 months: Adoptions with a Foreign Element Regulations 2005 (SI 2005/392) reg.9.

[458] Adoption and Children Act 2002 s.42(7).

Prior to their introduction, the courts could be faced with applications from unsuitable people with established relationships with the child so that there was no alternative to granting an adoption order.[459]

(4) Adoption overseas of UK-resident children[460]

As a consequence of concerns about the effects of the child migration programme,[461] adoption overseas is rarely considered appropriate for children in the United Kingdom and is subject to considerable safeguards. Such adoptions may be arranged with relatives overseas or where carers, temporarily resident in the United Kingdom, return overseas. Children may not be removed from the United Kingdom for adoption overseas except by parents, stepparents or relatives unless an order has been obtained granting the applicant parental responsibility.[462] Removing a child contrary to these provisions is an offence.

22–055

E. "In family" adoptions

Although never intended to re-order legal relationships within families, adoption orders have been used for this purpose since 1927. Some parents, stepparents, grandparents and other relatives have felt that the status of adoption provides advantages for them and their child relatives. At different times these adoptions have been favoured with less regulation or have been discouraged with increased controls. Alternative orders[463] were made available in the 1970s but were not popular; the majority of relative-carers look after children without formal arrangements, but approximately 500 stepparents obtained adoption orders in 2005.[464]

22–056

i. Adoption by a parent

In the 1950s when the stigma of illegitimacy was great, unmarried mothers were advised to adopt their own children in order to conceal the illegitimacy, improve the child's status and prevent the father interfering.[465] Adoption orders to

22–057

---

[459] "Except in the very unusual case where there is a claim for the return of the child by the natural family, in all reported cases welfare considerations have led the court to [grant the order]", *per* Johnson J. *Re C (Adoption: Legality)* [1999] 1 F.L.R. 370, 382; see also *Re R (No.1) (Intercountry Adoption)* [1999] 1 F.L.R. 1014, FD; *Re AW (Adoption Application)* [1993] 1 F.L.R. 62.

[460] The provisions also apply to Commonwealth citizens present in the UK. Such children may be in the UK because of the historic links between the countries, and children may need the same protection as those habitually resident here.

[461] See above, para.21–079.

[462] Adoption and Children Act 2002 ss.84, 85; Adoptions with a Foreign Element Regulations 2005 (SI 2005/392), Ch.2; DfES, *Guidance* (2005), Annex C. The order must be made by the High Court under s.84; *Re A (Adoption: Placement Outside Jurisdiction)* [2004] 2 F.L.R 337, CA; *Greenwich LBC v S* [2007] 2 F.L.R. 154

[463] Joint custody and custodianship introduced by the Children Act 1975, replaced by residence orders by the Children Act 1989 and supplemented special guardianship orders in Adoption and Children Act 2002 s.115.

[464] ONS, FM2 (2004), Table 6.3; a much larger number (850) is shown in *Judicial Statistics 2005*, Table 5.4.

[465] M. Kornitzer, *Child Adoption in the Modern World* (London: Putnam, 1952), pp.56, 319; M. Kornitzer, *Child Adoption* (London: Putnam, 1959), p.111.

unmarried mothers were anomalous since they did not end the father's obligation to support the child.[466] Although these parental adoptions were rare, the Houghton Committee recommended that they should be made only in exceptional circumstances and should end the father's obligation to maintain.[467] Provisions to this effect were introduced in the Children Act 1975 and have been repeated in subsequent legislation.[468] This use of adoption remains controversial:

> In *Re B (Adoption: Natural Parent)*[469] the mother requested that social services place her child for adoption, saying that the father was overseas. By chance, the father's whereabouts were known by the social worker; he was contacted and he offered to care for the child. The mother agreed to this arrangement and only expressed a slight reservation when he applied to adopt the child. The application was transferred to the High Court and the Official Solicitor was appointed. He opposed the application on the basis that it only served to end the mother's relationship with the child and did not therefore safeguard the child's welfare. The order was made; the mother's rejection of the child at birth justified making the order.[470] The Court of Appeal allowed the appeal by the Official Solicitor. Hale L.J. stated that only some reason such as death, disappearance or anonymous sperm donation could justify adoption by one parent. Ending in law, the mother-child relationship was a disproportionate response to the child's needs and contrary the child's art.8 rights.[471] A residence order was granted, the father was given unfettered powers to take the child abroad and the mother was barred from making any applications without leave. The father appealed. The House of Lords restored the adoption order on the basis that the Court of Appeal had exceeded its power to review the judge's discretion. It rejected the narrow interpretation of the circumstances in which adoption could be granted to a parent and, with less than convincing reasoning, held that an order that was in the child's best interests could not breach the child's rights.[472]

---

[466] Adoption Act 1958 s.15.

[467] Cmnd.5107, (1972) para.102; in 1970 there were 84 orders in favour of mothers and 11 in favour of fathers (App.B). Only 13 orders were made in 1978: *First Report to Parliament on the Children Act 1975* (HC 268)1979–80)), para.27.

[468] Adoption and Children Act 2002 s.51(4). The court must record the reason for granting the order.

[469] [2002] 1 F.L.R. 196, HL reversing [2001] 1 F.L.R. 589, CA and upholding the order made in *B v P (Adoption by Unmarried Father)* [2000] 2 F.L.R. 717, FD; see also Harris-Short [2002] C.F.L.Q. 325.

[470] [2000] 2 F.L.R. 721H, *per* Bracewell J.

[471] [2001] 1 F.L.R. 589 at paras 34–40. This assumes that "family life" exists between both a mother who has rejected the child at birth and her child, a point accepted by the House of Lords: [2002] 1 F.L.R. 196 at para.30, and see above, para.22–034.

[472] [2002] 1 F.L.R. 196 at paras 17–19, 23 and 31. The child's welfare was not paramount under the Adoption Act 1976; even if it were a marginal improvement in welfare, it would not necessarily justify a lifelong change of status, the effects of which could not possibly be determined when the order was made.

Such an adoption order in favour of a parent has no effect on the child's entitlement to property, which depends on a relationship with that parent.[473]

ii. Adoption by parent and stepparent

Stepparent adoptions are far more common,[474] but only a tiny minority of step- **22–058** families use adoption (or any other order) to regularise their position. Adoption orders in favour of a parent and stepparent are subject to most of the requirements that apply to other adoptions,[475] and have the same effect as other adoption orders. The child is legally integrated into the new family, cutting the links with the natural family. The birth parent and stepparent become the child's legal adoptive parents; the original birth certificate is replaced with an adoption certificate and, if the applicants are mother and step-father (as is most common),[476] the child's surname is usually changed. The Houghton Committee considered that such adoptions were inappropriate and could be damaging because they destroyed beneficial links with the non-adopting parent and could be used to conceal the child's past.[477] There was only very limited anecdotal evidence for this view,[478] which ignored the fact that many of the children had no contact with their other parent. Following recommendations by the Committee, the Children Act 1975 provided alternative orders—joint custody or custodianship—and required the court to make these where they were better than adoption.[479] This led to an immediate fall in stepparent adoption applications, even where no alternative was available, and a sharp increase in unsuccessful applications.[480] There were wide variations in the success rates in different courts; judges and social workers were uncertain when adoption was appropriate.[481] The Children Act 1989 repealed the specific restriction introduced in the 1975 Act; residence orders replaced joint custody and custodianship and were available to all stepparents. Following the general provision in the Children Act 1989, the 2002 Act s.1(6) requires the court to be satisfied that the order it makes is better than any alternative order or making no order at all.

Despite changes in law and practice emphasising the enduring nature of parenthood,[482] the *Review of Adoption Law* considered that it was inappropriate

---

[473] Adoption and Children Act 2002 s.67(4).

[474] 1,500 orders, just over a third of adoptions were in favour of a parent and stepparent in 2001, but there were over 14,000 orders in 1975: see Masson et al., *Mine*, p.12.

[475] The age limit for the child's parent (but not stepparent) is 18: Adoption and Children Act 2002 s.50(2)(a); the probationary period is six months: s.42(3).

[476] 96% of applications were made by mothers and step-fathers in the largest study of these adoptions: see Masson et al. *Mine*, p.46.

[477] Cmnd.5107 (1972), para.105. For a discussion of different approaches to stepparent adoption, see J. Masson, "Step-parent adoption", in P. Bean (ed.), *Adoption* (London: Tavistock, 1984).

[478] The report of the Association of Child Care Officers, *Adoption: The Way Ahead* (1969) and I. Goodacre, *Adoption Policy and Practice* (1966) were relied on by the Committee.

[479] Cmnd.5107 (1972), paras 106–110; ss.10(3) and 37(1); these sections were implemented on November 26, 1976 and December 1, 1985 respectively.

[480] Masson et al. *Mine*, Tables 7.5 and 7.6.

[481] See *Re S (Infants) (Adoption by Parent)* [1977] Fam. 173; *Re D (Adoption by Step Parent)* [1980] 2 F.L.R. 102. For a discussion of the judicial approaches in the case law, see J. Priest, "Step-parent adoptions: what is the law?" [1982] J.S.W.L. 285 and R.W. Rawlings, "Law reform with tears" (1982) 45 M.L.R. 637.

[482] Children Act 1989 ss.2, 3 and 33; Child Support Act 1991.

to prevent stepparent adoption. This could be a suitable arrangement where a child had no relationship with one side of his or her family. However, it was anomalous to require a birth parent to adopt their own children in order for their spouse to adopt, so a new form of adoption order needed to be provided.[483] The Adoption and Children Act 2002 enables the partner of the parent to adopt the child alone.[484] Where such an order is made, the stepparent becomes a legal parent but their spouse retains their status and relationship with the child.[485] The Act thus allows co-parenting arrangements between a parent and their gay, lesbian or heterosexual partner to be formalised through adoption and without changing the status of the birth parent. This form of order exists alongside the traditional form of stepparent adoption, and although the court can grant alternative orders under the Children Act, it is not clear that it can grant an adoption order in favour of only one of joint applicants. Couples seeking to create a legal relationship between a child and the parent's partner should be advised that only the partner need apply for adoption.[486]

22–059   The *Review of Adoption Law* also acknowledged that adoption might be inappropriate where the stepparent had little interest in the child or because adoption could undermine relationships with the extended family. It proposed a simpler alternative to discourage adoption applications.[487] Married stepparents should be able to share parental responsibility by an agreement with both natural parents, registered with the court, or under a court order. The Adoption and Children Act 2002 makes provision for this[488] and the Civil Partnership Act 2004 gives civil partners identical rights.[489]

The court is now provided with a confusing array of orders with quite similar effect in law but that may be viewed very differently by the applicants.[490] When hearing an adoption application, the court must consider the whole range of its powers and may make a residence order or special guardianship order (but not grant parental responsibility under s.4A), even though no application has been made.[491] The child's welfare is paramount, but the court will need to consider the impact of the order on the other parent, and the effect of granting an irrevocable adoption order to a stepparent whose relationship with the parent may break down, because these matters necessarily impact on the child's welfare. Both granting and refusing an order in favour of a stepparent may interfere with rights

---

[483] *Review of Adoption Law* (1992), paras 19.2–3.
[484] Adoption and Children Act 2002 s.52(2). Adoption is only available to one of the parents, and in practice this must be the parent with care: s.42(7).
[485] Adoption and Children Act 2002 s.67(2)(b).
[486] No explanation was given as to why both forms of stepparent adoption were thought desirable. The comparable provisions in the Adoption and Children (Scotland) Act 2007 ss.29, 30 only permits adoption by the parent's partner.
[487] *Review of Adoption Law* (1992), paras 19.2–19.3; Cm.2288 (1993), para.5.20.
[488] Adoption and Children Act 2002 s.112, adding Children Act 1989 s.4A.
[489] Civil Partnership Act 2004 s.75. The Government's original proposal, set out in a letter to Peers in June 2002, would have allowed s.4A agreements in favour of heterosexual partners, but required a court order for a same-sex partner.
[490] Applicants may not be satisfied if they are given a different order from that which they sought; adoption has emotional connotations derived from its established position in society: substitute orders have so far not been able to match this.
[491] Adoption and Children Act 2002 s.1(6); Children Act 1989 ss.4A(1)(b), 8(3), 10(1), 14A(6)(b).

to family life. The stepparent may have a relationship with the child that ought to be recognised, even though doing so will end a parent's legal relationship.[492] It is comparatively unusual for orders to be made, particularly where a parent, with parental responsibility objects, but there are cases where the child's need for security, the child's wish to be adopted, the strength of the relationship with the stepparent and the lack of positive involvement from the other natural parent justify adoption.[493] However, these adoptions are given thorough consideration.[494] Applicants may be counselled against seeking adoption,[495] and applications that undermine valuable relationships or do not include all the children are likely to be refused.[496]

iii. Adoption by grandparents or other relatives
Grandparents, aunts, uncles and other relatives[497] may also seek to adopt a child. **22–060** In most cases this will be the result of informal arrangements made in the family; local authorities do place children with relatives, these arrangements rarely lead to adoption[498] but there is no presumption in favour of special guardianship.[499] The Houghton Committee opposed adoption by relatives because of the possibility of distortion of family relationships (e.g. adoption by grandparents would turn the child's mother into a sister).[500] Custodianship was made available, but the Children Act 1989 replaced this with the residence order. The *Review of Adoption Law* did not want to rule out adoption by relatives, but considered that there were few situations where it provided clear advantages or that a residence order was inadequate.[501] The Adoption and Children Act 2002 requires adoption to be the better option[502] and applies the same restrictions to non-agency applications by relatives as apply to strangers. Relatives must have cared for the child for at least three of the previous five years or have the leave of the court before making an application.[503] They are required to notify the local authority and are subject to investigation.[504] The alternative of a residence order is

---

[492] *Soderback v Sweden* [1999] 1 F.L.R. 250; *Eski v Austria* [2007] 1 F.L.R. 1650.
[493] *Re B (Adoption: Father's Objection)* [1999] 2 F.L.R. 215, CA, *per* Butler-Sloss L.J. (order granted and appeal refused; father had twice kidnapped his son and been involved in over 140 court applications in respect of him). And see *Re PJ (Adoption: Practice on Appeal)* [1998] 2 F.L.R. 252, CA, where the violent father's appeal against dispensing with his consent was allowed, but the Court of Appeal exercising its own (pragmatic) discretion allowed the orders to stand.
[494] This was not the case in the past, and is not always expected by applicants; see Masson et al. *Mine.*
[495] DHSS Circular LAC84(10), para.60.
[496] *Re P (Minors) (Adoption)* [1989] 1 F.L.R. 1, CA.
[497] Adoption and Children Act 2002 s.144; great-uncles and great-aunts are not relatives; *Re C (minors) (wardship: adoption)* [1989] 1 F.L.R. 222.
[498] M. Murch et al., *Pathways to Adoption* (London: HMSO, 1993), p.11; only 7% of the sample of applications were by relatives; 80% of these resulted in orders: p.20.
[499] *Re A-J (Adoption or Special Guardianship)* [2007] 1 F.L.R. 507, CA.
[500] Cmnd.5107 (1973), para.111.
[501] *Review of Adoption Law* (1992), paras 6.3, 20.1–20.4.
[502] Adoption and Children Act 2002 s.1(6).
[503] Adoption and Children Act 2002 s.42(5), (6). Similar restrictions apply to applications for special-guardianship orders by those without a residence order: Children Act 1989 s.14A(5).
[504] Adoption and Children Act 2002 s.44(2)–(5).

available without satisfying these conditions, but applicants may need the leave of the court.[505]

The *Prime Minister's Review* also identified special guardianship as better than adoption for some children being cared for by their wider birth family.[506] Relatives will be able to strengthen their legal position by obtaining a special guardianship order if they already have a residence order, have cared for the child for three years or have the consent of everyone with parental responsibility.[507] The court may grant a residence order or a special guardianship order when considering an adoption application, and must give paramount consideration to the child's welfare throughout the child's life when choosing between these.[508] The determining factor could be the legal effects adoption has in adulthood:

> In *Re W (A Minor) (Adoption: Custodianship: Access)*[509] the Court of Appeal upheld a decision to dispense with the agreement of a mentally handicapped mother to the adoption of her child by her parents, although contact between the mother and child was continuing. The grandparents had cared for the child since birth. The mother's limited ability and lack of relationship with the child justified an order to secure the child's care. Adoption was more appropriate because it enabled the grandparents to appoint a testamentary guardian. However, this could now be achieved by special guardianship.[510]

Another factor could be the need to protect the child and carer from interference by the parent:

> In *Re A-J (Adoption Order or Special Guardianship Order)*[511] the child was removed when aged six months because of domestic violence and the father's significant criminality including drugs and firearms offences. He was placed with his paternal aunt and uncle as long-term foster parents. Later, the care plan was revised to adoption. The aunt favoured continuation of the care order so that the local authority would be responsible for liaison with the parents, who were unpredictable and aggressive. However, the judge rejected this and special guardianship and dispensed with the parents' agreement to adoption. Their appeal, arguing that this was a case for special guardianship, was dismissed. The child's need for security would not be met by special guardianship, even with additional restrictions on further applications by the parents.

---

[505] Children Act 1989 ss.9(3), 10(5). The court is to be given power to direct that the order lasts until the child is aged 18: Adoption and Children Act s.114, adding Children Act 1989 s.12(5)(6). There is no provision for inter vivos guardianship as proposed by Cm.2288 (1993), paras 5.4, 5.23–5.24.
[506] PIU, *Review* (2000), para.5.8. For an explanation of special guardianship, see para.17–046, above.
[507] Children Act 1989 s.14A(5)(b), (c).
[508] Children Act 1989 ss.10(1), 14A(6); Adoption and Children Act 2002 s.1(2)(6).
[509] [1988] 1 F.L.R. 175, CA.
[510] Children Act 1989 s.14G(4)(b), amending Children Act 1989 s.5(4).
[511] [2007] 1 F.L.R. 507, CA.

The Court of Appeal has acknowledged that parents and children are capable of "penetrating legal forms and retaining hold of the reality",[512] so the issue becomes which order will best meet the child's welfare. The carers' views are likely to be very important because the child's wellbeing will be dependent on theirs.

F. Open adoption

Adoption has traditionally been a closed and secretive process[513] in which birth **22–061** parents and adoptive parents are unaware of each other's identities, and the child's adoptive status is concealed from all but the child and the adoptive family.[514] Adoption law originally gave birth parents access to the identity of the adopters, but professional practices and legislation reinforced the closed nature of adoption.[515] In the 1970s there was increased recognition of the adopted person's need for information about their background in order to form a positive self-identity.[516] Later studies revealed the desire and need of those who had relinquished children for adoption to know that their child was placed successfully.[517] Adoption agencies began to develop more open-adoption practices; despite the lack of evidence of benefits to children,[518] it is now accepted that adoption plans should include arrangements for involving parents with adoption plans and maintaining the child's heritage.[519]

Openness can take many different forms, including greater involvement of the birth parents in the plan of adoption and selection of adoptive parents; indirect contact involving the passing of information after adoption between adults, with the adoption agency acting as a "letter box"; or direct contact between the child and natural parents or other relatives.[520] Arrangements in an individual case may become more or less open as time passes.[521] It has been suggested that where contact has survived the original care order, it is likely to survive into

---

[512] *Re S (Adoption Order of Special Guardianship Order)* [2007] 1 F.L.R. 819, *per* Wall L.J. at para.52.

[513] *Review of Adoption Law* (1992), para.4.1.

[514] The arrangements for court proceedings and for registration of adoption facilitate this.

[515] M. Ryburn, "Secrecy and openness in adoption—an historical perspective" (1995) 29 *Social Policy and Administration* 150; S. Cretney, *Family Law in the Twentieth Century* (2003) Ch.17.

[516] Following the publication of J. Triseliotis, *In Search of Origins* (1973) and the introduction of access to birth records; see above, para.22–011.

[517] Howe et al. *Half a Million Women*; D. Howe and J. Feast, *Adoption, Search and Reunion* (2000). These ideas have been accepted in the 2002 Act, with provision for intermediaries to assist parents to make contact with their adult birth children: s.98.

[518] A. Rushton, *Knowledge Review—The Adoption of Looked After Children* (SCIE, 2003), Ch.6; see also E. Neil and D. Howe, *Contact in Adoption and Permanent Foster Care* (BAAF, 2004).

[519] Adoption Standards (2003), Standards 7 and 8.

[520] *Review of Adoption Law* (1992), para.4.2; for details of the range of policies and practices, see SSI, *Moving Goalposts* (1995). Contact with maternal relatives is far more common than with paternal relatives: E. Neil, "The reasons why young children are placed for adoption" (2000) Child and Fam. Soc. Wk. 303, 314.

[521] *Review of Adoption Law* (1992), para.5.3 suggests that contact may diminish, but others have suggested that it is likely to develop as trust develops between the adopters and the birth parents: see E. Neil [2003] 2 *Adoption and Fostering* 32. The continuation of letterbox contact requires support: E. Brocklesby [2007] 2 *Seen and Heard* 12.

adoption.[522] At least 70 per cent of adopted children have some form of contact with their birth families.[523]

Openness is said to have the following advantages: it may facilitate better arrangements for the child's care, reduce the sense of rejection the adopted child feels, ensure the adopters and the child have more information about the child's background and encourages the birth family to support the adoption plan.[524] There is research evidence that some adopters feel their relationships with their adoptive children benefit from contact with birth relatives, but others feel their position is undermined.[525] Adopted children have indicated that they would like more contact with their families[526] but there is concern that contact is imposed to placate the birth parents, irrespective of the child's welfare,[527] that placements will be destabilised[528] and that prospective adopters will withdraw if they are expected to maintain contact.

22–062   Before making an adoption order, the court must consider contact arrangements and hear the views of all parties.[529] Unless children are represented in the adoption proceedings, the court may remain unaware of the importance of contact to them.[530] Where the effect of adoption is to terminate relationships with siblings, the court will need to be satisfied that formal arrangements for contact are not required to protect each child's art.8 rights.

Contact cannot be bargained for parental consent.[531] Although it is possible for the courts to make a s.8 contact order when making an adoption order,[532] they are extremely reluctant to do so. Where the adopters agree to contact, an order is regarded as unnecessary.[533] Where they do not, the imposition of contact is viewed as incompatible with adopters' complete parental responsibility.[534]

---

[522] M. Richards [1994] 4 *Adoption and Fostering* 5 at 6; In Ryburn's study of contested adoptions, nearly half had some ongoing contact: M. Ryburn (ed.), *Contested Adoption* (Aldershot: Arena, 1994), p.141; M. Ryburn [1994] 4 *Adoption and Fostering* 30. In Neil's study, contact was less common where children had been relinquished as babies: see (2000) Child and Fam. Soc. Wk. 303, 311.

[523] Unpublished research cited in DH, *Providing Effective Adoption Consultation Paper* (2002), p.15; see also Parker *Adoption Now*, p.47.

[524] *Review of Adoption Law* (1992), para.4.4. Lowe et al. *Supporting Adoption* p.324 also note that contact can help children to settle and allay their anxieties about the wellbeing of birth relatives.

[525] Thoburn *Success and Failure*, pp.85, 89; M. Ryburn, *Open adoption* (1994); Lowe et al. *Supporting Adoption* p.281. Lowe et al. suggest various conditions before adopters feel comfortable with contact and see the benefits for their children: birth relatives must approve of the adoption; adopters must accept that the child may need to see birth relatives; all parties must feel secure about the adoption and the adopters need to communicate pro contact attitudes to their children: p.324.

[526] C. Thomas et al., *Adopted Children Speaking* (1999), Ch.8.

[527] Lowe et al. (1999) p.313.

[528] SSI, *Moving Goalposts* (1995), p.28; for a case example of action to support the adoptive parents, see *Re O (contempt: committal)* [1995] 2 F.L.R. 767.

[529] Adoption and Children Act 2002 s.46(6). Courts need to consider both the potential advantages and the risks of contact.

[530] If children are not parties, the CAFCASS Children and Family Reporter reports on matters relating to welfare: see SI 2005/2795 rr.73 and 74; CAFCASS, *Guidance for Adoption Proceedings* (2007).

[531] Consent must be unconditional: s.52(5), and above para.22–029, but parents may feel more able to support adoption knowing that some contact will continue.

[532] For the position when a placement order is made, see above para.22–043.

[533] *Re T (Adoption: Contact)* [1995] 2 F.L.R. 251, CA.

[534] *Re C (Adoption: Conditions)* [1989] A.C. 1; adopters should be in the "driving seat": *Re T (Adoption: Contact)* [1995] 2 F.L.R. 251, CA at p.253, *per* Butler-Sloss L.J. The approach is quite

Agencies are encouraged to negotiate written agreements about contact between parents or relatives and prospective adopters, and to clarify their role in providing support for these.[535] These arrangements are not enforceable. Also, it is unclear that children's interests in maintaining contact with relatives, particularly siblings placed separately, are protected in such arrangements.

Applications for contact after adoption require leave and the court will only grant this where the adopters' decision is sufficiently contrary to the child's welfare or is unreasonable to justify overriding their discretion.[536] An appeal against refusal of leave was allowed where the adopters reneged on their agreement to provide an annual report to the adopted children's adult half-sister,[537] but leave was refused for an application on behalf of a nine-year-old adopted girl who wanted contact with her half-brother who was adopted into a different family.[538]

VI. Orders in Adoption Proceedings

A court hearing an adoption application must always consider the whole range of **22–063** powers available to it under the Adoption and Children Act 2002 and the Children Act 1989. It must not make an order unless this would be better for the child than not doing so[539] but may make s.8 orders or special guardianship orders without an application.[540] Three major decisions are involved: (1) whether to order adoption, special guardianship or residence or make no order at all; (2) whether or not to make orders for contact; and (3) whether to impose any other conditions on the adoption. These decisions must all be made giving paramount consideration to the child's welfare,[541] and in the case of a decision relating to the adoption of a child, this means welfare "throughout [the child's] life"[542] and includes (inter alia) the likely effect of ceasing to be a member of the original family and being an adopted person.[543]

The judge or magistrates considering the application will have reports from the agency or local authority[544] and may have the assistance of a CAFCASS officer.[545] They may also have evidence from the applicants, the birth parents,

different where birth parents separate: see CASC, *Making Contact Work* (2002); above para.18–056.

[535] Baroness Andrews, *Hansard Lords*, Vol.639, col.669 (Adoption and Children Bill, Report Stage) (October 15, 2002).

[536] *Re S (Contact: Application by Sibling)* [1998] 2 F.L.R. 897, FD.

[537] *Re T (Adopted Children: Contact)* [1995] 2 F.L.R. 792, CA. Applications for leave after adoption should be designed to ensure that the adopters are not disturbed: *per* Balcombe L.J. at pp.798–799; *Re E (Adopted Child: Contact Leave)* [1995] 1 F.L.R. 57, leave refused where a social worker had promised the birth parents a photograph of their child.

[538] *Re S (Contact: Application by Sibling)* [1998] 2 F.L.R. 897, FD.

[539] Adoption and Children Act 2002 subs.(6); Children Act 1989 s.1(5) and above, para.18–005.

[540] Children Act 1989 ss.10(1)(b), 14A(6)(b). A stepparent can get parental responsibility in this manner without an application, but an order under s.4A requires an application.

[541] Children Act 1989 s.1(1); Adoption and Children Act 2002 s.1(2), (7), and above, Ch.19.

[542] Adoption and Children Act 2002 s.1(2) and above, para.22–024.

[543] Adoption and Children Act 2002 s.1(4)(c).

[544] FPR 2005, r.29; These are known as Annex A reports.

[545] Either a children's guardian or a children and family reporter: s.102; SI 2005/2795 rr.59, 73.

relatives and, if they have been made parties, the children.[546] It is intended that most issues surrounding adoption are resolved before the final adoption hearing,[547] but this depends on the courts' approach to making alternative orders.

A. Adoption, special guardianship or residence?

22–064   It is important to recognise that there is more than one way of securing legal permanence,[548] and that special guardianship or residence, supported by other orders as required, may be more appropriate than adoption.[549] Special guardianship has been introduced with the intention of providing more security than long-term fostering but without the absolute legal severance from the birth family that occurs with adoption, and of providing a clear framework for support from the local authority.[550] It is likely to replace the residence order (but not adoption[551]) as a mechanism for providing permanency for children placed with relative-carers by local authorities.[552]

There are major differences between the effects of these orders. Adoption ends the child's legal relationship with the birth family and the status of the parents, and enables his or her full legal integration into the new family, with lifelong effect, giving a new and irrevocable status that affects citizenship and inheritance rights. Special guardians may appear very like parents during childhood; they can make almost all decisions about the child's upbringing and may be permitted to change the child's name,[553] but their power is limited in some respects.[554] Special guardianship does not change the child's status nor give inheritance rights, but provision for this may be made by will. There is considerable legal security for the arrangement; parents, children and some others can only apply for revocation of the order with the leave of the court,[555] and parents also require leave to seek a residence order during special guardianship.[556] The position of non-parents

---

[546] The parents must be notified of the proceedings: s.141(3), (4); SI 2005/2795 rr.32, 36, but unless the court requires, the person need not attend.

[547] Baroness Scotland, *Hansard Lords*, Vol.639 col.1345 (Adoption and Children Bill, Report Stage) (October 23, 2002).

[548] *Re B (Adoption Order)* [2001] 2 F.L.R. 26, 31, *per* Hale L.J. But in *Re O (Transracial Adoption)* [1995] 2 F.L.R. 597, at 607–608, Thorpe J. considered that the advice of the guardian that security could be achieved by residence was "inherently fallacious".

[549] See *Re A-J (Adoption Order or Special Guardianship Order)* [2007] 1 F.L.R. 507, CA; *Re M-J (Adoption Order or Special Guardianship Order)* [2007] 1 F.L.R 691, CA; *Re S (Adoption Order or Special Guardianship Order)* [2007] 1 F.L.R 819, CA and Selwyn and Quinton [2004] 2 *Adoption and Fostering* 6.

[550] DfES, *Special Guardianship Guidance* (2005), paras 4. 19.

[551] *Re A-J (Adoption Order or Special Guardianship Order)* [2007] 1 F.L.R. 507, CA, *per* Wall L.J. at para.44.

[552] The number of care orders appears to be declining: J. Masson et al., *Care Profiling Study* (2008). In 2006–7, 740 children left care under special guardianship orders, 490 in favour of former foster-carers and 1000 left under residence orders: ONS, SFR 27/2007, Table D1.

[553] But permission will not necessarily be granted: *Re L* [2007] EWCA Civ 196.

[554] For example they require consent of those with parental responsibility for a name change or to remove the child from the UK for more than three months: s.14C(3), added by Adoption and Children Act 2002 s.115.

[555] Children Act 1989 s.14D added by Adoption and Children Act 2002 s.115.

[556] Children Act 1989 s.10(7A), added by Adoption and Children Act 2002 Sch.3, para.56(d).

with residence orders is more limited,[557] but the court can direct that the order lasts until the child reaches age 18, and if it does so, the order cannot be varied or discharged without leave.[558] In either case, parents may continue to apply for contact, prohibited steps and specific issue orders without leave, unless the court has imposed restrictions under s.91(14).[559] Overall, those who obtain only special guardianship or residence orders have a more limited legal relationship with the child and less protection against further court proceedings by the parents than those who adopt. There are also differences in the regimes for support from the local authority, and each of these places far less responsibility on the local authority than it would have if the child remained subject to a care order with the child looked after by a foster carer.[560] Adopters have rights to assessment for post-adoption services, including financial support, but no rights to specific services.[561] There are similar provisions relating to special guardianship.[562] However, where there is only a residence order, the carers have no rights to be assessed for support services and can only seek family support under Children Act 1989 Pt III.[563] Local authorities may provide financial support where foster-carers obtain residence orders, but there is no statutory scheme; payments are discretionary and low.[564]

The choice between adoption and special guardianship involves balancing the **22–065** advantages and disadvantages of each for the child's welfare, and this may turn on the attitudes of the parties to each other and to each order. This is essentially a matter of judicial discretion; conclusions reached through hearing the parties will be difficult to challenge[565]:

> In *Re S*[566] the parents' relationship was marked by domestic violence and substance misuse. Care proceedings were begun when the child was three years old. Attempts at rehabilitation and family placement failed, and the child returned to the foster carer who had looked after her when she was first removed. The local authority planned adoption and the carer applied to be a party in the freeing proceedings and sought a residence order. There were further applications; particularly, the mother sought discharge of the care order and for contact and the carer applied to adopt. After hearing evidence from a child psychologist, the judge concluded that the child should remain with the applicant because the mother could not provide the quality of care

[557] See above, paras 17–044 and 18–016. The main difference is the length of time the child can be taken outside the UK without consent of those with parental responsibility or the court.
[558] Children Act 1989 s.12(5)(6). There is no restriction on applications for residence orders comparable to those applying where there is a special guardianship order.
[559] See above, para.18–028.
[560] A child who remains looked after by a local authority has rights to aftercare provision: Children Act 1989 ss.23A–24D: above, para.21–041.
[561] Adoption and Children Act 2002 ss.3, 4; Adoption Support Services Regulations 2005 (SI 2005/691) (England); SI 2005/1512 (Wales); DfES, *Guidance* (2005), Ch.9. Adopters who have children placed with them by agencies also have rights to Statutory Adoption Pay and Adoption Leave; see DfES, *Guidance* (2005) Annex E and above, Ch.7.
[562] DfES, *Special Guardianship Guidance* (2005); SI 2005/1109 (England); SI 2005/1513 (Wales).
[563] See above, paras 21–008 and 21–010.
[564] Children Act 1989 Sch.1, para.15; B. Broad and A Skinner, *Relative Benefits* (BAAF, 2005).
[565] *G v G (Custody: Appeal)* [1985] 1 F.L.R. 894, HL.
[566] [2007] 1 F.L.R. 819, CA; *Re S (No.2)* [2007] 1 F.L.R. 855, CA.

she needed. The judge considered submissions from the parties, including a balanced report from the CAFCASS guardian, noted the exceptionally good relationship between the mother and the carer and made a special guardianship order. The Court of Appeal dismissed the carer's appeal; the judge had heard the views of the parties and carefully considered the alternative orders so there was no basis for overturning the decision.

It has been said that a special guardianship order may be imposed on an unwilling party,[567] and that there is no requirement to make the least interventionist order.[568] The requirement for parental consent to adoption will not be a barrier; Wall L.J has suggested that where the child's welfare requires adoption dispensing consent is likely to be justified.[569] Consideration of the child's age and ability to understand the change of status that adoption brings means that in most cases greater weight is likely to be given to the applicant's views than those of the child. Security and status are matters where perception and feelings may be more important than the formal effect of orders. Carers may want adoption so as to be prepared for unlikely occurrences, such as emigration or their own premature deaths, and not merely to have an arrangement that will work in the ordinary course of events. If there is no prospect of return to the family of origin and the child is young, adoption may reflect the fact that the carers are the child's only effective parents.[570] Contact with parents is not a barrier to adoption,[571] but substantial contact may indicate a continued role as parent. Where the parents harbour unrealistic hopes of rehabilitation or are in conflict with the carers, special guardianship may not provide adequate security for the child,[572] but an adoption application may increase the conflict, at least in the short term. Adoption will alter the child's identity, which may be inappropriate, particularly where this damages links to culture or community. In some cases adoption may be essential because of the additional power it gives the adoptive parents.[573] Adoption remains attractive because the concept is well established and understood in the community.[574] Special guardianship may fit with more open family structures, but while adoption is well recognised and understood as a superior status, applicants are likely to seek it, not an alternative.

---

[567] *Re S (Adoption Order or Special Guardianship Order)* [2007] 1 F.L.R. 819, *per* Wall L.J. at para.73.
[568] *Re M-J (Adoption Order or Special Guardianship Order)* [2007] 1 F.L.R. 691, *per* Wall L.J. at para.19.
[569] *Re S (Adoption Order or Special Guardianship Order)* [2007] 1 F.L.R. 819, *per* Wall L.J. at paras 71–72. This was not necessarily the case under the previous law where the parent's refusal had to be unreasonable.
[570] *Re B (Adoption Order)* [2001] 2 F.L.R. 26, CA; *Re A (A Minor) (Adoption: Parental Consent)* [1987] 2 All E.R. 81, CA; *Re S (A Minor) (Adoption or Custodianship)* [1987] 2 F.L.R. 331, CA.
[571] *Re A-J (Adoption Order or Special Guardianship Order)* [2007] 1 F.L.R. 507, CA, *per* Wall L.J at para.52.
[572] *Re M (A minor) (Custodianship: Jurisdiction)* [1987] 1 W.L.R. 162, CA.
[573] *Re W (Adoption: Custodianship: Access)* [1988] 1 F.L.R. 175, CA (the need to appoint a guardian).
[574] Custodianship was not seen as attractive by foster carers, and there were few applications: see E. Bullard et al., *Custodianship: Caring for Other People's Children* (1991). Special guardianship may be more in keeping with Islamic law, which supports the retention of legal links with the birth family.

B. Contact orders

Before making an adoption order, the court must consider whether there should **22–066** be arrangements for allowing any person contact with the child[575]; this reflects a major change in policy,[576] recognising open adoption and the importance of maintaining relationships with members of the child's birth family.[577] The court may make s.8 contact orders but rarely does so, preferring that contact arrangements should be agreed by the adopters and under their control.[578] Contact orders may, of course, be made alongside special guardianship or residence orders, but there is no specific injunction on the court to consider doing so. Where contact arrangements are well established, an order may still be advantageous because it will make clear to all concerned that arrangements should continue despite the acquisition of parental responsibility by the carers. If the local authority played a major role in facilitating contact for a child in care before the adoption or special guardianship order was granted, this should be continued as part of the support package.[579]

C. Other conditions

Following the recommendation of the *Review of Adoption Law*, the power to **22–067** make adoption orders subject to "such terms and conditions as the court thinks fit"[580] has not been retained. Conditions were rarely used[581] and only exceptionally imposed on adopters without their consent because, by undermining them, the security of the child could be threatened.[582] Where conditions are appropriate, the court may impose them on the adopters or the birth parents by making prohibited steps or specific issue orders. The court may not include an injunction as a term of an adoption order.[583] Where it is necessary to protect the adopters and child against harassment by members of the birth family, the High Court may grant an injunction under its inherent jurisdiction[584]; any court could exercise

---

[575] Adoption and Children Act 2002 s.46(6).
[576] In *Re C (A Minor) (Adoption Conditions)* [1989] A.C. 1, the House of Lords accepted that a contact condition (in favour of contact with siblings) could be included in an adoption order.
[577] See above, para.22–062.
[578] See above, para.22–062. It thereby avoids any problems of enforcement; see above, para.19–052.
[579] ss.3, 4; Adoption Support Regulations 2005 reg.3(1)(c); Children Act 1989 s.14F; Special Guardianship Regulations 2005 (SI 2005/1109) reg.3(1)(c), and above, para.22–023. The court can make a family assistance order: *Re E (Family Assistance Order)* [1999] 1 F.L.R. 512, FD; above para.18–027.
[580] Review of Adoption Law (1992), para.5.8; Cm.2288, para.4.6; Adoption Act 1976 s.12(6).
[581] *Re J (A Minor) (Adoption Conditions)* [1973] Fam. 106; *Re C (A Minor) (Adoption Order: Conditions)* [1989] A.C. 1 are the leading examples; both concern conditions about contact.
[582] *Re S (A Minor) (Blood Transfusion)* [1994] 2 F.L.R. 416 at 421, *per* Waite L.J. (The appeal of adopters who were Jehovah's Witnesses against the imposition of a condition (given as an undertaking) to permit blood transfusions was allowed).
[583] *Re D (A Minor) (Adoption Order: Validity)* [1991] Fam. 137.
[584] *Re O (Minors) (Adoption: Injunction)* [1993] 2 F.L.R. 737, an injunction made in wardship proceedings prior to the adoption does not automatically survive the adoption order. (The parents were later imprisoned for breach of the injunction: *Re O (Contempt: Committal)* [1995] 2 F.L.R. 767, CA.) Where the adopters do not wish to apply the local authority has been allowed to do so on the basis that the Children Act 1989 s.100(4) was satisfied; *Re O* [1993] (above) and *Re X (A Minor) (Adoption Details: Disclosure)* [1994] 2 F.L.R. 450 at 453, CA.

powers under the Family Law Act 1996 Pt IV,[585] or action could be taken under the Protection from Harassment Act 1997.[586]

D. Interim orders

22–068 There is no power to grant interim adoption orders.[587] The *Review of Adoption Law* doubted whether an order with the emotional significance of adoption should ever be granted as a temporary measure, and considered interim orders to be unnecessary because the court can make residence orders.[588] In agency cases, the prospective adopters will already have parental responsibility under the placement order or agreement.[589]

E. Restrictions on making orders

22–069 Procedural requirements in non-agency cases for the notification of the local authority are enforced by precluding the making of adoption orders where notice has not been given.[590] However, there is no longer any statutory restriction on making an adoption order where an illegal payment has been made.[591] Although the court regarded permitting such adoptions as tantamount to ratifying the sale of a child for adoption,[592] it could authorise illegal payments and did so where it considered adoption in the child's interests.[593] The issue of payment remains relevant to determining whether adoption is in the child's interests,[594] and in Convention cases, the court could annul the adoption on the basis that it was contrary to public policy.[595]

Refusal of adoption no longer requires automatic return of the child. If the agency wishes to terminate the placement, it must serve notice in the normal way.[596] Where an adoption order has been refused, the court may not hear any further application for adoption by the same applicants unless it appears proper to do so because of a change in circumstances.[597] The ending of objections from the parents or the child, or even the passage of time, could justify a further application by long-term carers.

---

[585] See above, paras 9–025 *et seq.*
[586] See above, paras 9–025 *et seq.*
[587] cf. Adoption Act 1976 s.25.
[588] *Review of Adoption Law*, Discussion Paper No.3, *The Adoption Process* (1991), para.199.
[589] Adoption and Children Act 2002 s.25(3).
[590] Adoption and Children Act 2002 s.44.
[591] Adoption Act 1976 s.24(2); Adoption and Children Act 2002 s.95.
[592] *Per* Booth J. in *Re C (A Minor) (Adoption Application)* [1993] 1 F.L.R. 87 at 94, 101. (The application for adoption was withdrawn in this case and the child made a ward of court with a view to rehabilitation with her mother.)
[593] *Re Adoption Application* [1987] Fam. 81; *Re MW (Adoption: Surrogacy)* [1995] 2 F.L.R. 759.
[594] Being the subject of a commercial transaction is likely to be harmful to the child; past unscrupulous action on the part of prospective adopters may indicate likely future harm to the child: s.1(4)(e).
[595] Adoption and Children Act 2002 s.89.
[596] Adoption Act 1976 s.30—this was considered unsatisfactory by the Review of Adoption Law, Discussion Paper No.3, *The Adoption Process* (1991), para.174; Adoption and Children Act 2002 s.35.
[597] Adoption and Children Act 2002 s.48. This applies where the first application was made in any part of the UK or in the Isle of Man or Channel Islands.

A special guardianship orders can only be made if the court has received report about the suitability of the applicant. Local authorities must prepare reports when they have been notified by intending applicants, but those who require leave may only notify the local authority after leave has been given.[598] Although courts have power to grant this order without an application, including as an alternative to adoption, their use of it is hampered by the requirement for a report. The court can ask the local authority for a report to provide information not available in other reports, such as by a children's guardian,[599] and then make the order it thinks fit. In seeking to ensure that decisions are properly considered, a system has been created that adds complexity and delay. In this way it makes it more difficult for the courts to disappoint adoption applicants by making them special guardians.

VII. SURROGACY

A. Introduction

Surrogacy is the practice whereby one woman carries a child for another with the **22–070** intention that the child should be handed over after birth.[600] "Full" surrogacy arrangements involve semen and egg donation by the commissioning parents and use of in vitro fertilisation techniques so that the child is genetically related to both of them[601]; "partial" surrogacy, where the surrogate is inseminated artificially by the commissioning father, is more common.[602] Where surrogacy occurs, the commissioning parents want to be the child's social parents; although they may be the child's genetic parents, they can only acquire the legal status of parents[603] by taking further steps that, in the case of the mother (or a second parent of the same sex), necessitate court proceedings.

---

[598] Children Act 1989 s.14A(8), (11); Special Guardianship Regulations 2005 (SI 205/1109) Sch.; *Birmingham CC v R* [2007] 1 F.L.R. 564, CA. So as not to delay adoption hearings, notice is not required where leave has been given to apply for special guardianship in adoption proceedings: s.29(5)(6).

[599] Children Act 1989 s.14A(9); *Re S (Adoption Order or Special Guardianship Order) (No.2)* [2007] 1 F.L.R. 855, CA.

[600] *Report of the Committee of Inquiry into Human Fertilisation and Embryology (Warnock Report)* (Cmnd.9314 (1984)), para.8.1, p.216; G. Douglas, *Law, Fertility and Reproduction* (London: Sweet & Maxwell, 1991); D. Morgan, "Surrogacy: an introductory essay", in R. Lee and D. Morgan (eds), *Birth Rights: Law and Ethics at the Beginning of Life* (1989); R. Cook et al., *Surrogate Motherhood: International Perspectives* (Oxford: Hart, 2003).

[601] B. Steinbock, "Defining Parenthood", in J. Spencer and A Du Bois-Pedain, *Freedom and Responsibility in Reproductive Choice* (2006), p.107 gives case examples. F. Price and R. Cook, "The donor, the recipient and the child—human egg donation in UK licensed centres" [1995] C.F.L.Q. 145. For an explanation of some of the modern reproductive methods, see Lord Winston, *The IVF Revolution* (London: Vermillion, 1999) and the website of the Human Fertilisation and Embryology Authority: *http://www.hfea.gov.uk* [Accessed June 5, 2008].

[602] The child's legal status and the commissioning father's relationship with the child differ if artificial insemination or licensed treatment services are used: Human Fertilisation and Embryology Act 1990 s.28(2)(3); *Re D (Parental Responsibility: IVF Baby)* [2001] 1 F.L.R. 972, CA; *U v W (A-G Intervening)* [1997] 2 F.L.R. 282, FD and above, para.17–004.

[603] Human Fertilisation and Embryology Act 1990 ss.27, 28 and above, paras 17–003–17–004.

The extent to which surrogacy has been practised in the past is unknown, but it is likely that intrafamily arrangements were made; the provision of a baby for a childless relative is not uncommon in some Asian communities. In the early 1980s, commercial surrogacy agencies started to operate in the United States[604] and by the mid 1980s it looked as if they would develop in Europe.[605] In Britain, a committee, chaired by Dame Mary Warnock, was established in 1982 to examine the social, ethical and legal implications of developments in the field of assisted reproduction. Surrogacy was among the topics it considered. The majority of the committee was convinced that the danger of exploitation in surrogacy outweighed its potential benefits.[606] In order to minimise surrogacy, they proposed that all agencies involved in it and any professional who assisted (but not the parties) should be criminally liable.[607] They acknowledged that this would not eradicate private agreements, which they thought should be unenforceable, and recommended that the law should be clarified in this respect.[608] They made proposals about the parentage of children born through assisted reproduction, but not about the protection of children born following surrogacy arrangements. Two members of the committee dissented,[609] taking the view that surrogacy would be beneficial on some occasions, and thus gynaecologists should be able to refer couples to non-commercial, licensed agencies that would provide counselling and match prospective parties.[610] This would discourage unsatisfactory "do-it-yourself arrangements". The minority also recommended that adoption should be available to secure the status of the parents, even where the surrogate was paid for her services.[611] The *Warnock Report* was heavily criticised for failing to understand the complexity of the issues surrounding assisted reproduction and considering that the problems of surrogacy could be solved by making it illegal.[612] The incomplete implementation of either of the report's approaches to surrogacy created a policy vacuum and led to haphazard development.[613]

In January 1985 the birth of baby Cotton[614] following a commercial surrogacy arrangement produced a "moral panic". The Government introduced legislation, which became the Surrogacy Arrangements Act 1985.[615] This made it illegal for

---

[604] D. Morgan, "Surrogacy—giving it an understood name" [1985] J.S.W.L. 216 at 227.
[605] J. Zipper, "What else is new? Reproductive technologies and custody politics", in C. Smart and S. Sevenhuijsen (eds), *Child Custody and the Politics of Gender* (1989), p.264.
[606] *Warnock Report*, para.8.17.
[607] *Warnock Report*, para.8.18.
[608] *Warnock Report*, para.8.19.
[609] Dr David Davies and Dr Wendy Greengross.
[610] *Warnock Report, Expression of Dissent: A Surrogacy.*
[611] *Warnock Report, Expression of Dissent: A Surrogacy*, para.7.
[612] J. Priest (1985) 48 M.L.R. 73; M. Wright (1986) 16 Fam. Law 109.
[613] *Brazier Report: Surrogacy—Review for Health Ministers of Current Arrangements for Payment and Regulation* (Cm.4088 (1998)) i, para.3.
[614] *Re C (A Minor) (Ward Surrogacy)* [1985] F.L.R. 846. The local authority obtained a place of safety order (Children and Young Persons Act 1969 s.28), but the commissioning parents made the child a ward of court. They were permitted to take the child permanently to the US. The DHSS issued Circular (85)12 to advise local authorities of their responsibilities; see also K. Cotton and D. Winn, *Baby Cotton: For Love and Money* (London: Dorling Kindersley, 1985).
[615] M.D.A. Freeman, *Current Law Annotation to Surrogacy Arrangements Act 1985* (1985).

third parties to negotiate or facilitate any surrogacy for payment,[616] and banned advertisement for, or of, surrogacy services.[617] It appears to have prevented the growth of commercial surrogacy agencies in Britain. However, the Act does not affect non-commercial agencies; nor does it regulate negotiations directly between the carrying mother and the commissioning parents.

In 1986 a government Green Paper canvassed views on human infertility **22–071** services and embryo research.[618] The responses showed widespread agreement about the problems of surrogacy and the importance of the child's welfare, but there was no consensus about the most constructive role legislation might play in dealing with this.[619] The Government concluded that legislation should give no encouragement to non-commercial or private surrogacy but that it was not appropriate, nor in the child's best interests, to extend the criminal sanctions in the 1985 Act. However, it considered that views were still developing on these issues and that they should be kept under review. The Human Fertilisation and Embryology Act 1990[620] established a statutory licensing authority (the Human Fertilisation and Embryology Authority) to regulate research and treatment in human infertility and embryology.[621] The Act regulated surrogacy by bringing medicalised surrogacy services within the control of HFEA,[622] by determining who legally are the child's parents[623] and by enabling commissioning parents to become legal parents through obtaining a court order (the parental order).[624]

In 1998 the Brazier Committee reviewed the law relating to surrogacy. It justified further controls, backed by new legislation, on the basis of the potential risks to all parties, including the child. It considered that payments created a danger that women would be enticed to act as surrogates, commodified children and contravened society's norms. It proposed that only genuine, documented expenses should be permitted; surrogacy agencies should be registered, should operate only on a non-profit basis and be required to comply with a *Code of Practice*.[625] The committee did not seek to outlaw arrangements made without an agency, even between strangers,[626] but proposed that the commissioning adults should only be able to obtain a parental order where they had complied with the legislation and code.[627] No action was taken on these proposals. Surrogacy was

---

[616] Surrogacy Arrangements Act 1985 s.2. Payment could still be made to the mother for producing a diary about her pregnancy. A private Members' Bill, the Surrogacy Arrangements (Amendment) Bill that would have outlawed this, was unsuccessful.

[617] Surrogacy Arrangements Act 1985 s.3.

[618] *Legislation on Human Infertility Services and Embryo Research* (Cm.46 (1986)).

[619] *Human Fertilisation and Embryology: A Framework for Legislation* (Cm.259 (1987)), para.72.

[620] A comprehensive account of this Act is beyond the scope of this text: see D. Morgan, *Current Law Annotated Statutes* and G. Douglas, *Law, Fertility and Reproduction* (1991).

[621] Human Fertilisation and Embryology Act 1990 ss.5, 8.

[622] Human Fertilisation and Embryology Act 1990 s.8 and Sch.2. The HFEA keeps surrogacy under review but only has control over the activities of licensed clinics.

[623] Human Fertilisation and Embryology Act 1990 ss.27–29.

[624] Human Fertilisation and Embryology Act 1990 s.30.

[625] *Brazier Report: Surrogacy—Review for Health Ministers of Current Arrangements for Payment and Regulation* Cm.4068 (1998), i paras 4–9.

[626] This contrasts with the law of adoption; only placements with relatives can be made without an agency: Adoption and Children Act 2002 s.92(1), (4).

[627] Cm.4068 (1998), p.72, para.9(vii). Adoption would remain available subject to approval by the High Court.

briefly considered by the Select Committee on Science and Technology, which favoured further legislation, and in the Department of Health Review of the 1990 Act. The Government stated that surrogacy was now accepted by professionals as an appropriate response to infertility in some circumstances; it did not want to be unduly restrictive, and proposed minor changes to clarify the position of non-profit organisations advertising services and facilitating arrangements.[628] Provision was included to this effect in the Human Fertilisation and Embryology Bill 2007.[629] Concerns remain that agencies facilitating surrogacy are not registered, and there is insufficient protection for surrogate mothers and children born following surrogacy arrangements. Regulation is being considered.[630]

The extent to which surrogacy is practiced in the United Kingdom is unclear. A quarter of licensed fertility clinics have been involved in surrogacy arrangements, and each year about 40 parental orders are granted conferring status on the commissioning parents. The majority of these relate to arrangements made without a licensed clinic.[631] The numbers of British women who act as surrogates for couples elsewhere, and of British couples who use surrogates overseas, are not known; it has been estimated that in approximately 5 per cent of arrangements the birth mother refuses to hand over the child.[632]

B. Surrogacy and adoption

22–072   There are four main parallels that may be drawn between surrogacy and adoption.[633] First, surrogacy is seen as an alternative to adoption, which has become necessary because of the shortage of babies for adoption.[634] For some it is a preferred way of alleviating infertility because it enables them to have a child who is genetically related to one or both of them. Secondly, the practice of surrogacy, like adoption, is subject to control by professionals and regulatory bodies in order to safeguard the welfare of children.[635] Commercial arrangements for both surrogacy and adoption are illegal; payment of money other than expenses may preclude an order that gives the child's carers the status of

---

[628] Science and Technology Committee, *Human Reproductive Technologies Fifth Report* (HC 7 (2004–5)), paras 310–312; *Review of the Human Fertilisation and Embryology Act 1990* (Cm.6989 (2006)), paras 2.60–2.64.

[629] Bill 70 cl.59, amending Surrogacy Arrangements Act 1985 ss.1, 2.

[630] Joint Committee on the Human Tissue and Embryos draft Bill (HC 630 (2006–7)), para.289; *Government Response to the Report from the Joint Select Committee on the Human Tissue and Embryos (Draft) Bill 2007* (Cm.7207 (2000)), para.73.

[631] Cm.4068 (1998), paras 1.23, 1.27, 1.31.

[632] Cm.4068 (1998), para.3.5.

[633] See G. Douglas and N. Lowe, "Becoming a parent in English Law" (1992) 108 L.Q.R. 414; B. Hale, *From the Test Tube to the Coffin* (London: Sweet & Maxwell, 1996) 15, 28 *et seq.*; E. Blyth et al., "The implications of adoption for donor offspring following donor-assisted conception" [2001] Child and Family Soc. Wk. 295.

[634] See L. Harding, "The debate on surrogate motherhood" [1985] J.S.W.L. 37, 42.

[635] Human Fertilisation and Embryology Act 1990 s.13(5); Human Fertilisation and Embryology Authority, *Code of Practice*, 7th edn (2007); G. Douglas, "Assisted reproduction and the welfare of the child" [1993] C.L.P. 53, 67; E. Jackson, "Conception and the irrelevance of the welfare of the child" [2002] M.L.R. 176: scrutiny of those applying for assisted reproduction treatment is markedly less searching than for prospective adopters, and surrogacy agencies are not regulated.

parent.[636] Surrogacy arrangements may currently be made without the involvement of any agency,[637] but the Brazier Committee proposed in 1998 that surrogacy agencies should, like adoption agencies, be regulated.[638] Thirdly, the commissioning parents are not the child's legal parents[639] but can only acquire that status by a court process based on adoption, or adoption itself.[640] Fourthly, issues of secrecy and of access to information about birth arise in surrogacy arrangements and other forms of assisted reproduction as they do in adoption, but those who were born following gamete donation have more limited rights to knowledge of their origins.[641]

C. Enforceability of surrogacy contracts

The Surrogacy Arrangements Act 1985 s.1A[642] provides that "[n]o surrogacy **22–073** arrangement is enforceable by or against any of the persons making it". Thus no action may be brought to enforce payment or its return if the child is not handed over.[643] Agreements cannot be made to transfer parental responsibility[644]; any dispute about the residence of a child referred to the courts would be decided applying the welfare principle in s.1 of the Children Act 1989. The emphasis given to maintaining the status quo means that commissioning parents are unlikely to succeed in obtaining a court order transferring residence to them:

---

[636] *Re C (Application by Mr and Mrs X under s.30 of the Human Fertilisation and Embryology Act)* [2002] 1 F.L.R. 909, FD; *Re MW (Adoption: Surrogacy)* [1995] 2 F.L.R. 759, above, 23–062 and below.

[637] Although the use of *in vitro* fertilisation techniques is impractical outside a clinic, and offences will be committed by an unlicensed clinic using such techniques, partial surrogacy with artificial insemination or intercourse occurs legal but the legal effects may be different. Human Fertilisation and Embryology Act 1990 s.28(6) and *Re Q (Parental Order)* [1996] 1 F.L.R. 369.

[638] Cm.4068 (1998), p.72, para.9.

[639] See above, but the commissioning father could be the legal father: Human Fertilisation and Embryology Act 1990 s.28; *Re B (Parentage)* [1996] 2 F.L.R. 15; cf. *Re Q (Parental Order)* [1996] 1 F.L.R. 369, where the commissioning father was not the sperm donor, and the court found that he had not been treated "together with" the surrogate mother when she received AID. In *Re N* [2007] EWCA Civ 1053, Lloyd L.J. suggested that the surrogate's husband was the father because he had consented to her insemination: s.28(2).

[640] Human Fertilisation and Embryology Act 1990 s.30(9); Parental Orders (Human Fertilisation and Embryology) Regulations 1994 (SI 1994/2767). The Human Fertilisation and Embryology Bill 2008 cll.54 and 55 contain amendments.

[641] *Human Fertilisation and Embryology: A Framework for Legislation* (Cm.259 (1987)), paras 81–86. The Human Fertilisation and Embryology Authority (Disclosure of Donor Information) Regulations 2004 (SI 2004/1511), and below, para.22–080.

[642] Added by Human Fertilisation and Embryology Act 1990 s.36. The common-law offence of child sale may also be committed. The Warnock Committee took this view but wanted the matter clarified (Cmnd.9314 (1984), para.8.19).

[643] In *W and B v H (Child Abduction: Surrogacy)* [2002] 1. F.L.R. 1008; *(No.2)* [2002] 2 F.L.R. 252, Hedley J. dismissed a Hague Convention application for the return of twins born in England as a result of a surrogacy agreement in California even though, under Californian law, the commissioning parents were the legal parents and had obtained there a pre-birth determination of custody. The children were not habitually resident in California, and therefore were not unlawfully retained in England. In the second case, he ordered the children's summary return to California on the basis that they had no real connection with England (the only country they had ever lived in and of which they were citizens) so that the issue of their parentage and care could be determined by the Californian Court. The issues that this raised under the Human Rights Act 1998 were apparently not argued.

[644] Children Act 1989 s.2(9).

In *Re P (Minors) (Wardship Surrogacy)*[645] an Asian father commissioned a white single parent to bear a child for him and his wife. Twins were born following artificial insemination, but the mother refused to hand them over. The children, aged five months at the hearing, were made wards of court and the father applied for care and control. Arnold J. acknowledged that the father's home was materially and intellectually superior, and recognised the value of links with the children's Asian culture. However, he refused to order that the children should live with their father because these advantages did not outweigh the disadvantage of leaving their mother with whom they were bonded.

A very different view was taken where the mother set out to deceive the commissioning couple:

In *Re N*[646] the mother twice entered surrogacy agreements with the intention of keeping the children herself. She told the commissioning couples that she had miscarried, but her older daughter told the surrogacy agency. The first child was four years old when the father became aware. He began proceedings and contact was agreed. The second child was only 10 days old when the father began proceedings, but was 18 months when the court ruled that he should be handed to the father; the mother's appeal was dismissed. The judge's decision was fully supported by expert reports from a forensic child psychiatrist and the guardian ad litem. A transfer from a mother to a father in such circumstances looks like the enforcement of the agreement but was based on the child's welfare in the care of a deceptive mother.[647]

The likely outcome is also unclear if the surrogate mother changes her mind after handing over the baby:

In *Re W (A Minor) (Residence Order)*[648] the mother who had had a brief relationship with the father handed the baby to the father shortly after birth and signed a parental responsibility agreement. A few days later she regretted her actions and applied ex parte for a residence order. Her application was refused but her appeal was allowed so that she had care of the child pending a full hearing. Lord Donaldson M.R. stated that there was a "rebuttable presumption that a baby should be with its mother".[649]

---

[645] [1987] 2 F.L.R. 421; a similar approach was taken in the notorious American case *In Re Baby M*, 217 N.J. Super 313, 525 A. 2d 1128; (on appeal), 537 A.2d 1127, but the commissioning parents obtained custody of the child.
[646] [2007] EWCA Civ 1053.
[647] Such deception is unlikely to amount to significant harm that could result in a removal under a care order. Nor is it likely that a child who was well cared for by a mother would be transferred to a father who had not been involved in the care after 18 months in private law proceedings.
[648] [1992] 2 F.L.R. 332, CA. This was not a surrogacy case, although it is comparable to partial surrogacy.
[649] At p.336.

Disputes are decided under the Children Act 1989, but a commissioning parent who is not the child's legal parent will require leave.[650] Where there is a dispute, it is unlikely that a parental order could be obtained.[651]

D. Regulation of surrogacy practice

The creation in the United Kingdom of embryos outside the body and the storage **22–074** of gametes is prohibited except under a licence granted by the Human Fertilisation and Embryology Authority.[652] Consequently, full surrogacy and partial surrogacy using stored gametes[653] can only legally be undertaken in a licensed clinic. It is a condition of a licence that:

> "[A] woman shall not be provided with treatment services unless account has been taken of the welfare of any child who may be born as a result of the treatment (including the need of that child for a father), and of any other child who may be affected by the birth."[654]

This provision, which was introduced to neutralise opposition in Parliament from MPs concerned about the treatment of single or lesbian women, has been severely criticised.[655] The welfare of the child debate encapsulates arguments on the limits of reproductive freedom.[656] Jackson has argued that the provision is incompatible with the European Convention on Human Rights because it fails to respect art.8 rights and discriminates against those who use assisted conceptio services.[657] Even if there is a moral basis for requiring such assessments, clini can only undertake them with consent because they are forbidden fr communicating with third parties about provision of treatment.[658] The Hu Fertilisation and Embryology Authority provides guidance to clinics on welfare provision in its *Code of Practice*. It consulted on the operation c

[650] Children Act 1989 s.10(5).

[651] The application requires consent: Human Fertilisation and Embryology Act 1990 s.30(5) para.22–077.

[652] Human Fertilisation and Embryology Act 1990 ss.3(1), 4(1). The scope of regulation is e by the EU Human Tissue Directive (EU Directive 2004/23) implemented by Human Fertilisa Embryology (Quality and Safety) Regulations (SI 2007/1522). The provisions of the 2008 Bil limited to stored gametes but apply wherever artificial insemination techniques are used, inclu "basic partner treatment services" such as IUI, cl.14, amending Human Fertilisation and Emb Act 1990 s.13(5).

[653] The term "gamete" covers both sperm and eggs. Storage of gametes is required so that t be tested for HIV, etc.

[654] Human Fertilisation and Embryology Act 1990 s.13(5); and see B. Hale, *From the test tu* E. Blyth, "Children's welfare, surrogacy and social work" (1993) 23 Brit. J. Soc. Wk. 25 Jackson, "Conception and the irrelevance of welfare" [2002] M.L.R. 176.

[655] Jackson [2002] M.L.R. 176 p.195.

[656] Select Committee on Science and Technology, *Human Reproductive technologies and the* Report 2004–5 (HC 7), para.91. For example, debates on sex selection and "saviour sibli Laing and D. Oderberg, "Artificial reproduction, the 'welfare principle', and the commoi [2005] Med. L.Rev. 328.

[657] Jackson [2002] M.L.R. 176 pp.187, 193, 199. She also suggests that art.12 may be breac acknowledges that the Court of Appeal has suggested otherwise: *R. (on the application of A Secretary of State for the Home Department* [2001] 2 F.L.R. 1158, CA.

[658] Human Fertilisation and Embryology Act 1990 s.33; Douglas (1993), *op. cit.* p.65. Cent make inquiries of each prospective parent and, *with their consent*, may seek information fr sources. There is no requirement for police or other checks before treatment.

provision was hurriedly drafted to create parental orders,[677] but its implementation was delayed while a suitable process was devised. Section 30 was implemented on November 1, 1994; regulations based on adoption legislation explain the effects of a parental order.[678] The extension of adoption to unmarried and same-sex couples was not immediately mirrored in changes to parental orders. However, the Human Fertilisation and Embryology Bill 2008 makes provision for this so as to avoid obvious discrimination.[679]

i. Parental orders

22–077   Commissioning parents can apply for a parental order if at least one of them is the child's genetic parent.[680] A parental order gives the applicants the status of parents and extinguishes the parental responsibility of everyone else.[681] The parental order must be sought within six months of the birth of the child, the child must be living with the applicants and the legal parents (including a father who does not have parental responsibility) must agree unconditionally to the making of the order.[682] There are no provisions comparable to those in adoption for the dispensing of an agreement, but if a person cannot be found, or is incapable of giving it, their agreement is not required.[683] This means the use of anonymously donated gametes does not prevent the applicants from seeking a parental order.[684]

Regulations provide for the modification of adoption law and its application to these proceedings.[685] New regulations can be expected to replace the requirement that the child's welfare is the "first consideration" with paramountcy in line with the recommendations of the Brazier Committee[686] and the Adoption and Children Act 2002. Applications are made to the family proceedings court but may be transferred to a higher court.

A "parental order reporter" (a CAFCASS officer) is appointed to investigate the case,[687] including advising the court about alternatives; the role of the reporter is restricted by limited access to information from a clinic carrying out

---

[677] Human Fertilisation and Embryology Act 1990 s.30.

[678] Parental Orders (Human Fertilisation and Embryology) Regulations 1994 (SI 1994/2767).

[679] This is referred to as "fast track adoption" in the explanatory notes for the Human Fertilisation and Embryology Bill 2008 cl.54 and EN 181.

[680] Human Fertilisation and Embryology Act 1990 s.30(1); Human Fertilisation and Embryology Bill 2008 cl.54(1). Parental orders are available in either full or partial surrogacy.

[681] Parental Order (Human Fertilisation and Embryology) Regulations 1994 (SI 1994/2767), Sch.1; a useful account is provided in Department of Health Guidance LAC(94)25.

[682] Human Fertilisation and Embryology Act 1990 s.30(2), (3), (5); Human Fertilisation and Embryology Bill 2008 cl.54(3)–(5). The six month limit is waived for those (such as same-sex couples) who were not eligible to apply under s.30 and, cl.54(11).

[683] Human Fertilisation and Embryology Act 1990 s.30(6); Human Fertilisation and Embryology Bill 2008 cl.54(6).

[684] If the treatment occurred in a licensed clinic, the anonymous semen donor would not be the father: s.28; above para.17–004.

[685] Human Fertilisation and Embryology Bill 2008 cl.55(1).

[686] Cm.4068 (1998), ii para.7, but the report was not entirely consistent: see M.D.A. Freeman [1999] M.L.R. 1, 13.

[687] These are specified proceedings: Children Act 1989 s.42(6)(i). Only exceptionally difficult, unusual or sensitive cases should be referred to CAFCASS Legal: *CAFCASS Practice Note* [2001] F.L.R. 151, para.8.

the treatment,[688] but it has been said that reporters may presume that the child's welfare has been given adequate consideration where treatment occurred in a licensed clinic.[689] Guidance indicates that a recommendation against the making of an order is exceptional.[690] A parental order may not be made in any case where payments have been made other than to cover expenses, unless these payments have been authorised by the court.[691] However, the courts have been willing to authorise payments in order to safeguard the welfare of the child.[692] Parental-order proceedings are family proceeding, so the court may make any s.8 order with or without an application.[693] If an order is refused, an appeal may be made to the High Court.[694]

When a parental order is made, the child's birth is re-registered with the **22–078** commissioning parents as the child's legal parents.[695] The child's status is comparable with that obtained by adoption.[696] The making of a parental order does not affect the inheritance of honours, and other dispositions are construed as if the child was born on the date the parental order was obtained.[697]

All applicants who meet the basic qualifications for a parental order are likely to be successful. A number of factors account for this: sympathy for the applicants (they have usually only turned to surrogacy because of a misfortune of biology, which means the woman is unable to carry a pregnancy); a belief that they are entitled to the child (at least one of them is the child's genetic parent); recognition that it is only a legal device that defines others as the child's parents; and the general acceptance of the notion that biological reproduction is a qualification for parenthood—all combine to make substantial scrutiny of consensual and non-commercial arrangements unacceptable.[698] These arguments apply equally to same-sex couples.

---

[688] J. Timms, *Children's Representation* (London: Sweet & Maxwell, 1995), p.301; the 1990 Act was amended by the Human Fertilisation and Embryology (Disclosure of Information) Act 1992 s.1 to increase the information available for parental order proceedings.

[689] J. Timms, *Children's Representation* (1995), p.298, the *HFEA Code* (2007) requires more consideration of welfare issues, but Brazier found that the majority of parental order applicants had not used a clinic: Cm.4068 (1998), para.1.3.

[690] LAC(94)25.

[691] Human Fertilisation and Embryology Act 1990 s.30(7). See above, para.22–069, for the approach of the courts to comparable provisions in adoption. A survey for the Brazier Report found payments up to £12,000 and averaging nearly £4,000. In *Re MW (Adoption: Surrogacy)* [1995] 2 F.L.R. 759, the court authorised a payment of £7,500 to a surrogate mother, and made an adoption order after dispensing with her consent.

[692] *Re C (Application by Mr and Mrs X Under s.30 of the Human Fertilisation and Embryology Act 1990)* [2002] 1 F.L.R. 909, FD. If the child's welfare is paramount, there will be few if any circumstances where discretion would not be exercised to authorise the payment.

[693] Children Act 1989 s.10(1); Human Fertilisation and Embryology Act 1990 s.30(8)(a).

[694] Parental Orders (Human Fertilisation and Embryology) Regulations (1994) (SI 1994/2767) Sch.1, para.5(b), applying Adoption Act 1976 s.63(2).

[695] Parental Orders (Human Fertilisation and Embryology) Regulations 1994 (SI 1994/2767) Sch.1, para.4(a), applying Adoption Act 1976 s.50.

[696] Parental Orders (Human Fertilisation and Embryology) Regulations 1994 (SI 1994/2767) Sch.1, para.2, applying Adoption Act 1976 s.39.

[697] Parental Orders (Human Fertilisation and Embryology) Regulations 1994 (SI 1994/2767) Sch.1, para.3, applying Adoption Act 1976 ss.42–46.

[698] See D. Morgan, "A surrogacy issue: who is the other mother?" (1994) 8 Int. J. of Law and Fam. 386 and Jackson [2002] M.L.R. 176.

ii. Adoption

22–079 Where the conditions for a parental order are not satisfied (e.g. the birth mother refuses her agreement, the time limit has passed or neither of the commissioning adults is genetically related to the child), the status of parent can be acquired by adoption, but a placement with unrelated adopters breaches the law relating to private placements.[699] Applications for adoption are subject to more substantial scrutiny; the local authority must be notified of intention to adopt, must investigate the suitability of the prospective adopters and the welfare of the child and must report to the court hearing the application.[700] However, the court may be faced with a fait accompli so that it is necessary for the child's welfare to make the order.

Where neither a parental order nor adoption is available, the commissioning adults may secure their position through a residence order[701] or, if neither is the child's parent, special guardianship.

F. Knowledge of origins[702]

22–080 Access to information about genetic origins for those born as a result of assisted reproduction technologies is controversial. The Warnock Committee considered that non-identifying information about the donor should be made available to a child born as a result of AID at age 18.[703] The Government sought further views[704] and enacted a scheme that gave those born using donated gametes limited information about their origins, far less than is available to most adopted persons. The 1990 Act enables those over 18 to discover from the Human Fertilisation and Embryology Authority whether they were or may have been born in consequence of treatment services.[705] However, a person who has not been told of the circumstances of their conception will not know that the HFEA holds information.[706] Identifying information is not available; the applicant may only be told whether someone other than the legal parents is a genetic parent or whether an intended spouse is or may be a genetic relation.[707] Similarly, a child who is the subject of a parental order may, on reaching the age of 18, obtain a

---

[699] See above, para.22–014.

[700] Adoption and Children Act 2002 s.44(1), (5), (6).

[701] *Re H (A minor) (s.37 Direction)* [1993] 2 F.L.R. 541.

[702] See, generally, K. O'Donovan, "A right to know one's parentage?" (1988) 2 Int. J. Law & Fam. 27; E. Haimes, "'Secrecy': what can artificial reproduction learn from adoption?" (1988) 2 Int. J. Law & Fam. 46; M. Freeman, "The new birth right? Identity and the child of the reproduction revolution" (1996) 4 Int J. of Children's Rights 273; S. Wilson, "Identity, genealogy and the social family: the case of donor insemination" (1997) 11 Int. J. Law Pol. and Fam. 270; E. Blyth et al., "The implications of adoption for donor offspring following donor-assisted conception" [2001] Child and Family Soc. Wk. 295.

[703] *Warnock Report*, para.4.21.

[704] Cm.46 (1986), paras 31, 32; Cm.259 (1987), paras 81 *et seq.*

[705] Human Fertilisation and Embryology Act 1990 s.31 requires the authority to keep a register of treatment provided. The holding of information for treatment before then is unregulated.

[706] A large study of donor insemination families found that less than 10% of mothers had told the child by the age of 12 years, and 75% had decided not to do so: S. Golombok et al. cited in DH, *Donor Information Consultation* (2002), para.1.25.

[707] Human Fertilisation and Embryology Act 1990 s.31(4), (5).

copy of their original birth certificate, but this will not show the genetic parents where gamete donation was used.[708]

In 2002 the lack of access to information for those conceived through gamete donation was challenged, and art.8 was held to be engaged.[709] The Department of Health issued a consultation paper acknowledging that there were arguments for and against greater openness. The HFEA's response indicated that it supported moves towards ending donor anonymity, but that this should not be applied retrospectively[710] nor on an optional basis for future donors.[711] In 2004 the Minister announced that future anonymous donations would not be permitted. Access to identifying information about their donor would be available from 2023.[712] In addition, the Department of Health supported the setting up of a voluntary contact register through which those born as a result of donation and their genetic relatives might be able to establish relationships.[713]

The issues of anonymity and access to information were considered again by the Select Committee on Science and Technology. The Committee recognised that information about genetic origins could be valuable for identity and medical history, and that it was unethical for the state to hold information about a person that was unavailable to the person. Nevertheless, it was concerned that without anonymity there would be a shortage of donors, and parents would travel abroad or use unregulated services to secure an anonymous donor, or conceal the facts of their conception so that their children could not benefit from the available information. It recommended a twin-track approach so that donors and parents could choose whether identifying information would be available for children and access to non-identifying information before age 18 to assist parents telling their children about their conception.[714] In the 2006 White Paper, the Government re-iterated its commitment to donor identification and recognised that some donors wanted information about children born as a result of their donation. It also proposed reform to information rights so that those seeking to enter a civil partnership could also establish whether they were related to their intended partner.[715] Provisions to this effect were included in the draft Human Tissue and Embryos Bill and discussed by the Joint Committee on the Bill. The committee suggested further extension to information rights so that couples intending an intimate relationship could establish whether they were related, and children

---

[708] Parental Orders (Human Fertilisation and Embryology) Regulations 1994 (SI 1994/2767) Sch.1 para.4(b).

[709] *Rose v Secretary of State for Health and the HFEA* [2002] 2 F.L.R. 962, FD. The applications concerned persons conceived both before and after the introduction of the 1990 Act.

[710] There is no intention to make future disclosure rules retrospective: DH *Donor Information Consultation*, para.1.3. If any regulations were made under s.31 allowing disclosure of identifiable information, they would only apply to future donations.

[711] HFEA, *Response to the Department of Health's Consultation on Donor Information* (2002).

[712] Melanie Johnson MP, at the HFEA Annual Conference January 2004. Human Fertilisation and Embryology Authority (Disclosure of Donor Information) Regulations 2004 (SI 2004/1511), i.e. when those born following donations under the new regulations reached age 18.

[713] Cm.7087 (2007); Draft Bill EN para.143; HC 630 (2007), para.259; Human Fertilisation and Embryology Bill 2008 cl.24, adding s.31ZF.

[714] HC 7 (2004–5), paras 147–160.

[715] *Review of the Human Fertilisation and Embryology Act* (Cm.6989 (2006)), paras 2.57–2.59.

could obtain information at age 16.[716] It also considered whether parents should be required to inform children of their origins, and the marking of birth certificates to reflect this. Although it was clearly in favour of children having information, it rejected the idea of imposing a legal duty on parents and referred the issue of birth certificates back to the Government,[717] which has indicated its preference for educating parents about the benefits of openness rather than forcing the issue through the annotation of birth certificates.[718] The Human Fertilisation and Embryology Bill 2008 makes provision for non-identifying information such as the number of children born as a result of donations from the applicant's donor, their sex and the year of their birth to applicants aged 16 years or over. Similarly, for information about the possibility of a genetic relationship with an intended spouse, civil partner or intimate partner.[719] Donors may be informed that a child may have been born and that such requests have been made.[720] Also, where the register shows that two or more people aged over 18 were conceived from the same donor (one has agreed to information being shared and the other has requested information), the authority will be able to disclose this, providing that it does not lead to the identification of a donor who has not consented.[721]

Providing information about the sperm donor raises more complex legal issues than arise in relation to birth parents. This is not just a matter of breaking promises of confidentiality; it would also disrupt relationships, especially for those conceived before 1988. Prior to the Family Law Reform Act 1987, the sperm donor was the child's legal father with consequent rights of inheritance on intestacy and duties of support.[722] The man named on the birth certificate is not the father; the child could only have a right to inherit from him (and vice versa) under a will. Revealing that a child was conceived via donation also identifies infertility (medical information that could be expected to be kept confidential) and probably that a false declaration was made when the birth was registered. In some cases this information may have been concealed by the mother, who obtained treatment without discussing the issue with her husband. In addition, clinics were under no duty to keep or maintain records; for some of those born as a result of donation, any right to identifying information would be ineffective. Of course, maintaining anonymity does not resolve these difficulties but it does serve to conceal and contain them.

[716] HC 630 (2007), paras 256, 260. These proposals were accepted by the Government: Cm.7209 (2007), paras 63, 67 and 68.
[717] HC 630 (2007), paras 272, 276.
[718] Cm.7209 (2007), paras 69–70.
[719] Human Fertilisation and Embryology Act 1990 ss.31ZA and 31ZB, to be added by the 2008 Bill cl.24.
[720] Human Fertilisation and Embryology Act 1990 ss.31ZC and 31ZD, to be added by the 2008 Bill cl.24.
[721] Human Fertilisation and Embryology Act 1990 s.31ZE, to be added by the 2008 Bill cl.24.
[722] See above, para.17–004.

INDEX

Abduction of children
see **Child abduction**
Abuse of children
see **Child protection**
Access to information
adoption
Adoption Contact Register, 22–013
generally, 22–011—22–012
surrogacy, 22–080
Accommodation
see **Housing; Residential accommodation;
Secure accommodation**
Adoption
access to information
Adoption Contact Register, 22–013
generally, 22–011—22–012
adoption agencies
adoption societies, 22–016
local authorities, 22–015
adoption from care
foster carers, 22–045
introduction, 22–040—22–041
local authorities' duties, 21–070
placement orders, 22–043
planning, 22–042
revocation of placement orders, 22–044
adoption leave/pay, 6–032
adoption orders
conditions, 22–067
criteria for grant, 22–063—22–065
effect, 22–005—22–008
interim orders, 22–068
restrictions on making, 22–069
adoption services
adoption societies, 22–016
adoption support, 22–022—22–023
court's role, 22–017
eligibility of adopters, 22–019
introduction, 22–014
local authorities' duties, 22–015
matching, 22–021
suitability of adopters, 22–020
adoption societies, 22–016
adoption support, 22–022—22–023
baby placement
consent, 22–039
freeing for adoption, 22–038
introduction, 22–037
confidentiality, 22–035
consent
adoption orders, 22–029
dispensation, 22–031—22–033
introduction, 22–025
placement orders, 22–028
relevant persons, 22–026

Adoption—cont.
consent—cont.
scope, 22–027—22–029
timing, 22–030
contact orders, 22–066
court's role, 22–017
discrimination, 22–018
effect
citizenship, 22–007
introduction, 22–005
prohibited degrees, 22–008
succession, 22–006
eligibility of adopters, 22–019
grandparents, 22–060
history, 22–004
human rights, 22–034
"in family" adoption
grandparents, 22–060
introduction, 22–056
other relatives, 22–060
parents, 22–057
stepparents, 22–058—22–059
intercountry adoption
designated countries, 22–053
generally, 22–051
Hague Convention, 22–048—22–050
Hague Convention countries, 22–052
introduction, 22–046—22–047
other countries, 22–054
overseas adoption of UK resident
children, 22–055
introduction, 22–001—22–003
local authorities' duties, 22–015
matching, 22–021
open adoption, 22–061—22–062
parents, 22–057
placement orders
adoption from care, 22–043—22–044
generally, 22–027—22–028
revocation, 22–044
public law adoption
foster carers, 22–045
introduction, 22–040—22–041
placement orders, 22–043
planning, 22–042
revocation of placement orders, 22–044
refusal, 22–069
registration, 22–010
relatives, 22–060
relinquishment
consent, 22–039
freeing for adoption, 22–038
introduction, 22–037
residence orders, 22–063—22–065
revocation of adoption orders, 22–009

Adoption—*cont.*
special guardianship orders,
22–063—22–065
stepparents, 22–058—22–059
suitability of adopters, 22–020
surrogacy
generally, 22–079
relationship with adoption, 22–072
use, 22–036
welfare principle, 22–024
Adultery
see **Divorce**
After-care
local authorities' duties, 21–071
Age
ancillary relief, 13–075
capacity to marry, 2–012—2–013
majority, 16–001
welfare principle, 19–020
All port warnings
alerts on child abduction, 20–004
Ancillary relief
age of parties, 13–075
"all the circumstances"
age of parties, 13–075
conduct of parties, 13–082—13–084
contribution to welfare of family,
13–078—13–081
disabilities of parties, 13–077
duration of marriage, 13–075—13–076
financial needs, obligations and
responsibilities, 13–072—13–073
introduction, 13–063
loss of benefits, 13–085
resources of parties, 13–064—13–071
standard of living, 13–074
appeals
introduction, 13–102
permission to appeal out of time,
13–103—13–105
principles, 13–106
applicants
children, 13–016
spouses/civil partners, 13–014
third parties, 13–015
change of circumstances
introduction, 13–093
non-disclosure, 13–107—13–108
reopening clean break settlements,
13–102—13–106
variation of orders, 13–094—13–101
clean break
dismissal of periodical payments order
claims, 13–092
duty to consider, 13–088
introduction, 13–086—13–087
non-extension of periodical payments
orders, 13–091
reopening settlements, 13–102—13–106
specified term periodical payments orders,
13–089—13–090
concealment of facts, 13–107—13–108

Ancillary relief—*cont.*
conduct of parties, 13–082—13–084
consent orders, 13–005—13–007
contribution to welfare of family,
13–078—13–081
court's discretion
history, 13–032—13–035
introduction, 13–031
maintenance pending suit,
13–037—13–038
section 25 considerations,
13–039—13–092
statutory guidelines, 13–036
court's powers, 13–013
disabilities of parties, 13–077
duration of marriage, 13–075—13–076
earning capacity/potential, 13–067
enforcement
attachment of earnings, 14–012—14–013
bankruptcy orders, 14–005
charging orders, 14–008
committal, 14–011
courts, 14–003
introduction, 14–001
judgment summonses, 14–011
magistrates' courts, 14–015—14–019
periodical payment arrears, 14–002
receivership, 14–009
registration in magistrates' court, 14–014
restrictions on participation in
proceedings, 14–020
seizure and sale of goods, 14–006
sequestration, 14–010
third party debt orders, 14–007
enforcement (magistrates' courts)
attachment of earnings, 14–018
committal, 14–017
distress, 14–016
fines, 14–019
introduction, 14–015
financial needs, obligations and
responsibilities, 13–072—13–073
history
breakdown-based divorce law, 13–033
minimal loss principle, 13–034—13–035
offence-based divorce law, 13–032
housing-related orders
introduction, 13–109
local authority/housing association
tenancies, 13–118
Martin orders, 13–117
Mesher orders, 13–116
sale of property orders, 13–114
transfer of property orders,
13–110—13–113
introduction, 13–001—13–002
legislative framework, 13–012
loss of benefits, 13–085
lump sum orders
generally, 13–024
variation, 13–101
Martin orders, 13–117

Ancillary relief—*cont.*
Mesher orders, 13–116
needs, 13–072
new partners' resources, 13–068
non-disclosure, 13–107—13–108
obligations and responsibilities, 13–073
orders available, 13–017
pension sharing orders
effect, 13–125
generally, 13–029, 13–123
types, 13–124
pensions
offsetting, 13–121
orders available, 13–119
pension attachment orders, 13–122
pension sharing orders, 13–029,
13–123—13–125
resources of parties, 13–070
periodical payments orders
clean break, 13–086—13–092
death of payer, 13–020
introduction, 13–018
remarriage/formation of civil partnership
by payee, 13–021
secured orders, 13–018
specified term, 13–022
variation, 13–095—13–100
private agreements, 13–008—13–009
property adjustment orders
settlement of property orders, 13–026,
13–114
transfer of property orders, 13–025,
13–110—13–113
variation, 13–101
variation of settlement orders, 13–027
reopening clean break settlements
introduction, 13–102
permission to appeal out of time,
13–103—13–105
principles, 13–106
resources of parties
ascertainment, 13–064
earning capacity/potential, 13–067
expectations, 13–069
new partners, 13–068
pensions, 13–070
reality of financial situation, 13–066
rehousing entitlement, 13–071
sale of property orders, 13–028, 13–114
section 25 considerations
additional guidelines, 13–042—13–056
"all the circumstances", 13–063—13–085
clean break, 13–086—13–092
interpretation guidelines, 13–040
introduction, 13–039
overriding objective, 13–041
welfare principle, 13–058—13–062
setting aside orders, 13–107—13–108
settlement
consent orders, 13–005—13–007
costs, 13–011
facilitation, 13–010

Ancillary relief—*cont.*
settlement—*cont.*
introduction, 13–003
ouster of court's jurisdiction, 13–004
private agreements, 13–008—13–009
settlement of property orders
generally, 13–026
Martin orders, 13–117
Mesher orders, 13–116
standard of living, 13–074
tenancy transfer orders, 13–118
timing of orders, 13–030
transfer of property orders
deferred cash payments, 13–113
generally, 13–025
immediate cash payments, 13–112
reduction/extinction of periodical
payments, 13–111
variation of orders
introduction, 13–094
lump sum orders, 13–101
periodical payments orders,
13–095—13–100
property adjustment orders, 13–101
variation of settlement orders, 13–027
void marriages
financial provision after death, 2–057
financial provision after decree of nullity,
2–056
welfare principle
children of the family, 13–061
introduction, 13–058
minority of children, 13–062
paramountcy, 13–060
Annulment
see **Void civil partnerships; Voidable civil
partnerships; Void marriages;
Voidable marriages**
Ante-nuptial settlements
variation
ancillary relief applications, 13–027
child support applications,
15–043—15–045
Appeals
ancillary relief
introduction, 13–102
permission to appeal out of time,
13–103—13–105
principles, 13–106
care orders, 21–046
child support, 15–021
supervision orders, 21–046
welfare principle decisions,
19–024—19–025
Approbation
voidable marriages, 2–050—2–051
Assisted reproduction
see also **Surrogacy**
maternity, 17–003
paternity, 17–004—17–005

Attachment of earnings
enforcement of financial obligations
generally, 14–012—14–013
magistrates' courts, 14–018

Baby placement
see **Adoption**
Bankruptcy
enforcement of financial obligations, 14–005
sale of family home, 5–058—5–059
Banns
historical requirements, 1–002, 1–004
introduction, 1–021
publicity, 1–023
residence, 1–022
waiting time, 1–024
Behaviour
see **Divorce**
Beneficial interests
express declaration, 5–010—5–011
introduction, 5–009
mortgagees' position, 5–050—5–051
no express declaration, 5–012
Benefits
ancillary relief, effect of, 13–085
child support
income disregards, 15–027
parents in receipt of benefits, 15–012
history, 6–003—6–004
introduction, 6–008
means-tested benefits
cohabitation, 6–012—6–018
housing benefit, 6–020
income support, 6–009
jobseekers' allowance, 6–010
maintenance obligations of liable
relatives, 6–019
means test, 6–011
social fund, 6–021
non-means-tested benefits
child benefit, 6–023
contributory benefits, 6–025
guardian's allowance, 6–024
introduction, 6–022
Birth registration
birth certificates, 17–011
introduction, 17–009
parental responsibility of unmarried fathers,
17–039
procedure, 17–010
Breakdown of relationships
see **Ancillary relief; Dissolution; Divorce;
Domestic violence; Separation**

CAFCASS
role, 18–010
Calderbank **letters**
ancillary relief, 13–011
Canon law
history of marriage, 1–002—1–003

Capacity to form civil partnerships
see **Void civil partnerships; Voidable civil
partnerships**
Capacity to marry
see **Void marriages; Voidable marriages**
Care
see also **Care proceedings**
adoption from care
foster carers, 22–045
introduction, 22–040—22–041
local authorities' duties, 21–070
placement orders, 22–043
planning, 22–042
revocation of placement orders, 22–044
challenging local authorities' decisions
Commission for Local Administration in
England, 21–083
complaints procedures, 21–082
High Court jurisdiction, 21–085
human rights claims, 21–086—21–087
introduction, 21–081
judicial review, 21–085
Secretary of State's powers, 21–084
change of name, 21–080
children's rights, 21–073
contact, 21–074
court approval of local authorities' decisions
contact with children in care,
21–074—21–076
other decisions, 21–080
placement outside England and Wales,
21–079
secure accommodation, 21–077—21–078
local authorities' duties
accommodation, 21–068
adoption, 21–070
after-care, 21–071
introduction, 21–067
leaving care, 21–071
maintenance, 21–068
rehabilitation, 21–070
review of care, 21–069
marriage, 21–080
parents' position, 21–072
placement outside England and Wales,
21–079
secure accommodation, 21–077—21–078
Care proceedings
see also **Care**
care orders
appeals, 21–046
discharge, 21–045
generally, 21–041
interim orders, 21–043
introduction, 21–040
care plans, 21–039
children's guardians
practice, 21–059
provision, 21–057
role, 21–058
confidentiality, 21–038
domestic violence injunctions, 21–044

Care proceedings—*cont.*
  evidence, 21–036—21–038
  expert evidence, 21–037—21–038
  introduction, 21–030
  nature, 21–053
  orders available, 21–040
  Public Law Outline, 21–054—21–055
  representation
    children's guardians, 21–057—21–059
    children's solicitors, 21–060
    introduction, 21–056
  supervision orders
    appeals, 21–046
    discharge, 21–045
    generally, 21–042
    interim orders, 21–043
    introduction, 21–040
  threshold criteria
    child beyond parental control, 21–034
    harm attributable to care given to child,
      21–034
    introduction, 21–031
    likelihood of harm, 21–035
    present suffering of harm, 21–033
    significant harm, 21–032
Carers
  parental responsibility, 17–051
Case management directions
  family proceedings, 18–041
Change of circumstances
  ancillary relief
    introduction, 13–093
    non-disclosure, 13–107—13–108
    reopening clean break settlements,
      13–102—13–106
    variation of orders, 13–094—13–101
  child support, 15–021
Change of name
  children in care, 21–080
  parental rights, 17–025
Charging orders
  enforcement of financial obligations, 14–008
Chattels
  proprietary rights, 5–062—5–063
Child abduction
  conclusions, 20–026
  enforcement of contact, 20–024
  Hague Convention
    acquiescence, 20–019
    child's objections, 20–021
    consent, 20–019
    European Union, 20–022
    grave risk of harm, 20–020
    habitual residence, 20–015
    intolerable situation, 20–020
    introduction, 20–014
    proceedings, 20–018
    rights of custody, 20–017
    wrongful removal/retention, 20–016
  human rights, 20–025
  international child abduction
    central authorities, 20–013

Child abduction—*cont.*
  international child abduction—*cont.*
    European Union, 20–022
    Hague Convention countries,
      20–014—20–022
    introduction, 20–012
    non-Hague Convention countries, 20–023
  introduction, 20–001
  offences, 20–002
  preventative measures
    all ports warnings, 20–004
    introduction, 20–002
    "mirror" orders, 20–006
    passport control, 20–003
    security, 20–005
  recovery of children
    abduction between UK regions,
      20–010—20–011
    abduction within England and Wales,
      20–009
    introduction, 20–008
  removal from jurisdiction
    orders permitting removal, 18–026
    prohibition on removal, 18–021
  tracing children, 20–007
Child abuse
  see **Child protection**
Child assessment orders
  child protection, 21–052
Child benefit
  generally, 6–023
Child neglect
  see **Child protection**
Child protection
  see also **Care proceedings**
  child abuse/neglect
    generally, 21–016—21–018
    investigations, 21–022—21–028
  compensation for victims, 21–066
  criminal law
    children's evidence, 21–064—21–065
    decisions to prosecute, 21–063
    history, 21–061
    prosecution, 21–062
  emergencies
    child assessment orders, 21–052
    emergency protection orders,
      21–048—21–050
    introduction, 21–047
    police powers, 21–051
  intervention in family life, 21–019—21–020
  investigations
    child protection conferences, 21–025
    community notification, 21–028
    Contact Point, 21–026
    family group conferences, 21–025
    integrated children's system, 21–026
    local authorities' duties, 21–022—21–023
    negligence, 21–027
    police role, 21–024
    registers of offenders, 21–028
  system, 21–021

Child support
 see also **Periodical payments orders**
 appeals, 15–021
 assessment of system, 15–028
 benefits
   income disregards, 15–027
   parents in receipt of, 15–012
 capital provision
   applications by children, 15–045
   financial orders under Children Act 1989,
     15–046—15–052
   introduction, 15–042
   property adjustment orders,
     15–043—15–045
 change of circumstances, 15–021
 Child Support Act 1991, 15–002—15–004
 Children Act 1989 orders
   discretion of court, 15–051—15–052
   eligible applicants, 15–047
   introduction, 15–046
   liable persons, 15–048
   matters for consideration, 15–050
   orders available, 15–049
 collection, 15–023
 conclusions, 15–053
 court's role
   consent orders, 15–038
   disabled children, 15–036
   discretion, 15–040
   duration of orders, 15–041
   education expenses orders, 15–035
   introduction, 15–029
   jurisdiction, 15–030—15–038
   maintenance agreements, 15–038
   non-qualifying children, 15–031
   older children, 15–032
   orders against parents with care, 15–037
   powers, 15–039—15–041
   topping-up orders, 15–034
   UK residence, 15–033
 disabled children, 15–036
 duration of orders, 15–041
 education expenses orders, 15–035
 enforcement, 15–024—15–025
 fulfilment of responsibility
   introduction, 15–011
   parents in receipt of benefits, 15–012
   parents with existing court orders, 15–013
 impact, 15–027
 introduction, 15–001
 liable persons
   introduction, 15–007
   misattribution of parentage, 15–009
   non-residence, 15–010
   proof of parentage, 15–008
 parentage
   misattribution, 15–009
   proof, 15–008
 parents in receipt of benefits, 15–012
 parents with care, 15–037
 parents with existing court orders, 15–013

Child support—*cont.*
 property adjustment orders
   applications by children, 15–045
   discretion of court, 15–044
   orders available, 15–043
 qualifying children, 15–006
 quantification
   introduction, 15–014
   new system, 15–019
   original formula, 15–015
   revised formula, 15–016—15–018
 rates
   new system, 15–019
   old system, 15–016—15–018
 shared care, 15–017—15–018, 15–019
 special expenses, 15–020
 tenancy transfer orders, 15–049
 topping-up orders, 15–034
 variations, 15–020
 welfare principle, 15–026
Child tax credit
 generally, 6–007
Child trust funds
 generally, 6–026
Childcare
 employment rights, 6–028
Children
 see also **Care; Child abduction; Child
   protection; Child support; Children's
   rights; Family proceedings; Welfare
   principle**
 attendance at hearings, 18–042
 definition, 16–001
 introduction, 16–001—16–004
 legitimacy, 16–024—16–025
Children in care
 see **Care**
Children's guardians
 practice, 21–059
 provision, 21–057
 role, 21–058
Children's rights
 Children Act 1989, 16–019
 education law, 16–023
 European Convention on Human Rights,
   16–017—16–018
 Gillick competence
   generally, 16–011—16–014
   subsequent developments,
     16–015—16–016
 international law, 16–007—16–009
 legal proceedings, 16–020—16–022
 theoretical perspectives, 16–005—16–006
 UN Convention on the Rights of the Child,
   16–007—16–009
 unmarried parents, 16–024—16–025
Children's welfare
 see **Welfare principle**
Citizenship
 adoption, 22–007
 marriage/civil partnership, 3–040

Civil marriages
notice of intended marriage
appropriateness in modern society, 1–030
generally, 1–013
introduction, 1–012
registrar-general's licence, 1–019
superintendent registrar's certificate,
1–014—1–018
solemnisation
ceremony, 1–034
eligibility, 1–032
location, 1–033
Civil partnerships
see also **Civil partnerships (legal
consequences)**
death
decree of presumption of death and
dissolution, 12–003—12–004
introduction, 12–001
presumption of death at common law,
12–002
dissolution, 10–057
"engagement", 3–041
formalities, 1–049
parental consent, 17–023
separation orders, 11–001, 11–005
void/voidable civil partnerships
bars to annulment order, 2–061
conclusions, 2–063
effect of annulment order, 2–062
introduction, 2–058
void partnerships, 2–059
voidable partnerships, 2–060
Civil partnerships (legal consequences)
citizenship, 3–040
contract, 3–038
criminal law, 3–037
evidence, 3–039
home rights
introduction, 3–010
persons entitled, 3–011
third parties, effect on, 3–012—3–013
immigration status, 3–040
maintenance agreements
definition, 3–030
enforceability, 3–027
finality, 3–029
introduction, 3–026
public policy, 3–028
variation, 3–032
void contract terms, 3–031
maintenance orders
common law, 3–004
High Court/county courts, 3–021—3–024
introduction, 3–015
judicial separation, 3–025
magistrates' courts, 3–016—3–020
maintenance orders (High Court/county
courts)
duration, 3–024
factors for consideration, 3–022
introduction, 3–021

**Civil partnerships (legal
consequences)**—*cont.*
maintenance orders (High Court/county
courts)—*cont.*
types, 3–023
maintenance orders (magistrates' courts)
applications, 3–017
consent orders, 3–018
effect of cohabitation, dissolution or
remarriage, 3–019
introduction, 3–016
variation, 3–020
pensions, 3–035
property rights
generally, 3–006
home rights, 3–010—3–013
housekeeping allowances, 3–007
improvements to home, 3–008—3–009
taxation, 3–034
tort, 3–038
Clean break
see also **Ancillary relief**
dismissal of periodical payments order
claims, 13–092
duty to consider, 13–088
introduction, 13–086—13–087
non-extension of periodical payments orders,
13–091
reopening settlements
introduction, 13–102
permission to appeal out of time,
13–103—13–105
principles, 13–106
specified term periodical payments orders,
13–089—13–090
Cohabitation
benefits, 6–012—6–018
intestate succession, 7–008
maintenance orders, effect on, 3–019
proprietary rights, 8–006—8–007
**Commission for Local Administration in
England**
challenging local authorities' decisions,
21–083
Committal
breach of non-molestation orders,
9–035—9–036
enforcement of financial obligations
judgment summonses, 14–011
magistrates' courts, 14–017
Common licences
declaration, 1–027
impediments, 1–028
introduction, 1–025
publicity, 1–028
residence, 1–026
waiting time, 1–028
Compensation
child abuse victims, 21–066
Complaints
local authorities' decisions, 21–082

Concealment
ancillary relief, 13–107—13–108
Conduct
ancillary relief, 13–082—13–084
Confidentiality
adoption, 22–035
care proceedings, 21–038
family proceedings, 18–041
Consanguinity
see **Prohibited degrees**
Consent orders
ancillary relief, 13–005—13–007
child support, 15–038
magistrates' courts, 3–018
Consortium
generally, 3–003
Constructive trusts
common intention
express, 5–020—5–021
imputed, 5–024
inferred, 5–022—5–023
detrimental reliance, 5–025
introduction, 5–018
proprietary estoppel, relationship with,
5–037
quantification of interests, 5–026—5–031
Consummation
see **Voidable marriages**
Contact
children in care, 21–074
contact centres, 18–046
contact orders, 18–018—18–020
parental responsibility, 17–027
parental rights, 17–024
Contracts
effect of marriage/civil partnership, 3–038
family home
formalities, 5–006
intention to create legal relations, 5–005
introduction, 5–004
public policy, 5–007
maintenance and separation agreements
definition, 3–030
enforceability, 3–027
finality, 3–029
introduction, 3–026
public policy, 3–028
variation, 3–032
void contract terms, 3–031
parental right to contract on child's behalf,
17–026
Corporal punishment
parental rights, 17–017
Court proceedings
see **Family proceedings**
Criminal injuries compensation
child abuse victims, 21–066
Criminal law
child abduction, 20–002
child protection
children's evidence, 21–064—21–065
decisions to prosecute, 21–063

Criminal law—*cont.*
child protection—*cont.*
history, 21–061
prosecution, 21–062
domestic violence, 9–003—9–004
effect of marriage/civil partnership, 3–037
harassment
enforcement of orders, 9–041
introduction, 9–038
offences, 9–005—9–006
restraining orders, 9–039—9–040
parental responsibility in relation to child
offenders, 17–027
prohibited degrees, 2–011
reasonable punishment, 17–017
Death
see also **Family provision; Succession**
periodical payments orders, 13–020
termination of marriage/civil partnership
decree of presumption of death and
dissolution, 12–003—12–004
introduction, 12–001
presumption of death at common law,
12–002
"Deathbed marriages"
registrar-general's licence, 1–019
Decrees absolute
divorce, 10–012
Decrees *nisi*
divorce, 10–012
Deduction from earnings orders
child support, 15–023—15–024
**Department for Children, Schools and
Families**
functions, 21–006
Desertion
see **Divorce**
Disabilities
ancillary relief, 13–077
child support, 15–036
Discipline
see **Reasonable punishment**
Disclosure
family proceedings, 18–041
Dissolution
see also **Divorce**
civil partnerships, 10–057
Distress
enforcement of financial obligations, 14–016
Divorce
adultery
definition, 10–019
intolerability of further cohabitation,
10–020
introduction, 10–018
six months' continued cohabitation,
10–021
behaviour
continued cohabitation, 10–026
definition, 10–023
introduction, 10–022

Divorce—*cont.*
  behaviour—*cont.*
    reasonableness, 10–024—10–025
  children, 10–013
  conclusions, 10–058
  courts, 10–010
  criticisms of law, 10–047
  decrees *nisi* and absolute, 10–012
  desertion
    consensual separation, 10–030
    good cause for separation, 10–031
    intention, 10–029—10–032
    introduction, 10–027
    mental incapacity, 10–032
    separation, 10–028
    two years' separation, 10–033
  divorce rates, 10–002—10–003
  first year of marriage, 10–009
  five "facts"
    adultery, 10–018—10–021
    behaviour, 10–022—10–026
    desertion, 10–027—10–033
    introduction, 10–015—10–016
    judicial interpretation, 10–017
    living apart, 10–034—10–046
  ground, 10–015—10–016
  history
    irretrievable breakdown, 10–007
    matrimonial offence doctrine,
      10–004—10–005
    post-War reform, 10–006
  introduction, 10–001
  investigations, 10–011
  irretrievable breakdown
    generally, 10–015—10–016
    history, 10–007
  Jewish divorces, 10–014
  living apart
    calculation of time, 10–035
    consent to divorce, 10–041
    definition, 10–036—10–039
    financial arrangements, 10–045
    grave hardship, 10–042—10–044
    intention, 10–038—10–039
    introduction, 10–034
    reconciliation periods, 10–035
    refusal of decree, 10–042—10–045
    two-/five-year periods distinguished,
      10–040—10–045
  maintenance orders, effect on, 3–019
  mediation, 10–051
  reform proposals
    Family Advice and Information Service,
      10–054
    Family Law Act 1996, 10–049—10–053
    future developments, 10–055—10–056
    generally, 10–048
    information meetings, 10–052
    mediation, 10–051
  special procedure, 10–010

DNA tests
  determination of parentage,
    17–007—17–008
Domestic violence
  see also **Harassment; Non-molestation**
    orders; Occupation orders
  civil law's role, 9–007—9–008
  conclusions, 9–043
  contact orders, 18–019
  criminal law's role, 9–003
  injunctions
    care proceedings, 21–044
    general law, 9–042
  introduction, 9–001—9–002
  offences
    general law, 9–004
    harassment, 9–005—9–006
Duress
  voidable marriages
    effect of pressure, 2–041
    introduction, 2–038
    nature of pressure, 2–040
    source of pressure, 2–039

Education
  children's rights, 16–023
  education expenses orders, 15–035
  parental rights, 17–016
  welfare principle, 19–018
Emergency protection orders
  child protection, 21–048—21–050
Emigration
  parental right to prevent, 17–026
Employment
  adoption rights, 6–032
  childcare, 6–028
  flexible working, 6–034
  maternity rights, 6–030
  parental leave, 6–033
  paternity rights, 6–031
  work-life balance, 6–027
Enforcement
  see also **Ancillary relief**
  child support, 15–024—15–025
  non-molestation orders
    committal for contempt, 9–035—9–036
    introduction, 9–034
    prosecution, 9–037
  occupation orders, 9–024
  restraining orders, 9–041
  section 8 orders, 18–055—18–058
Engagement
  legal consequences, 3–041
European Convention on Human Rights
  see **Human rights**
European Court of Human Rights
  challenging local authority decisions,
    21–087
Evidence
  care proceedings, 21–036—21–038
  child protection, 21–064—21–065
  disclosure, 18–041

Evidence—*cont.*
spouses/civil partners, 3–039
Expert evidence
care proceedings, 21–037—21–038
family proceedings, 18–042—18–043

"Facts" of divorce
see **Divorce**
Family assistance orders
generally, 18–027
Family breakdown
see **Ancillary relief; Dissolution; Divorce;
Domestic violence; Separation**
Family home
see also **Occupation orders**
beneficial interests
express declaration, 5–010—5–011
introduction, 5–009
mortgagees' position, 5–050—5–051
no express declaration, 5–012
constructive trusts
detrimental reliance, 5–025
express common intention, 5–020—5–021
imputed common intention, 5–024
inferred common intention, 5–022—5–023
introduction, 5–018
proprietary estoppel, relationship with,
5–037
quantification of interests, 5–026—5–031
contractual arrangements
formalities, 5–006
intention to create legal relations, 5–005
introduction, 5–004
public policy, 5–007
disputes between co-owners
division of sale proceeds, 5–048
introduction, 5–039
sale of property orders, 5–045—5–047
severance of joint tenancies,
5–040—5–044
disputes with third parties
binding beneficial interests,
5–050—5–051
introduction, 5–049
sale of property orders, 5–057—5–061
setting aside transactions, 5–052—5–056
home rights
introduction, 3–010
persons entitled, 3–011
third parties, effect on, 3–012—3–013
improvements, 3–008—3–009
informal trusts
constructive trusts, 5–018—5–031
introduction, 5–013
resulting trusts, 5–014—5–017
intestate succession, 7–007
introduction, 5–001—5–002
legal title, 5–008
mortgagees
binding beneficial interests,
5–050—5–051
introduction, 5–049

Family home—*cont.*
mortgagees—*cont.*
sale of property orders, 5–060—5–061
setting aside transactions, 5–052—5–056
occupation rights
introduction, 3–010
persons entitled, 3–011
third parties, effect on, 3–012—3–013
proprietary estoppel
assurance, promise or representation,
5–033
constructive trusts, relationship with,
5–037
detrimental reliance, 5–034
introduction, 5–032
reform proposals, 5–038
remedies, 5–035—5–036
resulting trusts
contributions, 5–015
improper motive, 5–016
introduction, 5–014
quantification of interests, 5–017
sale of property orders
criteria for grant, 5–046
division of sale proceeds, 5–048
introduction, 5–045
occupation rent, 5–047
sale of property orders (third party
applications)
introduction, 5–057
secured creditors (property co-owned),
5–060
secured creditors (property solely owned),
5–061
trustees in bankruptcy, 5–058—5–059
setting aside transactions
constructive notice, 5–056
equity, 5–053
introduction, 5–052
misrepresentation, 5–054
undue influence, 5–055
severance of joint tenancies
acts operating on "share", 5–043
course of dealing, 5–044
introduction, 5–040
mutual agreement, 5–042
written notice, 5–041
Family law (general)
definition, A–001
key developments
civil partnerships, A–003—A–004
increase in cohabitation, A–005
introduction, A–002
private ordering, A–006
scope and arrangement of text,
A–007—A–008
Family proceedings
see also **Welfare principle**
applications with permission
criteria for permission, 18–036—18–039
introduction, 18–035

Family proceedings—*cont.*
applications without permission
contact/residence, 18–033—18–034
generally, 18–032
arrangements for children on divorce,
18–047
attendance of child at hearings, 18–042
CAFCASS, 18–010
case management directions, 18–041
children in respect of whom orders
available, 18–030
contact centres, 18–046
contact orders, 18–018—18–020
court system, 18–007—18–008
definition, 18–014
disclosure, 18–041
enforcement of orders, 18–055—18–058
expert evidence, 18–042—18–043
family assistance orders, 18–027
first dispute resolution hearing appointments,
18–040
hearings, 18–041
interim orders, 18–024
introduction, 18–001—18–002
investigations, 18–048
local authorities, 18–011—18–012
mediation, 18–045
"no order"
orders of "no order", 18–023
principle, 18–005
orders available, 18–015
orders restricting further applications,
18–028
permission
children's applications, 18–038
introduction, 18–035
local authority foster parents, 18–036
other persons, 18–039
relatives caring for child, 18–037
principles
avoidance of delay, 18–006
introduction, 18–003
"no order" principle, 18–005
welfare principle, 18–004
Private Law Programme, 18–040—18–043
procedure, 18–040—18–043
prohibited steps orders, 18–021
removal from jurisdiction
orders permitting removal, 18–026
prohibition on removal, 18–021
residence orders, 18–016—18–017
restrictions on making orders, 18–029
social services, 18–011—18–012
specific issue orders, 18–022
wardship
court's powers, 18–052—18–053
decline, 18–050
introduction, 18–049
procedure, 18–054
proceedings, 18–051
wasted costs orders, 18–041
welfare principle, 18–004

Family proceedings—*cont.*
welfare reports, 18–011—18–012
welfare services
CAFCASS, 18–010
introduction, 18–009
local authorities, 18–011—18–012
Family property
see also **Family home; Succession**
conclusions, 5–064
introduction, 4–001—4–002
personal property, 5–062—5–063
reform proposals
formalised relationships, 8–002—8–004
home-sharing relationships, 8–005
introduction, 8–001
non-formalised relationships,
8–006—8–007
socio-economic background, 4–003—4–004
Family provision
conditions for ordering
disposition by will or intestacy, 7–019
introduction, 7–018
reasonable financial provision not made,
7–020—7–022
eligible applicants
children, 7–014
former spouses/civil partners, 7–013
introduction, 7–011
persons living with deceased as spouse/
civil partner, 7–017
persons maintained by deceased, 7–016
persons treated as children of the family,
7–015
spouses/civil partners, 7–012
introduction, 7–009
matters for consideration
all cases, 7–024
children, 7–028
cohabitants, 7–030
former spouses/civil partners,
7–026—7–027
introduction, 7–023
persons maintained by deceased, 7–029
persons treated as children of the family,
7–028
spouses/civil partners, 7–026—7–027
orders available, 7–031
purpose, 7–010
reform proposals, 7–032
Fathers
see also **Unmarried fathers**
parentage, 17–004—17–005
Financial provision
see **Ancillary relief; Family provision**
Fines
enforcement of financial obligations, 14–019
Flexible working
employment rights, 6–034
Forced marriages
effect on petitioner, 2–041
introduction, 2–038
nature of pressure, 2–040

Forced marriages—*cont.*
source of pressure, 2–039
Foster care
adoption from care, 22–045
contact, 21–075
local authority placements, 21–068
section 8 order applications by carers, 18–036
Fraud
voidable marriages, 2–042
Funerals
parental rights, 17–026

Garnishee orders
see **Third party debt orders**
Gender reassignment
void marriages, 2–018—2–019
voidable marriages, 2–046
Gillick **competence**
generally, 16–011—16–014
subsequent developments, 16–015—16–016
Guardians
see also **Children's guardians**
appointment by court, 17–042
appointment by parents etc., 17–041
guardian's allowance, 6–024
introduction, 17–040
special guardians
generally, 17–046
special guardianship orders, 22–063—22–065

Hague Conventions
child abduction
acquiescence, 20–019
child's objections, 20–021
consent, 20–019
European Union, 20–022
grave risk of harm, 20–020
habitual residence, 20–015
intolerable situation, 20–020
introduction, 20–014
proceedings, 20–018
rights of custody, 20–017
wrongful removal/retention, 20–016
intercountry adoption
adoption from Hague Convention countries, 22–052
generally, 22–048—22–050
Harassment
enforcement of orders, 9–041
injunctions, 9–008, 9–039—9–040
introduction, 9–038
offences, 9–005—9–006
restraining orders, 9–039—9–040
Home rights
introduction, 3–010
persons entitled, 3–011
third parties, effect on, 3–012—3–013
Homelessness
eligible persons, 6–038
introduction, 6–036

Homelessness—*cont.*
local authorities' duties
generally, 6–037
relationship with other duties, 6–039
Housing
see also **Family home; Occupation orders**
generally, 6–035
homelessness
eligible persons, 6–038
introduction, 6–036
local authorities' duties, 6–037, 6–039
housing benefit, 6–020
orders relating to
introduction, 13–109
Martin orders, 13–117
Mesher orders, 13–116
sale of property orders, 13–114
tenancy transfer orders, 13–118
transfer of property orders, 13–110—13–113
Human rights
adoption, 22–034
child abduction, 20–025
children, 16–017—16–018
local authorities' decisions
claims in domestic courts, 21–086
ECtHR claims, 21–087
right to marry, 2–001
welfare principle, 19–004

Illegitimacy
abolition, 16–024—16–025
marriage after birth, 17–032
void marriages, 2–055, 17–031
Immigrants
effect of marriage/civil partnership on status, 3–040
marriage, 1–017
Incapacity to consummate
see **Voidable marriages**
Income support
benefits, 6–009
Indirect contact
contact orders, 18–017
Injunctions
domestic violence
care proceedings, 21–044
general law, 9–042
harassment, 9–008, 9–039—9–041
Intercountry adoption
see **Adoption**
Interim orders
adoption orders, 22–068
care orders, 21–043
section 8 orders, 18–024
supervision orders, 21–043
International child abduction
see **Child abduction**
International law
children's rights, 16–007—16–009
"Inter-sex" persons
void marriages, 2–020

Intestacy
see also **Family provision**
cohabitants, 7–008
critique of law, 7–008
family home, 7–007
introduction, 7–003
no surviving spouse/civil partner, 7–006
surviving spouse/civil partner and issue,
    7–004
surviving spouse/civil partner but no issue,
    7–005
Investigations
see also **Child protection**
divorce, 10–011
family proceedings, 18–048
Irretrievable breakdown
see **Divorce**

Jewish law
divorce, 10–014
marriage, 1–038
Jobseekers' allowance
benefits, 6–010
Joint tenancies
severance
    acts operating on "share", 5–043
    course of dealing, 5–044
    introduction, 5–040
    mutual agreement, 5–042
    written notice, 5–041
Judgment summonses
enforcement of financial obligations, 14–011
Judicial review
local authorities' decisions, 21–085
Judicial separation
see also **Separation**
effect, 11–003
grounds, 11–002
introduction, 11–001
uses, 11–004

Legal representation
care proceedings
    children's guardians, 21–057—21–059
    children's solicitors, 21–060
    introduction, 21–056
parental rights, 17–021
Legitimacy
abolition, 16–024—16–025
marriage after birth, 17–032
void marriages, 2–055, 17–031
Limitation periods
voidable marriages, 2–048
Living apart
see **Divorce; Separation**
Local authorities
see also **Care; Care proceedings; Child
    protection**
accommodation, 21–011—21–012
adoption services, 22–015
central government's role, 21–006

Local authorities—*cont.*
child protection investigations
    duties, 21–022—21–023
    negligence, 21–027
Children Act 1989, 21–005
children in need, 21–010
co-operation between authorities, 21–015
court's role, 21–007
family support, 21–008—21–009
history of children's services,
    21–002—21–003
homelessness duties
    generally, 6–037
    relationship with other duties, 6–039
introduction, 21–001
law reform, 21–004
parental responsibility, 17–047
removal from accommodation,
    21–013—21–014
voluntary agreements, 21–013—21–014
welfare services, 18–011—18–012
Looked-after children
see **Care**
Lump sum orders
child support
    applications by children, 15–045
    discretion of court, 15–044
    orders available, 15–043
generally, 13–024
variation, 13–101

Magistrates' courts
enforcement of financial obligations
    attachment of earnings, 14–018
    committal, 14–017
    distress, 14–016
    fines, 14–019
    registration, 14–014
maintenance orders
    applications, 3–017
    consent orders, 3–018
    effect of cohabitation, divorce or
        remarriage, 3–019
    introduction, 3–016
    variation, 3–020
Maintenance
see also **Child support; Periodical
    payments orders**
children in care, 21–068
effect of marriage/civil partnership, 3–004
maintenance pending suit, 13–037—13–038
Maintenance agreements
definition, 3–030
enforceability, 3–027
finality, 3–029
introduction, 3–026
public policy, 3–028
variation, 3–032
void contract terms, 3–031
Maintenance orders
common law, 3–004

Maintenance orders—*cont.*
High Court/county courts
duration, 3–024
factors for consideration, 3–022
introduction, 3–021
types, 3–023
introduction, 3–015
judicial separation, 3–025
magistrates' courts
applications, 3–017
consent orders, 3–018
effect of cohabitation, divorce or
remarriage, 3–019
introduction, 3–016
variation, 3–020
Maladministration
local authorities, 21–083
Marriage
see also **Marriage (formalities); Marriage
(legal consequences); Void marriages;
Voidable marriages**
children in care, 21–080
death
decree of presumption of death and
dissolution, 12–003—12–004
introduction, 12–001
presumption of death at common law,
12–002
"deathbed marriages", 1–019
"Fleet marriages", 1–003
history
canon law, 1–002—1–003
Lord Hardwicke's Act 1753, 1–004
Marriage Acts 1823 and 1836, 1–005
introduction, 1–001
proof, 1–043
right to marry, 2–001
Marriage (formalities)
see also **Solemnisation**
banns
historical requirements, 1–002, 1–004
introduction, 1–021
publicity, 1–023
residence, 1–022
waiting time, 1–024
common licences
declaration, 1–027
impediments, 1–028
introduction, 1–025
publicity, 1–028
residence, 1–026
waiting time, 1–028
"deathbed marriages", 1–019
detained persons, 1–018
housebound persons, 1–018
introduction, 1–006
irregularities
defects invalidating marriage, 1–045
defects not invalidating marriage, 1–046
introduction, 1–044
"non-marriage", 1–048
other defects, 1–047

Marriage (formalities)—*cont.*
notice of intended marriage (Anglican
marriages)
appropriateness in modern society, 1–030
banns, 1–021—1–024
common licences, 1–025—1–028
introduction, 1–020
special licences, 1–029
notice of intended marriage (civil marriages)
appropriateness in modern society, 1–030
generally, 1–013
introduction, 1–012
registrar-general's licence, 1–019
superintendent registrar's certificate,
1–014—1–018
parental consent
appropriateness in modern society, 1–011
dispensation, 1–010
generally, 1–007—1–008
parental rights, 17–023
relevant persons, 1–009
reform proposals, 1–050—1–051
Registrar General's licence, 1–019
registration, 1–043
special licences, 1–029
superintendent registrar's certificate
detained persons, 1–018
housebound persons, 1–018
notice, 1–014
objections and inquiries, 1–015
persons subject to immigration control,
1–017
waiting time, 1–016
Marriage (legal consequences)
citizenship, 3–040
common law
consortium, 3–003
introduction, 3–001
maintenance, 3–004
unity, 3–002
contract, 3–038
criminal law, 3–037
evidence, 3–039
home rights
introduction, 3–010
persons entitled, 3–011
third parties, effect on, 3–012—3–013
immigration status, 3–040
maintenance agreements
definition, 3–030
enforceability, 3–027
finality, 3–029
introduction, 3–026
public policy, 3–028
variation, 3–032
void contract terms, 3–031
maintenance orders
common law, 3–004
High Court/county courts, 3–021—3–024
introduction, 3–015
judicial separation, 3–025
magistrates' courts, 3–016—3–020

Marriage (legal consequences)—*cont.*
maintenance orders (High Court/county
   courts)
   duration, 3–024
   factors for consideration, 3–022
   introduction, 3–021
   types, 3–023
maintenance orders (magistrates' courts)
   applications, 3–017
   consent orders, 3–018
   effect of cohabitation, divorce or
      remarriage, 3–019
   introduction, 3–016
   variation, 3–020
pensions, 3 035
proprietary rights
   generally, 3–006
   home rights, 3–010—3–013
   housekeeping allowances, 3–007
   improvements to home, 3–008—3–009
   taxation, 3–034
   tort, 3–038
***Martin* orders**
generally, 13–117
Maternity rights
employment rights, 6–030
Matrimonial home
see **Family home**
Matrimonial home rights
see **Home rights**
Means-tested benefits
see **Benefits**
Mediation
divorce, 10–051
generally, 18–045
Medical treatment
Gillick competence
   generally, 16–011—16–014
   subsequent developments,
      16–015—16–016
parental consent, 17–022
Mental capacity
consent to marriage, 2–036—2–037
voidable marriages, 2–045
***Mesher* orders**
generally, 13–116
Misrepresentation
setting aside mortgages, 5–054
Mistake
voidable marriages, 2–042
Mortgagees
binding beneficial interests, 5–050—5–051
introduction, 5–049
sale of property orders, 5–060—5–061
setting aside transactions
   constructive notice, 5–056
   equity, 5–053
   introduction, 5–052
   misrepresentation, 5–054
   undue influence, 5–055

Mothers
parentage, 17–003

Names
children in care, 21–080
parental choice, 17–025
Neglect of children
see **Child protection**
Negligence
child protection investigations, 21–027
"No order"
orders of "no order", 18–023
principle, 18–005
Non-consummation
see **Voidable marriages**
Non-disclosure
ancillary relief, 13–107—13–108
"Non-marriage"
void marriages compared, 1–048, 2–004
Non-means-tested benefits
see **Benefits**
Non-molestation orders
associated persons, 9–028—9–030
court's own motion, 9–031
enforcement
   committal for contempt, 9–035—9–036
   introduction, 9–034
   prosecution, 9–037
introduction, 9–026
matters for consideration, 9–033
"molestation", 9–027
terms, 9–032
Notice of intended marriage
see **Marriage (formalities)**
Nullity
see **Void civil partnerships; Voidable civil
   partnerships; Void marriages;
   Voidable marriages**

Occupation of family home
see **Home rights; Occupation orders**
Occupation orders
ancillary provisions, 9–023
applicants
   entitled persons, 9–012—9–014
   introduction, 9–011
   non-entitled persons, 9–015
contents of property, 9–023
declaratory orders, 9–010
duration, 9–022
enforcement, 9–024
entitled persons
   introduction, 9–012
   persons entitled to occupy property, 9–013
   persons with home rights, 9–014
introduction, 9–009
matters for consideration
   entitled persons, 9–017—9–019
   introduction, 9–016
   non-entitled cohabitants/former
      cohabitants, 9–021

Occupation orders—*cont.*
 matters for consideration—*cont.*
  non-entitled former spouses/civil partners,
   9–020
 outgoings, 9–023
 regulatory orders, 9–010
 scope, 9–010
Offences
 see **Criminal law**
Offsetting
 pensions, 13–121
Ombudsmen
 challenging local authorities' decisions,
  21–083
Orders for sale
 see **Sale of property orders**
Orders restricting further applications
 generally, 18–028
Overseas marriages
 same sex partners, 2–017

Parentage
 birth registration
  birth certificates, 17–011
  introduction, 17–009
  procedure, 17–010
 determination
  birth registration, 17–009—17–011
  DNA tests, 17–007—17–008
  introduction, 17–006
  judicial procedures, 17–012
 fathers, 17–004—17–005
 introduction, 17–001—17–002
 mothers, 17–003
Parental leave
 employment rights, 6–033
Parental orders
 surrogacy, 22–076—22–078
Parental responsibility
 see also **Care; Parental rights**
 care, 17–027
 contact, 17–027
 de facto carers, 17–051
 definition, 17–013
 delegation, 17–050
 duration, 17–027
 guardians
  appointment by court, 17–042
  appointment by parents etc., 17–041
  introduction, 17–040
  special guardians, 17–046
 history, 17–001—17–002
 importance, 17–029
 local authorities, 17–047
 maintenance, 17–028
 married parents
  adoption, 17–033
  introduction, 17–030
  marriage after birth, 17–032
  surrogacy, 17–034
  void marriages, 17–031
 multiple persons, 17–048

Parental responsibility—*cont.*
 non-parents with residence orders, 17–044
 offences committed by children, 17–027
 persons without parental responsibility
  de facto carers, 17–051
  delegation, 17–050
  unmarried fathers, 17–052
 revocation, 17–049
 special guardians, 17–046
 stepparents, 17–045
 unmarried fathers
  birth registration, 17–039
  court orders, 17–037
  formal agreements, 17–038
  introduction, 17–035—17–036
  rights when parental responsibility not
   obtained, 17–052
Parental rights
 see also **Parental responsibility**
 administration of property, 17–020
 choice of name, 17–025
 consent to marriage/civil partnership,
  17–023
 consent to medical treatment, 17–022
 contact, 17–024
 contracts on children's behalf, 17–026
 discipline, 17–017
 education, 17–016
 funerals, 17–026
 history, 17–001—17–002
 legal representation, 17–021
 passports, 17–026
 possession of children, 17–014
 prevention of emigration, 17–026
 religion, 17–018
 services of children, 17–019
 upbringing, 17–015
Passports
 parental rights, 17–026
 prevention of child abduction, 20–003
Paternity
 determination
  birth registration, 17–009—17–012
  DNA tests, 17–007—17–008
  introduction, 17–006
 employment rights, 6–031
 generally, 17–004—17–005
 misattribution, 15–009
 proof, 15–008
Pensions
 effect of marriage/civil partnership, 3–035
 offsetting, 13–121
 orders available, 13–119
 pension attachment orders, 13–122
 pension sharing orders
  effect, 13–125
  generally, 13–029, 13–123
  types, 13–124
 resources of parties, 13–070
Periodical payments orders
 see also **Ancillary relief**
 arrears, 14–002

Periodical payments orders—*cont.*
  clean break
    dismissal of periodical payments order
      claims, 13–092
    duty to consider, 13–088
    introduction, 13–086—13–087
    non-extension of orders, 13–091
    specified term orders, 13–089—13–090
  death of payer, 13–020
  introduction, 13–018
  remarriage/formation of civil partnership by
    payee, 13–021
  secured orders, 13–018
  specified term, 13–022
  variation
    capital provision on variation application,
      13–100
    clean break on variation application,
      13–099
    court's powers, 13–096
    exercise of discretion, 13–098
    introduction, 13–095
    specified term orders, 13–097
Personal property
  proprietary rights, 5–062—5–063
Placement orders
  see also **Adoption**
  adoption from care, 22–043—22–044
  generally, 22–027—22–028
  revocation, 22–044
Police
  child abduction
    all ports warnings, 20–004
    recovery of children, 20–009
  child protection
    emergencies, 21–051
    investigations, 21–024
Polygamy
  void marriages, 2–022
Ports
  alerts on child abduction, 20–004
Post-nuptial settlements
  variation
    ancillary relief applications, 13–027
    child support applications,
      15–043—15–045
Prisoners
  marriage, 1–018
Prohibited degrees
  adoption, 2–009, 22–008
  criminal law, 2–011
  introduction, 2–007
  policy, 2–009—2–010
  restrictions, 2–008
  step-relationships, 2–009
Prohibited steps orders
  generally, 18–021
Property
  see also **Family property; Proprietary
    rights**
  parental administration, 17–020

Property adjustment orders
  see **Settlement of property orders;
    Transfer of property orders;
    Variation of settlement orders**
Proprietary estoppel
  assurance, promise or representation, 5–033
  constructive trusts, relationship with, 5–037
  detrimental reliance, 5–034
  introduction, 5–032
  reform proposals, 5–038
  remedies, 5–035—5–036
Proprietary rights
  see also **Family home; Family property**
  effect of marriage/civil partnership
    generally, 3–006
    home rights, 3–010—3–013
    housekeeping allowances, 3–007
    improvements to home, 3–008—3–009
  engagement, 3–041
Provision for family and dependants
  see **Family provision**

Quakers
  marriage, 1–038

Reasonable punishment
  parental rights, 17–017
Receivership
  enforcement of financial obligations, 14–009
Refusal to consummate
  see **Voidable marriages**
Registrar General
  marriage licences, 1–019
Registration
  see also **Birth registration**
  adoption, 22–010
  marriages, 1–043
Rehabilitation
  children in care, 21–070
Relationship breakdown
  see **Ancillary relief; Dissolution; Divorce;
    Domestic violence; Separation**
Religions
  parental right to choose religion, 17–018
  welfare principle, 19–020
Relinquishment
  see **Adoption**
Remarriage
  maintenance orders, 3–019
  periodical payments orders, 13–021
Removal from jurisdiction
  see also **Child abduction**
  orders permitting removal, 18–026
  prohibition on removal, 18–021
Representation
  care proceedings
    children's guardians, 21–057—21–059
    children's solicitors, 21–060
    introduction, 21–056
  parental rights, 17–021
Residence orders
  adoption, 22–063—22–065

Special licences
marriage, 1–029
Special measures for witnesses
child witnesses, 21–064—21–065
Specific issue orders
generally, 18–022
State benefits
see **Benefits**
State support for families
see **Benefits; Child trust funds;**
Employment; Housing; Local
authorities; Tax credits
Stepparents
adoption, 22–058—22–059
parental responsibility, 17–045
prohibited degrees, 2–009
Succession
see also **Family provision**
adoption, 22–006
intestacy
cohabitants, 7–008
critique of law, 7–008
family home, 7–007
introduction, 7–003
no surviving spouse/civil partner, 7–006
surviving spouse/civil partner and issue,
7–004
surviving spouse/civil partner but no
issue, 7–005
wills, 7–001—7–002
Superintendent registrar's certificate
see **Marriage (formalities)**
Supervised contact
contact orders, 18–018
Supervision orders
appeals, 21–046
discharge, 21–045
generally, 21–042
interim orders, 21–043
introduction, 21–040
Surrogacy
access to information, 22–080
adoption
generally, 22–079
relationship with surrogacy, 22–072
enforceability of contracts, 22–073
generally, 17–003
introduction, 22–070—22–071
parental orders, 22–076—22–078
regulation, 22–074—22–075

Tax credits
child tax credit, 6–007
introduction, 6–005
working tax credit, 6–006
Taxation
effect of marriage/civil partnership, 3–034
Tenancy transfer orders
see **Transfer of tenancies**
Third party debt orders
enforcement of financial obligations, 14–007

Tortious liability
effect of marriage/civil partnership, 3–038
Transfer of property orders
child support
applications by children, 15–045
discretion of court, 15–044
orders available, 15–043
deferred cash payments, 13–113
generally, 13–025
immediate cash payments, 13–112
reduction/extinction of periodical payments,
13–111
Transfer of tenancies
ancillary relief, 13–118
child support, 15–049
Truancy
care proceedings, 21–032

UN Convention on the Rights of the Child
generally, 16–007—16–009
Undue influence
setting aside mortgages, 5–055
Unmarried fathers
parental responsibility
birth registration, 17–039
court orders, 17–037
formal agreements, 17–038
introduction, 17–035—17–036
rights when parental responsibility not
obtained, 17–052
Unmarried parents
children's rights, 16–024—16–025
Unreasonable behaviour
see **Divorce**

Variation of settlement orders
child support
applications by children, 15–045
discretion of court, 15–044
orders available, 15–043
generally, 13–027
Venereal diseases
see **Sexually transmitted diseases**
Void civil partnerships
bars to annulment order, 2–061
conclusions, 2–063
effect of annulment order, 2–062
generally, 2–059
introduction, 2–058
Void marriages
see also **Voidable marriages**
conclusions, 2–063
defective formalities, 1–045, 2–014
effect of decree
financial provision after death, 2–057
financial provision after decree, 2–056
introduction, 2–052
legitimacy of children, 2–055
existing marriage/civil partnership, 2–015
grounds, 2–006
history
decrees of annulment, 2–003

Void marriages—*cont.*
history—*cont.*
generally, 2–002
"non-marriage", 2–004
introduction, 2–001
minimum age, 2–012—2–013
"non-marriage", 1–048, 2–004
parental responsibility, 17–031
polygamy, 2–022
prohibited degrees
adoption, 2–009
criminal law, 2–011
introduction, 2–007
policy, 2–009—2–010
restrictions, 2–008
step-relationships, 2–009
same sex partners
classification of "marriage", 2–021
gender reassignment, 2–018—2–019
inter-sex persons, 2–020
introduction, 2–016
overseas marriages, 2–017
Voidable civil partnerships
bars to annulment order, 2–061
conclusions, 2–063
effect of annulment order, 2–062
generally, 2–060
introduction, 2–058
Voidable marriages
see also **Void marriages**
bars to decree
approbation, 2–050—2–051
introduction, 2–047
knowledge, 2–049
limitation periods, 2–048
conclusions, 2–063
duress
effect on petitioner, 2–041
introduction, 2–038
nature of pressure, 2–040
source of pressure, 2–039
effect of decree, 2–052—2–053
fraud, 2–042
gender reassignment, 2–046
grounds, 2–023
history
decrees of annulment, 2–003
generally, 2–002
"non-marriage", 2–004
incapacity to consummate
incapacity, 2–026
introduction, 2–024
knowledge of incapacity, 2–028
policy, 2–029
requirements for consummation, 2–025
supervening incapacity, 2–027
introduction, 2–001
lack of consent
classification of "marriage", 2–044
duress, 2–038—2–041
fraud, 2–042
introduction, 2–034

Voidable marriages—*cont.*
lack of consent—*cont.*
mental capacity, 2–036—2–037
mistake, 2–042
outward/inward consent, 2–035
preventative steps, 2–043
mental illness, 2–045
mistake, 2–042
pregnancy by another, 2–045
sexually transmitted diseases, 2–045
wilful refusal to consummate
introduction, 2–030
just excuse, 2–032
requirements for consummation, 2–033
settled and definite decision, 2–031

Wardship
court's powers, 18–052—18–053
decline, 18–050
introduction, 18–049
procedure, 18–054
proceedings, 18–051
Wasted costs orders
family proceedings, 18–041
Welfare benefits
see **Benefits**
Welfare principle
adoption, 22–024
age, 19–020
ancillary relief
children of the family, 13–061
introduction, 13–058
minority of children, 13–062
paramountcy of welfare principle, 13–060
appeals against decisions, 19–024—19–025
application, 19–008—19–010
assessment of welfare, 19–005—19–007
assumptions, 19–003
checklist, 19–014—19–015
child support, 15–026
cultural background, 19–020
educational needs, 19–018
effect of change in circumstances, 19–019
emotional needs, 19–018
family proceedings, 18–004
harm suffered or likely to be suffered, 19–021
human rights, 19–004
introduction, 19–001—19–002
linguistic background, 19–020
parents' capabilities, 19–022
physical needs, 19–018
powers available to court, 19–023
presumptions, 19–003
problems, 19–011—19–013
racial origin, 19–020
religion, 19–020
review of decisions, 19–024—19–025
sex, 19–020

Welfare principle—*cont.*
  wishes and feelings of child,
    19–016—19–017
Welfare reports
  generally, 18–011—18–012
Wilful refusal to consummate
  see **Voidable marriages**

Wills
  generally, 7–001—7–002
Working tax credit
  generally, 6–006
Work-life balance
  see **Employment**